Fodor's

ESSENTIAL GERMANY

WELCOME TO GERMANY

From half-timber medieval towns to cosmopolitan cities, Germany offers a thoroughly engaging mix of tradition and modernity. You can explore Bavaria's magnificent baroque palaces one day, and immerse yourself in Hamburg's cool, redeveloped HafenCity the next. In hip Berlin, historic sites such as the Brandenburg Gate and contemporary art galleries create exciting contrasts. Throughout the country, discovering world-class museums and cutting-edge design is as quintessentially German as grabbing a stein of beer at a centuries-old *Biergarten*.

TOP REASONS TO GO

★ **Castles:** Majestic palaces such as Neuschwanstein seem straight out of a fairy tale.

★ **Fun Cities:** You can party all night in Berlin or soak up culture in Munich.

★ **Music:** From Bach to Beethoven to Wagner, Germany is the birthplace of the classics.

★ **Beer and Wine:** The home of Oktoberfest also surprises with top-notch regional wines.

★ **Markets:** Locally made crafts shine, especially during the Christmas season.

★ **Great Drives:** Scenic roads wind through the Alps and past vineyards and villages.

1 Rothenburg ob der Tauber

The best preserved town along the so-called "Romantic Road" is filled with cobblestone streets and buildings and churches that date to the 1400s. You can take the Night Watchman Tour, with a local guide dressed in Medieval garb. *(Ch. 4)*

2 Mainau

This Bodensee island is covered by a million colorful, fragrant, and rare tulips, hyacinths, roses, rhododendrons, as well as a conservatory with thousands of butterflies. *(Ch. 6)*

3 Oktoberfest

The world's largest annual party attracts more than six million visitors to Munich every fall to eat Bavarian pretzels and pork knuckle, sing songs, and drink beer in huge tents. *(Ch. 2)*

4 Beer Gardens

Indoor brewpubs and outdoor beer gardens are central to German life, and two of the best—the Hofbräuhaus and the Chinese pagoda in the Englischer Garten—are in Munich. *(Ch. 2)*

5 Baden Baden

The Romans discovered the extensive hot springs here, which still attracts visitors, but there are also theaters, a horse-racing track, and Germany's oldest casino. *(Ch. 7)*

6 German Wine

The Romans introduced grapes to this region, which is now dotted with small, family-owned vineyards. The most famous areas are the Mosel Valley, the Pfalz, and the Neckar Valley. *(Ch. 11)*

7 Christmas Markets

In late November Christmas Markets begin all over Germany, offering hand-made ornaments and such holiday foods as gingerbread and mulled wine. *(Ch. 5)*

8 The Black Forest

One of southern Germany's top regions offers miles of forested hiking trails, cuckoo clocks, top restaurants in Baiersbronn, spa towns, and delicious Black Forest Cake. *(Ch. 7)*

1933-1945

9 Heidelberg

This charming university town is overlooked by its Schloss (Castle). Take the funicular to see the romantic ruin that has enchanted writers from Goethe to Mark Twain. *(Ch. 8)*

10 Sobering Dachau

Once a thriving artist's colony, Dachau is most famous now as the site of Hitler's first concentration camp, an important reminder of the inhumanity of war. *(Ch. 2)*

11 Architecture in Weimar

In 1919, Walter Gropius founded the Bauhaus movement in the historic city where Goethe and Schiller are buried. *(Ch. 16)*

12 Baltic Beaches

Miles of white sand have drawn Germany's wealthy to summer elite to the Baltic coast since the 19th century, where Usedom Island is still a lovely, quiet escape. *(Ch. 14)*

13 A Trabant Tour of Berlin

The Trabant was the only car manufactured in the former East Germany, and popular tours are offered in surviving models, ideally with an experienced driver. *(Ch. 15)*

14 Royal Trappings

The palaces of Germany's fabulously wealthy rulers are now museums that showcase their royal trappings, from Dresden's Green Vault to Munich's Residenz, shown here. *(Ch. 2, 16)*

15 Schloss Neuschwanstein

Building this inconic, mountaintop castle nearly bankrupted Bavaria. Today it's the area's most popular attraction. *(Ch. 4)*

16 Stuttgart's Car Culture

Mercedes-Benz and Porsche both founded museums here that cover automotive design and technology, as well as company history. *(Ch. 8)*

17 Music in Bayreuth

The annual Wagner Festival, which he founded here in 1876, is Germany's most popular. But Bayreuth is a charming place to visit even if you aren't an opera lover. *(Ch. 5)*

18 Spring Asparagus

Each April and May, delicate, whilte Spargel (asparagus) shows up everywhere. Have it in Frankfurt with the popular Green Sauce. *(Ch. 9)*

19 Kölner Dom

Most major German cities have a cathedral, but this breathtaking Gothic example, dating from the 1200s, is the city's landmark and was briefly the world's tallest building. *(Ch. 11)*

20 Eating Like a Local

Berlin's currywurst is available on every street corner. In Munich, weisswurst are tender veal sausages that are boiled and served with a sweet mustard and soft pretzels. *(Ch. 2. 15)*

21 Garmisch-Partenkirchen

Site of the 1936 Winter Olympics, this resort has attracted skiers to the Zugspitze, Germany's highest mountain. *(Ch. 3)*

22 Historic Nuremberg

Known for the post-war international war crimes trials, this historic city also has the German National Museum and was the birthplace of artist Albrecht Dürer. *(Ch. 5)*

23 Cruising the Rhine

Germany's most scenic river is great for a long or short cruise, particularly the world heritage section near Rüdesheim *(Ch. 11)*

24 The Berlin Wall

Most of the wall has been demolished, but enough is left to help you visualize the desperation of those who tried to flee across the border between East and West. *(Ch. 15)*

25 Alpine Hiking

Berchtesgaden, Germany's first Alpine National Park, contains more than 200 miles of marked trails (both easy and challenging) through a lush green forest. *(Ch. 3)*

Fodor's ESSENTIAL GERMANY

Editorial: Douglas Stallings, *Editorial Director*; Margaret Kelly, Jacinta O'Halloran, *Senior Editors*; Kayla Becker, Alexis Kelly, Amanda Sadlowski, *Editors*; Teddy Minford, *Content Editor*; Rachael Roth, *Content Manager*

Design: Tina Malaney, *Design and Production Director*; Jessica Gonzalez, *Production Designer*

Photography: Jill Krueger, *Senior Photo Editor*

Maps: Rebecca Baer, *Senior Map Editor*; Mark Stroud (Moon Street Cartography) and David Lindroth, *Cartographers*

Production: Jennifer DePrima, *Editorial Production Manager*; Carrie Parker, *Senior Production Editor*; Elyse Rozelle, *Production Editor*

Business & Operations: Chuck Hoover, *Chief Marketing Officer*; Joy Lai, *Vice President and General Manager*; Stephen Horowitz, *Director of Business Development and Revenue Operations*; Tara McCrillis, *Director of Publishing Operations*

Public Relations and Marketing: Joe Ewaskiw, *Manager*; Esther Su, *Marketing Manager*

Writers: Joe Baur, Wibke Carter, Jennifer Ceaser, Christie Dietz, Lee A. Evans, Liz Humphreys, Evelyn Kanter, Chantal Pannozzo, Courtney Tenz

Editor: Douglas Stallings

Production Editor: Carrie Parker

1st Edition

ISBN 978-1-64097-110-3

ISSN 2578–3076

Library of Congress Control Number 2018954448

SPECIAL SALES

This book is available at special discounts for bulk purchases for sales promotions or premiums. For more information, e-mail SpecialMarkets@fodors.com.

PRINTED IN THE UNITED STATES OF AMERICA

10 9 8 7 6 5 4 3 2 1

CONTENTS

CONTENTS

CONTENTS

ABOUT THIS GUIDE

Fodor's Recommendations

Everything in this guide is worth doing—we don't cover what isn't—but exceptional sights, hotels, and restaurants are recognized with additional accolades. Fodor'sChoice★ indicates our top recommendations. Care to nominate a new place? Visit Fodors.com/contact-us.

Trip Costs

We list prices wherever possible to help you budget well. Hotel and restaurant price categories from $ to $$$$ are noted alongside each recommendation. For hotels, we include the lowest cost of a standard double room in high season. For restaurants, we cite the average price of a main course at dinner or, if dinner isn't served, at lunch. For attractions, we always list adult admission fees; discounts are usually available for children, students, and senior citizens.

Hotels

Our local writers vet every hotel to recommend the best overnights in each price category, from budget to expensive. Unless otherwise specified, you can expect private bath, phone, and TV in your room. For expanded hotel reviews, visit Fodors.com.

Top Picks	Hotels & Restaurants
★ Fodor'sChoice	⌂ Hotel
Listings	⌖ Number of rooms
✉ Address	⌖ Meal plans
✉ Branch address	⌖ Meal plans
☎ Telephone	✕ Restaurant
📠 Fax	⌖ Reservations
⊕ Website	⌖ Dress code
✉ E-mail	⊟ No credit cards
⌖ Admission fee	$ Price
☉ Open/closed times	**Other**
Ⓜ Subway	⇨ See also
⌖ Directions or Map coordinates	☞ Take note
	⌖ Golf facilities

Restaurants

Unless we state otherwise, restaurants are open for lunch and dinner daily. We mention dress code only when there's a specific requirement and reservations only when they're essential or not accepted.

Credit Cards

The hotels and restaurants in this guide typically accept credit cards. If not, we'll say so.

EUGENE FODOR

Hungarian-born Eugene Fodor (1905–91) began his travel career as an interpreter on a French cruise ship. The experience inspired him to write *On the Continent* (1936), the first guidebook to receive annual updates and discuss a country's way of life as well as its sights. Fodor later joined the U.S. Army and worked for the OSS in World War II. After the war, he kept up his intelligence work while expanding his guidebook series. During the Cold War, many guides were written by fellow agents who understood the value of insider information. Today's guides continue Fodor's legacy by providing travelers with timely coverage, insider tips, and cultural context.

EXPERIENCE GERMANY

GERMANY TODAY

About the size of Montana but home to Western Europe's largest population, Germany has once again taken a leading economic and political role from its position in the heart in Europe, where it often bridges the divide between East and West. The land of "Dichter und Denker" (poets and thinkers) is also one of the world's leading export countries, specializing in mechanical equipment, vehicles, chemicals, and household goods. Germany is both deeply conservative—valuing tradition, hard work, precision, and fiscal responsibility—and one of the world's most liberal countries—with a generous social welfare state, a strongly held commitment to environmentalism, and a postwar determination to combat xenophobia. Reunited after 45 years of division, it's a country that is always looking to redefine itself.

Migration and Integration

In the 1950s and 1960s, West Germany invited migrants ("guest workers") from Italy, Greece, the former Yugoslavia, and above all Turkey to provide cheap labor to rebuild the country and fuel its postwar economic boom. The Germans assumed these guest workers would only stay temporarily, providing little in the way of cultural integration. But many of these migrants had little formal education, and often they did not want to return to their economically depressed home countries. Instead, they brought their family to join them and settled in Germany, often forming parallel societies cut off from mainstream German life. Today, Berlin is home to the largest Turkish community outside of Turkey itself, and even claims to be the birthplace of the ubiquitous *döner kebab*. Germany has always been a land of emigrants, not immigrants, but its demographics are undergoing a radical shift: today, 20% of German residents have immigrant roots. Since the European migrant crisis started in 2015, about 1.4 million refugees (primarily from Syria, Afghanistan, and Iraq) have arrived in Germany. Increasing anti-immigrant sentiment has given rise to far-right nationalist parties, but their demonstrations are usually wildly outnumbered by much larger counterprotests.

Eurozone Enforcer

Germany, the world's fourth-largest economy, is the world's third-largest exporter, after China and the United States. The worldwide recession hit Germany squarely, though thanks to a strong social saftey-net, the unemployed and underemployed did not suffer on the level we are used to in the United States. In Germany, losing your job does not mean you lose your health insurance, and the unemployed receive financial help from the state to meet housing payments and other basic expenses. More recently, Germany has been a bastion of economic strength during the eurozone crisis, maintaining a solid economy while countries like Greece, Italy, Spain, and Portugal have entered into economic tailspins. By far the most important economy in the European Union, Germany, with its traditional, don't-spend-more-than-you-earn culture, has a strong voice in setting the EU's economic agenda along with France. However, the impact of Brexit and increasing anti-euro sentiment, especially with Italy's current populist government, mean that the eurozone, and Germany, are set to face many challenges ahead.

Engineer This

Germany has a well-deserved reputation as a land of engineers. The global leader in numerous high-tech fields, German companies are hugely successful on the world's export markets, thanks to lots of innovation, sophisticated technology, and quality manufacturing. German cars, machinery, and electrical and electronic equipment are all big sellers—though the fallout from Volkswagen's emissions scandal and the results of President Trump's June 2018 steel and aluminum tariffs remain to be seen. Recent years have also seen a series of bloopers. Three major building projects in Germany—the Elbphilharmonie concert hall in Hamburg; Stuttgart 21, a new train station in Stuttgart; and the new airport in Berlin—ran way over budget and dragged on for years. While Hamburg's concert hall opened in January 2017, Stuttgart's train station is not expected to become operational until 2021. The airport is the most egregious: originally planned to open in 2010, Berlin Brandenburg Airport has suffered delays due to poor construction planning, management, and execution. The projected opening date is now October 2020, though whether it will open at all is in question, and numerous politicians have expressed concern that failures like these will tarnish Germany's reputation as a country of can-do engineers.

Privacy, Please

The Germans are not big fans of Facebook. With good reason: following recent experiences of life in a police state under both the Nazi regime and the East German state, they don't like the idea of anyone collecting personal information about them. Germany has some of the most extensive data privacy laws in the world, with everything from credit card numbers to medical histories strictly protected. Germany was the first EU member state to draft legislation to implement the General Data Protection Regulation

(GDPR), which directs data protection and privacy across the EU and went into effect in May 2018.

To the Left, for Now

By American standards, German politics are distinctly left-leaning. One thing that's important to know is that the Germans don't have a two-party system; rather, they have several important parties, and these must form alliances after elections to pass initiatives. Thus, there's an emphasis on cooperation and deal-making—sometimes (but not always) making for odd bedfellows. In 2005, Germany elected the first female chancellor, center-right Christian Democratic Union party member Angela Merkel, a politician from the former East Germany. In the 2017 elections, many votes went to the smaller parties, and it was the first time since the 1950s that a far-right party, the Alternative for Germany (AfD), won seats in parliament. Forming a "grand coalition" of the Christian Democratic Union/Christian Social Union and the Social Democratic parties was necessary to form a government, with Merkel still at the helm but with her power somewhat weakened.

Going Green

In the early 2000s, Germany began moving away from fossil fuels toward renewable energy sources such as solar and wind, a policy known as *Energiewende*—literally, "energy transition." The transformation is a role model for many environmentalists, and thanks to aggressive government legislation over the past few decades, Germany is a leader in green energy technology (though the fact that prices for consumers have been steadily increasing is of great concern). In 2017, 36% of the electricity produced nationwide came from renewable sources.

WHAT'S WHERE

1 Munich. Beautiful Munich boasts wonderful opera, theater, museums, and churches—and the city's chic residents dress their best to visit them. This city also has lovely outdoor spaces, from parks, beer gardens, and cafés, to the famous Oktoberfest grounds.

2 The Bavarian Alps. Majestic peaks, lush green pastures, and frescoed houses brightened by flowers make for one of Germany's most photogenic regions. Quaint villages like Mittenwald, Garmisch-Partenkirchen, Oberammergau, and Berchtesgaden have preserved their charming historic architecture. Nature is the prime attraction here, with the country's finest hiking and skiing.

3 The Romantic Road. The Romantische Strasse is more than 355 km (220 miles) of soaring castles, medieval villages, *fachwerk* (half-timber) houses, and imposing churches, all set against a pastoral backdrop. Winding its way from Würzburg to Füssen, it features such top destinations as Rothenburg-ob-der-Tauber and Schloss Neuschwanstein, King Ludwig II's fantastical castle.

4 Franconia and the German Danube. Thanks to the centuries-old success of craftsmanship and trade, Franconia is a proud, independent-minded region in northern Bavaria. Franconia is home to historic Nuremberg, the well-preserved medieval jewel-box town of Bamberg, and Bayreuth, where Wagner lived and composed.

5 The Bodensee. The sunniest region in the country, the Bodensee (Lake Constance) itself is the highlight. The region is surrounded by beautiful mountains, and the dense natural surroundings offer an enchanting contrast to the picture-perfect towns and manicured gardens.

6 The Black Forest. Synonymous with cuckoo clocks and primeval woodland that is great for hiking, the Black Forest includes the historic university town of Freiburg—one of the most colorful and hippest student cities in Germany—and proud and elegant Baden-Baden, with its long tradition of spas and casinos.

7 Heidelberg and the Neckar Valley. This medieval town is quintessential Germany, full of cobblestone alleys, half-timber houses, vineyards, castles, wine pubs, and Germany's oldest university.

Oldenburg
Bremen
Hannover
Osnabrück
Braunschweig
Hildesheim
Magdeburg
Bielefeld
Potsdam
BERLIN
Oder
Weser
HARZ MTS
Göttingen
Halle
Leipzig
Elbe
Cottbus
Kassel
Weimar
Erfurt
Jena
Gera
Zwickau
Chemnitz
Dresden
Liberec
Siegen
Fulda
PRAGUE
Wiesbaden
Frankfurt
Mainz
Darmstadt
Würzburg
Bamberg
Bayreuth
Plzen
CZECH
REPUBLIC
Mannheim
Heidelberg
Nuremberg
Rhine
[7]
Heilbronn
Rothenburg-
ob-der-Tauber
Karlsruhe
Regensburg
Deggendorf
Baden-
Baden
Stuttgart
[3]
Ingolstadt
Danube
[4]
[6]
BLACK FOREST
Ulm
Augsburg
B A V A R I A
Passau
Memmingen
Munich
[1]
Inn
Salzburg
[5]
Konstanz
Oberammergau
[2]
Bad Reichenhall
Berchtesgaden
Zürich
Friedrichshafen
Füssen
Garmisch-Partenkirchen
Bodensee
Schloss
Neuschwanstein
BAVARIAN ALPS
SWITZERLAND
Mittenwald
Innsbruck
AUSTRIA
ALPS LIECHT
VADUZ

0   50 mi
0   50 km

WHAT'S WHERE

8 Frankfurt. Nicknamed "Mainhattan" because it is the only German city with appreciable skyscrapers, Frankfurt is Germany's financial center and transportation hub.

9 The Pfalz and Rhine Terrace. Wine reigns supreme here. Bacchanalian festivals pepper the calendar between May and October, and wineries welcome drop-ins for tastings year-round. Three great cathedrals are found in Worms, Speyer, and Mainz.

10 The Rhineland. The region along the mighty Rhine River is one of the most dynamic in Europe. Fascinating cities such as Köln (Cologne), steeped in Roman and medieval history, offer stunning Gothic architecture, such as the Kölner Dom. Visit during Karneval for boisterous celebrations.

11 The Fairy-Tale Road. The Märchenstrasse, stretching 600 km (370 miles) between Hanau and Bremen, is Brothers Grimm country. They nourished their dark and magical imaginations as children in Steinau an der Strasse, a beautiful medieval town in this region of misty woodlands and ancient castles.

12 Hamburg. Hamburg, with its long tradition as a powerful and wealthy Hanseatic port city, is quintessentially elegant. World-class museums of modern art; the wild red-light district along the Reeperbahn; and HafenCity, an environmentally and architecturally avant-garde quarter currently under construction, make Hamburg well worth a visit.

13 Schleswig-Holstein and the Baltic Coast. Off the beaten path, this region is scattered with medieval towns, fishing villages, unspoiled beaches, and summer resorts like Sylt, where Germany's jet set go to get away.

14 Berlin. No trip to Germany is complete without a visit to its capital, Europe's hippest urban destination. Cheap rents drew artists from all over the world to this gritty, creative, and broke city. Cutting-edge art exhibits, stage dramas, musicals, and bands compete for your attention with two cities' worth of world-class museums, three opera houses, eight state theaters, and two zoos.

15 Saxony, Saxony-Anhalt, and Thuringia. The southeast is a secret treasure trove of German high culture. Friendly, vibrant cities like Dresden, Leipzig, Weimar, and Eisenach are linked to Schiller, Goethe, Bach, Luther, and the like.

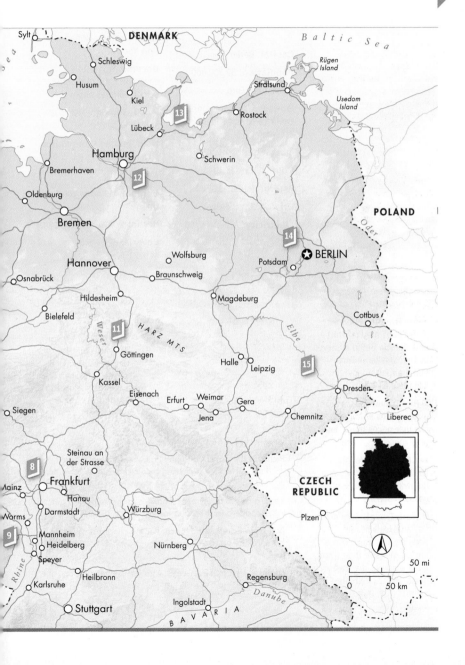

NEED TO KNOW

Berlin

GERMANY

AT A GLANCE
Capital: Berlin

Population: 82,300,000

Currency: Euro

Money: ATMs common; credit cards not widely accepted

Language: German

Country Code: 49

Emergencies: 110

Driving: On the right

Electricity: 220–240v/50 cycles; plugs have two round prongs

Time: Six hours ahead of New York

Documents: Up to 90 days with valid passport; Schengen rules apply

Mobile Phones: GSM (900 and 1800 bands)

Major Mobile Companies: T-Mobil, Vodafone, o2, E-Plus

WEBSITES
Germany: ⊕ www.germany.travel

Berlin: ⊕ www.visitberlin.de

Bavaria: ⊕ www.bavaria.us

GETTING AROUND

✈ **Air Travel:** Germany's major hubs are Frankfurt and Munich. Berlin is served by two smaller international airports, Tegel and Schönefeld.

🚌 **Bus Travel:** Buses cover major routes at much cheaper prices than trains or planes.

🚗 **Car Travel:** Renting a car is easy in any city and highways are top quality, but gas is expensive.

🚆 **Train Travel:** Germany has an excellent rail network, but trains can be more expensive than flying. Book early for the best deals. High-speed InterCity Express (ICE) trains connect major cities.

PLAN YOUR BUDGET

	HOTEL ROOM	MEAL	ATTRACTIONS
Low Budget	€90	€12	Bier & Oktoberfest Museum, €4
Mid Budget	€160	€25	Neuschwanstein and Hohenschwangau Castles admission, €25
High Budget	€220	€80	Berlin's Staatsoper performance, €80

WAYS TO SAVE

Picnic in the park. Germany has wonderful outdoor markets perfect for gathering picnic provisions. In winter, market halls offer indoor alternatives.

Book a rental apartment. Families and groups can get more space and a kitchen for less with a rental.

Buy train tickets in advance. For the cheapest rail fares, book online up to 90 days before travel. ⊕ www.bahn.de

Look for free museum days. Many museums are free one day a week.

PLAN YOUR TIME

Hassle Factor	Low. Flights to Germany are frequent, and it has a fantastic network of trains, buses, and cheap domestic flights.
3 days	Visit one major city, like Berlin or Munich, and venture out of town on a half- or full-day trip.
1 week	Combine two major destinations, visiting Hamburg, Dresden, or Leipzig along with Berlin, or the Bavarian Alps along with Munich. Enjoy a boat cruise along a scenic German river, like the Rhine, the Elbe, or the Mosel.
2 weeks	Pick a region to explore in depth, combining stops in major cities with a long weekend at the Baltic Sea's beaches and islands or a hiking trip through the legendary Black Forest.

WHEN TO GO

High Season: June through August is the most popular and expensive time to visit. In July and August, many Germans take vacation and leave the cities for the beach (in the north) or mountains and lakes (in the south). Flocks of tourists visit in December for Germany's charming Christmas markets.

Low Season: January to March is cold and dark, and locals may be in a sour mood from the seemingly endless string of gray days. Consequently, there are deals on lodging and airfare.

Value Season: September is gorgeous, with temperate weather and saner airfares. Temperatures start to drop by late November. Late April or early May is also a great time to visit, before crowds arrive but when the trees are in bloom and the locals are reveling in the return of spring. However, the weather can be unpredictable and wet.

BIG EVENTS

May: On May Day (May 1), there are street festivals and leftist protests for workers' rights.

June: Musicians perform throughout Berlin during the daylong festival Fête de la Musique. ⊕ www.fetedelamusique.de

September: Oktoberfest, the world's biggest beer festival, actually begins in September. ⊕ www.oktoberfest.de

February: Cologne celebrates Carnival with street parties and parades. ⊕ www.koelnerkarneval.de

READ THIS

■ *Five Germanys I Have Known,* Fritz Stern. Twentieth-century German historical memoir.

■ *Stasiland,* Anna Funder. Personal stories of life under East Germany's secret police.

■ *Germania,* Simon Winder. A satirical account of Germany and its people.

WATCH THIS

■ *The Lives of Others.* A Stasi agent in East Berlin spies on a playwright and his lover.

■ *Wings of Desire.* Angels watch over a divided Berlin.

■ *Cabaret.* An iconic film set in Weimar Germany.

EAT THIS

■ *Currywurst:* sliced sausage drenched in curry powder and ketchup

■ *Schweinshaxe:* Bavarian crispy pork knuckle

■ *Käsespätzle:* Swabian noodles topped with melted cheese and sometimes fried onions

■ *Weisser Spargel:* sweet white asparagus (April/May)

■ *Germknödel:* a dumpling filled with plum sauce and topped with poppy seeds

■ *Stollen:* fruitcake covered in powdered sugar, a favorite at Christmastime

FLAVORS OF GERMANY

Traditional German cuisine fell out of fashion several decades ago, and was replaced by Italian and Mediterranean food, Asian food, and Middle Eastern food. But there's a growing movement to go back to those roots, and even high-class German chefs are rediscovering old classics, from sauerkraut to *Sauerbraten* (traditional German pot roast). Traditional fruits and vegetables, from parsnips and pumpkins to black salsify, sunchoke, cabbage, yellow carrots, and little-known strawberry and apple varietals, are all making a comeback. That said, "German food" is a bit of a misnomer, as traditional cooking varies greatly from region to region. Look for the "typical" dish, wherever you are, to get the best sense of German cooking.

Generally speaking, regions in the south, like Baden-Württemberg and Bavaria, have held onto their culinary traditions more than states in the north. But with a little effort, you can find good German food just about anywhere you go.

Bavaria: White Sausage and Beer (for Breakfast)

In Bavaria, a traditional farmer's *Zweites Frühstück* (second breakfast) found at any beer hall consists of fat white sausages, called *Weisswurst,* made of veal and eaten with sweet mustard, pretzels, and, yes, a big glass of *Helles* or *Weissbier* (light or wheat beer). Other Bavarian specialties include *Leberkäse* (literally, "liver cheese"), a meat loaf of pork and beef that can be eaten sliced on bread, and tastes a lot better than it sounds. *Knödelgerichte,* or noodle dishes, are also popular.

Swabia: The Sausage Salad

Swabia (the area surrounding Stuttgart) is generally thought to have some of the best traditional food in Germany, having held onto its culinary heritage better than other areas. *Schwäbische Wurstsalat* (Swabian sausage salad), a salad of sliced sausage dressed with onions, vinegar, and oil, is a typical dish, as is *Käsespätzle* (Swabian pasta with cheese), a noodlelike dish made from flour, egg, and water topped with cheese. *Linsen mit Spätzle* (lentils and spätzle) could be considered the Swabian national dish: it consists of egg noodles topped with lentils and, often, a sausage.

Franconia: Nürnberger Bratwürste

Perhaps the most beloved of all *Bratwürste* (sausages) in a country that loves sausages is the small, thin sausage from the city of Nuremberg. Grilled over a beech-wood fire, it is served 6 or 12 at a time with horseradish and sauerkraut or potato salad. Fresh marjoram and ground caraway seeds give the pork-based sausage its distinctive flavor.

Hessen: Apfelwein in Frankfurt

Apfelwein (hard apple cider) is a specialty in and around Frankfurt. Look for an *Apfelweinkneipe* (cider bar), where you can spend a pleasant evening sipping this tasty alcoholic drink. Order *Handkäse,* traditional Hessian curdled milk cheese, to go with it. If you order *Handkäse mit Musik* (Handkäse with music), you'll get it with onions. Another winner is *Frankfurter Rippchen,* spare ribs served with sauerkraut.

Rhineland: Horse Meat and Kölsch

In Köln (Cologne), influenced by nearby Belgium and Holland, there's a traditional taste for horse meat, which they use in their local version of the pot roast, *Rheinische Sauerbraten.* Or try the *Kölsche Kaviar*—blood sausage with onions. Wash these dishes down with the local beer, *Kölsch.*

Northwest Germany: Herring with That?

States near the north coast, like Bremen, Hamburg, Westphalia, and Schleswig-Holstein, all have cuisines that are oriented toward the sea. Cod, crab, herring, and flatfish are all common traditional foods. *Labskaus,* a traditional fisherman's dish of choice, is made from corned beef, however. The salty meal comes with accompaniments such as fried egg, herring, pickle, and red beets. For your fix of vegetables, potatoes, cabbage, and rutabagas are all served stewed or pickled. *Rote Grütze,* a traditional dessert, is a berry pudding often served with whipped cream.

Northeast Germany: Currywurst and More

Berlin is known for its *Eisbein* (pork knuckle), *Kasseler* (smoked pork chop), *Bockwurst* (large sausage), and *Boulette* (a kind of hamburger made of beef and pork), but its most famous dish is *Currywurst,* a Berlin-born snack that consists of sausage cut in pieces and covered in ketchup and curry powder, often served with a side of fries. Brandenburg's idyllic Spreewald is famous for its pickled gherkins.

The East: Da, Soljanka

In former GDR states like Saxony, Saxony-Anhalt, and Thuringia, the Soviet influence can be felt in the popularity of traditionally Russian dishes like *Soljanka* (meat soup). *Rotkäppchen* sparkling wines come from Saxony-Anhalt, Germany's northernmost wine-making region (named for the company's bottles with red tops, Rotkäppchen is also the German name for Little Red Riding Hood). Another local treat is *Baumkuchen,* or "tree cake," which is formed by adding layer upon layer of batter on a spit and rotating it over a heat source. When you cut into the cake, it looks like the rings of a tree—hence the name.

The Döner Kebab: It's Fine Anytime

It would be hard to visit Germany without trying this Turkish sandwich, whether for lunch, dinner, or a snack after a night out on the town. Made from some combination of lamb, chicken, pork, or beef roasted on a spit then sliced into pita pockets with lettuce, chopped tomato, yogurt, and spicy sauce, the *döner kebab* is the indisputable king of snack food. An inexpensive alternative to German fare, they're available on almost any city corner.

Seasonal Favorites

Germans are very much attuned to seasonal fruits and vegetables. Traditional German produce like white asparagus, strawberries, plums, cherries, blueberries, and apples are for sale in supermarkets, farmers' markets, and from sidewalk sellers. When in season, these are delicious items to add to your diet and a healthy way to keep your blood sugar up as you set off to explore Germany.

BEERS OF GERMANY

Beer—or "liquid bread," as it was described by medieval monks who wanted to avoid God's anger—is not just a vital element of German cuisine, but of German culture. The stats say Germans are second only to the Czechs when it comes to per capita beer consumption, though they have been losing their thirst recently—from a peak of 146 liters (about 39 gallons) per head in 1980, each German now only manages 101.2 liters (roughly 27 gallons) every year. And yet the range of beers has never been wider.

Reinheitsgebot (Purity Law)

There are more than 1,300 breweries in Germany, offering more than 5,000 types of beer. Thanks to Germany's ancient "Beer Purity Law," or *Reinheitsgebot,* which allowed only three ingredients (water, malt, and hops), they are all very high quality. The water used in German beer also has to meet certain standards—a recent discussion about introducing fracking in certain parts of Germany was roundly criticized by the German Beer Association because the water in the area would become too dirty to use for making beer.

Germany's Major Beer Varieties

Pils: One effect of the Beer Purity Law was that Germany became dominated by one kind of beer: *Pils.* Invented in Bohemia (now the Czech Republic) in 1842, and aided by Bavarian refrigeration techniques, Pils was the first beer to be chilled and stored, thus allowing bottom fermentation, better clarity, and a longer shelf life. Today, the majority of German beers are brewed in the Pils, or Pilsner, style. German Pils tends to have a drier, more bitter taste than what you might be used to, but a trip to Germany is hardly complete without the grand tour along these

lines: Augustiner in Bavaria, Bitburger in the Rhineland, Flensburger in the north.

Helles: *Hell* is German for "light," but when it comes to beer, that refers to the color rather than the alcohol content. *Helles* is a crisp and clear Bavarian pale lager with between 4.5% and 6% alcohol. It was developed in the mid-19th century by a German brewer named Gabriel Sedlmayr, who adopted and adapted some British techniques to create the new beer for his famous Spaten Brewery in Bavaria. Another brewer, Josef Groll, used the same methods to produce one of the first German Pils, Pilsner Urquell. Spaten is still one the best brands for a good Helles, as are Löwenbräu, Weihenstephaner, and Hacker-Pschorr—all classic Bavarian beers.

Dunkelbier: At the other end of the beer rainbow from Helles is dark beer, or *Dunkelbier.* The dark, reddish color is a consequence of the darker malt that is used in the brewing. Despite suspicions aroused by the stronger, maltier taste, Dunkelbier actually contains no more alcohol than Helles. Dunkelbier was common in rural Bavaria in the early 19th century. All the major Bavarian breweries produce a Dunkelbier to complement their Helles.

Bock: Dunkelbier should not be confused with *Bock,* which also has a dark color and a malty taste but is a little stronger. It was first created in the Middle Ages in the northern German town of Einbeck, before it was later adopted by the Bavarian breweries, which had come to regard themselves as the natural home of German beer. In fact, the name Bock comes from the Bavarian interpretation of the word "Einbeck." Bock often has a sweeter flavor, and is traditionally drunk on public holidays. There are also subcategories, like *Eisbock* and *Doppelbock*, which have been refined to make an even stronger beverage.

Kölsch: If you're looking for lighter refreshment, then *Kölsch* is ideal. The traditional beer of Cologne, Kölsch is a mild, carbonated beer that goes down easily. It is usually served in a small, straight glass, called a *Stange*, which is much easier to wrangle than the immense Bavarian *Mass* (liter) glasses. If you're part of a big party, you're likely to get Kölsch served in a *Kranz*, or wreath—a circular wooden rack that holds up to 18 *Stangen*. Kölsch is very specific to Cologne and its immediate environs, so there's little point in asking for it anywhere else. Consequently, the major Kölsch brands are all relatively small; they include Reissdorf, Gaffel, and Früh.

Hefeweizen: Also known as *Weissbier* or *Weizenbier, Hefeweizen* is essentially wheat beer, and it was originally brewed in southern Bavaria. It has a very distinctive taste and cloudy color. It's much stronger than standard Pils or Helles, with an alcohol content of more than 8%. On the other hand, that content is slightly compensated for by the fact that wheat beer can be very filling. For a twist, try the clear variety called *Kristallweizen*, which tastes crisper, and is often served with half a slice of lemon. Hefeweizen is available throughout Germany, and the major Bavarian breweries all brew it as part of their range.

Top Brews by Region

Bavaria: Helles, Dunkelbier, Hefeweizen.

The six most famous brands are also the only ones allowed to be sold at Oktoberfest: Löwenbräu, Augustiner, Paulaner, Hacker-Pschorr, Spaten-Franziskanerbräu, and Hofbräu. Tegernseer Hell is also very good.

Rhineland: Kölsch, Pils.

Apart from Kölsch, which is impossible to avoid, look out for Krombacher and Bitburger.

Eastern Germany: Pils.

Radeberger and Hasseröder are two of the few beers in the region to have survived the fall of communism in former East Germany.

Berlin: Pils.

The most famous brands are Berliner Kindl, Schultheiss, and Berliner Pilsner, which are all worth trying.

Hamburg: Pils.

Astra—with its anchor-heart logo—is a cult Pils that is very much identified with Germany's biggest port city.

Northern Germany: Pils, Bock.

The best brands include Flensburger, Jever, and, of course, Beck's, which comes from the northern city of Bremen.

WINES OF GERMANY

Germany produces some of the finest white wines in the world. Although more and more quality red wine is being produced, the majority of German wines are white due to the northern continental climate. Nearly all wine production in Germany takes place by the River Rhine in the southwest. As a result, a single trip to this lovely and relatively compact wine region can give you a good overview of German wines.

German Wines: Then and Now
A BRIEF HISTORY
The Romans first introduced viticulture to the southernmost area of what is present-day Germany about 2,000 years ago. By the time of Charlemagne, winemaking centered on monasteries. A 19th-century grape blight necessitated a complete reconstitution of German grape stock, grafted with pest-resistant American vines, and formed the basis for today's German wines. With cold winters, a relatively northern climate, and less sun than other wine regions, the Germans have developed a reputation for technical and innovative panache. The result has traditionally been top-quality sweet Rieslings, though Germany has been making excellent dry and off-dry white wines and Rieslings in the past 30 years.

TODAY'S WINE SCENE
For years, German wines were known by their lowest common denominator, the cheap, sweet wine that was exported en masse to the United States, England, and other markets. However, more recently there has been a push to introduce the world to the best of German wines. Exports to the United States, Germany's largest export market, have grown steadily, followed by England, The Netherlands, Sweden, and Russia. Eighty-three percent of its exports are white wines. The export of *Liebfraumilch*, the sugary, low-quality stuff that gave German wine a bad name, has been steadily declining, and now 71% of exports are so-called *Qualitätswein*, or quality wines. This is a more accurate representation of German wine as it exists in Germany.

Germany's Dominant Varietals
WHITES
Müller-Thurgau: Created in the 1880s, this grape is a cross between a Riesling and a Madeleine Royale. Ripening early, it's prone to rot and, as the grape used in most Liebfraumilch, has a less than golden reputation.

Riesling: The most widely planted (and widely famous) of German grapes, Riesling ripens late. A hardy grape, it's ideal for late-harvest wines. High levels of acidity help wines age well. When young, grapes have a crisp, floral character.

Silvaner: This grape is dying out in most places, with the exception of Franconia, where it is traditionally grown. With low acidity and neutral fruit, it can be crossed with other grapes—like Kerner, Grauburgunder (pinot gris), Weissburgunder (pinot blanc), Bacchus, and others—to produce sweet wines.

REDS
Dornfelder: A relatively young varietal. Dornfelder produces wines with a deep color, which distinguishes them from other German reds, which tend to be pale, light, and off-dry.

Spätburgunder (Pinot Noir): This grape is responsible for Germany's full-bodied, fruity wines, and is grown in more southerly vineyards.

Terminology

German wine is a complex topic, even though the wine region is relatively small. Wines are ranked according to the ripeness of the grapes when picked, and instead of harvesting a vineyard all at once, German vineyards are harvested up to five times. The finest wines result from the latest harvests of the season, due to increased sugar content. Under the category of "table wine" fall *Deutscher Tafelwein* (German table wine) and *Landwein* (like the French Vin de Pays). Quality wines are ranked according to when they are harvested. *Kabinett* wines are delicate, light, and fruity. *Spätlese* ("late-harvest" wine) has more-concentrated flavors, sweetness, and body. *Auslese* wines are made from extra-ripe grapes, and are even richer, even sweeter, and even riper. *Beerenauslese* are rare and expensive, made from grapes whose flavor and acid has been enhanced by noble rot. *Eiswein* ("ice" wine) is made of grapes that have been left on the vine to freeze and may be harvested as late as January. They produce a sugary syrup that creates an intense, fruity wine. Finally, *Trockenbeerenauslese* ("dry ice" wine) is made in tiny amounts using grapes that have frozen and shriveled into raisins. These can rank among the world's most expensive wines. Other terms to keep in mind include *Trocken* (dry) and *Halbtrocken* (half-dry, or "off-dry").

Wine Regions

Mosel: The Mosel's steep, mineral-rich hillsides produce excellent Rieslings. With flowery rather than fruity top-quality wines, the Mosel is a must-stop for any wine lover. The terraced hillsides rising up along the banks of the River Mosel are as pleasing to the eye as the light-bodied Rieslings are to the palate.

Nahe: Agreeable and uncomplicated—this describes the wines made from Müller-Thurgau and Silvaner grapes of the Nahe region. The earth here is rich not just in grapes, but also in semiprecious stones and minerals, and you might just detect a hint of pineapple in your wine's bouquet.

Rheinhessen: The largest wine-making region of Germany, Rheinhessen's once grand reputation was tarnished in the mid-20th century, when large, substandard vineyards were cultivated and low-quality wine produced. Nonetheless, there's still plenty of the very good stuff to be found. Stick to the red sandy slopes over the river for the most full-bodied of Germany's Rieslings.

Rheingau: The dark, slaty soil of the Rheingau is particularly suited to the German Riesling, which is the major wine produced in this lovely hill country along the River Rhine. Spicy wines come from the hillsides, while the valley yields wines with body, richness, and concentration.

Pfalz: The second-largest wine region in Germany, the Pfalz stretches north from the French border. Mild winters and warm summers make for some of Germany's best pinot noirs and most opulent Rieslings. Wine is served here in a special dimpled glass called the *Dubbeglas*.

Baden: Farther to the south, Baden's warmer climate helps produce ripe, full-bodied wines that may not be well known but certainly taste delicious. The best ones, both red and white, come from Kaiserstuhl-Tuniberg, between Freiburg and the Rhine. But be forewarned: the best things in life do tend to cost a little extra.

GREAT ITINERARIES

Each of Germany's 16 states offers something different: tantalizing gastronomic adventures, medieval churches standing side by side with glassy high-rises, and local traditions kept alive despite being one of the most advanced economies in the world. Enjoy the lush countryside as you travel by train or car. *Below are three suggested itineraries—pick one or two, or combine elements from each.*

GERMANY FOR FIRST TIMERS, 10-DAY ITINERARY

See the best Germany has to offer: stunning landscapes, charming medieval towns, and cosmopolitan cities. Make the most of your trip by taking the train between stops. You'll enjoy views of rolling green countryside, towering wind turbines, and fairy-tale villages as you zip across the country. You'll also skip the hassle of finding parking and paying for high-cost gasoline.

Fly in: Munich Airport (MUC), Munich

Fly out: Tegel Airport (TXL), Berlin

Days 1 and 2: Munich

Fly into **Munich,** where you'll spend the first three nights. Get your bearings in Bavaria's capital city by standing in the center of the **Marienplatz** and watching the charming, twirling figures of the Glockenspiel in the tower of the **Rathaus** (Town Hall). Visit one of many world-class museums to see masterpieces in art, science, and technology, then wander through the sprawling **Englischer Garten** (English Garden). Throughout the city, you can sit elbow to elbow with genial Bavarians at long tables in sunny beer gardens, savoring a liter of cold Hefeweizen and a salty pretzel.

Day 3: Neuschwanstein

From Munich it's an easy day trip to Germany's fairy-tale castle, **Schloss Neuschwanstein,** in Schwangau. Though the 19th-century castle's fantastic silhouette has made it famous, this creation is more opera set than piece of history—the interior was never completed. A tour reveals why the king of Bavaria who built it earned the nickname "Mad" King Ludwig. Tickets come with a specific admission time and should be booked in advance by phone or online. You must pick them up from the ticket center in Hohenschwangau at least an hour before the tour starts—and before making your way up to the castle. Tours last about half an hour. Across the narrow wooded valley from Schloss Neuschwanstein is the ancient castle of the Bavarian Wittelsbach dynasty, **Schloss Hohenschwangau,** also open for tours. Return to Munich city center in the evening and treat yourself to a hearty meal of *Schweinshaxe* (roasted pork knuckle) and potatoes.

Logistics: Train from Munich's Hauptbahnhof to Füssen, then 15-minute bus ride to Hohenschwangau. From there it's a 30-minute walk to the castle; 4 hours and 30 minutes round-trip.

Day 4: Freiburg

Get an early start to arrive by late morning in **Freiburg,** one of Germany's most beautiful historic towns. Damaged during WWII, it has been rebuilt to preserve its delightful medieval character. Residents love to boast that Freiburg is the country's sunniest city. Its **cathedral** is a masterpiece of Gothic architecture, built over three centuries. Explore on foot, or by bike, and look out for the *Bächle,* or little brooks, that run for kilometers through this bustling university town. Check in

at the **Colombi**, the town's most luxurious hotel, for a stay with views of the old city.

Logistics: Train from Munich's Hauptbahnhof to Freiburg im Breisgau; 4 hours.

Day 5: The Black Forest

Freiburg puts you at the perfect point from which to explore the spruce-covered, low-lying mountains of the **Black Forest.** For a romp around the great outdoors, set out for **Titisee**, a placid glacial lake, passing deep gorges along the way. If your idea of relaxation includes getting off your feet, head toward the northern Black Forest. You can treat yourself to a spa day in tony **Baden-Baden**, relaxing in curative waters. In the evening return to Freiburg and rest up before the next day's train ride to the north.

Logistics: Train from Freiburg im Breisgau to Titisee or Baden-Baden; 1 hour and 20 minutes round-trip.

Days 6 and 7: Hamburg

Hamburg is one of Germany's wealthiest cities and the country's largest port. If you're in Hamburg on Sunday, wake up early to visit the open-air **Fischmarkt** (fish market) and see vendors set up their fresh wares while locals dance to live music as the sun comes up. Then, take a cruise through the city's canals with views of the Speicherstadt historic warehouse district,

a UNESCO World Heritage site. Exploring the harbor you'll see the enormous ocean liners that stop in Hamburg before crossing the Atlantic. The city offers exclusive shopping along the **Jungfernstieg**, a lakeside promenade. Try to get tickets for an evening concert at the Elbphilharmonie. Spend the night at the **Adina Apartment Hotel Hamburg Michel** and enjoy the amenities of your own apartment space.

Logistics: Train from Freiburg im Breisgau to Hamburg Hauptbahnhof; 5 hours and 45 minutes.

Days 8 and 9: Berlin

Start the day at two of the city's most iconic symbols, the **Reichstag** and the nearby **Brandenburg Gate** (note that if you want to visit the Reichstag dome, you need to register in advance). Head south to experience the moving silence in the maze of the Holocaust memorial, the **Denkmal für die Ermordeten Juden Europas.** Stop by Potsdamer Platz, which embodies the city's renaissance: once a no-go zone between East and West Berlin, the square now teems with glittering towers of optimism. A bit farther south is the **Topographie des Terrors,** an exhibition telling the story of the Nazi takeover in harrowing detail, built where the Gestapo headquarters used to be. Head back to Potsdamer

Platz, where you can hop on the double-decker public Bus 200, which travels down the grand, tree-lined boulevard Unter der Linden to the colossal **Berliner Dom** cathedral. You can then devote the entire afternoon to the stupendous collections of the **Museumsinsel**. The beautifully restored Neues Museum and the majestic Pergamon are standouts, as is the excellently curated Deutsches Historisches Museum (German History Museum).

Spend the second day exploring the young side of Berlin, in Kreuzberg. This is a good time to rent a bicycle. Browse vintage clothing stores and indie boutiques and have lunch at Markthalle Neun, home to a bevy of excellent local food stalls, then head south to **Tempelhofer Park,** the historic airfield-turned-park. Exit the park to Neukölln, a working-class neighborhood that has emerged as an epicenter of cool. For lunch, there are many Middle Eastern eateries as well as the popular Italian restaurant **Lavanderia Vecchia**. Continue east and cross the Spree over the redbrick Oberbaum Bridge, which served as a border crossing between East and West Berlin. On the other side of the river is Friedrichshain and the famous **East Side Gallery,** where international artists covered remnants of the Berlin Wall with colorful murals.

Logistics: Train from Hamburg Hauptbahnhof to Berlin Hauptbahnhof; 1 hour and 40 minutes.

Day 10: Potsdam
If you can tear yourself away from Berlin, take a day trip out to **Potsdam** and tour the opulent palaces and manicured gardens of **Sanssouci Park**. **Schloss Sanssouci,** a palace constructed to resemble Versailles, was used as a summer getaway for Frederick the Great and is a must-see (buy tickets in

advance if you can). Return to Berlin in the evening to explore more of its distinct neighborhoods, like Turkish Kreuzberg or lively Prenzlauer Berg. The next day, fly home from Berlin.

Logistics: Train from Berlin Hauptbahnhof to Potsdam Hauptbahnhof; 1 hour and 20 minutes round-trip.

GERMANY'S NORTHERN PORT CITIES AND BEACH TOWNS, 8-DAY ITINERARY

The North Sea and Baltic Sea lap the north coast of Germany, feeding a sprawling network of waterways that placed the country at the heart of historically important trade routes. Take in brickwork warehouses in old port cities, soak up the sun on sandy white beaches, float in Brandenburg's serene lakes, and cruise down the Rhine as you vacation like a local.

Fly in: Cologne Bonn Airport (CGN), Cologne

Fly out: Tegel Airport (TXL), Berlin

Day 1: Köln (Cologne)
Fly into **Cologne** and spend your first day in the heart of the Rhineland enjoying the city. Marvel at the **Kölner Dom** (cathedral), a UNESCO World Heritage site and Gothic masterpiece. Take a boat cruise down the River Rhine past the picturesque Altstadt (Old Town), then celebrate your first night in Germany by sipping a Kölsch beer at one of the city's sleek bars before getting some well-earned sleep.

Days 2 and 3: Hamburg
Hamburg is home to more canals than Venice, and is dotted with cafés and bars overlooking the accompanying locks and bridges. Start in front of the **Rathaus**

(Town Hall), a lavish structure built with the city's riches from its history as one of the most important trading ports in Europe. Stop to eat the traditional seafarer's favorite, *Labskaus,* a dish made of minced meat and served with a fried egg on top. Then head to the Speicherstadt, a UNESCO World Heritage site, to see traditional redbrick warehouses, and make a stop at **Miniatur Wunderland,** the world's biggest model railway—it's a must-see, even if you're not a train enthusiast. Spend two nights in the trendy neighborhood of Sternschanze.

Logistics: Train from Cologne to Hamburg Hauptbahnhof; 4 hours.

Day 4: Lübeck

Hop on an intercity train the next morning for a quick ride to **Lübeck.** Explore on foot through medieval alleyways in this 12th-century city founded by King Henry the Lion. Check out **Holstentor,** the western gate of the old city center, before making your way into the Altstadt, which boasts more 13th- to 15th-century buildings than the rest of Germany's major northern cities combined. Dine on large servings of seafood specialties from oak tables at **Schiffergesellschaft,** an old mariners' club. Stay the night in Lübeck.

Logistics: Train from Hamburg Hauptbahnhof to Lübeck; 35 minutes.

Days 5 and 6: Rostock and Warnemünde

Head east toward the city of **Rostock,** the former East German state's biggest shipbuilding center and your base for finding the perfect stretch of sandy white beach on the Baltic Sea. From there it's 9 miles north to the resort town of **Warnemünde,** a popular destination for German tourists. If you're there on the weekend, stop by the **Skybar** at night to watch ship lights under the stars. Stay in a 19th-century mansion in Rostock's Old Town, the **Pental Hotel.**

Logistics: Train from Lübeck to Rostock Hauptbahnhof; 1 hour and 50 minutes.

Days 7 and 8: Berlin

Spend your last days in Germany's capital, **Berlin,** a city with a fascinating history, particularly its recent division and shifting neighborhood dynamics after the fall of the **Berlin Wall** in 1989. Berlin is notorious for its late-night culture. You can even get some touring in in the evening: Sir Norman Foster's glass dome on the **Reichstag** (parliament building), the **TV tower** at Alexanderplatz, and the **Checkpoint Charlie Museum** don't close until 10 pm or later. Grab a beer and sit by the side of the **Spree** river, which winds through the middle of the city, before venturing out to the best nightlife in hip neighborhoods like Kreuzberg and Friedrichshain. Escape from the urban center the next morning to relax at one of the many lakes surrounding the city, such as **Wannsee.** Bring a picnic, rent a paddleboat, and swim in the cool, rejuvenating waters. Fly home the next day.

Logistics: Train from Rostock Hauptbahnhof to Berlin Hauptbahnhof; 2 hours and 40 minutes.

CASTLES IN WINE COUNTRY, 8-DAY ITINERARY

While frothy beers come to mind when you think of Germany, the country also produces a range of outstanding wines. It's best known for Riesling, but take a drive through the winding countryside past ancient fortresses and you'll get a taste of what German vineyards have to offer along with some of its history.

Fly in: Cologne Bonn Airport (CGN), Cologne

Fly out: Munich Airport (MUC), Munich

Day 1: Koblenz
Pick up a rental car in Cologne and start your tour in **Koblenz,** at the confluence of the Rhine and Mosel rivers. Once you have arrived in the historic downtown area, head straight for the charming little **Hotel Zum weissen Schwanen,** a half-timber inn and mill since 1693. Explore the city on the west bank of the **Rhine River** and then visit Europe's biggest fortress, the impressive **Festung Ehrenbreitstein** on the opposite riverbank.

Logistics: 90 km (60 miles); 1 hour and 10 minutes by car.

Day 2: Koblenz and Surrounding Castles
Get up early and spend the day driving along the most spectacular and historic section of "Vater Rhein." Stay on the left riverbank and you'll pass many mysterious landmarks on the way, including the **Loreley rock,** a 430-foot slate cliff named after the beautiful siren who lured sailors to their deaths with her song. Stay the night at **St. Goar** or **St. Goarshausen,** both lovely river villages.

Logistics: 35 km (22 miles); 40 minutes by car.

Day 3: Eltville and the Eberbach Monastery
The former Cistercian monastery **Kloster Eberbach** in **Eltville** is one of Europe's best-preserved medieval cloisters. Parts of the film *The Name of the Rose,* based on Umberto Eco's novel and starring Sean Connery, were filmed here. Spend the night at the historic wine estate **Schloss Reinhartshausen** and sample the fantastic wines of the region.

Logistics: 70 km (45 miles), 1 hour to Eltville, 15 minutes more to monastery by car.

Day 4: Heidelberg
On Day 4, leave early so you can spend a full day in **Heidelberg.** No other city symbolizes the German spirit and history better than this meticulously restored, historic town. Don't miss the impressive **Schloss Heidelberg,** one of Europe's greatest Gothic-Renaissance fortresses. Then head for the **Romantik Hotel zum Ritter St. Georg,** a charming 16th-century inn with a great traditional German restaurant.

Logistics: 110 km (70 miles); 1 hour and 15 minutes by car.

Days 5 and 6: The Burgenstrasse and the Neckar Valley

Head to the quaint little villages in the **Neckar Valley** just east of Heidelberg for superb food and wine. The predominant grapes here are Riesling (white) and Spätburgunder (red). Try to sample wines from small, private wineries—they tend to have higher-quality offerings. Sightseeing is equally stunning, with a string of castles and ruins along the famous **Burgenstrasse** (Castle Road). Since you have two days for this area, take your time and head to Eberbach and its romantic **Schloss Zwingenberg**, tucked away in the deep forest a 15-minute drive outside the village. In the afternoon, continue on to **Burg Hornberg** at Neckarzimmern, the home to the legendary German knight Götz von Berlichingen. Stay the night here, in the former castle stables.

The next morning, continue on another 20 minutes to **Bad Wimpfen**, the most charming valley town at the confluence of the Neckar and Jagst rivers. Spend half a day in the historic city center and tour the **Staufer Pfalz** (royal palace). Soaring high above the city, the palace was built in 1182, and was a popular retreat for the emperor Barbarossa.

Logistics: 60 km (40 miles); car via the B-37 to Eberbach; 1 hour to Neckarzimmern; 15 km (10 miles), 20 minutes to Bad Wimpfen.

Days 7 and 8: German Wine Route

Devote your last day to the **German Wine Route**, which winds its way through some of the most pleasant landscapes in Germany: the gentle slopes and vineyards of the Pfalz. The starting point for the route is **Bad Dürkheim**, a spa town and proud home of the world's largest wine cask, which holds 1.7 million liters (450,000 gallons). You can enjoy wine with lunch in the many Weinstuben here or wait until you reach **Neustadt** farther south, which is Germany's largest wine-making community. If time permits, try to visit **Burg Trifels** in the afternoon. Near Annweiler, the castle is a magnificent Hohenzollern residence, perched dramatically on three sandstone cliffs, and makes for a great photo op. Take it easy in the evening to prepare for the next day's drive to Munich and flight home.

Logistics: Car via A61 and A6 to Neustadt; 75 km (50 miles), 1 hour to Bad Dürkheim, then 20 km (12 miles), 20 minutes to Neustadt, then 40 km (25 miles), 40 minutes to Burg Trifels; from there it's a 4-hour drive to Munich.

WORLD WAR II SITES

After Adolf Hitler rose to power, he led the country into war in 1939 and perpetrated the darkest crimes against humanity. Nazi Germany systematically murdered 6 million Jews and millions of others deemed undesirable, including Roma and Sinti people, the disabled, and homosexuals. You can visit sites around the country that document and provide perspective on the extent of the horror.

Topography of Terror. This documentation center in Berlin takes a deep look at the political circumstances that led to the rise of the Nazi Party and the terror tactics they used. It stands on the former site of the headquarters for state security groups such as the Gestapo and the SS.

Obersalzburg. Upon his election, Hitler set about turning Obersalzburg into the southern headquarters for the Nazi party and a retreat for its elite. Located in the Bavarian Alps, the compound included luxurious homes for party officials. Today you can walk through the extensive bunker system while learning about the Nazis' takeover of the area.

Kehlsteinhaus. Not far from Obersalzburg you'll find the Kehlsteinhaus, Hitler's private home. Designed as a 50th birthday gift for Hitler by the Nazi party, the house is also known as *Adlerhorst* (Eagle's Nest). It's perched on a cliff, seemingly at the top of the world. The house's precarious location probably saved it from British bombing raids.

Bebelplatz. The Nazis organized mass burnings of books they considered offensive, including one in May 1933 at Bebelplatz in Berlin. Today a glass panel in the square looks down onto an underground room filled with empty shelves. A plaque also memorializes the event with the haunting words of the German poet Heinrich Heine, who wrote over one hundred years earlier that those who burn books will eventually burn people.

Nazi Party Rally Grounds. Masters of propaganda, the Nazis staged colossal rallies intended to impress the German people. Hitler considered Nuremberg so quintessentially German he developed an enormous complex here to host massive parades, military exercises, and major assemblies of the Nazi party. The Congress Hall, meant to outshine Rome's Colosseum, is the largest remaining building from the Nazi era. It houses a **Documentation Center** that explores the Nazis' tyranny.

Nürnberg Trials Memorial. War crimes trials took place here between November 1945 and October 1946. In this courthouse Nazi officials stood before an international military tribunal to answer for their crimes. The Allied victors chose Nuremberg on purpose—it's the place Germany's first anti-Semitic laws passed, decreeing the boycott of Jewish businesses.

KZ-Gedenkstätte Dachau. This is the memorial and site of the former notorious death camp. Hitler created Dachau soon after taking power, and it became the model for all other camps. Tens of thousands of prisoners died here. Today you'll see a few remaining cell blocks and the crematorium, along with shrines and memorials to the dead.

Bergen-Belsen. This is the concentration camp where Anne Frank perished along with more than 52,000 others. A meadow is all that remains of the camp, but it is still a chilling place to visit. The documentation center exhibits photos of the prisoners and interviews with survivors.

Other concentration camps include **Buchenwald, Sachsenhausen,** and **Dora-Mittelbau.**

MUNICH

WELCOME TO MUNICH

TOP REASONS TO GO

★ **Deutsches Museum:** The museum has an impressive collection of science and technology exhibits, and its location on the River Isar is perfect for a relaxing afternoon stroll.

★ **Englischer Garten:** With expansive greens, beautiful lakes, and beer gardens, the English Garden is a great place for a bike ride or a long walk.

★ **Gärtnerplatz:** Gärtnerplatz and the adjoining Glockenbachviertel are the hip 'hoods of the moment, with trendy bars, restaurants, cafés, and shops.

★ **Marienplatz:** In the heart of Munich everyone passes through this pretty medieval square at the center of everything. Be sure to take in the Glockenspiel's turning knights and musicians on the facade of the Rathaus at midday.

★ **Viktualienmarkt:** Experience farmers' market–style shopping, where there's fresh produce, finger food, and a beer garden. Dating back to 1823, this market should not be missed.

Munich (*München* in German) is the proud capital of the state of Bavaria.

1 Altstadt. Altstadt (Old Town) and its surrounding streets is a hub for locals and tourists alike.

2 Lehel. East of Marienplatz, down toward the River Isar, Lehel gently spreads out across the river.

3 Ludwigsvorstadt and Isarvorstadt. These neighborhoods south and west of Altstadt encompass several smaller quarters and are filled with cafés, bars, restaurants, and nightclubs.

4 Schwabing and Maxvorstadt. Maxvorstadt marks the northern boundary of Innenstadt (City Center). Schwabing starts north of the Victory Arch, and the Englischer Garten extends from Schwabing back down into the northeast part of Altstadt.

5 Au and Haidhausen. Across the Isar are fashionable Au and Haidhausen, conveniently located residential neighborhoods.

6 Outside Innenstadt. The western part of Munich, outside of the Innenstadt, is Nymphenburg, dominated by Nymphenburg Castle and its glorious grounds.

MUNICH'S BEER GARDENS

Take a bit of sunshine, a handful of picnic tables, and a few of the finest beers around, and you have yourself a *Biergarten* (beer garden). There are beer gardens throughout Germany, and many imitations across the world, but the most traditional, and the best, are still found in and around Munich. The elixir that transforms the traditional Munich beer garden into something special is the unbeatable atmosphere.

Beer gardens formed out of necessity. Brewers in the 18th and 19th centuries struggled to keep beer cool to prevent it from spoiling in warm weather. As early as 1724, Munich brewers dug cellars and began to store beer next to the shady shores of the Isar River. Local residents promptly took along their beer glasses for a cool drink and before long the odd table and bench appeared, and the beer-garden tradition was born.

(above and lower right) It's easy to make friends in the convivial atmosphere of a beer garden. (upper right) The Englischer Garten's Chinese Tower is one of the most famous beer gardens in Munich.

BIERGARTEN ETIQUETTE

Often, a beer garden is separated between where guests can bring food and where they must buy it. Simply ask to avoid confusion, or look for tablecloths—generally these are table-service only. The basis of a beer garden *Brotzeit* is delicious black bread, Obatzda, sausage, gherkin, and radish. As tradition dictates, remember to also order "Ein Mass Bier, bitte!" (A liter of beer, please!).

MUNICH'S BEST BEER GARDENS

AUGUSTINER KELLER BIERGARTEN

This is perhaps the most popular beer garden in Munich and certainly one of the largest. Located in Maxvorstadt, it is part of the **Augustiner Keller** restaurant, a few hundred yards from Hackerbrücke S-bahn station, or five minutes from the Hauptbahnhof. The main garden is separated in half between where you can bring your own food and where you buy food from the beer garden. The leaves of countless horse-chestnut trees provide a canopy covering, which adds to the dreamy atmosphere.

HOFBRÄUKELLER AM WIENER PLATZ

Some of the best beer gardens are found away from the City Center. This one in Haidhausen is a 15-minute walk (or take Tram No. 19 from the Hauptbahnhof) over the Isar River, past the Maximilianeum, to Wiener Platz, a delightful square well worth visiting. The beer garden attracts Münchners, as well as groups of British, Australian, and American expats. The staple beer-garden chicken, fries, roast pork, and spare ribs are better here than most.

KÖNIGLICHER HIRSCHGARTEN

With seating for 8,000, this is the biggest and most family-friendly beer garden in Munich. In a former royal hunting area outside the City Center (in Nymphenburg), it takes a little time and effort

to reach. Your best bet is to take the S-bahn, or rent a bike and cycle there. The rewards are clear: surrounded by trees and green parkland, the tables and benches seem to go on forever. The food and beer are good and there is even a small deer sanctuary, lending the "Deer Park" its name.

PARK CAFÉ

This is where trendsetters head for a more modern and sunny—there isn't as much shade here—take on the traditional beer garden. Set in Maxvorstadt in Munich's old botanical garden, five minutes from the Hauptbahnhof, this medium-size beer garden regularly has live bands on Friday and Saturday evenings, and live jazz often plays during Sunday-morning family breakfasts. It also has a good selection of cakes and a hip indoor bar.

SEEHAUS IM ENGLISCHEN GARTEN

Within Munich's very own oasis, the **Englischer Garten,** it was an inspired decision to build this beer garden next to a boating lake. A leisurely stroll through the garden to the Seehaus takes about an hour, but go early because it's popular after 11:30. Lots of people visit the Englischer Garten in Schwabing to play soccer and other sports, and if you want to join in you might choose to pass on the roast dinner and instead snack on a *Brezn* (pretzel), Obatzda, and salad.

Updated by Jennifer Ceaser

Known today as the city of laptops and Lederhosen, modern Munich is a cosmopolitan playground that nevertheless represents what the rest of the world incorrectly sees as "typically German": world-famous Oktoberfest, traditional *Lederhosen* (leather pants), busty Bavarian waitresses in *Dirndls* (traditional dresses), beer steins, and sausages.

Munich's cleanliness, safety, and Mediterranean pace give it a slightly rustic feel. The broad sidewalks, fashionable boutiques and eateries, views of the Alps, a sizable river running through town, and a huge green park make Munich one of Germany's most visited cities. When the first rays of spring sun begin warming the air, follow the locals to their beloved beer gardens, shaded by massive chestnut trees.

The number of electronics and computer firms—Siemens, Microsoft, and SAP, for starters—makes Munich a sort of mini–Silicon Valley of Germany, but for all its business drive, this is still a city with roots in the 12th century, when it began as a market town on the "salt road" between mighty Salzburg and Augsburg.

That Munich was the birthplace of the Nazi movement is a difficult truth that those living here continue to grapple with. To distance the city from its Nazi past, city leaders looked to Munich's long pre-Nazi history to highlight what they decreed was the real Munich: a city of great architecture, high art, and fine music. Many of the Altstadt's architectural gems were rebuilt postwar, including the lavish Cuvilliés-Theater, the Altes Rathaus, and the Frauenkirche.

The city's appreciation of the arts began under the kings and dukes of the Wittelsbach dynasty, which ruled Bavaria for eight centuries, until 1918. The Wittelsbach legacy is alive and well in many of the city's museums, which include the Alte Pinakothek and Neue Pinakothek, the Opera House, the philharmonic, and, of course, the Residenz, the city's royal palace. Any walk in the City Center will take you past ravishing baroque decoration and grand 19th-century neoclassical architecture.

PLANNING

WHEN TO GO

It's nicer to walk through the Englischer Garten when the weather's fine in summer. A few postsummer sunny days are usual, but the Oktoberfest is also an indication that fall is here, and the short march to winter has arrived. There are world-class museums and good restaurants to keep you entertained year-round, though, and theater and opera fans will especially enjoy winter, when the tour buses and the camera-toting crowds are gone.

FESTIVALS

Munich comes alive during Fasching, Germany's Mardi Gras, the week before Ash Wednesday in the pre-Easter season. The festival of festivals, Oktoberfest, takes place from the end of September to early October.

GETTING HERE AND AROUND

Munich's cream-color taxis are numerous. Hail them in the street, find them at a taxi stand, download their app, locate the nearest call box online, or phone the call center for one. Rates start at €3.70. Expect to pay around €12 for a 5-km (3-mile) trip within the city. There's a €0.60 charge for each piece of non–hand luggage and an additional charge of €1.20 if you call to order a cab.

AIR TRAVEL

Munich's International Airport is 35 km (22 miles) northeast of the City Center and has excellent air service from all corners of the world. An excellent train service links the airport with downtown. The S-1 and S-8 lines operate from a terminal directly beneath the airport's arrival and departure halls. Trains of both S-bahn lines leave at 20-minute intervals, and the journey takes around 45 minutes. Easiest is to buy a *Tageskarte* (day card) for the *Gesamtnetz* (whole network), costing €13, which allows you to travel anywhere on the system until 6 am the next morning. A one-way bus trip costs around €10.50 and takes about 45 minutes to the City Center. A taxi from the airport costs around €70. During rush hours (7–10 am and 4–7 pm), allow up to an hour of driving time. If you're driving to the city yourself, take the A-9 and follow the signs for "München Stadtmitte" (downtown). If you're driving to the airport from the City Center, head north through Schwabing, join the A-9 autobahn at the Frankfurter Ring intersection, and follow the signs for the "Flughafen" (airport).

Contacts Flughafen München. ✉ *Flughafen München 2* ☎ *089/97500* ⊕ *www.munich-airport.de/en* Ⓜ *Flughafen.*

BUS TRAVEL

The location of Munich's 2009 Central Bus Terminal (ZOB) means that many excursions and longer trips are now centralized in this futuristic hub five minutes from the main train station. As well as numerous shops and banks, it has travel firms offering bus tickets and destination advice.

Touring Eurolines buses arrive at and depart from the ZOB. Check their website for trips to Neuschwanstein and the Romantic Road.

DID YOU KNOW?

You can get an excellent panoramic view of Munich from the tower in Peter-skirche (Church of St. Peter). The 299-step climb up the tower and the viewing area can be crowded, but it only costs €3, and the views of Neues Rathaus and Frauen-kirche (Church of Our Lady), with its onion-dome cupolas, are fantastic.

Contacts Central Bus Station Munich (*ZOB*). ✉ *Arnulfstr. 21, Ludwigs-vorstadt* ⊕ *www.muenchen-zob.de/en* Ⓜ *Hackerbrücke.* **Touring Eurolines.** ✉ *DTG-Ticket-Center München (ZOB), Hackerbrücke 4, Ludwigsvorstadt* ☎ *089/5458–7000* ⊕ *www.eurolines.de/en/home* Ⓜ *Hackerbrücke.*

CAR TRAVEL

If you're driving to Munich from the north (Nuremberg or Frankfurt), leave the autobahn at the Schwabing exit. From Stuttgart and the west, the autobahn ends at Obermenzing, one of Munich's most westerly suburbs. The autobahns from Salzburg and the east, Garmisch and the south, and Lindau and the southwest all join the Mittlerer Ring (city beltway). When leaving any autobahn, follow the signs reading "Stadtmitte" for downtown Munich.

PUBLIC TRANSIT TRAVEL

Munich has one of the most efficient and comprehensive public transportation systems in Europe, consisting of the U-bahn (subway), the S-bahn (suburban railway), the Strassenbahn (streetcar, also called "Tram"), and buses. Marienplatz forms the heart of the U-bahn and S-bahn network, which operates regularly from around 5 am to 1 am (intermittently in the very early morning, so check times if you're expecting a long night or early start). The main MVV service counter under Marienplatz sells tickets and gives out information, also in English. The website ⊕ *www.mvv-muenchen.de* has excellent and extensive transportation information, also in English.

A basic *Einzelfahrkarte* (one-way ticket) costs under €2 for a journey of up to four stops (a maximum of two of them using U- or S-bahn), and under €3 for a longer ride in the inner zone. If you're taking a number of trips around the city, save money by buying a *Streifenkarte,* or multiple 10-strip ticket. On a journey of up to four stops validate one stripe, for the inner zone validate two stripes. If you plan to do several trips during one day, buy a *Tageskarte* (day card), which allows you to travel anywhere until 6 am the next morning. For a group of up to five there is a Tageskarte for the inner zone and one for all zones. There is also a three-day card for a single person and one for two people. See the MVV website for current prices and options. All tickets must be validated at one of the blue time-stamping machines at the station, or on buses and trams as soon as you board (don't wait till you've found a seat; if an inspector's around you'll get fined €60 that must be paid on the spot, and they don't care whether you're a tourist or a local). Spot checks for validated tickets are common. All tickets are sold at the blue dispensers at U- and S-bahn stations and at some bus and streetcar stops. Bus drivers have only single tickets (the most expensive kind). ■TIP→ **Holders of a EurailPass, a Youth Pass, or an Inter-Rail card can travel free on all suburban railway trains (S-bahn) and regional trains.** Be forewarned: if caught on a U-bahn, tram, or bus without a normal public-transport ticket, you will be fined €60, with no exceptions.

Contacts Munich Transport Corporation (*MVG*). ✉ *Hauptbahnhof (Central Station), Bahnhofpl. 1–3, Ludwigsvorstadt* ✛ *Underground in mezzanine of U- and S-bahn by exit to U1/U2* ☎ *0800/3442–26600 toll-free throughout Germany* ⊕ *www.mvg.de/en* Ⓜ *Hauptbahnhof.*

Munich Public Transit System

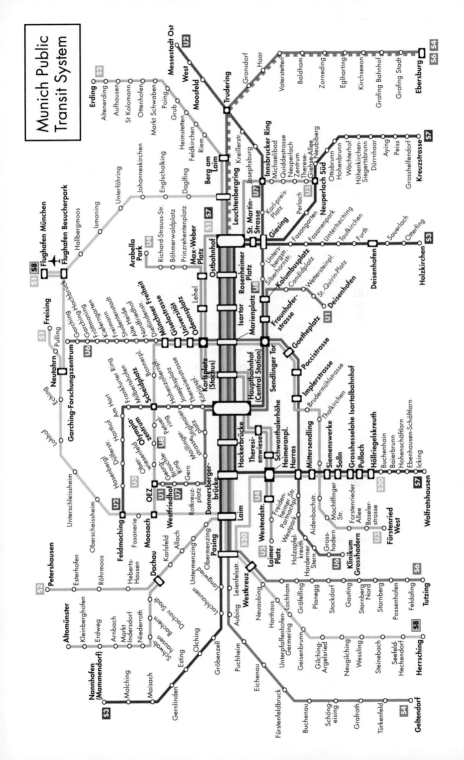

TAXI TRAVEL

Munich's cream-color taxis are numerous. Hail them in the street, find them at a taxi stand, download their app, locate the nearest call box online, or phone the call center for one. Rates start at €3.70. Expect to pay around €12 for a 5-km (3-mile) trip within the city. There's a €0.60 charge for each piece of non–hand luggage and an additional charge of €1.20 if you call to order a cab. Uber is available in Munich, however it is required that they are licensed livery drivers and that they use licenced livery cars, not private vehicles. Generally, the price for a ride tends to be the same as, or sometimes more than, the cost of a taxi.

Contacts Taxi München. ☏ *089/21610, 089/21610* ⊕ *www.taxi-muenchen. com.*

TRAIN TRAVEL

All long-distance rail services arrive at and depart from the Hauptbahnhof; trains to and from some destinations in Bavaria use the adjoining Starnberger Bahnhof, which is under the same roof. The high-speed InterCity Express (ICE) trains connect Munich, Nuremberg, Stuttgart, Frankfurt, Würzburg, Hamburg, and Berlin. Regensburg can be reached from Munich on Regio trains. You can purchase tickets by credit card at vending machines.

Contacts Deutsche Bahn. ✉ *Reisezentrum München Hauptbahnhof, Bahnhofpl. 2, Ludwigsvorstadt* ☏ *180/699–6633* ⊕ *www.bahn.de/p_en/view/index.shtml* Ⓜ *Hauptbahnhof.* **EurAide.** ✉ *Reisezentrum, Bahnhofpl. 2, Counter 1, Ludwigsvorstadt* ⊕ *www.euraide.com* Ⓜ *Hauptbahnhof.*

TOURS

There are several ways to experience a guided tour through Munich, on foot or by various modes of transportation, such as bus, rickshaw, octopus bike (an eight-person bicycle) and Segway.

City Segway Tours. Take a 2½-hour group Segway tour on a stop-and-go trek to see the main sights of the city, or a four-hour day tour to learn Munich's history from its humble beginnings, through tumultuous times, and up to the present day. Tours begin with a "driving" lesson. Participants must have a valid driver's license. ✉ *Karlspl. 4, Altstadt* ✛ *Look for shop in courtyard* ☏ *089/2388–8798* ⊕ *munich.citysegwaytours.com* ▨ *From €59* Ⓜ *Karlsplatz Stachus.*

FAMILY **Gray Line Sightseeing Munich.** The best way to get a feel for Munich is to board a double-decker sightseeing bus—look for *Stadtrundfahrten* (city sightseeing). These blue buses, run by Autobus Oberbayern, offer a hop-on, hop-off service throughout the City Center, with commentary headphones available in eight languages and a live host who offers commentary in English and German. The tour takes an hour. Buses run every 20 minutes April through October and every 30 minutes November through March. ■TIP➜ **Book online for the best price.** ✉ *Hauptbahnhof, Bahnhofpl. 7, Ludwigsvorstadt* ✛ *Wait outside Karstadt department store* ☏ *089/5490–7560* ⊕ *www.stadtrundfahrten-muenchen.de/en* ▨ *From €16* Ⓜ *Hauptbahnhof.*

FAMILY **Mike's Bike Tours.** The oldest bike-tour operation in Munich, Mike's humorous tours last four to seven hours, typically with an hour's break

2

at a beer garden, and cover roughly 4 miles. A daily 11:30 am tour takes place from mid-January through Christmas Eve, and starts at Marienplatz 15, next to the Toy Museum. From mid-April through mid-September a second tour starts at 4 pm. There are also three daily tours during Oktoberfest. Reserve to be sure, though you'll probably get a bike if you just show up. Bus Bavaria, part of the same company, also offers day-trips by bus to Neuschwanstein castle. ⊠ *Bräuhausstr. 10, Altstadt* ☎ *089/2554–3987* ⊕ *www.mikesbiketours.com* 🔄 *From €30* Ⓜ *Marienplatz, Isartor.*

FAMILY **Munich Tourist Office.** Munich's tourist office offers individual guided
Fodor's Choice tours with certified guides in 29 languages. Tours should be booked at
★ least six days ahead of time and should include all the specifics, such as the desired language, the number of people in your group, meeting place, time, date, and duration, and your address. You can include any specific sights if you have something in particular you want to see. Tours can last up to three hours. ⊠ *Marienpl. 2, Altstadt* ☎ *089/2333–0234* ⊕ *www.muenchen.de/rathaus/home_en/Tourist-Office/Service/Guided-Tours* 🔄 *From €120* Ⓜ *Marienplatz.*

FAMILY **Pedalheroes Munich.** A novel way of seeing the city is to hop on one of the bike-rickshaws with foldable rain canopies. The bike-powered two-seater cabs operate from Marienplatz and, besides the planned tours, you can also let a driver take you to a sight of your choosing. It's best to book a week ahead. Those traveling in a group, large or small, could consider taking an octopus bike tour on a circular tandem bicycle. ⊠ *Marsstr. 11, Altstadt* ☎ *089/5161–9911* ⊕ *www.pedalhelden. de* 🔄 *From €42* Ⓜ *Marienplatz.*

FAMILY **Radius Tours & Bike Rental.** Theme walks of Munich's highlights, Third Reich Munich, and the Dachau concentration camp are offered here, all departing from the Radius office in Hauptbahnhof. Third Reich tours start daily at 3 pm between April and mid-October and daily at 11:30 am the rest of the year. The Dachau tour starts daily at 9:15 am and 12:15 pm from April to mid-October, with a third tour added daily in June and July at 10:15 am. The rest of the year the Dachau tours run daily at 9:15 am. Advance booking is not necessary for individuals, but it is recommended. ⊠ *Hauptbahnhof, Arnulfstr. 3, Ludwigsvorstadt* ✛ *Office: in Hauptbahnhof opposite platforms 32–34* ☎ *089/5434–8777–40* ⊕ *www.radiustours.com* 🔄 *From €15* Ⓜ *Hauptbahnhof.*

Segway Tour Munich. Reserve your Segway online for the Classic Tour that stops at 20 key Bavarian sights around Munich, or the Third Reich Tour for the 22 most important places of the Nazi regime. With several starting times to choose from, standard tours of up to eight people begin at the Altes Rathaus at Marienplatz. Tours take about three hours, including a safety briefing. A valid driver's license is required to operate a Segway in Germany. ⊠ *Marienpl. 15, Altstadt* ✛ *Below archway of Altes Rathaus (Old Town Hall)* ☎ *089/2420–3401* ⊕ *www.seg-tour-munich.com* 🔄 *€75* Ⓜ *Marienplatz.*

FAMILY **Stadtrundfahrt CitySightseeing.** Yellow Cab's double-decker buses offer hop-on, hop-off service on one-hour tours leaving every 10–20 minutes between 10 am and 5 pm from April through October. From

November through March, the red and yellow buses leave between 10 am and 4 pm every 30–60 minutes on weekdays, and every 15–30 minutes on weekends. Commentary is in German over a loudspeaker and in several other languages with headsets. Tickets ordered online are cheaper. ⊠ *Luisenstr. 4, Ludwigsvorstadt* ⌖ *At Bahnhofsplatz across from Hauptbahhof Nord* ⊕ *www.citysightseeing-munich.com* ⊠ *From €15* Ⓜ *Hauptbahnhof.*

VISITOR INFORMATION

The Munich Tourist office has two locations. The Hauptbahnhof (main train station) tourist office is open Monday through Saturday 9–8 and Sunday 10–6. The Tourist office in Neues Rathaus (New Town Hall) in Marienplatz is open weekdays 9:30–7:30, Saturday 9–4, and Sunday 10–2. As well as tourist offices, a great way to start your Munich visit is to go to Infopoint in Alterhof's Münchner Kaiserburg, a comprehensive information center for all museums and palaces across Bavaria.

Contacts Infopoint Museen Bayern, Münchner Kaiserburg. ⊠ *Alter Hof 1, Altstadt* ☎ *089/2101–4050* ⊕ *www.muenchner-kaiserburg.de* Ⓜ *Marienplatz.* **Munich Tourist Office—Hauptbahnhof.** ⊠ *Hauptbahnhof, Bahnhofpl. 2, Ludwigsvorstadt* ⌖ *Entrance is from street, outside of Hauptbahnhof* ☎ *089/2339–6500* ⊕ *www.muenchen.de* Ⓜ *Hauptbahnhof.* **Munich Tourist Office—Rathaus.** ⊠ *Marienpl. 2, Altstadt* ☎ *089/2339–6500* ⊕ *www.muenchen. de* Ⓜ *Marienplatz.*

EXPLORING

Munich is a wealthy city—and it shows. At times this affluence may come across as conservatism. But what makes Munich so unique is that it's a new city superimposed on the old. The hip neighborhoods that make up the City Center (Innenstadt) are replete with traditional locales, and flashy materialism thrives together with a love of the outdoors.

ALTSTADT

The core of Munich's Innenstadt is Altstadt (Old Town), which has been rebuilt so often over the centuries that it no longer has the homogeneous look of so many other German towns. World War II leveled a good portion of the center, but unlike other cities that adopted more modern architectural styles, much of Munich's Altstadt was rebuilt as it was before the destruction. An amazing job has been done to restore the fairy-tale feel that prevailed here. From the modest palace of the Alter Hof in the Old Town, the Wittelsbachs expanded their quarters northward, away from the jumble of narrow streets. The new palace, the Residenz, is one of the stunning royal landmarks, and abuts the Englischer Garten, a present from the royal family to the locals. Although a few royal-themed sites can be found farther afield, most of the historical treasures are fairly concentrated in the Innenstadt, and mostly in Altstadt, making them easy to visit on foot.

Alter Hof (*Münchner Kaiserburg*). Alter Hof was the original home of the Wittelsbach dynasty of Bavaria (not to be confused with the adjacent

Residenz). Established in 1180, the **Münchner Kaiserburg** (Imperial Palace) at Alter Hof now serves various functions. Its **Infopoint** is a tourist-information center for Bavaria's castles and museums. In the vaulted hall beneath is a multimedia presentation about the palace's history. The west wing is home to **Restaurant Alter Hof,** offering Franconian delicacies and a wine bar. ⊠ *Alter Hof 1, Altstadt* ☎ *089/2101–4050* ⊕ *www. muenchner-kaiserburg.de* ◱ *Free* ☉ *Closed Sun.* Ⓜ *Marienplatz.*

FAMILY **Altes Rathaus** (*Old Town Hall*). Much of the work on Munich's first town hall was done in the 15th century, though various alterations were made through the centuries. Its great hall—destroyed in 1943–45 but now fully restored—was the work of the renowned architect Jörg von Halspach. Postwar, the tower was rebuilt as it looked in the 15th century and now it's used for official receptions and is not usually open to the public. The tower provides a fairy-tale-like setting for the **Spielzeugmuseum** (Toy Museum), accessible via a winding staircase. Its toys, dolls, and teddy bears are on display, together with a collection of Barbies from the United States. ⊠ *Marienpl. 15, Altstadt* ☎ *089/294–001 Spielzeugmuseum* ⊕ *www.muenchen.de/sehenswuerdigkeiten/orte/120398. html* ◱ *Spielzeugmuseum from €4* Ⓜ *Marienplatz.*

Fodor'sChoice **Asamkirche** (*St.-Johann-Nepomuk-Kirche*). Perhaps Munich's most
★ ostentatious church, it has a suitably extraordinary entrance, framed by raw rock foundations. The insignificant door, crammed between its craggy shoulders, gives little idea of the opulence and lavish detailing within the small 18th-century church (there are only 12 rows of pews). Above the doorway St. Nepomuk, the 14th-century Bohemian monk and patron saint of Bavaria who drowned in the Danube, is being led by angels from a rocky riverbank to heaven. The church's official name is Church of St. Johann Nepomuk, but it's more popularly known as the Asamkirche for its architects, the brothers Cosmas Damian and Egid Quirin Asam. The interior of the church is a prime example of true southern German late-baroque architecture. Frescoes by Cosmas Damian Asam and rosy marble cover the walls. The sheer wealth of statues and gilding is stunning—there's even a gilt skeleton at the sanctuary's portal. ⊠ *Sendlingerstr. 32, Altstadt* Ⓜ *Sendlingertor.*

FAMILY **Deutsches Jagd- und Fischereimuseum** (*German Museum of Hunting and Fishing*). This quirky museum is in the enormous former St. Augustus Church, and it contains a large collection of fishhooks, taxidermy animals (including a 6½-foot-tall brown bear and a grizzly from Alaska), and a 12,000-year-old megaloceros (giant deer) skeleton. You'll even find the *Wolpertinger,* a mythical creature with body parts of various animals. There are also rotating special exhibitions exploring native wildlife, as well as the history of hunting and fishing. ⊠ *Neuhauser Str. 2, Altstadt* ☎ *089/220–522* ⊕ *www.jagd-fischerei-museum.de* ◱ *€5* Ⓜ *Karlsplatz, Marienplatz.*

Dreifaltigkeitskirche (*Church of the Holy Trinity*). Take a quick look at this characteristic church built to commemorate Bavaria's part in the the War of Spanish Succession. A further motivation for its construction was a prophecy from the devout Maria Anna Lindmayr that if the city survived the war intact and a church was not erected in thanks, the city was doomed. The city was saved and a church was built between 1711 and 1718. It has a striking baroque exterior, and its interior is brought to life by frescoes by Cosmas Damian Asam depicting various heroic scenes. Remarkably, it is the only church in the city's Altstadt spared destruction in the war. ⊠ *Pacellistr. 6, Altstadt* ☎ *089/290–0820* ⊕ *www.muenchen.de/sehenswuerdigkeiten/orte/130940.html* Ⓜ *Karlsplatz, Lenbachplatz (Tram).*

Feldherrnhalle (*Field Marshals' Hall*). Erected in 1841–44, this open pavilion, fronted with three huge arches, was modeled on the 14th-century Loggia dei Lanzi in Florence. From Odeonsplatz, it faces Ludwigstrasse, with Siegestor in the distance, and was built to honor Bavarian military leaders and the Bavarian army. Two huge Bavarian lions are flanked by the larger-than-life statues of Count Johann Tserclaes Tilly, who led Catholic forces in the Thirty Years' War, and Prince Karl Philipp Wrede, hero of the 19th-century Napoleonic Wars. It was turned into a militaristic shrine in the 1930s and '40s by the Nazis, to whom it was significant because it marked the site of Hitler's failed coup, or *Putsch*, in 1923. Hitler installed a memorial in 1933 to commemorate the Nazis killed that day, and during the Third Reich, all who passed the guarded memorial had to give the Nazi salute. Viscardigasse, a passageway behind Feldherrnhalle linking Residenzstrasse and Theatinerstrasse, which became known as *Drückebergergasse* (Shirkers' Lane), was used as a bypass by those who didn't want to salute the memorial. The memorial was removed in 1945. ⊠ *Residenzstr. 1, Altstadt* ✛ *Odeonspl., between Theatinerkirche and Residenz* ☎ *089/290671* ⊕ *www.schloesser.bayern.de/englisch/palace/objects/mu_feldh.htm* ▨ *Free* Ⓜ *Odeonsplatz.*

Fodor'sChoice
★ **Frauenkirche** (*Church of Our Lady*). Munich's *Dom* (cathedral) is a distinctive late-Gothic brick structure with two huge towers, each 99 meters (325 feet) high (a Munich trademark but currently closed for renovations). The main body of the cathedral was completed in 20 years (1468–88)—a record time in those days, and the distinctive onion-dome-like cupolas were added by 1525. Shortly after the original work was completed in 1488, Jörg von Halspach, the Frauenkirche's architect, died, but he managed to see the project through. In 1944–45, the building suffered severe damage during Allied bombing raids, and was restored between 1947 and 1957. Inside, the church combines most of von Halspach's plans with a stark, clean modernity and simplicity of line. As you enter the church, look on the stone floor for the dark imprint of a large foot—the so-called *Teufelstritt* (Devil's Footprint). The cathedral houses the elaborate marble tomb of Duke Ludwig IV (1282–1347), who became Holy Roman Emperor Ludwig the Bavarian in 1328. One of the Frauenkirche's great treasures is the collection of wooden busts by Erasmus Grasser. ⊠ *Frauenpl. 12, Altstadt* ☎ *089/290–0820* ▨ *Free* Ⓜ *Marienplatz.*

FAMILY **Hofbräuhaus.** Duke Wilhelm V founded Munich's Hofbräuhaus (court brewery) in 1589; it's been at its present location since 1607, where the golden beer is consumed from 1-liter mugs called *Mass*. If the cavernous ground-floor hall or beer garden is too noisy, there's a quieter restaurant upstairs. Americans, Australians, and Italians far outnumber locals, who regard HBH as a tourist trap. The brass band that performs here most days adds modern pop and American folk music to the traditional German numbers. ⊠ *Platzl 9, Altstadt* ☏ *089/2901–36100* ⊕ *www.hofbraeuhaus.de/en/index_en.html* Ⓜ *Marienplatz, Isartor.*

Hofgarten (*Court Garden*). The formal court garden dates back to 1613 when it lay outside the Residenz moat. It's now bordered on two sides by arcades designed in the 19th century. On the east side of the garden is the state chancellery (office of the Bavarian prime minister), built in 1990–93 around the ruins of the 19th-century Army Museum and incorporating the remains of a Renaissance arcade. Bombed during World War II air raids, the museum stood untouched for almost 40 years as a reminder of the war. In front of the chancellery stands one of Europe's most unusual—some say, most effective—war memorials. Instead of looking up at a monument, you are led down to a **sunken crypt** covered by a massive granite block. In the crypt lies a German soldier from World War I. The crypt is a stark contrast to the **memorial** that stands unobtrusively in front of the northern wing of the chancellery: a simple cube of black marble bearing facsimiles of handwritten anti-Nazi manifestos. ⊠ *Hofgartenstr. 1, Altstadt* ✛ *North of Residenz* ⊕ *www.residenz-muenchen.de/englisch/garden/index.htm* Ⓜ *Odeonsplatz, Marienplatz.*

Jewish Center Munich (*Jüdisches Zentrum*). The striking Jewish Center at St.-Jakobs-Platz has transformed a formerly sleepy area into an elegant, busy modern square. The buildings signify the return of the Jewish community to Munich's City Center, six decades after the end of the Third Reich. The center includes a museum focusing on Jewish history in Munich (plus kosher café), and the impressive Ohel Jakob Synagogue, with its rough slabs topped by a latticelike cover, manifesting a thought-provoking sense of permanence. The third building is a community center, which includes the kosher Einstein restaurant (☏ *089/2024–00332* ⊕ *www.einstein-restaurant.de*). Guided tours of the synagogue are in great demand, and must be booked at least 10 days in advance (☏ *089/2024–00100*). ⊠ *St.-Jakobs-Pl. 16, Altstadt* ☏ *089/2339–6096* ⊕ *www.juedisches-museum-muenchen.de* 🎟 *€3* ⊗ *Museum closed Mon.* Ⓜ *Marienplatz, Sendlinger Tor.*

FAMILY **Karlsplatz** (*Stachus*). In 1728, Eustachius Föderl opened an inn and beer garden here, which might be how the square came to be called Stachus—it's still called that by the locals although both are long gone. One of Munich's most popular fountains is here. It's a magnet on hot summer days and makes way for an ice-skating rink in winter. Karlsplatz is a bustling meeting point, even more so because of the underground shopping center. ⊠ *Karlspl., Altstadt* ⊕ *www.muenchen.de/sehenswuerdigkeiten/orte/120328.html* ⊗ *Stachus Passage shops closed Sun.* Ⓜ *Karlsplatz.*

Fodor's Choice ★ **Kunsthalle der Hypo-Kulturstiftung** (*Hall of the Hypobank's Cultural Foundation*). Chagall, Giacometti, and Picasso, as well as contemporary artists like Peter Lindbergh and Robert Mapplethorpe t have been featured at this exhibition hall in the middle of the shopping pedestrian zone. It is set within the upscale **Fünf Höfe shopping mall,** designed by

Swiss architects Herzog and de Meuron, who also designed London's Tate Modern. Exhibitions at the Kunsthalle rarely disappoint, making it one of Germany's most interesting exhibition venues. ⊠ *Theatinerstr. 8, Altstadt* ☎ *089/224–412* ⊕ *www.kunsthalle-muc.de* 🎫 *€12* Ⓜ *Odeonsplatz, Marienplatz.*

FAMILY
Fodor'sChoice
★

Marienplatz. Bordered by the Neues Rathaus, shops, and cafés, this square is named after the gilded statue of the Virgin Mary that has watched over it for more than three centuries. It was erected in 1638 at the behest of Elector Maximilian I as an act of thanksgiving for the city's survival of the Thirty Years' War, the cataclysmic, partly religious struggle that devastated vast regions of Germany. When the statue was taken down from its marble column for cleaning in 1960, workmen found a small casket in the base containing a splinter of wood said to be from the cross of Christ. On the fifth floor of a building facing the Neues Rathaus is Café Glockenspiel. It overlooks the entire square and provides a perfect view of the glockenspiel. Entrance is around the back. ⊠ *Bounded by Kaufingerstr., Rosenstr., Weinstr., and Dienerstr., Altstadt* ⊕ *www.marienplatz.de* Ⓜ *Marienplatz.*

FAMILY **Maximilianstrasse.** Munich's most expensive and exclusive shopping street was named after King Maximilian II, who wanted to break away from the Greek-influenced classical architecture favored by his father, Ludwig I. He thus created this broad boulevard lined with majestic buildings culminating on a rise above the River Isar at the stately **Maximilianeum**. Finished in 1874, this building was conceived as an elite education foundation for the most talented young people across Bavaria, regardless of status or wealth. It is still home to an education foundation, but its principal role is as the grand, if slightly confined, home to the Bavarian state parliament. Rather than take the tram to see the Maximilianeum, the whole walk along Maximilianstrasse (from Max-Joesph-Platz) is rewarding. You'll pass various boutiques, plus the five-star Hotel Vier Jahreszeiten, the Upper Bavarian Parliament, the Museum Fünf Kontinente (State Museum of Ethnology), and cross the picturesque River Isar. Five minutes past the Maximilianeum, on the charming Wiener Platz, is the Hofbräukeller and its excellent beer garden. ⊠ *Maximilianstr., Altstadt* Ⓜ *Maximilianeum (Tram).*

FAMILY **Michaelskirche** (*St. Michael's Church*). A curious story explains why this hugely impressive Renaissance church, adjoining a former extensive Jesuit college, has no tower. Seven years after the start of construction, in 1583, the main tower collapsed. Its patron, pious Duke Wilhelm V, regarded the disaster as a heavenly sign that the church wasn't big enough, so he ordered a change in the plans—this time without a tower. Completed in 1597, the barrel vaulting of St. Michael's is second in size only to that of St. Peter's in Rome. The duke is buried in the crypt, along with 40 other Wittelsbach family members, including the eccentric King Ludwig II. A severe neoclassical monument in the north transept contains the tomb of Napoléon's stepson, Eugène de Beauharnais, who married a daughter of King Maximilian I and died in Munich in 1824. Once again a Jesuit church, it is the venue for performances of church music. A poster to the right of the front portal gives the dates. ⊠ *Neuhauser Str. 6, Altstadt* ☎ *089/231–7060* ⊕ *www.*

st-michael-muenchen.de ⌧ *Crypt €2, musical performances mostly free* Ⓜ *Karlsplatz, Marienplatz.*

FAMILY **Münchner Stadtmuseum** (*City Museum*). This museum is as eclectic inside as the architecture is outside. The buildings facing St.-Jakobs-Platz date to the 15th century, though they were destroyed in WWII and rebuilt. It houses the fabulous *Typical Munich!* exhibition, charting a riotous history few other cities can match: royal capital, brewery center, capital of art and classical music, and now wealthy, high-tech, and cultural center par excellence. There is also a separate, permanent exhibition dealing with the city's Nazi past. The museum is home to a puppet theater, a film museum showing rarely screened movies, and numerous photo and other temporary exhibitions. Check out the museum shop, servus.heimat, with the great and good of Munich kitsch and souvenirs. The entire museum is scheduled to close for renovations in late 2020 or early 2021 and will be closed until 2027. ⌧ *St.-Jakobspl. 1, Altstadt* ☎ *089/2332–2370* ⊕ *www.muenchner-stadtmuseum.de* ⌧ *From €4* ☺ *Closed Mon.* Ⓜ *Marienplatz, Sendlinger Tor.*

FAMILY **Münzhof** (*Mint*). Originally built between 1563 and 1567, the ground floor was home to Duke Albrecht V's stables, the second floor to living quarters for the servants, and the third to the ducal collection of high art and curiosities (6,000 pieces by 1600). Between 1809 and 1983 it housed the Bavarian mint, and a neoclassical facade, with allegories of copper, silver, and gold, was added in 1808–09. Today, with its slightly garish green exterior on three sides, it can appear to be little more than the somewhat undistinguished home to the Bavarian Land Bureau for the Conservation of Historic Monuments, but step inside the inner arcade to see a jewel of German Renaissance architecture. ⌧ *Hofgraben 4, Altstadt* ⚓ *Enter from Pfisterstr.* ⌧ *Free* ☺ *Closed weekends* Ⓜ *Marienplatz.*

FAMILY **Nationaltheater** (*National Theater*). Bavaria's original National Theater at Max-Joseph-Platz didn't last long. Opened in 1818, it burned to the ground in 1823 before it was completely finished. By 1825 it was rebuilt with its eight-column portico, and went on to premiere Richard Wagner's world-famous *Tristan und Isolde* (1865), *Meistersinger von Nürnberg* (1868), *Rheingold* (1869), and *Walküre* (1870). Allied bombs destroyed much of the interior in 1943, and its facade and elements of its interior were rebuilt as it was prewar. It finally reopened in 1963. Today, it is one of Europe's largest opera houses and contains some of the world's most advanced stage technologies. As the principal home to the Bavarian State Opera, it is considered one of the world's outstanding opera houses. Family opera is also available for children under 18 with an accompanying adult. The Munich Opera Festival takes place late June and July, including performances, free open-air Opera for All events, and live streaming opera online with Staatsoper TV. ⌧ *Max-Joseph-Pl. 2, Altstadt* ☎ *089/2185–1025* ⊕ *www.bayerische.staatsoper.de* ⌧ *From €5* Ⓜ *Odeonsplatz, Marienplatz.*

Fodor'sChoice ★ **Neues Rathaus** (*New Town Hall*). Munich's present neo-Gothic town hall was built in three sections and two phases between 1867 and 1905. It was a necessary enlargement on the nearby Old Town Hall, but city fathers also saw it as presenting Munich as a modern city, independent from the waning powers of the Bavarian Wittelsbach royal house. Architectural historians are divided over its merits, although its dramatic scale and lavish detailing are impressive. The main tower's 1908 **glockenspiel** (a chiming clock with mechanical figures), the largest in Germany, plays daily at 11 am and noon, with an additional performance at 5 pm March–October. As chimes peal out over the square, the clock's doors flip open and brightly colored dancers and jousting knights act out two events from Munich's past: a tournament held in Marienplatz in 1568 and the *Schäfflertanz* (Dance of the Coopers), which commemorated the end of the plague of 1515–17. You, too, can travel up there, by elevator, to an observation point near the top of one of the towers. On a clear day the view across the city with the Alps beyond is spectacular. ⊠ *Marienpl. 8, Altstadt* ⊕ *www.muenchen. de/int/en/sights/attractions/new-town-hall-neues-rathaus.html* 🎫 *Tower €3* Ⓜ *Marienplatz.*

Fodor'sChoice ★ **Peterskirche** (*Church of St. Peter*). The Altstadt's oldest parish church (called locally Alter Peter, or Old Peter) traces its origins to the 11th century, and has been restored in various architectural styles, including Gothic, baroque, and rococo. The rich baroque interior has a magnificent high altar and aisle pillars decorated with exquisite 18th-century figures of the apostles. In clear weather it's well worth the long climb up the approximately 300-foot-high tower, with a panoramic view of the Alps. ⊠ *Rindermarkt 1, Altstadt* ☎ *089/2102–37760* ⊕ *www. muenchen.de/int/en/sights/churches/church-of-st-peter.html* 🎫 *Tower €3* Ⓜ *Marienplatz.*

FAMILY Fodor'sChoice ★ **Residenz** (*Royal Palace*). One of Germany's true treasures, Munich's royal Residenz began in 1363 as the modest Neuveste (New Fortress) on the northeastern city boundary. By the time the Bavarian monarchy fell, in 1918, the palace could compare favorably with the best in Europe. With the Residenz's central location, it was pretty much inevitable that the Allied bombing of 1944–45 would cause immense damage, and subsequent reconstruction took decades. For tourists today, however, it really is a treasure chamber of delight. A wander around the Residenz can last anywhere from three hours to all day. The 16th-century, 70-meter-long arched Antiquarium, built for Duke Albrecht V's collection of antiques and library, is recognized as one of the most impressive Renaissance creations outside Italy (today it's used chiefly for state receptions). At a corner of the Residenz's Apothekenhof (courtyard) is the incomparable rococo Cuvilliés-Theater where Mozart's opera *Idomeneo* premiered in 1781. The Scatzkammer (Treasury) and Staatliche Münzsammlung (State Coin Museum) are also here. ■TIP→ The **Residenzmuseum comprises everything in the Residenz apart from the Schatzkammer (Treasury), Staatliche Münzsammlung, and the Cuvilliés-Theater, which have separate admission charges or can be visited on a combination ticket that covers everything.** ⊠ *Residenzstr. 1, Altstadt* ✛ *Enter from Max-Joseph-Pl. 3* ☎ *089/290–671* ⊕ *www.residenz-muenchen.de* 🎫 *From €7; Museum, Treasury, and Theater €13; audio guides free* Ⓜ *Odeonsplatz, Marienplatz.*

FAMILY **Staatliche Münzsammlung** (*State Coin Collection*). More than 300,000 coins, banknotes, medals, and precious stones, some 5,000 years old, star in the Staatliche Münzsammlung. ⊠ *Residenzstr. 1, Altstadt* ✛ *Enter from Kapellenhof (Chapel Courtyard)* ☎ *089/227–221* ⊕ *www. staatliche-muenzsammlung.de* ▦ *€3* ⊗ *Closed Mon.* Ⓜ *Odeonsplatz, Marienplatz.*

Theatinerkirche (St. Kajetan) (*Theatine Church*). This glorious baroque church owes its Italian appearance to its founder, Princess Henriette Adelaide of Savoy, who commissioned it in gratitude for the long-awaited birth of her son and heir, Max Emanuel, in 1662. A native of Turin, the princess mistrusted Bavarian architects and builders and thus summoned Agostino Barelli, a master builder from Bologna, to construct her church. It is modeled on Rome's Sant'Andrea della Valle. Barelli worked on the building for 12 years, but he was dismissed as too quarrelsome. It was another 100 years before the building was finished in a style similar to today's. Its striking yellow facade stands out, and its two lofty towers, topped by delightful cupolas, frame the entrance, with the central dome at the back. The superb stucco work on the inside has a remarkably light feeling owing to its brilliant white color. The expansive Odeonsplatz in front of the Feldherrnhalle and Theatinerkirche is often used for outdoor stage events. ⊠ *Theatinerstr. 22, Altstadt* ✛ *Facing Odeonspl.* ☎ *089/210–6960* ⊕ *www.theatinerkirche. de* ▦ *Free* Ⓜ *Odeonsplatz, Marienplatz.*

FAMILY

Fodor'sChoice

★

Viktualienmarkt (*Victuals Market*). The city's open-air market really is the beating heart of downtown Munich. It has just about every fresh fruit or vegetable you can imagine, as well as German and international specialties. All kinds of people come here for a quick bite, from well-heeled businesspeople and casual tourists to mortar- and paint-covered workers. It's also the realm of the garrulous, sturdy market women who run the stalls with dictatorial authority. Whether here, or at a bakery, *do not* try to select your pickings by hand: ask, and let it be served to you. There's a great beer garden (open pretty much whenever the sun is shining). The available beers rotate throughout the year among the six major Munich breweries, which are displayed on the maypole. These are also the only six breweries officially allowed to serve their wares at the Oktoberfest. ⊠ *Viktualienmarkt, Altstadt* ✛ *Just south of Marienpl.* ⊕ *www.muenchen.de/int/en/sights/attractions/viktualienmarkt.html* ⊗ *Closed Sun.* Ⓜ *Marienplatz.*

LEHEL

Seamlessly extending from Altstadt, Lehel is also home to some of Munich's royal-themed sights. While it mixes and mingles with the Old Town, it's a chic residential neighborhood as well, where locals come to escape from the crowded City Center.

FAMILY **Bayerisches Nationalmuseum** (*Bavarian National Museum*). Although the museum places emphasis on Bavarian cultural history, it has art and artifacts of international importance and regular exhibitions that attract worldwide attention. The museum is a journey through time, principally from the early Middle Ages to the 20th century, with medieval and

2

Renaissance wood carvings, works by the great Renaissance sculptor Tilman Riemenschneider, tapestries, arms and armor, a unique collection of Christmas crèches (the *Krippenschau*), Bavarian and German folk art, and a significant *Jugendstil* (art nouveau) collection. ✉ *Prinzregentenstr. 3, Lehel* ☎ *089/211–2401* ⊕ *www.bayerisches-nationalmuseum.de* 🎫 *From €7* ⊙ *Closed Mon.* Ⓜ *Lehel, Nationalmuseum/Haus d.Kunst (Tram).*

Fodor'sChoice
★
Haus der Kunst (*House of Art*). This colonnaded, classical-style building is one of Munich's most significant examples of Hitler-era architecture, and was officially opened as House of German Art by the Führer himself. During the Third Reich it only showed work deemed to reflect the Nazi aesthetic. One of its most successful postwar exhibitions was devoted to works banned by the Nazis. It now hosts cutting-edge exhibitions on art, photography, and sculpture, as well as theatrical and musical happenings, and P1 is one of the hottest bars in town. ✉ *Prinzregentenstr. 1, Altstadt* ☎ *089/2112–7113* ⊕ *www.hausderkunst.de/en* 🎫 *€14* Ⓜ *Odeonsplatz, Lehel, Nationalmuseum/Haus d.Kunst (Tram).*

Fodor'sChoice
★
Klosterkirche St. Anna (*Monastery Church of St. Anne*). This striking example of the two Asam brothers' work in the Lehel district impresses visitors with its sense of movement and heroic scale. The ceiling fresco from 1729 by Cosmas Damian Asam glows in all its original glory. The ornate altar was also designed by the Asam brothers. Towering over the delicate little church, on the opposite side of the street, is the neo-Romanesque bulk of the 19th-century Parish Church of St. Anne. Stop at one of the stylish cafés, restaurants, and patisseries gathered at the junction of St.-Anna-Strasse and Gewürzmühlstrasse, about 250 feet from the churches. ✉ *St.-Anna-Str. 19, Lehel* ☎ *089/211–260* ⊕ *www. erzbistum-muenchen.de/pfarrei/st-anna-muenchen/cont/64346* Ⓜ *Lehel.*

FAMILY
Museum Fünf Kontinente (*Five Continents Museum*). Founded in 1862, this museum houses an enormous quantity of ethnographic articles from around the world, including arts, crafts, photographs, and library material. The extensive museum takes a peek into non-European cultures from Africa, America, Asia, Australia, the Near and Middle East, and the South Seas to see how they differ (or not) from Europe with both permanent displays and special exhibits. ✉ *Maximilianstr. 42, Lehel* ☎ *089/2101–36100* ⊕ *www.museum-fuenf-kontinente.de/ services/english-summary.html* 🎫 *€5* ⊙ *Closed Mon.* Ⓜ *Isartor, Lehel, Maxmonument (Tram).*

Sammlung Schack (*Schack-Galerie*). Around 180 German 19th-century paintings from the Romantic era up to the periods of realism and symbolism make up the collections of the Sammlung Schack, originally the private collection of Count Adolf Friedrich von Schack. ✉ *Prinzregentenstr. 9, Lehel* ☎ *089/2380–5224* ⊕ *www.pinakothek. de/sammlung-schack* 🎫 *From €4* ⊙ *Closed Mon. and Tues.* Ⓜ *Lehel, Nationalmuseum/Haus d.Kunst (Tram).*

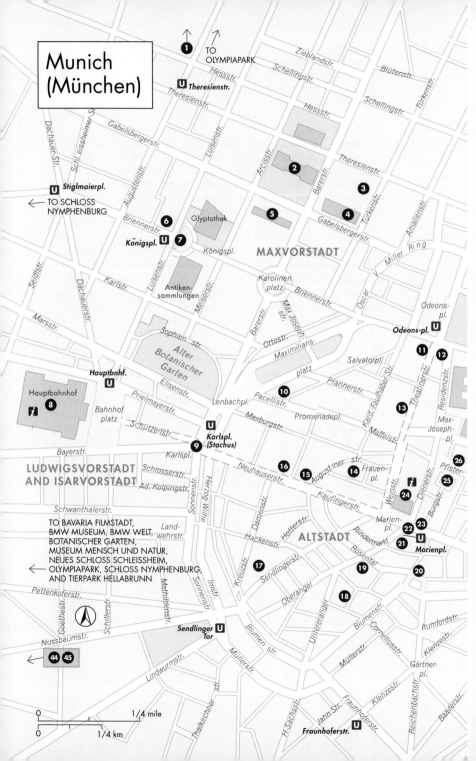

KEY

- Pedestrian Shopping Zone
- 🛈 Tourist information
- Ⓤ U-Bahn

LUDWIGSVORSTADT AND ISARVORSTADT

LUDWIGSVORSTADT

Oktoberfest and the Winter Tollwood Festival, not far from Hauptbahnhof, take place at the Theresienwiese meadow, which is located in Ludwigsvorstadt. This neighborhood, which includes the Hauptbahnhof (main train station), runs south from there, and is joined to the east by Isarvorstadt.

FAMILY **Bavaria Statue.** Overlooking the Theresienwiese, home of the Oktoberfest, is a 19th-century hall of fame (Ruhmeshalle) featuring busts of famous Bavarian scientists, artists, engineers, generals, and philosophers, and a monumental bronze statue of the maiden Bavaria. Unsurprisingly, it was commissioned by the art- and architecture-obsessed King Ludwig I, though not finished before his abdication in 1848. The Bavaria is more than 60 feet high and at the time was the largest bronze figure since antiquity. The statue is hollow, and an initial 48 steps take you up to its base. Once inside, there are 66 steps to her knee, and a further 52 all the way into the braided head, the reward being a view of Munich through Bavaria's eyes. ⊠ *Theresienhöhe 16, Ludwigsvorstadt* ⊕ *www.schloesser.bayern.de/englisch/palace/objects/ mu_ruhm.htm* 🎫€4 ⊙ *Bavaria Statue and Ruhmeshalle closed mid-Oct.–Mar.; Ruhmeshalle closed during Oktoberfest* Ⓜ *Theresienwiese, Theresienhöhe (Bus).*

Hauptbahnhof (*Central Station*). The train station isn't a cultural site, but it's a particularly handy starting point for exploring. The city tourist office here has maps and helpful information on events around town. On the underground level are all sorts of shops that remain open even on Sunday and holidays. There are also a number of places to get a late-night snack in and around the station. ⊠ *Bahnhofpl., Ludwigsvorstadt* Ⓜ *Hauptbahnhof.*

FAMILY **Oktoberfest Grounds at Theresienwiese.** The Oktoberfest and winter
Fodor's Choice Tollwood music fest grounds are named after Princess Therese von
★ Sachsen-Hildburghausen, who celebrated her marriage to the future King Ludwig I here in 1810 with thousands of Münchners. The event was so successful that it grew into a 16- to 18-day international beer and fair-ride bonanza attracting more than 6 million people annually. Oktoberfest originally began in October. As it grew, it extended into September for better weather. Follow the crowds to any of the several points of entry. ⊠ *Theresienwiese, Ludwigsvorstadt* ✛ *Some entrance points: in northeast at St.-Pauls-Pl. from Theresienwiese station; from east at Beethovenstr.; in southeast at Matthias-Pschorr-Str. from Goetheplatz station* ⊕ *www.oktoberfest.de/en* Ⓜ *Theresienwiese, Goetheplatz.*

ISARVORSTADT

Isarvorstadt, west of Ludwigsvorstadt and south of Altstadt and Lehel, continues eastward until just past the Isar River. Close to Altstadt, this neighborhood has happening restaurants and shops, as well as the world-famous Deutsches Museum.

The Aeronautics Hall of the Deutsches Museum displays aircraft from the early days of flight to jets and helicopters.

FAMILY
Fodor's Choice
★
Deutsches Museum (*German Museum*). Aircraft, vehicles, cutting-edge technology, and historic machinery fill this monumental building on an island in the Isar River, home to one of the best science and technology museums in the world. Though some areas are closed for renovation until 2020, there are still some 270,000 square feet and 35 exhibits to explore. The Centre for New Technologies includes interactive exhibitions, such as nanotechnology, biotechnology, and robotics. Children have their own "kingdom," the Kinderreich, where they can learn about modern technology and science through numerous interactive displays (parents must accompany their children). One of the most technically advanced planetariums in Europe has two to four shows daily, depending on the day, albeit in German only. The **Verkehrszentrum** (Center for Transportation), on the former trade fair grounds at the Theresienhöhe, has been completely renovated and houses an amazing collection of the museum's transportation exhibits. The museum's **Flugwerft Schleissheim** airfield is in Oberschleissheim, north of Munich. ✉ *Museumsinsel 1, Isarvorstadt* ☎ *089/217–9333* ⊕ *www.deutsches-museum.de* 🍴 *From €12* Ⓜ *Isartor.*

SCHWABING AND MAXVORSTADT

Some of the finest museums in Europe are in lower Schwabing and Maxvorstadt, particularly in the *Kunstareal* (Art Quarter). Schwabing, the former artists' neighborhood, is no longer quite the bohemian area where such diverse residents as Lenin and Kandinsky were once neighbors, and today is best known for the Englischer Garten. The cultural foundations of Maxvorstadt are immutable; the Kunstareal is rife with not-to-miss world-class museums and galleries. The area is also home to Ludwigs-Maximilians-Universität (LMU) and the Technical University (TUM) of Munich, two of Germany's top universities. Where the two areas meet, in the streets behind the university, life hums with a creative vibrancy, and Schwabing maintains a healthy selection of bars, clubs, and restaurants, which are frequented by students. The difficult part is having time to see it all.

Fodor'sChoice
★
Alte Pinakothek. With numerous Old Master paintings from the Netherlands, Italy, France, and Germany, the long redbrick Alte Pinakothek holds one of the most significant art collections in the world. It was originally constructed by Leo von Klenze between 1826 and 1836 to exhibit the collection of 14th- to 18th-century works (started by Duke Wilhelm IV in the 16th century). The collection comprises more than 700 pieces, including masterpieces by Dürer, Titian, Rembrandt, Da Vinci, Rubens (the museum has one of the world's largest Rubens collections), and two celebrated Murillos. Most of the picture captions are in German only, so it is best to rent an English audio guide. The Alte Pinakothek forms a central part of Munich's world-class *Kunstareal* (Art Quarter). Museums and collections here are of the highest quality, and are a few hundred yards apart. ⊠ *Barer Str. 27, entrance faces Theresienstr., Maxvorstadt* ☏ *089/2380–5216* ⊕ *www.alte-pinakothek. de* 🖾 *From €7* ⊘ *Closed Mon.* Ⓜ *Königsplatz.*

FAMILY
DenkStätte Weisse Rose (*Memorial to the White Rose Resistance Group*). Siblings Hans and Sophie Scholl, fellow students Alexander Schmorell and Christian Probst, and Kurt Huber, professor of philosophy, were the key members of the Munich-based resistance movement against the Nazis in 1942–43 known as the Weisse Rose (White Rose). All were executed by guillotine. A small exhibition about their work is in the inner quad of the university, where the Scholls were caught distributing leaflets and denounced by the janitor. A memorial to White Rose is just outside the university. ⊠ *Ludwig-Maximilians-Universität, Geschwister-Scholl-Pl. 1, Maxvorstadt* ☏ *089/2180–3053* ⊕ *www.weisse-rose-stiftung.de* 🖾 *Free* ⊘ *Closed Sun.* Ⓜ *Universität.*

Elisabethmarkt (*Elisabeth Market*). Founded in 1903, Schwabing's permanent outdoor market is smaller than the more famous Viktualienmarkt, but hardly less colorful. It has a pocket-size beer garden, where a jazz band performs on Saturday in summer. ⊠ *Elisabethpl., Arcisstr. and Elisabethstr., Schwabing* ⊕ *www.muenchen.de/int/en/shopping/ markets/elisabethmarkt.html* ⊘ *Closed Sun.* Ⓜ *Josephsplatz, Elisabethplatz (Tram).*

FAMILY
Fodor'sChoice
★
Englischer Garten (*English Garden*). This seemingly endless green space blends into the open countryside at the north of the city. Today's park covers nearly 1,000 acres and has 78 km (48 miles) of paths and more than 100 bridges. The open, informal landscaping—reminiscent of the English-style rolling parklands of the 18th century—gave the park its name. It has a boating lake, five beer gardens, and a series of curious decorative and monumental constructions. In the center of the park's most popular beer garden is a Chinese pagoda, erected in 1790 (reconstructed after World War II). The Englischer Garten is a paradise for

joggers, cyclists, musicians, soccer players, sunbathers, and, in winter, cross-country skiers. There's even surfing year-round, at the continuous man-made wave, Eisbachwelle, below the Eisbach bridge. The park has semi-official areas for nude sunbathing—the Germans have a positively pagan attitude toward the sun—so in some areas don't be surprised to see naked bodies bordering the flower beds and paths. ⊠ *There are various entrance points around garden, Schwabing* ⊕ *www.muenchen.de/ int/en/sights/parks/english-garden.html* Ⓜ *Chinesischer Turm (Bus), Seehaus: Münchner Freiheit (U-bahn), Hirschau: Herzogpark (Bus), Mini-Hofbräuhaus: Herzogpark (Bus), Aumeister: Studentenstadt (U-bahn).*

FAMILY **Königsplatz Museums.** Bavaria's greatest monarch, Ludwig I, was obsessed with antiquity, and the impressive buildings designed by Leo von Klenze that line this elegant square bear testament to his obsession. Two templelike structures face each other, the **Staatliche Antikensammlungen** (an acclaimed collection of Greek and Roman antiquities) and the **Glyptothek** (a fine collection of Greek and Roman statues). After WWII, Munich authorities restored the park. Today, the broad green lawns in front of the museums attract students and tourists in the warmer months for concerts, films, and other events. This area around became the national center of the Nazi Party in the 1930s and '40s. Destroyed in the war, the new **Munich Documentation Centre for the History of National Socialism** opened in 2015 on Brienner Strasse 34. On Arcisstrasse 12 is the Nazi-era building (now a music school) where in 1938 Britain's prime minister, Neville Chamberlain, infamously thought he had negotiated "peace in our time" with Hitler. ⊠ *Königspl. 1, Maxvorstadt* ☎ *089/5998–8830 Staatliche Antikensammlungen, 089/286–100 Glyptothek, 089/2336–7007 NS-Dokumentationszentrum* ⊕ *www. antike-am-koenigsplatz.mwn.de* 🌐 *From €6; €5 for NS-Dokumentationszentrum* ⊙ *Museums closed Mon.* Ⓜ *Königsplatz.*

Ludwigskirche (*Ludwig's Church*). Planted halfway along the stark, neoclassical Ludwigstrasse is this superb twin-towered Byzantine- and Italian-influenced church, built between 1829 and 1838 at the behest of King Ludwig I to provide his newly completed suburb with a parish church. From across the road, look up to see the splendidly colored, 2009 mosaic on the church's roof. Inside, see one of the great modern frescoes, the *Last Judgment* by Peter von Cornelius, in the choir. At 60 feet by 37 feet, it's also one of the world's largest. ⊠ *Ludwigstr. 22, Maxvorstadt* ☎ *089/287–7990* ⊕ *www.st-ludwig-muenchen.de* Ⓜ *Universität.*

Museum Brandhorst. This multicolor abstract box is filled with videos, paintings, sculptures, and installations by artists such as Andy Warhol, Damien Hirst, Gerhard Richter, and Joseph Beuys, and is a real treat for contemporary art fans. The location in the middle of the historic Kunstareal art district, although shocking to some less progressive art aficionados, highlights that the city has broken out of the shackles of its postwar conservatism. Königsplatz U-bahn is a simple way to get to the Kunstareal, though it involves a pleasant 15-minute walk. Tram 27 takes you directly from Karlsplatz to the Pinakothek stop, in the heart of the Kunstareal. ⊠ *Theresienstr. 35a, Maxvorstadt* ☎ *089/2380–52286*

⊕ *www.museum-brandhorst.de* 🖼 *From €7* ☉ *Closed Mon.* Ⓜ *Königsplatz, Pinakotheken (Tram).*

FAMILY

Fodor's Choice

★

Pinakothek der Moderne. Opened to much fanfare in 2002, this fascinating, light-filled building is home to four outstanding museums under one cupola-topped roof: art, graphic art, architecture, and design. The striking 130,000-square-foot glass-and-concrete complex by Stefan Braunfels has permanent and temporary exhibitions throughout the year in each of the four categories. The design museum is particularly popular, showing permanent exhibitions in vehicle design, computer culture, and other design ideas. ⊠ *Barer Str. 40, Maxvorstadt* ☎ *089/2380–5360* ⊕ *www.pinakothek.de* 🖼 *From €10* ☉ *Closed Mon.* Ⓜ *Königsplatz, Pinakotheken (Tram).*

Siegestor (*Victory Arch*). Built to bookend the Feldherrnhalle and mark the end of Ludwigstrasse, Siegestor nowadays also marks the beginning of Leopoldstrasse. Unsurprisingly, it has Italian origins and was modeled on the Arch of Constantine in Rome. It was built (1843–52) to honor the achievements of the Bavarian army during the Wars of Liberation (1813–15) against Napoléon. It received heavy bomb damage in 1944, and at the end of the war Munich authorities decided it should be torn down for safety reasons. Major Eugene Keller, the head of the U.S. military government in the postwar city, intervened and saved it. Its postwar inscription on the side facing the inner city is best translated as: "Dedicated to victory, destroyed by war, a monument to peace." ⊠ *Leopoldstr. 2, Schwabing* ✛ *Intersection of Leopoldstr., Ludwigstr., Shackstr., and Akademiestr.* ⊕ *www.siegestor.de* Ⓜ *Universität, Giselastrasse.*

FAMILY

Staatliche Sammlung Ägyptischer Kunst (*State Collection of Egyptian Art*). Various Bavarian rulers were fascinated with the ancient world and in the 19th century accumulated huge quantities of significant Egyptian treasures, part of which make up the Staatliche Sammlung Ägyptischer Kunst. The collection is housed in an impressive modern building in Munich's superb Kunstareal. ⊠ *Gabelsbergerstr. 35, Maxvorstadt* ☎ *089/2892–7630* ⊕ *www.smaek.de* 🖼 *€7* ☉ *Closed Mon.* Ⓜ *Königsplatz.*

Fodor's Choice

★

Städtische Galerie im Lenbachhaus. This exquisite late-19th-century Florentine-style villa is the former home and studio of Franz von Lenbach (1836–1904), one of the most famous artists in Germany in the 1880s. He painted Germany's Chancellor Bismarck around 80 times. A renovation and new extension designed by renowned British architecture firm Foster+Partners was unveiled in 2013. Lenbachhaus is home to a stunning assemblage of art from the early-20th-century *Blaue Reiter* (Blue Rider) group: Kandinsky, Klee, Jawlensky, Macke, Marc, and Münter. Indeed, only New York's Guggenheim comes close to holding as many works from a group that was at the forefront in the development of abstract art. There are also vivid pieces from the New Objectivity movement, as well as a significant Joseph Beuys collection. The adjoining **Kunstbau** (art building) within the Königsplatz U-bahn station hosts changing exhibitions of contemporary art. ⊠ *Luisenstr. 33, Maxvorstadt* ☎ *089/2333–2000* ⊕ *www.lenbachhaus.de* 🖼 *€10* ☉ *Closed Mon.* Ⓜ *Königsplatz.*

The Glyptothek museum on Königsplatz houses Greek and Roman statues.

AU AND HAIDHAUSEN

On the east side of the River Isar, bordered by Lehel and Isarvorstadt to the west, lie Au and Haidhausen, calm, green, and pleasant residential areas punctuated with a few cafés and restaurants, and very conveniently located to Munich's Altstadt.

FAMILY
Fodor'sChoice
★

Museum Villa Stuck. This dramatic neoclassical villa is the former home of one of Germany's leading avant-garde artists from the turn of the 20th century, Franz von Stuck (1863–1928). His work, at times haunting, frequently erotic, and occasionally humorous, covers the walls in many rooms. Stuck was prominent in the Munich art Secession (1892), though today the museum is famous for its fabulous art nouveau collections. The museum also features special exhibits of international modern and contemporary art. ⊠ *Prinzregentenstr. 60, Haidhausen* ☎ *089/455–5510* ⊕ *www.villastuck.de* ⊠ *From €4* ⊗ *Closed Mon.* Ⓜ *Prinzregentenplatz, Friedensengel, Villa Stuck (Tram).*

OUTSIDE INNENSTADT

FAMILY
Bavaria Filmstadt. For real movie buffs, Munich has its own Hollywood-like neighborhood, the Geiselgasteig, in the affluent Grünwald district, on the southern outskirts of the city. A number of notable films, such as *Das Boot (The Boat)* and *Die Unendliche Geschichte (The Neverending Story)*, were made here. It was also here that in 1925 British filmmaker Alfred Hitchcock shot his first film, *The Pleasure Garden.* There are a number of tours and shows, including a 4-D cinema (in English at 1 pm in high season), and extra events for kids. ⊠ *Bavaria Filmpl.*

Continued on page 82

CELEBRATING OKTOBERFEST

By Ben Knight

Oktoberfests are found around the world, but the original Munich Oktoberfest has never been equaled. Six million participants over 16–18 days make this one of Europe's largest and best-attended festivals. It's a glorious celebration of beer, Bavarian culture, beer, folk traditions, and still more beer. So tap a barrel, grab a *Mass*, and join the party with the immortal cry: *O'zapft is!* ("It's tapped!").

You could be forgiven for reducing the world's most famous beer festival to a string of clichés—drunken revelers, deafening brass bands, and red-faced men in leather shorts and feathered hunting hats singing uproariously. But Oktoberfest appeals to a broad range of people—it can be a great day out for families, a fun night for couples, or the scene of a spectacular party for larger groups—and provides enough entertainment to exhaust kids of all ages. Party aside, Oktoberfest is a cultural institution with costumes, parades, and traditions that play an important role in Oktoberfest and are an integral part of local identity.

OKTOBERFEST BY THE NUMBERS
More than 6.9 million liters (1.82 million gallons) of beer are put away, along with 280,000 sausages, 550,000 roast chickens, and around 116 oxen on the 103-acre Theresienwiese every year.

Left, Theresienwiese fairground. Top, Festival procession band.

OKTOBERFEST 101

HISTORY

The original Oktoberfest was a royal wedding party conceived in 1810 by Major Andreas Michael Dall'Armi, an officer in the Bavarian national guard. The major suggested a horse race to celebrate the wedding of Crown Prince Ludwig I (the future king) and Princess Therese of Saxony-Hildburghausen. The sports event proved popular, and was repeated every year, but in the long–term it did not prove as popular as the barrels of beer and wagons of roasted meat that came from the countryside to feed the onlookers. Out of these catering departments, the Oktoberfest was born.

The Oktoberfest grounds were named *Theresienwiese* after Princess Therese (literally "Therese meadow"), which gave rise to the popular nickname *Wiesn* now used to denote the grounds and sometimes the festival itself.

TOP EVENTS

Three not-to-miss Oktoberfest events are worth planning your trip around. First, there's the **ceremonial arrival of the brewers and landlords,** which starts at about 10:50 am on the first day of the festival. Setting off from Josephspital-strasse approximately a mile east of the Theresienwiese, the brewers and beer-tent landlords arrive at the Oktoberfest grounds on horse-drawn carriages festooned with flowers.

This is followed at noon by the **tapping of the first barrel,** performed by the mayor of Munich with a cry of "*O'zapft is!*" in the Schottenhamel tent.

The first Sunday of the festival sees the **Costume and Rifleman's Procession** (*Trachten- und Schützenzug*). This is Europe's biggest folk parade, consisting of almost 8,000 people promenading through Munich on horse-drawn wagons, in marching bands, or in formation, all in their full folk regalia. It begins between 9 and 10 am at the

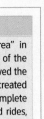

2

IN FOCUS CELEBRATING OKTOBERFEST

NOSTALGIA ZONE

The introduction of a "nostalgia area" in 2010, to mark the 200th anniversary of the first Oktoberfest, showed how well-loved the old sights and sounds remain. It recreated the Oktoberfests of simpler eras, complete with horse-racing, wooden fairground rides, and beer brewed using traditional recipes. It has now become a regular feature of the fest, known as the **Oide Wiesn** (Old Wiesn).

FOOD

The full range of hearty and surprisingly excellent Bavarian cuisine is available by table service in the tents. Tents that specialize in food, rather than beer (although they sell beer too), include sausage-centered **Zur Bratwurst;** fish emporium **Fischer-Vroni; Hochreiters Kalbsbraterei,** where you can try veal in myriad forms, among them the famous *Wiener Schnitzel;* and the **Ochsenbraterei,** which features ox meat.

The wide avenues between the tents are lined with stalls selling roast chicken, sugared almonds, *Lebkuchen* (decorated Bavarian gingerbread), and plenty of other baked or deep-fried treats for those who don't get a seat in a tent.

A main course in a tent can easily cost over €15, while half a chicken from a stall can cost over €10. Purchases are made in cash only, but there are ATMs near the main entrance, at the Theresienwiese U-bahn station, and throughout the Oktoberfest grounds.

COSTUMES

Walking to the Theresienwiese, you'll see more and more people wearing the traditional Oktoberfest costumes—*dirndls* (traditional dresses with a fitted bodice, blouse, skirt, and apron) for the ladies, and *lederhosen* (leather breeches) and leather waistcoats for the gentlemen. As a first-time visitor, you might be surprised by how many people of all ages actually wear the traditional Bavarian garb, also known as *Trachten.* Plenty of visitors wear it too; you can buy your Trachten from **Angermaier, Moser,** or more cheaply at department stores like **C&A** and **Galeria Kaufhof.**

GUIDE TO MAJOR BEER TENTS

The spectacular vista inside a beer tent is really what a trip to Oktoberfest is all about. There is something awe-inspiring about the sight of up to 10,000 people raising immense glasses of beer above their heads while a band leads a robust sing-along. This is a setting where the often reserved Germans let their inhibitions go, and since most of the seats are at long, communal tables, it's easy to make new friends. Below are descriptions of five of the 14 major tents. There are also 20 smaller beer tents. Altogether the tents, both large and small, provide some 100,000 seats.

SCHOTTENHAMEL
Scene: This is arguably the center of the Oktoberfest, because the mayor of Munich officially opens the festival here by tapping the first barrel. There's room for 9,000 people and it's considered the central party tent, where the young, single people of Munich gather.

Pros: Extremely lively, uninhibited atmosphere.

Cons: The emphasis is on drinking and dancing. This is not the place for a quiet, cozy chat.

Beer: Spaten-Franziskaner-Bräu has a fresh, malty taste with a clear amber color.

MARSTALL
Scene: New as a big tent since 2014, Marstall (meaning "royal riding school") has equipped their tent with an equestrian theme, evoking traditional horse imagery with carriages and carousels.

Pros: Happy to be in one of the big tents, the Able family's motivation to be a big player at Oktoberfest is palpable through the friendly service, and is a step up in class from some of the other tents.

Cons: With room for only 4,200 people, this is one of the smallest of the big beer tents, making it fairly hard to get a seat. Still, it's worth wandering around.

Beer: Spaten-Franziskaner-Bräu

Above, Revelers in the Hacker-Festzelt tent.

ABOUT THE BEER

Only the six Munich breweries (Spaten-Franziskaner-Bräu, Augustiner, Paulaner, Hacker-Pschorr, Hofbräu, and Löwenbräu) are allowed to sell beer at Oktoberfest. Each brews a special beer for the Oktoberfest with a higher alcohol percentage (6%, as opposed to 5%), and runs a major beer tent. Beer has surpassed €10 per *Mass* (liter).

HOFBRÄU-FESTZELT

Scene: This is the official Oktoberfest presence of the Hofbräuhaus, the immense beer hall in central Munich that has become one of the city's main tourist attractions. The proprietors take special pride in their international guests, and the tent has become an Oktoberfest launchpad for many U.S. and Australian revelers, with close to 10,000 seats.

Pros: This is the only main tent with a dance floor in front of the band. So you're spared precariously getting your groove on atop a wooden bench.

Cons: Since it's connected to the Hofbräuhaus, it can feel pretty touristy.

Beer: Hofbräu München has a sweet, yeasty flavor with a good frothy head.

LÖWENBRÄU-FESTZELT

Scene: The traditional home tent of Munich's soccer club TSV 1860 München, this 8,500-seat tent is the closest the Oktoberfest comes to a real, working-class Munich feel. Patrons are regaled at the entrance by a giant, beer-swilling plastic lion, who occasionally roars the name of his favorite beer—Löwenbräu—at new arrivals.

Pros: This tent has an unpretentious, what-you-see-is-what-you-get atmosphere.

Cons: Although the food here is good, it is pretty basic fare.

Beer: Löwenbräu is a strong beer with a slightly spicy flavor.

HACKER-FESTZELT

Scene: This tent is often nicknamed the "Bavarian heaven," mainly because of the painted clouds and other sky-related decor that hang from the ceiling (installed by Oscar-winning designer Rolf Zehetbauer). It has also become a favorite tent for native Bavarians.

Pros: This tent offers unique features including a rotating bandstand and a partially retractable roof for sunny days.

Cons: Because it's generally considered the most attractive of the tents, it fills up particularly quickly—so get a seat early.

Beer: Copper-colored Hacker-Pschorr has a bready taste and is one of the best of the Oktoberfest beers.

PLANNING FOR OKTOBERFEST

ADVANCE PLANNING Oktoberfest is one of Germany's biggest tourist events—it's estimated to contribute over one billion euros to Munich's economy—so you should plan everything at least six months in advance.

WHERE TO STAY Booking in advance is advisable for hotels, although you're unlikely to get a cheap deal anywhere in the immediate vicinity of Oktoberfest. For cheaper city-center options, especially if you're part of a bigger group, check out **Jaeger's Hotel** (⊕ *www.jaegershotel.de*) or **Smart Stay Hotels** (⊕ *smart-stay.de*). Otherwise book a hotel in Munich's outskirts and take public transit in.

RESERVATIONS The tents are free to enter, but if you want to sit and carouse into the evening, you need to reserve a seat at least six months in advance and up to ten months. Reservations are free, but the beer tents require you to buy food and drink vouchers with the reservation. Two liters of beer and half a chicken per seat is the usual standard minimum, and will cost a minimum of €30 per person, though could cost more depending on the tent and the time of day (evenings and weekends are more expensive). The vouchers can either be sent to you by mail (for a small fee), or picked up from special offices in Munich up to two weeks in advance. Reservations are only available through the individual beer tents, not through the Oktoberfest organizers. You can find the websites of the tents, plus addresses of the ticket offices on ⊕ *www. oktoberfest.de*.

WITHOUT RESERVATIONS There is only table service at the major tents, so in order to get served you must have a seat. If you don't have a reservation, come as early as you can; by mid-morning at the latest. One section of the central area of each tent (known as the *Mittelschiff*, or "mid-ship") is always reservation-free and you can snag a seat if you get there early. You can also sit in a reserved seat until its owner arrives.

HOURS Oktoberfest takes place the third weekend in September through the first weekend in October. It is open from 10 am to 11:30 pm every day, although the

Opposite, chain carousel at Oktoberfest fairground.

tents open at 9 am on weekends and public holidays. Last call is 10:30 pm.

RESTROOMS You can use the restrooms in any tent even if you're not drinking there. They are generally clean, well lit, and easy to find.

FAMILY DAYS Tuesdays are designated family days when there are discounts on all the fairground rides and food for kids. Rides range from old-fashioned carousels to vertiginous modern roller-coasters and cost under €10. There are also haunted houses, halls of mirrors, a flea circus, and many carnival games. Children are allowed in the beer tents, but kids under 6 years old must exit the tents after 8 pm.

PUBLIC TRANSIT The **Theresienwiese U-Bahn** (subway) stop is right outside Oktoberfest. However, this stop gets extremely crowded, particularly at closing time, so consider walking to either the nearby **Goetheplatz** or **Poccistrasse** stations. The **Hauptbahnhof**, where virtually all public transit lines converge, is just a 10- to 15-minute walk away.

TAXIS There is one taxi stand at the southern end of the Oktoberfest area, and taxis are easy to flag down in the city.

SAFETY Oktoberfest is generally very safe. There are plenty of security personnel in the tents and at the doors, and fights are rare. There is an information center, first aid, and police station behind the Schottenhamel tent. Sexual assault is not unknown at the Oktoberfest, but facilities have been revamped to increase safety, and a security point for women is located below the Bavaria statue in the service center next to the police and Red Cross. See ⊕ *www.sicherewiesn.de* for more safety information for women.

FOR MORE INFORMATION The official Oktoberfest website is ⊕ *www.oktoberfest.de*, which includes a useful English guide. The official "Oktoberfest.de" app offers news on upcoming events and a location feature in case you get lost.

7, Geiselgasteig ☎089/6499–2000 ⊕ *www.filmstadt.de* ☒ *From €6* Ⓜ *Grünwald, Bavariafilmplatz (Tram, Bus).*

FAMILY **BMW Museum.** Munich is the home of the famous BMW car company. The circular tower of its museum is one of the defining icons of Munich's modern cityscape. It contains not only a dazzling collection of BMWs old and new but also items and exhibitions relating to the company's social history and its technical developments. It's a great place to stop in if you're at the Olympiapark already. ⊠ *Am Olympiapark 2, Milbertshofen* ☎089/1250–16001 ⊕ *www.bmw-welt.com* ☒ *€10* ⊙ *Closed Mon.* Ⓜ *Olympiazentrum.*

FAMILY **BMW Welt.** Opened in 2007, the cutting-edge design of BMW Welt, with its sweeping, futuristic facade, is one structure helping to overcome the conservative image Munich has had in the realm of architecture since 1945. Even if you have just a passing interest in cars and engines, this showroom is a must—it has averaged 2 million visitors a year since its opening. In addition to tours of the building, there are readings, concerts, and exhibitions. Tours can only be booked via telephone or email. You can also visit the **BMW Plant** to see how a BMW car is made. It can be toured on weekdays (minimum age to participate is seven). Registration for plant tours, which last a maximum of 2½ hours, is only possible with a reservation. The tours start and finish at the north information counter at BMW Welt. Reserve at least two weeks in advance via phone or email; see the website for details. ⊠ *Am Olympiapark 1, Milbertshofen* ☎089/1250–16001 ⊕ *www.bmw-welt.com* ☒ *Tours from €8* ⊙ *BMW Plant closed weekends* Ⓜ *Olympiazentrum.*

FAMILY **Botanischer Garten** (*Botanical Garden*). On the northern edge of Schloss Nymphenburg, this collection of some 19,000 plants, including orchids, cacti, cycads, alpine flowers, and rhododendrons, makes up one of the most extensive botanical gardens in Europe. It is also used to provide a refuge for bee species, and for scientific research by local university students. ⊠ *Menzingerstr. 65, Nymphenburg* ☎089/1786–1310 ⊕ *www. botmuc.de* ☒ *€5* Ⓜ *Botanischer Garten (Tram).*

FAMILY
Fodor's Choice
★
Museum Mensch und Natur (*Museum of Man and Nature*). This popular museum in the north wing of Schloss Nymphenburg has nothing to do with the Wittelsbachs but is one of the palace's major attractions. Through interactive exhibits, the Museum Mensch und Natur looks at the variety of life on Earth, the history of humankind, and our place in the environment, as well as genetics and nature conservation. Main exhibits include a huge representation of the human brain and a chunk of Alpine crystal weighing half a ton. ⊠ *Schloss Nymphenburg, Nymphenburg* ☎089/179–5890 ⊕ *www.mmn-muenchen.de* ☒ *€3* ⊙ *Closed Mon.* Ⓜ *Schloss Nymphenburg (Tram or Bus).*

FAMILY **Neues Schloss Schleissheim** (*Schleissheim Palace*). Duke Wilhelm V found the perfect peaceful retreat outside Munich, and in 1598 built what is now known as the **Altes Schloss Schleissheim** (Schleissheim Old Palace). In 1685 Elector Max Emanuel added **Lustheim,** which houses one of Germany's most impressive collections of Meissen porcelain, and at the beginning of the 18th century the **Neues Schloss Schleissheim** (Schleissheim New Palace). This baroque palace's rooms display great works of art and outstanding interior decoration. ⊠ *Maximilianshof 1, Oberschleissheim* ☎ *089/315–8720* ⊕ *www.schloesser.bayern.de/englisch/palace/objects/schl_ns.htm* ⊡ *From €5* ☉ *Closed Mon.* Ⓜ *Oberschleissheim.*

FAMILY **Olympiapark** (*Olympic Park*). Built for the 1972 Olympic Games on the staggering quantities of rubble delivered from the wartime destruction of Munich, the Olympiapark was—and still is—considered an architectural and landscape wonder. The jewel in the crown is the **Olympic Stadium**, former home of Bayern Munich soccer team. With its truly avant-garde sweeping canopy roof, winding its way across various parts of the complex, it was an inspired design for the big events of the 1972 Olympic Games. Tragically, a bigger event relegated what was heading to be the most successful Games to date to the sidelines. It was from the adjacent accommodation area that a terrorist attack on the Israeli team began, eventually leaving 17 people dead.

Unlike many former Olympic sites around the world, today the area is heavily used; it's home to numerous concerts and sporting events, and is a haven for joggers, swimmers, and people just wishing to relax. Tours of the park are conducted on a Disneyland-style train throughout the day. For the more adventurous, how about climbing the roof of the Olympic Stadium and rappelling down or zip-lining 115 feet in the air across the stadium? For the best view of the whole city and the Alps, take the elevator up 623 feet to the viewing platform of the **Olympiaturm** (Olympic Tower) or try out the revolving **Restaurant 181**, at 181 meters (or 594 feet) above Munich. l. ⊠ *Spiridon-Louis-Ring 21, Milbertshofen* ☎ *089/3067–2414* ⊕ *www.olympiapark.de/en/olympiapark-munich* ⊡ *Stadium tour €8* Ⓜ *Olympiazentrum.*

FAMILY
Fodor'sChoice
★
Schloss Nymphenburg. This glorious baroque and rococo palace, the largest in Germany, grew in size and scope over more than 200 years. Begun in 1662 by the Italian architect Agostino Barelli, it was completed by his successor, Enrico Zuccalli. It represents a tremendous high point of Italian cultural influence, in what is undoubtedly Germany's most Italian city. Within the original building, now the central axis of the palace complex, is the magnificent **Steinerner Saal** (Great hall), extending over two floors and richly decorated with stucco and grandiose frescoes by masters such as François Cuvilliés the Elder and Johann Baptist Zimmermann. One of the surrounding royal chambers houses Ludwig I's famous **Schönheitsgalerie** (Gallery of Beauties), portraits of women who caught his roving eye. The palace park is laid out in formal French style, with low hedges and gravel walks extending into woodland. Among the ancient tree stands are three fascinating pavilions, including the **Amalienburg** hunting lodge by François Cuvilliés. It's also worth visiting the former royal stables, now the **Marstallmuseum**, which houses a fleet of carriages, coaches, and sleighs. In its upper rooms are examples of the world-renowned Nymphenburg porcelain, the electoral porcelain factory founded by Max III Joseph in 1747. ⊠ *Schloss Nymphenburg, Nymphenburg* ☎ *089/179–080* ⊕ *www.schloss-nymphenburg.de* ⊡ *From €5* ☉ *Amalienburg, Badenburg, Pagodenburg, and Magdalenenklause closed mid-Oct.–Apr.* Ⓜ *Schloss Nymphenburg (Tram or Bus).*

Wander the extensive grounds of Schloss Nymphenburg.

FAMILY **Tierpark Hellabrunn.** On the Isar, just upstream from the city, this attractive zoo has many parklike enclosures but a minimum of cages. Founded in 1911, the zoo is slightly different from most others in that it's a self-styled nature reserve, and it follows a concept called Geo-Zoo, which means care has been taken to group animals according to their natural and geographical habitats. Critics of the concept of zoos won't agree, but supporters appreciate the extra attention to detail. As well as the usual tours, there are also 90-minute nighttime guided tours with special night-vision equipment (register ahead of time at ⊕ *www.hellabrunn.de/anmeldeformular*; minimum age is 16). The huge zoo area also includes restaurants and children's areas, and some of the older buildings are in typical art nouveau style. ⊠ *Tierparkstr. 30, Harlaching* ✦ *From Marieneplatz, take U-bahn 3 to Thalkirchen, at southern edge of city* ☎ *089/625–080* ⊕ *www.hellabrunn.de/en* 🎟 *€15* Ⓜ *Thalkirchen (Tierpark), Tierpark (Alemannenstrasse) (Bus).*

WHERE TO EAT

Munich claims to be Germany's gourmet capital. It certainly has a large number of fine restaurants, but you won't have trouble finding a vast range of options in both price and style.

Typical, more substantial dishes in Munich include *Tellerfleisch,* boiled beef with freshly grated horseradish and boiled potatoes on the side, served on wooden plates. *Schweinebraten* (roast pork) is accompanied by dumplings and sauerkraut. *Hax'n* (ham hocks) are roasted until they're crisp on the outside and juicy on the inside. They are served with sauerkraut and potato puree. Game in season (venison or boar, for instance) and duck are served with potato dumplings and red cabbage. As for fish, the region has not only excellent trout, served either smoked as an hors d'oeuvre or fried or broiled as an entrée, but also the perchlike *Renke* from Lake Starnberg.

You'll also find soups, salads, casseroles, hearty stews, and a variety of baked goods—including *Breze* (pretzels). For dessert, indulge in a bowl of Bavarian cream, apple strudel, or *Dampfnudel,* a fluffy leavened-dough dumpling usually served with vanilla sauce.

The generic term for a snack is *Imbiss,* and thanks to growing internationalism you'll find a huge variety, from the generic *Wiener* (hot dogs) to the Turkish *döner kebab* sandwich (pressed and roasted lamb, beef, or chicken). Almost all butcher shops and bakeries offer some sort of *Brotzeit,* which can range from a modest sandwich to a steaming plate of goulash with potatoes and salad. A classic beer-garden Brotzeit is a Breze with Obatzda (a cheese spread made from Camembert and paprika served with freshly sliced rings of onion).

Some edibles come with social etiquette attached. The *Weisswurst,* a tender minced-veal sausage—made fresh daily, steamed, and served with sweet mustard and a crisp pretzel—is a Munich institution and, theoretically, should be eaten before noon with a *Weissbier* (wheat beer), supposedly to counteract the effects of a hangover. Some people use a knife and fork to peel off the skin, while others might indulge in *auszuzeln,* sucking the sausage out of the skin.

Another favorite Bavarian specialty is *Leberkäs*—literally "liver cheese," though neither liver nor cheese is among its ingredients. Rather, it's a sort of meat loaf baked to a crust each morning and served in pink slabs throughout the day. A *Leberkässemmel*—a wedge of the meat loaf between two halves of a bread roll slathered with a slightly spicy mustard—is the favorite Munich on-the-go snack.

Prices in the reviews are the average cost of a main course at dinner, or if dinner is not served, at lunch. Use the coordinates (✢ B3) at the end of each listing to locate a site on the corresponding map.

WHAT IT COSTS IN EUROS			
$	$$	$$$	$$$$
AT DINNER	under €15	€15–€20	€21–€25	over €25

Price per person for a main course or equivalent combination of smaller dishes at dinner.

ALTSTADT

$
FRENCH
✕ **Brasserie L'Atelier Art & Vin.** Take a seat by the wall of windows or at the long blond-wood bar, in this airy, casual brasserie, which specializes in French food and wine; the light, crisp quiches, in particular, are a delight. On nice days, tables are set outside on the sidewalk of the pleasant, relatively quiet street and the Bier & Oktoberfestmuseum is

right next door, highlighting the wonderful contrasts that are so typical of this city. **Known for:** regional French specialties like escargots from Burgundy; traditional boudin noir de l'atelier (Alsatian blood sausage); an extensive list of French wines by the glass. $ *Average main: €13* ✉ *Westenriederstr. 43, Altstadt* ☎ *089/2126–6782* ⊕ *www.brasserie-atelier.de* ▭ *No credit cards* ⊗ *Closed Sun. and Mon.* Ⓜ *Marienplatz, Isartor* ✛ *E5.*

$$
EUROPEAN

✕ **Brasserie OskarMaria.** Inside Literaturhaus, a converted Renaissance-style schoolhouse that is now a literary center, this stylish brasserie is named after Munich writer Oskar Maria Graf, who fled to New York after the Nazis took power. The vaulted ceiling and plate-glass windows create an airy, modern atmosphere to enjoy the eclectic international menu, ranging from saffron-and-crayfish risotto to beetroot dumplings with goat cheese, while its sprawling terrace is one of the city's best outdoor eating locations. **Known for:** top-quality seasonal fish and produce; in-house bakery; award-winning interior design. $ *Average main: €16* ✉ *Salvatorpl. 1, Altstadt* ☎ *089/2919–6029* ⊕ *www.oskarmaria.com* Ⓜ *Odeonsplatz, Marienplatz* ✛ *D3.*

$
GERMAN

✕ **Bratwurstherzl.** Tucked into a quaint little square off Viktualienmarkt, this delightful Bratwurst joint, dating from 1901, cooks up specialty sausages over an open grill right in the main red-brick vaulted dining room. For those looking for a bit less meat, there is also a hearty farmer's salad with veal strips and tasty oyster mushrooms. **Known for:** thin roasted Rostbratwurst sausages from Nuremberg; daily Bavarian specialties like Leberkäs; a good selection of Franconian wines by the glass. $ *Average main: €9* ✉ *Dreifaltigkeitspl. 1, Altstadt* ☎ *089/295–113* ⊕ *www.bratwurstherzl.de* ⊗ *Closed Sun.* Ⓜ *Marienplatz* ✛ *E5.*

$$$
INTERNATIONAL

✕ **Brenner Operngrill.** In an impressive columned hall that once was the stables of the royal residence, this sprawling restaurant features three distinct indoor dining spaces—the main grill room with an open fire, a smaller area serving homemade pasta, and a casual bar with lounge-like vibe—plus a small seasonal terrace. Particularly popular is the Sunday brunch, from 9:30 to 3, with a large selection of organic egg dishes and omelets. **Known for:** affordable daily lunch special; grilled beef and seafood; vegetarian and vegan options. $ *Average main: €24* ✉ *Maximilianstr. 15, Altstadt* ☎ *089/452–2880* ⊕ *www.brennergrill.de* Ⓜ *Marienplatz* ✛ *F4.*

$$$
EUROPEAN

✕ **Buffet Kull.** This chic yet comfortable Parisian-style bistro delivers a high-quality dining experience accompanied by an impressive variety of wines and friendly service. The daily specials are creative, portions are generous, and the prices are good value for the quality—all of which make this a very popular spot, so be sure to make a reservation. **Known for:** French-inspired dishes like coq au vin; homemade pastas; New York steak. $ *Average main: €25* ✉ *Marienstr. 4, Altstadt* ☎ *089/221–509* ⊕ *www.buffet-kull.de* Ⓜ *Marienplatz* ✛ *F5.*

$
BURGER

✕ **Cosmogrill.** Gourmet burgers made using organic beef, homemade sauces, and freshly baked buns make this casual spot a cut above typical fast-food joints—and it stays open until the wee hours should you need a late-night bite. For non-meat-eaters, there are plenty of choices, including three varieties of veggie burger, a spicy wasabi tuna burger, several salads, plus highly addictive potato wedges. **Known for:** wagyu burger topped with black truffles, Grana Padano and Dijon mustard aioli; BBQ bacon burger with onion rings; quick, affordable meals. [$] *Average main: €9* ✉ *Maximilianstr. 10, Altstadt* ✥ *Enter on Falkenturmstr.* ☎ *089/8905–9696* 🌐 *www.cosmogrill.de* ▭ *No credit cards* [M] *Nationaltheater (Tram)* ✥ *E4.*

$ ITALIAN Fodor's Choice ★ 🍴 **Due Passi.** So small it's easy to miss, this former dairy shop now offers a limited but fine selection of Italian fare, with a menu of fresh antipasti and pasta that changes daily. The high wooden tables and counters fill up fast at this lunch-only spot, so arrive early for the quieter, cooler window seat or take your food to go. **Known for:** signature penne "Due Passi"; two daily pasta specials; nostalgic setting. [$] *Average main: €8* ✉ *Ledererstr. 11, Altstadt* ☎ *089/224–271* 🌐 *duepassi.de* ▭ *No credit cards* ⏲ *Closed Sun. No dinner* [M] *Marienplatz* ✥ *E5.*

$ GERMAN FAMILY 🍴 **Hofbräuhaus.** The Hofbräuhaus is the most famous beer hall not just in Munich but in the world—a kitschy multiroom space with a pounding oompah band and singing and shouting drinkers contributing to the festive atmosphere. The courtyard beer garden provides an escape from the noise in good weather, and there's also a quieter upstairs restaurant where the food is fine, although there are better places in Munich for Bavarian cuisine. **Known for:** home-brewed original beer from the Hofbräuhaus brewery; seasonal specialty brews; Munich veal sausage with sweet mustard. [$] *Average main: €12* ✉ *Platzl 9, Altstadt* ☎ *089/2901–36100* 🌐 *www.hofbraeuhaus.de/en/welcome.html* [M] *Marienplatz, Isartor* ✥ *F5.*

$ GERMAN 🍴 **Jodlerwirt.** This cozy, alpine lodge–style restaurant in a small street behind the Rathaus is a treat for those craving an old-world tavern, complete with live accordion playing and yodelers who perform most nights, telling jokes and poking fun at their adoring guests in unintelligible Bavarian slang. The food is traditional Bavarian and the tasty beer is from the Ayinger brewery. **Known for:** homemade Käsespätzle (a hearty dish similar to macaroni and cheese); meal-size salads; festive atmosphere. [$] *Average main: €14* ✉ *Altenhofstr. 4, Altstadt* ☎ *089/221–249* 🌐 *www.jodlerwirt-muenchen.net* ▭ *No credit cards* ⏲ *Closed Sun. and Mon. except during Oktoberfest* [M] *Marienplatz* ✥ *E5.*

$$$$ ASIAN FUSION 🍴 **Matsuhisa Munich.** The only German outpost of the Japanese-Peruvian fusion concept from celebrated chef Nobuyuki (Nobu) Matsuhisa, this elegant, sleekly designed restaurant in the posh Mandarin Oriental hotel is a favorite of well-heeled locals. Along with top-notch sushi and sashimi, the menu features innovative flavor combinations like scallops layered with foie gras in a vanilla-miso sauce and for dessert, a matcha-dusted chocolate cake with green tea ice cream cleverly presented in a bento box. **Known for:** black cod miso; yellowtail sashimi with jalapeños; rare sake list. [$] *Average main: €40* ✉ *Mandarin Oriental Munich, Neuturmstr. 1, Altstadt* ☎ *089/2909–81875* 🌐 *www.mandarinoriental.de/munich/fine-dining/matsuhisa-munich* [M] *Marienplatz* ✥ *F5.*

$ ITALIAN 🍴 **Nero Pizza & Lounge.** On a side street between Gärtnerplatz and Isartor, Nero serves up excellent thin-crust pizzas with fresh ingredients imported straight from Italy—try the Diavolo, with spicy Neapolitan salami—as well as solid pastas and great steaks. The restaurant's high

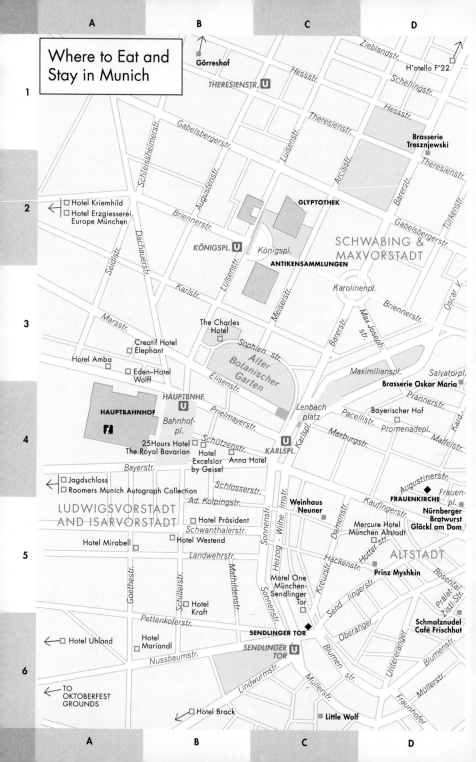

Where to Eat and Stay in Munich

A **B** **C** **D**

1

Görreshof

THERESIENSTR. U

H'otello F'22

Zieblandstr.

Schellingstr.

Hessstr.

Hessstr.

Theresienstr.

Brasserie
Tresznjewski

Theresienstr.

2

Hotel Kriemhild
Hotel Erzgiesserei
Europe München

Gabelsbergerstr.

Schleissheimerstr.

Luisenstr.

Arcisstr.

GLYPTOTHEK

Augustenstr.

Brienerstr.

KÖNIGSPL. U

Königspl.

ANTIKENSAMMLUNGEN

SCHWABING &
MAXVORSTADT

Gabelsbergerstr.

Türkenstr.

Barerstr.

Oscar V.

Dachauerstr.

Seidlstr.

Karlstr.

Luisenstr.

Meiserstr.

Karolinenpl.

Brienerstr.

3

Marsstr.

The Charles
Hotel

Sophien str.

Alter
Botanischer
Garten

Max-Joseph-str.

Barerstr.

Maximilianspl.

Salvatorpl.

Brasserie Oskar Maria

Creatif Hotel
Elephant

Hotel Amba

Eden–Hotel
Wolff

Elisenstr.

Lenbach
platz

Prannerstr.

Bayerischer Hof

Pacellistr.

Promenadepl.

Kard.

4

HAUPTBNHF.
U

HAUPTBAHNHOF

i

Bahnhof-
pl.

Prielmayerstr.

Schützenstr.

KARLSPL. U

Karlspl.

Maxburgstr.

Maffeistr.

25Hours Hotel
The Royal Bavarian

Hotel
Excelsior
by Geisel

Anna Hotel

Bayerstr.

5

Jagdschloss
Roomers Munich Autograph Collection

Schlosserstr.

Ad. Kolpingstr.

LUDWIGSVORSTADT
AND ISARVORSTADT

Hotel Präsident

Schwanthalerstr.

Hotel Mirabell

Hotel Westend

Landwehrstr.

Sonnenstr.

Herzog - Wilhe lmstr.

Weinhaus
Neuner

Damenstr.

Kaufingerstr.

Augustinerstr.

FRAUENKIRCHE

Frauen-
pl.

Nürnberger
Bratwurst
Glöckl am Dom

Mercure Hotel
München Altstadt

Hackenstr.

Sendlinger str.

Hotter str.

ALTSTADT

Rosental

Prinz Myshkin

6

Hotel Uhland

Hotel
Mariandl

Hotel
Kraft

Schillerstr.

Goethestr.

Mathildenstr.

Pettenkoferstr.

Nussbaumstr.

Motel One
München-
Sendlinger
Tor

Sonnenstr.

SENDLINGER TOR

SENDLINGER
TOR U

Lindwurmstr.

Müllerstr.

Kreuzstr.

Blumen str.

Oberanger

Unteranger

Fraunhofer

Blumenstr.

Müllerstr.

Prälat- Zistl- Str.

Schmalznudel
Café Frischhut

TO
OKTOBERFEST
GROUNDS

Hotel Brack

Little Wolf

A **B** **C** **D**

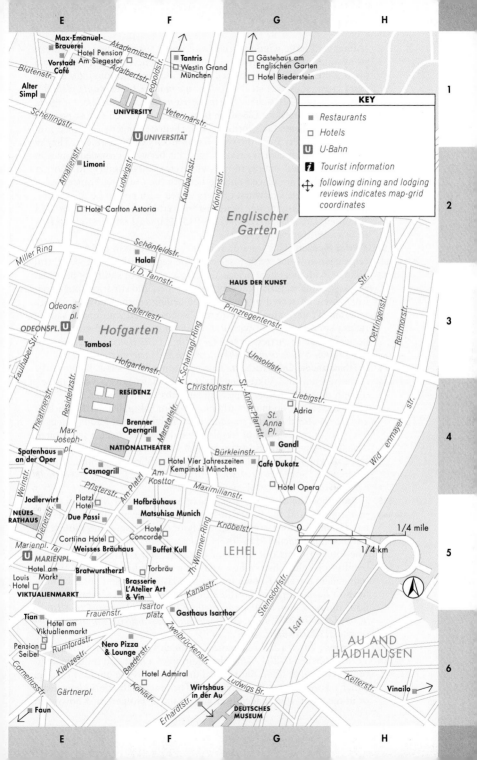

ceilings and large windows give it an open, spacious feel, or you can sit upstairs in the lounge for a cozier experience. **Known for:** bufala pizza with mozzarella imported from Campana; optional gluten-free pizza crust; sous vide steaks. $ Average main: €12 ⊠ Rumfordstr. 34, Altstadt ☎ 089/2101–9060 ⊕ www.nero-muenchen.de Ⓜ Isartor ✛ F6.

$
GERMAN

✕ **Nürnberger Bratwurst Glöckl am Dom.** One of Munich's most popular taverns is dedicated to Nürnberger Bratwürste (finger-size grilled sausages), a specialty from the rival Bavarian city of Nuremberg. They're served by dirndl-clad waitresses who flit between crowded tables in the dark-paneled dining rooms with remarkable agility; in warmer months, tables are placed outside beneath the towering Frauenkirche. **Known for:** huge Bratwurst platters served with potato salad and sauerkraut; fresh Augustiner beer; historic setting. $ Average main: €13 ⊠ Frauenpl. 9, Altstadt ☎ 089/291–9450 ⊕ www.bratwurst-gloeckl.de/en/home Ⓜ Marienplatz ✛ D5.

$$
VEGETARIAN
Fodor'sChoice
★

✕ **Prinz Myshkin.** This restaurant is one of the finest in the city, and it's vegetarian to boot, with a selection of vegan dishes. The delightful holiday from meat here brings an eclectic choice of skillfully prepared antipasti, quiche, pizza, gnocchi, tofu, crepes, and stir-fries, plus excellent wines, all served in an airy, high-ceiling room. **Known for:** tofu Stroganoff (marinated tofu with mushrooms in red wine cream sauce); ricotta spinach gnocchi with Parmesan and roasted pine nuts in sage butter; excellent curries. $ Average main: €16 ⊠ Hackenstr. 2, Altstadt ☎ 089/265–596 ⊕ prinzmyshkin.com/en Ⓜ Marienplatz ✛ D5.

$
GERMAN

✕ **Schmalznudel Café Frischhut.** This café, on a busy street between the Stadtmuseum and Viktualienmarkt, is as Bavarian as you can get, though it serves neither typical great slabs of meat nor Knödel. The fryers are turned on in the early morning for Viktualienmarkt workers and stay on for those still standing after a night out; at midday, lines of people wait for helpings of freshly cooked Schmalznudel, a selection of doughnut-type creations, from apple to sugar-coated to plain. **Known for:** cozy vintage setting; local favorite; plum-filled doughnuts. $ Average main: €2 ⊠ Prälat-Zistl-Str. 8, Altstadt ☎ 089/268–237 ▭ No credit cards ☉ Closed Sun. Ⓜ Marienplatz ✛ D5.

$$$
GERMAN

✕ **Spatenhaus an der Oper.** You'll have great views of Munich's grand opera house and the Bavarian National Theater, not to mention the hand-painted ceilings, on the second floor of this restaurant, though the outdoor tables facing Max-Joseph Square are best for people-watching. The kitchen turns out a mix of Bavarian and Austrian fare, plus a handful of lighter fish dishes, and what's considered the best Wiener schnitzel in the city. **Known for:** crispy roasted pork and potato dumplings in dark beer sauce; grilled or panfried fish; an elegant second-floor dining room. $ Average main: €21 ⊠ Residenzstr. 12, Altstadt ☎ 089/290–7060 ⊕ www.kuffler.de/en/restaurant/spatenhaus Ⓜ Odeonsplatz, Marienplatz ✛ E4.

$$$
ITALIAN

✕ **Tambosi.** After a full renovation, Munich's oldest café, dating from 1775, reopened in 2017 with the addition of a high-end Italian restaurant on its upper floor. But the real draw remains the outdoor seating, either on the terrace in full view of Theatinerkirche on Odeonsplatz or in the quiet, tree-shaded beer garden in the Hofgarten. **Known for:**

excellent location next to the Residenz and Hofgarten; good selection of salads; somewhat erratic service. $ *Average main: €24* ⊠ *Odeonspl. 18, Altstadt* ☎ *089/9018–3076* ⊕ *tambosi-odeonsplatz.de* Ⓜ *Odeonsplatz, Marienplatz* ✛ *E3.*

$$$$

VEGETARIAN

✕ **Tian.** This stylish vegetarian restaurant at the Viktualienmarkt uses whatever organic produce is in season to craft modern, brilliantly composed dishes, available à la carte or as part of a four- to eight-course tasting menu. The Light Lunch, served Tuesday to Friday from noon to 2, is well-priced with either two to three courses; for a speedier midday meal, choose from several excellent tarte flambée options, with seasonal, locally sourced toppings. **Known for:** organic vegetarian and vegan fare in an upscale setting; seasonal lunch and dinner tasting menus; fresh herb cocktails like the Sparkling Cucumber Mint Gin. $ *Average main: €52* ⊠ *Frauenstr. 4, Altstadt* ☎ *089/8856–56712* ⊕ *www.tianrestaurant.com* ⊗ *Closed Sun. and Mon.* Ⓜ *Marienplatz* ✛ *E6.*

$$$$

GERMAN

✕ **Weinhaus Neuner.** Munich's oldest wine tavern serves upscale food as well as superior wines in its two nooks: the wood-panel restaurant and the Weinstube (wine bar). The choice of food is remarkable, from roast duck to fish to modern interpretations of Bavarian and Austrian dishes. **Known for:** 4- and 5-course tasting menus (restaurant only); chicken fricassee with truffles in a puff pastry; interesting wine list. $ *Average main: €45* ⊠ *Herzogspitalstr. 8, Altstadt* ☎ *089/260–3954* ⊕ *www.weinhaus-neuner.de* Ⓜ *Marienplatz, Karlsplatz (Stachus)* ✛ *C5.*

$

GERMAN

✕ **Weisses Bräuhaus.** If you've developed a taste for Weissbier, this Munich institution—beautifully restored to something approaching how it would have looked when first opened in the 1870s—is the place to indulge. The tasty wheat beer from Schneider, a Bavarian brewery in existence since 1872, is served with hearty Bavarian dishes by famously straight-talking waitresses. **Known for:** 10 wheat beers on tap (plus specialty bottles); a "skirt steak kitchen" serving traditionally prepared offal; live Bavarian music. $ *Average main: €14* ⊠ *Tal 7, Altstadt* ☎ *089/290–1380* ⊕ *www.weisses-brauhaus.de* Ⓜ *Marienplatz, Isartor* ✛ *E5.*

LEHEL

$

FRENCH

✕ **Café Dukatz.** With two locations—one in Maxvorstadt on Klenzesstrasse 69 and this one in Lehel—Café Dukatz has made a name for itself with its delicious home-baked, French-style pastries. They also serve fine coffee and freshly pressed juices, as well as sandwiches, salads, and mainly vegetarian quiches for a quick lunch. **Known for:** flaky croissants, brioches, and tarts; freshly baked baguettes; excellent coffee. $ *Average main: €4* ⊠ *St.-Anna-Str. 11, Lehel* ☎ *089/2303–2444 St.-Anna-Str., 089/2006–2893 Klenzestr.* ⊕ *www.dukatz.de* ⊟ *No credit cards* Ⓜ *Lehel* ✛ *G4.*

$$$

FRENCH FUSION

✕ **Gandl.** This specialty shop, which stocks various European staples from French cheese to Belgian chocolate, doubles as a comfortable, relaxed restaurant; in summer, tables spill out onto St.-Anna-Platz in a charming setting. At lunch Gandl is ideal for a quick pasta or excellent antipasto misto before proceeding with the day's adventures, while dinner has more of a French flair. **Known for:** Saturday breakfast buffet;

spaghetti carbonara or bolognese (lunch only); the five-course tasting menu (dinner only). $ *Average main: €23* ✉ *St.-Anna-Pl. 1, Lehel* ☎ *089/2916–2525* 🌐 *www.gandl.de* ⏲ *Closed Sun.* [M] *Lehel* ✥ *G4.*

$ GERMAN 🍴 **Gasthaus Isarthor.** This old-fashioned *Wirtshaus* is one of the few places that serve Augustiner beer exclusively from wooden kegs, freshly tapped on a daily basis—beer simply doesn't get any better than this. Antlers and a wild boar look down on actors, government officials, apprentice craftspersons, journalists, and retirees, all sitting side by side at the simple wooden tables enjoying good traditional Bavarian fare. **Known for:** "Isarthor" plate with duck, roast pork, and red cabbage; Weisswurst breakfast with beer; inexpensive daily lunch dishes. $ *Average main: €11* ✉ *Kanalstr. 2, Lehel* ☎ *089/227–753* 🌐 *www.gasthaus-isarthor.de* 💳 *No credit cards* [M] *Isartor* ✥ *F5.*

LUDWIGSVORSTADT AND ISARVORSTADT

$ ECLECTIC 🍴 **Faun.** This happy combination of Munich tavern and international bistro is set on Hans-Sachs-Strasse, one of the city's most interesting streets. The Thai curries are wonderful, the juicy Schweinebraten will satisfy any meat cravings, and the beer served is Augustiner, so you can't go wrong there. **Known for:** affordable daily lunch menu; classic decor; seasonal outdoor seating. $ *Average main: €9* ✉ *Hans-Sachs-Str. 17, Ludwigsvorstadt* ☎ *089/263–798* 🌐 *www.faun.mycosmos.biz* 💳 *No credit cards* [M] *Frauenhoferstrasse* ✥ *E6.*

$ BARBECUE 🍴 **Little Wolf.** Step into the Deep South at this hip barbecue and soul food joint, decked out like an old-school American diner, with an open kitchen turning out slowly smoked meats including baby back ribs and brisket in homemade sauces. There are also fine renditions of such southern staples as spicy jambalaya and shrimp with creamy cheese grits, plus a host of tasty sides like collard greens and mac 'n' cheese. **Known for:** authentic smoked barbecue; homemade pastrami sandwich on rye; no reservations. $ *Average main: €14* ✉ *Pestalozzistr. 9, Ludwigsvorstadt* ☎ *089/8563–6152* 🌐 *little-wolf.de* ⏲ *Closed Sun.* 💳 *No credit cards* [M] *Sendlinger Tor* ✥ *C6.*

SCHWABING AND MAXVORSTADT

$ GERMAN 🍴 **Alter Simpl.** This cozy, atmospheric pub-restaurant has been a Munich institution since 1903, when it was a meeting place for leading writers, comedians, and artists whose pictures now hang on the dark, wood-panel walls. The beer's good and the equally good food, which includes filling options like roast pork, currywurst, and a bacon-cheeseburger with french fries, is served until 2 am (beer until 3 am) and even later on weekends. **Known for:** bohemian atmosphere; Munich- and Viennese-style schnitzel; late-night menu. $ *Average main: €11* ✉ *Türkenstr. 57, Maxvorstadt* ☎ *089/272–3083* 🌐 *www.eggerlokale.de* 💳 *No credit cards* [M] *Universität* ✥ *E1.*

$ INTERNATIONAL 🍴 **Brasserie Tresznjewski.** A good spot, especially if you're visiting the neighboring Pinakothek museums, this convivial corner bar and café attracts an interesting mix of students, artists, businesspeople, and trendy types from breakfast well into the wee hours. The menu features salads, sandwiches, and small selection of pastas—solid, affordable fare that won't exactly wow you—but the restaurant's art deco touches, funky artwork, and buzzy vibe are thoroughly enjoyable. **Known for:** Treszi's famous burger; loud late-night scene; excellent classic cocktails. $ *Average main: €14* ✉ *Theresienstr. 72, Maxvorstadt* ☎ *089/282–349* ⊕ *www.tresznjewski.com* Ⓜ *Pinakotheken (Tram)* ✛ *D2.*

$ ✕ **Görreshof.** In 1893 Augustiner, the oldest brewery in Munich, built
GERMAN   this sturdy Wirtshaus to sustain travelers on the 12-km (7-mile) trek from Munich to the castles at Schleissheim. Today it's as much a forum for good eating and drinking as it was more than 100 years ago, where you can enjoy hearty Bavarian food in a dining room festooned with antlers, in the cozy, quiet Bibliothek (library) or out on the covered terrace. **Known for:** "Little Alps Trio" platter with sausages and mini meat loaf; tavern stew of beef, pork, and veal in a spicy sauce; Rahm-schwammerl (dumplings in mushroom sauce). $ *Average main: €14* ✉ *Görresstr. 38, Maxvorstadt* ☎ *089/2020–9550* ⊕ *www.goerreshof. de* Ⓜ *Josephsplatz* ✛ *B1.*

$$$$ ✕ **Halali.** With nearly 100 years of history to its credit, polished wood
GERMAN   paneling, and antlers on the walls, the Halali is an old-style Munich restaurant that is *the* place to try traditional dishes of venison, pheasant, partridge, and other game in a quiet and elegant atmosphere. Save room for the crème brûlée with hazelnut ice cream. **Known for:** homemade fried blood and liver sausages; suckling pig; Bavarian smoked eel. $ *Average main: €31* ✉ *Schönfeldstr. 22, Maxvorstadt* ☎ *089/285–909* ⊕ *www.restaurant-halali.de* ⊘ *Closed Sun.* 🏛 *Jacket and tie* Ⓜ *Odeon-splatz* ✛ *F2.*

$$$ ✕ **Limoni.** There are a number of fine Italian restaurants around the
ITALIAN   city, but this is certainly one of the best, with excellent, often experi-
Fodor's Choice mental meat and fish dishes and lovely pastas that are a little more
★   budget-friendly. Be sure to reserve a table in good weather so you can sit on the charming patio in the back. **Known for:** four- and five-course tasting menus; seasonal homemade pastas; classic and creative Italian dishes. $ *Average main: €24* ✉ *Amalienstr. 38, Maxvorstadt* ☎ *089/2880–6029* ⊕ *www.limoni-ristorante.com* ⊘ *Closed Sun. No lunch* Ⓜ *Universität* ✛ *E2.*

$ ✕ **Max-Emanuel-Brauerei.** This historic brewery-tavern, first opened in
GERMAN   1880, offers great value Bavarian dishes. The best part about this place, however, is the cozy, secluded little beer garden (April–October) with huge chestnut trees, tucked in the back amid the apartment blocks in the heart of Munich's University district. **Known for:** Viennese-style schnitzels served weekends; good choice of vegetarian dishes; good selection of beers and wines by the glass. $ *Average main: €10* ✉ *Adalbertstr. 33, Schwabing* ☎ *089/271–5158* ⊕ *www.max-emanuel-brauerei.de* Ⓜ *Universität, Giselastrasse* ✛ *E1.*

$$$$ ✕ **Tantris.** Few restaurants in Germany can match the Michelin-starred
EUROPEAN   Tantris, which features unusual, sophisticated interpretations of classic
Fodor's Choice French cuisine by legendary chef Hans Haas. While it's possible to order
★   à la carte, you're better off opting (as the vast majority of guests do) for the tasting menu (three to five courses at lunch; five or eight courses at dinner) and let the skilled sommelier handle the wine pairings with

seasonal dishes such as confit of Dover sole with white asparagus and yuzu mousse. **Known for:** gourmet tasting menus; distinctive interior design; flawless service. $ *Average main: €195* ✉ *Johann-Fichte-Str. 7, Schwabing* ☎ *089/361–9590* ⊕ *www.tantris.de/en* ⊙ *Closed Sun.– Tues. Jan.–Sept.; closed Sun. and Mon. Oct.–Dec.* 🏛 *Jacket and tie* Ⓜ *Münchener Freiheit, Dietlindenstrasse* ✛ *F1.*

$ ✗ **Vorstadt Café.** Young professionals mix with students at this lively
INTERNATIONAL restaurant, a symphony in red and orange in an ode to the 1970s, whose 13 different breakfasts are a big draw: the Vorstadt Classic includes bacon and eggs, rolls, and several other kinds of bread, along with a plate of salami and homemade jam. Quick daily lunch specials are a good value, while the atmosphere at dinner is relaxed, complete with candlelight. **Known for:** sweet, savory, and vegetarian breakfast plates; fresh pastas; lengthy cocktail list. $ *Average main: €14* ✉ *Türkenstr. 83, Maxvorstadt* ☎ *089/272–0699* ⊕ *www.vorstadt-cafe.de* ▭ *No credit cards* Ⓜ *Universität* ✛ *E1.*

AU AND HAIDHAUSEN

$$$$ ✗ **Vinaiolo.** In the setting of an old apothecary, diners can enjoy special-
ITALIAN ties from Venice and other northern Italian regions, such as Florentine soup with tortellini and whole salt-crusted sea bass from chef Gianni Ianniccari. Service is good-humored and conscientious, and the menu changes regularly. **Known for:** daily changing lunch menu; extensive wine list; reservations required. $ *Average main: €28* ✉ *Steinstr. 42, Haidhausen* ☎ *089/4895–0356* ⊕ *www.vinaiolo.de* Ⓜ *Rosenheimer Platz* ✛ *H6.*

$$ ✗ **Wirtshaus in der Au.** *Wirtshaus* describes a kind of bar-restaurant serv-
GERMAN ing traditional Bavarian food and beer, and this one, with its great vaulted room lined with beer steins, has been doing so since 1901. It has a combination of fantastic service and outstanding local dishes, including *Hofente* (roast duck) and *Schweinsbraten* (roast pork), but the real specialty, and for which it is renowned, is *Knödel* (dumplings), which, in addition to traditional *Semmel* (bread) and *Kartoffel* (potato) varieties, come in spinach, cheese, and even red-beet flavors. **Known for:** Auer dark beer; homemade organic lemonades; weekend-only breakfast of Bavarian specialties. $ *Average main: €14* ✉ *Lilienstr. 51* ☎ *089/448– 1400* ⊕ *wirtshausinderau.de/en* Ⓜ *Isartor, Rosenheimerplatz* ✛ *F6.*

WHERE TO STAY

Although Munich has a vast number of hotels in all price ranges, booking can be a challenge, as this is a trade-show city as well as a prime tourist destination. If you're visiting during any of the major trade fairs such as the ISPO (sports, fashion) in February or the IHM (crafts) in March, or during Oktoberfest at the end of September, try to make reservations at least a few months in advance. It is acceptable here to request to see a room before committing to it, so feel free to ask at check-in.

2

Some of the large, upscale hotels that cater to expense-account business travelers offer attractive weekend discounts—sometimes as much as 50% below normal prices. Conversely, most hotels raise their regular rates by at least 30% during big trade fairs and Oktoberfest. Online booking sites like Hotel Reservation Service (⊕ *www.hrs.com*) often have prices well below the hotel's published prices (i.e., price ranges in this guide) in slow periods and on short notice. Look for the names we suggest here and search online for potential deals.

■ TIP➔ **Munich's tourist information office has two outlets that can help you with hotel bookings if you haven't reserved in advance. One is outside the Hauptbahnhof, or central station, and the other is at Marienplatz, in the Rathaus information office. Your best bet is to visit in person.**

Prices in the reviews are the lowest cost of a standard double room in high season. For expanded reviews, facilities, and current deals, visit Fodors.com. Use the coordinates (⊹ B3) at the end of each listing to locate a site on the corresponding map.

WHAT IT COSTS IN EUROS			
$	$$	$$$	$$$$
under €100	€100–€175	€176–€225	over €225

FOR TWO PEOPLE

Prices reflect the rack rate of a standard double room for two people in high season, including tax. Check online for off-season rates and special deals or discounts.

ALTSTADT

$$$$
HOTEL
Fodor's Choice
★

Bayerischer Hof. It would be easy to pigeonhole the Bayerische Hof as just another luxury hotel, but this property, opened in 1841, is a unique combination of luxury, history, and accessibility, offering minimalist-chic rooms in one wing refurbished in 2018 with the addition of two full floors as well as suites in the adjoining Palais Montgelas. **Pros:** superb public rooms with valuable oil paintings; roof garden restaurant has an impressive view of the Frauenkirche; Atelier restaurant has a habit of garnering Michelin stars. **Cons:** expensive accommodations; layout can be confusing; fee for higher-speed Wi-Fi. Ⓢ *Rooms from: €504* ⊠ *Promenadepl. 2–6, Altstadt* ☎ *089/21200* ⊕ *www.bayerischerhof.de/en* ➔ *411 rooms* ⦿ *No meals* Ⓜ *Karlsplatz, Marienplatz* ⊹ *D4.*

$$$$
HOTEL

Cortiina Hotel. This sleekly design, subtly luxurious hotel follows the minimalist gospel but also feels warm and inviting, with rooms decorated in neutral tones and subtle patterns and featuring wood floors throughout. **Pros:** welcoming, modern reception and bar; free fast Wi-Fi; excellent central location in Altstadt. **Cons:** rooms can be on the smaller side; some may find the beds uncomfortable; rooms above the restaurant can be noisy. Ⓢ *Rooms from: €250* ⊠ *Ledererstr. 8, Altstadt* ☎ *089/242–2490* ⊕ *www.cortiina.com* ➔ *75 rooms* ⦿ *No meals* Ⓜ *Marienplatz* ⊹ *F5.*

$$ HOTEL

🏨 **Hotel am Markt.** At this excellent location next to the Viktualienmarkt, you'll find simple rooms and fair prices, if not many frills. **Pros:** friendly and helpful staff; free Wi-Fi; decent restaurant. **Cons:** rooms are small and basic; rooms above restaurant can be noisy; breakfast costs extra. [$] *Rooms from: €122* ✉ *Heiliggeiststr. 6, Altstadt* ☎ *089/225–014* 🌐 *www.hotel-am-markt.eu* 🛏 *22 rooms* 🍴 *No meals* [M] *Marienplatz* ✥ *E5.*

$$ HOTEL

🏨 **Hotel Concorde.** Although the Concorde is just steps away from the Hofbräuhaus, it has a peaceful location on a side street near the Isartor station, a two-minute walk away. **Pros:** quiet rooms; friendly service; rates include continental breakfast buffet. **Cons:** no restaurant or bar; no air-conditioning in rooms; no international TV channels. [$] *Rooms from: €170* ✉ *Herrnstr. 38–40, Altstadt* ☎ *089/224–515* 🌐 *www.concorde-muenchen.de* 🛏 *72 rooms* 🍴 *Free Breakfast* [M] *Isartor* ✥ *F5.*

$$$$ HOTEL Fodor's Choice ★

🏨 **Hotel Vier Jahreszeiten Kempinski München.** Trend and tradition blend throughout this property, where flat-screen TVs hang on the walls alongside original oil paintings, and Bose stereos rest on antique cupboards in the guest rooms. **Pros:** luxurious sixth-floor spa with views of the city; Michelin-starred restaurant; free Wi-Fi. **Cons:** expensive accommodations; service can be spotty; rooms are on the small side for a luxury property. [$] *Rooms from: €390* ✉ *Maximilianstr. 17, Altstadt* ☎ *089/2125–2799* 🌐 *www.kempinski.com* 🛏 *297 rooms* 🍴 *No meals* [M] *Lehel, Kammerspiele (Tram)* ✥ *F4.*

$$$$ HOTEL Fodor's Choice ★

🏨 **Louis Hotel.** Combining subdued elegance, first-rate service, and a great location overlooking Viktualienmarkt, this upscale design hotel, a former bank, is aiming for a slightly more affluent clientele, though some room prices are competitive. **Pros:** brilliant location; attentive service; large rooms facing the marketplace. **Cons:** the bustle of the Viktualienmarkt is not for everyone; Wi-Fi can be spotty; some may find the mattresses too firm. [$] *Rooms from: €278* ✉ *Viktualienmarkt 6, Altstadt* ✥ *Enter from "Viktualienmarkt passageway" that runs from Rindermarkt street to Viktualienmarkt street* ☎ *089/4111–9080* 🌐 *www.louis-hotel.com* 🛏 *72 rooms* 🍴 *No meals* [M] *Marienplatz* ✥ *E5.*

$$ HOTEL

🏨 **Mercure Hotel München Altstadt.** There are a number of Mercure hotels in Munich, and all offer standard chain hotel rooms with limited service, but this location, between Marienplatz and Karlsplatz, is ideally situated in the Altstadt. **Pros:** very good breakfast buffet included; free minibar with nonalcoholic drinks refilled daily; free Wi-Fi. **Cons:** rooms are on the small side; no restaurant; public parking garage is a bit of a hike. [$] *Rooms from: €160* ✉ *Hotterstr. 4, Altstadt* ☎ *089/232–590* 🌐 *www.mercure-muenchen-altstadt.de* 🛏 *75 rooms* 🍴 *Free Breakfast* [M] *Marienplatz, Karlsplatz, Sendlinger Tor* ✥ *D5.*

$ HOTEL

🏨 **Motel One München-Sendlinger Tor.** Catering to the young, fast-paced professional, the Motel One chain boasts well-thought-out, slightly edgy design, free Wi-Fi, terrific service, and no hidden costs. **Pros:** children under 12 stay in parents' room for free; on-site bar/lounge; amiable, attentive service. **Cons:** staying in one is like staying in all of them; no full restaurant or room service; breakfast, parking, and pets cost extra. [$] *Rooms from: €94* ✉ *Herzog-Wilhelm-Str. 28, Altstadt* ☎ *089/5177–7250* 🌐 *www.motel-one.com* 🛏 *241 rooms* 🍴 *No meals* [M] *Sendlinger Tor* ✥ *C5.*

$$$$ ⌂ **Platzl Hotel.** The privately owned Platzl, which has won awards and
HOTEL   wide recognition for its environmentally friendly practices, stands in the
Fodor's Choice   historic heart of Munich, near the famous Hofbräuhaus beer hall and a
★   couple of minutes' walk from Marienplatz and many other landmarks.
Pros: excellent restaurant Pfistermühle; generous, comfortable beds;
free Wi-Fi. **Cons:** rooms facing the Hofbräuhaus get more noise; some
rooms are on the small side; breakfast not always included. $ *Rooms
from: €265* ⊠ *Sparkassenstr. 10, Altstadt* ☎ *089/237–030* ⊕ *www.
platzl.de* ⌂ *167 rooms* ⦿ *No meals* Ⓜ *Marienplatz* ✥ *E5.*

$$$$ ⌂ **Torbräu.** The welcoming Torbräu has been looking after guests in one
HOTEL   form or another since 1490, making it the oldest hotel in Munich, and
it has been run by the same family for more than a century. **Pros:** nice
rooms, air-conditioned and with free Wi-Fi; very attentive service; good
restaurant. **Cons:** underground parking difficult; front rooms a little
noisy; bathrooms are on the small side. $ *Rooms from: €235* ⊠ *Tal
41, Altstadt* ☎ *089/242–340* ⊕ *www.torbraeu.de* ⌂ *90 rooms* ⦿ *Free
Breakfast* Ⓜ *Isartor* ✥ *F5.*

LEHEL

$$ ⌂ **Adria.** This modern hotel is near a number of great museums and the
HOTEL   Englischer Garten, with large rooms that are tastefully decorated. **Pros:**
good location; attractive lobby; friendly staff. **Cons:** no full bar or res-
taurant; no air-conditioning; elevators do not go to all floors. $ *Rooms
from: €160* ⊠ *Liebigstr. 8a, Altstadt* ☎ *089/242–1170* ⊕ *www.adria-
muenchen.de* ⌂ *44 rooms* ⦿ *No meals* Ⓜ *Lehel* ✥ *G4.*

$$$$ ⌂ **Hotel Opera.** In the quiet residential district of Lehel, Hotel Opera
HOTEL   offers rooms decorated in an elegant style—lots of Empire, some art
Fodor's Choice   deco; some rooms even have glassed-in balconies. **Pros:** free Wi-Fi
★   throughout; pleasant courtyard; quiet location. **Cons:** bathrooms can
be on the smaller side; street noise in some rooms can be bothersome;
no on-site restaurant. $ *Rooms from: €240* ⊠ *St.-Anna-Str. 10, Lehel*
☎ *089/210–4940* ⊕ *www.hotel-opera.de/en* ⌂ *25 rooms* ⦿ *Free Break-
fast* Ⓜ *Lehel* ✥ *G4.*

LUDWIGSVORSTADT AND ISARVORSTADT

$$ ⌂ **Anna Hotel.** Modern, slightly minimalist decor and features are char-
HOTEL   acteristic of this design hotel. **Pros:** terrific location; beds are huge; free
Wi-Fi throughout. **Cons:** bar and restaurant get hectic from passersby
on the busy street; no single rooms; pricey breakfast buffet. $ *Rooms
from: €162* ⊠ *Schützenstr. 1, Ludwigsvorstadt* ☎ *089/599–940* ⊕ *www.
annahotel.de* ⌂ *75 rooms* ⦿ *No meals* Ⓜ *Karlsplatz* ✥ *B4.*

$$ ⌂ **Hotel Admiral.** The small, privately owned, tradition-rich hotel enjoys
HOTEL   a quiet side-street location and its own garden, close to the River Isar,
Fodor's Choice   minutes from the Deutsches Museum. **Pros:** attention to detail; quiet
★   setting; excellent service. **Cons:** no restaurant; no air-conditioning;
somewhat dated decor. $ *Rooms from: €170* ⊠ *Kohlstr. 9, Isarvorstadt*
☎ *089/216–350* ⊕ *www.hotel-admiral.de/en_index.html* ⌂ *32 rooms*
⦿ *Free Breakfast* Ⓜ *Isartor* ✥ *F6.*

$$ 🖵 **Hotel am Viktualienmarkt.** This design-forward hotel is perfectly
HOTEL located a few hundred yards from Viktualienmarkt and the Gärtner-
platz quarter. **Pros:** refreshing atmosphere; service attentive but not
overbearing; great location. **Cons:** no air-conditioning; no restaurant;
no parking on-site. $ *Rooms from: €149* ✉ *Utzschneiderstr. 14, Isar-*
vorstadt ☎ *089/231–1090* ⊕ *www.hotel-am-viktualienmarkt.de* 🗩 *26*
rooms ⦿*Free Breakfast* Ⓜ *Marienplatz, Isartor, Reichenbachplatz*
(Tram) ✛ *E6.*

$$ 🖵 **Hotel Brack.** A nice, light-filled lobby makes a good first impression,
HOTEL but Oktoberfest revelers value the Brack's proximity to the beer-festival
grounds, and its location—on a busy, tree-lined thoroughfare just south
of the city's center—is handy for city attractions. **Pros:** good location for
accessing Oktoberfest and city; free use of bicycles; free Wi-Fi. **Cons:**
front rooms can be noisy despite soundproof windows; no air-conditioning; the decor is somewhat dated. $ *Rooms from: €119* ✉ *Lind-*
wurmstr. 153, Ludwigsvorstadt ☎ *089/747–2550* ⊕ *www.hotel-brack.*
de/index_e.html 🗩 *50 rooms* ⦿*Free Breakfast* Ⓜ *Poccistrasse* ✛ *B6.*

$$$ 🖵 **Hotel Excelsior by Geisel.** Just a short walk along an underpass from
HOTEL the Hauptbahnhof station, the Excelsior welcomes you with rooms that
are spacious and inviting. **Pros:** welcoming reception; spacious rooms;
free Wi-Fi throughout. **Cons:** Schützenstrasse can get very busy; break-
fast not included in room price; per-night fee for pets, and additional
cleaning service after the stay. $ *Rooms from: €210* ✉ *Schützenstr. 11,*
Ludwigsvorstadt ☎ *089/551–370* ⊕ *www.excelsior-hotel.de* 🗩 *127*
rooms ⦿*No meals* Ⓜ *Hauptbahnhof, Karlsplatz* ✛ *B4.*

$$ 🖵 **Hotel Kraft.** Conveniently located between the City Center and the
HOTEL Oktoberfest grounds, this hotel has spacious rooms with an armchair,
an ample-size writing desk, and natural light from a large window. **Pros:**
hotel and rooms well cared for; quiet neighborhood; Wi-Fi and breakfast are included in the price. **Cons:** no air-conditioning; old-fashioned
decor; Wi-Fi can be spotty. $ *Rooms from: €110* ✉ *Schillerstr. 49, Lud-*
wigsvorstadt ☎ *089/550–5940* ⊕ *www.hotel-kraft.com* ☉ *Closed for*
Christmas holidays 🗩 *33 rooms* ⦿*Free Breakfast* Ⓜ *Sendlingertor,*
Theresienwiese ✛ *B5.*

$$ 🖵 **Hotel Mariandl.** The American armed forces commandeered this turn-
HOTEL of-the-20th-century neo-Gothic mansion in May 1945 and established
Munich's first postwar nightclub, the Femina, on the ground floor. **Pros:**
hotel and café are charmingly worn and a bit bohemian; rooms are spa-
cious; good restaurant. **Cons:** no elevator; no TV in rooms; some rooms
do not have private bathrooms. $ *Rooms from: €149* ✉ *Goethestr. 51,*
Ludwigsvorstadt ☎ *089/552–9100* ⊕ *www.mariandl.com* 🗩 *28 rooms*
⦿*Free Breakfast* Ⓜ *Hauptbahnhof* ✛ *A6.*

$$ 🖵 **Hotel Mirabell.** This modern hotel is used to American tourists who
HOTEL appreciate the friendly service, central location (between the main rail-
way station and the Oktoberfest fairgrounds), and reasonable room
rates. **Pros:** free Wi-Fi; modern design; personalized service. **Cons:** no
restaurant; this area of the Hauptbahnhof is not the most salubrious;
rooms are on the smaller side. $ *Rooms from: €106* ✉ *Landwehrstr. 42,*
entrance on Goethestr., Ludwigsvorstadt ☎ *089/549–1740* ⊕ *www.m-*
privathotels.de 🗩 *69 rooms* ⦿*Free Breakfast* Ⓜ *Hauptbahnhof* ✛ *A5.*

2

$$ HOTEL 🏨 **Hotel Präsident.** The location—just a block from the main train station—is the biggest draw of this hotel; the second draw is the price. **Pros:** central location; filling breakfast; pleasant service. **Cons:** rooms toward the street are noisy; streets around the hotel are not the most salubrious; no air-conditioning. [$] *Rooms from: €109* ✉ *Schwanthalerstr. 20, Ludwigsvorstadt* ☎ *089/549–0060* 🌐 *www.hotel-praesident.de* 🛏 *42 rooms* 🍴 *Free Breakfast* [M] *Hauptbahnhof, Karlsplatz* ✥ *B5.*

$$ HOTEL Fodor's Choice ★ 🏨 **Hotel Uhland.** This stately villa is a landmark building, in a quiet residential area, with pleasant rooms that are quite large and can accommodate three people. **Pros:** a real family atmosphere; care is given to details; free on-site parking. **Cons:** no restaurant or bar; the surrounding area is a bit quiet; no air-conditioning. [$] *Rooms from: €120* ✉ *Uhlandstr. 1, Ludwigsvorstadt* ☎ *089/543–350* 🌐 *www.hotel-uhland.de* 🛏 *29 rooms* 🍴 *Free Breakfast* [M] *Theresienwiese* ✥ *A6.*

$ HOTEL 🏨 **Hotel Westend.** Visitors have praised the friendly welcome and service they receive at this well-maintained and affordable lodging above the Oktoberfest grounds. **Pros:** good location; affordable breakfast buffet; free Wi-Fi. **Cons:** no restaurant; street noise; it's best to confirm your reservation. [$] *Rooms from: €88* ✉ *Schwanthalerstr. 121, Ludwigsvorstadt* ☎ *089/540–9860* 🌐 *www.westend-hotel.de* 🛏 *44 rooms* 🍴 *No meals* [M] *Hackerbrücke, Schwanthalerhöhe* ✥ *B5.*

$ HOTEL 🏨 **Pension Seibel.** If you're looking for an affordable little *Pension* a stone's throw from the Viktualienmarkt, this is the place. **Pros:** great location; pets are welcome for a small fee; some rooms are very spacious. **Cons:** tiny breakfast room; no elevator; Wi-Fi costs extra. [$] *Rooms from: €79* ✉ *Reichenbachstr. 8, Isarvorstadt* ☎ *089/231–9180* 🌐 *www.seibel-hotels-munich.de* 🛏 *15 rooms* 🍴 *Free Breakfast* [M] *Marienplatz, Isartor, Reichenbachplatz (Tram)* ✥ *E6.*

$$$ HOTEL Fodor's Choice ★ 🏨 **Roomers Munich Autograph Collection.** Bold design, a top-notch spa with Jacuzzi, a spacious gym, plus a slick Japanese-inspired bar and restaurant distinguish this upscale boutique hotel from most options in this area around busy Landsberger Strasse. **Pros:** excellent amenities; beautiful, spacious lobby invites lounging; located directly across from tram stop. **Cons:** on a busy street in a nondescript area; especially pricey breakfast; some may find the beds too firm. [$] *Rooms from: €220* ✉ *Landsberger Str. 68, Ludwigsvorstadt* ☎ *089/452–2020* 🌐 *www.roomers-munich.com* 🛏 *281 rooms* 🍴 *No meals* [M] *Schrenkstrasse (Tram)* ✥ *A4.*

$$$ HOTEL Fodor's Choice ★ 🏨 **25hours Hotel The Royal Bavarian.** Housed in a former post office opposite the city's main train station, this boutique hotel features plenty of fun, funky design touches, like refurbished typewriters and faux mounted deer heads in the lobby and lightboxes in the elevators that depict vintage scenes of Bavaria. **Pros:** outstanding, unique design; warm, friendly service; free fast Wi-Fi. **Cons:** the area around Hauptbahnhof (the main train station) can be unsavory; some may find the design too quirky; some rooms are on the smaller side. [$] *Rooms from: €220* ✉ *Bahnhofpl. 1, Ludwigsvorstadt* ☎ *089/904–0010* 🌐 *www.25hours-hotels.com* 🛏 *165 rooms* 🍴 *No meals* [M] *Hauptbahnhof* ✥ *B4.*

SCHWABING AND MAXVORSTADT

$$$$ HOTEL **The Charles Hotel.** With the Old Botanical Garden just outside the door, this modern hotel has a wonderfully peaceful setting, yet it's just a five-minute walk from the main train station and about 10 minutes to the museum quarter. **Pros:** impeccable service; excellent breakfast buffet with many healthy options (surcharge); some suites include limo service from the airport. **Cons:** can feel very businesslike, especially during corporate events; particularly pricey breakfast; room decor is a bit bland. [$] *Rooms from: €306* ✉ *Sophienstr. 28, Maxvorstadt* ☎ *089/544–5550* 🌐 *www.roccofortehotels.com* 🛏 *160 rooms* 🍴 *No meals* [M] *Hauptbahnhof* ✣ *B3.*

$ HOTEL **Creatif Hotel Elephant.** Tucked away on a quiet street near the train station, this hotel, easily distinguished by its colorful facade, appeals to a wide range of travelers, from businesspeople to tourists on a budget. **Pros:** close to Hauptbahnhof; great value; free Wi-Fi. **Cons:** no restaurant; modest furnishings; street noise can be bothersome. [$] *Rooms from: €59* ✉ *Lämmerstr. 6, Maxvorstadt* ☎ *089/555–785* 🌐 *www.creatif-hotel-elephant.de* 🛏 *44 rooms* 🍴 *Free Breakfast* [M] *Hauptbahnhof* ✣ *A3.*

$$$ HOTEL **Eden-Hotel Wolff.** Beyond a light-filled lobby, a spacious bar with dark-wood paneling beckons, contributing to the old-fashioned elegance of this downtown favorite. **Pros:** all rooms have air-conditioning; free Wi-Fi; nice spa facilities. **Cons:** close to the hustle and bustle of the main station; the modern design in some rooms may not appeal to everyone; not all rates include breakfast. [$] *Rooms from: €194* ✉ *Arnulfstr. 4, Maxvorstadt* ☎ *089/551–150* 🌐 *www.eden-hotel-wolff.de* 🛏 *214 rooms* 🍴 *No meals* [M] *Hauptbahnhof* ✣ *A3.*

$$ B&B/INN Fodor's Choice ★ **Gästehaus am Englischen Garten.** Reserve well in advance for a room at this popular converted water mill, more than 300 years old, adjoining the English Garden that's only a five-minute walk from the bars, shops, and restaurants of Schwabing, with a well-known Bavarian restaurant across the street. **Pros:** quiet location; wonderfully cozy rooms; free Wi-Fi. **Cons:** no elevator; no restaurant; no air-conditioning. [$] *Rooms from: €171* ✉ *Liebergesellstr. 8, Schwabing* ☎ *089/383–9410* 🌐 *hotelenglischergarten.de* 🛏 *31 rooms* 🍴 *No meals* [M] *Münchner Freiheit* ✣ *G1.*

$ HOTEL **Hotel Amba.** Right across the street from the main train station, Amba provides clean, bright rooms, good service, no expensive frills, and everything you need to plug and play. **Pros:** convenient to train station and sights; on-site parking (fee); clean, comfortable rooms. **Cons:** breakfast is extra; rooms that face the main street and the station are noisy; no air-conditioning. [$] *Rooms from: €88* ✉ *Arnulfstr. 20, Maxvorstadt* ☎ *089/545–140* 🌐 *www.hotel-amba.de* 🛏 *86 rooms* 🍴 *No meals* [M] *Hauptbahnhof* ✣ *A3.*

$$ HOTEL **Hotel Biederstein.** A modern block of a building, but covered with geraniums in summer, the Biederstein seems to want to fit into its wonderfully quiet Schwabing surroundings at the edge of the English Garden. **Pros:** all rooms have balconies; exemplary service; underground parking is available. **Cons:** not the most handsome building; no restaurant; U-bahn is four blocks away. [$] *Rooms from: €164* ✉ *Keferstr. 18, Schwabing* ☎ *089/3302–9390* 🌐 *www.hotel-biederstein.de* 🛏 *34 rooms* 🍴 *Breakfast* [M] *Münchner Freiheit* ✣ *G1.*

$$ HOTEL 🏨 **Hotel Carlton Astoria.** This family-run hotel, with an atmosphere of simple elegance, is a three- or four-minute walk to Amalienstrasse and Türkenstrasse, two of the most lively places in town, with dozens of restaurants, eateries, and student pubs, and it's near the Pinakotheken (art museums). **Pros:** good location; some rooms are quite spacious; free Wi-Fi. **Cons:** rooms on main street can be noisy; limited parking (prearrange with hotel); no air-conditioning. [$] *Rooms from: €150* ✉ *Fürstenstr. 12, Maxvorstadt* ☎ *089/383–9630* 🌐 *www.carlton-astoria.de/seiten/en/hotel.htm* 🛏 *49 rooms* 🍴 *Free Breakfast* [M] *Universität, Odeonsplatz* ✣ *E2.*

$$ HOTEL 🏨 **Hotel Erzgiesserei Europe München.** Rooms in this modern hotel are bright and some come with a balcony or terrace, but the rates vary greatly, even on the hotel's own website. **Pros:** relatively quiet location; nice courtyard; air-conditioning in all rooms. **Cons:** charm of a business hotel; breakfast area is cramped; bathrooms are on smaller side. [$] *Rooms from: €109* ✉ *Erzgiessereistr. 15, Maxvorstadt* ☎ *089/126–820* 🌐 *www.europe-hotels-international.de* 🛏 *106 rooms* 🍴 *Free Breakfast* [M] *Stiglmaierplatz* ✣ *A2.*

$$ HOTEL 🏨 **H'Otello F'22.** This is a high-caliber example of the design- and style-driven nature of the new Munich hotel scene—the style is minimalist, but with a roomy feel. **Pros:** parking available; some rooms have balconies; free Wi-Fi. **Cons:** no restaurant; breakfast costs extra; some may find the design a little too basic. [$] *Rooms from: €130* ✉ *Fallmerayerstr. 22, Schwabing* ☎ *089/4583–1200* 🌐 *www.hotello.de* 🛏 *74 rooms* 🍴 *No meals* [M] *Hohenzollernplatz, Kufürstenplatz (Tram)* ✣ *D1.*

$ B&B/INN 🏨 **Hotel Pension Am Siegestor.** Modest but appealing, this Pension—which takes up three floors of a fin de siècle mansion between the Siegestor monument on Leopoldstrasse and the university—is a great deal in one of Germany's most expensive cities. **Pros:** a delightful and homey place to stay; not far to walk to the Englischer Garten; free Wi-Fi. **Cons:** if elevators make you nervous, don't use this old one; no restaurant or bar; only some rooms have en suite bathrooms. [$] *Rooms from: €98* ✉ *Akademiestr. 5, Maxvorstadt* ☎ *089/399–550* 🌐 *www.siegestor.com* 💳 *No credit cards* 🛏 *20 rooms* 🍴 *Free Breakfast* [M] *Universität* ✣ *F1.*

OUTSIDE INNENSTADT

$$ HOTEL FAMILY 🏨 **Hotel Kriemhild.** This welcoming, family-run hotel is in a quiet western suburb, just a 10-minute walk from Schloss Nymphenburg and around the corner from the Hirschgarten Park, which houses Munich's biggest beer garden. **Pros:** quiet location; family-run; free Wi-Fi and parking. **Cons:** far from the sights in the City Center; rates don't include breakfast; only some larger suites have air-conditioning. [$] *Rooms from: €112* ✉ *Guntherstr. 16, Nymphenburg* ☎ *089/171–1170* 🌐 *www.kriemhild.de/en/* 🛏 *21 rooms* 🍴 *No meals* [M] *Laim, Kriemhildenstrasse (Tram)* ✣ *A2.*

$$ HOTEL 🏨 **Jagdschloss.** This century-old hunting lodge in Munich's leafy Obermenzing suburb is a delightful hotel. **Pros:** peaceful location; free, easy parking; free Wi-Fi in rooms. **Cons:** away from the City Center; convenient only with a car; no elevator. [$] *Rooms from: €140* ✉ *Alte Allee 21,*

Pasing-Obermenzing ☎ *089/820–820* 🌐 *www.jagd-schloss.com* 🛏 *36 rooms* 🍴 *Free Breakfast* ✥ *A4.*

$$$ HOTEL 🏨 **Westin Grand München.** The 23-story building may raise a few eyebrows as it stands on a slight elevation and is not the shapeliest of the Munich skyline, but what goes on inside, however, is sheer luxury. **Pros:** luxurious lobby and spa; rooms facing west toward the city have a fabulous view; multiple restaurant choices. **Cons:** hotel is difficult to reach via public transportation; expensive breakfast; free Wi-Fi in lobby only. [$] *Rooms from: €179* ✉ *Arabellastr. 6, Bogenhausen* ☎ *089/92640* 🌐 *www.westingrandmunich.com/en* 🛏 *627 rooms* 🍴 *No meals* [M] *Arabellapark* ✥ *F1.*

NIGHTLIFE AND PERFORMING ARTS

NIGHTLIFE

Munich has a lively night scene ranging from beer halls to bars to chic clubs. The fun areas for a night out are in Altstadt, Isarvorstadt (Gärtnerplatz and Glockenbachviertel are arguably the best in the city), and Schwabing around Schellingstrasse and Münchner Freiheit. Regardless of their size or style, many bars, especially around Gärtnerplatz, have DJs spinning either mellow background sounds or funky beats.

However many fingers you hold up, just remember the easy-to-pronounce "Bitte ein Bier" (Beer, please) when ordering a beer. The tricky part is, Germans don't just produce *one* beverage called beer; they brew more than 5,000 varieties. Germany has about 1,300 breweries.

In Munich you'll find the most famous breweries, the largest beer halls and beer gardens, the biggest and most indulgent beer festival, and the widest selection of brews. Even the beer glasses are bigger: a *Mass* is a 1-liter (almost 2-pint) serving; a *Halbe* is half a liter and the standard size. The Hofbräuhaus is Munich's best-known beer hall but considered strictly for tourists; you are more likely to find locals in one of the English Garden's four beer gardens or in a *Wirtshaus* (tavern).

In summer, last call at the beer gardens is around 11 pm. Most of the traditional places stay open until 1 am or so and are great for a few hours of wining and dining before heading out on the town. Most bars stay open until at least 3 am on weekends; some don't close until 5 or 6 am.

Munich has dozens of beer gardens, ranging from huge establishments that seat several hundred to small terraces tucked behind neighborhood pubs; the rest of the beer gardens are a bit farther afield and can be reached handily by bike or S- and U-bahn. Beer gardens are such an integral part of Munich life that a council proposal to cut down their hours provoked a storm of protest in 1995, culminating in one of the largest demonstrations in the city's history. They open whenever the thermometer creeps above 10°C (50°F) and the sun filters through the chestnut trees that are a necessary part of the scenery.

Everybody in Munich has at least one favorite beer garden, so you're usually in good hands if you ask someone to point you in the right direction.

You do not need to reserve. No need to phone either. If the weather says yes, then go. Most—but not all—allow you to bring your own food, but if you do, buy your drinks from the beer garden and don't defile this hallowed territory with something so foreign as pizza or a burger.

There are a few dance clubs in town worth mentioning, but the larger the venue, the more difficult the entry. In general, big nightclubs are giving way to smaller, more laid-back lounges and cocktail bars. Consider signing up for a tour of area bars with Bar Guide Munich (⊕ *www. barguide-muenchen.com*), whose guides take small groups to three or four hot spots for signature drinks; they also lead private beer garden/ brewery tours.

Munich also has a decent jazz scene, and some beer gardens have even taken to replacing their brass oompah bands with funky combos. Jazz musicians sometimes accompany Sunday brunch, too.

ALTSTADT

BARS

Bar Centrale. Around the corner from the Hofbräuhaus, Bar Centrale is a friendly Italian café by day, but come evening, it morphs into a dimly lit lounge, with cocktails (many with an Italian bent) served at cozy tables in the retro-looking interior. There's also a small, ever-changing menu of international dishes and a nice selection of Italian wines by the glass. ⊠ *Ledererstr. 23, Altstadt* ☎ *089/223–762* ⊕ *www.bar-centrale. com* Ⓜ *Marienplatz.*

Fodor's Choice ★ **Grapes Weinbar.** The young sommeliers here take a fresh, modern approach to wine, departing from the typical German Rieslings and French Pinot Noirs (though those are on the menu, too) and offering many lesser-known varietals, like say, a Rebula from Slovenia. The well-curated list of wines by the glass includes natural and biodynamic options; ask for the separate card of rare (and pricier) wines, also by the glass. The loungelike space and small garden terrace attract a well-heeled crowd; weekend evenings are particularly lively. ⊠ *Ledererstr. 8, Altstadt* ☎ *089/2422–49504* ⊕ *www.grapes-weinbar.de/en* Ⓜ *Marienplatz.*

Jahreszeiten Bar. Tucked inside the Hotel Vier Jahreszeiten Kempinski, this sophisticated spot, outfitted with plush carpeting, leather seating, and an open fireplace, serves a wide range of sparkling wines, whiskeys, and cocktails. There's live piano music every evening. ⊠ *Maximilianstr. 17, Altstadt* ☎ *089/2125–1745* ⊕ *www.kempinski.com* Ⓜ *Lehel, Marienplatz, Kammerspiele (Tram).*

Kilian's Irish Pub and Ned Kelly's Australian Bar. Just behind the Frauenkirche, Kilian's Irish Pub and Ned Kelly's Australian Bar (adjoining bars) offer an escape from the German tavern scene. Naturally, they have Guinness and Foster's, but they also serve Munich's lager, Augustiner, and regularly televise international soccer, rugby, and sports in general. There's also live music in the evenings at Kilian's starting at 9 pm. ⊠ *Frauenpl. 11, Altstadt* ☎ *089/2421–9899 both bars* ⊕ *www. kiliansirishpub.com; www.nedkellysbar.com* Ⓜ *Marienplatz.*

Pusser's Bar Munich. At the American-inspired, nautical-style Pusser's Bar Munich, great cocktails and Irish-German black-and-tans (Guinness and strong German beer) are poured to the sounds of live piano music. Try the "Painkiller," a specialty of the house. ⊠ *Falkenturmstr. 9, Altstadt* ☎ *089/220–500* ⊕ *www.pussersbar.de* Ⓜ *Marienplatz, Lehel.*

Fodor'sChoice ★ **Schumann's Les Fleurs du Mal.** At Munich's most famous bar, the bartenders are busy shaking cocktails after the curtain comes down at the nearby opera house. On the ground floor is Schumann's Bar am Hofgarten; one floor up, Les Fleurs du Mal has one 27-foot-long table for guests to share and converse with the barman, who will whip up bespoke cocktails based on your preferences. ⊠ *Odeonspl. 6–7, Altstadt* ☎ *089/229–060* ⊕ *www.schumanns.de* ☽ *Les Fleurs du Mal closed Sun.* Ⓜ *Marienplatz, Odeonsplatz.*

Trader Vic's. Exotic cocktails are the specialty at the Polynesian-themed Trader Vic's, a smart cellar bar in the Hotel Bayerischer Hof that's as popular among out-of-town visitors as it is with locals. It's open till 3 in the morning. ⊠ *Promenadenpl. 2–6, Altstadt* ☎ *089/212–0995* ⊕ *www. bayerischerhof.de* Ⓜ *Karlsplatz, Marienplatz.*

BEER GARDENS

FAMILY
Fodor'sChoice ★ **Biergarten am Viktualienmarkt.** The only true beer garden in the center of the city, and therefore the easiest to find, is the one at Viktualienmarkt. The beer on tap rotates among the six major Munich breweries to keep everyone happy throughout the year. ⊠ *Viktualienmarkt, Altstadt* ☎ *089/297–545* ⊕ *biergarten-viktualienmarkt.com* Ⓜ *Marienplatz.*

LEHEL

BARS

Goldene Bar. Everything glows golden at this aptly named bar within the Haus der Kunst. Among gilded wall paintings dating from 1937 and beneath a mod 1920s chandelier, hip locals sit on vintage furniture sipping classic cocktails with a modern twist. ⊠ *Prinzregentenstr. 1, Lehel* ☎ *089/5480–4777* ⊕ *www.goldenebar.de* Ⓜ *Odeonsplatz, Lehel, Nationalmuseum/Haus d.Kunst (Tram).*

DANCE CLUBS

P1. Bordering the Englischer Garten, in a wing of Haus der Kunst, P1 is definitely one of the most popular clubs in town for the see-and-be-seen crowd. It is chockablock with the rich and the wannabe rich and can be fun if you're in the mood. Seats on the seasonal terrace are highly coveted, so reservations are essential. The bouncers can be choosy about whom they let in, so you'll need to dress in style. ⊠ *Prinzregentenstr. 1, Lehel* ✛ *On west side of Haus der Kunst* ☎ *089/211–1140* ⊕ *www.p1-club.de.*

LUDWIGSVORSTADT AND ISARVORSTADT

Around Gärtnerplatz and Glockenbachviertel are a number of cool bars and clubs for a somewhat younger, hipper crowd.

BARS

Holy Home. For a New York City–style corner-bar experience, check out Holy Home, in the heart of the trendy Gärtnerplatz district. A hip local crowd frequents this hole-in-the-wall that books great low-key DJs.

✉ *Reichenbachstr. 21, Isarvorstadt* ☎ *089/201–4546* Ⓜ *Fraunhofer-strasse, Isartor.*

Wolf's Farmacy. This speakeasy-style "soda fountain," complete with a mini-barbershop in the back room, dispenses heady, whisky-infused barrel drinks alongside nonalcoholic ice cream floats, egg creams, and old-fashioned syrup sodas. ✉ *Klenzestr. 30, Isarvorstadt* ☎ *089/2694–9392* ⊕ *wolfsfarmacy.de* Ⓜ *Fraunhoferstrasse.*

GAY AND LESBIAN BARS
Munich's well-established gay scene stretches between Sendlingertor-platz and Isartorplatz in the Glockenbach neighborhood.

Ochsengarten. Opened in 1967, the Ochsengarten is Munich's men-only bar for lovers of leather and rubber. ✉ *Müllerstr. 47, Isar-vorstadt* ☎ *089/266–446* ⊕ *www.ochsengarten.de* Ⓜ *Sendlinger Tor, Fraunhoferstrasse.*

Paradiso Tanzbar. Formerly Old Mrs. Henderson, this is still one of the most lively clubs on the scene, combining dance, burlesque, cham-pagne, all kinds of music, all night long. ✉ *Rumfordstr. 2, Isarvorstadt* ☎ *089/263–469* ⊕ *www.paradiso-tanzbar.de* ☉ *Closed Sun.–Thurs.* Ⓜ *Blumenstrasse (Bus), Reichenbachplatz (Tram), Isartor.*

JAZZ
Fodor'sChoice **Jazzbar Vogler.** The Jazzbar Vogler is a nice bar with jam sessions
★ on Monday nights and regular jazz concerts. ✉ *Rumfordstr. 17, Isarvorstadt* ☎ *089/294–662* ⊕ *www.jazzbar-vogler.com* Ⓜ *Isartor, Reichenbachplatz (Tram).*

Mr. B's. The tiny Mr. B's is a treat. Featuring classic jazz performances, the club is run by New Yorker Alex Best, who also mixes great cocktails and, unlike so many other barkeeps, usually wears a welcoming smile. ✉ *Herzog-Heinrich-Str. 38, Ludwigsvorstadt* ☎ *089/534–901* ⊕ *www.misterbs.eu/index-e.html* ☉ *Closed Mon.* Ⓜ *Goetheplatz.*

SCHWABING AND MAXVORSTADT
BARS
Home. Cushy leather seating, brick walls, and flickering candles lend a warm, clubby vibe to this trendy bar near the Pinakotheken (art museums) and the university. There's a long list of classic and signature cocktails, plus a small-bites menu that includes an excellent currywurst. ✉ *Amalienstr. 23, Maxvorstadt* ☎ *089/4524–6140* ⊕ *home-munich.bar* Ⓜ *Universität, Pinakotheken (Tram).*

Schall und Rauch. Up on Schellingstrasse, this legendary student hangout, whose name literally means "Noise and Smoke," has great music and food. ✉ *Schellingstr. 22, Schwabing* ☎ *089/2880–9577* Ⓜ *Universität.*

Fodor'sChoice **Sophia's Bar.** Bow-tied bartenders sling creative cocktails at this botani-
★ cal-theme bar and lounge inside the Charles Hotel. Intricate, beautifully rendered drinks feature fresh and freeze-dried herbs, bold spices, and even seasonal vegetables like pumpkin and melon—justifying the steep prices. ✉ *The Charles Hotel, Sophienstr. 28, Maxvorstadt* ☎ *089/5445–551200* ⊕ *www.roccofortehotels.com* Ⓜ *Hauptbahnhof, Königsplatz.*

Türkenhof. The Türkenhof is a solid local pub that serves Augustiner and good food. ☒ *Türkenstr. 78, Schwabing* ☎ *089/280–0235* ⊕ *www. augustiner-braeu.de* Ⓜ *Universität, Türkenstrasse (Bus).*

BEER GARDENS

Fodor's Choice
★
Augustiner Keller Biergarten. Among Munich's largest beer gardens (5,000 seats)—and in fact its oldest—Augustiner Keller is one of the more authentic beer gardens, with excellent food, beautiful chestnut shade trees, a mixed local crowd, and Munich Augustiner beer. It's a few minutes from the Hauptbahnhof and Hackerbrücke. ☒ *Arnulfstr. 52, Maxvorstadt* ☎ *089/594–393* ⊕ *www.augustinerkeller.de* Ⓜ *Hacker-brücke, Hauptbahnhof.*

Biergarten am Chinesischen Turm. The famous Biergarten am Chinesischen Turm is at the five-story Chinese Tower in the Englischer Garten. Enjoy your beer to the strains of oompah music played by traditionally dressed musicians. ☒ *Englischer Garten 3, Schwabing* ☎ *089/383–8730* ⊕ *www. chinaturm.de* Ⓜ *Chinesischer Turm (Bus), Tivolistrasse (Tram).*

Hirschau. The Hirschau, pleasantly located in the Englischer Garten, has room for 2,500 guests, and it's about 10 minutes north of the Kleinhesseloher See. ☒ *Gysslingstr. 15, Englischer Garten, Schwabing* ☎ *089/3609–0490* ⊕ *www.hirschau-muenchen.de* Ⓜ *Herzogpark (Bus).*

Park Café. This is one of Munich's hippest cafés, restaurants, nightclubs, and beer gardens. It often draws a younger crowd, attracted by a thriving music scene in the café itself, which ranges from DJs to live bands, and the occasional celebrity spotting. There's a great atmosphere to go with the good food and drinks, even better when the sun is shining and the beer garden is open. ☒ *Sophienstr. 7, Maxvorstadt* ☎ *089/5161– 7980* ⊕ *www.parkcafe089.de* Ⓜ *Hauptbahnhof.*

Fodor's Choice
★
Seehaus im Englischen Garten. The Seehaus im Englischen Garten is on the banks of the artificial lake Kleinhesseloher See, where all of Munich converges on hot summer days. Take Bus 59 and exit at Osterwald-strasse or U-bahn 3/6 to Münchner Freiheit and stroll through the park. ☒ *Kleinhesselohe 3, Schwabing* ☎ *089/381–6130* ⊕ *www.kuffler. de* Ⓜ *Münchner Freiheit.*

AU AND HAIDHAUSEN
BEER GARDENS

FAMILY
Fodor's Choice
★
Hofbräukeller am Wiener Platz. This is one of the city's midsize beer gardens but undoubtedly one of the best. Its location off Wiener Platz makes it attractive enough, plus the food's good, and it serves the same beer as the Hofbräuhaus. Inside, the restaurant is well worth a look. There is a play area for the little'uns, and as usual a play area for children outdoors as well. There's also a lounge area with sand and sun loungers. ☒ *Innere Wiener Str. 19, Haidhausen* ☎ *089/459–9250* ⊕ *www.hofbraeukeller.de* Ⓜ *Max-Weber-Platz.*

FAMILY
Fodor's Choice
★
Paulaner am Nockherberg. Set atop "Holy Hill," so named because Pau-laner monks produced beer here as far back as 1627, this brewery/beer garden was entirely refurbished in early 2018. The sprawling shady beer garden, which seats 2,000 people, is a nice break from the touristy beer gardens found in much of the city. Sample handcrafted Paulaner beers made right on site, including the potent wheat beer Faustus; many are

specialty unfiltered brews you can't find elsewhere. The Bavarian cuisine here is particularly good. ⊠ *Hochstr. 77, Haidhausen* ☎ *089/459–9130* ⊕ *paulaner-nockherberg.com* Ⓜ *Kolumbusplatz, Mariahilfplatz (Tram).*

DANCE CLUBS

Muffathalle. One of the best live venues in the city, this club housed inside a historic power station puts on up-and-coming bands as well as ones on their second or third or more appearances after making it big. Many leading acts from the U.K. and U.S. scenes have played here. The café-bar here has different DJs nearly every night of the week, and the modest beer garden serves organic food. ⊠ *Muffatwerk, Zellstr. 4, behind Müllersches Volksbad near river, Haidhausen* ☎ *089/4587–5010* ⊕ *www.muffatwerk. de* Ⓜ *Isartor, Deutsches Museum (Tram), Gasteig (Tram).*

JAZZ

Fodor'sChoice ★ **Jazzclub Unterfahrt.** Unterfahrt is the place for the serious jazzolo-gist, though hip-hop is making heavy inroads into the scene. ⊠ *Einsteinstr. 42, Haidhausen* ☎ *089/448–2794* ⊕ *www.unterfahrt.de* Ⓜ *Max-Weber-Platz.*

OUTSIDE INNENSTADT

BEER GARDENS

Fodor'sChoice ★ **Königlicher Hirschgarten.** Out in the district of Nymphenburg is the huge Königlicher Hirschgarten, Munich's largest beer garden, with 8,000 seats. It's also a family-oriented beer garden; it even has a deer reserve. To get there, rent bikes and make a day of it in the park and beer garden, or take the S-bahn to Hirschgarten, then walk for 10 to 15 minutes. No matter how you get there, it'll be worth it. ⊠ *Hirschgarten 1, Nymphenburg* ☎ *089/1799–9119* ⊕ *www.hirschgarten.de* Ⓜ *Hirschgarten.*

FAMILY **Taxisgarten.** The crowd at Neuhausen's Taxisgarten, with 1,500 seats, is fairly white-collar and tame, but the food here is excellent, not to mention the beer. While parents refresh themselves, children exhaust themselves at the playground. ⊠ *Taxisstr. 12, Neuhausen-Nymphenburg* ☎ *089/156–827* ⊕ *www.taxisgarten.de* Ⓜ *Gern.*

DANCE CLUBS

Backstage. The Backstage is mostly a live-music venue for alternative music of all kinds, but there's also a chilled-out club and a beer garden. Purchase tickets at various websites, including **München Ticket** (⊕ *www.muenchenticket.de*). ⊠ *Reitknechtstr. 6, Neuhausen-Nymphenburg* ☎ *089/126–6100* ⊕ *www.backstage.eu* Ⓜ *Hirschgarten.*

PERFORMING ARTS

Bavaria's capital has an enviable reputation as an artistic hot spot. Details of concerts and theater performances are listed in *in münchen* (free) and *Monatsprogramm*, booklets available at most hotel reception desks, newsstands, and tourist offices. The official city website (⊕ *www.muenchen.de*) has listings. Otherwise, just keep your eye open for advertising pillars and posters.

Box Office of the Bavarian State Theaters. Tickets for performances at the Bavarian State Theater, Nationaltheater, Staatstheater am Gärtnerplatz, plus many other locations, are sold at the central box office. It's open

Monday to Saturday 10–7. ⊠ *Marstallpl. 5, Altstadt* ☎ *089/2185–1920* ⊕ *www.staatstheater-tickets.bayern.de/willkommen.html/language=en* Ⓜ *Marienplatz, Lehel, Odesonsplatz.*

München Ticket. This ticket agency has a German-language website where tickets for most Munich venues can be booked. ⊠ *Munich* ☎ *089/5481–8181* ⊕ *www.muenchenticket.de.*

Zentraler Kartenvorverkauf. Two Zentraler Kartenvorverkauf ticket kiosks are in the underground concourse: one at Marienplatz, and one at Karlsplatz (Stachus). ⊠ *Altstadt* ☎ *089/5450–6060 hotline* ⊕ *www. zkv-muenchen.de* Ⓜ *Marienplatz, Karlsplatz.*

CONCERTS

Munich and music go together. The city has two world-renowned orchestras. The Philharmonic was directed by Lorin Maazel, formerly of the New York Philharmonic, from the 2012 season until his death in 2014. Valery Gergiev filled the position in 2015. The Bavarian State Opera Company is managed by Russian conductor Kirill Petrenko, who will leave in autumn 2019 for the equivalent position in Berlin. The leading choral ensembles are the Munich Bach Choir, the Munich Motettenchor, and Musica Viva, the last specializing in contemporary music. The choirs perform mostly in city churches.

Bayerischer Rundfunk. The Bayerischer Rundfunk is the city's public radio and TV broadcaster, which also oversees three musical organizations— the Bavarian Radio Symphony Orchestra, the Munich Radio Orchestra, and the Bavarian Radio Choir. Performances take place at Bayerischer Rundfunk and at other city venues, such as Gasteig. The box office is open weekdays 9–5:30. ⊠ *Arnulfstr. 42, Maxvorstadt* ☎ *089/5900–10880 tickets* ⊕ *www.info.br-klassikticket.de* Ⓜ *Hauptbahnhof.*

Gasteig Culture Center. Hugely expensive to build and not particularly beautiful, this brick complex stands high above the Isar River, east of downtown. Its Philharmonic Hall is the permanent home of the Munich Philharmonic Orchestra and the largest concert hall in Munich. In 2021, the Gasteig is scheduled to close for renovations until the end of 2025 and the orchestra will relocate to another venue. The Gasteig also has several smaller concert and event spaces, as well as the public library. The sizeable open-kitchen Gast (⊕ *www.gast-muenchen.de*), part of the Gasteig complex, is a good option for a range of quick foods, from Thai curries to pizzas. ⊠ *Rosenheimerstr. 5, Haidhausen* ☎ *089/480–980* ⊕ *www.gasteig.de* Ⓜ *Rosenheimerplatz.*

Herkulessaal in der Residenz. This highly regarded orchestral and recital venue is in the former throne room of King Ludwig I. ⊠ *Residenzstr. 1, Altstadt* ☎ *089/5481–8181 München Ticket* ⊕ *www.muenchenticket. de* Ⓜ *Odeonsplatz, Marienplatz.*

Fodor'sChoice
★
Nationaltheater (*Bayerische Staatsoper*). The Bavarian State Orchestra is based at the Nationaltheater. ⊠ *Max-Joseph-Pl. 2, Altstadt* ☎ *089/218–501* ⊕ *www.staatsoper.de/en/index.html* Ⓜ *Odeonsplatz, Marienplatz.*

Fodor's Choice   **Olympiahalle.** One of Munich's major pop-rock concert venues is the
★   Olympiahalle, and the official ticket seller is München Ticket. ⊠ *Spiridon-Louis-Ring 21, Milbertshofen* ⊕ *www.olympiapark.de/en/olympi-
apark-munich* Ⓜ *Olympiazentrum.*

OPERA, BALLET, AND MUSICALS
Nationaltheater. Munich's Bavarian State Opera Company and its ballet
ensemble perform at the Nationaltheater. ⊠ *Max-Joseph-Pl. 2, Altstadt*
☎ *089/218–501* ⊕ *www.staatsoper.de/en/index.html* Ⓜ *Odeonsplatz,
Marienplatz.*

SPORTS AND THE OUTDOORS

BICYCLING

A bike is hands-down the best way to experience this flat, pedal-friendly
city. There are loads of bike lanes and paths that wind through its parks
and along the Isar River. The rental shop will give you maps and tips,
or you can get a map at any city tourist office.

RENTALS
Mike's Bike Tours. Besides offering guided tours, Mike's Bike Tours also
rents bikes. You can book your tour at the office around the corner
from the rear entrance of the Hofbräuhaus, at Bräuhausstrasse 10, but
the bike-rental location is a few hundred yards away, on the other side
of the Isar Tor. Return time is 7:30 pm mid-April–August, earlier in
other seasons. ⊠ *Thomas-Wimmer-Ring 16, Lehel* ☎ *089/2554–3987*
⊕ *www.mikesbiketours.com* ⚲ *Bikes from €18* Ⓜ *Isartor.*

Radius Tours and Bikes. Based at the main train station, Radius Tours
and Bikes rents all types of bikes, from seven- and eight-gear to 24-
and 27-gear to e-bikes. Helmets, child bikes, and child seats are also
available. ⊠ *Hauptbahnhof, opposite platform 32, Arnulfstr. 3, Ludwigsvorstadt* ☎ *089/5434–877730* ⊕ *www.radiustours.com* ⚲ *Bikes
from €4* Ⓜ *Hauptbahnhof.*

SHOPPING

Munich has three of Germany's most exclusive shopping streets, as well
as flea markets to rival those of any other European city. In between
are department stores, where acute German-style competition assures
reasonable prices and often produces outstanding bargains. Artisans
bring their wares of beauty and originality to the Christmas markets.
Collect their business cards—in summer you're sure to want to order
another of those little gold baubles that were on sale in December.

Munich has an immense central shopping area, a 2-km (1-mile) *Fuss-
gängerzone* (pedestrian zone) stretching from Karlsplatz to Marienplatz
along Neuhauser Strasse and Kaufingerstrasse, where most of the major
department stores are, and then north to Odeonsplatz. For upscale
shopping, Maximilianstrasse, Residenzstrasse, and Theatinerstrasse
are unbeatable. Schwabing, north of the university, has more offbeat

shopping streets—Schellingstrasse and Hohenzollernstrasse are two to try. ■ TIP➔ **The neighborhood around Gärtnerplatz also has lots of new boutiques.**

A few small shops around Viktualienmarkt sell Bavarian antiques, though their numbers are dwindling under the pressure of high rents. Antiques shoppers should also try the area north of the university— Türkenstrasse, Theresienstrasse, and Barerstrasse are all filled with antiques stores. Interesting and inexpensive antiques and assorted junk from all over Europe are laid out at the Friday and Saturday flea markets at Olympiapark (7 am–4 pm), not far from the Olympic Stadium, with hundreds of sellers.

If you want to deck yourself out in *Lederhosen* or a *Dirndl,* or acquire a green loden coat and little pointed hat with feathers, you have a wide choice in the Bavarian capital. ■ TIP➔ **There are a couple of shops along Tal street that have new and used lederhosen and dirndls at good prices in case you want to spontaneously get into the spirit of the 'Fest.**

Munich is a city of beer, and items related to its consumption are obvious choices for souvenirs and gifts. Munich is also the home of the famous Nymphenburg Porcelain factory. Between Karlsplatz and Viktualienmarkt there are loads of shops for memorabilia and trinkets.

■ TIP➔ **Nearly all stores, including drugstores and supermarkets, are closed on Sunday, except once every few months when they are allowed to have special Sunday opening hours because of a public holiday.**

ALTSTADT

ANTIQUES

Antike Uhren Eder. In Antike Uhren Eder, the silence is broken only by the ticking of dozens of highly valuable German antique clocks and by discreet negotiation over the high prices. ✉ *Lenbachpl. 7, Altstadt* ☎ *089/220–305* ⊕ *www.uhreneder.de* Ⓜ *Karlsplatz, Lenbachplatz (Tram).*

Roman Odesser. Antique German silver is the specialty at Roman Odesser. ✉ *Westenriederstr. 21, Altstadt* ☎ *089/226–388* ⊕ *roman-odesser.de* Ⓜ *Marienplatz.*

BOOKS

Hugendubel. This multistory bookshop has a good-size English-language section, with fiction and nonfiction selections. ✉ *Karlspl. 12, Altstadt* ☎ *089/3075–7575* ⊕ *www.hugendubel.de* Ⓜ *Karlsplatz.*

CERAMICS AND GLASS

F.S. Kustermann. In business since 1798, this large retailer stocks an impressive array of fine china, glassware, and ceramics, as well as everyday household goods. ✉ *Viktualienmarkt 8, Altstadt* ☎ *089/237–250* ⊕ *www.kustermann.de* Ⓜ *Marienplatz.*

Porzellan Manufaktur Nymphenburg. Nymphenburg's flaship store, this opulent space resembles a drawing room in the Munich palace of the same name. It has delicate, expensive porcelain safely locked away in bowfront cabinets. ⊠ *Odeonspl. 1, Altstadt* ☎ *089/282–428* ⊕ *www. nymphenburg.com* Ⓜ *Odeonsplatz.*

CRAFTS

Fodor's Choice ★ **Bayerischer Kunstgewerbe–Verein.** Bavarian craftspeople have a showplace of their own, the Bayerischer Kunstgewerbe–Verein. Here you'll find every kind of handicraft, from glass and pottery to textiles. ⊠ *Pacellistr. 6, Altstadt* ☎ *089/290–1470* ⊕ *www.bayerischer-kunstgewerbeverein. de* Ⓜ *Karlsplatz, Odeonsplatz.*

FOOD AND BEER

Chocolate & More. This tiny shop, located in the Viktualienmarkt, specializes in all things chocolate, with more than 120 varieties of chocolates and truffles. ⊠ *Westenrieder Str. 15, Altstadt* ☎ *089/2554–4905* ⊕ *www.chocolate-and-more.de* Ⓜ *Marienplatz.*

Dallmayr. Dallmayr is the city's most elegant and famous gourmet food store, with delights that range from exotic fruits and English jams to a multitude of fish and meats, all served by efficient Munich matrons in smart blue-and-white-linen uniforms. The store's famous specialty is coffee, with more than 50 varieties to blend as you wish. It even has its own chocolate factory. This is the place to prepare a high-class—if pricey—picnic. ⊠ *Dienerstr. 14–15, Altstadt* ☎ *089/21350* ⊕ *www.dallmayr.com* Ⓜ *Marienplatz.*

GIFTS AND SOUVENIRS

Max Krug. If you've been to the Black Forest and forgot to acquire a clock, or if you need a good Bavarian souvenir, like a *Krug* (stein) try Max Krug in the pedestrian zone. ⊠ *Neuhauser Str. 2, Altstadt* ☎ *089/224–501* ⊕ *www.max-krug.com* Ⓜ *Karlsplatz, Marienplatz.*

Sebastian Wesely. Besides a great variety of religious trinkets and candles, Sebastian Wesely is the place to come for beer-related vessels and *Stampferl* (schnapps glasses), walking sticks, scarves, and napkins with the famous Bavarian blue-and-white lozenges. ⊠ *Rindermarkt 1, at Peterspl., Altstadt* ☎ *089/264–519* ⊕ *www.wesely-schnitzereien.de* Ⓜ *Marienplatz.*

SHOPPING MALLS AND DEPARTMENT STORES

Breiter. For a classic selection of German clothing and hats, including some with a folk touch, try Munich's traditional family-run Breiter, with one of its stores on Altstadt's Kaufingerstrasse. ⊠ *Kaufingerstr. 26, Altstadt* ☎ *089/8905–8401* ⊕ *www.hutbreiter.de* Ⓜ *Marienplatz.*

Fünf Höfe. For a more upscale shopping experience, visit the many stores, boutiques, galleries, and cafés of the Fünf Höfe, a modern arcade carved into the block of houses between Theatinerstrasse and Kardinal-Faulhaber-Strasse. The architecture of the passages and courtyards is cool and elegant, in sharp contrast to the facades of the buildings. Along with outposts devoted to well-known international brands, there are German brands such as S. Baumeister (shoes and clothing) and Friendly Hunting for cashmere. ⊠ *Theatinerstr. 15, Altstadt* ✛ *Other entrances from Salvatorstr., Kardinal-Faulhaber-Str., and Maffeistr.* ⊕ *www.fuenfhoefe. de* Ⓜ *Marienplatz, Odeonsplatz.*

Galeria Kaufhof. With eight floors of offerings in this department store, you'll find midprice goods from cosmetics, fashion, and jewelry to greeting cards, office supplies, household items, and culinary delicacies. The end-of-season sales are bargains. ⊠ *Kaufingerstr. 1–5, Marienpl., Altstadt* ☎ *089/231–851* ⊕ *www.galeria-kaufhof.de* Ⓜ *Marienplatz.*

Hirmer. Spanning six floors, Hirmer has Munich's most comprehensive collection of German-made men's clothes, with a markedly friendly and knowledgeable staff. International brands are also here, such as Polo, Diesel, and Levi's. ⊠ *Kaufingerstr. 28, Altstadt* ☎ *089/236–830* ⊕ *www.hirmer-muenchen.de* Ⓜ *Marienplatz, Karlsplatz.*

Kaufinger Tor. Kaufinger Tor has several floors of boutiques and cafés packed neatly together along a passageway under a high glass roof. ⊠ *Kaufingerstr. 117, Altstadt* ⊕ *kaufingertor.de/en/home* Ⓜ *Marienplatz, Karlsplatz.*

Ludwig Beck. Ludwig Beck is considered a step above other department stores by Müncheners. It's packed from top to bottom with highly original wares and satisfies even the pickiest of shoppers. ⊠ *Marienpl. 11, Altstadt* ☎ *089/236–910* ⊕ *kaufhaus.ludwigbeck.de* Ⓜ *Marienplatz.*

Oberpollinger. The more-than-100-year-old Oberpollinger—one of Germany's finest upscale department stores—has seven floors packed with pricey and glamorous fashion, furniture, and beauty items. The large, open-plan self-service restaurant on the top floor, with an outdoor patio for the warm and sunny days, is well worth a visit, and isn't expensive. ⊠ *Neuhauser Str. 18, Altstadt* ☎ *089/290–230* ⊕ *www.oberpollinger. de/en* ⊙ *Closed Sun.* Ⓜ *Karlsplatz.*

Sporthaus Schuster. The focus here is on adventure sports, so if it's climbing, trekking, biking, or walking you're into, this huge store, just off Marienplatz, is the place. ⊠ *Rosenstr. 1–5, Altstadt* ☎ *089/237–070* ⊕ *www.sport-schuster.de* ⊙ *Closed Sun.* Ⓜ *Marienplatz.*

TRADITIONAL CLOTHING

Lederhosen Wagner. The tiny Lederhosen Wagner, right up against the Heiliggeist Church, carries Lederhosen, woolen sweaters called *Walk* (not loden), and children's clothing. ⊠ *Tal 2, Altstadt* ☎ *089/225–697* ⊕ *www.lederhosen-wagner.de* Ⓜ *Marienplatz, Isartor.*

Loden-Frey. Much of the fine loden clothing on sale at Loden-Frey is made at the company's own factory, on the edge of the Englischer Garten. ⊠ *Maffeistr. 7, Altstadt* ☎ *089/210–390* ⊕ *www.lodenfrey.com* ⊙ *Closed Sun.* Ⓜ *Marienplatz, Odeonsplatz.*

TOYS

Fodor's Choice ★ **Spielwaren Obletters.** Spielwaren Obletters has two extensive floors of toys, with the usual favorites plus many handmade playthings of great charm and quality. ⊠ *Karlspl. 12, Altstadt* ☎ *089/5508–9510* ⊕ *www.mueller.de* Ⓜ *Karlsplatz.*

LUDWIGSVORSTADT AND ISARVORSTADT

FOOD AND BEER

GötterSpeise. GötterSpeise is across the street from the restaurant Faun in Glockenbachviertel. The name of this delectable chocolate shop means "ambrosia," a fitting name for their gifts, delights, and hot drinks. ✉ *Jahnstr. 30, Isarvorstadt* ☎ *089/2388–7374* ⊕ *www.goetterspeise-muenchen.de* Ⓜ *Fraunhoferstrasse.*

SHOPPING MALLS AND DEPARTMENT STORES

Karstadt. Karstadt commands an entire city block between the main train station, Hauptbahnhof, and Karlsplatz. It is the largest and one of the best department stores in the city. On the fourth floor is a cafeteria with a great selection of excellent and inexpensive dishes. ✉ *Bahnhofpl. 7, Ludwigsvorstadt* ☎ *089/55120* ⊕ *www.karstadt.de* Ⓜ *Hauptbahnhof, Karlsplatz.*

TRADITIONAL CLOTHING

Almliebe Store Munich. Shop for traditional Bavarian attire including Dirndls and Lederhosen at this small shop in the Glockenbachviertel. ✉ *Ickstattstr. 22, Isarvorstadt* ☎ *089/5529–7471* ⊕ *www.almliebe.com* Ⓜ *Fraunhoferstrasse.*

Noh Nee. For a unique twist on the Dirndl, this shop in the Glockenbachviertel, owned by two sisters from Cameroon, combines bright African fabrics and embroidery with traditional Bavarian Dirndl styles. ✉ *Hans-Sachs-Str. 2, Isarvorstadt* ☎ *089/8898–1270* ⊕ *www.nohnee.com* Ⓜ *Fraunhoferstrasse.*

SCHWABING AND MAXVORSTADT

ANTIQUES

Die Puppenstube. For Munich's largest selection of dolls and marionettes, head to Die Puppenstube. ✉ *Luisenstr. 68, Maxvorstadt* ☎ *089/272–3267* Ⓜ *Theresienstrasse, Josephsplatz.*

BOOKS

Lehmkuhl. Lehmkuhl is Munich's oldest and one of its finest bookshops; it also sells beautiful cards. ✉ *Leopoldstr. 45, Schwabing* ☎ *089/380–1500* ⊕ *www.lehmkuhl.net* ⊙ *Closed Sun.* Ⓜ *Münchner Freiheit.*

FOOD AND BEER

Ludwig Mory. This pewter handcraft shop has everything from dinner plates and veal sausage to mugs and beer. Mugs come in all shapes and sizes, and are also available in ceramic. ✉ *Amalienstr. 16, Maxvorstadt* ☎ *089/224–542* ⊕ *www.zinn-mory.de.*

MARKETS

FAMILY **Elisabethplatz.** If you're in the Schwabing area, the daily market at Elisabethplatz is worth a visit—it's much smaller than the Victualien-markt but the range and quality of produce are comparable. Whereas at Viktualienmarkt you have visitors from many lands pushing past the stands, here life is more peaceful and local. There is a nicely shaded beer garden here as well. ✉ *Elisabethpl., Schwabing* ⊕ *www.muenchen.de* Ⓜ *Elisabethplatz (Tram).*

SIDE TRIPS FROM MUNICH

Munich's excellent suburban railway network, the S-bahn, brings several quaint towns and attractive rural areas within easy reach for a day's excursion. The two nearest lakes, Starnberger See and the Ammersee, are popular year-round. Dachau attracts overseas visitors mostly because of its concentration-camp memorial site, but it's a picturesque and historic town in its own right. Landshut, north of Munich, is way off the tourist track, but if it were the same distance south of Munich, this jewel of a Bavarian market town would be overrun. All these destinations have a wide selection of restaurants and hotels, and you can bring a bike on any S-bahn train. German Railways (DB) often has weekend specials that allow a family or group of five to travel inexpensively. Inquire at the main train station for a Bayern ticket, a cheap way for up to five people to travel in Bavaria for a day, and the *Wochenendticket* (weekend ticket), which is also at a reduced price. You can also opt for a *Tageskarte* (day ticket), in the ticket machines in the subway stations.

■TIP→ **Keep in mind that there are quite a few options for day trips to the famous castles built by King Ludwig, which are only a couple of hours away.** Mike's Bike Tours organizes trips, or ask at your hotel for bus-tour excursions. A train out to Füssen and Schloss Neuschwanstein takes two hours. *For more information on this fairy-tale castle and others, see Chapter 4, The Romantic Road.*

STARNBERGER SEE

27 km (25 miles) southwest of Munich's Innenstadt.

The Starnberger See is named after its chief town, Starnberg, the largest on the lake and the nearest to Munich; it was one of Europe's first pleasure grounds. Royal coaches were already trundling out from Munich to the lake's wooded shores in the 17th century. In 1663 Elector Ferdinand Maria threw a shipboard party at which 500 guests wined and dined as 100 oarsmen propelled them around the lake. Today pleasure steamers provide a taste of such luxury for the masses. The lake is still lined with the small baroque palaces of Bavaria's aristocracy (some of which are now hotels), but their owners now share the lakefront with public parks, beaches, and boatyards. Starnberger See is one of Bavaria's largest lakes—20 km (12 miles) long, 5 km (3 miles) wide, and 127 meters (416 feet) at its deepest point—so there's plenty of room for swimmers, sailors, and windsurfers. The water is very clean (like most Bavarian lakes), a testimony to stringent environmental laws and the limited number of motorboats allowed.

GETTING HERE AND AROUND

Starnberg and the north end of the lake are a 30-minute drive from Munich on the A-95 autobahn. Follow the signs to Garmisch and take the Starnberg exit. Country roads then skirt the west and east shores of the lake, but many are closed to the public.

The S-bahn 6 suburban line (direction Tutzing) runs from Munich's central Marienplatz to Starnberg and three other towns on the lake's west shore: Possenhofen, Feldafing, and Tutzing. The journey from Marienplatz to Starnberg takes around 40 minutes. The east shore of the lake can be reached by bus from the town of Wolfratshausen, the end of the S-bahn 7 suburban line.

The nicest way to visit the Starnberger See area is by boat or even by bicycle. Bayerische Seenschifffahrt (Bavarian Lakes Shipping Company) has a variety of boat tours.

VISITOR INFORMATION

CONTACTS   **Tourismusverband Starnberger Fünf-Seen-Land.** Starnberg Five-Lake-Region Tourist Information is the place to get all the information you need to enjoy trips to the lakes, towns, villages, and countryside between Munich and the Alps. ⊠ *Hauptstr. 1, Starnberg* ☎ *08151/90600* ⊕ *en. sta5.de* Ⓜ *Starnberg.*

EXPLORING

Buchheim Museum. The Buchheim Museum, on the western shore of the lake, has one of the finest private collections of German expressionist art in the form of paintings, drawings, watercolors, and prints. Among the artists represented are Otto Dix, Max Beckmann, Ernst Ludwig Kirchner, Karl Schmitt-Rotluff, and other painters of the so-called Brücke movement (1905–13). The museum is housed in an impressive modern building on the lakeside. Some areas of the museum are reserved for African cultic items and Bavarian folk art. The nicest way to get to the museum from Starnberg is by boat. ⊠ *Am Hirschgarten 1, Bernried, Starnberg* ☎ *08158/99700* ⊕ *www.buchheimmuseum.de* 💶 *€9* ⊙ *Closed Mon.* Ⓜ *Tutzing.*

Kaiserin Elisabeth Museum Possenhofen. The castle of Possenhofen, home of Ludwig's favorite cousin, Sissi, stands on the western shore, practically opposite Berg. Local lore says they used to send affectionate messages across the lake to each other. Sissi married the Austrian emperor Franz Joseph I, but spent more than 20 summers in the lakeside castle. The inside of the castle cannot be visited, but there is a nice park around it, and you can learn more about Sissi at the Kaiserin Elisabeth Museum (Sissi-Museum), set in the historical Possenhofen railway station (yards from S-bahn Possenhofen). ⊠ *Schlossberg 2, Poecking, Berg* ☎ *08157/924401* ⊕ *www.kaiserin-elisabeth-museum-ev.de/eng/index. php* 💶 *€4* ⊙ *Closed late Oct.–Apr.* Ⓜ *Possenhofen.*

König Ludwig II Votivkapelle Berg (*King Ludwig II Memorial Chapel*). On the lake's eastern shore, at the village of Berg, you'll find the König Ludwig II Votivkapelle Berg. A well-marked path leads through thick woods to the chapel, built near the point in the lake where the drowned king's body was found on June 13, 1886. He had been confined in nearby Berg Castle after the Bavarian government took action against his withdrawal from reality and his bankrupting castle-building fantasies. A cross in the lake marks the point where his body was recovered. ⊠ *near Berg Castle, Berg* Ⓜ *Tutzing.*

Roseninsel (*Rose Island*). Just offshore is the tiny island where King Maximilian II built a summer villa (called a casino). You can swim to the island's tree-fringed shores or sail across in a dinghy (rentals are available at Possenhofen's boatyard and at many other rental points along the lake). There is also a ferry service (⊕ *www.roseninsel.bayern*) to take you over. ⊠ *Possenhofen* ☎ *08158/2874–1905 ferry* ⊕ *www. sta5.de/reisefuehrer/wasser/roseninsel.html* ☉ *Ferry does not operate mid-Oct.–Apr. Casino closed Mon.* Ⓜ *Possenhofen.*

WHERE TO STAY

$$ 🖼 **Hotel Schloss Berg.** King Ludwig II spent his final days in the small cas-
HOTEL tle of Berg, from which this comfortable hotel gets its name. **Pros:** very nice view across the lake; spacious, elegantly furnished rooms; good, lively restaurant and lakefront beer garden. **Cons:** the reception desk is in the annex; you need a car to get here; the modern annex doesn't appeal to all. Ⓢ *Rooms from: €149* ⊠ *Seestr. 17, Berg* ☎ *08151/9630* ⊕ *www.hotelschlossberg.de* ⤳ *59 rooms* ⦿ *Free Breakfast* Ⓜ *Starnberg Nord, then Bus 961 or 975 to Berg/Grafstrasse stop.*

$$ 🖼 **Hotel Starnberger See.** This small hotel right next to the train sta-
HOTEL tion has several rooms with lake views. **Pros:** good lakefront location; free Wi-Fi throughout; excellent Italian restaurant attached. **Cons:** rooms facing the street are noisy; some rooms are simply furnished; prices can be high. Ⓢ *Rooms from: €140* ⊠ *Bahnhofpl. 6, Starnberg* ☎ *08151/908–500* ⊕ *www.hotelstarnbergersee.de* ⤳ *38 rooms* ⦿ *Free Breakfast* Ⓜ *Starnberg.*

AMMERSEE

40 km (25 miles) southwest of Munich.

Ammersee, known as "Peasants' Lake," is the country cousin of the better-known, more cosmopolitan Starnberger See (the "Princes' Lake"), and, accordingly, many Bavarians (and tourists, too) like it all the more. Munich cosmopolites of centuries past thought it too distant for an excursion—not to mention too rustic—so the shores remained relatively free of villas and parks. Though some upscale holiday homes claim some stretches of the eastern shore, Ammersee still offers more open areas for bathing and boating than the larger lake to the east. Bicyclists circle the 19-km-long (12-mile-long) lake (it's nearly 6 km [4 miles] across at its widest point) on a path that rarely loses sight of the water. Hikers can spread out the tour for two or three days, staying overnight in any of the comfortable inns along the way. Dinghy sailors and windsurfers zip across in minutes with the help of the alpine winds that swoop down from the mountains. A ferry cruises the lake at regular intervals in summer, stopping at several piers; board it at Herrsching.

Herrsching has a delightful promenade, part of which winds through the town's park. The 100-year-old villa that sits so comfortably there is a romantic and fanciful mixture of medieval turrets and Renaissance-style facades. It was actually built for the artist Ludwig Scheuermann in the late 19th century, and became a favorite meeting place for Bavarian artists. It's now a municipal cultural center and the setting for chamber-music concerts on some summer weekends.

GETTING HERE AND AROUND

Take A-96, follow the signs towards Lindau, and after about 20 km (12 miles) take the exit for Herrsching, the lake's principal town. Herrsching is also the end of S-bahn 8, about a one-hour ride from Munich's Hauptbahnhof.

Getting around by boat is the best way to visit. Each town on the lake has an *Anlegestelle* (pier).

EXPLORING

Fodor's Choice ★ **Andechs Monastery.** One of southern Bavaria's most famous pilgrimage sites, this Benedictine monastery is 5 km (3 miles) south of Herrsching. You can reach it on Bus 951 from the S-bahn station, but you can easily walk there too, as most people do. Surmounted by an octagonal tower and onion dome with a pointed helmet, Andechs has a history going back more than 1,000 years. The church, originally built in the 15th century, was entirely redone in baroque style in the early 18th century. The Heilige Kapelle contains the remains of the old treasure of the Benedictines in Andechs, including Charlemagne's "Victory Cross." One of the chapels contains the remains of composer Carl Orff, who works are performed on the grounds. The monastery also brews rich, almost black beer and makes its own cheese as well. ✉ *Bergstr. 2, 5 km (3 miles) south of Herrsching, Andechs* ☎ *08152/3760* 🌐 *andechs.de.*

Carl-Orff-Museum. Among the most famous artists who made their home here was the composer Carl Orff, author of numerous works inspired by medieval material, including the famous *Carmina Burana.* His life and work—notably the pedagogical Schulwerk instruments—are exhibited in the Carl-Orff-Museum. ✉ *Hofmark 3, Diessen* ☎ *08807/91981* 🌐 *www.orff.de/institutionen/carl-orff-museum.html* 🎟 *€3* ⏲ *Closed Mon.–Sat. Closed Jan. and Feb.*

Diessen am Ammersee. The little town of Diessen am Ammersee at the southwest corner of the lake has one of the most magnificent religious buildings of the whole region: the Augustine abbey church of St. Mary (aka Marienmünster). The great Munich architect Johann Michael Fischer designed this airy, early rococo structure. François Cuvilliés the Elder, whose work can be seen all over Munich, did the sumptuous gilt-and-marble high altar. Don't leave without at least peeping into neighboring St. Stephen's courtyard, its cloisters smothered in wild roses. Diessen has also attracted artists and craftspeople since the early 20th century. Among the most famous who made their home here was the composer Carl Orff. ✉ *Diessen.*

WHERE TO STAY

$$ HOTEL 🏨 **Ammersee Hotel.** This very comfortable, modern resort hotel is located on the Ammersee. **Pros:** prime location; good restaurant; great lake views. **Cons:** rooms facing the street are noisy; limited lake-facing balcony rooms; no air-conditioning. [$] *Rooms from: €130* ✉ *Summerstr. 32, Herrsching* ☎ *08152/96870* 🌐 *www.ammersee-hotel.de* 🛏 *40 rooms* 🍴 *Free Breakfast* [M] *Herrsching.*

$$ B&B/INN FAMILY 🏨 **Hotel Zur Post Garni-Andechs.** Not far from the Andechs Monastery, everything about this B&B is Bavarian country style—clean and functional, with solid-pine furnishings. **Pros:** convenient to Andechs

Monastery; free Wi-Fi; lovely terrace and lawn. **Cons:** no restaurant; room decor may not appeal to all; traffic noise from rooms facing road. [$] *Rooms from: €113* ✉ *Starnberger Str. 2, Andechs* ☎ *08152/91820* 🌐 *www.hotelzurpost-andechs.de* 🛏 *17 rooms* 🍴 *Breakfast.*

$$ HOTEL 🏨 **Seehof Herrsching.** The hotel's long lakefront turns into a huge beer garden in summer. **Pros:** great views; food in the restaurant is good; friendly staff. **Cons:** restaurant gets packed in summer; rooms above the restaurant and terrace can get noisy; Wi-Fi is spotty. [$] *Rooms from: €146* ✉ *Seestr. 58, Herrsching* ☎ *08152/9350* 🌐 *www.seehof-ammersee.de* 🛏 *43 rooms* 🍴 *Free Breakfast* [M] *Herrsching.*

DACHAU

20 km (12 miles) northwest of Munich.

Dachau predates Munich, with records going back to the time of Charlemagne. It's a handsome town, too, built on a hilltop with views of Munich and the Alps, which was why it became such a favorite of numerous artists. A guided tour of the town, including the castle and palace, leaves from the Rathaus (Konrad-Adenauer-Strasse 2–6) on Saturday at 11 am from May through October, in German, or rent an audio guide from the tourist information office. Dachau is infamous worldwide as the site of the "model" Nazi concentration camp, which was built just outside it. Dachau preserves the memory of the camp and the horrors perpetrated there with deep contrition while trying, with commendable discretion, to signal that the town has other points of interest.

GETTING HERE AND AROUND

From Munich take the Stuttgart autobahn (A8) to the Dachau-Fürstenfeldbruck exit, or the Nuremberg autobahn (A9) to the Oberschleissheim-Dachau exit. Dachau is also on S-bahn 2, a 25-minute ride from Munich's Marienplatz.

VISITOR INFORMATION

Contacts Tourist Information Dachau. ✉ *Konrad-Adenauer-Str. 1* ☎ *08131/75286* 🌐 *www.dachau.de/tourism.html?L=1* [M] *Dachau Rathaus (Bus) from Dachau train station.*

EXPLORING

Bezirksmuseum. To get a sense of the town's history, visit the Bezirksmuseum (district museum), which displays historical artifacts, furniture, and traditional costumes from Dachau and its surroundings. ✉ *Augsburger Str. 3* ☎ *08131/56750* 🌐 *www.dachauer-galerien-museen.de* 🎫 *€5* [M] *Dachau Rathaus (Bus) from Dachau train station.*

FAMILY Fodor's Choice ★ **Dachau Concentration Camp Memorial Site** (*KZ–Gedenkstätte Dachau*). The site of the infamous camp, now the KZ–Gedenkstätte Dachau, is just outside town. Photographs, contemporary documents, the few cell blocks, and the grim crematorium create a somber and moving picture of the camp, where more than 41,000 of the 200,000-plus prisoners lost their lives. A documentary film in English is shown five times daily. The former camp has become more than just a grisly memorial: it's now a place where people of all nations meet to reflect upon the past and on the present. By public transport take the S-2 from Marienplatz or Hauptbahnhof in the direction of Petershausen, and get off at Dachau. From there, take the clearly marked bus from right outside the Dachau S-bahn station (No. 726 toward Saubachsiedlung; it leaves about every 20 minutes). If you are driving from Munich, take the autobahn toward Stuttgart, get off at Dachau, and follow the signs. ✉ *Alte Römerstr. 75* ☎ *08131/6699–7135* 🌐 *www.kz-gedenkstaette-dachau.de* 🎟 *Free; English-language guided tours €4* [M] *Dachau, KZ-Gedenkstätte (Bus) from Dachau train station.*

Gemäldegalerie. An artists' colony formed here during the 19th century, and the tradition lives on. Picturesque houses line Hermann-Stockmann-Strasse and part of Münchner Strasse, and many of them are still the homes of successful artists. The Gemäldegalerie displays the works of many of the town's 19th-century artists. ✉ *Konrad-Adenauer-Str. 3* ☎ *08131/56750* 🌐 *www.dachauer-galerien-museen.de* 🎟 *€5* [M] *Dachau Rathaus (Bus) from Dachau train station.*

St. Jakob. St. Jakob, Dachau's parish church, was built in 1624–25 in late-Renaissance style on the foundations of a 13th-century Gothic structure. Baroque features and a characteristic onion dome were added in 1676–78. On the south wall you can admire a very fine sundial from 1699, which displays the month, the zodiac, and the time. ✉ *Pfarrstr. 7* ☎ *08131/36380* 🌐 *www.pv-dachau-st-jakob.de/st-jakob* [M] *Dachau Rathaus (Bus).*

FAMILY **Schloss Dachau.** This hilltop castle, built in 1715, dominates the town. During the Napoleonic Wars the palace served as a field hospital and then was partially destroyed. King Max Joseph lacked the money to rebuild it, so all that's left is a handsome cream-and-white building, with an elegant pillared and lantern-hung café on the ground floor and a former ballroom above. About once a month the grand Renaissance hall, with a richly decorated and carved ceiling, is used for chamber concerts. The east terrace affords panoramic views of Munich and, on fine days, the distant Alps. ✉ *Schlossstr. 7* ☎ *08131/87923* 🌐 *www.schloesser.bayern.de/englisch/palace/objects/dachau.htm* 🎟 *€2* 🕒 *Closed Mon.*

WHERE TO STAY

$$ HOTEL 🏨 **Hotel Fischer.** You can see this hotel across the square from the S-bahn station. **Pros:** free Wi-Fi; prime location; good restaurant. **Cons:** on nice evenings, noise from the patio may filter up to your room; decor is a bit dated; location isn't scenic. [$] *Rooms from: €125* ✉ *Bahnhofstr. 4* ☎ *08131/612–200* 🌐 *www.hotelfischer-dachau.de* 🛏 *29 rooms* 🍴 *Free Breakfast* [M] *Dachau.*

THE BAVARIAN ALPS

WELCOME TO THE BAVARIAN ALPS

TOP REASONS TO GO

★ **Herrenchiemsee:** Board a boat on the Chiemsee to visit the island housing King Ludwig II's last castle, a Bavarian take on Versailles.

★ **Remarkable nature:** From the crystalline waters of the Königssee to the grandiose Karwendel Mountains and the powdery snow atop the Zugspitze, it's everything a nature lover needs.

★ **Meditating in Ettal monastery:** Baroque ornamentation, a riot of frescoes, the fluid sound of the ancient organ that puts you in a deep, relaxing trance. A great brewery and distillery round out a deeply religious experience.

★ **Take a break on Tegernsee:** Hit the ski slopes or paddle out onto the quiet Alpine lake before pampering yourself at some of the country's best spa hotels.

★ **Berchtesgaden:** A national park attracts hikers and bikers; history buffs can explore the darkest chapter of German history at Obersalzberg, Hitler's mountain retreat.

While most locals wouldn't refer to their mountains as the "Bavarian Alps," there are several adjoining mountain ranges spanning the Ammergau, Wetterstein, and Karwendel Alps in the west to the Chiemgauer and Berchtesgadener Alpen in the east, and Germans will be quick to ask which range you mean.

1 Garmisch-Partenkirchen. This busy alpine spa and resort town hosted the 1936 Winter Olympics. The slopes here are typically open from December through April (and sometimes May on the Zugspitze).

2 Ettal. This small Bavarian town that hosts the largest Benedictine monastery in Germany, which has a magnificently painted 18th century ceiling.

3 Schloss Linderhof. The only castle that King Ludwig II completed during his lifetime is a mountain hunting lodge with gorgeous formal gardens.

4 Oberammergau. Home of the famous decennial passion play, which will be performed next in 2020.

5 Mittenwald. Widely considered the most beautiful town in the Bavarian Alps, Mittenwald is known for its beautiful 18th-century church and violin-making school.

6 Bad Tölz. Old-fashioned Bavarian spa resort that also offers good winter skiing om the Blomberg mountain.

7 Tegernsee. A beautiful Bavarian lake has drawn Germany's elite since the 19th century; its three main towns can be visted easily by ferry.

8 Chiemsee. The largest Bavarian lake has King Ludwig II's magnficent island castle Herrenchiemsee, which was modeled after Versailles.

9 Berchtesgaden. Gorgeous mountain town on the Austrian border is busy during both the summer (for hiking) and winter (for skiing). It also briefly hosted Hitler's weekend retreat.

10 Berchtesgaden National Park. Shared with Austria, 210 square km of beautiful mountains, forests, and alpine lakes are preserved for the benefit of more than one million tourists every year.

OUTDOORS IN THE BAVARIAN ALPS

Bursting up from the lowlands of southern Germany, the Bavarian Alps form both an awe-inspiring border with Austria and a superb natural playground for outdoors enthusiasts.

(above) Mountain bikers in the Bavarian foothills (upper right) Bavarian Alps (lower right) Backcountry skiers

Visible from Munich on a clear day, the northern front of the Alps stretches over 300 km (186 miles) from Lake Constance in the west to Berchtesgaden in the east, and acts as a threshold to the towering mountain ranges that lie farther south. Lower in altitude than their Austrian, Swiss, and French cousins, the Bavarian Alps have the advantage of shorter distances between the summits and the valleys below, forming an ideal environment for casual hikers and serious mountaineers alike.

In spring and summer, cowbells tinkle and wild flowers blanket meadows beside trails that course up and down the mountainsides. In winter, snow engulfs the region, turning trails into paths for cross-country skiers and the mountainsides into pistes for snowboarders and downhill skiers to carve their way down.

—Updated by Courtney Tenz

LEDERHOSEN

Along with sausages and enormous mugs of frothy beer, Lederhosen form the holy trinity of what many foreigners believe to be stereotypically "German." However, these embroidered leather breeches are traditionally worn only in Bavaria, where the durability and protection of leather are advantageous for those working as carpenters or farmers in the region. Handmade, tailored versions are worn on special occasions.

BEST WAYS TO EXPLORE

BY BIKE

You don't need to venture onto the slopes to appreciate the Alps' beauty; cycling through their foothills affords stunning views of the mountains combined with the luxury of refreshing stop-offs in beer gardens and dips in beautiful lakes like the Tegernsee. There's plenty of accommodation tailored to cyclists throughout the region and local trains are normally equipped with a bicycle carriage or two to transport you to more remote locations. The Alps also have thousands of miles of mountain-bike-friendly trails and a number of special bike parks serviced by cable cars.

BY FOOT

It's not without good reason that *Wanderlust* is a German word. The desire to travel and explore has been strong for hundreds of years in Germany, especially in places like the Alps where strenuous strolls are rewarded with breathtaking vistas. There are more than 7,000 km (4,350 miles) of walking trails in the Allgäu region alone to wander, conveniently divided into valley walks, mid-altitude trails, and summit hikes reflecting the varying altitude and difficulty. Hikes can be undertaken as day trips or as weeks-long endeavors, and there are campsites, mountain huts, farmhouses, and hotels to overnight in along the way, as well as a decent infrastructure of buses, trains, and cable cars to get you to your starting point. Get more information on hiking trails and current conditions from the Bavaria Tourism Office (🌐 *www.bavaria.by*) or the German Alpine Club (🌐 *www.alpenverein.de*).

BY SKIS

Neither as high nor as famous as their neighbors, the Bavarian Alps are frequently overlooked as a winter-sports destination. Resorts on the German side of the border may have shorter seasons than places like Zermatt and Chamonix, but they're also generally less expensive in terms of food and accommodations, and many, including the Zugspitze, are easily accessed from Munich for day trips.

3

BEST PHOTO OPS

No matter where you are around the Alps you'll be inundated with sights worth snapping. Here are a few:

■ **Neuschwanstein Castle** sits theatrically on the side of a mountain, its grand towers set against a background of tree- and snow-covered peaks.

■ The panoramic view from close to 10,000 feet at the peak of Germany's highest mountain, the **Zugspitze,** takes in 400 peaks in four countries.

■ Reputedly the cleanest lake in Germany, **Königssee** is also endowed with steep rock formations that soar thousands of meters up above the lake, beautifully framing its crystalline waters.

■ From **Tegernsee's** lovely Benedictine monastery, you can wander down to the lake for spectacular vistas of its glittering surface and the Alps beyond.

Updated by
Courtney Tenz

Fir-clad mountains, rocky peaks, Lederhosen, half-timber houses with geranium window boxes: villages in the Bavarian Alps embody what many of us envision as "Germany." Quaint towns are enlivened by houses carefully frescoed. Snow glistens on the mountain peaks in winter and lakes below shimmer all summer long. The castles of King Ludwig II, one of the last kings of Bavaria, are a favorite sight, as are the more modest monasteries of Benedictine monks. Sporting opportunities abound throughout the area year-round.

Upper Bavaria (Oberbayern) stretches south and east from Munich to the Austrian border. Leaving the city, you'll soon find yourself on a gently rolling plain leading to lakes surrounded by ancient forests. The plain merges into foothills, which suddenly give way to jagged Alpine peaks, and in Berchtesgadener Land, snowcapped mountains appear to rise straight up from the gemlike lakes.

Continuing south, you'll encounter cheerful villages with richly painted houses, churches, and monasteries filled with the especially sensuous Bavarian baroque and rococo styles, and several salt deposits in the area have created a spa culture where you can relax as you "take the waters." Some of the best sport in Germany can be enjoyed here: downhill and cross-country skiing, snowboarding, and ice-skating in winter; tennis, swimming, sailing, golf, and above all—sometimes literally—hiking, paragliding, and ballooning in summer.

MAJOR REGIONS

With Germany's highest peak and picture-perfect Bavarian villages, the **Wetterstein, Ammergau and Karwendel Mountains** offer a splendid mix of natural beauty combined with Bavarian art and culture. The region spreads out around the base of the Zugspitze, where the views from the top reach **Garmisch-Partenkirchen.** Just a stone's throw away are the serene **Kloster Ettal,** the frescoed houses of **Oberammergau,** and enchanting **Mittenwald.**

With its rolling hills and serene lakes in the shadow of the Alpine peaks, the **Upper Bavarian Lake District** is a natural paradise and a good transition into the mountains. Popular destinations include **Bad Tölz** and **Tegernsee,** but the main attraction is, without a doubt, the **Chiemsee** with the amazing palace on the Herreninsel, the biggest of the islands on the lake. The region is dotted with sparkling blue lakes and, although tourism is fairly well established, you may feel that you have much of the area all to yourself.

Berchtesgadener Land is the Alps at their most dramatic and most notorious. Although other peaks may be higher, the steep cliffs, hidden mountain lakes, and protected biospheres make the area uniquely beautiful. The salt trade brought medieval **Bad Reichenhall** and **Berchtesgaden** incredible wealth, which is still apparent in the large collection of antique houses and quaint streets. Berchtesgaden's image is a bit tarnished by its history and most infamous historical resident, Adolf Hitler. **Berchtesgaden National Park,** however, is a hiker's dream, and the resounding echo of the trumpet on the Königssee shouldn't be missed.

3

PLANNING

WHEN TO GO

This mountainous region is a year-round holiday destination. Snow is promised by most resorts from December through March, although there's skiing on the glacier slopes at the top of the Zugspitze at least through May. Spring and autumn are ideal times for leisurely hikes on the many mountain trails. November is a between-seasons time, when many hotels and restaurants close down or attend to renovations. Note, too, that locals are themselves sport lovers and in smaller towns, they may take a vacation after January 6, with businesses not related to sporting closed for anywhere up to a month. The lakes are extremely popular in summer as families set up camp in July and August.

GETTING HERE AND AROUND

AIR TRAVEL

Munich, 95 km (59 miles) northwest of Garmisch-Partenkirchen, is the gateway to the Bavarian Alps. If you're staying in Berchtesgaden, consider the closer airport in Salzburg, Austria—it has fewer international flights, but serves as a budget-airline and charter hub.

Contacts Salzburg Airport (*SZG*). ✉ *Innsbrucker Bundesstr. 95, Salzburg* ☎ *0662/85800* ⊕ *www.salzburg-airport.com.*

CAR TRAVEL

The Bavarian Alps are well connected to Munich by train, and an extensive network of buses links even the most remote villages. Because bus schedules can be unreliable and are timed for commuters, those in a hurry may want to visit the area by car. Three autobahns reach into the Bavarian Alps: A-7 comes in from the northwest (Frankfurt, Stuttgart, Ulm) and ends near Füssen in the western Bavarian Alps; A-95 runs from Munich to Garmisch-Partenkirchen; take A-8 from Munich for Tegernsee, Chiemsee, and Berchtesgaden. ■ TIP→ **The A-8 is statistically the most dangerous autobahn in the country, partially due to it being heavily traveled and without a set speed limit on stretches. The driving style is fast, and tailgating is common, although illegal. The recommended speed on the A-8 is 110 kph (68 mph); if an accident occurs at higher speeds, your insurance may not cover it.** It is a good idea to pick a town like Garmisch-Partenkirchen, Bad Tölz, or Berchtesgaden as a base and explore the area from there.

TRAIN TRAVEL

Most Alpine resorts are connected with Munich by regular express and slower service trains. Due to the rugged terrain, train travel in the region can be challenging, but with some careful planning—see ⊕ *www.bahn. de* for schedules and to buy tickets—you can visit this region without a car. The Bavarian Alps are furnished with cable cars, steam trains, and cog railways that whisk you to the tops of Alpine peaks, allowing you to see the spectacular views without hours of mountain climbing.

HOTELS

With few exceptions, a hotel or *Gasthof* in the Bavarian Alps and lower Alpine regions has high standards and is traditional in style, with balconies, pine woodwork, and gently angled roofs on which the snow sits and insulates. Many in the larger resort towns offer special packages, including spa or "wellness" packages online. Private homes all through the region offer Germany's own version of bed-and-breakfasts, indicated by signs reading "Zimmer frei" (rooms available). Their rates may be less than €25 per person for renting a room with a shared bathroom. As a general rule, the farther from the popular and sophisticated Alpine resorts you go, the lower the rates. Note, too, that many places offer a small discount if you stay more than one night. By the same token, some places frown on staying only one night, especially during the high seasons, in summer, at Christmas, and on winter weekends. In spas and many mountain resorts a *Kurtaxe* (spa tax) is added to the hotel bill. It amounts to no more than €3 per person per day and allows discounted use of spa facilities and may provide entry to local attractions and concerts, or use of local transportation.

RESTAURANTS

Restaurants in Bavaria run the gamut from the casual and *gemütlich* (cozy) Gasthof to formal gourmet offerings. More upscale establishments try to maintain a feeling of casual familiarity, but you will probably feel more comfortable at the truly upscale restaurants if you dress up a bit. Many restaurants take a break from serving in the afternoon, often closing between 2:30 and 6 pm. If you want to eat during these hours, look for the magic words *Durchgehend warme Küche,* indicating warm food is served throughout the day, although you may be limited in options during the off-hours. Most restaurants in the region don't accept credit cards.

Hotel prices in the reviews are the lowest cost of a standard double room in high season. Restaurant prices in the reviews are the average cost of a main course at dinner, or if dinner is not served, at lunch.

The Zugspitze is the highest mountain in Germany and is reachable from Garmisch-Partenkirchen.

	WHAT IT COSTS IN EUROS			
	$	$$	$$$	$$$$
Restaurants	under €15	€15–€20	€21–€25	over €25
Hotels	under €100	€100–€175	€176–€225	over €225

PLANNING YOUR TIME

The Alps are spread along Germany's southern border, but are fairly compact and easy to explore. A central base like Garmisch-Partenkirchen or Berchtesgaden, the largest towns, will have the most convenient transportation connections.

Although the Alps are a popular tourist destination, the smaller communities like Mittenwald and Ettal are quieter and make for more pleasant overnight stays. For an unforgettable experience, try spending the night in an Alpine hut, feasting on a simple but hearty meal and sleeping in the cool night air.

DISCOUNTS AND DEALS

One of the best deals in the area is the German Railroad's Bayern Ticket, which allows between one and five people to travel on any regional train and almost all buses in the Alps. Prices range between €25 for a single traveler to €49 for five people. Ticket holders also receive discounts on a large number of attractions in the area, including the Zugspitzbahn, a cog railroad and cable car that takes you up to the top of the Zugspitze. The city of Grainau's ZugspitzCard (three days, €57) offers discounts in almost every city near the Zugspitze. Visitors to spas or spa towns receive a Kurkarte, an ID that proves payment of the spa tax, either upon check-in (the nominal fee is already included in your bill) or by dropping in at the tourist office. The document allows discounts and often free access to sights in the town or area. If you've paid the tax, be sure to show the card everywhere you go.

VISITOR INFORMATION

Bavaria Tourism. ⊠ *Arabellastr. 17, Munich* ☎ *08921/23970* ⊕ *www. bavaria.by.*

GARMISCH-PARTENKIRCHEN

90 km (56 miles) southwest of Munich.

More commonly known by American travelers as simply "Garmisch," Garmisch-Partenkirchen is comprised of two separate communities that were fused together in 1935 to accommodate the Winter Olympics held the following year. Since then, it's grown into a bustling, year-round resort town. Today, with a population of 28,000, the area is the center of the Werdenfelser Land and large enough to offer every facility expected from a major Alpine resort. Garmisch is slightly closer to the ski lifts and a bit more urban, with a pedestrian zone, than the smaller Partenkirchen. In both parts of town pastel frescoes of biblical and bucolic scenes decorate facades.

Winter sports rank high on the agenda here. There are more than 60 km (37 miles) of downhill ski runs, 40 ski lifts and cable cars, and 180 km (112 miles) of *Loipen* (cross-country ski trails). One of the principal stops on the international winter-sports circuit, the area hosts World Cup races on two weekends every January. You can usually count on good skiing from December through April.

GETTING HERE AND AROUND

Garmisch-Partenkirchen is the cultural and transportation hub of the Werdenfelser Land. The autobahn A-95 links Garmisch directly to Munich. Regional German Rail trains head directly to Munich (90 minutes), Innsbruck (80 minutes), and Mittenwald (20 minutes). German Rail operates buses that connect Garmisch with Oberammergau, Ettal, and the Wieskirche. Garmisch is a walkable city; you probably won't need to use its frequent city-bus services.

Partenkirchen was founded by the Romans, and you can still follow the Via Claudia Augusta they built between Partenkirchen and neighboring Mittenwald, which was part of a major route between Rome and Germany well into the 17th century.

Bus tours can be coordinated by the local tourist office with one of the local agencies; regular trips are available to King Ludwig II's castles at Neuschwanstein and Linderhof and to the Ettal monastery, near Oberammergau, as well as into the neighboring Austrian Tyrol.

The Garmisch mountain railway company, the Bayerische Zugspitzbahn, offers special excursions to the top of the Zugspitze, Germany's highest mountain, on the world's fastest gondola, which opened in December 2017 (€45 per person).

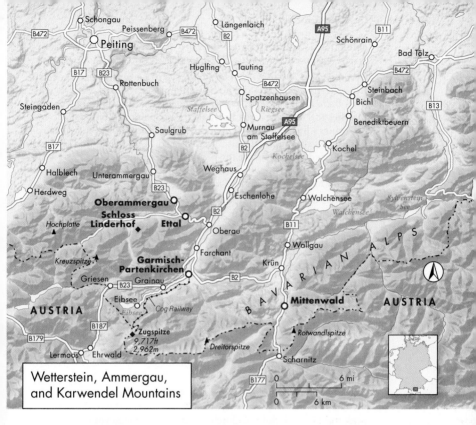

Wetterstein, Ammergau, and Karwendel Mountains

Contacts Bayerische Zugspitzbahn. ✉ *Olympiastr. 27* ☎ *08821/7970* ⊕ *www. zugspitze.de.*

TOURS

Weiss-Blau-Reisen. This local bus tour company organizes day trips to the neighboring sites, including Munich, Berchtesgaden, or the castles of King Ludwig II. Be sure to check the website for which tour is on, as the schedule changes daily and tickets should be reserved in advance. ✉ *Promenadestr. 5* ☎ *08821/6230* ⊕ *www.weiss-blau-reisen.de* 🚌 *From €20* 🕙 *Nov.–mid-May (groups can book for April).*

VISITOR INFORMATION

Contacts Garmisch-Partenkirchen. ✉ *Richard-Strauss-Pl. 2* ☎ *08821/180– 700* ⊕ *www.gapa.de.*

EXPLORING

Alte St. Martin Church. Across the Loisach River stands the original St. Martin church (aka "Die Alte Kirche," or the Old Church), whose original foundation was laid in the 9th century. Its current building dates to 1280 and showcases Gothic wall paintings from throughout the centuries, including a 7-meter-high (21-foot-high), larger-than-life figure of St. Christopher from 1330 and a Passion of the Christ fresco dating to the 1400s. ⌧ *Pfarrerhausweg 4* ⊕ *https://pv-zugspitze.de/st-martin-garmisch/alte-kirche-st-martin* 🎫 *Free.*

Richard Strauss Institut. On the eastern edge of Garmisch, at the end of Zöppritzstrasse, stands the home of composer Richard Strauss, who lived there until his death in 1949. The home itself is not open to visitors, but this institute across town offers a popular exhibition dedicated to Strauss's life; it becomes the center of activity during the *Richard-Strauss-Tage*, an annual music festival held in mid-June that features concerts and lectures on the town's most famous son. Other concerts are given year-round. ⌧ *Schnitzschulstr. 19* ⊕ *www.richard-strauss-institut. de* 🎫 *€4 for exhibit* ⊘ *Closed weekends.*

St. Martin Church. Beautiful examples of Upper Bavarian houses line Frühlingstrasse. A pedestrian zone begins at Richard-Strauss-Platz and at another end, just off Marienplatz, is this unassuming 18th-century parish church that contains significant stuccowork by the Wessobrunn artist Jospeh Schmutzer and rococo work by Matthäus Günther, restored to its original vibrancy. ⌧ *Marienpl.* ⊕ *pv-zugspitze.de* 🎫 *Free.*

Werdenfels Museum. The region's culture and history are intriguingly presented in this museum, part of which is housed in a building dating back to around 1200, with an addition and expansion completed in 2018 to make way for rotating art and local history exhibitions. Spread over 19 rooms and five floors, the exhibits explore traditional aspects of life in the Werdenfelser region, which was an independent state for more than 700 years, until 1802. ⌧ *Ludwigstr. 47* ☎ *08821/751–710* ⊕ *www.werdenfels-museum.de* 🎫 *€3* ⊘ *Closed Mon.*

Fodor's Choice
★

Zugspitze. The highest mountain (9,718 feet) in Germany is also the number-one attraction in the area. You can't see this world famous peak from Garmisch-Partenkirchen until you've made your way up the mountain—it's hidden from view on the ground and is often mistaken for the nearby Alpsspitze—so it's worth braving the glass-bottom cable car for the view both on the way up and for the Alpine panoramas once you've reached the peak. Opened in late 2017, the record-setting cable car ascends 6,381 feet over a distance of 10,451 feet in around 10 minutes. It's an engineering marvel on its own; combined with the view from one of two restaurants sunny terraces at the summit, the Zugspitze is awe-inspiring. To use the cable car, start in Grainau, 10 km (6 miles) outside town on the road to Austria. A unlimited one-day round-trip ticket costs €45 and is also valid for unlimited rides on the Gletscher Bahn, a gondola for skiers and hikers that covers the skiable "Zugspitzplatt," or flats. You can also combine a cable car ride with a leisurely 75-minute ride on a cog railroad, the Zahnradbahn. There are also a number of other peaks in the area with gondolas for both skiers in winter and hikers in summer, including the Hausberg Seilbahn, which takes you to a kid-friendly ski area. A four-seat cable car likewise will take you to the top of one of the lesser peaks: the 5,840-foot **Wank** for just €21.50. From there, you can tackle both mountains on foot, provided you're properly shod and physically fit. Or stop over at the **Alpspitze,** from where you can hike as well. ⌧ *Olympia Str. 27* ☎ *08821/7970* ⊕ *www.zugspitze.de* 🎫 *Funicular or cable car €45 round-trip (€50 in summer).*

EATING WELL IN THE BAVARIAN ALPS

Traditional Bavarian cuisine is rich and heavy, as it originated as staples for feeding farming families and those who spent their days outdoors doing manual labor. *Semmelknödel* (dumplings of old bread), pork dishes, sauerkraut, bread, and hearty soups helped sustain a person facing the elements. Those traditions live on, even as the menus have lightened up and some restaurants are finally incorporating vegetarian options. There's an abundance of local produce and meats to draw on for sustenance—including *Forelle* (fresh brook trout), *Renke* (pike-perch), venison, and, of course, pork. This substantial fare is often washed down with beer, nourishment in itself. Although local chefs are not immune to eclectic culinary trends, as of late, the trend has been a shift to creating menus based on whatever's locally grown and in season.

One area that remains rich is the dessert menu. Served at nearly every *Alm*, those quaint mountain-top huts where hikers can refresh, is *Kaiserschmarrn*, a panfried sweet dough often served with apple sauce. Or try a large portion of warm strudel (usually served with vanilla pudding) fresh from the oven.

Schnapps customarily ends a meal, and most communities have their own variant extracted from local fruit by virtuoso distillers.

WHERE TO EAT

$ ✕ **Bräustüberl.** Adorned with frescoes, this brewery fills up with large
GERMAN groups and families. The menu includes standard Bavarian pub fare and liters of beer in a more intimate atmosphere than a traditional beer hall, as dining is divided into smaller rooms. **Known for:** Bräustüberlpfanderl (a sampler that includes two types of pork and duck); duck legs with knoedel (dumplings); locally caught trout. $ *Average main:* €13 ✉ *Fürstenstr. 23* ☎ *08821/2312* ⊕ *www.braeustueberl-garmisch.de.*

$ ✕ **Vaun.** Offering healthier approach to regional cuisine, Vaun sources
GERMAN local ingredients for its small, seasonal menu that pays great attention
FAMILY to detail. Choices change monthly but will always include seasonal staples of German cuisine, including grilled asparagus, all served in a casual atmosphere in the heart of Garmisch, near Marienplatz. **Known for:** seasonal specialties including asparagus in spring or sweet potatoes in winter; fresh walleye (in season); homemade pesto and chutney that liven up the meals. $ *Average main:* €12 ✉ *Zugspitze Str. 2* ☎ *8821/730–8187* ⊘ *Closed Sun. No lunch* ⊟ *No credit cards.*

WHERE TO STAY

For information about accommodation packages with ski passes, call the Zugspitze or get in touch with the tourist office in Garmisch (☎ *08821/180–700* ⊕ *www.zugspitze.de*).

$$ ⛺ **Edelweiss Hotel.** Like its namesake, the "nobly white" Alpine flower
B&B/INN of *The Sound of Music* fame, this small downtown hotel (not to be confused with the military-members-only lodge in town) has plenty of

mountain charm. **Pros:** comfortable; homey; some rooms have mountain or river views. **Cons:** small hotel; furnishings appear a bit dated; staff can be brusque. [$] *Rooms from: €139* ✉ *Martinswinkelstr. 15–17* ☎ *08821/2454* 🌐 *www.hoteledelweiss.de* 🛏 *31 rooms* 🍴 *Free Breakfast.*

$$$ RESORT 🏨 **Hotel Waxenstein.** A bit outside of town, in the village of Grainau at the base of the Zugspitze cable car, is the delightful Waxenstein, with its unique take on Bavarian rustic. **Pros:** close to Zugspitze cable car; beautiful mountain views from north-facing rooms; excellent in-house restaurant. **Cons:** only accessible by car; all-inclusive option must be declined for price reduction; quiet, away from city. [$] *Rooms from: €200* ✉ *Höhenrainweg 3* ☎ *08821/9840* 🌐 *www.waxenstein.de* 🛏 *41 rooms* 🍴 *Free Breakfast.*

$$ HOTEL 🏨 **Reindl's Partenkirchner Hof.** Opened just before the 1936 Olympic games, Reindl's was an institution in its heyday, receiving royalty and celebrities in the quieter part of Partenkirchen. **Pros:** rooms renovated with modern local touches; great views; updated pool and wellness area. **Cons:** a few front rooms are on a busy street; underground parking costs extra; public areas reveal the hotel's age. [$] *Rooms from: €130* ✉ *Bahnhofstr. 15* ☎ *08821/943–870* 🌐 *www.reindls.de* ⏲ *Closed Nov.* 🛏 *52 rooms* 🍴 *Free Breakfast.*

$$$ HOTEL Fodor's Choice ★ 🏨 **Staudacherhof Hotel.** The Staudacher family has built a name for itself as a purveyor of Bavarian-style luxury at their sustainably renovated hotel. **Pros:** renovated, comfortable rooms; luxurious spa and pool areas; extensive dining options. **Cons:** some balcony views are not private; in city center; spa area not kid-friendly. [$] *Rooms from: €200* ✉ *Höllentalstr. 48* ☎ *08821/9290* 🌐 *www.staudacherhof.de* 🛏 *41 rooms* 🍴 *Free Breakfast.*

NIGHTLIFE AND PERFORMING ARTS

In season there's a busy après-ski scene. Many hotels have dance floors, and some have basement discos that pound away until the early hours. Bavarian folk dancing and zither music are regular nightlife features.

Gasthof Fraundorfer. Wednesday through Monday, the cozy tavern-restaurant at the Gasthof Fraundorfer hosts traditional music, yodeling, and folk dancing. ✉ *Ludwigstr. 24* ☎ *08821/9270* 🌐 *www.gasthof-fraundorfer.de.*

SPORTS AND THE OUTDOORS

HIKING AND CLIMBING

There are innumerable spectacular walks on 300 km (186 miles) of marked trails through the lower slopes' pinewoods and upland meadows. If you have the time and good walking shoes, try one of the two trails that lead to striking gorges (called *Klammen*). More expert hikers and climbers will find plenty of opportunities to explore, from the Herrgottschrofen and Gelbe Wände for all levels to the Jubiläumsgrat, which will test even the best climbers' limits. Before heading out, it's best to check with the DAV (the German Alpine Association) for passable routes and avalanche conditions; they can also assist with finding free mountain huts for multiple-day hikes and climbs.

Deutscher Alpenverein (*German Alpine Association*). The country's leading climbing and mountaineering organization, based in Munich, has all the details on hiking and on staying in the mountain huts and keeps updates on mountain conditions for climbers and skiers. ⊠ *Von-Kahr-Str. 2–4, Munich* ☎ *089/140–030* ⊕ *www.alpenverein.de.*

Höllentalklamm. A short but demanding hike at the base of the Zugspitze mountain range takes you on rugged paths alongside waterfalls and through grottoes to a magnificent gorge. It's a challenging uphill trek accessible only on foot and only open when there is no snowpack. Strollers, wheelchairs, and bicycles are not allowed. ⊠ *Höllentalstr. 18* ✛ *From Grainau parking, walk 30 mins along Klammweg from Hotel Haus Hammersbach* ☎ *08821/8895* ⊕ *www.hoellentalklamm-info.de* ☜ *From €2* ☼ *May–Oct. (weather permitting).*

Partnachklamm. A less challenging hike than the nearby Höllentalklamm, the Partnachklamm route is a spectacular short hiking trail that is easily accessible by bus or car. A 20-minute walk from the Olympic Ski Stadium will take you through a spectacular, tunneled water gorge ($), past a pretty little mountain lake, and 2,300 feet into the Zugspitze range. ⊠ *Karl-u.-Martin-Neuner-Pl. 1* ⊕ *www.partnachklamm.eu* ☜ *From €4.*

SKIING AND SNOWBOARDING

Garmisch-Partenkirchen was the site of the 1936 Winter Olympics, and remains Germany's premier winter-sports resort. The upper slopes of the Zugspitze and surrounding mountains challenge the best ski buffs and snowboarders, and there are also plenty of runs for intermediate skiers and families. The area is divided into two basic regions. The **Riffelriss** with the **Zugspitzplatt** is Germany's highest skiing area, with snow highly likely, though not guaranteed from December to May. Access is via the **Zugspitzbahn** funicular. Cost for a day pass is €45; a two-day pass is €83. The **Garmisch-Classic** has numerous lifts in the **Alpspitz, Kreuzeck,** and **Hausberg** regions. Day passes cost €43 for skiers and €27 for those on foot. The town has a number of ski schools and tour organizers, and information about all of them is available from the local tourist office. The Deutsche Alpenverein is another good contact for mountain conditions.

Alpine Auskunftstelle. The best local resource for information for all your snow sports needs is the Alpine office at the Garmisch tourist information office. ⊠ *Richard-Strauss-Pl. 2, Garmisch* ☎ *08821/180–700* ⊕ *www.gapa.de.*

Erste Skilanglaufschule Garmisch-Partenkirchen. Cross-country skiers can check on conditions or book a guided tour here. ⊠ *Olympia Skistadion, Osteingang, 1 OG, Karl-u.-Martin-Neuner-Pl. 1* ☎ *08821/1516* ⊕ *www.ski-langlauf-schule.de.*

FAMILY **Ski Schule GAP.** A full-service ski, cross-country, and snowboard rental office stands at the base of the Hausberg gondola; the shop offers daily lessons for all ages (snowboard lessons should be booked in advance). The Hausberg Resort is the shorter of the ski areas, with a kids zone at just around 4,500 feet. Lessons begin daily at 9 am, as soon as groups are sorted according to ability. Book online in advance for a discount. ⊠ *Hausberg 4* ☎ *08821/4931* ⊕ *skischule-gap.de/en.*

ETTAL

16 km (10 miles) north of Garmisch-Partenkirchen, 85 km (53 miles) south of Munich.

The village of Ettal is presided over by the massive bulk of Kloster Ettal, a great monastery and centuries-old distillery.

GETTING HERE AND AROUND

Ettal is easily reached by bus and car from Garmisch and Oberammergau. Consider staying in Oberammergau and renting a bike. The 4-km (2½-mile) ride along the river is clearly marked, relatively easy, and a great way to meet locals.

VISITOR INFORMATION

Contacts Tourist Information Ettal. ⊠ *Ammergauer Str. 8* ☎ *08822/923–634* ⊕ *www.ammergauer-alpen.de/ettal.*

EXPLORING

Fodor's Choice ★ **Kloster Ettal.** This remarkable monastery was founded in 1330 by Holy Roman Emperor Ludwig the Bavarian for a group of knights and a community of Benedictine monks. The largest Benedictine monastery in Germany, it still houses 33 monks; parts are a school. The original 10-sided church was brilliantly redecorated in 1744–53, becoming one of the foremost examples of Bavarian rococo, its chief treasure an enormous dome fresco, painted by Jacob Zeiller circa 1751–52. Today, the Kloster owns most of the surrounding land and directly operates the Hotel Ludwig der Bayer, the Kloster shop, and the Kloster market, as well as a brewery and distillery, all of which support its famous schools. Ettaler liqueurs, made from a centuries-old recipe, are still distilled at the monastery. The monks make seven different liqueurs, some with more than 70 mountain herbs. You can visit the distillery right next to the church and buy bottles of the libation from the gift shop. It's possible to tour the distillery and the brewery. However, English-language tours are available only for large groups. Brewery tours in German are given Friday at 10, and distillery tours are given Monday and Thursday at 4, both from May through October. ⊠ *Kaiser-Ludwig-Pl. 1* ☎ *08822/746–228 distillery, 08822/746–450 brewery* ⊕ *www.abtei.kloster-ettal.de* ⊠ *Free; brewery tour €12, distillery tour €9* ☉ *No tours Nov.–Apr.*

Schaukäserei. Besides its beer and spirits, Ettal has made another local industry into an attraction, namely cheese, yogurt, butter, and other milk derivatives. You can see them in the making at this public cheese-making plant. There is even a little buffet for a cheesy break. Tours are offered daily at 11 as long as there's a minimum five people to take part. ⊠ *Mandlweg 1* ☎ *08822/923–926* ⊕ *www.schaukaeserei-ettal.de* ⊠ *Tour from €2* ☉ *Closed Mon. Nov.–May.*

The dome fresco at Kloster Ettal (Ettal Monastery) was painted by Jacob Zeiller and is an excellent example of Bavarian rococo.

WHERE TO EAT

$ ✕ **Edelweiss.** This friendly café and restaurant next to the monastery
GERMAN is an ideal spot for a light lunch or coffee and homemade cakes.
Known for: spit-roasted pork; a wide selection of fresh cake and
apple strudel; venison with spätzle. $ *Average main: €11* ✉ *Kaiser-
Ludwig-Pl. 3* ☎ *08822/4509* ⊕ *www.edelweiss-ettal.de* ▭ *No credit
cards* ⊗ *Closed Fri.*

WHERE TO STAY

$$ 🏨 **Hotel Ludwig der Bayer.** Backed by mountains, this fine old hotel is run
RESORT by the Benedictine order, but there's little monastic about it, except for
FAMILY the exquisite religious carvings and motifs that adorn the walls. **Pros:**
good value; close to abbey; indoor pool and spa. **Cons:** can fill up
quickly with tour groups; books out during conventions; furnishings are
sparse. $ *Rooms from: €115* ✉ *Kaiser-Ludwig-Pl. 10* ☎ *08822/9150*
⊕ *www.ludwig-der-bayer.de* ⇥ *100 rooms* ❖ *Free Breakfast.*

SCHLOSS LINDERHOF

Fodor's Choice ★ The only one of King Ludwig's three castles to have reached completion
before his death, this gilded hunting lodge lies secluded in the moun-
tains, surrounded by well-manicured gardens. Though less visited than
his other castles, Schloss Linderhof tells a fantastic story about the life
of a king famous for his eccentricities.

EXPLORING

Fodor'sChoice   **Schloss Linderhof.** Built between 1870 and 1879 on the spectacular
★   grounds of his father's hunting lodge, the Linderhof Palace was the
only one of Ludwig II's royal residences to have been completed during the monarch's short life. It was the smallest of this ill-fated king's
castles, but the charming, French-style, rococo confection inspired by
the Petit Trianon at Versailles was his favorite country retreat. From
an architectural standpoint it's a whimsical combination of conflicting
styles: lavish on the outside, somewhat overly decorated on the inside.
The formal gardens contain whimsical touches, including a Moorish
pavilion—bought wholesale from the 1867 Paris Universal Exposition.
The palace is only accessible by guided tour. ⊠ *Linderhof 12, Linderhof* ☎ *08822/92030* ⊕ *www.schlosslinderhof.de* ⊠ *From €9; €5 for
grounds (Apr.–Sept.)* ☉ *Park grounds closed in winter.*

OBERAMMERGAU

*20 km (12 miles) northwest of Garmisch-Partenkirchen, 4 km (2½
miles) northwest of Ettal, 90 km (56 miles) south of Munich.*

Its location alone, in an Alpine valley beneath a sentinel-like peak,
makes this small town a major attraction. Its main streets are lined
with painted houses (such as the 1784 Pilatushaus on Ludwig-Thoma-
Strasse), and in summer the village bursts with color. Many of these
lovely houses are occupied by families whose men are highly skilled in
the art of wood carving, a craft that has flourished here since the early
12th century. Oberammergau is completely overrun by tourists during
the day, but at night you'll feel like you have a charming Bavarian village
all to yourself. The village is best known for its elaborate, decennial
presentation of the Passion of Christ; the next presentation is in 2020.

GETTING HERE AND AROUND
The B-23 links Oberammergau to Garmsich-Partenkirchen (allow a half-
hour for the drive) and to the A-23 to Munich. Frequent bus services
connect to Garmisch, Ettal, the Wieskirche, and Füssen. No long-distance trains serve Oberammergau, but a short ride on the Regional-Bahn
to Murnau will connect you to the long-distance train network.

VISITOR INFORMATION
Contacts Tourist Information Oberammergau. ⊠ *Eugen-Papst-Str. 9a*
☎ *08822/922–740* ⊕ *www.ammergauer-alpen.de/oberammergau.*

EXPLORING

Oberammergau Museum. This museum dedicated to local traditions displays historic examples of the wood craftsman's art and an outstanding collection of Christmas crèches dating from the mid-18th century.
There's a bit about Oberammergau's role in organ-building and the
influence local organs had on the design of U.S. churches. It's gotten a
modern update with multimedia storytelling from the region while maintaining the traditional exhibits of wood-carved animals and puppetry.
⊠ *Dorfstr. 8* ☎ *08822/94136* ⊕ *www.oberammergaumuseum.de* ⊠ *€6,*

DID YOU KNOW?

Schloss Linderhof, built by King Ludwig II, was modeled after Versailles. No visit to Linderhof is complete without a walk through its grounds, which include manicured gardens and tiered French fountains.

includes Pilatushaus and Passionsspielhaus 🕒 *Closed Mon.*

Oberammergau Passionsspielhaus. This immense theater is where the world-famous Passion Play showing the crucifixion is performed every 10 years. In the off-season (any year that's not 2020), the theater does host other concerts and plays. Tours providing a glimpse of the costumes, the sceneries, the stage, and even the auditorium are held in German at 2 pm Wednesday and Sunday. ✉ *Passionswiese, Theaterstr. 16* ☎ *08822/945–8833* 🌐 *www.passionstheater.de* 🎟 *€6, includes Oberammergau Museum and Pilatushaus* 🕒 *Closed Mon.*

LÜFTLMALEREI

The *Lüftlmalerei* style of fresco painting is unique to Bavaria and the Tyrol, where the opulently painted facades were used as a display of wealth. Commonly known by the French term, *trompe l'oeil,* the detailed frescoes give the illusion of three dimensions. They are painted directly onto fresh plaster, which preserves the painting for centuries. The term *Lüftlmalerei* originated in Oberammergau after the famous fresco artist Franz Seraph Zwinck painted a fresco on his house, the Zum Lüftl. Zwinck became the Lüftlmaler, or the painter of the Lüftl.

Pilatushaus. Wood carving is a centuries-old local tradition that carries on to this day. Here you can have a look at the local craftsmen in their workshop, alongside working potters and painters. Completed in 1775, the building itself is considered among the most beautiful in town due to the frescoes by Franz Seraph Zwinck, one of the greatest Lüftlmalerei painters. The house is actually named for the fresco over the front door depicting Christ before Pilate. ✉ *Ludwig-Thoma-Str. 10* ☎ *08822/949–511 tourist office* 🌐 *www.oberammergaumuseum.de* 🎟 *€6, includes Oberammergau Museum and Passionsspielhaus.*

St. Peter and St. Paul Church. Built in 1736, this is regarded as the finest work of rococo architect Josef Schmutzer, whose son, Franz Xaver Schmutzer, did a lot of the stuccowork. Striking frescoes by Matthäus Günther and Franz Seraph Zwinck depict Mary as the answerer of prayers as well as a scene from the crucifixion. The latter is said to date back to the 1633 promise by the elders of Oberammergau to hold the passion play every decade if the town were to be saved from the plague. ✉ *Pfarrpl. 1* 🌐 *www.ammergauer-alpen.de.*

WHERE TO EAT

$$ GERMAN 🍴 **Ammergauer Maxbrau.** A lively brewery located inside the Hotel Maximilian, this is an upscale meeting place for locally sourced Bavarian specialties; brewery tours can be booked as well. **Known for:** pork knuckle; beer crafted in-house; Bavarian-style platters full of pork specialties. [$] *Average main: €15* ✉ *Hotel Maximilian, Ettaler Str. 5* ☎ *08822/948–740* 🌐 *www.maximilian-oberammergau.de* 🕒 *No lunch weekdays.*

$ GERMAN 🍴 **Gasthaus zum Stern.** This is a traditional place (dating from the 16th century), with coffered ceilings, thick walls, smiling waitresses in

Dirndls, and an old *Kachelofen* (enclosed, tiled, wood-burning stove) that heats the dining room beyond endurance on cold winter days. The food is hearty, traditional Bavarian. $ *Average main: €13* ✉ *Dorfstr. 33* ☎ *08822/867* ⊕ *www.gasthaus-stern-oberammergau.de* ⊗ *Closed Wed.*

$
GERMAN ✕ **Mundart.** One of the best restaurants in town is known for its Bavarian cuisine based on regionally sourced seasonal ingredients. **Known for:** vegetarian dumplings (Maultasche); innovative takes on Bavarian "tapas"; local trout. $ *Average main: €14* ✉ *Bahnhofstr. 12* ☎ *08822/949–7565* ⊕ *www.restaurant-mundart.de* ⊗ *Closed Mon. and Tues.* ▭ *No credit cards.*

WHERE TO STAY

$$
B&B/INN **Gasthof zur Rose.** Everything is pretty rustic in this spacious remodeled barn, but the welcome and hospitality are genuine and gracious, even by Bavarian standards. **Pros:** quiet; affordable; right off the city center. **Cons:** rustic and worn; few amenities; basic rooms. $ *Rooms from: €100* ✉ *Dedlerstr. 9* ☎ *08822/4706* ⊕ *www.rose-oberammergau. de* ▭ *No credit cards* ⤴ *19 rooms* ⦿⃒ *Free Breakfast.*

$$$
HOTEL **Hotel Maximilian.** Modernized and luxurious, this spa retreat has won awards for both its hospitality and its gourmet restaurant, Ammergauer Maxbräu. **Pros:** nice views from front rooms; great in-house restaurant; warm, modern Bavarian aesthetic. **Cons:** pricey for the area; books out quickly; restaurant can get full. $ *Rooms from: €200* ✉ *Ettalerstr. 5* ☎ *08822/948–740* ⊕ *www.maximilian-oberammergau.de* ⤴ *19 rooms* ⦿⃒ *Free Breakfast.*

$$
HOTEL
FAMILY **Hotel Turmwirt.** Rich wood paneling reaches from floor to ceiling in this transformed 18th-century inn, set in the shadow of Oberammergau's mountain, the Kofel. **Pros:** great for families; good views of nearby mountains; central location. **Cons:** service can be brusque; nearby church bells ring frequently; small. $ *Rooms from: €101* ✉ *Ettalerstr. 2* ☎ *08822/92600* ⊕ *www.turmwirt.de* ⊗ *Closed 1 wk in early Dec.* ⤴ *23 rooms* ⦿⃒ *Free Breakfast.*

PERFORMING ARTS

Oberammergau Passionsspielhaus. Though the Passion Play theater was traditionally not used for anything other than the Passion Play (next performance: 2020), Oberammergauers have begun using it for opera or other theatrical events during the 10-year pause between the religious performances. Ticket prices for these events range between €19 and €50. ✉ *Theaterstr. 16* ☎ *008822/945–8888* ⊕ *www.passionstheater.de.*

Passion Play. Oberammergau is best known for its Passion Play, first presented in 1634 as an offering of thanks after the Black Death stopped just short of the village. In faithful accordance with a solemn vow, it will next be performed in the year 2020, as it has every 10 years since 1680. Its 16 acts, which take 5½ hours, depict the final days of Christ, from the Last Supper through the Crucifixion and Resurrection. It's presented daily on a partly open-air stage against a mountain backdrop from late May to late September. The entire village is swept up in the production, with some 1,500 residents directly involved in its preparation and presentation. Men grow beards in the hope of capturing a key role; young women have been known to put off their weddings—the role of Mary went only to unmarried girls until 1990, when, amid much local controversy, a 31-year-old mother of two was given the part. ✉ *Passionstheater, Theaterstr. 16* ⊕ *www.passionstheater.de.*

SPORTS AND THE OUTDOORS

BICYCLING

It's easy to bike to Schloss Linderhof (14 km [9 miles]) and to Ettal (4 km [2½ miles]) on the scenic paths along the river, where there are several good places to go swimming and have a picnic. The trail to Ettal branches off in the direction of Linderhof (marked as Graswang) where it becomes part of an old forestry road. Take the branch of the Ettal path that goes via the Ettaler-Mühle (Ettal Mill); it's quieter, the river is filled with trout, and the people you meet along the way will greet you with a friendly *Grüss Gott!* The path opens up at a restaurant with fantastic views of the Kloster.

Sport-Zentrale Papistock. You can rent bikes or e-bikes here. Located across the street from the train station, directly at the trailhead to Ettal and Linderhof, they even take credit cards. ✉ *Bahnhofstr. 6a* ☏ *08822/4178* ⊕ *www.sportzentrale-papistock.de* 🚲 *Bicycles from €12 per day, e-bikes from €24 per day* ⊙ *Closed Sun.*

MITTENWALD

20 km (12 miles) southeast of Garmisch-Partenkirchen, 105 km (65 miles) south of Munich.

Many regard Mittenwald as the most beautiful town in the Bavarian Alps. It has somehow avoided the architectural sins found in other Alpine villages by maintaining a balance between conservation and the needs of tourism. Its medieval prosperity is reflected on its main street, **Obermarkt,** which has splendid houses with ornately carved gables and brilliantly painted facades. Goethe called it "a picture book come alive," and it still is. The town has even re-created the stream that once flowed through the market square. In the Middle Ages, Mittenwald was the staging point for goods shipped from the wealthy city-state of Venice by way of the Brenner Pass and Innsbruck. From Mittenwald, goods were transferred to rafts, which carried them down the Isar River to Munich. By the mid-17th century the international trade routes shifted to a different pass, and the fortunes of Mittenwald evaporated.

In 1684, Matthias Klotz, a farmer's son turned master violin maker, returned from a 20-year stay in Cremona, Italy. There, along with Antonio Stradivari, he studied under Nicolo Amati, who developed the modern violin. Klotz taught the art of violin-making to his brothers and friends and before long, half the men in the village were crafting the instruments using wood from neighboring forests. Mittenwald became known as the Village of a Thousand Violins and the locally crafted instruments are still treasured around the world. In the right weather (sunny, dry) you may even catch the odd sight of laundry lines hung out with new violins, where they gain their naturally dark hue. The violin has made Mittenwald a small cultural oasis in the middle of the Alps. Not only is there an annual violin- (and viola-, cello-, and bow-) building contest each year in June, with concerts and lectures, but also an organ festival in the church of St. Peter and St. Paul held from the end of July to the end of September. The town also has a violin-making school.

GETTING HERE AND AROUND

The B-11 connects Mittenwald with Garmisch. Mittenwald is the last stop on the Munich–Garmisch train line.

VISITOR INFORMATION

Contacts Tourist Information Mittenwald. ✉ *Dammkarstr. 3* ☎ *08823/33981* 🌐 *www.alpenwelt-karwendel.de/en/mittenwald.*

EXPLORING

The Geigenbaumuseum. The violin-building and local museum describes in fascinating detail the history of violin making in Mittenwald. Ask the museum curator to direct you to the nearest of several violin makers—they'll be happy to demonstrate the skills handed down to them. ✉ *Ballenhausg. 3* ☎ *08823/2511* 🌐 *www.geigenbaumuseum-mittenwald.de* 🎫 *€6* 🕐 *Closed Mon. and Nov. 6–Dec. 13.*

St. Peter and St. Paul Church. On the back of the altar in this 18th-century church (as in Oberammergau, built by Josef Schmutzer and decorated by Matthäus Günther) you'll find Matthias Klotz's name, carved there by the violin maker himself. Note that on some of the ceiling frescoes, the angels are playing violins, violas da gamba, and lutes. In front of the church, Klotz is memorialized as an artist at work in vivid bronze sculpted by Ferdinand von Miller (1813–79), creator of the mighty Bavaria Monument in Munich. The church, with its elaborate and joyful stuccowork coiling and curling its way around the interior, is one of the most important rococo structures in Bavaria. The Gothic choir loft was added in the 18th century. The bold frescoes on its exterior are characteristic of Lüftlmalerei, where images, usually religious motifs, were painted on the wet stucco exteriors of houses and churches. On nearby streets you can see other fine examples on the facades of three famous houses: the Goethehaus, the Pilgerhaus, and the Pichlerhaus. Among the artists working here was the great Franz Seraph Zwinck. ✉ *Ballenhausg.* 🌐 *www.st-peter-und-paul-mittenwald.de.*

WHERE TO EAT

$ GERMAN 🍴 **Alpenrose.** Once part of a monastery and later given one of the town's most beautiful painted baroque facades, the Alpenrose features traditional Bavarian fare and is famous for featuring venison dishes the entire month of October. A sidewalk terrace is open on sunny days; a zither player strums away most evenings in the Josefi wine cellar. **Known for:** Knödel (dumplings); seasonal variations on pork; schnitzel. [$] *Average main: €14* ✉ *Obermarkt 1* ☎ *08823/92700* 🌐 *www.hotel-alpenrose-mittenwald.de.*

$ ✕**Gasthof Stern.** This white house with brilliant blue shutters in the middle of Mittenwald has a beer garden and small playground perfect for families. Locals love this dining room and its meat-heavy Bavarian cuisine. **Known for:** Bauernschmaus (a plate of sausage with sauerkraut and homemade liver dumplings); jaeger schnitzel; goulasch soup. ⓢ *Average main: €12* ✉ *Fritz-Plössl-Pl. 2* ☎ *08823/8358* ⊕ *www.stern-mittenwald.de* ◷ *Closed Mon.* ⊟ *No credit cards.*

GERMAN
FAMILY

WHERE TO STAY

$ ⛉ **Gasthof Stern.** A white house with brilliant blue shutters right in the middle of Mittenwald, the interiors are standard Bavarian style with loads of light wood and soft featherbeds. **Pros:** friendly service; clean, basic hotel with a great beer garden; central location. **Cons:** some rooms quite small; upper rooms warm in summer; events might detract from quiet. ⓢ *Rooms from: €70* ✉ *Fritz-Plössl-Pl. 2* ☎ *08823/8358* ⊕ *www.stern-mittenwald.de* ↷ *5 rooms* ⦿ *Breakfast.*

B&B/INN

$$$ ⛉ **Kranzbach.** This "English Castle," on 13 hectares (32 acres) surrounded by the Karwendel mountains, was commissioned in 1913 by an English aristocrat, Mary Portman. **Pros:** spa amenities; beautiful, quiet surroundings; distinguished historical setting. **Cons:** rooms in the garden wing are more contemporary and lose the old-fashioned touch; no children under 10 allowed; away from major sights. ⓢ *Rooms from: €197* ✉ *Kranzbach 1* ☎ *8823/928–000* ⊕ *www.daskranzbach.de* ↷ *129 rooms* ⦿ *Free Breakfast.*

HOTEL

$$ ⛉ **Post Hotel.** The hotel retains much of its historic charm—stagecoaches carrying travelers and mail across the Alps stopped here as far back as the 17th century—though the elegant rooms come in various styles, from modern to art nouveau to Bavarian rustic. **Pros:** art nouveau rooms in the back; great location near train station; nice pool area. **Cons:** no elevator; street noise in the evening; some staff have poor English. ⓢ *Rooms from: €117* ✉ *Obermarkt 9* ☎ *08823/938–2333* ⊕ *www.posthotel-mittenwald.de* ↷ *81 rooms* ⦿ *Free Breakfast.*

HOTEL

$$$$ ⛉ **Schloss Elmau.** This luxurious castle hotel became famous when it hosted the G7 summit in 2015, and its varied history, artistic heritage, and superior spa services have kept it popular despite high prices. **Pros:** gorgeous location; superior services, including above-standard spa; quiet atmosphere. **Cons:** expensive; rural location, removed from major sights; multiple-night stay required. ⓢ *Rooms from: €499* ✉ *Elmau 2* ☎ *08823/180* ↷ *123 rooms* ⦿ *All-inclusive.*

ALL-INCLUSIVE

SPORTS AND THE OUTDOORS

Mittenwald lies literally in the shadow of the mighty **Karwendel** Alpine range, which rises to a height of nearly 8,000 feet. There are a number of small lakes in the hills surrounding Mittenwald. You can either walk to the closer ones or rent bikes and venture farther afield. The information center across the street from the train station has maps, and they can help you select a route.

The **Dammkar** run is nearly 8 km (5 miles) long and offers some of the best skiing, telemarking, and snowboarding in the German Alps.

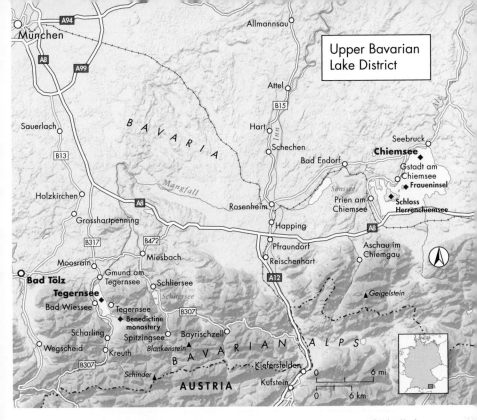

Erste Skischule Mittenwald. Skiers and snowboarders can find all they need, including equipment and instruction, at the Erste Skischule Mittenwald. ⊠ *Bahnhofspl. 14* ☎ *08823/3582.*

Karwendelbahn cable car. Hikers and skiers are carried to an altitude of 7,180 feet for the beginning of numerous trails down, or farther up into the Karwendel range. ⊠ *Alpenkorpsstr. 1* ☎ *08823/937–6760* ⊕ *www.karwendelbahn.de* 🎫 *From €20.*

SHOPPING

It's not the kind of gift every visitor wants to take home, but if you'd like a violin, a cello, or even a double bass, the Alpine resort of Mittenwald can oblige. There are more than 30 craftspeople whose work is coveted by musicians throughout the world.

Anton Maller. Anton Maller has been making violins and other stringed instruments for more than 25 years. ⊠ *Obermarkt 2* ☎ *08823/5865* ⊕ *www.violin-maller.de.*

BAD TÖLZ

14 km (8 miles) north of Sylvenstein Lake, 48 km (30 miles) south of Munich.

Bad Tölz's new town, dating from the mid-19th century, sprang up with the discovery of iodine-laden springs, which allowed the locals to call their town *Bad* (bath or spa) Tölz. You can take the waters, either by drinking a cupful from the local springs or going all the way with a full course of health treatments at a specially equipped hotel. **■ TIP→ If you can, visit on a Friday morning, when a farmers' market stretches along the main street to the Isar River and on the Jungmayr-Fritzplatz.**

This town clings to its ancient customs more tightly than any other Bavarian community. It is not uncommon to see people wearing traditional clothing as their daily dress. If you're in Bad Tölz on November 6, you'll witness one of the most colorful traditions of the Bavarian Alpine area: the Leonhardiritt equestrian procession, which marks the anniversary of the death in 559 of St. Leonhard of Noblac, the patron saint of animals, specifically horses. The procession ends north of town at an 18th-century chapel on the Kalvarienberg, above the Isar River.

GETTING HERE AND AROUND

Bad Tölz is on the B-472, which connects to the A-8 to Munich, and there are hourly trains from Munich. Once you're in Bad Tölz, it is easily walkable and has frequent city-bus services.

VISITOR INFORMATION

Contacts Bad Tölz Tourist Information. ✉ *Max-Höfler-Pl. 1* ☎ *08041/78670* 🌐 *www.bad-toelz.de.*

EXPLORING

The Stadtmuseum. Housed in the Altes Rathaus (Old Town Hall), the museum has a permanent exhibition containing many fine examples of *Bauernmöbel* (farmhouse furniture), as well as fascinating information on the history of the town and its environs as well as their patron saint, Leonhard. ✉ *Marktstr. 48* ☎ *08041/793–5156* 🌐 *www.bad-toelz.de* 🎫 *€2* 🕓 *Closed Mon.*

WHERE TO EAT

$ GERMAN FAMILY

🍴 **Reutbergstuberl.** A small restaurant set up for communal dining at large wooden tables, the Reutbergstuberl offers authentic Bavarian cuisine for lunch and dinner at fair prices. Located near the Kur park, it has a quiet,comfortable atmosphere both inside and on the fair-weather terrace. **Known for:** turkey medallions in cream sauce; Weisswurst (Bavarian white sausages); Schweinebraten (pork filets with sauerkraut). [$] *Average main: €10* ✉ *Schuetzenstr. 5* ☎ *08041/70839* 🌐 *www.reutbergstueberl.de* 🕓 *Closed Thurs.* 💳 *No credit cards.*

WHERE TO STAY

$$ ⊞ **Hotel Kolbergarten.** Near the Old Town and surrounded by a quiet
HOTEL garden with old trees, this hotel offers comfortable rooms, each care-
FAMILY fully done in a particular style, such as baroque or Biedermeier. **Pros:**
large, clean rooms; staff are great with children; nice views of the Isar.
Cons: often fully booked; paid public parking nearby; small. $ *Rooms
from: €108* ✉ *Fröhlichg. 5* ☎ *08041/78920* ⊕ *www.hotel-kolbergarten.
de* ⤸ *14 rooms* ⚬| *Free Breakfast.*

NIGHTLIFE AND PERFORMING ARTS

Tölzer Knabenchor Boys' Choir (*Knabenchor*). Bad Tölz is world renowned
for its outstanding boys' choir. When not in Munich or out on tour,
the choir gives regular concerts in the Kurhaus. ✉ *Kurhaus Bad Tölz,
Ludwigstr. 25* ⊕ *www.toelzerknabenchor.de.*

SPORTS AND THE OUTDOORS

FAMILY **Blomberg.** Bad Tölz's local mountain, the Blomberg, 3 km (2 miles) west
of town, has moderately difficult ski runs and can also be tackled on
a toboggan in winter and on a luge in summer. The winter run of 5
km (3 miles) is the longest in Bavaria. The concrete summer luge run
snakes 3,938 feet down the mountain and is great fun. ✉ *Am Blomberg
2* ☎ *08041/3726* ⊕ *www.blombergbahn.de* ▨ *€11 round-trip (sleds
not included).*

TEGERNSEE

16 km (10 miles) east of Bad Tölz, 50 km (31 miles) south of Munich.

The beautiful shores of the Tegernsee are among the most expensive
property in all of Germany. The interest in the region shown by King
Maximilian I of Bavaria at the beginning of the 19th century attracted
VIPs and artists, which led to a boom that has never really faded.
Most accommodations and restaurants, however, still have reason-
able prices, and there are plenty of activities for everyone. Tegernsee's
wooded shores, rising gently to scalable mountain peaks of no more
than 6,300 feet, invite hikers, walkers, and picnicking families. The
lake itself draws swimmers and sailors. In fall, the russet-clad trees
provide a colorful contrast to the snowcapped mountains. Beer lovers
are drawn to Tegernsee by one of the best breweries in Europe. There
are three main towns on the lake: Tegernsee, Rottach-Egern, and Bad
Wiessee. The town of Gmund, at the lake's northern end, also has a
number of attractions and is easily accessible by train or the public
boats on the lake.

GETTING HERE AND AROUND

The best way to reach all three towns is to take the BOB train from
Munich to Tegernsee (hourly) and then take a boat ride on one of
the eight boats that circle the lake year-round. The boats dock near
the Tegernsee train station and make frequent stops, including the

Benedictine monastery in Tegernsee, Rottach-Egern, Gmund, and Bad Wiessee. The monastery is a pleasant half-mile walk from the train station. Buses connect Tegernsee to Bad Tölz.

VISITOR INFORMATION

Contacts Rottach-Egern/Tegernsee Tourist Information. ✉ *Hauptstr. 2* ☎ *08022/927–380* 🌐 *www.tegernsee.com.*

EXPLORING

Benedictine monastery. On the eastern shore of the lake, the laid-back town of Tegernsee is home to a large Benedictine monastery. Founded in the 8th century, this was one of the most productive cultural centers in southern Germany; one of the *Minnesänger* (wandering lyrical poets), Walther von der Vogelweide (1170–1230), was a welcome guest. Not so welcome were Magyar invaders, who laid waste to the monastery in the 10th century. During the Middle Ages the monastery made a lively business producing stained-glass windows, thanks to a nearby quartz quarry, and in the 16th century it became a major center of printing. The late-Gothic **church** was refurbished in Italian baroque style in the 18th century and was where heirs to the Wittelsbach dynasty were married. The frescoes inside are by Hans Georg Asam, whose work also graces the Benediktbeuren monastery in Bavaria. Secularization sealed the monastery's fate at the beginning of the 19th century: almost half the buildings were torn down. Maximilian I bought the surviving ones and had Leo von Klenze redo them for use as a summer retreat, which is still used by members of the Wittelsbach family and therefore closed to the public.

Today there is a high school on the property, and students write their exams beneath inspiring baroque frescoes. The church and the **Herzogliches Bräustüberl,** a brewery and beer hall, are the only parts of the monastery open to the public. Try a *Mass* (a liter-size mug) of their legendary Tergernseer Helles or Spezial beer. ✉ *Schlosspl.*

Grosses Paraplui Hiking Path. Maximilian showed off this corner of his kingdom to Czar Alexander I of Russia and Emperor Franz I of Austria during their journey to the Congress of Verona in October 1821. You can follow their steps on a one hour hike along a well-marked 2½-km (1½-mile) path, starting just opposite Schlossplatz in Tegernsee, through the woods to the Grosses Paraplui, one of the loveliest lookout points in Bavaria. A plaque marks the spot where they admired the open expanse of the Tegernsee and the mountains beyond. ✉ *Asamweg 2.*

WHERE TO EAT

$$ EUROPEAN

🍴 **Freihaus Brenner.** Begun by proprietor Josef Brenner, who brought a taste of nouvelle cuisine to Tegernsee, the attractive restaurant commanding fine views from high above Bad Wiessee got new owners in 2018, but the menu has maintained the same assortment of seasonal specialties. **Known for:** fresh trout; steak and potatoes; Schweinebraten mit Knödel (roast pork with potato dumplings). [$] *Average main: €15* ✉ *Freihaus 4, Bad Wiessee* ☎ *08022/86560* 🌐 *www.freihaus-brenner.de* ⏲ *Closed Tues.*

$$$
GERMAN
FAMILY

✗**Gut Kaltenbrunn.** A series of farm buildings dating back to the 19th century on the lake's northern shore were converted into a self-sustaining restaurant with a focus on regional delicacies. A large terrace and walls of windows provide phenomenal views of the lake and a kid-friendly beer garden keeps young visitors happy until dusk. **Known for:** Tegernsee trout; steak from their own cattle; extensive dessert options. $ *Average main: €22* ⊠ *Kaltenbrunn 1, Gmund* ☎ *08022/187–0700.*

$
GERMAN

✗**Herzogliches Bräustüberl.** Once part of Tegernsee's Benedictine monastery, then a royal retreat, the Bräustüberl is now an immensely popular beer hall and brewery with tasty Bavarian snacks for under €10. In summer, quaff your beer beneath the huge chestnut trees and admire the delightful view of the lake and mountains. **Known for:** Bavarian pub fare; pork roast with fried potatoes; spare ribs. $ *Average main: €10* ⊠ *Schlosspl. 1* ☎ *08022/4141* ⊕ *www.braustuberl.de* ▭ *No credit cards.*

WHERE TO STAY

$$$$
RESORT

🛏**Althoff Seehotel Überfahrt.** Directly on the lakeshore, this trendy spa hotel has a Michelin-recognized chef helming one of three restaurants, and draws scenesters from around the world for "wellness" weekends. **Pros:** luxurious amenities; modern, updated rooms; relaxing spa. **Cons:** often full; fellow guests can be demanding; expensive. $ *Rooms from: €320* ⊠ *Überfahrtstr. 10, Rottach-Egern* ☎ *08022/6690* ⊕ *www.seehotel-ueberfahrt.com/de* ↩ *175 rooms* ⦿| *Free Breakfast.*

$$$$
HOTEL
Fodor'sChoice
★

🛏**Bachmair Weissach.** An upgrade in 2017 added an adults-only Japanese-style spa, Mizu Onsen (which can also be used by nonguests for a price), to this full-service luxurious resort. **Pros:** spacious rooms with balconies; friendly staff; very family-friendly. **Cons:** no lake views; at a busy intersection; can be booked out for business meetings. $ *Rooms from: €320* ⊠ *Wiesseerstr. 1, Rottach-Egern* ☎ *08022/2780* ⊕ *www.bachmair-weissach.com* ↩ *146 rooms* ⦿| *Free Breakfast.*

$$$$
HOTEL

🛏**Das Tegernsee Hotel & Spa.** The elegant, turreted hotel and its two spacious annexes sit high above the Tegernsee, backed by the wooded slopes of Neureuth Mountain. **Pros:** historical elegance accents updated rooms; excellent spa amenities; great views. **Cons:** a little away from the hub of the town; can get full if events are held; rooms with a view cost extra. $ *Rooms from: €345* ⊠ *Neureuthstr. 23* ☎ *08022/1820* ⊕ *www.dastegernsee.de* ↩ *73 rooms* ⦿| *Free Breakfast.*

NIGHTLIFE AND PERFORMING ARTS

Every resort town has its **spa orchestra**—in summer they play daily in the music-box-style bandstands that dot the lakeside promenades. A strong Tegernsee tradition is the summer-long program of **festivals,** some set deep in the forest. Tegernsee's lake festival in August, when sailing clubs deck their boats with garlands and lanterns, is unforgettable.

Casino (*Spielbank Bad Wiessee*). Bad Wiessee's casino is near the entrance of town coming from Gmund. The main playing rooms (daily from 3 pm) are not much to look at, but the panoramic views of the lake are worth a visit. ⊠ *Winner 1, Bad Wiessee* ☎ *08022/98350* ⊕ *www.spielbanken-bayern.de.*

SPORTS AND THE OUTDOORS

HIKING

Well-marked and well-groomed hiking trails lead from the glorious countryside, along rivers and lakes, through woods, and high into the Bavarian Alps. If you just want an afternoon stroll, head for the lower slopes. If you're a serious hiker, make for the mountain trails of the Zugspitze, in Garmisch-Partenkirchen; the heights above Oberammergau, Berchtesgaden, or Bad Reichenhall; or the lovely Walchensee. Well-marked trails near the Schliersee or Tegernsee (lakes) lead steadily uphill and to mountaintop inns. A special treat is a hike to the Tatzelwurm Gorge near Bayrischzell.

Wallberg. For the best vista in the area, climb the Wallberg, the 5,700-foot mountain at the south end of the Tegernsee. It's a hard four-hour hike or a short 15-minute cable-car ride up (€20 one-way, €11 round-trip). At the summit are a restaurant and sun terrace and several trailheads; in winter the nearby skiing is excellent. ⊠ *Wallbergstr. 28, Rottach-Egern* ⊕ *www.wallbergbahn.de.*

GOLF

Tegernseer Golfclub e.V. Besides swimming, hiking, and skiing, the Tegernsee area has become a fine place for golfing. The Tegernseer Golfclub e.V. has an 18-hole course in the valley of Bad Wiessee overlooking the lake and with a view to the mountains. With three tee possibilities, the course is surrounded by old forests and has a number of hazards to challenge even the most advanced golfer. ⊠ *Rohbognerhof, Bad Wiessee* ☎ 08022/271–130 ⊕ *www.tegernseer-golf-club.de* ✆*€45 weekdays, €55 weekends for 9 holes; €80 weekdays, €100 weekends for 18 holes* ⏱. *18 holes, 5500 yards, par 70.*

CHIEMSEE

80 km (50 miles) southeast of Munich, 120 km (75 miles) northeast of Garmisch-Partenkirchen.

Chiemsee is north of the Deutsche Alpenstrasse, but it demands a stop on your south of Munich to Berchtesgaden. The largest Bavarian lake, its main attraction is King Ludwig II's unfinished palace on one of the idyllic islands. The town of **Prien** is the lake's principal resort and where boats for the castle tour depart but other small lakeside villages are more worth your time if you stay.

GETTING HERE AND AROUND

Prien is the best jumping-off point if you'll be arriving by train or are only in town to see the Herrenchiemsee Castle. Frequent regional trains connecting Prien with Munich and Salzburg are met by a narrow-gauge steam train for the short trip to Prien-Stock, the boat dock. The only way to reach the Herreninsel (home to the castle) and the Fraueninsel (where the nunnery is located) is by boat.

VISITOR INFORMATION

Contacts **Chiemsee Chiemgau.** ⊠ *Haslacher Str. 30, Traunstein* ☎ *0861/909–5900* ⊕ *www.chiemsee-chiemgau.info.* **Chiemsee Infocenter.** ⊠ *Felden 10, Bernau am Chiemsee* ☎ *08051/965–550* ⊕ *www.chiemsee-alpenland.de.*

EXPLORING

Fraueninsel. Boats going between Stock and Herrenchiemsee Island also stop at this small retreat known as Ladies' Island. The **Benedictine convent** there, founded 1,200 years ago, now serves as a school. One of its earliest abbesses, Irmengard, daughter of King Ludwig der Deutsche, died here in the 9th century. Her grave in the convent chapel was discovered in 1961, the same year that early frescoes there were brought to light. The chapel is open daily from dawn to dusk. Otherwise, the island has just a few private houses, a couple of shops, and a guesthouse where visitors wishing to take part in the nuns' quiet lives can overnight. The Benedictine Sisters make delicious fruit liqueurs and marzipan. ✉ *Fraueninsel* ⊕ *www.frauenwoerth.de.*

Fodor's Choice
★
Schloss Herrenchiemsee. Despite its distance from Munich, the beautiful Chiemsee drew Bavarian royalty to its shores for its dreamlike, melancholy air. It was on one of the lake's three islands that King Ludwig built Schloss Herrenchiemsee, his third and last castle, which was modeled after Louis XIV's Versailles. As with most of Ludwig's projects, the building was never completed, and Ludwig spent only nine days there. Nonetheless, what remains is impressive—and ostentatious. Ferries leave from Stock, Prien's harbor. You can take an 1887 steam train from Prien to Stock to pick up the ferry. A horse-drawn carriage ($) takes you from the boat dock to the palace itself. Most spectacular is the Hall of Mirrors. Also of interest are the ornate bedrooms, the "self-rising" table, the elaborately painted bathroom, and the formal gardens. The south wing houses a museum. Also on the island is the **Alten Schloss,** where Germany's postwar constitution was drawn up in 1948; it is now a museum. English-language tours are timed to coincide with each ferry's arrival. ✉ *Herrenchiemsee* ☎ *08051/68870* ⊕ *www.herren-chiemsee.de* 🎫 *€11, includes Museum im Alten Schloss; €3 horse carriage from ferry dock.*

WHERE TO EAT

$
GERMAN
✕ **Schlosswirtschaft Herrenchiemsee.** Near the boat dock on the Herreninsel, home to King Ludwig II's famous palace, is this century-old-hotel-turned-beer garden and light restaurant with gorgeous views over the lake. **Known for:** cold sausage salad; Chiemsee whitefish; Käsespätzle (cheese dumplings). $ *Average main: €10* ✉ *Herrenchiemsee Island, Schlosshotel 5, Prien am Chiemsee* ☎ *08051/962–7670* ⊕ *schloss-wirtschaft-herrenchiemsee.de* ⊗ *Closed Jan. and when boats are not running* ▭ *No credit cards.*

WHERE TO STAY

$$$$
B&B/INN
FAMILY
Fodor's Choice
★
🏨 **Gut Ising.** In Ising, in the hills above the north shore of Chiemsee, this horse farm and hotel has become one of the area's most venerated addresses. **Pros:** family-friendly (with childcare during school holidays); superior spa services; all amenities on-site. **Cons:** a working horse farm, so dogs abound; not all rooms have been updated; not barrier-free. $ *Rooms from: €239* ✉ *Kirchberg 3* ☎ *08667/790* ⊕ *www.gut-ising.de* 🛏 *105 rooms* ⊝ *All-inclusive.*

Schloss Herrenchiemsee, King Ludwig II's last building project, lies in the middle of Lake Chiemsee on the Herreninsel.

$$ **Kloster Seeon.** A renovated abbey directly on Lake Seeon—just a
B&B/INN quick drive to the boat dock on Seebruck on Chiemsee or 20 minutes
Fodor's Choice to the boat docks at Prien—provides a unique, quiet atmosphere that
★ is also kid-friendly. **Pros:** modernized monk's rooms provide unique
atmosphere; private pier for swimming; gorgeous lake views. **Cons:** no
other amenities in the area; few touches of monastic life remain; very
quiet. $ *Rooms from: €105* ⊠ *Klosterweg 1, Seeon* ☎ *08624/897–429*
⊕ *www.kloster-seeon.de* ☞ *89 rooms* ⦿ *Free Breakfast.*

$$$ **Residenz Heinz Winkler.** Germany's youngest three-star Michelin chef
HOTEL started his own restaurant in 1989 and shortly after added this hotel,
which created a gourmet dining experience that is a destination in itself.
Pros: unparalleled gourmet meals; great service and attention to detail;
views of the mountains from back rooms. **Cons:** not on the lake; a
20-minute drive from the boat docks on Chiemsee; dated aesthetics.
$ *Rooms from: €224* ⊠ *Kirchpl. 1, Aschau* ☎ *08052/17990* ⊕ *www.
residenz-heinz-winkler.de* ☞ *32 rooms* ⦿ *Free Breakfast.*

SPORTS AND THE OUTDOORS

GOLF

Chiemsee Golf-Club Prien e.V. The gentle hills of the region are ideal for
golf and this parkland course makes good use of the undulating terrain,
along with well-placed water hazards, to provide a moderate-to-difficult
challenge. Fairways and greens have views of the distant mountains.
⊠ *Bauernberg 5, Prien am Chiemsee* ☎ *08051/62215* ⊕ *www.cgc-prien.
de/* ⊠ *€69 weekdays, €75 weekends* 🏌 *18 holes, 6300 yards, par 72.*

MULTISPORT OUTFITTERS

SportLukas. Equipment can be provided for any kind of sport imaginable, from skiing to kayaking, climbing to rafting, and it organizes tours. ⌧ *Hauptstr. 3, Schleching* ☎ *08649/243* ⊕ *www.sportlukas.de.*

Surfschule Chiemsee. For those wanting to learn windsurfing or to extend their skills, the Surfschule Chiemsee provides lessons for adults and kids and offers a package deal. You can also rent bikes or kayaks or take a lesson in stand-up paddleboarding. ⌧ *Ludwig-Thoma-Str. 15a, Bernau am Chiemsee* ☎ *08051/7777* ⊕ *www.surfschule-chiemsee.de.*

BERCHTESGADEN

18 km (11 miles) south of Bad Reichenhall, 20 km (12 miles) south of Salzburg.

Berchtesgaden is a gorgeous mountain town right on the border with Austria. From its location in a 2,300-foot-high valley, you can see Germany's second-highest mountain, the Watzmann, and embark on daylong or multiday hikes through the Alps. The nature and diversity of the forests surrounding it are unparalleled in Germany, as are its snowy winters; the small town becomes a hive of activity in high winter and high summer as tourists descend in search of sporting adventure, whether it be hiking or biking, skiing or bobsledding. Perhaps historically it's best known for its brief association as the second home of Adolf Hitler, who dreamed of his "1,000-year Reich" from the mountaintop where millions of tourists before and after him drank in the superb beauty of the Alpine panorama. But there is much more to the town than its dark past. The historic old market town and mountain resort has great charm. An ornate palace and working salt mine make up some of the diversions in this heavenly setting.

Salt was once the basis of Berchtesgaden's wealth. In the 12th century, Emperor Barbarossa gave mining rights to a Benedictine abbey that had been founded here a century earlier. The abbey was secularized early in the 19th century, when it was taken over by the Wittelsbach rulers. Salt is still important today because of all the local wellness centers. The entire area has been declared a *Kurgebiet* (health resort region), and was put on the UNESCO biosphere list.

GETTING HERE AND AROUND

The easiest way to reach Berchtesgaden is with the hourly regional train connection, or by bus, from Salzburg Hauptbahnhof. To get to Berchtesgaden from Munich requires a change in Freilassing or Salzburg. From Salzburg's renovated main train station there are regular connections to Berchtesgaden (choose the train without a Freilassing change). Once there, frequent local bus service makes it easy to explore the town and to reach Berchtesgaden National Park and the Königssee. Local bus services, except that from Dokumentation Obersalzberg to the Eagle's Nest, are included when you pay the *Kurtax*. The Schwaiger bus company runs tours of the area and across the Austrian border as far as Salzburg. An American couple runs Eagle's Nest Historical Tours out of the local tourist office, opposite the train station.

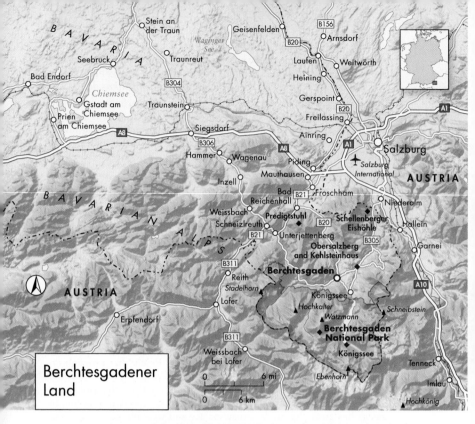

Berchtesgadener
Land

Contacts Schwaiger. ☎ 08652/2525 ⊕ www.bus-schwaiger.de/index.asp.

TOURS

Eagle's Nest Historical Tours. The recommended way to learn about Berchtesgaden's important role in World War II is via these tours run by English-speaking guides daily May–October at 1:15. The three-hour tour covers Obersalzberg, the bunkers, and the documentation center and offers unique insight into the city's historical role in the war. Children under eight years old are not permitted on the tour. ✉ *Königsseer Str. 2* ☎ *08652/64971* ⊕ *www.eagles-nest-tours.com* 🎫 *€55.*

VISITOR INFORMATION

Contacts Berchtesgaden Land Tourismus. ✉ *Maximilianstr. 9* ☎ *08652/656–5050* ⊕ *www.berchtesgaden.de.*

EXPLORING

Dokumentation Obersalzberg. This center documents the notorious history of the Third Reich, with a special focus on Obersalzberg and its role in the Holocaust and planning for World War II. The teaching museum includes some surprisingly rare archive material and access to the bunkers. English-language tours are only available for groups, but there is an audio guide in English. ✉ *Salzbergstr. 41* ☎ *08652/947–960* ⊕ *www.obersalzberg.de* 💶 *€3* ⊙ *Nov.–Mar., closed Mon.*

FAMILY **Haus der Berge.** Opened in 2015, this interactive museum brings the surrounding national park to life for children and adults alike with a rotating exhibition focusing on the wildlife and diverse nature to be found in the area. ✉ *Hanielstr. 7* ☎ *08652/979–0600* ⊕ *www.haus-der-berge.bayern.de* 💶 *€4.*

Obersalzberg and Kehlsteinhaus. The site of Hitler's luxurious mountain retreat is part of the north slope of the Hoher Goll, high above Berchtesgaden. It was a remote mountain community of farmers and foresters before Hitler's deputy, Martin Bormann, selected the site for a complex of Alpine homes for top Nazi leaders. Hitler's chalet, the Berghof, and all the others were destroyed in 1945, with the exception of a hotel that had been taken over by the Nazis, the Hotel zum Türken. Beyond Obersalzberg, the hairpin bends of Germany's highest road come to the base of the 6,000-foot peak on which sits the Kehlsteinhaus (aka the Adlerhorst, or "Eagle's Nest"), Hitler's personal retreat and his official guesthouse. To get the most out of your visit to the Kehlsteinhaus, consider taking a tour. To get there, you need to take a one-hour round trip from Berchtesgaden's post office by bus. A tunnel in the mountain will bring you to an elevator that whisks you up to the Kehlsteinhaus and what appears to be the top of the world, or you can walk up in about half an hour. ✉ *Königsseer Str. 2* ⊕ *www.kehlsteinhaus.de* 💶 *Bus ride €17 (round-trip); tour and bus ride €31* ⊙ *Closed Nov.–mid-May.*

FAMILY **Salzbergwerk.** One of the region's main attractions, this salt mine was once owned by Berchtesgaden's princely rulers. Where once only select guests were allowed to see how the source of the city's wealth was extracted from the earth, today an hour-long tour will transport you via a miniature train nearly 1 km (½ mile) into the mountain to an enormous chamber where the salt is mined. Included in the tour are rides down the wooden chutes used by miners to get from one level to another and a boat ride on an underground saline lake the size of a football field. You may wish to partake in the special four-hour **brine dinners** down in the mines ($$$$). These are very popular, so be sure to book early. ✉ *Bergwerkstr. 83* ☎ *08652/600–220* ⊕ *www.salzzeitreise.de* 💶 *€17.*

Schellenberger Eishöhle. Germany's largest ice caves lie 10 km (6 miles) north of Berchtesgaden. By car take B-305 to the village of Marktschellenberg and park at the Eishöhlenparkplatz near the B160 bus stop, or take Bus 2940 to the Eishöhle stop (€4) from the Berchtesgaden train station or Salzburg Hbf. From there you can reach the caves on foot by walking 3½ hours along the clearly marked route. A guided tour of the caves takes one hour. On the way to Marktschellenberg watch for the **Almbachklamm,** a narrow valley that is good for hikes. At its entrance is an old (1683) mill for making and polishing marbles. ✉ *Berchtesgaden* ☎ *08652/988-830* ⊕ *www.eishoehle.net* 💶 *€8* ⊙ *Closed in winter (usually Nov.–May).*

Schloss Berchtesgaden. The last royal resident of the Berchtesgaden abbey, Crown Prince Rupprecht (who died here in 1955), furnished it with rare family treasures that now form the basis of this permanent collection. Fine Renaissance rooms exhibit the prince's sacred art, which is particularly rich in wood sculptures by such great late-Gothic artists as Tilman Riemenschneider and Veit Stoss. There are two weaponry rooms exhibiting hunting tools, including rifles from the 19th century, and a beautiful rose garden out back. You can also visit the abbey's original, cavernous 13th-century dormitory and cool cloisters. Check in advance, as the Wittelsbach heir still occasionally stops by for a visit, at which times the castle is closed to visitors. ✉ *Schlosspl. 2* ☎ *08652/947–980* 🌐 *www.schloss-berchtesgaden.de* 🎟 *€10* 🕒 *Closed Sat.*

FAMILY **Watzmann Therme.** Here you'll find fragrant steam rooms, saunas with infrared cabins for sore muscles, an elegant pool, whirlpools, and a special pool for children. ✉ *Bergwerkstr. 54* ☎ *08652/94640* 🌐 *www.watzmann-therme.de* 🎟 *From €12.*

WHERE TO STAY

$$$ HOTEL Fodor's Choice ★ 🏨 **Berghotel Rehlegg.** In the heart of Ramsau, just outside of Berchtesgaden, this family-run Best Western hotel has a spa and pool and a special focus on sustainability. **Pros:** quiet location with views of Watzmann; swimming and spa area; friendly staff. **Cons:** perhaps too quiet for children; outside of town; restaurant gets busy. [$] *Rooms from: €198* ✉ *Holzeng. 16, Ramsau* ☎ *08657/98840* 🌐 *www.rehlegg.de* 🛏 *87 rooms* 🍴 *Free Breakfast.*

$$$$ RESORT FAMILY 🏨 **Kempinski Bavarian Alps.** In the hills outside of Berchtesgaden and surrounded by quiet woods, this five-star spa hotel, dripping with luxury, has a quiet, relaxed feel. **Pros:** stunning views; well-appointed modern furnishings; quiet location. **Cons:** can get busy with conferences; demanding guests; lunch meal service is limited. [$] *Rooms from: €260* ✉ *Hintereck 1* ☎ *08652/97550* 🌐 *www.kempinski.com* 🛏 *138 rooms* 🍴 *Free Breakfast.*

$$ HOTEL FAMILY 🏨 **Stoll's Hotel Alpina.** Set above the Königsee in the little village of Schönau, the Alpina offers rural solitude and easy access to Berchtesgaden. **Pros:** bedrooms are large and comfortable; good for families with children; great view of the Adlershorst. **Cons:** service can be brusque; bit outside the city; strict 21-day cancellation policy. [$] *Rooms from: €140* ✉ *Ulmenweg 14, Schönau* ☎ *08652/65090* 🌐 *www.stolls-hotel-alpina.de* 🕒 *Closed early Nov.–mid-Dec.* 🛏 *60 rooms* 🍴 *Free Breakfast.*

SPORTS AND THE OUTDOORS

Given its location in the Alps, Berchtesgaden is a place for the active. The Rossfeld ski area is one of the favorites, thanks to its abundance of natural snow. The piste down to Oberau is nearly 6 km (4 miles) long, with bus service at the end to take you back to Berchtesgaden. There is a separate snowboarding piste as well. Berchtesgaden also has many cross-country trails and telemark opportunities. The other popular area is on the slopes of the Götschenkopf, which is used for World Cup races. Snow is usually artificial, but the floodlit slopes at night and a lively après-ski scene make up for the lesser quality.

In summer, hikers, power-walkers, and paragliders take over the region. The Obersalzberg even has a summer luge track. Avid hikers should ask for a map featuring *Berghütten* (refuges) in the mountains, where

The gemlike Königsee Lake is the most photographed panorama in Germany.

one can spend the night either in a separate room or a bunk. Simple, solid meals are offered. In some of the smaller refuges you will have to bring your own food. For more information, check out ⊕ *www.* *berchtesgaden.de.* And though the Königsee is beautiful to look at, only cold-water swimmers will appreciate its frigid waters.

Consider walking along the pleasant mountain path from the Eagle's Nest back to Berchtesgaden.

Berchtesgadener Bergfuehrer. Professional mountaineers and rock climbers in this organization can help you find the right way up any of the surrounding mountains, including the Watzmann. ⊠ *Berchtesgadener-* *str. 21, Bischofswiesen* ☎ *08652/978–9690* ⊕ *www.berchtesgadener-* *bergfuehrer.de.*

Berchtesgaden Golf Club. Germany's highest course, the Berchtesgaden Golf Club, is on a 3,300-foot plateau of the Obersalzberg. Ten Berchtesgaden hotels offer their guests a 30% reduction on the greens fee—contact the tourist office or the club for details. ⊠ *Salzbergstr. 33* ☎ *08652/2100* ⊕ *www.golfclub-berchtesgaden.de* ▭ *€99 weekdays,* *€119 weekends* ⸙ *18 holes, 5680 yards, par 70.*

BERCHTESGADEN NATIONAL PARK

5 km (3 miles) south of Berchtesgaden.

The park covers 210 square km (81 square miles), and around two-thirds of its border is shared with Austria. Characterized by mountain vistas and the beautiful Königsee, the park has over 1.2 million visitors each year, which is a true testament to the area's popularity.

GETTING HERE AND AROUND
Berchtesgaden National Park is around 150 kilometers (93 miles) southeast of Munich by car. Many people find the train connection, with a change at Freilassing, and a 30-minute bus journey (total time is around two hours 50 minutes), a more rewarding, if adventurous journey.

EXPLORING

Berchtesgaden National Park. The deep, mysterious, and fabled Königssee is the most photographed panorama in Germany. Together with its much smaller sister, the Obersee, it's nestled within the Berchtesgaden National Park, 210 square km (81 square miles) of wild mountain country where flora and fauna have been left to develop as nature intended. No roads penetrate the area, and even the mountain paths are difficult to follow. The park administration organizes guided hikes from June through September. ⊠ *Nationalparkhaus, Franziskanerpl. 7, Berchtesgaden* ☎ *08652/64343* ⊕ *www.nationalpark-berchtesgaden.de*.

Königssee. One less strenuous way into the Berchtesgaden National Park is via electric boat. Only the skipper of these excursion boats is allowed to shatter the silence on the Königssee (King's Lake)—his trumpet fanfare demonstrates a remarkable echo as notes reverberate between the almost vertical cliffs that plunge into the dark green water. A cross on a rocky promontory marks the spot where a boatload of pilgrims hit the cliffs and sank more than 100 years ago. The voyagers were on their way to the tiny, twin-tower baroque chapel of St. Bartholomä, built in the 17th century on a peninsula where an early-Gothic church once stood. The princely rulers of Berchtesgaden built a hunting lodge at the side of the chapel; a tavern and restaurant now occupy its rooms.

Smaller than the Königssee but equally beautiful, the **Obersee** can be reached by a 15-minute walk from the second stop (Salet) on the boat tour. The lake's backdrop of jagged mountains and precipitous cliffs is broken by a waterfall, the Rothbachfall, which plunges more than 1,000 feet to the valley floor.

Boat service on the Königssee runs year-round, except when the lake freezes. A round-trip to St. Bartholomä and Salet, the landing stage for the Obersee, lasts almost two hours, without stops. A round-trip to St. Bartholomä lasts a little over an hour. In summer, the Berchtesgaden tourist office organizes evening cruises on the Königssee, which include a concert in St. Bartholomä Church and a four-course dinner in the neighboring hunting lodge. ⊠ *Boat service, Seestr. 29, Schönau* ☎ *08652/96360* ⊕ *www.bayerische-seenschifffahrt.de* 🎫 *€19 round-trip from Schonau to St. Bartholomä and Salet; €15 round-trip to St. Bartholomä only.*

4

THE ROMANTIC ROAD

WELCOME TO
THE ROMANTIC ROAD

TOP REASONS
TO GO

★ **Neuschwanstein:** Emerald lakes and the rugged peaks of the Alps surround what's become the world's most famous storybook castle.

★ **Rothenburg-ob-der-Tauber:** Stunning architecture and half-timber houses give this quaint walled village an authentic Middle Ages feel, which only increases as you patrol the city walls with the night watchman after the tour buses have left town.

★ **Wieskirche:** Rising up out of the pastoral countryside, this local pilgrimage church is a rococo gem.

★ **Ulm's Münster:** Climb the 768 steps of this church's tower to get a view over the city and take in the most elaborately designed evangelical church in Germany.

★ **Würzburg's Residenz:** Explore the gilt and crystal splendor of this lavish palace, once the home of prince-bishops.

The Romantic Road captures classic Germany in the 28 towns dotted along its route. At its southern most point is Füssen, directly on the mountainous Austrian border. From there, it winds northwest through pastoral countryside before ending in Würzburg in central Germany, an hour from Frankfurt.

1 Hohenschwangau. This small town near Füssen has two of King Ludwig II's casles: Hohenschwangau, where he grew up, and his more famous fairy-tale castle, Neuschwanstein, on a hill high above the town.

2 Füssen. Known for its musical heritage (in particular violin-making), Füssen was not bombed during World War II, retaining its medieval charm. The lovely rococo Wieskirche is nearby.

3 Augsburg. Bavaria's third-largest city has Roman roots and a lovely Gothic cathedral.

4 Ulm. Near but not on the Romantic road, Ulm is best known for its Münster, the largest and most elaborate evangelical church in Germany.

5 Nördlingen. This medieval-era walled city is built in two cocentric circles, with St. Georg's Church a the center.

6 Dinkesbühl. Offering much of the same Medieval-era charm as Rothenburg (but without the crowds), Dinkesbühl offers a quieter escape.

7 Rothenburg-ob-der-Tauber. The quintessential Medieval Bavarian town is filled with picturesque half-timber houses and remains one of the most Instagram-worthy towns in Germany.

8 Bad Mergentheim. For almost 300 years, Bad Mergentheim was home to the Teutonic Knights, but its current claim to fame is its sodium-sulfate-laden waters, which have made it a busy spa town.

9 Würzburg. This baroque-era city is the jewel of the Romantic Road, almost completely rebuilt and restored after World War II; the Residenz is UNESCO World Heritage Site.

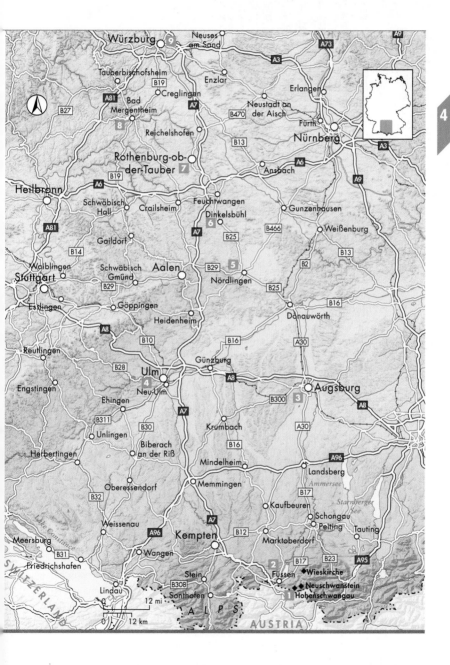

Würzburg **9**
Neuses am Sand
A73
A9
A3
Tauberbischofsheim
B19
Enzlar
Erlangen
B27
A81
Bad Mergentheim
Creglingen
A7
Neustadt an der Aisch
B470
Fürth
8
Reichelshofen
B13
Nürnberg
A3
Rothenburg-ob-der-Tauber **7**
Ansbach
A6
A9
Heilbronn
B19
A6
Schwäbisch Hall
Crailsheim
Feuchtwangen
Dinkelsbühl **6**
Gunzenhausen
A81
A7
B466
Weißenburg
B14
Gaildorf
B25
B13
Waiblingen
Schwäbisch Gmünd
Aalen
B29 **5**
B2
Stuttgart
B29
Nördlingen
B25
Esslingen
Göppingen
B16
Reutlingen
Heidenheim
Danauwörth
A8
B10
B16
A30
B28
Günzburg
Ulm **4**
A8
Augsburg
Engstingen
Neu-Ulm
B300 **3**
A8
Ehingen
A7
Krumbach
A30
B311
B30
Herbertingen
Biberach an der Riß
B16
Mindelheim
A96
Unlingen
Landsberg
Oberessendorf
Memmingen
B17
Ammersee
B32
Kaufbeuren
Starnberger See
Weissenau
A96
Schongau
Schongau
Pelting
Tauting
Meersburg
Kempten
B12
Marktoberdorf
B31
Wangen
B17
B23
A95
Friedrichshafen
Stein
Füssen **2**
◆Wieskirche
Lindau
B308
Sonthofen
◆ Neuschwanstein
1 Hohenschwangau

SWITZERLAND

A L P S

AUSTRIA

12 mi

0   12 km

4

Updated by
Courtney Tenz

Nowhere cries "quintessential German" quite as loudly as the Romantic Road, a 355-km (220-mile) drive through the south-central countryside. A mix of 28 traditional villages, some still brimming with medieval architecture, and larger cities like Ulm and Augsburg, the route through a pastoral landscape is memorable for the castles, abbeys, and churches tucked away beyond low hills, their spires and towers just visible through the greenery.

The Romantic Road began in 1950 as a bus tour through this corner of West Germany, then occupied by the American forces, as a way to promote this historic route through Bavaria and Baden-Württemberg. Don't let the name fool you—this isn't a road for lovebirds; rather the word *romantic* is a reference to the area's rich and diverse history, especially the Middle Ages.

Traveled by the Romans 2,000 years ago, the path of the Romantic Road criss-crosses centuries-old battlefields, most especially those of the Thirty Years' War, which destroyed the region's economic base in the 17th century. The depletion of resources prevented improvements that would have modernized the area—thereby assuring that these towns would become the quaint tourist destinations they are today.

MAJOR REGIONS

An hour west of Munich, the **Southern Romantic Road** climbs gradually toward the Alps, which burst into view between Landsberg and Schongau. **Hohenschwangau,** where the Hohenschwangau and Neuschwanstein castles are on most tourist itineraries. The pre-Alpine landscape grows more natural and rugged, with thick forests as you continue to the route's most southern tip—the town of **Füssen,** on the Austrian border near Hohenschwangau; just to the north is the **Wieskirche.**

The **Vineyards of South Franken** begin in in the Central Romantic Road, at **Augsburg,** which was founded by the Romans around 15 BC; today, it's Bavaria's third-largest city. It's worthwhile to take a short trip west to **Ulm** to see its magnificent protestant *Münster* (church). For a more intimate (and less touristy) experience, check out the medieval towns of **Nördlingen** or **Dinkelsbühl**. Picturesque **Rothenburg-ob-der-Tauber** is the highlight of this region, though certainly not the road less traveled.

After heading through the plains of Swabia in the south, the **Northern Romantic Road** skirts the wild, open countryside of the Spessart uplands. The spa town of **Bad Mergentheim** can make for a relaxing overnight stop before continuing on to **Würzburg** to see its UNESCO-recognized palace.

PLANNING

WHEN TO GO
Late summer and early autumn are the best times to travel the Romantic Road, as the grapes ripen on the vines around Würzburg and the geraniums run riot on the medieval walls of towns such as Rothenburg and Dinkelsbühl. You'll also miss the high-season summer crush of tourists. Otherwise, consider visiting the region in December, when Christmas markets fill the ancient town squares and snow gives the turreted Schloss Neuschwanstein a magical touch.

PLANNING YOUR TIME
While the two bigger cities of Augsburg and Würzburg can handle large influxes of visitors, it pays to visit any of the quaint villages lining the Romantic Road to get a feel for the laid-back local lifestyle. In the two most popular places, Rothenburg-ob-der-Tauber and Neuschwanstein, an overnight stay will help beat the crowds. On summer nights, you can follow the night watchman in Rothenburg as he makes his rounds, and stroll through the town in the early morning before the bus-tour groups push through the streets. At Neuschwanstein, it's even more important to get an early start, as tickets almost always sell out by late morning (even in the off-season); even after reserving your spot in advance online, expect a long wait during high season.

GETTING HERE AND AROUND
AIR TRAVEL
The major international airports serving the Romantic Road are Frankfurt and Munich.

BUS TRAVEL
Daily bus service from Frankfurt and Munich is provided by the Romantic Road Coach (operated by the tourist office), and covers the entire stretch of the Romantic Road from Würzburg to Füssen. It's a hop-on, hop-off service, and tickets bought online are valid for up to six months (€108 one-way, €158 round-trip). The buses run from early April through mid-October, come complete with audio guide and app to provide more information and stop at all the major sights along the road. Packages including bicycle transportation and hotel reservations can be booked directly online or through the Romantic Road official tourist office.

Contacts Romantic Road Coach. ✉ *Segringer Str. 19, Dinkelsbühl* ☎ *09851/551–387* ⊕ *www.romantic-road.com.*

CAR TRAVEL

Most easily traveled by car, the Romantic Road offers a number of opportunities to pause at scenic overlooks. Just be sure to follow brown landmark signs marking the Road instead of following a navigation system, as GPS will likely keep you on the faster, less scenic freeways, bypassing the many quaint villages lining the route. The rural routes are busy, and most have only two lanes, so figure on covering no more than 70 km (43 miles) each hour, particularly in summer. If you're coming up from the south and using Munich as a gateway, Augsburg is 70 km (43 miles) from Munich via A-8. Continue north from there and you'll end up in Würzburg, the northernmost city on the route, which is 124 km (77 miles) from Frankfurt. If you're traveling from the north, begin in Würzburg and follow country highway B-27 south to meet roads B-290, B-19, B-292, and B-25 along the Wörnitz River. The Romantic Road is just off the Frankfurt–Nuremberg highway (A-3), 115 km (71 miles) from Frankfurt. For route maps, with roads and sights highlighted, contact the Romantic Road Central Tourist Information Center based in Dinkelsbühl.

TRAIN TRAVEL

Frequent trains link the major cities on the Romantic Road. Würzburg, Ulm, and Augsburg all have both InterCity and high-speed InterCity Express (ICE) service with fast, near-hourly service to and from Munich, Stuttgart, and Frankfurt. Slower commuter trains to the smaller towns along the route are less frequent and more limited at night and on weekends.

HOTELS

With a few exceptions, Romantic Road hotels are quiet and rustic, and you'll find high standards of comfort and cleanliness. If you plan to stay in one of the bigger hotels in the off-season, ask about discounted weekend rates. Make reservations as far in advance as possible if you plan to visit in summer. Hotels in Würzburg, Augsburg, Rothenburg, and Füssen are often full year-round. Tourist information offices can usually help with accommodations, especially if you arrive early in the day.

RESTAURANTS

Restaurants in the heavily trafficked towns along the Romantic Road tend to be crowded during peak season, but if you plan your mealtimes around visits to smaller villages, you will be rewarded with Franconian or Swabian cuisine that is less expensive and may also be locally sourced. Some of the small, family-run restaurants close around 2 pm, or whenever the last lunch guests have left, and then open again at 5 or 5:30 pm. Some serve cold cuts or coffee and cake during that time, but no warm dishes.

Prices in restaurant reviews are the average cost of a main course at dinner, or if dinner is not served, at lunch. Prices in hotel reviews are the lowest cost of a standard double room in high season.

WHAT IT COSTS IN EUROS			
$	**$$**	**$$$**	**$$$$**
Restaurants	under €15	€15–€20	€21–€25	over €25
Hotels	under €100	€100–€175	€176–€225	over €225

TOURS
BIKE TOURS
Alpenlandtouristik. Specializing in hiking and biking tours, this company offers a number of multiday tours, including a "luggage-free" six-day castle tour from Landsberg am Lech to Neuschwanstein and Füssen (the Naturpfad) or the "King Ludwig" tour from Königssee to Chiemsee. ☎ *08191/308–620* ⊕ *www.alpenlandtouristik.de* ⌑ *From €420 for 6 days with hotel stays.*

Velotours. Offers a number of scenic days-long hiking and biking tours, including four along the Romantic Road (Würzburg to Rothenburg, Rothenburg to Donauwörth, or Donauwörth to Füssen). The first two trips can be combined for an eight-day tour. ✉ *Bücklestr. 13, Konstanz* ☎ *07531/98280* ⊕ *www.velotours.de* ⌑ *From €365.*

VISITOR INFORMATION
Contacts Bavaria Tourism Office. ✉ *Arabellastr. 17, Munich* ☎ *089/212–39743* ⊕ *www.bavaria.by.* **Romantische Strasse Touristik-Arbeitsgemeinschaft** *(Romantic Road Central Tourist Information).* ✉ *Segringerstr. 19, Dinkelsbühl* ☎ *09851/551–387* ⊕ *www.romantischestrasse.de.*

HOHENSCHWANGAU

103 km (64 miles) south of Augsburg, 121 km (75 miles) southwest of Munich.

This small town's famous castles belonging to the Wittelbachs are 1 km (½ mile) across a valley from each other, near the town of Schwangau. Bavaria's King Ludwig II (1845–86) spent many summers during his youth at Schloss Hohenschwangau. It's said that its neo-Gothic atmosphere provided the primary influences that shaped his wildly romantic Schloss Neuschwanstein, the more famous fairy-tale castle he built after he became king that has become one of Germany's most recognized sights.

GETTING HERE AND AROUND
From Schwangau, 5 km (3 miles) north of Füssen, follow the road signs marked "Königschlösser" (King's Castles). After 3 km (2 miles) you come to Hohenschwangau, a small village consisting of a few houses, some good hotels, lots of souvenir shops and restaurants, and four big parking lots (parking €6). You'll have to park and then walk up a small hill to the ticket center serving both castles. If you are staying in Füssen, it is easiest to take Bus 73 or 78 to Hohenschwangau, which leaves from the train station in Füssen every hour from morning to night, and

costs €1.80 per person one-way. Those arriving by train can use their Deutsche Bahn ticket to carry on the journey without paying extra.

Schloss Neuschwanstein itself is a strenuous, mile-long climb up a steep hill by paved trail. You can also take one of the horse-drawn carriages that leave from Hotel Müller next door to the ticket center (uphill €6, downhill €3), or a shuttle bus that departs near the ticket center (uphill €1.80, downhill €1) and takes you partway up the hill. Either way, a steep walk the last 500 yards cannot be avoided; strollers and wheelchairs are not allowed inside the castle itself, which contains stairs and is not handicapped accessible. Lines for both the bus and horse-drawn carriages can be long, even in the off-season, so allow plenty of time, as these cannot be booked in advance.

Schloss Hohenschwangau is a much less strenuous climb, or the trip can be done in a small horse-drawn carriage (€4.50 uphill, €2 downhill).

TICKETS

Castle Ticket Center. Tickets to both of the castles are for timed entry, so be sure to leave at least an hour, if not more, to get your tickets and take on the strenuous 1½-km (1-mile) uphill hike to Neuschwanstein from the ticket center (a bus or horse-drawn carriage is also available). Schloss Hohenschwangau is a much easier climb up a smaller hill immediately behind the ticket center that can be done on foot or by a small horse-drawn carriage. For a fee of €1.80, you can book your tickets up to two days in advance for either castle through the ticket center with a deposit or credit-card number; in high season be sure to book several weeks in advance. They almost always sell out, even in the off-season. You can change entrance times or cancel up to two hours before the confirmed entrance time. You can get a ticket for one castle, both castles, or both castles plus the Museum of Bavarian Kings. Each option includes an audio guide. ⊠ *Alpseestr. 12, Hohenschwangau* ☎ *08362/930–830* ⊕ *www.hohenschwangau.de.*

EXPLORING

Museum of the Bavarian Kings. Housed in the former Alpenrose Hotel, a museum chronicling the history of the Wittelsbach kings and queens from the 11th century to the present day opened in this grand building directly on the Alpensee in 2012. Focusing primarily on King Maximilian II and his son Ludwig, it details the family's story and the Wittelsbach family's influence in the region, from the development of Munich, their founding of the first Oktoberfest, and the family's role in the resistance to the Nazi regime, and their eventual imprisonment during World War II. The interactive exhibits couple state-of-the-art technology with the gold and gilt belongings of the royal family, including an elegant fur robe worn by King Ludwig II. The adjacent Alpenrose-am-See café overlooking the lake is a good spot to relax. ⊠ *Alpseestr. 27, Schwangau* ☎ *08362/926–4640* ⊕ *www.museumderbayerischenkoenige.de* 🎫 *From €11.*

Fodor'sChoice ★ **Schloss Neuschwanstein.** Bavaria's Fairy-Tale King, Ludwig II, commissioned a stage designer in 1868 to create this over-the-top architectural masterpiece overlooking the peaceful waters of the Alpsee. The

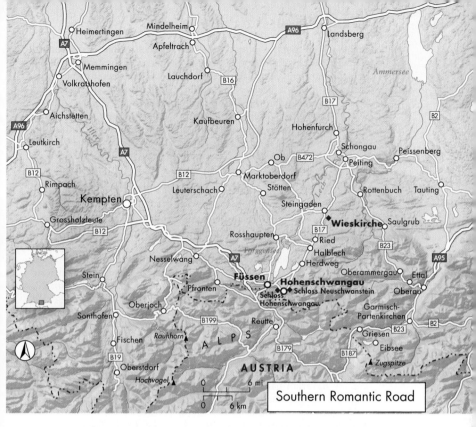

Southern Romantic Road

five-story castle was to pay tribute to the operas of Richard Wagner, and the interior contains numerous murals alluding to sagas and legends as Siegfried and the Swan Knight Lohengrin. Despite being largely incomplete—the extravagant Throne Room contains no throne—the castle is Germany's top tourist destinations, even inspiring Disney's *Sleeping Beauty* castle. Above the castle is the delicate **Marienbrücke** (Mary's Bridge) spun across a deep, narrow gorge. From this vantage point there are giddy views of the castle and the great Upper Bavarian Plain beyond. Tours almost always sell out, so booking in advance is strongly recommended. Room-by-room renovations will make some unviewable from 2018 through 2021; check ahead if you want to see a particular room. Pöllatschlucht gorge hiking trails are also closed. ⚠ **The castle is a very strenuous climb, so consider taking a bus or horse and carriage. The Marienbrücke and transportation often close on snowy days.** ✉ *Neuschwansteinstr. 20, Hohenschwangau* ☎ *08362/930–830* ⊕ *www.neuschwanstein.de* ✍ *From €13.*

Schloss Hohenschwangau. Built by the knights of Schwangau in the 12th century, this castle was later updated by King Ludwig II's father, the Bavarian crown prince Maximilian, between 1832 and 1836. Unlike Ludwig's more famous castle across the valley, Neuschwanstein, the mustard-yellow Schloss Hohenschwangau actually feels like a noble home, where comforts would be valued as much as outward splendor. Ludwig spent his childhood summers surrounded by the castle's murals, depicting ancient Germanic legends, including those that inspired the composer Richard Wagner in his *Ring* cycle of operas. The paintings remain untouched in the dining room, as does the "Women's floor," which looks just as it did at the death of Ludwig's mother, Marie, in 1889. The walk up to the castle from the ticket center is short but steep. The trip can also be done in a small horse-drawn carriage (€4.50 uphill, €2 downhill). ✉ *Alpseestr. 12, Schwangau* ☎ *08362/930–830* 🌐 *www.hohenschwangau.de* 🎫 *From €13.*

WHERE TO EAT

$$$ EUROPEAN 🍴 **Alpenrose am See.** There is no spot more idyllic in Hohenschwangau to enjoy excellent food and stunning views over the Alpsee and mountains beyond. The café next to the Museum of Bavarian Kings is a good choice to escape the tourist masses for lunch or afternoon coffee and cake on the terrace. **Known for:** vegetarian selections; wild boar ravioli; cakes and apple strudel. [$] *Average main: €22* ✉ *Alpseestr. 27, Hohenschwangau* ☎ *08362/926–4660* 🌐 *www.alpenrose-am-see.de* 🕒 *Closed daily 5–6 pm.*

WHERE TO STAY

$$ HOTEL 🏨 **Hotel Müller.** With a convenient location between the two Schwangau castles, the Müller fits beautifully into the stunning landscape, its creamy Bavarian baroque facade a contrast to the forested mountain slopes. **Pros:** personalized service; variety of rooms; right next to castles. **Cons:** crowded during the day; expensive in season; not many amenities. [$] *Rooms from: €120* ✉ *Alpseestr. 16, Hohenschwangau* ☎ *08362/81990* 🌐 *www.hotel-mueller.de* 🕒 *Closed Nov.–Dec. and early Jan.–mid-Feb.* 🛏 *43 rooms* 🍽 *Free Breakfast.*

FÜSSEN

5 km (3 miles) southwest of Schwangau, 129 km (80 miles) south of Munich.

A walled town left untouched by World War II bombs, Füssen's red roofs and turrets stand in picturesque contrast to the turquoise waters of the Lech River that rushes alongside the town, separating it from the Romantic Road. The only town with the infrastructure to accommodate the crush of tourists from the famous castles nearby, Füssen has a lot of charm of its own, with tidy, meandering streets lined with original architecture that offers an authentic slice of the past. The small town square is filled with cafés, restaurants, and shops; a centuries-old abbey and castle round out the sights. Home to violin makers for centuries, Füssen takes pride in its musical heritage, which it showcases during an annual summer jazz festival. At the foot of the mountains that separate Bavaria from the Austrian Tyrol, it is also a great starting point for hiking and bicycle tours in the area, and on the nearby Forggensee, a reservoir created to hold glacial runoff, you can take a boat ride with stunning views of Neuschwanstein.

GETTING HERE AND AROUND

On the border with Austria, Füssen is the last stop on the regional express train leaving every two hours from Munich, and using the train is a highly recommended way to get to this town in the Alpine foothills. From the tourist information center next to the main train station, you can get information about bus travel in and around the region; frequency varies based on the season, but buses run at least hourly to all of the nearby castles of King Ludwig. The pedestrian-only city center is just a few hundred yards' walk from the train station.

VISITOR INFORMATION

Contacts Füssen Tourismus und Marketing. ✉ *Kaiser-Maximilian-Pl. 1*
☎ *08362/93850* ⊕ *www.fuessen.de.*

4

EXPLORING

Hohes Schloss (*High Castle*). One of the best-preserved late-Gothic castles in Germany, Hohes Schloss was built on the site of the Roman fortress that once guarded this Alpine section of the Via Claudia, the trade route from Rome to the Danube. Evidence of Roman occupation of the area has been uncovered at the foot of the nearby Tegelberg Mountain, and the **excavations** next to the Tegelberg cable-car station are open for visits daily. The Hohes Schloss was the seat of Bavarian rulers before Emperor Heinrich VII mortgaged it and the rest of the town to the bishop of Augsburg for 400 pieces of silver. The mortgage was never redeemed, and Füssen remained the property of the Augsburg episcopate until secularization in the early 19th century. The bishops of Augsburg used the castle as their summer Alpine residence. It has a spectacular 16th-century **Rittersaal** (Knights' Hall) with a carved ceiling, and a princes' chamber with a Gothic tile stove. ✉ *Magnuspl. 10* ☎ *08362/903–146* ⊕ *www.stadt-fuessen.de/hohesschloss.html* 🎟 *€6* 🕓 *Closed Mon. Apr.–Oct., and Mon.–Thurs. Nov.–Mar.*

Kloster St. Mang. This baroque masterpiece dates back to the 8th century, when city patron Magnus, who spent most of his life ministering in the area, founded a monk's cloister here. The summer presence of the bishops of Augsburg ensured that Füssen would gain an impressive number of baroque and rococo churches, and after his death, the Benedictine abbey was built at the site of his grave. Although the abbey now houses civic offices and the Rathaus (Town Hall), the richly decorated Kaisersaal is only accessible via the City Museum (also housed here); the monastery gardens are open for a stroll during daylight hours, as is the baroque Annakapelle, which includes frescoes of the local legend, the Füssen Totentanz. A Romanesque crypt beneath the baroque abbey church has a partially preserved 10th-century fresco, the oldest in Bavaria. In summer, chamber concerts are held in the baroque splendor of the former abbey's soaring **Fürstensaal** (Princes' Hall). Program details are available from the tourist office. ✉ *Lechhalde 3* ☎ *08362/903–146* ⊕ *www.fuessen.de/kultur-und-kulinarik/kloster-st-mang.html* 🎟 *Abbey and church free; City Museum €6* 🕓 *Closed Mon. Apr.–Nov.; closed Mon.–Thurs. Nov.–Apr.*

Continued on page 178

FAIRY-TALE CASTLES OF KING LUDWIG II

By Catherine Moser

King Ludwig II's image permeates Bavarian culture—the picture of the raven-haired king with soulful eyes adorns everything from beer steins to the local autobahn. The fairy-tale palaces he built have drawn millions of visitors, but who was Ludwig II? Adopting the words of his favorite poet, Friedrich Schiller, he wrote: "I wish to remain an eternal enigma to myself and to others." A tour of his castles reveals a glimpse of the man behind the story of the "Dreamer King."

Born on August 25, 1845, in Nymphenburg Palace, Ludwig II became king at 18 after his father's, King Maximilian II's, sudden death in 1864. He would become the most famous king in the 900-year Wittelsbach dynasty, known not for his rule—he had little power, as Bavaria was governed by a constitutional monarchy—but for his eccentricities.

Ludwig attended Richard Wagner's *Lohengrin* at age 15. Identifying with the Swan Knight, he yearned for the heroic medieval world Wagner portrayed. As king, Ludwig became Wagner's greatest patron and funded the creation of his opera festival in Bayreuth. Wagner was so influential, and Ludwig's love for him so unabashed, that concerned Munich officials sent the composer away in 1865.

Seeking solace in the isolated, idealized world of his own creation, Ludwig embarked on three palace-building projects beginning in 1868. By 1885, he had amassed a personal debt of 14 million marks, putting a massive strain on the Wittelsbach fortune. A commission of doctors, enthralled with the emerging studies of psychology, was assembled to analyze the behavior of the recluse king. Led by Dr. von Gudden, the commission diagnosed the king with paranoia and declared him insane without ever examining Ludwig himself. Ludwig was arrested in the early-morning hours of June 12, 1886, and taken from Schloss Neuschwanstein to Castle Berg on the shores of Lake Starnberg. Just before midnight the following day, the bodies of Ludwig and Dr. von Gudden were found floating in the lake. Theories abound to this day about their deaths, but the truth of Ludwig's demise is unknown.

Opposite, Schloss Neuschwanstein. Above left, King Ludwig II. Above right, Golden angel fountain, Schloss Linderhof.

SCHLOSS LINDERHOF

Set in sylvan seclusion in Graswang Valley, high in the Alps, lies the royal palace of Linderhof. Built on the site of his father's hunting lodge, this was the first of Ludwig's building projects and the only one completed during his lifetime. Begun in 1868, the small villa based on the Petit Trianon of Versailles took six years to complete.

ENTRANCE HALL

Two lifesize Sèvres **peacocks** were placed outside the entry doors to signify when Ludwig was in residence. Upon entering the castle, there is a large bronze **statue of King Louis XIV**, Ludwig's idol. On the ceiling above the statue is a gold sun, symbolizing the "Sun King" of France, inscribed with his motto: *Nec Pluribus Impar* ("I stand above others").

THRONE ROOM AND BEDCHAMBER

With paintings of Louis XIV and XV watching over him, Ludwig spent hours meticulously overseeing the architectural plans of his other projects from the green and gold **throne room**. The **bedchamber**, with its three-dimensional golden tapestries set against his favorite color, royal blue, look out to a waterfall cascading down the hill to the **Neptune fountain**, with its 100-foot water jet.

DINING ROOM

Ludwig would eat alone in the adjoining **dining room**. His extreme sweet tooth had wreaked havoc on his mouth so that by the time he was 30, most of his teeth were missing and dining was a messy affair. For his privacy, the dining table could be lowered down through the floor by cables and pulleys to the kitchen below. It would then reappear with Ludwig's meal so that he never had to dine with servants in the room.

HALL OF MIRRORS

The reclusive king spent his time reading and literally reflecting in the **hall of mirrors,** with its optical illusion infinitely reflecting his image and vast collection of vases lining the walls.

LINDERHOF'S GROUNDS

In the **Venus grotto** (under renovation), Ludwig spent many evenings being paddled around in a scallop-shaped boat imagining he was in the world of Wagner's *Tannhäuser.* Ludwig would gather his equerries for decadent evenings spent in the **Moorish kiosk,** which was purchased wholesale from the 1867 Paris Universal Exposition, imagining himself as an Arabian knight lounging on his magnificent **peacock throne.** Deeper into the park is the **Hunding's hut,** a medieval-style lodge based on the set designs for the opening act of Wagner's *Die Walküre.* Ludwig took moonlit rides in winter to the original Hut, set deeply in the Alpine forest, in his gilt **gala sleigh.**

GETTING HERE AND AROUND

✉ Linderhof 12, Ettal-Linderhof

☎ 08822/92030 or -21

⊕ www.schlosslinderhof.de

🎫 €8.50, €7.50 winter

🕐 Open April–Oct. 15, daily 9-6; Oct. 16–March, daily 10-4:30; park buildings (grotto, Moorish kiosk, etc.) closed in winter

Car Travel: Take the A–95 motorway and the B–2 to Oberau. Follow the signs in Oberau to the B–23 (Ettaler Strasse). Outside Ettal turn left onto ST–2060. In Linderhof turn right to reach the palace.

Train Travel: Take the regional Deutsche Bahn train from Munich Hauptbahnhof to Oberammergau. Buy the Bayern Ticket, which allows for a full day of travel, including bus fare, from €25 for up to five people. From there, take bus 9622 to Linderhof.

Bus Tours: There are several tours combining both Linderhof and Neuschwanstein castles, but none that go just to Linderhof. Gray Line Tours (☎ 8954/907–560 ⊕ www. grayline.com) offers a day trip, including Linderhof, Neuschwanstein, and a short stop to shop in Oberammergau. It leaves daily at 8:30 am from the Karstadt Department store in front of the Munich Hauptbahnhof. Tickets are €62 for adults and €32 for children, not including castle admission.

SCHLOSS NEUSCHWANSTEIN

Neuschwanstein, the most famous of the three castles, was King Ludwig's crowning achievement. The castle soars from its mountainside like a stage creation—it should hardly come as a surprise that Walt Disney took it as the model for his castle in the movie *Sleeping Beauty* and later for the Disneyland castle itself.

Prince Ludwig spent idyllic childhood summers at **Hohenschwangau**, the neighboring medieval-style palace. The young prince was undoubtedly influenced by the vast murals of the legends of *Lohengrin* and romantic vision of these ancient times. Perhaps he envisioning his own, mightier palace when looking north to the mountains and the old ruins of a fortress of the Knights

of Schwangau. Upon commencing construction in 1868, Ludwig wrote to Wagner, "The Gods will come to live with us on the lofty heights, breathing the air of heaven."

THRONE ROOM

Wagner's *Tannhäuser* inspired the Byzantine-style **throne room**, drawn from plans for the original stage set for the opera; however, the actual throne was never constructed. The massive chandelier is styled after a Byzantine crown and surrounded by images of angels, apostles, and six kings of history who were canonized as saints. Look closely at the image of St. George, the patron saint of the Wittelsbachs, slaying a dragon in front of another medieval castle. That castle, Falkenstein, was set to be the next, even grander castle of Ludwig II. The elaborate mosaic floor contains two million stones.

Above, Schloss Neuschwanstein. Opposite (top) Singers' Hall, (bottom) Ludwig II's bedchamber.

BEDCHAMBER

The king spent his last days as ruler huddled in his late-Gothic-style **bedchamber** modeled after the nuptial chamber of *Lohengrin*. It took fourteen craftsmen more than four years to carve this room alone. The symbol of the swan occurs throughout Neuschwanstein, appearing here in the fixtures of the sink.

GROTTO

Reminiscent of the larger one at Linderhof, but stranger for its placement inside the palace, the **grotto** overlooking the Schwangau Valley once had a running waterfall lit by tinted lights.

SINGERS' HALL

Ludwig's favorite room, the **Singers' Hall,** was modeled after the stage design for the Forest of the Holy Grail from *Parsifal* and designed for the best acoustics. On moonless nights, the king would hike out to the Marienbrücke, over the rocky gorge, to watch the candlelit splendor of this hall. Ludwig never saw a performance here, but concerts are now held every September.

GETTING HERE AND AROUND

✉ Alpseestrasse 12, Hohenschwangau

☎ 8362/930–830

⊕ www.neuschwanstein.de

🎫 €13 tickets are for a set tour time, reserve ahead online (€1.80 extra). English tours every 15 minutes.

🕑 Open April–Oct. 15 daily 9–6; Oct. 16–March daily 10–4

Car Travel: Take the A–7 (direction Ulm-Kempten-Füssen) to the end. From Füssen, take B–17 to Schwangau, then follow signs to Hohenschwangau.

Train Travel: Take the regional Deutsche Bahn train from Munich Hauptbahnhof to Füssen (buy the Bayern Ticket). From Füssen, take either bus 73 toward Steingaden/Garmisch-Partenkirchen or bus 78 toward Schwangau until the Hohenschwangau/Alpseestrasse stop.

Getting to the Castle: Allow 30–40 minutes for the uphill walk from the ticket center to the castle. In summer, you can take a a bus (€1.80 uphill, €1 downhill) or horse-drawn carriage (€6 uphill, €3 downhill) up to the castle.

Bus Tours: Bus Bavaria (☎ 89255/43987 or -988 ⊕ mikesbiketours.com) leaves from central Munich daily from mid-April through mid-October. Tours cost €53–€59, not including admission.

SCHLOSS HERRENCHIEMSEE

The third and what would be the last of King Ludwig II's building projects, Herrenchiemsee, modeled after Louis XIV's Versailles, stands as a monument to the institution of the monarchy and the Bourbon kings he idolized. Ludwig never intended to use this palace as a place to live but rather a place to visit to transport himself to the days when the Sun King ruled the glorious court of Versailles. Ludwig stayed at this palace only once, for a brief ten-day visit in September 1885.

CONSTRUCTION OF HERRENCHIEMSEE
Ludwig purchased the Herreninsel, the biggest of the three islands on Lake Chiemsee in 1873. Work soon began on gardens to rival the ones at Versailles.

Above, Schloss Herrenchiemsee. Opposite (top) Hall of Mirrors, (bottom) fountain.

By the time the foundation stone of the palace was laid in 1878, the soaring fountains were already in use. Although 300 local craftsmen worked day and night to replicate the Sun King's palace, only 20 of the planned 70 rooms saw completion during the following eight years of construction. They abound with marble, gilt, and paintings of the Bourbon court, the French style replicated by skilled Bavarian artists.

PARADE BEDCHAMBER
The sumptuous red brocade bedspread and wall hangings in the **parade bedchamber**, which is twice the size of the original in Versailles, took 30 women seven years to embroider. Red silk curtains can be pulled over the bay windows to give the room a glow of regal red, the symbolic color of the Bourbon court. Ludwig never slept in this room; it was created in memory of Louis XIV. Instead, Ludwig slept in the **king's bed-**

chamber, softly lit by blue candlelight from the large blue orb over his bed.

HALL OF MIRRORS
In the **hall of mirrors,** longer than the original in Versailles, Ludwig held private concerts during his short stay here. A team of 35 servants took a half-hour to light the 2,000 candles of the chandeliers and candelabra lining the golden room.

LUDWIG II MUSEUM
Ludwig gave strict orders that no image of the Wittelsbach rulers or of himself should be found in his French palace. Today, however, this is the only one of his three palaces to have a museum devoted to the king. You can see his christening gown, uniforms, architectural plans for future building projects, and even sample his favorite cologne in the castle's **Ludwig II Museum.**

GETTING HERE AND AROUND

✉ Herrenchiemsee
☎ 8051/68870
🌐 www.herrenchiemsee.de
🎫 €11
🕐 Open April–Oct. 15, daily 9–6; Oct. 16–March, daily 9:40–4:15

Boat Travel: Herrenchiemsee lies on the island of Herreninsel in Lake Chiemsee. **Chiemsee Schifffahrt's** (✉ *Seestrasse 108, Prien am Chiemsee* ☎ *8051/6090* 🌐 *www.chiemsee-schifffahrt.de*) ferries leave regularly from Prien/Stock daily from 7 am–6:30 pm. Tickets cost €9.40 round-trip.

Car Travel: Take the A-8 motorway (Salzburg-Munich), leaving at the Bernau exit to continue to Prien am Chiemsee. At the roundabout outside Prien follow the signs to Chiemsee or Königsschloss.

Train Travel: Take the regional Deutsche Bahn train to Prien am Chiemsee, about an hour's ride from Munich (buy the Bayern Ticket). From the station, take the quaint **Chiemsee Bahn,** which winds through the town to the boats. It runs from April–October. Train and boat combination tickets cost €9.40.

Bus Tours: Gray Line Tours (☎ *8954/907-560* 🌐 *www.grayline.com*) offers a day trip, including the boat trip out to the castle (but not admission) and a visit to the Fraueninsel on Chiemsee for €47.

WHERE TO EAT

$ ✗ **Altstadthotel Zum Hechten.** Directly below the Hohes Schloss and flow-
GERMAN ering with geraniums is one of the town's oldest inns, which remains
family-run and serves hearty meals in a dining room with colorful
frescoed walls and an extensive menu of regional dishes. **Known for:**
Sauerkraut-Schupfnudeln (fried dough); liver dumplings; beer-soaked
beef tips. $ *Average main: €12 ✉ Ritterstr. 6 ☎ 08362/91600 ⊕ www.
hotel-hechten.com.*

$ ✗ **Markthalle.** In a building that opened in 1483 as the *Kornhaus* (grain
GERMAN storage) and then became the *Feuerhaus* (fire station), at this farmers'
market you can grab a quick lunch and a drink (or picnic supplies) at
reasonable prices. **Known for:** fish soup; good selection of food to-go;
Bavarian-style tapas. $ *Average main: €8 ✉ Schranneg. 12 ▭ No credit
cards ⊘ Closed Sun. No dinner.*

WHERE TO STAY

$$ 🏨 **Hotel Hirsch.** A family-run hotel right on main street pays homage
HOTEL to traditional Bavarian style with rooms uniquely decorated in trib-
ute to local sites—you can stay in the King Ludwig room, which has
pictures of him on the walls or a Spitzweg-decorated room based on
a Biedermeier-era artist who painted in Füssen. **Pros:** in the center of
town; good restaurant; some wheelchair-accessible rooms. **Cons:** front
rooms have street noise; pet-friendly so not allergy-free; evenings busy
with tour groups. $ *Rooms from: €120 ✉ Kaiser-Maximilian-Pl. 7
☎ 08362/93980 ⊕ www.hotelhirsch.de ↦ 71 rooms ❑ Free Breakfast.*

$$$ 🏨 **Schlossanger Alp.** A century of family tradition embraces guests at
B&B/INN this superb hotel combining the surroundings of a grand alpine hotel
FAMILY with the intimacy of a bed-and-breakfast. **Pros:** great food; updated
Fodor's Choice spa area; great for families. **Cons:** in the countryside, far from sights;
★ pet-friendly so not good for those with allergies; expensive. $ *Rooms
from: €219 ✉ Am Schlossanger 1, Pfronten ☎ 08363/914–550 ⊕ www.
schlossanger.de ↦ 35 rooms ❑ Free Breakfast.*

WIESKIRCHE

22 km (14 miles) north of Füssen, just outside of Steingaden.

Located among farmer's fields just off a rural highway, this popular
pilgrimage church in the village of Steingaden, a UNESCO World Heritage site, draws more than a million visitors annually. The mythology
surrounding the church has it that a local woman saw tears on the
face of Christ in a painting there, and then the church was designed to
accommodate pilgrims who wanted to bear witness to this miracle. An
outstanding example of the German rococo architecture that is prominent in Bavaria, it contains lavish frescoes depicting the life and death
of Christ and serves as the site of many gatherings by locals eager to
act out their traditions.

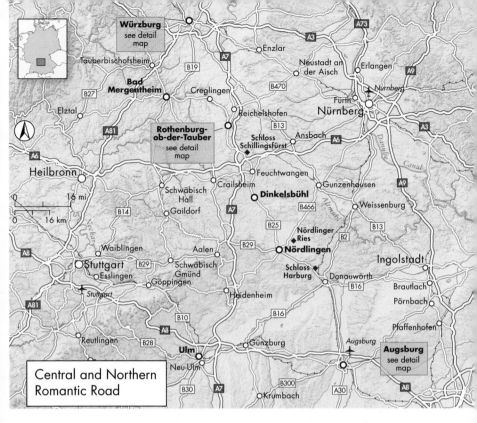

Central and Northern
Romantic Road

Buses 73 and 9651 leave from the train station in Füssen to Hohenste-
ingau and continue to Steingaden from 8 am through 2 pm; the journey
takes about 45 minutes (⊕ *www.rvo-bus.de* for detailed timetables and
to buy tickets).

Wieskirche. This church—a glorious example of German rococo architecture—stands in an Alpine meadow just off the Romantic Road. Its
yellow-and-white walls and steep red roof are set off by the dark backdrop of the Trauchgauer Mountains. The architect Dominicus Zimmermann, former mayor of Landsberg and creator of much of that town's
rococo architecture, built the church in 1745 on the spot where six years
earlier a local woman saw tears running down the face of a picture of
Christ. Although the church was dedicated as the Pilgrimage Church of
the Scourged Savior, it's now known simply as the Wieskirche (Church
of the Meadow). Visit it on a bright day if you can, when light streaming
through its high windows displays the full glory of the glittering interior.
A complex oval plan is animated by brilliantly colored stuccowork,
statues, and gilt. A luminous ceiling fresco completes the decoration.
Concerts are presented in the church from the end of June through the
beginning of August. ⊠ *Wies 12, Steingaden* ✢ *To get here from village
of Steingaden (22 km [14 miles] north of Füssen on B-17), turn east*

and follow signs to Wieskirche ☎ *8862/932–930* ⊕ *www.wieskirche. de* ✉ *Free (donations accepted)* ⊙ *Closed for tourists Sun. until 1 pm and during hrs of worship.*

AUGSBURG

70 km (43 miles) west of Munich.

Bavaria's third-largest city, Augsburg has long played a central role due to both its location and its religious history. It dates back to the Roman Empire, when in 15 BC a son of Augustus set up a military camp here on the banks of the Lech River. An important trading route, the Via Claudia Augusta, arose along the river connecting Italy to this silver-rich spot, and the settlement that grew up around it became known as Augusta, which is what Italians call the city to this day. The fashionable **Maximilianstrasse** lies on the Via Claudia Augusta, where the town's former wealth is still visible in its ornate architecture. City rights were granted Augsburg in 1156, and 200 years later, the Fugger family of bankers would become to Augsburg what the Medici were to Florence. Their wealth surpassed that of their Italian counterparts, and their influence is still felt throughout the city. It's easy to see the sights here, because signs on almost every street corner point the way to the main ones. See the tourist board's website for some additional walking-tour maps. You'll need a complete day to see Augsburg if you linger in any of the museums.

GETTING HERE AND AROUND

Augsburg is on a main line of the high-speed ICE trains, which run hourly and take 45 minutes to get here from Munich. The center of town and its main attractions can be visited on foot. To continue on the Romantic Road, take a regional train from the main train station to Ulm, Donauwörth, or Nördlingen.

VISITOR INFORMATION

Walking tours (€10) in English set out from the tourist office on the Rathaus square at 2 pm daily from April to October and on weekends November to March; there is an additional tour in German at 11 am. The tours include entrance to the Fuggerei and the Goldener Saal in the Rathaus.

Contacts Augsburg Tourist-Information. ✉ *Rathauspl. 1* ☎ *0821/324–9410* ⊕ *www.augsburg-tourismus.de.*

EXPLORING

FAMILY **Augsburg Puppenkiste.** This children's puppet theater next to Rotes Tor has been an institution in Germany from its inception in 1948, and it's still loved by kids and parents alike. The museum features puppets in historic or fairy-tale settings. Check the website for puppet-show times (held near-daily, though only in German). ✉ *Spitalg. 15* ☎ *0821/450–3450* ⊕ *www.augsburger-puppenkiste.de* ✉ *€5* ⊙ *Closed Mon.*

Dom St. Maria (*Cathedral of St. Mary*). Augsburg's cathedral contains the oldest cycle of stained glass in central Europe and five important

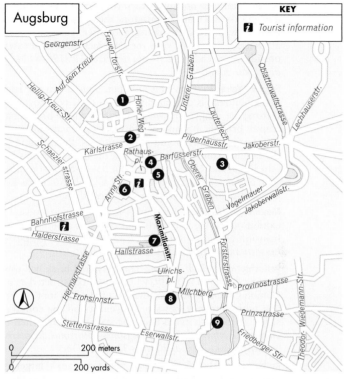

paintings by Hans Holbein the Elder, which adorn the altar. Originally built in the 9th century, the cathedral stands out because of its square Gothic towers, products of a 14th-century update. A 10th-century Romanesque crypt also remains from the cathedral's early years. Those celebrated stained-glass windows, from the 11th century, are on the south side of the nave, and depict the prophets Jonah, Daniel, Hosea, Moses, and David.

A short walk from the cathedral will take you to the quiet courtyards and small raised garden of the former episcopal residence, a series of 18th-century baroque and rococo buildings that now serve as the Swabian regional government offices. To the back of the cathedral at Kornhausg. 3–5 is the Diocese Museum of St Afra, where the cathedral's treasures are on display. ⊠ *Dompl., Johannisg. 8* ⊕ *www.museum-st-afra.de* ◰ *Cathedral free; museum €4* ⊘ *Museum closed Mon.*

Fuggerei and Fuggerhäuser. The world's oldest social housing project, this settlement was established by the wealthy Fugger family in 1516 to accommodate Augsburg's deserving poor. The 67 homes with 140 apartments still serve the same purpose and house about 150 people today. It's financed almost exclusively from the assets of the foundation, because the annual rent of "one Rhenish guilder" (€1) hasn't changed, either. Residents must be Augsburg citizens, Catholic, and destitute through no fault of their own—and they must pray three times daily for their original benefactors, the Fugger family. The most famous resident was Mozart's great-grandfather. You can view a showroom at Ochsengasse 51 or view the settlement from the exterior from the outside free of charge. ⊠ *Jakoberstr.* ☎ *0821/3198–8114* ⊕ *www.fugger. de* 🖼 *Museum €4.*

Fugger-Welser Museum. This museum, housed in a fine restored Renaissance building, is dedicated to two of the city's most influential benefactors, the Fugger and Welser families, whose banking and merchant empire brought Italian art and world artifacts along with wealth to Augsburg in the 15th and 16th centuries. Providing insight into how the families contributed to the city, the museum offers both a glimpse into life in the 15th century and a hands-on lesson in Augsburg history. ⊠ *Ausser Pfaffengässchen 23* ☎ *0821/502–070* ⊕ *www.fugger-und-welser-museum.de* 🖼 *€6* ☽ *Closed Mon.*

Maximilian Museum. Augsburg's main museum houses a permanent exhibition of Augsburg arts and crafts in a 16th-century merchant's mansion. ⊠ *Fuggerpl. 1* ☎ *0821/324–4102* ⊕ *www.kunstsammlungen-museen.augsburg.de* 🖼 *€9* ☽ *Closed Mon.*

Perlachturm (*Perlach Tower*). This plastered brick bell tower has foundations dating to AD 989, when it was constructed as a watchtower. Climbing the 258 stairs to the top of the 230-foot tower will provide you with gorgeous views of Augsburg and the countryside. Just be sure to time it to avoid being beneath the bells when they begin to chime. ⊠ *Rathauspl.* ⊕ *www.augsburg-tourismus.de/international* 🖼 *€2* ☽ *Closed Jan.–Apr., and Mon.–Thurs. in Dec.*

Rathaus. Augsburg's town hall was Germany's largest when it was built in the early 17th century; it's now regarded as the finest secular Renaissance structure north of the Alps. Its **Goldener Saal** (Golden Hall)—open to the public though closed during official city functions—was given its name because of its rich decoration: 8 pounds of gold are spread over its wall frescoes, carved pillars, and coffered ceiling. ⊠ *Rathauspl. 2* ⊕ *www.augsburg.de* 🖼 *€3.*

Sts. Ulrich and Afra. Standing at the highest point of the city, this Catholic basilica with an attached Protestant chapel symbolizes the Peace of Augsburg, the treaty that ended the religious struggle between the two groups. On the site of a Roman cemetery where St. Afra was martyred in AD 304, the original structure was built in the late-Gothic style in 1467. St. Afra is buried in the crypt, near the tomb of St. Ulrich, a 10th-century bishop who helped stop a Hungarian army at the gates of Augsburg in the Battle of the Lech River. The remains of a third patron of the church, St. Simpert, are preserved in one of the church's most elaborate side chapels. From the steps of the magnificent altar, look back along the high nave to the finely carved, wrought-iron-and-wood baroque railing that borders the entrance. As you leave, look into the separate but adjacent church of St. Ulrich, the baroque preaching hall that was added for the Protestant community in 1710, after the Reformation. ⊠ *Ulrichspl. 19* ⊕ *www.ulrichsbasilika.de* 🖼 *Free.*

Schaezlerpalais. This elegant 18th-century city palace was built by the von Liebenhofens, a family of wealthy bankers. Schaezler was the name of a baron who married into the family. Today the palace rooms contain the **Deutsche Barockgalerie** (German Baroque Gallery), a major art collection that features works of the 17th and 18th centuries. The palace adjoins the former church of a Dominican monastery. A steel door behind the banquet hall leads into another world of high-vaulted ceilings, where the **Staatsgalerie Altdeutsche Meister,** a Bavarian state collection, highlights old-master paintings, among them a Dürer portrait of one of the Fuggers. ✉ *Maximilianstr. 46* ☎ *0821/324–4102* 🌐 *www.kunstsammlungen-museen.augsburg.de* 🎟 *€7* 🕓 *Closed Mon.*

4

WHERE TO EAT

$$$ EUROPEAN Fodor's Choice ★

🍴 **Die Ecke.** On the small square behind the Augsburg town hall, this fine-dining restaurant offers an extensive wine list and an innovative, meat-heavy menu according to what's in season. In summer ask for a table on the patio. **Known for:** Zander fish fillet; seasonal venison dishes; rack of lamb. [$] *Average main: €21* ✉ *Elias-Holl-Pl. 2* ☎ *0821/510–600* 🌐 *www.restaurant-die-ecke.de* 🕓 *Closed Tues.*

$ GERMAN

🍴 **Ratskeller Augsburg.** In the cellar beneath the Rathaus is a popular local destination for Bavarian food and drink with a surprisingly airy feel. Lunches can be busy, as local workers head there for the wide array of traditional fare. **Known for:** Swabian specialties like Käsespätzle; panfried schnitzel; extensive cocktail menu. [$] *Average main: €12* ✉ *Ratshauspl. 2* ☎ *0821/3198–8238* 🌐 *www.ratskeller-augsburg.de* 💳 *No credit cards.*

WHERE TO STAY

$ HOTEL

🏨 **Dom Hotel.** Just around the corner from Augsburg's cathedral, this snug, quiet hotel has personality to spare, with a long history of hosting official church visitors, and an up-to-the-minute renovation that's provided good modern amenities. **Pros:** family-run, with good attention to detail; parking; nice view from upper rooms. **Cons:** stairs not wheelchair-friendly; no restaurant or bar; email response time can be slow. [$] *Rooms from: €99* ✉ *Frauentorstr. 8* ☎ *0821/343–930* 🌐 *www.domhotel-augsburg.de* 🛏 *52 rooms* 🍽 *Free Breakfast.*

$$$ HOTEL

🏨 **Steigenberger Drei Mohren Hotel.** Kings and princes, Napoléon, and the Duke of Wellington have all slept here, and these days all the rooms have been modernized and a spa area added without detracting from the 500-year-old building's traditional luxury. **Pros:** spacious lobby with inviting bar; good restaurants; spa amenities. **Cons:** can be booked out weekdays due to conventions; some rooms quite small; no air-conditioning. [$] *Rooms from: €200* ✉ *Maximilianstr. 40* ☎ *0821/50360* 🌐 *www.augsburg.steigenberger.de* 🛏 *131 rooms* 🍽 *Breakfast.*

ULM

85 km (53 miles) west of Augsburg.

Just off the Romantic Road, Ulm is worth a visit, if only briefly, to see its mighty Münster. The evangelical church is unusually ornate and has the world's tallest church tower (536 feet). Grown out of a medieval trading city thanks to its location on the Danube River, Ulm's Old Town is located directly on the river, which only adds to its charm. Each year, on the penultimate Monday in July—Schwörmontag—the townsfolk celebrate the mayor's "State of the Union" speech by parading down the Danube in homemade floating devices that make for a riotous sight. In the Fishermen's and Tanners' quarters the cobblestone alleys and stone-and-wood bridges over the Blau (a small Danube tributary) are especially picturesque. And down by the banks of the Danube, you'll find long sections of the old city wall and fortifications intact.

GETTING HERE AND AROUND

To get to Ulm from Augsburg, take A-8 west or take a 40-minute ride on one of the ICE (InterCity Express) trains that run to Ulm every hour.

TOURS

Ulm Tourist-Information Tours. The tourist office's 90-minute tours in German only include a visit to the Münster, the Old Town Hall, the Fischerviertel (Fishermen's Quarter), and the Danube riverbank. Offered twice-daily, the tours depart from the tourist office (Stadthaus) on Münsterplatz. For an English-speaking guide, book in advance or download the city's app to guide you. ⊠ *Ulm Tourist-Information, Münsterpl. 50* ☎ *0731/161–2830* ⊕ *www.tourismus.ulm.de* ⌨ *From €9.*

EXPLORING

Münster (*Minster*). Ulm's Minster, built by the citizens of their own initiative, is the largest evangelical church in Germany and one of the most elaborately decorated. Its church tower, just 13 feet higher than that of the Cologne Cathedral, is the world's highest, at 536 feet. It stands over the huddled medieval gables of Old Ulm with a single, filigree tower that challenges the physically fit to plod up the 768 steps of a spiral stone staircase to a spectacular observation point below the spire. On clear days, the steeple will reward you with views of the Swiss and Bavarian Alps, 100 miles to the south. Construction on the cathedral began in the late-Gothic age (1377) and took five centuries; it gave rise to the legend of the sparrow, which was said to have helped the townspeople in their building by inspiring them to pile the wood used in construction lengthwise instead of width-wise on wagons in order to pass through the city gates. Completed in the neo-Gothic years of the late 19th century, the church contains some notable treasures, including late-Gothic choir stalls and a Renaissance altar as well as images of the inspirational sparrow. Ulm itself was heavily bombed during World War II, but the church was spared. Its mighty organ can be heard in special recitals every Sunday at noon from Easter until November. ⊠ *Münsterpl. 21* ⊕ *www.ulmer-muenster.de* ⌨ *Free; tower €4.*

Climb the 258 steps of the Perlachturm (Perlach Tower) beside the Rathaus for a spectacular vantage point over Augsburg.

Rathaus. Built in 1370, the city hall maintains its original, opulently painted Renaissance facade despite its interior having been gutted by World War II bombs. Paintings depicting virtues, commandments, and vices dating back to the 1500s adorn the exterior and an astronomical clock to rival that in Prague was added in 1520. Still in official use, most of the interior is closed to tourists; however, inside hangs a reproduction of the local tailor Ludwig Berblinger's flying machine. In 1811 Berblinger, a local eccentric, cobbled together a pair of wings and made a big splash by trying to fly across the river. He didn't make it, but he grabbed a place in German history books for his efforts. ⊠ *Marktpl. 1* ⊕ *tourismus.ulm.de.*

Ulmer Museum (*Ulm Museum*). The recently discovered Löwenmensch, a 40,000-year-old figure of a half-man, half-lion found in a nearby cave, is the main attraction at this natural history and art museum, which also illustrates centuries of development in this part of the Danube Valley. Art lovers will appreciate its collection of works by such modern artists as Kandinsky, Klee, Léger, and Lichtenstein. ⊠ *Marktpl. 9* ☎ *0731/161–4330* ⊕ *www.museum.ulm.de* ⌨ *€8* ☉ *Closed Mon.*

WHERE TO EAT

$$
GERMAN

✕ **Zunfthaus der Schiffleute.** The sturdy half-timber Zunfthaus (Guildhall) has stood here for more than 500 years, first as a fishermen's pub and now as a charming tavern-restaurant. Ulm's fishermen had their guild headquarters here, and when the nearby Danube flooded, the fish swam right up to the door. **Known for:** Swabian cuisine like Maultaschen;

DID YOU KNOW?

Ulm's Münster has the world's highest church spire at 161 meters. You can climb the 768 steps to the top of the tower for views of Ulm and the Alps.

bratwurst and sauerkraut; Käsespätzle. $ *Average main: €15* ✉ *Fischerg. 31* ☎ *0731/64411* ⊕ *www.zunfthaus-ulm.de.*

$$
GERMAN
Fodor's Choice
★

✕ **Zur Forelle.** For more than 350 years Forelle (Trout) has stood over the small, clear River Blau, which flows through a large trout basin right under the restaurant. In addition to the trout, there are five other fish dishes available, as well as excellent venison in season. **Known for:** variations on trout; fresh Zander (pike-perch) fillets; beef tips. $ *Average main: €16* ✉ *Fischerg. 25* ☎ *0731/63924* ⊕ *www.zurforelle.com* ⊙ *Closed daily 2:30–5* ⊂ᵣ *Reserve in advance online.*

WHERE TO STAY

$
HOTEL

🏨 **Hotel am Rathaus/Reblaus.** Sister hotels (both family-owned) that are adjoined, the two buildings have unique decor; some of the rooms have vintage furniture, antique paintings, and dolls. **Pros:** location in heart of city; artistic touches; good value. **Cons:** no elevator; limited parking; not all rooms have a private en suite bath. $ *Rooms from: €98* ✉ *Kroneng. 8–10* ☎ *0731/968–490* ⊕ *www.rathausulm.de* ⊙ *Closed Christmas–early Jan.* ⤳ *34 rooms* ❍⏐ *Free Breakfast.*

$$
B&B/INN

🏨 **Hotel Restaurant Löwen.** Located a bit outside the city center, this converted monastery offers modern amenities to supplement small and simple, but comfortable, rooms. **Pros:** unique historical building; superb seasonal cuisine at restaurant; quiet, lovely terrace. **Cons:** a bit away from city center; books out quickly; some rooms have low ceilings. $ *Rooms from: €126* ✉ *Klosterhof 41* ☎ *0731/388–5880* ⊕ *www.hotel-loewen-ulm.de* ⤳ *20 rooms* ❍⏐ *Free Breakfast.*

NÖRDLINGEN

90 km (56 miles) northeast of Ulm, 72 km (45 miles) northwest of Augsburg.

In Nördlingen a medieval watchman's cry still rings out every night across the ancient walls and turrets. As in Rothenburg, its sister city, the medieval walls are completely intact, but here you can actually walk the entire circuit (about 4 km [2½ miles]) beginning at any of six original gates. Enjoy the peaceful atmosphere while taking in the riot of architecture, from the medieval to the Renaissance and the baroque, without the masses of tourists of its sister city. Or ask at the tourist office for accommodations in one of the small houses built into the city's wall for a unique overnight experience. The ground plan of the town is two concentric circles. The inner circle of streets, whose central point is St. Georg, marks the earliest medieval boundary. A few hundred yards beyond it is the outer boundary, a wall built to accommodate expansion. Fortified with 11 towers and punctuated by five massive gates, it's one of the best-preserved town walls in Germany. And if the Old Town looks a little familiar, it might be because the closing aerial shots in the 1971 film *Willy Wonka and the Chocolate Factory* were filmed over its red roofs.

Nördlingen was established along the same Roman road that goes through Augsburg, but its "foundation" goes much further back—the town is built in the center of a huge, basinlike depression, the Ries, which was at first believed to be the remains of an extinct volcano. In 1960 it was proven by two Americans that the crater, 24 km (15 miles) across, was caused by an asteroid at least 1 km (½ mile) in diameter that hit the spot some 15 million years ago. The compressed rock, or *Suevit,* formed by the explosive impact of the meteorite was used to construct many of the town's buildings, including St. Georg's tower.

GETTING HERE AND AROUND

About an hour's drive northwest from Ulm up the A-7, Nördlingen is also easily accessible from Donauworth via the B-25 by following the brown route signs directing you along the Romantic Road. During the week, a regional train can bring you from Donauworth into the city center twice-hourly; on weekends, the train runs every two hours.

VISITOR INFORMATION

Contacts Nördlingen Tourist-Information. ✉ *Marktpl. 2* ☎ *09081/84116* ⊕ *www.noerdlingen.de.*

EXPLORING

Nördlinger Ries. Nördlingen lies in the center of a huge, basinlike depression, the Ries, that until the beginning of this century was believed to be the remains of an extinct volcano. In 1960 it was proven by two Americans that the 24-km-wide (15-mile-wide) crater was caused by an asteroid at least 1 km (½ mile) in diameter. The compressed rock, or *Suevit,* formed by the explosive impact of the meteorite was used to construct many of the town's buildings, including St. Georg's tower. If you want, you can bike around the crater. ✉ *Dorfstr.* ✛ *9 km northeast of Nördlingen via B-466.*

Schloss Harburg. At the point where the little Wörnitz River breaks through the Franconian Jura Mountains, 20 km (12 miles) southeast of Nördlingen, you'll find one of southern Germany's best-preserved medieval castles. Schloss Harburg was already old when it passed into the possession of the counts of Oettingen in 1295; before that time it belonged to the Hohenstaufen emperors. The same family still owns the castle. The castle is on B-25, which runs under it through a tunnel in the rock. ✉ *Burg Str. 1, Harburg* ☎ *09080/96860* ⊕ *www.burg-harburg.de* 🎫 *Castle €5 (includes guided tour); garden from €3* ☉ *Closed Nov.–Easter.*

St. Georg's Church. Watchmen still sound out the traditional *So G'sell so* (All's well) message from the 300-foot tower of the central parish church of St. Georg at half-hour intervals between 10 pm and midnight. The tradition goes back to an incident during the Thirty Years' War, when an enemy attempted to slip into the town and was detected by a resident. You can climb the 365 steps up the tower—known locally as the Daniel—for an unsurpassed view of the town and countryside, including, on clear days, 99 villages. ✉ *Marktpl.* 🎫 *Tower €3.*

WHERE TO EAT

$ — Hotel Goldene Rose. A small, family-run hotel just inside the town
GERMAN wall is ideal for wholesome, inexpensive dishes and will happily fulfill
FAMILY special orders. Families feel welcome, and kids can roam the premises.
Known for: Franken bratwurst; roast beef; vegan dishes upon request.
$ *Average main: €12* ⊠ *Baldinger Str. 42* ☎ *09081/86019* ⊕ *www.*
goldene-rose-noerdlingen.de.

WHERE TO STAY

$ NH Kloesterle Hotel. Although part of the NH budget chain, this
HOTEL converted monastery within the city walls is less than monastic, with
FAMILY modern amenities, updated rooms, and two restaurants. **Pros:** unique
architecture; modern amenities; in the heart of the city. **Cons:** limited
street parking; no air-conditioning; some rooms are small. $ *Rooms*
from: €97 ⊠ *Beim Klösterle 1* ☎ *09081/87080* ⊕ *www.nh-hotels.com*
↝ *98 rooms* ⦿ *Free Breakfast.*

DINKELSBÜHL

32 km (20 miles) north of Nördlingen.

Within the walls of Dinkelsbühl, a beautifully preserved medieval town,
the rush of traffic seems a lifetime away. Although there is less to see
here than in Rothenburg, the town is a pleasant break from the crowds,
and you can relax among the locals at one of the Gasthauses in the
town's central Marktplatz. You can patrol the illuminated Old Town
with the night watchman at 9 pm free of charge, starting from the
Münster St. Georg.

When Dinkelsbühl was under siege by Swedish forces during the Thirty
Years' War and in imminent danger of destruction, a young girl led the
children of the town to the enemy commander and implored him in
their name for mercy. The commander of the Swedish army is said to
have been so moved by the plea that he spared the town. The story is
retold every year during the Kinderzech Festival, a children's pageant
that's held during a 10-day festival in July.

GETTING HERE AND AROUND

About 30 minutes' drive south of Würzburg on the Romantic Road,
Dinkelsbühl is best accessed by car, as it's right on the B-25. Once you
reach the city gates, however, the cobblestone streets are narrow, and
a maze of one-ways will have you lost in no time, so park outside one
of the city gates and walk.

VISITOR INFORMATION

Contacts Dinkelsbühl Tourist-Information. ⊠ *Marktpl., Altrathauspl. 14*
☎ *09851/902–440* ⊕ *www.dinkelsbuehl.de.*

EXPLORING

Minster St. Georg (*Cathedral St. George*). Dinkelsbühl's main church is the standout sight in town. At 235 feet long it's large enough to be a cathedral, and is among the best examples in Bavaria of the late-Gothic style. Note the complex fan vaulting that spreads sinuously across the ceiling. If you can face the climb, head up the 200-foot tower for amazing views over the jumble of rooftops any weekend that the weather allows. ✉ *Marktpl., Kirchhöflein 6* ☎ *09851/2245* 🌐 *www.st-georg-dinkelsbuehl.de* 🎫 *Free; tower €2* 🕒 *Closed Oct.–Apr.; closed weekdays May–Oct.*

WHERE TO EAT

$$ GERMAN 🍴 **Goldene Rose Restaurant.** Since 1450 visitors to Dinkelsbühl—among them Queen Victoria in 1891—have stopped at this half-timber house-turned-hotel, which has three distinct restaurants with menus that vary both in price and the complexity of offerings. Whereas the more upscale Ollmann's offers a five-course menu with dishes like foie gras, the more casual Zunftstube menu emphasizes fresh regional cuisine, especially fish and game alongside pastas and soups; the Bräustüberl, which is closed during winter months, has a pub menu. **Known for:** wild game in season; asparagus everything in spring; fresh fish. [$] *Average main: €19* ✉ *Hohtel Goldene Rose, Marktpl. 4* ☎ *09851/57750* 🌐 *www.hotel-goldene-rose.com.*

WHERE TO STAY

$$ HOTEL 🏨 **Hezelhof Hotel.** The upscale Hezelhof combines three charming, timber-frame buildings from the 16th century that are renovated inside to provide comfortable modern rooms with designer furnishings. **Pros:** quiet courtyard; some rooms have views of Minster; old Patrician House adds charm. **Cons:** parking and breakfast extra; pricey for area; facade looks historic, but interior is all modern. [$] *Rooms from: €129* ✉ *Segringer Str. 7* ☎ *09851/555–420* 🌐 *www.hezelhof.com* 🛏 *53 rooms* 🍽 *No meals.*

$$ HOTEL 🏨 **Hotel Deutsches Haus.** As you step into this medieval inn with a facade of half-timber gables and flower boxes, an old sturdy bar gives you a chance to register while sitting down and enjoying a drink. **Pros:** gorgeous historic building; views of church; great restaurant. **Cons:** some rooms noisy; service can be brusque; a few stairs. [$] *Rooms from: €129* ✉ *Weinmarkt 3* ☎ *09851/6058* 🌐 *www.deutsches-haus.net* 🛏 *18 rooms* 🍽 *Free Breakfast.*

ROTHENBURG-OB-DER-TAUBER

50 km (31 miles) north of Dinkelsbühl, 90 km (56 miles) west of Nuremberg.

Fodor's Choice ★ Rothenburg-ob-der-Tauber (literally, the "red castle on the Tauber") is the kind of medieval town that even Walt Disney might have thought too picturesque to be true, with half-timber architecture galore and

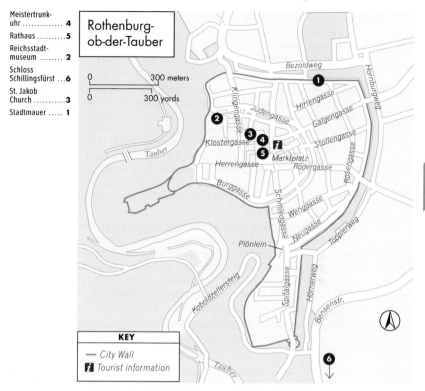

Rothenburg-
ob-der-Tauber

KEY

— *City Wall*

Tourist information

a wealth of fountains and flowers against a backdrop of towers and turrets. As late as the 17th century, it was a small but thriving market town that had grown up around the ruins of two 12th-century churches destroyed by an earthquake. Then it was laid low economically by the havoc of the Thirty Years' War, and with its economic base devastated, the town remained a backwater until modern tourism rediscovered it.

GETTING HERE AND AROUND

The easiest way to get here is via the Romantic Road bus from Augsburg via Donauwörth, Nördlingen, and Dinkelsbühl, with an optional layover on the way. If you arrive by car, there are large metered parking lots just outside the town wall. By local train it takes about 2½ hours from Augsburg, with two train changes. All attractions within the walled town can easily be reached on foot.

FESTIVALS

Der Meistertrunk Festspiel (*The Master Draught Historical Fest*). From Friday through Monday over Whitsun (Pentecost) weekend every year, the town celebrates the famous wager said to have saved it from destruction in 1631, at the height of the Thirty Years' War. A play of the events takes place every day, and handicraft and artisan markets, along with food stands, fill the town squares. ⊠ *Rothenburg ob der Tauber* ⊕ *www. meistertrunk.de.*

Reichsstadt Festage (*Imperial City Festival*). Locals in period costume gather in town over the first weekend in September to commemorate Rothenburg's being named Free Imperial City in 1274. Concerts are played throughout the city; the highlight is the Saturday fireworks show. ⊠ *Rothenburg ob der Tauber* ⊕ *www.meistertrunk.de.*

FAMILY **Schäfertanz** (*Shepherd's Dance*). A **Schäfertanz** (Shepherds' Dance) was once performed around the **Herterichbrunnen**, the ornate Renaissance fountain on the central Marktplatz, whenever Rothenburg celebrated a major event. Although its origins go back to local shepherds' annual gatherings, the dance is now celebrated with locals from the area costumed as maids, shepherds, soldiers, and nobility. It takes place in front of the Rathaus several times a year, chiefly at Easter, Pentecost, and in September as part of the Imperial City Festival. ⊠ *Am Marktpl., Rothenburg ob der Tauber* ⊕ *www.schaefertanzrothenburg.de.*

TOURS

Night Watchman Tour. A local legend, the costumed night watchman conducts a one-hour tour of the town nearly every night year-round, leading the way with a lantern. The tours, which run from Easter through Christmas, are offered in English at 8 pm at the Marktplatz or at 9:30 pm in German. ⊠ *Marktpl., Rothenburg ob der Tauber* ☏ *09861/404–800 tourist office* ⊕ *www.nightwatchman.de* ⌲ *€8.*

VISITOR INFORMATION

Contacts Rothenburg-ob-der-Tauber Tourist Information. ⊠ *Rathaus, Am Marktpl. 2, Rothenburg ob der Tauber* ☏ *09861/404–800* ⊕ *www.tourismus. rothenburg.de.*

EXPLORING

Meistertrunkuhr (*Master Draught Clock*). The tale of the Meistertrunk (Master Draught) and a prodigious civil servant dates to 1631, when the Protestant town was captured by Catholic forces during the Thirty Years' War. At the victory celebrations, the conquering general was embarrassed to find himself unable to drink a great tankard of wine in one go, as his manhood demanded. He volunteered to spare the town further destruction if any of the city councilors could drain the mighty six-pint draft. The mayor took up the challenge and succeeded, and Rothenburg was preserved. The tankard itself is on display at the Reichsstadtmuseum. On the north side of the main square is a fine clock, placed there 50 years after the mayor's feat. A mechanical figure acts out the epic Master Drink daily on the hour from 10 to 10. The feat is reenacted in the historical play "The Master Draught," and celebrated at the annual Meistertrunk festival. ⊠ *Am Marktpl., Rothenburg ob der Tauber.*

Rathaus. The heart of the city is the Rathaus, where a car-free square has become a gathering point with a great view. Half of the town hall is Gothic, begun in 1240; the other half is neoclassical, started in 1572, and renovated after its original facade was destroyed by a fire 500 years ago. You can climb the 220 stairs of the tower to get a good view of the Franken countryside. ⊠ *Rathauspl., Rothenburg ob der Tauber* ⊕ *www. rothenburg.de* ⌲ *Tower €3* ⊗ *Closed Jan.–Mar. Closed weekdays in Nov.*

FAMILY **Reichsstadtmuseum** (*Imperial Town Museum*). This city museum, in a former Dominican convent dating back to the 13th century, includes a cloister where one of the artifacts is the great tankard, or *Pokal,* of the Meistertrunk. A more recent addition, the Baumann Foundation, displays valuable weapons such as hunting weapons used by Marie Antoinette and a hunting rifle belonging to Frederick the Great of Prussia. ⊠ *Klosterhof 5, Rothenburg ob der Tauber* ☎ 09861/939–043 ⊕ *www. reichsstadtmuseum.rothenburg.de* 🖼€6.

FAMILY **Schloss Schillingsfürst.** This baroque castle of the Princes of Hohenlohe-Schillingsfürst is 20 km (12 miles) south of Rothenburg-ob-der-Tauber. Standing on an outcrop, it can be seen from miles away. You can watch eagles and falcons swoop down from high in the sky to catch their prey during one of the Bavarian falconry demonstrations held in the courtyard here, twice daily from April to October. ⊠ *Am Wall 14, Schillingsfürst* ☎ *09868/812* ⊕ *www.schloss-schillingsfuerst.de* 🖼 *From €5* ☾ *Closed Mon. Closed Nov.–Mar.*

St. Jakob Church. This Lutheran parish church, constructed from 1311 to 1485, showcases 600 years of stained-glass windows and has notable Riemenschneider sculptures, including the famous *Heiliges Blut* (Holy Blood of Christ) altar. Above the altar is a crystal capsule said to contain drops of Christ's blood. The Twelve Apostles Altar, by Friedrich Herlin, has the oldest depiction of the town of Rothenburg. ⊠ *Klosterg. 15, Rothenburg ob der Tauber* ☎ *09861/700–620* ⊕ *www.rothenburgtauber-evangelisch.de* 🖼 *Church free, audio guide €2.*

Stadtmauer (*City Wall*). Rothenburg's city walls are more than 4 km (2½ miles) long and dotted with 42 red-roofed watchtowers. Due to its age, only about half of the wall can be accessed on foot, but it provides an excellent way of circumnavigating the town from above. Let your imagination take you back 500 years as you explore the low, covered sentries' walkways, which are punctuated by cannons, turrets, and areas where the town guards met. Stairs every 200 or 300 yards provide ready access. There are superb views of the tangle of pointed and tiled red roofs and of the rolling country beyond. ⊠ *Stolleng. 8, Rothenburg ob der Tauber* ⊕ *www.rothenburg.de.*

WHERE TO EAT

$$ ✕ **Alter Keller.** On a side street, this guest house restaurant serves standard local cuisine but attracts a crowd thanks to its evening steak menu. The interior is traditional Bavarian and the family-run establishment has friendly personnel. **Known for:** wide assortment of steaks; venison goulash; pork schnitzel. 🛐 *Average main: €17* ⊠ *Alter Keller 8, Rothenburg ob der Tauber* ☎ *09861/2268* ⊕ *www.rothenburg-restaurant.de* ☾ *Closed Mon. and Tues.* ▭ *No credit cards.*

$$ ✕ **Restaurant-Zur Höll.** "To Hell" is in a building dating back to AD 900. With an extensive selection of Franconian wine and a delicious house beer, you'll have a nice late evening experience, but in summer be sure to reserve a table in advance. **Known for:** seasonal specialties, including delicious chanterelle mushroom soup; beef and pork platters; rack of lamb. 🛐 *Average main: €17* ⊠ *Burgg. 8, Rothenburg ob der Tauber* ☎ *098/614–229* ⊕ *www. hoell.rothenburg.de* ▭ *No credit cards* ☾ *Closed Sun. No lunch winter.*

WHERE TO STAY

$$ B&B/INN Fodor's Choice ★ 🏨 **Burg Hotel.** At this exquisite little hotel most rooms have a stunning, wide-angle view into the romantic Tauber Valley, and they also have plush furnishings, with antiques or fine reproductions. **Pros:** no crowds; terrific views from most rooms; plenty of parking. **Cons:** no restaurant; too quiet for kids; no air-conditioning. [$] *Rooms from: €165* ✉ *Klosterg. 1–3, Rothenburg ob der Tauber* ☎ *09861/94890* 🌐 *www.burghotel.eu* 🛏 *33 rooms* 🍴 *Free Breakfast.*

$$ HOTEL 🏨 **Hotel Eisenhut.** It's fitting that the prettiest small town in Germany should have one of the prettiest small hotels in its center. **Pros:** elegant lobby; exceptional service; good food. **Cons:** expensive; not for kids; breakfast not included. [$] *Rooms from: €100* ✉ *Herrng. 3–5/7, Rothenburg ob der Tauber* ☎ *09861/7050* 🌐 *www.eisenhut-rothenburg.com* 🛏 *78 rooms* 🍴 *No meals.*

$$ B&B/INN 🏨 **Hotel Reichs-Küchenmeister.** Master chefs in the service of the Holy Roman Emperor were the inspiration for the name of this historic hotel, occupying one of the oldest trader's houses in Rothenburg. **Pros:** central; excellent restaurant; well-kept. **Cons:** central location means it can get noisy from crowds of tourists; spa amenities extra; caters to tour groups. [$] *Rooms from: €118* ✉ *Kirchpl. 8, Rothenburg ob der Tauber* ☎ *09861/9700* 🌐 *www.reichskuechenmeister.com* 🛏 *45 rooms* 🍴 *Free Breakfast.*

$$ B&B/INN FAMILY 🏨 **Hotel-Restaurant Burg Colmberg.** East of Rothenburg, this 13th-century castle converted into a hotel maintains a high standard of comfort within its original medieval walls without sacrificing the atmosphere. **Pros:** romantic; you're staying in a real castle; antique furnishings. **Cons:** remote location; quite a few stairs to climb; can book out for weddings. [$] *Rooms from: €110* ✉ *An der Burgenstr., Colmberg* ✣ *18 km (11 miles) east of Rothenburg* ☎ *09803/91920* 🌐 *www.burg-colmberg.de* 🛏 *26 rooms* 🍴 *Free Breakfast.*

$$ B&B/INN 🏨 **Romantik Hotel Markusturm.** The Markusturm began as a 13th-century customs house, an integral part of the city defense wall, and has since developed over the centuries into an inn and staging post and finally into a luxurious small hotel. **Pros:** tasteful interior design; near the city gate; responsive owner. **Cons:** stairs, no elevator; some rooms under the eaves; central location can get loud with crowds of tourists. [$] *Rooms from: €145* ✉ *Röderg. 1, Rothenburg ob der Tauber* ☎ *09861/94280* 🌐 *www.markusturm.de* 🛏 *23 rooms* 🍴 *Free Breakfast.*

SHOPPING

Anneliese Friese. You'll find cuckoo clocks, beer tankards, porcelain, glassware, and much more at this old and atmospheric shop near the Rathaus, run by the delightful Anneliese herself. ✉ *Grüner Markt 7–8, Rothenburg ob der Tauber* ☎ *09861/7166.*

FAMILY **Käthe Wohlfahrt.** The Christmas Village part of this store is a wonderland of mostly German-made toys and decorations, particularly traditional ornaments. The Christmas museum, with a full history of the traditions over the centuries, is inside the store. ✉ *Herrng. 1, Rothenburg ob der Tauber* ☎ *09861/4090* 🌐 *www.wohlfahrt.com.*

With its half-timber houses, fountains, statues, and flowers, Rothenburg-ob-der-Tauber makes for great photo ops.

BAD MERGENTHEIM

24 km (15 miles) west of Creglingen.

Between 1525 and 1809, Bad Mergentheim was the home of the Teu-tonic Knights, one of the most successful medieval orders of chivalry. In 1809, Napoléon expelled them as he marched toward his ill-fated Russian campaign. The expulsion seemed to sound the death knell of the little town, but in 1826 a shepherd discovered mineral springs on the north bank of the river. They proved to be the strongest sodium sulfate and bitter spa waters in Europe, with supposedly health-giving properties that ensured the town's future prosperity as a health resort, which continues even today. Although soaking is on the agenda, it's the castle that's most worth your time due to its unique architecture.

GETTING HERE AND AROUND

A Deutsche Bahn train runs at least twice an hour from Würzburg and the journey takes nearly 50 minutes. By car, you can reach Bad Mer-gentheim either via the A-7 or by the more scenic B-19, which takes only about 10 minutes longer, depending on traffic.

VISITOR INFORMATION

Contacts Bad Mergentheim Tourist-Information. ⊠ *Marktpl. 1* ☎ *07931/57135* ⊕ *www.bad-mergentheim.de.*

EXPLORING

Deutschordensschloss. The Teutonic Knights' former castle, at the eastern end of the town, had its peak at from 1527 to 1809, when the highly influential and resident Deutschmeister received guests, including the Kaiser, here. Although it lost its luster after the Napoleonic wars, the medieval castle has remarkable architectural features: originally, a moated castle, the building was expanded beginning in 1568 and converted to a palace. Baroque features, including an intricately carved wooden staircase were added in the late 18th century. Post–World War II restoration work has converted the buildings into a museum that follows the history of the Teutonic Order. The castle also hosts classical concerts, lectures, and events for families and children. ✉ *Schloss 16* ☎ *07931/52212* 🌐 *www.deutschordensmuseum.de* 🎟 *From €6* 🕒 *Closed Mon.*

WHERE TO EAT

$$$$ GERMAN 🍴 **Weinstube Lochner.** Offering casual dining with white-table linens quality, the Weinstube offers a multicourse prix-fixe menu for lunch and dinner that features seasonal local products. They have both vegetarian and vegan offerings alongside fish and game. **Known for:** asparagus in season; venison dishes; cordon bleu, Lochner-style. [$] *Average main: €31* ✉ *Hauptstr. 39* ☎ *07931/9390* 🌐 *www.weinstube-lochner.de* 🕒 *Closed Mon.*

WÜRZBURG

200 km (124 miles) north of Ulm, 115 km (71 miles) east of Frankfurt.

Fodor's Choice ★ The baroque city of Würzburg, the pearl of the Romantic Road, shows what happens when great genius teams up with great wealth. Already a Celtic stronghold in 1000 BC, the city was founded as a bishopric in 742. Beginning in the 10th century, Würzburg was ruled by powerful (and rich) prince-bishops, who created the city with all the remarkable attributes you see today.

The city is at the junction of two age-old trade routes, in a calm valley backed by vineyard-covered hills. Festung Marienberg, a fortified castle on the steep hill across the Main River, overlooks the town. Constructed between 1200 and 1600, the fortress was the residence of the prince-bishops for 450 years.

Masterworks created by artists like Giovanni Battista Tiepolo abound in the city, including the Tilman Riemnschneider–designed tombstone of Prince-Bishop Rudolf von Scherenberg in the Romanesque St. Kilian church. The city is also home to the Residenz Palace, one of around 40 sites in Germany that has been recognized by UNESCO as a World Heritage site.

Present-day Würzburg is by no means completely original. On March 16, 1945, seven weeks before Germany capitulated, Würzburg was all but obliterated by Allied saturation bombing. The 20-minute raid destroyed 87% of the city and killed at least 4,000 people. Reconstruction has

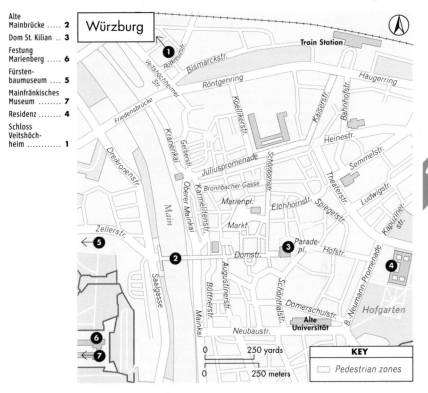

returned most of the city's famous sights to their former splendor. Except for some buildings with modern shops, it remains a largely authentic restoration.

GETTING HERE AND AROUND

Würzburg is on a main line of the superfast InterCity Express (ICE) trains, two hours from Munich and a bit more than an hour from Frankfurt. Most attractions in the old part of town are easily reached on foot. There's a bus to take you to Marienberg Castle, up on the hill across the river. A car is the best means of transportation if you want to continue your journey, but you can also use regional trains and buses.

FESTIVALS

Würzburg is well known for its wine festivals, with celebratory tastings held nearly every weekend at sites around the city and culminating with the Wine Parade in September. But wine isn't the only cultural connector here—there's a festival honoring Mozart's contributions to classical music every May and an annual jazz festival in November.

Mozartfest. The city of Würzburg hosts its annual Mozart Festival between May and July. More than 20 venues host events, but most concerts are held in the magnificent setting of the Residenz and feature world-class performers interpreting Mozart's works. Be sure to reserve

tickets early. ⊠ *Ticket Office, Rückermainstr. 2* ☏ *0931/372–336*
⊕ *www.mozartfest.de.*

Weindorf Würzburg (*Würzburg Wine Village*). During this annual festival, stands erected in the central square are stocked with wine and international foods in celebration of local agriculture. It's held the last week
in May and first week in June, with a kick-off ceremony at the Marien-
kapelle. ⊠ *Marktpl.* ☏ *0931/35170* ⊕ *www.weindorf-wuerzburg.de.*

Weinparade am Marktplatz. It is no surprise that a region known for its
wine and love of a good party has so many wine fests. This one, held
for a week in late August/early September, is the largest and one of the
best. More than 100 wineries gather on the Marktplatz and are joined
by some of the finest restaurants in the city. ⊠ *Marktpl.* ☏ *0931/35170*
⊕ *www.weinparade.de.*

TOURS

The tourist office maintains a thorough app that you can download for
a guided stroll through the Old Town. Or take a 40-minute City Train
ride and learn about the sites as you pass by them. The Würzburger
Schiffstouristik Kurth & Schiebe operates river excursions.

FAMILY **City Train Tour.** An English audio guide accompanies you on a 40-minute
ride on this tourist train, revealing both romantic and gruesome stories
from the city's history. Beginning at the Residenz, the train takes you
past all the major sites, including the Cathedral and the Castle of the
Thurn and Taxis. ⊠ *Residenz parking area, Balthasar Neumann Promenade* ☏ *09401/607–9977* ⊕ *www.city-tour.info* 🎫 *€9.*

Schiffstouristik Kurth & Schiebe. Departing from the Alte Kranen, 90-min-
ute boat tours along the Main River show you the city from a whole
new perspective; be sure to book in advance to ensure the tour takes
place. There are also day trips to Veitshöchheim (€9). ⊠ *Alter Kranen*
☏ *0931/58573* ⊕ *www.schiffstouristik.de* 🎫 *From €16 round-trip.*

VISITOR INFORMATION

Contacts Stadt Würzburg Tourist Information. ⊠ *im Falkenhaus am Markt*
☏ *0931/372–335* ⊕ *www.wuerzburg.de.*

EXPLORING

Alte Mainbrücke (*Old Main Bridge*). A stone bridge—Germany's first—
built in 1120 once stood on this site, over the Main River, but that
ancient structure was restored beginning in 1476. Twin rows of graceful
statues now line the bridge, placed here in 1730, at the height
of Würzburg's baroque period. They were largely destroyed in 1945, but
have been lovingly restored since then. Note the *Patronna Franconiae*
(commonly known as the Weeping Madonna). There's a beautiful view
of the Marienberg Fortress from the bridge. ⊠ *Würzburg.*

Dom St. Kilian (*St. Kilian Basilica*). Construction on Würzburg's Romanesque cathedral, the fourth-largest of its kind in Germany, began in
1045. Centuries of design are contained under one roof; the side wings
were designed in a late-Gothic style in the 16th century, followed by
extensive baroque stuccowork 200 years later. The majority of the

building collapsed in the winter following the bombing of the city near the end of World War II. Reconstruction, completed in 1967, brought a combination of modern design influences alongside a faithful restoration of the past thousand years of the church's history. Visit the side chapel designed by the baroque architect Balthasar Neumann, and a series of tombs of the bishops of Würzburg, designed by Tilman Riemenschneider. Tours (in German) are given daily at 12:30, mid-April through October. ⊠ *Domerpfarrg. 10* ☎ *0931/3866–2800* ⊕ *www.dom-wuerzburg.de* 🎫 *Free; guided tours €5.*

Festung Marienberg (*Marienberg Fortress*). This complex was the original home of the prince-bishops, beginning in the 13th century. The oldest buildings, including the **Marienkirche** (Church of the Virgin Mary) on the hilltop, date from around 700, although excavations have disclosed evidence that there was a settlement here in the Iron Age, 3,000 years ago. In addition to the rough-hewn medieval fortifications, there are a number of Renaissance and baroque apartments. Tours in English, held weekends at 3 pm, meet at the Pferdeschwemme. To reach the Marienberg, make the fairly steep climb on foot through vineyards or take Bus 9, starting at the Residenz, with several stops in the city. It runs about every 40 minutes from April to October. From April through October, tours around the fortress itself are offered, starting from the Scherenberg Tor. ⊠ *Oberer Burgweg* ⊕ *www.schloesser.bayern.de* 🎫 *Tours €4; museum from €5* 🕒 *Closed Mon., and Oct.–mid-Mar.*

Fürstenbaumuseum (*Princes' Quarters Museum*). The Marienberg collections are so vast that they spill over into another outstanding museum that's also part of the fortress. This one, the Fürstenbaumuseum, traces 1,200 years of Würzburg's history. The holdings include breathtaking exhibits of local goldsmiths' art. ⊠ *Festung Marienberg, Oberer Burgweg* ⊕ *www.schloesser.bayern.de* 🎫 *From €5.*

Mainfränkisches Museum (*Main-Franconian Museum*). A highlight of any visit to Festung Marienberg is likely to be this remarkable collection of art treasures. Be sure to visit the gallery devoted to Würzburg-born sculptor Tilman Riemenschneider (1460–1531). Also on view are paintings by Tiepolo and Cranach the Elder, as well as porcelain, firearms, antique toys, and ancient Greek and Roman art. Other exhibits showcase enormous old winepresses and narrate the history of Franconian wine making. ⊠ *Festung Marienberg, Oberer Burgweg* ☎ *0931/205–940* ⊕ *www.mainfraenkisches-museum.de* 🎫 *From €4* 🕒 *Closed Mon.*

Fodor'sChoice ★ **Residenz** (*Residence Palace*). Würzburg's prince-bishops lived in this baroque palace after moving down from the Festung Marienberg. Construction began in 1719 under Balthasar Neumann, who entrusted stuccowork to the Italian Antonio Bossi and Venetian painter Giovanni Battista Tiepolo. Thanks to their handiwork, the Residenz is considered one of Europe's most sumptuous palaces, though it was nearly completely destroyed by Allied bombing. Only a few rooms have been restored to their original glory, and you can view them on guided tours, which are held in English daily at 11 and 3 (starting in the **Vestibule**). The palace has the largest baroque staircase in the country; soaring above on the vaulting is Tiepolo's giant fresco *The Four Continents*,

The baroque Würzburg Residenz is a UNESCO World Heritage Site.

each quarter of which depicts the European outlook on the world in 1750—the savage Americas; Africa and its unusual creatures; cultured Asia, where learning and knowledge originated; and finally the perfection of Europe, with Würzburg as center of the universe. Then head to the grandest of the state rooms, the **Kaisersaal** (Throne Room) to glimpse Tiepolo's frescoes showing the 12th-century visit of Emperor Frederick Barbarossa to Würzburg to claim his bride. You'll also see private chambers of former residents and the reconstructed **Spiegelkabinett** (Mirror Cabinet). ⊠ *Residenzpl. 2* ☎ *0931/355–170* ⊕ *www. residenz-wuerzburg.de* 🖾 *€8; gardens free.*

Schloss Veitshöchheim. The first summer palace of the prince-bishops is 8 km (5 miles) north of Würzburg. Enlarged and renovated by Balthasar Neumann in 1753, the castle became a summer residence of the Bavarian kings in 1814. You reach the castle by walking down a long allée of trees on the extensive grounds. To your right are the "formal" rococo gardens, planned and laid out at the beginning of the 18th century. On the other side of the castle are the "utility" gardens, cared for by the Bavarian State College for Wines and Gardens. The college was founded here in 1902 as the Royal School for Gardening and Wine Culture. Walls, pavilions, a small lake teeming with fish, and gardens laden with fruit complete the picture of this huge park. From April to October fountains come to life every hour on the hour from 1 to 5. Inside the palace are the rooms of the Bavarian royal family, which can only be visited on the 30-minute guided tour, with a tour in German each hour. A bus service runs from Würzburg's Kirchplatz to the palace. From mid-April to mid-October there is also a boat operating between

Würzburg and the palace (daily 10–4). The 40-minute trip costs €9 round-trip. ✉ *Echterstr. 10, Veitshöchheim* ☎ *0931/915–82* 🌐 *www.schloesser.bayern.de* 🎟 *€5, including tour; gardens €2* ⏲ *Closed Mon., and mid-Oct.–Mar.*

WHERE TO EAT

$$ GERMAN 🍴 **Alte Mainmühle.** Sample Frankish bratwurst cooked over a wood grill and other regional dishes in this converted mill alongside the Main River. Sit outside on the terrace above the river for the best views of the Alte Mainbrücke and the Festung Marienberg. **Known for:** fresh trout; steak tartare; Frankische sauerbraten. [$] *Average main: €16* ✉ *Mainkai 1* ☎ *0931/16777* 🌐 *www.alte-mainmuehle.de* 💳 *No credit cards.*

$ GERMAN 🍴 **Backöfele.** More than 400 years of tradition are embedded in this old tavern, hidden away behind huge wooden doors on a back street. A surprisingly varied menu includes local favorites such as suckling pig and marinated pot roast, as well as good fish entrées, all at reasonable prices. **Known for:** veal tips; grandma's rouladen; cheese platters. [$] *Average main: €15* ✉ *Ursulinerg. 2* ☎ *0931/59059* 🌐 *www.backoefele.de.*

$$ GERMAN 🍴 **Juliusspital Weinstuben.** Giving a gastropub's twist to traditional Franconian fare, this restaurant is a draw for its private-label wines. While sampling local game and fish specialties, you can buy a bottle of wine to take home directly from the wait staff. **Known for:** veal schnitzel; bratwurst with sauerkraut; venison and wild game. [$] *Average main: €17* ✉ *Juliuspromenade 19, Ecke Barbarossapl.* ☎ *0931/54080* 🌐 *www.juliusspital-weinstuben.de* 💳 *No credit cards.*

$$ GERMAN 🍴 **Wein- und Speisehaus zum Stachel.** Have a seat in the ancient courtyard of the Stachel, which is shaded by a canopy of vine leaves and enclosed by tall, ivy-covered walls. The entrées are satisfyingly Franconian, from lightly baked onion cake to hearty roast pork served in a decidedly unstuffy atmosphere. **Known for:** fresh perch and trout; wild boar sausages; lamb's knuckle. [$] *Average main: €18* ✉ *Gresseng. 1* ☎ *0931/52770* 🌐 *www.weinhaus-stachel.de* 💳 *No credit cards* ⏲ *Closed Mon. No dinner Sun.*

WHERE TO STAY

$$ HOTEL 🏨 **Hotel Greifensteiner Hof.** The modern Greifensteiner offers comfortable, individually furnished rooms in a quiet corner of the city, just off the market square. **Pros:** center of town; excellent restaurants; nice bar. **Cons:** no spectacular views; parking extra; can be loud. [$] *Rooms from: €130* ✉ *Dettelbacherg. 2* ☎ *0931/35170* 🌐 *www.greifensteiner-hof.de* 🛏 *49 rooms* 🍽 *Free Breakfast.*

$$ HOTEL 🏨 **Hotel Rebstock zu Würzburg.** This hotel's rococo facade has welcomed guests for centuries, and inside, the rooms are all individually decorated and furnished in an English country-house style. **Pros:** historical building with modern amenities; quick access to the town's sights; attentive personnel. **Cons:** sometimes fills up with conferences and large groups; modern aesthetic lacks charm; some rooms have slanted ceilings. [$] *Rooms from: €140* ✉ *Neubaustr. 7* ☎ *0931/30930* 🌐 *www.rebstock.com* 🛏 *72 rooms* 🍽 *Free Breakfast.*

4

$$$ HOTEL **Schloss Steinburg.** Set atop vineyards and overlooking the towers of Würzburg, the Schloss Steinburg offers regal manor rooms as well as crisp and serene modern lodgings. **Pros:** beautiful views; nice variety of rooms; pool open year-round. **Cons:** outside the city center; can fill up with wedding parties; no air-conditioning. [$] *Rooms from: €210* ✉ *Mittlerer Steinburgweg 100* ☎ *0931/97020* 🌐 *www.steinburg.com* 💳 *No credit cards* 🛏 *69 rooms* 🍴 *Free Breakfast.*

SPORTS AND THE OUTDOORS

Stein-Wein-Pfad. Wine lovers and hikers should visit the Stein-Wein-Pfad, a signposted trail through the vineyards that rise up from the northwest edge of Würzburg. The starting point is the "info point" across from Weingut am Stein (Ludwig Knoll vineyard), 10 minutes on foot from the main train station. A two-hour round trip affords stunning views of the city as well as the chance to try the excellent local wines directly at the source. From May through mid-October, you can join a guided tour of the wineries in German every Saturday at 3 pm for €8, which includes a glass of wine. ✉ *Mittlerer Steinbergweg 5* ☎ *0931/946–00 Weingut Reiss* 🌐 *www.wuerzburger-steinweinpfad.de.*

5

FRANCONIA AND THE
GERMAN DANUBE

WELCOME TO FRANCONIA AND THE GERMAN DANUBE

TOP REASONS TO GO

★ **Bamberg's Altstadt:** This one isn't just for the tourists. Bamberg may be a UNESCO World Heritage Site, but it's also a vibrant town—the center of German brewing—living very much in the present.

★ **Vierzehnheiligen:** Just north of Bamberg, this church's swirling rococo decoration earned it the nickname "God's Ballroom."

★ **Nuremberg's Kaiserburg:** Holy Roman emperors once resided in the vast complex of this imperial castle, which has fabulous views over the entire city.

★ **Steinerne Brücke in Regensburg:** This 12th-century Stone Bridge was considered an amazing feat of engineering in its time.

★ **An organ concert in Passau:** You can listen to the mighty sound the 17,774 pipes of Dom St. Stephan's organ create at weekday concerts.

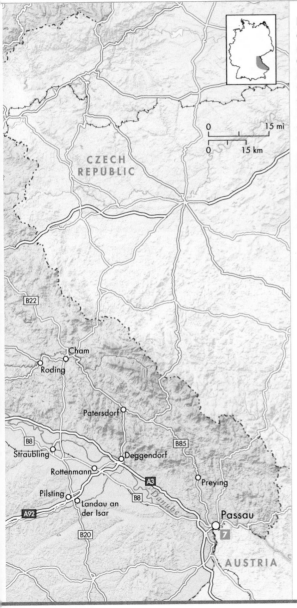

Franconia is seen as the dividing line between northern and southern Germany; below the Danube, which defintes the region as it passes through the Bavarian Forest toward Austria, is where Bavaria begins. West of Regensburg, river cruises and cyclists follow its path.

1 Coburg. The seat of the Saxe-Coburg-Gotha dynasty of whom Albert (husband of Victoria) is perhaps the best known member.

2 Bayreuth. Famous for its music and most famous resident, Richard Wagner; there's still an annual Wagner festival.

3 Bamberg. Built on seven hills, its Altstadt is a UNESCO World Heritage Site.

4 Bad Staffelstein. The small town has a famous abbey and rococo church.

5 Nuremberg (Nürnberg). Franconia's main city is full of history.

6 Regensburg. The medieval Old Town and its magnificent cathedral survived World War II.

7 Passau. The Old Town stands uniquely at the confluence of three rivers.

GERMANY'S CHRISTMAS MARKETS

Few places in the world do Christmas as well as Germany, and the country's Christmas markets, sparkling with white fairy lights and rich with the smells of gingerbread and mulled wine, are marvelous traditional expressions of yuletide cheer.

Following a centuries-old tradition, more than 2,000 *Weihnachtsmärtke* spring up outside town halls and in village squares across the country each year, their stalls brimming with ornate tree decorations and handmade pralines. Elegant rather than kitsch, the markets last the duration of Advent—the four weeks leading up to Christmas Eve—and draw festive crowds to their bustling lanes, where charcoal grills sizzle with sausages and cinnamon and spices waft from warm ovens. Among the handcrafted angels and fairies, kids munch on candy apples and ride old-fashioned carousels while their parents shop for stocking stuffers and toast the season with steaming mugs of *Glühwein* and hot chocolate.

—Jeff Kavanagh

(above and lower right) You can purchase handmade ornaments at the atmospheric Nürnberg Christkindlesmarkt. (upper right) The Spandau Christmas market is one of 60 in Berlin.

GLÜHWEIN

The name for hot spiced wine literally means "glowing wine" and a few cups of it will definitely add some color to your cheeks. It can be made from mulled red (the more popular) or white wine. Glühwein can be fortified with a *Schuss*, or shot of schnapps. *Feuerzangenbowle*, a supercharged version, is made by burning a rum-soaked sugar cone that drips caramelized sugar into the wine.

Dating from the late Middle Ages, Christmas markets began as a way to provide people with winter supplies; families came for the sugary treats and Christmas shopping. Now a bit more touristy, a visit to a traditional Christmas market is still a quintessential German experience. Starting on the first Sunday of Advent, the pace of life slows down when the cheerful twinkling lights are lit and the smell of hot wine lingers in the air, promising respite during the drab winter.

The most famous markets are in **Nuremberg** and **Dresden**, each drawing more than 2 million visitors every year. While these provide the essential market experience, it's well worth visiting a market in a smaller town to soak in some local flavor. **Erfurt's** market, set on the Cathedral Square, is the most picturesque. **Berlin's** immigrant communities offer themed markets on weekends, most notably the Hannumas Markt at the Jewish Museum or the Finnish Christmas Market in Templehof. No matter which you choose, keep in mind that the best time to visit is during the week when the crowds are the smallest; try to go in the early evening, when locals visit the markets with their friends and family. You'll experience a carnival-like atmosphere and won't be able to resist trying a mulled wine before heading home.

Despite the market theme, the real reason to visit is to snack on greasy, sweet, and warm market food. Each market has its own specialties—gingerbread in Nuremberg and stollen in Dresden—but the thread through all is candied almonds, warm chestnuts, and local sausages. Be sure to pair your snacks with a cup of hot spiced wine, which is served in small mugs that make great souvenirs. The wine varies from region to region, and special hot white wine is a trendy alternative. Other drinks include a warm egg punch, hot chocolate, and warm berry juices for children.

TIPS FOR VISITING

Always ask for local goods. Craftspeople, especially from the Ore Mountains in Saxony, produce some of the finest smoking-man incense burners, nativity scenes, candle pyramids, glass balls, and advent stars in the world.

Think about how you're getting your purchases home. Although some larger vendors will ship your purchases for you, it's wise to plan some extra baggage space and purchase some bubble wrap.

Dress warmly and wear comfortable shoes. All markets are outside, and even the smallest require walking.

Bring some small bills and coins. This will make food and wine transactions faster. Plastic dishes and cups require a deposit, which is refunded to you when you return the items.

5

Updated by
Lee A. Evans

All that is left of the huge, ancient kingdom of the Franks is the region known today as Franken (Franconia), stretching from the Bohemian Forest on the Czech border to the outskirts of Frankfurt. The Franks were not only tough warriors but also hard workers, sharp tradespeople, and burghers with a good political nose. The word *frank* means bold, wild, and courageous in the old Frankish tongue. It was only in the early 19th century, following Napóleon's conquest of what is now southern Germany, that the area was incorporated into northern Bavaria.

Although more closely related to Thuringia, this historic homeland of the Franks, one of the oldest Germanic peoples, is now begrudgingly part of Bavaria. Franconian towns such as Bayreuth, Coburg, and Bamberg are practically places of cultural pilgrimage. Rebuilt Nuremberg (Nürnberg in German) is the epitome of German medieval beauty, though its name recalls both the Third Reich's huge rallies at the Zeppelin Field and its henchmen's trials held in the city between 1945 and 1950.

Franconia is hardly an overrun tourist destination, yet its long and rich history, its landscapes and leisure activities (including skiing, golfing, hiking, and cycling), and its gastronomic specialties place it high on the enjoyment scale. Franconia is especially famous for its wine and for the fact that it's home to more than half of Germany's breweries.

MAJOR REGIONS

In **Northern Franconia,** three major German cultural centers lie within easy reach of one another, and you can easily take a detour to one of Germany's beer capitals: **Coburg,** a town with blood links to royal dynasties throughout Europe; **Bayreuth** is where composer Richard Wagner finally settled, making it a place of musical pilgrimage for Wagner fans from all over the world; and **Bamberg,** with its own claim to German royal history and an Old Town area designated a UNESCO World Heritage Site.

Nuremberg is Franconia's most important city and one of the most historic in Germany. There's plenty to see and do, and if you're here during the Christmas season, the Christkindelmarkt here is Europe's largest.

For many people, the sound of the Danube River (Donau in German) is the melody of *The Blue Danube,* the waltz written by Austrian Johann Strauss. The famous 2,988-km-long (1,857-mile-long) river, which is actually a pale green, originates in Germany's Black Forest and flows through 10 countries. The **German Danube** is mostly a rather unremarkable stream as it passes through cities such as Ulm on its southeasterly route. However, that changes at Kelheim, just west of **Regensburg,** where the Main–Donau Canal (completed in 1992) brings big river barges all the way from the North Sea. The river becomes sizable in Regensburg, where the ancient Steinerne Brücke (Stone Bridge) needs 15 spans of 30–48 feet each to bridge the water. Here everything from small pleasure boats to cruise liners joins the commercial traffic. In the university town of **Passau,** two more rivers join the waters of the Danube before Europe's longest river continues into Austria.

5

PLANNING

WHEN TO GO

Summer is the best time to explore Franconia, though spring and fall are also fine when the weather cooperates. Avoid the cold and wet months from November to March; many hotels and restaurants close, and no matter how pretty, many towns do seem quite dreary. If you're in Nuremberg in December, you're in time for one of Germany's largest and loveliest Christmas markets. Unless you plan on attending the Wagner Festival in Bayreuth, it's best to avoid this city in July and August.

PLANNING YOUR TIME

Nuremberg warrants at least a day of your time. It's best to base yourself in one city and take day trips to others. Bamberg is the most central of the northern Franconia cities and makes a good base. It is also a good idea to leave your car at your hotel and make the trip downstream to Regensburg or Passau by boat, returning by train.

GETTING HERE AND AROUND

AIR TRAVEL

The major international airport serving Franconia and the German Danube is Munich. Nuremberg's airport is served mainly by regional carriers.

Contacts Airport Nürnberg. ✉ *Flughafenstr. 100, Nürnberg* ☎ *0911/93700* ⊕ *www.airport-nuernberg.de.*

CAR TRAVEL

Franconia is served by five main autobahns: A-7 from Hamburg, A-3 from Cologne and Frankfurt, A-81 from Stuttgart, A-6 from Heilbronn, and A-9 from Munich. Nuremberg is 167 km (104 miles) north of Munich and 222 km (138 miles) southeast of Frankfurt. Regensburg and Passau are reached by way of the A-3 from Nuremberg.

CRUISE TRAVEL

Rising from the depths of the Black Forest and emptying into the Black Sea, the Danube is the queen of rivers; cloaked in myth and legend, it cuts through the heart and soul of Europe. The name Dānuvius, borrowed from the Celts, means swift or rapid, but along the Danube, there is no hurry. Boats go with the flow, and a river journey is a relaxed affair with plenty of time to drink in the history.

Whether you choose a one-hour, one-week, or the complete Danube experience, cruising Europe's historical waterway is a never-to-be-forgotten experience. On the map, the sheer length of the Danube is daunting at best; of the river's 2,848-km (1,770-mile) length, more than 2,400 km (1,500 miles) is navigable and the river flows through some of Europe's most important cities. You can head to major boating hubs, like Passau, Vienna, and Budapest or through historical stretches from Ulm to Regensburg.

The most interesting time to cruise the Danube is during the summer, when the river is abustle with passenger and commercial traffic. When the leaves start to change the river is awash in a sea of color, making autumn the most picturesque time to cruise. Many companies offer Christmas market tours from Nuremberg to Regensburg, Passau, Vienna, and Budapest. Spring is the least optimal time to go as the river often floods. You can board cruises from Passau, Regensburg, and Nuremberg among others with companies like Viking River Cruises, Uniworld, Tauck, AMA Waterways, and Crystal River Cruises.

Donauschifffahrt Wurm & Noe. This cruise line offers half a dozen day cruises through Franconia and the German Danube. With departures from Passau and Regensburg, boats travel to destinations up and down the Danube and the Ilm, especially to Valhalla and as far away as Linz in Austria ⊠ *Höllg. 26, Passau* ☎ *851/929–292* ⊕ *www. donauschifffahrt.eu.*

Regensburger Personen-Schifffahrt Klinger. With departures from Regensburg, Klinger serves the Danube basin with short excursions and longer trips. The highlight of the fleet is a medieval wooden cargo ship, rebuilt with the modern conveniences. ⊠ *Werftstr. 6, Regensburg* ☎ *941/52104* ⊕ *www.schifffahrtklinger.de.*

TRAIN TRAVEL

Franconia has one of southern Germany's most extensive train networks and almost every town is connected by train. Nuremberg is a stop on the high-speed InterCity Express (ICE) north–south routes, and there are hourly trains from Munich direct to Nuremberg. Regular InterCity services connect Nuremberg and Regensburg with Frankfurt and other major German cities. Trains run hourly from Frankfurt to Munich, with a stop at Nuremberg. The trip takes about three hours to Munich, two hours to Nuremberg. There are hourly trains from Munich to Regensburg.

Some InterCity Express trains stop in Bamberg, about midway between Berlin and Munich. Local trains from Nuremberg connect with Bayreuth and areas of southern Franconia. Regensburg and Passau are on the ICE line from Nuremberg to Vienna.

HOTELS

Make reservations well in advance for hotels in all the larger towns and cities if you plan to visit anytime between June and September. During the Nuremberg Toy Fair at the beginning of February, rooms are at a premium. If you're visiting Bayreuth during the annual Wagner Festival in July and August, consider making reservations up to a year in advance. Remember, too, that during the festival prices can be double the normal rates.

RESTAURANTS

Many restaurants in the rural parts of this region serve hot meals only between 11:30 am and 2 pm, and from 6 to 9 pm. ■ TIP→ **"Durchgehend warme Küche" means that hot meals are also served between lunch and dinner.**

Prices in dining reviews are the average cost of a main course at dinner, or if dinner is not served, at lunch. Prices in hotel reviews are the lowest cost of a standard double room in high season.

WHAT IT COSTS IN EUROS				
	$	**$$**	**$$$**	**$$$$**
Restaurants	under €15	€15–€20	€21–€25	over €25
Hotels	under €100	€100–€175	€176–€225	over €225

VISITOR INFORMATION

Franconia Tourist Board. ⊠ *Tourismusverband Franken e.V., Wilhelminenstr. 6, Nürnberg* ☎ *0911/941–510* ⊕ *www.frankentourismus.de.*

COBURG

105 km (65 miles) north of Nuremberg.

Coburg is a surprisingly little-known treasure in Northern Franconia that was founded in the 11th century and remained in the possession of the dukes of Saxe-Coburg-Gotha until 1918; the current duke still lives here. The remarkable Saxe-Coburg dynasty established itself as something of a royal stud farm, providing a seemingly inexhaustible supply of blue-blood marriage partners to ruling houses the length and breadth of Europe. The most famous of these royal mates was Prince Albert (1819–61), who married the English Queen Victoria, after which she gained special renown in Coburg. Their numerous children, married off to other kings, queens, and emperors, helped to spread the tried-and-tested Saxe-Coburg influence even farther afield. Despite all the history that sweats from each sandstone ashlar, Coburg is a modern and bustling town.

GETTING HERE AND AROUND

It takes a little more than an hour to drive to Coburg from Nuremberg, via A-73, or about 1¾ hours on the regional train service, which runs regularly throughout the day and costs €20–€25 one-way. Bus 29 runs twice-daily from Nuremberg's central bus station and takes two hours, with prices starting at €8 one-way.

FESTIVALS

Brazilian Samba Festival. In 1994 organizers Rolf Beyersdorf and Christof Pilarzyk had, in their own words, a "crazy idea" that has since become a huge three-day festival with more than 3,000 Sambistas. This weekend bacchanal, with food, drink, and dancing, is held in mid-July. ⊠ *Coburg* ☎ *09561/705–370* ⊕ *www.samba-festival.de.*

VISITOR INFORMATION

Contacts Tourismus Coburg. ⊠ *Herrng. 4* ☎ *09561/898–000* ⊕ *www.coburg-tourist.de.*

EXPLORING

Marktplatz (*Market Square*). A statue of Prince Albert, Victoria's high-minded consort, is surrounded by gracious Renaissance and baroque buildings in the Marktplatz. The **Stadhaus,** former seat of the local dukes, begun in 1500, is the most imposing structure here, with a forest of ornate gables and spires projecting from its well-proportioned facade. Opposite is the **Rathaus** (Town Hall). Look on the building's tympanum for the statue of the Bratwurstmännla (it's actually St. Mauritius in armor); the staff he carries is said to be the official length against which the town's famous bratwursts are measured. These tasty sausages, roasted on pinecone fires, are available on the market square. ⊠ *Coburg.*

Schloss Callenberg. Perched on a hill 5 km (3 miles) west of Coburg, this was, until 1231, the main castle of the Knights of Callenberg. In the 16th century it was taken over by the Dukes of Coburg. From 1842 on it served as the summer residence of the hereditary Coburg prince and later Duke Ernst II. It holds a number of important collections, including that of the Windsor gallery; arts and crafts from Holland, Germany, and Italy from the Renaissance to the 19th century; precious baroque, Empire, and Biedermeier furniture; table and standing clocks from three centuries; a selection of weapons; and various handicrafts. The best way to reach the castle is by car via Baiersdorf. City Bus No. 5 from Coburg's Marktplatz stops at the castle only on Sunday; on other days you need to get off at the Beirsdorf stop and walk for 25 minutes. ⊠ *Callenberger Str. 1* ☎ *09561/55150* ⊕ *www.schloss-callenberg.de* 🖾 *€5* ⊗ *Closed Mon.*

Schloss Ehrenburg. Prince Albert spent much of his childhood in this ducal palace. Built in the mid-16th century, it has been greatly altered over the years, principally following a fire in the early 19th century. Duke Ernst I invited Karl Friedrich Schinkel from Berlin to redo the palace in the then-popular neo-Gothic style. Some of the original Renaissance features were kept. The rooms of the castle are quite special, especially those upstairs, where the ceilings are heavily decorated with stucco and the floors have wonderful patterns of various woods. The Hall of Giants is named for the larger-than-life caryatids that support the ceiling; the favorite sight downstairs is Queen Victoria's flush

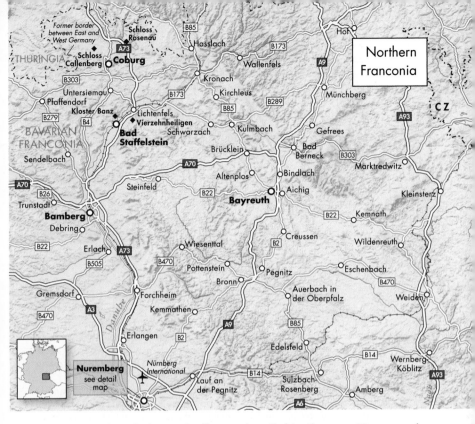

Nuremberg
see detail
map

toilet, which was the first one installed in Germany. Here, too, the ceiling is worth noting for its playful, gentle stuccowork. The baroque chapel attached to Ehrenburg is often used for weddings. ⌧ *Schlosspl. 1* ☎ *09561/80880* ⏣ *www.sgvcoburg.de* ⌦ *€5; combined ticket with Schloss Rosenau €7* ☺ *Closed Mon.*

Schloss Rosenau. Near the village of Rödental, 9 km (5½ miles) northeast of Coburg, the 550-year-old Schloss Rosenau sits in all its neo-Gothic glory in the midst of an English-style park. Prince Albert was born here in 1819, and one room is devoted entirely to Albert and his queen, Victoria. Much of the castle furniture was made especially for the Saxe-Coburg family by noted Viennese craftsmen. In the garden's Orangerie is the **Museum für Modernes Glas** (Museum of Modern Glass), which displays nearly 40 years' worth of glass sculptures (dating from 1950 to 1990) that provide an interesting juxtaposition with the venerable architecture of the castle itself. ⌧ *Rosenau 1, Rödental* ☎ *09563/1606* ⏣ *www.kunstsammlungen-coburg.de* ⌦ *From €3* ☺ *Closed Mon.*

Fodor's Choice ★ **Veste Coburg.** This fortress, one of the largest and most impressive in the country, is Coburg's main attraction. The brooding bulk of the castle guards the town from a 1,484-foot hill. Construction began around 1055, but with progressive rebuilding and remodeling today's predominantly late Gothic–early Renaissance edifice bears little resemblance to the original crude fortress. One part of the castle harbors the **Kunstsammlungen,** a grand set of collections including art, with works by Dürer, Cranach, and Hans Holbein, among others; sculpture from the school of the great Tilman Riemenschneider (1460–1531); furniture and textiles; magnificent weapons, armor, and tournament garb spanning four centuries (in the so-called **Herzoginbau,** or Duchess's Building); carriages and ornate sleighs; and more. The room where Martin Luther lived for six months in 1530 while he observed the goings-on of the Augsburg Diet has an especially dignified atmosphere. The **Jagdintarsien-Zimmer** (Hunting Marquetry Room), an elaborately decorated room that dates back to the early 17th century, has some of the finest woodwork in southern Germany. Finally, there's the **Carl-Eduard-Bau** (Carl-Eduard Building), which contains a valuable antique glass collection, mostly from the baroque age. Inquire at the ticket office for tours. ✉ *Festungshof* ☎ *09561/8790* 🌐 *www.kunstsammlungen-coburg.de* 🎫 *From €6* ⏲ *Closed Mon. Nov.–Mar.*

WHERE TO STAY

$ HOTEL 🏨 **Goldene Rose.** One of the region's oldest, this simple pleasant inn with modern rooms and a popular summer beer garden is in a small village about 5 km (3 miles) southeast of Coburg. **Pros:** family run; very good value; large parking lot behind the hotel. **Cons:** in a small village; front rooms overlooking the beer garden can be noisy; rooms plainly decorated. [$] *Rooms from: €55* ✉ *Coburgerstr. 31* ☎ *09560/92250* 🌐 *www.goldene-rose.de* 🛏 *14 rooms* 🍴 *Free Breakfast.*

$$ HOTEL 🏨 **Romantic Hotel Goldene Traube.** Rooms are individually decorated in this fine historical hotel (1756), and for dining you can choose between the elegant restaurant Esszimmer or the more casual Meer und Mehr (Sea and More), which serves fine seafood and regional specialties. **Pros:** welcoming, spacious lobby; two good restaurants and nice small wine shop; center of town. **Cons:** traffic noise in front rooms; stairs up to the lobby; some rooms allow smoking. [$] *Rooms from: €160* ✉ *Am Viktoriabrunnen 2* ☎ *09561/8760* 🌐 *www.goldenetraube.com* 🛏 *68 rooms* 🍴 *Free Breakfast.*

SHOPPING

Coburg is full of culinary delights; its *Schmätzen* (honey gingerbread) and *Elisenlebkuchen* (almond gingerbread cake) are famous. You'll find home-baked versions in any of the many excellent patisseries or at a Grossman store (there are three in Coburg).

Hummel Museum Store. Rödental, northeast of Coburg, is the home of the world-famous M. I. Hummel figurines. There's a Hummel Museum devoted to them, with 18th- and 19th-century porcelain from other manufacturers. Besides the museum's store, there are several retail outlets in the village. ✉ *Coburgerstr. 7, Rödental* ☎ *09563/92303* 🌐 *www.mihummel.de.*

BAYREUTH

24 km (15 miles) south of Kulmbach, 80 km (50 miles) northeast of Nuremberg.

The small town of Bayreuth (pronounced "bye- *roit*") owes its fame to the music giant Richard Wagner (1813–83). The 19th-century composer, musical revolutionary, ultranationalist, and Nazi poster child finally settled here after a lifetime of rootless shifting through Europe. Here he built his great theater, the Festspielhaus, as a suitable setting for his grand operas on Germanic mythological themes. The annual Wagner Festival dates to 1876, and brings droves of Wagner fans who push prices sky-high, fill hotels to bursting, and earn themselves much-sought-after social kudos in the process. The festival is held from late July until late August, so unless you plan to visit the town specifically for it, this is the time to stay away.

GETTING HERE AND AROUND

To reach Bayreuth, take the Bayreuth exit off the Nuremberg–Berlin autobahn. It's 1½ hours north of Nuremberg. The train trip is an hour from Nuremberg and costs from €33 one-way. In town you can reach most points on foot.

VISITOR INFORMATION

Contacts Bayreuth Kongress- und Tourismuszentrale. ⊠ *Luitpoldpl. 9* ☏ *0921/88588* ⊕ *www.bayreuth.de.*

EXPLORING

Bier Erlebnis Welt (*Beer Experience World*). Near the center of town, in the 1887 Maisel Brewery building, this brewery reveals the tradition of brewing over the past two centuries with a focus on the Maisel's trade in the Brewery Museum. The brewery operated here until 1981, when its much bigger current home was completed next door. After the 90-minute tour, which is offered daily at 2 and 6 pm, you can quaff a cool, freshly tapped traditional Bavarian *Weissbier* (wheat beer) in the museum's pub. The pub is also one of a handful of places to try Maisel & Friends Craft Beer, including the Citrilla Wheat, an experimental wheat-based IPA. ⊠ *Kulmbacherstr. 40* ☏ *0921/401–234* ⊕ *www. maisel.com* ⊠ *€8.*

Festspielhaus (*Festival Theater*). This high temple of the Wagner cult—where performances take place only during the annual Wagner Festival—is surprisingly plain. The spartan look is explained partly by Wagner's desire to achieve perfect acoustics. The wood seats have no upholstering, for example, and the walls are bare. The stage is enormous, capable of holding the huge casts required for Wagner's largest operas. The festival is still meticulously controlled by Wagner's family. You can see the theater on a guided tour except during Festival season. ⊠ *Festspielhügel 1* ☏ *0921/78780* ⊕ *www.bayreuther-festspiele.de* ⊠ *€7* ⊘ *No tours during Festival season (usually June–Aug.).*

Markgräfliches Opernhaus (*Margravial Opera House*). In 1745 Margravine Wilhelmine commissioned the Italian architects Giuseppe and

Carlo Bibiena to build this rococo jewel, sumptuously decorated in red, gold, and blue. Apollo and the nine Muses cavort across the baroque frescoed ceiling. It was this delicate 500-seat theater that originally drew Wagner to Bayreuth; he felt that it might prove a suitable setting for his own operas. In fact, it's a wonderful setting for the concerts and operas of Bayreuth's "other" musical festivals, which the theater hosts throughout the year. Due to restoration works, no performances are currently scheduled, but you can still visit the theater despite the ongoing work. ⊠ *Opernstr.* ☎ *0921/759–6922* ⊕ *www.bayreuth-wilhelmine.de* 🎟 *€8.*

Neues Schloss (*New Palace*). This glamorous 18th-century palace was built by the Margravine Wilhelmine, a woman of enormous energy and decided tastes. Though Wagner is the man most closely associated with Bayreuth, his choice of this setting is largely due to the work of this woman, who lived 100 years before him. Wilhelmine devoured books, wrote plays and operas (which she directed and, of course, acted in), and had buildings constructed, transforming much of the town and bringing it near bankruptcy. Her distinctive touch is evident at the palace, built when a mysterious fire conveniently destroyed parts of the original one. Anyone with a taste for the wilder flights of rococo decoration will love it. Some rooms have been given over to one of Europe's finest collections of faience. ⊠ *Ludwigstr. 21* ☎ *0921/759–6921* 🎟 *From €6.*

Richard-Wagner-Museum. "Wahnfried," built by Wagner in 1874 and the only house he ever owned, is now the Richard-Wagner-Museum. It's a simple, austere neoclassical building whose name, "peace from madness," was well earned. Wagner lived here with his wife Cosima, daughter of pianist Franz Liszt, and they were both laid to rest here. King Ludwig II of Bavaria, the young and impressionable "Fairy-Tale King" who gave Wagner so much financial support, is remembered in a bust before the entrance. The exhibits, arranged along a well-marked tour through the house, require a great deal of German-language reading, but it's a must for Wagner fans. The original scores of such masterpieces as *Parsifal, Tristan und Isolde, Lohengrin, Der Fliegende Holländer,* and *Götterdämmerung* are on display. You can also see designs for productions of his operas, as well as his piano and huge library. A multimedia display lets you watch and listen to various productions of his operas. The little house where Franz Liszt lived and died is right next door and can be visited with your Richard-Wagner-Museum ticket, but be sure to express your interest in advance. It, too, is heavy on the paper, but the last rooms—with pictures, photos, and silhouettes of the master, his students, acolytes, and friends—are well worth the detour. ⊠ *Richard-Wagner-Str. 48* ☎ *0921/757–2816* ⊕ *www.wagnermuseum. de* 🎟 *€8* ⊗ *Closed Mon.*

WHERE TO EAT

$$ ✕ **Oskar.** A huge glass ceiling gives the large dining room a light atmo-
GERMAN sphere even in winter. In summer, try for a table in the beer garden to enjoy fine Franconian specialties and Continental dishes. **Known for:** Franconian cuisine with fresh local produce; Sunday brunch; live jazz.

The torch-bearing figure of Apollo on his chariot adorns the Sonnentempel (Sun Temple) of Bayreuth's Neues Schloss.

Average main: €15 *Maximilianstr. 33* *0921/516–0553* *www.oskar-bayreuth.de* *No credit cards.*

$ GERMAN **Wolffenzacher.** This self-described "Franconian nostalgic inn" harks back to the days when the local *Wirtshaus* (inn-pub) was the meeting place for everyone from the mayor's scribes to the local carpenters. Beer and hearty traditional food are shared at wooden tables either in the rustic interior or out in the shady beer garden. **Known for:** Hefty Franconian cuisine balanced with Mediterranean influences; rustical ambience; traditional beer garden. *Average main: €12* *Sternenpl. 5* *0921/64552* *www.wolffenzacher.de* *No lunch.*

WHERE TO STAY

$$ HOTEL Fodor's Choice ★ **Goldener Anker.** No question about it, Bayreuth's grande dame is *the* place to stay; the hotel is right next to the Markgräfliches Opernhaus and has been entertaining composers, singers, conductors, and instrumentalists for hundreds of years. **Pros:** authentic historic setting with all modern amenities; exemplary service; excellent restaurant. **Cons:** no elevator; some rooms are on the small side; restaurant closed Monday and Tuesday, except during festival. *Rooms from: €168* *Opernstr. 6* *0921/65051* *www.anker-bayreuth.de* *40 rooms* *Free Breakfast.*

$$ HOTEL **Hotel Lohmühle.** The old part of this hotel is in Bayreuth's only half-timber house, a former sawmill by a stream, just a two-minute walk from the town center. **Pros:** pleasant rustic setting; reasonable prices; excellent restaurant. **Cons:** stairs between hotel and restaurant; front rooms let in traffic noise; spotty Internet. *Rooms from: €120* *Badstr. 37* *0921/53060* *www.hotel-lohmuehle.de* *42 rooms* *Free Breakfast.*

WAGNER: GERMANY'S TOP ROMANTIC

UNDERSTANDING WAGNER

Born in 1813, Richard Wagner has become modern Germany's most iconic composer. His music, which is best understood in its simple message of national glory and destiny, contributed greatly to the feeling of pan-Germanism that united Germany under the Prussian crown in 1871. However, his overtly nationalistic themes and blatant anti-Semitism also makes his music a bit controversial as it's also connected to the Nazi movement and Adolf Hitler; Hitler adored Wagner and saw him as the embodiment of his own vision for the German people. Wagner's focus on the cult of the leader and the glories of victory are prevalent in his works *Lohengrin* and *Parsifal.* Some of his most famous compositions are the four-opera cycle *The Ring of the Nibelung* (aka *Ring Cycle*), *Parsifal,* and *Lohengrin.*

WAGNER TODAY

In 1871 Wagner moved to the city of Bayreuth and began construction of the Festspielhaus, an opera house that would only perform Wagner's operas. The performance space opened its doors in 1876 with a production of *Das Rheingold* and the first full performance of the four-part *Ring Cycle.* The Festspielhaus continues to showcase Wagner's works during the annual Bayreuther Festspiel, a pilgrimage site for die-hard Wagner fans. The waiting list for tickets is years long; it's almost impossible for mere mortals to gain entrance to the holy temple. However, almost all German opera and symphony companies perform Wagner's works throughout the year. The best places to see Wagner's longer works are at Berlin's State Opera; the National Theater in Weimar; the Gewandhaus Orchestra and Opera in Leipzig; and Munich's Bavarian State Opera.

PERFORMING ARTS

Markgräfliches Opernhaus. If you don't get Wagner Festival tickets, console yourself with visits to the exquisite 18th-century opera house. In May the *Fränkische Festwochen* (Franconian Festival Weeks) take the stage with works of Wagner, of course, but also Paganini and Mozart. ⊠ *Opernstr.* ☎ *0921/759–6922.*

Wagner Festival. Opera lovers swear that there are few more intense operatic experiences than the annual Wagner Festival in Bayreuth, held July and August. You'll do best if you plan your visit several years in advance. It is nearly impossible to find a hotel room during the festival: try finding a room in a surrounding town instead of Bayreuth. For tickets, obtain an order form from the Bayreuther Festspiele Kartenbüro and submit the completed form by the middle of September the year before, at the latest. ■TIP→ The waiting list is years long, and they only offer tickets by mail or online and will ignore any other inquiries. ⊠ *Festspielhügel 1–2* ☎ *0921/78780* ⊕ *www.bayreuther-festspiele.de.*

BAMBERG

65 km (40 miles) west of Bayreuth, 80 km (50 miles) north of Nuremberg.

Fodor's Choice ★ Sitting majestically on seven hills above the Regnitz River, the entire Alstadt of this beautiful, historic town is a UNESCO World Heritage Site. It's a must-see because few towns in Germany survived the war with as little damage as Bamberg, and its canals and bridges make it a joy to stroll. Although it exploded onto the European political scene as the capital of the Holy Roman Empire under Emperor Heinrich II, its idyllic Old Town, with winding cobblestone streets, contains one of the best-preserved collections of early-medieval half-timber structures in Europe, dominated by the cathedral, consecrated in 1237.

GETTING HERE AND AROUND

Traveling to Bamberg by train will take about 45 minutes from Nuremberg; from Munich it takes about two hours, and it's a worthwhile five-hour train trip from Berlin. Bamberg's train station is a 30-minute walk from the Altstadt (Old Town). On the A-73 autobahn, Bamberg is two hours from Munich. Everything in town can be reached on foot.

TOURS

The Bamberg Tourist Information center offers an audio tour in English for €8.50 for four hours. It also offers brewery and beer-tasting tours of the nine Bamberg breweries.

Personenschiffahrt Kropf. Boats leave daily at 11 am, March through October, for short cruises on the Regnitz River and the Main–Donau Canal. ✉ *Kapuzinerstr. 5* ☎ *0951/26679* ⊕ *www.personenschiffahrt-bamberg.de* ⛴ *€7.*

VISITOR INFORMATION

Contacts Bamberg Tourismus und Congresservice. ✉ *Geyerswörthstr. 5* ☎ *0951/297–6200* ⊕ *www.bamberg.info.*

EXPLORING

Altes Rathaus (*Old Town Hall*). At Bamberg's historic core, the Altes Rathaus is tucked snugly on a small island in the Regnitz. To the west of the river is the so-called Bishops' Town; to the east, Burghers' Town. The citizens of Bamberg built this rickety, extravagantly decorated building on an artificial island when the bishop of Bamberg refused to give the city the land for a town hall. Its excellent collection of porcelain is a sampling of 18th-century styles, from almost sober Meissens with bucolic Watteau scenes to simple but rare Haguenau pieces from Alsace and faience from Strasbourg. ✉ *Obere Brücke 1* ☎ *0951/871–871* ⛴ *€5* ⊘ *Closed Mon.*

Dom (*Cathedral*). Bamberg's great cathedral is a unique building that tells not only the town's story but that of Germany as well. The first building here was begun by Heinrich II in 1003, and it was in this partially completed cathedral that he was crowned Holy Roman Emperor in 1012. In 1237 it was destroyed by fire, and replaced by the present late Romanesque–early Gothic building. The dominant features

EATING WELL IN FRANCONIA

Franconia is known for its good and filling food and for its simple and atmospheric *Gasthäuser*. Pork is a staple, served either as *Schweinsbraten* (a plain roast) or with *Knödel* (dumplings made from either bread or potatoes). The specialties in Nuremberg, Coburg, and Regensburg are the *Bratwürste*—short spiced sausages. The Nuremberg variety is known all over Germany; they are even on the menu on the ICE trains. You can have them grilled or heated in a stock of onions and wine (*Blaue Zipfel*). Bratwürste are traditionally served in denominations of 3, 6, or 8 with sauerkraut and potato salad or dark bread.

On the sweet side, try the *Dampfnudel*, a sweet yeast-dough dumpling that is tasty and filling. *Nürnberger Lebkuchen*, a sort of gingerbread eaten at Christmastime, is loved all over Germany. A true purist swears by *Elisenlebkuchen*, which are made with no flour. Both Lebkuchen and the small Bratwürste are protected under German law and are only "legal" when made in or around Nuremberg.

Not to be missed are Franconia's liquid refreshments from both the grape and the grain. Franconian wines, usually white and sold in distinctive flat bottles called *Bocksbeutel*, are renowned for their special bouquet. (Silvaner is the traditional grape.) The region has the largest concentration of local breweries in the world (Bamberg alone has nine, Bayreuth seven), producing a wide range of brews, the most distinctive of which is the dark, smoky *Rauchbier* and the even darker and stronger *Schwärzla*. Then, of course, there is Kulmbach, with the Doppelbock Kulminator 28, which takes nine months to brew and has an alcohol content of 12%.

are the massive towers at each corner. Heading into the dark interior, you'll find a striking collection of monuments and art treasures. The most famous piece is the **Bamberger Reiter** (Bamberg Horseman), an equestrian statue carved—no one knows by whom—around 1230 and thought to be an allegory of chivalrous virtue or a representation of King Stephen of Hungary. Compare it with the mass of carved figures huddled in the tympana above the church portals. In the center of the nave you'll find another masterpiece, the massive tomb of Heinrich and his wife, Kunigunde. It's the work of Tilman Riemenschneider. Pope Clement II is also buried in the cathedral, in an imposing tomb beneath the high altar; he's the only pope buried north of the Alps. ⊠ *Dompl.* ☎ *0951/502–330* ⊞ *Free.*

Diözesanmuseum (*Cathedral Museum*). Directly adjacent to the Bamberg Dom, this museum contains one of many nails and splinters of wood reputed to be from the cross of Jesus. The "star-spangled" cloak stitched with gold that was given to Emperor Heinrich II by an Italian prince is among the finest items displayed. More macabre exhibits in this rich ecclesiastical collection are the elaborately mounted skulls of Heinrich and Kunigunde. The building itself was designed by Balthasar Neumann (1687–1753), the architect of Vierzehnheiligen, and constructed between 1730 and 1733. ✉ *Dompl. 5* ☎ *0951/502–325* 🌐 *www.dioezesanmuseum-bamberg.de* 🎟 *€4* 🕓 *Closed Mon.*

Franconian Brewery Museum. Once a Benedictine monastery, the Kloster of St. Michael has been gazing over Bamberg since 1015. Due to renovation work, the monastery's lovely Church of St. Michael is closed to the public. The monastery itself is now used as a home for the aged. What's left is the museum, which exhibits everything that has to do with beer, from the making of malt to recipes and is worth a visit if the subject interests you. You'll learn the ins and outs of brewing and can arrange a tasting if you like. ✉ *Michelsberg 10f* ☎ *0951/53016 museum* 🌐 *www.brauereimuseum.de* 🎟 *€4* 🕓 *Closed Mon. and Tues., and Nov.–Mar.*

Neue Residenz (*New Residence*). This glittering baroque palace was once the home of the prince-electors. Their plan to extend the immense palace even further is evident at the corner on Obere Karolinenstrasse, where the ashlar bonding was left open to accept another wing. The most memorable room in the palace is the **Kaisersaal** (Throne Room), complete with impressive ceiling frescoes and elaborate stuccowork. The rose garden behind the Neue Residenz provides an aromatic and romantic spot for a stroll with a view of Bamberg's roofscape. You have to take a German-language tour to see the Residenz itself, but you can visit the **Staatsbibliothek** (library) at any time during its open hours. ✉ *Dompl. 8* ☎ *0951/519–390* 🌐 *www.residenz-bamberg.de* 🎟 *€5.*

5

WHERE TO EAT

$ GERMAN

🍴 **Bischofsmühle.** It doesn't always have to be beer in Bamberg. The old mill, its grinding wheel providing a sonorous backdrop for patrons, specializes in wines from Franconia and elsewhere. **Known for:** local Franconian specialties; extensive regional wine selection; rustic setting with outside seating. [$] *Average main: €10* ✉ *Geyerswörthstr. 4* ☎ *0951/27570* 🌐 *www.bischofsmuehle.com* 💳 *No credit cards.*

$ GERMAN

🍴 **Klosterbräu.** This massive old stone-and-half-timber house has been standing since 1533, making it Bamberg's oldest brewpub. The cuisine is basic, robust, filling, and tasty, with such items as a bowl of beans with a slab of smoked pork, or marinated pork kidneys with boiled potatoes. **Known for:** Klosterbraun, Bamberg's most famous brown beer; simple brewhouse cuisine; local charm. [$] *Average main: €10* ✉ *Obere Mühlbrücke* ☎ *0951/52265* 🌐 *www.klosterbraeu.de* 💳 *No credit cards.*

$ GERMAN

🍴 **Schlenkerla.** Set in the middle of the Old Town, this tavern has been serving beer inside an ancient half-timber house since 1405. The real reason to come here is to try the *Aecht Schenkerla Rauchbier,* a smoked beer brewed with smoked malt that tastes like liquid ham—it's an acquired taste but worth sampling—if you can choke down the first one, you'll be a fan for life. **Known for:** Rauchbier; hefty local specialties; traditional atmosphere and food. [$] *Average main: €10* ✉ *Dominikanerstr. 6* ☎ *951/56050* 🌐 *www.schlenkerla.de* 💳 *No credit cards.*

Bamberg's Altes Rathaus is perched precariously on an artificial island in the middle of the Regnitz River.

WHERE TO STAY

$$
B&B/INN
Fodor's Choice
★

⌂ **Hotel-Restaurant St. Nepomuk.** This half-timber house seems to float over the river Regnitz; many of the comfortable rooms have quite a view of the water and the Old Town Hall on its island. **Pros:** great views; an elegant dining room with excellent food; centrally located. **Cons:** hotel on a pedestrian-only street; public garage 700 feet away; the river can be disturbingly noisy. $ *Rooms from: €148* ✉ *Obere Mühlbrücke 9* ☎ *0951/98420* ⊕ *www.hotel-nepomuk.de* ⇆ *47 rooms* ⊙ *Free Breakfast.*

$$$$
HOTEL

⌂ **Romantik Hotel Weinhaus Messerschmitt.** This comfortable hotel, once the home of Willy Messerschmitt of aviation fame, has spacious and luxurious rooms, some with exposed beams and many of them lighted by chandeliers. **Pros:** elegant dining room with solid Franconian cuisine; variety of rooms to choose from; massive breakfast. **Cons:** older property; front rooms are noisy; expensive. $ *Rooms from: €239* ✉ *Langestr. 41* ☎ *0951/297–800* ⊕ *www.hotel-messerschmitt.de* ⇆ *67 rooms* ⊙ *Free Breakfast.*

PERFORMING ARTS

Capella Antiqua Bambergensis. The city's first-class ensemble, Capella Antiqua Bambergensis, specializes in ancient music featuring lute, harp, hurdy gurdy, and other early instruments. They perform (in medieval costume) at several venues in town. ✉ *Bamberg* ⊕ *www. capella-antiqua.de.*

E.T.A. Hoffmann Theater. Opera and operettas are performed here from September through July. ⊠ *E.T.A.-Hoffmann-Pl. 1* ☎ *0951/873–030* ⊕ *www.theater-bamberg.de.*

Kongresshalle Bamberg (*Sinfonie an der Regnitz*). This fine riverside concert hall is home to Bamberg's own world-class resident symphony orchestra, the Bamberger Symphoniker. ⊠ *Muss-Str. 1* ☎ *0951/964–7200* ⊕ *www.bamberg-ce.de, www.bamberger-symphoniker.de.*

SHOPPING

If you happen to be traveling around Christmastime, make sure you keep an eye out for crèches, a Bamberg specialty. Check the tourism website (⊕ *www.bamberg.info*) for the locations of nativity scenes and descriptions.

Café am Dom. For an edible souvenir, take home handmade chocolates like the only-in-Bamberg Rauchbier truffles made with Schlenkerla smoked beer. This café also has a roomy seating area to take a load off while you nibble on a delicious pastry. ⊠ *Ringleinsg. 2* ☎ *0951/519–290* ⊕ *www.cafeamdom.de.*

Magnus Klee. This shop sells nativity scenes, called *Krippen* in German, of all different shapes and sizes, including wood carved and with fabric clothes. ⊠ *Obstmarkt 2* ☎ *0951/26037.*

APFELWEIBLA

As you peruse the shops in Bamberg's Altstadt, you may notice an applelike face that adorns jewelry and housewares, the *Apfelweibla.* A replica of the Apfelweibla, a whimsical doorknob depicting an elderly woman's face, can be found at Eisgrube 14. The original doorknob is on display at the Museum of History at Domplatz. The doorknob inspired E. T. A. Hoffmann's novella *The Golden Pot.* It's said that rubbing the Apfelweibla will bring you good luck.

BAD STAFFELSTEIN

32.8 km (20 miles) north of Bamberg.

About 30 minutes north of Bamberg is Bad Staffelstein, which has two sights of interest. It's easily reached by train in about 20 minutes from Bamberg.

Kloster Banz (*Banz Abbey*). This abbey, which some call the "holy mountain of Bavaria," proudly crowns the west bank of the Main north of Bamberg. There had been a monastery here since 1069, but the present buildings—now a political-seminar center and think tank—date from the end of the 17th century. The highlight of the complex is the **Klosterkirche** (Abbey Church), the work of architect Leonard Dientzenhofer and his brother, the stuccoist Johann Dientzenhofer (1663–1726). Balthasar Neumann later contributed a good deal of work. Concerts are occasionally held in the church, including some by members of the renowned Bamberger Symphoniker. ⊠ *Kloster-Banz-Str. 1, Bad Staffelstein* ✛ *37.4 km (23 miles) north of Bamberg via A-73* ☎ *09573/7311.*

Fodor's Choice   **Vierzehnheiligen.** In Bad Staffelstein, on the east side of the Main north
★   of Bamberg, is a tall, elegant, yellow-sandstone edifice whose interior
represents one of the great examples of rococo decoration. The church
was built by Balthasar Neumann (architect of the Residenz at Würzburg) between 1743 and 1772 to commemorate a vision of Christ and
14 saints—*vierzehn Heiligen*—that appeared to a shepherd in 1445.
The interior, known as "God's Ballroom," is supported by 14 columns.
In the middle of the church is the *Gnadenaltar* (Mercy Altar) featuring the 14 saints. Thanks to clever play with light, light colors, and
fanciful gold-and-blue trimmings, the interior seems to be in perpetual
motion. Guided tours of the church are given on request; a donation is
expected. On Saturday afternoon and all day Sunday the road leading
to the church is closed and you have to walk the last half mile. ⊠ *Vierzehnheiligen 2, Bad Staffelstein ✛ 36 km (22 miles) north of Bamberg
via A-73* ☎ *09571/95080* ⊕ *www.vierzehnheiligen.de.*

NUREMBERG (NÜRNBERG)

60 km (37 miles) south of Bamberg.

With a recorded history stretching back to 1050, Franconia's main
city is among the most historic in all of Germany; the core of the
Old Town, through which the Pegnitz River flows, is still surrounded
by its original medieval walls. Year-round floodlighting adds to the
brooding romance of the moats, sturdy gateways, and watchtowers.
Nuremberg has always taken a leading role in German affairs. It
was here, for example, that the Holy Roman emperors traditionally
held the first Diet, or convention of the estates, of their incumbency.
And it was here, too, that Hitler staged the most grandiose Nazi rallies. With a sense of historical justice, Nuremberg in rubble was the
site of the Allies' war trials, where top-ranking Nazis were charged
with—and almost without exception convicted of—crimes against
humanity. The rebuilding of Nuremberg after the war was virtually
a miracle, considering the 90% destruction of the Old Town. As a
major intersection on the medi-
eval trade routes, Nuremberg
became a wealthy town where
the arts and sciences flowered.
Albrecht Dürer (1471–1528),
the first indisputable genius of
the Renaissance in Germany, was
born here. He married in 1509
and bought a house in the city
where he lived and worked for
the rest of his life. Other leading
Nuremberg artists of the Renaissance include painter Michael
Wolgemut (a teacher of Dürer),
stonecutter Adam Kraft, and the
brass founder Peter Vischer. The
tradition of the Meistersinger

UNDERGROUND NUREMBERG

Beer aficionados can get a deeper
look at Nuremberg's brewing
history with a tour into the cellars
where beer was made and stored
since the 1300s. The tour, offered
by Underground Nuremberg, costs
€7, which includes a beer tasting,
but is only offered in German.
English-language group tours are
available by appointment; see
⊕ *www.felsengaenge-nuernberg.
de.*

also flourished here in the 16th century, thanks to the high standard set by the local cobbler Hans Sachs (1494–1576). The Meistersinger were poets and musicians who turned songwriting into a special craft, with a wealth of rules and regulations. They were celebrated three centuries later by Wagner in his opera *Die Meistersinger von Nürnberg*.

The Thirty Years' War (1618–48) and the shift to sea routes for transportation led to a period of decline, which ended only in the early 19th century when the first railroad opened in Nuremberg. Among a great host of inventions associated with the city, the most significant are the pocket watch, gun casting, the clarinet, and the geographic globe. Among Nuremberg's famous products are *Lebkuchen* (gingerbread of sorts) and Faber-Castell pencils.

GETTING HERE AND AROUND

Nuremberg is centrally located and well connected, an hour north of Munich and two hours east of Frankfurt by train. With the extension of Germany's high-speed rail network, Nuremberg can be done as a day-trip from Berlin (3 hours each way) and Leipzig (2 hours each way). Five autobahns meet here: A-3 Düsseldorf–Passau, A-6 Mannheim–Nuremberg, A-9 Potsdam–München, A-73 Coburg–Feucht, and B-8 (four-lanes near Nuremberg) Würzburg–Regensburg. Most places in the Old Town can be reached on foot.

Nuremberg consists of a surprisingly compact city center that is easily explored on foot. All of the downtown historical sites, restaurants, and hotels are within easy walking distance from each other. Nuremberg's fantastic bus, trolley, or subway system will help you venture out to the Nazi sites farther afield. Information about city transportation is available at the VAG-KundenCenter at the main train station.

Essentials VAG-KundenCenter. ⊠ *U-Bahn Verteilergeschoss, Königstorpassage, Haltestelle Hauptbahnhof, Nürnberg* ⊕ *www.vgn.de.*

TOURS

Neukam-Reba. This company takes visitors on a combined bus tour with a short walking tour through the Nazi Party Grounds. Tours leave daily at 10 am, May through November and during the Christmas Market. ⊠ *Hallpl. 36, Nürnberg* ☎ *0911/200–1310* ⊕ *www.neukam-reba.de* 💷 *€17.*

Nuremberg Guide Association. An English-language walking tour through the Old Town departs from the Tourist Information Office on the Hauptmarkt daily at 1 pm, April through December. The tour lasts approximately two hours and covers all the essential Nuremberg sites, with some interesting, if not canned, commentary. ⊠ *Hauptmarkt, Nürnberg* ☎ *0911/3506–4631* ⊕ *www.nuernberg-tours.de* 💷 *€10.*

FESTIVALS

By far the most famous local festival is the **Christkindlesmarkt** (Christmas Market), an enormous pre-Christmas fair that runs from the Friday before Advent to Christmas Eve. One of the highlights is the candle procession, held every second Thursday of the market season, during which thousands of children parade through the city streets.

FAMILY
Fodor's Choice
★

Christkindlesmarkt. Perhaps the most famous Christmas Market in Germany, the Nürnberg Christkindlesmarkt sits on the town's cobblestone main square beneath the wonderful Frauenkirche. Renowned for its food, particularly *Nürnberger Bratwurstchen,* tasty little pork and marjoram sausages, and *Lebkuchen,* gingerbread made with cinnamon and honey, the market is also famed for its little figures made out of prunes called *Nürnberger Zwetschgenmännla* (Nuremberg Prune People). ⊠ *Hauptmarkt, Nürnberg* ⊕ *www.christkindlesmarkt.de.*

Kaiserburg Concerts. From May through July classical-music concerts are given in the Rittersaal of the Kaiserburg. ⊠ *Burg 13, Nürnberg* 🕾 *0911/244–6590* ⊕ *www.kaiserburg-nuernberg.de.*

Sommer in Nürnberg. Nuremberg holds this annual summer festival from May through July, with more than 200 events. Its international organ festival in June and July is regarded as Europe's finest. ⊠ *Nürnberg.*

VISITOR INFORMATION

Contacts Nürnberg Congress- und Tourismus-Zentrale. ⊠ *Frauentorgraben 3, Nürnberg* 🕾 *0911/23360* ⊕ *www.nuernberg.de.*

EXPLORING

Albrecht-Dürer-Haus (*Albrecht Dürer House*). The great painter Albrecht Dürer lived here from 1509 until his death in 1528. This beautifully preserved late-medieval house is typical of the prosperous merchants' homes that once filled Nuremberg. Dürer, who enriched German art with Renaissance elements, was more than a painter. He raised the woodcut, a notoriously difficult medium, to new heights of technical sophistication, combining great skill with a haunting, immensely detailed drawing style and complex, allegorical subject matter.. A number of original prints adorn the walls, and printing techniques using the old press are demonstrated in the studio. An excellent opportunity to find out about life in the house of Dürer is the tour with a guide role-playing Agnes Dürer, the artist's wife. ⊠ *Albrecht-Dürer-Str. 39, Nürnberg* 🕾 *0911/231–2568* 🖅 *€6* ⊘ *Closed Mon.*

Altes Rathaus (*Old Town Hall*). This ancient building on Rathausplatz was erected in 1332, destroyed in World War II, and subsequently reconstructed. Its intact medieval dungeons, consisting of 12 small rooms and one large torture chamber called the **Lochgefängnis** (the Hole), provide insight into the gruesome applications of medieval law. **Gänsemännchenbrunnen** (Gooseman's Fountain) faces the Altes Rathaus. This lovely Renaissance bronze fountain, cast in 1550, is a work of rare elegance and great technical sophistication. ⊠ *Rathauspl. 2, Nürnberg* 🕾 *0911/231–2690* 🖅 *€4, min. 5 people for tours* ⊘ *Closed Mon.*

Documentation Center Nazi Party Rally Grounds. On the eastern outskirts of the city, the **Ausstellung Faszination und Gewalt** (Fascination and Terror Exhibition) documents the political, social, and architectural history of the Nazi Party. The sobering museum helps illuminate the whys and hows of Hitler's rise to power during the unstable period after World War I and the end of the democratic Weimar Republic. This is one of the few museums that documents how the Third Reich's

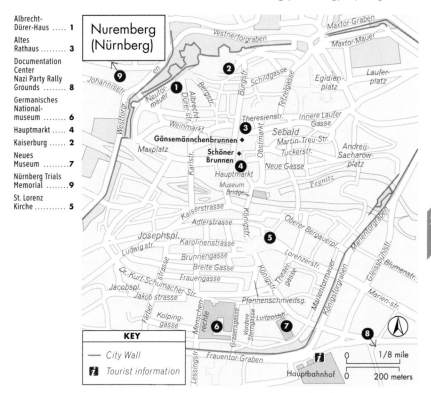

propaganda machine influenced the masses. The 19-room exhibition is inside a horseshoe-shape Congress Hall, designed for a crowd of 50,000, that the Nazis never completed. The Nazis did make infamous use of the nearby Zeppelin Field, the enormous parade ground where Hitler addressed his largest Nazi Party rallies. Today it sometimes shakes to the amplified beat of pop concerts. To get to the Documentation Center, take Tram 9 from the city center to the Doku-Zentrum stop. ⊠ *Bayernstr. 110, Nürnberg* ☎ *0911/231–5666* ⊕ *www.museen. nuernberg.de* ⊠ €6.

Fodor'sChoice **Germanisches Nationalmuseum** (*German National Museum*). You could
★ spend a lifetime exploring the largest museum of its kind in Germany. This vast museum showcases the country's cultural and scientific achievements, ethnic background, and history. Housed in a former Carthusian monastery, complete with cloisters and monastic outbuilding, the complex effectively melds the ancient with modern extensions, giving the impression that Germany is moving forward by examining its past. The exhibition begins outside, with the tall, sleek pillars of the Strasse der Menschenrechte (Street of Human Rights), designed by Israeli artist Dani Karavan. Thirty columns are inscribed with the articles from the Universal Declaration of Human Rights. There are few aspects of German culture, from the Stone Age to the 19th century, that

are not covered by the museum, and quantity and quality are evenly matched. One highlight is the superb collection of Renaissance German paintings (with Dürer, Cranach, and Altdorfer well represented). Others may prefer the exquisite medieval ecclesiastical exhibits—manuscripts, altarpieces, statuary, stained glass, jewel-encrusted reliquaries—the collections of arms and armor, the scientific instruments, or the toys. ⊠ *Kartäuserg. 1, Nürnberg* ☏ *0911/13310* ⊕ *www.gnm.de* ⊡ *€8* ⊗ *Closed Mon.*

Hauptmarkt (*Main Market*). Nuremberg's central market square was once the city's Jewish Quarter. In 1349, Emperor Charles IV instigated a pogrom that left the Jewish Quarter in flames and more than 500 dead. He then razed the ruins and resettled the remaining Jews so he could build this square. Towering over the northwestern corner, **Schöner Brunnen** (Beautiful Fountain) looks as though it should be on the summit of some lofty cathedral. Carved around the year 1400, the elegant 60-foot-high Gothic fountain is adorned with 40 figures arranged in tiers—prophets, saints, local noblemen, electors, Julius Caesar, and Alexander the Great. A gold ring set into the railing is said to bring good luck to those who touch it. A market still operates here on weekdays. Its colorful stands are piled high with produce, fruit, bread, homemade cheeses and sausages, sweets, and anything else you might need for a snack or picnic. It's also here that the Christkindlsmarkt is held. ⊠ *Hauptmarkt, Nürnberg.*

Fodor's Choice **Kaiserburg** (*Imperial Castle*). The city's main attraction is a grand yet
★ playful collection of buildings standing just inside the city walls; it was once the residence of the Holy Roman Emperor. The complex comprises three separate groups. The oldest, dating from around 1050, is the **Burggrafenburg** (Castellan's Castle), with a craggy old pentagonal tower and the bailiff's house. It stands in the center of the complex. To the east is the **Kaiserstallung** (Imperial Stables), built in the 15th century as a granary and now serving as a youth hostel. The real interest of this vast complex of ancient buildings, however, centers on the westernmost part of the fortress, which begins at the **Sinwell Turm** (Sinwell Tower). The **Kaiserburg Museum** is here, a subsidiary of the Germanisches Nationalmuseum that displays ancient armors and has exhibits relating to horsemanship in the imperial era and to the history of the fortress. This section of the castle also has a wonderful Romanesque **Doppelkappelle** (Double Chapel). The upper part—richer, larger, and more ornate than the lower chapel—was where the emperor and his family worshipped. Also visit the **Rittersaal** (Knights' Hall) and the **Kaisersaal** (Throne Room). Their heavy oak beams, painted ceilings, and sparse interiors have changed little since they were built in the 15th century. ⊠ *Burgstr., Nürnberg* ☏ *0911/2446–59115* ⊕ *www.kaiserburg-nuernberg. de* ⊡ *€7.*

Neues Museum (*New Museum*). Anything but medieval, this museum is devoted to international design since 1945. The collection, supplemented by changing exhibitions, is in a slick, modern edifice that achieves the perfect synthesis between old and new. It's mostly built of

Outside the Germanisches Nationalmuseum is the "Way of Human Rights," an outdoor sculpture consisting of 30 columns inscribed with the articles from the Universal Declaration of Human Rights.

traditional pink-sandstone ashlars, while the facade is a flowing, transparent composition of glass. The interior is a work of art in itself—cool stone, with a ramp that slowly spirals up to the gallery. Extraordinary things await, including a Joseph Beuys installation (*Ausfegen,* or *Sweep-out*) and *Avalanche* by François Morellet, a striking collection of violet, argon-gas-filled fluorescent tubes. The café-restaurant adjoining the museum contains modern art, silver-wrapped candies, and video projections. ⊠ *Luitpoldstr. 5, Nürnberg* ☎ *0911/240–200* ⊕ *www.nmn.de* 🖃 *From €5* ⊘ *Closed Mon.*

Nuremberg Trials Memorial. Nazi leaders and German organizations were put on trial here in 1945 and 1946 during the first international war-crimes trials, conducted by the victorious Allied forces of World War II. The trials were held in the Landgericht (Regional Court) in courtroom No. 600 and resulted in 11 death sentences, among other convictions. The actual courtroom is still in use and can only be visited when court is not in session. The guided tours in English take place on Saturday at 2 and an English-language audio guide is available. ⊠ *Bärenschanzstr. 72, Nürnberg* ☎ *0911/231–8411* ⊕ *www.memorium-nuremberg.de* 🖃 *€6* ⊘ *Closed Tues.* Ⓜ *Bärenschanze.*

St. Lorenz Kirche (*St. Laurence Church*). In a city with several striking churches, St. Lorenz is considered by many to be the most beautiful. Construction began around 1250 and was completed in about 1477; it later became a Lutheran church. Two towers flank the main entrance, which is covered with a forest of carvings. In the lofty interior, note the works by sculptors Adam Kraft and Veit Stoss: Kraft's great stone

Climb to the top of Nuremberg's Kaiserburg (Imperial Castle) for wonderful views of the city.

tabernacle, to the left of the altar, and Stoss's *Annunciation,* at the east end of the nave, are their finest works. There are many other carvings throughout the building, testimony to the artistic wealth of late-medieval Nuremberg. ✉ *Lorenzer Pl., Nürnberg.*

WHERE TO EAT

$$$$ GERMAN Fodor's Choice ★

🍴 **Essigbrätlein.** The oldest restaurant in Nuremberg, built in 1550 as a meeting place for the city's wine merchants, is also the top restaurant in the city and among the best in Germany. Today its tiny but elegant period interior caters to the distinguishing gourmet, but don't be put off if the restaurant looks closed—just ring the bell and a friendly receptionist will help you. **Known for:** four-course dinner menu; new German cuisine with uniquely blended spice mixes; perfect wine pairings. [$] *Average main: €30* ✉ *Weinmarkt 3, Nürnberg* ☎ *0911/225–131* 🌐 *www.essigbraetlein.de* 🕒 *Closed Sun. and Mon.*

$ GERMAN

🍴 **Hausbrauerei Altstadthof.** For traditional regional food, such as Nürnberg bratwurst, head to this atmospheric brewery. You can see the copper kettles where the brewery's organic *Rotbier* (red beer) is made. **Known for:** traditional Franconian cuisine served with craft brews; beer-related products such as beer vinegar, brandy, and soap; meeting point for cellar tours. [$] *Average main: €10* ✉ *Bergstr. 19–21, Nürnberg* ☎ *911/244–9859* 🌐 *www.hausbrauerei-altstadthof.de* 💳 *No credit cards.*

$ GERMAN FAMILY

🍴 **Historische Bratwurst-Küche Zum Gulden Stern.** The city council meets here—at the oldest bratwurst restaurant in the world—to decide the official size and weight of the Nürnberger bratwursts, so this should be your first stop to try the ubiquitous local delicacy. The sausages have to be small enough to fit through a medieval keyhole, which in earlier days enabled pub owners to sell them after hours. **Known for:** freshly roasted bratwurst, grilled on a beech-wood fire; Saure Zipfel (boiled sausages prepared in stock of Franconian wine and onions); medieval atmosphere. *$ Average main: €9 ⊠ Zirkelschmiedg. 26, Nürnberg ☎ 0911/205–9288 ⊕ www.bratwurstkueche.de.*

WHERE TO STAY

$ ⬚ **Agneshof.** This comfortable hotel is north of the Old Town, between
HOTEL the fortress and St. Sebaldus Church, and its interiors are very modern and tastefully done. **Pros:** many rooms have great views of the castle; warm yet professional welcome; pleasant wellness center. **Cons:** deluxe rooms overpriced; parking and hotel access difficult; no restaurant. *$ Rooms from: €85 ⊠ Agnesg. 10, Nürnberg ☎ 0911/214–440 ⊕ www. agneshof-nuernberg.de ⌁ 72 rooms ᵀᴼᵀ Free Breakfast.*

$ ⬚ **Burghotel Stammhaus.** At this quaint hotel the accommodations are
HOTEL small but cozy and the service is familial and friendly. **Pros:** great location in the city center; comfortable and good value; large swimming pool. **Cons:** small rooms; tiny lobby; parking not easy. *$ Rooms from: €70 ⊠ Schildg. 14, Nürnberg ☎ 0911/203–040 ⊕ www.invite-hotels.de ⌁ 22 rooms ᵀᴼᵀ Free Breakfast.*

$$ ⬚ **Hotel-Weinhaus Steichele.** An 18th-century bakery has been skill-
HOTEL fully converted into this comfortable hotel, which has been managed by the same family for four generations. **Pros:** Franconian charm; central location; good restaurants. **Cons:** small rooms and lobby; some rooms show their age; sporadic Wi-Fi. *$ Rooms from: €115 ⊠ Knorrstr. 2–8, Nürnberg ☎ 0911/202–280 ⊕ www.steichele.de ⌁ 56 rooms ᵀᴼᵀ Free Breakfast.*

$$$$ ⬚ **Le Meridien Grand Hotel.** Across the square from the central train sta-
HOTEL tion, this stately building with the calling card "Grand Hotel" arching over its entranceway has a spacious and imposing lobby with marble pillars, which feels grand and welcoming. **Pros:** luxury property; impressive lobby; excellent restaurant. **Cons:** expensive, with additional fees for every possible contingency; Germanic efficiency at reception desk; access from the station can be difficult with luggage (via an underpass with stairs). *$ Rooms from: €329 ⊠ Bahnhofstr. 1, Nürnberg ☎ 0911/23220 ⊕ www.nuremberg.lemeridien.com ⌁ 191 rooms ᵀᴼᵀ Free Breakfast.*

SHOPPING

Handwerkerhof. Step into this "medieval mall," in the tower at the Old Town gate (Am Königstor) opposite the main train station, and you'll think you're back in the Middle Ages. Craftspeople are busy at work turning out the kind of handiwork that has been produced in Nuremberg for centuries: pewter, glassware, basketwork, wood carvings, and, of course, toys. The Lebkuchen specialist **Lebkuchen-Schmidt** has a shop here as well. ⊠ *Am Königstor, Nürnberg ⊕ www. handwerkerhof.de.*

REGENSBURG

85 km (53 miles) southeast of Nuremberg, 120 km (75 miles) northwest of Munich.

Regensburg escaped World War II with no major damage, leaving it as one of the best-preserved medieval cities in Germany. The city's story begins with the Celts around 500 BC. In AD 179, as an original marble inscription in the Historisches Museum proclaims, it became a Roman military post called Castra Regina. The Porta Praetoria, or gateway, built by the Romans, remains in the Old Town, and whenever you see huge ashlars incorporated into buildings, you are looking at bits of the old Roman settlement. When Bavarian tribes migrated to the area in the 6th century, they occupied what remained of the Roman town and, apparently on the basis of its Latin name, called it Regensburg. Anglo-Saxon missionaries led by St. Boniface in 739 made the town a bishopric before heading down the Danube to convert heathens in even farther-flung lands. Charlemagne, first of the Holy Roman emperors, arrived at the end of the 8th century and incorporated Regensburg into his burgeoning domain. Regensburg benefited from the fact that the Danube wasn't navigable to the west, and thus it was able to control trade as goods traveled between Germany and Central Europe.

By the Middle Ages Regensburg had become a political, economic, and intellectual center. For many centuries it was the most important city in southeast Germany, serving as the seat of the Perpetual Imperial Diet from 1663 until 1806, when Napoléon ordered the dismantling of the Holy Roman Empire. Today the ancient and hallowed walls of Regensburg continue to buzz with life. Students from the university fill the restaurants and pubs, and locals tend to their daily shopping and run errands in the inner city, where small shops and stores have managed to keep international consumer chains out. While the city is a popular river-cruise stop, few visitors to Bavaria venture this far off the well-trodden tourist trails.

GETTING HERE AND AROUND

Regensburg is at the intersection of the autobahns 3 and 93. It is an hour away from Nuremberg and two hours from Munich by train. Regensburg is compact; its Old Town center is about 1 square mile. All of its attractions lie on the south side of the Danube, so you won't have to cross it more than once—and then only to admire the city from the north bank.

TOURS

English-language guided walking tours are conducted May through September and during the Christmas markets, Wednesday and Saturday at 1:30. They cost €6 and begin at the tourist office.

Personenschifffahrt Klinger. All boats depart from the Steinerne Brücke, and the most popular excursions are boat trips to Ludwig I's imposing Greek-style Doric temple of Walhalla. There are daily sailings at 10:30 and 2 to Walhalla from Easter through October. The round trip takes three hours, including about an hour to explore the temple. Don't

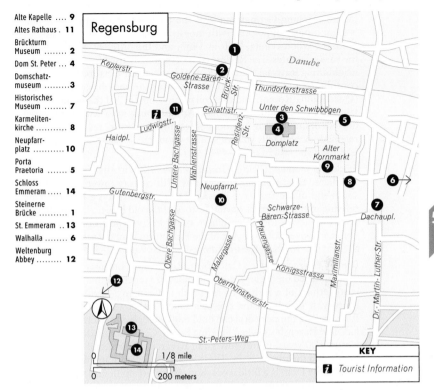

bother with the trip upriver from Regensburg to Kelheim. ☒ *Thundorf-str. 1* ☎ *0941/55359* ⊕ *www.schifffahrtklinger.de* ☒ *From €11.*

VISITOR INFORMATION

Contacts **Regensburg Tourismus.** ☒ *Altes Rathaus, Rathauspl. 4* ☎ *0941/507–4410* ⊕ *www.regensburg.de.*

EXPLORING

Alte Kapelle (*Old Chapel*). Erected by the Carolingian order in the 9th century, the Old Chapel's dowdy exterior hides joyous rococo treasures within—extravagant concoctions of sinuous gilt stucco, rich marble, and giddy frescoes, the whole illuminated by light pouring in from the upper windows. ☒ *Alter Kornmarkt 8* ☒ *Free.*

Altes Rathaus (*Old Town Hall*). The picture-book complex of medieval half-timber buildings, with windows large and small and flowers in tubs, is one of the best-preserved town halls in the country, as well as one of the most historically important. It was here, in the imposing Gothic **Reichssaal** (Imperial Hall), that the Perpetual Imperial Diet met from 1663 to 1806. This parliament of sorts consisted of the emperor, the electors (seven or eight), the princes (about 50), and the burghers, who assembled to discuss and determine the affairs of the far-reaching German lands of the Holy Roman Empire. The hall is sumptuously appointed with tapestries, flags, and heraldic designs. Note the wood ceiling, built in 1408, and the different elevations for the various estates. The Reichssaal is occasionally used for concerts. The neighboring **Ratssaal** (Council Room) is where the electors met for their consultations. The cellar holds the city's torture chamber; the **Fragstatt** (Questioning Room); and the execution room, called the **Armesünder-stübchen** (Poor Sinners' Room). Any prisoner who withstood three degrees of questioning without confessing was considered innocent and released—which tells you something about medieval notions of justice. ⊠ *Rathauspl.* ☎ *0941/507–4411* 🖵 *€8.*

Brückturm Museum (*Bridge Tower Museum*). With its tiny windows, weathered tiles, and pink plaster, this 17th-century tower stands at the south end of the Steinerne Brücke. The tower displays a host of items relating to the construction and history of the old bridge. It also offers a gorgeous view of the Regensburg roof landscape. The brooding building with a massive roof to the left of the Brückturm is an old salt warehouse. ⊠ *Steinerne Brücke, Weisse-Lamm-G. 1* ☎ *0941/507–5888* 🖵 *€2.*

Dom St. Peter (*St. Peter's Cathedral*). Regensburg's transcendent cathedral, modeled on the airy, powerful lines of French Gothic architecture, is something of a rarity this far south in Germany. Begun in the 13th century, it stands on the site of a much earlier Carolingian church. Remarkably, the cathedral can hold 6,000 people, three times the population of Regensburg when building began. Construction dragged on for almost 600 years, until Ludwig I of Bavaria, then ruler of Regensburg, finally had the towers built. These had to be replaced in the mid-1950s. Behind the Dom is a little workshop where a team of 15 stonecutters is busy full-time in summer recutting and restoring parts of the cathedral.

Before heading into the Dom, take time to admire the intricate and frothy carvings of its facade. Inside, the glowing 14th-century stained glass in the choir and the exquisitely detailed statues of the archangel Gabriel and the Virgin in the crossing (the intersection of the nave and the transepts) are among the church's outstanding features. ⚠ **Due to renovation work the Kreuzgang (Cloisters), reached via the garden, the Allerheiligenkapelle (All Saints' Chapel), and the ancient shell of St. Stephan's Church are inaccessible until 2020.** ⊠ *Dompl. 50* ☎ *0941/586–5500* 🖵 *Free; €3 for tour.*

Domschatzmuseum (*Cathedral Museum*). This museum contains valuable treasures going back to the 11th century. Some of the vestments and the monstrances, which are fine examples of eight centuries' worth of the goldsmith's trade, are still used during special services. The entrance is in the nave. ⊠ *Dompl.* ☎ *0941/597–2530* 🖵 *€3* ☉ *Closed Sun.*

Historisches Museum. The municipal museum vividly relates the cultural history of Regensburg. It's one of the highlights of the city, both for its unusual and beautiful setting—a former Gothic monastery—and for its wide-ranging collections, from Roman artifacts to Renaissance tapestries and remains from Regensburg's 16th-century Jewish ghetto. The most significant exhibits are the paintings by Albrecht Altdorfer (1480–1538), a native of Regensburg and, along with Cranach, Grünewald,

Regensburg's Dom St. Peter is an excellent example of the French Gothic style.

and Dürer, one of the leading painters of the German Renaissance. Altdorfer's work has the same sense of heightened reality found in that of his contemporaries, in which the lessons of Italian painting are used to produce an emotional rather than a rational effect. His paintings would not have seemed out of place among those of 19th-century Romantics. Far from seeing the world around him as essentially hostile, or at least alien, he saw it as something intrinsically beautiful, whether wild or domesticated. Altdorfer made two drawings of the old synagogue of Regensburg, priceless documents that are on exhibit here. ⊠ *Dachaupl. 2–4* ☎ *0941/507–2448* 🖼 *€5* 🕙 *Closed Mon.*

Karmelitenkirche (*Church of the Carmelites*). This lovely church, in the baroque style from crypt to cupola, stands next to the Alte Kapelle. It has a finely decorated facade designed by the 17th-century Italian master Carlo Lurago. ⊠ *Alter Kornmarkt* 🖼 *Free.*

Neupfarrplatz. Prior to 1519, this oversized square was once the heart of the Jewish ghetto. The **Neupfarrkirche** (New Parish Church) here, built as a pilgrimage church, was given to the Protestants, hence its barebones interior. In the late 1990s, excavation work (for the power company) on the square uncovered well-kept cellars and, to the west of the church, the old synagogue, including the foundations of its Romanesque predecessor. Archaeologists salvaged the few items they could from the old stones. Recovered items were carefully restored and are on exhibit in the Historisches Museum. Only one small underground area to the south of the church, the **Document,** accommodates viewing of the foundations. In a former cellar, surrounded by the original walls, visitors can watch a short video reconstructing life in the old Jewish ghetto. Over the old synagogue, the Israeli artist Dani Karavan designed a stylized plaza where people can sit and meet. VHS offers tour of the Document (reservations are requested). ⊠ *Neupfarrpl.* ☎ *0941/507–2433 for tours led by VHS* ⊕ *www.vhs-regensburg.de* ⊠ *Document €5.*

Porta Praetoria. The rough-hewn former gate to the old Roman camp, built in AD 179, is one of the most interesting relics of Roman Regensburg. Look through the grille on its east side to see a section of the original Roman road, about 10 feet below today's street level. ⊠ *Unter den Schwibbögen* ✛ *North side of Alter Kornmarkt.*

Schloss Emmeram (*Emmeram Palace*). Formerly a Benedictine monastery, this is the ancestral home of the princely Thurn und Taxis family, which made its fame and fortune after being granted the right to carry official and private mail throughout the empire and Spain by Emperor Maximilian I (1493–1519) and by Philip I, king of Spain. Their horn still symbolizes the post office in several European countries. After the death of her husband, Prince Johannes, in 1990, the young dowager Princess Gloria von Thurn und Taxis put many of the palace's treasures on display. A visit to the **State Rooms** include the splendid ballroom and throne room, allowing you to witness the setting of courtly life in the 19th century (guided tours only). A visit usually includes the fine **Kreuzgang** (cloister) of the former abbey. The items in the **Princely Treasury** have been carefully selected for their fine craftsmanship—be it dueling pistols, a plain marshal's staff, a boudoir, or a snuffbox. The palace's **Marstallmuseum** (former royal stables) holds the family's coaches and carriages as well as related items. ⊠ *Emmeramspl.* 5 ☎ *0941/504–8133* ⊕ *www.thurnundtaxis.de* ⊠ *From €5* ☉ *State Rooms closed weekdays mid-Nov.–mid-Mar. Princely Treasury and Marstallmuseum closed weekdays Nov.–Mar.*

Fodor's Choice ★ **Steinerne Brücke** (*Stone Bridge*). This impressive old bridge resting on massive pontoons is Regensburg's most celebrated sight. It was completed in 1146 and was rightfully considered a miraculous piece of engineering at the time. As the only crossing point over the Danube for miles, it effectively cemented Regensburg's control over trade. The significance of the little statue on the bridge is a mystery, but the figure seems to be a witness to the legendary rivalry between the master builders of the bridge and those of the Dom. ⊠ *Regensburg.*

St. Emmeram. The family church of the Thurn und Taxis family stands across from their ancestral palace, the Schloss Emmeram. The foundations of the church date to the 7th and 8th centuries. A richly decorated baroque interior was added in 1730 by the Asam brothers. St. Emmeram contains the graves of the 7th-century martyred Regensburg bishop Emmeram and the 10th-century saint Wolfgang. ⊠ *Emmeramspl.* 3 ☎ *0941/51030* ⊠ *Free.*

Walhalla. This is a sight you won't want to miss if you have an interest in the wilder expressions of newfound 19th-century pan-Germanic nationalism. Walhalla—a name resonant with Nordic mythology—was where the god Odin received the souls of dead heroes. Ludwig I erected this monumental pantheon temple in 1840 to honor important Germans from ages past, kept current with busts of Albert Einstein and Sophie

The Golden Gate Bridge may be better known today, but the 12th-century Steinerne Brücke (Stone Bridge) was its match in terms of engineering ingenuity and importance in its day.

Scholl. In keeping with the neoclassical style of the time, it is actually a copy of the Parthenon in Athens. The expanses of costly marble are evidence of both the financial resources and the craftsmanship at Ludwig's command. Walhalla may be kitschy, but the fantastic view it affords over the Danube and the wide countryside is definitely worth a look. A boat ride from the Steinerne Brücke in Regensburg is the best way to go. To get to the temple from the river, you'll have to climb 358 marble steps. ⊠ *Walhalla-Str. 48, Donaustauf* ✛ *Take Danube Valley country road (unnumbered) east from Regensburg 8 km (5 miles) to Donaustauf. Walhalla temple is 1 km (½ mile) outside village and well signposted* ⊕ *www.walhalla-regensburg.de* ⌦ *€4.*

Weltenburg Abbey (*Abbey Church of Sts. George and Martin*). Roughly 25 km (15 miles) southwest of Regensburg you'll find the great Weltenburg Benedictine Abbey sitting serenely on the bank of the Danube River. The most dramatic approach to the abbey is by boat (€10.50 round-trip) from Kelheim, 10 km (6 miles) downstream. On the stunning ride the boat winds between towering limestone cliffs that rise straight up from the tree-lined riverbanks. The abbey, constructed between 1716 and 1718, is commonly regarded as the masterpiece of the brothers Cosmas Damian and Egid Quirin Asam, two leading baroque architects and decorators of Bavaria. Their extraordinary composition of painted figures whirling on the ceiling, lavish and brilliantly polished marble, highly wrought statuary, and stucco figures dancing in rhythmic arabesques across the curving walls is the epitome of Bavarian baroque. Note especially the bronze equestrian statue of St. George above the high altar, reaching down imperiously with his flamelike, twisted gilt sword to dispatch the winged dragon at his feet. In Kelheim there are two boat companies that offer trips to Kloster Weltenburg every 30 minutes in summer. You cannot miss the landing stages and the huge parking lot. No Bavarian monastery is complete without a brewery and Kloster Weltenburg's is well worth visiting. ⊠ *Asamstr. 32, Kelheim* ⊕ *kloster-weltenburg.de* ✉ *Free.*

WHERE TO EAT

$ ✕ **Café Felix.** A modern two-level café and bar, Felix offers everything
CAFÉ   from sandwiches to steaks, and buzzes with activity from breakfast until the early hours. Light from an artsy chandelier and torchlike fixtures bounces off the many large framed mirrors. **Known for:** good, solid food for all meals; younger crowd; open early and late. $ *Average main: €10* ⊠ *Fröhliche-Türkenstr. 6* ☎ *0941/59059* ⊕ *www.cafefelix. de* ⊟ *No credit cards.*

$ ✕ **Historische Wurstküche.** At the world's oldest, and possibly smallest,
GERMAN   bratwurst grill, just by the Stone Bridge, succulent Regensburger sausages are prepared right before your eyes on an open beech-wood charcoal grill. If you want to eat them inside in the tiny dining room, you'll have to squeeze past the cook to get them. **Known for:** best Regensburger sausages in town; cozy atmosphere; meeting place for locals. $ *Average main: €9* ⊠ *Thundorferstr. 3* ☎ *0941/466–210* ⊕ *www. wurstkuchl.de* ⊟ *No credit cards* ⊗ *No dinner.*

$ ✕ **Leerer Beutel.** The "Empty Sack" prepares excellent international
ECLECTIC   cuisine—from antipasti to solid pork roast—served in a pleasant vaulted room supported by massive rough-hewn beams. **Known for:** rustic ambience; solid Franconian cuisine with international elements; a huge warehouse that's also a venue for concerts, exhibitions, and film screenings. $ *Average main: €14* ⊠ *Bertoldstr. 9* ☎ *0941/58997* ⊕ *www.leerer-beutel.de.*

WHERE TO STAY

$$ 🏨 **Grand Hôtel Orphée.** It's difficult to choose between the very spacious
HOTEL   rooms at the Grand, whether you decide to take an attic room with
Fodor's Choice   large wooden beams or an elegant room with stucco ceilings on the first
★   floor. **Pros:** tastefully apportioned rooms; excellent restaurant; center of town. **Cons:** difficult parking; front rooms are noisy; separate properties confusing. $ *Rooms from: €105* ⊠ *Untere Bachg. 8* ☎ *0941/596–020* ⊕ *www.hotel-orphee.de* ⇌ *34 rooms* ⦿| *Free Breakfast.*

$$ 🏨 **Hotel Münchner Hof.** This little hotel provides top service at a good
HOTEL   price, with Regensburg at your feet and the Neupfarrkirche nearby. **Pros:** some rooms with historic features; center of town; nice little lobby. **Cons:** not easy to find the entrance on narrow street; difficult parking; some rooms have thin walls. $ *Rooms from: €102* ⊠ *Tändlerg. 9* ☎ *0941/58440* ⊕ *www.muenchner-hof.de* ⇌ *53 rooms* ⦿| *Free Breakfast.*

$$ 🏨 **Hotel-Restaurant Bischofshof am Dom.** This is one of Germany's most his-
HOTEL   toric hostelries, a former bishop's palace where you can sleep in an apartment that includes part of a Roman gateway. **Pros:** historic building;

no-smoking rooms only; nice courtyard beer garden. **Cons:** restaurant not up to hotel's standards; no air-conditioning; some rooms showing their age. [$] *Rooms from: €150* ✉ *Krauterermarkt 3* ☎ *0941/58460* 🌐 *www.hotel-bischofshof.de* 🛏 *59 rooms* 🍴 *Free Breakfast.*

$ HOTEL 🏨 **Kaiserhof am Dom.** Renaissance windows punctuate the green facade of this historic city mansion, but the rooms are 20th-century modern. **Pros:** front rooms have a terrific view; historic breakfast room; pleasant staff. **Cons:** front rooms are noisy; no restaurant or bar; unimpressive breakfast buffet. [$] *Rooms from: €99* ✉ *Kramg. 10–12* ☎ *0941/585-350* 🌐 *www.kaiserhof-am-dom.de* 🕒 *Closed Dec. 21–Jan. 8* 🛏 *30 rooms* 🍴 *Free Breakfast.*

SHOPPING

The winding alleyways of the Altstadt are packed with boutiques, ateliers, jewelers, and other small shops offering a vast array of arts and crafts. You may also want to visit the Neupfarrplatz market (Monday through Saturday 9–4), where you can buy regional specialties such as *Radi* (juicy radish roots), which locals wash down with a glass of wheat beer.

5

PASSAU

137 km (85 miles) southeast of Regensburg, 179 km (111 miles) northeast of Munich.

Flanking the borders of Austria and the Czech Republic, Passau dates back more than 2,500 years. Originally settled by the Celts, then by the Romans, it later passed into the possession of prince-bishops whose domains stretched into present-day Hungary. In 752 a monk named Boniface founded the diocese of Passau, which at its height would be the largest church subdivision in the entire Holy Roman Empire.

Passau's location is truly unique. Nowhere else in the world do three rivers—the Ilz from the north, the Danube from the west, and the Inn from the south—meet. Wedged between the Inn and the Danube, the Old Town is a maze of narrow cobblestone streets lined with beautifully preserved burgher and patrician houses and riddled with churches. Many streets have been closed to traffic, making the Old Town a fun and mysterious place to explore.

GETTING HERE AND AROUND

Passau is on the A-3 autobahn from Regensburg to Vienna. It's an hour from Regensburg and about four hours from Vienna by train.

TOURS

The Passau tourist office leads tours May through October at 10:30 and 2:30 on weekdays and at 2:30 on Sunday; November through April the tours are held weekdays at noon. Tours start at the entrance to the cathedral. A one-hour tour costs €4.

Donauschiffahrt Wurm + Köck. In Passau cruises on the three rivers begin and end at the Danube jetties on Fritz-Schäffer Promenade. Donauschiffahrt Wurm + Köck runs 12 ships with capacity varying from 250 to 1,100 passengers. Options for tours include city sightseeing from the water, excursions with time ashore, an evening cruise with dinner, and a popular full-day excursion to the Austrian city of Linz, which departs at 9 am. ☒ *Passau* ☎ *0851/929–292* ⊕ *www.donauschiffahrt. de* ✉ *From €9; dinner cruises from €29.*

FESTIVALS

Christkindlmarkt. Passau's Christmas market is the biggest and most spectacular of the Bavarian Forest. It's held in the heart of the city's Altstadt, at the steps of Dom St. Stephan, from late November until just before Christmas. ☒ *Dompl.* ⊕ *www.passauer-christkindlmarkt.de.*

Europäische Wochen (*European Weeks*). Passau is the cultural center of Lower Bavaria. Its Europäische Wochen festival—featuring everything from opera to pantomime—is a major event on the European music calendar. The festival runs from mid-June to July or early August and is held in venues all over the city. ☒ *Dr.-Hans-Kapfinger-Str. 22* ⊕ *www. ew-passau.de.*

VISITOR INFORMATION

Contacts Tourist-Information Passau. ☒ *Rathauspl. 3* ☎ *0851/955–980* ⊕ *www.passau.de.*

EXPLORING

Fodor's Choice
★
Dom St. Stephan (*St. Stephan's Cathedral*). The cathedral rises majestically on the highest point of the earliest-settled part of the city. A baptismal church stood here in the 6th century, and 200 years later, when Passau became a bishop's seat, the first basilica was built. It was dedicated to St. Stephan and became the original mother church of St. Stephan's Cathedral in Vienna. A fire reduced the medieval basilica to ruins in 1662; it was then rebuilt by Italian master architect Carlo Lurago. What you see today is the largest baroque basilica north of the Alps, complete with an octagonal dome and flanking towers. Little in its marble- and stucco-encrusted interior reminds you of Germany, and much proclaims the exuberance of Rome. Beneath the dome is the largest church organ assembly in the world. Built between 1924 and 1928 and enlarged in 1979–80, it claims no fewer than 17,774 pipes and 233 stops. The church also houses the most powerful bell chimes in southern Germany. ☒ *Dompl.* ☎ *0851/3930* ✉ *Free; concerts from €4.*

Domplatz (*Cathedral Square*). This large square in front of the Dom is bordered by sturdy 17th- and 18th-century buildings, including the **Alte Residenz,** the former bishop's palace and now a courthouse. The neoclassical statue at the center is Bavarian King Maximilian I, who watches over the Christmas market in December. ☒ *Passau.*

Domschatz- und Diözesanmuseum (*Cathedral Treasury and Diocesan Museum*). The cathedral museum houses one of Bavaria's largest collections of religious treasures, the legacy of Passau's rich episcopal history. The museum is part of the **Neue Residenz,** which has a stately baroque entrance opening onto a magnificent staircase—a scintillating study in marble, fresco, and stucco. ☒ *Residenzpl.* ✉ *€2* ⊘ *Closed Sun.*

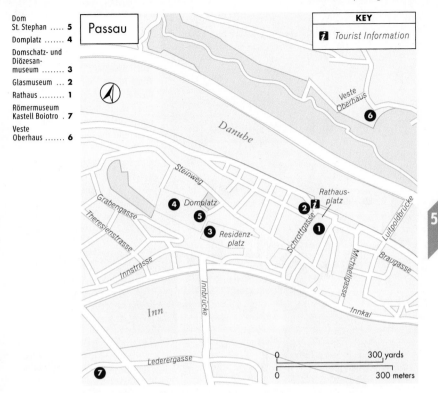

Glasmuseum (*Glass Museum*). The world's most comprehensive collection of European glass is housed in the lovely Hotel Wilder Mann. The history of Central Europe's glassmaking is captured in 30,000 items, from baroque to art deco, spread over 35 rooms. The museum also houses the world's largest collection of cookbooks. ✉ *Höllg. 1* ☎ *0851/35071* ⊕ *www.glasmuseum.de* 🖃 €7.

Rathaus. Passau's 14th-century Town Hall sits like a Venetian merchant's house on a small square fronting the Danube. It was the home of a wealthy German merchant before being declared the seat of city government after a 1298 uprising. Two assembly rooms have wall paintings depicting scenes from local history and legend, including the (fictional) arrival in the city of Siegfried's fair Kriemhild, from the Nibelungen fable. The Rathaus tower has Bavaria's largest glockenspiel, which plays daily at 10:30, 2, and 7:25, with an additional performance at 3:30 on Saturday. ✉ *Rathauspl.* ☎ *0851/3960* 🖃 €2.

Römermuseum Kastell Boiotro (*Roman Museum*). While excavating a 17th-century pilgrimage church, archaeologists uncovered a stout Roman fortress with five defense towers and walls more than 12 feet thick. The Roman citadel Boiotro was discovered on a hill known as the Mariahilfberg on the south bank of the river Inn, with its Roman well still plentiful and fresh. Pottery, lead figures, and other artifacts from

the area are housed in this museum at the edge of the site. ✉ *Ledererg. 43* ☎ *0851/34769* 🎟 *€4* 🕒 *Closed Mon.*

Veste Oberhaus (*Upper House Stronghold*). The powerful fortress and summer castle commissioned by Bishop Ulrich II in 1219 looks over Passau from an impregnable site on the other side of the river, opposite the Rathaus. Today the Veste Oberhaus is Passau's most important museum, containing exhibits that illustrate the city's 2,000-year history. From the terrace of its café-restaurant (open Easter–October), there's a magnificent view of Passau and the convergence of the three rivers. ✉ *Oberhaus 125* ✥ *To reach fortress, take bus from Rathauspl. (€5; Apr.–Nov., daily every ½ hr 10:30–5)* ☎ *0851/493–3512* 🌐 *www.oberhausmuseum.de* 🎟 *€5.*

WHERE TO EAT

5

$ GERMAN 🍴 **Hacklberger Bräustüberl.** Shaded by magnificent old trees, locals sit in this famous brewery's enormous beer garden (seating more than 1,000), sipping a Hacklberger and tucking into a plate of sausages. **Known for:** homemade beer since 1618; simple Bavarian brewhouse food; enormous beer garden that moves inside in the winter. [$] *Average main: €11* ✉ *Bräuhauspl. 7* ☎ *0851/58382* 🌐 *www.hacklbergers.de.*

$$ GERMAN 🍴 **Heilig-Geist-Stiftsschenke.** For atmospheric dining this 14th-century monastery-turned-wine cellar is a must. In summer eat beneath chestnut trees; in winter seek out the warmth of the vaulted, dark-paneled dining rooms. **Known for:** fish from the Stift's own ponds; wine from the Stift's own vineyards; traditional regional cuisine. [$] *Average main: €16* ✉ *Heilig-Geist-G. 4* ☎ *0851/2607* 🌐 *www.stiftskeller-passau.de* 🕒 *Closed Wed., and last 3 wks in Jan.*

$ GERMAN 🍴 **Peschel Terrasse.** The beer you sip on the high, sunny terrace overlooking the Danube is brought fresh from Peschl's own brewery below, which, along with this traditional Bavarian restaurant, has been in the same family since 1855. **Known for:** solid traditional Bavarian cuisine; homemade beer; extraordinary view. [$] *Average main: €11* ✉ *Rosstränke 4* ☎ *0851/2489* 🌐 *www.peschl-terrasse.de.*

$ GERMAN 🍴 **Zum Suppentopf.** Serving rustic home-style soups, just like your German grandmother makes, Zum Suppentopf is loved by locals and visitors alike, but keep a lookout: it's easy to walk by this small restaurant without noticing. The owner, Jacques, pours his soul into every bowl, and the large selection of daily offerings—rare in a venue this size—are all freshly prepared using local ingredients. **Known for:** simple delicious soups; creative uses of local produce; local hangout. [$] *Average main: €7* ✉ *Grabeng. 13/L* ☎ *0851/490–8560* 💳 *No credit cards.*

WHERE TO STAY

$$ HOTEL 🏨 **Hotel König.** Though built in 1984, the König blends successfully with the graceful Italian-style buildings alongside the elegant Danube waterfront. **Pros:** some rooms have an impressive view of the Danube; most rooms are spacious; incredible service and breakfast. **Cons:** no restaurant; uninspired bathrooms; some small rooms. [$] *Rooms from:*

€140 ✉ *Untere Donaulände 1* ☎ *0851/3850* ⊕ *www.hotel-koenig.de* ⟲ *61 rooms* ⦿| *Free Breakfast.*

$$ ⊞ **Hotel Weisser Hase.** The "White Rabbit" began accommodating travel-
HOTEL   ers in the early 16th century but is thoroughly modernized. **Pros:** good location in the heart of Passau; large marble bathrooms; great breakfast. **Cons:** street noise in the early morning; no air-conditioning; the hotel is in several buildings and sometimes feels cobbled together. Ⓢ *Rooms from: €170* ✉ *Heiliggeistg. 1* ☎ *0851/92110* ⊕ *www.weisser-hase.de* ⊘ *Closed Jan.–mid-Feb.* ⟲ *108 rooms* ⦿| *Free Breakfast.*

$ ⊞ **Hotel Wilder Mann.** Passau's most historic hotel dates from the 11th
HOTEL   century and is near the old Town Hall on the waterfront market square. **Pros:** historic hotel with some luxurious suites; center of town; some rooms with nice view of the river. **Cons:** some rooms showing their age; no restaurant or bar; spotty Wi-Fi. Ⓢ *Rooms from: €92* ✉ *Am Rathauspl. 1* ☎ *0851/35071* ⊕ *www.wilder-mann.com* ⟲ *54 rooms* ⦿| *Free Breakfast.*

THE BODENSEE

WELCOME TO THE BODENSEE

TOP REASONS TO GO

★ **The Bodensee:** Whether you're circling the lake on foot, or by bike, car, or train, crossing the water by boat, or dipping into it on a hot summer's day, the beautiful Bodensee affords myriad pleasures.

★ **Zeppelin Museum, Friedrichshafen:** Step inside the gracious passenger rooms of the airship, and you may question whether the air transport of today, though undeniably bigger and faster, is a real improvement.

★ **Altes Schloss in Meersburg:** Explore the oldest continuously inhabited castle in Germany, from the sinister dungeons to the imposing knights' hall.

★ **Schloss Salem, near Überlingen:** The castle itself offers plenty to see, with furnished rooms, stables, gardens, and museums.

★ **Mainau Island:** More than a million tulips and narcissi grace the flower island in spring—later they're followed by rhododendrons and azaleas, roses and dahlias.

The Bodensee (Lake Constance) is off the beaten path for most visitors, but for Germans it's a favorite summer vacation spot, so it's wise to reserve rooms in advance.

1 Lindau. A charming town a short ferry ride from Bregenz, Austria.

2 Friedrichshafen. Founded in the 19th century, this is where German zeppelins were built.

3 Meersburg. A romantic, old town with a car-free center.

4 Überlingen. A resort town with an almost Mediterranean feel.

5 Ravensburg. This medieval town has some of the best preserved walls and gates in Germany.

6 Weingarten. A small town known for its large baroque basilica.

7 Konstanz. This university town is the largest on the Bodensee.

8 Mainau. A tiny island covered with flower gardens.

9 Reichenau. A Bodensee island with three Romanesque churches and acres of greenhouses.

6

Updated
by Chantal
Panozzo

A natural summer playground, the Bodensee (Lake Constance) is ringed with little towns and busy resorts. Lapping the shores of Germany, Switzerland, and Austria, the Bodensee, at 63 km (39 miles) long and 14 km (9 miles) wide, is the largest lake in the German-speaking world.

Though called a lake, it's actually a vast swelling of the Rhine, gouged out by a massive glacier in the Ice Age and flooded by the river as the ice receded. The Rhine flows into its southeast corner, where Switzerland and Austria meet, and flows out at its west end. On the German side, the Bodensee is bordered almost entirely by the state of Baden-Württemberg (a small portion of the eastern tip, from Lindau to Nonnenhorn, belongs to Bavaria).

It's one of the warmest areas of the country, not just because of its southern latitude but also owing to the warming influence of the water, which gathers heat in summer and releases it in winter. The lake itself practically never freezes over—it has done so only once in the past two centuries. The climate is excellent for growing fruit, and along the roads you'll find stands and shops selling apples, peaches, strawberries, jams, juices, wines, and schnapps, much of it homemade.

MAJOR REGIONS

There's a feeling on **The Northern Shore,** in the midst of a peaceful Alpine landscape, that the Bodensee is part of Germany and yet separated from it—which is literally the case for **Lindau,** which sits in the lake tethered to land by a causeway. **Friedrichshafen** was once the center for the German zeppelin program. **Meersburg,** with its pedestrianized core, is one of the most romantic destinations on the lake. **Überlingen,** a beautiful resort at the northwestern finger of the lake, attracts many vacationers and spa goers. Clear days reveal the snowcapped mountains of Switzerland to the south and the peaks of the Austrian Vorarlberg to the east.

From Friedrichshafen, B-30 leads north along the valley of the little River Schussen and links up with one of Germany's lesser-known but most attractive scenic routes. The Oberschwäbische Barockstrasse (**Upper Swabian Baroque Road**) follows a rich series of baroque churches and abbeys. **Ravensburg,** once a thriving economic center in southern Germany, has a well-preserved medieval core. Germany's largest baroque church can be found in **Weingarten.**

The area **Around the Bodanrück Peninsula** on the northwestern edge of the lake has several places that are worth a visit. The immense Bodensee owes its name to a small, insignificant town, Bodman, on the peninsula. The university town **Konstanz** is the largest on the Bodensee. The tiny island of **Mainau** has been turned into a botanical garden and also has an extensive children's play area and a small farm. **Reichenau,** another island, is a farming center that is also known for its Romanesque churches. The peninsula's most popular destinations, Konstanz and Mainau, are reachable by ferry from Meersburg—by far the most romantic way to get to the area. The other option is to take the road (B-31, then B-34, and finally B-33) that skirts the western arm of the Bodensee and ends its German journey at Konstanz.

PLANNING

WHEN TO GO

6

The Bodensee's temperate climate makes for pleasant weather from April to October. In spring, orchard blossoms explode everywhere, and on Mainau, the "island of flowers," more than a million tulips, hyacinths, and narcissi burst into bloom. Holiday crowds come in summer, and autumn can be warm and mellow. Some hotels and restaurants as well as many tourist attractions close for winter.

GETTING HERE AND AROUND

AIR TRAVEL

The closest major international airport is in Zürich, Switzerland, 60 km (37 miles) from Konstanz, connected by the autobahn. There are also direct trains from the Zürich airport to Konstanz. There are several domestic and international (primarily of United Kingdom and European origin) flights to the regional airport at Friedrichshafen—these are mostly operated by budget airlines.

Contacts Flughafen Friedrichshafen (FDH). ✉ *Am Flugpl. 64, Friedrichshafen* ☎ *07541/2840* ⊕ *www.bodensee-airport.eu.* **Zürich Airport (ZRH).** ✉ *Flughafenstr., Kloten* ☎ *043/8162211 for general info, 0900/300–313 for flight info (CHF 1.99 per min)* ⊕ *www.zurich-airport.com.*

BOAT AND FERRY TRAVEL

Car and passenger ferries have different docking points in the various towns. The car ferries run all year; in summer you may have to wait in line. The passenger routes, especially the small ones, often do not run from November to March. Sailing on a car ferry as a passenger can be cheaper than taking a passenger ferry—and most car ferries are reasonably comfortable. Bicycles can be taken on both types of ferry, and because one of the best ways to experience the Bodensee area is by bike, taking one is highly recommended. ■ TIP➔ **Note that the English pronunciation of "ferry" sounds a lot like the German word "fähre," which means car ferry. "Schiffe" is the term used for passenger ferries.**

The Weisse Flotte line of boats, which is run by the Bodensee-Schiffs-betriebe (BSB), links most of the larger towns and resorts. One of the nicest trips is from Konstanz to Meersburg and then on to the island of Mainau. Excursions around the lake last from one hour to a full day. Many cross to Austria and Switzerland; some head west along the Rhine to Schaffhausen and the Rheinfall, the largest waterfall in Europe. Information on lake excursions is available from all local tourist offices and travel agencies.

Contacts Bodensee-Schiffsbetriebe. ⊠ *Hafenstr. 6, Konstanz* ☎ *07531/36400* ⊕ *www.bsb.de.*

BUS TRAVEL

Buses serve most smaller communities that have no train links, but service is infrequent. Along the shore there are buses that run regularly throughout the day from Überlingen to Friedrichshafen, stopping in towns such as Meersburg, Hagnau, and Immenstaad.

CAR TRAVEL

The A-96 autobahn provides the most direct route between Munich and Lindau. For a more scenic, slower route, take B-12 via Landsberg and Kempten. For another scenic and slower route from Frankfurt, take B-311 at Ulm and follow the Oberschwäbische Barockstrasse (Upper Swabian Baroque Road) to Friedrichshafen. From Stuttgart, follow the A-81 autobahn south. At Exit 40 take B-33 to Konstanz, or the A-98 autobahn and B-31 for the northern shore. Lindau is also a terminus of the picturesque Deutsche Alpenstrasse (German Alpine Road), running east–west from Salzburg to Lindau.

Lakeside roads, particularly those on the northern shore, boast won-derful vistas but experience occasional heavy traffic in summer, and on weekends and holidays year-round. Stick to the speed limits in spite of tailgaters—speed traps are frequent, especially in built-up areas. For-malities at border-crossing points are few. However, in addition to your passport you'll need insurance and registration papers for your car. For rental cars, check with the rental company to make sure you are allowed to take the car into other countries. Crossing into Switzerland, you're required to have an autobahn tax sticker (CHF 40 or €40, payable in euros or Swiss francs) if you plan to drive on the Swiss autobahn. These are available from border customs offices, and from petrol sta-tions and post offices in Switzerland. This sticker is not necessary if you plan to stick to nonautobahn roads. Car ferries link Romanshorn, in Switzerland, with Friedrichshafen, as well as Konstanz with Meersburg. Taking either ferry saves substantial mileage. The fare depends on the size of the car.

TRAIN TRAVEL

From Frankfurt to Friedrichshafen and Lindau, take the ICE (InterCity Express) to Ulm and then transfer (total time four hours). A combina-tion of ICE and regional train gets you to Konstanz from Frankfurt in 4½ hours, passing through the beautiful scenery of the Black Forest. From Stuttgart to Konstanz, take the IC (InterCity) to Singen, and transfer to an RE or IRE (Regional/InterRegio Express) for the brief last leg to Konstanz (total time 2½ hours). From Munich to Lindau, the EC (Europe Express) train or the ALX (Alex) train takes 2½ hours. From Zürich to Konstanz, the trip lasts 1½ hours. Local trains encircle the Bodensee, stopping at most towns and villages.

HOTELS

Accommodations in the towns and resorts around the lake include venerable wedding-cake-style, fin de siècle palaces as well as more modest *Gasthöfe*. If you're visiting in July and August, make reservations in advance. For lower rates in a more rural atmosphere, consider staying a few miles away from the lake.

RESTAURANTS

In this area, international dishes are not only on the menu but also on the map—you have to drive only a few miles to try the Swiss or Austrian dish you're craving in its own land. *Seeweine* (lake wines) from vineyards in the area include Müller-Thurgau, Spätburgunder, Ruländer, and Kerner.

Prices in restaurant reviews are the average cost of a main course at dinner, or if dinner is not served, at lunch. Prices in hotel reviews are the lowest cost of a standard double room in high season.

WHAT IT COSTS IN EUROS			
$	**$$**	**$$$**	**$$$$**
Restaurants	under €15	€15–€20	€21–€25	over €25
Hotels	under €100	€100–€175	€176–€225	over €225

TOURS

Most of the larger tourist centers have city tours with English-speaking guides. The Bodensee is a great destination for bike travelers, with hundreds of miles of well-signposted paths that keep riders safe from cars. You can go on your own or enjoy the comfort of a customized tour with accommodations and baggage transport (and a rental bike, if need be). Wine-tasting tours are available in Überlingen, Konstanz, and Meersburg. Call the local tourist offices for information. Zeppelin tours operated by the Deutsche Zeppelin Reederei (DZR) are not cheap (sightseeing trips cost €245–€845), but they do offer a special experience and a reminder of the grand old days of flight. The zeppelins depart from the airport in Friedrichshafen.

Deutsche Zeppelin Reederei. Perfect for aviation enthusiasts, and those looking for a unique way to experience the Bodensee: glide silently above it in a Zeppelin. ⊠ *Messestr. 132, Friedrichshafen* ☎ *07541/59000* ⊕ *www.zeppelinflug.de* ✈ *From €245.*

Radweg-Reisen GmbH. This cycle-hire company's most popular tour circumnavigates the Bodensee in a relaxed eight days, with hotel accommodation and breakfast included. ⊠ *Fritz-Arnold-Str. 16a, Konstanz* ☎ *07531/819–930* ⊕ *www.radweg-reisen.com* ✈ *From €529.*

Velotours Touristik GmbH. Velotours offers a variety of cycle-tour options around the Bodensee. Their Eastern Bodensee route begins and ends in Konstanz, taking in highlights in Germany, Austria, and Switzerland, including a ferry "shortcut" from Konstanz to Meersburg. ⊠ *Bücklestr. 13, Konstanz* ☎ *07531/98280* ⊕ *www.velotours.de* ⊠ *From €475.*

PLANNING YOUR TIME

Choosing a place to stay is a question of finance and interest. The closer you stay to the water, the more expensive and lively it becomes. Many visitors pass by on their way from one country to another, so during the middle of the day, key hubs like Konstanz, Mainau, Meersburg, and Lindau tend to be crowded. Try to visit these places either in the morning or in the late afternoon, and make your day trips to the lesser-known destinations: the baroque churches in upper Swabia, the Swiss towns along the southern shore, or the nearby mountains.

VISITOR INFORMATION

Contacts Internationale Bodensee Tourismus. ⊠ *Hafenstr. 6, Konstanz* ☎ *07531/133–030* ⊕ *www.bodensee.eu.*

LINDAU

180 km (112 miles) southwest of Munich.

By far the best way to get to know this charming old island town is on foot. Lose yourself in the maze of small streets and passageways flanked by centuries-old houses. Wander down to the harbor for magnificent views, with the Austrian shoreline and mountains close by to the east. Just 13 km (8 miles) away, they are nearer than the Swiss mountains visible to the southwest.

Lindau was made a Free Imperial City within the Holy Roman Empire in 1275. It had developed as a fishing settlement and then spent hundreds of years as a trading center along the route between the rich lands of Swabia and Italy. The Lindauer Bote, an important stagecoach service between Germany and Italy in the 18th and 19th centuries, was based here; Goethe traveled via this service on his first visit to Italy in 1788. The stagecoach was revived a few years ago, carrying passengers on a 13-day journey to Italy. This service only runs occasionally—ask at the Lindau tourist office.

As the German empire crumbled toward the end of the 18th century, battered by Napoléon's revolutionary armies, Lindau fell victim to competing political groups. It was ruled by the Austrian Empire before passing into Bavarian control in 1805. Lindau's harbor was rebuilt in 1856.

GETTING HERE AND AROUND

Lindau is halfway between Munich and Zürich, and about two hours from both on the EC (European Express) train. From Frankfurt it takes about four hours—change from the ICE (InterCity Express) train in Ulm to the IRE (InterRegio Express) train. You can also reach Lindau by boat: it takes about 20 minutes from Bregenz across the bay. Once in Lindau, you can reach everything on foot. Its *Altstadt* (Old Town) is a maze of ancient streets with half-timber and gable houses making up most of the island. The center and main street is the pedestrian-only Maximilianstrasse.

TOURS

The best way to see Lindau is from the lake. Take one of the pleasure boats of the Bodensee-Schiffsbetriebe (sometimes referred to locally as the Weisse Flotte, or "white fleet"), which leave Lindau's harbor several times a day for the 20-minute ride to Bregenz in Austria. These large boats carry up to 800 people on three decks. A round trip costs €12.40

VISITOR INFORMATION

Contacts Lindau Tourist-Information. ⊠ Alfred-Nobel-Pl. 1 ☎ 08382/260–030 ⊕ www.lindau.de.

EXPLORING

Altes Rathaus (*Old Town Hall*). The Old Town Hall is the finest of Lindau's handsome historic buildings. It was constructed between 1422 and 1436 in the midst of a vineyard and given a Renaissance face-lift 150 years later, though the original stepped gables remain. Emperor Maximilian I held an imperial diet (deliberation) here in 1496; a fresco on the south facade depicts the scene. The building retains city government functions, thus its interior is closed to the public. ⊠ Bismarckpl. 4 ⊕ www.lindau.de.

Der Bayerische Löwe (*Bavarian Lion*). A proud symbol of Bavaria, the lion is Lindau's most striking landmark. Carved from Bavarian marble and standing 20 feet high, the lion stares out across the lake from a massive plinth. ⊠ *Lindau Harbor entrance, Römerschanze* ⊕ *www. lindau.de.*

Haus zum Cavazzen (*Stadtmuseum Lindau*). Dating to 1729, this house belonged to a wealthy merchant and is now considered one of the most beautiful in the Bodensee region, owing to its rich decor of frescoes. Today it serves as a local history museum, with collections of glass and pewter items, paintings, and furniture from the past five centuries, alongside touring exhibitions. ⊠ *Marktpl. 6* ☎ *08382/944–073* ⊕ *www. lindau.de* 🎫 *€3* ⊙ *Closed Sept.–Feb.*

FAMILY **Mangenturm** (*Mangturm*). At the harbor's inner edge, across the water from the Neuer Leuchtturm, stands this 13th-century former light-house, one of the lake's oldest. After a lightning strike in the 1970s, the roof tiles were replaced, giving the tower the bright top it now bears. The interior of the tower can be visited as part of organized storytelling events—contact Lindau Tourist-Information. ⊠ *Seeprom-enade* ⊕ *www.lindau.de.*

Marktplatz. Lindau's market square is lined by a series of sturdy and attractive old buildings. The Gothic **Stephanskirche** (St. Stephen's Church) is simple and sparsely decorated, as befits a Lutheran place of worship. It dates to the late 12th century but went through numerous transformations. One of its special features is the green-hue stucco orna-mentation on the ceiling, which immediately attracts the eye toward the heavens. In contrast, the Catholic **Münster Unserer Lieben Frau** (St. Mary's Church), which stands right next to the Stephanskirche, is exuberantly baroque. ⊠ *Marktpl.* ⊕ *www.lindau.de.*

Neuer Leuchtturm (*New Lighthouse; Neuer Lindauer Leuchtturm*). Ger-many's southernmost lighthouse stands sentinel with the Bavarian Lion across the inner harbor's passageway. A viewing platform at the top is open in good weather from April until the end of September. Climb the 139 steps for views over the harbor. ⊠ *Schützingerweg* 🎫 *€3* ⊙ *Closed Oct.–Mar.*

Schloss Montfort (*Montfort Castle*). Twelve km (7½ miles) west of Lindau (about midway between Lindau and Friedrichshafen) is the small, pretty town of Langenargen, famous for the region's most unusual castle, Schloss Montfort. Named for the original owners, the counts of Mont-fort-Werdenberg, this structure was a conventional medieval fortifica-tion until the 19th century, when it was rebuilt in pseudo-Moorish style by its new owner, King Wilhelm I of Württemberg. If you can, see it from a passenger ship on the lake; the castle is especially memorable in the early morning or late afternoon. The castle houses a restaurant, open for dinner from Tuesday to Sunday, April through October, and on weekends during the colder months. The restaurant is also open for Sunday brunch year-round (10–2, all-you-can-eat German buffet-style brunch). A wine bar features in the atmospheric cellar, open Friday night. You can also climb the wooden spiral staircase to the top of the tower for views across the lake to Switzerland, Austria, and over the rolling German countryside. ✉ *Untere Seestr. 3, Langenargen* ☎ *07543/912–712* 🌐 *www.vemax-gastro.de* 🎫 *Tower €2* ⏲ *Tower closed Nov.–Feb.*

Wasserburg. Six kilometers (4 miles) west of Lindau lies Wasserburg, whose name means "water castle," a description of what this enchanting island town once was—a fortress. It was built by the St. Gallen monastery in 924, and the owners, the counts of Montfort zu Tettnang, sold it to the Fugger family of Augsburg. The Fuggers couldn't afford to maintain the drawbridge that connected the castle with the shore and instead built a causeway. In the 18th century the castle passed into the hands of the Habsburgs, and in 1805 the Bavarian government took it over. Wasserburg has some of the most photographed sights of the Bodensee: the yellow, stair-gabled presbytery; the fishermen's St. Georg Kirche, with its onion dome; and the little Malhaus museum, with the castle, Schloss Wasserburg (now a luxury hotel), in the background. ✉ *Lindau* 🌐 *www.wasserburg-bodensee.de.*

BREGENZ, AUSTRIA

Bregenz is a mere 13 km (8 miles) from Lindau, on the other side of the bay. It's a 20-minute boat ride to get there, which makes for a great side trip. Wander around the lakeshore and the lovely, romantic remains of the once-fortified medieval town. An enormous floating stage is the site for performances of grand opera and orchestral works under the stars. Ascend Pfänder Mountain, in Bregenz's backyard, via the *Pfänderbahn* cable tramway for views that stretch as far as the Black Forest and the Swiss Alps.

6

WHERE TO EAT

$$ GERMAN 🍴 **Gasthaus zum Sünfzen.** This ancient inn was serving warm meals to the patricians, officials, merchants, and other good burghers of Lindau back in the 14th century. Today you can sit under the building's arches on the cobblestoned street or in the traditional warm wooden interior and enjoy authentic home-style cooking featuring fish from the lake in season, venison from the mountains, and apples—pressed to juice or distilled to schnapps—from local orchards. **Known for:** regional menu; fresh ingredients; local wine. [$] *Average main: €15* ✉ *Maximilianstr. 1* ☎ *08382/5865* 🌐 *www.suenfzen.de* ⏲ *Closed mid-Jan.–mid-Feb. and Wed. Nov.–Dec.*

WHERE TO STAY

$$ HOTEL 🏨 **Gasthof Engel.** Tucked into one of the Old Town's ancient, narrow streets, this ancient property with a pedigree dating back to 1390 positively exudes history with renovated rooms that maintain a rustic elegance. **Pros:** historic building; central location; redecorated rooms. **Cons:** no elevator; steep, narrow stairs; hard to find parking. [$] *Rooms from: €128* ✉ *Schafg. 4* ☎ *08382/5240* 🌐 *www.engel-lindau.de* 🛏 *10 rooms* 🍽 *Free Breakfast.*

EATING WELL BY THE BODENSEE

On a nice day you could sit on the terrace of a Bodensee restaurant forever, looking across the sparkling waters to the imposing heights of the Alps in the distance. The fish on your plate, possibly caught that very morning in the lake, is another reason to linger. Fish predominates on the menus of the region; 35 varieties swim in the lake, with *Felchen* (whitefish) the most highly prized. Felchen belongs to the salmon family and is best eaten *blau* ("blue"—poached in a mixture of water and vinegar with spices, called *Essigsud*) or *Müllerin* (baked in almonds). A white *Seewein* (lake wine) from one of the vineyards around the lake provides the perfect pairing. Sample a German and a Swiss version. Both use the same kind of grape, from vineyards only a few miles apart, but they produce wines with very different tastes. The Swiss like their wines very dry, whereas the Germans prefer them slightly sweeter.

One of the best-known Swabian dishes is *Maultaschen*, a kind of ravioli, usually served floating in a broth strewn with chives. Another specialty is *Pfannkuchen* (pancakes), generally filled with meat, or chopped into fine strips and scattered in a clear consommé known as *Flädlesuppe*. Hearty *Zwiebelrostbraten* (beef steak with lots of fried onions) is often served with a side of *Spätzle* (hand-cut or pressed, golden soft-textured egg noodles) and accompanied by a good strong Swabian beer.

$$$
HOTEL

Hotel Bayerischer Hof. This is *the* address in town, a stately hotel directly on the edge of the lake, its terrace lush with semitropical, long-flowering plants, trees, and shrubs and its luxuriously appointed rooms featuring lake and mountain views. **Pros:** pretty lake view from many rooms; elegant dining room with good food; majority of rooms air-conditioned. **Cons:** not all rooms have a lake view; no free parking; on weekends in summer parking is difficult. $ *Rooms from: €190* ⊠ *Hafenpl.* ☎ *08382/9150* ⊕ *www.bayerischerhof-lindau.de* ⌁*104 rooms* ○*Free Breakfast.*

$$
HOTEL

Insel-Hotel. In fine weather, you can enjoy breakfast alfresco as you watch the town come alive at this friendly central hotel on the pedestrian-only Maximilianstrasse. **Pros:** center of town; family-run; excellent breakfast. **Cons:** no free parking; some rooms are small; no air-conditioning. $ *Rooms from: €130* ⊠ *Maximilianstr. 42* ☎ *08382/5017* ⊕ *www.insel-hotel-lindau.de* ⌁*28 rooms* ○*Free Breakfast.*

NIGHTLIFE AND PERFORMING ARTS

Fodor'sChoice
★

Bregenzer Festspiele (*Bregenz Music Festival*). A dramatic floating stage supports orchestras and opera stars during the famous Bregenzer Festspiele from mid-July to the end of August. Make reservations well in advance. The Austrian town of Bregenz is 13 km (8 miles) from Lindau, on the other side of the bay. ⊠ *Pl. Der Wiener Symphoniker 1, Bregenz* ☎ *0043/5574–4076* ⊕ *www.bregenzerfestspiele.com.*

FAMILY **Lindauer Marionettenoper.** Enjoy opera in an intimate setting at the Lindauer Marionettenoper, where puppets do the singing. Tickets are available at the Stadttheater box office. ⊠ *Fischerg. 37* ☎ *08382/911–3911* ⊕ *www.marionettenoper.de.*

SPORTS AND THE OUTDOORS

Bodensee Yachtschule. This sailing school in Lindau charters yachts and offers sailing courses for all ages, from beginner to advanced levels. ⊠ *Schiffswerfte 2* ☎ *08382/944–588* ⊕ *www.bodensee-yachtschule.de.*

Surfschule Kreitmeir. You can rent boards and take windsurfing and stand-up paddleboarding lessons at Surfschule Kreitmeir from May through September. ⊠ *Strandbad Eichwald, Eichwaldstr. 20* ☎ *08382/997–6566* ⊕ *www.surfschulelindau.de.*

SHOPPING

Almost all stores are closed on Sunday.

Biedermann en Vogue. This high-end boutique carries various luxury fashion brands, as well as custom-made clothing, cashmere sweaters, and Italian shoes. ⊠ *Maximilianstr. 2* ☎ *08382/944–913.*

Böhm. A destination for interior decorators, Böhm consists of three old houses full of lamps, mirrors, precious porcelain, and elegant furniture. ⊠ *Maximilianstr. 21* ☎ *08382/94880* ⊕ *www.boehmdieeinrichtungen.de.*

FRIEDRICHSHAFEN

24 km (15 miles) west of Lindau.

Named for its founder, King Friedrich I of Württemberg, Friedrichshafen is a relatively young town (dating to 1811). In an area otherwise given over to resort towns and agriculture, Friedrichshafen played a central role in Germany's aeronautics tradition, which saw the development of the zeppelin airship before World War I and the Dornier seaplanes in the 1920s and '30s. The zeppelins were once launched from a floating hangar on the lake, and the Dornier water planes were tested here. The World War II raids on its factories virtually wiped the city off the map. The current layout of the streets is the same, but the buildings are all new and not necessarily pretty. The atmosphere, however, is good and lively, and occasionally you'll find a plaque with a picture of the old building that stood at the respective spot. The factories are back, too. Friedrichshafen is home to such international firms as EADS (airplanes, rockets, and helicopters) and ZF (gear wheels).

GETTING HERE AND AROUND

It takes about two hours from Ulm on the IRE (InterRegio Express) train, then a bus or BOB (Bodensee Oberschwaben Bahn). Most trains stop at Friedrichshafen airport. The car ferry takes you on a 40-minute run across the lake to Romanshorn in Switzerland, where you have direct express trains to the airport and Zürich. In town you can reach most places on foot.

TOURS

Deutsche Zeppelin Reederei GmbH. For an unforgettable experience, take a scenic zeppelin flight out of Friedrichshafen airport. The flying season runs from March to November. For those who prefer to stay grounded, you can also tour the Zeppelin NT (New Technology) in its hangar. ⊠ *Friedrichshafen* ☎ *07541/59000* ⊕ *www.zeppelinflug. de* ☑ *From €195.*

Konair. Konair provide scenic flights, flight lessons, and an air-taxi service around the Bodensee region. ⊠ *Riedstr. 82, Konstanz* ☎ *07531/361– 6905* ⊕ *www.konair.aero.*

VISITOR INFORMATION

Contacts Friedrichshafen Tourist-Information. ⊠ *Bahnhofpl. 2* ☎ *07541/2035–5444* ⊕ *www.friedrichshafen.info.*

EXPLORING

Dornier Museum. Explore a century of pioneering aviation history. Alongside the main focuses on Claude Dornier and his company, restored classic Dornier aircraft and Dornier's explorations into aerospace technology, temporary exhibitions on various aviation themes are shown. A special Dornier Museum/Zeppelin Museum combination ticket provides a discount for those exploring the major aviation attractions of Friedrichshafen. ⊠ *Claude-Dornier-Pl. 1* ⊹ *At Friedrichshafen Airport* ☎ *07541/487–3600* ⊕ *www.dorniermuseum.de* ☑ *€11.*

Schloss Hofen (*Hofen Castle*). A short walk from town along the lakeside promenade is a small palace that served as the summer residence of Württemberg kings until 1918. The palace was formerly a priory—its foundations date from the 11th century. Today it is the private home of Duke Friedrich von Württemberg and isn't open to the public. You can visit the adjoining priory **church,** a splendid example of regional baroque architecture. The swirling white stucco of the interior was executed by the Schmuzer family from Wessobrunn whose master craftsman, Franz Schmuzer, also created the priory church's magnificent marble altar. ⊠ *Klosterstr. 3* ☾ *Closed Nov.–Mar.*

Zeppelin Museum. Graf Zeppelin (Ferdinand Graf von Zeppelin) was born across the lake in Konstanz, but Friedrichshafen was where, on July 2, 1900, his first "airship"—the LZ 1—was launched. The story is told in the Zeppelin Museum, which holds the world's most significant collection of artifacts pertaining to airship history. In a wing of the restored Bauhaus **Friedrichshafen Hafenbahnhof** (harbor railway station), the main attraction is the reconstruction of a 108-foot-long section of the legendary *Hindenburg*, the LZ 129 that exploded at its berth in Lakehurst, New Jersey, on May 6, 1937. (The airships were filled with hydrogen, because in 1933 the United States had passed an act banning helium sales to foreign governments due to its military usefulness and scarcity at that time.) Climb aboard the airship via a retractable stairway and stroll past the authentically furnished passenger room, the original lounges, and the dining room. The illusion of traveling in a zeppelin is followed by exhibits on the history and technology of airship aviation: propellers, engines, dining-room menus, and films of the airships traveling or at war. Car fans will appreciate the great Maybach standing on the ground floor; passengers once enjoyed being transported to the zeppelins in it. The museum's restaurant, a good place to take a break, is open for lunch and dinner. ✉ *Seestr. 22* ☎ *07541/38010* 🌐 *www.zeppelin-museum.de* 🎫 *€9* 🕓 *Closed Mon. Nov.–Apr.*

WHERE TO EAT

$$ ECLECTIC 🍴 **Lukullum.** This lively, novel restaurant is divided into seven *Stuben* (rooms), all themed: sit in a wine barrel, dine in Tyrol, relax under the image of an airship in the Zeppelin Bräustüble—or enjoy the beer garden in summer. Service is friendly and dishes are good and basic, with some international touches. **Known for:** late dining options; schnitzel; lager from house brewery. [$] *Average main: €16* ✉ *Friedrichstr. 21* ☎ *07541/6818* 🌐 *www.lukullum.de* 🕓 *Closed Mon. No lunch Tues.–Fri.*

$$ ECLECTIC 🍴 **Zeppelin-Museumrestaurant.** A grand view of the harbor and the lake is only one of the attractions of this art deco–style restaurant in the Zeppelin Museum. Soak up the retro airship travel theme as you enjoy cakes and drinks, and a range of Swabian, Italian, and Asian-influenced meals. **Known for:** amazing views; fair prices; friendly service. [$] *Average main: €16* ✉ *Seestr. 22* ☎ *07541/953–0088* 🌐 *www.zeppelinmuseum-restaurant.de* 🕓 *Closed Mon. Nov.–Apr. No dinner Sun. and Mon.*

WHERE TO STAY

$$ HOTEL 🏨 **Buchhorner Hof.** This traditional family-run hotel near the train station is decorated with hunting trophies, leather armchairs, and Turkish rugs; bedrooms are large and comfortable, and many have nice views. **Pros:** business floor; cozy and big lobby; excellent restaurant. **Cons:** many rooms look onto a busy main street; parking is difficult; breakfast is at additional cost. [$] *Rooms from: €120* ✉ *Friedrichstr. 33* ☎ *07541/2050* 🌐 *www.buchhorn.de* 🛏 *96 rooms* 🍽 *No meals.*

$$ HOTEL 🏨 **Flair Hotel Gerbe.** A former farm and tannery that's about 5 km (3 miles) from the city center, is now a pleasant, spacious hotel; its rooms (many with balconies) overlook the gardens, the countryside, and—on a clear day—the Swiss mountains. **Pros:** spacious rooms with good views; ample parking; indoor swimming pool. **Cons:** 5 km (3 miles) from center of town; some rooms have street noise; old-fashioned decor. [$] *Rooms from: €116* ✉ *Hirschlatterstr. 14, Ailingen* ☎ *07541/5090* 🌐 *www.hotel-gerbe.de* 🛏 *59 rooms* 🍽 *Free Breakfast.*

$$$ HOTEL 🏨 **Ringhotel Krone.** This large Bavaria-themed hotel in the Schnetzenhausen district's semirural surroundings, 6 km (4 miles) from the center of town, has a lot to offer active guests, including tennis, minigolf, bicycles to rent, a gym, saunas, and indoor and outdoor pools. **Pros:** great variety of rooms; good food; lots of parking. **Cons:** not near the center of town; a few rooms have street noise; single rooms are small. [$] *Rooms from: €200* ✉ *Untere Mühlbachstr. 1, Schnetzenhausen* ☎ *07541/4080* 🌐 *www.ringhotel-krone.de* 🛏 *140 rooms* 🍽 *Free Breakfast.*

6

The Altes Schloss in Meersburg, a true medieval castle, has a museum with armor and jousting equipment.

NIGHTLIFE AND PERFORMING ARTS

Café Bar Belushi. College students and a mostly young crowd raise their glasses and voices above the din at Café Bar Belushi. ⊠ *Montfortstr. 3* ☎ *07541/32531* ⊕ *www.cafe-bar-belushi.de.*

Graf-Zeppelin-Haus. This modern convention center on the lakeside promenade also functions as a cultural center, where musicals, light opera, and classical as well as pop-rock concerts take place several times a week. The Graf-Zeppelin-Haus has a good modern restaurant with a big terrace overlooking the harbor. ⊠ *Olgastr. 20* ☎ *07541/2880* ⊕ *www.gzh.de.*

SHOPPING

Weber & Weiss. Excellent chocolates are sold at Weber & Weiss. Look for the special zeppelin airship–shape chocolates and candies. ⊠ *Charlottenstr. 11* ☎ *07541/21771* ⊕ *www.weber-weiss.de.*

MEERSBURG

18 km (11 miles) west of Friedrichshafen.

Meersburg is one of the most romantic old towns on the German shore of the lake. Seen from the water on a summer afternoon with the sun slanting low, the steeply terraced town looks like a stage set, with its bold castles, severe patrician dwellings, and a gaggle of half-timber houses arranged around narrow streets. It's no wonder that cars have been banned from the center: the crowds of people who come to visit the sights on weekends fill up the streets. The town is divided into the Unterstadt (Lower Town) and Oberstadt (Upper Town), connected by several steep streets and stairs.

VISITOR INFORMATION

Contacts Tourism Meersburg. ⊠ *Kirchstr. 4* ☎ *07532/440–400* ⊕ *www. meersburg.de.*

EXPLORING

Altes Schloss (*Old Castle; Burg Meersburg*). Majestically guarding the town is the Altes Schloss, the original "Meersburg" (Sea Castle). It's Germany's oldest inhabited castle, founded in 628 by Dagobert, king of the Franks. The massive central tower, with walls 10 feet thick, is named after him. The bishops of Konstanz used it as a summer residence until 1526, at which point they moved in permanently. They remained until the mid-18th century, when they built themselves what they felt to be a more suitable residence—the baroque Neues Schloss. Plans to tear down the Altes Schloss in the early 19th century were shelved when it was taken over by Baron Joseph von Lassberg, a man much intrigued by the castle's medieval romance. He turned it into a home for like-minded poets and artists, among them the Grimm brothers and his sister-in-law, the poet Annette von Droste-Hülshoff (1797–1848). The Altes Schloss is still private property, but much of it can be visited, including the richly furnished rooms where Droste-Hülshoff lived and the chamber where she died, as well as the imposing knights' hall, the minstrels' gallery, and the sinister dungeons. The **Altes Schloss Museum** (Old Castle Museum) contains a fascinating collection of weapons and armor, including a rare set of medieval jousting equipment. ⊠ *Schlosspl. 10* ☎ *07532/80000* ⊕ *www.burg-meersburg.de* 🎫 *€13.*

Fürstenhäusle (*Prince's Little House, Droste Museum*). An idyllic retreat almost hidden among the vineyards, the Fürstenhäusle was built in 1640 by a local vintner and later used as a holiday house by the poet Annette von Droste-Hülshoff. It's now the Droste Museum, containing many of her personal possessions and giving a vivid sense of Meersburg in her time. You'll need to join a guided tour to enter the museum. ⊠ *Stettener- str. 11, east of Obertor, town's north gate* ☎ *07532/807–9410* ⊕ *www. fuerstenhaeusle.de* 🎫 *€5* ⊘ *Closed Mon., and Nov.–Mar.*

Neues Schloss. The spacious and elegant "New Castle" is directly across from its predecessor. Designed by Christoph Gessinger at the beginning of the 18th century, it took nearly 50 years to complete. The grand double staircase, with its intricate grillwork and heroic statues, was the work of Balthasar Neumann. The interior's other standout is the glittering **Spiegelsaal** (Hall of Mirrors). ⊠ *Schlosspl. 12* ☎ *07532/807–9410* ⊕ *www.neues-schloss-meersburg.de* 🎫 *€5* ⊘ *Closed weekdays Nov.–Mar.*

Pfahlbauten. As you proceed northwest along the lake's shore, a settle- ment of "pile dwellings"—a reconstructed village of Stone Age and Bronze Age houses built on stilts—sticks out of the lake. This is how the original lake dwellers lived, surviving off the fish that swam outside their humble huts. Real dwellers in authentic garb give you an accurate picture of prehistoric lifestyles. The on-site **Pfahlbaumuseum** (Lake Dwelling Open-Air Museum and Research Institute) contains actual finds excavated in the area. Admission includes a 45-minute tour. ✉ *Strandpromenade 6, Unteruhldingen* ☎ *07556/928–900* 🌐 *www.pfahlbauten.com* 🎫 *€10* 🕑 *Closed weekends Dec.–Feb.*

Vineum Bodensee (*Museum of Wine, Culture and History*). Take a fascinating look into Meersburg's cultural—and vinicultural—history at this museum space housed in the city's historic hospital building, the Heilig Geist Spital (Hospital of the Holy Spirit). ✉ *Vorburgg. 11* ☎ *07532/440–2632* 🌐 *www.vineum-bodensee.de* 🎫 *€6* 🕑 *Closed Mon. Closed weekdays Nov.–Mar.*

WHERE TO EAT

$$$ GERMAN 🍴 **Winzerstube zum Becher.** Fresh fish from the lake is a specialty at this traditional restaurant near the New Castle, which has been in the Benz family for three generations. You can pair the day's catch with white wine from their own vineyard. **Known for:** historic ambience; quality wines; friendly service. [$] *Average main: €25* ✉ *Höllg. 4* ☎ *07532/9009* 🌐 *www.winzerstube-zum-becher.de* 🕑 *Closed Mon., and 1 wk in Jan.*

WHERE TO STAY

$ HOTEL 🏨 **Gästehaus am Hafen.** This family-run, half-timber pension is in the middle of the Old Town, near the harbor. **Pros:** close to the harbor; in the center of the Lower Town; good value. **Cons:** small rooms; no credit cards; parking is five minutes away on foot. [$] *Rooms from: €78* ✉ *Spitalg. 3–4* ☎ *07532/7069* 🌐 *www.amhafen.eu* 💳 *No credit cards* 🕑 *Closed Nov.–Mar.* 🛏 *7 rooms* 🍽 *Free Breakfast.*

$ HOTEL 🏨 **Hotel Weinstube Löwen.** Rooms at this local landmark—a centuries-old, ivy-clad tavern on Meersburg's market square—have their own corner sitting areas, some with genuine Biedermeier furniture. **Pros:** center of town; pleasant rooms; good food in a cozy restaurant. **Cons:** lots of daytime noise from tourists; no elevator; no on-site parking. [$] *Rooms from: €95* ✉ *Marktpl. 2* ☎ *07532/43040* 🌐 *www.hotel-loewen-meersburg.de* 🛏 *25 rooms* 🍽 *Free Breakfast.*

$$ HOTEL 🏨 **Romantik Hotel Residenz am See.** This tastefully modern hotel overlooking the lake features two restaurants, including the Michelin-starred Casala, and Residenz Restaurant, which specializes in regional fare. **Pros:** good food; pleasant rooms with lake view; quiet rooms toward the vineyards. **Cons:** not in center of town; must pay for parking; poor Wi-Fi connection. [$] *Rooms from: €131* ✉ *Uferpromenade 11* ☎ *07532/80040* 🌐 *www.hotel-residenz-meersburg.com* 🛏 *25 rooms* 🍽 *Breakfast; Some meals.*

$$ HOTEL 🏨 **See Hotel Off.** Nearly all rooms at this bright, airy and crisply renovated hotel just a few steps from the shore offer balconies with views across the lake or vineyards. **Pros:** close to the lake; individually decorated rooms; away from center of town. **Cons:** not in center of town; no air-conditioning; some rooms on small side. [$] *Rooms from: €123*

⊠ *Uferpromenade 51* ☏ *07532/44740* ⊕ *www.seehotel-off.de* ⊘ *Closed Jan.* ⇆ *21 rooms* ⦿ *Free Breakfast.*

$$ ⬚ **Zum Bären.** Individually furnished rooms lend character to this his-
HOTEL toric hotel, whose ivy-covered facade, with its characteristic steeple, hasn't changed much over the centuries. **Pros:** center of town; good value; own parking garage. **Cons:** no elevator; some rooms are small; no credit cards. **$** *Rooms from: €110* ⊠ *Marktpl. 11* ☏ *07532/43220* ⊕ *www.baeren-meersburg.de* ▭ *No credit cards* ⊘ *Closed mid-Nov.–mid-Mar.* ⇆ *21 rooms* ⦿ *Free Breakfast.*

SPORTS AND THE OUTDOORS

FAMILY **Meersburg Therme** (*Meersburg Spa*). This lakeside pool complex east of the harbor has three outdoor pools, an indoor "adventure" pool, an indoor-outdoor thermal bath (34°C [93.2°F]), and an indoor-outdoor "sauna world" with a wide variety of saunas, including two "Pfahl-bau saunas" built to look like traditional *Pfahlbauten* (lake dwellings). ⊠ *Uferpromenade 12* ☏ *07532/440–2850* ⊕ *www.meersburg-therme. de* ⊑ *From €18.*

SHOPPING

FAMILY **Omas Kaufhaus.** If you can't find something at this incredible gift shop (with nostalgic retro toys, enamelware, books, dolls, model cars, and much more), then you should at least see the exhibition of toy trains and tin boats on the first floor. The boats are displayed in a long canal filled with real water. ⊠ *Corner Kirchstr. and Steigstr.* ☏ *07532/433–9611* ⊑ *Entry to the exhibition €2.*

ÜBERLINGEN

13 km (8 miles) west of Meersburg, 24 km (15 miles) west of Friedrichshafen.

This Bodensee resort has an attractive waterfront and an almost Medi-terranean feel. It's midway along the north shore of the Überlingersee, a narrow finger of the Bodensee that points to the northwest. Über-lingen is ancient—it's first mentioned in records dating back to 770. In the 14th century it earned the title of Free Imperial City and was known for its wines. No fewer than seven of its original city gates and towers remain from those grand days, as well as substantial por-tions of the old city walls. What was once the moat is now a grassy walkway, with the walls of the Old Town towering on one side and the Stadtpark stretching away on the other. The **Stadtgarten** (city garden), which opened in 1875, cultivates exotic plants and has a famous col-lection of cacti, a fuchsia garden, and a small deer corral. The heart of the city is the Münsterplatz.

VISITOR INFORMATION

Contacts Überlingen Tourist-Information. ⊠ *Landungspl. 5* ☏ *07551/947–1522* ⊕ *www.ueberlingen-bodensee.de.*

EXPLORING

FAMILY **Affenberg** (*Monkey Mountain*). On the road between Überlingen and Salem, the Affenberg (Monkey Mountain) is a 50-plus-acre park that serves as home to more than 200 free-roaming Barbary apes, as well as deer, aquatic birds, gray herons, ducks, coots, and—during nesting time—a colony of white storks. ⊠ *Mendlishauser Hof* ✛ *On road between Überlingen and Salem* 🕾 *07553/381* ⊕ *www.affenberg-salem. de* 🖃 *€9* 🛇 *Closed Nov.–mid-Mar.*

Altes Rathaus (*Old Town Hall*). Inside the late-Gothic Altes Rathaus is a high point of Gothic decoration, the **Rathaussaal**, or council chamber, which is still in use today. Its most striking feature amid the riot of carving is the series of figures, created between 1492 and 1494, representing the states of the Holy Roman Empire. To visit the interior, you'll need to take the short guided tour. Tours are free; simply show up shortly before the set start time. ⊠ *Münsterstr. 15* 🕾 *07551/991–011* ⊕ *www. ueberlingen-bodensee.de* 🛇 *No tours Fri.–Tues.*

Münster St. Nikolaus (*Church of St. Nicholas*). The huge Münster St. Nikolaus was built between 1512 and 1563 on the site of at least two previous churches. The interior is all Gothic solemnity and massiveness, with a lofty stone-vaulted ceiling and high, pointed arches lining the nave. The single most remarkable feature is not Gothic at all but opulently Renaissance—the massive high altar, carved by Jörg Zürn from lime wood that almost looks like ivory. The subject of the altar carvings is the Nativity. ⊠ *Münsterpl.* 🕾 *07551/92720* 🖃 *Free.*

FAMILY
Fodor's Choice
★
Schloss Salem (*Salem Castle*). This huge castle in the tiny inland village of Salem, 10 km (6 miles) north of Überlingen, began its existence as a convent and large church. After many architectural permutations, it was transformed into a palace for the Baden princes, though traces of its religious past can still be seen. You can view the royally furnished rooms of the abbots and princes, a library, stables, and the church. The castle also houses an interesting array of museums, workshops, and activities, including a museum of firefighting, a potter, a musical instrument builder, a goldsmith shop, a glassblowing shop, pony farms, a golf driving range, and a fantasy garden for children. There is a great path that leads from the southwestern part of the grounds through woods and meadows to the pilgrimage church of Birnau. The route was created by the monks centuries ago and is still called the Prälatenweg (path of the prelates) today. It's an 8-km (5-mile) walk (no cars permitted). ⊠ *Salem* 🕾 *07553/916–5336* ⊕ *www.salem.de* 🖃 *€9* 🛇 *Closed Nov.–Mar.*

Städtisches Museum (*City Museum*). This museum is housed in the Reichlin-von-Meldegg house, built in 1462, one of the earliest Renaissance dwellings in Germany. It displays exhibits tracing Bodensee history and Germany's largest collection of antique dollhouses. ⊠ *Krummebergstr. 30* 🕾 *07551/991–079* ⊕ *www.museum-ueberlingen.de* 🖃 *€5* 🛇 *Closed Mon.*

Wallfahrtskirche Birnau (*Pilgrimage Church; Basilika Birnau*). Just northwest of Unteruhldingen, the Wallfahrtskirche Birnau stands among vineyards overlooking the lake. The church was built by the master architect Peter Thumb between 1746 and 1750. Its exterior consists of pink-and-white plaster and a tapering clock-tower spire above the

Near Überlingen, Schloss Salem was constructed as a convent and then transformed into a palace. Leading from the palace grounds is a 5-mile path to Wallfahrtskirche Birnau (Pilgrimage Church).

main entrance. The interior is overwhelmingly rich, full of movement, light, and color. It's hard to single out highlights from such a profusion of ornament, but look for the Honigschlecker (Honey Sucker), a gold-and-white cherub beside the altar, dedicated to St. Bernard of Clairvaux, "whose words are sweet as honey" (it's the last altar on the right as you face the high altar). The cherub is sucking honey from his finger, which he's just pulled out of a beehive. The fanciful spirit of this play on words is continued in the small squares of glass set into the pink screen that rises high above the main altar; the gilt dripping from the walls; the swaying, swooning statues; and the swooping figures on the ceiling. A free tour is offered on Thursday at 3 pm from mid-May through mid-September. ⊠ *Birnau-Maurach 5, Uhldingen-Mühlhofen* ☎ *07556/92030* ⊕ *www.birnau.de.*

WHERE TO STAY

$$ 🏨 **Bad Hotel mit Villa Seeburg.** This stately hotel with a charming 19th-
HOTEL century villa annex is both on the lake and in town, with oak-floor modern rooms done in crisp white with small bursts of color. **Pros:** on the lake; in the center of town; quiet. **Cons:** rooms in the main building on the busy street can be noisy and hot; expensive breakfast; Wi-Fi connection is poor. ⓢ *Rooms from: €130* ⊠ *Christophstr. 2* ☎ *07551/8370* ⊕ *www.bad-hotel-ueberlingen.de* 🛏 *78 rooms* ⦿⦿ *No meals.*

$ 🏨 **Landgasthof zum Adler.** This unpretentious, rustic country inn in a vil-
HOTEL lage a few miles north of Überlingen has a blue-and-white half-timber
FAMILY facade, scrubbed wooden floors, maple-wood tables, and thick down comforters on the beds. **Pros:** good food in old wooden restaurant;

modern rooms in annex; family-friendly. **Cons:** rooms on the street side can be noisy; a bit far from Überlingen; family-oriented. $ *Rooms from: €98 ⊠ Hauptstr. 44, Lippertsreute ☎ 07553/82550 ⊕ www.adler-lippertsreute.de ⊅ 16 rooms ¹⊙¹ Free Breakfast.*

$$ 🏨 **Romantik Hotel Johanniter Kreuz.** Parts of this family-run, half-timber
HOTEL hotel in a small village north of Überlingen date from the 17th century, setting a romantic tone that's further enhanced by the huge fireplace in the center of the cozy restaurant. **Pros:** rooms are spacious; modern and welcoming lobby; golf course close by. **Cons:** 3 km (2 miles) from center of town; long corridors from historic part of hotel to reach elevator in new part; limited public transport from hotel to town. $ *Rooms from: €134 ⊠ Johanniterweg 11, Andelshofen ☎ 07551/937–060 ⊕ www.johanniter-kreuz.de ⊅ 29 rooms ¹⊙¹ Free Breakfast.*

$$ 🏨 **Schäpfle.** The charm of this vine-covered hotel in the center of town
HOTEL has been preserved and supplemented through time—in the hallways you'll find quaint furniture and even an old Singer sewing machine painted with flowers. **Pros:** center of town; local atmosphere in restaurant; annex with lake view. **Cons:** parking nearby, but for a fee; no credit cards; very basic breakfast. $ *Rooms from: €118 ⊠ Jakob-Kessenringstr. 12 and 14 ☎ 07551/83070 ⊕ www.schaepfle.de ▭ No credit cards ⊅ 32 rooms ¹⊙¹ Free Breakfast.*

SHOPPING

The beauty and charm of Überlingen is one reason so many artists work and live here; there are more than 20 workshops and artists' shops where you can browse and buy at reasonable prices. ■ **TIP→** Ask at the **tourist office for the brochure listing all the galleries.**

Holzer Goldschmiede. You'll find this master goldsmith's studio near the city's Franziskanertor. ⊠ *Turmg. 8, Am Franziskanertor ☎ 07551/61525 ⊕ www.goldschmiede-holzer.de.*

RAVENSBURG

20 km (12 miles) north of Friedrichshafen.

The Free Imperial City of Ravensburg once competed with Augsburg and Nuremberg for economic supremacy in southern Germany. The Thirty Years' War put an end to the city's hopes by reducing it to little more than a medieval backwater. The city's loss proved fortuitous only in that many of its original features have remained much as they were built (in the 19th century, medieval towns usually tore down their medieval walls and towers, which were considered ungainly and constraining). Fourteen of Ravensburg's town gates and towers survive, and the Altstadt is among the best preserved in Germany.

GETTING HERE AND AROUND

Consider taking an official tour of the city, which grants you access to some of the towers for a splendid view of Ravensburg and the surrounding countryside. Tours are available at the tourist office.

VISITOR INFORMATION
Contacts **Ravensburg Tourist-Information.** ⊠ *Marienpl. 35* ☎ *0751/82800* ⊕ *www.ravensburg.de.*

EXPLORING

Blasersturm (*Trumpeter's Tower*). Ravensburg is home to a remarkable collection of well-preserved medieval towers and city gates. Highlights include the **Grüner Turm** (Green Tower), so called for its green tiles, many of which are 14th-century originals. Another stout defense tower is the massive **Obertor** (Upper Tower), the oldest gate in the city walls. The curiously named **Mehlsack** (Flour Sack) tower—so called because of its rounded shape and whitewash exterior—stands 170 feet high and sits upon the highest point of the city. From April to October, visitors can climb to the top of the **Blaserturm** (Trumpeter's Tower) for rooftop views over the city. ⊠ *Ravensburg* ☎ *0751/82800* ⊕ *www.ravensburg. de* ⊡ *€2* ⊘ *Closed Oct.–Mar.*

Humpis-Quartier Museum. Glass walkways, stairways, and a central court-yard connect the well-preserved medieval residences at this museum, where visitors can take a close look into the lives of Ravensburgers in the Middle Ages. The residences once belonged to the Humpis family, who were traders in the 15th century. ⊠ *Marktstr. 45* ☎ *0751/82820* ⊕ *www.museum-humpis-quartier.de* ⊡ *€5* ⊘ *Closed Mon.*

Marienplatz. Many of Ravensburg's monuments that most recall the town's wealthy past are concentrated on this central square. To the west is the 14th-century **Kornhaus** (Granary); once the corn exchange for all of Upper Swabia, it now houses the public library. The late-Gothic **Rathaus** is a staid, red building with a Renaissance bay window and imposing late-Gothic rooms inside. Next to it stands the 15th-century **Waaghaus** (Weighing House), the town's weigh station and central warehouse. Its tower, the **Blaserturm** (Trumpeter's Tower), which served as the watchman's abode, was rebuilt in 1556 after a fire and now bears a pretty Renaissance helmet. Finally there's the colorfully frescoed **Lederhaus,** once the headquarters of the city's leather workers, and now home to a café. On Saturday morning the square comes alive with a large market. ⊠ *Ravensburg.*

FAMILY **Museum Ravensburger.** Ravensburg is a familiar name to all jigsaw-puzzle fans, because the Ravensburg publishing house produces the world's largest selection of puzzles, as well as many other children's games. Here you can explore the history of the company, founded in 1883 by Otto Robert Maier. Be sure to try out new and classic games via the interactive game stations throughout the museum. ⊠ *Marktstr. 26* ☎ *0751/861–377* ⊕ *www.museum-ravensburger.de* ⊡ *€9* ⊘ *Closed Mon. Sept.–July.*

WHERE TO EAT

$ ✕**Firenze Caffé e Gelateria.** This bustling multilevel café opens early and ITALIAN closes late and offers a mind-boggling array of ice-cream dishes and other sweet and savory fare. For a quick and inexpensive meal, consider

DID YOU KNOW?

The Weingarten Basilica's altar is said to hold a vial of Christ's blood. On the day after Ascension Thursday, a huge procession of pilgrims makes its way to the basilica.

the tasty breakfasts, sandwiches, and German- and Italian-influenced items on offer. **Known for:** quick service; good prices; German and Italian influences. Ⓢ *Average main: €10* ✉ *Marienpl. 47* ☎ *0751/24665* 🖃 *No credit cards.*

WHERE TO STAY

$$ 🛏 **Gasthof Ochsen and Ochsen Hotel am Mehlsack.** A typical, family-owned
HOTEL Swabian inn, the Ochsen consists of a traditional Gasthof, and the adjoining, newly renovated Ochsen Hotel am Mehlsack featuring more modern (and pricier) rooms. **Pros:** warm atmosphere and good Swabian food in two cozy restaurants; many rooms refurbished; clean. **Cons:** parking not on-site; on-site restaurant closed Sunday; difference in room quality between inn and hotel. Ⓢ *Rooms from: €114* ✉ *Burgstr. 1* ☎ *0751/25480* ⊕ *www.ochsen-rv.de* 🗫 *25 rooms* ⦿| *Free Breakfast.*

WEINGARTEN

5 km (3 miles) north of Ravensburg.

Weingarten is famous throughout Germany for its huge and hugely impressive basilica, which you can see up on a hill from miles away, long before you get to the town. The city has grown during the last century, as several small and midsize industries settled here. It's now an interesting mixture, its historic Old Town surrounded by a small, prosperous industrial city.

VISITOR INFORMATION

Contacts Weingarten Amt für Kultur- und Tourismus. ✉ *Münsterpl. 1* ☎ *0751/405–232* ⊕ *www.weingarten-online.de.*

EXPLORING

Alemannenmuseum. If you want to learn about early Germans—residents from the 6th, 7th, and 8th centuries whose graves are just outside town—visit the Alemannenmuseum in the Kornhaus, which was once a granary. Archaeologists discovered the hundreds of Alemannic graves in the 1950s. ✉ *Karlstr. 28* ☎ *0751/49343* ⊕ *www.weingarten-online. de* 🖙 *€2* ☉ *Closed Mon. and Tues.*

Weingarten Basilica (*St. Martin Basilica*). At 220 feet high and more than 300 feet long, Weingarten Basilica is the largest baroque church in Germany. It was built as the church of one of the oldest and most venerable convents in the country, founded in 1056 by the wife of Guelph IV. The Guelph dynasty ruled large areas of Upper Swabia, and generations of family members lie buried in the church. The majestic edifice was renowned because of its little vial said to contain drops of Christ's blood. First mentioned by Charlemagne, the vial passed to the convent in 1094, entrusted to its safekeeping by the Guelph queen Juditha, sister-in-law of William the Conqueror. Weingarten then became one of Germany's foremost pilgrimage sites. To this day, on the day after Ascension Thursday—the anniversary of the day the vial of Christ's blood was entrusted to the convent—a huge procession of pilgrims wends its way to the basilica. It's well worth seeing the procession, which is headed by nearly 3,000 horsemen (many local farmers breed horses just for this occasion). The basilica was decorated by leading early-18th-century German and Austrian artists: stuccowork by Franz Schmuzer, ceiling frescoes by Cosmas Damian Asam, and a Donato Frisoni altar—one of the most breathtakingly ornate in Europe, with nearly 80-foot-high towers on either side. The organ, installed by Josef Gabler between 1737 and 1750, is among the largest in the country. ⊠ *Kirchpl. 6* ⊕ *www.st-martin-weingarten.de.*

KONSTANZ

A ½-hr ferry ride from Meersburg.

The university town of Konstanz is the largest on the Bodensee; it straddles the Rhine as it flows out of the lake, placing it both on the Bodanrück Peninsula and the Switzerland side of the lake, where it adjoins the Swiss town of Kreuzlingen. Konstanz is among the best-preserved medieval towns in Germany; during the war the Allies were unwilling to risk inadvertently bombing neutral Switzerland. On the peninsula side of the town, east of the main bridge connecting Konstanz's two halves, runs **Seestrasse,** a stately promenade of neoclassical mansions with views of the Bodensee. The Old Town center is a labyrinth of narrow streets lined with restored half-timber houses and dignified merchant dwellings. This is where you'll find restaurants, hotels, pubs, and much of the nightlife.

It's claimed that Konstanz was founded in the 3rd century by Emperor Constantine Chlorus, father of Constantine the Great. The story is probably untrue, though it's certain there was a Roman garrison here. In the late 6th century Konstanz was made a bishopric; in 1192 it became a Free Imperial City. What put it on the map was the Council of Constance, held between 1414 and 1418 to settle the Great Schism (1378–1417), the rift in the church caused by two separate lines of popes, one ruling from Rome, the other from Avignon. The Council resolved the problem in 1417 by electing Martin V as the true, and only, pope. The church had also agreed to restore the Holy Roman emperor's (Sigismund's) role in electing the pope, but only if Sigismund silenced the rebel theologian Jan Hus, of Bohemia. Even though Sigismund had allowed Hus safe passage to Konstanz for the Council, he won the church's favor by having Hus burned at the stake in July 1415. In a satiric short story, the French author Honoré de Balzac created the character of Imperia, a courtesan of great beauty and cleverness, who raised the blood pressure of both religious and secular VIPs during the council. No one visiting the harbor today can miss the 28-foot statue of **Imperia** standing out on the breakwater. Dressed in a revealing and alluring style, in her hands she holds two dejected figures: the emperor and the pope. This hallmark of Konstanz, created by Peter Lenk, caused controversy when it was unveiled in April 1993.

Most people enjoy Konstanz for its worldly pleasures—the elegant Altstadt, trips on the lake, walks along the promenade, elegant shops,

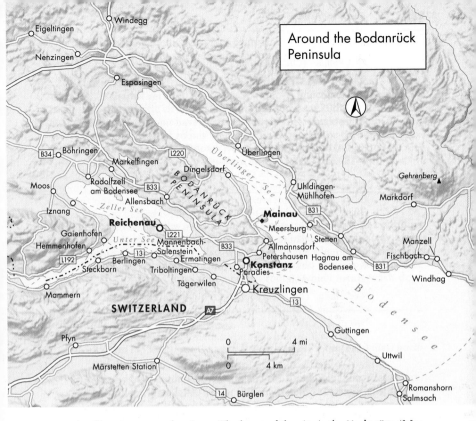

Around the Bodanrück Peninsula

the restaurants, the views. The heart of the city is the **Marktstätte** (Marketplace), near the harbor, with the simple bulk of the Konzilgebäude looming behind it. Erected in 1388 as a warehouse, the **Konzilgebäude** (Council Hall) is now a concert hall. Beside the Konzilgebäude are statues of Jan Hus and native son Count Ferdinand von Zeppelin (1838–1917). The Dominican monastery where Hus was held before his execution is still here, doing duty as a luxurious hotel, the Steigenberger Insel-Hotel.

GETTING HERE AND AROUND

Konstanz is in many ways the center of the lake area. You can reach Zürich airport by direct train in about an hour, and Frankfurt in 4½ hours. Swiss autobahn access to Zürich is about 10 minutes away, and you can reach the autobahn access to Stuttgart in about the same time. To reach the island of Mainau, you can take a bus, but a much more pleasant way to get there is by boat, via Meersburg. You can take another boat downriver to Schaffhausen in Switzerland, or east to the northern shore towns as well as Bregenz in Austria. The Old Town is manageable on foot.

VISITOR INFORMATION

Contacts Tourist-Information Konstanz. ✉ *Bahnhofpl. 43* ☎ *07531/133–030* 🌐 *www.konstanz-tourismus.de.*

EXPLORING

Altes Rathaus (*Old Town Hall*). This old town hall was built during the Renaissance and painted with vivid frescoes—swags of flowers and fruits, shields, and sturdy knights wielding immense swords. Walk into the courtyard to admire its Renaissance restraint. ✉ *Kanzleistr. 13.*

Münster. Konstanz's cathedral, the Münster, was the center of one of Germany's largest bishoprics until 1827, when the seat was moved to Freiburg. Construction on the cathedral continued from the 10th through the 19th century, resulting in an interesting coexistence of architectural styles: the twin-tower facade is sturdily Romanesque; the elegant and airy chapels along the aisles are full-blown 15th-century Gothic; the complex nave vaulting is Renaissance; and the choir is severely neoclassical. The Mauritius Chapel behind the altar is a 13th-century Gothic structure, 12 feet high, with some of its original vivid coloring and gilding. It's studded with statues of the Apostles and figures depicting the childhood of Jesus. Climb the **Münsterturm** (Münster Tower) for views over the city and lake. ✉ *Münsterpl. 4* 🎟 *€2* 🕒 *Tower closed Nov.–Mar.*

Niederburg. The Niederburg, the oldest part of Konstanz, is a tangle of twisting streets leading to the Rhine. From the river take a look at two of the city's old towers: the **Rheintorturm** (Rhine Tower), the one nearer the lake, and the aptly named **Pulverturm** (Powder Tower), the former city arsenal. ✉ *Konstanz.*

Rosgartenmuseum (*Rose Garden Museum*). Within the medieval guildhall of the city's butchers, this museum has a rich collection of art and artifacts from the Bodensee region. Highlights include exhibits of the life and work of the people around the Bodensee, from the Bronze Age through the Middle Ages and beyond. There's also a collection of sculpture and altar paintings from the Middle Ages. ✉ *Rosgartenstr. 3–5* ☎ *07531/900–245* 🌐 *www.rosgartenmuseum-konstanz.de* 🎟 *€3 (free Wed. after 2 pm and 1st Sun. of month)* 🕒 *Closed Mon.*

FAMILY **Sealife.** This huge aquarium has gathered all the fish species that inhabit the Rhine and the Bodensee, from the river's beginnings in the Swiss Alps to its end in Rotterdam and the North Sea. Also check out the **Bodensee Naturmuseum** at the side entrance, which gives a comprehensive overview of the geological history of the Bodensee and its fauna and flora right down to the microscopic creatures of the region. You can buy tickets in advance online for a significantly cheaper price. ✉ *Hafenstr. 9* ☎ *07531/128–270* 🌐 *www.sealife.de* 🎟 *€19 (€14 booked online).*

WHERE TO EAT

$$ GERMAN 🍴 **Brauhaus Joh. Albrecht.** This small brewery with shiny copper cauldrons, part of a chain of five throughout Germany, serves simple dishes as well as regional specialties and vegetarian food on large wooden tables. **Known for:** Swabian dishes; schnitzel; house-brewed beer. [$] *Average main: €16* ✉ *Konradig. 2* ☎ *07531/25045* 🌐 *konstanz.brauhaus-joh-albrecht.de.*

For views of the Bodensee from Konstanz, head to the Seestrasse promenade.

$$ GERMAN 🍴 **Hafenhalle.** Enjoy eclectic cooking—including Italian, Bavarian, and Swabian fare—on the terrace at this warm-weather spot on the harbor. Sit outside and watch the busy harbor traffic, or enjoy the beer garden with sandbox for children and big TV screen for watching sports. **Known for:** beer garden; great views; televised sports. [$] *Average main: €18* ✉ *Hafenstr. 10* ☎ *07531/21126* 🌐 *www.hafenhalle.com* 🕒 *Closed Jan. and Feb.*

WHERE TO STAY

$ HOTEL 🏨 **ABC Hotel.** This hotel offers large, comfortable, individually furnished rooms, all with kitchen facilities; book the unusual Turmsuite (Tower Suite) for an especially memorable stay among exposed beams and steeply sloping walls, and with private access to the top of the tower. **Pros:** warm welcome; quiet location; free on-site parking and Wi-Fi. **Cons:** not in the center of town; no elevator; quality varies by room. [$] *Rooms from: €99* ✉ *Steinstr. 19* ☎ *07531/8900* 🌐 *www.abc-hotel.de* 🛏 *37 rooms* 🍽 *Free Breakfast.*

$$ HOTEL 🏨 **Barbarossa.** This historic hotel in the heart of Old Town has been modernized inside, but such original elements as wooden support beams lend a romantic, authentic feel. **Pros:** historic building; cozy restaurant with good food; free Wi-Fi. **Cons:** some rooms simply furnished; parking available but a third-of-a-mile walk away; no air-conditioning. [$] *Rooms from: €115* ✉ *Obermarkt 8–12* ☎ *07531/128–990* 🌐 *www.hotelbarbarossa.de* 🛏 *50 rooms* 🍽 *Free Breakfast.*

$$ ⊡ **Stadthotel.** It's a five-minute walk to the lake from this friendly hotel,
HOTEL where rooms are modern, airy, and decorated in bright colors. **Pros:** center of town; quiet location with little traffic; excellent breakfast. **Cons:** no restaurant; parking garage five minutes away on foot; no elevator. $ *Rooms from: €120* ⊠ *Bruderturmg. 2* ☎ *07531/90460* ⊕ *www.stadthotel-konstanz.com* ⊋ *24 rooms* |◎| *Free Breakfast.*

$$$$ ⊡ **Steigenberger Insel-Hotel.** With its original cloisters intact, this former
HOTEL 16th-century monastery, filled with spacious and stylish bedrooms with
Fodor's Choice lake views, is now the most luxurious lodging in town. **Pros:** luxurious;
★ good restaurants; some renovated rooms. **Cons:** a few rooms look out
on railroad tracks; some rooms need refurbishing; expensive. $ *Rooms from: €230* ⊠ *Auf der Insel 1* ☎ *07531/1250* ⊕ *www.konstanz.steigenberger.com* ⊋ *102 rooms* |◎| *Free Breakfast.*

NIGHTLIFE AND PERFORMING ARTS

K9 (*Kommunales Kunst-und Kulturzentrum K9*). This cultural center
draws all ages with its music and dance club, theater, comedy, and
cabaret. It's in the former Church of St. Paul. ⊠ *Hieronymusg. 3*
☎ *07531/16713* ⊕ *www.k9-kulturzentrum.de.*

Kulturladen (*Kula*). Concerts and variously themed DJ nights are held
at Kulturladen. ⊠ *Joseph Belli Weg 5* ☎ *07531/52954* ⊕ *www.kulturladen.de.*

Seekuh. This cozy and crowded Italian restaurant ($) and bar features
the occasional live jazz night and also screens live football games from
time to time. ⊠ *Konzilstr. 1* ☎ *07531/27232* ⊕ *www.seekuh.de.*

Seenachtfest (*Lake Night Festival*). In August, Konstanz shares this one-day city festival with neighboring Kreuzlingen in Switzerland, with
street events, music, clowns, and magicians, and ending with fireworks
over the lake. ⊠ *Lakefront* ⊕ *www.seenachtfest.de* ⊠ *€19.*

Stadttheater (*Theater Konstanz*). The Stadttheater, Germany's oldest
active theater, has staged plays since 1609 and has its own repertory
company. ⊠ *Konzilstr. 11* ☎ *07531/900–150 tickets* ⊕ *www.theaterkonstanz.de.*

SPORTS AND THE OUTDOORS

BICYCLING
Bike rentals generally cost €13 per day.

Kultur-Rädle. This friendly store rents bikes at the main train station from
April through September. A two-day rental costs €25. ⊠ *Bahnhofpl. 29*
☎ *07531/27310* ⊕ *www.kultur-raedle.de.*

Velotours Touristik GmbH. You can book bicycle tours and rent bikes at
Velotours Touristik GmbH. ⊠ *Bücklestr. 13* ☎ *07531/98280* ⊕ *www.velotours.de.*

BOATING

Wilde Flotte—Segel & Wassersportschule Konstanz Wallhausen (*Wild Fleet*). This sailing school offers boat charters—both skippered and solo—as well as lessons in sailing, wakeboarding, and waterskiing. ⊠ *Uferstr. 21, Wallhausen* ☎ *07533/997–8802* ⊕ *www.wilde-flotte.de.*

Yachtcharter Konstanz. Sail and motor yachts are available at Yachtcharter Konstanz. ⊠ *Hafenstr. 7b* ☎ *07531/363–3970* ⊕ *www.yachtcharter-konstanz.de.*

SHOPPING

It's worthwhile to roam the streets of the old part of town, where there are several gold- and silversmiths and jewelers.

Modehaus Fischer. This elegant fashion store has enough style for a city 10 times the size of Konstanz. Much of its business comes from Swiss who visit Konstanz for what they consider bargain prices. Modehaus Fischer deals in well-known international fashion stock, including handbags and exquisite shoes. The store is actually spread over three branches a few blocks apart—two for women, and one for men at Obermarkt. ⊠ *Rosgartenstr. 36, Hussenstr. 29, and Obermarkt 1* ☎ *07531/363–250* ⊕ *www.modefischer.de* ☉ *Closed Sun.*

MAINAU

7 km (4½ miles) north of Konstanz by road; by ferry, ½–1 hr from Konstanz (depending on route), or 20 mins from Meersburg.

Fodor's Choice ★ One of the most unusual sights in Germany, Mainau is a tiny island given over to the cultivation of rare plants and splashy displays of more than a million tulips, hyacinths, and narcissi. Rhododendrons and roses bloom from May to July; dahlias dominate the late summer. A greenhouse nurtures palms and tropical plants.

The island was originally the property of the Teutonic Knights, who settled here during the 13th century. In the 19th century Mainau passed to Grand Duke Friedrich I of Baden, a man with a passion for botany. He laid out most of the gardens and introduced many of the island's more exotic specimens. His daughter Victoria, later queen of Sweden, gave the island to her son, Prince Wilhelm, and it has remained Swedish ever since. Today it's owned by the family of Prince Wilhelm's son, Count Lennart Bernadotte. In the former main reception hall of the castle are changing art exhibitions.

GETTING HERE AND AROUND

Ferries to the island from Meersburg and Konstanz depart from April to October approximately every 1½ hours between 9 and 5. You must purchase a ticket to enter the island, which is open year-round from dawn until dusk. There's a small bridge to the island; at night you can drive across it to the restaurants. Ferry/admission tickets cost €21 from March through October (half price after 5 pm), €10 from November through February.

Mainau Island, on the Bodensee, is covered with flowering gardens.

VISITOR INFORMATION
Contacts **Insel Mainau.** ✉ *Mainaustr. 1, Konstanz* ☎ *07531/3030* ⊕ *www. mainau.de.*

EXPLORING

Das Schmetterlinghaus. Beyond the flora, the island of Mainau's other colorful extravagance is Das Schmetterlinghaus, Germany's largest butterfly conservatory. On a circular walk through a semitropical landscape with water cascading through rare vegetation, you'll see hundreds of butterflies flying, feeding, and mating. The exhibition in the foyer explains the butterflies' life cycle, habitats, and ecological connections. Like the park, this oasis is open year-round. ✉ *Insel Mainau, Mainaustr. 1, Konstanz* ⊕ *www.mainau.de.*

Gärtnerturm. At the middle of the island, the Gärtnerturm (Gardener's Tower) contains an information center, a shop, and an exhibition space. Several films on Mainau and the Bodensee are also shown. ✉ *Gärtnerturm.*

WHERE TO EAT

There are nine restaurants and cafés on the island, but nowhere to stay overnight.

$$
SCANDINAVIAN
✕ **Schwedenschenke.** Lunch is quick and reasonably priced at this country-inspired restaurant, while dinner adds candlelight and Swedish flair. The resident Bernadotte family is Swedish, and so are the

specialties of the chef. **Known for:** local ingredients and fish from the lake; regional wine selection; vegan options available. $ *Average main: €18* ⊠ *Insel Mainau* ☎ *07531/303–156* ⊕ *www.mainau.de* ⊙ *Closed Nov.–Dec. No dinner Jan.–Mar.*

REICHENAU

10 km (6 miles) northwest of Konstanz, 50 mins by ferry from Konstanz.

Reichenau is an island rich in vegetation, but unlike Mainau, it features vegetables, not flowers. In fact, 15% of its area—the island is 5 km (3 miles) long and 1½ km (1 mile) wide—is covered by greenhouses and crops of one kind or another. It also has three of Europe's most beautiful Romanesque churches, a legacy of Reichenau's past as a monastic center in the early Middle Ages. The churches are in each of the island's villages—**Oberzell, Mittelzell,** and **Niederzell,** which are separated by only 1 km (½ mile). Along the shore are pleasant pathways for walking or biking.

VISITOR INFORMATION

Contacts Reichenau Tourist-Information. ⊠ *Pirminstr. 145* ☎ *07534/92070* ⊕ *www.reichenau-tourismus.de.*

6

EXPLORING

Münster of St. Maria and St. Markus. Begun in 816, the Münster of St. Maria and St. Markus, the monastery's church, is the largest and most important of Reichenau's Romanesque churches. Perhaps its most striking architectural feature is the roof, whose beams and ties are open for all to see. The monastery was founded in 725 by St. Pirmin and became one of the most important cultural centers of the Carolingian Empire. It reached its zenith around 1000, when 700 monks lived here. It was then probably the most important center of manuscript illumination in Germany. The building is simple but by no means crude. Visit the **Schatzkammer** (Treasury) to see some of its more important holdings. They include a 5th-century ivory goblet with two carefully incised scenes of Christ's miracles, and some priceless stained glass that is almost 1,000 years old. ⊠ *Münsterpl. 4, Mittelzell* ☎ *07534/92070* ⊕ *www.reichenau-tourismus.de/kultur3/kirchen.*

Stiftskirche St. Georg (*Collegiate Church of St. George*). The Stiftskirche St. Georg, in Oberzell, was built around 900; now cabbages grow in ranks up to its rough plaster walls. Small round-head windows, a simple square tower, and massive buttresses signal the church's Romanesque origin from the outside. The interior is covered with frescoes painted by the monks in around 1000. They depict the eight miracles of Christ. Above the entrance is a depiction of the Resurrection. From May through September you can only visit by taking one of the daily guided tours at 12:30 and 4. ⊠ *Seestr. 4, Oberzell* ⊕ *www.reichenau-tourismus.de/kultur3/kirchen* ⊠ *Free; tours €2.*

Stiftskirche St. Peter und Paul (*St. Peter and Paul Parish Church*). The Stiftskirche St. Peter und Paul, at Niederzell, was revamped around 1750. The faded Romanesque frescoes in the apse contrast with bold rococo paintings on the ceiling and flowery stucco. ✉ *Corner Eginostr. and Fischerg., Niederzell* 🌐 *www.reichenau-tourismus.de/kultur3/kirchen.*

WHERE TO EAT

$ GERMAN 🍴 **Kiosk am Yachthafen.** This kiosk-style restaurant at Reichenau's yacht harbor provides an ideal lunch, drink, or snack stop when wandering the island. In good weather, you can sit outside and watch the boats come and go. **Known for:** fresh pretzels; pike-perch bites; coffee and cake. [$] *Average main: €10* ✉ *Yacht Harbor, Hermannus-Contractus-Str. 30* ☎ *07534/999–655* 🌐 *www.sbrestaurant-reichenau.de* 💳 *No credit cards* 🕒 *Closed Nov.–Mar.*

WHERE TO STAY

$$ HOTEL 🏨 **Strandhotel Löchnerhaus.** Standing commandingly on the water's edge fronted by its own boat pier, the Strandhotel (Beach Hotel) Löchnerhaus offers wonderful views of Switzerland over the lake and exudes a retro Riviera feel. **Pros:** nice location; quiet; free bicycle rental. **Cons:** closed in winter; some rooms expensive; additional cost for balcony and terrace rooms. [$] *Rooms from: €160* ✉ *An der Schiffslände 12* ☎ *07534/8030* 🌐 *www.loechnerhaus.de* 🕒 *Closed Nov.–mid-Mar.* 🛏 *41 rooms* 🍽 *Free Breakfast.*

THE BLACK FOREST

WELCOME TO THE BLACK FOREST

TOP REASONS TO GO

★ **Excellent eats:** Enjoy extraordinary regional specialties like Black Forest cake, Schwarzwald ham, and incredible brews from the Alpirsbach Brewery before feasting on Baiersbronn's gourmet offerings.

★ **Freiburg Münster:** One of the most beautiful Gothic churches in Germany, the Cathedral of Freiburg survived the war unscathed. The view from the bell tower is magnificent.

★ **Stunning scenery:** From the country's largest waterfall in Triberg to the glacially carved Titisee Lake, the landscape in the Black Forest National Park is unparalleled.

★ **Healing waters:** The region is home to more than 30 spas, including the legendary scrub-down at the Friedrichsbad in Baden-Baden, the ultimate place for relaxation.

★ **Libations at Kaiserstuhl:** With a diversity of wine like nowhere else in Germany, the sunny border region is especially pretty when the grapes are being harvested.

Germany's Black Forest, in the southwestern corner of the country, grows thick as you leave the bigger cities behind and escape up winding mountain roads dotted with picturesque villages.

1 Karlsruhe. Founded only in the early 18th century, Karlsruhe is best known for being the seat of Germany's supreme court.

2 Baden-Baden. One of Europe's most famous and fashionable spa towns has Germany's oldest casino a well as Europe's second-largest performing arts center, which is housed in a former train station.

3 Calw. One of the Black Forest's prettiest towns, this is the birthplace of writer Hermann Hesse.

4 Baiersbronn. A mountain resort that actually encompasses nine villages, this little town has the highest concentration of Michelin starred restaurants in all of Germany, making it a popular location to unwind—and eat.

5 Freudenstadt. The Duke Frederick I of Württemberg intended (before he died) to build a palace here. It's now known more for its lovely summer climate.

6 Alpirsbach. A small village known for its brewery, Alpirsbacher Klosterbräu.

7 Gutach. You can see a few of Germany's remaining thatched roofs here.

8 Triberg. The cuckoo clock was invented here, and the clocks are still made in the area's workshops. Tourists also enjoy the scenic Black Forest Railway and the large waterfalls.

9 Titisee. The most scenic lake in the Black Forest is a popular summertime escape.

10 Freiburg. Founded as a free-trading city in the 12th century, Freiburg is better known these days for its magnificent cathedral.

11 Staufen. Geothe's *Faust* is set here, and you can visit the guesthouse where he allegedly lived (and died).

12 Kaiserstuhl. Close to the borders of both France and Switzerland, this wine-making region in Germany's southwest region is known for its *sekt* (sparkling wine).

13 Rust. Europapark, located here, is Europe's largest amusement parks—bigger than Disneyland Paris.

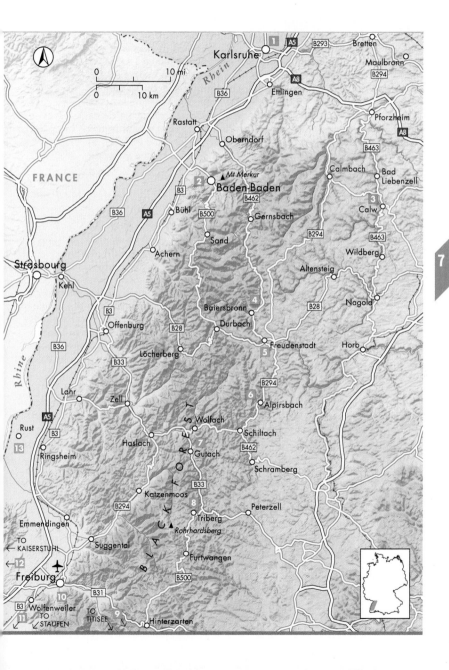

Updated by
Courtney Tenz

A wood so dense that the sun couldn't penetrate the thick pine trees—that's how the Black Forest (*Schwarzwald* in German) got its name. Stretching west to the Rhine River and south into the Alpine foothills in Switzerland, this southwest corner of Baden-Württemberg (partially in the larger region known as Swabia) has one of Germany's most beautiful natural landscapes.

The Romans arrived in southern Germany nearly 2,000 years ago, bringing with them a spa culture that has remained since the Roman emperor Caracalla and his army rested and soothed their battle wounds in the natural-spring waters at what later became Baden-Baden. Though the area has changed hands several times over the course of history, the Black Forest really came into its own in the 19th century, as the dark woods opened up to the outside world.

Europe's upper-crust discovered Baden-Baden for itself around 1797–1799 after they convened nearby for the Congress of Rastatt, which attempted to end the wars of the French Revolution. In the 19th century kings, queens, emperors, princes, princesses, members of Napoléon's family, and the Russian nobility, along with actors, writers, and composers, flocked to the little spa town. Turgenev, Dostoyevsky, and Tolstoy were among the Russian contingent. Victor Hugo was a frequent visitor. Brahms composed lilting melodies in this calm setting. Queen Victoria spent her vacations here. Mark Twain put the Black Forest on the map for Americans by stating, "Here ... you lose track of time in ten minutes and the world in twenty," in his 1880 book *A Tramp Abroad*.

While today the city has become a favorite getaway for movie stars and millionaires, it's the national park surrounding Baden-Baden that is the area's biggest draw for the everyday traveler. Within its protected areas, an adventurous sporting scene has arisen, with possibilities for kayaking, biking, and hiking. The Schwarzwald-Verein, an outdoors association in the region, maintains no fewer than 30,000 km (18,000 miles) of hiking trails. In winter the terrain is ideally suited for cross-country skiing. A river cruise along the nearby Rhine is worthwhile at any time of year, with its unique perspective on the landscape.

MAJOR REGIONS

The **Northern Black Forest** is densely wooded, and dotted with little lakes such as the Mummelsee and the Wildsee. **Karlsruhe** is an important industrial and administrative center; nearby, the magnificent abbey at Maulbronn is a regional treasure. The Black Forest Spa Route (270 km [168 miles]) links many of the spas in the region, including **Baden-Baden** (the best known). **Calw** is one of the area's prettiest towns. **Freudenstadt**'s convenient location (not to mention its many inviting spas) makes it a good base. **Baiersbronn** is a lovely mountain resort with gourmet dining.

The **Central Black Forest** is hilly, a rural forest that includes the Simonswald, Elz, and Glotter valleys. It's where the clichés all come together—pom-pom hats, thatch-roof farmhouses, and cuckoo clocks abound. Major stops in the area include **Alpirsbach** and **Gutach.** However, the area around the Triberg Falls—the highest falls in Germany—is especially scenic. The Schwarzwaldbahn (Black Forest Railway; Offenburg–Villingen line), which passes through **Triberg,** is one of the most scenic in all of Europe.

In the **Southern Black Forest** you'll find the most spectacular mountain scenery in the area, culminating in the Feldberg—at 4,899 feet it is the highest mountain in the Black Forest. The region also has two large lakes, **Titisee** and Schluchsee. **Freiburg** is a romantic university city with a superb Gothic cathedral. Other popular destinations include **Staufen** and **Kaiserstuhl.**

PLANNING

WHEN TO GO

The Black Forest is one of the most visited mountain regions in Europe and despite its name, one of the sunniest places in Germany. Be sure to make reservations well in advance for spas and hotels, especially from June to August. The area around Titisee is particularly crowded then. In early fall and late spring, when the weather turns more temperate, the Black Forest is less crowded, but just as beautiful. Some hotels in small towns close for up to a month in winter so be sure to check ahead.

GETTING HERE AND AROUND

AIR TRAVEL

The closest international airport in Germany is Frankfurt. Strasbourg, in neighboring French Alsace, and the Swiss border city of Basel, the latter just 70 km (43 miles) from Freiburg, are also reasonably close. An up-and-coming airport is the Baden-Airpark, now known more commonly as Karlsruhe-Baden, near Baden-Baden. It is used by European budget carriers including Ryanair (⊕ *www.ryanair.com*) and Tui Fly (⊕ *www.tuifly.com*), serving short-haul international destinations such as London, Edinburgh, and Mallorca.

Contacts Aeroport International de Strasbourg. ☎ *00333/8864–6767* ⊕ *www.strasbourg.aeroport.fr.* **EuroAirport Basel-Mulhouse-Freiburg.** ✉ *Saint*

Louis Cedex ☎ *0389/903–111 France country code required* ⊕ *www.euroairport. com.* **Flughafen Frankfurt Main.** ☎ *01805/372–4636* ⊕ *www.frankfurt-airport. de.* **Karlsruhe-Baden.** ✉ *Halifax Ave.* ☎ *07229/662–000* ⊕ *www.badenairpark.de.*

BUS TRAVEL

Long-distance bus lines including Eurolines and Flix Bus have added more destinations in recent years. Regionally, the bus system is partially owned by and coordinated with the German Railways, so it's easy to reach every corner of the Black Forest by combining bus with train travel, since regional bus stations can usually be found at or near the train station. For more information, contact the Regionalbusverkehr Südwest (Regional Bus Lines) in Karlsruhe or look at the extensive Deutsche Bahn website (⊕ *www.bahn.de*) for travel planning that includes bus journeys.

Contacts Regionalbusverkehr Südwest (*Regional Bus Lines*). ☎ *0721/966– 8610* ⊕ *www.bahn.de/suedwestbus/view/index.shtml.*

CAR TRAVEL

The main autobahns are the A-5 (Frankfurt–Karlsruhe–Basel), which runs through the Rhine Valley along the western length of the Black Forest; A-81 (Stuttgart–Bodensee) in the east; and A-8 (Karlsruhe–Stuttgart) in the north. Good two-lane highways crisscross the entire region. B-3 runs parallel to A-5 and follows the Baden Wine Road. Traffic jams on weekends and holidays are not uncommon. Taking the side roads might not save time, but they are a lot prettier. The Schwarzwald-Hochstrasse is one of the area's most scenic routes, running from Freudenstadt to Baden-Baden. The region's tourist office has mapped out thematic driving routes: the Valley Road, the Spa Road, the Baden Wine Road, the Asparagus Road, and the Clock Road. Most points along these routes can also be reached by train or bus.

Freiburg, the region's major city, is 275 km (170 miles) south of Frankfurt and 410 km (254 miles) west of Munich.

TRAIN TRAVEL

Karlsruhe, Baden-Baden, and Freiburg are served by fast ICE trains zipping between Frankfurt-am-Main and Basel in Switzerland. Regional express trains also link these hubs with many other places locally, including Freudenstadt, Titisee, and, in particular, the spectacular climb from Baden-Baden to Triberg, one of the highest railroads in Germany.

Local lines connect most of the smaller towns. Two east–west routes, the Schwarzwaldbahn (Black Forest Railway) and the Höllental Railway, are among the most spectacular in the country. Many small towns participate in the KONUS program that allows you to travel for free on many Black Forest train lines while staying in the region. Details are available from Deutsche Bahn.

Contacts Deutsche Bahn. ☎ *0180/699–6633 €0.20–€0.60 per call* ⊕ *www. bahn.de.*

HOTELS

Accommodations in the Black Forest are varied and plentiful, from simple rooms in farmhouses to five-star luxury. Some properties have been passed down in the same family for generations. *Gasthöfe* offer low prices and local color. Keep in mind that many hotels in the region do not offer air-conditioning.

RESTAURANTS

Restaurants in the Black Forest range from award-winning dining rooms to simple country inns. Old *Kachelöfen* (tile stoves) are still in use in many area restaurants; try to sit near one if it's cold outside.

Prices in restaurant reviews are the average cost of a main course at dinner, or if dinner is not served, at lunch. Prices in hotel reviews are the lowest cost of a standard double room in high season.

WHAT IT COSTS IN EUROS			
$	$$	$$$	$$$$
Restaurants	under €15	€15–€20	€21–€25	over €25
Hotels	under €100	€100–€175	€176–€225	over €225

PLANNING YOUR TIME

The lively, student-driven city of Freiburg—Germany's "greenest" town—is the largest, most obvious base from which to explore the Black Forest, but you may do well to stay in one of the smaller nearby villages in Kaiserstuhl or Titisee, where the accommodations are nicer and the scenery more breathtaking. Don't miss "taking the waters" at a spa in Baden-Baden, a charming place with loads of cultural offerings and luxury to spare. Bear in mind that the winding, often steep Black Forest highways can make for slow driving, so you may want to consider adding overnight stays at other locations. Freudenstadt's vast market square lends it a uniquely pleasant atmosphere, and Triberg's mountain location is picturesque. Baiersbronn has gained a reputation as one of the country's leading high-end resort towns, with good reason. If there is one place in the region to go out of your way to get a beer, head to Alpirsbach.

TOURS

Bicycles can be rented in nearly all towns and many villages, as well as at the Deutsche Bahn train stations. Several regional tourist offices sponsor tours on which the biker's luggage is transported separately from one overnight stop to the next and you may be able to secure an e-bike for a bit of help in getting up the hills. Six- to 10-day tours are available at reasonable rates, including bed-and-breakfast and bike rental. This region is also ideal for hikers. Similar to the bike tours, *Wandern ohne Gepäck* (hike without luggage) tours are available; get details from tourist offices.

VISITOR INFORMATION

Contacts Schwarzwald Tourismus GmbH. ⊠ *Hapsburger Str. 132, Freiburg* ☎ *0761/896–460* ⊕ *www.schwarzwald-tourismus.info.*

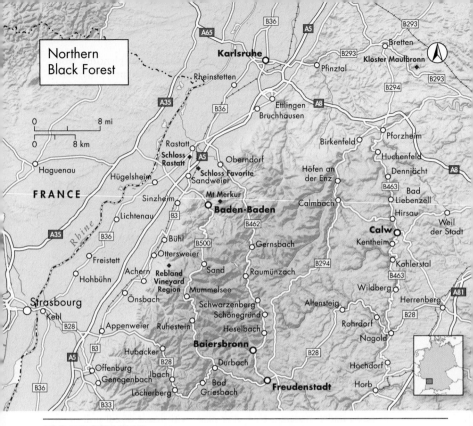

Northern
Black Forest

0   8 mi
0   8 km

FRANCE

KARLSRUHE

78 km (48 miles) northwest of Stuttgart, 52 km (32 miles) south of Speyer.

Karlsruhe, founded at the beginning of the 18th century, is a young upstart, but what it lacks in years it makes up for in industrial and administrative importance, sitting as it does astride a vital autobahn and rail crossroads. It's best known as the seat of Germany's Supreme Court, and has a high concentration of legal practitioners.

GETTING HERE AND AROUND

The autobahn A-5 connects Freiburg, Baden-Baden, and Karlsruhe. Karlsruhe's train station is an easy 15-minute walk from the city center and trains run frequently throughout the region; south to Baden-Baden (15 minutes) and Freiburg (1 hour), and east to Pforzheim (25 minutes) and Frankfurt (1 hour).

VISITOR INFORMATION

Contacts Tourist-Information Karlsruhe. ⊠ *Bahnhofpl. 6* ☎ *0721/3720–5383* ⊕ *www.karlsruhe-tourismus.de.*

EXPLORING

Badisches Landesmuseum (*Baden State Museum*). Housed in the Schloss Karlsruhe, this museum has a large number of Greek and Roman antiquities and trophies that Ludwig the Turk brought back from campaigns in Turkey in the 17th century. Most of the other exhibits are devoted to local history. ⊠ *Schloss, Schlossbezirk 10* ☎ *0721/926–6514* ⊕ *www. landesmuseum.de* 🖾 *From €4; free Fri. after 2 pm* ⊗ *Closed Mon.*

Kloster Maulbronn (*Maulbronn Monastery*). The little town of Maulbronn, 45 km (28 miles) due east of Karlsruhe, is home to the best-preserved medieval monastery north of the Alps; its entire complex of 30 buildings is on UNESCO's World Heritage list. The name Maulbronn (Mule Fountain) derives from a legend. Monks seeking a suitably watered site for their monastery considered it a sign from God when one of their mules discovered and drank at a spring. The Kloster is also known for inventing the *Maultasche,* a kind of large ravioli. The monks thought that by coloring the meat filling green by adding parsley and wrapping it inside a pasta pocket, they could hide it from God on fasting days. Today the Maultasche is the cornerstone of Swabian cuisine. An audio guide in English is available. ⊠ *Off B-35, Klosterhof 5, Maulbronn* ✚ *Trains to Maulbronn from Karlsruhe require several changes and can take up to 2 hrs; Bus 735 from Pforzheim will get you to abbey in 45 mins* ☎ *07043/926–610* ⊕ *www.kloster-maulbronn.de* 🖾 *€8* ⊗ *Closed Mon. Nov.–Feb.*

Schloss Karlsruhe. The town quite literally grew up around the former Schloss of the Margrave Karl Wilhelm, which was begun in 1715 and was in use for more than 200 years. Thirty-two avenues radiate from the palace, 23 leading into the extensive grounds, and the remaining nine forming the grid of the Old Town. Today, the palace is home to the Badisches Landmuseum. ⊠ *Schlossbezirk 10.*

Staatliche Kunsthalle (*State Art Gallery*). One of the most important collections of paintings in the Black Forest region hangs in this gallery. Look for masterpieces by Grünewald, Holbein, Rembrandt, and Monet, and also for work by the Black Forest painter Hans Thoma. The **Kunsthalle Orangerie** next door houses work by such modern artists as Braque and Beckmann. ⊠ *Hans-Thoma-Str. 2–6* ☎ *0721/926–3359* ⊕ *www.kunsthalle-karlsruhe.de* 🖾 *€8* ⊗ *Closed Mon.*

FAMILY **Zentrum für Kunst und Medientechnologie/Museum für Neue Kunst** (*Center for Art and Media Technology/Museum of Modern Art*). In a former munitions factory, the vast Zentrum für Kunst und Medientechnologie, or simply ZKM, is an all-day adventure consisting of two separate museums. At the **Medienmuseum** (Media Museum) you can watch movies, listen to music, try out video games, flirt with a virtual partner, or sit on a real bicycle and pedal through a virtual New York City. The **Museum für Neue Kunst** houses a top-notch collection of media art, in all genres, from the end of the 20th century. ⊠ *Lorenzstr. 19* ☎ *0721/81000* ⊕ *www.zkm.de* 🖾 *From €6* ⊗ *Closed Mon. and Tues.*

7

WHERE TO STAY

$$ HOTEL 🏨 **Hotel Der Blaue Reiter.** Named after the short-lived prewar art movement, Der Blaue Reiter is a colorful place to stay in a lovely residential neighborhood on Karlsruhe's eastern outskirts. **Pros:** quiet location near beer garden; uniquely designed; good value for money. **Cons:** some doubles are two twin beds pushed together; modern furnishings give it a chain vibe; some rooms allow smoking. [$] *Rooms from: €118* ✉ *Amalienbadstr. 16* ☎ *0721/942–660* 🌐 *www.hotelderblauereiter.de* 🛏 *83 rooms* 🍴 *Free Breakfast.*

BADEN-BADEN

51 km (32 miles) north of Freudenstadt, 24 km (15 miles) north of Mummelsee.

Fodor's Choice ★ Perhaps best known as Europe's most fashionable spa town, Baden-Baden is more than its name implies. With a storied history, original 19th-century French-influenced architecture, world-class cultural offerings, and a sunny location in a valley at the edge of the Black Forest, the city has more to offer than just a relaxing soak. It sits atop extensive underground hot springs and can trace its spa heritage back to the time of the Roman emperor Caracalla, whose legions discovered the springs and named the area Aquae Aureliae. The ruins of these Roman baths can still be seen in the city center, next to the historic Friedrichsbad and Caracalla Therme. The spa tradition continues, making it a nice last stop on the way home, as Baden-Baden is just 1½ hours from Frankfurt Airport by train.

In the 19th century, Baden-Baden attracted the upper classes from around Europe, thanks to its comfortable climate. Seeking leisurely pursuits, cultural power players like Fyodor Dostoyevsky joined European royal families at their unofficial summer residence. Palatial homes and stately villas from that time survived the war unscathed and continue to grace the tree-lined avenues, and the town's role as a cultural center carries on today. As home to Europe's second-largest performing arts center—the Festpielhaus, or Festival Hall—Baden-Baden hosts some of the world's best symphonies, opera singers, and ballet troupes each year, from St. Petersburg's Mariinsky Ballet to the Berlin Philharmonie to violin soloist Anne-Sophie Mutter. Five museums add to the city's unique cultural repertoire.

GETTING HERE AND AROUND

High-speed ICE trains stop at Baden-Baden en route between Frankfurt and Basel. The station is some 4 km (2½ miles) northwest of the center. To get downtown, take one of the many buses that leave from outside the station. Once in the center, Baden-Baden is manageable on foot, but there is a range of alternatives available if you get tired, including a hop-on, hop-off tourist train and horse-drawn carriages.

VISITOR INFORMATION

Contacts Baden-Baden Tourism. ✉ *Schwarzwaldstr. 52* ✥ *Trinkhalle* ☎ *07221/275–200* 🌐 *www.baden-baden.de.*

EXPLORING

Casino. Germany's oldest casino, this testament to 19th-century decadence was the brainchild of Parisian Jacques Bénazet, who persuaded the sleepy little Black Forest spa town to build gambling rooms to enliven its evenings after gambling was banned in France (just a few miles away). Opened in 1855, the sumptuous interior was modeled on Versailles, right down to the Pompadour Room, home to a "practice" roulette table, and the luminous Winter Garden, with white marble and antique Chinese vases. The richly decorated gaming rooms could make even an emperor feel at home—Kaiser Wilhelm I was a regular patron, as was his chancellor, Bismarck. Russian novelist Dostoyevsky related his experiences here in his novella, *The Gambler,* and Marlene Dietrich reputedly called it the most beautiful casino in the world. Passports are necessary as proof of identity. Come in the morning before the doors open to players for a guided tour (40 minutes), available in English on request. To try your hand at either French or American roulette, blackjack, or Texas hold'em, you'll need to be over 21 and follow a strict dress code (jacket for men, no sneakers). ⊠ *Kaiserallee 1* ☎ *07221/30240* ⊕ *www.casino-baden-baden.de* 🎟 *From €5.*

Fabergé Museum. The first museum dedicated to the work of Russian jeweler Carl Peter Fabergé holds up to 700 masterpieces from the private collection of Muscovite businessman A. Ivanov. Priceless pieces from the late 19th century include several of the 52 unique eggs gifted to members of Russian royalty, including the first of its kind, a modest egg made of white enamel inside of which a gold yolk, tiny chick, and diamond-emblazoned crown are nested. A Buddha made of nephrite—a green stone unique to Russia—with ruby eyes was originally a gift to the King of Siam. Multilingual staff are on hand to explain the collection in detail. ⊠ *Sophienstr 30* ☎ *07221/970–890* ⊕ *www.faberge-museum. de* 🎟 *€18* ⊗ *Closed Mon.–Thurs. in Jan.–Mar.*

Lichtentaler Allee. A well-groomed park bordering the slender Oos River, this green, tree-lined pedestrian boulevard is a perfect place to stroll, take in the atmosphere, and forget you're in a city. Lined with 19th-century villas, it's home to four museums and an extensive rose garden, the **Gönneranlage**, which contains more than 400 types of roses. ⊠ *Baden-Baden.*

Mount Merkur. The road to Gernsbach, a couple of miles east of Baden-Baden, skirts this 2,000-foot-high mountain peak, named after a monument to the god Mercury that dates from Roman times and still stands just below the mountain summit. You can take the Berg Bahn cable car to the summit, but it's not a trip for the fainthearted—the incline (54 degrees) is one of Europe's steepest. ⊠ *2 Merkuriusberg* 🎟 *Cable car €5 round-trip.*

Museum Frieder Burda. Built as an exhibition hall for the private collection of businessman Frieder Burda, this modern structure was created by acclaimed New York architect Richard Meier. Continually rotating, the private collection focuses on classic modern and contemporary art. Highlights include a number of pieces by Gerhard Richter as well as works by Picasso, German expressionists, the New

York School, and American abstract expressionists. ✉ *Lichtentaler Allee 8b* ☎ *07221/398–980* 🌐 *www.museum-frieder-burda.de* 🎟 *€13* 🕒 *Closed Mon.*

Rebland Vineyard Region. The soft slopes between the Rhine plains and the Black Forest on the outskirts of Baden-Baden enjoy a mild climate that's perfect for the vineyards growing Riesling here. A part of the Baden Wine Route, the Rebland area is home to a number of small, family-run vineyards that offer tours and tastings. ✉ *Mauerbergstr. 32* ☎ *07223/96870 to arrange group tours at any member of wine growers' association* 🌐 *www.baden-badener-wg.de.*

Russian church. The sandstone church is on the corner of Robert Koch Strasse and Lichtentaler Strasse. The Russian diaspora community in Baden-Baden consecrated it in 1882; it's identifiable by its gold onion dome. ✉ *Lichtentaler Str. 76* 🎟 *€1* 🕒 *Closed Dec. and Jan.*

Schloss Favorite. Five kilometers (3 miles) south of Rastatt, in Förch, Ludwig the Turk's Bohemian-born wife, Sibylle Augusta, constructed her own charming little summer palace after his death. Inside, in an exotic, imaginative baroque interior of mirrors, tiles, and marble, her collection of miniatures, mosaics, and porcelain is strikingly displayed. One of the only original palaces left unscathed by the war, the opulent interior includes a one-of-a-kind, 18th-century Florentine cabinet with 758 colorful panels. ✉ *Am Schloss Favorite 5* ☎ *07222/41207* 🌐 *www.schloss-favorite.de* 🎟 *€8* 🕒 *Closed Mon., and mid-Nov.–mid-Mar.*

Schloss Rastatt. A pink-sandstone, three-wing Schloss forms the centerpiece of the small town of Rastatt. Built at the end of the 17th century by Margrave Ludwig Wilhelm of Baden (known as Ludwig the Turk for his exploits in the Turkish wars), its highlights include the chapel, gardens, and a pagoda. It played a pivotal role in history at the turn of the 18th century, when a meeting called to end the fighting between France and the Holy Roman Empire and declare the existence of the state of Germany ended in the death of the French envoy. Inside the palace itself are museums of German defense history. ✉ *Herrenstr. 18* ☎ *07222/34244* 🌐 *www.wgm-rastatt.de* 🎟 *€8* 🕒 *Closed Mon.*

WHERE TO EAT

$ CAFÉ 🍴 **Cafe König.** A small chocolate and macaroon shop is attached to this ornate café specializing in breakfast, light lunches and sweet cakes. It's a centrally located place that's perfect for people-watching and indulging in the German coffee-and-cake tradition. **Known for:** omelets; asparagus in season; chocolate eclairs. [$] *Average main: €12* ✉ *Lichtentalerstr. 12* ☎ *07221/23573* 🌐 *www.chocolatier.de* 🕒 *No dinner* 💳 *No credit cards.*

$$$$ FRENCH 🍴 **Le Jardin de France.** This clean, crisp little French restaurant, whose owners are actually French, emphasizes elegant, imaginative dining in a modern setting. The restaurant sits in a quiet courtyard away from the main street, offering the possibility of alfresco dining in summer. **Known for:** milk-fed suckling pig; steak tartare; foie gras. [$] *Average main: €40* ✉ *Lichtentalerstr. 13* ☎ *07221/300–7860* 🌐 *www.lejardindefrance.de* 🕒 *Closed Sun. and Mon. Mar.–Dec. Closed Sun.–Tues. Jan. and Feb.*

$$ **Rizzi.** This trendy lounge with an eclectic menu focusing on seafood
FUSION has become a beloved institution thanks to its oversize patio. Although
the food is noteworthy, the service could use a course in proper table
etiquette; this is a see-and-be-seen kind of place. **Known for:** oversize
burgers with everything; mussels with risotto; salmon. $ *Average main:*
€17 ⊠ Augustapl. 1 ☎ 07221/25838 ⊕ www.rizzi-baden-baden.de.

$$ **Weinstube im Baldreit.** A lively little wine bar in the middle of the Old
WINE BAR Town enchants you with its lovely terraces and courtyard. Excellent
local wines and simple seasonal meals are served before a cozy fireplace
in the huge barrel-vaulted cellar. **Known for:** Flammkuchen (Alsatian
tart); Maultaschen (pasta stuffed with meat and spinach); asparagus
with ham in season. $ *Average main: €15 ⊠ Küferstr. 3 ☎ 07221/23136*
⊙ Closed Sun. and Mon. No lunch.

WHERE TO STAY

$$$$ **Brenner's Park Hotel & Spa.** This stately and exclusive hotel on the
HOTEL Lichtentaler Allee is one of Germany's most celebrated and storied
retreats—a favorite of royalty, from Queen Victoria to Czar Alexander
II, and their contemporaries. **Pros:** elegant rooms; good location; quiet.
Cons: fellow guests can be aloof; expensive; spa area a bit medicinal.
$ *Rooms from: €390 ⊠ Schillerstr. 6 ☎ 07221/9000 ⊕ www.brenners.*
com ⊷ 104 rooms ⦿ Free Breakfast.

$$$ **Der Kleine Prinz.** The Rademacher family opened this hotel using patri-
HOTEL arch Norbert's experience as a veteran of New York's Waldorf-Astoria,
FAMILY and his wife, Edeltraud's interior design skills to elegantly combine
two elegant city mansions into a unique, antiques-filled lodging. **Pros:**
friendly and welcoming staff; some rooms have wood-burning fireplaces
or balconies; most bathrooms have whirlpool tubs. **Cons:** stairs required
to get to elevator; some rooms may get noisy; uninspired breakfast.
$ *Rooms from: €179 ⊠ Lichtentalerstr. 36 ☎ 07221/346–600 ⊕ www.*
derkleineprinz.de ⊷ 40 rooms ⦿ Free Breakfast.

$$$$ **Hotel Belle Epoque.** Evoking the beauty of its namesake era (and a
HOTEL touch classier than its sister hotel Der Kleine Prinz), the Belle Epoque
Fodor's Choice offers large rooms, soaring ceilings, spacious beds, genuine antiques,
★ luxurious baths, and a beautiful enclosed garden. **Pros:** beautiful gar-
dens; room price includes breakfast and afternoon tea; personal and
friendly service. **Cons:** only the newer wing has an elevator; some older
furnishings; can book out easily. $ *Rooms from: €230 ⊠ Maria-Vikto-*
riastr. 2c ☎ 07221/300–660 ⊕ www.hotel-belle-epoque.de ⊷ 20 rooms
⦿ Free Breakfast.

NIGHTLIFE AND PERFORMING ARTS

Nightlife revolves around Baden-Baden's elegant **casino.**

PERFORMING ARTS

Fodor's Choice **Festspielhaus** (*Festival Hall Baden-Baden*). The entryway to Europe's sec-
★ ond-largest performing arts center is the renovated former train station,
whose grand foyer down to the ticketing window was retained. A mod-
ern, state-of-the-art theater with 2,500 seats and a 900-square-meter

stage was attached where the former train tracks had once lain. More than 120 events annually draw culture lovers and performers from the world over, including the Gewandhausorchester Leipzig and John Neumeier's Hamburg Ballet. ⊠ *Beim Alten Bahnhof 2* ☎ *07221/301–3101* ⊕ *www.festspielhaus.de.*

Theater Baden-Baden. Baden-Baden has one of Germany's most beautiful performance halls in the Theater Baden-Baden, a late-baroque jewel built in 1860–62 in the style of the Paris Opéra. It opened with the world premiere of Berlioz's opera *Beatrice et Benedict.* Today the theater presents a regular series of dramas. ⊠ *Goethepl. 1* ☎ *07221/932–700* ⊕ *www.theater.baden-baden.de.*

SPORTS AND THE OUTDOORS

GOLF

Eight golf courses, spread across Germany and France—but none more than an hour's drive from Baden-Baden—comprise the golf region "Baden Elsass" that includes 18-hole courses designed by the Canadian Royal Air Force and with views of Baden-Baden's old castle, depending on which course you opt for. Greens fees are discounted for those staying in local hotels, which can also book tee times for you.

SPAS

The history of "taking the waters" in Baden-Baden dates back to AD 75, when the Roman army established the city of Aquae Aureliae. The legions under Emperor Caracalla soon discovered that the region's salty underground hot springs were just the thing for aching joints. In a modern sense, bathing became popular within the upper-class elite when Friedrich I banned gambling in 1872. Everyone from Queen Victoria to Karl Marx dangled their feet in the pool and sang the curative praises of the salty warm water bubbling from the ground.

FAMILY **Caracalla Therme.** Less of a relaxing "forget-the-outside-world" experience than the neighboring Friedrichsbad, the Caracalla Therme maintains a series of indoor–outdoor swimming pools with temperatures between 18°C and 38°C (64°F–100°F) that are ideal for the more modest traveler and those with families, since bathing suits are required here. Though children under seven are not allowed in the spa upstairs and those under 14 must be accompanied by an adult, the swimming area offers whirlpools, Jacuzzis, and waterfalls to complement the warm waters. A series of adults-only saunas on the upper level are clothing-free and provide an escape from the hustle and bustle of the pool area below. Be sure to bring your own robe and bath towel, as they are not a part of the package here. Childcare is offered on-site if your kids are too young to use the facilities. ⊠ *Römerpl. 1* ☎ *07221/275–940* ⊕ *www. carasana.de* ⊠ *From €15.*

Fodor's Choice **Friedrichsbad.** Also known as the Roman-Irish Baths, Friedrichsbad ★ offers a one-of-a-kind spa experience. With 17 stations that take you through warm and hot dry saunas, ice baths, and thermal pools, there is a method to the ultimate relaxation on offer. Housed in a building dating back to 1877, this "temple of well-being" was considered the most modern bathing establishment in Europe and its ornate copper and terra-cotta temple only adds to the unique ambience. As with all spas in Germany, this one is textile-free; the 3½-hour spa treatment package includes a honey peeling or soap-and-brush massage. Note that no cameras or children under 14 are allowed (though on-site childcare is available). Mixed bathing is offered Tuesday, Wednesday, Friday, and Sunday; gender-separate bathing is offered on Monday, Thursday, and Saturday. ⊠ *Römerpl. 1* ☎ *07221/275–920* ⊕ *www.carasana.de* 🖾 *From €25.*

CALW

28 km (17 miles) south of Pforzheim on B-463.

Calw, one of the Black Forest's prettiest towns, is the birthplace of Nobel Prize–winning novelist Hermann Hesse (1877–1962). The town's market square, with its two sparkling fountains, is surrounded by 18th-century half-timber houses whose sharp gables pierce the sky. It's an ideal spot for relaxing, picnicking, or people-watching, especially during market time.

GETTING HERE AND AROUND
Calw is best reached by car, as it's no longer serviced by trains. Bus connections to nearby destinations, including Weil and Boebelingen, are available daily by several companies, including the Deutsche Bahn's Südwest Bus.

VISITOR INFORMATION
Contacts Tourist Information Calw. ⊠ *Sparkassenpl. 2* ☎ *07051/167–399* ⊕ *www.calw.de.*

EXPLORING

Hermann Hesse Museum. The museum recounts the life of the Nobel Prize–winning writer Hermann Hesse, author of *Steppenwolf* and *Siddharta,* who rebelled against his middle-class German upbringing to become a pacifist and the darling of the Beat Generation. The museum tells the story of his life in personal belongings, photographs, manuscripts, and other documents. ⊠ *Marktpl. 30* ☎ *07051/7522* ⊕ *www.calw.de/museum-hermann-hesse* 🖾 *€5* ⊗ *Closed Mon.*

Hirsau. Three kilometers (2 miles) north of Calw, Hirsau has ruins of a 9th-century monastery, now the setting for a weekend festival in June and the Klostersummer open-air concerts in July and August. Buy advance tickets at the Calw tourist office. ⊠ *Calw* ⊕ *www.klostersommer.de* ⊗ *Closed Sept.–June.*

WHERE TO STAY

$$
HOTEL
🖾 **Hotel Kloster Hirsau.** A model of comfort and gracious hospitality, this hotel is in Hirsau, 3 km (2 miles) from Calw. **Pros:** quiet location; homey atmosphere; near abbey ruins. **Cons:** a bit out of town;

personnel a tad unfriendly; kids over 7 cost extra. [$] *Rooms from: €124* ✉ *Wildbaderstr. 2, Hirsau* ☎ *07051/96740* 🌐 *www.hotel-kloster-hirsau.de* 🛏 *42 rooms* 🍴 *Breakfast.*

$$ HOTEL 🏨 **Hotel Therme Bad Teinach.** In the northern Black Forest a few miles from Calw, this modern hotel connected to thermal baths is a somewhat isolated getaway with all amenities in house, including a restaurant serving local *Badische* cuisine and a hiking hut a few kilometers away serving some meals. **Pros:** access to thermal bads; natural environment; gorgeous forest views. **Cons:** outside of Calw town; can book out for conferences; too quiet for kids. [$] *Rooms from: €145* ✉ *Otto-Neidhart-Allee 5, Bad Teinach-Zavelstein* ☎ *07053/290* 🌐 *www.hotel-therme-teinach.de* 🛏 *58 rooms* 🍴 *Free Breakfast.*

BAIERSBRONN

6 km (4 miles) northwest of Freudenstadt.

The mountain resort of Baiersbronn—actually comprised of nine separate villages, all named after the valleys they inhabit—has become a high-end destination thanks to an incredible collection of hotels and bed-and-breakfasts providing not only rest and relaxation in beautiful surroundings, but also a gourmet experience. With eight Michelin stars among three of the restaurants and spa resorts, the village has become a favorite location to unwind and indulge in culinary delights; head to the Bareiss Restaurant, the Restaurant Schlossberg, or the Schwarzwaldstube, all in area hotels. The natural surroundings in the midst of the national park make this an ideal place to walk, ski, golf, and ride horseback.

GETTING HERE AND AROUND

On one of the most scenic roads in all of Germany, the Schwarzwaldstrasse (Black Forest Highway), Baiersbronn is best accessed by car. There is also regular weekday regional train service every two hours from nearby Karlsruhe.

VISITOR INFORMATION

Contacts Baiersbronn Touristik. ✉ *Rosenpl. 3* ☎ *07442/84140* 🌐 *www.baiersbronn.de.*

WHERE TO EAT

Both the Hotel Bareiss and Hotel Traube Tonbach have much-lauded, three–Michelin star restaurants, while the restaurant at the Hotel-Café Sackmann has a single Michelin star. It's a heady and expensive dining scene for such a small town, but you can also eat quite well here without spending down your 401K.

$$ GERMAN 🍴 **Hotel Lamm.** With a log-cabin look and traditional Black Forest architecture, there's little clue this restaurant is inside a spa hotel. A moderately priced gourmet menu focuses on local ingredients, including fresh rainbow trout from their own pond. **Known for:** veal schnitzel; rainbow trout; Käsespätzle. [$] *Average main: €15* ✉ *Ellbacherstr. 4* ☎ *07442/4980* 🌐 *www.lamm-mitteltal.de.*

Baden-Baden's Festspielhaus (Festival Hall) hosts concerts, operas, and ballets throughout the year; outside is a sculpture by Henry Moore.

$
GERMAN
FAMILY

✕ **Sattelei.** One of several restaurants run by the team behind the five-star Hotel Bareiss, this hiker's hut is more moderately priced than many of the towns more famous Michelin-starred gourmet restaurants, but the quality of the regional specialties served remains high. It's the perfect place for coffee and cake or a simple lunch, and it's also open for dinner on Sunday; atop a 700-meter-high hill near hiking trails, it has loads of outdoor seating from which to enjoy the natural surroundings. **Known for:** Black forest cake; thick potato soup; Flammkuchen (Alsatian tart). $ *Average main: €8* ⊠ *An der Sattelei* ☎ *4974/424–7320 for hotel* ⊕ *www.bareiss.com/sattelei/wanderhuette-sattelei.html* ⊟ *No credit cards.*

WHERE TO STAY

$$$$
RESORT
FAMILY

🛏 **Bareiss.** A much-loved luxury hotel founded by Hermione Bareiss in 1951, this is one of the top hotels in Europe and one of the very best in Germany. **Pros:** beautiful, secluded location; excellent pools and sauna; excellent restaurants. **Cons:** expensive; too quiet for some; minimum stays in high season. $ *Rooms from: €510* ⊠ *Hermine-Bareiss-Weg 1, Mitteltal* ☎ *07442/470* ⊕ *www.bareiss.com* ↵ *99 rooms* ❍ *Free Breakfast* ↝ *Rates include breakfast and dinner.*

$$
HOTEL
FAMILY

🛏 **Hotel-Café Sackmann.** An imposing cluster of white houses in the narrow Murg Valley north of Baiersbronn, this country-style hotel has broad appeal: families can nest here thanks to children's programs, wellness-seekers can take advantage of the spa facilities, and sightseers can use this as a base for exploring much of the Black Forest. **Pros:** good for families; beautiful location; gourmet restaurant on-site. **Cons:**

furnishings could use updating; some rooms face to the street, can be a bit louder; restaurants are pricey. [$] *Rooms from: €170* ✉ *Murgtalstr. 602, Schwarzenberg* ☎ *07447/2980* 🌐 *www.hotel-sackmann.de* 🛏 *65 rooms* 🍴 *Free Breakfast.*

$$ HOTEL 🏨 **Hotel Lamm.** With a large indoor pool and sauna, a good restaurant, and comfortable rooms, this boutique hotel offers a nice alternative to the luxury of some of the other local options if you don't mind the plaid-filled, 1970s aesthetic of the room decor. **Pros:** beautiful traditional building; friendly staff; fireplaces. **Cons:** can feel remote in winter; some rooms have stairs; furnishings have a unique aesthetic. [$] *Rooms from: €150* ✉ *Ellbacherstr. 4, Mitteltal* ☎ *07442/4980* 🌐 *www.lamm-mitteltal.de* 🛏 *46 rooms* 🍴 *Free Breakfast.*

$$$$ HOTEL FAMILY Fodor's Choice ★ 🏨 **Traube Tonbach.** One of the best hotels in Baiersbronn (and Germany), the Traube Tonbach offers a relaxing atmosphere with sweeping views of the Black Forest from each of its contemporary, stylish rooms, not to mention an outstanding spa and swimming pool, along with on-site child care. **Pros:** beautiful countryside setting; friendly and efficient staff; superior dining. **Cons:** expensive; credit cards only accepted in restaurants; may require minimum stay. [$] *Rooms from: €249* ✉ *Tonbachstr. 237* ☎ *07442/4920* 🌐 *www.traube-tonbach.de* 💳 *No credit cards* 🛏 *118 rooms* 🍴 *Free Breakfast* ☞ *Half-board available.*

FREUDENSTADT

65 km (40 miles) south of Calw, 22 km (14 miles) southwest of Altensteig.

At an altitude of 2,400 feet, Freudenstadt claims to be the "better climate" in Germany and it has the sunny days to prove it. Founded in 1599 by Duke Frederick I of Württemberg, the "city of joy" has the country's largest market square, more than 650 feet long and edged with arcaded shops. The square still awaits the palace that was supposed to be built here for the city's founder, who died before its construction began, though it is difficult to admire its vastness, since a busy, four-lane street cuts it nearly in half. The city's location along three scenic driving routes (the Valley Route, the Spa Route, and the Black Forest Mountain Route) makes it an ideal place for an overnight stay. ■ TIP→ **When the fountains all spout on this square, it can be quite a sight, and a refreshing one as well.**

GETTING HERE AND AROUND

Freudenstadt is served by regular trains from both Karlsruhe and Stuttgart. The huge main square makes the city feel larger than it actually is. The central zone can easily be covered on foot.

VISITOR INFORMATION

Contacts Freudenstadt. ✉ *Marktpl. 64* ☎ *07441/864–730* 🌐 *www.freudenstadt.de.*

EXPLORING

Stadtkirche. Don't miss Freudenstadt's Protestant Stadtkirche, a Gothic-influenced Renaissance church just off the Market Square. Its lofty L-shape nave is a rare architectural feature built in 1608, constructed this way so that male and female worshippers would be separated and unable to see each other during services. ✉ *Marktpl. 36* 🎫 *Free.*

WHERE TO EAT

$ GERMAN 🍴 **Berghütte Lauterbad.** This traditional mountain hut in the woods is run by the nearby Hotel Lauterbad. The restaurant has an outdoor seating area and a beautiful panoramic view that you can enjoy while munching regional delicacies after a hike. **Known for:** seasonal salads; cheese boards; cold-cut platters. [$] *Average main: €10* ✉ *Am Zollernblick 1* ☎ *07441/950–990* 🌐 *www.berghuette-lauterbad.de* 💳 *No credit cards.*

$ GERMAN 🍴 **Turmbräu Freudenstädter.** Lots of wood paneling, exposed beams, and a sprinkling of old sleds and hay wagons give this place on the main square its rustic atmosphere. A brewery with its own beer, the restaurant has fondue night on Wednesday and turns into a disco on weekends. **Known for:** fondue; steak with sauerkraut; pumpkin goulash in season. [$] *Average main: €11* ✉ *Brauhaus am Markt, Marktpl. 64* ☎ *07441/905–121* 🌐 *www.turmbraeu.de.*

EATING WELL IN THE BLACK FOREST

Don't pass up the chance to try *Schwarzwälder Schinken* (pinecone-smoked ham) and *Schwarzwälder Kirschtorte* (a dense, layered cake with chocolate sponge soaked in cherry liqueur and covered in a fluffy whipped-cream frosting). *Kirschwasser,* locally called *Chriesewässerle* (from the French *cerise,* meaning "cherry"), is cherry brandy, the most famous of the region's excellent schnapps varieties. If traveling from May to June, keep an eye out for the "king of vegetables," white asparagus. Most restaurants create special menus that feature this locally grown delicacy.

$$$ GERMAN 🍴 **Warteck.** With leaded, stained-glass windows, vases of flowers, and beautifully upholstered banquettes, this hotel's two dining rooms are a bright spot in local cuisine. Pricey multicourse menus feature seasonal organic products. **Known for:** mussels; duck breast with potato dumplings (Knödel); extensive wine list. [$] *Average main: €25* ✉ *Stuttgarterstr. 14* ☎ *07441/919–20* 🌐 *www.warteck-freudenstadt.de* 🕒 *Closed Tues. and Wed.*

WHERE TO STAY

$ HOTEL 🏨 **Hotel Adler.** Between the main square and the train station, this hotel is comprised of two buildings: one modern with glass features and one historic section, each with comfortable, affordable rooms. **Pros:** friendly personnel; some rooms are accessible; centrally located. **Cons:** some rooms are small; not all rooms updated; balcony views aren't phenomenal. $\boxed{\$}$ *Rooms from: €100* ✉ *Forststr. 15–17* ☎ *07441/91520* ⊕ *www.adler-fds.de* ⌁ *21 rooms* ⊙ *Free Breakfast.*

$$ ⊡ **Hotel Schwanen.** Just a few steps from the main square, this historic
HOTEL   building has been renovated to appeal to both tourists and business travelers. **Pros:** great location near pedestrian area; excellent-value restaurant; comfortably furnished. **Cons:** no elevator in historic building; some bathrooms small; somewhat charmless modern interiors. $\boxed{\$}$ *Rooms from: €104* ✉ *Forststr. 6* ☎ *07441/91550* ⊕ *www.schwanen-freudenstadt.de* ⌁ *18 rooms* ⊙ *Free Breakfast.*

$$ ⊡ **Hotel Warteck.** A small, family-run hotel in the city center with
HOTEL   gourmet dining and delicate touches that lend the modern place warmth. **Pros:** large bathrooms with tubs; modern updates; gourmet dining. **Cons:** modern furnishings a bit stiff; in-house restaurants are pricey; no air-conditioning in rooms. $\boxed{\$}$ *Rooms from: €105* ✉ *Stuttgarterstr. 14* ☎ *07441/91920* ⊕ *www.warteck-freudenstadt.de* ⌁ *13 rooms* ⊙ *Free Breakfast.*

ALPIRSBACH

16 km (10 miles) south of Freudenstadt.

The hamlet of Alpirsbach was founded in 1035 and developed around the Benedictine monastery Kloster Alpirsbach. Although the Reformation forced the abbey to close its doors in 1535, its brewing tradition lives on. Locals claim that it's the pristine artesian water that makes the Alpirsbacher Klosterbräu so incredible. The village maintains a charming, well-preserved historic core with a fine collection of half-timber houses.

GETTING HERE AND AROUND

Alpirsbach is on the direct train line between Freudenstadt and Offenburg, and is a great day trip by train from Freiburg (two hours with a change in Offenburg).

VISITOR INFORMATION

Contacts Alpirsbach Tourist-Information. ✉ *Hauptstr. 20* ☎ *07444/951–6281* ⊕ *www.alpirsbach.de.*

EXPLORING

Brauerei Museum (*Brewery Museum*). The Brauerei was once part of the monastery, and has brewed beer since the Middle Ages. The unusually soft water gives the beer a flavor that is widely acclaimed. There are guided tours of the brewery museum daily at 2:30 (in German only). If there is one place in Germany to go out of your way for a beer, Alpirsbach is it! ✉ *Marktpl. 1* ☎ *07444/67149* ⊕ *www.alpirsbacher.de* ▣ *Tour €7.*

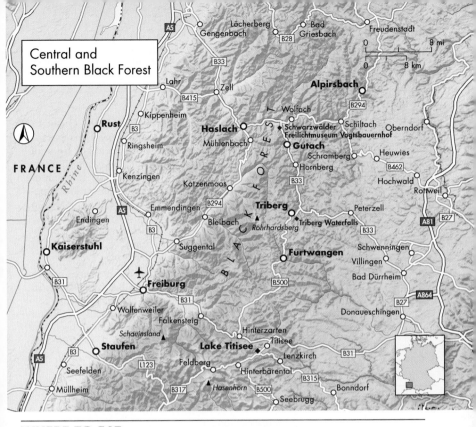

Central and
Southern Black Forest

WHERE TO EAT

$

GERMAN

✕ **Zwickel & Kaps.** The name is a highly sophisticated brewing term describing the means by which the brewmaster samples the fermenting product. That's a good description of the atmosphere here, too: a brewery with service that takes its time to prepare burgers, steaks, and other heavy dishes that wash down well with beer. **Known for:** Nebraska porterhouse steaks; extensive burger menu; Flammkuchen. $ *Average main: €13* ⊠ *Marktstr. 3* ☎ *07444/917–8407* ⊕ *www.vivamisi.com* ⊘ *Closed Mon., and late Dec.–mid-Jan.*

GUTACH

17 km (11 miles) north of Triberg.

Gutach lies in Gutachtal, a valley famous for the traditional costumes, complete with pom-pom hats, worn by women on feast days and holidays. Married women wear black pom-poms, unmarried women red ones. The village is one of the few places in the Black Forest where you can still see thatch roofs. However, escalating costs caused by a decline in skilled thatchers (and soaring fire-insurance premiums) have made them rare.

GETTING HERE AND AROUND
Gutach is a 20-minute train ride from Freiburg. Trains leave once per hour.

EXPLORING

Schwarzwälder Freilichtmuseum Vogtsbauernhof (*Black Forest Open Air Museum*). Near Gutach, this is one of the most appealing museums in the Black Forest. Farmhouses and other rural buildings from all parts of the region have been transported here and reassembled, complete with traditional furniture, to create a living-history museum of Black Forest architecture through the centuries. Demonstrations ranging from traditional dances to woodworking capture life as it was in centuries past; be sure to check the website for daily shows. ⊠ *B-33, Vogtsbauernhof* 🕾 *07831/93560* ⊕ *www.vogtsbauernhof.org* 🖾 *€10* ☺ *Closed Nov.–Mar.* ☞ *When traveling by train, be sure to stop at Gutach (Schwarzwaldbahn), not Gutach im Breisgau.*

Schwarzwalder Trachtenmuseum. Regional traditional costumes can be seen at this museum in a former monastery in the village of Haslach, 10 km (6 miles) northwest of Gutach. The village is quaint, with a fine collection of half-timber houses. Pom-pom-topped straw hats, bejeweled headdresses, embroidered velvet vests, and *Fasnet* (Carnival) regalia of all parts of the forest are on display. ⊠ *Klosterstr. 1* 🕾 *07832/706–172* ⊕ *www.haslach.de* 🖾 *€3* ☺ *Closed Jan., Mon. Apr.–mid-Oct., and Sat.– Mon. mid-Oct.–Mar.*

TRIBERG

16 km (10 miles) south of Gutach.

The cuckoo clock, that symbol of the Black Forest, is at home in the Triberg area. It was invented here, it's made and sold here, it's featured in two museums, and the world's largest cuckoo clock is here.

GETTING HERE AND AROUND
Triberg is accessible via one of the prettiest train rides in Germany, with direct services to Lake Constance and Karlsruhe. The train station is at the lower end of the long main street, and the waterfalls are a stiff uphill walk away. You can take a bus up the hill from the train station to the entrance to the waterfalls, relieving most of the uphill struggle.

VISITOR INFORMATION
Contacts Triberg Tourist Information. ⊠ *Wahlfahrtstr. 4* 🕾 *07722/866–490* ⊕ *www.triberg.de.*

EXPLORING

TOP ATTRACTIONS
Schwarzwaldbahn (*Black Forest Railway*). The Hornberg–Triberg–St. Georgen segment of the Schwarzwaldbahn is one of Germany's most scenic train rides. The 149-km (93-mile) Schwarzwaldbahn, built from 1866 to 1873, runs from Offenburg to Lake Constance via Triberg. It

CLOSE UP

Cuckoo for Cuckoo Clocks

"In Switzerland they had brotherly love—they had 500 years of democracy and peace, and what did that produce? The cuckoo clock."

So says Harry Lime, played by Orson Welles in the classic 1949 film *The Third Man.* He misspoke in two ways. First, the Swiss are an industrious, technologically advanced people. And second, they didn't invent the cuckoo clock. That was the work of the Germans living in the adjacent Black Forest.

CUCKOO HISTORY

The first *Kuckucksuhr* was designed and built in 1750 by Franz Anton Ketterer in Schönwald near Triberg. He cleverly produced the cuckoo sound with a pair of wooden whistles, each attached to a bellows activated by the clock's mechanism.

The making of carved wooden clocks developed rapidly in the Black Forest. The people on the farms needed ways to profitably occupy their time during the long snowbound winters, and the carving of clocks was the answer. Wood was abundant, and the early clocks were entirely of wood, even the works.

Come spring, one of the sons would don a traditional smock and hat, mount the family's winter output on a big rack, hoist it onto his back, and set off into the world to sell the clocks. In 1808 there were 688 clock makers and 582 clock peddlers in the districts of Triberg and Neustadt. The *Uhrenträger* (clock carrier) is an important part of the Black Forest tradition. Guides often wear the traditional costume.

CLOCK STYLES

The traditional cuckoo clock is made with brown stained wood with a gabled roof and some sort of woodland motif carved into it, such as a deer's head or a cluster of leaves. The works are usually activated by cast-iron weights, in the form of pinecones, on chains.

Today's clocks can be much more elaborate. Dancing couples in traditional dress automatically move to the sound of a music box, a mill wheel turns on the hour, a farmer chops wood on the hour, the Uhrenträger even makes his rounds. The cuckoo itself moves its wings and beak and rocks back and forth when calling.

The day is long past when the clocks were made entirely of wood. The works are of metal and therefore more reliable and accurate. Other parts of the clock, such as the whistles, the face, and the hands, are usually of plastic now, but hand-carved wood is still the rule for the case. The industry is still centered in Triberg. There are two museums in the area with sections dedicated to it, and clocks are sold everywhere, even in kiosks.

7

has no fewer than 39 tunnels, and at one point climbs almost 2,000 feet in just 11 km (6½ miles). It's part of the German Railway, and you can make inquiries at any station. ✉ *Triberg* ☎ *0180/699–6633 20 euro-cents per call* ⊕ *www.bahn.de.*

Schwarzwaldmuseum (*Black Forest Museum*). Triberg's famous Schwarzwaldmuseum is a treasure trove of the region's traditional arts: wood carving, costumes, and handicrafts. The Schwarzwaldbahn is described, with historical displays and a working model. The Black Forest was also a center of mechanical music, and, among many other things, the museum has an "Orchestrion"—a cabinet full of mechanical instruments playing like an orchestra. ✉ *Wallfahrtstr. 4* ☎ *07722/4434* 🌐 *www.schwarzwaldmuseum.de* 🎫 *€6* 🕒 *Closed Mon. Oct.–Easter.*

Stadtmuseum. Rottweil, 26 km (16 miles) east of Triberg, has the best of the Black Forest's Fasnet celebrations, which here are pagan, fierce, and steeped in tradition. In the days just before Ash Wednesday, usually in February, "witches" and "devils" roam the streets wearing ugly wooden masks and making fantastic gyrations as they crack whips and ring bells. If you can't make it to Rottweil during the Carnival season, you can still catch the spirit of Fasnet. There's an exhibit on it at the Stadtmuseum, and tours are organized to the shops where they carve the masks and make the costumes and bells—just be aware that the museum is only open Tuesday through Sunday, from 2 to 4. The name *Rottweil* may be more familiar as the name for a breed of dog. The area used to be a center of meat production, and locals bred the Rottweiler to herd the cattle. ✉ *Hauptstr. 20, Rottweil* ☎ *0741/494–330* 🌐 *www.rottweil.de* 🎫 *€2* 🕒 *Closed Mon.*

Triberg Waterfalls. At the head of the Gutach Valley, the Gutach River plunges more than 500 feet over seven huge granite cascades at Triberg's waterfall, Germany's highest. The pleasant 45-minute walk from the center of town is well signposted. A longer walk goes by a small pilgrimage church and the old Mesnerhäuschen, the sacristan's house. You can do much of the hike free of charge but to climb to the top, you'll need to pay a fee. ✉ *Hauptstr. 85* 🌐 *www.triberg.de* 🎫 *From €5.*

Uhren Museum (*Clock Museum*). In the center of Furtwangen, 16 km (10 miles) south of Triberg, drop in on the Uhren Museum, the largest such museum in Germany. It charts the development of Black Forest clocks and exhibits all types of timepieces—from cuckoo clocks, church clock mechanisms, kinetic wristwatches, and old decorative desktop clocks to punch clocks and digital blinking objects. ✉ *Robert-Gerwig-Pl. 1* ☎ *07723/920–2800* 🌐 *www.deutsches-uhrenmuseum.de* 🎫 *€6.*

WHERE TO EAT

$$ GERMAN FAMILY

🍴 **Inselklause.** Inside a small family-run hotel done up in Black Forest decor, the Inselklause uses only regional ingredients in season when creating their ever-changing menu, which features German delights like boar in fall and asparagus in spring. Sit in the lovely garden out back or peer into their stream to see the *Forelle* (trout) caught fresh for your plate. **Known for:** home-grown trout; chanterelles with pasta; Black Forest ham. [$] *Average main: €15* ✉ *Triberger Str. 7* ☎ *07722/7743422* 🌐 *www.inselklause.com* 🕒 *Closed Tues. No lunch Wed.* 💳 *No credit cards.*

WHERE TO STAY

$ HOTEL **Hotel Restaurant Pfaff.** Rooms at this hotel-restaurant are very comfortable, and some have balconies overlooking the famous waterfall. **Pros:** friendly service; close to waterfall; charming architecture. **Cons:** some rooms quite small; no elevator; some furnishings a bit frayed. [$] *Rooms from: €84* ✉ *Hauptstr. 85* ☎ *07722/4479* 🌐 *www.hotel-pfaff.com* 🛏 *10 rooms* 🍴 *Breakfast.*

$$ HOTEL **Parkhotel Wehrle.** This large mansion, which dominates the town center, has a wisteria-covered facade, steep eaves, and individually furnished, wood-accented rooms. **Pros:** elegant rooms; friendly service; small swimming pool and spa area. **Cons:** main street outside can be noisy; no elevators; bar can be loud on weekends. [$] *Rooms from: €155* ✉ *Gartenstr. 24* ☎ *07722/86020* 🌐 *www.parkhotel-wehrle.de* 🛏 *52 rooms* 🍴 *Free Breakfast.*

TITISEE

37 km (23 miles) south of Furtwangen, 40 km (25 miles) south of Triberg.

Beautiful Titisee, carved by a glacier in the last Ice Age, is the most scenic lake in the Black Forest. The heavily wooded landscape is ideal for long bike tours, which can be organized through the Titisee tourist office. The lake measures 2½ km (1½ miles) long and is invariably crowded in summer, but it's a refreshing place to swim as it is closed to motorboats. A public beach with outdoor pool ensures everyone has lake access. On rainy days, head to the indoor water park on the outskirts of town to stay refreshed. Stop by one of the many lakeside cafés to enjoy some of the region's best Black Forest cherry cake with an unparalleled waterside view. ■ TIP→ **Paddleboats and stand-up paddleboards can be rented at several points along the shore.**

GETTING HERE AND AROUND

East of Freiburg, just beyond the Höllental (Hell Valley), Titisee is best reached via the picturesque twice-hourly regional train, which stops in the center of the resort area, just a short walking distance from the lake. By car it's a winding 30-km (19-mile) drive along the B-31, which can be treacherous in fresh snowfall.

VISITOR INFORMATION

Contacts Titisee-Neustadt Tourist-Information. ✉ *Strandbadstr. 4, Titisee-Neustadt* ☎ *07652/1206–8100* 🌐 *www.hochschwarzwald.de.*

WHERE TO STAY

$ B&B/INN FAMILY **Neubierhäusle.** This small guesthouse on the road between Titisee and Neustadt offers a unique charm just a few kilometers away from the crowded lakeshore. **Pros:** large rooms, some of which can be adjoined; friendly service; views of the Black Forest. **Cons:** a short bus ride or drive to the lake; modern furnishings; a bit out of town. [$] *Rooms from: €74* ✉ *Neustadter Str. 79, Titisee-Neustadt* ☎ *07651/8230* 🌐 *www.neubierhaeusle.com* 🛏 *24 rooms* 🍴 *Free Breakfast* 💳 *No credit cards.*

$$ 🔲 **Treschers Schwarzwald Romantikhotel.** Right on the lake, this hotel has
RESORT   the best location in town, and most rooms have a balcony with great
FAMILY   views. **Pros:** large rooms, many with lake views; spa and pool area;
Fodor'sChoice   great on-site restaurant. **Cons:** several rooms face the pedestrian zone,
★   which can get loud in summer; souvenir shop gets busy with tourists;
not all rooms have a good view. $ *Rooms from: €117* ✉ *Seestr. 10,
Titisee-Neustadt* ☎ *07651/8116* ⊕ *www.schwarzwaldhotel-trescher.de*
↩ *83 rooms* ⏐◯⏐ *Free Breakfast.*

FREIBURG

34 km (21 miles) west of Titisee.

Duke Berthold III founded Freiburg im Breisgau in the 12th century as a
free trading city. World War II left extensive damage, but skillful restora-
tion helped re-create the original and compelling medieval atmosphere
of one of the loveliest historic towns in Germany. The 16th-century
geographer Martin Waldseemüller was born here; in 1507 he was the
first to put the name "America" on a map.

For an intimate view of Freiburg, wander through the car-free streets
around the Münster or follow the main shopping artery of Kaiser-
Joseph-Strasse. After you pass the city gate (Martinstor), follow Gerbe-
rau off to the left. You'll come to quaint shops along the banks of one
of the city's larger canals, which continues past the former Augustinian
cloister to the equally picturesque area around the *Insel* (island). This
canal is a larger version of the *Bächle* (brooklets) running through
many streets in Freiburg's Old Town. The Bächle, so narrow you can
step across them, were created in the 13th century to bring fresh water
into the town. Legend has it that if you accidentally step into one of
them—and it does happen to travelers looking at the sights—you will
marry a person from Freiburg. The tourist office sponsors English walk-
ing tours daily at 10:30, with additional tours on Friday and Saturday
at 10. The two-hour tour costs €8.

If you are approaching Freiburg—the largest city in the southern Black
Forest—from the east, you have to brave the curves of the winding road
through the **Höllental** (Hell Valley). In 1770 Empress Maria Theresa's
15-year-old daughter—the future queen Marie Antoinette—made her
way along what was then a coach road on her way from Vienna to
Paris. She traveled with an entourage of 250 officials and servants in
some 50 horse-drawn carriages. The first stop at the end of the valley
is a little village called **Himmelreich**, or Kingdom of Heaven. Railroad
engineers are said to have given the village its name in the 19th century,
grateful as they were to finally have laid a line through Hell Valley. At
the entrance to Höllental is a deep gorge, the **Ravennaschlucht**. It's worth
scrambling through to reach the tiny 12th-century chapel of **St. Oswald**,
the oldest parish church in the Black Forest (there are parking spots off
the road). Look for a bronze statue of a deer high on a roadside cliff,
5 km (3 miles) farther on. It commemorates the legend of a deer that
amazed hunters by leaping the deep gorge at this point. Another 16 km
(10 miles) will bring you to Freiburg. If you aren't coming from this
direction, a detour is worthwhile.

Visitors light candles at the Münster Unserer Lieben Frau (Cathedral of Our Dear Lady) in Freiburg.

GETTING HERE AND AROUND

Freiburg is on the main railroad line between Frankfurt and Basel, and regular ICE (InterCity Express) trains stop here. The train station is a short walk from the city center. Although Freiburg is a bustling metropolis, the city center is compact. In fact, the bulk of the Old Town is closed to traffic, so walking is by far the most practical and pleasurable option. The Old Town is ringed with parking garages for those who arrive by car.

VISITOR INFORMATION

Contacts **Visit Freiburg.** ⊠ *Rathausg. 33* ☎ *0761/388–1880* ⊕ *visit.freiburg.de.*

EXPLORING

Augustinermuseum. A visit to Freiburg's cathedral is not really complete without also exploring the Augustinermuseum, in the former Augustinian cloister. Original sculpture from the cathedral is on display, as well as gold and silver reliquaries. The collection of stained-glass windows, dating from the Middle Ages to today, is one of the most important in Germany. ⊠ *Augustinerpl.* ☎ *0761/201–2531* ⊕ *www.museen.freiburg. de* ⊠ *€7* ⊘ *Closed Mon.*

Fodor'sChoice
★ **Münster Unserer Lieben Frau** (*Cathedral of Our Dear Lady*). The Münster Unserer Lieben Frau, Freiburg's most famous landmark, towers over the medieval streets. The cathedral took three centuries to build, from around 1200 to 1515. You can easily trace the progress of generations of builders through the changing architectural styles, from the fat columns and solid, rounded arches of the Romanesque period to the lofty

Gothic windows and airy interior of the choir. A daily hour-long tour at 2 pm points out the architectural details. The delicately perforated 380-foot spire, the finest in Europe, can be climbed. In addition to a magnificent view, you'll get a closer look at the 16 bells, including the 1258 "Hosanna," one of Germany's oldest functioning bells. ⊠ *Münsterpl. 1* ☎ *0761/388–101* ⊕ *www.freiburgermuenster.info* 🖃 *From €2.*

Museum für Stadtgeschichte (*Museum of City History*). The former home of painter, sculptor, and architect Johann Christian Wentzinger (1710–97) houses the City History Museum, which contains fascinating exhibits, including the poignant remains of a typewriter recovered from a bombed-out bank. The ceiling fresco in the stairway, painted by Wentzinger himself, is the museum's pride and joy. ⊠ *Münsterpl. 30* ☎ *0761/201–2515* ⊕ *www.museen.freiburg.de* 🖃 *€3* ⊘ *Closed Mon.*

Rathaus. Freiburg's famous Rathaus (Town Hall) is actually two 16th-century patrician houses joined together. Destroyed in the war, it was faithfully reconstructed in the 1950s. Among its attractive Renaissance features is an oriel, or bay window, clinging to a corner and bearing a bas-relief of the romantic medieval legend of the Maiden and the Unicorn. ⊠ *Rathauspl. 2–4* ⊕ *www.freiburg.de* ⊘ *Closed weekends.*

WHERE TO EAT

$$$
GERMAN

✕**Oberkirchs Weinstube.** Across from the cathedral and with a terrace on the market square in summer, this hotel, restaurant, and wine cellar is a bastion of tradition and *Gemütlichkeit* (comfort and conviviality). The proprietor personally bags some of the game that ends up on the menu, which features simple but filling dishes and includes around 20 Baden wines served by the glass, many supplied from the restaurant's own vineyards. **Known for:** venison stew; fresh fish; veal schnitzel. ⓢ *Average main: €22* ⊠ *Münsterpl. 22* ☎ *0761/202–6868* ⊕ *www.hotel-oberkirch.de.*

WHERE TO STAY

$$$$
HOTEL
Fodor's Choice
★

🖾 **Colombi Hotel.** Freiburg's most luxurious hotel has tastefully furnished rooms with floor-to-ceiling windows overlooking the romantic Old Town as well as a great restaurant. **Pros:** air-conditioning in all rooms; quiet location; comfortable rooms. **Cons:** business hotel; often fully booked; furnishings could use an update. ⓢ *Rooms from: €264* ⊠ *Rotteckring 16* ☎ *0761/21060* ⊕ *www.colombi.de* ⌂ *112 rooms* ❙◉❙ *Free Breakfast.*

$$
HOTEL

🖾 **Hotel Rappen.** This hotel's brightly painted rooms are on the sunny side of the cobblestone cathedral square and marketplace, and some rooms have beautiful views of the cathedral's flying buttresses. **Pros:** ideal central location; rooms for allergy-sensitive; clean rooms. **Cons:** hard to find your way in—go through restaurant to find lobby; can be loud on holidays if bells are ringing in church; some rooms only have showers. ⓢ *Rooms from: €129* ⊠ *Münsterpl. 13* ☎ *0761/31353* ⊕ *www.hotel-rappen-freiburg.de* ⌂ *24 rooms* ❙◉❙ *Free Breakfast.*

For a break from cathedrals and historic sites, take the kids to Europa Park in Rust.

$ **HOTEL** **Hotel Schwarzwälder Hof.** Located in a former mint in the Old Town's pedestrian zone, this family-run hotel has contemporary-style rooms with dark-wood floors and cool white walls and bed linens, and there's a two-room family suite in the attic with a balcony overlooking the Münster and Old Town. **Pros:** central location; clean rooms; good on-site restaurant. **Cons:** can be noisy; modern rooms belie historic character; no air-conditioning. [$] *Rooms from: €99* ✉ *Herrenstr. 43* ☎ *0761/38030* 🌐 *www.schwarzwaelder-hof.com/en* 🛏 *45 rooms* 🍴 *Free Breakfast.*

$$ **HOTEL** **Park Hotel Post.** This century-old building near the train station has seen a lot of writers come through its historic doors, and editions signed by visiting authors—including Teju Cole, children's illustrator Janusch, and Alice Schwarzer—line the halls. **Pros:** friendly service; some rooms have park views; within walking distance of main train station yet quiet. **Cons:** outside the medieval center; very modern aesthetic; some furnishings could use updating. [$] *Rooms from: €149* ✉ *Eisenbahnstr. 35–37* ☎ *0761/385–480* 🌐 *www.park-hotel-post.de* 🛏 *45 rooms* 🍴 *Free Breakfast.*

$$ **HOTEL** **Zum Roten Bären.** The "Red Bear" claims to be the oldest inn in Germany, with its history traced back 50 generations and documented in a book. **Pros:** dripping with history; great location. **Cons:** some rooms are quite small. [$] *Rooms from: €158* ✉ *Oberlinden 12* ☎ *0761/387–870* 🌐 *www.roter-baeren.de* 🛏 *22 rooms, 3 suites* 🍴 *Breakfast.*

NIGHTLIFE

Nightlife in Freiburg takes place in the city's *Kneipen* (pubs), wine bars, and wine cellars, which are plentiful on the streets around the cathedral. For student pubs, wander around Stühlinger, the neighborhood immediately south of the train station.

STAUFEN

20 km (12 miles) south of Freiburg via B-31.

Once you've braved Hell Valley to get to Freiburg, visit the nearby town of Staufen, where Dr. Faustus is reputed to have made his pact with the devil. The Faustus legend is remembered today chiefly because of Goethe's *Faust* (published in two parts, 1808–32). In this account, Faust sells his soul to the devil in return for eternal youth and knowledge. The historical Faustus was actually an alchemist whose pact was not with the devil but with a local baron who convinced him that he could make his fortune by converting base metal into gold. The explosion leading to his death at Gasthaus zum Löwen produced so much noise and sulfurous stink that the townspeople were convinced the devil had carried him off.

GETTING HERE AND AROUND

To reach Staufen, take the twice-hourly train from Freiburg and change at Bad Krozingen. The train station is a 15-minute walk northwest of the town center. The B-31 highway connects Staufen with Freiburg and the A-5 motorway.

EXPLORING

Gasthaus zum Löwen. You can visit the ancient Gasthaus zum Löwen, where Faust lived—allegedly in room No. 5—and died. Guests can stay overnight in the room, which has been decked out in period furniture with all modern conveniences removed (including the telephone) to enhance the effect. The inn is right on the central square of Staufen, a town with a visible inclination toward modern art in ancient settings. ⊠ *Rathausg. 8* ☎ *07633/908–9390* ⊕ *www.fauststube-im-loewen.de.*

WHERE TO STAY

$ **Landgasthaus zur Linde.** Guests have been welcomed here for more than 350 years, but the comforts inside the inn's old walls are contemporary. **Pros:** friendly; quiet; good restaurant. **Cons:** remote; no elevator; some rooms have showers only. $ *Rooms from: €93* ⊠ *Krumlinden 13, 14 km (9 miles) southeast of Staufen, Münstertal* ☎ *07636/447* ⊕ *www.landgasthaus.de* ⌲ *14 rooms* ⦿ *Free Breakfast.*

KAISERSTUHL

20 km (12 miles) northwest of Freiburg on B-31.

The southwesternmost corner of Germany, nestled on the borders of France and Switzerland is the Kaiserstuhl (Emperor's Chair) region, a volcanic outcrop clothed in vineyards that produce some of Baden's best wines—reds from the Spätburgunder grape and whites that have an uncanny depth. A third of Baden's wines are produced in this single area, which has the warmest climate in Germany and some of the country's most beautiful countryside. The especially dry and warm microclimate has given rise to a diversity of wildlife and vegetation, including sequoias and a wide variety of orchids, as well as dragonflies found nowhere else in the world.

VISITOR INFORMATION

Contacts Kaiserstuhl Tourist-Information. ✉ *Rhine Tourist Information Office, Marktpl. 16* ☎ *07667/940–155* 🌐 *www.naturgarten-kaiserstuhl.de.*

EXPLORING

Breisach am Rhine. The largest of several towns comprising the Kaiserstuhl region, Breisach am Rhine is a typical German village, with a cathedral atop a hill and an impressive city hall. The exceptional thing here is the views from the square beside the cathedral, which show the Black Forest to the east and France to the west (just beyond the River Rhine). It's a sister city to the UNESCO-recognized Neuf-Breisach across the border and a beautiful stopover for many Rhine river cruises. 🌐 *www.breisach.de.*

Endingen. Officially founded in 1285, this small town in the center of the wine-growing Kaiserstuhl changed hands several times, most notably when it became a tributary to the Hapsburg Empire. This history is documented in the free Museum of Ancient Austria in the town's tourist information center. Largely spared from the ravages of war, the town center still maintains timber-frame houses dating back to the 15th century that give it a quaint, traditional look complemented by a series of churches within the city walls. ☎ *07642/689–990* 🌐 *www.endingen.de.*

Geldermann Sektkellerei. A wine cellar specializing in turning white wine into the sparkling white wine known as *Sekt* in German, this 600-year-old building with an arched eave basement was used as a bomb shelter during the war and adapted for the years-long in-bottle fermentation process. Tours are held every day at 2 pm; arrive 30 minutes early to watch the DVD introduction in English. ☎ *07667/834–258* 🌐 *www.geldermann.de* 🎟 *Tours €8* 🕒 *Closed Sun. Nov.–Feb.*

7

WHERE TO STAY

$$ B&B/INN 🏨 **Hotel Zur Krone.** The building dates to 1561, and the Höfflin-Schüssler family, now in its fourth generation as hoteliers, know how to make visitors feel welcome. **Pros:** friendly; quiet; quaint village views. **Cons:** can feel remote; modern, sparse furnishings; service can be brusk. [$] *Rooms* *from: €120 ✉ Schlossbergstr. 15, Achkarren, Vogtsburg ☎ 07662/93130 🌐 www.hotel-krone-achkarren.de 🛏 23 rooms 🍴 Breakfast.*

$$ HOTEL Fodor's Choice ★ 🏨 **Zollhaus.** A converted customs house, this design hotel only has four rooms but luxury to spare, and the interaction of modernity with old beams and exposed brickwork is very striking. **Pros:** quiet despite central location; friendly service; designer feel. **Cons:** only four rooms; no one on-site; no credit cards. [$] *Rooms from: €109 ✉ Hauptstr. 3 ☎ 07642/920–2343 🌐 www.zollhaus-endingen.de ⏲ Closed 2 wks in early Aug. 🛏 4 rooms 🍴 Free Breakfast 💳 No credit cards.*

RUST

35 km (22 miles) north of Freiburg.

The town of Rust, on the Rhine almost halfway from Freiburg to Strasbourg, has a castle dating from 1577 and painstakingly restored half-timber houses. But its big claim to fame is Germany's biggest amusement park, with its own autobahn exit.

EXPLORING

FAMILY Fodor's Choice ★ **Europa Park.** Covering 160 acres, Europa Park is the continent's largest and busiest amusement park and one of Germany's best-loved attractions. It has a quaint walk-through replica of European villages as well as roller coasters and rides, like the Eurosat, a virtual journey past clusters of meteors and falling stars and the Silver Star, Europe's highest roller coaster. Take part in a Spanish jousting tournament or a "4-D" movie in which you might get damp in the rain or be rocked by an earthquake. *✉ Europa-Park-Str. 2 ☎ 01805/776–688 🌐 www.europapark.de 🎟 €43 ⏲ Closed Nov.–Easter.*

WHERE TO STAY

$$ HOTEL FAMILY 🏨 **Hotel am Park.** This handy hotel, with a waterfall and a statue of a "friendly dragon" in the lobby, is just across the road from the entrance to Europa Park. **Pros:** child-friendly; convenient to Europa Park; packages include tickets to Europa Park and parking. **Cons:** it can get noisy; very full in season; directly at amusement park. [$] *Rooms from: €110 ✉ Austr. 1 ☎ 07822/444–900 🌐 www.hotel-am-freizeitpark-rust.de 🛏 47 rooms 🍴 Free Breakfast.*

HEIDELBERG AND
THE NECKAR VALLEY

WELCOME TO HEIDELBERG AND THE NECKAR VALLEY

TOP REASONS TO GO

★ **Heidelberg Castle:** The architectural highlight of the region's most beautiful castle is the Renaissance courtyard—harmonious, graceful, and ornate.

★ **Heidelberg's Alte Brücke:** Walk under the twin towers that were part of medieval Heidelberg's fortifications, and look back for a picture-postcard view of the city and the castle.

★ **Burg Hornberg:** With its oldest parts dating from the 12th century, this is one of the best of more than a dozen castles between Heidelberg and Stuttgart.

★ **Stuttgart's museums:** Top art collections in the Staatsgalerie and the Kunstmuseum contrast with the Mercedes and Porsche museums, where the history of the automobile is illustrated by historic classic cars and sleek racing cars.

★ **Tübingen Altstadt:** With its half-timber houses, winding alleyways, and hilltop setting overlooking the Neckar, Tübingen is the quintessential small-town German experience.

Although not as well known as the Rhine, the Neckar River has a wonderful charm of its own. After Heidelberg, it winds through a small valley guarded by castles. It then flows on, bordered by vineyards on its northern slopes, passing the interesting and industrious city of Stuttgart, before it climbs toward the Swabian Hills. You follow the Neckar until the old half-timber university town of Tübingen. The river continues toward the eastern slopes of the Black Forest, where it originates less than 80 km (50 miles) from the source of the Danube.

1 Heidelberg. The natural beauty of Heidelberg is created by the embrace of mountains, forests, vineyards, and the Neckar River, all crowned by the city's famous ruine castle.

2 Neckargemünd. If you are looking for a quieter (and cheaper) place to base yourself along the Neckar, this small town is a quick 10-minute train ride from its more famous neighbor.

3 Neckarzimmern. Burg Hornburg, located here, is the largest castle on the Neckar and also a hotel where you can spend a comfortable night.

4 Bad Wimpfen. This spa town that dates back to Roman times, is one of the most charming on the Neckar.

5 Ludwigsburg. With its huge barqoue castle and flower gardens, this city near Stuttgart is almost as famous for its summer music festival, held since the early 1930s.

6 Stuttgart. The Swabian capital has elegant streets, shops, hotels, and museums, as well as some of Germany's top industries, among them Mercedes, Porsche, and Bosch.

7 Bebenhausen. This small town between Stuttgart and Tübingen is known for its monastery and a particularly well known restaurant, the Waldhorn.

8 Tübingen. With its half-timber houses, this charming university town is quintessentially German and wholly charming.

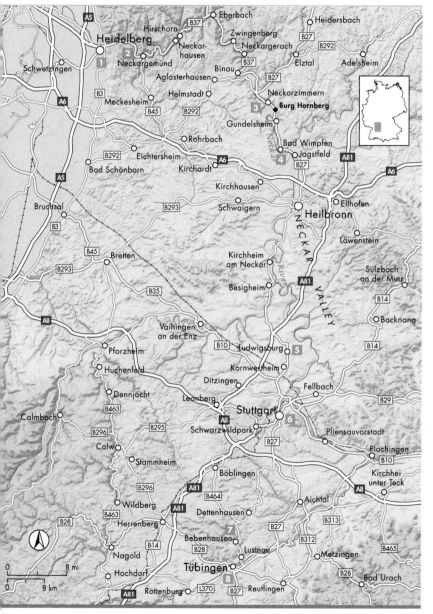

Updated by
Evelyn Kanter

Heidelberg remains one of the best-known and most visited cities in Germany, identifiable by its graceful baroque towers and the majestic ruins of its red-sandstone castle. From this grand city, the narrow and quiet Neckar Valley makes its way east, then turns to the south, taking you past villages filled with half-timber houses and often guarded by their own castle—sometimes in ruins but often revived as a museum or hotel. This part of Germany is aptly named the *Burgenstrasse* (Castle Road).

The valley widens into one of the most industrious areas of Germany, with Stuttgart at its center. In this wealthy city, world-class art museums like the Staatsgalerie or the Kunstmuseum in the center of town contrast with the new and striking Mercedes and Porsche museums in the suburbs, adjoining their sprawling manufacturing facilities.

A bit farther south, the rolling Swabian Hills cradle the university town of Tübingen, a center of learning in a beautiful historic setting on the banks of the Neckar River. Overlooking the town is, of course, a mighty castle.

MAJOR REGIONS

The natural beauty of **Heidelberg** is created by the embrace of mountains, forests, vineyards, and the Neckar River, all crowned by the famous ruined castle. The Neckar and the Rhine meet at nearby Mannheim, the biggest train hub for the superfast ICE (InterCity Express) trains of Germany, a major industrial center, and the second-largest river port in Europe.

The Neckar Valley narrows upstream from Heidelberg, presenting a landscape of orchards, vineyards, and wooded hills crowned with castles rising above the gently flowing stream. It's one of the most impressive stretches of **The Burgenstrasse (Castle Road)**. Along the B-37 are small valleys—locals call them *Klingen*—that cut north into the Odenwald and are off-the-beaten-track territory. Among the picturesque Neckar Valley towns are **Neckargemünd, Neckarzimmern,** and **Bad Wimpfen.**

Ludwigsburg, Stuttgart, and Tübingen are all part of the ancient province of **Swabia,** a region strongly influenced by Protestantism and Calvinism. The inhabitants speak the Swabian dialect of German. **Ludwigsburg** is known for its two splendid castles. **Stuttgart,** the capital of the state of Baden-Württemberg, is one of Germany's leading industrial cities, home to both Mercedes and Porsche, and is cradled by hills on three sides, with the fourth side opening up toward its river harbor. Tiny **Bebenhausen** has a rare medieval Cistercian monastery. The medieval town of **Tübingen** clings to steep slopes and hilltops above the Neckar.

PLANNING

WHEN TO GO

If you plan to visit Heidelberg in summer, make reservations well in advance and expect to pay top rates. To get away from the crowds, consider staying out of town and driving or taking the bus or train into the city. Hotels and restaurants are much cheaper just a little upriver. A visit in late fall, when the vines turn a faded gold, or early spring, with the first green shoots of the year, can be captivating. In the depths of winter, river mists creep through the narrow streets of Heidelberg's Old Town and awaken the ghosts of a romantic past.

GETTING HERE AND AROUND

AIR TRAVEL

From the Frankfurt and Stuttgart airports, there's fast and easy access, by car and train, to all major centers along the Neckar.

BUS AND SHUTTLE TRAVEL

From Frankfurt Airport to Heidelberg, hop aboard the Lufthansa Airport Bus, which takes about an hour and is not restricted to Lufthansa passengers. Buses depart every 90 minutes from the charter bus lane at Arrivals Hall B of Terminal 1. Airport-bound buses leave the Crowne Plaza Heidelberg between 5:30 am and 8 pm. One-way tickets are €25 per person. With advance reservations you can also get to downtown Heidelberg via the shuttle service TLS. The trip costs €35 per person. Vans leave hourly, 8 am to 6 pm weekdays and 8 am to 1 pm on Saturday.

Contacts Lufthansa Airport Bus. ☎ *06152/976–9099* ⊕ *www.frankfurt-airport-shuttles.de.* **TLS.** ☎ *06221/770–077* ⊕ *www.tls-heidelberg.de.*

CAR TRAVEL

Heidelberg is a 15-minute drive (10 km [6 miles]) on A-656 from Mannheim, a major junction of the autobahn system. The Burgenstrasse (Route B-37) follows the north bank of the Neckar River from Heidelberg to Mosbach, from which it continues south to Heilbronn as B-27, the road parallel to and predating the autobahn (A-81). B-27 still leads to Stuttgart and Tübingen.

TRAIN TRAVEL

Heidelberg is 17 minutes from Mannheim, by S-bahn regional train, or 11 minutes on hourly InterCity Express (ICE) trains. These sleek, super-high-speed trains reach 280 kph (174 mph), so travel time between Frankfurt Airport and Mannheim is just 30 minutes. From Heidelberg to Stuttgart, direct InterCity (IC) trains take 40 minutes. Local services link many of the smaller towns.

HOTELS

This area is full of castle-hotels and charming country inns that range in comfort from upscale rustic to luxurious. For a riverside view, ask for a *Zimmer* (room) or *Tisch* (table) *mit Neckarblick* (with a view of the Neckar). The Neckar Valley offers idyllic alternatives to the cost and crowds of Heidelberg. Driving or riding the train from Neckargemünd, for example, takes 20 minutes.

RESTAURANTS

Mittagessen (lunch) in this region is generally served from noon until 2 or 2:30, *Abendessen* (dinner) from 6 until 9:30 or 10. *Durchgehend warme Küche* means that hot meals are also served between lunch and dinner. While credit cards are widely accepted, many small family-owned restaurants, cafés, and pubs will accept only cash or debit cards issued by a German bank. Casual attire is typically acceptable at restaurants here, and reservations are generally not needed.

Prices in restaurant reviews are the average cost of a main course at dinner, or if dinner is not served, at lunch. Prices in hotel reviews are the lowest cost of a standard double room in high season.

WHAT IT COSTS IN EUROS				
	$	$$	$$$	$$$$
Restaurants	under €15	€15–€20	€21–€25	over €25
Hotels	under €100	€100–€175	€176–€225	over €225

PLANNING YOUR TIME

To fully appreciate Heidelberg, try to be up and about before the tour buses arrive. After the day-trippers have gone and many shops have closed, the good restaurants and the nightspots open up. Visit the castles on the Burgenstrasse at your leisure, perhaps even staying overnight. Leaving the valley toward the south, you'll drive into wine country. Even if you are not a car enthusiast, the museums of Mercedes and Porsche in Stuttgart are well worth a visit. Try to get to Tübingen during the week to avoid the crowds of Swabians coming in for their *Kaffee und Kuchen* (coffee and cake). During the week, try to get a room and spend a leisurely evening in this charming half-timber university town.

VISITOR INFORMATION

Visitor Information State Tourist Board Baden-Württemberg. ⊠ *Esslinger-str. 8, Stuttgart* ☎ *0711/238–580* ⊕ *www.tourism-bw.com.*

HEIDELBERG

57 km (35 miles) northeast of Karlsruhe.

If any city in Germany encapsulates the spirit of the country, it is Heidelberg. Scores of poets and composers—virtually the entire 19th-century German Romantic movement—have sung its praises. Goethe and Mark Twain both fell in love here: the German writer with a beautiful young woman, the American author with the city itself. Sigmund Romberg set his operetta *The Student Prince* in the city; Carl Maria von Weber wrote his lushly Romantic opera *Der Freischütz* here. Composer Robert Schumann was a student at the university. The campaign these artists waged on behalf of the town has been astoundingly successful. Heidelberg's fame is out of all proportion to its size (population 140,000); more than 3½ million visitors crowd its streets every year.

Heidelberg was the political center of the Lower Palatinate. At the end of the Thirty Years' War (1618–48), the elector Carl Ludwig married his daughter to the brother of Louis XIV in the hope of bringing peace to the Rhineland. But when the elector's son died without an heir, Louis XIV used the marriage alliance as an excuse to claim Heidelberg, and in 1689 the town was sacked and laid to waste. Four years later he sacked the town again. From its ashes arose what you see today: a baroque town built on Gothic foundations, with narrow, twisting streets and alleyways.

Above all, Heidelberg is a university town, with students making up some 20% of its population. And a youthful spirit is felt in the lively restaurants and pubs of the Altstadt (Old Town). In 1930 the university was expanded, and its buildings now dot the entire landscape of Heidelberg and neighboring suburbs. Modern Heidelberg changed as U.S. Army barracks and industrial development stretched into the suburbs, but the old heart of the city remains intact, exuding the spirit of romantic Germany.

GETTING HERE AND AROUND

Heidelberg is 15 minutes from Mannheim, where four ICE trains and five autobahn routes meet. Everything in town may be reached on foot, but wear sturdy, comfortable shoes, since much of the Old City is uneven cobblestones. A funicular takes you up to the castle and Heidelberg's Königstuhl Mountain, and a streetcar runs from the city center to the main train station. From April through October there are daily walking tours of Heidelberg in German (Friday and Saturday also in English) at 10:30 am; from November through March, tours are in German only, Friday at 2:30 and Saturday at 10:30; the cost is €7. They depart from the main entrance to the Rathaus (Town Hall). Bilingual bus tours run April through October on Thursday and Friday at 1:30 and on Saturday at 1:30 and 3. From November through March, bus tours are on Saturday at 1:30. They cost €17 and depart from Universitätsplatz.

DISCOUNTS AND DEALS

The two-day HeidelbergCARD, which costs €14.50 per person or €31.50 for a family of up to five people, includes free or reduced admission to most tourist attractions as well as free use of all public transportation—including the *Bergbahn* (funicular) to the castle—and other extras such as free entrance to the castle courtyard, free guided walking tours, discounts on bus tours, and a city guidebook. It can be purchased at the tourist-information office at the main train station or the Rathaus, and at many local hotels.

VISITOR INFORMATION

Contacts Heidelberg Tourist Information. ⌧ *Willy-Brandt-Pl.* ☎ *06222/581–0580* ⊕ *www.heidelberg-marketing.de.*

EXPLORING

Alte Brücke (*Old Bridge*). Framed by two Spitzhelm towers (so called for their resemblance to old German helmets), this bridge was part of Heidelberg's medieval fortifications. In the west tower are three dank dungeons that once held common criminals. Above the portcullis you'll see a memorial plaque that pays warm tribute to the Austrian forces that helped Heidelberg beat back a French attempt to capture the bridge in 1799. As you enter the bridge from the Old Town, you'll also notice a statue of an animal that appears somewhat catlike. It's actually a monkey holding a mirror. Legend has it the statue was erected to symbolize the need for both city-dwellers and those who lived on the other side of the bridge to take a look over their shoulders as they cross—that neither group was more elite than the other. The pedestrian-only bridge is at the end of Steingasse, not far from the Marktplatz. ⌧ *End of Steing.*

Alte Universität (*Old University*). The three-story baroque structure was built between 1712 and 1735 at the behest of the elector Johann Wilhelm, although Heidelberg's Ruprecht Karl University was originally founded in 1386. Today it houses the **University Museum**, with exhibits that chronicle the history of Germany's oldest university. The present-day Universitätsplatz (University Square) was built over the remains of an Augustinian monastery that was destroyed by the French in 1693. ⌧ *Grabeng. 1–3* ☎ *06221/542–152* ⌨*€3* ⊗ *Closed Mon. Apr.–Oct.; closed Sun. and Mon. Nov.–Mar.*

Heiliggeistkirche (*Church of the Holy Ghost*). The foundation stone of this Gothic church was laid in 1398, but it was not actually finished until 1544. The gargoyles looking down on the south side (where Hauptstrasse crosses Marktplatz) are remarkable for their sheer ugliness. The church fell victim to plundering by the Catholic League during the Thirty Years' War, when the church's greatest treasure—the Bibliotheca Palatina, at the time the largest library in Germany—was loaded onto 500 carts and trundled off to the Vatican. Few volumes found their way back. At the end of the 17th century, French troops plundered the church again, destroying the tombs; only the 15th-century tomb of Elector Ruprecht III and his wife, Elisabeth von Hohenzollern, remain. Today, the huge church is shared by Heidelberg's Protestant and Catholic populations. ⌧ *Marktpl.* ☎ *06221/21117.*

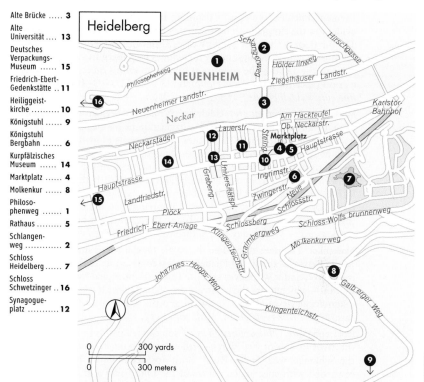

Königstuhl (*King's Throne*). The second-highest hill in the Odenwald range—1,800 feet above Heidelberg—is only a hop, skip, and funicular ride from Heidelberg. On a clear day you can see as far as the Black Forest to the south and west to the Vosges Mountains of France. The hill is at the center of a close-knit network of hiking trails. Well-marked trails from the top lead hikers through the woods of the Odenwald. ✉ *Heidelberg*.

Fodor'sChoice
★ **Königstuhl Bergbahn** (*funicular*). Hoisting visitors to the summit of the Königstuhl in 17 minutes, the funicular stops on the way at the ruined Heidelberg Schloss and Molkenkur. A modern funicular usually leaves every 10 minutes, and a historical train comes every 20 minutes. ✉ *Kornmarkt* ⊕ *www.bergbahn-heidelberg.de* ✉ *Königstuhl €12 round-trip; Schloss €7 round-trip (additional charge to visit Schloss)*.

Kurpfälzisches Museum (*Palatinate Museum*). This baroque palace was built as a residence for a university professor in 1712, and since turned into an art and archeology museum with two standout exhibits worth the visit. One is a replica of the jaw of Heidelberg Man, a key link in the evolutionary chain thought to date from a half-million years ago (the original was unearthed near the city in 1907). The larger attraction is the *Windsheimer Zwölfbotenaltar* (*Twelve Apostles Altarpiece*), one of the largest and finest works of early Renaissance sculptor Tilman

Riemenschneider. Its exquisite detailing and technical sophistication are evident in the simple faith that radiates from the faces of the Apostles. The top floor of the museum showcases 19th-century German paintings, sculptures, and drawings, many depicting Heidelberg from the Middle Ages to the 1800s. The restaurant in the museum's quiet courtyard is a good place for a break. ⊠ *Hauptstr. 97* ☎ *06221/583–4020* ⊕ *www. museum-heidelberg.de* 🎟 *€3* ⊗ *Closed Mon.*

Marktplatz (*Market Square*). Heidelberg's main square, with the Rathaus (Town Hall) on one side and the Heiliggeistkirche on the other, has been its focal point since the Middle Ages. Public courts of justice were held here in earlier centuries, and those accused of witchcraft and heresy were burned at the stake. The baroque fountain in the middle, the *Herkulesbrunnen* (Hercules Fountain), is the work of 18th-century artist Heinrich Charrasky. Until 1740 a rotating, hanging cage stood next to it. For minor crimes, people were imprisoned in it and exposed to the abuse of their fellow citizens. Today the Marktplatz hosts outdoor markets every Wednesday and Saturday. ⊠ *Heidelberg.*

Molkenkur. The next stop after the castle on the Königstuhl funicular, Molkenkur was the site of Heidelberg's second castle. Lightning struck it in 1537, and it was never rebuilt. Today it's occupied by a small restaurant—which bears the creative name Molkenkur Restaurant—with magnificent views of the Odenwald and the Rhine plain from the terrace. ⊠ *Off Klingenteichstr., Molkenkurweg.*

Philosophenweg (*Philosophers' Path*). You can reach this trail high above the river in one of two ways—either from Neuenheim or by taking the **Schlangenweg** (Snake Path). Both are steep climbs, but you'll be rewarded with spectacular views of the Old Town and castle. From Neuenheim, turn right after crossing the bridge and follow signs to the walking path. ⊠ *Heidelberg.*

Rathaus (*Town Hall*). Work began on the town hall in 1701, a few years after the French destroyed the city. The massive coat of arms above the balcony is the work of Heinrich Charrasky, who also created the statue of Hercules atop the fountain in the middle of the square. ⊠ *Marktpl.*

Schlangenweg (*Snake Path*). This walkway starts just above the Alte Brücke opposite the Old Town and cuts steeply through terraced vineyards until it reaches the woods, where it crosses the Philosophenweg (Philosophers' Path). ⊠ *Off Ziegelhäuser Landstr.*

Fodor's Choice
★

Schloss Heidelberg (*Castle*). What's most striking is the architectural variety of this great complex. The oldest parts still standing date from the 15th century, though most of the castle was built during the Renaissance in the baroque styles of the 16th and 17th centuries, when the castle was the seat of the Palatinate electors. The "English wing," built in 1612 by the elector Friedrich V, is positively foreign compared to the castle's more opulent styles. The architectural highlight remains the Renaissance courtyard—harmonious, graceful, and ornate. Even if you have to wait, make a point of seeing the *Grosses Fass* (Great Cask) in the cellar, possibly the world's largest wine barrel, made from 130 oak trees and capable of holding 58,500 gallons. The Deutsches Apotheken-Museum is also included in your ticket and worth a look to see six re-created apothecaries dating back as far as the 17th century. Take the Königstuhl Bergbahn, or funicular—faster and less tiring than hiking to the castle on the Burgweg. Audio guides are available in seven languages. ✉ *Schlosshof* ☎ *06221/654429* 🌐 *www.heidelberg-schloss.de* 🎫 *€6; audio guide €4.*

LOCAL LEGEND

During the rule of the elector Carl Philip, the Great Cask in the Schloss was guarded by the court jester, a Tyrolean dwarf called Perkeo. When offered wine, he always answered, "*Perche no?*" (Why not?), hence his nickname. Legend has it that he could consume frighteningly large quantities of wine and that he died when he drank a glass of water by mistake. A statue of Perkeo stands next to the two-story-high barrel.

Schloss Schwetzingen. This formal 18th-century palace was constructed as a summer residence by the Palatinate electors. It is a noble rose-color building, imposing and harmonious; a highlight is the rococo theater in one wing. The extensive park blends formal French and informal English styles, with neatly bordered gravel walks trailing off into the dark woodland. Fun touches include an exotic mosque—complete with minarets and a shimmering pool (although they got a little confused and gave the building a very baroque portal)—and the "classical ruin" that was de rigueur in this period. The palace interior can only be visited by tour. It's one of Germany's many UNESCO World Heritage sites. ✉ *Schloss Mittelbau, Schwetzingen* ✣ *11 km (7.3 miles) west of Heidelberg; most trains require a change in Mannheim* ☎ *06202/742–770* 🌐 *www.schloss-schwetzingen.de* 🎫 *€9 Apr.–Oct., €7 Nov.–Mar. (includes palace tour and gardens); gardens only: €5 Apr.–Oct., €3 Nov.–Mar.* ⊗ *No English-language tours weekdays.*

Synagogueplatz. The site of the former Heidelberg Synagogue, built in 1877 and burned down in 1938, is now a memorial to the local Jewish population lost in World War II, their names listed on a bronze plaque on an adjoining building. On this residential corner, 12 stone blocks represent the synagogue's pews and the 12 tribes of Israel. ✉ *Corner of Lauerstr. and Grosse Mantelg.* 🌐 *www.tourism-heidelberg.com.*

8

WHERE TO EAT

$ CAFÉ 🍴 **Café Knösel.** Heidelberg's oldest (1863) coffeehouse has always been a popular meeting place for students and professors, and offers traditional Swabian food, pastries, and ambience. A historic change is that the café no longer produces café founder Fridolin Knösel's *Heidelberger Studentenkuss*. This iconic "student kiss" is a chocolate wrapped in paper showing two sets of touching lips—an acceptable way for 19th-century students to "exchange kisses" in public. **Known for:** fresh baked pastries; cheese platters; varieties of coffees and hot chocolate. [$] *Average main: €10* ✉ *Haspelg. 20* ☎ *06221/727–2754* 🌐 *www.cafek-hd.de.*

$$$$ GERMAN 🍴 **Scharff's Schlossweinstube.** This baroque dining room inside the famous Heidelberg castle specializes in *Ente von Heidelberg* (roast duck), but there's always something new on the seasonal menu. Whatever you

EATING WELL IN THE NECKAR VALLEY

Fish and *Wild* (game) from the streams and woods lining the Neckar Valley, as well as seasonal favorites—*Spargel* (asparagus), *Pilze* (mushrooms), *Morcheln* (morels), *Pfifferlinge* (chanterelles), and *Steinpilze* (porcini)—are regulars on menus. Pfälzer specialties are also common, but the penchant for potatoes yields to *Knödel* (dumplings) and pasta farther south. The latter includes the Swabian and Baden staples *Maultaschen* ("pockets" of pasta stuffed with meat or spinach) and *Spätzle* (roundish egg noodles), as well as *Schupfnudeln* (finger-size noodles of potato dough), also called *Buwespitzle.* Look for *Linsen* (lentils) and sauerkraut in soups or as sides. *Schwäbischer Rostbraten* (beefsteak topped with fried onions) and *Schäufele* (pickled and slightly smoked pork shoulder) are popular meat dishes, along with a variety of *Würste.*

Considerable quantities of red wine are produced along the Neckar Valley. Crisp, light Trollinger is often served in the traditional *Viertele*, a round, quarter-liter (8-ounce) glass with a handle. Deeper-color, more substantial reds include Spätburgunder (Pinot Noir) and its mutation Schwarzriesling (Pinot Meunier), Lemberger, and Dornfelder. Riesling, Kerner, and Müller-Thurgau (synonymous with Rivaner), as well as Grauburgunder (Pinot Gris) and Weissburgunder (Pinot Blanc), are the typical white wines. A birch broom or wreath over the doorway of a vintner's home signifies a *Besenwirtschaft* (broomstick inn), a rustic pub where you can enjoy wines with snacks and simple fare. Many vintners offer economical B&Bs. These places are ideal spots to try out your newly learned German phrases; you'll be surprised how well you speak German after the third glass of German wine.

order, pair it with a bottle from the extensive selection of international wines. **Known for:** elegant and romantic setting; international wine List; gourmet versions of popular German dishes. $ *Average main: €75 ⊠ Schlosshof, on castle grounds ☎ 06221/872–7010 ⊕ www.heidelberger-schloss-gastronomie.de ⊗ Closed late Dec.–Jan., and Wed. No lunch ⛺ Jacket required.*

$ ✕ **Schnitzelbank.** Little more than a hole in the wall, this former cooper's
GERMAN   workshop has been transformed into a candlelighted pub. No matter
Fodor's Choice   when you go, it seems to be filled with people seated around the wooden
★   tables (so dinner reservations are strongly advised). **Known for:** cozy atmosphere; Saumagen (a spicy meat-and-potato mixture encased in a sow's stomach, definitely an acquired taste); Wurst platters. $ *Average main: €14 ⊠ Bauamtsg. 7 ☎ 06221/21189 ⊕ www.schnitzelbank-heidelberg.de ⊗ No lunch weekdays.*

$$$ ✕ **Simplicissimus.** Saddle of lamb and sautéed liver in honey-pepper
MEDITERRANEAN   sauce are specialties here, as are seasonal preparations with asparagus and mushrooms. The menu changes every six weeks. **Known for:** Dessertsteller (sweets sampler); saddle of lamb in honey-pepper sauce; attentive service. $ *Average main: €25 ⊠ Ingrimstr. 16 ☎ 06221/673–2588 ⊕ www.simplicissimus-restaurant.de ⊗ Closed Sun. and Mon. No lunch.*

$ ✕**Trattoria Toscana.** Traditional Italian fare is on offer here, including
ITALIAN antipasti, pasta dishes, pizzas, and special daily offerings. The restaurant is in a central location in the main square, and in warm weather you can opt for a table outside on the cobblestones—perfect for people-watching with your meal. **Known for:** generous portions; individual pizzas; homemade tiramisu and panna cotta. $ *Average main: €12* ✉ *Marktpl. 1* ☎ *06221/28619* ⊕ *www.trattoria-toscana-hd.de.*

$$ ✕**Zum Roten Ochsen.** Many of the rough-hewn oak tables here have initials carved into them, a legacy of the thousands who have visited Heidelberg's most famous old tavern. Mark Twain, Marilyn Monroe, and John Wayne may have left their mark—they all ate here, and Twain's photo is on one of the memorabilia-covered walls. **Known for:** local specialties including Maultaschen (meat-filled ravioli); popular with both locals and visitors; kitchen open late. $ *Average main: €15* ✉ *Hauptstr. 217* ☎ *06221/20977* ⊕ *www.roterochsen.de* ⊙ *Closed Sun., and mid-Dec.–mid-Jan. No lunch Nov.–Mar.*

GERMAN
Fodor's Choice
★

$$ ✕**Zum Weissen Schwan.** Founded in 1398 and in this location on Heidelberg's Hauptstrasse (main street) since 1778—so you know they are doing something right—the White Swan specializes in regional fare. The menu includes several versions of Maultaschen (traditional Swabian ravioli) and local mushrooms and asparagus are featured in season. **Known for:** regional specialties; kitchen open late; beer and wine list. $ *Average main: €15* ✉ *Hauptstr. 143* ☎ *06221/659–692* ⊕ *weisser-schwan.de* ▬ *No credit cards.*

GERMAN

$$$$ ✕**Zur Herrenmühle.** A 17th-century grain mill has been transformed into this romantic restaurant in the heart of Altstadt (Old Town). The old beams add to the warm atmosphere. **Known for:** homemade pasta; fish and lamb dishes; historic ambience. $ *Average main: €28* ✉ *Near Karlstor, Hauptstr. 239* ☎ *06221/602–909* ⊕ *www.herrenmuehle-heidelberg.de* ⊙ *Closed Mon. No lunch.*

EUROPEAN

8

WHERE TO STAY

$$ ☷ **Bergheim 41.** This sleek and trendy hotel in the "new" part of Heidelberg is built into one side of the Alten Hallenbad, the covered former city pool that is now a popular upscale international food court. **Pros:** roof garden; some rooms have views of the Schloss; parking available. **Cons:** 15 minutes from Old City; on a busy street (although windows are soundproofed); no restaurant. $ *Rooms from: €110* ✉ *Bergheim 41* ☎ *06221/750–040* ⊕ *www.bergheim41.de* ▬ *No credit cards* ⤚ *34 rooms* ¶○¶ *Free Breakfast.*

HOTEL

$$ ☷ **Crowne Plaza Heidelberg.** This grand hotel has stylish furnishings, soaring ceilings, and an enviable location, minutes on foot from Old Town. **Pros:** parking garage; pool and fitness center; direct shuttle from Frankfurt airport (80 km [50 miles] away). **Cons:** chain-hotel feel; impersonal lobby; oriented toward business travelers, not leisure. $ *Rooms from: €125* ✉ *Kurfürsten-Anlage 1* ☎ *06221/9170* ⊕ *www.crowneplaza.com* ⤚ *236 rooms* ¶○¶ *No meals.*

HOTEL

$$$$ 🖼 **Der Europäische Hof–Hotel Europa.** On secluded grounds next to the Old
HOTEL Town, this most luxurious of Heidelberg hotels has been welcoming
Fodor'sChoice guests since 1865. **Pros:** indoor pool; castle views from the two-story
★ fitness and spa center; central location. **Cons:** restaurant dinner-only
October–June; limited parking; expensive. $ *Rooms from: €228*
✉ *Friedrich-Ebert-Anlage 1* ☎ *06221/515–512* ⊕ *www.europaeischer-hof.com* ⌐ *118 rooms* ⦿ *Free Breakfast.*

$$ 🖼 **Gasthaus Backmulde.** This traditional family-owned Gasthaus on a
B&B/INN residential street in the heart of Heidelberg has very nice modern rooms
at affordable prices. **Pros:** quiet rooms; nice restaurant for dinner only;
cooking classes with chef in restaurant kitchen. **Cons:** difficult parking;
some rooms have shared baths; restaurant closed Sunday and Monday.
$ *Rooms from: €135* ✉ *Schiffg. 11* ☎ *06221/53660* ⊕ *www.gasthaus-backmulde.de* ⌐ *26 rooms* ⦿ *Free Breakfast.*

$$ 🖼 **Holländer Hof.** Opposite the Alte Brücke, and with views across
HOTEL the busy Neckar River to the forested hillside beyond, this ornate
19th-century building is in a prime Old Town location. **Pros:** nice
view of river and beyond; comfortable accommodations; some rooms
are wheelchair-accessible. **Cons:** noisy at times; no restaurant or bar
(although both are in adjoining building); small rooms. $ *Rooms
from: €120* ✉ *Neckarstaden 66* ☎ *06221/60500* ⊕ *www.hollaender-hof.de* ⌐ *39 rooms* ⦿ *Free Breakfast.*

$$$ 🖼 **Hotel Die Hirschgasse.** A stunning castle view, fine restaurants, a liter-
HOTEL ary connection, and a touch of romance distinguish this historic inn
Fodor'sChoice (1472) across the river from the Old Town, opposite Karlstor. **Pros:** ter-
★ rific view; very good food in both restaurants; close to "museum row".
Cons: limited parking; 15-minute walk to Old Town; restaurant closed
Sunday and Monday. $ *Rooms from: €205* ✉ *Hirschg. 3* ☎ *06221/4540*
⊕ *www.hirschgasse.de* ⌐ *20 suites* ⦿ *Free Breakfast.*

$$ 🖼 **Hotel zum Ritter.** If this is your first visit to Germany or to Hei-
HOTEL delberg, try to stay here, since it's the only surviving Renaissance
Fodor'sChoice building in Heidelberg—and one of the oldest—built in 1592 as
★ the private home of a wealthy merchant, and it has an unbeatable
location opposite the market square in the heart of Old Town. **Pros:**
charm and elegance; nice views; spacious rooms. **Cons:** off-site parking; rooms facing the square can be noisy; slow elevator. $ *Rooms
from: €125* ✉ *Hauptstr. 178* ☎ *06221/1350* ⊕ *www.hotel-ritter-heidelberg.com* ⌐ *37 rooms* ⦿ *Free Breakfast.*

$$ 🖼 **KulturBrauerei Heidelberg.** Rooms with warm, sunny colors and mod-
HOTEL ern style are brilliantly incorporated into this old brewery in the heart
of Old Town. **Pros:** lively restaurant; Wi-Fi in most rooms; beer gar-
den. **Cons:** noisy in summer; difficult parking; rooms above Zum Seppl
restaurant are accessed by steep, narrow stairs and dark hallways,
and you have to walk a block to get breakfast. $ *Rooms from: €115*
✉ *Leyerg. 6* ☎ *06221/502–980* ⊕ *www.heidelberger-kulturbrauerei.de* ⌐ *43 rooms* ⦿ *Free Breakfast.*

$$ 🖼 **NH Heidelberg.** The glass-covered entrance hall of this primarily busi-
HOTEL ness hotel is spacious—not surprising, as it was the courtyard of a former
brewery. **Pros:** gym and spa; underground garage; wheelchair-accessible
rooms. **Cons:** lacks charm; 15-minute walk to Old Town; breakfast

expensive. $ *Rooms from: €125* ⊠ *Bergheimerstr. 91* ☎ *06221/13270* ⊕ *www.nh-hotels.com* ⥂ *174 rooms* ⦿ *No meals.*

$

HOTEL

⊡ **Star Inn Hotels & Suites Premium.** The city's largest hotel opened Spring 2018, with spacious modern rooms and individually controlled air-conditioning, still a rarity in Germany. **Pros:** lobby bar open 24/7; 90 parking spaces, free electric vehicle charging stations; pet-friendly. **Cons:** no restaurant; busy street; distance from Altstadt. $ *Rooms from: €80* ⊠ *Speyerer Str. 9* ☎ *6221/36000* ⊕ *starinnhotels.com* ⥂ *299 rooms* ⦿ *Free Breakfast.*

$$

HOTEL

⊡ **Weisser Bock.** Exposed beams, stucco ceilings, warm wood furnishings, and individually decorated, comfortable rooms are all part of this hotel's charm. **Pros:** nicely decorated rooms; exceptional food; smoke-free facility. **Cons:** parking difficult to find; not all rooms accessible by elevator; breakfast not included in room rate. $ *Rooms from: €115* ⊠ *Grosse Mantelg. 24* ☎ *06221/90000* ⊕ *www.weisserbock.de* ⥂ *23 rooms* ⦿ *No meals.*

NIGHTLIFE AND PERFORMING ARTS

Information on all upcoming events can be found in the monthly *Heidelberg aktuell,* free and available from the tourist office or on the Internet (⊕ *www.heidelberg-aktuell.de*).

NIGHTLIFE

Heidelberg nightlife is concentrated in the area around the Heiliggeistkirche (Church of the Holy Ghost), in the Old Town. Don't miss a visit to one of the old student taverns that have been in business for generations.

Today's students, however, are more likely to hang out in one of the dozen or more cafés and bars on **Untere Strasse,** which runs parallel to and between Hauptstrasse and the Neckar River, starting from the market square.

Billy Blues (im Ziegler). This restaurant, bar, and disco, popular with university students, has live music most Thursdays and a salsa party on Wednesday. There also are a few small, efficiently decorated, budget-priced rooms upstairs. ⊠ *Bergheimer Str. 1b* ☎ *06221/25333* ⊕ *www.billyblues.de* ⊘ *Closed Sun.–Tues.*

Destille. This club plays rock music until 2 am on weekdays and 3 am on weekends, and the young crowd that packs the place is always having a good time. A tree in the middle of this club is decorated according to season. This is also an art gallery; paintings by local artists decorate the walls and are for sale. ⊠ *Untere Str. 16* ☎ *06221/22808* ⊕ *www.destilleonline.de.*

Halle 02. The old railway freight terminal has been reborn as an art gallery and music club for concerts and dance parties. There's a beach atmosphere in summer on the outdoor patio. Concerts generally begin at 8 pm, dance parties at 11 pm or later. ⊠ *Zollhofgarten* ☎ *06621/398–9990* ⊕ *www.halle02.de.*

8

Kulturhaus Karlstorbahnhof. This 19th-century train station has been transformed into a vibrant complex of music, theater, cabaret and cinema. Thanks in part to its central location, there's always something happening, although hours and ticket prices vary. ⊠ *Am Karlstor* ☎ *06221/97894* ⊕ *www.karlstorbahnhof.de.*

Schnookeloch. In the same location since 1703, it was a favorite of the Burschenschaften, or dueling fraternities, for two centuries. These days it's popular with Heidelberg's university students, locals and visitors for its traditional ambience and well-priced food and beer that starts flowing at 7:30 am daily. The wood-panel walls are filled with historic photos and maps. There also are budget-price rooms upstairs. ⊠ *Haspelg. 8* ☎ *06221/138–080.*

Vetters Alt-Heidelberger Brauhaus. It's worth elbowing your way into this bar for the brewed-on-the-premises beer. Try the Dunkles Hefeweizen, or dark wheat beer, which is not produced as widely as the lighter version. As with most German brewpubs, there's a full menu, too, including a long list of Wurst dishes. ⊠ *Steing. 9* ☎ *06221/165–850* ⊕ *www.brauhaus-vetter.de.*

Fodor's Choice ★ **Zum Roten Ochsen.** Mark Twain rubbed elbows with students here during his 1878 stay in Heidelberg—look for his photo on one of the memorabilia-covered walls. Zum Roten Ochsen is popular with students and local residents for its friendly atmosphere and hearty meals at reasonable prices. The Red Ox has been operated by the Spengel family for more than 170 years. A pianist plays German and international favorites, starting at 7:30 pm, likely to turn into a sing-along after several refills of regional German wines and local Heidelberg beer. ⊠ *Hauptstr. 217* ☎ *06221/20977* ⊕ *www.roterochsen.de.*

Zum Seppl. When this traditional restaurant and bar opened at the end of the 17th century, it had its own brewery on the premises; now the brewery is a block away and called Kulturbrauerei Heidelberg. The Seppl crowd is a mix of Heidelberg students, local residents, and visitors, all attracted by the old-world charm and ample servings of traditional German specialties. Every inch of wall space is covered with historic photos, menus, and other memorabilia. ⊠ *Hauptstr. 213* ☎ *06221/502–980* ⊕ *www.heidelberger-kulturbrauerei.de/en/scheffels-wirtshaus-zum-seppl.*

SHOPPING

Heidelberg's **Hauptstrasse,** or Main Street, is a pedestrian zone lined with shops, sights, and restaurants that stretches more than 1 km (½ mile) through the heart of town. But don't spend your money before exploring the shops on such side streets as **Plöck, Ingrimstrasse,** and **Untere Strasse,** where there are candy stores, bookstores, and antiques shops on the ground floors of baroque buildings. If your budget allows, the city can be a good place to find reasonably priced German antiques, and the Neckar Valley region produces fine glass and crystal.

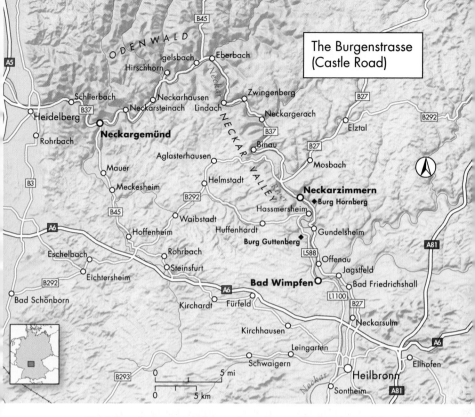

The Burgenstrasse (Castle Road)

Heidelberg has open-air farmers' markets on Wednesday and Saturday mornings on Marktplatz and Tuesday and Friday mornings, as well as Thursday afternoon, on Friedrich-Ebert-Platz.

Fodor'sChoice
★ **Heidelberger Zuckerladen.** The old glass display cases and shelves here are full of lollipops and "penny" candy. If you're looking for an unusual gift or special sweet treat, the shop fashions colorful, unique items out of sugary ingredients such as marshmallow and sweetened gum. Avoid early afternoon, when the tiny shop is crowded with schoolchildren. ✉ *Plöck 52* ☎ *06221/24365* ⊕ *www.zuckerladen.de.*

NECKARGEMÜND

11 km (7 miles) from Heidelberg.

Coming from the hustle and bustle of Heidelberg, you'll find the hamlet of Neckargemünd is a quiet place where you can relax by the Neckar River and watch the ships go by. The town also makes a good base from which to visit Heidelberg. Leave the car here and enjoy the 10-minute ride by bus or train.

GETTING HERE AND AROUND

The S1, S2, S5, and S51 commuter trains from Heidelberg run every few minutes and will get you here in less than 10 minutes. By car, it will take 25 minutes via the B-37. Once here, the Altstadt (Old Town) and Neckar River views are walkable, but you'll need a car or take a taxi to visit the Schloss Zwingennberg, about a half-hour distant via the S1 (toward Osterburken) or the B-37 and B-45.

WHERE TO STAY

$ B&B/INN FAMILY 🏨 **Art Hotel.** In a historic building in the heart of the Altstadt (Old City), this stylish hotel has spacious rooms and suites, including three- and four-bed junior suites that are perfect for families. **Pros:** good for families; reasonable rates; quiet. **Cons:** on a busy street; no elevator; no restaurant. [$] *Rooms from: €95* ✉ *Hauptstr. 40* ☎ *06223/862–768* 🌐 *www.art-hotel-neckar.de* 🛏 *13 rooms* 🍴 *Free Breakfast.*

$ B&B/INN 🏨 **Gasthaus Reber.** If you're looking for a clean, simple, and inexpensive room, this small inn is an ideal candidate, conveniently located opposite the railway station for trips to or from Heidelberg. **Pros:** unbeatable rates; close to public transportation; owner-operated. **Cons:** on busy street; not all rooms have an en suite bathroom; restaurant closed for lunch on weekdays. [$] *Rooms from: €70* ✉ *Bahnhofstr. 52* ☎ *06223/8779* 🌐 *www.gasthaus-reber.de* 💳 *No credit cards* 🛏 *10 rooms* 🍴 *Free Breakfast.*

NECKARZIMMERN

83 km (52 miles) from Heidelberg.

The main attraction here is the Burg Hornberg castle high above the town, but visitors will find the village itself to be a charming respite, with a traditional town square surrounded by historic buildings, and pleasant riverfront walks.

GETTING HERE AND AROUND

By road from Heidelberg, take the E-5 autobahn south (toward Bruschal) then the E-6 east to Sinsheim, where you connect with local road 292 northeast past Mossbach to Neckarzimmern, then follow signs. If you have time en route, stop off at the Sinsheim Auto & Technik Museum for displays including Formula 1 racecars and a Concorde supersonic jet.

EXPLORING

FAMILY **Burg Guttenberg.** One of the best-preserved Neckar castles is the 15th-century Burg Guttenberg. Within its stone walls are a museum and a restaurant (closed January, February, and Monday) with views of the river valley. The castle also is home to Europe's leading center for the study and protection of birds of prey, the German Raptor Research Center, with 100 falcons and other birds of prey. There are demonstration flights from the castle walls from April through October, daily at 11 and 3. ✉ *Burgstr., Neckarmühlbach* ✣ *15 km (9.3 miles) south of*

You can tour Burg Hornberg or spend the night at this spectacular castle.

Neckarzimmern ☎ *06266/388* 🌐 *www.burg-guttenberg.de* 🎫 *Castle €5; castle and flight demonstration €11* ⏲ *Closed Nov.–Feb.*

8

Fodor's Choice ★ **Burg Hornberg.** The largest and oldest castle in the Neckar Valley, the circular bulk of Burg Hornberg rises above the town of Neckarzimmern. The road to the castle leads through vineyards that have been providing dry white wines for centuries. These days, the castle is part hotel (24 rooms and part museum). In the 16th century it was home to the larger-than-life Götz von Berlichingen (1480–1562). When the knight lost his right arm in battle, he had a blacksmith fashion an iron replacement. Original designs for this fearsome artificial limb are on view in the castle, as is his suit of armor.

For many Germans, this larger-than-life knight is best remembered for a remark that was faithfully reproduced in Goethe's play *Götz von Berlichingen*. Responding to an official reprimand, Von Berlichingen told his critic, more or less, to "kiss my ass" (the original German is a bit more earthy: *Er kann mich am Arsche lecken*). To this day the polite version of this insult is known as a *Götz von Berlichingen*. Inquire at the hotel reception about visiting the castle, or just enjoy the walking trails and views from the top of the hill. ✉ *Hornbergerweg* ☎ *06261/5001* 🌐 *www.burg-hornberg.de* 🎫 *€5.*

WHERE TO STAY

$$ HOTEL Fodor's Choice ★ **Burg Hornberg Hotel.** Your host at this antiques-filled hotel with comfortable, modern rooms is the present Baron of the Burg Hornberg. **Pros:** historic setting; nice restaurant; on-site wineshop. **Cons:** no elevator; restaurant can be crowded in season on weekends; not enough parking. [$] *Rooms from: €110* ✉ *Marcus Freiherr von Gemmingen* ☎ *06261/92460* 🌐 *www.castle-hotel-hornberg.com* 🕒 *Closed late Dec.–late Jan.* 🛏 *24 rooms* 🍴 *Free Breakfast.*

BAD WIMPFEN

8 km (5 miles) south of Neckarzimmern.

Fodor's Choice ★ At the confluence of the Neckar and Jagst rivers, Bad Wimpfen is one of the most stunning towns of the Neckar Valley. The Romans built a fortress and a bridge here, on the riverbank site of an ancient Celtic settlement, in the 1st century AD. A millennium later, the Staufen emperor Barbarossa chose this town as the site of his largest *Pfalz* (residence). The ruins of this palace still overshadow the town and are well worth a stroll, as are the streets with historic half-timber houses, including one from 1580 with inscriptions in Hebrew.

GETTING HERE AND AROUND

There's a direct regional commuter train from Heidelberg that will get you to Bad Wimpfen in 45 minutes, and from Neckarzimmern there's an hourly service that takes 30 minutes. By road, take the B-27 east from Neckarzimmern to the L-1100. The old city is good for walking, but wear comfortable shoes for the uneven cobblestones.

TOURS

Medieval Bad Wimpfen offers a town walk year-round, Sunday at 2 (€2), departing from the visitor center inside the old train station.

DISCOUNTS AND DEALS

On arrival, ask your hotel for a free *Bad Wimpfen à la card* for reduced or free admission to historic sights and museums.

FESTIVALS

FAMILY **Zunftmarkt.** On the last weekend in August, the Old Town's medieval past comes alive during the Zunftmarkt, a historical market dedicated to the *Zünfte* (guilds). "Artisans" in period costumes demonstrate the old trades and open the festivities with a colorful parade on horseback. ✉ *Bad Wimpfen* 🌐 *www.zunftmarkt.de.*

VISITOR INFORMATION

Contacts Bad Wimpfen–Gundelsheim Tourist-Information. ✉ *Hauptstr. 45* ☎ *07063/97200* 🌐 *www.badwimpfen.de.*

EXPLORING

FAMILY **Deutsches Zweirad–Museum** (*German Motorcycle Museum*). Displays include the 1885 Daimler machine that started us on the road to motorized mobility, the world's first mass-produced motorcycles (Hildebrand and Wolfmüller), and exhibits on racing. Also here is the NSU Museum, an early motorbike manufacturer acquired by the predecessor of the company now called Audi, which has an auto production facility in Neckarsulm. The collections are arranged over five floors in a handsome 400-year-old castle that belonged to the Teutonic Knights until 1806. The Audi factory in nearby Neckarsulm offers tours. ⊠ *Urbanstr. 11, Neckarsulm* ☎ *07132/35271* ⊕ *www.zweirad-museum.de* 🎟️ *€6* 🕑 *Closed Mon.*

Ritterstiftskirche St. Peter. Wimpfen im Tal (Wimpfen in the Valley), the oldest part of town, is home to the Benedictine monastery of Gruessau and its church, Ritterstiftskirche St. Peter, which dates from the 10th and 13th centuries. The cloisters are an example of German Gothic at its most uncluttered. ⊠ *Lindenpl.* ⊕ *www.badwimpfen.de.*

Stadtkirche (*City Church*). The 13th-century stained glass, wall paintings, medieval altars, and the stone pietà in the Gothic Stadtkirche are worth seeing, as are the Crucifixion sculptures (1515) by Rhenish master Hans Backoffen on Kirchplatz, behind the church. ⊠ *Kirchsteige 8* ⊕ *www.kirche-badwimpfen.de.*

Steinhaus. Germany's largest Romanesque living quarters and once the imperial women's apartments, this is now a history museum with relics from the Neolithic and Roman ages along with the history of the Palatinate, including medieval art, armor and weapons, and ceramics. Next to the Steinhaus are the remains of the northern facade of the palace, an arcade of superbly carved Romanesque pillars that flanked the imperial hall in its heyday. The imperial chapel, next to the Red Tower, holds a collection of religious art. ⊠ *Burgviertel 25* ☎ *07063/97200* 🎟️ *€3* 🕑 *Closed Mon. Closed mid-Oct.–mid-Apr.*

8

WHERE TO EAT

$ ✕ **Weinstube Feyerabend.** There are three adjoining eateries here: the
GERMAN Weinstube for a glass of good Swabian wine with a snack, the Restaurant for a full meal at lunch or dinner, or let yourself be tempted by the good-looking cakes from their own bakery in the Konditerei/Cafe. **Known for:** homemade pretzels; seasonal asparagus; seasonal menus. 💲 *Average main: €12* ⊠ *Hauptstr. 74* ☎ *07063/950–566* ⊕ *www.friedrich-feyerabend.de* ⊟ *No credit cards* 🕑 *Closed Mon.*

LUDWIGSBURG

15 km (9 miles) north of Stuttgart.

Although its residents would never call it a suburb of Stuttgart, its proximity to the modern industrial and commercial center of Baden-Württenberg has made it one. Ludwigsburg's main attraction is its fabulous baroque castle, with more than 450 rooms spread over 18 buildings, surrounded by the beautiful Schlosspark (gardens). A music festival, held each summer since 1932, features performances both outdoors and in the original palace theater.

GETTING HERE AND AROUND

There is regular commuter rail service from Stuttgart's Hauptbahnhof (main train station). Take the S4 or S5 for the journey of around 45 minutes. The castle is close enough to the station to walk, or you can take a taxi.

EXPLORING

Fodor's Choice
★

Residenzschloss Ludwigsburg. One of Europe's largest palaces to survive in its original condition, Residenzschloss Ludwigsburg certainly merits a visit for its sumptuous interiors and exquisite gardens. The main palace is also home to the **Keramikmuseum,** a collection of historical treasures from the porcelain factories in Meissen, Nymphenburg, Berlin, Vienna, and Ludwigsburg, as well as an exhibit of contemporary ceramics. The **Barockgalerie** is a collection of German and Italian baroque paintings from the 17th and 18th centuries. The **Modemuseum** showcases three centuries of fashion, particularly royal clothing of the 18th century. The castle is surrounded by the fragrant, colorful 74-acre park **Blühendes Barock** (Blooming Baroque), filled with thousands and thousands of tulips, huge masses of rhododendrons, and fragrant roses. A **Märchengarten** (fairy-tale garden) delights children of all ages. Guided tours in English are weekdays at 1:30, and weekends at 11, 1:30, and 3:15.

✉ *Schloss Str. 30* ☎ *07141/182–004* ⊕ *www.schloesser-und-gaerten.de*
🎫 *Palace €7, park €9; museums with audio guide €4; museum tour
with audio guide €7; combination ticket €18.*

STUTTGART

50 km (31 miles) south of Heilbronn.

Stuttgart is a city of contradictions. It has been called, among other
things, "Germany's biggest small town" and "the city where work is a
pleasure." For centuries Stuttgart, whose name derives from *Stutengar-
ten,* or "stud farm," remained a pastoral backwater along the Neckar,
despite being the seat of the fabulously powerful and wealthy Württemberg dukes and all the money and prestige that meant. Then the
Industrial Revolution propelled the city into the machine age. Leveled
in World War II, Stuttgart has regained its position as one of Germany's
top industrial centers.

This is Germany's can-do city, whose natives have turned out Mercedes-
Benz and Porsche cars, Bosch electrical equipment, and a host of other
products exported worldwide. Yet Stuttgart is also a city of culture and
the arts, with world-class museums, opera, and ballet. Moreover, it's
the domain of fine local wines; the vineyards actually approach the city
center in a rim of green hills. Forests, vineyards, meadows, and orchards
compose more than half the city, which is enclosed on three sides by
woods. Each year in October, Stuttgart is home to Germany's second-
largest Oktoberfest (after Munich), called the Canstatter Volksfest.

An ideal introduction to the contrasts of Stuttgart is a guided city bus
tour. Included is a visit to the needle-nose TV tower, high on a mountaintop above the city, affording stupendous views. Built in 1956, it was
the first of its kind in the world. The tourist office also offers superb
walking tours. On your own, the best place to begin exploring Stuttgart
is the Hauptbahnhof (main train station); from there walk down the
pedestrian street Königstrasse to Schillerplatz, a small, charming square
named after the 18th-century poet and playwright Friedrich Schiller,
who was born in nearby Marbach. The square is surrounded by historic
buildings, many of which were rebuilt after the war.

DISCOUNTS AND DEALS

The three-day **StuttCard** (€9.70) offers discounts to museums and attractions, with or without a free public-transit pass (€17–€27 for 24–72
hours, includes a transit card valid in the whole city; €18 for the city
center only). All the cards are available from the Stuttgart tourist office
opposite the main train station, and include free admission to nearly all
the city's museums and points of interest.

GETTING HERE AND AROUND

Stuttgart is the major hub for the rail system in southwestern Germany,
and two autobahns cross here. It's about 2½ hours away from Munich
and a bit more than an hour from Frankfurt. The downtown museums
and the main shopping streets are doable on foot. For the outlying
attractions and to get to the airport, there is a very efficient S-bahn
and subway system.

8

TOURS

The tourist office (i-Punkt Information kiosk) opposite the Hauptbahnhof (main train station) is the meeting point for city walking tours in German (year-round, Saturday at 10) for €8. There are daily bilingual walks April–October at 11 am for €18. Bilingual bus tours costing €8 depart from the bus stop around the corner from the tourist office, in front of Hotel am Schlossgarten (April–October, daily at 1:30; November–March, Friday–Sunday at 1:30). All tours last from 1½ to 2½ hours. Stuttgart Tourist-Information offers 12 different special-interest tours altogether. Call for details.

VISITOR INFORMATION

Contacts Stuttgart Touristik-Information i-Punkt. ⊠ *Königstr. 1A* ☎ *0711/222–8246* ⊕ *www.stuttgart-tourist.de.*

EXPLORING

FAMILY
Fodor'sChoice
★
Altes Schloss (*Old Castle*). This former residence of the counts and dukes of Württemberg was originally built as a moated castle around 1320. Wings were added in the mid-15th century, creating a Renaissance palace. The palace now houses the **Landesmuseum Württemberg** (Württemberg State Museum), with exhibits tracing the area's development from the Stone Age to modern times and a floor of jaw-dropping family jewels of the fabulously rich and powerful Württemberg royals There's also a separate floor dedicated to a children's museum. ⊠ *Schillerpl. 6, Mitte* ☎ *0711/8953–5111* ⊕ *www.landesmuseum-stuttgart.de* 🎫 *€12* ⊙ *Closed weekends.*

Kunstmuseum Stuttgart (*Stuttgart Art Museum*). This sleek structure encased in a glass facade is a work of art in its own right. The museum contains artwork of the 19th- and 20th centuries and the world's largest Otto Dix collection, including the *Grossstadt* (*Metropolis*) triptych, which captures the essence of 1920s Germany. The bistro-café on the rooftop terrace affords great views; the lobby houses another café and the museum shop. ⊠ *Kleiner Schlosspl. 1, Mitte* ☎ *0711/216–19600* ⊕ *www.kunstmuseum-stuttgart.de* 🎫 *From €6* ⊙ *Closed Mon.*

FAMILY
Fodor'sChoice
★
Mercedes-Benz Museum. The stunning futuristic architecture of this museum is an enticement to enter, but the equally stunning historic and futuristic vehicles inside are the main attraction. Visitors are whisked to the top floor to start this historical timeline tour of motorized mobility in the 1880s, with the first vehicles by Gottlieb Daimler and Carl Benz. Other museum levels focus on a particular decade or category of vehicle, such as trucks and buses, race cars, concept cars, and future technology, including autonomous driving. Historic photos and other artifacts line the walls of the circular walkway that links the levels. A restaurant on the lower level serves mostly German cuisine with a modern twist, and stays open after the museum has closed, and there's a huge gift shop with all kinds of Mercedes-Benz–branded items. In the adjoining new-car showroom you can muse over appealing models that are sold in Europe but not in North America. Guided tours of the factory are also available. ⊠ *Mercedesstr. 100, Untertürkheim*

The postmodern Neue Staatsgalerie (New State Gallery) is where you'll find 20th-century masterpieces by artists including Picasso and Chagall.

☎ *0711/173–0000* ⊕ *www.mercedes-benz-classic.com* ✉ *From €10 (€5 after 4:30)* ⊙ *Closed Mon.*

FAMILY
Fodor's Choice
★

Porsche Museum. In the center of the Porsche factory complex in the northern suburb of Zuffenhausen, the architecturally dramatic building expands outward and upward from its base, like a sports stadium. Inside is a vast collection of legendary and historic Porsche cars including racing cars, nearly 1,000 racing trophies and design and engineering awards, and several vehicles designed by Ferdinand Porsche that eventually became the VW Beetle. It is astounding how some 1930s models still look contemporary today. The museum includes a coffee shop, a snack bar, and the sophisticated Christophorus restaurant, regarded as the best American-style steak house in Stuttgart, open for lunch and dinner beyond museum hours. The gift shop sells some Porsche logo clothing, but mostly miniature collectibles. Stand under the special "cones" on the upper level to hear the different engine sounds of various Porsche models, and try out the interactive "touch wall" timeline to explore nine decades of automotive history. Factory tours are available with advance arrangement. ✉ *Porschepl. 1, Zuffenhausen* ☎ *0711/911–20911* ⊕ *www.porsche.com/museum* ✉ *€8* ⊙ *Closed Mon.*

Schlossplatz (*Palace Square*). A huge area enclosed by royal palaces and planted gardens, the square has elegant arcades branching off to other stately plazas. The magnificent baroque **Neues Schloss** (New Palace), now occupied by Baden-Württemberg state government offices, dominates the square. Schlossplatz is the extension of the Koenigstrasse pedestrian shopping street, dotted with outdoor cafés in season. It borders the Schlossgarten (Palace Garden), which extends across Schillerstrasse all the way to Bad Canstatt on the Neckar River (where the annual Canstatter Volksvest, or Oktoberfest, is held). The adjoining parks also include an exhibition hall, planetarium, and the mineral hot springs that attracted the Romans. ✉ *Corner of Koenigstr. and Planie, Mitte.*

Fodor's Choice ★ **Staatsgalerie** (*State Gallery*). This not-to-be-missed museum displays one of the finest art collections in Germany. The old part of the complex, dating from 1843, has paintings from the Middle Ages through the 19th century, including works by Cranach, Holbein, Hals, Memling, Rubens, Rembrandt, Cézanne, Courbet, and Manet. Connected to the original building is the **Neue Staatsgalerie** (New State Gallery), designed by British architect James Stirling in 1984 as a melding of classical and modern, sometimes jarring, elements (such as chartreuse window mullions). Considered one of the most successful postmodern buildings, it houses works by such 20th-century artists as Braque, Chagall, de Chirico, Dalí, Kandinsky, Klee, Mondrian, and Picasso. Visit both sections on the same ticket. ✉ *Konrad-Adenauer-Str. 30–32, Mitte* ☎ *0711/470–400, 0711/4704–0249 info-line* 🌐 *www.staatsgalerie.de* 🎫 *Permanent collection €7 (free Wed.); special exhibitions €10–€12; guided tours €5* 🕒 *Closed Mon.*

WHERE TO EAT

$$ GERMAN Fodor's Choice ★ 🍴 **Alte Kanzlei.** Steps from the Altes Schloss, the building dates from 1565, but the menu is modern, offering both pastas and traditional Swabian specialties. In a nod to Bavarian neighbors, the menu also offers *Weisswurst,* or veal sausages, but only on weekends. **Known for:** regional specialties including Maultaschen (meat-filled ravioli); feaured wine of the month specials; seasonal specialties including Spargel (white asparagus). [$] *Average main: €15* ✉ *Schillerpl. 5A, Mitte* ☎ *0711/294–457* 🌐 *www.alte-kanzlei-stuttgart.de.*

$$ GERMAN 🍴 **Paulaner am Alten Postplatz** (*Paulaner Brewpub*). The motto here is "wurst and bier are friends," and there's plenty of both consumed in this popular brewpub. Paulaner is a Munich beer, so you'll find traditional Bavarian fare, including Weisswurst,on the menu along with Swabian favorites such as house-made Maultaschen. **Known for:** generous portions; outdoor beer garden in season; Bavarian and Swabian specialties. [$] *Average main: €15* ✉ *Calwerstr. 45, Mitte* ☎ *711/214450* 🌐 *www.paulaner-stuttgart.de.*

$$$$ ECLECTIC Fodor's Choice ★ 🍴 **Top Air.** Top Air distinguishes itself as Europe's only Michelin-starred airport restaurant. A respite of calm in a busy location, travelers with time and money can opt for a four-course chef's tasting menu, but you don't have to have a ticket to dine here. **Known for:** extensive wine list and a sommelier to explain it; free parking; pan-European menu. [$] *Average main: €40* ✉ *Stuttgart Airport, Terminal 1, Level 4* ☎ *711/948–2137* 🌐 *www.restaurant-top-air.de* 🕒 *Closed Sun. and Mon. No lunch Thurs.–Tues.*

$$$$ EUROPEAN 🍴 **Wielandshöhe.** One of Germany's top chefs, Vincent Klink, and his wife, Elisabeth, are very down-to-earth, cordial hosts, offering artfully plated cuisine using locally grown ingredients in the ever-changing menu

The fountain in Schlossplatz (Palace Square) is a great place for people-watching, or to contemplate the surrounding architecture.

wherever possible. House specialties, such as saddle of lamb with a potato gratin and green beans or the Breton lobster with basil potato salad, are recommended. **Known for:** additive-free meats and veggies only; classic, attentive service; exemplary wine list. [$] *Average main: €45* ✉ *Alte Weinsteige 71, Degerloch* ☎ *0711/640–8848* 🌐 *www.wielandshoehe.de* 🕒 *Closed Sun. and Mon.* 👔 *Jacket required.*

8

WHERE TO STAY

$$$ HOTEL 🏨 **Am Schlossgarten.** Stuttgart's top accommodations are in a modern structure surrounded by spacious gardens, a stone's throw from many of the top sights and opposite the main station. **Pros:** views of the park; welcoming lobby; close to museums, ballet, opera. **Cons:** not all rooms face the park; expensive room rates; limited and expensive parking. [$] *Rooms from: €200* ✉ *Schillerstr. 23, Mitte* ☎ *0711/20260* 🌐 *www.hotelschlossgarten.com* 🛏 *116 rooms* 🍴 *Free Breakfast.*

$$$ B&B/INN 🏨 **Der Zauberlehrling.** The "Sorcerer's Apprentice" is aptly named, as Karen and Axel Heldmann have conjured up an unusual luxury hotel with each room's decor based on a different theme. **Pros:** fabulous rooms with lots of surprises; enjoyable restaurant; free Wi-Fi. **Cons:** minuscule lobby; no elevator; reserve far in advance to get choice of themed room style. [$] *Rooms from: €200* ✉ *Rosenstr. 38, Bohnenviertel* ☎ *0711/237–7770* 🌐 *www.zauberlehrling.de* 🛏 *17 rooms* 🍴 *Free Breakfast.*

$$ HOTEL 🏨 **Hotel Wartburg.** This comfortable hotel is on a quiet side street a five-minute walk from the Konigstrasse pedestrian mile and the museums around Schlossplatz. **Pros:** free parking; close to shopping and theaters;

free Wi-Fi. **Cons:** rooms facing street can be noisy; residential neighborhood can feel isolated late at night; restaurant closed weekends. [$] *Rooms from: €125* ✉ *Langestr. 49, Mitte* ☎ *0711/20450* 🌐 *www.hotel-wartburg-stuttgart.de* 🛏 *74 rooms* 🍴 *Free Breakfast.*

$$ HOTEL 🏨 **Mövenpick Hotel Stuttgart Airport.** Across the street from Stuttgart Airport, the doors of this hotel open into a completely soundproof glass palace with airy rooms and a convenient location for the fairgrounds. **Pros:** discount for booking online; spacious rooms; gym, sauna, steam room. **Cons:** swells with business travelers; 15 minutes from downtown museums, theater, or shopping; expensive. [$] *Rooms from: €175* ✉ *Flughafenstr. 50, Flughafen* ☎ *0711/553–440* 🌐 *www.movenpick.com/Stuttgart* 🛏 *326 rooms* 🍴 *No meals.*

$$ RESORT Fodor's Choice ★ 🏨 **Waldhotel.** On the edge of a forest (*Wald*) with miles of hiking and biking trails, yet just a 10-minute streetcar ride from downtown, this modern resort hotel offers lots of amenities and peaceful nights. **Pros:** free Wi-Fi; ample free parking; spacious modern bathrooms. **Cons:** walk from streetcar after dark is not well lit; distance from center city; extra charge for children sharing room. [$] *Rooms from: €175* ✉ *Guts-Muths-Weg 18, Degerloch* ☎ *0711/185–720, 0711/185–72120* 🌐 *www.waldhotel-stuttgart.de* 🛏 *96 rooms* 🍴 *Free Breakfast.*

NIGHTLIFE AND PERFORMING ARTS

NIGHTLIFE

There's no shortage of rustic beer gardens, wine pubs, and sophisticated cocktail bars in and around Stuttgart. Night owls should head for the **Schwabenzentrum** on Eberhardstrasse; the **Bohnenviertel,** or "Bean Quarter" (Charlotten-, Olga-, and Pfarrstrasse); the "party mile" along **Theodor-Heuss-Strasse; Calwer Strasse**; and **Wilhelmsplatz.**

PERFORMING ARTS

You can buy discounted tickets for most arts events at the i-Punkt tourist office in front of the main train station.

SI-Centrum. Built to showcase big-budget musicals, including American imports, this entertainment complex contains theaters, hotels, bars, restaurants, a casino, a wellness center, movie theaters, and shops. ✉ *Plieninger Str. 100, Möhringen* ☎ *0711/721–1111* 🌐 *www.si-centrum.de.*

Staatstheater. Stuttgart's internationally renowned ballet company performs at this elegant historic theater. The ballet season—including works choreographed by Stuttgart Ballet's John Cranko—is September through July and alternates with the highly respected State Opera. The box office is open weekdays 10–7, Saturday 10–2. ✉ *Oberer Schlossgarten 6, Mitte* ☎ *0711/202090* 🌐 *www.staatstheater.stuttgart.de.*

SPORTS AND THE OUTDOORS

BOAT TRIPS

Necckar-Kapt'n. From the pier close to the entrance to the Wilhelma Zoo, Neckar-Käpt'n offers a wide range of boat trips, as far north as scenic Besigheim. ✉ *Off Neckartalstr., Anlegestelle Wilhelma,*

Wilhelma ☎ *0711/5499–7060* ⊕ *www.neckar-kaeptn.de* ☑ *From €7* Ⓜ *U14 to Rosensteinbrucke.*

SHOPPING

Stuttgart is a shopper's paradise, from the department stores on the Königstrasse to the boutiques in the Old Town's elegant passages and the factory outlet stores.

Some of Stuttgart's more unique shops, including secondhand shops, are found in this Boheniertel (Bean Quarter); a stroll through the neighborhood's smaller streets reveals many tucked-away shops specializing in fashion, jewelry, artwork, and gifts, especially along Wagnerstrasse and Eslingerstrasse.

You'll find several blocks of boutiques, cafés, and restaurants on Calwerstrasse, between the main shopping streets of Koenigstrasse and Theodore-Heuss-Strasse, but far less busy. The restaurants spill into the pedestrian-only street in warm weather.

Breuninger. The flagship store of this upscale regional department-store chain has glass elevators that rise and fall under the dome of the central arcade, whisking you to multiple floors of designer boutiques. There is also a clearance Breuninger Outlet at Rotebühlplatz 25. ⊠ *Marktstr. 1–3, Mitte* ☎ *0711/2110* ⊕ *www.breuninger.de.*

Fodor's Choice ★ **Markthalle.** The beautiful art nouveau Markthalle on Dorotheenstrasse is one of Germany's finest market halls, with a curved glass ceiling for natural light to show off a mouthwatering selection of exotic fresh fruits, spices, meats, cheeses, chocolates, honeys, flowers, and handmade jewelry and crafts, including holiday decorations in season. Check out the huge ceramic fountain, which spouts water from the original well. The restaurant balcony overlooks the action, which starts at 7:30 am weekdays ⊠ *Dorotheenstr. 4* ⊕ *www.markthalle-stuttgart.de.*

BEBENHAUSEN

6 km (4 miles) north of Tübingen.

Between Stuttgart and Tübingen lies this small hamlet consisting of a few houses, a monastery, and the Waldhorn, an excellent and well-known restaurant. The monastery was founded in the 12th century by the count of Tübingen. Today it belongs to the state.

GETTING HERE AND AROUND

To get here by public transportation, take the train from Stuttgart to Tübingen (45 minutes) then a bus to Bebenhausen (15 minutes). Trains and bus connections are several times an hour on weekdays, less on weekends. If you're driving, take the B-27 and B-464 south from Stuttgart.

EXPLORING

Fodor's Choice ★ **Bebenhausen Monastery and Palace** (*Bebenhausen Monastery and Palace*). This is a rare example of a well-preserved medieval monastery from the late 12th century, becoming one of the weslthiest in the region, with a boarding school added in 1504. It was annexed by the local government in 1806, and in 1868 parts of the complex were rebuilt as a hunting castle for King Frederick of Württemberg. Expansion and restoration continued as long as the palace and monastery continued to be a royal residence. Visits to the palace are available only on a guided tour; and English-language tours are available only by special arrangement (usually for groups). ✉ *Im Schloss* ☎ *07071/602–802* 🌐 *www.kloster-bebenhausen.de* 🎟 *Monastery €5; palace €7* ⏲ *Palace closed Mon.*

WHERE TO EAT

$$$$ EUROPEAN Fodor's Choice ★ 🍴 **Waldhorn.** Old favorites such as the *Vorspeisenvariation* (a medley of appetizers), local fish, and goose keep people coming back to this historic eatery. Garden tables have a castle view. **Known for:** seasonal specialties including Spargel (white asparagus) and Pfifferling (wild mushrooms); rhubarb strudel with ice cream; wine list with a well-chosen selection of top local wines. [$] *Average main: €40* ✉ *Schönbuchstr. 49* ☎ *07071/61270* 🌐 *www.waldhorn-bebenhausen.de* ⏲ *Closed Mon. and Tues.*

TÜBINGEN

40 km (25 miles) south of Stuttgart.

With its half-timber houses, winding alleyways, and hilltop setting overlooking the Neckar, Tübingen provides the quintessential German experience. The medieval flavor is quite authentic, as the town was untouched by wartime bombings. Dating to the 11th century, it flourished as a trade center; its weights and measures and currency were the standard through much of the area. The town declined in importance after the 14th century, when it was taken over by the counts of Württemberg. Between the 14th and the 19th century, its size hardly changed as it became a university and residential town, its castle the only symbol of ruling power.

Yet Tübingen hasn't been sheltered from the world. It resonates with a youthful air. Even more than Heidelberg, Tübingen is virtually synonymous with its university, a leading center of learning since it was founded in 1477. The best way to see and appreciate Tübingen is simply to stroll around, soaking up its age-old atmosphere of quiet erudition.

GETTING HERE AND AROUND

By regional train or by car on the autobahn, Tübingen is an hour south of Stuttgart on B-27. Trains run several times an hour on weekdays, less often on weekends. In the Old Town you reach everything on foot.

TOURS

The Tübingen tourist office runs guided city tours year-round at 2:30. From March through October tours take place daily and cost €9. From November through February, tours are on weekends only. Tours start at the Rathaus on the market square.

VISITOR INFORMATION

Contacts Verkehrsverein Tübingen. ☏ *07071/91360* ⊕ *www.tuebingen-info.de.*

EXPLORING

FAMILY
Fodor's Choice
★

Boxenstop Museum. A wealth of vintage toys, model trains, and vehicles, including motorcycles, awaits children of all ages. This private collection, open to the public, includes Porsche, Ferrari, and Maserati race cars, an original 1957 VW Beetle, and a rare 1954 Lloyd. Ask a docent to start up the HO trains or one of the antique musical toys. Kids can ride one of the old pedal cars. There's also a small café. ✉ *Brunnenstr. 18* ☏ *7071/929–090* ⊕ *www.boxenstop-tuebingen.de* ☞ *€7* ☉ *Closed Mon. and Tues., and Mon.–Sat. in Nov. and Dec.*

Fodor's Choice
★

Burg Hohenzollern. The majestic silhouette of this massive castle is visible from miles away. The Hohenzollern House of Prussia was the most powerful family in German history. It lost its throne when Kaiser William II abdicated after Germany's defeat in World War I. The Swabian branch of the family owns one-third of the castle, the Prussian branch two-thirds. Today's neo-Gothic structure, perched high on a conical wooded hill, is a successor of a castle dating from the 11th century. On the fascinating 45-minute castle tour you'll see the Prussian royal crown and beautiful period rooms, all opulent from floor to ceiling, with such playful details as door handles carved to resemble peacocks and dogs. The restaurant on the castle grounds, Burgschänke (closed January, and Monday in February and March) serves regional food, and there's an outdoor beer garden in season. From the castle parking lot it's a 20-minute walk to the entrance, or in summer take the shuttle bus. English-language tours are offered on weekdays at 2 pm from April through October. ✉ *25 km (15 miles) south of Tübingen on B–27, Hechingen* ☏ *07471/2428* ⊕ *www.burg-hohenzollern.com* ☞ *From €7; shuttle bus €3 round-trip, €2 one-way.*

Marktplatz (*Market Square*). Houses of prominent burghers of centuries gone by surround this square. At the open-air market on Monday, Wednesday, and Friday from 7 to 5 in the summer and 9 to 3 in winter, you can buy flowers, bread, pastries, poultry, sausage, and cheese. ✉ *Tübingen.*

Rathaus (*Town Hall*). Begun in 1433, this building slowly expanded over the next 150 years. Its ornate Renaissance facade is bright with colorful murals and a marvelous astronomical clock dating from 1511. The half-timber halls and reception rooms are adorned with paintings from the late 19th century. ✉ *Marktpl.*

Schloss Hohentübingen. The original castle of the counts of Tübingen (1078) was significantly enlarged and altered by Duke Ulrich during the 16th century. Particularly noteworthy is the elaborate Renaissance

portal patterned after a Roman triumphal arch. The coat of arms of the duchy of Württemberg depicted in the center is framed by the emblems of various orders, including the Order of the Garter. Today the castle's main attraction is its magnificent view over the river and town. It's a 90-minute walk from Schlossbergstrasse, over the Spitzberg, or via the Kapitänsweg that ends north of the castle. ⊠ *Burgsteige 11* ⊕ *burg-hohenzollern.com/admission-fees.html* 🎫 *€7* ⊙ *Closed Mon. and Tues.*

Stiftskirche (*Collegiate Church*). The late-Gothic church has been well preserved; its original features include the stained-glass windows, the choir stalls, the ornate baptismal font, and the elaborate stone pulpit. The windows are famous for their colors and were much admired by Goethe. The dukes of Württemberg, from the 15th through the 17th century, are interred in the choir. ⊠ *Holzmarkt* 🕾 *0707/43151* ⊕ *www.stiftskirche-tuebingen.de.*

WHERE TO EAT

$$
GERMAN
Fodor'sChoice
★

✕ **Forelle.** Beautiful ceilings painted with vine motifs, exposed beams, wooden wainscotting and an old tile stove make for a *gemütlich* (cozy) atmosphere. This small restaurant fills up fast, not least because of the Swabian specialties which dominate the menu and fresh, regional ingredients. Save room for dessert, especially the house-made *Schwäbische Apfelküchle* (Swabian apple cake) with vanilla sauce. **Known for:** Maultaschen (meat-filled ravioli), a regional favorite; the inn's namesake trout, often served as French-style amandine; daily lunch specials. 💲 *Average main: €20* ⊠ *Kronenstr. 8* 🕾 *07071/568–8980* ⊕ *www.weinstube-forelle.de* ⊙ *Closed Tues.*

$$
GERMAN
Fodor'sChoice
★

✕ **Wurstküche.** For more than 200 years, this wood-panel inn has been a favorite of students attracted by filling yet inexpensive selections; locals, because the food is the typical Swabian fare their mothers made; and out-of-town visitors, who love the old-fashioned atmosphere. In summer try to get a seat at one of the sidewalk tables. **Known for:** regional favorites including Maultaschen (meat-filled ravioli) and Spätzle and lentils with sausages; vegetarian dishes including veggie strudel; inventive cocktails. 💲 *Average main: €15* ⊠ *Am Lustnauer Tor 8* 🕾 *07071/92750* ⊕ *www.wurstkueche.com.*

WHERE TO STAY

$$
B&B/INN

🏨 **Hotel Am Schloss.** There are lovely views of the Old Town from the rooms in this charming small hotel, and it's close to the castle that towers over the town. **Pros:** lovely views of castle and valley; excellent restaurant; charging station for EVs in garage. **Cons:** no elevator; difficult parking; rooms facing street can be noisy. 💲 *Rooms from: €118* ⊠ *Burgsteige 18* 🕾 *07071/92940* ⊕ *www.hotelamschloss.de* ⇗ *37 rooms* ❙⊙❙ *Free Breakfast.*

FRANKFURT

WELCOME TO FRANKFURT

TOP REASONS TO GO

★ **Sachsenhausen:** Frankfurt's South Bank, with its riverbank row of world-class museums, upscale restaurants, fast-food joints, bars with live music, and traditional Apfelwein pubs, is one big outdoor party in summer.

★ **Paleontology paradise:** Beyond a huge dinosaur skeleton, the Senckenberg Natural History Museum has exhibits of many other extinct animals and plants, plus dioramas of animals in their habitats.

★ **Enjoy the outdoors:** The parks and riverbanks are popular with locals and tourists for strolls, sunbathing, and picnics.

★ **Get some wheels:** Hop on and tour the city sites from a bike; you'll be in good company alongside locals.

★ **Exotic experience:** Head to the Frankfurt Zoo's "exotarium," where coral, fish, snakes, alligators, amphibians, insects, and spiders are on display.

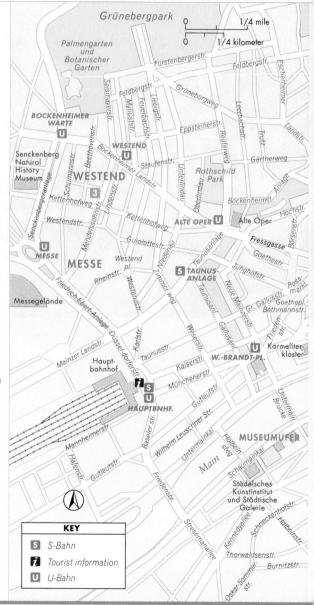

KEY

S S-Bahn

𝑖 Tourist information

U U-Bahn

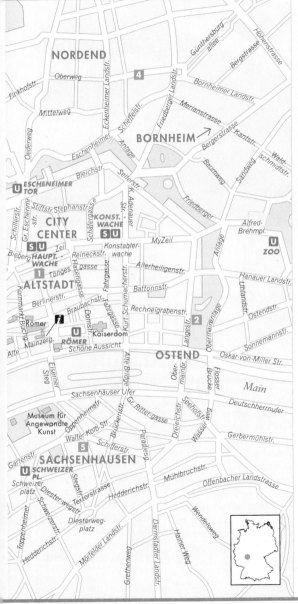

Frankfurt is Germany's most important center of business and finance.

1 Altstadt and City Center. Frankfurt's downtown includes the Altstadt (Old City), the Zeil, the Fressgass ("Pig-Out Alley"), and the bank district.

2 Ostend. This area near the East Harbor is where you'll find lots of corporations and banks, but also some sights and the zoo.

3 Messe and Westend. The Westend is a mix of the villas of the prewar rich and a skyscraper extension of the business district. Messe is the area around Frankfurt's huge and busy convention center.

4 Nordend and Bornheim. These residential areas are a great place to get away from the crowds and enjoy small neighborhood restaurants and shops.

5 Sachsenhausen. Just across the river from downtown, Sachsenhausen is distinguished by the *Apfelwein* (Apple Wine) district and the *Museumufer* (Museum Riverbank).

9

GERMAN SAUSAGES

The one thing you're guaranteed to find wherever your travels in Germany take you: sausages. Encased meats are a serious business here, and you could spend a lifetime working your way through 1,500 varieties of German sausage, also known as *Wurst*.

(above) Landjäger sausage (lower right) Thüringer Rostbratwurst (upper right) Frankfurter

The tradition of making sausages goes back centuries, both as a method to preserve food long before refrigeration and as the best way to use every last piece of precious meat. Sausage recipes go back for generations, and like most German cooking, sausage types vary from region to region. There's also an abundance of ways to serve a sausage: grilled sausages are served up in a small roll, essentially just a sausage "holder"; Weisswursts come to the table after a gentle bath in warm water; cured sausages often are served sliced, while other cooked sausages are dished up with sauerkraut. Germans don't mess around when it comes to their love for sausage, eating about 62 pounds of sausage per person each year.

WEISSWURST ETIQUETTE

Weisswurst is a delicate white sausage made with veal, bacon, lemon, and parsley. It's traditional in the southern state of Bavaria, where they are sticklers about the way to eat them. The casing is never eaten; instead, you *zuzeln* (suck) out the meat. Make a slit at the top, dunk it in sweet mustard, and suck out the insides. It's all right to slit and peel it as well.

FRANKFURTER

In Germany a *Frankfurter* isn't something that must be doused in condiments to make it palatable, like a subpar ballpark frank; instead, you'll immediately notice the crisp snap of the Frankfurter's skin and a delicious smoky taste. Frankfurters are long and narrow by design, to absorb as much flavor as possible during cold smoking. When served on a plate for lunch or dinner, they're normally served in a pair, and you should eat them dipped in mustard, with your fingers. Frankfurters and other *Würste* also are served inside a small roll, called a *Brotchen*. The only condiment used is mustard, never sauerkraut or other toppings.

THÜRINGER ROSTBRATWURST

This *Bratwurst* dates back to 1613, and it's clear why it has stood the test of time: it's one of Germany's most delicious sausages. The *Rostbratwurst* is a mix of lean pork belly, veal, and beef, seasoned with herbs and spices. Most families closely guard their recipes, but often use garlic, caraway, or nutmeg. You'll smell the scent of grilled *Thüringer* wafting through the streets because they're popular at street markets and festivals.

LANDJÄGER

This small, narrow, and dense rectangular sausage is sold in pairs. It's cured by air-drying, so it resembles a dry salami in color and texture. *Landjäger* are made of beef—sometimes with pork—and red wine and spices. Historically, fieldworkers and wine-grape harvesters liked to eat these salty sausages. Landjäger keep well, so they're a great snack to tuck in your backpack when you head out for a day of hiking in the mountains.

BLUTWURST

Sometimes called *Rotwurst* (red sausage), *Blutwurst* is a combination of ground pork, spices, and—the key ingredient—blood, fresh from the slaughter. After it's been cooked and smoked, the blood congeals, and the sausage takes on a dark hue and looks almost black. Depending on the region, it can be studded with bacon, pickled ox tongue, or potatoes. For most of its history Blutwurst has been considered a luxury item.

BOCKWURST

This sausage got its name when hungry students ordered it with a round of *Bockbier*, a style of beer, in Berlin in 1889. The sausage came from a nearby Jewish butcher, who made it with veal and beef. *Bockwurst* is a thick sausage seasoned with salt, white pepper, and paprika, in a natural casing. It's usually boiled and served hot, but it can also be grilled. It's one of Germany's most popular sausages, so you'll find it on menus all over the country.

9

Updated by
Evelyn Kanter

Although many consider Frankfurt more or less a gateway to their European travels, the city's rich culture and history, dining, and amusement options might just surprise you.

Standing in the center of the Römerberg (medieval town square), you'll see the city's striking contrasts at once. Re-creations of neo-Gothic houses and government buildings enfold the square, while just beyond them modern skyscrapers pierce the sky. The city cheekily nicknamed itself "Mainhattan," using the name of the Main River that flows through it to suggest that other famous metropolis across the Atlantic. Although only fifth in size among German cities, with a population of nearly 700,000, Frankfurt is Germany's financial powerhouse. The German Central Bank (*Bundesbank*) is here, as is the European Central Bank (ECB), which manages the euro. Some 300 credit institutions (more than half of them foreign banks) have offices in Frankfurt, including the headquarters of five of Germany's largest banks. You can see how the city acquired its other nickname, "Bankfurt am Main." It's no wonder that Frankfurt is Europe's financial center. The city's stock exchange, one of the most important in the world, was established in 1585, and the Rothschild family opened their first bank here in 1798.

The long history of trade might help explain why the temperament of many Frankfurters is competitive but open-minded. It's also one of the reasons Frankfurt has become Germany's most international city. Close to a quarter of its residents are foreign, with a growing number from Eastern Europe and the Middle East.

Because of its commercialism, Frankfurt has a reputation for being cold and boring, but people who know the city think this characterization is unfair. The district of Sachsenhausen is as *gemütlich* (fun, friendly, and cozy) as you will find anywhere. The city has world-class ballet, opera, theater, and art exhibitions; an important piece of Germany's publishing industry (and the world's largest annual book fair); a large university (43,000 students); and two of the three most important daily newspapers in Germany. Despite the skyscrapers, especially in the *Hauptbahnhof* (main train station) area and adjoining Westend district, there's much here to remind you of the old world, along with much that explains the success of postwar Germany.

PLANNING

DISCOUNTS AND DEALS

The Frankfurt tourist office offers a one- or two-day ticket—the Frankfurt Card (€10.50 for one day, €15.50 for two days)—allowing unlimited travel on public transportation in the inner zone, and to the airport. It also includes a 50% reduction on admission to 24 museums, the zoo, and the Palmengarten, and price reductions at some restaurants and stores.

GETTING HERE AND AROUND

AIR TRAVEL

There are two airports with the name "Frankfurt": Flughafen Frankfurt Main (FRA), one of Europe's largest, receives direct flights from many U.S. cities and from all major cities in Europe, Africa, Asia, and the Mideast; and Frankfurt-Hahn (HHN), a former U.S. air base a full 112 km (70 miles) west of Frankfurt, handles some bargain flights, mainly to and from secondary European airports.

Contacts **Flughafen Frankfurt Main** (FRA). ✉ *200 Flughafen Frankfurt am Main* ☏ *180/6372–4636 toll call* ⊕ *www.frankfurt-airport.de.* **Frankfurt-Hahn** (HHN). ✉ *1 Saonestr., Hahn-Flughafen* ☏ *06543/509–113* ⊕ *www.hahn-airport.de.*

AIRPORT TRANSFERS

Flughafen Frankfurt Main is 10 km (6 miles) southwest of downtown via the A-5 autobahn, and has its own railway station for high-speed InterCity (IC) and InterCity Express (ICE) trains. Getting into Frankfurt from the airport is easy via S-bahn lines 8 and 9, which run between the airport and downtown. Most travelers get off at the Hauptbahnhof (main train station, or HBF) or at Hauptwache, in the heart of Frankfurt. Trains run at least every 15 minutes, and the trip takes about 15 minutes. The one-way fare is €5.50. A taxi from the airport into the City Center normally takes around 25 minutes (double that during rush hours). The fare is around €35. If you are driving a rental car from the airport, take the main road out of the airport and follow the signs reading "Stadtmitte" (downtown).

Bohr Busreisen offers regular bus service to and from Frankfurt-Hahn Airport. It leaves every hour to every 1½ hours, 3 am to 8 pm, from the south side of the Frankfurt Hauptbahnhof, with a stop 15 minutes later at the new long-distance coach parking area, P36, between Terminal 1 and 2 at Flughafen Frankfurt Main. The trip to Frankfurt-Hahn takes an hour and 45 minutes, and costs €15.

BUS AND SUBWAY TRAVEL

Frankfurt's smooth-running, well-integrated public transportation system (called RMV) consists of the U-bahn (subway), S-bahn (suburban railway), Strassenbahn (streetcars), and buses. Buses are the only public-transit option between 1 am and 4 am.

Fares for the entire system, which includes an extensive surrounding area, are uniform, though they are based on a complex zone system. Within the time that your ticket is valid (one hour for most inner-city destinations), you can transfer from one part of the system to another.

9

Tickets may be purchased from automatic vending machines, which are at all U-bahn and S-bahn stations. Weekly and monthly tickets are sold at central ticket offices and newsstands. A basic one-way ticket for a ride in the inner zone costs €2.60 during the peak hours of 6 am–9 am and 4 pm–6:30 pm weekdays (€2.30 the rest of the time). There's also a reduced *Kurzstrecke* (short-stretch) fare of €1.60 the whole day. A day ticket for unlimited travel in the inner zones costs €6.60. A seven-day pass costs €25.70 and includes travel to and from the airport. If you're caught without a ticket, there's a fine of €40.

Some 200 European cities have bus links with Frankfurt, largely through Deutsche Touring. Buses arrive at and depart from the south side of the Hauptbahnhof and Terminal 1 at the Frankfurt Main airport. Eurolines provides tours to nearby cities, including Mannheim, Hamburg, and Hanover.

Contacts Bohr Busreisen. ☎ *0654/350–190* ⊕ *www.omnibusse.bohr.de.* **Eurolines.** ✉ *Mannheimerstr. 15, City Center* ☎ *069/21303* ⊕ *www.eurolines. de/en.* **Verkehrsgesellschaft Frankfurt am Main** (*Municipal Transit Authority*). ☎ *069/19449* ⊕ *www.vgf-ffm.de.*

CAR TRAVEL

Frankfurt is the meeting point of a number of major autobahns. The most important are A-3, running south from Cologne and then on east to Würzburg and Nuremberg, and A-5, running south from Giessen and then on toward Heidelberg and Basel.

There are many reasonably priced parking garages around the downtown area and a well-developed park-and-ride system with the suburban train lines. The transit map shows nearly 100 outlying stations with a blue "P" symbol beside them, meaning there is convenient parking there. A 2006 anti-air-pollution law requires vehicles to have a special environmental sticker or badge (*Umweltplakette*) to enter the "green zone" of most German cities of any size, including Frankfurt. It applies to anyone driving in Germany, whether a resident or a foreigner. Even if the car meets German/EU pollution standards, a driver can still be fined if there is no sticker on the car's windshield. If you are renting a vehicle, be sure your vehicle has a green zone sticker or badge in the windshield.

TAXI TRAVEL

Cabs are not always easy to hail from the sidewalk; some stop, but others will pick up only from the city's numerous taxi stands or outside hotels or the train station. You can always order a cab. Fares start at €2.80 (€3.30 in the evening) and increase by a per-kilometer (½ mile) charge of €1.75 (€1.60 after 10 km). Frankfurt also has Velotaxis, covered tricycles seating two passengers and a driver that are useful for sightseeing or getting to places on the traffic-free downtown streets. They charge €2.50 per km.

Contacts Taxis. ☎ *069/230–001.* **Velotaxi.** ☎ *069/7158–8855* ⊕ *www. velotaxi.de.*

TRAIN TRAVEL

EuroCity, InterCity (IC), and InterCity Express (ICE) trains connect Frankfurt with all German cities and many major European ones. The InterCity Express line links Frankfurt with Berlin, Hamburg, Munich, and a number of other major hubs. All long-distance trains arrive at and depart from the Hauptbahnhof, and many also stop at the long-distance train station at the main airport.

Contacts **Deutsche Bahn** (*German Railways*). ✉ *Bahnhof* ☎ *01805/996–633* ⊕ *www.bahn.de.*

VISITOR INFORMATION

Tourismus und Congress GmbH Frankfurt–Main has its main office at Römerberg 27, in Old Town. It's open weekdays 9:30–5:30 and weekends 9–4.

The airport's information office is on the first floor of Arrivals Hall B and open daily 5:30 am–11 pm. Another information office in the main hall of the railroad station is open weekdays 8 am–9 pm, weekends 9–6. Both can help you find accommodations.

Contacts **Tourismus und Congress GmbH Frankfurt/Main.** ✉ *Römerberg 27, City Center* ☎ *069/2123–8800* ⊕ *www.frankfurt-tourismus.de.*

TOURS

Two-hour city bus tours with English-speaking guides are available from the Frankfurt Tourist Office throughout the year.

Ebbelwei Express. The one-hour Apple Wine Express tour in a vintage streetcar is offered hourly on weekends and some holidays. It gives you a quick look at the city's neighborhoods, a bit of Frankfurt history, and a chance to sample Apfelwein (a bottle, along with pretzels, is included in the fare). ☎ *069/2132–2425* ⊕ *www.ebbelwei-express. com* 🎟 *From €8.*

Frankfurt Personenschiffahrt Primus-Linie. Day trips on the Main River and Rhine excursions run from April through October and leave from the Frankfurt Mainkai am Eiserner Steg, just south of the Römer complex. ✉ *Mainkai 36, Altstadt* ☎ *069/133–8370* ⊕ *www.primus-linie. de* 🎟 *From €9.*

WHEN TO GO

The weather in Frankfurt is moderate throughout the year, though often damp and drizzly. Summers are mild, with the occasional hot day, and it rarely gets very cold in winter and hardly ever snows. Because Frankfurt is one of the biggest trade-fair cities in all of Europe, high season at all hotels is considered to be during trade shows throughout the year. Be sure to check dates to avoid paying premium price for a room or even finding yourself without a place to stay.

EXPLORING

ALTSTADT

Altstadt (Old City) is the historic, cultural, and culinary heart of Frankfurt, with restored medieval buildings around a huge town square, notable churches and museums, and historic restaurants serving traditional local fare. Be sure to walk to Fressgasse ("Pig-Out Alley"), a pedestrian-only street of cafés, gourmet food shops, and jazz clubs.

Alte Oper (*Old Opera House*). Kaiser Wilhelm I traveled from Berlin for the gala opening of this opera house in 1880. Gutted in World War II, it remained a hollow shell for 40 years while controversy raged over its reconstruction. The exterior and lobby are faithful to the original, though the remainder of the building is more like a modern multipurpose hall. Although classical music and ballet performances are held here, most operas these days are staged at the Frankfurt Opera. ⊠ *Opernpl. 1, Altstadt* ☎ *069/13400* ⊕ *www.alteoper.de* ✆ *Tours from €7* Ⓜ *Alte Oper (U-bahn).*

Archäologisches Museum (*Archeology Museum*). The soaring vaulted ceilings make the former Gothic Karmeliterkirche (Carmelite Church) an ideal setting for huge Roman columns and other local and regional artifacts, including Stone Age and Neolithic tools and ancient papyrus documents. Modern wings display Greek, Roman, and Persian pottery, carvings, and more. The main cloister displays the largest religious fresco north of the Alps, a 16th-century representation of Christ's birth and death by Jörg Ratgeb. Adjacent buildings house the Institut für Stadtgeschichte (Institute of City History). The basement, called *Die Schmiere* (The Grease), is a satirical theater. ⊠ *Karmeliterg. 1, Altstadt* ☎ *069/2123–5896* ⊕ *www.archaeologisches-museum.frankfurt.de* ✆ *Museum €7; free last Sat. of month* ☽ *Closed Mon.* Ⓜ *Willy-Brandt-Platz (U-bahn).*

Fodor's Choice ★ **Fressgass.** Grosse Bockenheimer Strasse is the proper name of this pedestrian street, but it's nicknamed "Pig-Out Alley" because of its amazing choice of delicatessens, wine merchants, cafés, and restaurants, offering everything from crumbly cheeses and smoked fish to vintage wines and chocolate creams. Check the side streets for additional cafés and restaurants. ⊠ *Grosse Bockenheimerstr., Altstadt* ⊕ *www.frankfurt-fressgass.de* Ⓜ *Hauptwache (U-bahn and S-bahn), Alte Oper (U-bahn).*

Goethehaus und Goethemuseum (*Goethe's Residence and Museum*). The house where Germany's most famous poet was born is furnished with many original pieces that belonged to his family, including manuscripts in his own hand. The original house, which was destroyed by Allied bombing, has been carefully rebuilt and restored. Johann Wolfgang von Goethe (1749–1832) studied law and became a member of the bar in Frankfurt, but he was quickly drawn to writing, and in this house he eventually wrote the first version of his masterpiece, *Faust*. The adjoining museum contains works of art that inspired Goethe (he was an amateur painter) and works associated with his literary contemporaries. ⊠ *Grosser Hirschgraben 23–25, Altstadt* ☎ *069/138–800* ⊕ *www.goethehaus-frankfurt.de* ✆ *€7* Ⓜ *Hauptwache or Willy-Brandt-Platz (U-bahn and S-bahn).*

Hauptwache. The attractive baroque building with a steeply sloping roof is the actual Hauptwache (Main Guardhouse), from which the square takes its name. The 1729 building was partly demolished to permit excavation for a vast underground shopping mall. It was then restored to its original appearance and is now considered the heart of the Frankfurt pedestrian shopping area. The outdoor patio of the building's restaurant-café is a popular people-watching spot on the Zeil. ⊠ *An der Hauptwache 15, Altstadt* Ⓜ *Hauptwache (U-bahn and S-bahn).*

FAMILY **Historisches Museum** (*Historical Museum*). This fascinating museum in a building in Römer Square that dates from the 1300s doubled in size with the addition of an adjoining wing in 2015. The city's oldest museum explores two millennia of Frankfurt history through a collection of some 630,000 objects, including what the city of the future might look like. Standout exhibits include scale models of historic Frankfurt at various periods, with every street, house, and church, plus photos of the devastation of World War II. The new wing blends in with the surrounding historic architecture with its gabled roof and carved sandstone sides, and offers both a café and city views from the top floor. ⊠ *Fahrtor 2 (Römerberg), Altstadt* ☎ *069/2123–5599* ⊕ *www.historisches-museum. frankfurt.de* ⊠ *€6; scale models €1* ⊙ *Closed Mon.* Ⓜ *Römer (U-bahn).*

Junges Museum (Youth Museum). This modern stand-alone museum opened in 2018, replacing the Kindermuseum (Children's Museum) that was once part of the Historisches Museum. Interactive historical and cultural exhibits invite exploration (and it's free for children under 18). ⊠ *Saalhof 1, Altstadt* ☎ *069/2123–5154* ⊕ *www.kindermuseum.frankfurt.de* ⊙ *Closed Mon.* Ⓜ *Hauptwache.*

Kaiserdom. Because the Holy Roman emperors were chosen and crowned here from the 16th to the 18th century, the church is known as the Kaiserdom (Imperial Cathedral), even though it isn't the seat of a bishop. Officially the Church of St. Bartholomew, but called simply "The Dom" by locals, it was built largely between the 13th and 15th centuries and survived World War II with the majority of its treasures intact. The most impressive exterior feature is the tall, red-sandstone tower (almost 300 feet high), which was added between 1415 and 1514. Climb it for a good view. The **Dommuseum** (Cathedral Museum) occupies the former Gothic cloister. ⊠ *Dompl. 1, Altstadt* ☎ *069/297–0320* ⊕ *www.dom-frankfurt.de* ⊠ *Dommuseum €4* Ⓜ *Römer (U-bahn).*

Museum für Moderne Kunst (*Museum of Modern Art*). Austrian architect Hans Hollein (born in 1934) designed this distinctive triangular building, shaped like a wedge of cake. The collection features works by artists such as Andy Warhol and Joseph Beuys. There are free guided tours in English on Saturday at 4 pm. ⊠ *Domstr. 10, Altstadt* ☎ *069/2123–0447* ⊕ *www.mmk-frankfurt.de* ⊠ *€16* ⊙ *Closed Mon.* Ⓜ *Willy-Brandt-Platz (U-bahn).*

Paulskirche (*St. Paul's Church*). The first all-German parliament was held here in 1848 but lasted only a year, achieving little more than offering the Prussian king the crown of Germany. Today the church, which has been extensively restored, remains a symbol of German democracy and is used mainly for ceremonies. The most striking feature of the interior

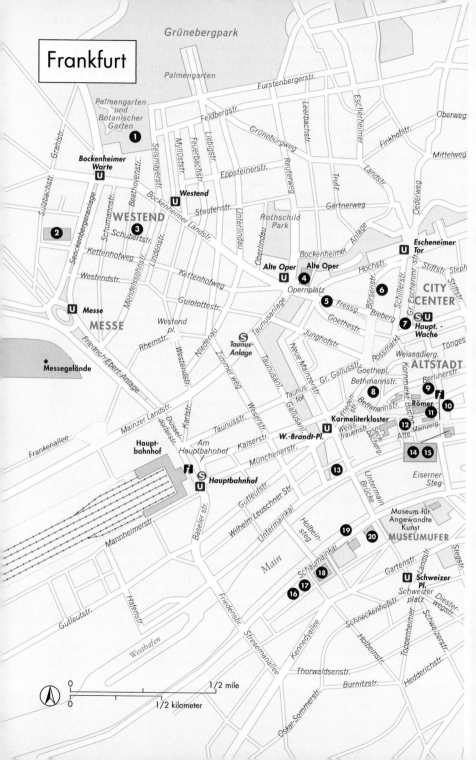

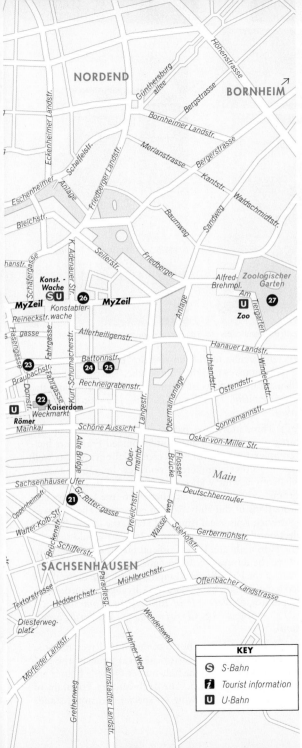

Goethe's House and Museum is filled with the manuscripts and paintings of Germany's best-loved poet.

is a giant, completely circular mural showing an "endless" procession of the people's representatives into the Paulskirche. The plenary chamber upstairs is flanked by the flags of Germany, the 16 states, and the city of Frankfurt. ⊠ *Paulspl. 11, Altstadt* ☎ *069/2123–70658* ✉ *Free* Ⓜ *Römer (U-bahn).*

Fodor's Choice
★
Römer (*City Hall*). Three individual patrician buildings make up the Römer, Frankfurt's town hall. The mercantile-minded Frankfurt burghers used the complex for political and ceremonial purposes as well as for trade fairs and other commercial ventures. Its gabled facade with an ornate balcony is widely known as the city's official emblem. The most important events to take place here were the festivities celebrating the coronations of the Holy Roman emperors. The first was in 1562 in the glittering **Kaisersaal** (Imperial Hall), the last in 1792 to celebrate the election of the emperor Francis II, who would later be forced by Napoléon to abdicate. Unless official business is being conducted, you can see the impressive, full-length 19th-century portraits of the 52 emperors of the Holy Roman Empire, which line the walls of the reconstructed banquet hall, but you have to arrange a tour through a private local operator. ⊠ *West side of Römerberg, Römerberg 27, Altstadt* ☎ *069/2123–4814* ✉ *€3* ⊙ *Closed weekends and during events* Ⓜ *Römer (U-bahn).*

Römerberg. This square a few blocks north of the Main River, restored after wartime bomb damage, is the historical focal point of the city. The Römer, the Nikolaikirche, and the half-timber Ostzeile houses are all clustered around this huge plaza. The 16th-century Fountain of Justitia (Justice), which flows with wine on special occasions, stands in the center of the Römerberg. The square is also the site of many public festivals throughout the year, including the Christmas market in December. Kleine Krame is a pedestrian street just north of the square that's lined with snack shops and cafés. ⊠ *Between Braubachstr. and Main River, Altstadt* Ⓜ *Römer (U-bahn).*

Zeil. The heart of Frankfurt's shopping district is this bustling pedestrian street running east from Hauptwache Square. It's lined with a mix of department stores, boutiques, drugstores, camera and elecgronics shops, restaurants, and more. Stop in at the outdoor farmers' market every Thursday and Saturday for a freshly grilled Bratwurst and a beer. ⊠ *Hauptwache Square, Altstadt* Ⓜ *Hauptwache, Konstablerwache (U-bahn and S-bahn).*

CITY CENTER

Frankfurt was rebuilt after World War II with little attention paid to the past. Nevertheless, important historical monuments can still be found among the modern architecture. The city is very walkable—its growth hasn't encroached on its parks, gardens, pedestrian arcades, or outdoor cafés. The riverbank paths make for great strolls or bike rides.

Alter Jüdischer Friedhof (*Old Jewish Cemetery*). Containing hundreds of moss-covered gravestones, this cemetery was in use between the 13th- and mid-19th centuries and is one of the few reminders of prewar Jewish life in Frankfurt. It suffered minimal vandalization in the Nazi era, even though its adjoining grand Börneplatz Synagogue was destroyed on Kristallnacht, in 1938. That space is now part of Museum Judengasse; ask the admissions desk for the key to open the vandal-proof steel gates to the cemetery. Mayer Amschel Rothschild, founder of the banking family, who died in 1812, is buried here, along with some family members (the Rothschild mansion is now the main Jewish Museum). The wall around the cemetery is dotted with more than 1,000 small memorial plaques, each with the name of a Jewish Frankfurter and the concentration camp where they died. The newer Jewish cemetery on Rat-Beil-Strasse in the North End contains more than 800 graves dating from 1828 to 1929, including that of Nobel Prize winner Paul Ehrlich. ⊠ *Battonnstr. 2, City Center* ☏ *069/2127–0790* ⊕ *juedischesmuseum. de/museumjudengasse* 🎟 *Free* 🕙 *Closed Sat.* Ⓜ *Börneplatz (S-bahn).*

Börse (*Stock Exchange*). This is the center of Germany's stock and money market. The Börse was founded in 1585, but the present domed building dates from the 1870s. These days computerized networks and telephone systems have removed much of the drama from the dealers' floor, but it's still fun to visit the visitor gallery and watch the hectic activity. You must reserve your visit 24 hours in advance. ⊠ *Börsenpl. 4, City Center* ☏ *069/211–11515* ⊕ *www.boerse-frankfurt.de* 🎟 *Free* 🕙 *Closed weekends* Ⓜ *Hauptwache (U-bahn and S-bahn).*

Jüdisches Museum (*Jewish Museum*). The story of Frankfurt's Jewish community is told in the former Rothschild Palais, which overlooks the river Main. Prior to the Holocaust, Frankfurt's Jewish quarter was the second-largest in Germany (after Berlin), and the silver and gold household items on display are a testament to its prosperity. The museum

9

contains a library of 5,000 books, a large photographic collection, and a documentation center. Be sure to check out the wall of ceremonial menorahs. The museum reopens in spring 2019 after a two-year renovation that includes the addition of a new wing. ⊠ *Untermainkai 14/15, City Center* ☏ *069/2123–5000* ⊕ *www.juedischesmuseum.de* 🎫 *€6* ⊙ *Closed Mon.* Ⓜ *Willy-Brandt-Platz (U-bahn).*

Museum Judengasse. This branch of the Jewish Museum (the main museum reopens in early 2019 after a major renovation) is built on the site of the Bornerplatz Synagogue, which was destroyed in 1938, and the foundations of mostly 18th-century buildings that were once part of the Jewish quarter, or Judengasse. ⊠ *Battonstr. 46, City Center* ☏ *069/297–7419* ⊕ *www.juedischesmuseum.de* 🎫 *€3* ⊙ *Closed Mon., Thurs., and Sat.* Ⓜ *Bornerplatz (U-bahn).*

OSTEND

Named for its location around the city's East Harbor, the business-oriented Ostend is sprouting new restaurants and cafés, attracted by the 2014 opening of the new European Central Bank headquarters building.

FAMILY **Zoologischer Garten** (*Zoo*). Founded in 1858, this is one of the most important and attractive zoos in Europe. Its remarkable collection includes some 4,500 animals of 500 different species, an exotarium (an aquarium plus reptiles), a large ape house, and an aviary, one of the largest in Europe. Nocturnal creatures move about in a special section. ⊠ *Bernhard-Grimek-Allee 1, Ostend* ☏ *069/2123–3735* ⊕ *www.zoo-frankfurt.de* 🎫 *From €10* Ⓜ *Zoo (U-bahn).*

MESSE AND WESTEND

The city's huge, sprawling convention center (Messe) is one of the busiest in Europe, and the area around it isn't especially interesting. Westend, on the other hand, is a charming residential neighborhood dotted with some good restaurants.

FAMILY
Fodor's Choice
★
Naturkundemuseum Senckenberg (*Natural History Museum*). The important collection of fossils, animals, plants, and geological exhibits here is upstaged by the permanent dinosaur exhibit: it's the most extensive of its kind in all of Germany. The diplodocus dinosaur, imported from New York, is the only complete specimen of its kind in Europe. Many of the exhibits of prehistoric animals, including a series of dioramas, have been designed with children in mind. ⊠ *Senckenberganlage 25, Westend* ☏ *069/75420* ⊕ *www.senckenberg.de* 🎫 *€9* Ⓜ *Bockenheimer Warte (U-bahn).*

FAMILY **Palmengarten und Botanischer Garten** (*Botanical Gardens*). The splendid cluster of tropical and semitropical greenhouses here contains cacti, orchids, palms, and other plants. The surrounding park, which can be surveyed from a miniature train, has many recreational facilities, including a small lake where you can rent rowboats, a play area for children, and a wading pool. The Palmengarten offers free tours on a variety of topics on Sunday. In summer there's also an extensive concert program that takes place in an outdoor pavilion. ⊠ *Siesmayerstr. 63,*

Climb to the top of Kaiserdom, officially called the Church St. Bartholomew, for a fantastic view of the city.

Westend ☎ *069/2123–6689* ⊕ *www.palmengarten.de* ✉ *€7* Ⓜ *Westend (U-bahn).*

FAMILY **Struwwelpeter Museum** (*Slovenly Peter Museum*). This charming little museum honors the Frankfurt physician who created the sardonic children's classic *Struwwelpeter,* or Slovenly Peter. Heinrich Hoffmann wrote the poems and drew the rather amateurish pictures in 1844, to warn children of the dire consequences of being naughty. The book has seen several English translations, including one by Mark Twain, which can be purchased at the museum. The kid-friendly museum has a puppet theater and game room, and is popular for birthday parties. After years in a historic mansion, it will reopen in a new location nearby in spring 2019. ✉ *Hinter den Lammchen 2–4, Westend* ☎ *069/747–969* ⊕ *www. struwwelpeter-museum.de* ✉ *€5* 🕒 *Closed Mon.* Ⓜ *Westend (U-bahn).*

9

NORDEND AND BORNHEIM

Nordend was the center of antigovernment student demonstrations in the 1960s and 1970s and still retains its slightly shabby, bohemian flavor. For its part, Bornheim holds on to some of the liveliness it had as the city's red-light district a century ago. Both have some pleasant small shops and restaurants.

SACHSENHAUSEN

The old quarter of Sachsenhausen, on the south bank of the Main River, has been sensitively preserved, and its cobblestone streets, half-timber houses, and beer gardens make it a popular area to stroll.

Sachsenhausen's two big attractions are the **Museumufer** (Museum Riverbank), with nine museums almost next door to one another and beautiful views of the Frankfurt skyline, as well as the famous Apfelwein taverns around the Rittergasse pedestrian area. For a reasonable price, you can eat and drink well in one of these small, traditional establishments.

FAMILY
Fodor's Choice
★

Deutsches Filmmuseum (*German Film Museum*). Germany's first museum of cinematography, set in a historic villa on "museum row," offers visitors a glimpse at the history of film, with artifacts that include "magic lanterns" from the 1880s, costume drawings from Hollywood and German films, and multiple screens playing film clips. Interactive exhibits show how films are photographed, given sound, and edited, and let visitors play with lighting and animation. A theater in the basement screens every imaginable type of film, from historical to avant-garde to *Star Wars.* ⊠ *Schaumainkai 41, Sachsenhausen* ☏ *069/9612–20220* ⊕ *www.deutschesfilmmuseum.de* 🎫 *€5* ⊙ *Closed Mon.* Ⓜ *Schweizer Platz (U-bahn).*

Ikonen-Museum (*Icon Museum*). One of very few museums in the world to exhibit a wide spectrum of the Christian Orthodox world of images, the art and ritual of icons from the 15th to the 20th century on display here are part of a collection that totals more than 1,000 artifacts. Admission is free on the last Saturday of the month. ⊠ *Brückenstr. 3–7, Sachsenhausen* ☏ *069/2123–6262* ⊕ *www.ikonenmuseumfrankfurt.de* 🎫 *€5* ⊙ *Closed Mon.*

Museum für Kommunikation (*Museum for Communication*). This is the place for visiting the past and the future of communication technology, in an airy, modern glass building. Exhibitions on historic methods include mail coaches, a vast collection of stamps from many countries and eras, and ancient dial telephones, with their clunky switching equipment. ⊠ *Schaumainkai 53, Sachsenhausen* ☏ *069/606–0320* ⊕ *www. museumsstiftung.de* 🎫 *€4* ⊙ *Closed Mon.* Ⓜ *Schweizer Platz (U-bahn).*

Museum Giersch. This museum, part of Goethe University, is set in a beautiful neoclassical villa along the strip of museums in Sachsenhausen and focuses on paintings from the 19th century and early 20th century. The artists are drawn mainly from the Rhine-Main region. ⊠ *Schaumainkai 83, Sachsenhausen* ☏ *069/138–21010* ⊕ *www.museum-giersch.de* 🎫 *€6* ⊙ *Closed Tues. and Fri.*

Fodor's Choice
★

Städelsches Kunstinstitut und Städtische Galerie (*Städel Art Institute and Municipal Gallery*). This is one of Germany's most important art collections, covering 700 years of paintings and sculpture, with a vast collection of paintings by Dürer, Vermeer, Rembrandt, Rubens, Monet, Renoir, and other masters. The downstairs annex features a large collection of works from contemporary artists, including a huge portrait of Goethe by Andy Warhol. The section on German expressionism is particularly strong, with representative works by the Frankfurt artist Max Beckmann and Ernst Ludwig Kirchner. A free smartphone app with a built-in audio guide enhances the experience. There is also a café-restaurant, Holbein's. ⊠ *Schaumainkai 63, Sachsenhausen* ☏ *069/605–0980* ⊕ *www.staedelmuseum.de* 🎫 *€14* ⊙ *Closed Mon.* Ⓜ *Schweizer Platz (U-bahn).*

Sachsenhausen comes alive at night with a lively restaurant and bar scene.

Städtische Galerie Liebieghaus (*Liebieg Municipal Museum of Sculpture*). The sculpture collection here represents 5,000 years of civilization and is considered one of the most important in Europe. Ancient Greece and Rome, the Middle Ages, the Renaissance, classicism, and the baroque are all represented. Some pieces are exhibited in the lovely gardens surrounding the historic brick villa with its signature turret tower. Don't miss out on the freshly baked German cakes in the museum café. ⊠ *Schaumainkai 71, Sachsenhausen* ☎ *069/6050–98200* ⊕ *www. liebieghaus.de* 🎫 *€10* 🕐 *Closed Mon.* Ⓜ *Schweizer Platz (U-bahn).*

WHERE TO EAT

Many international cuisines are represented in the financial hub of Europe. For vegetarians there's usually at least one meatless dish on a German menu, and substantial salads are popular, too (though often served with *Speck,* or bacon). The city's most famous contribution to the world's diet is the *Frankfurter Würstchen*—a thin smoked pork sausage—served with bread and mustard, but not with sauerkraut like the American hot dog also called a frankfurter. *Grüne Sosse* is a thin cream sauce of herbs served with potatoes and hard-boiled eggs. The oddly named *Handkäs mit Musik* (literally, "hand cheese with music") consists of slices of cheese covered with raw onions, oil, and vinegar, served with dark bread and butter (an acquired taste for many). There is the *Rippchen,* or cured pork chop, served on a mound of sauerkraut, and the *Schlachtplatte,* an assortment of sausages and smoked meats.

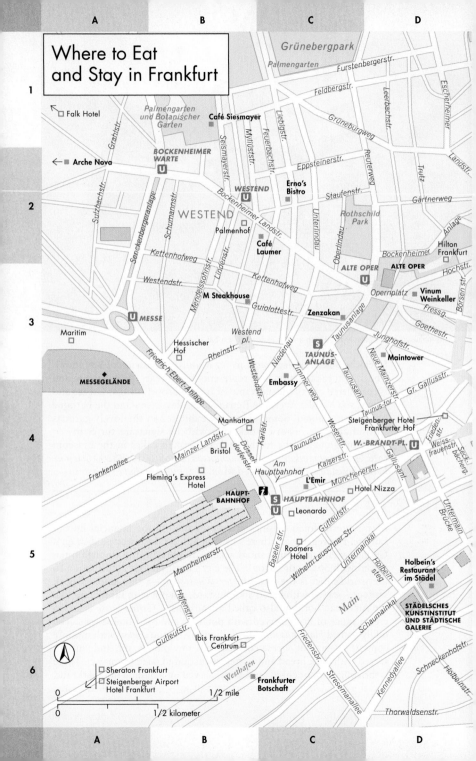

Where to Eat and Stay in Frankfurt

A   **B**   **C**   **D**

Grünebergpark

Palmengarten

Furstenbergerstr.

Feldbergstr.

Grüneburgweg

1

□ Falk Hotel

Palmengarten und Botanischer Garten

■ Café Siesmayer

Leerbachstr.

Escherheimer

Landstr.

Liebigstr.

Feuerbachstr.

Myliusstr.

Eppsteinerstr.

Reuterweg

Trutz

BOCKENHEIMER WARTE
Ⓤ

←■ **Arche Nova**

WESTEND

■ Erno's Bistro

Staufenstr.

Gärtnerweg

2

Sulzbachstr.

Grästr.

Schumannstr.

Senckenbergeranlage

Bockenheimer Landstr.

Seismayerstr.

WESTEND

□ Palmenhof

Unterlindau

Oberlindau

Rothschild Park

Anlage

Hilton Frankfurt

□

Bockenheimer

Hochstr.

Börsstr.

Kettenhofweg

□ Café Laumer

Lindenstr.

Kettenhofweg

ALTE OPER
Ⓤ

ALTE OPER
■

Opernplatz

■ **Vinum Weinkeller**

Fressg.

3

□ Maritim

Ⓤ **MESSE**

Mendelssohnstr.

■ **M Steakhouse**

Guiolottestr.

Westend pl.

■ **Zenzakan**

Taunusanlage

Junghofstr.

Goethestr.

Neue Mainzerstr.

■ **Maintower**

◆ **MESSEGELÄNDE**

Friedrich Ebert Anlage

□ Hessischer Hof

Rheinstr.

Niedenau

Westendstr.

Zimmerweg

Ⓢ **TAUNUS- ANLAGE**

Taunusanl.

Taunus-tor-

Gr. Gallusstr.

4

Frankenallee

Mainzer Landstr.

□ Manhattan

□ Bristol

Karlstr.

Düsseldorferstr.

Taunusstr.

Weserstr.

Kaiserstr.

Münchenerstr.

Gallusanl.

Steigenberger Hotel Frankfurter Hof

W.-BRANDT-PL. Ⓤ

Friedens- str.

Weissfrauenstr.

Seck- bacher

□ Fleming's Express Hotel

Am Hauptbahnhof

■ L'Emir

□ Hotel Nizza

HAUPT- BAHNHOF

🚹

Ⓢ **HAUPTBAHNHOF**
Ⓤ

□ Leonardo

Gutleutstr.

Untermain Brücke

5

Mannheimerstr.

Hafenstr.

Baseler str.

□ Roomers Hotel

Wilhelm Leuschner Str.

Untermainkai

Holbein steg

Main

Schaumainkai

■ **Holbein's Restaurant im Städel**

STÄDELSCHES KUNSTINSTITUT UND STÄDTISCHE GALERIE

Untermainkai

Schneckenhofstr.

6

🧭

□ Ibis Frankfurt Centrum

Gutleutstr.

Westhafen

□ Sheraton Frankfurt

□ Steigenberger Airport Hotel Frankfurt

■ **Frankfurter Botschaft**

Friedensbr.

Stresemannallee

Kennedyallee

Thorwaldsenstr.

Holbeinstr.

0   1/2 mile

0   1/2 kilometer

A   **B**   **C**   **D**

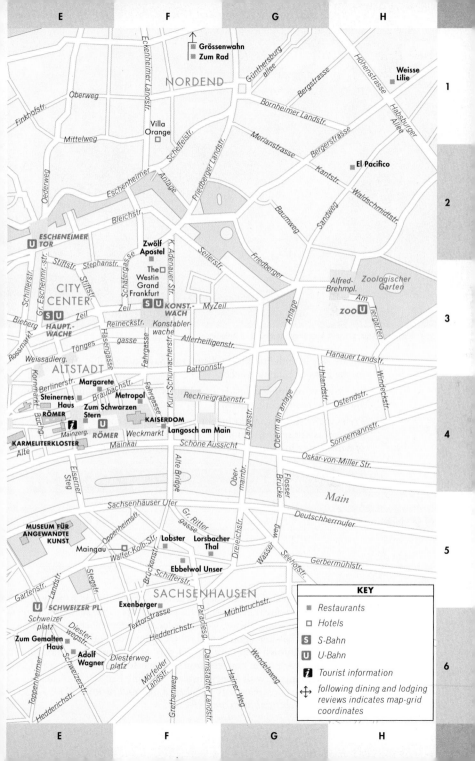

Don't leave Frankfurt without sampling a tall glass of Apfelwein.

All are served with Frankfurt's distinctive hard-cider drink, Apfelwein, by the glass or ceramic pitcher.

Smoking is prohibited inside Frankfurt's bars and restaurants, but allowed in most beer gardens.

Prices in the reviews are the average cost of a main course at dinner, or if dinner is not served, at lunch. Use the coordinates (⊕ C3) at the end of each listing to locate a site on the corresponding map.

	WHAT IT COSTS IN EUROS			
	$	$$	$$$	$$$$
AT DINNER	under €15	€15–€20	€21–€25	over €25

ALTSTADT

$ VEGETARIAN 🍴 **Langosch am Main.** This eclectic vegetarian and vegan spot, a rarity in Frankfurt, serves breakfast, lunch, dinner, and late-night snacks made only with organic ingredients. Centrally located a few blocks from the Dom, the café has low lighting and rough-hewn wood tables; the rock 'n' roll and Motown tunes are played here at a volume low enough not to discourage quiet conversation. **Known for:** organic wine and beer; desserts made with honey instead of refined sugar; homemade lemonade. [$] *Average main: €10* ✉ *Fahrg. 3, Altstadt* ☎ *069/9203–9510* 🌐 *www.langosch-frankfurt.com* ⊕ *F4.*

CLOSE UP

Apfelwein

Apfelwein, the local hard cider and the quintessential Frankfurt drink, is more sour than the sweet versions you may be used to. To produce Apfelwein, the juice of pressed apples is fermented for approximately eight weeks. Its alcohol content of 5%–7% makes it comparable to beer. Straight up, it is light and slightly fizzy. You can also try it carbonated with seltzer (*Sauergespritzer*), or sweetened with lemonade (*Süssgespritzer*).

Apfelwein is drunk from a lattice-patterned glass called a *Gerippte*. When among friends, it is poured from blue stoneware pitchers called *Bembels*, which range in size from big (a liter) to enormous (4 liters and up).

Popular throughout the state of Hesse, locals drink Apfelwein with pride. The largest concentration of Frankfurt's Apfelwein establishments is in the old neighborhood of Sachsenhausen. Look for establishments with a pine wreath hanging over the door; this signifies that Apfelwein is sold. There is also an annual weeklong Apfelwein Festival in Rossmarkt square in mid-August.

$$$ INTERNATIONAL
🍴 **Margarete.** This modern restaurant with an open-kitchen design is named for the Viennese architect Margarete Scütte-Lihotzky, who created the style in the 1920s. There are three-course prix-fixe menus both for lunch and dinner, or order à la carte from an eclectic and creative menu including homemade soups, risotto, and meats with the ubiquitous Frankfurter green herb sauce. **Known for:** extensive bar bites menu; regional specialties including lentil dishes; desserts including chocolate tart with bitter orange marmalade and berry sorbet. [$] *Average main: €25* ✉ *Braubachstr. 18–22, Altstadt* ☎ *069/1306–6500* 🌐 *www.margarete-restaurant.de* [M] *Willy-Brandt-Platz (U-bahn), Dom (U-bahn)* ✥ *E4.*

$ CAFÉ
🍴 **Metropol.** Breakfast is the main attraction at this café near the Römerberg and Dom. The dining room is large, and in the warmer months there are also tables on a garden patio. **Known for:** cakes and pastries; pastas and traditional German dishes; no credit cards accepted. [$] *Average main: €12* ✉ *Weckmarkt 13–15, Altstadt* ☎ *069/288–287* 🌐 *www.metropolcafe.de* 💳 *No credit cards* 🕒 *Closed Mon.* [M] *Römer (U-bahn)* ✥ *F4.*

$ GERMAN
🍴 **Steinernes Haus.** At this friendly spot, diners share long wooden tables beneath traditional clothing mounted on the walls. The house specialty is a raw steak brought to the table with a heated rock tablet (*Stein* is the German word for stone) where you do your own cooking. **Known for:** traditional, meat-centric German menu; old-fashioned ambience; kitchen open late. [$] *Average main: €14* ✉ *Braubachstr. 35, Altstadt* ☎ *069/283–491* 🌐 *www.steinernes-haus.de* [M] *Römer (U-bahn)* ✥ *E4.*

$$ GERMAN
🍴 **Zum Schwarzen Stern.** This restaurant in a historic half-timber house that dates from 1453 offers a menu focusing on traditional Hessian food, but presented in a modern way, with carefully arranged plating. Try to get a table by the windows for people-watching across the busy square. **Known for:** "Frankfurter Teller" sampler with sausages, pork loin, and crispy pork knuckle; chicken and local pike-perch; mushroom and

aparagus dishes in season. $ *Average main: €20* ⊠ *Römerberg 6, Altstadt* ☎ *069/291–979* ⊕ *www.schwarzerstern.de* Ⓜ *Römer (U-bahn)* ✛ *E4.*

CITY CENTER

$$
ECLECTIC
✕ **Embassy.** This modern restaurant, bar, and lounge near many of the city's largest banks makes it a natural for business lunches, but it also attracts many young professionals for after-work socializing and dinner. The moderately priced menu of contemporary dishes includes nearly two dozen varieties of pizza. **Known for:** some two dozen pizza options; pastas; happy-hour specials. $ *Average main: €15* ⊠ *Zimmerweg 1, corner of Mainzer Landstr., City Center* ☎ *069/7409–0844* ⊕ *www.embassy-frankfurt.de* ⊘ *Closed weekends* Ⓜ *Taunusanlage (S-bahn)* ✛ *C3.*

$$$
ECLECTIC
✕ **Frankfurter Botschaft.** Frankfurt's Westhafen (West Harbor), once busy and commercial, has been transformed into an upscale neighborhood of apartments, a yacht club, and waterfront restaurants. One of the most chic is Frankfurter Botschaft, with a glass facade and a big terrace overlooking the Main River. **Known for:** international, primarily organic, menu; sandy beach area with folding chairs and umbrellas; beautifully designed place settings. $ *Average main: €24* ⊠ *Westhafenpl. 6–8, City Center* ☎ *069/2400–4899* ⊕ *www.frankfurterbotschaft.de* ⊘ *Closed Sun. No lunch Sat.* 🏛 *Jacket required* Ⓜ *Hauptbahnhof (U-bahn and S-bahn)* ✛ *B6.*

$$
MIDDLE EASTERN
✕ **L'Emir.** The atmosphere is right out of *One Thousand and One Nights* at this restaurant near the train station, with belly dancers performing every Saturday night and urging patrons to join in. The Middle Eastern menu is largely vegetarian and heavy on garlic, olive oil, and lemon juice. **Known for:** meze, including delicious falafel; lamb dishes, including the homemade lamb sausage and marinated chops grilled over charcoal; party atmosphere. $ *Average main: €20* ⊠ *Ramada Hotel, Weserstr. 17, City Center* ☎ *069/2400–8680* ⊕ *www.lemir.de* Ⓜ *Hauptbahnhof (U-bahn and S-bahn)* ✛ *C4.*

$$$$
GERMAN
✕ **Maintower.** On the 53rd floor of the skyscraper that houses the Helaba Landesbank Hessen-Thüringen, this popular cocktail bar and high-end restaurant captures an unbeatable views through 25-foot floor-to-ceiling windows, from where you can take in all of "Mainhattan." The cuisine is part global, part regional, served at dinner as a three-course prix fixe. Lunch is an open menu with no minimum, as is the lounge for drinks and bar snacks, which opens at 9 pm. **Known for:** impeccable service; extensive wine list; €4.50 per person elevator fee. $ *Average main: €45* ⊠ *Neue Mainzerstr. 52–58, City Center* ☎ *069/3650–4770* ⊕ *www.maintower-restaurant.de* ⊘ *Closed Sun. and Mon. No lunch Tues. and Sat.* 🏛 *Jacket required* Ⓜ *Alte Oper (U-Bahn), or Taunusanlage (S-Bahn)* ✛ *D3.*

$$
GERMAN
Fodor's Choice
★
✕ **Vinum Weinkeller.** Housed in a former wine cellar that dates from 1893 in one of the alleys off Fressgasse, Vinum specializes in regional wines, by the glass or bottle to accompany a regional prix-fixe menu. The burnished brickwork and low lighting adds to the charm. **Known for:** wine-friendly dishes, including cheese platters; German specialties, including Würste; Sauerbraten with dumplings and red cabbage.

$ *Average main: €15* ⊠ *Kleine Hochstr. 9, City Center* ☎ *069/293–037* ⊕ *www.vinum-frankfurt.de* ☯ *Closed Sun., Oct.–Apr. No lunch* ⊹ *D3.*

$ ✕ **Zwölf Apostel.** There are few inner-city restaurants that brew their
GERMAN own beer, and the Twelve Apostles is one of the pleasant exceptions. Enjoy homemade pilsners in the dimly lighted, cavernous cellar, and sample traditional international and Croatian dishes. **Known for:** large servings; reasonable prices; regional specialties including Wurst platters. $ *Average main: €13* ⊠ *Rosenbergerstr. 1, City Center* ☎ *069/288–668* ⊕ *www.12aposteln-frankfurt.de* Ⓜ *Konstablerwache (U-bahn and S-bahn)* ⊹ *F2.*

MESSE AND WESTEND

$ ✕ **Café Laumer.** The ambience of an old-time Viennese café pervades
CAFÉ this popular spot, where there's a lovely garden in summer—as well as some of the city's best freshly baked pastries and cakes year-round, best teamed with a *Kaffee mit Schlag* (coffee with whipped cream). It closes early, by 7 pm. **Known for:** Viennese-style pastries and cakes; home-made soups; quiches and Wurst platters. $ *Average main: €8* ⊠ *Bockenheimer Landstr. 67, Westend* ☎ *069/727–912* ⊕ *www.cafelaumer.de* ☯ *No dinner* Ⓜ *Westend (U-bahn)* ⊹ *C2.*

$ ✕ **Café Siesmayer.** This sleek establishment at the Palmengarten is acces-
GERMAN sible either from the botanical garden or from the street, offering fresh-baked pastries throughout the day and a limited prix-fixe lunch menu that changes daily. It closes at 7 pm. **Known for:** splendid garden views; cheese and Wurst platters; daily lunch specials. $ *Average main: €14* ⊠ *Siesmayerstr. 59, Westend* ☎ *069/9002–9200* ⊕ *www.cafe-siesmayer. de* ☯ *No dinner* Ⓜ *Westend (U-bahn)* ⊹ *B1.*

$$$$ ✕ **Erno's Bistro.** This tiny, unpretentious place in a quiet Westend neigh-
FRENCH borhood seems an unlikely candidate for the best restaurant in Ger-
Fodor's Choice many, yet that's what one French critic called it. Fresh seafood, the
★ specialty, is often flown in from France, as are the wines (the wine list boasts 600 choices). **Known for:** elegant service; duck and seafood also from France; chef's tasting menus. $ *Average main: €45* ⊠ *Liebigstr. 15, Westend* ☎ *069/721–997* ⊕ *www.ernosbistro.de* ☯ *Closed weekends and for 6 wks during Hesse's summer school vacation* 🎩 *Jacket required* Ⓜ *Westend (U-bahn)* ⊹ *C2.*

$$$$ ✕ **M Steakhouse.** Many say the M Steakhouse serves the best steak in
STEAKHOUSE Germany, all of it imported Nebraska prime beef. Prices are in line with
Fodor's Choice the quality of meat, and the sides complement the dishes perfectly, but if
★ you're looking for non-meat options, you won't find them here. **Known for:** rib-eye and porterhouse steaks; American-style sides including fries and onion rings; large portions. $ *Average main: €30* ⊠ *Feuerbachstr. 11a, Westend* ☎ *069/7103–4050* ⊕ *www.mook-group.de* ☯ *Closed Sun. No lunch Sat.* 🎩 *Jacket required* ⊹ *C3.*

$$$$ ✕ **Zenzakan.** Hailed as a sort of pan-Asian supper club, this large restau-
JAPANESE rant with Asian decor has a bar scene that's just as good a reason to visit as its exceptional menu of both Japanese and Chinese dishes. Beef lovers will find plenty to choose from, including sliced hangar steak with Japa-nese barbecue sauce, and there's a smokers' lounge, rare in smoke-free Frankfurt, featuring Japanese vodka. **Known for:** innovative cocktails

9

CLOSE UP

Riesling: Try It Dry

Germany's mild, wet climate and a wine-making tradition that dates back 2,000 years combine to produce some of the world's finest white wines.

The king of German varietals is Riesling. Grown on the banks of Germany's many rivers, most notably the Rhine, the grape produces wines of stunning variety and quality. Rieslings are noted for their strong acidity, sometimes-flowery aroma, and often mineral-tasting notes—stemming from the grape's susceptibility to influences from the soil. Riesling made its name throughout the world through sweet (*lieblich*) wines, but many Germans prefer them dry (*trocken*). Importers, especially in the United States, don't bring over many dry German Rieslings, so take the opportunity to sample some while in Frankfurt.

SIP IT HERE
The **Bockenheimer Weinkontor** (⊠ *Schlossstr. 92* ☎ *069/702–031* ⊕ *www.bockenheimer-weinkontor.de* Ⓜ *Bockenheimer Warte [U-bahn]*) is nearby the Messegelände (Exhibition Center), in the Bockenheim area. Through a courtyard and down a set of stairs, the cozy bar offers 15–20 reasonably priced local wines by the glass. The trellis-covered back garden is a treat.

For prestige wines, head to **Piccolo** (⊠ *Bornheimer Landstr. 56* ☎ *069/9441–1277* ⊕ *www.weinbar-piccolo.de* Ⓜ *Merianplatz [U-bahn]*), where the bilingual staff make solid recommendations. Try a glass from the Markus Molitor or Alexander Freimuth wineries. Along with wine, they serve a range of snacks and main courses. The space is small, so make reservations if you plan to dine here.

such as a lemongrass martini; excellent sushi; kitchen open late. $ *Average main: €30* ⊠ *Taunusanlage 15, Westend* ☎ *069/9708–6908* ⊕ *www.mook-group.de/zenzakan* ⊘ *Closed Sun. No lunch* ✚ *C3.*

NORDEND AND BORNHEIM

$ ✕ **El Pacifico.** Some of Frankfurt's best Mexican cuisine is found in this
MEXICAN festive little place. Warm and colorful, this restaurant serves a variety of fruity margaritas and is well known for its extensive selection of tequilas. **Known for:** hearty chicken wings appetizers; good fajitas; seven types of salsa. $ *Average main: €14* ⊠ *Sandweg 79, Bornheim* ☎ *069/446–988* ⊕ *www.el-pacifico-ffm.de* ⊘ *No lunch Mon.–Sat.* Ⓜ *Merianplatz (U-bahn)* ✚ *H2.*

$$ ✕ **Grössenwahn.** The Nordend is noted for its trendy establishments,
ECLECTIC and this corner restaurant, which is often crowded, is one of the best. The name translates as "megalomania," which may refer to its menu, which changes daily, incorporating German, Greek, Italian, and French elements. **Known for:** fresh seasonal ingredients; quick service; busy on weekends, when reservations are essential. $ *Average main: €15* ⊠ *Lenaustr. 97, Nordend* ☎ *069/599–356* ⊕ *www.cafe-groessenwahn.de* ⊘ *No lunch* Ⓜ *Glauburgstrasse (U-bahn)* ✚ *F1.*

$ ✕**Weisse Lilie.** Come to this Bornheim favorite for the delicious selec-
SPANISH   tion of tapas, paella, and other Spanish specialties. The dark interior
Fodor'sChoice   has wooden tables brightened by fresh-cut flowers and candles, mak-
★   ing it a good spot for an intimate dinner. **Known for:** seafood; grilled
meats; reasonably priced red wines. Ⓢ *Average main: €11* ✉ *Bergerstr.
275, Bornheim* ☎ *069/453–860* ⊕ *www.weisse-lilie.com* ☉ *No lunch*
Ⓜ *Bornheim Mitte (U-bahn)* ✛ *H1.*

SACHSENHAUSEN

$ ✕**Adolf Wagner.** With sepia-toned murals of merrymaking above the
GERMAN   dark-wood wainscoting, this Apfelwein classic succeeds in being tour-
FAMILY   isty and traditional all at once, and it's a genuine favorite of local resi-
Fodor'sChoice   dents. The kitchen produces the same hearty German dishes as other
★   nearby taverns, only better. Cider is served in large quantities in the
noisy, crowded dining room. **Known for:** schnitzel; Tafelspitz mit Frankfurter grüner Sosse (stewed beef with a sauce of green herbs); fresh fish
(a Friday special). Ⓢ *Average main: €13* ✉ *Schweizerstr. 71, Sachsenhausen* ☎ *069/612–565* ⊕ *www.apfelwein-wagner.com* Ⓜ *Schweizer
Platz (U-bahn)* ✛ *E6.*

$ ✕**Ebbelwol Unser.** This friendly Apfelwein restaurant offers typical decor,
GERMAN   with traditional wood paneling and coat hooks on the wall. It's popular
with locals, who come for regional favorites, including dishes with the
ubiquitous Frankfurter green sauce, but also a rarity: beer. **Known for:**
slaughter plate (with sausage and liver dumplings); generous-size pork
and veal schnitzels; Appelkranzen (battered and fried apple rings dusted
with cinnamon sugar and served with ice cream). Ⓢ *Average main:
€12* ✉ *Abtsgaesschen 8, Sachsenhausen* ☎ *069/153–45128* ⊕ *www.
ebbelwol-unser.de* ☉ *No lunch* ✛ *F5.*

$ ✕**Exenberger.** The menu is typical of Old Sachsenhausen—apple wine
GERMAN   and sauerkraut are served—but the interior is bright and modern and
the Frankfurt specialties are a cut above the rest. As proprietor Kay
Exenberger puts it: "We're nearly as fast as a fast-food restaurant, but
as *gemütlich* (quaint) as an apple wine locale must be." It's so popular
that reservations are a good idea, even at lunch, and everything can
be wrapped up to go. **Known for:** lentil soup with Frankfurters; Himmel und Erde (Heaven and Earth) Wurst platter; chocolate pudding
with vanilla sauce. Ⓢ *Average main: €9* ✉ *Bruchstr. 14, Sachsenhausen*
☎ *069/6339–0790* ⊕ *www.exenberger-frankfurt.de* ▭ *No credit cards*
☉ *Closed Sun.* Ⓜ *Südbahnhof (U-bahn and S-bahn)* ✛ *F5.*

$$$ ✕**Holbein's Restaurant im Städel.** The restaurant on the ground floor of the
ECLECTIC   Städel art museum changes from a casual bistro at lunch to an elegant
restaurant open until midnight. Lunch features pastas and panini, or a
three-course prix-fixe business lunch. **Known for:** elegant setting; Irish
prime beefsteaks and tartare; surprisingly good sushi. Ⓢ *Average main:
€24* ✉ *Städelsches Kunstinstitut und Städtische Galerie, Holbeinstr. 1,
Sachsenhausen* ☎ *069/6605–6666* ⊕ *www.meyer-frankfurt.de* ☉ *Closed
Mon. in July* Ⓜ *Schweizer Platz (U-bahn)* ✛ *D5.*

$$ ✕**Lobster.** This small restaurant and wine bistro is a favorite of locals
SEAFOOD   and visitors alike. The menu, dramatically different from those of its
neighbors, focuses mostly on seafood, including lobster. **Known for:**

9

pasta with seafood; shrimp prepared several ways; busy weekends (reservations almost essential then). $ *Average main: €17* ✉ *Wallstr. 21, Sachsenhausen* ☎ *069/612–920* ⊕ *www.lobster-weinbistrot.de* ⊘ *Closed Sun. No lunch* Ⓜ *Schweizer Platz (U-bahn)* ✛ *F5.*

$$
GERMAN

✕ **Lorsbacher Thal.** This is a traditional-looking restaurant that has been reinvented with a modern vibe; it also claims to have the largest Apfelwein and cider selection in Germany. More than 200 labels are represented, including those from other countries, and cellar tours are offered to diners who request one. **Known for:** apple wine; vegetarian dishes; Wurst platters. $ *Average main: €15* ✉ *Great Ritterg. 49, Sachsenhausen* ☎ *069 /616–459* ⊕ *www.lorsbacher-thal.de* ✛ *F5.*

$
GERMAN
Fodor's Choice
★

✕ **Zum Gemalten Haus.** There aren't many classic Apfelwein locales left, but this is one of them. It's just as it has been since the end of the 19th century: walls covered with giant paintings darkened with age, giant stoneware pitchers called *Bembels,* glasses that are ribbed to give greasy hands traction, long tables that can seat 12 people, schmaltzy music, hearty food with daily specials, and, as is traditional, no beer. **Known for:** favored by locals; apple wine and other fruit wines and liqueurs; sausage platters and cheese platters. $ *Average main: €8* ✉ *Schweizerstr. 67, Sachsenhausen* ☎ *069/614–559* ⊕ *www.zumgemaltenhaus.de* ⊘ *Closed Mon., and 1st 2 wks of Aug.* Ⓜ *Schweizer Platz (U-bahn)* ✛ *E6.*

OUTER FRANKFURT

$$
VEGETARIAN

✕ **Arche Nova.** This sunny establishment is a feature of Frankfurt's Ökohaus, which was built according to environmental principles (solar panels, catching rainwater, etc.). The menu is mainly vegetarian, with such dishes as a vegetable platter with feta cheese or curry soup with grated coconut and banana. **Known for:** vegetarian and vegan dishes; good curries; organic wines and beers. $ *Average main: €16* ✉ *Kasselerstr. 1a, Bockenheim* ☎ *069/707–5859* ⊕ *www.arche-nova.de* ⊘ *No dinner Sun.* Ⓜ *Westbahnhof (S-bahn)* ✛ *A2.*

$
GERMAN

✕ **Zum Rad.** Named for the huge *Rad* (wagon wheel) that serves as a centerpiece, this is one of the few Apfelwein taverns in Frankfurt that still makes its own apple wine, which it's been doing since 1806. It's located in the villagelike district of Seckbach, on the northeastern edge of the city. **Known for:** pork and veal schnitzels; Wurst platters; cash only. $ *Average main: €10* ✉ *Leonhardsg. 2, Seckbach* ✛ *U-4 to Seckbacher Landstr. then Bus 43 to Draisbornstr.* ☎ *069/479–128* ⊕ *www.zum-rad. de* ☰ *No credit cards* ⊘ *Closed Tues. No lunch Mon.–Sat.* ✛ *F1.*

WHERE TO STAY

Businesspeople descend on Frankfurt year-round, so most hotels in the city are frequently booked up well in advance and are expensive (though many offer significant reductions on weekends). Many hotels add as much as a 50% surcharge during trade fairs (*Messen*), of which there are about 30 a year. The majority of the larger hotels are close to the main train station, fairgrounds, and business district (*Bankenviertel*). The area around the station has a reputation as a red-light district, but

In summer, riverside bars and DJs spinning music are all part of the local scene.

is well policed. More atmosphere is found at smaller hotels and pensions in the suburbs; the efficient public transportation network makes them easy to reach. Hotels in Germany are not always smoke-free, particularly if they don't belong to a large international chain; public spaces are always smoke-free.

Prices in the reviews are the lowest cost of a standard double room in high season. For expanded reviews, facilities, and current deals, visit Fodors.com. Use the coordinates (✥ C3) at the end of each listing to locate a site on the corresponding map.

9

	WHAT IT COSTS IN EUROS			
	$	**$$**	**$$$**	**$$$$**
FOR TWO PEOPLE	under €100	€100–€175	€176–€225	over €225

CITY CENTER

$$ HOTEL 🏨 **Bristol.** One of the nicest hotels in the neighborhood around the main train station, this stylish choice features modern, minimalist decor in soothing earth tones, and air-conditioning adds to the appeal. **Pros:** lobby bar is open 24 hours; beautiful garden patio; central location. **Cons:** minimalist decor; small rooms; can be noisy. [$] *Rooms from: €150* ✉ *Ludwigstr. 15, City Center* ☎ *069/242–390* 🌐 *www.bristol-hotel.de* 🛏 *145 rooms* 🍴 *Free Breakfast* [M] *Hauptbahnhof (U-bahn and S-bahn)* ✥ *B4.*

$ HOTEL

Fleming's Express Hotel. If there ever was a hotel at the vortex of arrivals and departures, it's this centrally located one in an elegant old-world building across the street from the main train station, where new owners have completely refurbished the rooms and facilities. **Pros:** underground parking at train station; clean, modern decor; central location. **Cons:** on a busy, noisy street; no restaurant; small rooms and bathrooms. [$] *Rooms from: €100* ✉ *Poststr. 8, City Center* ☎ *069/273–910* 🌐 *www.flemings-hotels.com* 🛏 *384 rooms* 🍴 *Free Breakfast* [M] *Hauptbahnhof (U-bahn and S-bahn)* ✥ *B4.*

$$$ HOTEL FAMILY Fodor's Choice ★

Hilton Frankfurt. This international chain's downtown Frankfurt outpost has all the perks the business traveler wants, from secretarial services to video conferencing facilities and a hip lobby bar (Gekkos) that is definitely worth a visit. **Pros:** child-friendly and pet-friendly facilities; indoor pool; large terrace overlooking a park. **Cons:** expensive; small bathrooms; international chain decor. [$] *Rooms from: €225* ✉ *Hochstr. 4, City Center* ☎ *069/133–8000* 🌐 *www.frankfurt.hilton.com* 🛏 *342 rooms* 🍴 *No meals* [M] *Eschenheimer Tor (U-bahn)* ✥ *D2.*

$$ HOTEL

Hotel Nizza. This beautiful Victorian building close to the main train station is filled with antiques and hand-painted murals by the owner, and features a lovely roof garden with a view of the skyline. **Pros:** antique furnishings; roof garden with shrubbery and a view of the skyline; very comfortable. **Cons:** Bahnhof district can be a bit seedy at night; not all rooms have a private bath; elevator goes only to 4th floor. [$] *Rooms from: €110* ✉ *Elbestr. 10, City Center* ☎ *069/242–5380* 🌐 *www.hotelnizza.de* 🛏 *26 rooms* 🍴 *Free Breakfast* [M] *Willy-Brandt-Platz (U-bahn and S-bahn) or Hauptbahnhof (U-bahn and S-bahn)* ✥ *C5.*

$$ HOTEL FAMILY Fodor's Choice ★

Ibis Frankfurt Centrum. The Ibis is a reliable budget hotel chain, and this location offers simple, straightforward rooms on a quiet street near the river. **Pros:** short walk from the station and museums; 24-hour bar; family rooms and wheelchair-accessible rooms available. **Cons:** far from stores and theaters; small rooms and bathrooms; no restaurant. [$] *Rooms from: €110* ✉ *Speicherstr. 4, City Center* ☎ *069/273–030* 🌐 *www.ibishotel.com* 🛏 *233 rooms* 🍴 *No meals* [M] *Hauptbahnhof (U-bahn and S-bahn)* ✥ *B6.*

$ HOTEL

Leonardo. Across the street from the main train station, this modern, sparkling hotel has its own underground garage. **Pros:** underground garage; quiet summer garden; central location. **Cons:** on a busy street; parking expensive; can be noisy. [$] *Rooms from: €75* ✉ *Münchenerstr. 59, City Center* ☎ *069/242–320* 🌐 *www.leonardo-hotels.com* 🛏 *108 rooms* 🍴 *Free Breakfast* [M] *Hauptbahnhof (U-bahn and S-bahn)* ✥ *C5.*

$ HOTEL

Manhattan. Get to all parts of town quickly from this centrally located hotel. **Pros:** close the Messe (convention center); all rooms no-smoking and air-conditioned; free high-speed Wi-Fi. **Cons:** no restaurant; not close to museums; on a busy street. [$] *Rooms from: €100* ✉ *Düsseldorferstr. 10, City Center* ☎ *069/269–5970* 🌐 *www.manhattan-hotel.com* 🛏 *55 rooms* 🍴 *Free Breakfast* [M] *Hauptbahnhof (U-bahn and S-bahn)* ✥ *B4.*

$$$ HOTEL Fodor's Choice ★ **Roomers Hotel.** This lively boutique hotel features modern and sleek designs everywhere you look, including rooms heavy on black lacquer furniture offset by white bedspreads and chairs and large, airy windows. **Pros:** trendy design; convenient location close to train station and museums; underground parking. **Cons:** expensive; not good for families; distance from Altstadt. [$] *Rooms from: €220* ✉ *Gutleutstr. 85, City Center* ☎ *069/271–3420* 🌐 *www.roomers.frankfurt.com* 🛏 *116 rooms* 🍴 *No meals* ✣ *C5.*

$$$$ HOTEL Fodor's Choice ★ **Steigenberger Hotel Frankfurter Hof.** The neo-Gothic Frankfurter Hof is the first choice of visiting heads of state and business moguls, who keep coming back because of its impeccable service, luxurious rooms, and endless-seeming amenities. **Pros:** old-fashioned elegance; central location close to Altstadt and museums; marble baths with whirlpool tubs. **Cons:** expensive rates; on a busy street; limited parking. [$] *Rooms from: €249* ✉ *Am Kaiserpl., City Center* ☎ *069/21502* 🌐 *www.frankfurter-hof.steigenberger.de* 🛏 *303 rooms* 🍴 *No meals* [M] *Willy-Brandt-Platz (U-bahn)* ✣ *D4.*

$$ HOTEL FAMILY **The Westin Grand Frankfurt.** Those who like downtown Frankfurt will appreciate the Westin's location, just steps from the famous Zeil shopping street, plus all the features of a high-end chain hotel, including a fitness room, spa, pool, and sauna. **Pros:** kids stay free; indoor pool; loaner work-out gear for the gym. **Cons:** on a noisy street; chain hotel feel, including large, impersonal lobby; free in-room Wi-Fi only for members of Starwood frequent-stay rewards program. [$] *Rooms from: €175* ✉ *Konrad Adenauer Str. 7, City Center* ☎ *069/29810* 🌐 *www.westingrandfrankfurt.com* 🛏 *371 rooms* 🍴 *No meals* [M] *Konstablerwache (U-bahn and S-bahn)* ✣ *F3.*

MESSE AND WESTEND

$$$$ HOTEL **Hessischer Hof.** This is the choice of many businesspeople, not just for its location across from the convention center but also for the air of class that pervades its handsome interior. **Pros:** adjacent to the convention center and public transportation; site of Jimmy's, one of the town's cult bars; roof garden. **Cons:** lobby can be crowded; expensive; far from Altstadt and museums. [$] *Rooms from: €250* ✉ *Friedrich-Ebert-Anlage 40, Messe* ☎ *069/75400* 🌐 *www.hessischer-hof.de* 🛏 *117 rooms* 🍴 *No meals* [M] *Messe (S-bahn)* ✣ *B3.*

$$$ HOTEL **Maritim.** It's so close to the Messegelände (Exhibition Center) that you can reach the exhibition halls, as this top-notch business hotel puts it, "with dry feet." It has its own underground garage, a sauna, steam bath, and indoor pool, and a sushi bar that draws many nonguests. **Pros:** direct access to the convention center; indoor pool; Sky Lounge and lobby bar open late. **Cons:** online booking site is in German only; hectic during fairs; far from museums and theaters. [$] *Rooms from: €190* ✉ *Theodor-Heuss-Allee 3, Messe* ☎ *069/75780* 🌐 *www.maritim.de* 🛏 *524 rooms* 🍴 *No meals* [M] *Messe (S-bahn)* ✣ *A3.*

$$$ HOTEL **Palmenhof.** This luxuriously modern hotel, held in the same family for three generations, occupies a renovated art nouveau building dating from 1890. **Pros:** near the Palmengarten; less expensive than similar hotels; spacious rooms. **Cons:** no restaurant; top floor can get very hot;

isolated feel after dark. $ *Rooms from: €190* ⊠ *Bockenheimer Landstr. 89–91, Westend* ☎ *069/753–0060* ⊕ *www.palmenhof.com* ⌇ *38 rooms* ¶◯¶ *Free Breakfast* Ⓜ *Westend (U-bahn)* ✛ *B2.*

NORDEND AND BORNHEIM

$$
HOTEL
◌ **Villa Orange.** Frankfurt's first eco-hotel features modern, natural-wood furniture, including canopy beds, and organic cotton sheets and towels. **Pros:** everything organic, from furnishings to food; on a quiet residential street; all rooms are smoke-free. **Cons:** hard beds; not close to museums, shopping, or public transportation; limited parking. $ *Rooms from: €165* ⊠ *Hebelstr. 1, Nordend* ☎ *069/405–840* ⊕ *www.villa-orange.de* ⌇ *38 rooms* ¶◯¶ *Breakfast* Ⓜ *Musterschule (U-bahn)* ✛ *F1.*

SACHSENHAUSEN

$$
HOTEL
◌ **Maingau.** This pleasant hotel in the middle of the lively Sachsenhausen quarter has recently renovated rooms that are modest but comfortable; the nightly rate includes a substantial breakfast buffet. **Pros:** close to nightlife; fantastic (but expensive) restaurant; overlooks a small park. **Cons:** on a busy street; small rooms; must request no-smoking floors. $ *Rooms from: €120* ⊠ *Schifferstr. 38–40, Sachsenhausen* ☎ *069/609–140* ⊕ *www.maingau.de* ⌇ *78 rooms* ¶◯¶ *Free Breakfast* Ⓜ *Schweizer Platz (U-bahn)* ✛ *F5.*

OUTER FRANKFURT

$$
HOTEL
◌ **Falk Hotel.** In the heart of Bockenheim—and near numerous cafés, bars, shops, and the *Messe* (trade center)—this hotel is a good deal, especially on weekends. **Pros:** fairly low rates, especially on weekends; quiet residential neighborhood; convenient to public transportation. **Cons:** small rooms; no restaurant or bar; far from museums, theater, and shopping. $ *Rooms from: €134* ⊠ *Falkstr. 38A, Bockenheim* ☎ *069/7191–8870* ⊕ *www.hotel-falk.de* ⌇ *29 rooms* ¶◯¶ *Free Breakfast* Ⓜ *Leipzigerstrasse (U-bahn)* ✛ *A1.*

$$$$
HOTEL
◌ **Sheraton Frankfurt.** This huge hotel is connected to one of Frankfurt Airport's terminals. **Pros:** directly connected to the airport; 24-hour amenities including business center and gym; sports bar open to 1am daily. **Cons:** smoke-free rooms not always available; very expensive; free Wi-Fi in lobby only. $ *Rooms from: €559* ⊠ *Hugo-Eckener-Ring 15, Flughafen Terminal 1, Airport* ☎ *069/69770* ⊕ *sheraton.marriott.com* ⌇ *1,036 rooms* ¶◯¶ *Free Breakfast* Ⓜ *Flughafen (S-bahn)* ✛ *A6.*

$$$
HOTEL
FAMILY
◌ **Steigenberger Airport Hotel Frankfurt.** The sylvan beauty of this family-friendly hotel is surprising, considering that it's just a half mile from the airport and connected to it by a steady stream of shuttle buses that operate 24 hours. **Pros:** many rooms overlook park; indoor pool and gym; four restaurants, including a 24-hour bistro. **Cons:** restaurants are expensive; far from downtown; far from public transportation. $ *Rooms from: €200* ⊠ *Unterschweinstiege 16, Airport* ☎ *069/69750* ⊕ *www.steigenberger.com* ⌇ *570 rooms* ¶◯¶ *No meals* Ⓜ *Flughafen (S-bahn)* ✛ *A6.*

NIGHTLIFE AND PERFORMING ARTS

NIGHTLIFE

Most bars close between 2 am and 4 am. Nightclubs typically charge entrance fees ranging from €5 to €20. In addition, some trendy places, such as King Kamehameha, enforce dress codes—usually no jeans, sneakers, shorts, or khaki pants admitted.

Sachsenhausen (Frankfurt's "Left Bank") is a good place for bars, clubs, and traditional Apfelwein taverns. The fashionable Nordend has an almost equal number of bars and clubs but fewer tourists. Frankfurt was a real pioneer in the German jazz scene, and also has done much for the development of techno music. Jazz musicians make the rounds from smoky backstreet cafés all the way to the Old Opera House, and the local broadcaster Hessischer Rundfunk sponsors the German Jazz Festival in fall. The Frankfurter Jazzkeller has been the most noted venue for German jazz fans for decades.

CITY CENTER

DANCE CLUBS

Gibson Club. This nightclub in the heart of the Zeil attracts a mostly young crowd with its live music performances by international musicians. It's open Thursday and Sunday from 8 pm and Friday and Saturday from 11 pm. Concert tickets from €21. ⊠ *Zeil 85–93, City Center* ☎ *069/9494–7770* ⊕ *www.gibson-club.de.*

Odeon. The type of crowd depends on the night. The large club hosts student nights on Thursday, a "27 Up Club" on Friday (exclusively for guests 27 or older), disco nights on Saturday, as well as "Black Mondays"—a night of soul, hip-hop, and R&B. It's housed in a beautiful white building that looks like a museum. There's lots of neon and pulsing lights, including under the see-through dance floor. ⊠ *Seilerstr. 34, City Center* ☎ *069/285–055* ⊕ *www.theodeon.de.*

JAZZ CLUBS

Der Frankfurter Jazzkeller. The oldest jazz cellar in Germany, Der Frankfurter Jazzkeller was founded by legendary trumpeter Carlo Bohländer. The club, which once hosted such luminaries as Louis Armstrong and Ella Fitzgerald, now offers hot, modern jazz, at a cover of €5–€25. There are jam sessions on Wednesday and "Latin-funky" dances on Friday. Jazzkeller is located on a difficult-to-find alleyway off Fressgasse, which just adds to its charm and legend. ⊠ *Kleine Bockenheimerstr. 18, City Center* ☎ *069/284–927* ⊕ *www.jazzkeller.com.*

Zoom. Sinkkasten, a Frankfurt musical institution, was renamed Zoom in 2013. By any name it is a great place for blues, jazz, pop, and rock. Saturday nights are Hit Happens, with hip-hop and techno-electro music. Zoom is open from 9 pm to 1 am every day but Monday, and live shows often begin at 11 pm. ⊠ *Brönnerstr. 5, City Center* ☎ *069/280–385* ⊕ *www.zoomfrankfurt.de.*

9

OSTEND
JAZZ CLUBS
Jazzlokal Mampf. With posters of Chairman Mao on the walls, time seems to have stood still at the Jazzlokal Mampf. It looks straight out of the 1970s, but with live music to match, many don't think that's so bad. Since it opens at 6 pm for dinner and drinks, there's a lively after-work crowd on weekdays. Live jazz performances begin at 8 pm. ⊠ *Sandweg 64, Ostend* ☎ *069/448–674* ⊕ *www.mampf-jazz.de* Ⓜ *Merianplatz (U-bahn).*

HAUSEN
LIVE MUSIC
Brotfabrik. An important address for jazz, rock, salsa, and disco, the "Bread Factory" really is set in a former bakery in an area of town that's still primarily industrial. The building houses two stages, a concert hall, two restaurants, three not-for-profit projects, an ad agency, and a gallery. ⊠ *Bachmannstr. 2–4, Hausen* ☎ *069/2479–0800* ⊕ *www.brotfabrik.info* Ⓜ *Fischstein (U-bahn).*

MESSE AND WESTEND
BARS
Fox and Hound. Frankfurt is teeming with Irish pubs, but this is an example of a great English pub, too. Its patrons, mainly British, come to watch the latest football (soccer to Americans), rugby, and cricket matches. Enjoy the authentic British pub food; 35 whiskies, bitters, and stout; and the basket of chips. Monday is steak night, with American-style sirloins and rib eyes. ⊠ *Niedenau 2, Westend* ☎ *069/9720–2009* ⊕ *www.foxandhound.de* Ⓜ *Festhalle/Messe (U-bahn).*

Jimmy's Bar. The meeting place of business executives since 1951, Jimmy's Bar is classy and expensive, just like the hotel it's in. There is live piano music, mostly jazz, every evening from 10 pm to 3 am, and the kitchen is open just as late. You must ring the doorbell to get in, although regulars have their own keys. ⊠ *Hessischer Hof, Friedrich-Ebert-Anlage 40, Messe* ☎ *069/7540–2461* ⊕ *www.hessischer-hof.de/en/hotel-bar-frankfurt.*

SACHSENHAUSEN
LIVE MUSIC
Balalaika. The spacious club has an intimate feel, as candles are just about the only source of light. The proprietor is Anita Honis, an American singer from Harlem, who likes to get out her acoustic guitar and perform on occasion. Everyone is invited to sing or play on the piano, which is set up for impromptu and scheduled performances, and there's usually music nightly from 8 pm. ⊠ *Schifferstr. 3, Sachsenhausen* ☎ *069/612–226* ⊕ *www.balalaikafrankfurt.de* Ⓜ *Bus 36 to Affentorplatz.*

PERFORMING ARTS

The Städtische Bühnen—municipal theaters, including the city's opera company—are the prime venues for Frankfurt's cultural events. The city has what is probably the most lavish theater in the country, the

The Eiserner Steg (Iron Bridge) was Europe's very first suspension bridge, and a walk across promises great photo ops of Frankfurt's skyline.

Alte Oper, a magnificently ornate 19th-century opera house that's now a multipurpose hall for pop and classical concerts, as well as dances. (These days operas are presented at the Städtische Bühnen.)

TICKETS

Best Tickets. Tickets for theater, concerts, and sports events can be purchased from Best Tickets downtown in the Zeilgalerie. ⊠ *Zeil 106, Room 77, City Center* ☎ *069/20228, 069/20228* ⊕ *www.journal-ticketshop.de.*

Frankfurt Ticket. Theater, concert, and sports event tickets are all available here. ⊠ *Hauptwache Passage, City Center* ☎ *069/134–0400* ⊕ *www. frankfurtticket.de* ⊙ *Weekdays 9–7, Sat. 10–3.*

BALLET, CONCERTS, AND OPERA

Alte Oper. The most glamorous venue for classical and contemporary music concerts and ballet is the Alte Oper, one of the most beautiful buildings in Frankfurt, which opened in 1880. Tickets to performances can range from €20 to nearly €150. There is a bar or bistro on each level for drinks, coffee, and pastries during intermission, and the elegant Restaurant Opera for dining before or after performances. ⊠ *Opernpl., City Center* ⊕ *www.alteoper.de.*

Bockenheimer Depot. Frankfurt's ballet company performs in the Bockenheimer Depot, a former trolley barn also used for other theatrical performances and music events. ⊠ *Carlo-Schmidt-Pl. 1, Bockenheim.*

Frankfurt Opera. Widely regarded as one of the best in Europe, the Frankfurt Opera is known for its dramatic artistry. Richard Wagner and Richard Strauss both oversaw their own productions for the

The elegant illumination of the Alte Oper (Old Opera House) and fountain make for magical nighttime viewing.

company, now housed in a modern glass-walled building in the city center. In an effort to introduce a new generation to opera, there are special family programs with free tickets for children and teens up to 19 years. Ticket prices from €15. ✉ *Städtische Bühnen, Untermainanlage 11, City Center* ☎ *069/2124–9494* ⊕ *www.oper-frankfurt.de* Ⓜ *Willy-Brandt-Platz (U-bahn).*

SHOPPING

Frankfurt, along with the rest of Germany, no longer has the restrictive laws that once kept stores closed evenings and Saturday afternoon, the very times working people might want to shop. Stores now can stay open until 10 pm, but pretty much everything is still closed on Sunday except for restaurants and bakeries.

The tree-shaded pedestrian zone of the **Zeil** is said to be one of the richest shopping strips in Germany. The section between Hauptwache and Konstablerwache is famous for its incredible variety of department and specialty stores. But there's much more to downtown shopping. The subway station below the Hauptwache also doubles as a vast underground mall. West of the Hauptwache are two parallel streets highly regarded by shoppers. One is the luxurious **Goethestrasse,** lined with trendy boutiques, art galleries, jewelry stores, and antiques shops. The other is **Grosse Bockenheimer Strasse,** better known as the Fressgass ("Pig-Out Alley"), an extension of the Zeil that's lined with cafés, restaurants, and pricey food shops.

One gift that's typical of the city is the Apfelwein. You can get a bottle of it at any grocery store, but more enduring souvenirs would be the Bembel pottery pitchers and ribbed glasses that are an equal part of the Apfelwein tradition. Then there is the sausage: you can get the "original hot dog" in cans or vacuum-packed at any grocery store.

CITY CENTER

CLOTHING

August Pfüller. Find upscale designer day wear, evening wear, jeans, handbags, and other accessories for men, women, and kids, ranging from classic to trendy, at three adjoining Pfüller shops. Everything is displayed elegantly, and personal service is impeccable in this three-story shopping destination. Pfüller has separated its equally upscale children's collection to a separate multifloor store directly across the street, called Pfüller Kids. ⊠ *Goethestr. 15–17, City Center* ☎ *069/1337–8060* ⊕ *www.august-pfueller.de/en/women.*

Peek & Cloppenburg. At this huge branch of the clothing chain, men and women can find what they need for the office, gym, and nightclub. Prices range from easily affordable to sky-high for top designer labels. There's also a branch at the Skyline Plaza shopping mall near the Messe. ⊠ *Zeil 71–75, City Center* ☎ *069/298–950* ⊕ *www.peek-cloppenburg. de* ⊗ *Closed Sun.*

Schillerpassage. The Schillerpassage shopping area is lined with men's and women's fashion boutiques. ⊠ *Rahmhofstr. 2, City Center.*

FOOD AND WINE

Kleinmarkthalle. The large and airy Kleinmarkthalle is a treasure trove of stands selling spices, herbs, teas, exotic fruits, cut flowers, meats, live fish flown in from the Atlantic, and more varieties of Wurst and cheese than you can count. Plus, it offers all kinds of snacks in case you need a break while shopping. ⊠ *Haseng. 5–7, City Center* ☎ *069/2123–3696* ⊕ *www.kleinmarkthalle.com* Ⓜ *Hauptwache (S-bahn), Dom (U-bahn).*

Weinhandlung Dr. Teufel. Weinhandlung Dr. Teufel is well known for its wide selection of regional wines, many priced under €10, plus rare vintages costing three figures or more. There are also chocolate and cigars, a complete line of glasses, carafes, corkscrews, and other accessories, and books on all aspects of viticulture. The store also has a location in the Westend. ⊠ *Kleiner Hirschgraben 4, City Center* ☎ *069/448–989* ⊕ *www.weinteufel.de.*

SHOPPING MALLS AND DEPARTMENT STORES

Galeria Kaufhof. One of Germany's biggest and most popular department stores, the Galeria Kaufhof carries clothing, jewelry, sports equipment, cosmetics, toys, and more. The Frankfurt branch has a food hall on the lower floor; the restaurant on the top floor has great city views. ⊠ *Zeil 116–126, City Center* ☎ *069/21910* Ⓜ *Hauptwache (U-bahn).*

Karstadt. One of Germany's biggest department store chains, Karstadt is known for both its upscale brand-name designer offerings, including popular German designers Betty Buckley and Gerry Weber (for women), and its splendid food and drink department, with plenty

9

of opportunity to sample the offerings. ⊠ *Zeil 90, City Center* ☎ *069/929–050* ⊕ *www.karstadt.de.*

Skyline Plaza. This multilevel shopping mall connected to the *Messe* (convention center) contains more than 170 shops, including clothing, shoes, jewelry, and accessories, and the biggest food court in Frankfurt. Unfortunately, it feels like an American mall, with all its familiar international food and fashion chains dominating the German brands. Head to the roof garden for a picture-postcard view of the skyline year-round, and for outdoor dining in season. ⊠ *Europa-Allee 6, Messe* ☎ *069/2972–8700* Ⓜ *Festhalle/Messe (U-bahn).*

WESTEND

FOOD

Café Laumer. The pastry shop at Café Laumer has local delicacies such as *Bethmännchen und Brenten* (marzipan cookies) and *Frankfurter Kranz* (a kind of creamy cake). It's open daily. ⊠ *Bockenheimer Landstr. 67, Westend* ☎ *069/727–912* ⊕ *www.cafelaumer.de.*

SIDE TRIPS FROM FRANKFURT

Destinations reachable by the local transportation system include Höchst and the Taunus Hills, which include Bad Homburg and Kronberg. Just to the northwest and west of Frankfurt, the Taunus Hills are an area of mixed pine and hardwood forest, medieval castles, and photogenic towns many Frankfurters regard as their own backyard. It's home to Frankfurt's wealthy bankers and business executives, and on weekends you can see them enjoying their playground: hiking through the hills, climbing the Grosse Feldberg, taking the waters at Bad Homburg's health-enhancing mineral springs, or just lazing in elegant stretches of parkland.

BAD HOMBURG

12 km (7 miles) north of Frankfurt.

Emperor Wilhelm II, the infamous "Kaiser" of World War I, spent a month each year at Bad Homburg, the principal city of the Taunus Hills. Another frequent visitor to Bad Homburg was Britain's Prince of Wales, later King Edward VII, who made the name *Homburg* world-famous by associating it with a hat.

GETTING HERE AND AROUND

Bad Homburg is reached easily by the S-bahn from Hauptwache, the main station, and other points in downtown Frankfurt. The S5 goes to Bad Homburg. There's also a Taunusbahn (from the main station only) that stops in Bad Homburg and then continues into the far Taunus, including the Römerkastell-Saalburg and Wehrheim, with bus connections to Hessenpark. Bad Homburg is about a 30- to 45-minute drive north of Frankfurt on A-5.

VISITOR INFORMATION

Contacts Kur- und Kongress GmbH Bad Homburg. ✉ *Louisenstr. 58, Bad Homburg vor der Höhe* ☎ *06172/1000* ⊕ *www.bad-homburg.de.*

EXPLORING

FAMILY **Freilichtmuseum Hessenpark.** This open-air museum is about an hour's walk through the woods along a well-marked path from the Römerkastell-Saalburg is an open-air museum at Hessenpark, near Neu-Anspach. The museum presents a clear picture of the world in which 18th- and 19th-century Hessians lived, using 135 acres of rebuilt villages with houses, schools, and farms typical of the time. The park, 15 km (9 miles) outside Bad Homburg in the direction of Usingen, can also be reached by public transportation. ✉ *Laubweg 5, Neu-Anspach* ⊕ *Take Taunusbahn from Frankfurt main station to Wehrheim; then transfer to Bus 514* ☎ *06081/5880* ⊕ *www.hessenpark.de* ▣ *€9.*

Kurpark (*spa*). Bad Homburg's greatest attraction has long been the Kurpark, in the heart of the Old Town, with more than 31 fountains. Romans first used the springs, which were rediscovered and made famous in the 19th century. In addition to the popular (and highly salty) Elisabethenbrunnen spring, look for a Thai temple and a Russian chapel, mementos left by royal guests—King Chulalongkorn of Siam and Czar Nicholas II. ✉ *Bad Homburg vor der Höhe* ⊕ *www.bad-homburg-tourismus.de/en/entdecken/freizeit_kurpark.htm.*

FAMILY **Römerkastell-Saalburg** (*Saalburg Roman Fort*). The remains of a Roman fortress built in AD 120, the Römerkastell-Saalburg could accommodate a cohort (500 men) and was part of the fortifications along the Limes Wall, which ran from the Danube to the Rhine and was meant to protect the Roman Empire from barbarian invasion. It was restored in the early 1900s under the direction of the Kaiser. The site, which includes a museum of Roman artifacts, is 6½ km (4 miles) north of Bad Homburg on Route 456 in the direction of Usingen; there's a direct bus from Bad Homburg. There's also a small café. ✉ *Archäologischer Park, Saalburg 1, Bad Homburg vor der Höhe* ☎ *06175/93740* ⊕ *www.saalburgmuseum.de* ▣ *€5.*

Schloss Homburg. The most historically noteworthy sight in Bad Homburg is the 17th-century Schloss, where the kaiser stayed when he was in town. The state apartments are exquisitely furnished, and the **Spiegelkabinett** (Hall of Mirrors) is especially worthy of a visit. In the surrounding park look for two cedars from Lebanon, both now about 200 years old. The museum holds artifacts from much earlier, including from archeological digs on the site. ✉ *Schloss, Bad Homburg vor der Höhe* ☎ *02293/91010* ⊕ *www.schloss-homburg.de* ▣ *€5.*

Spielbank Bad Homburg. This casino boasts with some justice that it is the "Mother of Monte Carlo." The first *Spielbank* (casino) in Bad Homburg, and one of the first in the world, was established in 1841, but closed in 1866 because Prussian law forbade gambling. Proprietor François Blanc then established the famous Monte Carlo casino on the French Riviera, and the Bad Homburg casino wasn't reopened until 1949. Classic table games such as roulette and blackjack have been joined by poker variations Texas Hold 'Em and Three Card Poker, plus slot machines and other electronic games including electronic roulette. A bus from the south side of Frankfurt's Hauptbahnhof leaves every 60–90 minutes between 2 pm and 1 am. Buses back to Frankfurt run every one to two hours from 4:30 pm to 4 am. The trip takes one hour each way. The €10 fare is refunded after the casino's full entry fee has been deducted. Note that a passport or other government-issued identification is required for admission (and you must be 21 or over). There is also dining and weekend events with live music and dancing to DJs ⊠ *Kisseleffstr. 35, Bad Homburg vor der Höhe* ☎ *06172/17010* ⊕ *www. spielbank-bad-homburg.de* ⊠ *Slot-machine area free; gaming area €3.*

WHERE TO EAT

$ ✕**Kartoffelküche.** This simple restaurant serves traditional dishes accom-
GERMAN panied by potatoes cooked every way imaginable. The potato-and-broccoli gratin and the potato pizza are excellent. **Known for:** good kids menu; potato soup with and without sausage or bacon; schnitzels. Ⓢ *Average main: €9* ⊠ *Audenstr. 4, Bad Homburg vor der Höhe* ☎ *06172/21500* ⊕ *www.kartoffelkueche.com* ☉ *No lunch Mon.–Thurs.*

WHERE TO STAY

$$$ ⊡ **Steigenberger Bad Homburg.** This hotel, which opened in 1883, was
HOTEL renowned for catering to Europe's royalty in its pre–World War I heyday, and it's still good at pleasing a well-heeled clientele. **Pros:** old-world class; handy to the Kurpark; fitness equipment and sauna. **Cons:** expensive; parking is difficult; access to pool, sauna, and steam room is a whopping €60 daily fee. Ⓢ *Rooms from: €180* ⊠ *Kaiser-Friedrich-Promenade 69–75, Bad Homburg vor der Höhe* ☎ *06172/1810* ⊕ *www. bad-homburg.steigenberger.de* ⇄ *165 rooms* ⏍*No meals.*

THE PFALZ AND
RHINE TERRACE

WELCOME TO
THE PFALZ AND RHINE TERRACE

TOP REASONS TO GO

★ **Wine:** German Rieslings are some of the most versatile white wines in the world. If you've only tried sweet German wines, the rest may be a revelation.

★ **Festivals:** Wine is a great excuse for merrymaking, and there are wine festivals in almost every town and village across the region from May through October. The largest wine festival in the world takes place in the town of Bad Dürkheim, in front of a wine barrel the size of a building.

★ **Pfälzerwald:** The Palatinate Forest is a paradise for hiking and cycling. Even a short stroll under the beautiful pine and chestnut trees is a relaxing way to spend an afternoon.

★ **Castles:** Burg Trifels and Schloss Villa Ludwigshöhe contrast strikingly in style, inside and out. Both are wonderful settings for concerts.

★ **Cathedrals:** The cathedrals in Speyer, Worms, and Mainz are the finest examples of grand-scale Rhenish Romanesque architecture in Germany.

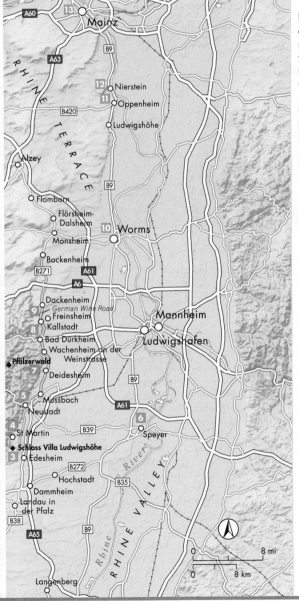

If you're arriving from the dramatic stretch of the river Rhine centered on the Loreley and Koblenz to the north, you'll notice that the landscape here is far gentler. So, too, is the climate: this region, guarded at its northern edge by the medieval city of Mainz and touching the French border at its southern extreme, is one of Germany's warmest. This helps the land give birth to plentiful fruits such as apricots and figs, and to some of Germany's greatest wines.

1 Bad Bergzabern

2 Gleiszellen

3 Schloss Villa Ludwigshöhe

4 St. Martin

5 Neustadt

6 Speyer

7 Deidesheim

8 Bad Dürkheim

9 Freinsheim

10 Worms

11 Oppenheim

12 Nierstein

13 Mainz

10

DRIVING THE GERMAN WINE ROAD

With its warm weather and fertile fields, the Pfalz is often referred to as Germany's Tuscany. In addition to vineyards, the mild climate fosters fig, lemon, and chestnut trees.

(above) Autumn is a gorgeous time of year to tour the region. (upper right) Vineyards in Pfalz (lower right) Winery-hopping by bike is a nice alternative to driving.

Summers here get very hot and sticky, so the best time to visit is early spring, when the route is awash with almond blossoms, or early fall, when sweet young wines are available. The Deutsche Weinstrasse begins in Schweigen-Rechtenbach on the French border and runs alongside *Bundesstrassen* (highways) B-38 and B-271. Yellow signs depicting a cluster of grapes guide visitors north through medieval villages and rolling vineyards to the end of the route at the "House of the German Wine Road" in Bockenheim. The entire road is just more than 50 miles and can be driven in just a few hours, but, if you stop to sample the local food and wines, explore the charming villages, or hike through vineyards along the way, you can easily turn it into a proper road trip.

—Updated by Christie Dietz

DRINKING AND DRIVING

Germany has strict laws against driving (and biking) under the influence, so if you're planning to take advantage of the numerous *Weinprobe* (wine samples) offered along the route, make sure you have a designated driver. Alternatively, just let the vintner know what you like, and he can help you pick a bottle to enjoy when you reach your final destination.

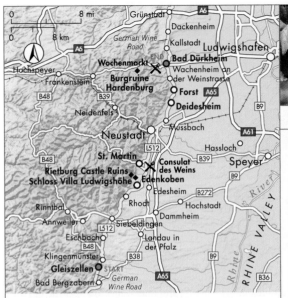

QUICK BITES

Consulat des Weines.
Oenophiles won't want to miss this Vinothek in the charming village of St. Martin. It offers more than 80 varieties of wine from its vineyards in St. Martin and nearby Edenkoben (cash only). The sheer variety makes it easy to overindulge—good thing there's a hotel and restaurant on-site. There's a second location, also on Maikammerer Strasse near the St. Martiner Castell hotel (closed Sunday). ✉ *Maikammerer Str. 44, St. Martin* ☎ *06323/8040* ⊕ *www.consulat-des-weins.de.*

Wochenmarkt. If you're in Bad Dürkheim on a Wednesday or Saturday morning, head to the farmers' market for flowers, bread, wine, meats, cheeses, and vinegars. ✉ *Am Obermarkt, Bad Dürkheim* ☎ *06323/8040* ⊕ *www.wochenmarkt-duerkheim.de.*

Start your journey at the *Deutsches Weintor* (German Wine Gate) in Schweigen-Rechtenbach, or pick up the route in **Gleiszellen,** pausing for a glass of the hard-to-find, floral Muskateller wine at homey **Weinstube Wissing.**

Stop to stretch your legs at the Pompeian-style palace **Schloss Villa Ludwigshöhe** in **Edenkoben,** then take the Rietburgbahn chairlift to admire the views from the **Rietburg Castle Ruins.** If you're planning a two-day drive, the neighboring village of **St. Martin** is approximately halfway through the journey and an ideal place to overnight.

Continue north, stopping for lunch in **Deidesheim,** home to three of the region's most famous wineries. Drive leisurely through the vineyards of **Forst,** pausing at the imposing ruins of **Burgruine Hardenburg** (Hardenburg Fortress), and end with a visit to the world's biggest wine barrel in **Bad Dürkheim.**

10

Updated by
Christie Dietz

The Pfalz and wine go hand in hand. This region of vineyards and picturesque villages is the home of the German Wine Road and the country's greatest wine festival at Bad Dürkheim. Six of Germany's 13 wine-growing regions are in the area.

The Pfalz has a mild, sunny climate, and that seems to affect the mood here, too. Vines carpet the foothills of the thickly forested Haardt Mountains, an extension of the Alsatian Vosges. The Pfälzerwald (Palatinate Forest) with its pine and chestnut trees is the region's other natural attraction. Hiking and cycling trails lead through the vineyards, the woods, and up to castles on the heights.

The border between the Pfalz and Rheinhessen is invisible, but you begin to get a sense of Rheinhessen's character soon after crossing it. It's a region of gentle, rolling hills and expansive farmland, where grapes are but one of many crops; vineyards are often scattered miles apart. The slopes overlooking the Rhine between Worms and Mainz—the so-called Rhine Terrace—are a notable exception, with a nearly uninterrupted ribbon of vines, including the famous vineyards of Oppenheim, Nierstein, and Nackenheim on the outskirts of Mainz.

The southernmost wine village of the Pfalz lies on the French border. During the economically depressed 1930s, local vintners established a route through the vineyards to promote tourism. The German Wine Road was inaugurated in 1935; a year later, the massive stone Deutsches Weintor (German Wine Gate) was erected to add visual impact to the marketing concept. Halfway up the gateway is a platform that offers a fine view of the vineyards—to the south, French, to the north, German. Schweigen-Rechtenbach's 1-km (½-mile) Weinlehrpfad (educational wine path) wanders through the vineyards and, with signs and exhibits, explains the history of viticulture from Roman times to the present.

MAJOR REGIONS

The Germany Wine Road spans the length of the **Pfalz** wine region, north to south, and makes for a memorable road trip in either direction. Given its central location, the Pfalz is convenient to visit before or after a trip to the Black Forest, Heidelberg, or the northern Rhineland. It encompasses (from south to north) **Schweigen-Rechtenbach, Bad Bergzabern, Gleiszellen, Schloss Villa Ludwigshöhe, St. Martin, Neustadt, Speyer, Deidesheim,** and **Bad Dürkheim.**

The **Rhine Terrace** is a broad, fertile valley along the Rhine and immediately east of the Pfalz region. It's known for its medieval cities that were powerhouses in their day, including **Worms, Oppenheim, Nierstein,** and **Mainz.** Like Speyer, the cities of Worms and Mainz were Free Imperial Cities and major centers of Christian and Jewish culture in the Middle Ages. Germany's first synagogue and Europe's oldest surviving Jewish cemetery, both from the 11th century, are in Worms. The imperial Diet of Worms in 1521 and 1529 stormed around Martin Luther (1483–1546) and the rise of Protestantism. In 1455, Johannes Gutenberg (1400–68), the inventor of the printing press and of movable type in Europe, printed the first Gutenberg Bible in Mainz.

PLANNING

WHEN TO GO
After countless celebrations of the *Mandelblüten* (blossoming of the almond trees) along the Wine Road in March, wine festival season picks up in May and continues through October. The landscape alters dramatically in May as the vines' tender shoots and leaves begin to appear, and as the wine harvest progresses in September and October, foliage takes on reddish-golden hues.

FESTIVALS
Attending a wine festival is a fun and memorable part of any vacation in wine country. You can sample local food and wine inexpensively, and meet winegrowers at their stands without making an appointment. Wine, *Sekt* (sparkling wine), and *Weinschorlen* (wine spritzers) flow freely at festivals all over the region, from tiny villages to the larger towns. The bigger events often involve live music, parades, fireworks, and rides. See ⊕ *www.germanwines.de* for an events calendar with an up-to-date overview of the many smaller, local wine festivals that take place in virtually every village.

Brezelfest (*Pretzel Festival*). Beer and pretzels are central to this annual celebration held in Speyer over the second weekend in July. Other highlights include carnival rides and games, fireworks, and a grand parade. ⊠ *Festpl., Speyer* ⊕ *www.brezelfest-speyer.de.*

Deidesheim Weinkerwe. For two long weekends in August, the wine town of Deidesheim fills up with stalls where visitors can sample local wines and hearty cuisine. Deidesheim's wineries also stay open late, offering live entertainment most nights during the festival. ⊠ *Marktpl., Deidesheim.*

Deutsches Weinlesefest (*German Wine Harvest Festival*). In Neustadt, the German Wine Queen is crowned during this 10-day wine festival in late September–early October. The festival includes wine tastings, the largest wine festival parade in Germany, and a huge fireworks display on the final night. ⊠ *Various locations including Saalbau, Heztelpl., and Bahnhofsvorpl., Neustadt* ⊕ *www.neustadt.eu.*

Dürkheimer Wurstmarkt (*Sausage Market*). The Pfalz is home to the world's largest wine festival, held in Bad Dürkheim in mid-September in front of the world's largest wine barrel. Some 400,000 pounds of sausage are consumed during eight days of merrymaking. ⊠ *Sankt-Michaels-Allee 1, Bad Dürkheim* ⊕ *www.duerkheimer-wurstmarkt.de.*

Mainzer Johannisnacht (*The Mainz Midsummer St. John's Night Festival*). In addition to carnival rides, a craft market, fireworks, and plenty of food and drink, live performances from local and international bands, as well as theater and cabaret performances, take place on six stages in the city center in late June. Since the festival is at least nominally in honor of Johannes Gutenberg, printers' apprentices are dunked in water in front of the Gutenberg Museum as part of a "printers' baptism" ceremony. ⊠ *Various locations, Mainz* ⊕ *www.mainz.de.*

Wormser Backfischfest (*Fried Fish Festival*). Carnival rides, traditional folk music and dance, jousting on the Rhine, and fireworks create a jovial atmosphere at this annual festival, starting in late August, which honors the city's fishermen. Don't pass up the chance to taste more than 400 wines at the festival's Wonnegauer Wine Cellar. ⊠ *Festpl., Worms* ⊕ *www.backfischfest.de.*

PLANNING YOUR TIME

Central hubs such as Bad Dürkheim or Neustadt make good bases for exploring the region; smaller towns such as St. Martin, Deidesheim, and Gleiszellen are worth an overnight stay because of their charm. Driving the Wine Road takes longer than you might expect, and will probably involve spur-of-the-moment stops, so you may want to consider a stopover in one of the many country inns en route.

GETTING HERE AND AROUND

AIR TRAVEL

Frankfurt Main is the closest major international airport for the entire Rhineland. International airports in Stuttgart and France's Strasbourg are closer to the southern end of the German Wine Road. If you're traveling from within Europe, the frequently disparaged Ryanair hub in the remote Frankfurt suburb of Hahn is actually a convenient jumping-off point for a tour of the region, with bus services to Mainz, Koblenz, Heidelberg, and Karlsruhe.

BIKE TRAVEL

There's no charge for transporting bicycles on local trains throughout Rheinland-Pfalz; carriages suitable for traveling with them are indicated by stickers depicting bicycles. For maps, suggested routes, bike-rental locations, and details on *Pauschalangebote* (package deals) or *Gepäck-transport* (luggage-forwarding service), contact the Pfalz or Rhine Terrace tourist service centers.

CAR TRAVEL

It's 162 km (100 miles) between Schweigen-Rechtenbach and Mainz, the southern- and northernmost points of this region. The main route is the Deutsche Weinstrasse, which is a Bundesstrasse, abbreviated "B," as in B-38, B-48, and B-271. The route from Worms to Mainz is the B-9.

TRAIN TRAVEL

Mainz is on the high-speed ICE (InterCity Express) train route linking Wiesbaden, Frankfurt, and Dresden, and so forms a convenient gateway to the region. The excellent networks of public transportation called the **Rheinland-Pfalz-Takt** and **Rhein-Main Verkehrsverbund** operate throughout the region with well-coordinated **RegioLinie** (buses) and **Nahverkehrszüge** (local trains). Regional trains link Mainz with other towns along the Rhine Terrace, including Worms and Speyer, while local branch lines serve key hubs along the Wine Road such as Neustadt and Bad Dürkheim. Smaller towns and villages connect with these hubs by an excellent network of local buses.

■TIP→ **The Rheinland-Pfalz Ticket is a great value if you plan to travel on the train.** The ticket costs €24 for the first person and €5 for each additional person, up to five people. It's valid for a whole day, beginning at 9 am on weekdays and midnight on weekends and holidays, until 3 am the following morning. It can be used on all regional trains and buses, but not the high-speed ICE trains; ensure you write your name on your ticket after purchase.

HOTELS

Family hotels and B&Bs abound in these regions, but book in advance if your visit coincides with a large festival. Look for signs reading "Fremdenzimmer" or "Zimmer frei" (rooms available). A *Ferienwohnung* (holiday apartment), abbreviated "FeWo" in tourist brochures, is an economical option if you plan to stay in one location for several nights.

RESTAURANTS

Lunch in this region is generally served from noon until 2 or 2:30, dinner from 6 until 9:30 or 10. Credit cards have gained a foothold, but many restaurants will accept only cash or debit cards issued by a German bank. Casual attire is typically acceptable at restaurants here, and reservations are generally not needed.

Prices in hotel reviews are the lowest cost of a standard double room in high season. Prices in restaurant reviews are the average cost of a main course at dinner, or if dinner is not served, at lunch.

WHAT IT COSTS IN EUROS			
	$	$$	$$$	$$$$
Restaurants	under €15	€15–€20	€21–€25	over €25
Hotels	under €100	€100–€175	€176–€225	over €225

10

VISITOR INFORMATION

Contacts Pfalz Touristik. ✉ *Martin-Luther-Str. 69, Neustadt* 🌐 *www.pfalz.de.* **Rheinhessen-Touristik.** ✉ *Friedrich-Ebert-Str. 17, Ingelheim am Rhein* 🌐 *www.rheinhessen.de.* **Rheinland-Pfalz Tourismus.** ☎ *01805/757–4636 €0.14/min, mobile max €0.42/min* 🌐 *www.romantic-germany.info.*

BAD BERGZABERN

10 km (6 miles) north of Schweigen-Rechtenbach on B-38.

The landmark of this little spa town, situated where the forests and vineyards meet, is the baroque **Schloss** (palace) of the dukes of Zweibrücken. The Gasthaus Zum Engel (Königstrasse 45) is an impressive Renaissance house with elaborate scrolled gables and decorative oriels. ■ **TIP→ Visit Café Herzog (Marktstrasse 48) for scrumptious, homemade chocolates, cakes, and ice creams made with unexpected ingredients, such as wine, pepper, cardamom, curry, thyme, or fig vinegar. The café is closed Monday and Tuesday.**

GETTING HERE AND AROUND

From Landau, you can take the regional train to Bad Bergzabern, which takes about 30 minutes and requires a change in Winden (Pfalz). Bus No. 543 also connects Bad Bergzabern along the Wine Road to Schweigen-Rechtenbach, over the French border to Wissembourg. The Rheinland-Pfalz ticket is valid on both train and bus as far as the French border.

WHERE TO STAY

$$$ HOTEL **Hotel–Restaurant Krone.** East of Bad Bergzabern, behind a simple, half-timber facade, is a hotel with modern facilities, upscale and tasteful furnishings, a well-regarded restaurant, and a warm welcome from the Kuntz family. **Pros:** use of bicycles and tennis courts included; excellent food; free Wi-Fi. **Cons:** a detour off the Wine Road (about a half-hour drive); not many activities in the surrounding area; expensive. [$] *Rooms from: €190* ✉ *Hauptstr. 62–64, Hayna* ✣ *20 km (12 miles) east of Bad Bergzabern* ☎ *07276/5080* 🌐 *www.hotelkrone.de* 🛏 *66 rooms* 🍴 *Free Breakfast.*

GLEISZELLEN

4 km (2½ miles) north of Bad Bergzabern on B-48.

Gleiszellen's Winzergasse (Vintners' Lane) is a little vine-canopied street lined with a beautiful ensemble of half-timber houses. Try a glass of the town's specialty wine: spicy, aromatic Muskateller, a rarity seldom found elsewhere in Germany.

GETTING HERE AND AROUND

Gleiszellen is on the No. 543 bus line that runs from Landau to the French border town of Wissembourg. The bus runs hourly.

The Wines of Rheinland-Pfalz

CLOSE UP

The Romans planted the first Rhineland vineyards 2,000 years ago, finding the mild, wet climate hospitable to grape growing. By the Middle Ages, viticulture was flourishing and a bustling wine trade had developed. Winemaking and splendid Romanesque cathedrals are the legacies of the bishops and emperors of Speyer, Worms, and Mainz. This area, now the state of Rheinland-Pfalz (Rhineland Palatinate), remains a major wine center, home to two of the largest wine regions in the country: Rheinhessen and the Pfalz.

In the Pfalz, you can follow the Deutsche Weinstrasse as it winds its way north from the French border. Idyllic wine villages beckon with vine-draped facades and courtyards full of palms, oleanders, and fig trees. "Weinverkauf" (wine for sale) and "Weinprobe" (wine tasting) signs are posted everywhere—an invitation to stop in to sample the wines.

Most of the wines from both the Pfalz and Rheinhessen are white, and those from Rheinhessen are often fragrant and sweeter than their counterparts in the Pfalz. Many are sold in restaurants as *offene Weine* (wines by the glass). The classic white varieties are Riesling, Silvaner, Müller-Thurgau (also called Rivaner), Grauburgunder (Pinot Gris), and Weissburgunder (Pinot Blanc). Spätburgunder (Pinot Noir), Dornfelder, and Portugieser are the most popular red wines. The word *Weissherbst*, after the grape variety, indicates a rosé wine.

Riesling is the king of German grapes. It produces wines that range widely in quality and character. Rieslings are noted for their strong acidity, sometimes-flowery aroma, and often mineral-tasting notes—all reflections of the soil in which they're grown. Riesling made its name throughout the world as a sweet (*lieblich*) wine, but many Germans (and, increasingly, others) prefer dry (*trocken*) or semi-dry (*halbtrocken*) versions.

EXPLORING

10

Fodor'sChoice ★ **Burg Trifels.** Burg Trifels is on the highest of three sandstone bluffs overlooking Annweiler, 15 km (9 miles) northwest of Gleiszellen. Celts, Romans, and Salians all had settlements on this site, but it was under the Hohenstaufen emperors (12th and 13th centuries) that Trifels was built on a grand scale. It housed the crown jewels from 1125 to 1274 (replicas are on display today). It was also an imperial prison, perhaps where Richard the Lion-Hearted was held captive in 1193–94. Although it was never conquered, the fortress was severely damaged by lightning in 1602. Reconstruction began in 1938, shaped by visions of grandeur to create a national shrine to the imperial past. The monumental proportions of some parts of today's castle bear no resemblance to those of the original Romanesque structure. The imperial hall is a grand setting for summer concerts. **Arriving on foot:** From Annweiler, follow the local signs for Burg Trifels. The hike is about an hour. **Arriving by car:** Follow the A-65 direction Karl-Ludwigshafen, take exit Landau-Sued, then B-10 to Annweiler west. From there follow the local signs. Parking is at

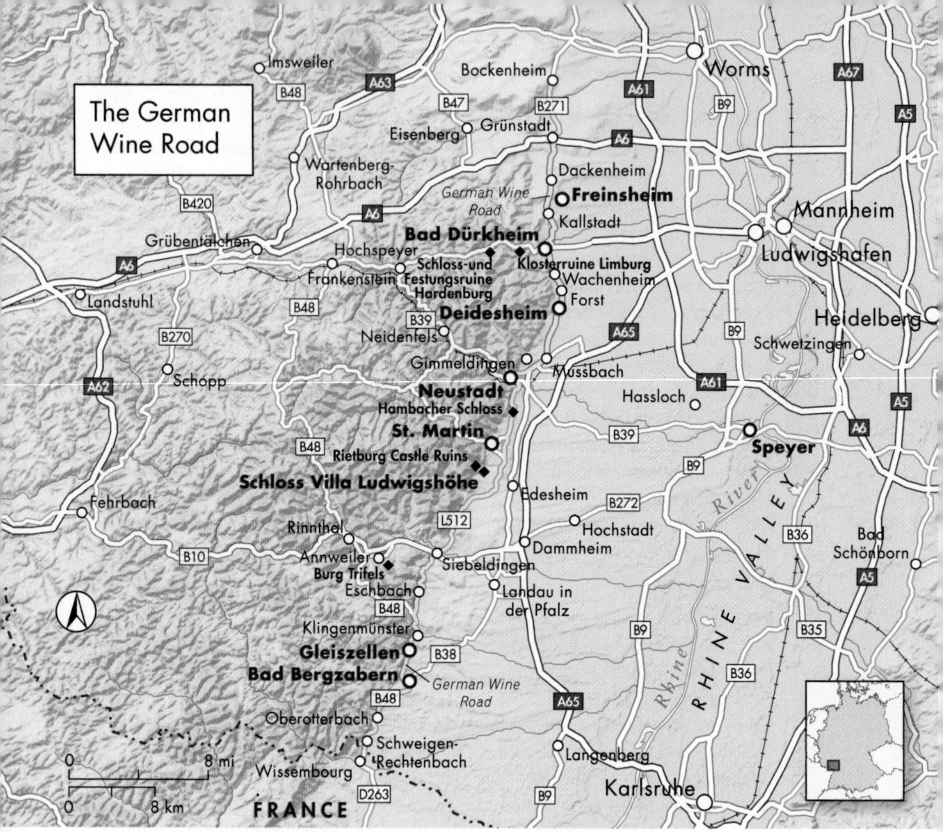
The German Wine Road
Imsweiler
Bockenheim
Worms
Grünstadt
Eisenberg
Wartenberg-Rohrbach
Dackenheim
German Wine Road
Freinsheim
Mannheim
Kallstadt
Bad Dürkheim
Grübentälchen
Hochspeyer
Schloss-und Festungsruine Hardenburg
Klosterruine Limburg
Ludwigshafen
Frankenstein
Wachenheim
Landstuhl
Forst
Deidesheim
Heidelberg
Neidenfels
Schwetzingen
Gimmeldingen
Mussbach
Schopp
Neustadt
Hassloch
Hambacher Schloss
St. Martin
Speyer
Rietburg Castle Ruins
Schloss Villa Ludwigshöhe
Edesheim
Rhine River
Fehrbach
Hochstadt
Rinnthal
Dammheim
Bad Schönborn
Annweiler
Siebeldingen
Burg Trifels
Eschbach
Landau in der Pfalz
Klingenmünster
RHINE VALLEY
Gleiszellen
Bad Bergzabern
German Wine Road
Oberotterbach
Schweigen-Rechtenbach
Langenberg
Wissembourg
Karlsruhe
FRANCE
0
8 mi
0
8 km
A63
B48
B47
B271
A61
B9
A67
A5
A6
B420
B270
A65
A62
B39
L512
B272
B36
B10
B35
B38
D263

the foot of the fortress, a 20-minute walk from the top. ✉ *Burg Trifels, Annweiler* ☎ *06346/8470* 🌐 *www.reichsburg-trifels.de* 🎫 *€5* 🕓 *Closed Dec. and Jan. Closed weekdays mid-Feb.–mid-Mar. and mid-Oct.–Nov.*

WHERE TO EAT

$$ 🍴 **Weinstube Wissing.** Wines, fine spirits, and regional delicacies are
WINE BAR offered in the former premises of the family-owned distillery. Don't miss a chance to sample their fruity Muskateller wine, and you might also want to pick up a bottle of their fresh red or white *Pfälzer Traubensaft* (grape juice) as a tasty souvenir. **Known for:** good service; friendly atmosphere; popular with hikers. [$] *Average main: €15* ✉ *Winzerg. 34* ☎ *06343/610–0505* 🌐 *www.weingut-wissing.de* 💳 *No credit cards* 🕓 *No lunch Mon., Tues., Thurs., and Fri. and varying periods in summer and winter.*

WHERE TO STAY

$ 🏨 **Gasthof Zum Lam.** Flowers cascade from the windowsills of this
B&B/INN 250-year-old half-timber inn in the heart of town, where the good
Fodor's Choice ★ rates include free Wi-Fi and a breakfast buffet. **Pros:** quiet location; charming courtyard; beautiful old building. **Cons:** no elevator; no

air-conditioning; some complaints of slow service at the restaurant. $ *Rooms from: €53* ✉ *Winzerg. 37* ☎ *06343/939–212* ⊕ *www.zum-lam.de* ⇨ *20 rooms* ⦿ *Free Breakfast.*

SCHLOSS VILLA LUDWIGSHÖHE

24 km (15 miles) north of Annweiler, slightly west of Edenkoben on the Wine Road.

For a cultural break from all that wine tasting, head to this Pompeiian-style palace, the former summer residence of King Ludwig I, which overlooks what he described as "the most beautiful square mile of my realm," where the Palatinate vineyards end and the forests begin. The layout and decor of the neoclassical palace—Pompeian-style murals, splendid parquet floors, and Biedermeier and Empire furnishings—are quite a contrast to those of medieval castles elsewhere in the Pfalz. Follow up your visit with a chairlift ride to the vantage point of the Rietburg Castle Ruins, or get your heart racing by following the example of the hardy German tourists who can often be seen hiking uphill between the two sights.

GETTING HERE AND AROUND

Arriving by car, exit the A65 at Edenkoben and follow the signs for Villa Ludwigshöhe. By bus/on foot, take the No. 500 Palatina bus from Neustadt train station to bus stop Edenkoben/Ludwigshöhe and walk the remaining 30 minutes to the palace. On Sunday and holidays, the Palatina Bus No. 506 goes directly to the palace from Edenkoben train station.

EXPLORING

FAMILY **Rietburg Castle Ruins.** From Schloss Villa Ludwigshöhe you can hike (30 minutes) or ride the Rietburgbahn chairlift (10 minutes) up to the Rietburg ruins for a sweeping view of the Pfalz. During a festive *Lampionfahrt* in July and August (dates vary each year), the chairlift operates until midnight on Saturday, and the route is lit by dozens of Chinese lanterns. A restaurant, game park, and playground are on the grounds. ✉ *Villastr. 67, Edenkoben* ☎ *06323/1800* ⊕ *www.rietburgbahn-edenkoben.de* ⛓ *Chairlift from €5* ☉ *Closed early Nov.–early Mar. Closed Mon.–Sat. early–mid-Mar.*

Fodor'sChoice **Schloss Villa Ludwigshöhe.** Bavaria's King Ludwig I's Italian-style villa ★ sits on the slopes overlooking Edenkoben and Rhodt unter Rietburg. The house is now used as a space for art exhibitions and musical events: the former dining room is used for classical concerts; the cellars house exhibitions of 20th-century ceramics; and an extensive collection of paintings and prints by the leading German impressionist Max Slevogt (1868–1932) is also on display. Hourly tours are included in the admission fee.

Schloss Villa Ludwigshöhe is reachable by car, bus, or foot; the No. 506 Palatina bus goes directly from Edenkoben on Sunday and holidays. If you opt to walk, the *Weinlehrpfad* (educational trailpath) takes about 45 minutes. Historical winepresses and vintners' tools are displayed at

10

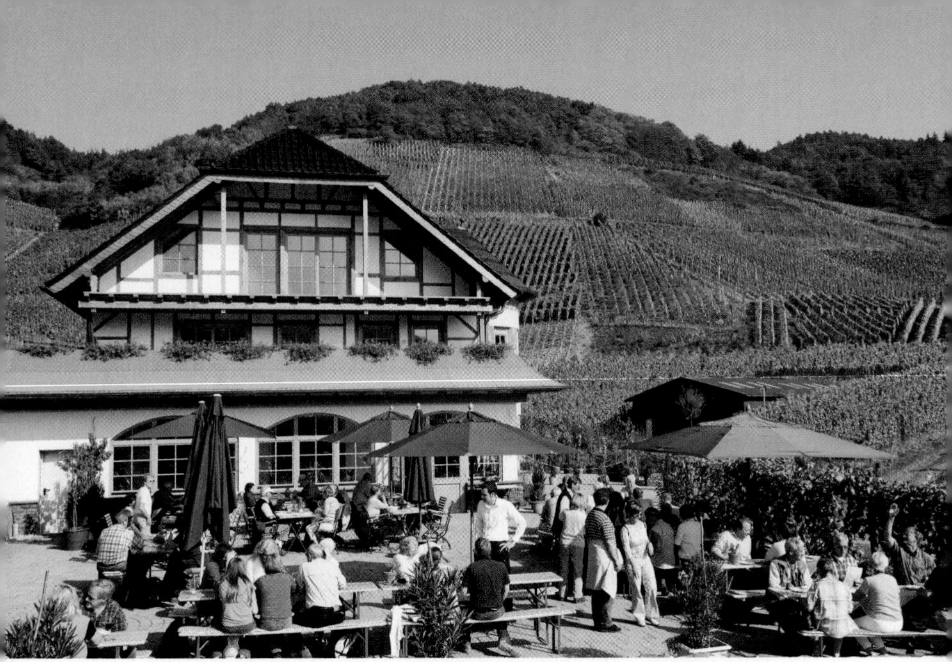

Some wineries offer seasonal outdoor seating areas where guests can enjoy samples.

intervals along the path, which starts at the corner of Landauer Strasse and Villa Strasse in Edenkoben. ✉ *Schloss Villa Ludwigshöhe, Villastr. 64, Edenkoben* ☎ *06323/93016* 🌐 *www.schloss-villa-ludwigshoehe.de* 🎟 *€6* 🕘 *Closed Dec.–mid-Mar. Closed Mon. mid-Mar.–Oct. Closed weekdays in Nov.*

WHERE TO STAY

$$ 🏨 **Alte Rebschule.** Fireside seating in the lobby lounge and spacious
HOTEL rooms (all with a balcony) make for a pleasant, peaceful stay in this former *Rebschule* (vine nursery) on the edge of the forest. **Pros:** beautiful vineyard views; quiet; good range of wellness treatments available. **Cons:** room decor a bit old-fashioned; restaurant expensive; sauna a bit cramped. [$] *Rooms from: €141* ✉ *Theresienstr. 200, 3 km (2 miles) west of Schloss Villa Ludwigshöhe, Rhodt unter Rietburg* ☎ *06323/70440* 🌐 *www.alte-rebschule.de* 🛏 *37 rooms* 🍴 *Free Breakfast.*

ST. MARTIN

26 km (16 miles) north of Annweiler, slightly west of the Wine Road. Turn left at the northern edge of Edenkoben.

This is one of the most charming wine villages in the Pfalz. Narrow cobblestone streets are lined by historic half-timber houses that are now home to inns, restaurants, and wineshops, making the compact, historically preserved *Altstadt* (Old Town) a pleasure to stroll.

EATING WELL IN THE PFALZ

Wine has a big influence on the cuisine here, turning up both in dishes and as an accompaniment to them. *Weinkraut* is sauerkraut braised in white wine; *Dippe-Has'* is hare and pork belly baked in red wine; and *Backes Grumbeere* is scalloped potatoes cooked with bacon, sour cream, white wine, and a layer of pork. Among the regional dishes well suited to wine is the *Pfälzer Teller*, a platter of bratwurst, *Leberknödel* (liver dumplings), and slices of *Saumagen* (a spicy meat-and-potato mixture cooked in a sow's stomach) served with *Sauerkraut* and *Kartoffelpüree* (mashed potatoes) on the side. Seasonal favorites include *Spargel* (white asparagus), *Wild* (game), *Maronen* (chestnuts), and mushrooms, particularly *Pfifferlinge* (chanterelles) and *Steinpilz* (porcini). During the grape harvest, from September through November, try a slice of *Zwiebelkuchen* (onion tart) with a glass of *Federweisser*, fermenting young grape juice—just drink it slowly as it tastes nonalcoholic but can be very potent.

GETTING HERE AND AROUND

The easiest way to reach St. Martin is by car. There's no train station, but Bus Nos. 500 and 501 connect St. Martin with Neustadt and Edenkoben. The trip takes about 20 minutes from Neustadt, a further five to Edenkoben in the same direction, and the buses run approximately every half hour. Alight at "St. Martin, Ort."

EXPLORING

Katholische Pfarrkirche St. Martin (*Catholic church of St. Martin*). Perched dramatically on the northern edge of St. Martin against a backdrop of vineyards, this late-Gothic church was thought to have been built around 1200 (the interior was renovated in the mid-1980s). Renaissance tombstones and a Madonna sculpture carved from a single piece of oak are among the intriguing artworks found inside. ⊠ *Am Pfarrgarten 10* ☎ *02621/628–9822* ⊕ *www.pfarrei-stmartin.de.*

Schloss Kropsburg. Now romantic ruins, this castle was originally constructed in the early 13th century and used by the bishops of Speyer; during the 15th to the 19th century, the Knights of Dalberg resided there. You can see Schloss Kropsburg from the hills above St. Martin. It's not open to the public, but if you hike up to the castle's outskirts, you can enjoy a traditional sausage lunch at the charming inn and restaurant **Burgschänke an der Kropsburg** ($, closed Tuesday) while admiring the views. ⊠ *Kropsburg.*

10

WHERE TO STAY

$$

B&B/INN

Landhaus Christmann. This bright, modern house in the midst of the vineyards outside of St. Martin has stylish rooms and apartments decorated with both antiques and modern furnishings, and is close enough to walk into town. **Pros:** excellent value; quiet location; free Wi-Fi. **Cons:** rooms are very simple; extra charge for breakfast and daily room cleaning for apartments; no elevator. $ *Rooms from: €104* ⊠ *Riedweg 1* ☎ *06323/94270* ⊕ *www.landhaus-christmann.de* ⤴ *9 rooms* ❍❘ *No meals.*

$$
HOTEL
Fodor's Choice
★

⊡ **St. Martiner Castell.** The Mücke family transformed a simple vintner's house into a fine, family-friendly hotel and restaurant, retaining many of the original features, such as exposed beams and an old winepress. **Pros:** free Wi-Fi; free parking; breakfast included. **Cons:** can be noisy; fee for cots; fee for extra bed. $ *Rooms from: €125* ⊠ *Maikammerer Str. 2* ☎ *06323/9510* ⊕ *www.martinercastell. de* ⤴ *24 rooms* ❍❘ *Free Breakfast.*

PERFORMING ARTS

Schloss Villa Ludwigshöhe, Kloster Heilsbruck (a former Cistercian convent near Edenkoben), and **Schloss Edesheim** serve as backdrops for concerts and theater in summer. For a calendar of events, contact the Südliche Weinstrasse regional tourist office in Landau (☎ *06341/940–407* ⊕ *www.suedlicheweinstrasse.de*).

SHOPPING

Weinessiggut Doktorenhof. Artist Georg Wiedemann is responsible for both the contents and the design of the beautiful glass bottles at Germany's premier wine-vinegar manufacturer. The wide range of creatively named vinegars are of organic quality, but are not labeled as such because Georg doesn't want to make public his secret recipes. Vinegar tastings and cellar tours take place on Saturday morning (90 minutes, €25); the shop is in Venningen, 2 km (1 mile) east of Edenkoben. ⊠ *Raiffeisenstr. 5, Venningen* ☎ *06323/5505* ⊕ *www.doktorenhof. de* ⊘ *Closed Sun.*

NEUSTADT

8 km (5 miles) north of St. Martin, 5 km (3 miles) north of Hambach on the Wine Road.

Neustadt and its nine wine suburbs are at the midpoint of the Wine Road and the edge of the district known as Deutsche Weinstrasse–Mittelhaardt. With around 5,000 acres of vines, they together make up Germany's largest wine-making community.

GETTING HERE AND AROUND

Regular trains connect Neustadt with Ludwigshafen (which connects further to Worms and Mainz). Coming from Speyer, change in Schifferstadt. Local buses connect Neustadt to other towns along the Wine Road. Once you're in Neustadt, the best way to get around is on foot.

VISITOR INFORMATION

Contacts Tourist-Information. ⊠ *Tourist-Information, Hetzelpl. 1* ☎ *06321/926–892* ⊕ *www.neustadt.eu.*

Pink and white almond blossoms line the roads of the region in spring.

EXPLORING

FAMILY **Eisenbahn Museum.** Thirty historic train engines and railway cars are on display at the Eisenbahn Museum behind the main train station. Take a ride through the Palatinate Forest on one of the museum's historic steam trains, the *Kuckucksbähnel*, which departs from Track 5 around 10:45 am on intermittent days between May and mid-October, and in December (check the website for the latest schedule). There are special seasonal trips during wine season and during the run up to Christmas. It takes a little more than an hour to cover the 13-km (8-mile) stretch from Neustadt to Elmstein. ⊠ *Neustadt Hauptbahnhof, close to Schillerstr. entrance* ☎ *06321/30390* ⊕ *www.eisenbahnmuseum-neustadt. de* 🖀 *Museum €5; Kuckucksbähnel €14* ⊗ *Closed Jan.–Apr. and Nov.*

Hambacher Schloss. On the Wine Road, it's a brief drive to the Neustadt suburb of Hambach. The sturdy block of Hambacher Schloss is considered the cradle of German democracy. It was here, on May 27, 1832, that 30,000 patriots demonstrated for German unity, raising the German colors for the first time. Inside there are exhibits about the uprising and the history of the castle. The French destroyed the 11th-century imperial fortress in 1688. Reconstruction finally began after World War II, in neo-Gothic style, and the castle is now an impressive setting for theater and concerts. On a clear day, you can see the spire of Strasbourg Cathedral and the northern fringe of the Black Forest from the terrace restaurant. Audio guides are available. ⊠ *Hambacher Schloss* ☎ *06321/926–290* ⊕ *www.hambacher-schloss.de* 🖀 *€6; tours €9.*

BIKING, HIKING, AND WALKING

Country roads and traffic-free vineyard paths make the area perfect for cyclists. There are also well-marked cycling trails, such as the **Radwanderweg Deutsche Weinstrasse**, which runs parallel to its namesake from the French border to Bockenheim, and the **Radweg** (cycling trail) along the Rhine between Worms and Mainz. The Palatinate Forest, Germany's largest single tract of woods, has more than 10,000 km (6,200 miles) of paths.

The **Wanderweg Deutsche Weinstrasse**, a walking route that traverses vineyards, woods, and wine villages, covers the length of the Pfalz. It connects with many trails in the Palatinate Forest that lead to Celtic and Roman landmarks and dozens of castles dating primarily from the 11th to 13th century. In Rheinhessen, you can hike two marked trails parallel to the Rhine: the **Rheinterrassenwanderweg** and the **Rheinhöhenweg** along the heights.

FAMILY **Holiday Park.** The Holiday Park, in Hassloch, 10 km (6 miles) east of Neustadt, is one of Europe's largest amusement parks. The admission fee covers all attractions, shows, special events, and the children's world. The free-fall tower, hell barrels, and Thunder River rafting are long-standing favorites, and Expedition GeForce is one of the largest roller coasters in Europe, with a steep drop of 82 degrees. For a great panoramic view of the surroundings, whirl through the air on Lighthouse-Tower, Germany's tallest carousel (265 feet). On Saturday in summer, the "Party Summer Nights" spectacular features live music and an outdoor laser light show. Hours vary, so be sure to check the web site if you want to go. ⊠ *Holiday Parkstr. 1–5* ☎ *06324/59930* ⊕ *www. holidaypark.de* ⌑ *€33* ⊘ *Closed early Nov.–late Mar.*

Marktplatz (*Market square*). The Marktplatz is the focal point of the Old Town and a beehive of activity when farmers come to sell their wares on Tuesday and Saturday, plus Thursday from April to October. The square itself is ringed by baroque and Renaissance buildings (Nos. 1, 4, 8, and 11) and the Gothic **Stiftskirche** (Collegiate Church), built as a burial church for the Palatinate counts. In summer, concerts take place in the church (Saturday 11:30–noon). Afterward, you can ascend the southern tower (187 feet) for a bird's-eye view of the town. The world's largest cast-iron bell—weighing more than 17 tons—hangs in the northern tower. Indoors, see the elaborate tombstones near the choir and the fanciful grotesque figures carved into the baldachins and corbels. ⊠ *Marktpl.* ⊕ *www.stiftskirche-nw.de.*

Otto Dill Museum. The impressionist painter Otto Dill (1884–1957), a native of Neustadt, is known for his powerful animal portraits (especially lions, tigers, and horses) and vivid landscapes. The museum dedicated to his work displays some 100 oil paintings and 50 drawings and watercolors from the Manfred Vetter collection. ⊠ *Manfred-Vetter-Str. 8, at Rathausstr.* ☎ *06321/398–321* ⊕ *www.otto-dill-museum.de* ⊘ *Closed Mon., Tues., and Thurs.*

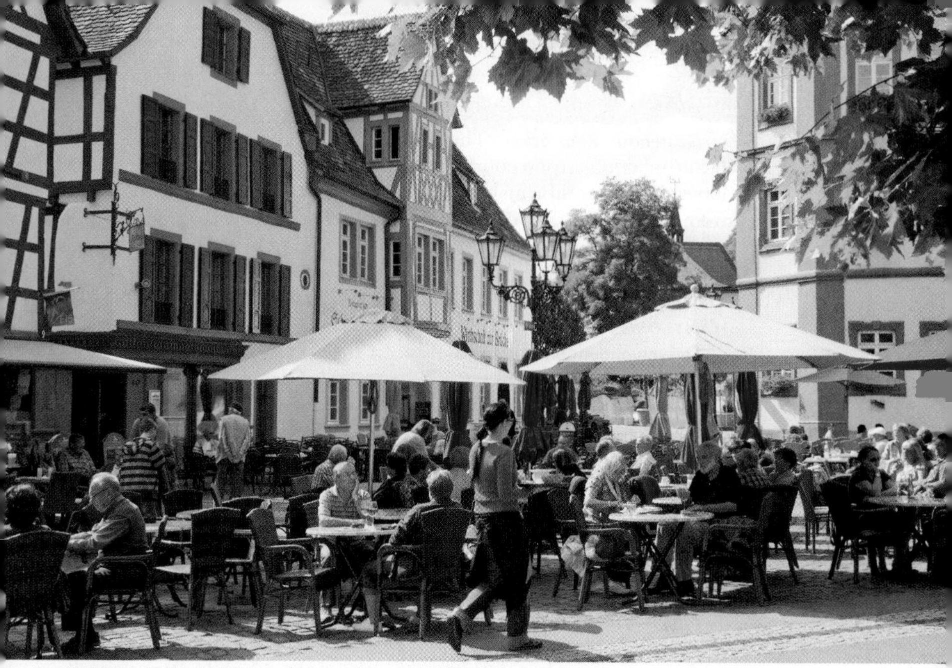

The Marktplatz in Neustadt is your best bet for a meal alfresco.

WHERE TO EAT

$$ GERMAN 🍴 **Altstadtkeller bei Jürgen.** Tucked behind a wooden portal on a cobblestone street, this vaulted sandstone "cellar" (it's actually on the ground floor) feels very cozy, but equally inviting is the Tuscan-style terrace, with its citrus, olive, palm, and fig trees. The regular menu includes rustic regional dishes as well as Mediterranean-inspired options. **Known for:** very friendly owner; well-chosen wine list; welcoming atmopshere. [$] *Average main: €19* ✉ *Kunigundenstr. 2* ☎ *06321/32320* 🌐 *www.altstadtkeller-neustadt.de* 🕒 *Closed Mon. No dinner Sun.*

10

$$$$ GERMAN Fodor's Choice ★ 🍴 **Urgestein.** Dine inside the cozy brick-lined former horse stables or outside on the lovely patio at this restaurant inside the historic stone houses of the Steinhauser Hof. There's no à la carte ordering here, only ambitious tasting menus: choose from one of two five-course menus (extra for wine pairings), or splurge even more on the seven-course surprise menu, which includes the wine. **Known for:** using local ingredients; wine list with more than 350 Pfalz wines; vegetarian menu. [$] *Average main: €100* ✉ *Steinhauser Hof, Rathausstr. 6* ☎ *06321/489–060* 🌐 *www.restaurant-urgestein.de* 🕒 *Closed Sun. and Mon. No lunch.*

$ WINE BAR 🍴 **Weinstube Eselsburg.** The *Esel* (donkey) lends its name to his wine pub and one of its specialties, *Eselssuppe,* a hearty soup of pork, beef, and vegetables. The excellent menu of regional specialties is dictated by the seasons, and the ingredients—from cheese and meat to fruit and vegetables—are all sourced locally. **Known for:** open hearth in winter; flower-filled courtyard in summer; wine list featuring some of the best local wineries. [$] *Average main: €14* ✉ *Kurpfalzstr. 62* ☎ *06321/66984* 🌐 *www.eselsburg.de* 🕒 *Closed Sun. and Mon. No lunch.*

WHERE TO STAY

$ B&B/INN 🏨 **Gästehaus Rebstöckel.** This 17th-century stone guesthouse has a beautiful cobblestone courtyard and magnificent fig tree; all the rooms have blond-wood furnishings, and some have kitchenettes. **Pros:** quiet; friendly; rustic location. **Cons:** no hotel services or real reception; additional fee for baby bed, room charge for children; online reservations but you still have to pay cash. [$] *Rooms from: €89* ✉ *Kreuzstr. 11, Diedesfeld* ☎ *06321/484–060* 🌐 *www.rebstoeckel.eu* 💳 *No credit cards* 🛏 *5 rooms* 🍴 *Breakfast.*

$ RENTAL 🏨 **Ferienwohnungen Mithras Stuben.** In the picturesque village of Gimmeldingen, the convivial proprietor and wine devotee Bernd Hagedorn rents four spacious apartments with contemporary furnishings, Oriental rugs, and modern baths. **Pros:** spacious accommodations; perfect for longer stays; very good restaurant with extensive local and international wine list. **Cons:** no elevator; no air-conditioning; restaurant closed Wednesday and Thursday; breakfast is available in the restaurant opposite. [$] *Rooms from: €70* ✉ *Loblocherstr. 34, Gimmeldingen* ☎ *06321/679–0335, 06321/6796–8200 after 6 pm* 🌐 *www.weinstube-kommerzienrat.de* 💳 *No credit cards* 🛏 *4 apartments* 🍴 *No meals.*

$$ HOTEL 🏨 **Steinhäuser Hof.** This architectural gem dates back to 1276 and is one of the oldest preserved stone mansions in Rhineland-Palatinate and is in a prime location in the center of the Altstadt. **Pros:** friendly staff; Michelin-starred restaurant in hotel; free Wi-Fi. **Cons:** small, basic rooms; some street noise; no parking (though a public lot is nearby). [$] *Rooms from: €100* ✉ *Rathausstr. 6* ☎ *06321/489–060* 🌐 *www.steinhaeuserhof.de* 🛏 *6 rooms* 🍴 *No meals.*

SPEYER

25 km (15 miles) east of Neustadt via B-39, 22 km (14 miles) south of Mannheim via B-9 and B-44.

Speyer is a picturesque and easily walkable town filled with interesting sights and a wonderful Christmas market in the winter. It's also a must-visit for those who like to eat well: there's a huge choice of traditional German restaurants and pretty beer gardens, and in summer, the main street (Maximilianstrasse) is packed with the tables and chairs of the plethora of cafés that line it. It was one of the great cities of the Holy Roman Empire, founded in pre-Celtic times, taken over by the Romans, and expanded in the 11th century by the Salian emperors. Between 1294, when it was declared a Free Imperial City, and 1570, no fewer than 50 imperial diets were convened here. The term *Protestant* derives from the Diet of 1529, referring to those who protested when the religious freedom granted to evangelicals at the Diet of 1526 was revoked and a return to Catholicism was decreed. The neo-Gothic **Gedächtniskirche** on Bartolomäus-Weltz-Platz commemorates those 16th-century Protestants.

GETTING HERE AND AROUND

Speyer is a little way off the German Wine Road. It is served by regular trains from Mannheim (around 30 minutes) and Mainz (approximately 1 hour). Buses go down the main street, but the center is compact enough that getting around on foot is not a problem.

TOURS

From April to October, you can take a short river cruise through the network of branching arms of the river to the north or south of Speyer to discover the idyllic landscape of the ancient, forested islands along the *Altrhein,* the original course of the Rhine. The islands are home to rare flora, fauna, and many birds. There are grand views of the cathedral from the boat.

Fahrgastschiff Pfälzerland. Enjoy a peaceful tour of the Speyer harbor and its surrounding river network on a ship built for 250 passengers. Coffee and homemade cakes are available on board. There are two 90-minute tours are offered from Tuesday to Sunday and on holidays, departing from the Leinpfad. ⊠ *Leinpfad 1a, On Rheinuferpromenade* 🕿 *06232/71366* ⊕ *www.personenschifffahrt-streib.de* 🖅 *From €8* ⊘ *Closed Mon.*

MS Sea Life Speyer. Seasonal boat tours depart from just outside the Sea Life Aquarium at noon, 2, and 4. The trip lasts about 1½ hours and offers a unique look at Speyer's old harbor and its fascinating network of rivers. ⊠ *Hafenstr. 22* 🕿 *06232/291–150* ⊕ *www.ms-sealife.de* 🖅 *€10* ⊘ *Closed Nov.–late Mar.*

VISITOR INFORMATION

Pick up a SpeyerCARD (€4, €10 family card) at the Altpörtel, Judenhof, or the Tourist-Information Office, and enjoy free entry to various sites as well as discounts for a variety of museums, tours, shops, and restaurants. A free three-day pass is also available with a two-night stay at certain hotels. A variety of guided tours are available; ask at the Tourist Office for details.

Contacts Speyer Tourist-Information Office. ⊠ *Maximilianstr. 13* 🕿 *06232/142–392* ⊕ *www.speyer.de.*

10

EXPLORING

Altpörtel. Ascend the Altpörtel, the impressive town gate, for a grand view of Maximilianstrasse, the now busy shopping street that once led kings and emperors straight to the cathedral. ⊠ *Postpl.* 🖅 *€3* ⊘ *Closed Nov.–Mar.*

Historisches Museum der Pfalz (*Palatinate Historical Museum*). Opposite the cathedral, the museum houses the **Domschatz** (Cathedral Treasury). Other collections chronicle the art and cultural history of Speyer and the Pfalz from the Stone Age to modern times. Don't miss the Golden Hat of Schifferstadt, a Bronze Age headdress used in religious ceremonies dating back to approximately 1300 BC. The **Wine Museum** houses the world's oldest bottle of wine, which is still liquid and dates to circa AD 300. The giant 35-foot-long wooden winepress from 1727 is also worth a look. ✉ *Dompl. 4* ☎ *06232/13250* 🌐 *www.museum.speyer.de* 🎟 *From €7* 🕓 *Closed Mon.*

Fodor's Choice ★ **Jewish Quarter.** Speyer was an important medieval Jewish cultural center. Behind the Palatinate Historical Museum is the Jewish quarter, where you'll find synagogue remains from 1104; Germany's oldest (circa 1126) ritual baths, the 33-foot-deep *Mikwe*; and the **Museum SchPIRA,** which displays objects such as gravestones and coins from the Middle Ages . ✉ *Kleine Pfaffeng. 21, near Judeng.* ☎ *06232/291–971 Museum SchPIRA* 🎟 *€3* 🕓 *Closed Mon., and Nov.–Mar.*

Fodor's Choice ★ **Kaiserdom** (*Imperial Cathedral*). The Kaiserdom, one of the finest Romanesque cathedrals in the world and a UNESCO World Heritage site, conveys the pomp and majesty of the early Holy Roman emperors. It was built between 1030 and 1061 by the emperors Konrad II, Henry III, and Henry IV. The last replaced the flat ceiling with groin vaults in the late 11th century, an innovative feat in its day. A restoration program in the 1950s returned the building to almost exactly its original condition. The four towers symbolize the four seasons and the idea that the power of the empire extends in all four directions. Look up as you enter the nearly 100-foot-high portal; it's richly carved with mythical creatures. In contrast to Gothic cathedrals, whose walls are supported externally by flying buttresses, allowing for a minimum of masonry and a maximum of light, at Speyer the columns supporting the roof are massive. The **Krypta** lies beneath the chancel. It's the largest crypt in Germany and is strikingly beautiful in its simplicity. Four emperors, four kings, and three empresses are buried here. ✉ *Edith-Stein-Pl.* ☎ *06232/1020* 🎟 *Donation requested; crypt €4; audio guide €8.*

Fodor's Choice ★ **Technik Museum** (*The Technical Museum of Speyer*). Built on the site of a former aircraft works just outside the city center (about a 10-minute walk from the Kaiserdom), the Technik Museum houses 300 exhibits including space suits, a landing capsule, and an original Russian BURAN space shuttle as part of Europe's largest aerospace exhibition. In addition, there are walk-in exhibits including a Boeing 747 and a 46-meter-long U9 submarine; and there's also a collection of vintage cars, ships, locomotives, and motorcycles. While you're here, don't miss one of the world's biggest collections of mechanical musical instruments at the Wilhelmsbau Museum (entry included in ticket price) or a movie on the curved screen of the IMAX DOME theater. Allow at least three hours to visit this extensive museum, which covers several large buildings. ✉ *Am Technik Museum 1* ☎ *06232/67080* 🌐 *speyer.technik-museum.de* 🎟 *From €16.*

WHERE TO EAT

$ GERMAN 🍴 **Alter Hammer.** Speyer's oldest beer garden, a 15-minute stroll through the gardens behind the cathedral, is a popular, leafy spot to pass the afternoon. There's a good selection of beer, and the portions of rustic, regional fare are enormous. **Known for:** riverside location; friendly service; Wurstsalat mit Pommes (salad with bologna sausage, onions, and gherkins served with fries). [$] *Average main: €13* ✉ *Leinpfad 1c* ☎ *06232/75539* 🌐 *www.alter-hammer.de* 💳 *No credit cards.*

$$ ✕ **Ratskeller.** Friendly service and fresh seasonal dishes make for an
GERMAN   enjoyable dining experience in the town hall's vaulted cellar (from
1578). The frequently changing menu offers entrées such as *Sauerbraten nach Grossmutters Art* (sour pot roast the way grandma used to make it) or *Bachsaibling* (brook trout) in a red-wine-butter sauce. **Known for:** good service; cozy atmosphere; shady terrace. $ *Average main: €17* ✉ *Maximilianstr. 12* ☎ *06232/78612* ⊕ *www.ratskeller-speyer.de* ☾ *Closed Mon. No dinner Sun.*

$ ✕ **Weinstube Rabennest.** It's small and often packed with local families,
GERMAN   but the rustic cooking in this cozy restaurant is worth the wait: hearty portions of regional specialties will delight both your mouth and your wallet. The *Leberknödel* (liver dumplings) and *Rumpsteak* (rump steak) are both excellent, and there's also a nice selection of fresh salads. **Known for:** good value; patio seating in summer; cozy atmosphere. $ *Average main: €11* ✉ *Korng. 5* ☎ *06232/623–857* ⊕ *www.weinstube-rabennest.de* ▭ *No credit cards.*

$$ ✕ **Wirtschaft Zum Alten Engel.** This 19th-century vaulted brick cellar has
GERMAN   rustic wood furnishings and cozy niches perfect for settling down for an evening of hearty Pfälzer and wider German food. The restaurant has long been a promoter of the global Slow Food movement, and its dishes, created using locally sourced ingredients, include *Blutwurst* (blood sausage), *Maultaschen* (large ravioli), and *Tafelspitz* (slow-cooked rump cap of beef, with horseradish sauce). **Known for:** seasonal menu; good selection of wines, brandies, and German liqueurs; friendly service. $ *Average main: €18* ✉ *Mühlturmstr. 7* ☎ *06232/70914* ⊕ *www.zum-altenengel.de* ☾ *No lunch.*

WHERE TO STAY

$$ ▦ **Hotel Domhof.** Positioned a very short walk from the cathedral end
HOTEL   of Maximilianstrasse, the Domhof makes for an ideal base for exploring the town. **Pros:** very central; breakfast can be eaten on the terrace in summer; lots of care taken over details. **Cons:** cathedral bells may disturb light sleepers; no air-conditioning; decor rather outdated. $ *Rooms from: €126* ✉ *Bauhof 3* ☎ *06232/13290* ⊕ *www.domhof.de* ⇆ *49 rooms* ⦿❘ *Free Breakfast.*

$ ▦ **Hotel Goldener Engel.** A scant two blocks west of the Altpörtel is
HOTEL   the "Golden Angel," a friendly, family-run hotel offering individually furnished rooms (with antiques and innovative metal-and-wood designer furniture). **Pros:** friendly; good location; free Wi-Fi. **Cons:** some rooms are a little small; no air-conditioning; noise from the main street may disturb light sleepers. $ *Rooms from: €92* ✉ *Mühlturmstr. 5–7* ☎ *06232/13260* ⊕ *www.goldener-engel-speyer.de* ⇆ *46 rooms* ⦿❘ *Free Breakfast.*

10

NIGHTLIFE AND PERFORMING ARTS

City highlights for music lovers are **Orgelfrühling,** the organ concerts in the Gedächtniskirche (Memorial Church) in spring, the jazz festival in mid-August, and the concerts in the cathedral during September's **Internationale Musiktage.** Contact the Speyer tourist office for program details and tickets.

Kulturhof Flachsgasse. Walk into the town-hall courtyard to enter the Kulturhof Flachsgasse, home of the city's art collection and special exhibitions. ⊠ *Flachsg. 3* ☎ *06232/142–399.*

DEIDESHEIM

8 km (5 miles) north of Neustadt via the Wine Road, B-271.

The immaculately preserved half-timber houses and historical facades lining its narrow streets fit perfectly with Deidesheim's reputation as one of the most renowned wine towns in the Pfalz. The grapes have made winemakers here a great deal of money over the centuries, and it shows: despite its size, it's a town that boasts Michelin-starred restaurants and world-class hotels owned by each of its biggest wine producers, Bassermann, Buhl, and Bürklin-Wolf. Sites of interest include the Gothic Church of St. Ulrich, the Rathaus (Town Hall), and the elegant Hotel Deidesheimer Hof. In August, the **Deidesheim Weinkerwe** (wine festival) begins at the Marktplatz, and in December, it's the site of a lively Christmas market. The main reason to visit, however, remains the opportunity to taste some of the best wines the Pfalz has to offer. Most of the local *Weingüter* (wineries) lining the streets are open to visitors year-round.

VISITOR INFORMATION

Contacts Deidesheim Tourist Service Center. ⊠ *Bahnhofstr. 5* ☎ *06326/96770* ⊕ *www.deidesheim.de.*

EXPLORING

Church of St. Ulrich. A Gothic gem inside and out, this is the only 15th-century church in the Palatinate region whose walls have been entirely preserved, though the interior has changed according to the style of the times. Despite having been looted during the French Revolution and turned first into a wine warehouse and later a military prison, the basic exterior structure of the church hasn't been altered. The interior includes stained glass that dates from the Middle Ages and wooden figures from around 1500. ⊠ *Marktpl.*

Rathaus und Museum für Weinkultur (*Town Hall and Museum of Viniculture*). The old Rathaus, whose doorway is crowned by a baldachin and baroque dome, is at the Marktplatz. The attractive open staircase leading up to the entrance is the site of the festive *Geissbock-Versteigerung* (billy-goat auction) every Pentecost Tuesday, followed by a parade and folk dancing. The goat is the tribute neighboring Lambrecht has paid Deidesheim since 1404 for grazing rights. Inside, in addition to a richly appointed *Ratssaal* (council chamber) is a museum of wine culture, which examines the importance of wine throughout history. ✉ *Historisches Rathaus, Marktpl. 9* ☎ *06326/981–561* ⊕ *www.weinkultur-deidesheim.de* 🖃 *Donation requested* 🕑 *Closed Sun.–Tues. and Thurs.*

Schloss Deidesheim. Vines, flowers, and fig trees cloak the houses behind St. Ulrich on Heumarktstrasse and its extension, Deichelgasse (nicknamed Feigengasse because of its *Feigenbäume*—fig trees). To see the workshops and ateliers of about a dozen local artists, sculptors, and goldsmiths, follow the *Künstler-Rundweg,* a signposted trail (black on yellow signs). Cross the Wine Road to reach the grounds of Schloss Deidesheim, now a pub-restaurant (open April–October). The bishops of Speyer built a moated castle on the site in the 13th century. Twice destroyed and rebuilt, the present castle dates from 1817, and the moats have been converted into gardens. ✉ *Schlossstr. 4* ☎ *06326/96690* ⊕ *www.schloss-deidesheim.de* 🕑 *Closed Mon.–Thurs. Nov.–Mar.; closed Tues. and Wed. Apr.–Oct. No lunch Mon. and Thurs.*

WHERE TO EAT

$$$$
FUSION
Fodor's Choice
★
✕ **L.A. Jordan im Ketschauer Hof.** An 18th-century complex is the home to the Bassermann-Jordan wine estate and an elegant restaurant, which has one Michelin star. Choose a five- or seven-course menu from the selection of Mediterranean-influenced Asian dishes, or order à la carte; and select a wine from more than 500 bottles from all over the world, including every vintage of Bassermann-Jordan wine since 1870. **Known for:** sleek, modern decor in historic buildings; creative modern cooking; excellent service. $ *Average main: €35* ✉ *Ketschauerhofstr. 1* ☎ *06326/70000* ⊕ *www.ketschauer-hof.com* 🕑 *Closed Sun. and Mon. No lunch.*

$$$
GERMAN
✕ **Restaurant St. Urban.** Named after the patron saint of the wine industry, this upscale restaurant offers traditional Palatinate cuisine and what is probably the best wine list in the regions. An inviting outdoor terrace offers an affordable lunch menu while the restaurant offers an excellent dinner, including a prix-fixe menu with wine pairings. **Known for:** historic setting; selection of banqueting rooms; excellent service. $ *Average main: €23* ✉ *Hotel Deidesheimer Hof, Marktpl. 1* ☎ *06326/96870* ⊕ *www.deidesheimerhof.de.*

WHERE TO STAY

$$$
HOTEL
Fodor's Choice
★
🏨 **Hotel Deidesheimer Hof.** Despite the glamour of some of its clientele—heads of state, entertainers, and sports stars line the guest book—this hotel retains its country charm and friendly service. **Pros:** some rooms have whirlpool baths; friendly staff; rooms for allergy sufferers available. **Cons:** breakfast is expensive; nearby church bells ring hourly all night; some complaints of slow Wi-Fi. $ *Rooms from: €177* ✉ *Marktpl. 1* ☎ *06326/96870* ⊕ *www.deidesheimerhof.de* 🕑 *Closed 2 wks in Jan.* ⤴ *28 rooms* ⊙⏴ *No meals.*

$$$$
HOTEL
🏨 **Hotel Ketschauer Hof.** This sleek, sophisticated former manor house, one of the few modern design hotels in the region, attracts a discerning crowd. **Pros:** high-speed Wi-Fi; spa facilities; air-conditioned. **Cons:**

10

expensive; few public spaces in the hotel; fee for additional beds and baby beds. $ *Rooms from: €230 ⊠ Ketschauerhofstr. 1 ☎ 06326/70000 ⊕ www.ketschauer-hof.com ⇄ 18 rooms ⊙❘ Free Breakfast.*

$$ 🍽 **Kaisergarten.** At the younger, trendier sister of the nearby
HOTEL Ketschauer Hof, the ambience is relaxed but classy: rooms are
Fodor's Choice decorated in earthy tones, and the deluxe doubles and suites have
★ private balconies. **Pros:** free high-speed Wi-Fi; use of gym, spa, and pool included; all rooms are air-conditioned. **Cons:** breakfast costs extra; parking costs extra; cots and extra beds cost extra. $ *Rooms from: €140 ⊠ Weinstr. 12 ☎ 06326/700–077 ⊕ www.kaisergarten-deidesheim.com ⇄ 85 rooms ⊙❘ No meals.*

$ 🍽 **Weingut & Landhotel Lucashof.** The beautifully decorated, modern guest
HOTEL rooms are named after famous vineyards in Forst, and six have balconies—the Pechstein room is particularly nice. **Pros:** quiet location; friendly; rooms have a balcony or terrace. **Cons:** outside of Deidesheim; difficult to reach without a car; no Wi-Fi. $ *Rooms from: €75 ⊠ Wiesenweg 1a, Forst ☎ 06326/336 ⊕ www.lucashof.de ⊟ No credit cards ⇄ 7 rooms ⊙❘ Free Breakfast.*

BAD DÜRKHEIM

6 km (4 miles) north of Deidesheim on B-271.

This pretty spa town is nestled into the hills at the edge of the Palatinate Forest and ringed by vineyards. The saline springs discovered here in 1338 are the source of today's drinking and bathing cures, and at harvest time there's a detoxifying *Traubenkur* (grape-juice cure). The town is the site of the Dürkheimer Wurstmarkt, the world's largest wine festival, held in mid-September. Legendary quantities of *Weck, Worscht, und Woi* (dialect for "bread rolls, sausage, and wine") are consumed at the fair, including enough wine to fill half a million *Schoppen*, the region's traditional glasses, which hold a half liter (about a pint). The festival grounds are also the site of the world's largest wine cask, the **Dürkheimer Riesenfass,** which has a capacity of 450,000 gallons. Built in 1934 by an ambitious cooper, the cask is now a restaurant that can seat more than 450 people.

GETTING HERE AND AROUND
Regional trains link Bad Dürkheim with Freinsheim and Neustadt. Once in town, all the hotels and restaurants are within easy walking distance.

VISITOR INFORMATION
Contacts Bad Dürkheim Tourist Information. ⊠ *Kurbrunnenstr. 14* ☎ *06322/935–140 ⊕ www.bad-duerkheim.com.*

EXPLORING

Schloss- und Festungsruine Hardenburg (*Hardenburg Castle Ruins*). The massive ruins of 13th-century Hardenburg Castle lie 3 km (2 miles) west of Kloster Limburg (via B-37). In its heyday, it was inhabited by more than 200 people, but it burned down in 1794. In the visitor center there's an exhibit about the fascinating history of the castle, and various events are held here throughout the year, including a medieval fair in September. ✉ *Kaiserslauterer Str.* ☎ *06322/7530* 🌐 *www.schloss-hardenburg.de* 🎟 *€5* 🕒 *Closed Dec. and Jan. Closed weekdays Feb.–mid-Mar. and Nov. Closed Mon. mid-Mar.–Oct.*

Heidenmauer (*Heathen Wall*). One kilometer (½ mile) northwest of town lies the Heidenmauer, the remains of an ancient Celtic ring wall more than 2 km (1 mile) in circumference and up to 20 feet thick in parts. The remnants are on the Kastanienberg, above the quarry. Nearby are the rock drawings at **Kriemhildenstuhl,** an old Roman quarry where the legionnaires of Mainz excavated sandstone. ✉ *Schloss- und Festungsruine Hardenburg.*

Klosterruine Limburg (*Limburg Abbey Ruins*). Overlooking the suburb of Grethen are the ruins of Kloster Limburg. Emperor Konrad II laid the cornerstone in 1030, supposedly on the same day that he laid the cornerstone of the Kaiserdom in Speyer. The monastery was never completely rebuilt after a fire in 1504, but it's a majestic backdrop for open-air performances in summer. ✉ *Luitpoldweg 1.*

WHERE TO EAT

$ GERMAN 🍴 **Dürkheimer Riesenfass.** Sure, it's a bit of a tourist trap, but then again, how often do you get the chance to eat in the world's biggest wine barrel? The two-story "giant cask" is divided into various rooms and niches with rustic wood furnishings, but you can also sit outside to enjoy the restaurant's regional wines, Pfälzer specialties, and international dishes. **Known for:** wine tastings; banquet hall (venture upstairs for a look); location of world's largest annual wine festival. [$] *Average main: €14* ✉ *St. Michael Allee 1* ☎ *06322/2143* 🌐 *www.duerkheimer-fass.de* 🕒 *Closed Wed.*

$$ ECLECTIC 🍴 **Weinstube Petersilie.** Behind a group of lush, potted plants and a sign on a pink-and-white house reading "Bier- und Weinstube Tenne" is Petersilie, a traditional wine tavern in the heart of the town on the Römerplatz. The menu offers both homey Pfälzer fare and international cuisine, from *Saumagen* (stuffed pig's stomach) to chili con carne. **Known for:** outdoor patio; dozy interior; central location. [$] *Average main: €16* ✉ *Römerpl. 12* ☎ *06322/4394* 🌐 *www.weinstube-petersilie.de* 💳 *No credit cards.*

10

WHERE TO STAY

$$ HOTEL 🏨 **Mercure Hotel Bad Dürkheim an den Salinen.** Within walking distance to the center of town, this well-maintained chain hotel offers free admission to the Salinarium water park and spa next door, where there are indoor and outdoor pools and wellness treatments. **Pros:** free Wi-Fi; plenty of free parking; three restaurants and two bars in the hotel. **Cons:** not a lot of character; dated decor; in summer, some noise from the open-air bar. [$] *Rooms from: €160* ✉ *Kurbrunnenstr. 30–32* ☎ *06322/6010* 🌐 *www.accorhotels.com* 🛏 *100 rooms* 🍽 *Free Breakfast.*

$ RENTAL 🏠 **Weingut Fitz-Ritter.** At the Fitz-Ritter wine estate there are two different places to stay: a centuries-old stone cottage that sleeps up to four people and has its own pool on the parklike grounds, and a suite that sleeps four, plus four further rooms with shared bathroom and kitchen facilities in a courtyard full of oleanders, palms, fig trees, and nesting swallows. **Pros:** quiet location amid the vines; friendly staff; short walk to the town center. **Cons:** additional cleaning charge for cottage; on weekends April–October, all four rooms need to be rented together; no breakfast. [$] *Rooms from: €45* ✉ *Weinstr. Nord 51* ☎ *06322/5389* 🌐 *www.fitz-ritter.de* 🛏 *6 rooms* 🍴 *No meals.*

$ B&B/INN 🏠 **Weingut und Gästehaus Ernst Karst und Sohn.** Rooms at this cheerful guesthouse in the middle of the vineyards are airy and furnished mostly in pine; all of them have splendid views of the countryside, which you are invited to explore on bikes that you can borrow. **Pros:** quiet vineyard location; friendly staff; excellent spot for cycle tours and hiking. **Cons:** apartments do not include breakfast; far from the sights; use of the sauna costs extra. [$] *Rooms from: €80* ✉ *In den Almen 15* ☎ *06322/2862* 🌐 *www.weingut-karst.de* 💳 *No credit cards* 🕑 *Closed Nov.–Feb.* 🛏 *4 rooms* 🍴 *Free Breakfast.*

NIGHTLIFE

Spielbank (*Casino*). This casino, which first opened in 1949, opens daily at 11 am for the slot machines, 2 pm for roulette and poker, and 6 pm for blackjack; jacket and tie are no longer required, but tennis shoes, T-shirts, and shorts are not allowed. Be certain to bring your passport for identification; the minimum age is 18. On a sunny day, take a walk around the pebbled garden and down the steps into the beautiful Kurpark. ✉ *Schlosspl. 6–7* 🌐 *spielbank-bad-duerkheim.de* 🕑 *Check website for holiday closing times.*

SHOPPING AND SPAS

Freizeitbad Salinarium. The Freizeitbad Salinarium houses all kinds of bathing facilities, including thermal baths, herbal steam baths, a sauna, and a hammam (Turkish bath). The sauna is mixed apart from on women-only Thursday. Prices are very reasonable ✉ *Kurbrunnenstr. 14* ☎ *06322/935–865* 🌐 *www.salinarium.de.*

Weindom. This small shop next to the Dürkheimer Riesenfass offers a selection of more than 200 wines from Bad Dürkheim and around, available by the bottle or box. It also sells other grape-related products and accessories. ✉ *St.-Michaels-Allee 10* ☎ *06322/949–222* 🌐 *www.weindom.de.*

FREINSHEIM

7 km (4½ miles) northeast of Bad Dürkheim, via Kallstadt, right turn to Freinsheim is signposted midway through Kallstadt.

The small, very pretty town of Freinsheim is known for its 1.3-km (0.8-mile) fortification wall, which was built between 1350 and 1514 and surrounds its medieval Old Town. Most of the wall—though only five of its original towers—remains intact, and a stroll around its inner perimeter makes for a fascinating walk (speak to the very helpful tourism office for tours in English). The town was partially destroyed a number of times until it was completely burned down by the French in 1689. It was later rebuilt in the baroque style, and when the almond trees blossom in Spring and leaves cover the ubiquitous vines, Freinsheim could not be more picturesque. Surrounded by vineyards, the area is well known for its gastronomy and viticulture, with wine festivals and wine walks taking place throughout the warmer months.

GETTING HERE AND AROUND

Freinsheim is located directly on the German Wine Route, so it is convenient to reach by car or bicycle; however, it's also well-connected by direct trains from Neustadt, Bad Dürkheim, and Mainz. The train station is a 10-minute walk from the center of the old town, but once you're there, Freinsheim's cobbled streets are easily navigable by foot.

VISITOR INFORMATION

i-Punkt Freinsheim. Drop in to the tourist office for inspiration for things to do in Freinsheim and around: there are brochures galore listing events including cycling tours, almond blossom festivals and wine and gourmet hikes. ✉ *Hauptstr. 2* ☎ *06353/989–294* 🌐 *www.freinsheim.de.*

EXPLORING

Freinsheim's Christmas market, with its nativity scene complete with live animals, is one of the region's loveliest; the town's food and wine festival takes place in September, offering a 7-km (4.3-mile) hike through the vineyards, with 20 food and wine stands to pause at along the way.

Kallstadt. From Freinsheim, it's a gentle if slightly hilly 3-km (1.8-mile) walk (or cycle) through the vineyards to Kallstadt, a village known outside of Germany for two very famous exports to the United States: food entrepreneur Henry J. Heinz and the family Drumpf (now known as Trump). In the Pfalz, however, Kallstadt is best known for *Saumagen,* both the local dish (stuffed pig's stomach) and the vineyard of the same name. Enjoy a glass at **Weinhaus Henninger** along the very cute Weinstrasse (no lunch Monday), and take a short stroll around the tiny village before returning to Freinsheim. ✉ *Kallstadt.*

WHERE TO EAT

$ INTERNATIONAL

🍴 **Hofschänke Im Zwinger.** Tucked away off the street through an easy-to-miss entrance just inside the outer iron gate, this restaurant offers a leafy, decorated courtyard in which to sit and enjoy a glass of local wine, coffee, and homemade cake, or lunch or dinner from a short but varied international menu that includes Mediterranean antipasti, burgers, and salads. The *Flammkuchen* (Tarte flambée) are freshly made to order and cooked with your chosen toppings in a stone oven, and they're absolutely delicious. **Known for:** relaxed atmosphere; homemade dishes and light bites; special Christmas-market menu during Advent. [$] *Average* *main: €10* ✉ *Herrenstr. 14* ☎ *06353/959–8998* 🌐 *www.imzwinger.de* ⏲ *Closed Mon.–Thurs.* 💳 *No credit cards.*

$ GERMAN 🍴 **Strausswirtschaft Weisenborn.** Situated right on the road as you arrive in Kallstadt from Freinsheim, this cozy, traditional little *Strausswirtschaft* (a seasonal pop-up run by vintners) with its leafy courtyard is perfect for restoring yourself after a cycle or hike, whatever the weather. If you don't think you'll have space for a *Pfälzer Teller* (*Saumagen* with a sausage, a liver dumpling and sauerkraut), there's a variety of bread and cold meat or cheese combinations to choose from. **Known for:** good, simple, hearty cooking; easy to find; friendly service. [$] *Average main: €8* ✉ *Freinsheimer Str. 41, Kallstadt* ☎ *06322/8930* 🌐 *www.weingut-weisenborn.de* ⏲ *Closed mid-Dec.–mid-Mar. Closed Mon. and Tues. mid-Mar.–June and Sept.–mid-Dec. No lunch Wed.–Fri.*

WHERE TO STAY

$ RENTAL FAMILY 🏨 **Wein- und Feriengut Altes Landhaus.** A great deal of love and thought went into transforming this old family hotel into five apartments just outside the center of the town; all are well equipped, individually decorated, and carefully maintained. **Pros:** very friendly and welcoming; lovely outdoor spaces; relaxed atmosphere. **Cons:** three-night minimum in some seasons; no air-conditioning; outside the medieval wall. [$] *Rooms from: €86* ✉ *Hauptstr. 37* ☎ *06353/93630* 🌐 *www.altes-landhaus.de* 🛏 *5 apartments* 🍽 *No meals.*

SHOPPING

Alte Bäckerei. In the tiny, picturesque courtyard of these lovingly restored former stables is the fig tree, which, thanks to a windfall of fruit one year, inspired the beginnings of the even tinier shop in the corner. The chutneys and mustard jams made and sold at the Alte Bäckerei are all made using traditional methods, without preservatives or artificial flavors, from apricots, peaches, quinces, rhubarb, berries, and other fruits from around the region. ✉ *Hauptstr. 22* ☎ *06353/508–649* 🌐 *www.altebaeckerei-freinsheim.de.*

WORMS

15 km (9 miles) east of Bockenheim via B-47 from Monsheim, 45 km (28 miles) south of Mainz on B-9.

In addition to having a striking Romanesque cathedral, Worms is a center of the wine trade and one of the most storied cities in Germany, with a history going back some 6,000 years. Settled by the Romans, Worms (pronounced "*vawrms*") later became one of the imperial cities of the Holy Roman Empire. More than 100 Imperial diets (assemblies) were held here, including the 1521 meeting where Martin Luther pleaded his cause.

Worms developed into an important garrison town under the Romans, but it's better known for its greatest legend, the *Nibelungenlied,* derived from the short-lived kingdom established by Gunther and his

Burgundian tribe in the early 5th century. The complex and sprawling story was given its final shape in the 12th century and tells of love, betrayal, greed, war, and death. It ends when Attila the Hun defeats the Nibelungen (Burgundians), who find their court destroyed, their treasure lost, and their heroes dead. One of the most famous incidents tells how Hagen, treacherous and scheming, hurls the court riches into the Rhine. Near the Nibelungen Bridge there's a bronze statue of him caught in the act. The Nibelungenlied may be legend, but the story is based on fact. A Queen Brunhilda, for example, is said to have lived here. It's also known that a Burgundian tribe was defeated in 436 by Attila the Hun in what is present-day Hungary.

Not until Charlemagne resettled Worms almost 400 years later, making it one of the major cities of his empire, did the city prosper again. Worms was more than an administrative and commercial center—it was a great ecclesiastical city as well. The first expression of this religious importance was the original cathedral, consecrated in 1018. Between 1130 and 1181 it was rebuilt in three phases into the church you see today.

GETTING HERE AND AROUND
Worms can be reached by direct trains from both Mannheim and Mainz (approximately 30 minutes from each). The city center is quite compact and negotiable on foot.

VISITOR INFORMATION
Contacts Worms Tourist Information. ⊠ *Neumarkt 14* ☎ *06241/8537–304* ⊕ *www.worms.de.*

EXPLORING

Heylshofgarten. An imperial palace once stood in this park just north of the cathedral. It was the site of the fateful 1521 meeting between Luther and Emperor Charles V that ultimately led to the Reformation. Luther refused to recant his theses demanding Church reforms and went into exile in Eisenach, where he translated the New Testament in 1521 and 1522. ⊠ *Stephansg. 9* ☎ *022/000* 🖙 *€4.*

Judenfriedhof Heiliger Sand (*Holy Sand Jewish Cemetery*). This is the oldest Jewish cemetery in Europe and also one of the most atmospheric and picturesque. The oldest of some 2,000 tombstones date from 1076. Entry is via the gate on Willy-Brandt-Ring. *Male visitors must cover their heads to enter the cemetery.* ⊠ *Willy-Brandt-Ring 21* ☉ *Closed Sat. and Jewish holidays.*

Fodor's Choice ★ **Kunsthaus Heylshof** (*Heylshof Art Gallery*). Located in the Heylshofgarten, this is one of the leading art museums of the region. It has an exquisite collection of German, Dutch, and French paintings as well as stained glass, glassware, porcelain, and ceramics dating from the 15th to the 19th century. ⊠ *Stephansg. 9* ☎ *06241/22000* ⊕ *www.heylshof. de* 🖙 *€4* ☉ *Closed Jan. and Feb. Closed Mon. Mar.–Dec.*

Liebfrauenkirche (*Church of Our Lady*). This twin-towered Gothic church sits in a vineyard on the northern outskirts of Worms. It's the namesake of the popular, sweet white wine *Liebfraumilch* (literally,

10

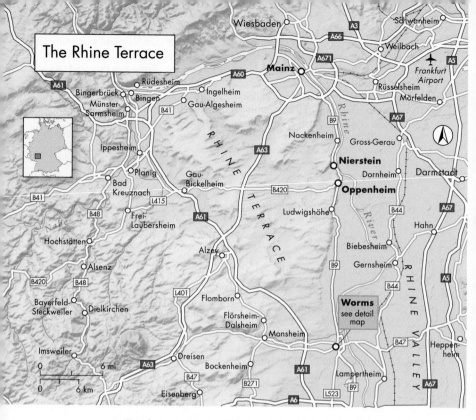

The Rhine Terrace

"Milk of Our Lady"). The wine (Blue Nun is the most well known brand) was originally made from the grapes of the small vineyard surrounding the church, but today it's produced throughout Rheinhessen, the Pfalz, the Nahe, and the Rheingau wine regions. ⊠ *Liebfrauenring 21* ⊕ *www.liebfrauen-worms.de*.

Lutherdenkmal. This monument commemorates Luther's appearance at the Diet of Worms. He ended his speech with these words: "Here I stand. I have no choice. God help me. Amen." The 19th-century monument includes a large statue of Luther ringed by other figures from the Reformation. It's set in a small park on the street named Lutherring. ⊠ *Lutherpl./Lutherring*.

Nibelungen Museum. This stunning sight-and-sound exhibition is dedicated to *Das Nibelungenlied (Song of the Nibelungs)*, the epic German poem dating to around 1200. Cleverly installed in two medieval towers and the portion of the Old Town wall between them, the exhibition brings to life the saga of the dragon slayer Siegfried. The architecture of the structure itself is also fascinating, and the rampart provides a wonderful view of the town. The tour script (via headphones and printed matter) is offered in English. Allow 1½ hours for a thorough visit. ⊠ *Fischerpförtchen 10* ☎ *06241/202–120* ⊕ *www.nibelungen-museum. de* 🎫 €6 🕙 *Closed Mon.*

Synagogue and Raschi Haus. This first synagogue in Worms was built in 1034, rebuilt in 1175, and expanded in 1213 with a synagogue for women. Destroyed in 1938, it was rebuilt in 1961 using as much of the original masonry as had survived. It is located in the Jewish quarter, which is along the town wall between Martinspforte and Friesenspitze and between Judengasse and Hintere Judengasse. Next door to the synagogue is a former study hall, dance hall, and Jewish home for the elderly, which now houses the city archives and the Jewish Museum. The well-written, illustrated booklet *Jewish Worms* chronicles a millennium of Jewish history in Worms. ✉ *Synagogenpl.* ☎ *06241/8534–707 Jewish Museum* 🎟 *Museum €2* ⏲ *Museum closed Mon.*

Fodor's Choice ★ **Wormser Dom St. Peter** (*Cathedral of St. Peter*). In contrast to Speyer's Romanesque cathedral, the Worms Cathedral of St. Peter is much more Gothic. In part this is simply a matter of chronology, since Speyer Cathedral was finished in 1061, nearly 70 years before the one in Worms was even begun—and long before the lighter, more vertical lines of the Gothic style evolved. In addition, Speyer Cathedral was left largely untouched, but the Worms Cathedral underwent frequent remodeling. The Gothic influence here can be seen both inside and out, from the elaborate tympanum with biblical scenes over the southern portal (today's entrance) to the great rose window in the west choir and the five sculptures in the north aisle recounting the life of Christ. The cathedral was gutted by fire in 1689 in the War of the Palatinate Succession. For this reason many of the furnishings are baroque, including the magnificent gilt high altar from 1742, designed by the master architect Balthasar Neumann (1687–1753). The choir stalls are no less decorative. They were built between 1755 and 1759 in rococo style. Walk around the building to see the artistic detail of the exterior. ✉ *Lutherring 9* ☎ *06241/6115* 🌐 *pg-dom-st-peter-worms.bistummainz.de* 🎟 *Donation requested.*

WHERE TO EAT

$$ GERMAN 🍴 **Gasthaus Hagenbräu.** Located a little to the west of the center, by the banks of the Rhine, this house brewery serves a good range of classic German dishes such as meat loaf with *Spätzle* (egg noodles) as well as regional specialties. Service and decor are bright and cheery, and you will be surrounded by copper vats and oak barrels as you dine. **Known for:** good beer selection; summer terrace with river view; generous portions. [$] *Average main: €15* ✉ *Am Rhein 3* ☎ *06241/921–100* 🌐 *www.hagenbraeu.de* ⏲ *Closed Mon. Nov.–Feb.*

WHERE TO STAY

$$ HOTEL 🏨 **Dom-Hotel.** The appeal of this hotel, with comfortable if somewhat bland rooms, lies in its friendly staff and its terrific location in the heart of the pedestrian zone (a parking garage is available for free), perfect for sightseeing and/or shopping. **Pros:** central location; breakfast included; free Wi-Fi. **Cons:** building design doesn't have much charm; hotel in need of a refresh; fee for extra bed or baby bed. [$] *Rooms from: €105* ✉ *Obermarkt 10* ☎ *06241/9070* 🌐 *www.dom-hotel.de* 🛏 *55 rooms* 🍽 *Free Breakfast.*

10

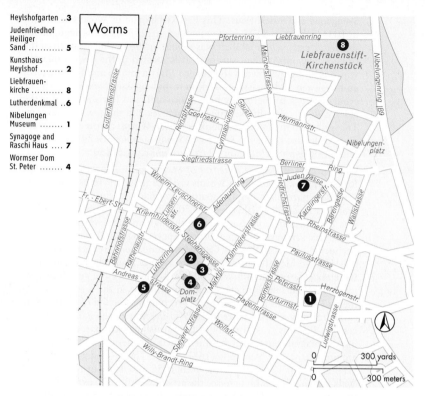

$ 🏨 **Landhotel Zum Schwanen.** Bärbel Berkes runs this lovingly restored
HOTEL   country inn in Osthofen, 10 km (6 miles) northwest of Worms. **Pros:**
quiet location; inviting beer garden; free Wi-Fi in rooms. **Cons:** far
from the sights; no elevator; breakfast a little basic. $ *Rooms from:*
€94 ✉ *Friedrich-Ebert-Str. 40, west of B-9, Osthofen* ☎ *06242/9140*
⊕ *www.zum-schwanen-osthofen.de* ⤳ *30 rooms* ❑ *Free Breakfast.*

SHOPPING

Star Region. Eat, drink, and shop: this store and restaurant specializes in
regional culinary items, including gift baskets, from Rheinhessen, Odenwald, and Pfalz. They also offer wine seminars, such as guided wine
and cheese or chocolate tastings ✉ *Kammererstr. 60* ☎ *06241/269–796*
⊕ *www.starregion.de* ☉ *Closed Sun.*

OPPENHEIM

*26 km (16 miles) north of Worms, 23 km (14 miles) south of Mainz
on B-9.*

Oppenheim is slightly off the beaten path, making it an ideal destination
if you're looking to avoid the hordes of tourists that often descend on

One of the focal points of the Gothic Wormser Dom St. Peter (Worms Cathedral of St. Peter) is the rose window.

the Wine Road in midsummer. It's a steep walk from the train station up to the picturesque old town and market square, but worth the effort to reach the Katharinenkirche, Oppenheim's obvious crown, and the town's mysterious hidden gem: the Oppenheimer Kellerlabyrinth.

GETTING HERE AND AROUND

An excellent network of regional trains connect Oppenheim with Mainz and Worms. Both journeys take about 20 minutes, and trains depart every half hour. Nierstein is just one stop away on the same regional train.

VISITOR INFORMATION

Contacts Oppenheim Tourist Office. ⊠ *Merianstr. 2a* ☎ *06133/490–910* ⊕ *www.stadt-oppenheim.de.*

EXPLORING

Deutsches Weinbaumuseum (*German Viticultural Museum*). Oppenheim and its neighbors to the north, Nierstein and Nackenheim, are home to some of Rheinhessen's best-known vineyards. The Deutsches Weinbaumuseum has wine-related artifacts that chronicle the region's 2,000-year-old winemaking tradition, not to mention the world's largest collection of mousetraps and more than 2,000 corkscrews. ⊠ *Wormser Str. 49* ☎ *06133/2544* ⊕ *www.dwm-content.de* 🎫 *€4* ⊗ *Closed Nov.– Mar. Closed Mon. Apr.–Oct.*

Katharinenkirche (*St. Catherine's Church*). On the way to Oppenheim, the vine-covered hills parallel to the Rhine gradually steepen. Then, unexpectedly, the spires of Oppenheim's Gothic St. Catherine's Church come into view. The contrast of its pink sandstone facade against a bright blue sky is striking. Built between 1225 and 1439, it's the most important Gothic church between Strasbourg and Cologne. The interior affords a rare opportunity to admire magnificent original 14th-century stained-glass windows including two rose windows, the Lily Window and the Oppenheim Rose. The church houses masterfully carved tombstones, and the chapel behind it has a *Beinhaus* (charnel house) containing the bones of 20,000 citizens and soldiers from the 15th to 18th century. ⊠ *Katharinenstr. 1* ☎ *06133/2381* ⊕ *www.katharinen-kirche. de* ☉ *Shop closed Mon. Easter–Oct.*

Fodor's Choice   **Oppenheimer Kellerlabyrinth** (*Oppenheim cellar labyrinth*). Beneath
★   Oppenheim's surface, there are five layers of cellars, tunnels, and stairways. Thought to have been built in the 14th century, their purpose remains unknown. Of the 40 km (24 miles) of complex underground passageways, today ¾ km (½ mile) is open to the public; contact the Oppenheim tourist office to arrange a tour. ⊠ *Merianstr. 2a* ☎ *06133/490–919 Oppenheim Tourismus* ⊕ *www.stadt-oppenheim. de* ☜ *Tour €8.*

PERFORMING ARTS

FAMILY   **Burgruine Landskron.** During the Oppenheim Festival, from the end of August till the end of September, concerts are held at St. Catherine's, and open-air theater takes place in the Burgruine Landskron, the 12th-century imperial fortress ruins. From here, there's a wonderful view of the town and the vineyards, extending all the way to Mannheim and Frankfurt on a clear day. The castle ruins are northwest of the church. Follow Dalbergerstrasse north; from there it's a short, steep walk up to the ruins. For tickets to the open-air theater performances contact the Oppenheim tourist office. ⊠ *Oppenheim.*

NIERSTEIN

3 km (2 miles) north of Oppenheim on B-9.

Surrounded by 2,700 acres of vines, Nierstein is a small, quaint town that's home to the largest wine-growing community on the Rhine. It is also home to Glöck, Germany's oldest documented vineyard (AD 742), which surrounds St. Kilian's Church.

GETTING HERE AND AROUND
Regional trains leave every 30 minutes between Nierstein and both Mainz and Worms. The journey takes about 20 minutes.

EXPLORING

Niersteiner Winzergenossenschaft (*Cooperative winery*). The Niersteiner Winzergenossenschaft (Nierstein Wine Cooperative) can be the starting point of an easy hike or drive to the vineyard heights and the vantage point at the *Wartturm* (watchtower). When you return to the bottom of the hill, drop in to the **Weintreff Nierstein** to try some wines, including Silvaner, the typical specialty of the Rheinhessen wine region. In the summer, the Niersteiner *Weinwanderung* (wine walk) takes place along the roten Hang, or "red slope," of the vineyards—the soil here has a lot of red clay in it—with food and wine-tasting stands set up along the way. From up there, there's a stunning view of the Rhine. ⊠ *Karolingerstr. 6* ☎ *06133/971–720 Weintreff Nierstein* ⊕ *www.weintreff-nierstein. de* ⊗ *Weintreff Nierstein closed Sun.*

WHERE TO STAY

$

B&B/INN

Fodor'sChoice

★

🏠 **Jordan's Untermühle.** The spacious grounds of an old mill are home to a restaurant, a wine store, and this comfortable country inn with two types of rooms: country-style with wood floors in the main building, and bright and modern in a newer annex. **Pros:** beautiful buildings; great value; very quiet. **Cons:** a long way from anywhere; difficult to reach without a car; beer garden very busy during summer. $ *Rooms from: €65* ⊠ *Ausserhalb 1, Köngernheim* ✛ *West of B-9, at Nierstein turn left on B-420 (toward Wörrstadt), drive through Köngernheim and turn right toward Selzen* ☎ *06737/71000* ⊕ *www.jordans-untermuehle. de* ⤶ *38 rooms* ❙❍❙ *Free Breakfast.*

MAINZ

14 km (9 miles) north of Nackenheim, 45 km (28 miles) north of Worms on B-9, and 42 km (26 miles) west of Frankfurt on A-3.

Mainz is the capital of the state of Rheinland-Pfalz. It's a lively university town with friendly locals renowned for their community spirit, whether it be in supporting the local soccer team, Mainz 05, enjoying wine-tavern culture in the cobbled Old Town, or partying at *Karneval* (carnival). Today's city was built on the site of a Roman citadel dating back to 38 BC, and given its central location at the confluence of the Main and Rhine rivers, it's not surprising that Mainz has always been an important trading center, rebuilt time and again in the wake of wars.

GETTING HERE AND AROUND

As the regional hub, Mainz is well served by trains, with fast connections to Frankfurt (40 minutes) and Cologne (one hour, 40 minutes). The station is a short walk west of the center. A comprehensive network of local buses makes getting around the city a breeze (route maps and timetables are posted at bus stops), while the upper areas of town are also served by trams. Although the sights are fairly spread out, they're manageable on foot if you're in reasonably good shape.

DISCOUNTS AND DEALS

◼ TIP➜ **Head to the Tourist Service Center to pick up a mainzcardplus for €11.95, or €25 for up to five people.** The card covers 48 hours of unlimited public transportation in the specified area, free entry to museums and the casino, free walking tours, plus discounts on theater tickets and trips with the Cologne-Düsseldorf Rheinschiffahrt and Gutenberg-Express sightseeing train.

10

VISITOR INFORMATION

Mainz offers year-round tours of the city, including its Roman and medieval areas, the cathedral, and the modern city center, departing Saturday at 2 pm from outside the Tourist Service Center. Drop in to ask about arranging a personalized tour at a different time or a guided visit to the Gutenberg Museum or St. Stephen's Church.

Contacts Mainz Tourist Service Center. ⊠ *Brückenturm am Rathaus, Rheinstr. 55* ☎ *06131/242–888* ⊕ *www.mainz-tourismus.com.*

EXPLORING

Fodor'sChoice   **Dom** (*St Martin's Cathedral*). This cathedral's interior is a virtual sculp-
★   ture gallery of elaborate monuments and tombstones of archbishops, bishops, and canons, many of which are significant artworks in their own right. Emperor Otto II began building the oldest of the Rhineland's trio of grand Romanesque cathedrals in 975, the year in which he named Willigis archbishop and chancellor of the empire. Henry II, the last Saxon emperor of the Holy Roman Empire, was crowned here in 1002, as was his successor, Konrad II, the first Salian emperor, in 1024. In 1009, on the very day of its consecration, the cathedral burned to the ground. It was the first of seven fires the Dom has endured. Today's cathedral dates mostly from the 11th to 13th century. During the Gothic period, remodeling diluted the Romanesque identity of the original; an imposing baroque spire was added in the 18th century. Nevertheless, the building remains essentially Romanesque, and its floor plan demonstrates a clear link to the cathedrals in Speyer and Worms. Individual and group tours can be arranged through the Tourist Service Center. ⊠ *Domstr. 3, on Marktpl.* ☎ *06131/253–412* ⊕ *mainzerdom.bistummainz.de* ⊠ *Donations requested* ☉ *Closed Sun.*

Dom und Diözesanmuseum. From the Middle Ages until secularization in the early 19th century, the archbishops of Mainz, who numbered among the imperial electors, were extremely influential politicians and property owners. The wealth of religious art treasures they left behind can be viewed in the cathedral cloisters. ⊠ *Domstr. 3* ☎ *06131/253–344* ⊕ *www.dommuseum-mainz.de* ⊠ *€5.*

Gutenberg Museum. Opposite the east end of the cathedral (closest to the Rhine) stands this fascinating museum, which is devoted to the history of writing, printing, and books. Exhibits include historical printing presses, incunabula (books printed in Europe before 1501), and medieval manuscripts with illuminated letters, as well as two precious 42-line Gutenberg bibles printed circa 1455. A replica workshop demonstrates how Gutenberg implemented his invention of movable type. ⊠ *Liebfrauenpl. 5* ☎ *06131/122–640* ⊕ *www.gutenberg-museum. de* ⊠ *€5* ☉ *Closed Mon.*

Kupferberg Terrasse. These hillside sparkling wine cellars were built in 1850 on a site where the Romans had cultivated vines and cellared wine. The Kupferberg family expanded them to create 60 seven-story-deep vaulted cellars—the deepest in the world. The winery has a splendid collection of glassware; posters from the belle époque period (1898–1914);

richly carved casks from the 18th and 19th centuries; and the **Trauben-saal** (Grape Hall), a tremendous example of the art nouveau style. Tours of the cellars and museum last one hour plus time for a sparkling wine tasting, and involve lots of stairs! Reservations for group or public tours are required, and can be made by emailing. The Kupferberg Terrassen restaurant ($$$) here is a lovely place to dine before or after your tour, and offers an excellent-value two-course lunch menu. ✉ *Kupferbergter-rasse 17–19* ☎ *06131/693–8363* ✉ *g.bals@sektkellerei-kupferberg.de* ⊕ *www.restaurant-kupferberg.de* ⚓ *Tours from €16.*

Landesmuseum. The various collections of the Museum of the State of Rheinland-Pfalz are in the former electors' stables, easily recognized by the statue of a golden stallion over the entrance. Exhibits range from the Middle Ages to the 20th century. Among the highlights are paintings by Dutch masters, artworks from the baroque to art nouveau periods, and collections of porcelain and faience. ✉ *Grosse Bleiche 49–51* ☎ *06131/28570* ⊕ *www.landesmuseum-mainz.de* ⚓ *€6* ⊙ *Closed Mon.*

FAMILY **Marktplatz.** The area around the cathedral is the focal point of the city. The *Marktplatz* (market place) is especially colorful on Tuesday, Friday, and Saturday from 7 am to 2 pm, when farmers, butchers, cheesemongers, and florists set up stands to sell their produce. On Saturdays from March to November, join friendly Mainzers in the adjoining Liebfrauenplatz for the legendary *Marktfrühstück* (Market Breakfast), where you can sample local wines alongside a traditional local breakfast of *Fleischwurst* (German bologna sausage) with mustard and a crusty bread roll. ✉ *Marktpl.*

Museum für Antike Schiffahrt (*Museum of Ancient Navigation*). The main attractions at this bright, airy museum are the fascinating remains of five 4th-century wooden Roman warships, on display with two full-size replicas. The remains were unearthed in 1981, when the foundation for an expansion to the Hilton hotel was dug. For more than a decade, the wood was injected with a water-and-paraffin mixture to restore its stability. There's also an extensive exhibit dedicated to the history of shipbuilding and an educational area for children. To arrange a tour, contact the service office. ✉ *Neutorstr. 2b* ☎ *06131/912–4170 service office (for tours)* ⊕ *web.rgzm.de* ⚓ *Free* ⊙ *Closed Mon.*

Fodor'sChoice **St. Stephanskirche** (*St. Stephen's Church*). It's just a short walk up Gaus-★ trasse from Schillerplatz to the church, which affords a hilltop view of the city. Nearly 200,000 people make the trip each year to see the nine magnificent blue stained-glass windows designed by the Russian-born artist Marc Chagall. ✉ *Kleine Weissg. 12* ☎ *06131/231–640* ⊕ *www.st-stephan-mainz.de.*

WHERE TO EAT

$ ✕ **Eisgrub-Bräu.** It's loud, it's busy, and the small selection of high-quality GERMAN beer is brewed on-site in a labyrinth of vaulted cellars. The menu offers regional snacks as well as hearty Bavarian fare, from *Schweinehaxen* (pork knuckle) to sauerkraut. **Known for:** good-value weekday lunch specials; free brewery tours (must be arranged in advance); fun spot to

10

In addition to Bibles printed circa 1455, the Gutenberg Museum has artifacts that tell the story of the printed word, including ancient manuscripts and presses.

watch soccer on a big screen. $ *Average main: €10* ⊠ *Weisslilieng. 1a* ☎ *06131/221–104* ⊕ *www.eisgrub.de.*

$$$
GERMAN
✕ **Gebert's Weinstuben.** Gebert's smart yet traditional wine tavern serves refined versions of regional favorites and modern European cuisine using fresh, seasonal ingredients. The *geeister Kaffee* (coffee ice cream and a chocolate praline in a cup of coffee) uses delicious, handmade chocolate pralines. **Known for:** excellent list of German wines; appealing courtyard; friendly service. $ *Average main: €21* ⊠ *Frauenlobstr. 94* ☎ *06131/611–619* ⊕ *www.geberts-weinstuben. de* ⊗ *Closed Mon. and Tues.*

$$
GERMAN
Fodor's Choice
★
✕ **Weinhaus Schreiner.** It's one of the more formal Mainz wine taverns, yet Schreiner still attracts a mixed, jovial clientele who come to enjoy excellent local wines and delicious, refined takes on regional German cuisine, often with a Mediterranean twist. During periods of warm weather, you can sit in the garden (check website for opening times). **Known for:** Saumagen (sliced stuffed pig's stomach); regularly changing seasonal menu; good list of wines and German spirits. $ *Average main: €17* ⊠ *Rheinstr. 38* ☎ *06131/225–720* ⊕ *www.weinhausschreiner.de* ⊗ *Closed Sun., and Mon. Sept.–July. No lunch weekdays* ▭ *No credit cards.*

$$
GERMAN
✕ **Weinstube zum Bacchus.** A tiny wine tavern with a narrow, rickety staircase up to a tightly packed, wood-paneled room, Bacchus offers traditional Mainzer appetizers such as Handkäs mit Musik as well as as salads and elegant versions of classic seasonal German dishes, from schnitzel with green sauce in the spring to goose with dumplings at Christmastime. There are also good vegetarian options. **Known for:** Flammkuchen (tarte flambé); small selection of German craft beer; cozy

atmosphere. $ *Average main: €16* ✉ *Jakobsbergstr. 7* ☎ *06131/487–5548* ⊕ *www.weinstube-zum-bacchus.de* �9 *Closed Mon. No lunch.*

$$
GERMAN
× **Zum Goldstein.** This cozy wine tavern offers simple, traditional German fare, from pickled herrings with sour cream, apple, and vinegar to schnitzel with fried potatoes and mushroom sauce, as well as a handful of international dishes. Pick a glass of Riesling from their wine list and enjoy a leisurely summer's evening in the popular walled garden, which sits in the shade of an enormous tree lit with fairy lights. **Known for:** rump steak with herb butter and fried potatoes; beer garden; relaxed atmosphere. $ *Average main: €15* ✉ *Kartäuserstr. 3* ☎ *06131/236–576* ⊕ *www.zum-goldstein.de* �9 *No lunch weekdays.*

WHERE TO STAY

$$$
HOTEL
🏨 **FAVORITE parkhotel.** Mainz's city park is a lush setting for this amenity-filled hotel about a half hour away from the Old Town. **Pros:** quiet location; good views; some rooms have balconies. **Cons:** a bit far from the sights; you can hear the train from some rooms; air-conditioning only in the park wing. $ *Rooms from: €205* ✉ *Karl-Weiser-Str. 1* ☎ *06131/80150* ⊕ *www.favorite-mainz.de* �9 *Restaurant closed Mon. and Tues.* ⇌ *147 rooms* ⦿ *Free Breakfast.*

$$$$
HOTEL
FAMILY
Fodor's Choice
★
🏨 **Hyatt Regency Mainz.** From the spacious atrium lobby to the luxurious rooms and spa, everything is sleek, modern, and comfortable at this award-winning hotel. **Pros:** grand public spaces; friendly staff; riverside location. **Cons:** expensive; breakfast is extra and expensive; the smell from the coffee factory across the river can be unpleasant. $ *Rooms from: €289* ✉ *Malakoff-Terrasse 1* ☎ *06131/731–234* ⊕ *www.hyatt.com* ⇌ *268 rooms* ⦿ *No meals.*

NIGHTLIFE AND PERFORMING ARTS

Mainz supports a broad spectrum of cultural events—classical as well as avant-garde music, dance, opera, and theater performances—at many venues throughout the city. Music lovers can attend concerts in venues ranging from the cathedral and the Rathaus to the market square and historic churches.

Nightlife centers on its numerous *Weinstuben* (wine taverns). Rustic and cozy, they're packed with locals who come to enjoy a meal or snack with a glass (or more) of local wine—expect to share your table when they're busy. Most are on the Old Town's main street, Augustinerstrasse, and its side streets (Grebenstrasse, Kirschgarten, Kartäuserstrasse, Jakobsbergstrasse).

Weinhaus Wilhelmi. This tiny, historic wood-paneled pub close to the river is a favorite with locals young and old, who come to enjoy glasses of regional wine with traditional Mainzer snacks such as Handkäse (a sour milk cheese marinated in vinegar and caraway). Hearty mains include fried pork steak with onions, and liver sausage from the Pfalz. ✉ *Rheinstr. 53* ☎ *06131/224–949* ⊕ *www.weinhaus-wilhelmi.de* �9 *No lunch.*

10

CLOSE UP

Gutenberg: The Father of Modern Printing

His invention—printing with movable type—transformed the art of communication, yet much about the life and work of Johannes Gutenberg is undocumented, starting with his year of birth. It's conjectured that he was born in Mainz circa 1400, into a patrician family that supplied the city mint with metal for coining. Gutenberg's later accomplishments attest to his own skill in working with metals. Details about his education are unclear, but he probably helped finance his studies by copying manuscripts in a monastic scriptorium. He moved to Strasbourg around 1434, where he was a goldsmith by day and an inventor by night. It was here that he worked—in great secrecy—to create movable type and develop a press suitable for printing by adapting the screw press conventionally used for making wine. By 1448, Gutenberg

had returned to Mainz. Loans from a wealthy businessman enabled him to set up a printer's workshop and print the famous 42-line Bible. The lines of text are in black ink, yet each of the original 180 Bibles printed from 1452 to 1455 is unique, thanks to the artistry of the hand-painted illuminated letters.

Despite its significance, Gutenberg's invention was not a financial success. His quest for perfection rather than profit led to a legal battle during which his creditor was awarded the workshop and the Bible type. Gutenberg's attempts to set up another print shop in Mainz failed, but from 1465 until his death in 1468 he received an allowance for service to the archbishop of Mainz, which spared the "father of modern printing" from dying in poverty.

SHOPPING

The Old Town is full of boutiques selling clothes, jewelry, and gifts, and the shopping district stretches between Schillerplatz, the Marktplatz, Höfchen, and **Am Brand,** an ancient marketplace that is now a pedestrian zone full of clothes stores.

Fodor's Choice ★ **Gutenberg-Shop.** The Gutenberg-Shop, in the building of the local newspaper, *Allgemeine Zeitung Mainz,* offers splendid souvenirs and gifts, including pages from the Bible, books, posters, pens, and stationery. The friendly staff will also arrange to ship your purchases outside the country. There's a similar selection at the shop in the Gutenberg Museum. ⊠ *Markt 17* ☎ *06131/143–666* ⊕ *www.gutenberg-shop.de.*

Krempelmarkt. Antiques and perhaps a few hidden treasures await the patient shopper at Krempelmarkt. The flea market is on the banks of the Rhine (Rheinufer) between the Hilton hotel and Kaiserstrasse. At the Theodor Heuss Bridge is the children's flea market, where the youngest sellers offer clothes, toys, and books. ⊠ *Rheinufer.*

THE RHINELAND

WELCOME TO THE RHINELAND

TOP REASONS TO GO

★ **Drachenfels:** This dramatic castle in Königswinter crowns a high hill overlooking the Rhine.

★ **Fastnacht:** Germany's Carnival season culminates with huge parades, around-the-clock music, and dancing in Düsseldorf, Cologne, and Mainz the week leading up to Ash Wednesday.

★ **Rhine in Flames:** These massive displays of fireworks take place the first Saturday in May in Linz/Bonn; the first Saturday in July in Bingen/Rüdesheim; the second Saturday in August in Koblenz; the second Saturday in September in Oberwesel; and the third Saturday in September in St. Goar/St. Goarshausen.

★ **The romance of the Rhine:** From cruises to Rhine-view rooms, castles to terraced vineyards, the romantic Rhine region does not disappoint.

★ **Spectacular wine:** Some of Germany's most highly regarded wineries can be found in this region, producing the country's distinctive white wines.

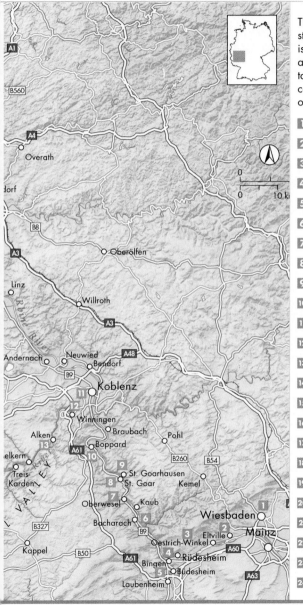

The most spectacular stretch of the Rhineland is between Mainz and Koblenz, which takes in the historical castles and vineyards of the Rhine Gorge.

1 **Wiesbaden**

2 Eltville

3 **Oestrich-Winkel**

4 **Rüdesheim**

5 Bingen

6 Bacharach

7 Oberwesel

8 St. Goar

9 St. Goarhausen

10 Boppard

11 Koblenz

12 Winningen

13 Alken

14 Cochem

15 Ediger-Eller

16 Traben-Trarbach

17 Bernkastel-Kues

18 Trier

19 Bonn

20 Königswinter

21 Brühl

22 Cologne (Köln)

23 Aaachen

24 Düsseldorf

Updated by
Christie Dietz
and Joe Baur

The hills along the Rhine are crowned by castle after castle and covered in the vineyards that provide the livelihood of many of the villages dotted along the banks of the river. In the words of French poet Victor Hugo, "The Rhine combines everything. The Rhine is swift as the Rhône, wide as the Loire, winding as the Seine … royal as the Danube and covered with fables and phantoms like a river in Asia."

The importance of the Rhine cannot be overestimated. Although not the longest river in Europe (the Danube is more than twice as long), the Rhine has been the main river-trade artery between the heart of the continent and the North Sea (and Atlantic Ocean) throughout recorded history. The Rhine runs 1,230 km (764 miles) from the Bodensee (Lake Constance) west to Basel, then north through Germany, and, finally, west through the Netherlands to Rotterdam.

Vineyards, a legacy of the Romans, are an inherent part of the Rhine landscape from Wiesbaden to Bonn. The Rhine tempers the climate sufficiently for grapes to ripen this far north, and the world's finest Rieslings come from the Rheingau and the Rhine's most important tributary, the Mosel. Thanks to the river, these wines were shipped far beyond the borders of Germany, giving rise to the wine trade that shaped the fortune of many riverside towns. Rüdesheim, Bingen, and Koblenz remain important commercial wine centers to this day.

The river is steeped in legend and myth. The Loreley, a jutting sheer slate cliff, was once believed to be the home of a beautiful and bewitching maiden who lured boatmen to a watery end in the swift currents. Heinrich Heine's poem *Song of Loreley* (1827), inspired by Clemens Brentano's *Legend of Loreley* (1812) and set to music in 1837 by Friedrich Silcher, has been the theme song of the landmark ever since. The Nibelungen, a legendary Burgundian people said to have lived on the banks of the Rhine, serve as subjects for Wagner's epic opera cycle *Der Ring des Nibelungen* (1852–72).

William Turner captured misty Rhine sunsets on canvas. Famous literary works, such as Goethe's *Sankt-Rochus-Fest zu Bingen* (*The Feast of St. Roch*; 1814), Lord Byron's *Childe Harold's Pilgrimage* (1816), and Mark Twain's *A Tramp Abroad* (1880), captured the spirit of Rhine romanticism on paper, encouraging others to follow in their footsteps.

MAJOR REGIONS

The heart of the **Rheingau** region begins in Wiesbaden, where the Rhine makes a sharp bend and flows east to west for some 30 km (19 miles) before resuming its south to north course at Rüdesheim. **Wiesbaden** is a good starting point for touring any of the well-marked cycling, hiking, and driving routes through the Rheingau's villages and vineyards. The largest town in the Rheingau is **Eltville**, while the largest vineyard is in **Oestrich-Winkel**. However, the town at the very center of the region's wine tourism is arguably **Rüdesheim**. ■TIP➔ **In summer, nearly every Rheingau village has an outdoor Weinprobierstand (wine-tasting stand), usually near the riverbank. It is staffed and stocked by a different wine estate every weekend.**

The romance of the Rhine is most apparent in the **Mittlerhein** (Middle Rhine), which stretches for 65 km (40 miles). The area was designated a UNESCO World Heritage site in 2002, with its concentration of magnificent castles, medieval towns, and the vineyards of the Rhine Gorge. It begins in **Bingen** and includes **Bacharach, Oberwesel, St. Goar, St. Goarshausen,** and **Boppard,** ending in **Koblenz,** at the confluence of the Rhine and Mosel rivers.

Koblenz and Trier aren't very far apart as the crow flies, but the driving distance along the twists and turns of the **Mosel Valley** is 201 km (125 miles). The journey is worth it, though. The region is unspoiled, and most of the towns, including **Winningen, Alken, Cochem, Ediger-Eller, Traben-Trarbach, Bernkastel-Kues,** and **Trier** are absolute joys to explore. The scenery is a medley of vineyards and forests, and there's a wealth of Roman artifacts, medieval churches, and castle ruins to admire.

North of Koblenz, the Rhine is less picturesque as it passes through **Bonn and the Köln (Cologne) Lowlands. Bonn,** the former capital of West Germany and of reunified Germany until 1999, is the next major stop along the Rhine after Koblenz. It's close to the legendary Siebengebirge (Seven Hills), a national park and the site of western Germany's northernmost vineyards. According to German mythology, Siegfried (hero of the Nibelungen saga) killed a dragon here and bathed in its blood to make himself invincible. The lowland, a region of gently rolling hills north of Bonn, lacks the drama of the Rhine Gorge upstream but offers the urban pleasures of **Königswinter; Brühl; Köln** (Cologne), an ancient cathedral town; **Aachen,** which though not technically in the Rhineland, has one of the great storehouses of Carolingian art and architecture in Europe; and **Düsseldorf,** an elegant city of art and fashion.

PLANNING

WHEN TO GO

The peak season for cultural, food, and wine festivals is March through mid-November, followed by colorful Christmas markets in December. The season for many hotels, restaurants, riverboats, cable cars, and sights is from Easter through October, particularly in smaller towns. Opening hours at many castles, churches, and small museums are shorter in winter. Orchards blossom in March, and the vineyards are verdant from May until late September, when the vines turn a shimmering gold.

GETTING HERE AND AROUND

AIR TRAVEL

The Rhineland is served by three international airports: Frankfurt, Düsseldorf, and Köln/Bonn. Bus and rail lines connect each airport with its respective downtown area and provide rapid access to the rest of the region. There are direct trains from Frankfurt airport to downtown Cologne (Köln) and Düsseldorf.

No-frills carriers that fly within Europe are based at the tiny Frankfurt-Hahn Airport in Lautzenhausen, between the Rhine and Mosel valleys (a one-hour drive from Wiesbaden or Trier; a 90-minute bus ride from Frankfurt Airport). The Luxembourg Findel International Airport (a 30-minute drive from Trier) is close to the upper Mosel River valley.

Contacts Flughafen Düsseldorf. ☎ *0211/4210* ⊕ *www.dus.com.* **Flughafen Frankfurt.** ☎ *01806/372–4636* ⊕ *www.frankfurt-airport.com.* **Flughafen Frankfurt-Hahn.** ☎ *06543/509–113* ⊕ *www.hahn-airport.de.* **Flughafen Köln/Bonn.** ☎ *02203/404–001* ⊕ *www.koeln-bonn-airport.de.* **Luxembourg Findel International Airport.** ☎ *00352/24640* ⊕ *www.lux-airport.lu.*

CRUISE TRAVEL

While the fastest way to get around the region is by car or train, the Rhine and Mosel rivers have been navigated by ship for thousands of years, and this option remains the most scenic, not to mention the safest for visitors looking to drink wine while soaking up a little history. The Rhine is the more popular of the two rivers, but many find its little sister, the Mosel, even more beautiful.

Many Rhine trips are available from Cologne and Düsseldorf, but the river doesn't truly turn scenic until south of Bonn. The most popular starting point is Koblenz, where the Rhine and Mosel converge. The area between Koblenz and Bingen, the Rhine Gorge, offers the shortest cruises with the highest concentration of castles.

Trips along the Rhine and Mosel range in length from a few hours to days or weeks. Day-trippers don't generally need advance reservations, and the tourist offices in the major Rhine or Mosel towns can provide information about short round-trip cruises (*Rundfahrten*) or hop-on, hop-off waterbuses (*Linienfahrten*), which generally run on the Rhine daily from Easter to late October and on the Mosel from June through September. Some multiday cruises also make extra trips in November and December to stop at Christmas markets.

SHORT
CRUISES

Bingen-Rüdesheimer. Short Loreley and castle cruises along the Middle Rhine, plus a ferry service between Bingen and Rüdesheim. ☎ 06721/308–080 ⊕ www.bingen-ruedesheimer.de.

Köln-Düsseldorfer Deutsche Rheinschiffahrt. One of the region's most popular short-journey lines, this company offers day trips on the Rhine, Main, and Mosel, and cruises combined with experiences such as city, brewery, mountain, or castle tours. ☎ 0221/208–8318 ⊕ www.k-d.com.

Mosel-Schiffstouristik Hans Michels. Short cruises on the middle Mosel including round-trip tours from Bernkastel-Kues (one hour) and single trips between there and Traben-Trarbach (two hours). Check website for departure times and staggered prices. ⊠ Goldbachstr. 47, Bernkastel-Kues ☎ 06531/8222 ⊕ www.mosel-personenschifffahrt.de.

Personenschiffahrt Merkelbach. This line offers a variety of trips on the Rhine and Mosel, including castle cruises from Koblenz to Schloss Stolzenfels (60 minutes) or to the Marksburg (100 minutes). ☎ 0261/76810 ⊕ www.merkelbach-personenschiffe.de.

Primus-Linie. Frankfurt-originating short cruises down the Rhine and Main rivers include day cruises, short sightseeing trips, and dinner and evening cruises as well as themed Oktoberfest and Christmas excursions. ⊠ Mainkai 36, Frankfurt ☎ 069/133–8370 ⊕ www.primus-linie.de.

Rheinschifffahrt Hölzenbein. This is a Koblenz-based line, with regular short Rhine cruises to Rüdesheim. ⊠ Rheinzollstr. 4, Koblenz ☎ 0261/37744 ⊕ www.hoelzenbein.de.

Rösslerlinie. Middle Rhine cruises including the castle-rich stretch between Rüdesheim and Assmanshausen. ☎ 06722/2353 ⊕ www.roesslerlinie.de.

TRAIN TRAVEL

InterCity and EuroCity expresses connect all the cities and towns of the area. Hourly InterCity routes run between Düsseldorf, Cologne, Bonn, and Mainz, with most services extending as far south as Munich and as far north as Hamburg. German Rail Passes are valid on these and all Deutsche Bahn trains; passes come in many configurations and include Rhineland-specific bonuses like discounts on KD Rhine Line cruises. The city transportation networks of Bonn, Cologne, and Düsseldorf are linked by S-bahn, regional, and local trains (for information contact the KVB).

Train Contacts Deutsche Bahn. ☎ 646/883–3246 in U.S. ⊕ www.bahn.com.
Kölner Verkehrs-Betriebe (KVB). ☎ 01806/504–030 ⊕ www.kvb-koeln.de.

HOTELS

The most romantic places to lay your head are the old riverside inns and castle hotels. Ask for a Rheinblick (Rhine view) room. Hotels are often booked well in advance, especially for festivals and when there are trade fairs in Cologne, Düsseldorf, or Frankfurt, making rooms even in Wiesbaden and the Rheingau scarce and expensive. Many hotels close for winter.

RESTAURANTS

Although Düsseldorf, Cologne, and Wiesbaden are home to many talented chefs, some of Germany's most creative classic and contemporary cooking can be found in smaller towns or country inns.

Prices in restaurant reviews are the average cost of a main course at dinner, or if dinner is not served, at lunch. Prices in hotel reviews are the lowest cost of a standard double room in high season.

WHAT IT COSTS IN EUROS			
$	$$	$$$	$$$$
Restaurants	under €15	€15–€20	€21–€25	over €25
Hotels	under €100	€100–€175	€176–€225	over €225

VISITOR INFORMATION

Contacts Rheingau-Taunus Kultur & Tourismus. ⊠ *Probeck´scher Hof, Rhein-weg 30, Oestrich-Winkel* ☎ *06723/602–720* ⊕ *www.rheingau.de.* **Romantic Germany Rhineland-Palatinate.** ⊠ *Rheinland-Pfalz Tourismus GmbH, Löhrstr. 103–105, Koblenz* ☎ *01805/757–4636* ⊕ *www.romantic-germany.info.*

WIESBADEN

40 km (25 miles) west of Frankfurt.

Wiesbaden, the capital of the state of Hesse, is a small city of tree-lined avenues with elegant shops and handsome facades. Its hot mineral springs have been a drawing card since the days when it was known as Aquis Mattiacis (the waters of the Mattiaci)—the words boldly inscribed on the portal of the Kurhaus—and Wisibada (the bath in the meadow).

In the 1st century AD, the Romans built thermal baths here, a site then inhabited by a Germanic tribe, the Mattiaci. Modern Wiesbaden dates from the 19th century, when the dukes of Nassau and, later, the Prussian aristocracy commissioned the grand public buildings and parks that shape the city's profile today. Wiesbaden developed into a fashionable spa town that attracted the rich and the famous. Their ornate villas on the Neroberg and turn-of-the-20th-century town houses are part of the city's flair.

GETTING HERE AND AROUND

If you're driving, take the A-66 from Frankfurt.

TOURS

Thermine. For a one-hour ride around the city, board this little train. A one-day ticket, purchased from the driver or in advance at Tourist Information, enables you to get on and off at the Greek Chapel and the Neroberg funicular railway station in order to explore the sights. From April through October—and on select dates during November and December—it departs numerous times daily between 10 and 4:30,

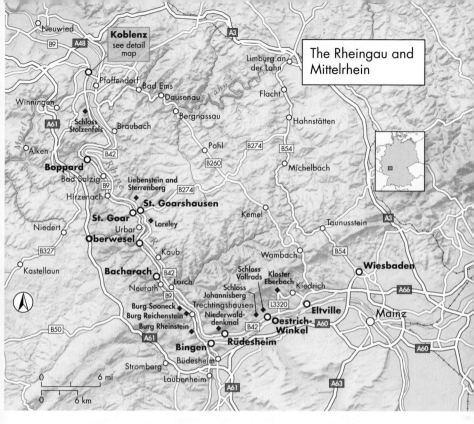

The Rheingau and Mittelrhein

from Café Lumen (behind the Marktkirche, opposite Tourist Information). ☎ *0611/5893–9464* ⊕ *www.thermine.de* ✉ *€9 for all-day ticket.*

VISITOR INFORMATION

Small-group English-language guided walking tours of Wiesbaden can be arranged in advance through the Tourist Office.

Contacts Wiesbaden Tourist-Information. ✉ *Marktpl. 1* ☎ *0611/172–9930* ⊕ *www.wiesbaden.eu.*

EXPLORING

Altstadt. Called *Schiffchen* (Little Ship) for its boatlike shape, Wiesbaden's pretty Old Town is packed with restaurants, cafés and shops. It's located just behind the Stadtschloss (a former duke's palace, now the seat of state parliament, the Hessischer Landtag) on Grabenstrasse, Wagemannstrasse, and Goldgasse. ✉ *Wiesbaden.*

Kochbrunnen Fountain. Fifteen of Wiesbaden's 26 springs converge at the steaming Kochbrunnen Fountain, where the sulfurous but at least theoretically healthful waters are there for the tasting. ✉ *Kochbrunnenpl.*

Fodor's Choice ★ **Kurhaus.** Built in 1907, the neoclassical Kurhaus is the cultural center of the city. It houses the casino, the Thiersch-Saal, a splendid setting for concerts, and a Parisian-style bistro. The Staatstheater (1894), opulently appointed in baroque and rococo revival styles, and two beautifully landscaped parks—one with a boating pond—flank the Kurhaus. ✉ *Kurhauspl. 1* 🌐 *www.wiesbaden.de/kurhaus.*

Museum Wiesbaden. Nature and culture come together under one roof at the Museum Wiesbaden. The natural history section exhibits a wealth of geological finds and preserved animals, and the art collection ranges from 12th-century polychromes to present-day installations. The museum is best known for its expressionist paintings, particularly the works of Russian artist Alexej Jawlensky, who lived in Wiesbaden for the last 20 years of his life. ✉ *Friedrich-Ebert-Allee 2* ☎ *0611/335–2250* 🌐 *www.museum-wiesbaden.de* 🎫 *€6* 🕒 *Closed Mon.*

WHERE TO EAT

$$$$ ECLECTIC 🍴 **Käfer's Bistro.** This bistro has a striking art nouveau interior, the walls crammed with paintings, a grand piano (live music nightly), and a good-size bar, attracting an upscale clientele and the post-theater crowd. Käfer's is well known for its Black Angus steaks as well as its very popular (and expensive!) Sunday brunch. **Known for:** lovely veranda for good weather; relaxed but sophisticated crowd; good service. [$] *Average main: €28* ✉ *Kurhauspl. 1* ☎ *0611/536–200* 🌐 *www.kuffler.de.*

$$ GERMAN 🍴 **Weihenstephaner Wiesbaden.** High ceilings, chandeliers, and traditional wooden furnishings help shape Wiesbaden's answer to a Bavarian beer hall, with a good selection of draft and bottled Weihenstephaner beers to match. The classic Bavarian food comes in generous portions, from the best crispy pork knuckle (*Schweinshaxe*) in town—worth ordering in advance as they only make a set number each day—to schnitzel, fried chicken (*Backhendl*), and sausages with sauerkraut and fried potatoes. **Known for:** good beer; friendly atmosphere; excellent food. [$] *Average main: €17* ✉ *Taunusstr. 46* ☎ *0611/2059–035* 🌐 *weihenstephaner-wiesbaden.de* 🕒 *No lunch.*

WHERE TO STAY

$$ HOTEL 🏨 **Hotel Klemm.** If you like a bit of personality in your accommodation, you'll love the individually decorated rooms at the peaceful and welcoming Hotel Klemm. **Pros:** very friendly, helpful staff; definitely not a bland chain; quiet yet central location close to the antique shops and restaurants on Taunusstrasse. **Cons:** short but steep uphill walk to reach hotel; extra charge for cots or additional beds; garage parking costs extra and must be reserved in advance. [$] *Rooms from: €115* ✉ *Kapellenstr. 9* ☎ *0611/5820* 🌐 *www.hotel-klemm.de* 🛏 *70 rooms* 🍽 *No meals.*

$$$ HOTEL 🏨 **Hotel Nassauer Hof.** Situated opposite the Kurhaus, Wiesbaden's premier address for well over a century—and the first hotel in Germany to be awarded five stars—is home to three restaurants, including the gorgeous Orangerie for breakfast, and Wiesbaden's only Michelin-starred restaurant, the Ente. **Pros:** excellent service; Germany's only rooftop thermal pool; well-equipped gym with a view of the city. **Cons:** the cigar lounge can get very smoky; expensive breakfast not included; some

rooms feel a little dated. [$] *Rooms from: €225* ✉ *Kaiser-Friedrich-Pl. 3–4* ☎ *0611/1330* 🌐 *www.nassauer-hof.de* 🛏 *159 rooms* 🍴 *No meals.*

$$ HOTEL Fodor's Choice ★ **Radisson Blu Schwarzer Bock Hotel.** The Schwarzer Bock first opened as a bathhouse in 1486 and is now a sophisticated hotel that maintains stunning architectural features such as marble columns and an exceptionally charming wood-paneled room adjacent to the classically decorated bar. **Pros:** fully air-conditioned; excellent location; wonderful old furnishings. **Cons:** extra cost for cots; parking is expensive and 100 meters away; rooms on the first floor facing the street can be noisy at night. [$] *Rooms from: €134* ✉ *Kranzpl. 12* ☎ *0611/1550* 🌐 *www.radissonblu.com* 🛏 *142 rooms* 🍴 *No meals.*

$$ HOTEL **Town Hotel.** Its central location (a five-minute walk from the Kurhaus, Old Town, and shopping district), particularly friendly and helpful staff, and affordability make the Gerbers' modern hotel an excellent choice. **Pros:** a good deal; free telephone calls to North America and most of Europe; very friendly and helpful staff. **Cons:** often full during the week; no air-conditioning; rooms are rather basic. [$] *Rooms from: €119* ✉ *Spiegelg. 5* ☎ *0611/360–160* 🌐 *www.townhotel.de* 🛏 *24 rooms* 🍴 *No meals.*

NIGHTLIFE AND PERFORMING ARTS

In addition to the casino, restaurants, bars, and beer garden at the Kurhaus, nightlife is centered on the many bistros and pubs on Taunusstrasse and in the Old Town. The tourist office provides schedules and sells tickets for most venues listed here.

PERFORMING ARTS

CONCERTS

Kurhaus. Throughout the year, a number of high-class events are offered at the Kurhaus, including performances from the Hessian State Orchestra, and the annual Wine Ball and New Year's Eve party. In addition, there are very occasional organ concerts in the Friedrich-von-Thiersch-Saal, which has been home to an organ since the Kurhaus was built in 1907. On organ open days, you can visit the organ room, which is usually closed to the public. ✉ *Kurhauspl. 1* ☎ *0611/172–9100* 🌐 *www.wiesbaden.de.*

Marktkirche. The Marktkirche is a striking, red neo-Gothic church built between 1853 and 1862, and is Wiesbaden's main protestant church. The Walcker organ has a total of 6,198 pipes, which can be heard during the free organ recitals that are held on Saturday at 11:30 am. ✉ *Schlosspl. 4* ☎ *0611/900–1612* 🌐 *www.marktkirche-wiesbaden.de.*

RheinMain CongressCenter. The impressive modern RheinMain CongressCenter was completely rebuilt using a mix of natural stone, wood, glass, and metal, and reopened in 2018. Its events listings include concerts, cultural events, and trade fairs. The Italian restaurant bagutta housed within offers pizza, pasta, antipasti, and sweets, and has a sun terrace out front as well as a glass-fronted upstairs interior, from where you can watch what's going on in the banqueting hall below. ✉ *Rheinstr. 20* ☎ *0611/172–9400* 🌐 *www.rmcc.de.*

SHOPPING

Broad, tree-lined Wilhelmstrasse, with designer boutiques housed in its fin de siècle buildings, is one of Germany's most elegant shopping streets. Taunusstrasse and Nerostrasse offer between them a small selection of excellent—and expensive—antiques shops. Head to the Altstadt for a handful of upscale boutiques; Kirchgasse and its extension, Langgasse, are the heart of the shops-filled pedestrian zone.

Der Kakaobaum. This tiny chocolate shop offers a delicious selection of high-quality pralines, both homemade and created by master chocolatiers including Alsace's Daniel Rebert; there are also wonderful chocolate creations around Christmastime. The friendly staff will be happy to guide you in selecting a sparkling wine to pair with your pralines. ⊠ *Neug. 13* ☎ *0611/3608–6960* ⊕ *der-kakaobaum.de.*

RSA Antiquitäten. Regine Schmitz-Avila specializes in antique German and some French furniture from the 18th and 19th centuries. The beautiful art deco, baroque, and Biedermeier pieces are lovingly displayed in her welcoming shop on Taunusstrasse. ⊠ *Taunusstr. 34* ☎ *0611/529–0570* ⊕ *www.antiquitaeten-wiesbaden.de.*

Stadtstück. From locally made condiments and beverages such as mustard or seven-herb gin, to traditional Frankfurt ceramics and fun T-shirts, Stadtstück offers out-of-the-ordinary contemporary souvenirs, design objects, and culinary treats all related to Wiesbaden and the Hessen region. ⊠ *Goldg. 5* ☎ *0611/8904–4223* ⊕ *www.stadtstueck.de.*

SPAS

Kaiser-Friedrich-Therme. The Kaiser-Friedrich-Therme was built in the art nouveau style at the beginning of the 20th century and was extensively renovated at the end of it to restore and preserve the elegant decorations of the Irish-Roman bath. Pamper yourself in this historic setting with the thermal-spring and cold-water pools, Russian steam bath and saunas, two solaria, and a score of health- and wellness treatments. Towels and robes can be rented on-site, but come prepared for bathing nude. Children under 16 are not admitted. On Tuesday (except holidays) the facility is for women only. ⊠ *Langg. 38–40* ☎ *0611/317–060* ⊕ *www. wiesbaden.de* 💰 *€7 per hr, Sept.–Apr.; €5 per hr, May–Aug.*

Thermalbad Aukammtal. There's year-round swimming indoors and out thanks to the thermal springs (32°C [90°F]) that feed the two large pools connected by a swim-through canal. The facility also includes an activity pool, six saunas, a steam room, a whirlpool, water massage, and various other treatments. The sauna is for ladies only on Monday (except holidays). ⊠ *Leibnizstr. 7* ✛ *Bus No. 18 from Wilhelmstr. to "Thermalbad" stop* ☎ *0611/317–080* ⊕ *www.wiesbaden.de* 💰 *From €10; €15 deposit for chip bracelet not included.*

ELTVILLE

11

14 km (9 miles) west of Wiesbaden.
The largest town in the Rheingau,
Eltville rose to prominence in the
Middle Ages as the residence of
the archbishops of Mainz. Today,
it's cherished for its sparkling wines
and its roses, the latter of which are
celebrated most colorfully during
the town's *Rosentage* (Rose Days),
held the first weekend of June,
when the romantic Kurfürstliche
Burg and the old town on the banks
of the Rhine are transformed into a
veritable sea of flowers.

Burg Crass (Crass Castle), located
on the riverbank, is well worth a
look, as are the half-timber houses
and aristocratic manors on the
lanes between the river and Rhe-
ingauer Strasse (B-42), notably the
Bechtermünzer Hof (Kirchgasse 6),
Stockheimer Hof (Ellenbogengasse 6), and Eltzer Hof (at the Martinstor
gateway).

> ## TAKE A HIKE!
>
> The Rheinhöhenweg (Rhine
> Heights Path) gives its hikers
> splendid views and descents
> into the villages en route. These
> marked trails run between Oppen-
> heim on the Rhine Terrace and
> Bonn for 240 km (149 miles) and
> between Wiesbaden and Bonn-
> Beuel for 272 km (169 miles).
> The most extensive hiking trail is
> the Rheinsteig, from Wiesbaden
> to Bonn on the right side of the
> Rhine. It comprises 320 km (199
> miles) of well-marked paths that
> offer everything from easy walks
> to challenging stretches on a par
> with Alpine routes.

There are a number of prominent wineries in the area, and some offer
tours and tastings. The Nussbrunnen, Wisselbrunnen, and Marcobrunn
estates get their name from the *Brunnen* (wells) that are beneath the
vineyards.

GETTING HERE AND AROUND

Just 9 miles from Wiesbaden, via A-66 and B-42, and 12 from
Mainz via A-643, Eltville is easily accessible by road, rail, or
bus service using the local public transport network, the RMV
(Rhein-Main-Verkehrsverbund).

Contacts RMV (Rhein-Main-Verkehrsverbund). ☎ *069/2424–8024* ⊕ *www.
rmv.de.*

VISITOR INFORMATION

Contacts Eltville Tourist Information. ⊠ *Kurfürstliche Burg, Burgstr. 1*
☎ *06123/90980* ⊕ *www.eltville.de.*

EXPLORING

Fodor'sChoice ★ **Kloster Eberbach.** The former Cistercian monastery is idyllically set in
a secluded forest clearing 3 km (2 miles) west of Kiedrich. Its Romanesque and Gothic buildings (12th–14th century) look untouched by
time—one reason why the 1986 film of Umberto Eco's medieval mur-
der mystery *The Name of the Rose* was filmed here. The monastery's
impressive collection of old winepresses bears witness to a viticultural
tradition that spans nearly nine centuries. The wines can be sampled

year-round in the atmospheric wine cellar (or on a roving tasting around the abbey), in the **Vinothek,** or in the restaurant on the grounds; in warmer months, you can enjoy them outside at Kloster Eberbach's premier vineyard, the Steinberg, which is surrounded by a 3-km (2-mile) stone wall (dating from the 13th–18th centuries). The church, with its excellent acoustics, and the large medieval dormitories, are the settings for concerts, wine auctions, and festive wine events. English audio guides are available for self-guided tours. ⊠ *Kloster Eberbach* ☎ *06723/917–8100* ⊕ *www. kloster-eberbach.de* 🖅 *€9.*

HESSIAN STATE WINE DOMAINS

Sekt (sparkling wine) production in the Rheingau is concentrated in Eltville, Wiesbaden, and Rüdesheim. The administrative headquarters and main cellars of the Hessian State Wine Domains, Germany's largest wine estate, are in the town itself. The estate owns about 500 acres of vineyards throughout the Rheingau and in the Hessische Bergstrasse wine region south of Frankfurt. Its shops in the early-Gothic hospital at Kloster Eberbach stock a comprehensive selection of regional sparkling wines.

Kurfürstliche Burg (*Electors' Castle*). Eltville flourished as a favorite residence of the archbishops of Mainz in the 14th and 15th centuries, and it was during this time that the castle—which now houses Eltville's tourist-information center—was built. The museum includes an exhibition commemorating Johannes Gutenberg, the inventor of modern letterpress printing, who was appointed courtier here in 1465; the Count's Chamber with its impressive 14th-century murals; an observation deck with a lovely view of the city; and a dungeon that is accessed by a narrow spiral staircase. More than 300 varieties of roses grow in the castle's courtyard garden, its walls, and out along the Rhine promenade. ⊠ *Burgstr. 1* ☎ *06123/909–80* ⊕ *www. eltville.de* 🖅 *Tower €4; rose garden free.*

Weingut Robert Weil. Built by the English aristocrat John Sutton, this beautiful villa south of St. Valentine's Church is home to one of Germany's leading wine estates. Its famed Rieslings can be sampled in the tasting room at no cost (but with the expectation that a bottle or two of wine is purchased afterward). For 10 people or more, an exclusive tasting including a two-hour cellar tour can be arranged in advance for a fee. ⊠ *Mühlberg 5, Kiedrich* ☎ *06123/2308* ⊕ *www.weingut-robert-weil.com.*

WHERE TO EAT

$
GERMAN

✕**Klosterschänke und Gästehaus Kloster Eberbach.** Beneath the vaulted ceiling of the Klosterschänke you can pair local wines with seasonal German cuisine. Menu highlights include their hearty winter soups, a bread-and-cold cuts platter (*Eberbacher Winzerbrett*), and the delectable *Apfelstrudel* (apple strudel). **Known for:** cozy, friendly atmosphere; plentiful outside seating on the garden terrace; traditional food. $ *Average main: €12* ⊠ *Kloster Eberbach* ✛ *Via Kiedrich or Hattenheim* ☎ *06723/993–299* ⊕ *www.klostereberbach.de* ▭ *No credit cards.*

11

$$ ✕ **Weingut J. Koegler.** The quiet, walled, rose-filled wine garden at
INTERNATIONAL Koegler's is a wonderful spot to enjoy some of their excellent food,
which includes German and Russian specialties as well as some very
good options for kids. If you fall for their quality wines—the classic
Alta Villa Riesling is particularly pleasing—you can purchase them at
the neighboring Koegler Vinothek as you leave. **Known for:** friendly
service; "cult classic" carpaccio of Handkäse with a trio of paired wines;
live guitar music on Sunday (outside only, in good weather). $ *Average
main: €18* ✉ *Kirchg. 5, Wiesbaden* ☎ *06123/2437* ⊕ *www.weingut-
koegler.de* ⊗ *No lunch weekdays.*

$$$ ✕ **Zum Krug.** Winegrower Josef Laufer more than lives up to the hospi-
GERMAN tality promised by the wreath and *Krug* (an earthenware pitcher) hang-
ing above the front door of his hotel and restaurant. The wood-paneled
restaurant, with its old tiled stove, is cozy; the service warm and welcoming; and the regularly changing seasonal German fare includes trout
from the Wisper river and game. **Known for:** traditional menu; attentive
service; list of more than 600 Rheingau wines, plus liqueurs. $ *Average
main: €25* ✉ *Hauptstr. 34, Hattenheim* ☎ *06723/99680* ⊕ *www.hotel-
zum-krug.de* ⊗ *Closed Mon. No lunch Tues.; no dinner Sun.*

WHERE TO STAY

$$ ⬚ **Weinhotel Hof Bechtermünz.** Within a 15th-century structure on Elt-
HOTEL ville's Weingut Koegler complex, Weinhotel Hof Bechtermünz brings
modern style to its historic setting (Johannes Gutenberg printed the
world's first dictionary here in 1467). **Pros:** historic and central setting;
quiet location; right next door to the excellent Koegler restaurant and
Vinothek. **Cons:** no air-conditioning; often booked up for weddings
and events; upper floors accessible by stairs only. $ *Rooms from: €155*
✉ *Kirchg. 5* ☎ *06123/2437* ⊕ *www.weingut-koegler.de* ⇄ *16 rooms*
⦿ *Free Breakfast.*

OESTRICH-WINKEL

21 km (13 miles) west of Wiesbaden, 7 km (4½ miles) west of Eltville.

Oestrich-Winkel's vineyard area is the largest in Hesse, and there are
wineries on every street in this small riverside town. From April to
September, you can sample the wines of weekly changing wineries at
the outdoor wine-tasting stands down by the river, including at Wein-
probierfass Oestrich, which is opposite the town's landmark, an 18th-
century wine-loading crane.

GETTING HERE AND AROUND
By road from Wiesbaden or Eltville go west on B-42.

VISITOR INFORMATION
Oestrich Winkel's Tourist Information reopened in the newly reno-
vated wine press house of the historical Brentano estate in early 2018,
and includes a museum shop with range of souvenirs relating to the
Brentanohaus and Rhine romanticism. Ask here about the town's
festivals and various tourist programs; you can also purchase tickets
for various events.

Kloster Eberbach, a former Cistercian monastery, is worth a stop for its well-preserved architecture and its winery.

Contacts Tourist-Information Oestrich-Winkel. ⊠ *Am Brentanohaus, Haupt-str. 87* ☎ *06723/601–2806* ⊕ *www.oestrich-winkel.de.*

EXPLORING

Fodor's Choice ★ **Schloss Johannisberg.** The origins of this grand wine estate date from 1100, when Benedictine monks built a monastery and planted vines on the slopes below. The striking early-18th-century palace is closed to the public, but wine tastings and cellar tours take place from Monday to Saturday, and there is an excellent wine shop, which also offers the estate's gin. The excellent restaurant, Schlossschänke, offers stunning views over the vineyards. ⊠ *Weinbaudomäne Schloss Johannisberg, Geisenheim* ✛ *From Winkel, turn off main street at Schillerstr. and drive north all the way uphill. After road curves to left, watch for left turn to castle* ☎ *06722/70090* ⊕ *www.schloss-johannisberg.de.*

Fodor's Choice ★ **Schloss Vollrads.** Built in 1211, Schloss Vollrads is the oldest of Germany's major wine estates. The tower, built in 1330 and surrounded by a moat, was the Greiffenclau residence for 350 years until the present palace was built in the 17th century. There is a wineshop, and the castle's period rooms can be toured during concerts, festivals, and wine tastings. It's 3 km (2 miles) north of town. In addition to the restaurant, you can sit outside on the patio in the warmer months and order very good Flammkuchen and sausages from the food truck. ⊠ *Vollradser Allee* ✛ *North on Kirchstr., continue on Vollradser Allee* ☎ *06723/660* ⊕ *www.schlossvollrads.com* ⊗ *Castle courtyard closed weekdays. Restaurant closed Wed.; no dinner Sun.*

WHERE TO EAT

$$ | **✕ Die Wirtschaft.** Beate and Florian Kreller give you a warm welcome
GERMAN | to their historic building full of cozy niches and exposed beams, where
local dishes are the specialty, with emphasis placed on fresh, local, seasonal ingredients. Vegan and vegetarian options are available alongside the schnitzel and sausages. **Known for:** pretty courtyard; friendly service; rustic atmosphere. $ *Average main: €16* ✉ *Hauptstr. 70, Winkel* ☎ *06723/7426* ⊕ *www.die-wirtschaft.net* ⚍ *No credit cards* ☉ *Closed Mon. and Tues. No dinner weekdays.*

$$ | **✕ Gutsrestaurant Schloss Vollrads.** Great care is taken over the light, seasonal international dishes here, which are made with fresh, carefully chosen ingredients and served with the estate's wines. Choose to dine in the Kavalierhaus (squire's house, 1650), the orangery, or in the summer, on the flower-lined terrace facing the garden. **Known for:** creative menu; knowledgeable service; relaxed atmosphere. $ *Average main: €20* ✉ *Schloss Vollrads, Vollradser Allee, north of Winkel* ☎ *06723/5270* ⊕ *www.schlossvollrads.com* ☉ *Closed Wed. No dinner Sun.*
MEDITERRANEAN
Fodor'sChoice
★

$$$$ | **✕ Schlossschänke auf dem Johannisberg.** Sit on the patio, in the restaurant, or the glassed-in terrace, which affords a spectacular view of the Rhine and the vineyards where the Schloss Johannisberg wines originate. Seasonal specialties include wild garlic soup, white asparagus with schnitzel, and duck with cabbage and potato dumplings. **Known for:** exceptional views; creative dishes; excellent wines. $ *Average main: €26* ✉ *Schloss Johannisberg, Geisenheim* ☎ *06722/96090* ⊕ *www.schloss-johannisberg.de.*
GERMAN

WHERE TO STAY

$$ | **⌂ Hotel Schwan.** Owned by the Wenckstern family since it was built in
B&B/INN | 1628, this green-and-white half-timber inn offers considerable comfort, with the adjacent Gasthaus Ilse offering simpler, more budget-friendly rooms than those in the historic main building. **Pros:** lovely location right at the 18th-century crane on the river; free Wi-Fi and parking; three-bed family rooms available. **Cons:** not all rooms can be accessed with the lift; terrace gets some traffic noise from the road; reception not 24 hours. $ *Rooms from: €129* ✉ *Rheinallee 5, Oestrich* ☎ *06723/8090* ⊕ *www.hotel-schwan.de* ↵ *58 rooms* ⦿ *Free Breakfast.*

RÜDESHEIM

30 km (19 miles) west of Wiesbaden, 9 km (5½ miles) west of Oestrich-Winkel.

Tourism and wine are the heart and soul of Rüdesheim. With south-facing slopes reaching down to the riverbanks, wine growing has thrived here for 1,000 years. Since being discovered by English and German romanticists in the early 19th century for its picturesque solitude, Rüdesheim has long lost its quiet innocence, as the narrow, medieval alleys fill with boatloads of cheerful visitors from all over the world.

GETTING HERE AND AROUND
The town is on the B-42.

TOURS
Luftsport-Club Rheingau. With the wings of a glider you can silently soar over the Rhine Valley. At the Luftsport-Club Rheingau you can catch a 30- to 60-minute sightseeing *Segelflug* (glider flight) between Rüdesheim and the Loreley; allow 90 minutes for pre- and postflight preparations. ✉ *Flugpl. Eibinger Forstwiesen über Kammerforster Str.* ✛ *3 km (2 miles) north of Niederwald-Denkmal and Landgut Ebenthal* ☎ *06722/2979* ⊕ *www.lsc-rheingau.de* ✉ *Glider from €15; power glider from €30* ⊗ *Closed Nov.–Mar., and weekdays Apr.–Oct. (except holidays).*

VISITOR INFORMATION
Contacts Rüdesheim Tourist-Information. ✉ *Rheinstr. 29a* ☎ *06722/906–150* ⊕ *www.ruedesheim.de.*

EXPLORING

Drosselgasse (*Thrush Alley*). Less than 500 feet long, Drosselgasse is a narrow, pub-lined lane between Rheinstrasse and Oberstrasse that buzzes with music and merrymaking from 10 am until well past midnight every day, all year round. The first wine tavern here, the Drosselhof, opened in 1727. ✉ *Rüdesheim.*

Niederwalddenkmal. High above Rüdesheim and visible for miles stands Germania, a colossal female statue crowning the Niederwald Monument. This tribute to German nationalism was built between 1877 and 1883 to commemorate the rebirth of the German Empire after the Franco-Prussian War (1870–71). Germania faces across the Rhine toward its eternal enemy, France. At her base are the words to a stirring patriotic song: "Dear Fatherland rest peacefully! Fast and true stands the watch, the watch on the Rhine!" There are splendid panoramic views from the monument and from other vantage points on the edge of the forested plateau. You can reach the monument on foot, by car (via Grabenstrasse), or over the vineyards in the *Seilbahn* (cable car). There's also a *Sessellift* (chairlift) to and from Assmannshausen, a red-wine enclave, on the other side of the hill; a "Ring-ticket" will take you from the Old Town to Niederwald by cable car, from Niederwald to Assmannshausen by chairlift, and back to Rüdesheim by boat. Allow three to four hours for the trip. ✉ *Oberstr. 37* ☎ *06722/2402* ⊕ *www.seilbahn-ruedesheim.de* ✉ *Cable car or chair lift from €6; Ring Ticket €15* ⊗ *Closed for 2 wks in Nov., and late Dec.–mid-Mar.*

Weinmuseum Brömserburg (*Brömsburg Wine Museum*). Housed in one of the oldest castles on the Rhine, which dates from around the year 1000, the museum displays wine-related artifacts and drinking vessels dating from Roman times. There are great views from the roof and the terrace, where there are occasionally wine tastings (ask at the desk). The entrance fee includes an audio-visual guide, tasting glass, and savory baked treats. ✉ *Rheinstr. 2* ☎ *06722/2348* ⊕ *www.rheingauer-weinmuseum.de* ✉ *€5* ⊗ *Closed Nov.–Feb.*

Take the Seilbahn over picturesque vineyards to the Niederwald-Denkmal monument above Rüdesheim.

WHERE TO STAY

$$ 🏨 **Breuer's Rüdesheimer Schloss.** Vineyard views grace most of the rooms
HOTEL   at this stylish, historic hotel, where guests are welcomed with a drink
from the family's Rheingau wine estate. **Pros:** right off the Drosselgasse;
numerous rate packages; very welcoming. **Cons:** noisy, touristy area;
extra fee (on sliding scale dependent on age) for cots and kids' beds;
parking difficult. $ *Rooms from: €149* ✉ *Steing. 10* ☎ *06722/90500*
⊕ *www.ruedesheimer-schloss.com* ⏱ *Closed late Dec.–Jan.* ⇌ *26 rooms*
🍽️ *Free Breakfast.*

$$$ 🏨 **Hotel Krone Assmannshausen.** From its humble beginnings in 1541
HOTEL   as an inn for sailors and ferrymen, the Krone evolved into an elegant,
Fodor's Choice   antiques-filled hotel with a fine restaurant. **Pros:** very old-world, tradi-
★   tional feel; pool with panoramic view; spacious free parking. **Cons:** right
on a main railroad line; rooms at the back have a less than spectacular
view; 6 km (3.7 miles) from Rüdesheim. $ *Rooms from: €180* ✉ *Rhe-
inuferstr. 10, Assmannshausen* ☎ *06722/4030* ⊕ *www.hotel-krone.com*
⇌ *66 rooms* 🍽️ *Free Breakfast.*

BINGEN

35 km (22 miles) west of Wiesbaden.

Bingen overlooks the Nahe-Rhine conflux near a treacherous stretch
of shallows and rapids known as the Binger Loch (Bingen Hole). This
small town developed into an important commercial center early on,
for it was here—as with Rüdesheim on the opposite shore—that goods
were moved from ship to shore to circumvent the impassable waters.

Bingen was also the crossroads of Roman trade routes between Mainz, Koblenz, and Trier. Thanks to this central location, as well as its situation at the meeting point of three of Germany's wine regions—Rheinhessen, Mittelrhein and Nahe—Bingen grew into a major center of the wine trade and remains so today. Wine is celebrated during 11 days of merrymaking in late August and early September at the annual **Winzerfest.**

GETTING HERE AND AROUND

From Wiesbaden by road, take A-60 via Mainz. If you're coming from Rüdesheim, you can hop on a ferry from the wharf opposite the train station (€4.50 one-way by car; €2.50 as a foot passenger).

VISITOR INFORMATION

Contacts **Bingen Tourist-Information.** ⊠ Rheinkai 21 ☎ 06721/184–205 ⊕ www.bingen.de.

EXPLORING

Basilika St. Martin. The Basilika St. Martin was built on the site of a Roman temple and first mentioned in 793. It's been destroyed and rebuilt a number of times since then and as a result is a real mix of architectural styles; the 11th-century crypt and Gothic and baroque furnishings make it worth a visit. It's a ten-minute walk from here to the 12th-century Drususbrücke, Germany's oldest medieval stone bridge, which runs over the Nahe. ⊠ Basilikastr. 1.

Burg Klopp. Bingen was destroyed repeatedly by wars and fires; thus there are many ancient foundations but few visible architectural remains of the past. Since Celtic times the Kloppberg (Klopp Hill), in the center of town, has been the site of a succession of citadels, all named Burg Klopp, since 1282. Here you'll find a terrace with good views of the Rhine, the Nahe, and the surrounding hills, and from April to October you can climb the tower for a more lofty view. ⊠ Kloppg. 1 ⊕ www. bingen.de ☾ Closed Nov.–Mar.

Burg Reichenstein. Under new ownership since 2014 and on the fast track to becoming a stylish castle hotel with two restaurants, Reichenstein also has an interesting museum with collections of decorative cast-iron slabs (from ovens and historical room-heating devices), hunting weapons and armor, period rooms, and paintings. It's the only one of the area's three castles directly accessible by car. ⊠ Burgweg 7, Trechtingshausen ☎ 06721/6117 ⊕ www.burg-reichenstein.com ☎ €5.

Fodor'sChoice
★

Burg Rheinstein. This castle was the home of Rudolf von Habsburg from 1282 to 1286. To establish law and order on the Rhine, he destroyed the neighboring castles of Burg Reichenstein and Burg Sooneck and hanged their notorious robber barons from the oak trees around the Clemens Church, a late-Romanesque basilica near Trechtingshausen. The Gobelin tapestries, 15th-century stained glass, wall and ceiling frescoes, a floor of royal apartments, and antique furniture—including a rare "giraffe spinet," which Kaiser Wilhelm I is said to have played—are the highlights here. All of this is illuminated by candlelight on some summer Fridays. Rheinstein was the first of many a Rhine ruin to be rebuilt by a royal Prussian family in the 19th century. ✉ *Trechting-shausen* ✛ *From A-61, take exit AS Bingen center. Continue on B-9 through Bingerbrück toward Trechtingshausen; parking is below castle* ☎ *06721/6348* ⊕ *www.burg-rheinstein.de* 🎫 *€6.*

Burg Sooneck. Perched on the edge of the Soon (pronounced *"zone"*) Forest, this imposing 11th-century castle houses a valuable collection of Empire, Biedermeier, and neo-Gothic furnishings, medieval weapons, and paintings from the Rhine Romantic era. ✉ *Sooneckstr. 1, Nieder-heimbach* ☎ *06743/6064* ⊕ *www.burgen-rlp.de* 🎫 *€4* ⊗ *Closed Dec. and Jan. Closed Mon.–Thurs. Feb.–mid-Mar. and Nov. Closed Mon. mid-Mar.–Oct.*

Hildegard Forum. Near the St. Roch Chapel, the Hildegard Forum has exhibits related to St. Hildegard, a medicinal medieval herb garden, and a restaurant serving tasty, wholesome foods (many based on Hildegard's theories of nutrition) and a substantial selection of local wines. The lunch buffet of soups, salads, mains, and sweets, is a very good value. ✉ *Rochusberg 1* ☎ *06721/181–000* ⊕ *www.hildegard-forum.de* ⊗ *Restaurant closed Mon. Nov.–Apr.*

Historisches Museum am Strom (*History Museum*). At this small but very well cared-for museum, you can see the most intact set of Roman surgical tools ever discovered (2nd century), period rooms from the Rhine Romantic era, and displays about Abbess St. Hildegard von Bingen (1098–1179), one of the most remarkable women of the Middle Ages. An outspoken critic of papal and imperial machinations, she was a highly respected scholar, naturopath, and artist whose mystic writings and (especially) music became very popular from the 1990s onward. An excellent illustrated booklet in English on Rhine Romanticism, *The Romantic Rhine,* is sold at the museum shop. The museum is housed in a former power station (1898) on the riverbank. ✉ *Museumsstr. 3* ☎ *06721/184–353* ⊕ *www.bingen.de* 🎫 *€3* ⊗ *Closed Mon.*

Mäuseturm (*Mouse Tower*). Looking west along the river from Bingen, you can just about spot the Mäuseturm, perched on a rocky island near the Binger Loch. The name derives from a gruesome legend. One version tells that during a famine in 969 the miserly Archbishop Hatto hoarded grain and sought refuge in the tower to escape the peasants' pleas for food. The stockpile attracted scads of mice to the tower, where they devoured everything in sight, including Hatto. In fact, the tower was built by the archbishops of Mainz in the 13th and 14th centuries as a *Mautturm* (watch tower and toll station) for their fortress, Ehrenfels, on the opposite shore (now a ruin). It was restored in neo-Gothic style by the king of Prussia in 1855, who also rebuilt Burg Sooneck, but you can't go inside. ✉ *Mäuseturminsel, Trechtingshausen* ✛ *5 km (3 mile) drive northwest of Bingen on B-9* ⊕ *www.bingen.de.*

WHERE TO EAT

$$ ✗ Geniesserei Alte Wache. With its position right on the market place
INTERNATIONAL in the center of town, you'd be mistaken for thinking this might be
FAMILY a tourist trap. But good regional cuisine such as local trout (*Forelle*)
with potato and apple salad as well as salads, sandwiches, and a very
popular spaghetti bolognese are on the reasonably priced menu in this
spacious, friendly, air-conditioned café. **Known for:** good-value daily
lunch special; attentive service; central location. $ *Average main: €15*
✉ *Speisemarkt 3* ☎ *06721/987–280* ⊕ *www.altewache.org.*

$$ ✗ Weinstube Kruger-Rumpf. It's well worth the 10-minute drive from Bin-
GERMAN gen (just across the Nahe River) to enjoy the refined country cooking
and wines produced by the Rumpf family, whether inside the 1790s
house, or outside on the large, wisteria-draped suntrap of a patio. Seasonal house specialties include *geschmorte Schweinebacken* (braised
pork jowls) with kohlrabi, boiled beef with green herb sauce, and *Win-
zerschmaus* (a casserole of potatoes, sauerkraut, bacon, cheese, and
herbs). **Known for:** regional specialties; exquisite Nahe wines; excellent
service. $ *Average main: €18* ✉ *Rheinstr. 47, Münster-Sarmsheim* ✛ *4
km (2½ miles) southwest of Bingen* ☎ *06721/43859* ⊕ *www.kruger-
rumpf.com* ⊗ *Closed Mon. No lunch weekdays.*

BACHARACH

*16 km (10 miles) north of Bingen, ferry 3 km (2 miles) north of town,
to Kaub.*

Bacharach, whose name may derive from the Latin *Bacchi ara* (altar of
Bacchus), has long been associated with wine. Like Rüdesheim, Bingen,
and Kaub, it was a shipping station where barrels would interrupt
their Rhine journey for land transport. Riesling wine from the town's
most famous vineyard, the Bacharacher Hahn, is served on the KD
Rhine steamers, and Riesling is used in local cooking for marinades and
sauces; you can even find Riesling ice cream. In June you can sample
wines at the **Weinblütenfest** (Vine Blossom Festival) in the side-valley
suburb of Steeg, and, in late August, at **Kulinarische Sommernacht** in
Bacharach proper (⊕ *www.kulinarische-sommernacht.de*).

Park on the riverbank and enter the town through one of its medieval
gateways. You can ascend the 14th-century town wall for a walk along
the ramparts around the town, then stroll along the main street (one
street but three names: Koblenzer Strasse, Oberstrasse, and Mainzer
Strasse) for a look at patrician manors, typically built around a *Hof*
(courtyard), and half-timber houses. Haus Sickingen, Posthof, Zollhof,
Rathaus (Town Hall), and Altes Haus are all fine examples.

VISITOR INFORMATION

Contacts Bacharach Tourist-Information. ✉ *Oberstr. 10* ☎ *06743/919–303*
⊕ *www.bacharach.de.*

EXPLORING

11

St. Peters Kirche. The massive tower in the center of town belongs to the parish church of St. Peter. A good example of the transition from Romanesque to Gothic styles, it has an impressive four-story nave. ⊠ *Oberstr. 45.*

Wernerkapelle. From the parish church a set of stone steps (signposted) leads to Bacharach's landmark, the sandstone ruins of the Gothic Wernerkapelle, highly admired for its filigree tracery. The chapel's roof succumbed to falling rocks in 1689, when the French blew up Burg Stahleck. Originally a Staufen fortress (11th century), the castle lay dormant until 1925, when a youth hostel was built on the foundations. The sweeping views from there are worth the 10-minute walk. ⊠ *Bacharach* ✛ *Climb stairs to left of St. Peter's church on Oberstr.; route is signposted.*

WHERE TO EAT

$
GERMAN
✗**Altes Haus.** This wonderfully charming medieval half-timber house (1368) is Bacharach's oldest one standing and a favorite setting for films and photos. It doesn't disappoint with its food and wine, either: the kitchen uses the freshest ingredients possible and buys meat and game from local butchers and hunters, serving up local classics such as *Rieslingrahmsuppe* (Riesling cream soup) and *Reibekuchen* (potato pancakes) in addition to the seasonal specialties. **Known for:** good regional wine list; friendly service; cozy atmosphere. $ *Average main: €14* ⊠ *Oberstr. 61* ☎ *06743/1209* ⊗ *Closed Wed., Dec.–Easter, and weekdays in Apr. and Nov. No lunch Mon.*

$
GERMAN
✗**Gutsausschank Zum Grünen Baum.** The Bastian family (also owners of the vineyard Insel Heyles'en Werth, on the island opposite Bacharach) runs this cozy tavern in a half-timber house dating from 1421. The "wine carousel" is a great way to sample a full range of wine flavors and styles (15 wines) alongside light snacks that include delicious *Wildsülze* (game in aspic), with potato salad, sausages, and cheese. **Known for:** very pretty inner courtyard; excellent wines; friendly service. $ *Average main: €12* ⊠ *Oberstr. 63* ☎ *06743/1208* ⊕ *www.weingut-bastian-bacharach.de.*

WHERE TO STAY

$
HOTEL
▦ **Altkölnischer Hof.** Flowers line the windows of country-style rooms in this pretty half-timber hotel near the market square. **Pros:** half-timber romance; great breakfast; friendly, welcoming staff. **Cons:** noisy, touristy area; parking a block away; restaurant very popular (reservations strongly advised). $ *Rooms from: €90* ⊠ *Blücherstr. 2* ☎ *06743/947–780* ⊕ *www. altkoelnischer-hof.de* ⊗ *Closed Nov.–Mar.* ⤳ *24 rooms* ⦿ *Free Breakfast.*

$
HOTEL
▦ **Rhein Hotel Bacharach.** The modern rooms in this friendly, family-run operation, each of them named after a vineyard, come with stunning views; there's also a "wellness suite" complete with its own sauna. **Pros:** Rhine and castle views; free bike loans for hotel guests; wonderful outside seating at the restaurant. **Cons:** no elevator; next to railroad; no air-conditioning. $ *Rooms from: €75* ⊠ *Langstr. 50* ☎ *06743/1243* ⊕ *www.rhein-hotel-bacharach.de* ⤳ *14 rooms* ⦿ *Free Breakfast.*

OBERWESEL

8 km (5 miles) north of Bacharach.

Oberwesel retains its medieval silhouette. Sixteen of the original 21 towers and much of the town wall still stand in the shadow of Schönburg Castle. The "town of towers" is also renowned for its Riesling wines, which are celebrated during a festival held the first half of September. Both Gothic churches, on opposite ends of town, are worth visiting.

VISITOR INFORMATION

Contacts Oberwesel Tourist-Information. ✉ *Rathausstr. 3* ☎ *06744/710–624* ⊕ *www.oberwesel.de.*

EXPLORING

Liebfrauenkirche (*Church of Our Lady*). Popularly known as the "red church" because of its brightly colored exterior, Liebfrauenkirche has superb sculptures, tombstones and paintings, and one of Germany's oldest high gothic shrine altars (1331). ✉ *Kirchstr. 1.*

Pfarrkirche St. Martin. Set on a hill and with a fortresslike tower, the Roman Catholic so-called white church has beautifully painted vaulting and a magnificent baroque altar. ✉ *Martinsberg 1.*

Stadtmuseum Oberwesel. Oberwesel's city museum—a former winery—offers a virtual tour of the town, as well as a multimedia "journey through time" showing the area from the Stone Age to the present day. It also houses a fine collection of old etchings and drawings of the Rhine Valley, including one by John Gardnor, an English clergyman and painter, who published a book of sketches upon his return to England and kicked off a wave of Romantic tourism in the late 18th century. ✉ *Rathausstr. 23* ☎ *06744/714–726* ⊕ *www.kulturhaus-oberwesel.de* 🎫 *€3* ⊙ *Closed weekends, and Mon. Nov.–Mar.*

> ### BIKE THE MIDDLE RHINE
>
> There is a 132-km (82-mile) cycle path called the Rheinradweg running through the Middle Rhine Valley parallel to the road and the railroad tracks from Bingen to Bonn. It's an ideal way of combining sightseeing with some not-so-strenuous exercise, unless you attempt to reach the castles on the hills. Watch out for pedestrians and other bicyclists.

WHERE TO EAT

$$
GERMAN
✕ **Historische Weinwirtschaft.** Tables in the flower-laden garden in front of this lovingly restored half-timber house are at a premium in summer, though the seats in the nooks and crannies indoors are just as inviting. From generous portions of sour pot roast beef (*Sauerbraten*) and spit roast pork (*Spiessbraten*), the menu—in local dialect, but you can ask for a version in English—is country cooking at its best. **Known for:** vaulted cellar, which houses art exhibitions; extensive list of Mittelrhein wine by the glass; wonderfully welcoming owner. 💲 *Average main: €16*

✉ Liebfrauenstr. 17 ☎ 06744/8186 ⊕ www.historische-weinwirtschaft. de ⊗ Closed Tues. and Wed. No lunch Mon. and Thurs.–Sat.

WHERE TO STAY

$$$$
B&B/INN
Fodor's Choice
★

🏨 **Burghotel "Auf Schönburg".** Antique furnishings and historic rooms—a library, chapel, and prison tower—make for an unforgettable stay at this lovingly restored hotel and restaurant in the 12th-century Schönburg Castle complex. **Pros:** castle right out of a storybook; stunning views; free entrance to the tower museum for hotel guests. **Cons:** lots of climbing (the hotel is nearly 300 yards up a cobblestoned hill from the parking lot); train tracks nearby; very expensive. 💲 *Rooms from: €290 ✉ Auf Schönburg ☎ 06744/93930 ⊕ www.hotel-schoenburg.com ⊗ Closed mid-Jan.–mid-Mar. ➦ 25 rooms ⊚ Free Breakfast.*

ST. GOAR

7 km (4½ miles) north of Oberwesel.

St. Goar and St. Goarshausen, its counterpoint on the opposite shore, are named after a Celtic missionary who settled here in the 6th century. He became the patron saint of innkeepers—an auspicious sign for both towns, which now live off tourism and wine. The town is busy with various events throughout the year, but the splendid fireworks display, "Rhine in Flames," is a highlight in September.

GETTING HERE AND AROUND

Highway B-9 and train service link St. Goar to other towns on the Mittelrhein's west side; ferries to St. Goarshausen connect it to the east.

VISITOR INFORMATION

Contacts **St. Goar Tourist-Information.** ✉ *Heerstr. 127* ☎ *06741/383* ⊕ *www. st-goar.de.*

EXPLORING

FAMILY **Burg Rheinfels.** The castle ruins overlooking the town bear witness to the fact that St. Goar was once the best-fortified town in the Mittelrhein. From its beginnings in 1245, it was repeatedly enlarged by the counts of Katzenelnbogen, a powerful local dynasty, and their successors, the Landgraviate of Hesse. Rheinfels was finally blasted by the French in 1797. Take time for a walk through the impressive ruins and the museum, which has a detailed model of how the fortress looked in its heyday. It's a steep ascent by foot, but between 11 am to 5 pm, the cab company Papst will take you from the Katholische Kirche to the castle and back, ✉ *Off Schlossberg Str. ⊕ Use "Schlossberg 47, 56329 St. Goar" for GPS. By foot, it's a signposted 20-min walk from St. Goar's pedestrianized zone. ☎ 06741/7753 ⊕ www. burg-rheinfels.com ⊠ €5 ⊗ Closed mid-Nov.–mid-Mar.*

Stiftskirche. This 15th-century collegiate church was built atop the tomb of St. Goar, despite the fact that the tomb itself (an ancient pilgrimage site) was discovered to be empty during the church's construction. The

DID YOU KNOW?

The Gothic Liebfrauenkirche (Church of Our Lady), which dominates Oberwesel's skyline, is worth a look inside for its gilt altar, intricate carvings, and paintings.

11th-century crypt has been called the most beautiful to be found on the Rhine between Cologne and Speyer. ✉ *Marktpl.*

WHERE TO EAT

$$ GERMAN 🍴 **Weinhotel Landsknecht.** Martina Lorenz and her winemaker husband Joachim operate the Vinothek at this hotel and restaurant north or St. Goar, where you can sample his delicious Bopparder Hamm wines. These go well with the hearty local dishes, such as Rhine-style Sauerbraten or seasonal specialties (asparagus, game), at the Ausblick restaurant. **Known for:** friendly, welcoming staff; the hotel is an official Rheinsteig and Rhein-Burgen trail partner, so perfect for hikers; family-friendly. [$] *Average main: €16* ✉ *Aussiedlung Landsknecht 4–6* ☎ *06741/2011* 🌐 *www.hotel-landsknecht.de* 🕒 *Closed mid-Dec.–Mar.*

WHERE TO STAY

$$ HOTEL Fodor's Choice ★ 🏨 **Romantik Hotel Schloss Rheinfels.** Directly opposite Burg Rheinfels, this hotel offers modern comfort and expansive views from rooms furnished in country-manor style. **Pros:** marvelous views of the Rhine and the town; lovely outdoor dining area; excellent breakfast. **Cons:** villa section some distance from main hotel and lacks charm; restaurant very busy in summer; parking costs extra. [$] *Rooms from: €175* ✉ *Schlossberg 47* ☎ *06741/8020* 🌐 *www.schloss-rheinfels.de* 🛏 *64 rooms* 🍽 *Free Breakfast.*

ST. GOARSHAUSEN

29 km (18 miles) north of Rüdesheim.

The town closest to the famous Loreley rock, pretty St. Goarshausen even calls itself *Die Loreleystadt* (Loreley City), and it's a popular destination for Rhineland travelers, especially during the **Weinwoche** (Wine Week) festival, which takes place in September.

Overlooking the town are two 14th-century castles whose names, Katz (Cat) and Maus (Mouse), reflect but one of the many power plays on the Rhine in the Middle Ages. Territorial supremacy and the privilege of collecting tolls fueled the fires of rivalry. In response to the construction of Burg Rheinfels, the archbishop of Trier erected a small castle north of St. Goarshausen to protect his interests. In turn, the masters of Rheinfels, the counts of Katzenelnbogen, built a bigger castle directly above the town. Its name was shortened to Katz, and its smaller neighbor was scornfully referred to as Maus. Neither castle is open to the public.

GETTING HERE AND AROUND

Roads (B-42 and B-274) and rail service connect St. Goarshausen to neighboring towns on the east side of the Mittelrhein. Ferries to St. Goar link it to the west.

EXPLORING

Liebenstein and Sterrenberg. Some 10 km (6 miles) north of the Maus castle, near Kamp-Bornhofen, is a castle duo separated by a "quarrel wall": Liebenstein and Sterrenberg, known as the *Feindliche Brüder* (enemy brothers) in reference to the feuding descendants who inherited the castles from the king who built them. Liebenstein is now home to a charming medieval-style hotel, and Sterrenberg offers a traditional German restaurant with garden and terrace that offer wonderful panoramic views. ⊠ *Hotel Castle Liebenstein, Zu den Burgen 1, Kamp-Bornhofen* ⊕ *www.castle-liebenstein.com.*

Loreley. One of the Rhineland's main attractions lies 4 km (2½ miles) south of St. Goarshausen: the steep (430-foot-high) slate cliff named after the beautiful blonde nymph Loreley. Here she supposedly sat, singing songs so lovely that sailors and fishermen were lured to the treacherous rapids—and their demise. The rapids really were treacherous; the Rhine is at its narrowest here and the current the swiftest. The Loreley nymph was invented in 1801 by author Clemens Brentano, who drew his inspiration from the sirens of Greek legend. Her tale was retold as a ballad by Heinrich Heine and set to music by Friedrich Silcher at the height of Rhine Romanticism in the 19th century. The haunting melody is played on the PA systems of the Rhine boats whenever the Loreley is approached. ⊠ *St. Goarshausen.*

Loreley Besucherzentrum. The 20-minute 3-D film and hands-on exhibits at this visitor center are entertaining ways to learn about the region's flora and fauna, geology, wine, shipping, and, above all, the myth of the Loreley. You can stock up on souvenirs in the shop and have a snack at the bistro before heading for the nearby vantage point at the cliff's summit. The center is on the Rheinsteig trail, and other hiking trails are signposted in the landscaped park. From Easter to October there's hourly bus service to and from the KD steamer landing in St. Goarshausen. ⊠ *Auf der Loreley (Loreleyplateau)* ☎ *06771/599–093* ⊕ *www. loreley-besucherzentrum.de* 🎫 *€3 for 3-D film* ⊙ *Closed Nov.–Feb.*

BOPPARD

17 km (11 miles) north of St. Goar, ferry to Filsen.

Boppard is a pleasant little resort that evolved from a Celtic settlement into a Roman fortress, Frankish royal court, and Free Imperial City. Contact the tourist office to arrange a walking tour of the town or guided tours through the wider region.

VISITOR INFORMATION

Contacts Tourist Information Boppard. ⊠ *Altes Rathaus, Am Marktpl.* ☎ *06742/3888* ⊕ *www.boppard-tourismus.de.*

EXPLORING

Karmeliterkirche (*Carmelite Church*). Two baroque altars dominate the interior of the Gothic Karmeliterkirche on Karmeliterstrasse, near the Rhine. It houses intricately carved choir stalls and tombstones and several beautiful Madonnas. Winegrowers still observe the old custom of laying the first-picked *Trauben* (grapes) at the foot of the Traubenmadonna (1330) to ensure a good harvest. ✉ *Karmeliterstr.*

Marksburg. On the eastern shore overlooking the town of Braubach is the Marksburg. Built in the 13th century to protect the silver and lead mines in the area, it's the only land-based castle on the Rhine to have survived the centuries intact. Within its massive walls are a collection of weapons and manuscripts, a medieval botanical garden, and a self-service restaurant with a terrace that has stunning views. The castle can only be visited as part of a 50-minute guided tour: individual English tours take place daily during the summer months at 1 pm and 4 pm; call ahead if you'd like to join a pre-arranged tour at a different time. ✉ *Braubach* ☎ *02627/206* 🌐 *www.marksburg.de* 🎫 *€7.*

Römer-Kastell Bodobrica. The Roman garrison (*Römer-Kastell*) Bodobrica, established here in the 4th century, was enclosed by a 26-foot-high rectangular wall (1,010 by 505 feet) with 28 defense towers. You can see portions of these in a fascinating open-air archaeological park. ✉ *Angertstr. corner Kirchg.* ✥ *Near B-9 and the railroad tracks* 🎫 *Free.*

Severuskirche (*Church of St. Severus*). Excavations in the 1960s revealed ancient Roman baths beneath the twin-tower, Romanesque Severuskirche on the market square. The large triumphal crucifix over the main altar and a lovely statue of a smiling Madonna date from the 13th century. ✉ *Marktpl.*

Vierseenblick. From the Mühltal station, let the *Sesselbahn* (chairlift) whisk you a half-mile uphill to the Vierseenblick (Four-Lake View), from where the Rhine looks like a chain of four lakes. The journey takes approximately 20 minutes. ✉ *Mühltal 12* ☎ *06742/2510* 🌐 *www.sesselbahn-boppard.de* 🎫 *€9 round-trip* 🕓 *Closed Nov.–Mar.*

WHERE TO EAT

$ GERMAN 🍴 **Weingut Heilig Grab.** This wine estate's tavern and hotel, Boppard's oldest, is full of smiling faces: the wines are excellent, the food is simple and hearty, and the welcome is warm. Old chestnut trees shade tables in the courtyard. **Known for:** rustic atmosphere; charming staff; pretty garden in the summer. [$] *Average main: €10* ✉ *Zelkesg. 12* ☎ *06742/2371* 🌐 *www.heiliggrab.de* 🕓 *Closed Mon. No lunch.*

WHERE TO STAY

$$ HOTEL 🏨 **Bellevue Rheinhotel.** In this traditional hotel now run by the fourth and fifth generations of the same family, you can enjoy a Rhine view from many of the rooms, or from the terrace next to the waterfront promenade. **Pros:** secure parking close by; longer stays include free cable-car tickets; very atmospheric. **Cons:** not all rooms are air-conditioned;

breakfast costs extra; night street noise in some rooms at the back. [$] *Rooms from: €125* ✉ *Rheinallee 41* ☎ *06742/1020* 🌐 *www.bellevue-boppard.de* 🛏 *94 rooms* 🍴 *No meals.*

SPORTS AND THE OUTDOORS

Mittelrhein Klettersteig. If you have Alpine hiking ambitions, try this climbing path—a "via ferrata" complete with cables, steps, and ladders to help reach heights more quickly. It's an alternate route of the Rhein-Burgen-Wanderweg (hiking trail from Koblenz to Bingen). The trail starts at St.-Remigius-Platz, about 1 km (½ mile) from Boppard Hauptbahnhof. Allow two to three hours for the climb, though there are several possibilities to return to the "normal" path in-between climbs. Rent the necessary gear at the Aral gas station on Koblenzer Strasse in Boppard (€25 plus €5 fee and €20 deposit; ID required). ✉ *St.-Remigius-Pl.* ☎ *06742/2447 Aral gas station.*

Weinlehrpfad Bopparder Hamm (*Wine Hiking Trail*). This 11.3-km wine trail takes you along paved paths through the Bopparder Hamm vineyards. The route begins and ends at the large wine barrel by the Peternach level crossing on the B-9 just outside Boppard in the direction of Koblenz. There are lots of benches and resting spots along the trail, from which you can enjoy glorious panoramic views of the river. Many other marked trails in the vicinity are outlined on maps and in brochures available from the tourist office. 🌐 *www.boppard-tourismus.de.*

KOBLENZ

20 km (12 miles) north of Boppard.

The ancient city of Koblenz is at a geographic nexus known as the Deutsches Eck (German Corner) in the heart of the Mittelrhein region. Rivers and mountains converge here: the Mosel flows into the Rhine on one side; the Lahn flows in on the other a few miles south; and three mountain ridges intersect.

Founded by the Romans in AD 9, the city was first called Castrum apud Confluentes (Fort at the Confluence). It became a powerful center in the Middle Ages, when it controlled trade on both the Rhine and the Mosel. Air raids during World War II destroyed 87% of the city, but extensive restoration has done much to re-create its former atmosphere. As the host of Germany's Federal Horticultural Show in 2011, the city saw widespread urban development, including the new Seilbahn that transports visitors across the river and up to the Ehrenbreitstein fortress.

GETTING HERE AND AROUND

You can get here speedily by autobahn or train, or via a leisurely scenic drive along the Rhine (or even more mellow, by cruise boat). The Koblenz tourist office has guided English-language tours on Saturday at 3 from April to October. Tours are €7 and depart from the Tourist-Information office.

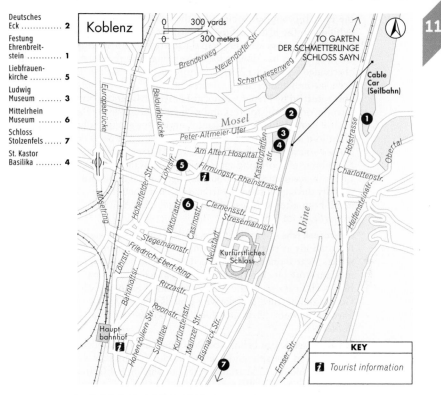

VISITOR INFORMATION

Contacts Koblenz Tourist-Information. ✉ *Forum Confluentes, Zentralpl. 1*
☎ *0261/19433* ⊕ *www.koblenz-tourism.com.*

EXPLORING

Deutsches Eck (*German Corner*). This pointed bit of land, jutting into the river like the prow of an early ironclad warship, is at the sharp intersection of the Rhine and Mosel rivers. One of the more effusive manifestations of German nationalism—an 1897 equestrian statue of Kaiser Wilhelm I, first emperor of the newly united Germany—was erected here. It was destroyed at the end of World War II and replaced in 1953 with a ponderous monument to Germany's unity. After German reunification a new statue of Wilhelm was placed atop this monument in 1993. Pieces of the Berlin Wall stand on the Mosel side—a memorial to those who died as a result of the partitioning of the country.

Fodor's Choice **Festung Ehrenbreitstein.** Europe's largest fortress, towering 400 feet above
★ the left bank of the Rhine, offers a magnificent view over Koblenz and where the Mosel and the Rhine rivers meet. The earliest buildings date from about 1100, but the bulk of the fortress was constructed in the 16th century. In 1801 it was partially destroyed by Napoléon, and

the French occupied Koblenz for the next 18 years. The museum has exhibits on the history of local industries, from wine growing to technology. Pride of place is given to the fortress's 16th-century Vogel Greif cannon, which has done a lot of traveling over the years. The French absconded with it in 1794, the Germans took it back in 1940, and the French commandeered it again in 1945. The 15-ton cannon was peaceably returned by French president François Mitterrand in 1984. For an introduction to the fortress and its history, head for the *Besucherdienst* (visitor center). English-language tours are for groups only, but you can often join a group that is registered for a tour. A *Seilbahn* (cable car) carries you a half mile from Konrad-Adenauer-Ufer over the river to Ehrenbreitstein, offering spectacular views of the Deutsches Eck below. Lifts can accommodate 7,000 passengers in an hour, and operate continually throughout the day from a half hour before the site opens until a half hour after it closes. ⊠ *Felsenweg* ☎ *0261/6675–4000* ⊕ *tor-zum-welterbe.de* ⤳ *From €7.*

Liebfrauenkirche (*Church of Our Lady*). This church stands on Roman foundations at the Old Town's highest point, where, on surrounding streets, war damage is evidenced by the blend of old buildings and modern store blocks. The bulk of the church is of Romanesque design, but its choir is one of the Rhineland's finest examples of 15th-century Gothic architecture, and the west front is graced with two 17th-century baroque towers. ⊠ *An der Liebfrauenkirche 16* ⊕ *www.liebfrauen-koblenz.de.*

Ludwig Museum. Just behind the Deutsches Eck, this modern art museum is housed in the spic-and-span Deutschherrenhaus, a restored 13th-century building. Industrialist Peter Ludwig, one of Germany's leading contemporary-art collectors, has filled this museum with part of his huge collection. ⊠ *Danziger Freiheit 1* ☎ *0261/304–0412* ⊕ *www.ludwigmuseum.org* ⤳ *€6* ☉ *Closed Mon.*

Mittelrhein Museum. Relocated in 2013 to the new Forum Confluentes, this museum, founded in 1835, houses the city's excellent art collection, including extensive holdings of landscapes focusing on the Rhine. It also has a notable collection of secular medieval art and contemporary works by regional artists. ⊠ *Zentralpl. 1* ☎ *0261/129–2520* ⊕ *www.mittelrhein-museum.de* ⤳ *From €6* ☉ *Closed Mon.*

Schloss Stolzenfels. On the outskirts of Koblenz, the neo-Gothic towers of Schloss Stolzenfels come into view. The castle's origins date to the mid-13th century, when the archbishop of Trier sought to counter the influence (and toll rights) of the archbishop of Mainz, who had just built Burg Lahneck, a castle at the confluence of the Lahn and Rhine rivers. Its superbly furnished period rooms and beautiful gardens are well worth a visit. From B-9 (curbside parking) it's about a 15-minute walk to the castle entrance. ⊠ *Koblenz* ☎ *0261/51656* ⊕ *www.schloss-stolzenfels.de* ⤳ *€5* ☉ *Closed Dec. and Jan. Closed weekdays Feb.–mid-Mar. and Nov. Closed Mon. mid-Mar.–Oct.*

St. Kastor Basilika (*St. Castor Basilica*). It was in this sturdy Romanesque basilica, consecrated in 836, that plans were drawn for the Treaty of Verdun a few years later, formalizing the division of Charlemagne's great empire and leading to the creation of Germany and France as separate states. Inside Koblenz's oldest church, compare the squat Romanesque columns in the nave with the intricate fan vaulting of the Gothic sections. The **St. Kastor Fountain** outside the church is an intriguing piece of historical one-upmanship. It was built by the occupying French to mark the beginning of Napoléon's ultimately disastrous Russian campaign of 1812. ✉ *Kastorhof* 🌐 *www.sankt-kastor-koblenz.de.*

WHERE TO EAT

$ GERMAN 🍴 **Altes Brauhaus.** For a classic brewery pub experience, look no further than this traditional German restaurant with its classic chequered flooring, wooden furniture, and welcoming owner. The hearty food here comes in large portions: if you're feeling hungry, order the *Haxentopf "Spezial,"* chunks of pork knuckle meat braised with onions and vegetables and served in a cast-iron pan with potatoes and a fried egg; wash it down with a glass of Königsbacher Pilsener. **Known for:** good selection of beers; friendly service; welcoming atmosphere. [$] *Average main: €10* ✉ *Braug. 4* ☎ *0261/133–0377* 🌐 *www.altesbrauhaus-koblenz.de* 💳 *No credit cards.*

$ INTERNATIONAL 🍴 **eGeLoSIa.** Ice-cream fans can't miss a visit to this ice-cream shop opposite the Liebfrauenkirche. Inventive flavors and natural ingredients mean that the cold sweets here, from bitter chocolate and fig or panna cotta caramel ice cream to sour cherry sorbet or eggnog gelato, are hugely popular: be prepared to stand in a long line, but the efficient, friendly staff will have you served as quickly as they can. **Known for:** ice-cream laboratory on show; seasonal flavors; cash only. [$] *Average main: €5* ✉ *Braug. 6* ☎ *0261/133–4264* 🌐 *www.egelosia.de* 💳 *No credit cards.*

$ GERMAN 🍴 **Weinhaus Hubertus.** Hunting scenes and trophies line the wood-paneled walls of this cozy wine restaurant, named after the patron saint of hunters and built in 1689. Hearty portions of fresh, traditional fare (à la *Wildschwein Würstchen,* or wild boar sausages) are what you'll find on offer here. **Known for:** friendly atmosphere; excellent selection of wines; historic hand-painted murals. [$] *Average main: €14* ✉ *Florinsmarkt 6/Ecke Gemüseg.* ☎ *0261/31177* 🌐 *www.weinhaus-hubertus.de* 🕓 *Closed Tues. No lunch Mon.–Thurs.*

$$ GERMAN 🍴 **Zum Weissen Schwanen.** Guests have found a warm welcome in this half-timber inn and mill since 1693, a tradition carried on by the Kunz family, who continue to offer a charming place to enjoy a dinner of well-prepared, contemporary German cuisine with regional specialties. Brasserie Brentano serves lighter dishes as well as lunch and Sunday brunch. **Known for:** official Rheinsteig trail partner; historic restaurant; lovely outdoor seating. [$] *Average main: €20* ✉ *Brunnenstr. 4, Braubach* ✥ *12 km (7½ miles) south of Koblenz via B-42, next to 13th-century town gateway of Braubach, just below Marksburg* ☎ *02627/9820* 🌐 *www.zum-weissen-schwanen.de* 🕓 *Closed Wed. and Thurs. No lunch.*

WHERE TO STAY

$$ HOTEL 🏨 **GHOTEL hotel & living Koblenz.** What this modern block lacks in character it more than makes up for with its location, being ideally positioned for accessing trains, the city center, and Koblenz's main sights. **Pros:** three-minute walk from train station; underground garage; air-conditioned. **Cons:** extra charge for parking; some rooms a little small; restaurant gets very busy during peak times. [$] *Rooms from: €118* ✉ *Neversstr. 15* ☎ *0261/200–2450* 🌐 *www.ghotel.de* 🛏 *120 rooms* 🍴 *Free Breakfast.*

$$ HOTEL 🏨 **Hotel Kleiner Riesen.** You can literally watch the Rhine flowing by from the four front rooms of this friendly, family-operated hotel, about a 10-minute walk from the station. **Pros:** quiet; very good breakfast buffet; good location near most sights. **Cons:** some rooms a little dated; kettles provided but no cups; parking must be booked in advance for an extra charge. [$] *Rooms from: €105* ✉ *Januarius-Zick Str. 11* ☎ *0261/303–460* 🌐 *www.hotel-kleinerriesen.de* 🛏 *22 rooms* 🍴 *Free Breakfast.*

SHOPPING

Koblenz's most pleasant shopping is in the Old Town streets around the market square, Am Plan, where there are plenty of independent boutiques to explore.

Forum Mittelrhein. Built in 2012, this spacious shopping mall offers a wide variety of stores, including well-known brands and smaller boutiques, plus a food court and plentiful parking. ✉ *Zentralpl. 2* ☎ *0261/293–5870* 🌐 *www.forum-mittelrhein.com.*

Pfeffersack und Söhne. A bit of a cult destination for German foodies, Pfeffersack und Söhne create their own dried herb and spice blends from regionally grown plants where possible, as well as dried produce from farther afield. You can buy the gorgeous ceramic pots the spices are sold in separately; also on offer are various gourmet specialties such as mustard, oil, and tea. The staff are friendly, knowledgeable, and very happy to advise you on your spice purchases. ✉ *Schenkendorfstr. 22* ☎ *0261/4509–9290* 🌐 *www.pfeffersackundsoehne.de.*

WINNINGEN

11 km (7 miles) southwest of Koblenz.

Winningen is a gateway to the Terrassenmosel (Lower Mosel), the portion of the river characterized by steep, terraced vineyards. Winches help haul miniature monorails, with the winegrowers and their tools aboard, up the steep incline, but tending and harvesting the vines are all done by hand. **TIP→ For a bird's-eye view of the valley, drive up Fährstrasse to Am Rosenhang, the start of a pleasant walk along the Weinlehrpfad (Educational Wine Path).**

As you head upstream toward Kobern-Gondorf, you'll pass the renowned vineyard site, Uhlen. In Kobern, the Oberburg—a hill castle—and the St. Matthias Kapelle, a 12th-century chapel, are good vantage points. Half-timber houses reflecting the architectural styles of three centuries ring the town's pretty market square.

Stroll through Koblenz's Old Town, stopping for a bite at a sidewalk café along one of the squares, such as Jesuitenplatz.

WHERE TO EAT

$$$ ✕ **Alte Mühle Thomas Höreth.** Thomas and Gudrun Höreth's enchant-
GERMAN   ing country inn—a former mill dating back to 1026—is a labyrinth of little rooms and cellars grouped around oleander-lined courtyards. Highlights of the menu include homemade cheeses, terrines, pâtés, and *Entensülze* (goose in aspic), served with the Höreths' own wines. **Known for:** excellent wine and Sekt (sparkling wine); beautiful loca-tion; eclectic, charming decor. $ *Average main: €22* ✉ *Mühlental 17, Kobern-Gondorf* ⊹ *Via B-416* ☎ *02607/6474* ⊕ *www.thomashoereth. de* ⊙ *No lunch weekdays.*

WHERE TO STAY

$ 🏨 **Hotel Simonis.** Two of the suites in this traditional hotel on Kobern-
B&B/INN   Gondorf's market square, 6 km (4 miles) from Winningen, are across the courtyard, in what might be Germany's oldest half-timber house (1321). **Pros:** historic building; breakfast can also be served in-room (ask at time of booking); free Wi-Fi. **Cons:** no elevator; decor a little outdated; close to the train tracks (can be loud at night). $ *Rooms from: €89* ✉ *Marktpl. 4, Kobern-Gondorf* ☎ *02607/974–8537* ⊕ *www.hotel-simonis.com* ⊙ *Closed Jan. and Feb.* ⤳ *15 rooms* ❗ *Free Breakfast.*

ALKEN

22 km (14 miles) southwest of Koblenz.

One of the Mosel's oldest towns (the Celts were here by 450 BC), today Alken is best known for its 12th-century castle, Burg Thurant. With a pretty waterside setting backdropped by rolling vineyards and the castle above, Alken's among the loveliest wine village stops along the Terassenmosel between Koblenz and Pünderich.

GETTING HERE AND AROUND

The B-49 connects Alken to Koblenz. The nearest train stop, on the Regionalbahn from Koblenz, is at Löf, across the river and linked to Alken by a bridge and a 2½-km (1½-mile) walk.

EXPLORING

Fodor's Choice
★
Burg Eltz (*Eltz Castle*). Genuinely medieval (12th–16th century) and genuinely stunning, Burg Eltz deserves as much attention as King Ludwig's trio of castles in Bavaria. Tours begin every 10 to 15 minutes: for the 40-minute English-language tour, which guides you through the period rooms and massive kitchen, as well as a treasure vault filled with gold and silver, ask at the souvenir shop. To get here, exit B-416 at Hatzenport (opposite and southwest of Alken), proceed to Münstermaifeld, and follow signs to the parking lot near the Antoniuskapelle. From here it's a 15-minute walk, or take the shuttle bus (€2). Hikers can reach the castle from Moselkern in about an hour. ⊠ *Burg Eltz, Münstermaifeld* ☎ *02672/950–500* ⊕ *www.burg-eltz.de* 🎫 *Tour and treasure vault €10* ⊗ *Closed Nov.–Mar.*

Burg Thurant. This 12th-century castle towers over the village and the Burgberg (castle hill) vineyard. Castle tours include the chapel, cellar, tower, and a weapons display, and wine and snacks are served in the courtyard. Allow a good half hour for the climb from the riverbank. ⊠ *Alken* ☎ *02605/2004* ⊕ *www.thurant.de* 🎫 *€4* ⊗ *Closed mid-Nov.–Feb.*

COCHEM

51 km (32 miles) southwest of Koblenz, approximately 93 km (58 miles) from Trier.

Cochem is one of the most attractive towns of the Mosel Valley, with a riverside promenade to rival any along the Rhine. It's especially lively during the wine festivals in June and late August. If time permits, savor the landscape from the deck of a boat—many excursions are available, lasting from one hour to an entire day. From the **Enderttor** (Endert Town Gate) you can see the entrance to one of Germany's longest railroad tunnels, the Kaiser-Wilhelm, an astonishing example of 19th-century engineering. The 4-km (2½-mile) tunnel saves travelers a 21-km (13-mile) detour along one of the Mosel's great loops.

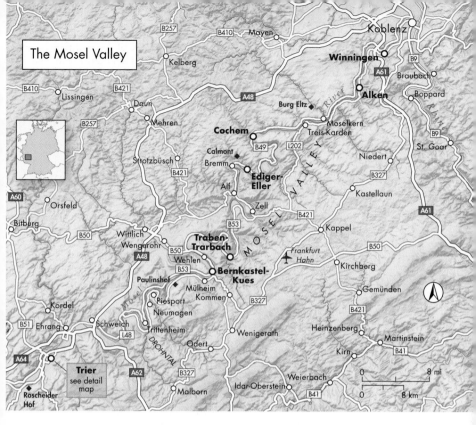

The Mosel Valley

Trier
see detail
map

Contacts **Tourist-Information Ferienland Cochem.** ✉ *Endertpl. 1*
☎ *02671/60040* ⊕ *www.cochem.de.*

EXPLORING

Cochemer Sesselbahn (*Cochem Chairlift*). A ride on the chairlift to the
Pinner Kreuz provides great vistas, which you can enjoy from the terrace of the café at the top ✉ *Endertstr. 44* ☎ *02671/989–063* ⊕ *www.
cochemer-sesselbahn.de* 🎫 *€7 round-trip* ⊗ *Closed early Nov.–mid-Mar.*

Historische Senfmühle. Wolfgang Steffens conducts half-hour daily tours
at 11, 2, 3, and 4, showing how he produces the gourmet mustard at
his 200-year-old mill. Garlic, cayenne, honey, curry, and Riesling wine
are among the flavors you can sample and buy in the shop. From the
Old Town, walk across the bridge toward Cond. The mill is to the left
of the bridgehead. ✉ *Endertstr. 18* ☎ *02671/607–665* ⊕ *www.senfm-
uehle.net* 🎫 *Tours €3.*

Reichsburg (*Imperial Fortress*). The 15-minute walk to this 1,000-year-
old castle overlooking the town will reward you with great views of
the area. English guided tours lasting 40 minutes take place daily at
noon and 3 pm throughout the summer; check the website for tours

during the winter months. During the first week of August, there's a medieval festival including colorful tournaments. On Friday (7 pm) and Saturday (6 pm) evenings, medieval banquets take place in German but with English translation sheets to accompany the feasting and merriment; the price includes a castle tour. ✉ *Schlossstr. 36* ☎ *02671/255* 🌐 *www.reichsburg-cochem.de* 🎫 *€6; medieval banquets €49* ⏲ *Castle restaurant closed mid-Nov.–Dec. 25.*

WHERE TO EAT

$ GERMAN 🍴 **Alte Gutsschänke.** Locals and tourists mingle naturally here, near the open fireplace and antique winemaking equipment; as the night progresses, locals might unpack their musical instruments and start playing. The food is local and fortifying: sausages, cheeses, ham, and homemade soups served with the wines from host Arthur Schmitz's own estate. **Known for:** very friendly atmosphere; simple, rustic dishes; excellent wine list. [$] *Average main: €10* ✉ *Schlossstr. 6* ☎ *02671/8950* 💳 *No credit cards* ⏲ *No lunch.*

$$$ GERMAN FAMILY 🍴 **Restaurant Müllerstube.** The rustic family inn Moselromantik Hotel Weissmühle is set amid the forested hills of the Enderttal (Endert Valley) on the site of a historic mill that belonged to the current proprietor's great-great-grandfather. Beneath the exposed beams and painted ceiling of Restaurant Müllerstube, trout from the hotel's own fish farm will grace your table, served alongside German and French wines. **Known for:** underground bar filled with 1970s kitsch; seasonal specialties; quiet location despite being only a short drive from Cochem. [$] *Average main: €22* ✉ *Im Enderttal* ☎ *02671/8955* 🌐 *www.hotel-weissmuehle.de.*

EDIGER-ELLER

61 km (38 miles) southwest of Koblenz.

Ediger-Eller, once two separate hamlets, is another photogenic wine village with well-preserved houses and remnants of a medieval town wall. It's particularly romantic at night, when the narrow alleys and half-timber buildings are illuminated by historic streetlights.

EXPLORING

Calmont. As you continue along the winding course of the Mosel, you'll pass Europe's steepest vineyard site, Calmont, just before the loop at Bremm. Opposite Calmont are the romantic ruins of a 12th-century Augustinian convent. 🌐 *www.calmont-region.de.*

Martinskirche (*St. Martin's Church*). The church is a remarkable amalgamation of art and architectural styles, inside and out. Take a moment to admire the 117 carved bosses in the star-vaulted ceiling of the nave. Among the many fine sculptures throughout the church and the chapel is the town's treasure: a Renaissance stone relief, *Christ in the Winepress.* ✉ *Kirchstr.*

Zell. This popular village is full of pubs and wineshops that ply the crowds with Zeller Schwarze Katz, or "Black Cat" wine, a commercially successful product and the focal point of a large wine festival in late June. Some 6 million vines hug the slopes around Zell, making it one of Germany's largest wine-growing communities. The area between Zell and Schweich (near Trier), known as the Middle Mosel, is home to some of the world's finest Riesling. 🌐 *www.zell-mosel.com.*

WHERE TO STAY

$ HOTEL 🏨 **Zum Löwen.** This simply furnished hotel comes with friendly service and a splendid terrace overlooking the Mosel. **Pros:** fine view of the Mosel; some rooms have balconies; good restaurant. **Cons:** on a busy street; no elevator; suite only bookable for two nights or more. [$] *Rooms from: €99* ✉ *Moselweinstr. 23* ☎ *02675/208* 🌐 *www.mosel-hotel-loewen.de* 🕒 *Closed late Dec.–Mar.* 🛏 *20 rooms* 🍴 *Free Breakfast.*

TRABEN-TRARBACH

30 km (19 miles) south of Cochem.

The Mosel divides Traben-Trarbach, which has pleasant promenades on both sides of the river. Its wine festivals are held in July. Traben's art nouveau buildings are worth seeing, including the Hotel Bellevue, the gateway on the Mosel bridge, the post office, the train station, and the town hall.

After passing Traben-Trarbach—and during the next 24 km (15 miles) down the Mosel—you'll pass by world-famous vineyards, such as Erdener Treppchen, Ürziger Würzgarten, the *Sonnenuhr* (sundial) sites of Zeltingen and Wehlen, and Graacher Himmelreich, before reaching Bernkastel-Kues.

EXPLORING

Mittelmosel Museum. For a look at some 20 fine 18th- and 19th-century rooms visit the Mittelmosel Museum in the baroque villa Haus Böcking (1750), which exhibits a number of works of art as well as a collection on the historical development of the area. ✉ *Casino Str. 2* ☎ *06541/9480* 🕒 *Closed Mon. Easter–Oct.*

WHERE TO STAY

$$ HOTEL 🏨 **Jugendstilhotel Bellevue.** Traben-Trarbach's premier hotel has a first-class reputation that derives from its belle époque architecture, fine cuisine, professional, knowledgeable staff, and superb wine list. **Pros:** fantastic art nouveau surroundings; prime Mosel-side location; wonderful breakfast. **Cons:** expensive; some rooms lack river views; some rooms accessed by stairs only. [$] *Rooms from: €170* ✉ *An der Mosel 11* ☎ *06541/7030* 🌐 *www.bellevue-hotel.de* 🛏 *68 rooms* 🍴 *Free Breakfast.*

Continued on page 471

In the heart of the Mosel Valley lies the Mittelmosel (Middle Mosel), where vineyards tumble down steep slate slopes to riverside villages full of half-timbered, baroque, and belle époque architecture. Famed for its warm climate and 2,000-year-old winemaking tradition, it produces some of the best Rieslings in the world. The Middle Mosel's many wineries and tasting rooms are concentrated along a meandering 75-mile stretch of lush river valley, picturesque towns, and rural estates between the ancient town of Trier and the village of Zell, allowing for multiple sips in a short amount of time.

By Jeff Kavanagh

Above, Dr Pauly-Bergweiler bottle.
Left, Vineyards in the Mosel Valley.

Wine Tasting
in the
Mosel Valley

TWO DAYS IN THE MIDDLE MOSEL

DAY 1

Traben-Trarbach

Small, family-run wineries that have been producing high-quality wines for generations dominate the Middle Mosel. Starting in Trier, just across the border from Luxembourg, the tour follows the B-53 and the Mosel River as it flows northwest through a succession of pretty wine villages and steep-sloped estates.

Map labels:
Alf
Velschbill
Kordel
Ehrang
Kenn
Schweich
Mehring
Fell
Trier
Episcopal Wine Estates
Weinstube Kesselstatt
Leiwen
Dhronfal
Sektgut St. Laurentius
Klüsserath
Neumagen
Weingut Lehnert-Veit
Piesport
Mülheim
Braueberg
Weingut Karp-Schreiber
Weingut Bauer
Weinromantik Richtershof Hotel
Wengerohr
Rachtig-Zeltingen
Rebenhof
Schmitges
Kröv
Enkirch
Weingut Martin Mül
Jugendstilho
Bellevue
Kerpen
Wehlen
Traben-Trarbac
Der Ratskeller
Bernkastel-Kues
Dr. Pauly-Bergweiler
Monzelfeld
Kommen
MOSEL VALLEY
Moselle

Bischöfliche Weingüter
Drop down into a labyrinth of cellars beneath Trier's streets or visit the estate's elegant *vinothek* (wine store) to sample fine Rieslings built upon almost two millennia of priestly tradition. **Try:** fruity and elegant Scharzhofberger Riesling.
✉ Gervasiusstrasse 1, Trier
☎ 0651/145–760
🌐 www.bischoeflichewe-ingueter.de

Mosel grape harvest

Sektgut St. Laurentius
Whether in the spacious tasting room, on the outdoor terrace, or in the modern little wine bar near the river, there are plenty of places to taste this winery's *sekt* (sparkling wine), considered some of the best in the region. **Try:** fruity, creamy, and yeasty Crémant.
✉ Laurentiusstrasse 4, Leiwen
☎ 06507/3836
🌐 www.st-laurentius-sekt.de

Weingut Lehnert-Veit
In addition to Riesling, visitors can sample Merlot, Pinot Noir, and Chardonnay in this winery's Mediterranean-style garden on the banks of the Mosel. **Try:** playfully fruity Felsenwingert Goldtröpfchen Riesling.

✉ In der Dur 6–10, Piesport
☎ 06507/2123
🌐 www.weingut-lv.net

Weingut Karp-Schreiber
This welcoming winery's varietals include Riesling and Weissburgunder; Regent; it also produces a nice Rotling, a *cuvée* (blend) of Müller-Thurgau and Regent. When the sun's shining, the best place to taste them is on the winery's little trellised veranda. **Try:** fresh, elegant "my karp" Riesling.
✉ Moselweinstrasse 186, Braueberg
☎ 06534/236
🌐 www.karp-schreiber.de

Weingut Bauer
An extension of the family home, where four generations reside beneath the same roof, the Bauer's simple, modern tasting room is a good place to sample award-winning still and sparkling white wines presented with old-fashioned hospitality. **Try:** fruity, refreshing Winzersekt Riesling Brut.
✉ Moselstrasse 3, Mülheim
☎ 06534/571
🌐 www.weingut-bauer.de

| Wine barrels at Kerpen | Weingut Karp-Schreiber | Vineyards in the Mosel Valley |

DAY 2

From the quiet village of Mül-heim, the Mosel makes a couple of sweeping loops up the val-ley, passing through the towns of Bernkastel-Kues and Traben-Trarbach as it winds along.

Dr. Pauly-Bergweiler
This winery's presence in the Mosel includes vineyards in seven different villages and a grand villa in the center of Bernkastel, where its cozy vinothek finds space within the mansion's vaulted cellars. **Try:** racy, flinty Alte Badstube am Doctorberg Riesling.
✉ Gestade 15, Bernkastel
☎ 06531/3002
⊕ www.pauly-bergweiler.com

Kerpen
A friendly husband-and-wife-run winery, Kerpen has eight generations of winemaking tra-dition, a special collection of Rieslings with labels designed by visiting artists, and an un-pretentious tasting room within a stone's throw of the river. **Try:** dry Graacher Himmelreich Riesling Kabinett Feinherb.
✉ Uferallee 6, Bernkastel-Wehlen
☎ 06531/6868
⊕ www.weingut-kerpen.de

Rebenhof
You'll find only Rieslings in Rebenhof's stylish, contempo-rary tasting room, which shares space with stainless-steel fermentation tanks. **Try:** flinty, old-vine Ürziger Würtgarten Riesling Spätlese.
✉ Hüwel 2-3, Ürzig
☎ 06532/4546
⊕ www.rebenhof-schmitz.de

Schmitges
Located on an unassuming village lane, Schmitges spe-cializes in the production of high-quality dry whites that, along with the modern, wine-bar style of their vinothek, distinguishes them from many other local establishments.
Try: light, summery Rivaner.
✉ Hauptstrasse 4, Erden
☎ 06532/2743
⊕ www.schmitges-weine.de

Weingut Martin Müllen
Established in 1991, this win-ery is a mere infant compared to many others here, but its success has its roots in mod-ern and traditional winemaking principles, and one of the best *Grand Cru* (great growth) vine-yards in the region. **Try:** light but complex Trarbacher Hüh-nerberg Riesling Spätlese.
✉ Alte Marktstrasse 2, Traben-Trarbach
☎ 06541/9470
⊕ www.muellen.de

STOP FOR A BITE

✖ Weinstube Kesselstatt
Sitting beneath vines in the shadow of the Liebfrauen-kirche and the Trier Dom you can sip Kesselstatt estate wines and snack on wild boar and locally produced cheese.
✉ Liebfrauenstrasse 10, Trier
☎ 0651/41178
⊕ weinstube-kesselstatt.de

✖ Weinromantik Richters-hof Hotel
An ideal place for lovers of the grape, this stately hotel has a bistro that serves sea-sonal dishes such as white as-paragus and ham, a gourmet restaurant offering contempo-rary cuisine, and a wine list that runs to 350 bottles, 150 of which are from the Mosel.
✉ Hauptstrasse 81-83, Mül-heim
☎ 06534/9480
⊕ www.weinromantikhotel.de

✖ Der Ratskeller
Just off Bernkastel's main square, Der Ratskeller's un-complicated regional fare can be enjoyed at an outside table with a view of the action or in-side cozily surrounded by dark wood and leadlight windows.
✉ Markt 30, Bernkastel-Kues
☎ 06531/973–1000
⊕ www.ratskeller-bernkastel.de

✖ Jugendstilhotel Bellevue
Traben-Trarbach's premier hotel has a first-class repu-tation that derives from its belle époque architecture, fine cuisine, professional, knowledgeable staff, and su-perb wine list.
✉ An der Mosel 11, Traben-Trarbach
☎ 06541/7030
⊕ www.bellevue-hotel.de

WINE TOURING AND TASTING

WHEN TO GO
The best time to visit the region is between May and September, when a lightly chilled glass or two of wine is the perfect complement to a sunny spring day or a warm summer evening. This coincides with high season in the valley, when roads and cycle paths swell with tourists, particularly in the warmer months, and in September during the wine harvest. Fortunately, the next wine village is never far along the Mosel River. If you arrive and find a tasting room that's too busy, there's invariably another just around the corner.

IN THE TASTING ROOM
While varietals such as Müller-Thurgau, Weissburgunder, and Pinot Noir are produced in the Middle Mosel, the staple of most estates is Riesling. Given that the wineries are predominantly small, family-owned operations, there tends to be an emphasis on the production of high-quality, low-quantity wines. Their tasting rooms, when not part of the winery itself, are frequently extensions of family homes, affording visitors intimate contact with the winemakers. Naturally, German is the dominant language spoken by local tourists and many of the Dutch, Belgians, and Luxembourgers who pop across the border for a visit, but most winemakers speak English at least well enough to describe their wines. Opening hours vary, and although you can drop into most tasting rooms outside of these times, there may not always be someone around to serve you. To avoid disappointment it's worth checking websites for opening times first.

BOTTLE PRICES AND TASTING FEES
Once the most expensive wines in the world, Mosel Valley Rieslings have come down significantly in price since their heyday in the early 20th century, yet they remain world class. Quality bottles of Riesling start at about €10; each winery's price list is generally detailed in brochures found in its tasting room. Most wineries won't charge to taste a couple of their wines, but will expect you to purchase a bottle or two if you try more. Those that do have tasting fees, which are commonly between €5 and €15, will often waive them if you purchase a bottle.

Left, Romantic wine village on the Mosel River.
Right, Bottle display from Mosel-Weinmuseum in Bernkastel-Kues

BERNKASTEL-KUES

22 km (14 miles) southwest of Traben-Trarbach, 100 km (62 miles) southwest of Koblenz.

Bernkastel and Kues straddle the Mosel, on the east and west banks, respectively. Bernkastel is home to famed Bernkasteler Doctor, a small, especially steep vineyard that makes one of Europe's most expensive wines. Early German humanist Nikolaus Cusanus (1401–64) was from Kues; today his birthplace and St.-Nikolaus-Hospital are popular attractions.

GETTING HERE AND AROUND

By car, Bernkastel-Kues is about 45 minutes northeast of Trier and 90 minutes southwest of Koblenz. The closest train station (Regionalbahn) is in Wittlich, about a 20-minute taxi ride away.

VISITOR INFORMATION

Contacts Bernkastel-Kues Tourist-Information. ⌧ *Gestade 6* ☏ *06531/500– 190* ⊕ *www.bernkastel.de.*

EXPLORING

Burgruine Landshut. From the hilltop ruins of this 13th-century castle there are splendid views. It was here that Trier's Archbishop Boemund II is said to have recovered from an illness by drinking the local wine. This legendary vineyard, still known as "the Doctor," soars up from Hinterm Graben street near the town gate, Graacher Tor. You can purchase these well-regarded wines at some of the shops around town. ⌧ *Bernkastel-Kues.*

Jüdischer Friedhof. Bernkastel's former Jewish population was well assimilated into town society until the Nazis took power. You can ask at the tourist center to borrow a key to the town's Jewish cemetery, reachable by a scenic half-hour hike through the vineyards in the direction of Traben-Trarbach. Opened in the mid-19th century, it contains a few headstones from a destroyed 17th-century graveyard. ⌧ *Str. "Unter Thanisch"* ⊹ *About 1 km (½ mile) from Graacher Tor.*

Mittelalterlicher Marktplatz. Elaborately carved half-timber houses (16th–17th century) and a Renaissance town hall (1608) frame St. Michael's Fountain (1606) on Bernkastel's photogenic medieval market square. From late August to early September, the square and riverbank are lined with wine stands for one of the region's largest wine festivals, the Weinfest der Mittelmosel. ⌧ *Bernkastel-Kues.*

Mosel Wein Museum (*The Mosel Wine Museum*). Within St.-Nikolaus-Hospital is a wine museum as well as a bistro. There's also a *Vinothek* (wineshop) in the vaulted cellar, where you can sample more than 150 wines from the entire Mosel-Saar-Ruwer region. ⌧ *St.-Nikolaus-Hospital, Cusanusstr. 2* ⊕ *www.moselweinmuseum.de* ⌦ *Museum €5; Vinothek free, wine tasting €15.*

Paulinshof. The 55-km (34-mile) drive from Bernkastel to Trier takes in another series of outstanding hillside vineyards, including the Braune-berg, 10 km (6 miles) upstream from Bernkastel. On the opposite side of the river is the Paulinshof, where Thomas Jefferson was impressed by a 1783 Brauneberger Kammer Auslese during his visit here in 1788. You can sample contemporary vintages of this wine in the beautiful chapel on the estate grounds. ✉ *Paulinsstr. 14, Kesten ✢ 10.4 km (6½ miles) down river from Berkastel-Kues* ☎ *06535/544* 🌐 *www.paulinshof.de* 🕒 *Closed Sun.*

Piesport. On a magnificent loop 12 km (7½ miles) southwest of Brauneberg stands the famous village of Piesport, whose steep, slate cliff is known as the Loreley of the Mosel. The village puts on a fireworks display for its Loreleyfest the first weekend in July. Wines from its 35 vineyards are collectively known as Piesporter Michelsberg. The finest individual vineyard site, and one of Germany's very best, is the Goldtröpfchen (little droplets of gold). ✉ *Piesport ✢ 18.7 km (11½ miles) down river from Bernkastel-Kues.*

St.-Nikolaus-Hospital. The Renaissance philosopher and theologian Nikolaus Cusanus (1401–64) was born in Kues. The St.-Nikolaus-Hospital is a charitable *Stiftung* (foundation) he established in 1458, famous for his library that contains more than 300 handwritten manuscripts from the 9th through 15th centuries, and it still operates today as a home for the elderly and a wine estate. ✉ *Cusanusstr. 2* ☎ *06531/2260* 🌐 *www.cusanus.de* 🎫 *Tours €7* 🕒 *Closed Nov.–Mar.*

WHERE TO EAT

$$ FRENCH
🍴 **Rotisserie Royale.** This French restaurant is housed in one of Burgstrasse's charming listed half-timber houses. The fish menu, vegetarian selection, and fancy twists on traditional and regional dishes are what set tit apart from the crowd. **Known for:** five-course menu for two people or more; historic setting; local wines. [$] *Average main: €17* ✉ *Burgstr. 19* ☎ *06531/6572* 🌐 *www.rotisserie-royale.de* 💳 *No credit cards* 🕒 *Closed Wed.*

$$$$ FRENCH
Fodor's Choice ★
🍴 **Waldhotel Sonnora.** At this elegant country hotel in the forested Eifel Hills, guests are offered one of Germany's absolute finest dining experiences in a room plush with gold and white wood furnishings and red carpet. Choose a five-, seven-, or eight-course menu or dine à la carte: the chef is renowned for transforming truffles, foie gras, and Persian caviar into masterful dishes, and challans duck in an orange-tarragon sauce is his specialty. **Known for:** elegant surroundings; excellent wine list; numerous accolades. [$] *Average main: €70* ✉ *1 Auf dem Eichelfeld, Dreis* ☎ *06578/406* 🌐 *www.hotel-sonnora.de* 🕒 *Closed Mon. and Tues., and 2 wks in summer and winter.*

$$$ EUROPEAN
🍴 **Weinhotel St. Stephanus.** Rita and Hermann Saxler operate a comfortable, modern hotel and upscale restaurant in a 19th-century manor house on the *Ufer* (riverbank) at Zeltingen. Whether you opt for the handsome dining room or the terrace overlooking the Mosel, Saxler's restaurant is a good destination for refined regional cooking with a Mediterranean touch. **Known for:** seasonal menus; three- and four-course menus in addition to à la carte; premium wine list. [$] *Average main: €22* ✉ *Uferallee 9, Zeltingen-Rachtig* ☎ *06532/680* 🌐 *www.hotel-stephanus.de* 🕒 *No lunch Mon.–Thurs. Jan.–Mar.*

WHERE TO STAY

$$ B&B/INN **Wein- & Landhaus S. A. Prüm.** The spacious rooms and baths at this welcoming hotel are all individually decorated with a winning mixture of contemporary and antique furnishings and thoughtful touches such as fresh flowers and an honesty bar. **Pros:** some rooms have vineyard and Mosel views; very good breakfast; charging point for electric cars (at an extra cost). **Cons:** no elevator; reception not manned 24 hours; no air-conditioning. [$] *Rooms from: €130* ✉ *Uferallee 25* ☎ *06531/3110* 🌐 *www.sapruem.com* 🕑 *Closed 2 wks in winter* 🛏 *10 rooms* 🍴 *Free Breakfast.*

$$ HOTEL Fodor's Choice ★ **Weinromantikhotel Richtershof.** This renovated 17th-century manor in a shady park offers comfortable rooms and first-class friendly service. **Pros:** garden terrace; on-site parking; 24-hour room service. **Cons:** thin walls; no air-conditioning; decor a little dated. [$] *Rooms from: €165* ✉ *Hauptstr. 81–83, Mülheim* ✥ *5 km (3 miles) south of Bernkastel via B-53* ☎ *06534/9480* 🌐 *www.weinromantikhotel.de* 🛏 *43 rooms* 🍴 *Free Breakfast.*

TRIER

55 km (34 miles) southwest of Bernkastel-Kues, 150 km (93 miles) southwest of Koblenz.

Thanks to its deep history, the Trier of today holds a wealth of ancient sites. It's also an important university town, and accordingly boasts a surprisingly rich modern cultural landscape for a city of its size (just over 100,000 residents).

Its roots reach back to at least 400 BC, by which time a Celtic tribe, the Treveri, had settled the Trier Valley. Eventually, Julius Caesar's legions arrived at this strategic point on the river, and Augusta Treverorum ("the town of [Emperor] Augustus in the land of the Treveri") was founded in 16 BC. It was described as an opulent city, as beautiful as any outside Rome.

Around AD 275 an Alemannic tribe stormed Augusta Treverorum and reduced it to rubble. But it was rebuilt in even grander style and renamed Treveris. Eventually it evolved into one of the leading cities of the empire, and was promoted to *Roma secunda* (a second Rome) north of the Alps. As a powerful administrative capital it was adorned with all the noble civic buildings of a major Roman settlement, as well as public baths, palaces, barracks, an amphitheater, and temples. The Roman emperors Diocletian (who made it one of the four joint capitals of the empire) and Constantine both lived in Trier for years at a time.

Trier survived the collapse of Ancient Rome and became an important center of Christianity and, ultimately, one of the most powerful archbishoprics in the Holy Roman Empire. The city thrived throughout the Renaissance and baroque periods, taking full advantage of its location at the meeting point of major east–west and north–south trade routes and growing fat on the commerce that passed through.

GETTING HERE AND AROUND

The area is excellent for biking. Rentals are available from the cycling station near track 11 of the main train station (from €12 per day). Cyclists can follow the marked route of the *Radroute Nahe-Hunsrück-Mosel* between Trier and Bingen.

FESTIVALS

Altstadtfest. On the last weekend in June, more than 100,000 people come out for this music festival in Trier's Old Town, which features several music stages as well as a citywide run, markets, a parade and 120 food and drink stalls. Major venues include the Trier Arena and Trier Europahalle, hosting the likes of André Rieu, James Last, and Deep Purple. ⊠ *Trier ⊕ www.altstadtfest-trier.de.*

Moselfest Zurlauben. Also known as *Mosel in Flammen* (Mosel on fire), this annual July celebration along the Zurlauben riverbank (as part of the several days-long festival, the *Zurlaubener Heimatfest*) involves much wine, sparkling wine, and beer, and an impressive display of fireworks. ⊠ *Trier ⊕ www.zurlaubener-heimatfest.de.*

Trier Weinfest (*Wine Festival*). This traditional wine festival takes place in early August in the Olewig district of Trier. As well as local wine, there's live music and various regional culinary specialties to be enjoyed. ⊠ *Trier ⊕ www.trier-info.de.*

Trierer Weihnachtsmarkt. Trier's Christmas market features nearly a hundred wooden huts selling Christmas decorations, toys and candles, as well as *Glühwein* (mulled wine), sausages, and potato cakes. It takes place on the main market square and in front of the impressive backdrop of Trier cathedral. ⊠ *Trier ⊕ www.trierer-weihnachtsmarkt.de.*

TOURS

BUS TOURS

Römer-Express. You can circumnavigate the town with the multilingual narrated tours of the Römer-Express trolley. It departs from Porta Nigra, near the tourist office. ⊠ *An der Porta Nigra* ☎ *0651/9935–9525* ⊕ *www.roemer-express.de* ⊠ *From €9.*

WALKING TOURS

City Tours. Various city tours are offered by the tourist office, by bike, foot or bus. The English-language walking tour takes place Saturday at 1 pm, May through October. Reservations are essential; tickets are available from the tourist office. ⊠ *Tourist Information Trier, An der Porta Nigra* ☎ *0651/978–080 Tourist Information Trier* ⊕ *www.trier-info.de* ⊠ *From €8.*

VISITOR INFORMATION

Contacts Tourist Information Trier. ⊠ *An der Porta Nigra* ☎ *0651/978–080* ⊕ *www.trier-info.de.*

EXPLORING

11

Fodor's Choice
★
Amphitheater. The sheer size of Trier's oldest Roman structure (circa AD 100) is impressive; in its heyday it seated 20,000 spectators. You can climb down to the cellars beneath the arena—animals were kept in cells here before being unleashed to do battle with gladiators. Gladiatorial performances (1¼ hours) take place Friday through Sunday and holidays at 6 pm (also 8 pm during very busy times) from April through September, at 5 pm in October. Tickets can be booked in advance at Tourist Information. ⊠ *Oleweiger Str.* ⚏*€3; Gladiator performances €14.*

Bischöfliche Weingüter (*Episcopal Wine Estates*). Drop down into a labyrinth of cellars beneath Trier's streets or visit the estate's elegant *Vinothek* (wine store) to sample fine Rieslings, which were built on almost two millennia of priestly tradition. Tastings are available for four wines, including one sparkling. ⊠ *Gervasiusstr.1* ☎ *0651/145–760* ⊕ *www.bischoeflicheweingueter.de* ⚏ *Wine tastings from €15* ⊙ *Closed Sun.*

Fodor's Choice
★
Kaiserthermen (*Imperial Baths*). This enormous 4th-century bathing palace once housed cold- and hot-water baths and a sports field. Although only the masonry of the Calderium (hot baths) and the vast basements remain, they are enough to give a fair idea of the original splendor and size of the complex. Originally 98 feet high, the walls you see today are just 62 feet high. ⊠ *Weberbach 41* ☎ *0651/436–2550* ⊕ *www.zentrum-der-antike.de* ⚏ *€4.*

Karl-Marx-Haus. Marx was born on May 5, 1818, in this bourgeois house built in 1727. Visitors with a serious interest in social history will be fascinated by its small museum. Some of Marx's personal effects, as well as first-edition manifestos are on display. Audio guides are available in English. ⊠ *Brückenstr. 10* ☎ *0651/970–680* ⊕ *www.fes.de/karl-marx-haus* ⚏ *€5.*

Konstantin Basilika (*Constantine Basilica*). An impressive reminder of Trier's Roman past, this edifice, now the city's major Protestant church, was built by the emperor Constantine around AD 310 as the imperial throne room of the palace. At 239 feet long, 93 feet wide, and 108 feet high, it demonstrates the astounding ambition of its Roman builders and the sophistication of their building techniques. The basilica is one of the two largest Roman interiors in existence (the other is the Pantheon in Rome). Look up at the deeply coffered ceiling; more than any other part of the building, it conveys the opulence of the original structure. An ornate rococo garden now separates the basilica from the Landesmuseum. ⊠ *Konstantinpl. 10* ☎ *0651/9949–1200* ⊕ *ekkt.ekir.de.*

Museum am Dom Trier (*Museum at the Trier Cathedral*). This collection, just behind the Dom, focuses on medieval sacred art, and there are also fascinating models of the cathedral as it looked in Roman times. Look for the 15 Roman frescoes, discovered in 1946, that may have adorned the Emperor Constantine's palace. ⊠ *Bischof-Stein-Pl. 1* ☎ *0651/710–5255* ⊕ *www.bistum-trier.de/museum* ⚏ *From €4* ⊙ *Closed Mon.*

Porta Nigra (*Black Gate*). The best-preserved Roman structure in Trier was originally a city gate, built in the 2nd century (look for holes left by the iron clamps that held the structure together). The gate served as part of Trier's defenses and was proof of the sophistication of Roman military might and its ruthlessness. Attackers were often lured into the two innocent-looking arches of the Porta Nigra, only to find themselves enclosed in a courtyard. In the 11th century the upper stories were converted into two churches, in use until the 18th century. The tourist office is next door. ⊠ *Porta-Nigra-Pl.* ☎ *0651/978–080 Tourist Information* ⊕ *www.trier-info.de* ⊠ *€4.*

Rheinisches Landesmuseum (*Rhenish State Museum*). The largest collection of Roman antiquities in Germany is housed here. The highlight is the 4th-century stone relief of a Roman ship transporting barrels of wine up the river. This tombstone of a Roman wine merchant was discovered in 1874, when Constantine's citadel in Neumagen was excavated. Have a look at the 108-square-foot model of the city as it looked in the 4th century—it provides a sense of perspective to many of the sights you can still visit today. ⊠ *Weimarer-Allee 1* ☎ *0651/97740* ⊕ *www.landesmuseum-trier.de* ⊠ *€8* ⊗ *Closed Mon.*

Roscheider Hof. For a look at 19th- and 20th-century rural life in the Mosel-Saar area, visit this hilltop *Freilichtmuseum* (open-air museum) near Konz-Saar, 10 km (6 miles) southwest of Trier via B-51. Numerous farmhouses and typical village buildings in the region were saved from the wrecking ball by being dismantled and brought to the Roscheider Hof, where they were rebuilt and refurnished as they appeared decades ago. Old schoolrooms, a barbershop and beauty salon, a tavern, a shoemaker's workshop, a pharmacy, a grocery, and a dentist's office have been set up in the rooms of the museum proper, along with period rooms and exhibitions on local trades and household work, such as the history of laundry. A large collection of tin figures is here too, and there's also a Biedermeier rose garden, museum shop, and restaurant with beer garden (closed Monday) on the grounds. ⊠ *Roscheiderhof 1, Konz* ☎ *06501/92710* ⊕ *www.roscheiderhof.de* ⊠ *€7* ⊗ *Closed Mon. mid-Dec.–Jan.*

Trierer Dom (*Trier Cathedral*). The oldest Christian church north of the Alps, the Dom stands on the site of the Palace of Helen. Constantine tore the palace down in AD 330 and put up a large church in its place. The church burned down in 336, and a second, even larger one was built. Parts of the foundations of this third building can be seen in the east end of the present structure (begun in about 1035). The cathedral you see today is a weighty and sturdy edifice with small round-head windows, rough stonework, and asymmetrical towers, as much a fortress as a church. Inside, Gothic styles predominate—the result of remodeling in the 13th century—although there are also many baroque tombs, altars, and confessionals. The highlight of the **Schatzkammer** (Cathedral Treasury) is the 10th-century Andreas Tragaltar (St. Andrew's Portable Altar), constructed of oak and covered with gold leaf, enamel, and ivory by local craftsmen. It's a reliquary for the soles of St. Andrew's sandals, as signaled by the gilded, life-size foot on the top of the altar. You can also visit the Cathedral

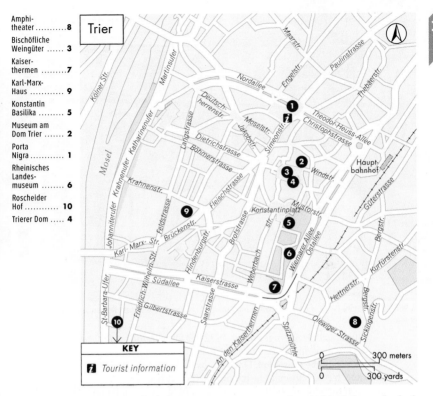

KEY

🛈 *Tourist information*

Museum, which has a separate entrance just behind the cathedral. ✉ *Liebfrauenstr. 12* ☏ *0651/979–0792* ⊕ *www.dominformation.de* 💶 *Cathedral free; Schatzkammer from €2* ⊘ *Schatzkammer closed Mon. in Nov. and Jan.–Mar.*

WHERE TO EAT

$$$$ ✕ **Becker's Hotel.** This wine estate in the peaceful suburb of Olewig fea-
GERMAN tures a gourmet restaurant with prix-fixe menus, a wine bar serving regional cuisine, and a casual wine tavern. Bordeaux and Burgundy wines are available in addition to the estate's own wines, and wine tastings, cellar visits, cooking classes and guided tours on the wine path can be arranged. **Known for:** superb food; beautiful terrace; numerous accolades. 💲 *Average main: €30* ✉ *Olewiger Str. 206* ☏ *0651/938–080* ⊕ *www.beckers-trier.de* ⊘ *Closed Sun.–Tues. No lunch.*

$$$$ ✕ **Schlemmereule.** The name means "gourmet owl," and, indeed, the
GERMAN chef caters to gourmets in the 19th-century Palais Walderdorff complex opposite the cathedral. Truffles are a specialty, and the fish is always excellent; wines from top German estates, particularly from the Mosel, as well as an extensive selection of red wines are available. **Known for:** light-filled dining room; decorated with a replica of one of Michaelangelo's Sistine Chapel ceiling paintings; courtyard seating during the

Trier's Porta Nigra (Black Gate), a city gate dating from the 2nd century, is the largest Roman structure north of the Alps.

summer. $ *Average main: €32* ✉ *Domfreihof 1B* ☎ *0651/73616* ⊕ *www.schlemmereule.de* ☾ *Closed Sun.*

$$
GERMAN ✗ **Weinstube Kesselstatt.** Daily soups and stews, hearty fare, cold snacks, and fresh, regional cuisine are served with wines from the Reichsgraf von Kesselstatt estate. The *Tagesgericht* (daily special) and *Aktionsmenü* (prix-fixe menu) are a good bet; *Das Beste der Region* (the region's best) is an ample selection of local hams, cheeses, fish, and breads, served on a wooden board for two. **Known for:** great wine selection; changing seasonal menus; shady terrace in summer. $ *Average main: €15* ✉ *Liebfrauenstr. 10* ☎ *0651/41178* ⊕ *www.weinstube-kesselstatt.de.*

$$
GERMAN ✗ **Zum Domstein.** Whether you dine inside or out, don't miss the collection of Roman artifacts displayed in the cellar. In addition to the German dishes on the regular menu, you can order à la carte or prix-fixe based on recipes attributed to the Roman gourmet Marcus Gavius Apicius in the evening. **Known for:** great location; cozy atmosphere; good outdoor seating for people-watching. $ *Average main: €15* ✉ *Hauptmarkt 5* ☎ *0651/74490* ⊕ *www.domstein.de.*

WHERE TO STAY

$$
B&B/INN 🏨 **Hotel Ambiente.** Markus and Monika Stemper—a passionate cook and a gracious hostess—bring modern style to their country inn near the Luxembourg border. **Pros:** country atmosphere; legendary garden; free parking. **Cons:** removed from city center; breakfast costs extra; reservations essential for restaurant. $ *Rooms from: €109* ✉ *In der Acht 1–2* ☎ *0651/827–280* ⊕ *www.ambiente-trier.de* ⇌ *12 rooms* ⦿❘ *No meals.*

$$ 🏨 **Hotel Petrisberg.** The Pantenburgs' friendly, family-run hotel is high
HOTEL on Petrisberg hill overlooking Trier, not far from the amphitheater and
a 20-minute walk to the Old Town. **Pros:** fine view of Trier; extremely
quiet; attentive service. **Cons:** somewhat removed from the city cen-
ter; no bathtubs; not all rooms have balconies. $ *Rooms from: €110*
⊠ *Sickingenstr. 11–13* ☎ *0651/4640* ⊕ *www.hotelpetrisberg.de* ⤳ *26
rooms* ⦿ *Free Breakfast.*

$$ 🏨 **Römischer Kaiser.** Centrally located near the Porta Nigra, this hand-
HOTEL some patrician manor from 1885 offers well-appointed rooms with
attractive baths. **Pros:** near the Porta Nigra; some rooms have nice
views; very friendly staff. **Cons:** some rooms are dark due to a neighboring building; no air-conditioning; patchy Wi-Fi. $ *Rooms from:
€120* ⊠ *Porta-Nigra-Pl. 6* ☎ *0651/977–0100* ⊕ *www.friedrich-hotels.
de* ⤳ *43 rooms* ⦿ *Free Breakfast.*

BONN

*61 km (38 miles) north of Koblenz, 28 km (17 miles) south of Cologne
(Köln).*

Bonn was the postwar seat of the federal government and parliament
until Berlin became its capital again in 1999. Aptly described by the title
of John le Carré's spy novel *A Small Town in Germany,* the quiet university town was chosen as a stopgap measure to prevent such weightier
contenders as Frankfurt from becoming the capital, a move that would
have lessened Berlin's chances of regaining its former status. With the
exodus of the government from Bonn, the city has become a bit less cosmopolitan. Still, Bonn thrives as the headquarters of two of Germany's
largest multinational corporations (Deutsche Telekom and Deutsche
Post/DHL), and the UN has expanded its presence in the city as well.
The fine museums and other cultural institutions that once served the
diplomatic elite are still here to be enjoyed.

GETTING HERE AND AROUND

The town center is a car-free zone; an inner ring road circles it with
parking garages on the perimeter. A convenient parking lot is just across
from the train station and within 50 yards of the tourist office, which
is on Windeckstrasse near the Hauptbahnhof. Bonn has extensive bike
paths downtown; these are designated paths (often demarcated with
blue-and-white bicycle symbols) on the edges of roads or sidewalks.
■ TIP→ **Pedestrians, beware: anyone walking on a bike path risks getting mowed down.** Bicyclists are expected to follow the same traffic rules
as cars. In Bonn the Radstation, at the main train station, will not only
rent you a bike and provide maps, but will also fill your water bottle
and check the pressure in your tires for free.

Contacts Radstation. ⊠ *Quantiusstr. (opposite Nos. 4–6)* ☎ *0228/981–4636*
⊕ *www.radstationbonn.de.*

FESTIVALS

Beethoven-Festival. Concerts are held at numerous indoor and outdoor
venues during September's monthlong Beethoven-Festival. ⊠ *Bonn*
☎ *0228/201–0345* ⊕ *www.beethovenfest.de.*

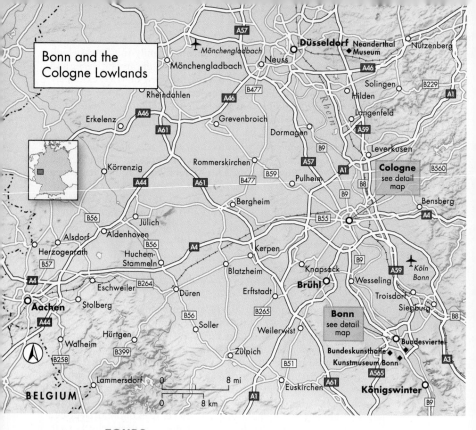

Bonn and the
Cologne Lowlands

TOURS

A variety of walking tours are also available, including the "Bonn zu
Fuss" city tour (€9), offered Saturday at 11 am from late April to
October.

Bus Tours. Bilingual bus tours of Bonn start from the tourist office daily
at 2, Easter through the first weekend in November and on Saturday
in March and November. ⊠ *Bonn* 🚌*€16.*

VISITOR INFORMATION

Contacts Bonn Information. ⊠ *Windeckstr. 1, on Münsterpl.* ☎ *0228/775–000*
🌐 *www.bonn.de.*

EXPLORING

Alter Friedhof (*Old Cemetery*). This ornate, leafy cemetery is the resting
place of many of the country's most celebrated sons and daughters.
Look for the tomb of composer Robert Schumann (1810–56) and his
wife, Clara, also a composer and accomplished pianist. ⊠ *Bornheimer-
str.* ✚ *From main train station, follow Quantiusstr. west (parallel to
tracks) until it becomes Herwarthstr.; before street curves to left, turning
into Endenicherstr., take underpass below railroad track. You'll then be
on Thomastr., which borders cemetery* 🚌 *Tours €5.*

Altes Rathaus (*Old Town Hall*). This 18th-century rococo town hall looks somewhat like a pink dollhouse. Its elegant steps and stair entry have seen a great many historic figures, including French president Charles de Gaulle and U.S. president John F. Kennedy. It's now the seat of the Lord Mayor of Bonn and can only be admired from the outside. ⊠ *Am Markt.*

Beethoven-Haus (*Beethoven House*). Beethoven was born in Bonn in 1770 and, except for a short stay in Vienna, lived here until the age of 22. You'll find scores, paintings, a grand piano (his last, in fact), and an ear trumpet or two. Thanks to the modern age, there's now a *Stage for Music Visualization,* an interactive exhibit involving 3-D glasses that shows Beethoven's best-loved works. The museum shop carries everything from kitsch to elegant Beethoven memorabilia. ⊠ *Bonng. 20* ☎ *0228/981–7525* ⊕ *www.beethoven-haus-bonn.de* ☜ *€6.*

Bundeskunsthalle (*Art and Exhibition Hall of the German Federal Republic*). This is one of the Rhineland's most important venues for major temporary exhibitions about art, culture, and archaeology. Its modern design, by Viennese architect Gustave Peichl, is as interesting as anything on exhibit in the museum. It employs three enormous blue cones situated on a lawnlike rooftop garden. ⊠ *Friedrich-Ebert-Allee 4* ☎ *0228/91710* ⊕ *www.bundeskunsthalle.de* ☜ *From €10; reduced to €7 2 hrs before closing* ⊙ *Closed Mon.*

Bundesviertel (*Federal Government District*). Walking through the pleasant area that was once the government district is like taking a trip back in time, to an era when Bonn was still the sleepy capital of West Germany. Bordered by Adenauerallee, Kaiser-Friedrich-Strasse, Franz-Josef-Strasse, and the Rhine, the quarter boasts sights such as the **Bundeshaus**, which includes the Plenarsaal (Plenary Hall). Designed to serve as the new Federal Parliament, the Bundeshaus was completed only seven years before the capital was relocated to Berlin in 1999. A few steps away, you'll find the historic **Villa Hammerschmidt,** the German equivalent of the White House. This stylish neoclassical mansion began serving as the federal president's permanent residence in 1950, and is still his home when he stays in Bonn. Equally impressive is the **Palais Schaumburg,** another fine example of the Rhein Riveria estates that once housed the Federal Chancellery (1949–76). It became the center of Cold War politics during the Adenauer administration. ⊠ *U-Bahn Heussallee.*

Haus der Geschichte (*House of History*). German history since World War II is the subject of this museum, which begins with "hour zero," as the Germans call the unconditional surrender of 1945. The museum displays an overwhelming amount of documentary material organized on five levels and engages various types of media. It's not all heavy either—temporary exhibits have featured political cartoonists, Cold War–era sporting contests pitting East Germany versus West Germany, and an in-depth examination of the song "Lili Marleen," sung by troops of every nation during World War II. An audio guide in English is available. ⊠ *Willy-Brandt-Allee 14* ☎ *0228/91650* ⊕ *www.hdg.de* ☜ *Free* ⊙ *Closed Mon.*

Bonn is the city of Beethoven: he was born here, you can tour his home, there is a concert hall named after him, and a monument to him on Münsterplatz.

Kunstmuseum Bonn (*Art Museum*). Changing exhibits are generally excellent at this large museum that focuses on Rhenish expressionists and German art since 1945 (Beuys, Baselitz, and Kiefer, for example). The museum's airy and inexpensive café is better than the stuffier version across the plaza at the Kunst- und Ausstellungshalle. ✉ *Friedrich-Ebert-Allee 2* ☎ *0228/776–260* ⊕ *www.kunstmuseum-bonn.de* ✉ *€7* ☺ *Closed Mon.*

Kurfürstliches Schloss (*Prince-Electors' Palace*). Built in the 18th century by the prince-electors of Cologne, this grand palace now houses Bonn's university. If the weather is good, stroll through Hofgarten park in front of it. When Bonn was a capital, this patch of grass drew tens of thousands to antinuclear demonstrations. Today it's mostly used for games of pickup soccer and ultimate Frisbee. ✉ *Am Hofgarten.*

Münster (*Minster*). The 900-year-old church is vintage late Romanesque, with a massive octagonal main tower and a soaring spire. It stands on a site where two Roman soldiers were executed in the 3rd century for being Christian. It saw the coronations of two Holy Roman Emperors (in 1314 and 1346) and was one of the Rhineland's most important ecclesiastical centers in the Middle Ages. The 17th-century bronze figure of St. Helen and the ornate rococo pulpit are highlights of the interior. Outside you'll find two giant stone heads: those of Cassius and Florentius, the martyred soldiers. ✉ *Münsterpl.* ☎ *0228/985–880* ⊕ *www.bonner-muenster.de* ✉ *Free* ☺ *Closed Sun.*

Poppelsdorfer Schloss (*Poppelsdorf Palace*). This former electors' palace, built in the baroque style between 1715 and 1753, now houses the university's mineralogical collection. Its botanical gardens are home to

12,000 species, among the largest variety in Germany. ✉ *Meckenheimer Allee 171* ☎ *0228/732–764* 🌐 *www.steinmann.uni-bonn.de/museen; www.botgart.uni-bonn.de* 🎟 *Mineralogical collection €3; botanical garden free weekdays, €3 Sun.* ⏰ *Closed Sat.*

WHERE TO EAT

$ GERMAN 🍴 **Em Höttche.** Beethoven was a regular at this tavern, which has been around since the late 14th century. Today it offers one of the best-value lunches in town, and the kitchen stays open until 1 am. **Known for:** Halver Hahn (an open-face sandwich of soft cheese on rye bread); Bonner Zwiebelmett (minced raw pork with onions); Rheinischer Brauhausteller (fried potatoes with bacon and onions). [$] *Average main: €10* ✉ *Markt 4* ☎ *0228/690–009* 🌐 *www.em-hoettche.de.*

$$$ ITALIAN 🍴 **Ristorante Sassella.** When the Bundestag was still in town, this Bonn institution used to be cited in the press as frequently for its backroom political dealings as for its Lombardy-influenced food. Locals, prominent and otherwise, still flock to the restaurant, in an 18th-century house in the suburb of Kessenich. **Known for:** Nudeltaschen (radicchio and scarmo cheese stuffed with fried walnuts and brussel sprouts); garganelli with bolognese and sliced Parmesan; veal meatballs in mushroom sauce on cheese-filled ravioli. [$] *Average main: €25* ✉ *Karthäuserpl. 21* ☎ *0228/530–815* 🌐 *www.ristorante-sassella.de* ⏰ *Closed Mon. No lunch Sat., no dinner Sun.*

$$$$ EUROPEAN Fodor's Choice ★ 🍴 **Strandhaus.** On a quiet residential street, and hidden from view in summer by an ivy-covered patio, this restaurant feels like a true escape—befitting its laid-back name, Beach House. The chef insists on local produce, and presents her delicate, innovatively spiced food with elegance, but no fuss. **Known for:** roasted duck breast; roasted lamb fillet; carefully crafted wine list. [$] *Average main: €27* ✉ *Georgstr. 28* ☎ *0228/369–4949* 🌐 *www.strandhaus-bonn.de* ⏰ *Closed Sun. and Mon. No lunch.*

WHERE TO STAY

$$$ HOTEL 🏨 **Best Western Domicil.** A group of buildings around a quiet, central courtyard has been converted into a charming and comfortable hotel, with rooms individually furnished and decorated in styles ranging from fin de siècle romantic to Italian modern. **Pros:** quiet courtyard; handy to the train station; excellent, central location. **Cons:** plain exterior; small rooms; noisy for light sleepers thanks to passing trams. [$] *Rooms from: €195* ✉ *Thomas-Mann-Str. 24–26* ☎ *0228/729–090* 🌐 *domicil-bonn.bestwestern.de* 🛏 *44 rooms* 🍴 *Free Breakfast.*

$$ HOTEL 🏨 **Hotel Mozart.** Elegant on the outside and simple on the inside, this small, attractive hotel is often recommended to friends by locals. **Pros:** quiet tree-lined street; close to the train station; charming boutique hotel. **Cons:** thin walls; complaints about the staff; relatively basic hotel. [$] *Rooms from: €105* ✉ *Mozartstr. 1* ☎ *0228/659–071* 🌐 *www.hotel-mozart-bonn.com* 🛏 *38 rooms* 🍴 *Free Breakfast.*

Alter Friedhof 1
Altes Rathaus ... 3
Beethoven-Haus 2
Bundes-kunsthalle 8
Bundes-viertel 9
Haus der Geschichte 7
Kunstmuseum Bonn 10
Kurfürstliches Schloss 4
Münster 5
Poppelsdorfer Schloss 6

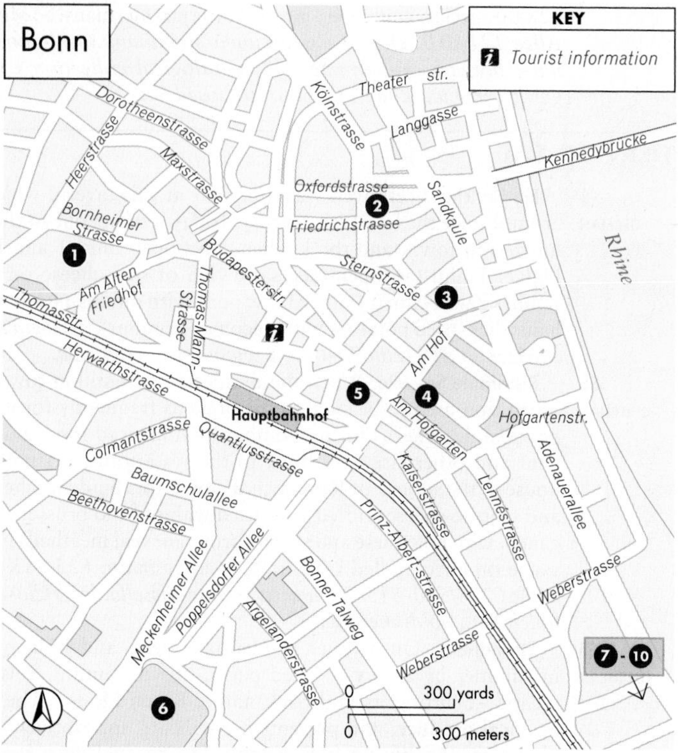

$$$ HOTEL 🏨 **Sternhotel.** For solid comfort and a picturesque, central location, the Sternhotel is tops—and their weekend rates are a bargain. **Pros:** in the center of town; partnership with gym across the square, allowing guests free entry; nicest hotel in central Bonn. **Cons:** market square location can be noisy in the morning and evening; expensive for the area; doesn't seem like a four-star hotel. [$] *Rooms from: €185* ✉ *Markt 8* ☎ *0228/72670* 🌐 *www.sternhotel-bonn.de* 🛏 *80 rooms* 🍴 *Free Breakfast.*

PERFORMING ARTS

Beethovenhalle. The Bonn Beethoven Orchestra opens its season in grand style every year in late summer as part of Beethovenfest Bonn. Many of its concerts are held in the Beethovenhalle. ✉ *Wachsbleiche 16* ☎ *0228/72220* 🌐 *www.beethovenhalle.de.*

Beethoven-Haus. In the Beethoven-Haus, recitals are sometimes given on a 19th-century grand piano, and concerts take place regularly in the chamber music hall. ✉ *Bonng. 20* ☎ *0228/981–750* 🌐 *www.beethoven-haus-bonn.de.*

Pantheon Theater. This is a major venue for comedy and cabaret. ✉ *Siegburger Str. 42* ☎ *0228/212–521* 🌐 *www.pantheon.de.*

11

Schumannhaus. Chamber-music concerts are given regularly at the Schumannhaus, where composer Robert Schumann spent his final years. ✉ *Sebastianstr. 182* ☎ *0228/773–656* ⊕ *www.schumannhaus-bonn.de.*

Theater Bonn. Operas are staged regularly at the Theater Bonn, which also hosts musicals and performances by world-renowned dance companies, including ballet. ✉ *Am Boeselagerhof 1* ☎ *0228/778–000* ⊕ *www.theater-bonn.de.*

KÖNIGSWINTER

12 km (7 miles) southeast of Bonn.

Home to one of Germany's most popular castles, Drachenfels, Königswinter is also the gateway to the 30 large and small hills that make up the Siebengebirge, the country's oldest nature reserve. In early May, festivities and fireworks light up the town as part of the "Rhine in Flames" fireworks display.

GETTING HERE AND AROUND

Königswinter is 20 minutes south of Bonn by train (Regionalbahn) or 40 minutes from Cologne.

VISITOR INFORMATION

Contacts Siebengebirge Tourist Office. ✉ *Drachenfelsstr. 51* ☎ *02223/917–711* ⊕ *www.siebengebirge.com.*

EXPLORING

Drachenfels. The town of Königswinter has one of the most visited castles on the Rhine, the Drachenfels. Its ruins crown one of the highest hills in the Siebengebirge, with a spectacular view of the Rhine. It's also part of Germany's oldest nature reserve, with more than 100 km (62 miles) of hiking trails. The castle was built in the 12th century by the archbishop of Cologne, and takes its name from a dragon said to have lived in a nearby cave. (The dragon was slain by Siegfried, hero of the epic *Nibelungenlied.*)

The castle ruins can be reached via two different hikes, each of about 45 minutes. One route begins at the Drachenfelsbahn station, and passes the Nibelungenhalle reptile zoo along the way. The other route starts at Rhöndorf on the other side of the hill. The Siebengebirge Tourist Office at Drachenfelsstrasse 51 in Königswinter can provide a map that includes these and other local hiking trails. ✉ *Königswinter* ⊡ *Free.*

> **BIER AM RHEIN**
>
> When it's warm out, most Germans like nothing better than to sit outside with a beer in hand. In Bonn, the best beer gardens are right on the River Rhine, which runs through the city. On the Bonn city center side, there's the **Alter Zoll** (*Brassertufer 1*) and **Schänzchen** (*Rosental 105*). Across the Kennedy Bridge in Beuel, however, is where the late-afternoon sun shines best. On either side of the bridge are **Rheinlust** (*Rheinaustr. 134*) and **Bahnhöfchen** (*Rheinaustr. 116*).

Drachenfelsbahn. If hiking to Drachenfels isn't for you, you can also reach the castle ruins by taking the Drachenfelsbahn, a steep, narrow-gauge train that makes trips to the summit every half hour from March through October, and hourly in January and February. ⊠ *Drachenfelsstr. 53* ☎ *02223/92090* ⊕ *www.drachenfelsbahn-koenigswinter.de* 🖃 *€10 round-trip* ⊗ *Closed mid-Nov.–Dec.*

FAMILY **Sea Life.** Königswinter's huge aquarium features 2,000 creatures from the sea. The biggest pool has a glass tunnel that enables you to walk on the "bottom of the sea." ⊠ *Rheinallee 8* ☎ *0180/6666–90101 tickets, €0.20–€0.60 per call* ⊕ *www.visitsealife.com* 🖃 *€15.*

BRÜHL

20 km (12 miles) northwest of Bonn.

In the center of Brühl stands the Rhineland's most important baroque palace, the Augustusburg. Brühl is also home to one of Germany's most popular theme parks, Phantasialand.

EXPLORING

Jagdschloss Falkenlust. This small castle, at the end of an avenue leading under the tracks across from Schloss Augustusburg's grounds, was built as a getaway where the prince could indulge his passion for falconry. ⊠ *Otto-Wels-Str.* ☎ *02232/44000* ⊕ *www.schlossbruehl.de* 🖃 *€7 (without guide)* ⊗ *Closed Mon.*

Schloss Augustusburg. This castle and the magnificent pleasure park that surrounds it were created in the time of Prince Clemens August, between 1725 and 1768. The palace contains one of the most famous achievements of rococo architecture, a staircase by Balthasar Neumann. The castle can be visited only on guided tours, which leave the reception area every hour or so. An English-language recorded tour is available. ⊠ *Max-Ernst-Allee* ☎ *02232/44000* ⊕ *www.schlossbruehl.de* 🖃 *Guided tours from €9* ⊗ *Closed Mon., and Dec. and Jan.*

COLOGNE (KÖLN)

28 km (17 miles) north of Bonn, 47 km (29 miles) south of Düsseldorf, 70 km (43 miles) southeast of Aachen.

Cologne (Köln in German) is the largest city on the Rhine (the fourth-largest in Germany) and one of the most interesting. The city is vibrant and bustling, with a lightness and cheerfulness that's typical of the Rhineland. At its heart is tradition, manifested in the abundance of bars and brew houses serving the local Kölsch beer and old Rhine cuisine. These are good meeting places to start a night on the town. Tradition, however, is mixed with the contemporary, found in a host of elegant shops, sophisticated restaurants, modern bars and dance clubs, and a contemporary-art scene that's now just hanging on against unstoppable competition from Berlin.

Although not as old as Trier, Cologne has been a dominant power in the Rhineland since Roman times, and it remains a major commercial, intellectual, and ecclesiastical center. Cologne was first settled in 38 BC. For nearly a century it grew slowly, in the shadow of imperial Trier, until a locally born noblewoman, Julia Agrippina, daughter of the Roman general Germanicus, married the Roman emperor Claudius. Her hometown was elevated to the rank of a Roman city and given the name Colonia Claudia Ara Agrippinensium (Claudius Colony at the Altar of Agrippina). For the next 300 years Colonia (hence Cologne, or Köln) flourished; evidence of the Roman city's wealth resides in the Römisch-Germanisches Museum. In the 9th century Charlemagne, the towering figure who united the sprawling German lands (and ruled much of present-day France) as the first Holy Roman Emperor, restored Cologne's fortunes and elevated it to its preeminent role in the Rhineland by appointing the first archbishop of Cologne. The city's ecclesiastical heritage is one of its most striking features; it has a full dozen Romanesque churches and one of the world's largest and finest Gothic cathedrals. In the Middle Ages it was a member of the powerful Hanseatic League, occupying a position of greater importance in European commerce than either London or Paris.

Cologne was a thriving modern city until World War II, when bombings destroyed 90% of it. Only the cathedral remained relatively unscathed. Like many other German cities that rebounded during the "Economic Miracle" of the 1950s, Cologne is a mishmash of old and new, sometimes awkwardly juxtaposed. A good part of the former Old Town along the Hohe Strasse (the old Roman "High Road") was turned into a remarkably charmless pedestrian shopping mall. It's all framed by six-lane expressways winding along the rim of the city center—barely yards from the cathedral—illustrating the problems of postwar reconstruction. However, much of the Altstadt, ringed by streets that follow the line of the medieval city walls, is closed to traffic. Most major sights are within this area and are easily reached on foot. Here, too, you'll find the best shops.

DISCOUNTS AND DEALS

The Cologne Tourist Board Service Centre across from the cathedral and most central hotels sell the **KölnCard** (€9 for one day, €18 for two days), which entitles you to discounts on sightseeing tours, admissions to all the city's museums, free city bus and tram travel, and other reductions.

GETTING HERE AND AROUND

As one of Germany's most important railroad hubs, Cologne is connected by fast trains to cities throughout northwestern Europe, including Paris, Brussels, and Frankfurt. The German railroad network links Cologne to the entire nation. You can reach Cologne from Bonn in about 20 minutes, and Brühl in about 15.

FESTIVALS

Weihnachtsmarkt am Kölner Dom. Of Cologne's four main Christmas markets the Weihnachtsmarkt am Kölner Dom, in the shadow of the city's famed cathedral, is the most impressive. Set against the backdrop of the church's magnificent twin spires, a giant Christmas tree stands proudly in the middle of the market's 160 festively adorned stalls, which sell mulled wine, roasted chestnuts, and many other German yuletide treats. ⊕ *www.koelnerweihnachtsmarkt. com.*

TOURS

Bus trips into the countryside (to the Eifel Hills, the Ahr Valley, and the Westerwald) are organized by several city travel agencies.

City Bus Tours. The 90-minute tours, conducted in English and nine other languages, leave year-round from the tourist office next to the cathedral. There are daily departures every half hour between 10 am and 5:30 pm from late March to early January and hourly between 10:30 am and 5:30 pm until late March. ⊠ *Cologne* ☎ *0211/346–430* ⊕ *www.citytour.de* 🎫 *From €13.*

Radstation Köln Bike Tours. In addition to their bike rentals, Radstation Köln conduct three-hour bike tours of the city, departing daily at 1:30 pm. ⊠ *Köln Hauptbahnhof (Cologne Central Station) or Markmannsg. next to Deutzer Brücke* ☎ *0221/139–7190* ⊕ *www.radstationkoeln.de* 🎫 *Rentals from €6; tours from €23.*

Walking Tours. From mid-June to September, a 90-minute English-language walking tour leaves from the tourist office every Saturday at 3 pm. Additional walking tours in English are often available by arrangement with the tourist office. ⊠ *Köln Tourismus Office, Kardinal-Höffner-Pl. 1* 🎫 *From €11.*

VISITOR INFORMATION

Contacts Köln Tourismus Office. ⊠ *Kardinal-Höffner-Pl. 1* ☎ *0221/346–430* ⊕ *www.cologne-tourism.com.*

EXPLORING

Alter Markt (*Old Market*). The square has an eclectic assembly of buildings, most of them postwar. However, two 16th-century houses survived the war intact—Nos. 20 and 22, which are today a Kölsch brewpub. The oldest structure dates from 1135. In late November and December, Alter Markt is the site of one of the city's prettiest Christmas markets. ⊠ *Altstadt.*

Altes Rathaus (*Old Town Hall*). The Rathaus is worth a look, even from the outside. It's the oldest town hall in Germany, with elements remaining from the 14th century. The famous bell tower rings its bells daily at 9, noon, 3, and 6. Standing on pedestals at one end of the town hall

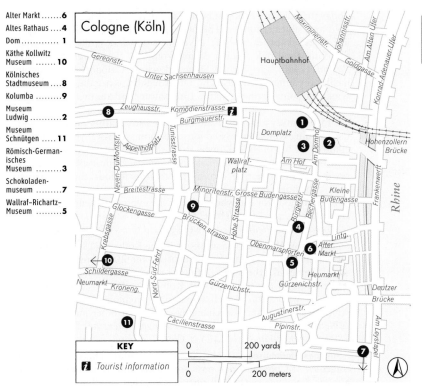

Cologne (Köln)

KEY

🅸 *Tourist information*

0 — 200 yards

0 — 200 meters

are figures of prophets made in the early 15th century. Ranging along the south wall are nine additional statues, the so-called Nine Good Heroes, carved in 1360. ⊠ *Rathauspl. 2, Altstadt* ☎ *0221/2212–3332.*

Fodor's Choice
★

Dom (*Cathedral*). Cologne's landmark embodies one of the purest expressions of the Gothic spirit in Europe. The cathedral, meant to be a tangible expression of God's kingdom on Earth, was conceived with such immense dimensions that construction, begun in 1248, was not completed until 1880, after the original plan was rediscovered. At 515 feet high, the two west towers of the cathedral were briefly the tallest structures in the world when they were finished (before being eclipsed by the Washington Monument). The cathedral was built to house what are believed to be the relics of the Magi, the three kings who paid homage to the infant Jesus (the trade in holy mementos was big business in the Middle Ages—and not always scrupulous). The size of the building was not simply an example of self-aggrandizement on the part of the people of Cologne, however; it was a response to the vast numbers of pilgrims who arrived to see the relics. The ambulatory (the passage that curves around the back of the altar) is unusually large, allowing cathedral authorities to funnel large numbers of visitors up to the crossing (where the nave and transepts meet and where the relics were originally displayed), around the back of the altar, and out again.

Today the relics are kept just behind the altar, in the original, enormous gold-and-silver **reliquary**. The other great treasure of the cathedral, in the last chapel on the left as you face the altar, is the **Gero Cross**, a monumental oak crucifix dating from 971. The *Altar of the City Patrons* (1440), a triptych by Stephan Lochner, Cologne's most famous medieval painter, is to the right. Other highlights are the stained-glass windows, some dating from the 13th century and another, designed by Gerhard Richter with help from a computer program, from the 21st; the 15th-century altarpiece; and the early-14th-century high altar, with its glistening white figures and intricate choir screens. If you're up to it, climb to the top of the bell tower to get the complete vertical experience (but be aware that viewing Cologne from the Dom itself removes the skyline's most interesting feature). The treasury includes the silver shrine of Archbishop Engelbert, who was stabbed to death in 1225. Allow at least an hour for the whole tour of the interior, treasury, and tower climb. ⊠ *Dompl., Altstadt* ☎ *0221/9258–4730* ⊕ *www.koelner-dom.de* 🎫 *Tower €4; cathedral treasury €6; guided tours €7.*

Käthe Kollwitz Museum. The works of Käthe Kollwitz (1867–1945), the most important German female artist of the 20th century, focus on social themes like the plight of the poor and the atrocities of war. This is the larger of the country's two Kollwitz collections and comprises all of her woodcuts, as well as paintings, etchings, lithographs, and sculptures. There are also changing exhibits of other modern artists. ⊠ *Neumarkt 18–24, in Neumarkt Passage, Innenstadt* ☎ *0221/227–2899* ⊕ *www.kollwitz.de* 🎫 *€5* ⊘ *Closed Mon.*

Kölnisches Stadtmuseum (*Cologne City Museum*). The triumphs and tragedies of Cologne's rich past are packed into this museum at the historic *Zeughaus*, the city's former arsenal. Here you'll find an in-depth chronicle of Cologne's history—including information about the lives of ordinary people and the destruction incurred during World War II. For those who've always wanted to be privy to the inside stories surrounding local words such as *Klüngel, Kölsch,* and *Karneval,* the answers are waiting to be discovered within the museum's walls. ⊠ *Zeughausstr. 1–3, Altstadt* ☎ *0221/2212–5789* ⊕ *www.koelnisches-stadtmuseum. de* 🎫 *€5* ⊘ *Closed Mon.*

Kolumba. The origins of the official art museum of the Archdiocese of Cologne stretch back to 1853, but the institution received a big boost in 2007, with the opening of a new home atop the ruins of the Gothic parish church of St. Kolumba. Designed by the Swiss architect Peter Zumthor, the new building pays homage to the site's Roman, Gothic, and medieval heritage, while unstuffily presenting a collection of art spanning from late antiquity to the present. ⊠ *Kolumbastr. 4, Innenstadt* ☎ *0221/933–1930* ⊕ *www.kolumba.de* 🎫 *€5* ⊘ *Closed Tues.*

Museum Ludwig. This museum is dedicated to art from the beginning of the 20th century to the present day. Its American pop-art collection (including Andy Warhol, Jasper Johns, Robert Rauschenberg, Claes Oldenburg, and Roy Lichtenstein) rivals that of most American museums. ⊠ *Heinrich-Böll-Pl., Innenstadt* ☎ *0221/2212–6165* ⊕ *www. museum-ludwig.de* 🎫 *€12* ⊘ *Closed Mon.*

11

Museum Schnütgen. A treasure house of medieval art from the Rhine region, the museum has an ideal setting in a 12th-century basilica. Don't miss the crucifix from the St. Georg Kirche or the original stained-glass windows and carved figures from the Dom. Other exhibits include intricately carved ivory book covers, rock-crystal reliquaries, and illuminated manuscripts. ⌂ *Cäcilienstr. 29, Innenstadt* ☎ *0221/2213–1355* ⊕ *www.museum-schnuetgen.de* 🎟 *€6* ◷ *Closed Mon.*

EAU DE COLOGNE

The original "eau de Cologne" was first produced here in the early 18th century from an Italian formula. It's made from a secret formula and aged in oak barrels. The most famous cologne is 4711, which derives its name from the firm's address at 4711 Glockengasse. The building itself is equipped with a carillon, a museum, and (naturally) a gift shop. The light scent, primarily derived from citrus, rosemary, and lavender, may seem a little old-fashioned to some, but it comes in an elegant bottle with a turquoise-and-gilt label, and makes a nice souvenir.

Fodor's Choice ★ **Römisch-Germanisches Museum** (*Roman-Germanic Museum*). This cultural landmark was built in the early 1970s around the famous Dionysius mosaic discovered here during the construction of an air-raid shelter in 1941. The huge mosaic, more than 800 square feet, once formed the dining-room floor of a wealthy Roman trader's villa. Its millions of tiny earthenware and glass tiles depict some of the adventures of Dionysius, the Greek god of wine. The pillared 1st-century tomb of Lucius Publicius (a prominent Roman officer), some stone Roman coffins, and everyday objects of Roman life are among the museum's other exhibits. Bordering the museum on the south is a restored 90-yard stretch of the old Roman harbor road. ⌂ *Roncallipl. 4, Altstadt* ☎ *0221/2212–4438* ⊕ *www.roemisch-germanisches-museum.de* 🎟 *€8* ◷ *Closed Mon.*

FAMILY **Schokoladenmuseum** (*Chocolate Museum*). This riverside museum south of the cathedral is a real hit. It recounts 3,000 years of civilization's production and enjoyment of chocolate, from the Central American Maya to the colonizing and industrializing Europeans. It's also a real factory, with lava flows of chocolate and a conveyer belt jostling thousands of truffles. The museum shop, with a huge variety of chocolate items, does a brisk business, and the riverside panorama café serves some of the best cake in town. ⌂ *Am Schockoladenmuseum 1a, Rheinufer* ☎ *0221/931–8880* ⊕ *www.schokoladenmuseum.de* 🎟 *€12.*

Wallraf-Richartz-Museum. This museum contains paintings spanning the years 1300 to 1900. The Dutch and Flemish schools are particularly well represented, as is the 15th- to 16th-century Cologne school of German painting. Its two most famous artists are the Master of the St. Veronica (whose actual name is unknown) and Stefan Lochner, represented by two luminous works, *The Last Judgment* and *The Madonna in the Rose Bower.* Large canvases by Rubens, who spent his youth in Cologne, hang prominently on the second floor. There are also outstanding works by Rembrandt, Van Dyck, and Frans Hals, and the largest collection

DID YOU KNOW?

The 515-foot-high west towers of Cologne's Dom were the tallest structures in the world until they were eclipsed by the Washington Monument.

of French impressionism in Germany. ✉ *Obenmarspforten, Altstadt* ☎ *0221/2212–1119* 🌐 *www.wallraf.museum* 🎟 *€9* 🕒 *Closed Mon.*

WHERE TO EAT

$ EUROPEAN 🍴 **Café Elefant.** For three decades, writers and artists from Cologne's elegant Agnesviertel neighborhood have been meeting at this cozy locale on a quiet, tree-lined street. Inside, the ambience—like a little corner of Montmartre—is just right for thinking deep thoughts, or simply chatting over a slice of chocolate cake. **Known for:** Königin Pastete (puff pastry with homemade chicken ragout); Kürbiscreme Suppe (pumpkin soup); Elefantentoast (bread toasted with fresh ham, cheese, and vegetables). [$] *Average main: €7* ✉ *Weissenburgstr. 50* ☎ *0221/734–520* 🌐 *www.cafe-zum-elefanten.de* 💳 *No credit cards.*

$$$ FRENCH Fodor's Choice ★ 🍴 **Capricorn i Aries.** This corner brasserie—part neighborhood bistro, part upscale restaurant—serves the staples of French rural cuisine with a Rhineland twist, whether it's a simple soup or a five-course dinner. The owners' highly regarded four-table restaurant across the street is also available for special events. **Known for:** veal cutlet with herbs, carrots and thyme sauce; confit de canard with cannellini beans; fried monkfish with crustacean sauce and lentils. [$] *Average main: €22* ✉ *Alteburger Str. 31, Neustadt-Süd* ☎ *0221/397–5710* 🌐 *www.capricorniaries.com* 💳 *No credit cards* 🕒 *Closed Wed. and Sun. No lunch Sat.*

$$$$ ITALIAN Fodor's Choice ★ 🍴 **Casa di Biase.** The sophisticated Italian cuisine is served here in a warm, elegant setting on the city's southwest side. The seasonally changing menu focuses on fish and game, and the wine list is interesting and extensive—although sometimes pricey. **Known for:** tagliere with fine ham and salami; spaghetti Chelucci (with tuna and salmon); risotto Carnaroli (with raw veal strips and black garlic). [$] *Average main: €26* ✉ *Eifelpl. 4, Südstadt* ☎ *0221/322–433* 🌐 *www.casadibiase.de* 🕒 *Closed Sun. No lunch Sat.*

$ GERMAN 🍴 **Früh am Dom.** For real down-home German cooking, few places in Cologne compare to this time-honored former brewery in the shadow of the Dom. It's often crowded, but the mood's fantastic. **Known for:** Rheinischer Sauerbraten with dumplings and homemade apple sauce; Schweinehaxe (Pork knuckle) with fried potatoes and mixed salad; Himmel un Ääd (heaven and earth), or fried black pudding with potato-apple mash and fried onions. [$] *Average main: €14* ✉ *Am Hof 12–18, Altstadt* ☎ *0221/261–3215* 🌐 *www.frueh-am-dom.de* 💳 *No credit cards.*

$$$ ECLECTIC 🍴 **Heising und Adelmann.** A young crowd gathers here to do what people along the Rhine have done for centuries—talk, drink, and enjoy good company. There's a party every Friday and Saturday with a DJ. **Known for:** mushroom risotto with braised cheek of Duroc pork; Norwegian salmon with green asparagus, mashed potatoes, and white butter; duck breast with asparagus, broccoli, sweet potatoes, and Madeira jus. [$] *Average main: €22* ✉ *Friesenstr. 58–60, Neustadt-Nord* ☎ *0221/130–9424* 🌐 *www.heising-und-adelmann.de* 🕒 *Closed Sun. and Mon. No lunch.*

$ GERMAN 🍴 **Päffgen.** There's no better Bräuhaus in Cologne for drinking Kölsch, the city's home brew. You won't sit long in front of an empty glass before a blue-aproned waiter sweeps by and places another one before you. **Known for:** pork shank with malt sauce,

KARNEVAL IN COLOGNE

As the biggest city in the traditionally Catholic Rhineland, Cologne puts on Germany's most exciting and rowdy carnival. The Kölsch starts flowing on November 11 at 11:11 am with screams of the famous motto *Kölle alaaf!* (Cologne is alive!). Karneval then calms down for a few months, only to reach a fever pitch in February for the last five days before Lent. On Fat Thursday, known as *Weiberfastnacht,* women roam the streets with scissors and exercise merciless precision in cutting off the ties of any men foolish enough to wear them. Starting then, bands, parades, and parties go all night, and people of all ages don silly costumes, including the customary red clown nose. It's a good time to meet new people; in fact, it is practically impossible not to, as kissing strangers is considered par for the course. ■TIP➔ During this time, visitors who are claustrophobic or who don't want to risk having beer spilled on them should avoid the Heumarkt area in the Old Town, and possibly the whole city. The festivities come to an end Tuesday at midnight with the ritual burning of the "Nubbel"—a dummy that acts as the scapegoat for everyone's drunken, embarrassing behavior. Note: many museums are closed during Karneval.

apple red cabbage, and Röggelchen dumplings; beer-marinated pork roast with fried potatoes and coleslaw; Meter Bratwurst (fresh and homemade) with Päffgen mustard and dumplings. $ *Average main: €11* ✉ *Friesenstr. 64–66, Friesenviertel* ☎ *0221/135–461* ⊕ *www. paeffgen-koelsch.de* ▭ *No credit cards.*

WHERE TO STAY

The tourist office, across from the cathedral, can make hotel bookings for you for the same night, at a cost of €3 per booking. If you plan to be in town for Karneval, be sure to reserve a room well in advance.

$$$$
HOTEL
Excelsior Hotel Ernst. Old Master paintings, including a Van Dyck, grace this 1863 hotel's sumptuous Empire-style lobby, while Gobelins tapestries hang in the ballroom; the rooms are spacious, and the deluxe category of rooms melds old-world elegance with modern sophistication. **Pros:** Van Dyck paintings and Gobelins tapestries; steps from both the train station and Dom; famous piano bar is always a crowd-pleaser. **Cons:** expensive; styling and design could use an update; hard beds for some. $ *Rooms from: €270* ✉ *Dompl., Trankg. 1, Altstadt* ☎ *0221/2701* ⊕ *www.excelsiorhotelernst.de* ⤳ *140 rooms* ¡©¡ *No meals.*

$$
HOTEL
Hopper Hotel et cetera. The rooms in this former monastery in the Belgian Quarter are spare but not spartan, though a startlingly realistic sculpture of a bishop, sitting in the reception area, serves as a constant reminder of the building's ecclesiastic origins. **Pros:** chic renovation; attractive neighborhood; affordable. **Cons:** not centrally located; showers tricky for older guests; complaints of uncomfortable mattresses. $ *Rooms from: €130* ✉ *Brüsselerstr. 26, Belgisches Viertel* ☎ *0221/924–400* ⊕ *www.hopper.de* ⤳ *50 rooms* ¡©¡ *Free Breakfast.*

$
HOTEL
◻ **Hotel Chelsea.** This designer hotel with classic modern furnishings has a strong following among artists and art dealers, as well as with the musicians who come to play at the nearby Stadtgarten jazz club. **Pros:** an artsy clientele and neighborhood; great location in the Belgian Quarter; spacious rooms. **Cons:** some rooms need freshening up; a few rooms don't have their own bathroom; overall a bit shabby. ⓈＲooms from: €98 ✉ Jülicherstr. 1, Belgisches Viertel ☎ 0221/207–150 ⊕ www.hotel-chelsea.de ⟿ 39 rooms ⓄNo meals.

$
HOTEL
◻ **Hotel im Kupferkessel.** The best things about this small, unassuming, family-run hotel are its immaculate housekeeping—the very model of German fastidiousness—and the price (small single rooms with shared bath are very inexpensive). **Pros:** inexpensive, and breakfast is included; short walk to the main train station; comfortable hotel. **Cons:** no elevator and four stories; some rooms don't have their own bathroom; basic amenities and decor. Ⓢ Rooms from: €82 ✉ Probsteig. 6, Altstadt ☎ 0221/270–7960 ⊕ www.im-kupferkessel.de ⟿ 12 rooms Ⓞ Free Breakfast.

$$
HOTEL
◻ **Hotel im Wasserturm.** What used to be Europe's tallest water tower is now an independent, 11-story luxury hotel that's welcomed guests like Brad Pitt and fashion mogul Wolfgang Joop. **Pros:** modern luxury at its finest; unique hotel in an old water tower; generally favorable service. **Cons:** expensive breakfast; a few blocks outside of the Altstadt; some rooms don't have a great view as you might expect. Ⓢ Rooms from: €174 ✉ Kayg. 2, Altstadt ☎ 0221/20080 ⊕ www.hotel-im-wasserturm. de ⟿ 78 rooms Ⓞ No meals.

$$
HOTEL
◻ **Pullman Cologne.** One of the city's favorite business hotels, the 12-story Pullman Cologne draws travelers from around the world with its welcoming vibe and unexpectedly lighthearted flair. **Pros:** great location; many rooms with Dom views; very helpful and friendly staff. **Cons:** standard rooms are small; rooms can be a bit dated; expensive for what you're getting. Ⓢ Rooms from: €148 ✉ Helenenstr. 14, Altstadt ☎ 0221/275–2200 ⊕ www.pullmanhotels.com ⟿ 275 rooms Ⓞ No meals.

EHRENFELD: THE WORLD IN COLOGNE

If you ever needed proof of Cologne's multiethnic mix, head to Ehrenfeld, just beyond the city center's western edge. Within a square mile you'll find restaurants serving home-style versions of a host of world cuisines. Two of the best are **Yadaary-Orienthaus** (Sömmerlingstr. 48), which serves flavorful Arab dishes in an intimate atmosphere, and **Saudade** (Wahlenstr. 2), a Portuguese wine bar and café where the *vinho verde* comes fresh from the cask. Ehrenfeld is also home to Cologne's most exclusive sauna and spa, **Neptunbad** (Neptunpl. 1).

NIGHTLIFE AND PERFORMING ARTS

Kölnticket. Tickets to most arts events can be purchased through Kölnticket. ☎ *0221/2801* ⊕ *www. koelnticket.de.*

NIGHTLIFE

Cologne's nightlife is centered on three distinct areas: along the river in the Old Town, which seems to be one big party on weekends; on Zulpicherstrasse near the university; and around the Friesenplatz U-bahn station. Many streets off the Hohenzollernring and Hohenstaufenring, particularly Roonstrasse and Aachenerstrasse, also provide a broad range of nightlife. In summer the Martinsviertel, a part of the Altstadt around the Gross St. Martin church, which is full of restaurants, brew houses, and *Kneipen* (pubs), is a good place to go around sunset.

> ### KÖLSCH, BITTE!
>
> It is said that the city's beloved beer can only be called Kölsch if it's brewed within sight of the cathedral. The beverage is served in traditional *Kölschkneipen.* Your waiter, called a *Köbes,* is likely to tease you (that's the Rhenish humor) and will replace your empty glass with a full one whether you order it or not. (If you want to avoid this, leave a swallow in the nearly empty glass or cover it with a coaster.) This automatic replacement is justified by the fact that the glass, called a *Stange* (pole), is quite small due to the belief that Kölsch doesn't stay fresh for long after it has been poured.

Papa Joe's Em Streckstrump. For live jazz, head to the tiny Papa Joe's Jazzlokale, where there's never a cover charge. ⊠ *Buttermarkt 37, Altstadt* ☎ *0221/257–7931* ⊕ *www.papajoes.de.*

Papa Joe's Klimperkasten. This classic, kitschy, roaring twenties–style Altstadt *Biersalon* plays oldies from Piaf to Porter. ⊠ *Alter Markt 50–52, Altstadt* ☎ *0221/258–2132* ⊕ *www.papajoes.de.*

Stadtgarten. In summer, head straight for the Stadtgarten and sit in the Biergarten for some good outdoor *Gemütlichkeit* (coziness). At other times of the year it's still worth a visit for its excellent jazz club. Stadtgarten also runs a beer garden with cheap, tasty eats in the shaded Rathenauplatz park, by Cologne's synagogue. ⊠ *Venloerstr. 40, Altstadt* ☎ *0221/952–9940* ⊕ *www.stadtgarten.de.*

PERFORMING ARTS

Antoniterkirche. Organ recitals and chamber concerts are presented in many of the Romanesque churches around town, and in the Gothic Antoniterkirche. ⊠ *Schilderg. 57, Innenstadt* ☎ *0221/9258–4615* ⊕ *www.antonitercitykirche.de.*

Oper Köln. Cologne's opera company is known for exciting classical and contemporary productions, including collaborative efforts with the French fashion designer Christian Lacroix. The opera house on Offenbachplatz, originally scheduled to reopen in the fall of 2015 after a major multiyear renovation, remains delayed until 2022. Their interim location is the StaatenHaus am Rheinpark in Cologne-Deutz. ⊠ *Offenbachpl., Innenstadt* ☎ *0221/2212–8256* ⊕ *www.oper.koeln.*

Philharmonie. Cologne's WDR Sinfonieorchester performs regularly in the city's excellent concert hall. ✉ *Bischofsgartenstr. 1, Altstadt* ☎ *0221/204–080* ⊕ *www.koelner-philharmonie.de.*

Schauspielhaus. Cologne's principal theater is the Schauspielhaus, home to the 20 or so private theater companies in the city. Until its main space on Offenbachplatz reopens in 2016 after a major renovation, Schauspielhaus productions take place at an industrial space (Carlswerk, Schanzenstrasse 6–20) in the Mülheim neighborhood. ✉ *Offenbachpl., Innenstadt* ☎ *0221/2212–8400* ⊕ *www.schauspielkoeln.de.*

GO BELGIAN

Among Cologne's most enticing areas for a drink or light meal is the leafy and attractive Belgian Quarter. German soap stars and media power brokers flock to eateries like **Pepe** (*Antwerpenerstr. 63*). There's a hipper crowd at cafés like **Hallmackenreuther** (*Brüsselerpl. 9*) and **Salon Schmitz** (*Aachenerstr. 30*)—a place to see and be seen.

SHOPPING

A good shopping loop begins at the Neumarkt Galerie. From there, head down the charmless but practical pedestrian shopping zone of the Schildergasse. From Schildergasse, go north on Herzogstrasse to arrive at Glockengasse. A block north is Breite Strasse, another pedestrian shopping street. At the end of Breite Strasse is Ehrenstrasse, where the young and young-at-heart can shop for hip fashions and trendy housewares. After a poke around here, explore the small boutiques on Benesisstrasse, which will lead you to Mittelstrasse, best known for high-tone German fashions and luxury goods. Follow Mittelstrasse to the end to return to the Neumarkt. For some of the city's coolest shopping, head a few blocks farther west to the Belgian Quarter, where you'll find a hodgepodge of indie fashion designers, concept shops, and secondhand stores.

Glockengasse. Cologne's most celebrated product, Eau de Cologne No. 4711, was first concocted here by the 18th-century Italian chemist Johann Maria Farina. At the company's flagship store there's a small exhibition of historical 4711 bottles, as well as a perfume fountain in which you can dip your fingers. ✉ *House of 4711, Glockeng. 4, Innenstadt* ☎ *0221/2709–9910* ⊕ *www.4711.com.*

Neumarkt Galerie. This bright, modern indoor shopping arcade has a web of shops and cafés (including the city's only Primark) surrounding an airy atrium. Just look for the huge sculpture of an upside-down ice cream cone above the entrance. ✉ *Richmodstr. 8* ⊕ *www.neumarkt-galerie.com.*

Peek & Cloppenburg. This big clothing store is a highlight of Schildergasse. Designed by the architect Renzo Piano, the building looks like a spaceship, and its selection of fashions—for men and women, from budget to couture—is out of this world. ✉ *Schilderg. 65–67, Innenstadt* ☎ *0221/453–900* ⊕ *www.peek-cloppenburg.com.*

AACHEN

70 km (43 miles) west of Cologne (Köln).

At the center of Aachen, the characteristic three-window-wide facades give way to buildings dating from the days when Charlemagne made Aix-la-Chapelle (as it was then called) the great center of the Holy Roman Empire. Thirty-two German emperors were crowned here starting with Charlemagne in 800, gracing Aachen with the proud nickname "Kaiserstadt" (Emperors' City). Roman legions had been drawn here for the healing properties of the sulfur springs emanating from the nearby Eifel Mountains. (The name "Aachen," based on an old Frankish word for water, alludes to this.) Charlemagne's father, Pepin the Short, also settled here to enjoy the waters, and to this day the city is also known as Bad Aachen and is still drawing visitors in search of a cure.

VISITOR INFORMATION

One-and-a-half-hour walking tours (€7) of the Altstadt depart from the tourist office throughout the year at 11 on weekends, as well as at 2 on weekdays from April to December. The Saturday tours are conducted in English (€9) as well as German.

Contacts Tourist Info Elisenbrunnen. ⊠ *Friedrich-Wilhelm-Pl.* ☎ *0241/180–2960* ⊕ *www.aachen-tourismus.de.*

EXPLORING

Carolus-Thermen Bad Aachen. If you're a steam-lover, try this high-tech spa with a venerable history. In Dürer's time there were regular crackdowns on the orgiastic goings-on at the baths. Today taking the waters is done with a bathing suit on, but be aware that the sauna area is a clothes-free zone. ⊠ *Passstr. 79* ☎ *0241/182–740* ⊕ *www.carolus-thermen.de* 🎫 *From €12.*

Centre Charlemagne. Despite its name, this museum, which opened in 2014, doesn't just pay homage to Charlemagne, the man who put Aachen on the map in the 8th century. It also reveals Aachen's much broader history, from Neolithic times to the present, including its Celto-Roman and baroque-era stints as a spa town, and its centuries as Holy Roman imperial coronation city. Multimedia stations help bring the past to life, and the interactive audio guide is highly recommended. ⊠ *Katschhof 1* ☎ *0241/432–4998* ⊕ *www.centre-charlemagne.eu* 🎫 *€6* ☉ *Closed Mon.*

Fodor'sChoice **Dom** (*Cathedral*). Aachen's stunning cathedral, the "chapelle" of the
★ town's earlier name of Aix-la-Chapelle, remains the single greatest storehouse of Carolingian architecture in Europe, and it was the first place in Germany to be named a UNESCO World Heritage site. Though it was built over the course of 1,000 years and reflects architectural styles from the Middle Ages to the 19th century, its commanding image remains the magnificent octagonal royal chapel, rising up two arched stories to end in the cap of the dome. It was this section, the heart of the church, that Charlemagne saw completed in AD 800. His bones now lie

in the Gothic choir, in a golden shrine surrounded by wonderful carvings of saints. Another treasure is his marble throne. Charlemagne had to journey all the way to Rome for his coronation, but the next 32 Holy Roman emperors were crowned here in Aachen (with some exceptions), and each marked the occasion by presenting a lavish gift to the cathedral. In the 12th century Emperor Frederick I (aka Barbarossa) donated the great chandelier now hanging in the center of the Palatine chapel; his grandson, Friedrich II, donated Charlemagne's shrine. English-language guided tours of the cathedral (€4) are offered daily at 2. ⊠ *Münsterpl., Domhof 1* ☎ *0241/477–090* ⊕ *www.aachenerdom.de* ☒ *Free.*

Domschatzkammer (*The Cathedral Treasury*). The cathedral houses sacred art from late antiquity and the Carolingian, Ottonian, and Hohenstaufen eras. A bust of Charlemagne on view here was commissioned in the late 14th century by Emperor Karl IV, who traveled here from Prague for the sole reason of having it made. The bust incorporates a piece of Charlemagne's skull. Other highlights include the Cross of Lothair and the Persephone Sarcophagus. ⊠ *Papst-Johannes-Paul-II.-Str.* ☎ *0241/4770–9127* ⊕ *www.aachener-domschatz.de* ☒ *€5.*

Elisenbrunnen (*Elisa Fountain*). Southeast of the cathedral and the site of the city's tourist-information center is an arcaded, neoclassical structure built in 1822. The central pavilion contains two fountains with thermal water—the hottest north of the Alps—that is reputed to help cure a wide range of ailments in those who drink it. If you can brave a gulp of the sulfurous water, you'll be emulating the likes of Dürer, Frederick the Great, and Charlemagne. ⊠ *Friedrich-Wilhelm-Pl.*

Ludwig Forum für Internationale Kunst. One of the world's most important art collectors, chocolate magnate Peter Ludwig, endowed two museums in the town he called home. The Forum, the larger of the two, holds a portion of Ludwig's enormous collection of contemporary art and hosts traveling exhibits. ⊠ *Jülicher Str. 97–109* ☎ *0241/180–7104* ⊕ *www.ludwigforum.de* ☒ *€5* ☾ *Closed Mon.*

Rathaus (*Town Hall*). Aachen's town hall sits behind the Dom, across Katschhof Square. It was built in the early 14th century on the site of the *Aula Regia,* or "great hall," of Charlemagne's palace. Its first major official function was the coronation banquet of Emperor Karl IV in 1349, held in the great Gothic hall you can still see today (though this was largely rebuilt after World War II). On the north wall of the building are statues of 50 emperors of the Holy Roman Empire. The greatest of them all, Charlemagne, stands in bronze atop the Karlsbrunnen in the center of the market square. ⊠ *Marktpl.* ☎ *0241/432–7310* ⊕ *rathaus-aachen.de* ☒ *€5.*

Suermondt-Ludwig Museum. The smaller of the two Ludwig art institutions in town (the Ludwig Forum is the larger one) has a collection that concentrates paintings from the 12th to the early 20th century, including a sizable holding of 17th-century Dutch and Flemish works by the likes of Anthony Van Dyck and Frans Hals. It's also home to one of Germany's largest sculpture collections. ⊠ *Wilhelmstr. 18* ☎ *0241/479–8040* ⊕ *www.suermondt-ludwig-museum.de* ☒ *€5* ☾ *Closed Mon.*

WHERE TO EAT

$$ ✕ **Am Knipp.** At this Bierstube dating from 1698, you can dig into
GERMAN regional dishes like *Zwiebelrahmrostbraten* (onion meat loaf) at low
wooden tables next to the tile stove. Pewter plates and beer mugs line
the walls. **Known for:** schnitzel with onions and mushrooms in cream
sauce; Zwiebelrahmrostbraten (onion meat loaf); slices of turkey breast
with a warm mustard dressing. $ *Average main: €16* ✉ *Bergdriesch 3*
☎ *0241/33168* ⊕ *www.amknipp.de* ⊘ *Closed Tues. Closed Dec. 24–
Jan. 2, and 2 wks in Apr. and Oct. No lunch.*

$$ ✕ **Der Postwagen.** Sitting at one of the low wooden tables in Der Post-
GERMAN wagen, surveying the marketplace through the wavy old glass, you
Fodor's Choice can dine well on solid German fare. If you really want to go local, try
★ *Himmel en Erd* (mashed potatoes and apple sauce topped by pan-fried
slices of blood sausage and onions). **Known for:** Himmel en Erd (with
black pudding, mashed potatoes, apples, and fried onions); Grillhaxe
(grilled pork shank on sauerkraut with mashed potatoes and caraway);
cod fillet on risotto with mustard sauce. $ *Average main: €15* ✉ *Markt
40* ☎ *0241/35001* ⊕ *www.ratskeller-aachen.de.*

$$$$ ✕ **La Becasse.** The sophisticated French nouvelle cuisine and attentive
FRENCH staff here are a hit with upscale locals. The restaurant, which is named
for the woodcock, has been in operation just outside the Old Town
by the Westpark since 1981. **Known for:** Japanese wagyu steak, seasoned with truffle pesto; lobster tempura and veal dressing; eel and
goose liver terrine, yuzu-citron jelly, tuna sauce. $ *Average main: €37*
✉ *Hanbrucherstr. 1* ☎ *0241/74444* ⊕ *www.labecasse.de* ⊘ *Closed Sun.
No lunch Sat. and Mon.*

WHERE TO STAY

$ 🛏 **ibis Styles Aachen City.** A 15-minute walk from the Dom, this colorfully
HOTEL furnished modern budget hotel is a good value, especially for families
FAMILY with children. **Pros:** kids under 16 get their own room for half-price;
welcoming modern aesthetic; solid budget hotel. **Cons:** on a busy street
somewhat removed from the center; might be a bit basic for some; beds
a bit small for two people. $ *Rooms from: €89* ✉ *Jülicherstr. 10–12*
☎ *0241/51060* ⊕ *www.ibis.com* ⤴ *102 rooms* ❑ *Free Breakfast.*

$$ 🛏 **Pullman Aachen Quellenhof.** This old-fashioned and grand hotel has
HOTEL rooms with high ceilings, a Roman-style spa area, and an inviting
pool. **Pros:** spacious rooms; elegant setting; formal service. **Cons:** on a
busy street; some renovations needed; old hotel. $ *Rooms from: €173*
✉ *Monheimsallee 52* ☎ *0241/91320* ⊕ *www.pullmanhotels.com* ⤴ *183
rooms* ❑ *Free Breakfast.*

SHOPPING

Don't leave Aachen without stocking up on the traditional local ginger-
bread, *Aachener Printen.* Each bakery in town offers its own varieties
(topped with whole or crushed nuts, milk or dark chocolate, etc.), and
guards its recipe like a state secret.

Café Van den Daele. Some of the best Aachener Printen can be found here, at one of Aachen's most beloved cafés, as can another tasty Aachen specialty, *Reisfladen* (a sort of tart filled with milk rice and often topped with fruit—pears, apricots, or cherries). Also known as Alt Aachener Kaffeestuben, the café is worth a visit if for nothing more than its atmosphere and tempting aromas. They can also mail their goods to you (or others) back home. ⊠ *Büchel 18* ☎ *0241/35724* ⊕ *www.van-den-daele.de.*

DÜSSELDORF

47 km (29 miles) north of Cologne (Köln).

Düsseldorf, the state capital of North Rhine–Westphalia is a diverse city of immigrants with an elegant old town center with plenty of charm. By contrast to Cologne's boisterous, working-class charm, Düsseldorf is known as one of the country's richest cities, with a reputation that epitomizes the economic success of postwar Germany. Because 80% of Düsseldorf was destroyed in World War II, the city has since been more or less rebuilt from the ground up—and that includes re-creating landmarks of long ago and restoring a medieval riverside quarter.

At the confluence of the Rhine and Düssel rivers, this dynamic city started as a small fishing town. The name means "village on the Düssel," but obviously this *Dorf* is a village no more. Trams and subways speed past the towering glass-and-steel structures of the modern MedienHafen and Königsalle; showcasing the finest clothes, furs, jewelry, and other goods that money can buy.

GETTING HERE AND AROUND

Trains connect Düsseldorf to the Rhineland region's main cities; a trip from Cologne takes under 25 minutes. The impressive Flughafen Düsseldorf, Germany's third-largest airport, serves more than 180 destinations.

TOURS

Düsseldorf Bus Tours. Hop-on, hop-off bus tours of Düsseldorf depart from the main train station every hour daily between 10 and 5 every (every half-hour Friday through Sunday) from late March to late October; hourly 10 to 4 from late October to late December; and at 11, 1, and 3 from late December to late March. Tickets can be purchased on the bus or at the information center ⊠ *Düsseldorf* ☜ *€15.*

Old Town Walking Tour. A walking tour of the Old Town leaves from the Altstadt tourist-info center (corner of Marktstrasse and Rheinstrasse) daily from April to October: Sunday at 11 am, weekdays at 3, and Saturday at 11 and 1. From November to March, tours depart Sunday at 11, Friday at 3, and Saturday at 1. ⊠ *Tourist Information Office Altstadt, Marktstr. 6d, at Rheinstr.* ☎ *211/1720–2854* ⊕ *www.duesseldorf-tourismus.de* ☜ *€12.*

VISITOR INFORMATION

Contacts Düsseldorf Tourist-Information. ⊠ *Marktstr. 6d, at Rheinstr.* ☎ *211/1720–2844* ⊕ *www.duesseldorf-tourismus.de.*

Düsseldorf's elegant high-end malls are great for window-shopping.

EXPLORING

Altstadt (*Old Town*). This party-hearty district has been dubbed "the longest bar in the word" by locals. Narrow alleys thread their way to some 300 restaurants and taverns. All crowd into the 1-square-km (½-square-mile) area between the Rhine and Heinrich-Heine-Allee. When the weather cooperates, the area really does seem like one big sidewalk café. ✉ *Düsseldorf.*

Heinrich-Heine-Institut. This museum and archive houses significant manuscripts of the German poet and man of letters, Heinrich Heine. Part of the complex was once the residence of the composer Robert Schumann. ✉ *Bilkerstr. 12–14* ☎ *0211/899–5571* ⊕ *www.duesseldorf.de/heineinstitut* 🎟 *€4* 🕐 *Closed Mon.*

Hofgarten Park. The oldest remaining parts of the Hofgarten date back to 1769, when it was transformed into Germany's first public park. The promenade leading to what was once a hunting palace, Schloss Jägerhof, was all the rage in late-18th-century Düsseldorf before the park was largely destroyed by Napoléon's troops. Today it's an oasis of greenery at the heart of downtown. ✉ *Düsseldorf.*

Kaiserswerth. It is one of the most historic corners of Düsseldorf but feels like a storybook German town completely separate from the city, with its cobblestone streets and neatly packed stone and brick buildings. The U79 U-bahn provides easy access to central Klemensplatz, or if the weather is agreeable, a bike ride along the Rhine will work up your appetite before indulging in traditional German fare. ✉ *Düsseldorf* ⊕ *www.duesseldorf-tourismus.de* Ⓜ *U79.*

11

Fodor's Choice **Königsallee.** Düsseldorf's main shopping avenue epitomizes the city's
★ affluence, lined as it is with designer boutiques and stores. Known as
"the Kö," this wide, double boulevard is divided by an ornamental
waterway fed by the River Düssel. Rows of chestnut trees line the Kö,
shading a string of sidewalk cafés. Beyond the Triton Fountain, at the
street's north end, begins a series of parks and gardens. In these patches
of green you can sense a joie de vivre that might be surprising in a city
devoted to big business. ⊠ *Düsseldorf.*

Kunstsammlung Nordrhein-Westfalen: K20. This important fixture on Düsseldorf's art scene is split into two parts, plus an installation space.
Behind the sleek, polished black stone facade of K20 is a treasure trove
of art (*Kunst*, hence the K) of the 20th century, including works from
masters like Picasso, Klee, and Richter. (The K21 museum of modern
art is in a separate location.) Rounding things off is the quirky, modern
Schmela Haus (1967), a former commercial gallery, which the museum
uses as a space for special events and exhibitions. ⊠ *K20, Grabbepl. 5*
☎ *0211/838–1204* ⊕ *www.kunstsammlung.de* 🖾 *From €12; free entry
1st Wed. of month, 6–10; Schmela Haus: free* ☉ *Closed Mon.*

Kunstsammlung Nordrhein-Westfalen: K21. Within the more conservative 19th-century architecture of K21 is edgier fare—international
art since about 1980, including the works of Thomas Ruff and Nam
June Paik. (The K20 has a separate location.) ⊠ *K21, Ständehausstr. 1*
☎ *0211/838–1204* ⊕ *www.kunstsammlung.de* 🖾 *From €12; free entry
1st Wed. of month* ☉ *Closed Mon.*

MedienHafen. This stylish, revamped district is a mix of late-19th-cen-
tury warehouses and ultramodern restaurants, bars, and shops: it's
one of Europe's masterpieces in urban redevelopment. Surrounding
the historic commercial harbor, now occupied by yachts and leisure
boats, are the many media companies that have made this area their
home. On the riverbank you'll find Frank Gehry's **Neuer Zollhof,** a
particularly striking ensemble of three organic-looking high-rises. The
best way to tackle the buzzing architecture is to take a stroll down the
promenade. ⊠ *Düsseldorf.*

Museum Kunstpalast. This impressive art museum lies at the northern
extremity of the Hofgarten, close to the Rhine. Its excellent German
expressionist collection (Beckmann, Kirchner, Nolde, Macke, among
others) makes it worth a trip, as does its collection of glass art—one
of the largest in Europe. ⊠ *Ehrenhof 4–5* ☎ *0211/899–2460* ⊕ *www.
smkp.de* 🖾 *Permanent collection €5; special exhibition prices vary*
☉ *Closed Mon.*

Neanderthal Museum. Just outside Düsseldorf, the Düssel River forms
a valley, called the Neanderthal, where the bones of a Stone Age relative of modern man were found. The impressive museum, built at the
site of the discovery in the suburb of Mettmann, includes models of
the original discovery, replicas of cave drawings, and life-size models
of Neanderthal Man. Many scientists think he was a different species
of human; short, stocky, and with a sloping forehead. The bones were
found in 1856 by workers quarrying the limestone cliffs to get flux for

blast furnaces. ✉ *Talstr. 300, Mettmann* ☎ *02104/97970* ⊕ *www.nean-derthal.de* 🖾 *Permanent exhibition €9; special exhibitions from €7.*

Rhine Promenade. Traffic is routed away from the river and underneath this pedestrian strip, which is lined by chic shopping arcades and cafés. Joggers, rollerbladers, and folks out for a stroll make much use of the promenade as well. ✉ *Düsseldorf.*

Schloss Jägerhof. At the far-east edge of the Hofgarten, this baroque structure is more a combination town house and country lodge than a palace. It houses the **Goethe-Museum**, featuring original manuscripts, first editions, personal correspondence, and other memorabilia of Germany's greatest writer. A collection of Meissen porcelain, the Sammlung Ernst Schneider Collection, is also here. ✉ *Jacobistr. 2* ☎ *0211/899–6262* ⊕ *www.goethe-museum.com* 🖾 *€4* ⊙ *Closed Mon.*

Schlossturm (*Palace Tower*). A squat tower is all that remains of the palace built by the Berg family, which ruled Düsseldorf for more than five centuries. The tower also houses the **SchifffahrtMuseum**, which charts 2,000 years of Rhine boatbuilding and navigation. ✉ *Burgpl. 30* ☎ *0211/899–4195* ⊕ *www.freunde-schifffahrtmuseum.de* 🖾 *€3* ⊙ *Closed Mon.*

St. Lambertus. This Gothic church is near the palace tower on Carlsplatz. Its spire became distorted because unseasoned wood was used in its construction. The Vatican elevated the 14th-century brick church to a basilica minor (small cathedral) in 1974 in recognition of its role in church history. Built in the 13th century, with additions from 1394, St. Lambertus contains the tomb of William the Rich and a graceful late-Gothic tabernacle. ✉ *Stiftspl. 7* ⊕ *www.lambertuspfarre.de* 🖾 *Free.*

WHERE TO EAT

$$$$
FRENCH
✕ **Berens am Kai.** This glass-and-steel building with ceiling-to-floor windows looks more like a modern office complex than the sleek restaurant it is. Head here for creative French recipes, a wine list with vintages from around the world, and tempting desserts—it's a good option if you're hankering for a change from old-style German cooking. **Known for:** smoked eel; goose liver; blanquette of rabbit. Ⓢ *Average main: €40* ✉ *Kaistr. 16* ☎ *0211/300–6750* ⊕ *www.berensamkai.de* ⊙ *Closed Sun. No lunch Sat.*

$
FRENCH
✕ **Bistro Zicke.** Weekend brunch (served until 4 pm) can get busy at this French-inspired artists' café on a quiet square one block from the riverfront. Otherwise, the bistro—with its big windows and walls plastered with old movie and museum posters—is an oasis from the hustle and bustle of the busy Altstadt. **Known for:** potatoes and herbal quark; Swabian ravioli; baked camembert. Ⓢ *Average main: €14* ✉ *Bäckerstr. 5a* ☎ *0211/327–800* ⊕ *www.bistro-zicke.de* ⊟ *No credit cards.*

$
GERMAN
✕ **Brauerei im Füchschen.** Füchsen is a traditional Düsseldorf Alt Bier brewery set back away from the commotion of the central Alt Stadt on scenic Rattingerstrasse. Here you'll find traditional German cuisine paired with one of the city's favorite takes on the local beer, as well as a recently launched Pilsner. **Known for:** Wiener schnitzel with cranberry marmalade and roasted potatoes; pork knuckle (Schweinshaxe);

Sauerbraten "Rhein Style." $ *Average main: €13* ⊠ *Ratinger Str. 28* ☏ *0211/137–470* ⊕ *www.fuechschen.de* ⊟ *No credit cards.*

$$ ╳ **Hausmann's.** This Altstadt restaurant offers a modern take on tra-
GERMAN ditional German cuisine in an updated environment that takes the Bratwurst and Rinderfilet out of the timber buildings of yesteryear and into the 21st century, with German craft beer to help savor the experience. **Known for:** Rhineland-style Sauerbraten (Rheinischer Art); Riesling-hühchenkeule (Riesling-braised chicken leg); Senfi-Ei (mustard egg). $ *Average main: €20* ⊠ *Hafenstr. 9* ☏ *0211/2610–1210* ⊕ *www. hausmanns-duesseldorf.de.*

$$$$ ╳ **Im Schiffchen.** This is grande luxe, with cooking turned into fine art
ITALIAN through the skills of chef Jean-Claude Bourgueil and his staff. The
Fodor'sChoice restaurant Enzo im Schiffchen on the ground floor features lighter Con-
★ tinental fare created by the same chef but at lower prices. **Known for:** ravioli del plin; grilled lobster sausages on spumante risotto; extensive selection of wines by the glass. $ *Average main: €48* ⊠ *Kaiserswerther Markt 9* ☏ *0211/401–050* ⊕ *www.im-schiffchen.de* ☉ *Closed Sun. and Mon. No lunch.*

$ ╳ **Naniwa Noodles and Soups.** Düsseldorf has one of the largest Japanese
GERMAN communities outside of mainland Japan, and Naniwa is a standout in the heart of the community near Immermanstrasse. Lines can stretch down the block, but service is quick and worth the wait for traditional soup and noodle dishes. **Known for:** curry noodle soup; toriteri-Don (chicken with teriyaki sauce, rice, and vegetables); tenshin-han (rice with sweet-and-sour roasted crab and vegetables). $ *Average main: €12* ⊠ *Oststr. 55* ☏ *0211/866–990* ⊕ *www.uerige.de* ⊟ *No credit cards* ☉ *Closed Tues.*

WHERE TO STAY

$$$$ ▦ **Breidenbacher Hof, a Capella Hotel.** The original, two-centuries-old Bre-
HOTEL idenbacher Hof was rebuilt from the ground up in 2008 to create this opulent, high-tech hotel, adding a luxurious new 6,500-square-foot spa to its basement in 2014. **Pros:** luxurious accommodation; consistently positive ratings from guests; great location on the Kö. **Cons:** expensive for most budgets; some complaints about customer service; some rooms are loud. $ *Rooms from: €360* ⊠ *Königsallee 11* ☏ *0211/1609–0909* ⊕ *www.capellahotels.com/dusseldorf* ⇨ *106 rooms* ⦿| *Free Breakfast.*

$$ ▦ **carathotel Düsseldorf.** Besides bright, good-size rooms, the true
HOTEL strength of this modern hotel is its location, near the market in the Altstadt. **Pros:** near the main train station; free Wi-Fi; high level of cleanliness. **Cons:** style is a bit dated; some complaints of noisy rooms; advertised park view is of a courtyard. $ *Rooms from: €129* ⊠ *Ben-ratherstr. 7a* ☏ *0211/13050* ⊕ *www.carat-hotel-duesseldorf.de* ⇨ *73 rooms* ⦿| *Free Breakfast.*

$$ ▦ **Hotel Orangerie.** Steps away from Altstadt action and the Rhine, this
HOTEL small hotel on a cobblestone road offers simple comfort and a surprising amount of quiet. **Pros:** unbeatable location; free Wi-Fi; hospitable staff. **Cons:** small rooms; small bathroom towels; caters to business travelers. $ *Rooms from: €130* ⊠ *Bäckerg. 1* ☏ *0211/866–800* ⊕ *www.hotel-orangerie-mcs.de* ⊟ *No credit cards* ⇨ *27 rooms* ⦿| *Free Breakfast.*

$$$ RENTAL 🏨 **Steigenberger Parkhotel.** Miraculously quiet despite its central location on the edge of the Hofgarten and at the beginning of the Königsallee, this old hotel is anything but stodgy, especially after a major face-lift in 2013. **Pros:** central location; quiet despite the busy area; consistent guest favorite. **Cons:** fairly high rates; some complaints about service; amenities don't match the price. [$] *Rooms from: €225* ✉ *Königsallee 1a* ☎ *0211/13810* 🌐 *www.steigenberger.de* 🛏 *130 rooms* 🍴 *Free Breakfast.*

NIGHTLIFE AND PERFORMING ARTS

The **Altstadt** is a landscape of pubs, dance clubs, ancient brewery houses, and jazz clubs in the vicinity of the Marktplatz and along cobblestone streets named Bolker, Kurze, Flinger, and Mühlen. These places may be crowded, but some are very atmospheric. The local favorite for nightlife is the **Hafen** neighborhood. Its restaurants and bars cater to the youngish professionals who work and party there.

Even straitlaced Düsseldorf knows how to get funky when it comes to the Flingern district. Cool indie cafés, galleries, and local designer shops line Ackerstrasse between Hermannstrasse and Birkenstrasse. At night, youngsters flock to **Edge Bar** (Bruchstr. 34), a popular watering hole with craft beer and music. But the neighborhood's not all hipster yet; there's still a neat mix of people and businesses, as evidenced by places like **Okra** (Ackerstr. 119), a simple Ethiopian restaurant with a retired bowling alley in its basement.

Fodor's Choice ★ **Deutsche Oper am Rhein.** The city's highly regarded opera company and ballet troupe are showcased here. ✉ *Heinrich-Heine-Allee 16a* ☎ *0211/892–5211* 🌐 *www.operamrhein.de.*

HOLY CRAFT Beer Bar. Thanks to the (in)famous Rheinheitsgebot that's regulated German beer for centuries, "craft beer" has been something of an anomaly with purists preferring the beer of their city, like Alt in Düsseldorf or Kölsch in Cologne. That's rapidly changing with the likes of this bar, which serves up the latest concoctions from German microbreweries across the country, inspired by distinctly non-German styles, including IPAs and even sours. Tasty appetizers are also on the menu so you're not drinking on an empty stomach. ✉ *Lieferg. 11* ☎ *0211/3004–9600.*

Robert-Schumann-Saal. Classical and pop concerts, symposia, film, and international theater are presented at the Robert-Schumann-Saal. ✉ *Ehrenhof 4–5* ☎ *0211/899–0200* 🌐 *www.smkp.de.*

Tonhalle. The finest concert hall in Germany after Berlin's Philharmonie is a former planetarium on the edge of the Hofgarten. It's the home of the Düsseldorfer Symphoniker, which plays from September to June. ✉ *Ehrenhof 1* ☎ *0211/899–6123* 🌐 *www.tonhalle.de.*

THE FAIRY-TALE ROAD

WELCOME TO
THE FAIRY-TALE ROAD

TOP REASONS
TO GO

★ **Valley Road:** Drive or bike the scenic highway between Hannoversch-Münden and Hameln (Hamelin)—it's a landscape of green hills, Weser Renaissance towns, and inviting riverside taverns.

★ **Marburg:** Staircase streets cover the steep hillsides of this half-timber university town; sit outdoors and soak up the atmosphere.

★ **Bremen:** Browse the shops and galleries lining the picturesque Böttcherstrasse and Schnoorviertel, then savor the city's rich coffee tradition.

★ **Dornröschenschloss Sababurg:** With its spiral staircases, imposing turrets, and fairy-tale setting, this castle was said to have inspired the Grimm brothers' tale of Sleeping Beauty.

★ **Schlosspark Wilhelmshöhe:** Home to a stunning, crescent-moon palace and a fairy-tale castle, the park's trees, ponds, and wide-open spaces offer a dramatic contrast to the urbanity below.

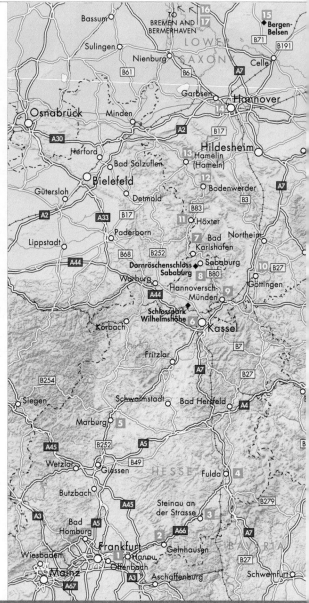

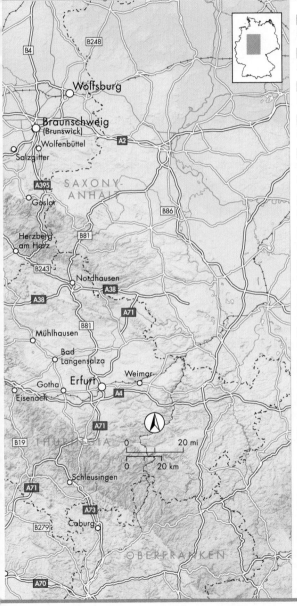

1 Hanau. Where the brothers Grimm were born.

2 Gelnhausen. A charming historic town.

3 Steinau an der Strasse. Where the Grimms grew up.

4 Fulda. Famed for its cathedral and palace.

5 Marburg. Its university was attended by the Grimms.

6 Kassel. Has beautiful Schloss Wilhelmshöhe.

7 Bad Karlshafen. Spa town popular with campers.

8 Sababurg. Home of "Sleeping Beauty's Castle."

9 Hannoversch-Münden. Delightful half-timber town.

10 Göttingen. Univeristy where the Grimm's worked.

11 Höxter. Known for Schlooss Corvey.

12 Bodenwerder. Home of Baron von Münchhausen.

13 Hamelin (Hameln). Of pied piper fame.

14 Hannover. Has the Hannover summer palace.

15 Bergen-Belsen. Where Anne Frank died.

16 Bremen. River port.

17 Bremerhaven. North Sea port city.

Updated by
Courtney Tenz

With a name evocative of magic and adventure, the Fairy-Tale Road (Märchenstrasse) takes its travelers on a path through the land of the Brothers Grimm and a rolling countryside of farmland and forests that inspired tales of sleeping princesses, hungry wolves, and gingerbread houses. Flowing through the heart of western Germany to its North Sea coast, the Märchenstrasse stops along the way at towns and villages where the brothers spent much of their lives two centuries ago.

It was here among medieval castles and witch towers that the brothers, first as young boys, and then later as students and academics, listened to legends told by local storytellers, and adapted them into the fairy tales that continue to be read around the world today; enchanted and frequently dark tales that include "Sleeping Beauty," "Little Red Riding Hood," and "Hansel and Gretel."

Following the Grimms' footsteps through a landscape of river valleys and wide-open skies, or down cobblestone streets flanked by half-timber houses and baroque palaces, it's possible to imagine things haven't changed that much since the brothers' time. Traditional taverns serving strong German beers and thick slabs of beef and pork dot the way, and storytelling continues to be a major attraction along the Fairy-Tale Road, though nowadays more commonly in the form of guided tours and interactive museum displays.

The Fairy-Tale Road, of course, is also a modern route, and its wide, smooth roads pass through larger urban areas, such as Kassel and Bremen, full of contemporary hotels, eateries, and stores. Like large parts of the rest of the country, many of these towns and cities were greatly damaged during World War II, and their hurried reconstruction often favored functionality over form, so that many buildings are much more stark than those they replaced. This contrast, however, often only serves to emphasize the beauty of what remained.

Not every town on the road can lay claim to a connection to the Brothers Grimm or the inspiration for a specific tale, but many continue to celebrate the region's fairy-tale heritage with theme museums, summer festivals, and outdoor plays.

It's this heritage, the natural appeal of the countryside, and the tradition and culture found in its towns and cities that attract travelers along the Märchenstrasse; that, mixed with the promise of adventure and the opportunity to create some tales of their own.

MAJOR REGIONS

The first portion of the Fairy-Tale Road, from Hanau to Bad Karlshafen, lies within the state of **Hesse.** Much of the state's population is concentrated in the south; here in the northern part it is quieter, with a pretty, rural, hilly, and forested landscapes. Here you'll find **Hanau,** where the Fairy Tale Road begins; **Gelnhausen,** overlooking the Kinzig River; **Steinau an der Strasse;** the cathedral city **Fulda;** the almost vertical city of **Marburg; Kassel,** where the Grimm brothers lived as teenagers; **Bad Karlshafen,** a pretty spa town; and **Sababurg** and its beautiful Renaissance castle.

Lower Saxony was formed from an amalgamation of smaller states in 1946. Its picturesque landscape includes one of Germany's most haunting river roads, along the Weser River between **Hannoversch-Münden,** passing through **Göttingen,** and **Bodenwerder,** on the way to **Hameln** (Hamelin). This road, part of the Fairy-Tale Road, follows green banks where it's hard to see where the water ends and the land begins. Standing sentinel are superb little towns whose half-timber architecture gave rise to the term *Weser Renaissance*. The Lower Saxon landscape also includes the juniper bushes and flowering heather of the Lüneburg Heath. The region also includes **Hannover, Bergen-Belsen, Bremen,** and **Bremerhaven.**

PLANNING

WHEN TO GO

Summer is the ideal time to travel through this varied landscape, although in spring you'll find the river valleys carpeted in the season's first flowers, and in fall the sleepy Weser is often blanketed in mist. Keep in mind that retail stores and shops in the smaller towns in this area often close for two to three hours at lunchtime.

GETTING HERE AND AROUND
AIR TRAVEL

The closest international airports to this region are in Frankfurt, Hannover, and Hamburg. Frankfurt is less than a half-hour from Hanau, and Hamburg is less than an hour from Bremen.

Contacts City Airport Bremen. ✉ *Flughafenallee 20, Bremen* ☎ *0421/55950* ⊕ *www.bremen-airport.com.* **Hannover-Langenhagen Airport.** ✉ *Petzelstr. 84, Hannover* ☎ *0511/9770* ⊕ *www.hannover-airport.de.*

BIKE TRAVEL

The Fulda and Werra rivers have 190 km (118 miles) of bike paths, and you can cycle the whole length of the Weser River from Hannoversch-Münden to the North Sea at Cuxhaven without making too many detours from the river valley.

BUS TRAVEL

Contacts Eurolines. ☎ 069/7903–501 ⊕ www.eurolines.de.

CAR TRAVEL

The best way to travel is by car. The A-1 and A-7 autobahn network connects most major stops on the route, including Hanau, Fulda, Kassel, Göttingen, and Bremen, but you can't savor the fairy-tale country from this high-speed superhighway. Bremen is 60 km (35 miles) northwest of Hannover.

The Fairy-Tale Road incorporates one of Germany's loveliest scenic drives, the Wesertalstrasse, or Weser Valley Road (B-80 and B-83), between Hannoversch-Münden and Hameln; the total distance is approximately 103 km (64 miles).

TRAIN TRAVEL

Hanau, Fulda, Kassel, Göttingen, Hannover, and Bremen are reachable via InterCity Express (ICE) trains from Frankfurt and Hamburg. Rail service, but not ICE service, is available to Hannoversch-Münden, Marburg, and Hameln.

Contacts Deutsche Bahn. ☎ 0800/699–6633 €0.20 per call ⊕ www.bahn.de.

HOTELS

Make hotel reservations in advance if you plan to visit in summer. Though it's one of the less-traveled tourist routes in Germany, the main destinations on the Fairy-Tale Road are popular. Hannover is particularly busy during trade-fair times and Kassel can book out a year in advance during Documenta years.

RESTAURANTS

In this largely rural area many restaurants serve hot meals only between 11:30 am and 2 pm, and 6 and 9 pm. You rarely need a reservation here, and casual clothing is generally acceptable.

Prices in restaurant reviews are the average cost of a main course at dinner, or if dinner is not served, at lunch. Prices in hotel reviews are the lowest cost of a standard double room in high season.

WHAT IT COSTS IN EUROS			
$	$$	$$$	$$$$
Restaurants under €15	€15–€20	€21–€25	over €25
Hotels under €100	€100–€175	€176–€225	over €225

12

PLANNING YOUR TIME

The Fairy-Tale Road isn't really for the traveler in a hurry. If you only have a day or two to savor it, concentrate on a short stretch. A good suggestion is the Weser River route between Hannoversch-Münden and Hameln (Hamelin). The landscape is lovely, and the towns are romantic. If you have more time, but not enough to travel the whole route, focus on the southern half of the road. It's more in character with the fairy tales.

TOURS

BIKE TOURS

Five- and seven-day cycle tours of the Fulda and Werra river valleys are available. These typically include bike rentals, overnight accommodations, and luggage transport between stops.

SRJ. This bike-tour company offers a number of packages for those interested in cycling north along the Weser River. You can choose anything from a four-day package along the Weser to a longer tour over nine days. ⊠ *Hermannstr 46, Minden* ☎ *0571/889–1900* ⊕ *www.srj. de* 🖾 *From €255.*

BOAT TOURS

Flotte Weser. The eight boats of Flotte Weser operate short summer excursions along a considerable stretch of the Weser River between Bremen and Bad Karlshafen. The trip between Corvey and Bad Karlshafen, for example, takes four hours; the entire route will take 10½ hours. ⊠ *Am Stockhof 2, Hamelin* ☎ *05151/939–999* ⊕ *www.flotte-weser.de* 🖾 *From €15.*

VISITOR INFORMATION

Contacts Deutsche Märchenstrasse. ⊠ *Kurfürstenstr. 9, Kassel* ☎ *0561/9204–7910* ⊕ *www.deutsche-maerchenstrasse.de.*

HANAU

16 km (10 miles) east of Frankfurt.

The Fairy-Tale Road begins in Hanau, the town where the Brothers Grimm were born. Although Grimm fans will want to start their pilgrimage here, Hanau is now a traffic-congested suburb of Frankfurt, with post–World War II buildings that are not particularly attractive.

GETTING HERE AND AROUND

Less than a 50-minute S-bahn (Line No. 9) journey from Frankfurt Airport, Hanau is also reachable by high-speed ICE trains from Berlin and Munich, or a combination of ICE and regional trains from Hannover, Bremen, and Hamburg.

VISITOR INFORMATION

Contacts Tourist Information Hanau. ⊠ *Am Markt 14–18* ☎ *06181/295–950* ⊕ *www.hanau.de.*

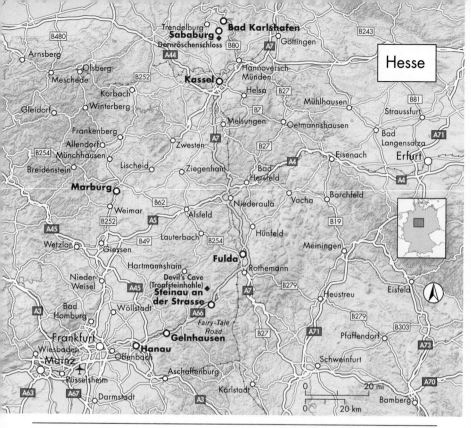

EXPLORING

Brüder Grimm Nationaldenkmal (*Brothers Grimm Memorial*). Hanau's main attraction can be reached only on foot. The bronze memorial, erected in 1898, is a larger-than-life-size statue of the brothers, one seated, the other leaning on his chair, the two of them pondering an open book. ☒ *Marktpl.* ☒ *Free.*

Neustädter Rathaus (*New Town Hall*). The solid bulk of Hanau's 18th-century Rathaus stands behind the Grimm brothers statue. Every day at noon its bells play tribute to another of the city's famous sons, the composer Paul Hindemith (1895–1963), by chiming out one of his canons. On Wednesday and Sunday, a farmer's market fills the square in front of the baroque building. ☒ *Marktpl. 14.*

Schloss Philippsruhe. Completed in 1880, this palace mixes a bit of rococo, neo-Renaissance, and neoclassism in its design; a museum inside has a small Grimm exhibit that includes clothing, artifacts, and writings. It's on the bank of the Main in the suburb of Kesselstadt. Historical Hanau treasures, including a priceless collection of faience, are also on display here. ☒ *Philippsruher Allée 45* ☎ *06181/295–564* ⊕ *www. museen-hanau.de* ☒ *€4* ☉ *Closed Mon.*

GELNHAUSEN

20 km (12 miles) northeast of Hanau, 35 km (21 miles) northeast of Frankfurt.

Perched elegantly on the side of a hill above the Kinzig River, Gelnhausen's picturesque Altstadt (Old Town) offers the first taste of the half-timber houses and cobblestone streets that lie in abundance farther north. In spring and summer, school children dressed in traditional garb are guided down its winding streets and through lively little squares flanked by ice cream parlors and outdoor cafés, to listen to tales of Red Beard, and the fate of those poor townswomen suspected of being witches.

GETTING HERE AND AROUND

If you're flying into Frankfurt, Gelnhausen is an ideal spot for your first night on the Fairy-Tale Road. It's smaller and more charming than Hanau, and is still less than an hour's drive from Frankfurt's main airport. Trains to Gelnhausen leave from Frankfurt's main station every half hour and take approximately 35 minutes, with frequent connections to and from Hanau. Once here, the historic Old Town is hilly, but small enough to walk around. April through October, a walking tour leaves from the town hall at 2 on Sunday.

VISITOR INFORMATION

Contacts Gelnhausen. ⊠ *Tourist Information, Obermarkt 8* ☎ *06051/830–300* ⊕ *www.gelnhausen.de.*

EXPLORING

Hexenturm (*Witches' Tower*). The Hexenturm was originally constructed in the 15th century as a watchtower to protect the town from invaders. What remains today is an imposing 9 meters in diameter and 24-meter-high tower, which was used as a grim prison during the time when Gelnhausen was the center of a witch hunt in the late 16th century. Dozens of women were either burned at the stake or bound hand-and-foot and then thrown into the Kinzig River after being held prisoner here. ⊠ *Am Fratzenstein* ☎ *06051/830–300* ⊕ *www.gelnhausen.de* ⊠ *Free.*

Kaiserpfalz. On an island in the gentle little Kinzig River you'll find the remains of the Kaiserpfalz. Emperor Friedrich I—known as Barbarossa, or "Red Beard"—built the castle in this idyllic spot in the 12th century; in 1180 it was the scene of the first all-German Imperial Diet, a gathering of princes and ecclesiastical leaders. Today only parts of the russet walls and colonnaded entrance remain. Still, you can stroll beneath the castle's ruined ramparts and you'll get a tangible impression of the medieval importance of the court of Barbarossa. ⊠ *Burgstr. 14* ☎ *06051/830–300* ⊕ *www.schloesser-hessen.de* ⊠ *€4* ⊘ *Closed Mon. and Dec. 24–Feb.*

To begin your tour of the Grimm brothers' fairy-tale landscape, head to the Brüder Grimm Nationaldenkmal (Brothers' Grimm Memorial) in Hanau.

WHERE TO STAY

$ HOTEL **Romantisches Hotel Burg Mühle.** This peaceful hotel, a few steps from the Kaiserpfalz and within an easy walk of the Altstadt, was once the castle's mill (*Mühle*) and sawmill. **Pros:** large rooms (many with balconies); unique building; central location. **Cons:** furnishings a bit worn; must call for late check-in (after 10 pm); some rooms could use updating. [$] *Rooms from: €77* ✉ *Burgstr. 2* ☎ *06051/82050* 🌐 *www.burgmuehle.de* 🛏 *40 rooms* 🍴 *Free Breakfast.*

STEINAU AN DER STRASSE

30 km (18 miles) northeast of Gelnhausen, 65 km (40 miles) northeast of Frankfurt.

The little town of Steinau—full name Steinau an der Strasse (Steinau "on the road," referring to an old trade route between Frankfurt and Leipzig)—had a formative influence on the Brothers Grimm as they arrived in the town as preschoolers and stayed until they were aged 10 and 11, when they left after their father's death.

Steinau dates from the 13th century, and is typical of villages in the region. Marvelously preserved half-timber houses are set along cobblestone streets; an imposing castle bristles with towers and turrets. In its woodsy surroundings you can well imagine encountering Little Red Riding Hood, Snow White, or Hansel and Gretel. A major street is named after the brothers; the building where they lived is now named after them.

CLOSE UP

The Brothers Grimm

The Grimm fairy tales originated in the southern part of the Märchenstrasse. This area, mainly in the state of Hesse, was the home region of the brothers Jacob (1785–1863) and Wilhelm (1786–1859) Grimm. They didn't create the stories they are famous for. Their feat was to mine the great folklore tradition that was already deeply ingrained in local culture.

COLLECTING THE STORIES

For generations, eager children had been gathering at dusk around the village storyteller to hear wondrous tales of fairies, witches, and gnomes, tales passed down from storytellers who had gone before. The Grimms sought out these storytellers and recorded their tales.

The result was the two volumes of their work *Kinder- und Hausmärchen* (*Children's and Household Tales*), published in 1812 and 1814 and revised and expanded six times during their lifetimes. The last edition, published in 1857, is the basis for the stories we know today. Earlier versions contained more violence and cruelty than was deemed suitable for children.

That is how the world got the stories of Cinderella, Sleeping Beauty, Hansel and Gretel, Little Red Riding Hood, Snow White and the Seven Dwarfs, Rumpelstiltskin, Puss-in-Boots, Mother Holle, Rapunzel, and some 200 others, many of which remain unfamiliar.

THE BROTHERS' OTHER WORK

Both Jacob and Wilhelm Grimm had distinguished careers as librarians and scholars, and probably would be unhappy to know that they are best remembered for the fairy tales. Among other things, they began what would become the most comprehensive dictionary of the German language and produced an analysis of German grammar.

The brothers were born in Hanau, near Frankfurt, which has a statue memorializing them as well as a Grimm exhibit at Schloss Philippsruhe. They spent their childhood in Steinau, 30 km (18 miles) to the north, where their father was magistrate. There are two Grimm museums there, one in their home. On their father's untimely death they moved to their mother's home city of Kassel, where they found the best of their stories. Kassel has an important Grimm museum, the GRIMMWELT, which opened in 2015 and is dedicated to promoting the brothers' role in enhancing the German language as we know it today. Although they attended the university at Marburg from 1802 to 1805, they later returned to Kassel to work as librarians before they went on to work in the university town of Göttingen; the brothers spent their last years as academics in Berlin.

12

GETTING HERE AND AROUND

Regional trains leave hourly from Gelnhausen and take about 15 minutes to reach Steinau an der Strasse. The train station is just over a kilometer (½ mile) from the Old Town's center and, should the walk be too far, the MKK90 bus goes into the town, albeit at irregular and sometimes lengthy intervals (get off at Ringstrasse). Or you can take a taxi. A city walking tour takes place April to October, the first Sunday of the month, leaving at 2 from the Märchenbrunnen (fountain).

VISITOR INFORMATION

Contacts Steinau an der Strasse. ⊠ *Verkehrsbüro, Brüder-Grimm-Str. 70* ☎ *06663/96310* ⊕ *www.steinau.eu.*

EXPLORING

In case you don't get enough half-timber on the Fairy-Tale Road there is also the **German Half-Timber Road** (Deutsche Fachwerkstrasse), with lots more storybook architecture. A map and brochure can be obtained from the Deutsche Fachwerkstrasse (⊕ *www.deutsche-fachwerkstrasse.de*).

FAMILY **Brüder Grimm Haus and Museum Steinau.** Occupying both the house where the Brothers Grimm lived for much of their childhoods as well as the house's old barn, the Brüder Grimm Haus and Museum Steinau are fun and engaging museums. Featuring a reconstruction of the family's old kitchen, the brothers' former house also displays old personal possessions such as letters and reading glasses, and has an upper floor divided into nine rooms with interactive displays that celebrate the Grimms' stories and other fairy tales from around Europe. Across a small courtyard, the town's museum documents what life was like on the old trade route that ran through Steinau, incorporating into its exhibits a coach, inn signs, milestones, and the type of pistol travelers used to defend themselves from bandits. ⊠ *Brüder-Grimm-Str. 80* ☎ *06663/7605* ⊕ *www.museum-steinau.de* 🖾 *€6.*

Devil's Cave (Tropfsteinhöhle). On this half-hour tour through a 2½-million-year-old cave on the outskirts of Steinau, you may stumble upon sleeping bats as you explore the unique geological formations, including stalactites and stalagmites that reach up to 82 feet (25 meters) high and 36 feet (11 meters) in circumference as well as a so-called chapel room with ceilings up to 26 feet (8 meters) tall. ⊠ *Mooshecke 1* ⊹ *Free parking off L3179; must walk 10 mins to cave entrance* ☎ *06663/96310* ⊕ *www.tropfstein-hoehle-steinau.de* 🖾 *€4* ☼ *Closed Mon.–Thurs. and Oct.–mid-Apr.*

Schloss Steinau (*Steinau Castle*). Schloss Steinau is straight out of a Grimm fairy tale. It stands at the top of the town, with a "Fairy-tale Fountain" in front of it. Originally an early-medieval fortress, it was rebuilt in Renaissance style between 1525 and 1558 and first used by the counts of Hanau as their summer residence. Later it was used to guard the increasingly important trade route between Frankfurt and Leipzig. It's not difficult to imagine the young Grimm boys playing in the shadow of its great gray walls or venturing into the encircling dry moat.

The castle houses a **Grimm Museum,** one of two in Steinau, which exhibits the family's personal effects, including portraits of the Grimm relatives, the family Bible, an original copy of the Grimms' dictionary (the German equivalent of the *Oxford English Dictionary*), and all sorts of mundane things such as spoons and drinking glasses. Climb the tower for a breathtaking view of Steinau and the countryside. ⊠ *Schloss an der Steinau* ☎ *06663/6843* ⊕ *www.schloesser-hessen.de* 🖾 *From €4* ☼ *Closed Jan. and Feb. Closed Mon. Mar.–Nov. Closed Mon.–Sat. in Dec.*

12

WHERE TO EAT

$ 🍴 **Brathähnchenfarm.** A cheery hotel-restaurant a long uphill hike from GERMAN the center of Steinau, the "Roast Chicken Farm" is unique to Steinau. Get your fill of rotisserie chicken in the open dining room, or take a room in the attached guesthouse. **Known for:** rotisserie chicken; chicken livers and gizzards; potato soup with blutwurst. [$] *Average main: €14* ✉ *Im Ohl 1* ☎ *06663/228* 🌐 *www.brathaehnchenfarm.de* 💳 *No credit cards* 🕓 *Closed Mon. and late Dec.–mid-Feb.*

WHERE TO STAY

$ 🏨 **Burgmannenhaus.** Previously a 16th-century customs house, sitting on B&B/INN 1,000-year-old foundations and a secret tunnel that runs to the nearby Schloss and church, this friendly travelers' inn is the type of place made for history buffs. **Pros:** in the center of town; tasty regional beer and wild game meals; historical building. **Cons:** very simple furnishings; restaurant closed Wednesday and Thursday; no air-conditioning. [$] *Rooms from: €82* ✉ *Brüder Grimm Str. 49* ☎ *06663/911–2902* 🌐 *www.burgmannenhaus-steinau.de* 💳 *No credit cards* 🛏 *5 rooms* 🍽 *No meals.*

FULDA

32 km (20 miles) northeast of Steinau an der Strasse, 100 km (62 miles) northeast of Frankfurt.

The cathedral city of Fulda is worth a brief detour off the Fairy-Tale Road. There are two distinct parts to its downtown area. One is a stunning display of baroque architecture, with the cathedral, orangery, and formal garden, which grew up around the palace. The other is the Old Town, where the incredibly narrow and twisty streets are lined with boutiques, bistros, and a medieval tower. ■ **TIP→ You'll find Kanalstrasse and Karlstrasse in the Old Town lined with good, inexpensive cafés and restaurants, serving German, Mediterranean, and other dishes.**

GETTING HERE AND AROUND

InterCity Express trains connect Fulda with Frankfurt, Hannover, and Hamburg, while regional trains link the city with many other Fairy-Tale Road destinations. Within Fulda itself, the Old Town and the city's other main attractions are all in walking distance of each other.

VISITOR INFORMATION

Contacts Tourismus und Kongressmanagement Fulda. ✉ *Bonifatiuspl. 1* ☎ *0661/102–1813* 🌐 *www.tourismus-fulda.de.*

EXPLORING

Dom zu Fulda. Fulda's 18th-century cathedral, an impressive baroque building with an ornate interior, has two tall spires and stands on the other side of the broad boulevard that borders the palace park. The basilica accommodated the ever-growing number of pilgrims who converged on Fulda to pray at the grave of the martyred St. Boniface, the "Apostle of the Germans." A black alabaster bas-relief depicting his death marks the martyr's grave in the crypt. ✉ *Dompl. 1* 🌐 *www.bistum-fulda.de.*

Cathedral Museum. The Cathedral treasury contains a document bearing St. Boniface's writing, along with several other treasures, including Lucas Cranach the Elder's fine 16th-century painting *Christ and the Adulteress.* ✉ *Dompl. 2* ☎ *0661/87207* 🌐 *www.bistum-fulda.de/bistum_fulda* 🎟 *€3* 🕒 *Closed Mon. and mid-Jan.–mid-Feb.*

FAMILY **Kinder-Akademie-Fulda.** Germany's first children's museum has interactive exhibits to help explain science and technology, including a walk-through heart. ✉ *Mehlerstr. 4* ☎ *0661/902–730* 🌐 *www.kaf.de* 🎟 *From €4* 🕒 *Closed Sat. May–Sept.*

Michaeliskirche. Dating back to AD 819, this is one of Germany's oldest churches. Formerly a part of the Benedictine order, the church's interior is bare bones and yet impressive with its domed ceiling and arched cupola. ✉ *Michaelsberg 1* 🌐 *www.bistum-fulda.de* 🎟 *Free.*

Fodor's Choice ★ **Stadtschloss** (*City Palace*). The city's grandest example of baroque design is the immense Stadtschloss, formerly the residence of the prince-bishops. The **Fürstensaal** (Princes' Hall), on the second floor, provides a breathtaking display of baroque decorative artistry, with ceiling paintings by the 18th-century Bavarian artist Melchior Steidl, and fabric-clad walls. The palace also has permanent displays of fine Fulda porcelain.

Also worth seeing is the **Spiegelsaal,** with its many tastefully arranged mirrors. Pause at the windows of the Grünes Zimmer (Green Chamber) to take in the view across the palace park to the **Orangery,** a large garden with summer-flowering shrubs and plants. ✉ *Schlossstr. 1* ☎ *0661/102–1814* 🌐 *www.fulda.de/kultur/stadtschloss-fulda.html* 🎟 *€6 tour* 🕒 *Closed Mon.*

FAMILY **Vonderau Museum.** The Vonderau Museum is housed in a former Jesuit seminary. Its exhibits chart the cultural and natural history of Fulda and eastern Hesse. A popular section of the museum is its **planetarium,** which has a variety of shows, including one for children. Since it has only 35 seats, an early reservation via email or telephone is advisable. Shows take place Friday at 7, and on weekends at 2:30 and 3:30. ✉ *Jesuitenpl. 2* ☎ *0661/102–3212* 🌐 *www.museum-fulda.de* 🎟 *From €4* 🕒 *Closed Mon.*

WHERE TO EAT

$$ GERMAN 🍴 **Dachsbau.** An intimate atmosphere in a 350-year-old house with a sunny terrace near the city's baroque quarter complements the gourmet menu, which focuses on using regional, in-season ingredients in its traditional German dishes. An extensive wine list ensures you'll always have the right glass to go with your locally caught trout or grilled pork loin. **Known for:** grilled pork loin; homemade pasta with truffles; rack of lamb. [$] *Average main: €21* ✉ *Pfandhausstr. 8* ☎ *0661/74112* 🌐 *www.dachsbau-fulda.de* 🕒 *Closed Mon. and Tues.* 💳 *No credit cards.*

12

EATING WELL ON THE FAIRY-TALE ROAD

A specialty of northern Hesse is sausages with *Beulches,* made from potato balls, leeks, and black pudding. *Weck,* which is local dialect for "heavily spiced pork," appears either as *Musterweck,* served on a roll, or as *Weckewerk,* a frying-pan concoction with white bread. Heading north into Lower Saxony, you'll encounter the ever-popular *Speckkuchen,* a heavy and filling onion tart. Another favorite main course is *Pfefferpothast,* a sort of heavily browned goulash with lots of pepper. Trout and eels are common in the rivers and streams around Hameln, and by the time you reach Bremen, North German cuisine has taken over the menu. *Aalsuppe grün,* eel soup seasoned with dozens of herbs, is a must in summer, and the hearty *Grünkohl mit Pinkel,* a cabbage dish with sausage, bacon, and cured pork, appears in winter. Be sure to try the coffee. Fifty percent of the coffee served in Germany comes from beans roasted in Bremen. The city has been producing the stuff since 1673, and knows just how to serve it in pleasantly cozy—or, as locals say, *gemütlich*—surroundings.

WHERE TO STAY

$ B&B/INN 🏨 **Hotel zum Ritter.** Centrally located but tucked away on a side alley, this charming hotel and restaurant has quiet, comfortable rooms and very friendly staff, making it a great base for city exploring or for business travelers. **Pros:** friendly staff; great central location; traditional character. **Cons:** rooms are charmlessly modern; older furnishings; no air-conditioning. [$] *Rooms from: €99* ✉ *Kanalstr. 18–20* ☎ *0661/250–800* 🌐 *www.hotel-ritter.de* 🛏 *33 rooms* 🍴 *Free Breakfast.*

$$ HOTEL 🏨 **Maritim Hotel am Schlossgarten.** At the luxurious showpiece of the Maritim chain, guests can breakfast beneath frescoed ceilings and enormous chandeliers in a stunning 18th-century orangery overlooking Fulda Palace Park. **Pros:** gorgeous restaurants; lovely terrace with views of park and nearby cathedral; best location in town. **Cons:** no air-conditioning; rooms are rather dull; chain feel outside of public areas. [$] *Rooms from: €175* ✉ *Paulusspromenade 2* ☎ *0661/2820* 🌐 *www.maritim.de* 🛏 *112 rooms* 🍴 *No meals.*

$$ HOTEL Fodor'sChoice ★ 🏨 **Romantik Hotel Goldener Karpfen.** An institution in Fulda for more than 100 years, the Goldener Karpfen has remained family owned and run, with an elegant disposition and engaging hosts that have brought singers, actors, and archbishops through its doors. **Pros:** luxury lodging; a short stroll to the town's major attractions; excellent breakfast buffet. **Cons:** public spaces can feel cluttered; parking extra; not all windows have darkening blinds. [$] *Rooms from: €165* ✉ *Simpliziusbrunnen 1* ☎ *0661/86800* 🌐 *www.hotel-goldener-karpfen.de* 🛏 *50 rooms* 🍴 *Free Breakfast.*

Many of Marburg's cobblestone streets are pedestrian-only zones, perfect for strolling and people-watching.

MARBURG

60 km (35 miles) northwest of Fulda.

"I think there are more steps in the streets than in the houses." That is how Jacob Grimm described the half-timber hillside town of Marburg, which rises steeply from the Lahn River to the spectacular castle that crowns the hill. Many of the winding, crooked "streets" are indeed stone staircases, and several of the hillside houses have back doors five stories above the front doors. The town's famous university and its students are the main influence on its social life, which pulses through the many cafés, restaurants, and hangouts around the marketplace. The Grimms themselves studied here from 1802 to 1805.

Many of the streets are closed to traffic, and are filled with outdoor tables when the weather cooperates. There is a free elevator near the tourist-information office on Pilgrimstein that can transport you from the level of the river to the Old Town.

GETTING HERE AND AROUND

Two hours from Fulda by train, the cheapest way to get here is by taking a regional train to the town of Giessen and changing there; every two hours a regional train runs between Marburg and Kassel. By car, take the B-254 and then B-62 from Fulda.

VISITOR INFORMATION

Contacts Marburg Tourismus. ⊠ *Biegenstr. 15* ☏ *06421/99120* ⊕ *www.marburg-tourismus.de.*

EXPLORING

Elisabethkirche (*St. Elizabeth Church*). Marburg's most important building is the Elisabethkirche, which marks the burial site of St. Elizabeth (1207–31), the town's favorite daughter. She was a Hungarian princess, betrothed at age 4 and married at 14 to a member of the nobility, Ludwig IV of Thuringia. In 1228, when her husband died in the Sixth Crusade, she gave up all worldly pursuits. She moved to Marburg, founded a hospital, gave her wealth to the poor, and spent the rest of her very short life (she died at the age of 24) in poverty, caring for the sick and the aged. She is largely responsible for what Marburg became. Because of her selflessness she was made a saint four years after her death. The Teutonic Knights built the Elisabethkirche, which quickly became a pilgrimage site, enabling the city to prosper. You can visit the shrine in the sacristy that once contained her bones, a masterpiece of the goldsmith's art. The church is a veritable museum of religious art, full of statues and frescoes. Walking tours of Marburg begin at the church on Saturday at 3, year-round. Tours inside the church are held Monday to Friday at 3 from April to October, and Sunday shortly after Mass (around 11:15). ⌧ *Elisabethstr. 1* ☎ *06421/65573* ⊕ *www.elisabethkirche.de* ⌧ *€3; tours €4.*

Landgrafenschloss. Sitting at the highest point in the town, this castle was finished in 1500 and survived the war unscathed. It offers panoramic views of Marburg below. ⌧ *Landgrafenschloss* ☎ *06421/282–5871* ⊕ *www.uni-marburg.de/uni-museum.*

Wendelgasse. Fascinating narrow lanes, crooked steps, superbly restored half-timber houses, and venerable old churches abound in the old town of Marburg; the narrow Wendelgasse takes you up 175 stairs through the city, surrounded by old timber-framed houses. ⌧ *Wendelg.* ⌧ *Free.*

WHERE TO EAT

$ ✕ **Cafe Vetter.** This café has the most spectacular view in town—and
CAFÉ Marburg is famous for its panoramas. Both an outdoor terrace and a glassed-in terrace take full advantage of the site. **Known for:** layer cakes; ice cream coffee floats; bread-heavy breakfasts. $ *Average main: €7* ⌧ *Reitg. 4* ☎ *06421/25888* ⊕ *www.cafe-vetter-marburg.de* ▭ *No credit cards* ⊗ *No dinner.*

$$ ✕ **Weinlädele.** This half-timber wine bar's fine selection of German
WINE BAR wines, and light, crispy *Flammkuchen* (a flambéed tart with bacon, onions, and crème fraîche) is a welcome break from traditional German dining. Just up the street from the Old Town's main marketplace, it's a busy spot, popular with patrons of all ages. with a little terrace for a view down the hill. **Known for:** cheese platters; Flammkuchen (Alsatian tart); beef Rouladen. $ *Average main: €15* ⌧ *Schlosstreppe 1* ☎ *06421/14244* ⊕ *weinlädele.de* ▭ *No credit cards.*

WHERE TO STAY

$$ HOTEL **Marburger Hof.** A modern hotel in the center of town, the Marburger Hof has comfortable, updated rooms that still carry some charm. **Pros:** some rooms with cathedral view; recently upgraded rooms are well-kept; good on-site restaurant. **Cons:** a bit sterile due to its size; not all rooms are air-conditioned; some rooms need updating. [$] *Rooms from: €124* ✉ *Elisabeth Str. 12* ☎ *06421/590–750* 🌐 *www.marburgerhof.de* 🛏 *102 rooms* 🍴 *Free Breakfast.*

KASSEL

100 km (62 miles) northeast of Marburg.

The Brothers Grimm lived in Kassel, their mother's hometown, as teenagers, and also worked there as librarians at the court of the king of Westphalia, Jerome Bonaparte (Napoléon's youngest brother), and for the elector of Kassel. In researching their stories and legends, their best source was not books but storyteller Dorothea Viehmann, who was born in the Knallhütte tavern, which is still in business in nearby Baunatal.

Much of Kassel was destroyed in World War II, and the city was rebuilt with little regard for its architectural past. The city's museums and the beautiful Schloss Wilhelmshöhe and Schlosspark, however, are well worth a day or two of exploration.

FESTIVALS

documenta. Every five years, a 100-day contemporary and modern art show takes over the city of Kassel. Begun in 1955, the next exhibit will take place in 2022. ✉ *Friedrichspl. 18* ☎ *0561/707–270* 🌐 *www.documenta.de.*

GETTING HERE AND AROUND

On a main InterCity Express line between Munich and Hamburg, you can also travel to Kassel-Wilhelmshöhe from Hannover and Bremen by high-speed train. By car, travel northeast from Marburg on the B-3 to Borken, then take autobahn A-49 into Kassel.

TOURS

Guided bus tours of Kassel set off from the Stadttheater on Saturday at 11.

VISITOR INFORMATION

Contacts Kassel Marketing GmbH. ✉ *Wilhelmsstr. 23* ☎ *0561/707–707* 🌐 *www.kassel-marketing.de.*

EXPLORING

GRIMMWELT (*Grimm's World*). Opened in 2015, this museum and exhibition space brings the world of the Grimm brothers to life with a combination of artifacts from their time in Kassel and interactive exhibitions devoted to furthering awareness of their important role in the development of the German language. Temporary exhibits include video art installations focusing on language or take a playful view of the brothers' fairy tales. ✉ *Weinbergstr. 21* ☎ *0561/598–6190* ⊕ *www. grimmwelt.de* 💶 *From €8* ⊙ *Closed Mon.*

Fodor'sChoice
★ **Schloss und Bergpark Wilhelmshöhe** (*Wilhelmshöhe Palace and Palace Park*). The magnificent grounds of the 18th-century Schloss and the Bergpark Wilhelmshöhe, at the western edge of Kassel, are said to be Europe's largest hill park. If you have time, plan to spend an entire day at this UNESCO World Heritage site, exploring its wonderful gardens, water features, museums, and castle. Wear good walking shoes and bring some water if you want to hike all the way up to the giant statue of Hercules that crowns the hilltop.

The Wilhelmshöher Park was laid out as a baroque park in the early 18th century, its elegant lawns separating the city from the thick woods of the Habichtswald (Hawk Forest). Schloss Wilhelmshöhe was added between 1786 and 1798. The great palace stands at the end of the 5-km-long (3-mile-long) Wilhelmshöher Allée, an avenue that runs straight as an arrow from one side of the city to the other.

Kassel's leading art gallery and the state art collection lie within Schloss Wilhelmshöhe as part of the **Museumslandschaft Hessen Kassel**. Its collection includes 11 Rembrandts, as well as outstanding works by Rubens, Hals, Jordaens, Van Dyck, Dürer, Altdorfer, Cranach, and Baldung Grien.

The giant 18th-century statue of Hercules that crowns the Wilhelmshöhe heights is an astonishing sight. You can climb the stairs of the statue's castlelike base—and the statue itself—for a rewarding look over the entire city. At 2:30 pm on Sunday and Wednesday from May through September, water gushes from a fountain beneath the statue, rushes down a series of cascades to the foot of the hill, and ends its precipitous journey in a 175-foot-high jet of water. A café lies a short walk from the statue. ✉ *Schloss Wilhelmshöhe, Schlosspark 1* ☎ *0561/316–800* ⊕ *www.museum-kassel.de* 💶 *Park free; Hercules and Octagon €3.*

Löwenburg (*Lion Fortress*). Amid the thick trees of the Wilhelmshöher Park, it comes as something of a surprise to see the turrets of a medieval castle breaking the harmony. There are more surprises at the Löwenburg, for this is not a true medieval castle but a fanciful, stylized copy of a Scottish castle, built in 1793 (70 years after the Hercules statue that towers above it). The Löwenburg contains a collection of medieval armor and weapons, tapestries, and furniture. ✉ *Schlosspark 9* ☎ *0561/3168–0244* ⊕ *www.museum-kassel.de* 💶 *€2 (includes tour)* ⊙ *Closed Mon. Closed Mon.–Thurs. mid-Nov.–Feb.*

WHERE TO EAT

$ ✕ **Brauhaus Knallhütte.** This brewery and inn, established in 1752, was
GERMAN the home of the village storyteller Dorothea Viehmann, who supplied the Grimms with some of their best stories, including "Little Red Riding Hood," "Hansel and Gretel," and "Rumpelstiltskin." It's a tradition carried on to this day as "Dorothea" tells her stories here (in German only) every first and third Saturday of the month at 5:30. If you're planning on visiting on the weekend, it's best to book ahead or call to

Climb to the top of the Schloss und Bergpark Wilhelmshöhe, where a giant statue of Hercules and a fantastic view of Kassel await.

arrange a tour of the brewery and then eat and drink as much as you want for a set price. **Known for:** Bauerbraten (pork chops with dumplings); Thursday grilled meat special; assorted schnitzels. $\boxed{\$}$ *Average main: €14* ⊠ *Rengershausen, Knallhütte. 1, Baunatal* ☎ *0561/492–076* ⊕ *www.knallhuette.de.*

WHERE TO STAY

$$ 🖼 **Hotel Gude.** It may be 10 minutes by tram away from the city center, but this modern, friendly hotel and its comfortable, spacious rooms with modern furnishings and excellent restaurant ($$$) justify the journey. **Pros:** close to the autobahn; easy parking; comfortable beds. **Cons:** removed from the city center; on a busy street; prices notably higher in documenta years. $\boxed{\$}$ *Rooms from: €119* ⊠ *Frankfurter Str. 299* ☎ *0561/48050* ⊕ *www.hotel-gude.de* ⟿ *85 rooms* ⫿⊘⫿ *Free Breakfast.*

HOTEL
Fodor's Choice
★

$$ 🖼 **Schlosshotel Wilhelmshöhe.** Positioned beside the lovely baroque gardens and woodland paths of the hilltop Wilhelmshöhe park, this comfortable, modern hotel and its rooms take in views on the park grounds on one side and stunning vistas over Kassel on the other. **Pros:** tranquil atmosphere; historic setting; park views are stunning. **Cons:** not all rooms renovated to meet modern aesthetic standards; modern hotel (not itself a castle); far from city center. $\boxed{\$}$ *Rooms from: €129* ⊠ *Am Schlosspark 8* ☎ *0561/30880* ⊕ *www.schlosshotel-kassel.de* ⟿ *130 rooms* ⫿⊘⫿ *Free Breakfast.*

HOTEL

BAD KARLSHAFEN

50 km (31 miles) north of Kassel.

Popular with holidaymakers in mobile homes and trailers, who park up on the banks of the Weser directly across from its historic center, Bad Karlshafen's a pretty little spa town with baroque architecture that is best viewed from the campsite side of the river, as the town is surrounded by hills covered in dense forest. Its elevation and rural location provide fresh air, and there are salt springs that the locals believe can cure just about whatever ails you.

GETTING HERE AND AROUND

Regional trains run here from Göttingen, but only infrequently, so check train timetables well ahead of any visit.

VISITOR INFORMATION

Contacts **Bad Karlshafen Kur- und Touristik-Information.** ⊠ *Weserstr. 19* ☎ *05672/922–6140* ⊕ *www.bad-karlshafen-tourismus.de.*

EXPLORING

Fodor's Choice ★ **Fürstenberg Porcelain factory.** Germany's second-oldest porcelain factory is at Fürstenberg, 24 km (14 miles) north of Bad Karlshafen and 8 km (5 miles) south of Höxter, in a Weser Renaissance castle high above the Weser River. The crowned Gothic letter *F*, which serves as its trademark, is known worldwide. You'll find Fürstenberg porcelain in Bad Karlshafen and Höxter, but it's more fun to journey to the 18th-century castle itself, where production first began in 1747, and buy directly from the manufacturer. Fürstenberg and most dealers will take care of shipping arrangements and any tax refunds. Porcelain workshops can be booked ahead of time, and there's also a sales outlet, museum, and café. The view from the castle is a pastoral idyll, with the Weser snaking through the immaculately tended fields and woods. You can also spot cyclists on the riverside paths. ⊠ *Schloss Fürstenberg, Meinbrexener Str. 2, Fürstenberg* ☎ *05271/401–161* ⊕ *www.fuerstenberg-porzellan.com* ⊠ *€9* ⊘ *Closed Mon., and Tues.–Thurs. Nov.–Feb.*

Rathaus. Bad Karlshafen's baroque beauty, the town's best example of the stunning architectural style, stands in surprising contrast to the abundance of half-timber houses found along the rest of the Weser. Inside, the building is still used for administrative purposes, so it is not accessible to the public. ⊠ *Hafenpl. 8* ⊕ *www.bad-karlshafen.de.*

FAMILY **Weser Therme.** This huge spa facility sitting on the banks of the Weser River has whirlpools, sauna and steam baths, thermal saltwater pools, and an outdoor pool that is said to be as salty as the Dead Sea. The spa's waters are famed for their therapeutic benefits, and a couple of hours bathing in them often helps relieve aches and stress. Massages are available to further aid the relaxation process. ⊠ *Kurpromenade 1* ☎ *05672/92110* ⊕ *www.wesertherme.de* ⊠ *Pools from €13.*

WHERE TO STAY

$ HOTEL **Hessischer Hof.** Located in the heart of town, this inn started as a tavern and now includes several comfortably furnished bedrooms, plus an apartment for larger families and the numerous cycling groups that visit. **Pros:** centrally located; reasonable rates; friendly staff. **Cons:** no elevator; decor quite dated; attic rooms have slanted ceilings. [$] *Rooms from: €88* ✉ *Carlstr. 13–15* ☎ *05672/1059* 🌐 *www.hess-hof.de* 🛏 *20 rooms* 🍴 *Free Breakfast.*

$ HOTEL **Hotel zum Weserdampfschiff.** From the snug riverside rooms of this popular hotel-tavern, guests can watch passengers step directly off Weser pleasure boats and into the hotel's welcoming beer garden below. **Pros:** river view; low rates; near spa and city center. **Cons:** early check-out (10:30 am); no credit cards accepted; dated furnishings. [$] *Rooms from: €92* ✉ *Weserstr. 25* ☎ *05672/2425* 🌐 *www.zumweserdampfschiff.de* 💳 *No credit cards* 🛏 *14 rooms* 🍴 *Breakfast.*

SABABURG

50 km (31 miles) west of Göttingen, 100 km (62 miles) south of Hannover.

Sababurg's not really a village as such, but it is the location of an enchanting, 700-year-old Renaissance castle, an impressive animal park, and Germany's oldest forest nature reserve, all of which lie within the peaceful, wooded surrounds of the Reinhardswald. The castle, which sits proudly on the crest of a hill in the forest, is also known as Dornröschenschloss, widely believed to be the source of inspiration for the Grimms Brothers' tale of Sleeping Beauty.

GETTING HERE AND AROUND

Removed from the main highway and with no rail connection, Sababurg, Dornröschenschloss, and the nearby Sababurg Tierpark are best visited by car.

EXPLORING

Fodor's Choice ★ **Dornröschenschloss** (*Sleeping Beauty's Castle*). The story goes that after Sleeping Beauty had slumbered for 100 years, the thick thorn hedge surrounding her castle suddenly burst into blossom, thereby enabling a daring prince to find a way in to lay a kiss upon her lips and reawaken her. This handsome castle hotel is said to be the inspiration for the original tale. The stony exterior of Dornröschenschloss continues to be clad in colorful roses, and its walled garden is home to an impressive collection of the flowers. Even if you don't stay the night, a drive here is scenic, as it overlooks the nearby animal park. There are ruins as well as the garden to explore for a small fee, or enjoy a coffee on the pleasant outdoor terrace with views over forest-covered hills to enjoy afterward. Every Sunday afternoon there is a reenactment of the fairy tale in the castle courtyard for hotel guests; nonguests can partake of the performance for a fee. Call ahead to request it in English. ✉ *Sababurg 12* 🌐 *www.sababurg.de* 🎫 *From €4; free for hotel guests.*

FAMILY **Tierpark Sababurg.** The Tierpark Sababurg is one of Europe's oldest wildlife refuges. Bison, red deer, wild horses, and all sorts of waterfowl populate the park. There's also a petting zoo for children. ⊠ *Sababurg 1* ☏ *05671/766–4990* ⊕ *www.tierpark-sababurg.de* ⤳ *€8.*

12

WHERE TO STAY

$$ ⚑ **Dornröschenschloss Sababurg.** The medieval fortress thought to have
HOTEL inspired the tale of Sleeping Beauty was renovated after a fire into a family-run hotel, complete with domed turrets and spiral staircases. **Pros:** sylvan setting with views; romantic; quiet. **Cons:** some dated rooms; not easy to find; quality of rooms is not the same across the board. $ *Rooms from: €165* ⊠ *Sababurg 12, Hofgeismar* ☏ *05671/8080* ⊕ *www.sababurg.de* ⤳ *17 rooms* ☉⦿ *Free Breakfast.*

$$ ⚑ **Hotel Burg Trendelburg.** Ivy-bedecked towers, a shadowy foyer deco-
HOTEL rated with suits of armor and swords, and guest rooms with four-poster
Fodor'sChoice beds and little bathrooms hidden behind cupboard doors endow this
★ establishment with an atmosphere of fairy-tale adventure. **Pros:** great views; authentic castle experience; rooms have furnishings to match the castle atmosphere. **Cons:** some rooms small; in a otherwise uninspiring village; tower not always open to visitors. $ *Rooms from: €155* ⊠ *Steinweg 1, Trendelburg* ☏ *05675/9090* ⊕ *www.burg-hotel-trendelburg. com* ⤳ *24 rooms* ☉⦿ *Free Breakfast.*

HANNOVERSCH-MÜNDEN

24 km (15 miles) north of Kassel, 150 km (93 miles) south of Hannover.

You'll have to travel a long way through Germany to find a grouping of half-timber houses as harmonious as those in this delightful town, seemingly untouched by the modern age—there are some 700 of them. Hannoversch-Münden is surrounded by forests and the Fulda and Werra rivers, which join here and flow northward as the Weser River.

GETTING HERE AND AROUND

Regional trains linking Hannoversch Münden to both Kassel and Göttingen run every hour.

VISITOR INFORMATION

Contacts Hannoversch-Münden. ⊠ *Touristik Naturpark Münden, Lotzestr. 2, Hannoversch Münden* ☏ *05541/75313* ⊕ *www.hann.muenden-tourismus.de.*

EXPLORING

Johann Andreas Eisenbart Glockenspiel. Dr. Johann Andreas Eisenbart (1663–1727) would be forgotten today if a ribald 19th-century drinking song ("Ich bin der Doktor Eisenbart, widda, widda, wit, boom! boom!") hadn't had him shooting out aching teeth with a pistol, anesthetizing with a sledgehammer, and removing boulders from kidneys. He was, as the song has it, a man who could make "the blind walk and the lame see." This is terribly exaggerated, of course, but the town, where he died, takes advantage of it. The good Dr. Eisenbart has "office hours" in the town hall at 1:30 on Saturday from May through

December. Throughout the year, a glockenspiel on the town hall depicts Eisenbart's feats, to the tune of the Eisenbart song three times daily: at noon, 3, and 5. There's a statue of the doctor in front of his home at Langestrasse 79, and his grave is outside the St. Ägidien Church. ✉ *Lotzestr. 2, Hannoversch Münden* ☎ *05541/75313* ⊕ *www.hann. muenden-tourismus.de.*

GÖTTINGEN

30 km (19 miles) northeast of Hannoversch-Münden, 110 km (68 miles) south of Hannover.

Distinguished by its famous university, where the Brothers Grimm served as professors and librarians between 1830 and 1837, the fetching town of Göttingen buzzes with student life. Young people on bikes zip past bookshops and secondhand boutiques; when night falls, the town's cozy bars and cafés swell with students making the most of the drinks specials.

In the streets around the Rathaus you'll find magnificent examples of Renaissance architecture. Many of these half-timber, low-gable buildings house businesses that have been here for centuries. It's also a large and modern place and boasts the shiny stores, chain coffee shops, and other trappings you'd expect of a 21st-century German town. Though not strictly on the Fairy-Tale Road (despite its association with the Grimms), Göttingen is still well worth visiting.

GETTING HERE AND AROUND
Göttingen is a stop on the same InterCity Express line between Munich and Hamburg as Kassel-Wilhelmshöhe, and is also easily reached from Bremen.

VISITOR INFORMATION
Contacts Göttingen Tourist Information. ✉ *Altes Rathaus, Markt 9* ☎ *0551/499–800* ⊕ *www.goettingen-tourismus.de.*

EXPLORING

Altes Rathaus (*Old Town Hall*). The Old Town Hall was begun in the 13th century and houses a completely preserved Gothic heating system in the part-medieval, part-Renaissance building. The tourist information office is on the first floor. ✉ *Markt 9* ☎ *0551/499–800* ⊕ *www. goettingen.de* 🆓 *Free* ⊗ *Closed Sun. Nov.–Mar.*

Gänseliesel. The statue of Gänseliesel, the little Goose Girl of German folklore, stands in Göttingen's central market square, symbolizing the strong link between the students and their university city. The girl, according to the story, was a princess who was forced to trade places with a peasant, and the statue shows her carrying her geese and smiling shyly into the waters of a fountain. The students of Göttingen gave her a ceremonial role: traditionally, graduates who earn a doctorate bestow a kiss of thanks upon Gänseliesel. Göttingen's citizens say she's the most kissed girl in the world. ✉ *Altes Rathaus, Markt 9* ⊕ *denkmale. goettingen.de* 🆓 *Free.*

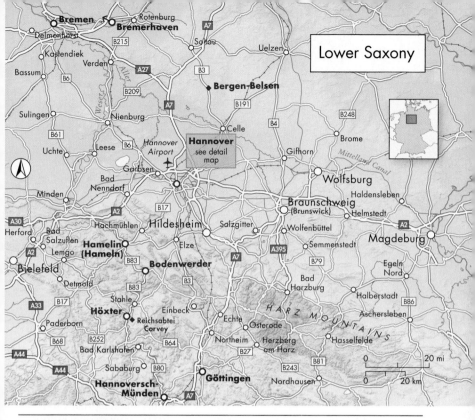

WHERE TO EAT

$$$
MEDITERRANEAN

✕ **Gaudi.** In a town rich with cozy taverns and hearty local food, the appearance of this Mediterranean restaurant, with its terra-cotta-and-blue color scheme, arty chandeliers, and light, airy spaces, stands out as much as its cuisine. Right in the middle of Göttingen's historic Börner Viertel, the restaurant is a favorite with staff from the university and its food and excellent service are worth the extra cost. **Known for:** consommé; Spanish-style shrimp; lasagna with goat's cheese. $ *Average main: €24* ⊠ *Rote Str. 16* ☎ *0551/531–3001* ⊕ *www.restaurant-gaudi. de* ☉ *Closed Sun., and 1st 2 wks of Jan. No lunch Mon.*

$$
GERMAN

✕ **Landgasthaus Lockemann.** If you like to walk and hike, consider heading to the *Stadtwald* (city forest) and then eating a meal at this half-timber lodge where locals go for the friendly service and hearty German cooking. A bit off the beaten path, the trip will take 20 minutes, but you'll be rewarded with wild game and steak options. **Known for:** surf and turf; rack of lamb; beef goulash. $ *Average main: €20* ⊠ *Im Beeke 1* ☎ *0551/209–020* ⊕ *www.landgasthaus-lockemann.de* ▭ *No credit cards* ☉ *Closed Mon. No lunch weekdays.*

The virgin forests of Sababurg, where Sleeping Beauty slumbered for 100 years, are still wild and dense.

WHERE TO STAY

$$$ HOTEL

Romantik Hotel Gebhards. Though within walking distance to the main train station, this family-run hotel stands aloof and serene on its own grounds, a modernized 18th-century building that's something of a local landmark. **Pros:** across from the train station; historic building; charming country-style furnishings. **Cons:** on a busy street; expensive for quality; some rooms need updating. [$] *Rooms from: €180* ✉ *Goethe-Allée 22–23* ☎ *0551/49680* 🌐 *www.gebhardshotel.de* 🛏 *50 rooms* 🍴 *Free Breakfast.*

HÖXTER

24 km (14 miles) north of Bad Karlshafen, 100 km (62 miles) south of Hannover.

Höxter is not actually in Lower Saxony, but just over the border in North Rhine-Westphalia. The town's appeal lies in its proximity to the impressive Reichsabtei Corvey, an abbey that's a short drive away. There's not much Grimm here; Höxter's connection to a fairy tale is limited to a small Hansel and Gretel fountain in the middle of town. Its downtown has charming examples of timber-framed buildings and its Rathaus is a perfect example of the Weser Renaissance style.

GETTING HERE AND AROUND

Every couple of hours buses and regional trains run from Bad Karlshafen to Höxter Rathaus and take about 45 minutes, or you can take a combination of regional trains from Göttingen that take from 90 minutes to 2½ hours.

VISITOR INFORMATION

Contacts Höxter Tourist-Info. ✉ *Weserstr. 11* ☎ *05271/963–431* ⊕ *www. hoexter-tourismus.de.*

EXPLORING

Fodor'sChoice ★ **Reichsabtei Corvey** (*Imperial Abbey of Corvey*). The impressive Reichsabtei Corvey, or Schloss Corvey, is idyllically set between the wooded heights of the Solling region and the Weser River. During its 1,200-year history it has provided lodging for several Holy Roman emperors. Heinrich Hoffmann von Fallersleben (1798–1874), author of the poem "Deutschland, Deutschland über Alles," worked as librarian here in the 1820s. The poem, set to music by Joseph Haydn, became the German national anthem in 1922. A music festival is held in the church and great hall, the Kaisersaal, in May and June of every even-numbered year. Corvey is reached on an unnumbered road heading east from Höxter (3 km [2 miles]) toward the Weser. There are signposts to "Schloss Corvey." ✉ *Schloss Corvey* ☎ *05271/694–010* ⊕ *www.schloss-corvey. de* 🎫 *€10; abbey church from €2* ⊙ *Closed Nov.–mid-Mar.*

BODENWERDER

34 km (21 miles) north of Höxter, 70 km (43 miles) south of Hannover.

The charming Weser town of Bodenwerder is the home of the Lügenbaron (Lying Baron) von Münchhausen (1720–97), who was known as a teller of whoppers and whose fantastical tales included a story about riding a cannonball toward an enemy fortress but then, having second thoughts, returning to where he started by leaping onto a cannonball heading the other way. Stretched out along a peaceful valley, the nicest part of the town is around the baron's old home, now the town hall, its half-timber architecture set against a backdrop of the river and surrounding hills. A regular stop for cyclists on the Wesertal route, the town also attracts canoeists, and anglers who can tell their own whoppers about the one that got away.

GETTING HERE AND AROUND

Reachable from Höxter by a combination of bus and regional train, or by bus from Hameln (Hamelin), changes are required along the way, and any visits requiring public transport should be planned in advance.

VISITOR INFORMATION

Contacts Bodenwerder Tourist-Information. ✉ *Münchausenpl. 1* ☎ *05533/40541* ⊕ *www.muenchhausenland.de.*

EXPLORING

Münchhausen Museum. Housed in an old, renovated farm building right next to the imposing family home in which Baron von Münchhausen grew up (it's now the Rathaus), the Münchhausen Museum is crammed with mementos of his adventurous life, including his cannonball. A fountain in front of the house represents another story. The baron, it seems, was puzzled when his horse kept drinking insatiably at a trough. Investigating, he discovered that the horse had been cut in two by a closing castle gate and that the water ran out as fast as the horse drank. The water in the fountain, of course, flows from the rear half of a horse. ✉ *Münchhausenpl. 1* ☎ *05533/409–147* 🌐 *www.muenchhausenland.de* 🎟 *Museum €3* 🕒 *Closed Nov.–Easter.*

WHERE TO EAT

$$ GERMAN
🍴 **Burg Ottenstein.** An isolated castle just a few miles up the road from Bodenwerder in the hamlet of Ottenstein has a small dining room done up with knights' armor and other medieval gear. It's got charming character and an extensive menu of meaty dishes with sides. **Known for:** Rittermahl (their meaty take on what knights may have once eaten); steak and potatoes; chicken breasts. [$] *Average main: €20* ✉ *Amtstr. 2* ☎ *05286/945–330* 🕒 *Closed Wed.* 💳 *No credit cards.*

WHERE TO STAY

$$$ HOTEL Fodor's Choice ★
🏨 **Schlosshotel Münchhausen.** This 17th-century castle was converted into a top-class luxury hotel in a manner that retains much of the original charm and decoration without sacrificing modern amenities, including a spa and swimming area. **Pros:** accommodations in a real castle; gorgeous park surroundings; pool. **Cons:** several rooms are in the Zehntscheune (former barn) out back; not all rooms have air-conditioning; can be booked out when dignitaries are present. [$] *Rooms from: €200* ✉ *Schwöbber 9* ☎ *05154/70600* 🌐 *www.schlosshotel-muenchhausen.com* 🛏 *68 rooms* 🍽 *Free Breakfast.*

HAMELIN (HAMELN)

24 km (15 miles) north of Bodenwerder, 47 km (29 miles) southwest of Hannover.

Given their relationship with one of the most famous fairy-tale characters of all time, it's unsurprising that Hameln's townsfolk continue to take advantage of the Pied Piper. Known locally as the *Rattenfänger*, or "rat-catcher," these days he tends to be celebrated more than exploited (even if his name does adorn everything from coffee mugs to restaurants), and regular costumed tours through the town re-create his deeds, while a bronze statue of him stands proudly in the town's lovely pedestrian zone. Not as exciting as Hannover to the north or as relaxing as Bodenwerder to the south, Hameln is still one of the top places to visit along the Fairy-Tale Road thanks to its fairy-tale legacy, elegantly painted and inscribed half-timber buildings, and laid-back atmosphere.

GETTING HERE AND AROUND

At 45 minutes away from Hannover by S-bahn (Line No. 5), Hamelin is within easy reach of the Lower Saxon capital.

VISITOR INFORMATION

Contacts Hameln Marketing und Tourismus. ✉ *Deisterallee 1, Hamelin* ☎ *05151/957–823* 🌐 *www.hameln.de.*

EXPLORING

Hochzeitshaus (*Wedding House*). On central Osterstrasse you'll see several examples of Weser Renaissance architecture, including the Rattenfängerhaus (Rat-Catcher's House) and the Hochzeitshaus, a beautiful 17th-century sandstone building now used for city offices. From mid-May to mid-September the Hochzeitshaus terrace is the scene of two free open-air events commemorating the Pied Piper legend. From May to September, local actors and children present a half-hour reenactment each Sunday at noon, and there is also a 40-minute musical, *Rats*, each Wednesday at 4:30 during the same months. The carillon of the Hochzeitshaus plays tunes every day at 9:35 and 11:35, and mechanical figures enact the piper story on the west gable of the building at 1:05, 3:35, and 5:35. ⊠ *Osterstr. 2, Hamelin.*

FAMILY **Museum Hameln.** The story of the city of Hamelin comes to life in this museum, which contains the **Rattenfänger Theater,** a unique mechanical theater that shows the Pied Piper in action with a sound-and-light show that lasts 12 minutes and occurs hourly from 11:30 to 5:15 each day. ⊠ *Osterstr. 8–9, Hamelin* ☎ *05151/202–1215* ⊕ *www.museum-hameln. de* ⊠€5 ⊗ *Closed Mon.*

WHERE TO EAT

$ ✕ **Rattenfängerhaus.** This brilliant example of Weser Renaissance archi-
GERMAN tecture is Hamelin's most famous building, where the Pied Piper supposedly stayed during his rat-extermination assignment (it wasn't actually built until centuries after his supposed exploits). "Rats" are all over the menu, from the "rat-killer liqueur" to a "rat-tail flambé," but don't be put off by the names: the traditional dishes are excellent. **Known for:** "rat's tails" (breaded pork chops); seasonal asparagus with Hollandaise; fresh North Sea fish. $ *Average main: €13* ⊠ *Osterstr. 28, Hamelin* ☎ *05151/3888* ⊕ *www.rattenfaengerhaus.de.*

WHERE TO STAY

$$ 🛏 **Hotel zur Krone.** On the Old Town's pedestrian zone, Hotel zur Krone
HOTEL has a terrace that lets you watch locals coming and going, and afternoon coffee here is a summer delight. **Pros:** a half-timber marvel; lovely terrace; nice location. **Cons:** modern annex lacks charm; some guest rooms a little small; furnishings simple, outdated. $ *Rooms from: €102* ⊠ *Osterstr. 30, Hamelin* ☎ *05151/9070* ⊕ *www.hotelzurkrone.de* 🛏 *32 rooms* ❑ *Free Breakfast.*

HANNOVER

47 km (29 miles) northeast of Hameln.

A little off the Fairy-Tale Road—and better known internationally as a trade-fair center than a tourist destination—the Lower Saxon capital holds an attractive mix of culture, arts, and nature. With several leading museums, an opera house of international repute, and the finest baroque park in the country, it's a place that packs a surprising amount into a city of only half a million people. Conveniently centered between the city's main train station and its pleasant inner city lake, most of Hannover's major attractions, including its fine New and Old Town Halls, are within an easy walk of one another. In spring and summer the city's parks fill with picnicking families, while fall and winter are celebrated first with the second-biggest Oktoberfest in the world and then cheery Christmas markets.

GETTING HERE AND AROUND

Travel northeast from Hameln on autobahn A-33 to Hannover in under an hour. There is also frequent direct rail service from Hameln and InterCity Express (ICE) trains run to and from larger cities nearby. Hannover has an airport and is served by Eurolines buses.

VISITOR INFORMATION

Contacts Hannover Tourismus. ⊠ *Ernst-August-Pl. 8* ☎ *0511/1684–9700* ⊕ *www.visit-hannover.com.*

EXPLORING

Altes Rathaus (*Old Town Hall*). It took nearly 100 years, starting in 1410, to build this gabled brick edifice that once contained a merchants' hall and an apothecary. In 1844 it was restored to the style of about 1500, with its exceptional Gothic gables and the ornamental frieze. The facade's fired-clay frieze depicts coats of arms and representations of princes, and a medieval game similar to arm wrestling using only the fingers. This marvelous picture above the outer right arched window in the Schmiedestrasse can only be seen by following the "red line" around the Old Town Hall. Inside is a modern interior with boutiques and a restaurant. ⊠ *Karmarschstr. 42* 🔁 *Free.*

Fodor's Choice ★ **Herrenhausen Palace and Gardens.** The gardens of the former Hannoverian royal summer residence are the city's showpiece, unmatched in Germany for its formal precision, with patterned walks, gardens, hedges, and chestnut trees framed by a placid moat. There is a fig garden with a collapsible shelter to protect it in winter and dining facilities behind a grotto. The mausoleum in the Berggarten houses the remains of local royalty, including those of King George I of Britain. From Easter until October there are fireworks displays and fountains play for a few hours daily (weekdays 10–noon and 3–5, weekends 10–noon and 2–5). The 17th-century palace on the grounds was completely destroyed in 1943, leaving only the fountains and stairs remaining. In 2013, a relatively faithful reconstruction replaced the castle, which now houses a museum dedicated to its history and is used frequently as an event location. Herrenhausen is outside the city, a short ride on Tram Line 4 or 5. ⊠ *Herrenhauserstr. 5* ☎ *0511/1684–4543* ⊕ *www.hannover.de/herrenhausen* 🔁 *Museum and gardens €8 Apr.–Oct., €6 Nov.–Mar.* ☉ *Closed Mon. Nov.–Mar.*

Landesmuseum Hannover. The priceless art collection of this regional museum includes works by Tilman Riemenschneider, Veit Stoss, Hans Holbein the Younger, Claude Monet, and Lucas Cranach. There are also historical and natural history sections. ⊠ *Willy-Brandt-Allée 5*

DID YOU KNOW?

The story of the Pied Piper of Hamelin (Rattenfänger von Hameln), who led the rats out of town and then, when the townspeople refused to pay him, also led their children away, may refer to historical events. Theories abound that Hameln's children were lost to the plague or a children's crusade.

☏ *0511/980–7686* ⊕ *www.landesmuseum-hannover.niedersachsen.de*
🎫 *€5 for permanent exhibition only* 𝄐 *Closed Mon.*

Leineschloss. The former royal palace of the Hanovers—whose members sat on the British throne from 1714 to 1837 as Kings George I–IV—stands grandly beside the River Leine, and is now home to the Lower Saxony State Parliament. Although the interior of the palace is largely closed to the public, its imposing Corinthian columns and river setting provide some excellent photo ops. ✉ *Hinrich-Wilhelm-Kopf-Pl. 1.*

Neues Rathaus (*New Town Hall*). The massive New Town Hall was built at the start of the 20th century in Wilhelmine style (named for Kaiser Wilhelm). The pomp and circumstance were important ingredients of the German bureaucracy of the time. Four scale models on the ground floor depict Hannover in various stages of development and destruction: as a medieval walled city, in the years before World War II, immediately following World War II, and in its present-day form. An elevator rises diagonally to the dome for a splendid view. Tours are held in German every third Sunday at 11. ✉ *Trammpl. 2* ☏ *0511/1684–5333* 🎫 *Tour €6; dome €4* 𝄐 *Dome closed mid-Nov.–Mar.*

Opernhaus (*Staatsoper Hannover*). Hannover's neoclassical opera house, completed in 1852, has two large wings and a covered, colonnaded portico adorned with statues of great composers and poets. The building originally served as the court theater, but now is used almost exclusively for opera. It was gutted by fire in a 1943 air raid and restored in 1948. Unless you have tickets to a performance, the only part of the interior you can visit is the foyer (official tours are held on a near-monthly basis). ✉ *Opernpl. 1* ☏ *0511/9999–1111* ⊕ *www.staatstheater-hannover.de/oper.*

Sprengel Museum. An important museum of modern art, the Sprengel holds major works by Max Beckmann, Max Ernst, Paul Klee, Emil Nolde, Oscar Schlemmer, Hans Arp, and Pablo Picasso. A recent addition to the museum known as *Ten Rooms, Three Loggias and a Hall,* added space to feature contemporary artists reflecting on space, light, and perception. The street where it's located is named after Kurt Schwitters, a native son and prominent Dadaist, whose works are also exhibited. ✉ *Kurt-Schwitters-Pl. 1* ☏ *0511/1684–3875* ⊕ *www.sprengel-museum.de* 🎫 *€7* 𝄐 *Closed Mon.*

Fodor's Choice
★ **Wilhelm Busch Museum.** This section of the Georgenpalais, near Herrenhausen, is devoted to the works of cartoonists and caricaturists with an emphasis on Wilhelm Busch, the "godfather of the comic strip," whose original drawings and effects are on display. More than a century ago, Busch (1832–1908) wrote and illustrated a popular children's book, *Max und Moritz,* which tells the story of two boys who mixed gunpowder into the village tailor's pipe tobacco and, with fishing lines down the chimney, filched roasting chickens off the fire. The first American comic strip, *The Katzenjammer Kids* (1897), drew not only on Busch's naughty boys (they even spoke with a German accent) but also on his loose cartoon style. ✉ *Georgengarten 1* ☏ *0511/1699–9916* ⊕ *www. karikatur-museum.de* 🎫 *€6* 𝄐 *Closed Mon.*

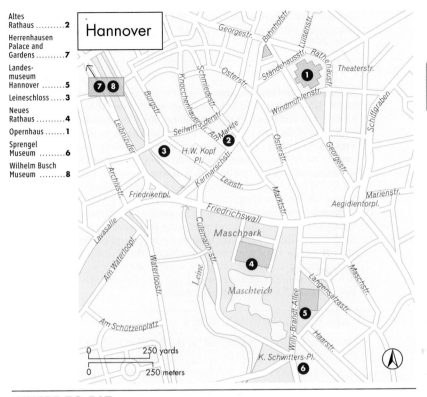

Altes
Rathaus **2**

Herrenhausen
Palace and
Gardens **7**

Landes-
museum
Hannover **5**

Leineschloss **3**

Neues
Rathaus **4**

Opernhaus **1**

Sprengel
Museum **6**

Wilhelm Busch
Museum **8**

WHERE TO EAT

$$$ ✕ **Basil.** Constructed in 1867 as a riding hall for the Royal Prus-
ECLECTIC   sian military, this upmarket restaurant's home is as striking as the
menu, which is Mediterranean-inspired. Cast-iron pillars support the
vaulted brick ceiling, and two-story drapes hang in the huge win-
dows. **Known for:** three-course meals featuring asparagus in season;
veal and wild game; seafood, including mussels. $ *Average main:
€22* ✉ *Dragonerstr. 30* ☎ *0511/622–636* ⊕ *www.basil.de* ☾ *Closed
Sun. No lunch.*

$ ✕ **Brauhaus Ernst August.** This brewery has so much artificial greenery
GERMAN   that you could imagine yourself in a beer garden, but with live music
and DJs on the weekends, it's got more of a club atmosphere. Han-
noverian pilsner is brewed on the premises, and regional specialties
are the menu's focus. **Known for:** pub fare like schnitzel with fries;
hearty egg-heavy breakfasts; traditional German dishes like Rouladen.
$ *Average main: €13* ✉ *Schmiedstr. 13* ☎ *0511/365–950* ⊕ *www.
brauhaus.net.*

$$ ✕ **Broyhan Haus.** The claim of "Hannoverian hospitality over three
GERMAN   floors" written on the exterior of this half-timber tavern in the middle
of town isn't made frivolously. Convivial waitstaff ferry plates to tables
outside on the pedestrian zone in summer, or pull up a seat on the

ground floor, where there's a well-stocked bar. **Known for:** pork and sauerkraut; rump steak; herring fillets. [$] *Average main: €16* ✉ *Kramerstr. 24* ☎ *0511/323–919* 🌐 *www.broyhanhaus.de* 💳 *No credit cards.*

WHERE TO STAY

$$ HOTEL 🏨 **Concorde Hotel am Leineschloss.** Near the elegant Altes Rathaus and the stately Leineschloss, and only a leisurely stroll from the Neues Rathaus, Opernhaus, and the city's main museums, this simple, modern hotel has easily one of the best locations in the city and has a lot of single rooms. **Pros:** in the middle of the shopping district; close to the U-bahn (U3, 7, and 9); every double room has a bath. **Cons:** no restaurant; dated furnishings; public areas can be loud. [$] *Rooms from: €136* ✉ *Am Markte 12* ☎ *0511/357–910* 🌐 *www.concordehotel-am-leineschloss.de* 🛏 *81 rooms* 🍴 *Free Breakfast.*

$$ HOTEL Fodor's Choice ★ 🏨 **Kastens Hotel Luisenhof.** Antiques are everywhere in this elegant hotel, which is traditional both in appearance and service; tapestries adorn the lobby walls, oil paintings hang in the foyer, and copper engravings enliven the bar. **Pros:** near the train station; helpful staff; elegant. **Cons:** expensive; on a narrow, ordinary street; rooms are small for price. [$] *Rooms from: €169* ✉ *Luisenstr. 1–3* ☎ *0511/30440* 🌐 *www.kastens-luisenhof.de* 🛏 *149 rooms* 🍴 *No meals.*

NIGHTLIFE AND PERFORMING ARTS

Hannover's nightlife is centered on the Bahnhof and the Steintor red-light district.

FAMILY **Opera.** Hannover's opera company is internationally known, with productions staged in one of Germany's finest 19th-century classical opera houses. Completed in 1852, the neoclassical opera house has two large wings and a covered, colonnaded portico adorned with statues of great composers and poets. The building originally served as the court theater, but now is used almost exclusively for opera and you can only view its interior beauty with tickets to a performance. It was gutted by fire in a 1943 air raid and restored in 1948. ✉ *Opernpl. 1* ☎ *0511/9999–1111* 🌐 *www.staatstheater-hannover.de/oper.*

BERGEN-BELSEN

58 km (36 miles) northeast of Hannover.

A visit to the site of the infamous prisoner-of-war and concentration camp where Anne Frank, along with tens of thousands of others, perished isn't an easy undertaking. All that remains are foundations and burial mounds, but the interpretive center helps to contextualize what you'll see.

GETTING HERE AND AROUND

Although it's possible to get here via public transport, it requires traveling first to the town of Celle by train, and then taking an hour-long bus journey. Buses run every two hours and require multiple changes. By car, take autobahn exits Mellendorf or Solltau Süd and follow the signposts to the memorial.

EXPLORING

Gedenkstätte Bergen-Belsen (*Bergen-Belsen Memorial*). The site of the infamous POW and concentration camp is now a memorial to the victims of World War II and the Holocaust. Anne Frank was among the more than 70,000 Jews, prisoners of war, homosexuals, Roma, and others who died here.

12

A place of immense suffering, the camp was burned to the ground by British soldiers, who liberated it in April 1945, arriving to find thousands of unburied corpses and typhus, typhoid, tuberculosis, and other diseases spreading rapidly among the survivors. Today, all that physically remains of the camp, which is inside a nature preserve, are the foundations of some of its prisoner barracks and a number of burial mounds overgrown with heather and grass and bearing stark inscriptions such as "Here lie 1,000 dead."

The history of the camp and its victims is explained further through a series of moving video, audio, photo, and text exhibits within the slender, minimalist structure of the 200-meter-long (656-foot-long), 18-meter-wide (59-foot-long) Documentation Center. Built almost entirely of plain concrete panels, the center is softly lit and peaceful inside, its floor sloping gently upward from the entrance and beyond the exhibits to windows that let in light and views of the trees outside.

Visitors to the Memorial should plan to stay at least two or three hours. Ninety-minute tours of the site in German and English leave the Documentation Center information desk at 11:30 and 2:30 on weekends from March to September. Don't try to see everything when visiting the memorial, but do take some time to walk around outside, visiting the site of the barracks to gain a better understanding of the atrocious living conditions inmates of the camp were forced to suffer.

Bear in mind that the memorial is not recommended for children under the age of 14. Older children should be in the company of an adult. ✉ *Anne-Frank-Pl., Lohheide* ☎ *05051/47590* ⊕ *www.bergenbelsen.de* 🎫 *Free; tour €3.*

BREMEN

110 km (68 miles) northwest of Hannover.

Germany's smallest city-state, Bremen, is also Germany's oldest and second-largest port (only Hamburg is larger). Together with Hamburg and Lübeck, Bremen was an early member of the merchant-run Hanseatic League, and its rivalry with the larger port on the Elbe River is still tangible. Though Hamburg may still claim its title as Germany's "gateway to the world," Bremen likes to boast, "But we have the key." Bremen's symbol is, in fact, a golden key, which you will see displayed on flags and signs throughout the city.

DID YOU KNOW?

Schnoorviertel is Bremen's oldest quarter, dating from the 15th and 16th centuries. Today, it is filled with crafts-people's studios, boutiques, cafés, and souvenir shops.

12

GETTING HERE AND AROUND

Bremen's international airport is a gate to many European destinations, and InterCity (IC) and InterCity Express (ICE) trains connect the city with much of the rest of Germany, including Hamburg and Hannover in just one hour.

VISITOR INFORMATION

Contacts Bremen Tourist Information. ⊠ *Böttcherstr. 4* ☎ *0421/308–0010* ⊕ *www.bremen-tourism.de.*

EXPLORING

Marktplatz. Bremen's impressive market square sits in the charming Altstadt. It's bordered by the St. Petri Dom, an imposing 900-year-old Gothic cathedral; an ancient Rathaus; a 16th-century guildhall; and a modern glass-and-steel state parliament building, with gabled town houses finishing the panorama. Alongside the northwest corner of the Rathaus is the famous bronze statue of the four **Bremen Town Musicians,** one atop the other in a sort of pyramid. Their feats are reenacted in a free, open-air play at the Neptune Fountain near the cathedral, at noon each Sunday, from May to September. Another well-known figure on the square is the stone statue of **Roland,** a knight in service to Charlemagne, erected in 1404. Three times larger than life, the statue serves as Bremen's good-luck piece and a symbol of freedom and independence. It is said that as long as Roland stands, Bremen will remain a free and independent state. ⊠ *Marktpl.*

Museen Böttcherstrasse (*Museums on Barrel Makers' Street*). Don't leave Bremen's Altstadt without strolling down this street that was once lined by coopers (barrel makers). Between 1924 and 1931 the houses were torn down and reconstructed in a style at once historically sensitive and modern by the Bremen coffee millionaire Ludwig Roselius. (He was the inventor of decaffeinated coffee and held the patent for decades.) Many of the restored houses are used as galleries for local artists. At one end are two separate museums housed in the 17th-century **Ludwig Roselius-Haus,** one which showcases late-medieval art and a silver treasury, and a unique collection of German and Dutch art; these pieces contrast with the paintings of **Paula Modersohn-Becker,** a noted early expressionist of the Worpswede art colony whose work is housed in the same building. Notice also the arch of Meissen bells at the rooftop. Except when freezing weather makes them dangerously brittle, the bells chime daily on the hour from noon to 6 from May to December (only at noon, 3, and 6 from January to April) ⊠ *Böttcherstr. 6* ☎ *0421/336–5077* ⊕ *www. pmbm.de* 🎫*€8* 🕙 *Closed Mon.*

Rathaus. A 15th-century statue of Charlemagne, together with seven princes, adorns the Gothic town hall, the only European town hall built in the late Middle Ages that has not been destroyed or altered, managing to survive in its original form over the centuries. It was Charlemagne who established a diocese here in the 9th century. The Rathaus acquired a Weser Renaissance facade during the early 17th century. Tours, given when no official functions are taking place, are in German and English and take you into the upper hall as well as the Golden Chamber, a magnificent plenary hall. Inside, the model ships that hang from the ceiling bear witness to the importance of commerce and maritime trade for the city. Their miniature cannons can even be fired if the occasion demands. ⊠ *Am Markt 21* 🎫 *Tour €7.*

Fodor'sChoice   **Schnoorviertel.** Stroll through the narrow streets of this idyllic district,
★   a jumble of houses, taverns, and shops. This is Bremen's oldest district, dating back to the 15th and 16th centuries. The neighborhood is fashionable among artists and craftspeople, who have restored the tiny cottages to serve as galleries and workshops. Other buildings have been converted into popular antiques shops, cafés, and pubs. The area's definitely a great source for souvenirs, with incredibly specialized stores selling porcelain dolls, teddy bears, African jewelry, and smoking pipes, among many other things. There's even a year-round Christmas store. ⊠ *Bremen.*

St. Petri Dom (*St. Peter's Cathedral*). Construction of the cathedral began in the mid-11th century. Its two prominent towers, one of which can be climbed, are Gothic, but in the late 1800s the cathedral was restored in the Romanesque style. It served as the seat of an archbishop until the Reformation turned the cathedral Protestant. It has a small museum and five functioning organs. ⊠ *Sandstr. 10–12* 🎫 *0421/365–0447* 🎫 *Free; tower €1.*

WHERE TO EAT

$$$$ ✕ **Grashoffs Bistro.** An enthusiastic crowd, willing to put up with the
FRENCH   extremely cramped conditions, descends on this small restaurant
Fodor'sChoice   and deli. The menu has a French touch, with an emphasis on fresh
★   fish from the Bremerhaven market while the deli has a whole wall of teas, another of cheeses, and a huge assortment of wines. **Known for:** liver and onions; seafood pasta; vitello tonnato. $ *Average main: €27* ⊠ *Contrescarpe 80* 🎫 *0421/147–49* ⊕ *www.grashoff.de* ⊙ *Closed Sun. and Mon. No dinner Sat.*

$$ ✕ **Ratskeller.** This cavernous cellar with vaulted ceilings is said to be
GERMAN   Germany's oldest and most renowned town-hall restaurant—it's been here for 600 years. Its walls are lined with wine casks, and there are small alcoves with sliding wooden doors, once shut tight by merchants as they closed their deals. **Known for:** extensive fresh seafood options; Seemannslabskaus (corned beef hash with beets); open-face sandwiches. $ *Average main: €15* ⊠ *Am Markt 1* 🎫 *0421/321–676* ⊕ *www.ratskeller-bremen.de.*

WHERE TO STAY

$$ 🏨 **Dorint Park Hotel Bremen.** This palatial hotel comes with an enviable
HOTEL   location between a small lake and an extensive area of park and forest
Fodor'sChoice   not far from the main train station. **Pros:** traditional luxury; on a lake;
★   inviting public areas. **Cons:** expensive; outside the city; some furnishings a bit worn. $ *Rooms from: €150* ⊠ *Im Bürgerpark* 🎫 *0421/340–800* ⊕ *www.parkhotel-bremen.de* ⇥ *175 rooms* ◯I No meals.

12

$ HOTEL **Hotel Classico.** A small hotel in the heart of the city, this well-loved lodging just a few steps off the main square has small, uniquely themed rooms, including those dedicated to Alexander the Great, Napoléon, and other heroes that add to its charm. **Pros:** convenient location on market square; historic building; air-conditioning. **Cons:** no two rooms alike, and some are on the smaller side; showers only; reception only open 8–8 (must call ahead for late arrival). [$] *Rooms from: €99* ✉ *Hinter dem Schuetting 1A* ☎ *0421/244–00867* 🌐 *www.hotel-classico-bremen.de* 🛏 *12 rooms* 🍴 *No meals.*

BREMERHAVEN

66 km (41 miles) north of Bremen.

This busy port city, where the Weser empties into the North Sea, is technically part of Bremen, which is an hour to the south. You can take in the enormity of the port from a promenade that runs its length. In addition to being a major port for merchant ships, it is the biggest fishery pier in Europe, and its promenade is lined with excellent seafood restaurants.

GETTING HERE AND AROUND

Regional trains run every hour from Bremen to this North Sea port, and take 35 minutes to get here. Reederei Hafenrundfahrt offers a one-hour trip around the Bremerhaven harbor for €11 (March to November only). If you'd like to go farther afield and view Schnoorviertel, there's a down-river tour; to see the stark, red-cliff island of Helgoland, "My Fair Lady" has a daily round-trip ferry for €39.90 per person or take an OFD charter flight for €220.

Contacts HafenRundFahrt. ✉ *Hermann-Henrich-Meier-Str. 4* ☎ *0471/415–850* 🌐 *www.hafenrundfahrt-bremerhaven.de.* **OFD Airlines.** ✉ *Flughafen, Am Luneort 15* ☎ *0471/89920* 🌐 *www.fliegofd.de.*

VISITOR INFORMATION

Contacts Bremerhaven Tourism. ✉ *Hermann-Henrich-Meier-Str. 6* ☎ *0471/8093–6100* 🌐 *www.bremerhaven-touristik.de.*

EXPLORING

Fodor's Choice ★ **Deutsches Auswandererhaus** (*German Emigration Center*). Located at the point where 7 million Europeans set sail for the New World, the Deutsches Auswandererhaus is made to order for history buffs and those wanting to trace their German ancestry. "Passengers" get boarding passes, wait on dimly lit docks with costumed mannequins and piles of luggage, and once on board navigate their way through cramped and creaky sleeping and dining cabins. After being processed at Ellis Island, visitors can then research their genealogy using the museum's emigration database and its extensive collection of passenger lists. Further on, there is a section of the museum dedicated to immigrants to Germany, complete with an impressive 1970s-era shopping mall; a retro movie theater screens short films about German emigrants and their families. ✉ *Columbusstr. 65* ☎ *0471/902–200* 🌐 *www.dah-bremerhaven.de* 🎟 *€15.*

Deutsches Schifffahrtsmuseum (*German Maritime Museum*). The country's largest and most fascinating maritime museum, the Deutsches Schifffahrtsmuseum, includes a harbor, open from April through October, that shelters seven old trading ships as well as a separate submarine-turned-technology-museum. ✉ *Hans-Scharoun-Pl. 1* ✥ *From Bremen take A-27 to exit for Bremerhaven-Mitte* ☎ *0471/482–070* 🌐 *www.dsm.museum* 🎟 *From €1* 🕒 *Closed Mon. mid-Nov.–mid-Mar.*

Klimahaus Bremerhaven 8° Ost. This unique interactive museum takes visitors through nine stations covering the various climatic regions of the Earth. The history of the climate—ranging from the origins of the Earth 3.9 billion years ago and looking forward to the year 2050—is on display in this museum dedicated to helping visitors understand what factors determine the weather and the climate. Located directly on the seafront, it also has information about an offshore wind farm that will put the city's relationship to the sea and the changing climate into perspective. ✉ *Hermann-Henrich-Meier-Str.* ☎ *0471/902–0300* 🌐 *www.klimahaus-bremerhaven.de* 🎟 *€16.*

WHERE TO STAY

$ HOTEL 🏨 **Atlantic Hotel SailCity.** Designed in the shape of a sail catching the wind, this glass skyscraper located directly on the harbor and within walking distance to all the major sights is popular with travelers hoping to catch a glimpse of the Atlantic—which they can from most rooms. **Pros:** friendly staff; great location; sea views. **Cons:** can fill up with convention-goers; chain-style modern interiors; parking extra. [$] *Rooms from: €99* ✉ *Am Strom 1* ☎ *0471/309–900* 🌐 *www.atlantic-hotels.de/sailcity/de/Start.html* 🛏 *120 rooms* 🍴 *Free Breakfast.*

$$ HOTEL 🏨 **Hotel Haverkamp.** Not far from Bremerhaven's harbor and world-class museums, this modern hotel may not look like much from the outside, but its enviable reputation is built on excellent service, a fine restaurant, and small, tidy guest rooms with modern furnishings. **Pros:** convenient location; quiet area; good restaurant. **Cons:** plain exterior; pool is very small; views look onto other building facades. [$] *Rooms from: €129* ✉ *Pragerstr. 34* ☎ *0471/48330* 🌐 *www.hotel-haverkamp.de* 🛏 *85 rooms* 🍴 *Free Breakfast.*

HAMBURG

WELCOME TO HAMBURG

TOP REASONS TO GO

★ **Alster cruises:** Marvel at the luxurious villas gracing the shores of the Alster lakes and its canals while relaxing with a *Glühwein* (mulled wine) or cool beer and listening to tidbits of trivia about the city.

★ **Hamburger Kunsthalle and the Deichtorhallen:** Spend an afternoon admiring the fantastic art collections at two of Germany's leading galleries of modern art.

★ **Historic harbor district:** Travel back in time and walk the quaint cobblestone alleys around Deichstrasse and the Speicherstadt.

★ **Retail therapy:** Indulge your inner shopper as you weave your way through the streets behind the elegant Jungfernstieg, amble up and down Mönckebergstrasse, stroll through Altona and the Schanzenviertel, and end the afternoon at one of the quarters' funky cafés.

★ **Sin City:** Adventure along the Reeperbahn, browse its quirky sex shops, and dive into the nightlife of Europe's biggest party district.

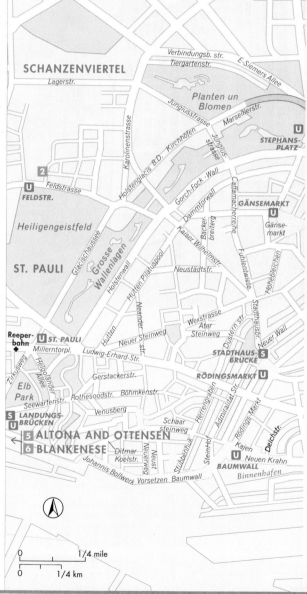

13

Moorweidenstr.
Theodor
Heuss-
pl.

S **DAMMTOR**

Mittelweg

Alsterglacis

Warburgstr.

Alsterufer

Aussenalster

Esplanade

Kennedybrücke

Colonnaden

An der Alster

Alster Lakes

Lombardsbrücke

Neuer Jungfernstieg

ST. GEORG

Holzdamm

Binnenalster

3

Hamburger
Kunsthalle

Ernst-Merck-Str.

Kirchen Allee

fi U S **HBF.-**
NORD

HBF.-SÜD S

Grosse
Bleichen

Jungfernstieg

Postttr.

U **JUNGFERN-**
STIEG
S

Ballindamm

Ferdinandstr.

Brandsende

Hermannstr.

Raboisen

Gloctengiesser wall

Kurte

Lange-Mührenstr.

Gerh
Hauptm
Pl.

Mühren

Steintor-
wall

Klosterwall

NEUSTADT

MÖNCKEBERGSTR. U

Mönckebergstrasse U
RATHAUS U
Mönckebergstr.

1

Kurt-Schumacher-Allee

Adolph.
Alter Wall

Gr.
Johannsstr.

Pelzerstr.

Schmiedst.

Speer sort

Steinstr.

Johannis
Wall

Mönke-
damm

Burchard-
pl.

STEINSTR. U

ALTSTADT

Gr.
Burstah

Domstrasse

Burchardstr.

Kl. Reichenstr.

Deichtor
Pl.

MESSBERG U

Willy-Brandt-Strasse

Dovenfleet

Deichtorhallen

Oberbaumbrücke

Deichtorstr.

Burstah

B.D.
Mühren

Zippelhaus

Alter Wandrahm

Neuer Wandrahm

Zollkanal

SPEICHERSTADT

4

HAFENCITY

KEY

S *S-Bahn*

fi *Tourist information*

U *U-Bahn*

1 **Altstadt and Neustadt.**
Together, the Old Town and
New Town make up the
Innenstadt, or inner city.

2 **St. Pauli and**
Schanzenviertel.
An entertainment district
since the 17th century, St.
Pauli continues to draw fun
seekers and night owls. Just
down the road, is the
Schanzenviertel.

3 **St. Georg.** The center of
Hamburg's gay and lesbian
scene and also home to a
large Turkish community.

4 **Speicherstadt and**
HafenCity. The old and the
new are both part of
Hamburg's inner city port,
with formidable
19th-century redbrick
warehouses at the UNESCO-
listed Speicherstadt and
state-of-the-art riverside
apartment and office
complexes at HafenCity.

5 **Altona and Ottensen.**
These former working-class
areas are now particularly
desirable places to live and
visit.

6 **Blankenese and**
Beyond. Many of Hamburg's
outlying suburbs have their
own distinct atmosphere
and feel—none more so
than the elegant riverside
neighborhood of
Blankenese.

COFFEE AND CAKE

When the afternoon rolls around, it's time for *Kaffee und Kuchen,* one of Germany's most beloved traditions. In villages and cities alike, patrons still stroll into their favorite *Konditorei* (pastry shop) for a leisurely cup of coffee and slice of cake.

(above) Cake is serious business in Germany, and you'll have your pick of many at any Konditorei worth its salt. (upper right) Mohnkuchen (lower right) Gugelhupf

The tradition stretches back hundreds of years, when coffee beans were first imported to Germany in the 17th century. Coffee quickly became the preferred hot drink of the aristocracy, who paired it with cake, their other favorite indulgence. In time, the afternoon practice trickled down to the bourgeoisie, and was heartily embraced. Now everyone can partake in the tradition.

There are hundreds of German cakes, many of which are regional and seasonal with an emphasis on fresh fruits in summer, and spiced cakes in winter. Due to modern work schedules, not as many Germans take a daily coffee and cake break anymore. Families will have theirs at home on the weekend, and it's often an occasion for a starched tablecloth, the best china, and candles.

VISITING THE KONDITOREI

Seek out the most old-fashioned shops, as these tend to have the best cakes. Check out what's in the glass case, since most Konditoreien don't have printed menus. Don't worry about a language barrier—when it comes time to order, just point to the cake of your choice.

BEST CAKES TO TRY

FRANKFURTER KRANZ

The *Frankfurter Kranz,* or Frankfurt wreath, is a butter cake flavored with lemon zest and a touch of rum. It's then split into three layers and spread with fillings of buttercream and red preserves. The cake's exterior is generously coated with crunchy cookie crumbs or toasted nuts, and each slice is graced with a swirl of buttercream frosting and a bright red cherry.

GUGELHUPF

Of all cakes, the *Gugelhupf* has the most distinctive shape, one that you'll likely recognize as a bundt cake. It tends to be more popular in southern Germany. Gugelhupf had its start as a bready yeast cake, studded with raisins and citrus peel, but today you're just as likely to have it as a marble cake. During the Biedermeier period, in the early 19th century, the wealthy middle class regarded the Gugelhupf as a status symbol.

HERRENTORTE

A layer cake of dark chocolate, *Herrentorte* means "gentleman's cake." It's not as sweet or creamy as most layer cakes, and thus meant to appeal to a man's palate. A *Torte* refers to a fancier layered cake, as opposed to the more humble *Kuchen,* which is more rustic. The Herrentorte has a rich and refined taste—in Germany, all chocolate is required to have a high cocoa content, improving its overall taste and texture.

MOHNKUCHEN

Mohnkuchen is a poppy seed cake—in fact, this is a cake so completely brimming with poppy seeds you could mistake it for a piece of chocolate cake. You'll come across it as a tall wedge, sprinkled with powdered sugar, or a fat square glazed with a lick of icing. The poppy seeds are mixed with sugar, butter, and sometimes milk. Lightly crushed they make for a very moist filling.

STREUSELKUCHEN

This cake became especially popular in the 19th century, in Prussia. Owing to its versatility, you'll find it today all over Germany. The simple, buttery yeast cake's selling point is its sugary, crunchy topping of pebbled *Streusel,* which can stand on its own or be combined with rhubarb, apricots, cherries, apples, or other fruit. *Streuselkuchen* is baked on large sheet pans and cut into generous squares

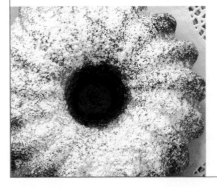

13

Updated by
Wibke Carter

Frequently described as "the gateway to the world" by its proud citizens, the handsome port city of Hamburg has for centuries welcomed merchants, traders, and sailors to a rich assortment of grand hotels, fine restaurants, and, yes, seedy bars and brothels.

This vibrant, affluent city's success began with its role as a founding member of the Hanseatic League, a medieval alliance of northern European cities that once dominated the shipping trade in the North and Baltic Seas. To this day, the city is known as "the Free and Hanseatic City of Hamburg," reflecting both its association with the league and its status as an independent city-state.

Shipping continues to be a major industry. Straddling the mighty Elbe River, more than 100 km (62 miles) inland from the North Sea, Hamburg's inner city harbor is the third-biggest port in Europe. The city is now also one of Germany's major media hubs, serving as headquarters for the publishing giants Axel Springer, Gruner + Jahr, and Bauer Verlag; and for such influential publications as *Die Zeit, Der Spiegel,* and *Stern.*

The profits of these endeavors are apparent throughout Hamburg, from its imposing neo-Renaissance town hall, to the multitude of luxury boutiques studding the adjacent Neuer Wall, to the Elbchaussee, a long, leafy stretch of road lined with Hollywood-like mansions and overlooking the Elbe. Hamburg has more millionaires per capita than any other German city.

Like many other of the country's urban centers, however, the city has suffered a tumultuous history. Since its founding as "Hammaburg" in 811, Hamburg has been destroyed by Vikings, burned down by Poles, and occupied by Danish and French armies. The Great Fire of 1842 devastated much of its commercial center, and in 1943 the Allied Forces' Operation Gomorrah bombing raids and the resulting firestorms left 40,000 people dead and large swaths of Hamburg in ruins.

Scars from World War II still remain, and you need only walk down a residential street to see the plain, functional apartment buildings that were built to replace those destroyed by bombs. There are also frequent reminders of the terrible fate suffered by Hamburg's Jews, and others considered enemies of the state during this time. Memorials in HafenCity and near Dammtor train station mark where those persecuted by Nazis were deported to concentration camps. As part of a Germany-wide project, small brass plaques set into sidewalks outside apartment buildings commemorate former residents executed by the regime.

Modern-day Hamburg is a progressive city endowed with attractive architecture, cultural diversity, and liberal attitudes. It's notable for its parks and trees and a pair of beautiful inner city lakes, but it's famous for its enormous red-light party district, which fans off from the seamy, neon-lit Reeperbahn. Shabby but chic quarters such as St. Pauli and the Schanzenviertel are as beloved by locals as the affluent Blankenese and Eppendorf, and the city's annual schedule of spring and summer festivals has enough room for a huge gay-pride parade in the middle of town, as well as a celebration of *Hafengeburtstag*—the harbor's birthday.

As you'd expect in such a wealthy city, Hamburg has more than its share of world-class museums and art galleries, as well as an assortment of grand theaters and music venues, an opera company, and an internationally renowned ballet company. Not content to rest on its laurels, the city is also steaming ahead with the ambitious HafenCity, an urban-renewal project that has transformed a significant section of the city's port front. The Elbphilharmonie—a futuristic concert hall and new landmark of Hamburg—is its centerpiece.

PLANNING

DISCOUNTS AND DEALS

Hamburg is one of Germany's most expensive cities, but the several citywide deals can make attractions more affordable.

The **Hamburg Card** allows unlimited travel on all public transportation (including express buses) within Hamburg and more than 150 discounts at many of the city's museums, cruises, restaurants, and stores. A one-day card, which is valid until 6 am the following day, costs €10.50 for one adult and up to three children under 15. The three-day card will set you back €25.90. A *Gruppenkarte* costs €18.50 for one day, €44.90 for three days, and covers five people. The Hamburg Card is available from HVV buses, vending machines, and service centers; tourist offices; and many hotels and hostels; as well as online at ⊕ *www.hvv.de* and ⊕ *www.hamburg-travel.com*.

WHEN TO GO

Known for its long, gray winters, Hamburg is frequently treated to a pleasant spring come late March or early April. Once the weather warms, the city's mood visibly improves. One of the highlights of the season is *Hafengeburtstag,* in early May, when the Elbe comes alive with a long parade of ships and riverside festivities.

Summer may be the best time of the year to visit. Temperatures rarely exceed the mid-80s, and the days are long, with the sun rising at around 5 am and light still in the sky till after 10 pm. Tables outside cafés and bars fill up with alfresco diners and drinkers; plumes of smoke rise from grills in parks and beaches along the Elbe. From mid-June to early September, the *Schlemmersommer* (Gourmet Summer) comes to tempt food lovers. During this time, more than 120 restaurants throughout the city, including a number of award winners, offer multicourse dinners for two for €64.

September and October are usually good months to visit, despite the fact that October can often be quite cold and wet. September's *Reeperbahn Festival* is great for music fans hoping to see the next big thing, and Hamburg's small but popular film festival (held the same month) usually attracts one or two of the leading lights of European and world cinema.

The mercury drops quickly once the clocks go back an hour at the end of October. Happily, Christmas markets selling Glühwein begin to spring up on street corners and in public squares around the last week of November, and many continue on to *Silvester* (New Year's Eve). December, despite temperatures frequently dropping below zero, is a fun time to visit the city. January and February, however, are quiet and fairly uneventful.

FESTIVALS

Fodor's Choice ★ **Historischer Weihnachtsmarkt.** Hamburg's Historischer Weihnachtsmarkt enjoys a spectacular backdrop—the city's Gothic town hall. The market's stalls are filled with rows of candy apples, chocolates, and doughnuts. Woodcarvers from Tyrol, bakers from Aachen, and gingerbread makers from Nuremberg (Nürnberg) come to sell their wares. And in an appearance arranged by the circus company Roncalli, Santa Claus ho-ho-hos his way along a tightwire high above the market every evening at 4, 6, and 8. The Hamburg Christmas market runs from late November until December 23. ⊠ *Rathausmarkt 1, Altstadt* ⊕ *www. hamburger-weihnachtsmarkt.com* Ⓜ *Rathaus (U-bahn).*

GETTING HERE AND AROUND

AIR TRAVEL

Hamburg Airport is 8 km (5 miles) northwest of the city. S-bahn Line No. 1 runs about every 10 minutes from the airport to Hamburg's main station (*Hauptbahnhof*) on its way to Altona. The trip takes 25 minutes, and tickets are €3.30. A taxi to the center of the city (Alstadt and Neustadt) costs €29. If you're driving a rental car from the airport, follow the signs to "Zentrum" (Center). ■ TIP→ There is an Edeka supermarket on the arrivals level between Terminal 1 and 2. It's a bit smaller than a full-size German supermarket, and the prices are a bit higher than they would be in town. However, it is a great place to pick up some snacks or drinks for your hotel room or some food for an extended journey.

Contacts Hamburg Airport (*HAM*). ⊠ *Flughafenstr. 1–3* ☎ *040/50750* ⊕ *www. hamburg-airport.de.*

BUS AND SUBWAY TRAVEL

The HVV, Hamburg's public transportation system, includes the U-bahn (subway), the S-bahn (commuter train), ferries, buses, and express buses (which cost an additional €2.10). Distance determines fares; a single trip costs €3.30 for longer journeys (such as the airport into Hamburg's main station); €2.20 for shorter distances (for instance, from St. Pauli or Altona into the center of town); and €1.60 if you're only traveling a couple of stops. If you're planning to make multiple trips about the city, then you may want to get the *Tageskarte*, or day pass, which for an adult and three children under 15 costs €7.70 when purchased before 9 am and €6.40 after that. A €12 *Gruppenkarte* is the best option for those traveling in a group. A group of five adults can use this card after 9 am on weekdays and all day on weekends.

Tickets and passes are available on all buses and from vending machines in every U- or S-bahn station. HVV is partially based on the honor system. You only need to show a ticket to the bus driver after 9 pm and all day on Sunday, but not on trains or ferries unless asked by a ticket inspector during random checks; those caught without a ticket are fined €60 on the spot. Subway and commuter trains run throughout the night on weekends, but stop running around 12:30 am during the week. After that, night buses (Nos. 600–688) take over.

Information is available in English on the HVV website. The trip planner function gives the times, prices, walking directions, and maps for each journey. If you don't know the address of a site, you can simply type in the name of the popular destination, such as "Hamburg airport." Prepared commuters can buy tickets and passes from the website and print them out, or use HVV's smart-phone app.

Don't be afraid to take the bus. Buses have dedicated traffic lanes, and most of their stops aren't too close together, so travel tends to be fast. It's a good way to see more of this beautiful city.

Hamburg's intercity bus station, the Zentral-Omnibus-Bahnhof (ZOB), is located diagonally across from the south exit of the main train station.

Contacts HVV (*Hamburg Transportation Association*). ✉ *Johanniswall 2, Altstadt* ☎ *040/3288–2924* ⊕ *www.hvv.de/en* Ⓜ *Steinstrasse (U-bahn).* **Zentral-Omnibus-Bahnhof** (*ZOB*). ✉ *Adenauerallee 78, St. Georg* ☎ *040/247–576* ⊕ *www.zob-hamburg.de.*

CAR TRAVEL

With its popular public transportation system, Hamburg is easier to negotiate by car than many other German cities, and traffic here is relatively free-flowing outside of rush hours. Several autobahns (A-1, A-7, A-23, A-24, and A-250) connect with Hamburg's three beltways, which then lead to the downtown area. Follow the "Zentrum" (Center) signs.

TAXI TRAVEL

Taxi meters start at €3.50, then add €2.45 per km for the first 4 km (2½ miles), €2.20 per km for the next 5 km (3 miles), and €1.50 per km after that. You can hail taxis on the street, outside subway and train stations, and at popular locations (like along Mönckebergstrasse). You can also order one by phone or online.

Contacts Hansa-Taxi. ☎ *040/211–211* ⊕ *www.taxi211211.de.*

TRAIN TRAVEL

Hamburg Hauptbahnhof (Hamburg Main Station) is the city's central hub for local, regional, long-distance, and international trains. InterCity Express (ICE) trains going to and from Basel, Stuttgart, and Munich all start and terminate in Hamburg-Altona, and pass through Hauptbahn-hof and Dammtor stations on the way.

Contacts Deutsche Bahn. ☎ *0180/699–6633* ⊕ *www.bahn.de.*

TOURS
BOAT TOURS
There are few better ways to get to know the city than by taking a trip on its waters. Alster Touristik, Rainer Abicht, and Maritime Circle Line offer a wide variety of tour options, or you can simply take the HADAG ferry for great harbor views. Visits of the historic Speicherstadt depend on the tides; at high and low water levels boats are unable to operate there.

■ TIP→ **An HVV public transport day pass is valid for trips on the No. 62 HADAG ferry between Landungsbrücken Pier 1 and Finkenwerder, a suburb on the south side of the Elbe river. There's no commentary on the ferry, but on a fine day the top deck's a great spot to watch ships sailing in and out of the harbor, and for superb views of the city from the river.**

Alster Touristik. This company operates a variety of picturesque boat trips around the Alster lakes and through the canals, leaving from a small dock at the Jungfernstieg. The one-hour round-trip Alster cruise leaves every half hour. The Winter Warmer Trip, from November through March, offers hot chocolate and Glühwein (for an additional charge) several times a day. You can also get a two-hour twilight tour through the canals to the bucolic Harvestehude neighborhood May through September. A two-hour Speicherstadt canal tour runs April through October three times a day. Audio guides in English are available for all tours. ⊠ *Anleger Jungfernstieg, Neustadt* ☎ *040/357–4240* ⊕ *www.alstertouristik.de* ⊠ *From €15* Ⓜ *Jungfernstieg (U-bahn and S-bahn).*

Barkassen-Meyer. Operating launches on Hamburg's waterways, this long-running company offers one- and two-hour cruises in English. Visitors can follow audio information during every tour (approximately every hour) on their smartphone. ⊠ *Landungsbrücken 6, St. Pauli* ☎ *040/317–7370* ⊕ *www.barkassen-meyer.de* ⊠ *From €18.*

HADAG. Harbor ferries have been operating around Hamburg's docks since 1888 and offer an inexpensive way to get out on the water. Either take one of the scheduled ferries, or opt for the harbor tour or one of the hop-on, hop-off cruises. Ticket prices depend on the route taken. ☎ *040/311–7070* ⊕ *www.hadag.de* ⊠ *From €2.*

Maritime Circle Line. The Maritime Circle Line tours major attractions on the Elbe. Passengers embark at St Pauli Landungsbrücken Pier 10 and can hop on and hop off at a number of stops including Bal-linStadt, Hamburg Harbor Museum, HafenCity, and the historic ship MV *Cap San Diego*. The tours run every two hours daily from 11 to 3, April through October, and on weekends only from November to March. Tickets, which can be bought at the pier or online, include discounts at all the venues. ⊠ *Landungsbrücken 10, St. Pauli* ☎ *040/2849–3963* ⊕ *www.maritime-circle-line.de* ⊠ *€16* Ⓜ *Hamburg Landungsbrücken (S-bahn).*

Take a relaxing boat cruise on the Alster lakes and through the canals of the city.

Rainer Abicht. One-hour tours of the harbor with live commentary in English are offered daily at noon aboard one of Rainer Abicht's fleet of boats, which include its famous *Louisiana Star* riverboat. The tours leave from Landungsbrücken Pier 4. ☎ *040/317–8220* ⊕ *www.abicht. de* ✉ *€20* Ⓜ *Hamburg Landungsbrücken (S-bahn).*

ORIENTATION TOURS

Hamburger Stadtrundfahrt. Sightseeing bus tours of the city, all with guides, who rapidly narrate in both English and German, leave from Kirchenallee by the main train station and St. Pauli Landungsbrücken 1–2. A 90-minute bus tour and a hop-on, hop-off service set off at varying times daily; departure times vary according to season. The company also offers bus tours in combination with harbor or lakes cruises, a twilight tour and a Hamburg Dungeon Combo. ☎ *040/792–8979* ⊕ *www. die-roten-doppeldecker.de* ✉ *From €18* Ⓜ *Hauptbahnhof Süd (U-bahn) or Landungsbrücken (S-bahn).*

WALKING TOURS

A great way to learn more about the city while also getting some exercise is on a walking tour. There are plenty of tours to choose from, although many only run from April through November. In addition to guided walks of the Altstadt and Neustadt, the harbor district, HafenCity, and St. Pauli, there are also themed excursions, such as Beatles tours and a red-light walking tour of the Reeperbahn. To find a guided walk in English, contact Hamburg Tourismus, the tourist office (⊕ *www. hamburg-travel.com*).

VISITOR INFORMATION

Hamburg Tourismus (Hamburg Tourism Office) has several outlets around the city which are open daily. The main office is in the Hauptbahnhof. The airport branch sits on the departure level between Terminals 1 and 2. At the harbor there's an office at the St. Pauli Landungsbrücken between Piers 4 and 5. All tourist offices can help with accommodations, and there's a central call-in booking office for hotel and ticket reservations and general information, the Hamburg-Hotline.

Contacts Hamburg Tourismus Main Office. ⊠ *Hamburg Hauptbahnhof, Kirchenallee (main exit), Altstadt* ☎ *040/3005–1701* ⊕ *www.hamburg-tourism.de* Ⓜ *Hauptbahnhof (U-Bahn and S-Bahn).*

EXPLORING HAMBURG

Despite being a large, sprawling city that covers almost as much ground as Berlin, Hamburg feels a lot more compact. The bulk of its major attractions and sights are between the Alster lakes to the north and the city's harbor and the Elbe River to the south. At the center of the city are the Altstadt and Neustadt—the city's historical core. East of the Altstadt is St. Georg, a major gay neighborhood. To the west of the Neustadt lie the nightlife district of St. Pauli and its neighbor the Schanzenviertel, while farther down the river are the more multicultural areas of Altona and Ottensen, and the quaint settlement of Blankenese. Just south of the Altstadt are the portside districts of the Speicherstadt and the HafenCity.

ALTSTADT AND NEUSTADT

Divided by the Binnenalster (Inner Alster Lake) and the Kleine Alster canal, the Altstadt (Old Town) and Neustadt (New Town) form the heart of Hamburg's Innenstadt (Inner City).

ALTSTADT

Stretching from Hauptbahnhof to Hamburg's town hall and down to the canals of the Speicherstadt and the Elbe, the Altstadt was heavily bombed during World War II (as was the Neustadt). Much of its splendor was restored during the postwar reconstruction of the city. Sprinkled between its office blocks and modern department stores are a number of majestic churches, handsome museums, and stately government buildings.

GETTING HERE AND AROUND

The best way to get to the center of the Altstadt is to take the U-bahn or S-bahn to the Hauptbahnhof or the U-bahn stations of Mönckebergstrasse and Rathaus. Once here, most of the sights and attractions are within an easy walk of each other.

Fodor'sChoice ★ **Alster Lakes.** The twin lakes of the Binnenalster (Inner Alster) and Aussenalster (Outer Alster) provide Hamburg with some of its most celebrated vistas. The two lakes meet at the Lombardsbrücke and Kennedybrücke (Lombard and Kennedy bridges). The boat landing at the Jungfernstieg, below the Alsterpavillon, is the starting point for lake and canal cruises. Small sailboats and rowboats, rented from yards on the shores of the Alster, are very much a part of the summer scene.

Every Hamburger dreams of living within sight of the Alster, but only the wealthiest can afford it. Those that can't still have plenty of opportunities to enjoy the waterfront, however, and the outer Alster is ringed by 7 km (4½ miles) of tree-lined public pathways. ■ TIP→ **Popular among joggers, these paths are also a lovely place for a stroll.** ⊠ *Altstadt* Ⓜ *Jungfernstieg (U-bahn).*

Fodor'sChoice
★

Chilehaus (*Chile House*). Almost 5 million bricks went into the construction of this marvelous building at the heart of the Kontorhausviertel, a collection of handsome office buildings that were built in the 1920–40s and now, together with the nearby Speicherstadt, form a UNESCO World Heritage site. Built in a brick expressionist style in 1924 for expat Brit Henry Brarens Sloman, who emigrated to Chile from Hamburg as a young man, made a considerable fortune trading saltpeter and returned to the city to make his mark, the Chilehaus stands 10 stories high, its impressive, jutting tip resembling the prow of a ship. Still a home to business offices, it also counts a number of small cafés and shops, and a bar as residents, and is well worth a visit, particularly at night when illuminated. ⊠ *Fischertwiete 2, Altstadt* Ⓜ *Messberg (U-bahn), Mönckebergstrasse (U-bahn).*

Fodor'sChoice
★

Deichstrasse. The oldest residential area in the Old Town of Hamburg now consists of lavishly restored houses from the 17th through the 19th century. Many of the original, 14th-century houses on Deichstrasse were destroyed in the Great Fire of 1842, which broke out in No. 38 and left approximately 20,000 people homeless; only a few of the early dwellings escaped its ravages. These days the narrow cobblestone street is flanked by a number of lovely little restaurants specializing in fish or German cuisine, which have taken residence inside its historic buildings. ⊠ *Altstadt* Ⓜ *Rödingsmarkt (U-bahn).*

Deichtorhallen. A pair of large markets built in 1911–12, not far from the main train station, now house two of Germany's largest exhibition halls for contemporary art and photography. One of the Deichtorhallen's modern, airy interiors resembles an oversize loft space, and its changing exhibits have presented the works of such artists as Andy Warhol, Roy Lichtenstein, and Miró. ⊠ *Deichtorstr. 1–2, Altstadt* ☎ *040/321–030* ⊕ *www.deichtorhallen.de* ⊠ *€10* ⊙ *Closed Mon.* Ⓜ *Steinstrasse (U-bahn).*

Hamburger Kunsthalle. One of the most important art museums in Germany, the Kunsthalle has 3,500 paintings, 650 sculptures, and a coin and medal collection that includes exhibits from the ancient Roman era. In the postmodern, cube-shaped building designed by Berlin architect O.M. Ungers, the **Galerie der Gegenwart** has housed a collection of international modern art since 1960, including works by Andy Warhol, Joseph Beuys, Georg Baselitz, and David Hockney. With 1,200 drawings and other works, graphic art is well represented, including works by Pablo Picasso and Horst Janssen, a Hamburg artist famous for his satirical worldview. In the other areas of the museum, you can view works by local artists dating from the 16th century. The outstanding

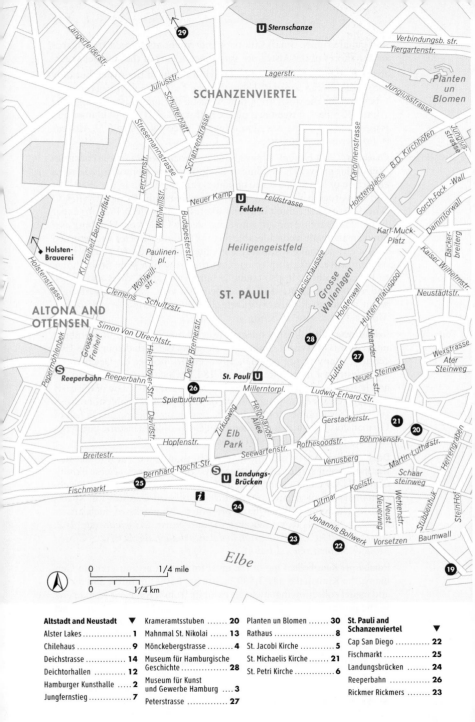

Altstadt and Neustadt ▼

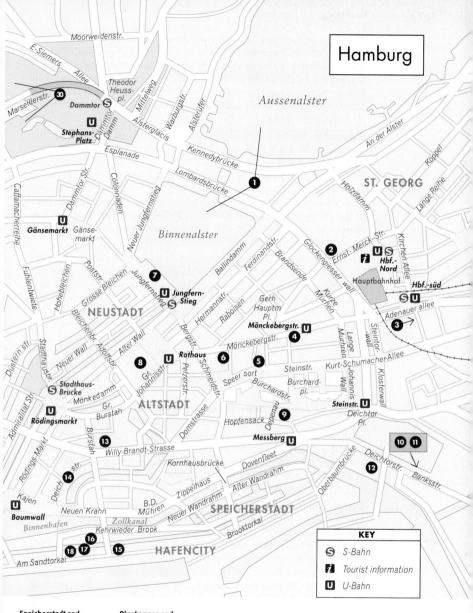

Hamburg

Aussenalster

Moorweidenstr.

E-Siemers Allee

Marseillerstr.

Theodor Heuss-pl.

Mittelweg

Walburgstr.

Alsteruferstr.

30 Dammtor Ⓢ

Dammtor Ⓤ

Stephans-Platz Ⓤ

Dammtor Damm

Alsterglacis

Esplanade

Colonnaden

Kennedybrücke

Lombardsbrücke

1

ST. GEORG

Holzdamm

An der Alster

Lange Reihe

Koppel

Calfamacherreihe

Gänsemarkt Ⓤ Gänse-markt

Dammtorstr.

Poststr.

Neuer Jungfernstieg

Binnenalster

Ballindamm

Ferdinandstr.

Brandsende

Glockengiesser wall

2

Ernst-Merck-Str.

Hbf.-Nord Ⓤ Ⓢ

🛈

Hauptbahnhof

Kirchen Allee

Hbf.-süd

Fuhlentwiete

Hohenbleichen

Grosse Bleichen

Jungfernstieg

Jungfernstieg Ⓤ Ⓢ Jungfern-Stieg

7

NEUSTADT

Bleichenbr. Adolfstr.

Alter Wall

Hermannstr.

Raboisen

Gerh Hauptm Pl.

Mönckebergstr.

4 Ⓤ

Kurze Mühren

Lange Mühren

Steintor-wall

Adenauer allee

Ⓢ Ⓤ

3 →

Kurt-Schumacher-Allee

Klosterwall

Stadthausbr.

Neuer Wall

Rathaus

8 Gr. Johannisstr.

Bergstr.

Schmeidstr.

Pelzerstr.

Mönckebergstr.

6

5

Steinstr.

Speer sort

Burchardstr.

Burchard-pl.

Lange Johannis Wall

Steinstr. Ⓤ

Deichtor Pl.

Admiralität Str.

Düstern str.

Stadthaus-Brücke Ⓢ

Rödingsmarkt Ⓤ

Mönkedamm

Gr. Burstah

Burstah

ALTSTADT

Domstrasse

Hopfensack

Depenau

9

Messberg Ⓤ

10 **11**

Rödings-Markt

Deichstr.

13

Willy-Brandt-Strasse

Kornhausbrücke

Dovenfleet

Oberbaumbrücke

Deichtorstr.

12

Banksstr.

Kajen Ⓤ

14

Baumwall Ⓤ

Neuen Krahn

B.D. Mühten

Zippelhaus

Neuen Wandrahm

Alter Wandrahm

SPEICHERSTADT

Binnenhafen

Zollkanal

Kehrwieder Brook

Brooktorkai

16

18 **17** **15**

HAFENCITY

Am Sandtorkai

KEY

Ⓢ S-Bahn

🛈 Tourist information

Ⓤ U-Bahn

562 <   **Hamburg**

collection of German Romantic paintings includes pieces by Caspar David Friedrich. Paintings by Holbein, Rembrandt, Van Dyck, Tiepolo, and Canaletto are also on view, while late-19th-century impressionism is represented by works by Leibl, Liebermann, Manet, Monet, and Renoir. ⊠ *Glockengiesserwall, Altstadt* ☎ *040/4281–31200* ⊕ *www. hamburger-kunsthalle.de* ⬚*€14* ۞ *Closed Mon.* Ⓜ *Hauptbahnhof (U-bahn and S-bahn).*

Mahnmal St. Nikolai (*St. Nicholas Memorial*). Burned down during the air raids of World War II, neo-Gothic church serves as a memorial for the victims of war and persecution from 1933 to 1945. The museum features an exhibition on the air raids and the destruction of Hamburg and other European cities. A glass elevator on the outside of the building takes visitors 250 feet up to the steeple, which offers magnificent views of the surrounding historic streets. ⊠ *Willy-Brandt-Str. 60 at Hopfenmarkt, Altstadt* ☎ *040/371–125* ⊕ *www.mahnmal-st-nikolai.de* ⬚ *€5* Ⓜ *Rödingsmarkt (U-bahn).*

Mönckebergstrasse. This broad street of shops, which cuts through the city's Altstadt, is Hamburg's major thoroughfare. Built between 1908 and 1911 to connect the main train station to the town hall, but only open to taxis and buses, the street is perfect for a stroll. Home to the Karstadt and Galeria Kaufhof department stores, electronics megastore Saturn, as well as a host of global brand stores from Adidas to Zara, it swells with local and out-of-town shoppers on Saturday and public holidays. The best cafés and restaurants tend to be found on side streets off Mönckebergstrasse, where the rents for shop space are generally not as high. ⊠ *Altstadt* Ⓜ *Mönckebergstrasse (U-bahn), Hauptbahnhof (U-bahn and S-bahn).*

Museum für Kunst und Gewerbe Hamburg (*Arts and Crafts Museum*). The museum houses a wide range of exhibits, from 15th- to 18th-century scientific instruments to an art nouveau interior complete with ornaments and furnishings. Its founder, Justus Brinckmann, amassed a wealth of unusual objects, including ceramics from around the world. ⊠ *Steintorpl., Altstadt* ☎ *040/4281–34880* ⊕ *www.mkg-hamburg.de* ⬚*€12* ۞ *Closed Mon.* Ⓜ *Hauptbahnhof (U-bahn and S-bahn).*

Fodor'sChoice **Rathaus** (*Town Hall*). To most Hamburgers this impressive neo-Renais-
★ sance building is the symbolic heart of the city. The seat of the city's *Senate* (state government) and *Bürgerschaft* (parliament), it was constructed between 1886 and 1897, with 647 rooms and an imposing clock tower. Along with much of the city center, the Rathaus was heavily damaged during World War II, but was faithfully restored to its original beauty in the postwar years, and it's now one of the most photographed sights in Hamburg. The 40-minute tours of the building (in English on demand) begin in the ground floor *Rathausdiele*, a vast pillared hall. Although visitors are shown only the state rooms, their tapestries, glittering chandeliers, coffered ceilings, and grand portraits give you a sense of the city's great wealth in the 19th century and the Town Hall's status as an object of civic pride. Outside, the Rathausmarkt (Town Hall Square) is the site of regular festivals and events. ⊠ *Rathausmarkt*

Hamburg's neo-Renaissance Rathaus (Town Hall) is worth a peek inside for its opulent interiors.

1, Altstadt ☎ 040/42831–2064 ⊕ www.hamburg.de ✉ Free; tours €5 Ⓜ *Rathaus (U-bahn), Jungfernstieg (U-bahn and S-bahn).*

St. Jacobi Kirche (*St. James's Church*). This 15th-century church was almost completely destroyed during World War II. Only the interiors survived, and reconstruction was completed in 1963. The interior is not to be missed—it houses such treasures as a massive baroque organ and three Gothic altars from the 15th and 16th centuries. ⊠ *Jacobikirchhof 22, at Steinstr., Altstadt* ☎ *040/303–7370* ⊕ *www.jacobus.de* ✉ *Free* ☉ *Closed Sun.* Ⓜ *Mönckebergstrasse (U-bahn).*

St. Petri Kirche (*St. Peter's Church*). This church was created in 1195 and has been in continuous use since then. St. Petri is the only one of the five main churches in Hamburg that came out of World War II relatively undamaged. The current building was built in 1849, after the previous building burned down in the Great Fire of 1842. Every Wednesday at 5:15 pm is the *Stunde der Kirchenmusik*, an hour of liturgical organ music. ⊠ *Bei der Petrikirche 2, Altstadt* ☎ *040/325–7400* ⊕ *www.sankt-petri.de* ✉ *Free* Ⓜ *Rathaus (U-bahn), Jungfernstieg (U-bahn and S-bahn).*

NEUSTADT

To the west of the Altstadt, and bordered by the Aussenalster (Outer Alster) to the north and the Elbe to the south, lies the Neustadt. The area dates back to the 17th century, when a second wall was built to protect the city during the Thirty Years' War. These days, the Neustadt is more or less indistinguishable from its older neighbor. Similarly blessed with a number of stunning buildings, including those that line the pretty lakeside promenade of Jungfernstieg, the Neustadt is also famed for its wealth of shopping opportunities.

On the edge of the harbor, tucked in between Landungsbrücken and Baumwall, lies a small slice of Iberia in Hamburg. Famed for its cluster of tapas restaurants and little cafés on and around Ditmar-Koel-Strasse, the Portugiesenviertel is a great place to go to feast on a plate of grilled sardines or have a creamy *galão* (espresso with foamed milk). Head here in summer, when the streets are flooded with tables and diners making the most of the good weather.

GETTING HERE AND AROUND

The Neustadt is served by a number of U-bahn stops, but Gänsemarkt and Jungfernstieg are the most central. Hamburg's downtown area isn't particularly large, and strolling to Jungfernstieg from the main train station via Mönckebergstrasse won't take much more than 10 minutes, assuming you're not going on a Saturday or during the school holidays.

> **DID YOU KNOW?**
>
> Although Germans love to compare Hamburg to Venice, it's a bit of a stretch. Still, Hamburg is threaded with countless canals and waterways spanned by about 2,500 bridges, even more than you'll find in Venice, Amsterdam, and London combined. Swans glide on the canals and arcaded passageways run along the waterways. In front of the Rathaus is a grand square that some say resembles the Piazza San Marco in Venice.

Jungfernstieg. This wide promenade looking out over the Alster lakes is the beginning of the city's premier shopping district. Laid out in 1665, it used to be part of a muddy millrace that channeled water into the Elbe. Hidden from view behind the sedate facade of Jungfernstieg is a network of several small shopping centers that together account for almost a mile of shops selling everything from souvenirs to haute couture. Many of these passages have sprung up in the past two decades, but some have been here since the 19th century; the first glass-covered arcade, called Sillem's Bazaar, was built in 1845. ⊠ *Neustadt* Ⓜ *Jungfernstieg (U-bahn and S-bahn).*

Krameramtsstuben (*Grocers' Houses*). The grocers' guild built this tightly packed group of courtyard houses between 1620 and 1626 for members' widows. The half-timber, two-story dwellings, with unusual twisted chimneys and decorative brick facades, were restored in the 1970s. A visit inside the Kramer-Witwen-Wohnung—part of the Museum of Hamburg History—gives you a sense of what life was like in these 17th-century dwellings. ⊠ *Historic House C, Krayenkamp 10, Neustadt* ☎ *040/3750–1988* ⚏ *€3* ⊙ *Closed Mon. Apr.–Oct.; closed weekdays Nov.–Mar.* Ⓜ *Rödingsmarkt (U-bahn), Stadthausbrücke (S-bahn).*

FAMILY **Museum für Hamburg Geschichte** (*Museum of Hamburg History*). The museum's vast and comprehensive collection of artifacts gives you an excellent overview of Hamburg's development, from its origins in the 9th century to the present. Pictures and models portray the history of the port and shipping here, from 1650 onward. ⊠ *Holstenwall 24, Neustadt* ☎ *040/4281–32100* ⊕ *www.hamburgmuseum.de* ⚏ *€10* ⊙ *Closed Tues.* Ⓜ *St. Pauli (U-bahn).*

Peterstrasse. This elegant street lies steps away from the site of the former city wall, and is of great historical interest. At No. 35–39, for example, is a replica of the baroque facade of the Beylingstift complex, built in 1751. The composer Johannes Brahms's former home, now a museum in his honor, is at No. 39. All the buildings in the area have been painstakingly designed to follow the style of the original buildings, thanks largely to nonprofit foundations. ⊠ *Neustadt* Ⓜ *St. Pauli (U-bahn).*

FAMILY **Planten un Blomen** (*Plants and Flowers Park*). In 1821, a botanist planted a sycamore tree in a park near Dammtor train station. From this tree, a sanctuary for birds and plants evolved and a botanical garden that resembles the current park opened in 1930. This 116-acre inner-city oasis features a grand Japanese garden, a minigolf course, an outdoor roller-skating and ice-skating rink, trampolines, and water features. If you visit between May and August, you'll see the *Wasserlichtkonzerte,* the play of an illuminated fountain set to organ music. Make sure you get to the lake in plenty of time for the nightly show, which begins at 10 pm. ⊠ *Marseiller Str. 7, Neustadt* ☎ *040/4285–44723* ⊕ *www.plantenunblomen.hamburg.de* ☜ *Free* Ⓜ *Dammtor (S-bahn), Messehallen (U-bahn).*

Fodor'sChoice **St. Michaelis Kirche** (*St. Michael's Church*). The Michel, as it's called
★ locally, is Hamburg's principal church and northern Germany's finest baroque-style ecclesiastical building. Its first incarnation, built between 1649 and 1661 (the tower followed in 1669), was razed after lightning struck almost a century later. It was rebuilt between 1750 and 1786 in the decorative Nordic baroque style, but was gutted by a terrible fire in 1906. The replica, completed in 1912, was demolished during World War II and the present church is a reconstruction. The distinctive 436-foot brick-and-iron tower bears the largest tower clock in Germany, 26 feet in diameter. Just above the clock is a viewing platform (accessible by elevator or stairs) that affords a magnificent panorama of the city, the Elbe River, and the Alster lakes. ∎TIP➔ **For a great view of Hamburg's skyline, head to the clock tower at night.** ⊠ *Englische Planke 1, Neustadt* ☎ *040/376–780* ⊕ *www.st-michaelis.de* ☜ *Tower €5; crypt and movie €4; combined ticket €7* Ⓜ *Rödingsmarkt (U-bahn), Stadthausbrücke (S-bahn).*

ST. PAULI AND SCHANZENVIERTEL

The harborside quarter of St. Pauli is perhaps the city's best-known neighborhood, its web of narrow streets branching off the bright neon vein of the Reeperbahn. Named after the rope makers that once worked here, the long street runs the length of St. Pauli's extensive red-light district—one of the largest in Europe. The broad sidewalks here are lined with strip joints, sex shops, and bars. In the early 1960s, the Beatles famously cut their teeth in clubs just off the street, playing 12-hour-long gigs in front of drunken revelers. These days St. Pauli's all-night bars, nightclubs, and pubs continue to be a big draw. Despite the seediness of its sex industry, however, the area has undergone some serious gentrification over the years, and those dive bars and flophouses now rub shoulders with trendy eateries and design hotels.

The neighboring Schanzenviertel has also experienced a significant makeover in the last decade. Once filled with artists, punks, and students, and infused with an antiestablishment culture, the "Schanze" remains a neighborhood where the most recognizable building is the Rote Flora, an old theater occupied by squatters who use it for concerts and cultural events. Now, however, it's also a place where cool young Hamburgers go to browse through clothing boutiques and then drink and dine in laid-back, reasonably priced bars and restaurants. Ten minutes from the center of town by S-bahn, Schanzenviertel has elegant old apartment buildings that have found favor with Hamburg's media and finance professionals. This has driven the rents up, and forced out many of the same tenants who once imbued the Schanzenviertel with its original edginess.

GETTING HERE AND AROUND

The harbor can be reached by taking a U-bahn or S-bahn train to Landungsbrücken. The mile-long Reeperbahn is bookended by the Reeperbahn S-bahn and St. Pauli U-bahn stations. The Schanzenviertel is served by the Sternschanze U-bahn and S-bahn station.

TIMING

You can easily spend a full day and a long night here, starting with breakfast and shopping in the Schanzenviertel, then lunch and a river cruise at the harbor, and a night on the Reeperbahn after dinner.

Cap San Diego. Close to the *Rickmer Rickmers* ship at Hamburg's piers sits the handsome 1960s freighter *Cap San Diego*, nowadays a seaworthy museum and hotel. Before it docked at Hamburg permanently, it regularly sailed between Germany and South America. ⊠ *Übersee- brücke, Landungsbrücken, St. Pauli* ☎ *040/364–209* ⊕ *www.capsandi- ego.de* ☜ €7 Ⓜ *Landungsbrücken (U-bahn and S-bahn).*

Fischmarkt (*Fish Market*). A trip to the Altona Fischmarkt is definitely worth getting out of bed early—or staying up all night—for. The Sunday markets hark back to the 18th century, when fishermen sold their catch before church services. Today, freshly caught fish sold to the locals by salty auctioneers from little stalls is only a part of the scene. You can find almost anything here: live parrots and palm trees, armloads of flowers and bananas, valuable antiques, and fourth-hand junk. Those keen to continue partying from the night before can get down to live bands rocking the historic Fischauktionshalle. ⊠ *Grosse Elbestr. 9, St. Pauli* Ⓜ *Reeperbahn (S-Bahn).*

FAMILY **Landungsbrücken** (*Piers*). Hamburgers and tourists flock to the city's impressive port—Germany's largest—to marvel at the huge container and cruise ships gliding past, pick up maritime-themed gifts from souvenir stores, and treat themselves to something from the many snack and ice-cream stands. It's best to take a tour to get a complete idea of the massive scale of the place, which is one of the most modern and efficient harbors in the world. Barge tours leave from the main passenger terminal, along with a whole range of ferries and boats heading to other destinations on the Elbe and in the North Sea. There's frequently a breeze here, so it's worth packing something warm, particularly if

Grosse Freiheit, a side street off the Reeperbahn, comes alive at night with crowds looking for a good time.

you're planning on taking an open-top harbor tour. ⊠ *Bei den St. Pauli Landungsbrücken, St. Pauli* Ⓜ *Landungsbrücken (U-bahn and S-bahn).*

FodorsChoice
★

Reeperbahn. The hottest nightspots in town are concentrated on and around St. Pauli's pulsating thoroughfare, the Reeperbahn, and a buzzing little side street known as Grosse Freiheit ("Great Freedom"). It was there, in the early 1960s, that a then-obscure band called the Beatles polished their live act. The Kiez, as the area is known colloquially, is a part of town that never sleeps. It has long been famed for its music halls and drinking holes, but also for its strip clubs, sex shops, and brothels. Street walkers still line Davidstrasse; around the corner, on Herbert-strasse, skimpily dressed women sit in windows and offer their services to passersby. The Kiez is about more than just its red-light activities, however, and the Reeperbahn swells on evenings and weekends with bar hoppers and nightclubbers, concert- and theatergoers, and locals and out-of-towners out for dinner and a few drinks. ⊠ *St. Pauli* Ⓜ *St. Pauli (U-bahn), Reeperbahn (S-bahn).*

Rickmer Rickmers. This majestic 19th-century sailing ship once traveled as far as Cape Town. Now it's permanently docked at Hamburg's piers, where it serves as a museum and site for painting and photography exhibitions. ⊠ *St. Pauli Landungsbrücken Ponton 1a, St. Pauli* ☎ *040/319–5959* ⊕ *www.rickmer-rickmers.de* 🎫 *€5* Ⓜ *Landungsbrücken (U-bahn and S-bahn).*

CLOSE UP

The Beatles in Hamburg

It was on the mean streets of St. Pauli, and specifically Grosse Freiheit, that four young lads from Liverpool cut their teeth playing to frequently hostile crowds of sailors, prostitutes, and thugs before going on to become the biggest band in the world. Signed by Bruno Koschmider, a nightclub owner and entrepreneur of dubious character, the Beatles first arrived in Hamburg in August 1960. Their first gig was at Koschmider's Indra Club, a seedy joint that doubled as a strip club, and their first lodgings consisted of a couple of windowless rooms in the back of a movie theater, the Bambi Kino. Over the next 2½ years, the young Beatles would visit Hamburg five times and play almost 300 concerts in the city. During one stint in 1961, they performed 98 nights in a row, often starting at 8:30 at night and playing their last song around the same time the next morning.

Perhaps surprisingly, some of the venues where the Beatles strutted their stuff remain. The Star Club, the site of their last Hamburg concert, on New Year's Eve 1962, may be gone, but the **Indra Club** is still at Grosse Freiheit 64. Down the road, at No. 36, is the **Kaiserkeller**, where the boys moved after the Indra was closed down for being too rowdy. In addition to hitting the clubs, fans of the Fab Four can pose beside the life-size metal sculptures of the five original Beatles on the **Beatles-Platz,** and also retrace the band's steps on a number of walking tours, which take in the **Bambi Kino** and other venues they played at, along with the **Gretel und Alfons** pub, a favorite haunt.

ST. GEORG

First-time visitors to Hamburg may have some trouble, at least initially, getting their heads around this vibrant quarter. Fanning out to the northeast of the Altstadt, St. Georg is a place whose rich diversity is best understood by trips down its three main streets: Steindamm, Lange Reihe, and An der Alster. Just across the main station, Steindamm begins as a one-way street full of sex shops and prostitutes lurking in doorways and turns into a busy road lined with Middle Eastern restaurants and minimarkets and a large mosque. A few blocks over, in the middle of the three, is Lange Reihe, a long, narrow thoroughfare brimming with gay and lesbian bars and cafés and some of the best places to drink and eat in town. Lastly, a short walk from Lange Reihe to the outer Alster lake's edge, sits An der Alster and a row of luxury hotels and penthouse apartments that come with million-euro views.

GETTING HERE AND AROUND
The closest station for U-bahn and S-bahn trains is Hauptbahnhof, and the No. 6 bus runs the length of Lange Reihe. St. Georg is compact, making it easy enough to stroll around.

SPEICHERSTADT AND HAFENCITY

No two places in Hamburg embody the changing commerce of the city and its love affair with the Elbe as vividly as the harbor districts of the Speicherstadt and the HafenCity. Built around a series of narrow canals, the stunning redbrick, Gothic architecture of the former's warehouses (which make up the largest complex of integrated warehouses in the world and have recently been named a UNESCO World Heritage site) sits next to the gleaming glass and steel of Europe's largest urban renewal development project. The Speicherstadt's 100-year-old warehouses continue to store and trade in everything from coffee to Oriental carpets, but now count restaurants, museums, and the world's largest model railway amongst their tenants. The HafenCity, meanwhile, has become a popular site for the headquarters of many of the city's largest firms, as well as home to a number of new apartment blocks, hotels and restaurants. Hamburg's new landmark, the impressive Elbphilharmonie concert hall is the jewel in its crown.

GETTING HERE AND AROUND

To get to the Speicherstadt, take the U-bahn to Messberg or Baumwall stations, or walk or bike over from the Altstadt. The HafenCity is served by the city's U4 train line, which stops at the U-bahn stations of Überseequartier and HafenCity Universität. Both areas are close enough to each other to walk between.

Elbphilharmonie (*Elbe Philharmonic Hall*). Hamburg's new landmark (and tallest building) is an impressive merger between the distinctive northern redbrick architecture and a modern glass facade. The Elbphilharmonie, or Elphi as the locals call it, sits on top of an old warehouse building and its wavelike rooftop, resembling a hoisted sail or quartz crystal can be from seen miles away. Inside are two concert halls, a hotel, and residential apartments, in addition to the public viewing area (Plaza) that extends around the whole building, offering spectacular 360-degree views of the city and harbor and has proved to be so popular that it requires a timed entry ticket, which is free if booked in person but has a fee if reserved in advance. The public waited nine years for what is now considered one of the largest and most acoustically advanced concert halls in the world. ⊠ *Pl. der Deutschen Einheit 1, Speicherstadt* ☎ *040/3576–6666* ⊕ *www.elbphilharmonie.de* ☜ *Plaza free (if booked in person); €2 (online reservation fee)* Ⓜ *Baumwall (U-bahn).*

HafenCity Infocenter Kesselhaus (*HafenCity Information Center*). In an old 19th-century boiler house, this popular information center documents the HafenCity urban development project. In addition to changing photographic and architectural exhibitions, the center also has an impressive 1:500 scale model of the HafenCity. Free two-hour walking and cycling tours of the HafenCity are also available. Tours in English are offered for groups of 10 people or more and can be booked ahead of time on the center's website. ⊠ *Am Sandtorkai 30, Hafen-City* ☎ *040/3690–1799* ⊕ *www.hafencity.com* ☜ *Free* Ⓜ *Baumwall (U-bahn), Überseequartier (U-bahn).*

Check out HafenCity for a look at the Hamburg of the future, a planned development with offices, apartments, restaurants, museums, and entertainment spaces all in one neighborhood.

FAMILY
Fodor's Choice
★

Miniatur Wunderland. You don't need to be a model-railroad enthusiast or a 10-year-old to be blown away by the sheer scale and attention to detail of the Miniatur Wunderland. The largest model railroad in the world features more than 14,000 square feet of little trains click-clacking their way through wonderfully faithful miniature replicas of Hamburg itself as well as foreign towns in Switzerland, Austria, the United States, Italy, and Scandinavia; a new Venice section was added in 2018. Planes land at a little airport; every 15 minutes, day turns into night and hundreds of thousands of LED lights illuminate the trains, buildings, and streets. Unsurprisingly, it's one of Hamburg's most popular attractions, so it's best to book ahead, particularly on weekends and school holidays, when waiting times for entry can stretch to a couple of hours. If you do have to wait, free drinks and ice cream for children, and videos to watch ease the pain. ⊠ *Kehrwieder 2–4, Block D, Speicherstadt* ☎ *040/300–6800* ⊕ *www.miniatur-wunderland.com* 🎫 *€15* ⊗ *Hrs vary; call or check website before setting out* Ⓜ *Baumwall (U-bahn), Messberg (U-bahn).*

Speicherstadtmuseum. An excursion to this little museum, inside an original 19th-century warehouse, gives you a sense of the trade that flowed through the Speicherstadt in its heyday. Sacks of coffee and spices, chests of tea, and scales and mills are scattered throughout the museum, and there is information detailing the history and architecture of the district, as well as historical photographs and diagrams. ⊠ *Am Sandtorkai 36, Speicherstadt* ☎ *040/321–191* ⊕ *www.speicherstadtmuseum. de* 🎫 *€4* ⊗ *Closed Mon. Dec.–Feb.* Ⓜ *Baumwall (U-bahn).*

Spicy's Gewürzmuseum. Hamburg's proud past as Europe's gateway to the world comes to life at the tiny but fascinating Spicy's Gewürzmuseum, where you can smell and touch more than 50 spices. More than 900 objects chronicle five centuries of the once-prosperous spice trade in Hamburg. ✉ *Am Sandtorkai 34, Speicherstadt* ☎ *040/367–989* ⊕ *www. spicys.de* 🎫 *€5* Ⓜ *Baumwall (U-bahn).*

ALTONA AND OTTENSEN

Generally the closer an area is to water in Hamburg, the more desirable a place it is to live. This is particularly true of the borough of Altona and Ottensen, an upscale neighborhood. Bordered by the Elbe, where Altona forms part of the port, and centered on a large domestic and international train station, the area has an allure heightened by a lively shopping boulevard and narrow side streets with bakeries, boutiques, and bars.

Much of this predominantly working-class area has been transformed over the last few decades. Nineteenth-century factories and industrial plants now accommodate cultural centers, movie theaters, offices, and hotels. Despite its increasingly middle-class makeup the quarter remains multicultural, and a large Turkish population continues to live and run all sorts of businesses here. It's a part of Hamburg that in many ways feels separate from the city surrounding it, which is unsurprising given its history. Part of Denmark until 1864, Altona was an independent city as late as 1937, and its stately town hall above the river is a reminder of its distinguished past.

GETTING HERE AND AROUND
The Altona train station, 15 minutes from Hauptbahnhof, is the starting and finishing point for all domestic and international InterCity Express trains that pass through the main station. It's also a stop on a number of local S-bahn lines. The main shopping area surrounds the station.

BLANKENESE AND ELSEWHERE

Thirty or so minutes along the Elbe by car or by S-bahn from the middle of the city lies the lovely riverside suburb of Blankenese. It's nicely situated on the side of a hill, with steep flights of narrow steps that snake between its handsome villas. It makes a popular destination for weekend walks and coffee and cake afterward.

Other parts of town within easy reach of the main station, and worth a visit, include the upscale neighborhood of Eppendorf, its more modest, less self-conscious neighbor Eimsbüttel, and the lakeside suburbs of Harvestehude, Winterhude, and Uhlenhorst.

Farther afield are the BallinStadt emigration museum in Veddel and the Neuengamme Concentration Camp.

GETTING HERE AND AROUND
Other than driving, the best way to get to Blankenese and Veddel is to take the S-bahn to their respective stations. Neuengamme is reachable by a combination of S-bahn and bus. The other suburbs are 15 to 30 minutes away from the center of town by U-bahn.

BallinStadt. This museum and family-research center tells the story of European emigration to the United States and elsewhere. The complex on the Elbe island Veddel, completed in 1901, was built by the HAPAG shipping line for its passengers and named after Alfred Ballin, its then general director. To accommodate visitors for several days or months, Ballinstadt featured a hospital, church, music hall, housing, and hotels. For approximately 5 million European emigrants, Hamburg was the "Gateway to the World" between 1850 and 1939. Their experience comes to life with artifacts; interactive displays; detailed reproductions of the buildings (all but one was demolished); and firsthand accounts of oppression in Europe, life in the "city," conditions during the 60-day ocean crossing, and life in their new home. The main draw is the research booths, where you can search the complete passenger lists of all ships that left the harbor. ■**TIP→ Research assistants are available to help locate and track your ancestors.** ⊠ *Veddeler Bogen 2, Veddel* ☎ *040/3197–9160* ⊕ *www.ballinstadt.de* 🎫 *€13* Ⓜ *Veddel (S-bahn).*

Konzentrationslager Neuengamme (*Neuengamme Concentration Camp*). Hamburg is a city of great beauty but also tragedy. On the southeastern edge of the city, between 104,000 and 106,000 people, including children, were held at Neuengamme concentration camp in its years of operation from December 1938 to May 1945. It was primarily a slave-labor camp, not an area focused on extermination, where bricks and weapons were the main products. Neuengamme held German political prisoners, Europeans pushed into servitude, gays, Roma (gypsies), and Jews. Jewish children were the subjects of cruel medical experiments; others worked with their parents or simply grew up in prison. To keep people in line, there were random acts of violence, including executions, and atrocious living conditions. Officials estimate that as many as 43,000 people died at Neuengamme. A memorial opened on the site in 2005. Where the dormitories, dining hall, and hospital once sat, there are low pens filled with large rocks. The main area has exhibits describing working conditions in an actual factory as well as a museum with interactive displays about the prisoner experience. Firsthand accounts, photographs from prisoners, furniture, clothing, and possessions make the experience even more affecting. ⊠ *Jean-Dolidier-Weg 75, Neuengamme* ☎ *040/4281–31500* ⊕ *www. kz-gedenkstaette-neuengamme.de* 🎫 *Free* Ⓜ *KZ-Gedenkstätte, Mahnmal (Bus 227 or 327 from Bergedorf station [S-bahn]).*

FAMILY **Tierpark Hagenbeck** (*Hagenbeck Zoo*). One of the country's oldest and most popular zoos, the Tierpark Hagenbeck was founded in 1907 and is family owned. It was the world's first zoo to let wild animals such as lions, elephants, chimpanzees, and others roam freely in vast, open-air corrals. The **Tropen-Aquarium**, on the same property as the zoo, is like a trip around the world. Detailed re-creations of deserts, oceans, rain forests, and jungles are home to sea life, marvelous birds, fish, exotic mammals, insects, and curious reptiles from almost every continent. ⊠ *Lokstedter Grenzstr. 2, Stellingen* ☎ *040/530–0330* ⊕ *www.hagenbeck.de* 🎫 *Zoo €20; aquarium €14; combination ticket €30* Ⓜ *Hagenbecks Tierpark (U-bahn).*

WHERE TO EAT

Hamburg has plenty of chic restaurants to satisfy the fashion-conscious local professionals, as well as the authentically salty taverns typical of a harbor town. There may not be a huge range of restaurants, but what they serve is delicious.

Prices in the reviews are the average cost of a main course at dinner, or if dinner is not served, at lunch. Use the coordinates (✢ B2) at the end of each listing to locate a site on the corresponding map.

13

WHAT IT COSTS IN EUROS			
	$	$$	$$$	$$$$
AT DINNER	under €15	€15–€20	€21–€25	over €25

ALTSTADT AND NEUSTADT

$$$ **Alt Hamburger Aalspeicher.** The Alt Hamburger Aalspeicher specializes
GERMAN in fish, including Hamburg's famous *Aalsuppe* (a clear broth with a variety of vegetables, seafood, and meat—basically everything that is leftover). Over time the Low German word for everything (*all*) became mistaken for the word for eel (*Aal*), so some restaurants make eel the focus, while others stick with creating their own versions of the soup. **Known for:** 16th-century building; old family recipes; Nikolaifleet canal views. $ *Average main: €25* ✉ *Deichstr. 43, Altstadt* ☎ *040/362–990* ⊕ *www.aalspeicher.de* ☾ *Closed Tues.* Ⓜ *Rödingsmarkt (U-bahn)* ✢ *E6.*

$$$ ✕ **Café Paris.** A slice of Paris in the heart of Hamburg, this turn-of-
FRENCH the-19th-century café's unfailing popularity derives from its superb traditional French fare, which naturally includes steak frites and beef tartare, served by crisply polite staff beneath a tiled art nouveau ceiling. The café's bar is an ideal spot to take in the atmosphere and sample something off the superb wine list until a table becomes free. **Known for:** intimate dining in the salon; breakfast, which is a treat; noisy and busy atmosphere. $ *Average main: €23* ✉ *Rathausstr. 4, Altstadt* ☎ *040/3252–7777* ⊕ *www.cafeparis.net* ▭ *No credit cards* Ⓜ *Rathaus (U-bahn)* ✢ *F5.*

$$$ ✕ **Deichgraf.** Located in an old merchant house decorated with oil paint-
GERMAN ings featuring 19th-century sailing ships, this small and elegant seafood restaurant is a Hamburg classic. It's one of the best places to get traditional dishes such as *Hamburger Pannfisch* (fried catch of the day in a wine-and-mustard sauce) at a very reasonable price. **Known for:** lunch special for under €10; busy weekends (reservations are essential); outdoor summer terrace. $ *Average main: €24* ✉ *Deichstr. 23, Altstadt* ☎ *040/364–208* ⊕ *www.deichgraf-hamburg.de* ☾ *Closed Sun. and Mon.* Ⓜ *Rödingsmarkt (U-bahn)* ✢ *E6.*

$$$$ ✕ **Die Bank.** Venture beyond the grand exterior of this 19th-century
FRENCH bank building and you'll find yourself in an elegant bar and brasserie lighted by opulent chandeliers set in a ceiling supported by handsome black columns. Diners can feast on steaks, goose, and sashimi at

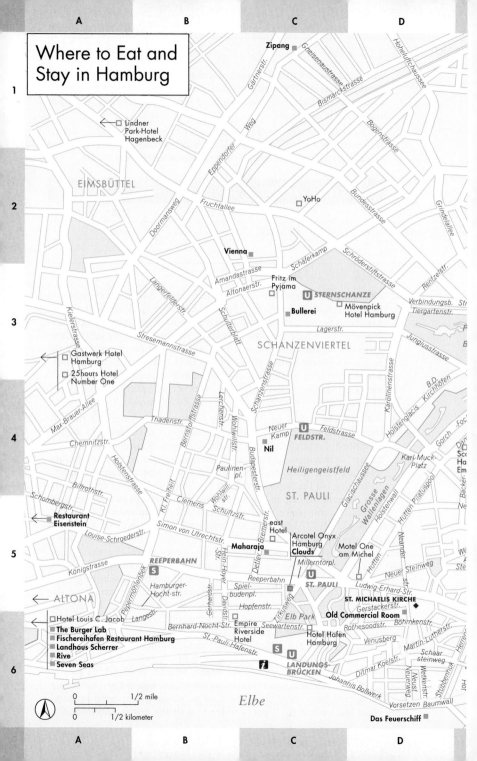

Where to Eat and Stay in Hamburg

A **B** **C** **D**

1

Zipang ▪
Gneisenaustrasse
Gärtnerstr.
Hoheluftchaussee
Bismarckstrasse
Bogenstrasse

□← Lindner
Park-Hotel
Hagenbeck
Weg
Eppendorfer

EIMSBÜTTEL
Fruchtallee
Bundesstrasse
Grindelallee

2
□ YoHo
Doormansweg
Schäferkamp
Langenfelderstr.

Vienna ▪
Amandastrasse
Schröderstiftstrasse
Rentzelstr.
Fritz im
Pyjama
Altonaerstr.
Schulterblatt
U STERNSCHANZE
Verbindungsb. Str

Bullerei ▪
Mövenpick
Hotel Hamburg
Tiergartenstr.

3
Kielerstrasse
Stresemannstrasse
Lagerstr.
SCHANZENVIERTEL
Junghusstrasse
B

□ Gastwerk Hotel
Hamburg
Schanzenstrasse
B.D.
Kirchhöfen

□ 25hours Hotel
Number One
Thadenstr.
Leichenstr.
Bernstorffstrasse
Karolinenstrasse
Holstenglacis. Kirchhöfen
Gorch- Foc

Max-Brauer-Allee
Wohlwillstr.
Gorch- Foc

4
Chemnitzstr.
Paulinen-
pl.
Neuer
Kamp
U
FELDSTR.
Feldstrasse
Karl-Muck-
Platz
Da
Sc
Ha
Em

Nil ▪
Heiligengeistfeld
Glashütte

Billrothstr.
Wohlwill-
str.
ST. PAULI
Grosse
Wallanlagen
Holstenwall
Backer
Ne

Schombergstr.
Kl. Freiheit
Clemens
Schultzstr.
Hütten Pilatuspool

←▪ Restaurant
Eisenstein
Simon von Utrechtstr.
east
Hotel
Hütten

5
Louise-Schroederstr.
Hein-Hoyer-
Str.
Detlev
Bremerstr.
Maharaja ▪
Arcotel Onyx
Hamburg
Clouds
Neander
Motel One
am Michel
Neuer Steinweg
We
Ste

Königstrasse
REEPERBAHN
S
Millerntorpl.
U
ST. PAULI
Ludwig-Erhard-Str.

← ALTONA
Hamburger-
Hocht-str.
Reeperbahn
Spiel-
buden-
pl.
ST. MICHAELIS KIRCHE ◆
Old Commercial Room

□ Hotel Louis C. Jacob
Peperm.öhlenbek
Langestr.
Gerhardstr.
Davidstr.
Hopfenstr.
Trikusweg
Elb Park
Rothesoodstr.
Böhmkenstr.
Venusberg
Gerstackerstr.
Martin-Luther-Str.

▪ The Burger Lab
▪ Fischereihafen Restaurant Hamburg
▪ Landhaus Scherrer
▪ Rive
▪ Seven Seas
Bernhard-Nocht-Str.
St.-Pauli-Hafenstr.
Empire
Riverside
Hotel
Seewartenstr.
Hotel Hafen
Hamburg
S
U

6
LANDUNGS-
BRÜCKEN
i
Johannis Bollwerk
Ditmar Koel-str.
Schaar
steinweg
Werkhenstr.
Neust.
Neuerweg
Stubbenhuk
Here

Elbe
Das Feuerschiff ▪
Vorsetzen Baumwall

0 ——— 1/2 mile
0 ——— 1/2 kilometer

A **B** **C** **D**

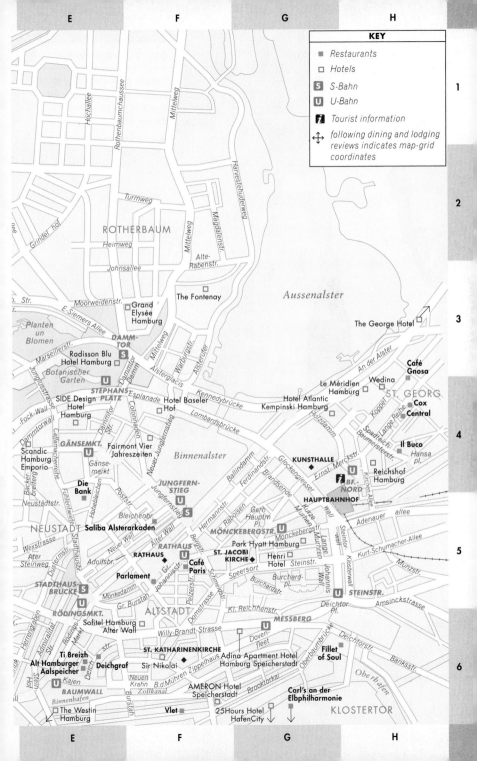

KEY

- ■ Restaurants
- □ Hotels
- **S** S-Bahn
- **U** U-Bahn
- **i** Tourist information
- ↔ following dining and lodging reviews indicates map-grid coordinates

E   **F**   **G**   **H**

1
2
3
4
5
6

ROTHERBAUM
Heimweg
Turmweg
Johnsallee
Hochallee
Rothenbaumchaussee
Mittelweg
Magdalenstr.
Harvestehuderweg
Alte-Rabenstr.

Aussenalster

The Fontenay

The George Hotel

Grand Elysée Hamburg

Moorweidenstr.
E-Siemers Allee
Str.
Grindel hof

Planten un Blomen

DAMM-TOR **S**

Radisson Blu Hotel Hamburg **S**
Marseillerstr.
Jungiusstrasse
Botanischer Garten **U**
STEPHANS-PLATZ **U**
SIDE Design Hotel Hamburg

Café Gnosa

Le Méridien Hamburg
Wedina
ST. GEORG
Cox
Central
Koppel
Lange Reihe

Hotel Atlantic
Kempinski Hamburg

Il Buco
Hansa pl.

Reichshof Hamburg

Hotel Baseler Hof
Mittelweg
Warburgstr.
Alsteruter
Kennedybrücke
Lombardsbrücke
Esplanade
Colonnaden
Dammtor Damm
Alsterglacis

GÄNSEMKT. **U**
Gänse-markt
Fairmont Vier Jahreszeiten
Binnenalster
Ballindamm
Ferdinandstr.
Brandsende
Glockengiesser
Ernst-Merckstr.
Kirchen Allee
Spadteich
Baumeisterstr.
Holzdamm
An der Alster

Scandic Hamburg Emporio
Bäcker-breitergang
Caffamacherreihe
Fuhlentwiete
Neustädtstr.
Die Bank
Hohe Bleichen
Poststr.
Neuer Wall
Neuer Jungfernstieg
JUNGFERN-STIEG **S**
Jungfernstieg

KUNSTHALLE ♦
i BF.-NORD
HAUPTBAHNHOF

NEUSTADT
Wexstrasse
Alter Steinweg
Adolfsbr.
Stadthausbr.
Dammtorwall
Saliba Alsterarkaden
Bleichenbr.
Alter Wall
Bergstr.
Hermannstr.
Raboisen
Gerh Hauptm Pl.
MÖNCKEBERGSTR.
Mönckebergstr.
Kurze Mühren
Lange Mühren
Steintor-wall
Steintor-wall
Adenauer allee
Kurt-Schumacher-Allee
Munzstr.

Park Hyatt Hamburg
ST. JACOBI KIRCHE ♦
Henri Hotel
Steinstr.
Burchard-pl.
Johannis Wall
Klosterwall
STEINSTR. **U**
Amsinckstrasse

RATHAUS **U**
Café Paris
Parlament
RATHAUS
Gr. Johannisstr.
Pelzerstr.
Speersort
Burchardstr.
Kl. Reichnstr.
Domstrasse

STADTHAUS-BRÜCKE **S U**
RÖDINGSMKT. **U**
Herrengraben
Stadthausbr.
Düsternstr.
Gr. Burstah
Mönkedamm
Deichtor Pl.
Oberbaumbrücke
MESSBERG
Deichtorstr.
Fillet of Soul
Bankstr.

ALTSTADT
Sofitel Hamburg Alter Wall
Willy-Brandt-Strasse
Dovenfleet **U**

Ti Breizh
Alt Hamburger Aalspeicher
Deichgraf
Deichstr.
ST. KATHARINENKIRCHE
Sir Nikolai ♦
Zippelhaus
Adina Apartment Hotel Hamburg Speicherstadt
B.D.Mühren
Brooktorkai

BAUMWALL **U**
Kajen
Admiralität
Neuen Krahn
Steinhöft
Binnenhafen
Zollkanal
Bei den Mühren
Burstah
AMERON Hotel Speicherstadt

The Westin Hamburg
Vlet
25Hours Hotel HafenCity ↓
Carl's an der Elbphilharmonie
Oberhafen
KLOSTERTOR

E   **F**   **G**   **H**

DID YOU KNOW?

You can get a great view of
the Rathaus and a bite to eat
at one of the cafés that line
the Rathausmarkt.

white-clothed tables or out on the restaurant's spacious, sunny terrace. **Known for:** traditional dishes with a modern twist; freshly squeezed juices; great cocktail bar. [$] *Average main: €32* ⊠ *Hohe Bleichen 17, Neustadt* ☎ *040/238–0030* ⊕ *www.diebank-brasserie.de* ⊘ *Closed Sun.* Ⓜ *Gänsemarkt (U-bahn)* ✣ *E4.*

$$$
GERMAN
Fodor's Choice
★

✕ **Fillet of Soul.** The art of fine contemporary European cuisine is on display at this hip, yet casual restaurant set among the modern art exhibits of the Deichtorhallen. The minimalist dining room fills rapidly for lunch and dinner every day, its guests drawn to dishes that use fresh, organic produce such as baked cod with quinoa and spinach cream. **Known for:** small but excellent menu; open kitchen; great value lunch. [$] *Average main: €24* ⊠ *Deichtorstr. 2, Altstadt* ☎ *040/7070–5800* ⊕ *www.fillet-of-soul.de* ⊘ *Closed Mon. No dinner Sun.* Ⓜ *Steinstrasse (U-bahn)* ✣ *H6.*

$$$
GERMAN

Old Commercial Room. Just opposite St. Michaelis Kirche, this is one of Hamburg's most traditional and best-loved restaurants, in existence since 1795. Book a table in one of its cozy booths to sample a local specialty such as *Labskaus* (a curious mixture of potato, corned beef, beet, and herring) or Altona Lobster Soup. **Known for:** daily fresh fish; seating on three levels (not wheelchair-accessible); extensive wine list. [$] *Average main: €21* ⊠ *Englische Planke 10, Neustadt* ☎ *040/366–319* ⊕ *www.oldcommercialroom.de* Ⓜ *Rödingsmarkt (U-bahn), Stadthausbrücke (S-bahn)* ✣ *D5.*

$$$
GERMAN

✕ **Parlament.** Snugly sited beneath vaulted ceilings in the cellar of the city's town hall, this elegant old pub turned restaurant and cocktail bar serves no-nonsense meat and seafood meals, including shrimp fresh from the North Sea, with a light touch of German nouvelle cuisine. Popular with local businesspeople during and after work, it's also a nice spot for a frothy beer and some *Flammkuchen*, Alsace's take on pizza, between traipsing around the nearby sights. **Known for:** historical setting; inexpensive two-course business lunch; hangout for politicians. [$] *Average main: €24* ⊠ *Rathausmarkt 1, Altstadt* ☎ *040/7038–3399* ⊕ *www.parlament-hamburg.de* ⊘ *Closed Sun.* Ⓜ *Rathaus (U-Bahn)* ✣ *F5.*

$$$
MIDDLE EASTERN

✕ **Saliba Alsterarkaden.** On the edge of a canal and beneath the arches of the elegant Alster arcade, this popular Syrian meze restaurant enjoys superb views of Hamburg's town hall. While it specializes in lamb, including homemade lamb sausages, Saliba's menu also caters to vegetarian and vegan diners with offerings of falafel and eggplant dishes. **Known for:** canalside tables; red wines from Lebanon; Damascene bakery desserts. [$] *Average main: €21* ⊠ *Neuer Wall 13, Neustadt* ☎ *040/345–021* ⊕ *www.saliba.de* Ⓜ *Jungfernstieg (U-bahn and S-bahn)* ✣ *F5.*

$
FRENCH
Fodor's Choice
★

✕ **Ti Breizh.** Stepping into this 18th-century merchant's house turned Breton crepe restaurant, with its sky-blue window frames and waitstaff in striped fishermen's shirts, is a little like being transported to a seaside eatery in northern France. Ti Breizh wows with fantastically good galettes (buckwheat crepes) topped with ham, cheese, mushrooms, and fried eggs, and its caramelized apple, banana, almond, and vanilla ice-cream crepe is worth a visit alone. **Known for:** sweet buckwheat crepes;

13

mostly French staff; pontoon terrace in summer. $ *Average main: €10* ✉ *Deichstr. 39, Altstadt* ☎ *040/3751–7815* ⊕ *www.tibreizh.de* Ⓜ *Röd-ingsmarkt (U-bahn), Baumwall (U-bahn)* ✛ *E6.*

ST. PAULI AND SCHANZENVIERTEL

$$$$
STEAKHOUSE

✕ **Bullerei.** The success of this extremely popular café and restaurant derives from its celebrity-chef ownership—Tim Mälzer, an old friend of Jamie Oliver, is a regular TV presence—its location in a former livestock hall in the heart of the Schanze, and its heavy emphasis on quality cuts of meat. Every night, the busy but friendly waitstaff ferry large plates of steak and pork through an interior of exposed brickwork and pipes, while diners dig into bowls of lamb, pork, and veal Bolognese in the white-tiled "deli" next door. **Known for:**

> ### CAFÉ CULTURE
>
> The area around the Alster lakes and the canals is dotted with small restaurants with outside dining and an excellent selection of wine. They make good places to discover a refreshing *Grauburgunder* (Pinot Gris) while watching swans glide on the canal waters, sample classic French fare, or sip a perfect cup of coffee at one of the cafés sprinkled throughout central Hamburg.

popular lunch at on-site deli; steaks (T-bone, porterhouse, and flank steak); rustic interior with comic-like paintings. $ *Average main: €27* ✉ *Lagerstr. 34 B, Schanzenviertel* ☎ *040/3344–2100* ⊕ *www.bullerei. com* Ⓜ *Sternschanze (U-bahn and S-bahn)* ✛ *C3.*

$$$$
INTERNATIONAL

✕ **Clouds.** Hamburg's highest restaurant and bar awaits you on the 23rd floor of the "Tanzende Türme" (Dancing Towers) scycrapers, dazzling with floor-to-ceiling views over the city, excellent cocktails, and creative crossover cuisine. The culinary focus here is on a variety of different steaks and cuts of meat. **Known for:** open kitchen; Italian and Asian delicacies; innovative desserts. $ *Average main: €37* ✉ *Reeperbahn 1, St. Pauli* ☎ *040/3099–3280* ⊕ *www.clouds-hamburg.de* ☾ *No lunch weekends* Ⓜ *St. Pauli (U-bahn)* ✛ *C5.*

$
INDIAN

✕ **Maharaja.** Such is the popularity of this occasionally hectic little Indian restaurant in the heart of St. Pauli that a table booking doesn't always mean you'll be seated at the time you booked, especially if it's the weekend. The high quality of its vegetable and meat dishes—Himalayan *kofta* (vegetables and cheese mixed into balls and served with a tomato, cashew nut, and fruit sauce) and *rogan josh* (lamb cooked with red onions, peppers, and paneer) among them—combined with the coziness of its shabby-chic styling is enough to forgive the inconvenience, however. **Known for:** ayurvedic recipes; eating with your hands the Indian way (if you want to); homemade paneer. $ *Average main: €14* ✉ *Detlev-Bremer-Str. 25–27, St. Pauli* ☎ *040/3009–3466* ⊕ *www.maha-raja-hamburg.de* ☾ *No lunch weekends* Ⓜ *St. Pauli (U-bahn)* ✛ *C5.*

$$$
GERMAN

✕ **Nil.** The simple but cool style, excellent service, and high-quality food (seasonal variations using local produce) at this busy bistro keep the locals coming back. Inventive four-course menus merge typical German cuisine with international flavors. **Known for:** modern German dishes; seafood; weekend cooking courses. $ *Average main:*

€22 ✉ Neuer Pferdemarkt 5, St. Pauli ☎ 040/439–7823 🌐 www.restaurant-nil.de 💳 No credit cards 🕐 Closed Tues. No lunch [M] Feldstrasse (U-bahn) ✣ C4.

$$ EUROPEAN Fodor's Choice ★ 🍴 **Vienna.** The kitchen at this much-loved little bistro in Eimsbüttel officially opens for business at 7 pm, but Vienna opens its doors early in the afternoon for those wanting an espresso or apertif from their tiny bar. Early arrivers might still be asked to share a table in the dining room or outside in the courtyard, but given the lovingly prepared sausages, fresh fish dishes, and hearty desserts coming out of the kitchen, it will matter little to most. **Known for:** people drinking aperitifs while queuing; only 10 tables; Wiener schnitzel. [$] *Average main: €18 ✉ Fettstr. 2, Eimsbüttel ☎ 040/439–9182 🌐 www.vienna-hamburg.de 💳 No credit cards 🕐 Closed Mon. No lunch [M] Christuskirche (U-bahn) ✣ C2.*

13

ST. GEORG

$ GERMAN 🍴 **Café Gnosa.** A stalwart of Hamburg's gay and lesbian neighborhood, this local favorite is probably best known for its friendly service and outrageously good cakes—spiced apple; rhubarb; and Black Forest gâteau among them—that are baked on-site in the café's own Konditorei. Beyond its sweet treats, the café whips up solid German breakfasts of bread rolls with smoked salmon and herring or cold cuts and cheeses and has a dependable if somewhat unexciting lunch and dinner menu. **Known for:** delicious desserts and cakes; breakfast treats; occasional drag performances. [$] *Average main: €11 ✉ Lange Reihe 93, St. Georg ☎ 040/243–034 💳 No credit cards [M] Lohmühlenstrasse (U-bahn), Gurlittstrasse (Bus M6) ✣ H3.*

$$$ MODERN EUROPEAN 🍴 **Central.** Aptly situated in the middle of St. Georg's main drag, this trendy yet friendly eatery justifies a visit for its good-size yet varied menu that includes the likes of teriyaki steak and wasabi burgers and homemade gnocchi with mushrooms, sage butter, and apple chutney. All the meat and fish served here is organic, and the Mediterranean-style vegetarian dishes are prepared with seasonal produce. **Known for:** minimalist decor; late-night food; outdoor tables on the sidewalk. [$] *Average main: €22 ✉ Lange Reihe 50, St. Georg ☎ 040/2805–3704 🌐 www.central-hamburg.de 🕐 No lunch weekends [M] Gurlittstrasse (Bus M6), Hauptbahnhof (U-bahn and S-Bahn) ✣ H4.*

$$$ GERMAN 🍴 **Cox.** Cox has delighted guests with its nouvelle German cuisine for years, and with a cool, dark interior and red-leather banquettes reminiscent of a French brasserie, it remains one of the hippest places around. Friday and Saturday night sees its two large rooms swell with diners, and consequently service can slow a little. **Known for:** steamed catfish fillet with mussel tartare; innovative desserts; stylish yet relaxed atmosphere. [$] *Average main: €22 ✉ Lange Reihe 68/Greifswalder Str. 43, St. Georg ☎ 040/249–422 🌐 www.restaurant-cox.de 💳 No credit cards 🕐 No lunch weekends [M] Gurlittstrasse (Bus M6), Hauptbahnhof (U-bahn and S-Bahn) ✣ H4.*

$$ ITALIAN 🍴 **Il Buco.** Hidden down a side street off Hansaplatz, this neighborhood favorite is easily missed, but it's worth seeking out for its excellent plates of *vitello tonnato* (cold sliced veal with a creamy tuna sauce), *saltimbocca* (marinated veal with prosciutto and herbs), and truffle

pasta. The restaurant's intimate atmosphere, similar to grandmother's living room, extends beyond the candlelight and banquette seating to the amicable staff and spoken menu, which features many of the filling and comforting pasta, meat, and fish dishes typical of rustic Italian cuisine. **Known for:** personable service; small, cozy dining room; delicious desserts, especially the tiramisu. [$] *Average main: €18* ✉ *Zimmerpforte 5, St. Georg* ☎ *040/247–310* 🌐 *www.ristoranteilbuco.juisyfood.com* 💳 *No credit cards* 🕒 *Closed Sun. and Mon. No lunch* [M] *Hauptbahnhof (U-bahn and S-bahn)* ✥ *H4.*

SPEICHERSTADT AND HAFENCITY

$$$$ FRENCH

🍴 **Carl's an der Elbphilharmonie.** This extension of the Hotel Louis C. Jacob consists of a relaxed Bistro restaurant that serves quiche, tartines, and other small dishes, and a more formal Brasserie that boasts a large bay window with excellent views of ships gliding up the Elbe. The French menu has touches of German flavors, and local seafood. **Known for:** warm and knowledgeable service; classic French and north German cuisine; three-course preconcert menu. [$] *Average main: €27* ✉ *Am Kaiserkai 69, HafenCity* ☎ *40/3003–22400* 🌐 *www.carls-brasserie.de* [M] *Baumwall (U-bahn)* ✥ *G6.*

$$$ EUROPEAN

🍴 **Das Feuerschiff.** This bright-red lightship served in the English Channel before it retired to the city harbor in 1989 and became a landmark restaurant, guesthouse, and pub. Local favorites such as Hamburger *Pannfisch* (panfried fish with mustard sauce) and *Labskaus* (a mixture of corned beef, potato, onion, beet, and gherkins) are on the ship's extensive menu, along with Argentine steaks and rack of lamb. **Known for:** live Jazz on Monday evening; Sunday breakfast buffet; views of Elbphilharmonie and Hamburg port. [$] *Average main: €24* ✉ *City Sporthafen, Vorsetzen, Speicherstadt* ☎ *040/362–553* 🌐 *www.das-feuerschiff.de* [M] *Baumwall (U-bahn)* ✥ *D6.*

$$$$ GERMAN

🍴 **Vlet.** Much like its setting inside a Speicherstadt warehouse, where exposed bricks and beams are offset by sleek furniture and lighting, Vlet's menu blends traditional German methods with new techniques. The kitchen offers two tasting menus that can be accompanied by corresponding glasses of wine, and the permanent "Vlet Classics" menu, which includes beef tartare prepared at the table. **Known for:** formal service; North German cheese selection; twist on old Hamburg favorites like Labskaus. [$] *Average main: €26* ✉ *Am Sandtorkai 23/24, Speicherstadt* ✥ *Entrance at Kibbelstegbrücke* ☎ *040/3347–53750* 🌐 *www.vlet.de* 🕒 *Closed Sun. No lunch* [M] *Überseequartier (U-bahn)* ✥ *F6.*

ALTONA AND OTTENSEN

$ BURGER
Fodor's Choice ★

🍴 **The Burger Lab.** Somewhat ironically, for a long time it was very hard to find a decent hamburger in Hamburg; however, this small restaurant sandwiched between the Schanzenviertel and Altona is perhaps the best of the newly sprouted burger joints. Set up by two Germans and a Kiwi, The Burger Lab grinds the beef for its gourmet burgers as well as whipping up their own excellent sauces, which include chipotle aioli and burned onion cream **Known for:** outside dining in summer;

lamb burgers and sweet potato fries; no reservations. [$] *Average main: €9* ✉ *Max-Brauer-Allee 251, Altona* ☎ *040/4149–4529* 🌐 *www.theburgerlab.de* 💳 *No credit cards* [M] *Sternbrücke (Bus 3, 15, 602)* ✣ *A6.*

$$$$ SEAFOOD 🍴 **Fischereihafen Restaurant Hamburg.** For some of the best fish in Hamburg, book a table at this splendid portside restaurant, which looks plain from the outside, but feels like a dining room aboard a luxury liner inside. The menu changes daily according to what's available in the fish market that morning; the elegant oyster bar here is a favorite with the city's beau monde. **Known for:** great views of the Elbe from the sun terrace; oil paintings of nautical scenes on the walls; imperial caviar. [$] *Average main: €36* ✉ *Grosse Elbstr. 143, Altona* ☎ *040/381–816* 🌐 *www.fischereihafenrestaurant.de* [M] *Altona (S-bahn), Dockland (Fischereihafen) (Bus No. 111)* ✣ *A6.*

$$$$ GERMAN Fodor's Choice ★ 🍴 **Landhaus Scherrer.** A proud owner of a Michelin star since it opened its doors in 1978, Landhaus Scherrer continues to be one of the city's best-known and most celebrated restaurants. The focus is on the use of organic, sustainable ingredients to produce classic and modern German cuisine with international touches, and unsurprisingly, the accompanying wine list is exceptional. **Known for:** Vierländer duck; parklike setting; on-site bistro for similar fare at lower prices. [$] *Average main: €40* ✉ *Elbchaussee 130, Ottensen* ☎ *040/8830–70030* 🌐 *www.landhausscherrer.de* 🕑 *Closed Sun.* [M] *Hohenzollernring (Bus Nos. M15 and 36)* ✣ *A6.*

$ ITALIAN 🍴 **Restaurant Eisenstein.** A long-time neighborhood favorite, Eisenstein sits inside a handsome 19th-century industrial complex turned art center and serves fantastic Italian and Mediterranean cuisine at affordable prices. Sharing space with a movie theater, the restaurant is popular with pre- and postmovie crowds and probably best known for its gourmet wood-fired pizzas like the Pizza Helsinki (salmon, crème fraîche, and onions) and the Blöde Ziege (Stupid Goat) with rosemary-tomato sauce, crispy bacon, and goat cheese. **Known for:** modern, international cuisine; popular with artists and movie industry people; high ceilings and brick walls invoking rustic charm. [$] *Average main: €14* ✉ *Friedensallee 9, Ottensen* ☎ *040/390–4606* 🌐 *www.restaurant-eisenstein.de* 💳 *No credit cards* [M] *Altona (S-bahn)* ✣ *A5.*

$$$$ SEAFOOD 🍴 **Rive.** It would be difficult to find a better spot in town than this handsome seafood restaurant to watch big boats cruise by while satisfying your appetite for fresh lobster, sashimi, bouillabaisse, Scottish salmon, Dover sole, and oysters. Its ample sun terrace sits just above the Elbe, while the large open-plan dining room has ceiling-high windows facing downstream toward the city and the Elbe Philharmonic Hall. **Known for:** flavorsome seafood and grilled meats; great value two- and three-course lunch options; excellent service. [$] *Average main: €27* ✉ *Kreuzfahrt-Center, Van-der-Smissen Str. 1, Altona* ☎ *040/380–5919* 🌐 *www.rive.de* [M] *Königstrasse (S-bahn), Dockland (Fischereihafen) (Bus No. 111)* ✣ *A6.*

BLANKENESE AND ELSEWHERE

$$$$
EUROPEAN
Fodor'sChoice
★

✕ **Seven Seas.** With a couple of Michelin stars, Karlheinz Hauser—one of Europe's premier chefs at the helm—and a spot high on a hill overlooking the Elbe, this restaurant of the Süllberg Hotel literally and figuratively is a cut above the competition. Dishes can only be ordered in five- to eight-course set menus, and the full degustation menu features scallops with Imperial caviar and Iberian pork with oysters and accompanying glasses of wine. **Known for:** elegant, Hanseatic interior; exclusive wines by the glass; expensive but outstanding dining. $ *Average main: €165* ✉ *Süllbergsterrasse 12, Blankenese* ☎ *040/866–2520* ⊕ *www.karlheinzhauser.de* ☾ *Closed Mon. and Tues. No lunch* Ⓜ *Blankenese (S-bahn), Kahlkamp (Bus No. 48)* ✛ *A6.*

$$$
JAPANESE

✕ **Zipang.** Hamburg may not have many good Japanese restaurants, but this modern bistro-style restaurant has developed a loyal clientele of locals and Japanese expats through its warm service and modern interpretation of Japanese haute cuisine. As well as the typical offerings of sushi and tempura udon, the menu here features such treats as wagyu beef with dipping sauces and duck and eggplant in red miso sauce. **Known for:** reasonably priced lunch; Japanese/German fusion cuisine; rare Koshu-grape wines. $ *Average main: €23* ✉ *Eppendorfer Weg 171, Eppendorf* ☎ *040/4328–0032* ⊕ *www.zipang.de* ☾ *Closed Sun. and Mon.* Ⓜ *Hoheluftbrücke (U-bahn)* ✛ *C1.*

WHERE TO STAY

Hamburg has simple pensions as well as five-star luxury enterprises. Nearly year-round conference and convention business keeps most rooms booked well in advance, and the rates are consistently high during the week. But many of the more expensive hotels lower their rates on weekends, when businesspeople have gone home. The tourist office can help with reservations if you arrive with nowhere to stay. In Hamburg, independent hotels may not have coffeemakers or an information book in the guest rooms, but, in general, you will find generously sized rooms and staff willing to answer questions about the hotel. Hotels without business centers will fax and copy for you. At hotels without concierges, front-desk staff will whip out a map and give recommendations.

All accommodations offer no-smoking rooms. Although breakfast is not generally included, those who opt for the meal are usually greeted with an all-you-can-eat masterpiece with hot food options that sometimes includes an omelet station.

Keep in mind that you'll probably encounter nudity in coed saunas at most hotels. Also, most double beds are made of two single beds on a large platform and an individual blanket for each mattress.

Prices in the reviews are the lowest cost of a standard double room in high season. For expanded reviews, facilities, and current deals, visit Fodors.com. Use the coordinates (✛ B3) at the end of each listing to locate a site on the corresponding map.

	WHAT IT COSTS IN EUROS			
	$	$$	$$$	$$$$
FOR TWO PEOPLE	under €100	€100–€175	€176–€225	over €225

ALTSTADT AND NEUSTADT

$$$$ HOTEL Fodor's Choice ★ **Fairmont Vier Jahreszeiten.** Some claim that this beautiful 19th-century town house on the edge of the Binnenalster is the best hotel in Germany. **Pros:** luxury hotel with great view of Alster lakes; close to shopping on Jungfernstieg; large, charming rooms. **Cons:** high prices even in off-season; not much in way of nightlife outside of the hotel; some consider bathrooms too small. [$] *Rooms from: €251* ✉ *Neuer Jungfernstieg 9–14, Neustadt* ☎ *040/34940* 🌐 *www.fairmont.com* 🛏 *156 rooms* 🍴 *No meals* [M] *Jungfernstieg (U-bahn and S-bahn)* ✥ *F4.*

$$$$ HOTEL Fodor's Choice ★ **The Fontenay.** On the shores of Lake Alster and surrounded by a park, this newly built, upscale hotel combines sculptural architecture, a classic yet modern interior, two restaurants, and a rooftop bar with outstanding views. **Pros:** exceptional, friendly service; indoor/outdoor infinity pool on the top floor; first-class dining. **Cons:** in-room technology can be overwhelming; about 20-minute walk from the city center; not much nightlife in vicinity. [$] *Rooms from: €320* ✉ *Fontenay 10, Rotherbaum* ☎ *040/6056–6050* 🌐 *www.thefontenay.de* 🛏 *130 rooms* 🍴 *No meals* [M] *Dammtor (S-bahn)* ✥ *F3.*

$$$ HOTEL **Grand Elysée Hamburg.** The "grand" here refers to its size, from the nearly 11,000-square-foot spa area and five restaurants to the 511 guest rooms and extra-wide beds. **Pros:** large, quiet guest rooms; close to tourist sites; diverse art throughout hotel. **Cons:** rooms' tasteful beiges won't set many hearts racing; public spaces can feel a little cold; no kettle in rooms. [$] *Rooms from: €190* ✉ *Rothenbaumchaussee 10, Altstadt* ☎ *040/414–120* 🌐 *www.grand-elysee.com* 🛏 *511 rooms* 🍴 *No meals* [M] *Dammtor (S-bahn)* ✥ *F3.*

$$ HOTEL **Henri Hotel.** Concealed down a side street not far from the main station, this small boutique hotel, with its retro rooms, furniture, and phones, will undoubtedly please fans of film noir and *Mad Men.* **Pros:** intimate, friendly service; very quiet; excellent house cocktail. **Cons:** may seem a little masculine for some tastes; on an otherwise uninspiring side street; limited nightlife in the area. [$] *Rooms from: €155* ✉ *Bugenhagenstr. 21, Altstadt* ☎ *040/554–3570* 🌐 *www.henri-hotel.com* 🛏 *65 rooms* 🍴 *No meals* [M] *Hauptbahnhof (U-bahn and S-bahn), Mönckebergstrasse (U-bahn)* ✥ *G5.*

$$ HOTEL **Hotel Baseler Hof.** It's hard to find fault with this handsome central hotel near the Binnenalster and the opera house; the service is friendly and efficient, the rooms are neatly albeit plainly furnished, and the prices are reasonable for such an expensive city. **Pros:** directly across from the casino; walking distance from Dammtor train station; complimentary three-day pass for public transport. **Cons:** small rooms; rooms at the front of the hotel face onto a busy street; lobby sometimes crowded

when groups check in. $ *Rooms from: €121* ✉ *Esplanade 11, Neustadt* ☎ *040/359–060* ⊕ *www.baselerhof.de* ⤳ *173 rooms* ⦿ *Breakfast* Ⓜ *Stephansplatz (U-bahn)* ✛ *F4.*

$ 🛏 **Motel One Am Michel.** Perched at the end of the Reeperbahn, this
HOTEL   branch of the Motel One chain is ideal for those looking for a trendy, design-minded, central yet inexpensive base. **Pros:** close to the best nightlife in town; bar open 24 hours; hard-to-beat value for money. **Cons:** no amenities; no restaurant; rooms too small for longer stays. $ *Rooms from: €96* ✉ *Ludwig-Erhard-Str. 26, Altstadt* ☎ *040/3571–8900* ⊕ *www.motel-one.com* ⤳ *437 rooms* ⦿ *No meals* Ⓜ *St. Pauli (U-bahn), Landungsbrücken (U-bahn and S-bahn)* ✛ *D5.*

$$$$ 🛏 **Park Hyatt Hamburg.** Housed within the historic Levantehaus, the Park
HOTEL   Hyatt Hamburg delivers the hospitality and comfort expected of one of Germany's best hotels, with plush beds, marble bathrooms, and peace and quiet. **Pros:** close to museums and shopping; large, quiet rooms with all modern amenities; friendly and helpful service. **Cons:** area can feel dead on Sunday, when all the stores are closed; far from most nightlife; too few power outlets. $ *Rooms from: €237* ✉ *Bugenhagenstr. 8, Neustadt* ☎ *040/3332–1234* ⊕ *park.hyatt.com* ⤳ *283 rooms* ⦿ *No meals* Ⓜ *Mönckebergstrasse (U-bahn)* ✛ *G5.*

$$ 🛏 **Scandic Hamburg Emporio.** Just around the corner from the shopping
HOTEL   district Gänsemarkt and the idyllic Alster River, the Scandic Hamburg Emporio features colorful rooms with wooden floors and large windows. **Pros:** close to city center and main sights; great value for money; good, inexpensive breakfast. **Cons:** some rooms facing main street have noise issues; sterile Scandinavian design is not for everyone; rooms can get hot in summer. $ *Rooms from: €134* ✉ *Dammtorwall 19, Neustadt* ☎ *040/4321870* ⊕ *www.scandichotels.de* ⤳ *340 rooms* ⦿ *No meals* Ⓜ *Gänsemarkt (U-bahn)* ✛ *E4.*

$$$ 🛏 **SIDE Design Hotel Hamburg.** Futuristic, minimalistic—call it what you
HOTEL   like—hip five-star hotel SIDE stands out from the rest of the crowd because of what's on the inside, including a soaring, glass-paneled atrium and sleek, space-age interiors decorated with brightly colored cubes and pebble-shape furniture. **Pros:** rooftop terrace lounge; close to the opera and major sights but a quiet location; inner-city cool. **Cons:** some might find interior design sterile; most guest rooms lack views; no tea and coffee facilities in room. $ *Rooms from: €189* ✉ *Drehbahn 49, Neustadt* ☎ *040/309–990* ⊕ *www.side-hamburg.de* ⤳ *178 rooms* ⦿ *No meals* Ⓜ *Gänsemarkt (U-bahn)* ✛ *E4.*

$$$ 🛏 **Sofitel Hamburg Alter Wall.** Behind the facade of a centrally located,
HOTEL   former Deutsche Post building hides the sleek style and famously comfortable beds of one of the city's finest business hotels. **Pros:** in the historic downtown area; close to luxury shops; large rooms. **Cons:** somewhat cold design; no real nightlife within walking distance; some noise issues due to close tram. $ *Rooms from: €211* ✉ *Alter Wall 40, Altstadt* ☎ *040/369–500* ⊕ *www.sofitel.com* ⤳ *259 rooms* ⦿ *No meals* Ⓜ *Rödingsmarkt (U-bahn)* ✛ *F6.*

ST. PAULI AND SCHANZENVIERTEL

$$ | **Arcotel Onyx Hamburg.** Moored at the start of the Reeperbahn, this
HOTEL | black-glass monolith houses a welcoming design hotel ideal for those who want to just dip their toes into the waters of the red-light district. **Pros:** close to a number of attractions, including St. Michaelis and the harbor; just across from St. Pauli U-bahn; exciting part of town. **Cons:** no real views, even from upper floors; buffet area in breakfast room can get overcrowded; designer furniture and carpets won't be to everyone's taste. $ *Rooms from: €125* ⊠ *Reeperbahn 1 A, St. Pauli* ☎ *040/209–4090* ⊕ *www.arcotelhotels.com* ⟿ *215 rooms* ⦵ *No meals* Ⓜ *St. Pauli (U-bahn)* ✛ *C5.*

$$ | **east Hotel.** Not content to limit itself to merely being a place to sleep,
HOTEL | this chic landmark hotel combines a buzzing cocktail bar with a simi-
Fodor'sChoice | larly trendy sushi and steak restaurant to create one of the hottest
★ | spots in town. **Pros:** unique design and atmosphere; popular nightclub on fourth floor (Friday and Saturday only); excellent service. **Cons:** area around the hotel can be frenetic on weekends; parking garage is removed from main building; open bathrooms not for those who prefer privacy. $ *Rooms from: €109* ⊠ *Simon-von-Utrecht-Str. 31, St. Pauli* ☎ *040/309–930* ⊕ *www.east-hamburg.de* ⟿ *129 rooms* ⦵ *No meals* Ⓜ *St Pauli (U-bahn)* ✛ *C5.*

$$ | **Empire Riverside Hotel.** The prime location between the Reeperbahn
HOTEL | and the harbor, the clever use of space and light, and a top-floor cocktail
Fodor'sChoice | joint, 20up, that attracts thousands every weekend make this a favorite
★ | with locals and out-of-towners alike. **Pros:** close to nightlife; excellent views of city and port; contemporary design. **Cons:** a steep hill separates the hotel from the harbor; top-floor bar gets crowded after 9 pm on weekends; staff are polite but not friendly. $ *Rooms from: €139* ⊠ *Bernhard-Nocht-Str. 97, St. Pauli* ☎ *040/311–190* ⊕ *www.empire-riverside.de* ⟿ *327 rooms* ⦵ *No meals* Ⓜ *Reeperbahn (S-bahn)* ✛ *B6.*

$$ | **Fritz im Pyjama.** This little hotel squeezed into an old apartment build-
HOTEL | ing in the center of the Schanzenviertel has been transformed into fun, swinging-'60s-style accommodations. **Pros:** unique, funky accommodations; S- and U-bahn stations directly across the street; myriad eating and drinking options nearby. **Cons:** noise from nearby train tracks; area crowded on weekend nights; difficult to find parking. $ *Rooms from: €118* ⊠ *Schanzenstr. 101–103, Schanzenviertel* ☎ *040/8222–2830* ⊕ *www.fritz-im-pyjama.de* ⟿ *17 rooms* ⦵ *No meals* Ⓜ *Sternschanze (U-bahn and S-bahn)* ✛ *C3.*

$ | **Hotel Hafen Hamburg.** This harbor landmark, just across from the
HOTEL | famous St. Pauli Landungsbrücken and a few streets back from the Reeperbahn, is a great value considering its central location. **Pros:** top location for harbor and St. Pauli sightseeing; in the heart of the city's best nightlife; Port restaurant serves good-quality Hanseatic fare. **Cons:** hotel spread between three separate buildings; a bit of a climb to reach hotel from the pier; no gym. $ *Rooms from: €80* ⊠ *Seewartenstr. 7–9, St. Pauli* ☎ *040/311–130* ⊕ *www.hotel-hafen-hamburg.de* ⟿ *380 rooms* ⦵ *No meals* Ⓜ *Landungsbrücken (U-bahn and S-bahn)* ✛ *C6.*

13

$$ **Mövenpick Hotel Hamburg.** For its Hamburg outpost, the Mövenpick
HOTEL chain transformed a 19th-century water tower on a hill in the middle
of the leafy Schanzenpark into a state-of-the-art hotel. **Pros:** in the
middle of a quiet park; unique building; English-language newspaper
available in restaurant. **Cons:** modern styling will feel a little sterile to
some; some lower-level rooms have ordinary views; "alternative neigh-
borhood". $ *Rooms from: €121* ⊠ *Sternschanze 6, Schanzenviertel*
☎ *040/334–4110* ⊕ *www.movenpick.com* ⮌ *236 rooms* ⧄ *No meals*
Ⓜ *Sternschanze (U-bahn and S-bahn)* ✛ *C3.*

ST. GEORG

$$ **The George Hotel.** At the end of a strip of funky cafés and bars that
HOTEL stretches down from the central station, the George, with its groovy
New British styling and renowned gin and whisky bar, fits right in.
Pros: bar serves some of the best G&Ts in town; DJs play in the hotel
on weekends; afternoon tea at 3. **Cons:** can be noisy, particularly for
guests on the first floor; rooftop bar's lounge music won't be to everyone's taste; no gym. $ *Rooms from: €134* ⊠ *Barcastr. 3, St. Georg*
☎ *040/280–0300* ⊕ *www.thegeorge-hotel.de* ⮌ *125 rooms* ⧄ *No
meals* Ⓜ *Lohmühlenstrasse (U-bahn)* ✛ *H3.*

$$$ **Hotel Atlantic Kempinski Hamburg.** There are few hotels in Germany
HOTEL more sumptuous than this gracious Edwardian palace facing the Aus-
senalster, which draws both celebrities and the not-so-famous search-
ing for a luxe retreat. **Pros:** great views of lakeside skyline; impeccable
service; historic flair. **Cons:** public areas can be crowded; faces onto a
busy thoroughfare; service can be slow. $ *Rooms from: €188* ⊠ *An der
Alster 72–79, St. Georg* ☎ *040/28880* ⊕ *www.kempinski.com* ⮌ *221
rooms* ⧄ *No meals* Ⓜ *Hauptbahnhof (U-bahn and S-bahn)* ✛ *G4.*

$$$ **Le Méridien Hamburg.** This luxury hotel along the Alster oozes beauty
HOTEL inside and out, with contemporary art on view throughout—includ-
ing the elevator. **Pros:** great location with views of the Alster; smartly
designed, large rooms; more than 650 art works decorate the hotel.
Cons: basic gym facilities; top-floor bar and restaurant can be crowded;
rooms a bit dated. $ *Rooms from: €189* ⊠ *An der Alster 52–56, St.
Georg* ☎ *040/21000* ⊕ *www.leroyalmeridienhamburg.com* ⮌ *284
rooms* ⧄ *No meals* Ⓜ *Hauptbahnhof (U-bahn and S-bahn)* ✛ *H4.*

$$ **Reichshof Hamburg.** Opposite the main train station, the completely
HOTEL renovated Reichshof, part of the Hilton Group, blends the so-called
Golden Twenties with present-day elements. **Pros:** very central loca-
tion; one-of-a-kind hotel bar; great breakfast in historic setting. **Cons:**
lack of good views; some rooms on the smaller side; no concierge desk.
$ *Rooms from: €152* ⊠ *Kirchenallee 34–36, St. Georg* ☎ *040/370–
2590* ⊕ *www.reichshof-hotel-hamburg.de* ⮌ *278 rooms* ⧄ *No meals*
Ⓜ *Hauptbahnhof (U-bahn, S-bahn)* ✛ *H4.*

$$ **Wedina.** A laid-back oasis in the bustling neighborhood of St. Georg,
HOTEL the Wedina's red, blue, green, pink, and yellow houses have themes
Fodor'sChoice that include "Tuscany" and "Literature." It's renowned for the famous
★ authors, including J. K. **Pros:** cozy, comfortable, and quiet rooms; free
rental bikes; great breakfast. **Cons:** hotel spread over several buildings;
minimalist furniture; no elevator. $ *Rooms from: €155* ⊠ *Gurlittstr.*

23, St. Georg ☎ 040/280–8900 ⊕ www.hotelwedina.com ⌧ 54 rooms ⦿ Free Breakfast Ⓜ Hauptbahnhof (U-bahn and S-bahn), Gurlittstrasse (Bus No. 6) ✛ H4.

SPEICHERSTADT AND HAFENCITY

$$
HOTEL
▣ **Adina Apartment Hotel Speicherstadt.** These modern, handsome apartments with fully equipped kitchens will appeal to those who appreciate a few home comforts when they travel. **Pros:** kids age 11 and under stay free with parents; home away from home; close to subway station. **Cons:** busy road in front so some noise on lower floors; breakfast area can be crowded; few bar and food options nearby. Ⓢ *Rooms from: €144* ✉ *Willy-Brandt-Str. 25, Speicherstadt* ☎ *040/334–6080* ⊕ *www.adinahotels.com* ⌧ *202 apartments* ⦿ *No meals* Ⓜ *Messberg (U-bahn)* ✛ *G6.*

$$
HOTEL
▣ **AMERON Hotel Speicherstadt.** Paying homage to its history as an office building for coffee traders, the only hotel in the UNESCO-designated Speicherstadt zone combines vintage features like 1950s dial room telephones with modern amenities such as flat-screen TVs, walk-in wardrobe, complimentary minibar, and yacht-style decor. **Pros:** large outdoor terrace on top floor; stunning view from upper floors, spa area, and gym; historic and maritime features throughout. **Cons:** about eight-minute walk to subway station; long corridors of a former office building; small gym. Ⓢ *Rooms from: €148* ✉ *Am Sandtorkai 4, Speicherstadt* ☎ *040/638–5890* ⊕ *www.ameronhotels.com* ⌧ *192 rooms* ⦿ *No meals* Ⓜ *Überseequartier (U-bahn)* ✛ *F6.*

$$
HOTEL
▣ **Sir Nikolai.** Right next to the Nikolaifleet canal on an unassuming, quiet residential street stands this sophisticated boutique hotel. **Pros:** outstanding Japanese/Peruvian restaurant; attention to detail in room design; latest technologies like mood lighting. **Cons:** no balconies, terraces, or any other outdoor space; not much nightlife in vicinity; rooms facing the street lack views. Ⓢ *Rooms from: €146* ✉ *Katharinenstr. 29* ☎ *040/2999–6666* ⊕ *www.sirhotels.com* ⌧ *94 rooms* ⦿ *No meals* Ⓜ *Rödingsmarkt (U-bahn)* ✛ *F6.*

$$
HOTEL
▣ **25Hours Hotel HafenCity.** This trendy HafenCity hotel is full of fun, from guest rooms that resemble designer ship cabins to a chill-out room with retro couches. **Pros:** has a little shop selling magazines and souvenirs; up-and-coming part of town; something outside the norm. **Cons:** quiet, but directly across from a construction site; not a lot of other nightlife options within walking distance; rooms on the smaller side. Ⓢ *Rooms from: €130* ✉ *Überseeallee 5, Speicherstadt* ☎ *040/257–7770* ⊕ *www.25hours-hotels.com* ⌧ *170 rooms* ⦿ *No meals* Ⓜ *Überseequartier (U-bahn)* ✛ *G6.*

$$$$
HOTEL
Fodor's Choice
★
▣ **The Westin Hamburg.** Located inside Hamburg's new landmark, the Elbphilharmonie, the Westin offers lodging on 10 floors soaring above the Elbe River. **Pros:** unique building; perfect hotel when attending Elbphilharmonie concerts; hotel with the most suites in Hamburg. **Cons:** windows can only be opened a tiny bit; not for people uncomfortable with heights; some areas overlooked by tourists visiting the Elbphilharmonie. Ⓢ *Rooms from: €270* ✉ *Pl. der Deutschen Einheit 2, Speicherstadt* ☎ *040/800–0100* ⊕ *www.westinhamburg.com* ⌧ *244 rooms* ⦿ *No meals* Ⓜ *Baumwall (U-bahn)* ✛ *E6.*

ALTONA AND OTTENSEN

$$ ⬚ **Gastwerk Hotel Hamburg.** Proudly dubbing itself Hamburg's first
HOTEL design hotel, the Gastwerk, named after the 120-year-old gasworks
it's housed inside, is certainly one of the most stylish places to stay
in town. **Pros:** complimentary parking; shuttle service to musicals on
Friday and Saturday evenings; friendly, welcoming staff. **Cons:** removed
from downtown area and most sightseeing spots; breakfast room, bar,
and other public spaces can get crowded; some rooms have no exte-
rior windows. ⓢ *Rooms from: €103* ✉ *Beim Alten Gaswerk 3, Altona*
☎ *040/890–620* ⊕ *www.gastwerk.com* ⮐ *141 rooms* ⦿ *No meals*
Ⓜ *Bahrenfeld (S-bahn)* ✛ *A3.*

$ ⬚ **25hours Hotel Number One.** Packing fun and retro design into a
HOTEL relaxed package that includes beanbag chairs, shag carpets, and bold
wallpapers, this is the type of place for travelers seeking something
a bit different. **Pros:** 1960s and '70s retro style sets it apart; shop-
ping center and supermarket nearby; sunset views from roof terrace.
Cons: removed from the city center; a 10-minute walk to the nearest
train station; no on-site spa. ⓢ *Rooms from: €84* ✉ *Paul-Dessau-Str.
2, Altona* ☎ *040/855–070* ⊕ *www.25hours-hotels.com* ⮐ *128 rooms*
⦿ *No meals* Ⓜ *Bahrenfeld (S-bahn)* ✛ *A3.*

BLANKENESE AND ELSEWHERE

$$$ ⬚ **Hotel Louis C. Jacob.** Those who make the effort to travel 20 minutes
HOTEL from the center of town to this small yet luxurious hotel perched above
Fodor's Choice Elbe will gain a mixture of sophistication, Michelin-starred dining, and
★ fine Hanseatic hospitality. **Pros:** outstanding service with attention to
personal requests; quiet, serene setting; extremely comfortable beds.
Cons: lounge is a little stuffy; away from downtown area and most
nightlife, restaurants, and shopping; expensive. ⓢ *Rooms from: €208*
✉ *Elbchaussee 401–403, Blankenese* ☎ *040/8225–5405* ⊕ *www.hotel-
jacob.de* ⮐ *85 rooms* ⦿ *No meals* Ⓜ *Hochkamp (S-bahn)* ✛ *A6.*

$$ ⬚ **Lindner Park-Hotel Hagenbeck.** Inspired by its location right next to
HOTEL the zoo, the hotel features artwork, furnishings, and even aromas from
FAMILY Asia and Africa to create spaces reminiscent of 19th-century safari out-
posts. **Pros:** smartly designed Africa and Asia theme carried throughout
hotel; air-conditioning in guest rooms; great restaurant with Indian
and African dishes. **Cons:** removed from the city center; not much else
going on in the immediate area; aimed at families. ⓢ *Rooms from: €129*
✉ *Hagenbeckstr. 150, Stellingen* ☎ *040/8008–08100* ⊕ *www.lindner.de*
⮐ *134 rooms* ⦿ *No meals* Ⓜ *Hagenbecks Tierpark (U-bahn)* ✛ *A1.*

$$ ⬚ **YoHo.** Housed in a historic villa that's an easy walk from the Schan-
HOTEL zenviertel, this friendly, modern little hotel attracts a young, cosmopoli-
tan crowd, families and business travelers. **Pros:** quiet neighborhood;
reasonable prices without skimping on quality; free parking. **Cons:**
sometimes noisy due to young travelers; removed from all major sights;
small bathrooms. ⓢ *Rooms from: €119* ✉ *Moorkamp 5, Eimsbüttel*
☎ *040/284–1910* ⊕ *www.yoho-hamburg.de* ⮐ *30 rooms* ⦿ *No meals*
Ⓜ *Christuskirche (U-bahn), Schlump (U-bahn)* ✛ *C2.*

NIGHTLIFE AND PERFORMING ARTS

NIGHTLIFE

ALTSTADT AND NEUSTADT
JAZZ AND LIVE MUSIC
Cotton Club. A visit to the Cotton Club, Hamburg's oldest jazz club, is worth it for the house beer alone. Throw in the club's relaxed vibe and nights devoted to jazz, blues, soul, and Dixieland, and it's not difficult to find a reason to drop in. ⊠ *Alter Steinweg 10, Neustadt* ☎ *040/343–878* ⊕ *www.cotton-club.de* Ⓜ *Stadthausbrücke (S-bahn).*

ST. PAULI AND SCHANZENVIERTEL
Whether you think it sexy or seedy, the Reeperbahn and its nightlife defines Hamburg as much as as the upscale department stores and boutiques on Jungfernstieg. St. Pauli's main drag is peppered with bars and clubs, while its most famous side street, Grosse Freiheit, heaves with dance clubs every night of the week. Hans-Elber-Platz also has a cluster of bars, some with live music.

BARS
Unsurprisingly for an area known as an entertainment district, St. Pauli has an enormous spectrum of places to get a drink, from cheap beer-and-shot dive bars to high-rise cocktail joints and everything in between.

Christiansen's. Discreetly positioned on a quiet corner an easy meander down from the Reeperbahn is one of St Pauli's coziest cocktail bars. Inside, red leather stools flank an enormously well-stocked bar staffed by knowledgeable and friendly bartenders. ⊠ *Pinnasberg 60, St. Pauli* ☎ *040/317–2863* ⊕ *www.christiansens.de* Ⓜ *Reeperbahn (S-bahn).*

The Chug Club. Opened in 2015, this cocktail bar is considered one of the best in Germany and firmly rooted in St. Pauli's nightlife. Tequila, in an infinite variety of aromas, flavors, and combinations, is the signature drink served in small glasses, the so-called chugs. ⊠ *Taubenstr. 13, St. Pauli* ☎ *040/3573–5130* Ⓜ *St. Pauli (U-bahn).*

Mandalay. With its fancy cocktails and "reservations recommended" exclusivity, the Mandalay verges on being out of place among the shabby-chic pubs and bars typical of the Schanzenviertel, but its sleek styling and eclectic mix of swing, ambient, and disco nights ensures its enduring popularity. ⊠ *Neuer Pferdemarkt 13, Schanzenviertel* ☎ *040/4321–4922* ⊕ *www.mandalay-hamburg.de* Ⓜ *Feldstrasse (U-bahn).*

Tower Bar at Hotel Hafen Hamburg. Facing stiff competition from a number of newly opened and similarly loftily perched cocktail joints, the Tower Bar may have aged a tad since its opening in 1987, but its service, reasonably priced drinks, and views over the harbor and city all remain good reasons to reserve a window table for a sundowner or two. ⊠ *Seewartenstr. 9, St. Pauli* ☎ *040/31113–70450* ⊕ *www.hotel-hafenhamburg.de* Ⓜ *Landungsbrücken (U-bahn and S-bahn).*

20up at the Empire Riverside Hotel. For a smooth cocktail, cool lounge music, and jaw-droppingly good views over the city and harbor, try this bar, which is one of the most popular nightspots in town. It's best to book ahead, particularly on weekends. ⊠ *Empire Riverside Hotel, Bernhard-Nocht-Str. 97, St. Pauli* ☏ *040/31119–70470* ⊕ *www.empireriverside.de* Ⓜ *Reeperbahn (S-bahn).*

Yakshi's Bar at the east Hotel. With its combination of exposed brickwork, soft lighting, and soothing, curvy shapes—not to mention a drinks menu that runs to more than 250 different drinks, shots, and cocktails—it's little wonder that this popular cocktail bar draws fashionable people of all ages. ⊠ *east Hotel, Simon-von-Utrecht-Str. 31, St. Pauli* ☏ *040/309–930* ⊕ *www.east-hamburg.de* Ⓜ *St. Pauli (U-bahn).*

CABARET THEATER
Schmidt Theater and Schmidts Tivoli. The quirky Schmidt Theater and Schmidts Tivoli has become Germany's most popular variety theater, presenting a classy repertoire of live music, vaudeville, and cabaret. ⊠ *Spielbudenpl. 27–28, St. Pauli* ☏ *040/3177–8899* ⊕ *www.tivoli.de* Ⓜ *Reeperbahn (S-bahn), St. Pauli (U-bahn).*

DANCE CLUBS
Mojo Club. After changing locations, the storied Mojo Club has been reborn and is now located beneath a spaceship-like hatch, which rises out of the sidewalk to allow in revelers who come to see live local and international acts, as well as DJs spinning jazz, funk, soul, and electronic beats. ⊠ *Reeperbahn 1, St. Pauli* ☏ *040/319–1999* ⊕ *www.mojo.de* Ⓜ *St. Pauli (U-bahn), Reeperbahn (S-bahn).*

JAZZ AND LIVE MUSIC
Docks. There's a stylish bar here, as well as one of Hamburg's largest venues for live music acts from around the world. Once the stage has been cleared, techno and house parties keep Docks rocking late into the night. ⊠ *Spielbudenpl. 19, St. Pauli* ☏ *040/317–8830* ⊕ *www.docksprinzenbar.de* Ⓜ *St. Pauli (U-bahn), Reeperbahn (S-bahn).*

Grosse Freiheit 36. One of the best-known nightspots in town, Grosse Freiheit 36 has made its name as both a popular venue for big names from around the world and as the location of the **Kaiserkeller,** a nightclub where the Beatles once played that's still going strong. ⊠ *Grosse Freiheit 36, St. Pauli* ☏ *040/317–7780* ⊕ *www.grossefreiheit36.de* Ⓜ *Reeperbahn (S-bahn), St. Pauli (U-bahn).*

Indra Club. The Beatles' first stop on the road to fame was the Indra Club. The club's owner, Bruno Koschmider, asked for one thing, and that was a wild show. These days, the Indra is still a nightclub, with live music acts nearly every night. ⊠ *Grosse Freiheit 64, St. Pauli* ⊕ *www.indraclub64.de* Ⓜ *Reeperbahn (S-bahn), St. Pauli (U-bahn).*

PUBS
Altes Mädchen. Beer fans will be hard-pressed to find a better spot in town to sample that amber nectar. With a number of local beers on tap and more than 60 craft beers to order from, plus a decent selection of German pub food, it's unsurprising that this gastropub has maintained a glowing reputation since opening in early 2013. ⊠ *Lagerstr.*

28b, Schanzenviertel ☎ 040/8000–77750 ⊕ www.altes-maedchen.com Ⓜ *Sternschanze (U-bahn and S-bahn).*

Gretel und Alfons. Northern Germans are not best known for mingling, but at this small pub in the middle of Grosse Freiheit, you can strike up a conversation with the person sitting next to you. Perhaps that's why it was a firm favorite with the Beatles, who could often be found here when not performing at a number of clubs on the street. ⊠ *Grosse Freiheit 29, St. Pauli* ☎ *040/313–491* Ⓜ *Reeperbahn (S-bahn), St. Pauli (U-bahn).*

ST. GEORG

BARS

Bar DaCaio at the George Hotel. This bar has a black-on-black design, good looks all over, great service, and endless drink options. It's also within one of the hottest hotels in town. ⊠ *Barcastr. 3, St. Georg* ☎ *040/2800–301810* ⊕ *www.thegeorge-hotel.de* Ⓜ *Hauptbahnhof (U-bahn and S-bahn), AK St. Georg (Bus No. 6).*

PERFORMING ARTS

The arts flourish in this cosmopolitan city. Hamburg's ballet company is one of the finest in Europe, and the Hamburger Ballett-Tage, its annual festival, brings the best from around the world to the city.

At the end of September, the city comes alive with movie showings. The Hamburg Film Festival features the best feature films, documentaries, short films, and children's movies. About 80% of the films are in English or have English subtitles. For two weeks, thousands of people watch mainstream and quirky films in various theaters around town.

Information on all major events is available on the Hamburg Tourism Office website. ■ TIP→ The best way to order tickets for all major Hamburg theaters, musicals, and most cultural events is through the Hamburg-Hotline (040/3005–1300).

TICKETS

Funke Konzertkassen. Hamburg's largest ticket seller has box offices throughout Hamburg, including one in the main train station (Stage Ticket Shop). The website is only in German, but a ticket hotline will connect you with English-speaking representatives. ⊠ *Wandelhalle Hauptbahnhof, Neustadt* ☎ *040/3038–2758* ⊕ *www.funke-ticket.de* Ⓜ *Hauptbahnhof (U-bahn, S-bahn).*

Hamburg-travel.com. The city's official website is a good source for information about cultural and arts events in the city. Just click on "Events" in the "Experience" section. Tickets for plays, concerts, and the ballet can be bought online, via the hotline in English or at the Hamburg tourist office at Landungsbrücken (between Piers 4 and 5). ⊠ *Hamburg* ☎ *040/300–51701* ⊕ *www.hamburg-travel.com.*

BALLET AND OPERA

Hamburgische Staatsoper. One of the most beautiful theaters in the country, the Hamburgische Staatsoper is the leading northern German venue for opera and ballet. The Hamburg Ballet has been directed by the renowned American choreographer John Neumeier since 1973.

✉ *Grosse Theaterstr. 25, Neustadt* ☎ *040/356–868* ⊕ *www.staatsoperhamburg.de* Ⓜ *Stephansplatz (U-bahn), Gänsemarkt (U-bahn).*

Stage Operettenhaus. The Stage Operettenhaus stages productions of top musicals including the musical adaptation of *Rocky,* and *Love Never Dies,* the follow-up to *The Phantom of the Opera.* Tours of the theater are also available. ✉ *Spielbudenpl. 1, St. Pauli* ☎ *01805/4444 ticket hotline (pay per minute), 040/311–170 theater* ⊕ *www.stage-entertainment.de* Ⓜ *St. Pauli (U-bahn), Reeperbahn (S-bahn).*

CONCERTS

Laeiszhalle. Both the Philharmoniker Hamburg (Hamburg Philharmonic) and the Hamburger Symphoniker (Hamburg Symphony) appear regularly in the magnificent neo-baroque interior of the Laeiszhalle, which also hosts international orchestras and some of the biggest names in contemporary music. ✉ *Johannes-Brahms-Pl., Neustadt* ☎ *040/3576–6666* ⊕ *www.elbphilharmonie.de* Ⓜ *Messehallen (U-bahn), Gänsemarkt (U-bahn).*

SHOPPING

Although not appearing as rich or sumptuous as Düsseldorf or Munich, Hamburg is nevertheless expensive, and ranks first among Germany's shopping experiences. Some of the country's premier designers, such as Karl Lagerfeld, Jil Sander, and Wolfgang Joop, are native Hamburgers, or at least worked here for quite some time. Hamburg has the greatest number of shopping malls in the country—they're mostly small, elegant downtown arcades offering entertainment, fashion, and fine food.

All the big luxury names—Chanel, Versace, Armani, Prada, Louis Vuitton, Cartier, Tiffany—are found in the warren of streets bounded by Jungfernstieg, the Rathaus, and Neue ABC-Strasse. International chain stores, like Fossil, Adidas, and MAC, and European chains, such as Görtz shoe stores, Zara clothing stores, and Christ jewelry stores, and German department stores mingle on Mönckebergstrasse. Independent boutiques sell primarily distinguished and somewhat conservative fashion; understatement is the style here. Eppendorf offers miles of unique shops for shoes, clothes, home design, and housewares with quaint cafés sprinkled among them. Sternschanze offers a funky mix of stores selling cool home accessories and fashion, with dive bars and small restaurants for pit stops.

SHOPPING DISTRICTS

Hamburg's shopping districts are among the most elegant on the continent, and the city has Europe's largest expanse of covered shopping arcades, most of them packed with small, exclusive boutiques. The streets **Grosse Bleichen** and **Neuer Wall,** which lead off Jungfernstieg, are a big-ticket zone. The Grosse Bleichen holds four malls with the most sought-after labels, and several of these shopping centers are connected. The marble-clad **Galleria** is reminiscent of London's Burlington Arcade. Daylight streams through the immense glass ceilings of the

Hanse-Viertel, an otherwise ordinary reddish-brown brick building. At No. 103, **Kaufmannshaus** is one of the oldest malls in Hamburg. Steps away from these retail giants are the fashionable **Hamburger Hof,** the historic Alte Post with a beautiful, waterfront promenade, the posh Bleichenhof, and the stunningly designed, larger **Europa Passage** mall.

In the fashionable Rotherbaum district, take a look at Milchstrasse and Mittelweg. Both are filled with small boutiques, restaurants, and cafés.

Walk down Susannenstrasse and Schanzenstrasse in Sternschanze to find unique clothes, things for the home, and even LPs. Eppendorfer Landstrasse and Eppendorfer Weg are brimming with stores that sell clothing in every flavor—high-end labels, casual wear, sportswear, German designers—and elegant and fun home decor.

Running from the main train station to Gerhard-Hauptmann-Platz, the boulevard Spitalerstrasse is a pedestrian-only street lined with stores. ■ TIP➔ **Prices here are noticeably lower than those on Jungfernstieg.**

ALTSTADT AND NEUSTADT

ANTIQUES

Neustadt and St. Georg. ABC-Strasse in the Neustadt is a happy hunting ground for antiques lovers, as are the shops in the St. Georg district behind the train station, especially those along Lange Reihe and Koppel. You'll find a mixture of genuine antiques (*Antiquitäten*) and junk (*Trödel*) there. You'll also be lucky if you find many bargains, however. ⊠ *Hamburg.*

DEPARTMENT STORES AND SHOPPING MALLS

Alsterhaus. Hamburg's large and high-end department store is a favorite with locals, as well as an elegant landmark. A food hall and a champagne bar on the top level are both worth a stop. ⊠ *Jungfernstieg 16–20, Neustadt* ☎ *040/3590–1218* ⊕ *www.alsterhaus.de* Ⓜ *Jungfernstieg (U-bahn).*

Europa Passage. With 120 shops over five stories, a food hall, an ice-cream stand and even a Michelin-starred restaurant, this shopping mall slap-bang in the middle of town almost literally has something for everyone. ⊠ *Ballindamm 40, Altstadt* ☎ *040/3009–2640* ⊕ *www. europa-passage.de* Ⓜ *Jungfernstieg (U-bahn).*

Hamburger Hof. The historic Hamburger Hof is one of the most beautiful, upscale shopping complexes in town, with a wide variety of designer clothing, jewelry, and gift stores that cater primarily to women. ⊠ *Jungfernstieg 26–30/Grosse Bleichen 8+16, Neustadt* ⊕ *www.hhof-passage. de* Ⓜ *Jungfernstieg (U-bahn and S-bahn).*

Karstadt. Germany's leading department-store chain isn't as posh as the Alsterhaus, but it still has a good and varied selection of clothing, perfume, watches, household goods, and food. Hamburg's downtown Karstadt Sports, which is up the street from the main store at Lange Mühren 14, is the city's best place to shop for sports clothing and gear. ⊠ *Mönckebergstr. 16, Altstadt* ☎ *040/30940* ⊕ *www.karstadt.de* Ⓜ *Mönckebergstrasse (U-bahn), Rathaus (U-bahn).*

13

JEWELRY

Wempe. Germany's largest seller of fine jewelry has two locations in Hamburg, and this is its flagship. The selection of watches here is particularly outstanding. ⊠ *Jungfernstieg 8, Neustadt* ☎ *040/3344–8824* ⊕ *www.wempe.com* Ⓜ *Jungfernstieg (U-bahn and S-bahn).*

MEN'S CLOTHING

Thomas-I-Punkt. Occupying the entire five floors of a handsome Dutch Renaissance building in the middle of town, Thomas-I-Punkt has long been supplying the fashion-conscious with trendy brand and private-label clothes and shoes. ⊠ *Mönckebergstr. 21, Altstadt* ☎ *040/327–172* ⊕ *www.thomasipunkt.de* Ⓜ *Rathaus (U-bahn), Mönckebergstrasse (U-bahn).*

Wormland. The Hamburg outlet of the chain store is the city's largest store for men's clothes. Wormland offers both affordable yet very fashionable clothes, as well as (much more expensive) top designer wear. ⊠ *Europa Passage, Ballindamm 40, Altstadt* ☎ *040/4689–92700* ⊕ *www.wormland.de* Ⓜ *Jungfernstieg (U-bahn and S-bahn).*

WOMEN'S CLOTHING

& other stories. A part of the ever-expanding H&M empire, this recent addition to Neuer Wall specializes in premium-brand yet alternative clothes, bags, jewelry, and cosmetics, designed to be mixed and matched. ⊠ *Neuer Wall 20, Neustadt* ☎ *040/5003–2251* ⊕ *www.stories.com* Ⓜ *Jungfernstieg (U-bahn and S-bahn).*

ST. PAULI AND SCHANZENVIERTEL

ANTIQUES

Flohschanze. Germans in search of a great deal love a good *Flohmarkt* (Flea market). These markets unfold every weekend throughout Hamburg, and the best of the lot may be the one at Flohschanze. With acres of clothes, furniture, books, CDs, records, home accessories, jewelry, and art, the market attracts both collectors and bargain hunters every Saturday from 8 until 4. ⊠ *Neuer Kamp 30, Schanzenviertel* ☎ *040/270–2766* ⊕ *www.marktkultur-hamburg.de* Ⓜ *Feldstrasse (U-bahn).*

GIFTS

Baqu. The two storefronts here are filled with wacky knickknacks, useful home appliances, and modern home accessories, all at reasonable prices. ⊠ *Susannenstr. 39, Schanzenviertel* ☎ *040/433–814* Ⓜ *Sternschanze (U-bahn and S-bahn).*

Captain's Cabin. Don't miss this Hamburg institution, which is the best place for all of the city's specialty maritime goods, including elaborate model ships and brass telescopes. ⊠ *Landungsbrücken 3, St. Pauli* ☎ *040/316–373* ⊕ *www.captains-cabin.de* Ⓜ *Landungsbrücken (U-bahn and S-bahn).*

MEN'S CLOTHING

Herr von Eden. Fine tailored suits and everything else you need to look like a true gentleman are sold at this elegant and ultrahip store on the vintage-clothing paradise of Marktstrasse. ✉ *Marktstr. 33, Schanzenviertel* ☎ *040/6506–5200* ⊕ *www.herrvoneden.com* Ⓜ *Feldstrasse (U-bahn).*

PERFUME AND COSMETICS

Mimulus Naturkosmetik. The all-natural cosmetics and toiletries here, as well as the facial and body treatments, are available at surprisingly reasonable prices. ✉ *Schanzenstr. 39a, Schanzenviertel* ☎ *040/430–8037* ⊕ *www.mimulus-kosmetik.de* Ⓜ *Sternschanze (U-bahn and S-bahn).*

WOMEN'S CLOTHING

Fräuleinwunder. This small emporium sells trendy sportswear, shoes, accessories, and jewelry for women. There's also a small selection of casual clothing for men. ✉ *Susannenstr. 13, Schanzenviertel* ☎ *40/3619–3329* Ⓜ *Sternschanze (U-bahn and S-bahn).*

Kauf dich glücklich. With a name that translates to "Shop yourself happy," this inviting store—one of two in the Schanzenviertel—sells clothes and shoes for men and women, as well as sunglasses, jewelry, scarves, hats, and other accessories. ✉ *Susannenstr. 4, Schanzenviertel* ☎ *040/4922–2221* ⊕ *www.kaufdichgluecklich-shop.de* Ⓜ *Sternschanze (U-bahn and S-bahn).*

Purple Pink. The tiny shop sells a good selection of cool Scandinavian labels, such as Stine Goya, Carin Wester, and Minimarket. It's also great for jewelry and bags. ✉ *Weidenallee 21, Schanzenviertel* ☎ *040/4321–5379* ⊕ *www.purple-pink.de* Ⓜ *Schlump (U-bahn), Sternschanze (U-bahn and S-bahn).*

Weide. Primarily known for its funky wallpapers, handmade lamps, and retro-style furniture, this great little design store on the increasingly trendy Weidenallee also sells stylish modern clothes and accessories. ✉ *Weidenallee 23, Schanzenviertel* ☎ *040/2878–1227* ⊕ *www.weide-hamburg.de* Ⓜ *Schlump (U-bahn), Sternschanze (U-bahn and S-bahn).*

ALTONA AND OTTENSEN

VINTAGE CLOTHING

Pick N Weight. The concept here is fairly simple: paying for vintage clothes and accessories by how much they weigh rather than a fixed price per item. The store has a huge collection of pre-loved jeans, jackets, bags, and belts, which cost between €25 and €85 per kilo, depending on their label and quality. ✉ *Beim Grünen Jäger 16, Altona* ☎ *040/4319–3334* ⊕ *www.picknweight.de* Ⓜ *Feldstrasse (U-bahn).*

BLANKENESE AND ELSEWHERE

FOOD MARKETS

Wochenmarkt Blankenese. This small but top-class food market in the heart of Blankenese manages to preserve the charm of a small village. It sells only fresh produce from what it considers environmentally friendly farms. ⊠ *Blankeneser Bahnhofstr., Blankenese* Ⓜ *Blankenese (S-bahn).*

GIFTS

WohnDesign Così. The most interesting pieces of contemporary design from around the world are on view at this home-furnishings store. ⊠ *Eppendorfer Landstr. 48, Eppendorf* ☎ *040/470–670* ⊕ *www. wohndesign-cosi.de* Ⓜ *Kellinghusenstrasse (U-bahn), Eppendorfer Baum (U-bahn).*

WOMEN'S CLOTHING

Anita Hass. This impressive store covers several storefronts and carries the newest apparel, shoes, jewelry, handbags, and accessories, such as iPhone covers. It's a Hamburg classic that carries both international brands and several German designers. ⊠ *Eppendorfer Landstr. 60, Eppendorf* ☎ *040/465–909* ⊕ *www.anitahass.com* Ⓜ *Kellinghusenstrasse (U-bahn).*

Kaufrausch. The upscale shop on the handsome suburban thoroughfare of Isestrasse carries mostly clothing and accessories for women. ⊠ *Isestr. 74, Harvestehude* ☎ *040/477–154* ⊕ *www.kaufrausch-hamburg.de* Ⓜ *Eppendorfer Baum (U-bahn).*

SCHLESWIG-HOLSTEIN
AND THE BALTIC COAST

WELCOME TO SCHLESWIG-HOLSTEIN AND THE BALTIC COAST

TOP REASONS TO GO

★ **Brick Gothic architecture:** The historic towns of Lübeck, Wismar, and Stralsund have some of the finest redbrick Gothic architecture in northern Europe. A walk through medieval Stralsund, in particular, is like a trip into the proud past of the powerful Hanseatic League.

★ **Rügen:** One of the most secluded islands of northern Europe, Rügen is a dreamy Baltic oasis where endless beaches, soaring chalk cliffs, and a quiet pace of life have charmed painters, writers, and artists for centuries.

★ **Schwerin:** Nestled in a romantic landscape of lakes, rivers, forests, and marshland, the Mecklenburg state capital and its grand water palace make a great place to relax.

★ **Sylt:** A windswept outpost in the rough North Sea, Sylt is home to Germany's jet set, who come here for the tranquillity, the white beaches, the gourmet dining, and the superb hotels throughout the year.

The Baltic Sea Coast is conveniently broken down into three major areas of interest: the western coastline of Schleswig-Holstein; the lakes inland in Western Mecklenburg; and Vorpommern's secluded, tundralike landscape of sandy heath and dunes.

1 Husum. A popular summer resort town was once an important port for the Hanseatic League.

2 Sylt. This long, narrow island near the border between Germany and Denmark is famed for its unspoiled, white-sand beaches and charming villages. It's the Hamptons of northern Germany.

3 Schleswig. The region's oldest city has been a stronghold since Viking days.

4 Kiel. The capital of Schleswig-Holstein has always been an important seaport, and its ocean-going heritage is celebrated in a local museum.

5 Lübeck. Lübeck has been important since the Middle Ages. It's Altstadt is a UNESCO World Heritage Site, and its Holstentor, a two-faced city gate, is famous around the world.

Thomas Mann's novel *Buddenbrooks* is set here.

6 Wismar. This old city in Mecklenburg was one of the founding members of the Hanseatic League.

7 Schwerin. The second-largest city in Meklenburg is famous for it's island castle, as well as a Gothic cathedral.

14

8 Bad Doberan. This small town has Germany's oldest seaside resort, the Grand Hotel Heiligendamm.

9 Rostock. The biggest port on Germany's eastern Baltic coast is a popular stop for cruise ships in the summer, with its direct rail connections to Berlin.

10 Warnemünde. Near Rostock, this seaside resort town comes alive in summer due to its beautiful beaches, lined with good hotels and restaurants.

11 Stralsund. Once controlled by Sweden, Stralsund retains much of its historic charm.

12 Rügen Island. This Vorpommern island has inspired generations of poets and painters, drawn to its beautiful beaches and landscapes. It's been a popular resort since the 19th century, and many mansions and resorts of that era have survived.

13 Usedom Island. East of Rügen, near the border with Poland, much of Usedom is preserved as a nature reserve.

BALTIC COAST BEACHES

Although Germany may not be the first place on your list of beach destinations, a shore vacation on the Baltic never disappoints. The coast here ranges from the remote bucolic shores of Usedom to the chic beaches of Sylt.

(above) You can rent one of the colorful Strandkorb on Usedom Island's beaches. (upper right) Stroll along Ahlbeck's beach and pier. (lower right) The "it" crowd hangs out on Sylt.

Be sure to rent a *Strandkorb,* a kind of beach chair in a wicker basket, which gives you all of the sun, but protects you from the wind and flying sand. You can rent these chairs by the hour, half day, or day. There is usually an office near the chairs; look for the kiosk that sells sundries and beach toys nearest the chair you want.

A blue flag on the beach indicates that the water is safe for swimming. But, be aware that water temperatures even in August rarely exceed 20°C (65°F). There's a *Kurtaxe* (a tax that goes to the upkeep of the beaches) of €1.50–€5 for most resort areas; the fees on Sylt average €3.50 per day. Fees are usually covered by your hotel; you should get a card indicating that you've paid the tax. You can use the card for discounted services, but don't need to present it to visit the beach.

BALTIC AMBER

It is believed that about 40 million years ago a pine forest grew in the area that is now the Baltic Sea. Fossilized resin from these trees, aka amber, lies beneath the surface. In fact, this area has the largest known amber deposit—about 80% of the world's known accessible deposits. The best time for amber "fishing," dipping a net into the surf, is at low tide after a storm when pieces of amber dislodge from the seabed.

BALTIC COAST BEST BEACHES

HIDDENSEE ISLAND
If you're partial to the bucolic and tranquil, head to the car-free island of **Hiddensee,** Rügen's neighbor to the west. With a mere 1,000 inhabitants, Hiddensee is the perfect place to look for washed-up amber.

RÜGEN ISLAND
Germany's largest island, Rügen has picture-perfect beaches, chalk cliffs, and pristine nature. It also served as the stomping ground for the likes of Albert Einstein, Christopher Isherwood, and Caspar David Friedrich. An easy day trip from Berlin, the town of **Binz** is the perfect Rügen getaway. Binz has a nice boardwalk, a pretty beach dotted with Strandkörbe, and fine mansions.

You'll find a wonderful white-sand beach at **Prora** and a smattering of artists' studios; the hulking abandoned resort here was designed by the Nazis to house 20,000 vacationers in the *Kraft durch Freude* (Strength Through Joy) program.

SYLT
Germany's northernmost island is the granddaddy of all beach resorts and by far the most popular seaside destination in Germany. Sylt is chic and trendy, but, despite being overrun by tourists, it is still possible to find your own romantic abandoned stretch of beach. **Westerland**

is the most popular beach, with its long promenade and sun-drenched sand. The "Fun-Beach Brandenburg" bursts at the seams with family-friendly activities, volleyball, and other sporting contests. Farther afield, the red cliffs of **Kampen** are the perfect backdrop for a little mellow sun and schmoozing with the locals. It's a lovely place for a walk along the shore and up the cliffs, where the view is spectacular. The best beach for families is at **Hörnum,** where a picture-perfect red-and-white lighthouse protects the entrance to the bay.

USEDOM ISLAND
The towns of **Ahlbeck** and **Heringsdorf** are the most popular on Usedom Island, with pristine 19th-century villas and mansions paired with long boardwalks extending into the sea. For the true and unspoiled experience, head west to **Ückeritz,** where the beach feels abandoned.

WARNEMÜNDE
A resort town popular with German tourists and local day-trippers from Rostock, the 20 km (12 miles) of windswept white-sand beach can't be beat. A fun promenade stretches the length of the beach and features daily music performances and restaurants ranging from high-end dining to fish shacks where you can get a paper bag filled with fried mussels.

Updated by
Wibke Carter

Germany's true north is a quiet and peaceful region that belies, but takes a great deal of pride in, its past status as one of the most powerful trading centers in Europe. The salty air and lush, green landscape of marshlands, endless beaches, fishing villages, and lakes are the main pleasures here, not sightseeing. The Baltic coast is one of the most visited parts of Germany, but because most visitors are German, you'll feel like you have discovered Germany's best-kept secret. On foggy November evenings, or during the hard winter storms that sometimes strand islanders from the mainland, you can well imagine the fairy tales spun by the Vikings who once lived here.

In Schleswig-Holstein, Germany's most northern state, the Danish-German heritage is the result of centuries of land disputes, flexible borders, and intermarriage between the two nations—you could call this area southern Scandinavia. Since the early 20th century its shores and islands have become popular weekend and summer retreats for the well-to-do from Hamburg. The island of Sylt, in particular, is known throughout Germany for its rich and beautiful sunbathers.

The rest of Schleswig-Holstein, though equally appealing in its green and mostly serene landscape, is far from rich and worldly. Most people farm or fish, and often speak *Plattdütsch*, or "low German," which is difficult for outsiders to understand. Cities such as Husum, Schleswig, Kiel (the state capital), and even Lübeck all exude a laid-back, small-town charm.

The neighboring state of Mecklenburg-Vorpommern includes the Baltic Coast and is even more rural. On the resort islands of Rügen and Usedom, the clock appears to have stopped before World War II. Though it has long been a popular summer destination for families and city-weary Berliners, few foreign tourists venture here.

MAJOR REGIONS

Schleswig-Holstein once thrived, thanks to the Hanseatic League (a trading confederation of Baltic towns and cities) and the Salzstrasse (Salt Route), a merchant route connecting northern Germany's cities. The kings of Denmark warred with the dukes of Schleswig and, later, the German Empire over the prized northern territory of Schleswig-Holstein. The northernmost strip of land surrounding Flensburg became German in 1864. The quiet, contemplative spirit of the region's people, the marshland's special light, and the ever-changing face of the sea are inspiring. Today the world-famous Schleswig-Holstein-Musikfestival ushers in classical concerts to farmhouses, palaces, and churches. Major destinations include **Husum**; the resort town of **Sylt**; **Schleswig**, the region's oldest city; **Kiel**; and the Hanseatic city of **Lübeck**.

14

Mecklenburg is a long-forgotten Baltic Coast region, pinned between two sprawling urban areas—the state capital of Schwerin, in the west, and Rostock, in the east—and is thriving with trade, industry, and tourism. Though the region is close to the sea, it's made up largely of seemingly endless fields of wheat and yellow rape and a hundred or so wonderful lakes. "When the Lord made the Earth, He started with Mecklenburg," wrote native novelist Fritz Reuter. Major destinations of note include **Wismar,** one of the founding members of the Hanseatic League; **Schwerin,** the region's second-largest town; **Bad Doberan,** famous for its cathedral; **Rostock,** the area's busiest port; and **Warnemünde,** a quaint seaside resort.

The best description of **Vorpommern** is found in its name, which simply means "before Pomerania." This area, indeed, seems trapped between Mecklenburg and the authentic, old Pomerania farther east, now part of Poland. Its remoteness ensures an unforgettable view of unspoiled nature, primarily attracting families and younger travelers. **Stralsund** is a jewel of the Baltic; **Rügen Island** has long been popular with poets and painters; and **Usedom Island** is a popular beach resort.

PLANNING

WHEN TO GO

The region's climate is at its best when the two states are most crowded with vacationers—in July and August. Winter can be harsh in this area, and even spring and fall are rather windy, chilly, and rainy. ■ TIP→ **To avoid the crowds, schedule your trip for June or September. But don't expect tolerable water temperatures or hot days on the beach.**

GETTING HERE AND AROUND

AIR TRAVEL

The international airport closest to Schleswig-Holstein is in Hamburg. For an eastern approach to the Baltic Coast tour, use Berlin's Tegel or Schönefeld Airports.

BOAT AND FERRY TRAVEL

The Weisse Flotte (White Fleet) line operates ferries linking the Baltic ports, as well as running short harbor and coastal cruises. Boats depart from Warnemünde, Zingst (to Hiddensee), Stahlbrode (to Rügen), and

Stralsund. In addition, Scandlines ferries run from Puttgarden and Rostock to destinations in Sweden and Denmark. Almost all Baltic Sea cruises dock in Warnemünde.

Contacts Scandlines. ☎ *0381/7788–7766* ⊕ *www.scandlines.de.* **Weisse Flotte.** ☎ *03831/26810* ⊕ *www.weisse-flotte.de.*

BUS TRAVEL

Local buses link the main train stations with outlying towns and villages, especially the coastal resorts. Buses operate throughout Sylt, Rügen, and Usedom islands.

CAR TRAVEL

The two-lane roads (*Bundesstrassen*) along the coast can be full of traffic in summer. The ones leading to Usedom Island can be extremely log-jammed, as the causeway bridges have scheduled closings to let ships pass. Using the Bundesstrassen takes more time, but these often tree-lined roads are by far more scenic than the autobahn.

Sylt island is 196 km (122 miles) from Hamburg via autobahn A-7 and bundesstrasse B-199 and is ultimately reached via train. B-199 cuts through some nice countryside, and instead of A-7 or B-76 between Schleswig and Kiel you could take the slow route through the coastal hinterland (B-199, B-203, or B-503). Lübeck, the gateway to Mecklenburg-Vorpommern, is 56 km (35 miles) from Hamburg via A-1. B-105 leads to all sightseeing spots in Mecklenburg-Vorpommern. A faster route is the A-20, connecting Lübeck and Rostock. From Stralsund, B-96 cuts straight across Rügen Island, a distance of 51 km (32 miles). From Berlin, take A-11 and head toward Prenzlau for B-109 all the way to Usedom Island, a distance of 162 km (100 miles). A causeway connects the mainland town of Anklam to the town of Peenemünde, on Usedom Island; coming from the west, use the causeway at Wolgast.

TRAIN TRAVEL

Trains connect almost every notable city in the area and it's much more convenient than bus travel. Sylt, Kiel, Lübeck, Schwerin, and Rostock have InterCity train connections to either Hamburg or Berlin, or both.

A north–south train line links Schwerin and Rostock. An east–west route connects Kiel, Hamburg, Lübeck, and Rostock, and some trains continue through to Stralsund and Sassnitz, on Rügen Island.

TOURS

Although tourist offices and museums have worked to improve the English-language literature about this area, English-speaking tours are infrequent and must be requested ahead of time through the local tourist office. Because most tours are designed for groups, there's usually a flat fee of €20–€30. Towns currently offering tours are Lübeck, Stralsund, and Rostock. Schwerin has two-hour boat tours of its lakes. Many of the former fishermen in these towns give sunset tours of the harbors, shuttle visitors between neighboring towns, or take visitors fishing in the Baltic Sea, which is a unique opportunity to ride on an authentic fishing boat. In Kiel, Rostock, and on Sylt, cruise lines make short trips through the respective bays and/or islands off the coast, sailing even as far as Denmark and Sweden. Inquire at the local tourist office about companies and times, as well as about fishing-boat tours.

HOTELS

In northern Germany you'll find both small *Hotelpensionen* and fully equipped large hotels; along the eastern Baltic Coast, some hotels are renovated high-rises dating from GDR (German Democratic Republic, or East Germany) times. Many of the small hotels and pensions in towns have been restored to the romantic, quaint splendor of German *Bäderarchitektur* (spa architecture) from the early 20th century. In high season all accommodations, especially on the islands, are in great demand.

RESTAURANTS

Don't count on eating a meal at odd hours or after 10 pm in this largely rural area. Many restaurants serve hot meals only between 11:30 am and 2 pm, and from 6 to 9 pm. You rarely need a reservation here, and casual clothing is generally acceptable.

Prices in hotel reviews are the average cost of a main course at dinner, or if dinner is not served, at lunch. Prices in hotel reviews are the lowest cost of a standard double room in high season.

WHAT IT COSTS IN EUROS			
$	$$	$$$	$$$$
Restaurants	under €15	€15–€20	€21–€25	over €25
Hotels	under €100	€100–€175	€176–€225	over €225

VISITOR INFORMATION

Tourismusverband Mecklenburg-Vorpommern. ✉ *Konrad-Zuse-Str. 2, Rostock* ☎ *0381/403–0500* ⊕ *www.off-to-mv.com.*

HUSUM

158 km (98 miles) northwest of Hamburg.

The town of Husum is the epitome of northern German lifestyle and culture. Immortalized in a poem as the "gray city upon the sea" by its famous son, Theodor Storm, Husum is actually a popular vacation spot in summer.

The central **Marktplatz** (Market Square) is bordered by 17th- and 18th-century buildings, including the historic Rathaus (Town Hall), which houses the tourist-information office. The best impression of Husum's beginnings in the mid-13th century is found south of the Marktplatz, along **Krämerstrasse**; the **Wasserreihe**, a narrow and tortuous alley; and **Hafenstrasse**, right next to the narrow **Binnenhafen** (city harbor).

VISITOR INFORMATION

Contacts Husum Tourist Office. ✉ *Grossstr. 27* ☎ *04841/89870* ⊕ *www. husum-tourismus.de.*

EXPLORING

Schloss vor Husum (*Husum Castle*). Despite Husum's remoteness, surrounded by the stormy sea, wide marshes, and dunes, the city used to be a major seaport and administrative center. The Husum Castle, which was originally built as a Renaissance mansion in the late 16th century, was transformed in 1752 by the dukes of Gottorf into a redbrick baroque country palace. ✉ *König-Friedrich V.-Allee* ☎ *04841/897–3130* 💶 *€4* 🕐 *Closed Mon. Mar.–Oct., and weekdays Nov.–Feb.*

Theodor-Storm-Haus. This is the most famous house on Wasserreihe, where writer Theodor Storm (1817–88) lived between 1866 and 1880. It's a must if you're interested in German literature or if you want to gain insight into the life of the few well-to-do people in this region during the 19th century. The small museum includes the poet's living room and a small *Poetenstübchen* (poets' parlor), where he wrote many of his novels. ✉ *Wasserreihe 31* ☎ *04841/803–8630* ⊕ *www.storm-gesellschaft.de* 💶 *€4* 🕐 *Closed Mon., Wed., Fri., and Sun. Nov.–Mar.*

WHERE TO STAY

$$$ HOTEL Fodor's Choice ★ 🏨 **Geniesser Hotel Altes Gymnasium.** In a former redbrick high school behind a pear orchard, you'll find a surprisingly elegant country-style hotel. **Pros:** stylish and quiet setting; a perfect overnight stop on the way to Sylt; great spa. **Cons:** far from any other sights; more vintage than modern ambience; breakfast buffet average. [$] *Rooms from: €195* ✉ *Süderstr. 2–10* ☎ *04841/8330* 🌐 *www.geniesserhotel-altes-gymnasium.de* 🛏 *72 rooms* 🍴 *Free Breakfast.*

SYLT

44 km (27 miles) northwest of Husum, 196 km (122 miles) northwest of Hamburg.

Fodor's Choice ★ Sylt (pronounced "ts-oo- *lt*") is a long, narrow island (38 km [24 miles] by as little as 220 yards) of unspoiled beaches and marshland off the western coast of Schleswig-Holstein and Denmark. Famous for its clean air and white beaches, Sylt is the hideaway for Germany's rich and famous.

A popular activity here is *Wattwanderungen* (walking in the Watt, the shoreline tidelands), whether on self-guided or guided tours. The small villages with their thatch-roof houses, the beaches, and the nature conservation areas make Sylt one of the most enchanting German islands.

GETTING HERE AND AROUND

Trains are the *only* way to access Sylt (other than flying from Hamburg or Berlin). The island is connected to the mainland via the train causeway Hindenburgdamm, and Deutsche Bahn will transport you and your car in 35 minutes directly to the Westerland station on the island. The daily shuttle car train leaves Niebüll roughly every 30–90 minutes from 5:05 am to 9:05 pm (Friday and Saturday 5:05 am to 9:35 pm). There are no reservations on this train.

VISITOR INFORMATION

Contacts Sylt Marketing GmbH. ✉ *Stephanstr. 6, Rantum* ☎ *04651/82020* 🌐 *www.sylt.de.* **Tourismus-Service Kampen.** ✉ *Hauptstr. 12, Kampen* ☎ *04651/46980* 🌐 *www.kampen.de.* **Westerland.** ✉ *Strandstr. 35, Westerland* ☎ *04651/9988* 🌐 *www.insel-sylt/westerland.*

EXPLORING

Kampen. The Sylt island's unofficial capital is the main destination for the wealthier crowd and lies 9 km (6 miles) northeast of Westerland. Redbrick buildings and shining white thatch-roof houses spread along the coastline. The real draw—aside from the fancy restaurants and chic nightclubs—is the beaches. ✉ *Kampen* 🌐 *www.kampen.de.*

Rotes Kliff (*Red Cliff*). One of the island's best-known features is this dune cliff on the northern end of the Kampen beaches, which turns an eerie dark red when the sun sets. ✉ *Kampen.*

St. Severin Church. The 800-year-old church was built on the highest elevation in the region. Its tower once served the island's fishermen as a beacon. Strangely enough, the tower also served as a prison until 1806. Now a Lutheran church, it is a popular site for weddings. ⊠ *Pröstwai 20, Keitum* ☎ *04651/31713* ⊕ *www.st-severin.de* ⊠ *Free.*

Sylter Heimatmuseum (*Sylt Island Museum*). This small museum tells the centuries-long history of the island's seafaring people. It presents traditional costumes, tools, and other gear from fishing boats and relates stories of islanders who fought for Sylt's independence. In the same street (at No. 13) stands the **Altfriesisches Haus** (Old Frisian House), which offers a glimpse of the rugged lives of 19th-century fishermen and a time when most seamen thrived on extensive whale hunting. ⊠ *Am Kliff 19, Keitum* ☎ *04651/31669* ⊠ *€5* ⊙ *Closed Sun.–Tues. Nov.–Mar.*

FAMILY **Westerland.** The island's major town is not quite as expensive as Kampen, but it's more crowded. An ugly assortment of modern hotels lines an undeniably clean and broad beach. Each September windsurfers meet for the Surf Cup competition off the **Brandenburger Strand,** the best surfing spot. ⊠ *Westerland.*

BEACHES

FAMILY **Buhne 16 and Rotes Kliff.** Kampen's beach—divided into the **Buhne 16** and the **Rotes Kliff**—is the place where the rich and famous meet average joes. Buhne 16 is Germany's most popular nudist beach, and Germans call this section "the great equalizer," as social inequalities disappear with the clothing. The Red Cliff section is less crowded than Buhne 16 and clothing is required. The beach access point offers one of the best views of the Cliffs and North Sea; the viewing platform is wheelchair accessible. The beaches are surrounded by a ring of dunes that beg for exploration. **Amenities:** food and drink; lifeguards; parking; showers; toilets; water sports. **Best for:** partiers; sunset; swimming; walking. ⊠ *Kampen.*

FAMILY **Fun Beach am Brandenburger Strand.** Westerland's beach bursts at the seams in the summer months. More than 6 km (4 miles) of pristine white sand is filled with more than 4,000 *Strandkörbe,* a kind of beach chair in a wicker basket, which are all for rent. There's also volleyball, soccer, darts, and other beach sports, and everyone is invited to participate in the Beach Olympics, which are held every Friday at 2 pm in the summer months. Despite its popularity, it is easy to find some privacy on the many secluded bike and footpaths. **Amenities:** food and drink; lifeguards; parking; showers; toilets; water sports. **Best for:** partiers; snorkeling; walking; windsurfing. ⊠ *Brandenburger Strand, Westerland.*

FAMILY **Hörnum Beach.** The town of Hörnum is bordered on three sides by a rock-free, fine-white-sand beach that is perfect for paddling, quick dips in the sea, or simply lounging in one of the ever-present *Strandkörbe* beach chairs. The main beach is one of the most family-friendly on the island, and it's easily accessible from the promenade. A magnificent red-and-white lighthouse looms over the beach. Hörnum is the best place to take long walks along the Wattenmeer. **Amenities:** food and drink; lifeguards; parking; showers; toilets; water sports. **Best for:** surfing; swimming; walking; windsurfing. ⊠ *An der Düne, Hörnum.*

The beach at Westerland on Sylt is clean and wide.

WHERE TO EAT

$$$$ GERMAN Fodor's Choice ★ 🍴 **Restaurant "JM".** Owner Jörg Müller, considered by many to be the island's leading chef, serves haute cuisine in the gracious and friendly setting of an old thatch-roof farmhouse, which doubles as a small hotel. Restaurant "JM" offers outstanding dining with a seasonal menu that incorporates a diverse locally sourced selection of produce and fish. **Known for:** rustic Frisian atmosphere; local seafood, lamb, and beef; Michelin star. [$] *Average main: €48* ✉ *Süderstr. 8, Westerland* ☎ *04651/27788* 🌐 *www.hotel-joerg-mueller.de* 🕒 *Closed Mon. and Tues.*

$$$$ ECLECTIC 🍴 **Sansibar.** Sansibar is the island's most popular restaurant where a diverse clientele—basically everyone ever on Sylt—often make it a rambunctious night out by imbibing drinks with no regard for the morning after under the bar's maverick logo of crossed pirates' sabers. To get a table, you must reserve at least six weeks in advance, and no reservations are possible between noon and 6 pm. **Known for:** Sunday brunch; seafood and fondue; extensive wine list. [$] *Average main: €30* ✉ *Hörnumer Str. 80, Rantum* ☎ *04651/964–646* 🌐 *www.sansibar.de.*

WHERE TO STAY

$$$$ RESORT Fodor's Choice ★ 🏨 **Dorint Söl'ring Hof.** This luxurious resort sits directly *on* the dunes in a white, thatch-roof country house, and the view from most of the rooms is magnificent—with some luck you may even spot frolicking harbor porpoises. **Pros:** one of the few luxury hotels on the island with perfect service and a top-notch restaurant; right on the beach; private beach

chairs. **Cons:** remote location; often fully booked; rooms tend to be small. $ *Rooms from: €490* ⊠ *Am Sandwall 1, Rantum* ☎ *04651/836–200* ⊕ *www.soelring-hof.de* ⇨ *15 rooms* ⦿*Free Breakfast.*

$$$
B&B/INN
FAMILY

▥ **Ulenhof Wenningstedt.** One of Sylt's loveliest old thatch-roof apartment houses, this is a quiet alternative to the busier main resorts in Kampen and Westerland. **Pros:** a great, but small, spa; dogs allowed; private garden for some apartments. **Cons:** off the beaten track and away from the main action in Kampen and Westerland; credit cards are not accepted; spa and pool access for young children only until 5 pm. $ *Rooms from: €190* ⊠ *Friesenring 14, Wenningstedt* ☎ *04651/94540* ⊕ *www.ulenhof. de* ⊟ *No credit cards* ⇨ *28 apartments* ⦿*Free Breakfast.*

NIGHTLIFE

Club Rotes Kliff. The nightspots in Kampen are generally more upscale and more expensive than the pubs and clubs of Westerland. This is one of the most classic clubs on Sylt—a bar and dance club that attracts a hip crowd of all ages. ⊠ *Braderuper Weg 3, Kampen* ☎ *04651/43400* ⊕ *www.club-rotes-kliff.de.*

SCHLESWIG

82 km (51 miles) southeast of Sylt, 114 km (71 miles) north of Hamburg.

Schleswig-Holstein's oldest city is also one of its best-preserved examples of a typical north German town. Once the seat of the dukes of Schleswig-Holstein, it has not only their palace but also ruins left by the area's first rulers, the Vikings. The Norse conquerors, legendary and fierce warriors from Scandinavia, ruled northern Germany between 800 and 1100. Although they brought terror and domination to the region, they also contributed commerce and a highly developed social structure. Under a wide sky, Schleswig lies on the Schlei River in a landscape of freshwater marshland and lakes, making it a good departure point for bike or canoe tours.

GETTING HERE AND AROUND

Schleswig's train station is 3 km (2 miles) from the city center. It's easiest to take Bus No. 1505 or 1506 into town. You'll find the buses across the street from the front of the train station, and all stop at Schloss Gottorf.

EXPLORING

The Holm. The fishing village comes alive in the Holm neighborhood, an old settlement with tiny and colorful houses. The windblown buildings give a good impression of what villages in northern Germany looked like 150 years ago. ⊠ *Süderholmstr.*

Schloss Gottorf. The impressive baroque Schloss Gottorf, dating from 1703, once housed the ruling family. It has been transformed into the **Schleswig-Holsteinisches Landesmuseum** (State Museum of Schleswig-Holstein) and holds a collection of art and handicrafts of northern Germany from the Middle Ages to the present, including paintings by

EATING WELL IN SCHLESWIG-HOLSTEIN

The German coastline is known for fresh and superb seafood, particularly in summer. A few of the region's top restaurants are on Sylt and in Lübeck. Eating choices along the Baltic Coast tend to be more down-to-earth. However, restaurants in both coastal states serve mostly seafood such as *Scholle* (flounder) or North Sea *Krabben* (shrimp), often with fried potatoes, eggs, and bacon. Mecklenburg specialties to look for are *Mecklenburger Griebenroller,* a custardy casserole of grated potatoes, eggs, herbs, and chopped bacon; *Mecklenburger Fischsuppe,* a hearty fish soup with vegetables, tomatoes, and sour cream; *Gefüllte Ente* (duck with bread stuffing); and *Pannfisch* (fish patty). A favorite local nightcap since the 17th century is *Grog,* a strong blend of rum, hot water, and local fruits.

Lucas Cranach the Elder. ✉ *Schlossinsel 1* ☎ *04621/813–222* 🌐 *www.schloss-gottorf.de* 🎟 *€9* 🕒 *Closed Mon.*

FAMILY **Wikinger Museum Haithabu** (*Haithabu Viking Museum*). The most thrilling museum in Schleswig is at the site of an ancient Viking settlement. This was the Vikings' most important German port, and the boats, gold jewelry, and graves they left behind are displayed in the museum. Be sure to walk along the trail to the Viking village, to see how the Vikings really lived. The best way to get there is to take the ferry across the Schlei from Schleswig's main fishing port. ✉ *Haddeby, Am Haddebyer Noor 2, Busdorf* ☎ *04621/813–222* 🌐 *www.schloss-gottorf.de/haithabu* 🎟 *€7.*

WHERE TO EAT

$$ GERMAN 🍴 **Asgaard Brauerei.** Taste the "Divine beer of the Vikings," a malty cold-fermented amber lager, at Schleswig's only brewery. While the Luzifer Restaurant offers typical brewpub fare, it is the small Viking twists, like roast meat served only with a knife and horned glasses that make this place worth a visit. **Known for:** specialty beers; outside beer garden; central location. [$] *Average main: €15* ✉ *Königstr. 27* ☎ *04621/488–213* 🌐 *www.asgaard.de* 🕒 *No dinner.*

$$ GERMAN 🍴 **ODINS HADDEBY.** This restaurant dates back to 1828, when it was a pub serving villagers at the gates of Schleswig. Today, it specializes in seasonal and regional dishes with fresh ingredients sourced exclusively from local farmers. **Known for:** historical setting; northern German cuisine; homemade rolls for breakfast. [$] *Average main: €17* ✉ *Haddebyer Chaussee 13, Busdorf* ☎ *04621/850–500* 🌐 *www.odins-haddeby.de.*

WHERE TO STAY

$$ HOTEL 🏨 **Hotel Strandhalle.** A modern hotel (now part of the Azkent hotel group) overlooking the small yacht harbor, this establishment has surprisingly low rates. **Pros:** central spot in the heart of Schleswig; great views of Schlei River; clean and comfortable. **Cons:** lack of flair; rather bland

rooms; no elevator. [$] *Rooms from: €103* ✉ *Strandweg 2* ☎ *04621/9090* 🌐 *www.hotel-strandhalle.de* 🛏 *30 rooms* 🍴 *Free Breakfast.*

SHOPPING

Keramikstube. The tiny Keramikstube offers craft work and beautiful traditional handmade pottery. ✉ *Rathausmarkt 14* ☎ *04621/24757* 🌐 *www.keramikstube-schleswig.de.*

KIEL

53 km (33 miles) southeast of Schleswig, 130 km (81 miles) north of Hamburg.

The state capital of Schleswig-Holstein, Kiel, is known throughout Europe for the annual Kieler Woche, a regatta that attracts hundreds of boats from around the world. Despite the many wharves and industries concentrated in Kiel, the **Kieler Förde** (Bay of Kiel) has remained mostly unspoiled. Unfortunately, this cannot be said about the city itself. Because of Kiel's strategic significance during World War II—it served as the main German submarine base—the historic city, founded more than 750 years ago, was completely destroyed. Sadly, due to the modern reconstruction of the city, there is no real reason to spend more than half a day in Kiel.

VISITOR INFORMATION

Contacts Kiel Marketing e.V. GmbH. ✉ *Andreas-Gayk-Str. 31* ☎ *0431/679–100* 🌐 *www.kiel-sailing-city.de.*

EXPLORING

FAMILY **Kieler Hafen** (*Kiel Harbor*). At Germany's largest passenger-shipping harbor, you can always catch a glimpse of one of the many ferries leaving for Norway from the **Oslokai** (Oslo Quay) or for Göteborg from the **Schwedenkai** (Sweden Quay). ✉ *Oslokai* 🌐 *www.portofkiel.com.*

Kunsthalle zu Kiel (*Kiel Art Gallery*). One of northern Germany's best collections of modern art can be found here. Russian art of the 19th and early 20th centuries, German expressionism, and contemporary international art are on display. ✉ *Düsternbrooker Weg 1* ☎ *0431/880–5756* 🌐 *www.kunsthalle-kiel.de* 🎟 *€7* 🕒 *Closed Mon.*

FAMILY **Schifffahrtsmuseum Fischhalle** (*Maritime Museum*). Housed in a hall of the old fish market, this museum pays tribute to Kiel's impressive maritime history. The exhibit includes two antique fishing boats and an impressive collection of multimedia workstations that detail Kiel's role as a center of the fishing industry. ✉ *Wall 65* ☎ *0431/901–3428* 🌐 *www.kiel.de* 🎟 *Free* 🕒 *Closed Mon.*

U-Boot-Museum (*Submarine Museum*). A grim reminder of one aspect of Kiel's marine past is exhibited at this museum in Kiel-Laboe. The vessels of the much-feared German submarine fleet in both World Wars were mostly built and stationed in Kiel before leaving for the Atlantic, where they attacked American and British supply convoys.

Today the submarine U995, built in 1943, serves as a public-viewing model of a typical World War II German submarine. The 280-foot-high **Marineehrenmal** (Marine Honor Memorial), in Laboe, was built in 1927–36. You can reach Laboe via ferry from the Kiel harbor or take B-502 north. ⊠ *Strandstr. 92, Laboe* ☎ *04343/4948–4962* ⊠ *Memorial €6; museum from €5.*

WHERE TO EAT

$ ✕ **Kieler Brauerei.** Kiel has been a center of German brewing since the
GERMAN   Middle Ages, when industrious citizens brewed around the clock for export and visiting merchant seamen. In this brauhaus you can try the *Naturtrübes Kieler* and other north German beers in pitchers, or order a small barrel for your table and tap it yourself (other patrons will cheer you). **Known for:** local beer straight from the tap; hearty food, mostly fish, pork and potato dishes; massive oak tables and benches. $ *Average main: €12* ⊠ *Alter Markt 9* ☎ *0431/906–290* ⊕ *www.kieler-brauerei.de.*

14

WHERE TO STAY

$$$ 🏨 **Hotel Kieler Yachtclub.** This traditional hotel overlooking the Kieler
HOTEL   Förhde provides standard yet elegant refurbished rooms in the main building and completely new, bright accommodations in the Villentrakt. **Pros:** central location in the heart of Kiel; nice views; modern maritime style. **Cons:** service and attitude can feel a bit too formal at times; quite pricey for Kiel; catered to business travelers. $ *Rooms from: €202* ⊠ *Kiellinie 70* ☎ *0431/88130* ⊕ *www.hotel-kyc.de* ➴ *21 rooms* ⏀ *Free Breakfast.*

NIGHTLIFE

TraumGmbH. A college crowd goes to industrial-style cultural center TraumGmbH to eat pizza, watch a movie, or dance (Friday is best for dancing). ⊠ *Grasweg 19* ☎ *0431/544–450* ⊕ *www.traumgmbh.de.*

LÜBECK

60 km (37 miles) southeast of Kiel, 56 km (35 miles) northeast of Hamburg.

Fodor's Choice   The ancient island core of Lübeck, dating from the 12th century, was
★   a chief stronghold of the Hanseatic merchant princes, until its almost complete destruction in 1942. It was the roving Heinrich der Löwe (King Henry the Lion) who greatly enhanced the town's position and, in 1173, laid the foundation stone of the redbrick Gothic cathedral. The town's famous landmark gate, the **Holstentor,** built between 1464 and 1478, is flanked by two round squat towers and serves as a solid symbol of Lübeck's prosperity as a trading center.

GETTING HERE AND AROUND

Lübeck is accessible from Hamburg in 45 minutes either by InterCity trains or by car via the A-24 and A-1, which almost takes you from one city center to the other. Lübeck is also well connected by autobahns and train service to Kiel, Flensburg, and the neighboring eastern coastline. The city, however, should be explored on foot or by bike, as the many tiny, medieval alleys in the center cannot be accessed by car. English tours of Old Lübeck depart from the tourist Welcome Center on Holstentorplatz (€10; *May–Oct. and Dec., Sat. at 11:30*).

VISITOR INFORMATION

Contacts Lübeck Tourist Office. ⊠ *Holstentorpl. 1* ☎ *0451/889–9700* ⊕ *www. luebeck-tourismus.de.*

EXPLORING

Fodor'sChoice ★ **Altstadt** (*Old Town*). Proof of Lübeck's former position as the golden queen of the Hanseatic League is found at every step in the Altstadt, which contains more 13th- to 15th-century buildings than all other large northern German cities combined. This fact has earned the Altstadt a place on UNESCO's register of the world's greatest cultural and natural treasures. ⊠ *Lübeck.*

Buddenbrookhaus. Named after Thomas Mann's saga *Buddenbrooks,* the patrician house was once home to the Mann family and now houses the Heinrich and Thomas Mann Zentrum, a literary museum documenting the brothers' lives. A tour and video in English are offered. ⊠ *Mengstr. 4* ☎ *0451/122–4243* ⊕ *www.buddenbrookhaus. de* ☜ *€7* ⊗ *Closed Mon. Jan.–Mar.*

Günter Grass-Haus. This mansion contains a museum devoted to wide-ranging exhibits on literature and visual arts, prominently featuring the work of one of Germany's most famous postwar writers and winner of the Nobel Prize for Literature (1999), Günter Grass (1927–2015). ⊠ *Glockengiesserstr. 21* ☎ *0451/122–4230* ⊕ *www.grass-haus.de* ☜ *€7* ⊗ *Closed Mon. Jan.–Mar.*

Fodor'sChoice ★ **Holstentor** (*Holsten Gate*). Lübeck's famous gate was part of the medieval fortifications of the city. It has two faces: one it shows the world and one it shows the city. The "field side," which faces away, appears as if it is made of two defensive towers connected by a middle gate. The "city side" looks like one smooth building and has more windows, arcades, and friezes. The inscription on the field side, added in 1871, reads, "Concordia domi foris pax," an abbreviated version of the statement, "Harmony within and peace outside are indeed the greatest good of all." It houses a museum with ship models, suits of armor, and other artifacts from Lübeck's heyday. ⊠ *Holstentorpl.* ☎ *0451/122–4129* ⊕ *www.museum-holstentor.de* ☜ *€7* ⊗ *Closed Mon. Jan.–Mar.*

Lübecker Dom (*Lübeck Cathedral*). Construction of this, the city's oldest building, began in 1173. This Lutheran cathedral was built by Heinrich der Löwe and was partially destroyed in WWII. ⊠ *Domkirchhof* ☎ *0451/74704* ⊕ *www.domzuluebeck.de* ☜ *Free.*

Marienkirche (*St. Mary's Church*). The impressive redbrick Gothic structure, which has the highest brick nave in the world, looms behind the Rathaus. Look for the old bells, as they are still in the spot where they fell during the bombing of Lübeck. ✉ *Marienkirchhof 1* ☎ *0451/397–700* 🌐 *www.st-marien-luebeck.de.*

Rathaus (*Town Hall*). Dating from 1240, the Rathaus is among the buildings lining the arcaded Marktplatz, one of Europe's most striking medieval market squares. ✉ *Breitestr. 62* ☎ *0451/122–1005* 🌐 *www.luebeck-tourism.de* 🎟 *Guided tour in German €4* ⏲ *Closed Sun.*

WHERE TO EAT

$$ GERMAN Fodor's Choice ★ 🍴 **Schiffergesellschaft.** This dark, wood-panel restaurant dating back to 1535 is the city's old Mariners' Society house, which was off-limits to women until 1870. Today locals and visitors alike enjoy freshly brewed beer and great seafood in church-style pews at long 400-year-old oak tables. **Known for:** ship lanterns, old model ships; historical setting; traditional fish dishes. [$] *Average main: €20* ✉ *Breitestr. 2* ☎ *0451/76776* 🌐 *www.schiffergesellschaft.de.*

$$$$ GERMAN 🍴 **Wullenwever.** Committed to the city's maritime heritage, Wullenwever serves fish such as bass, halibut, plaice, pike, and trout, which is fried or sautéed according to local country cooking. It's certainly one of the most attractive establishments in town, with dark furniture, chandeliers, and oil paintings on pale pastel walls. **Known for:** sophisticated dining; extensive wine list; set menus only. [$] *Average main: €65* ✉ *Beckergrube 71* ☎ *0451/704–333* 🌐 *www.wullenwever.de* ⏲ *Closed Sun. and Mon. No lunch.*

WHERE TO STAY

$$ B&B/INN FAMILY 🏨 **Hotel zur Alten Stadtmauer.** This historic town house in the heart of the city is Lübeck's most charming hotel with small, modest, well-kept guest rooms for up to five people on two floors. **Pros:** cozy hotel with personal, friendly service; suitable for people with allergies; great value for money. **Cons:** rather simply furnished rooms; when it's full, the hotel feels cramped; narrow staircase. [$] *Rooms from: €114* ✉ *An der Mauer 57* ☎ *0451/73702* 🌐 *www.hotelstadtmauer.de* 🛏 *24 rooms* 🍽 *Free Breakfast.*

$$ HOTEL 🏨 **Ringhotel Friederikenhof.** A lovely country hotel set in 19th-century, redbrick farmhouses 10 minutes outside Lübeck, the family-run Friederikenhof is a perfect hideaway with a soothing garden and great view of the city's skyline. **Pros:** charming, old-style farmhouse typical of the region; personal and very friendly service; free parking. **Cons:** outside Lübeck; charge for sauna use; limited food options in surroundings. [$] *Rooms from: €115* ✉ *Langjohrd 15–19* ☎ *0451/800–880* 🌐 *www.friederikenhof.de* 🛏 *30 rooms* 🍽 *Free Breakfast.*

$ HOTEL 🏨 **Ringhotel Jensen.** Only a stone's throw from the Holstentor, this hotel is close to all the main attractions and faces the moat surrounding the Old Town. **Pros:** perfect location in the heart of Lübeck's downtown area; major sights are all within walking distance; dogs welcome. **Cons:** small pensionlike hotel without many of the amenities of larger hotels;

bland decoration in rooms; parking at extra cost nearby. $ *Rooms from: €93* ✉ *An der Obertrave 4–5* ☎ *0451/702–490* ⊕ *www.hotel-jensen-luebeck.de* ⤸ *42 rooms* ⦿ *Free Breakfast.*

$$
HOTEL

☎ **SAS Radisson Senator Hotel Lübeck.** Close to the famous Holstentor, this ultramodern hotel, with its daring architecture, still reveals a north German heritage: the redbrick building, with its oversized windows and generous, open lobby, mimics an old Lübeck warehouse. **Pros:** luxury hotel in a central location; some rooms with river views; indoor pool and sauna. **Cons:** lacks the historic charm typical of medieval Lübeck; car park charges; pricey food. $ *Rooms from: €145* ✉ *Willy-Brandt-Allee 6* ☎ *0451/1420* ⊕ *www.senatorhotel.de* ⤸ *224 rooms* ⦿ *Free Breakfast.*

14

SHOPPING

Local legend has it that marzipan was invented in Lübeck during the great medieval famine. According to the story, a local baker ran out of grain for bread and, in desperation, began experimenting with the only four ingredients he had: almonds, sugar, rose water, and eggs. The result was a sweet almond paste known today as marzipan. The story is more fiction than fact; it is generally agreed that marzipan's true origins lie in the Middle East. ■ **TIP→ Lübecker Marzipan, an appellation that has been trademarked, is now considered among the best in the world. Any marzipan that uses the appellation Lübecker must be made within the city limits.**

Holstentor-Passage. The city's largest downtown shopping mall is next to the Holstentor and is filled with stores selling clothing or home accessories. ✉ *An der Untertrave 111* ☎ *0451/75292.*

Konditorei-Café Niederegger. Lübeck's most famous marzipan maker, Niederegger, sells the delicacy molded into a multitude of imaginative forms at its Konditorei-Café flagship store. Upstairs is a small museum about marzipan, as well as some life-size marzipan figures. ✉ *Breitestr. 89* ☎ *0451/5301–126* ⊕ *www.niederegger.de.*

WISMAR

60 km (37 miles) east of Lübeck.

The old city of Wismar was one of the original three sea-trading towns, along with Lübeck and Rostock, which banded together in 1259 to combat Baltic pirates. From this mutual defense pact grew the great and powerful private-trading bloc, the Hanseatic League (the *Hanse* in German), which dominated the Baltic for centuries. The wealth generated by the Hanseatic merchants can still be seen in Wismar's ornate architecture.

VISITOR INFORMATION

Contacts Tourist-Information Wismar. ✉ *Lübsche Str. 23a* ☎ *03841/19433* ⊕ *www.wismar.de.*

EXPLORING

Fürstenhof (*Princes' Court*). The home of the former dukes of Mecklenburg stands next to the Marienkirche. It's an early-16th-century Italian Renaissance palace with touches of late Gothic. The facade is a series of fussy friezes depicting scenes from the Trojan War. ✉ *Fürstenhof 1.*

Marienkirche (*St. Mary's Church*). All that remains of the oldest sacral building in Wismar is the 250-foot tower. Although only partially damaged in the war, the East German government demolished the hall of the church in 1960. At noon, 3, and 7, listen for one of 14 hymns played on its carillon. ✉ *St.-Marien-Kirchhof.*

Marktplatz (*Market Square*). One of the largest and best-preserved squares in Germany is framed by patrician gabled houses. Their style ranges from redbrick late Gothic through Dutch Renaissance to 19th-century neoclassical. The square's **Wasserkunst,** the ornate pumping station built in Dutch Renaissance style, was constructed between 1580 and 1602 by the Dutch master Philipp Brandin. ✉ *Wismar.*

St. Georgen zu Wismar. One of northern Germany's biggest Gothic churches, built between 1315 and 1404, St. Georgen zu Wismar stands next to the Fürstenhof. It was a victim of the war, but has been almost completely restored. ✉ *St.-Georgen-Kirchhof 1a.*

WHERE TO EAT

$$ GERMAN 🍴 **Alter Schwede.** Located in Wismar's oldest patrician house and regarded as one of the most attractive, authentic taverns on the Baltic—and correspondingly busy—this eatery focuses on Mecklenburg's fish, game and poultry dishes, such as the traditional *Mecklenburger Ente* (Mecklenburg duck). This filling dish is filled with baked plums, apples, and raisins, and served with red cabbage and potatoes. **Known for:** historical setting; regional fish dishes; small but excellent menu. [$] *Average main: €17* ✉ *Am Markt 22* ☎ *03841/283–552* 🌐 *www.alter-schwede-wismar.de.*

$$ GERMAN 🍴 **Brauhaus am Lohberg.** Wismar's first brewery (1452) is the only place that still brews *Wismarer Mumme,* a dark beer with enough alcohol to keep it fresh for export as far away as St. Petersburg. The restaurant serves good-value typical pub food in an old half-timber house near the harbor. **Known for:** homemade beer; regional and international food; live music every Saturday. [$] *Average main: €15* ✉ *Kleine Hohe Str. 15* ☎ *03841/250–238* 🌐 *brauhaus-wismar.de.*

WHERE TO STAY

$$$ B&B/INN 🏨 **Seehotel Neuklostersee.** Set at the dreamy Naun Lake, this country hotel is a hidden gem 15 km (9 miles) east of Wismar. **Pros:** great rural setting in quaint surroundings; some rooms have lake views, others a private conservatory; includes use of beach chairs, bikes, and other amenities. **Cons:** outside Wismar; many day-trip visitors; expensive for Mecklenburg. [$] *Rooms from: €185* ✉ *Seestr. 1, Nakenstorf* ☎ *038422/4570* 🌐 *www.seehotel-neuklostersee.de* ⏲ *Closed 2nd and 3rd wks in Jan.* 🛏 *26 rooms* 🍽 *Free Breakfast.*

The Baltic Coast
FERRY TO COPENHAGEN, DENMARK
FERRY TO YSTAD, SWEDEN
FERRY TO RØNNE, DENMARK
FERRY TO TRELLEBORG, SWEDEN
FERRY TO TRELLEBORG, SWEDEN
DENMARK
Baltic Sea
Sakskøbing
A9
Nykøbing Falster
E55
Rødbyhavn
Gedser
Puttgarden
0 20 mi
0 20 km
Mecklenburger Bucht
Kap Arkona
Putgarten
Hiddensee
Schaprode
Rügen Island
L29
Sassnitz
Prora
Binz
Bergen
Jagdschloss Granitz
Prerow
Wustrow
Barth
B96
Putbus
Göhren
Stralsund
B105
Greifswalder Bodden
Deutsches Bernsteinmuseum
Ribnitz-Damgarten
B194
B105
Peenemünde
Historisch-Technisches Museum Peenemünde
Usedom Island
Heiligendamm
Kühlungsborn
Warnemünde
Wolgast
Ückeritz
Rostock
Bad Doberan
A20
Greifswald
B111
Bansin
Heringsdorf
Ahlbeck
Neubukow
Loitz
Bandelin
A20
A19
Laage
B110
VORPOMMERN
Swinoujscie
Demmin
Wismar
A20
Anklam
A20
WESTERN MECKLENBURG
Güstrow
Teterow
Reuterstadt Stavenhagen
B197
B109
A14
Sternberg
B104
Schwerin
A19
B104
Neubrandenburg
A20
Pasewalk
Karow
Waren
B192

$ 🏨 **Steigenberger–Hotel Stadt Hamburg.** This first-class hotel hides behind a
HOTEL rigid gray facade dating back to the early 19th century, but the interior is surprisingly open and airy, with skylights and a posh lobby. **Pros:** the only upscale hotel in town; great package deals available; appealing interior design. **Cons:** lacks atmosphere and personal touches; no air-conditioning; rooms facing square can be a bit noisy on market days. [$] *Rooms from: €85* ✉ *Am Markt 24* ☎ *03841/2390* 🌐 *www.wismar.steigenberger.de* 🛏 *104 rooms* 🍴 *Free Breakfast.*

SCHWERIN

32 km (20 miles) south of Wismar on Rte. 106.

Schwerin, the second-largest town in the region after Rostock and the capital of the state of Mecklenburg-Vorpommern, is worth a trip just to visit its giant island castle.

TOURS

FAMILY **Weisse Flotte.** The quintessential experience in Schwerin is one of the Weisse Flotte boat tours of the lakes—there are seven in the area. A trip to the island of Kaninchenwerder, a small sanctuary for more than 100 species of waterbirds, is an unforgettable experience. Boats for this 1½-hour standard tour depart from the pier adjacent to the Schweriner

Schloss. ⊠ *Anlegestelle Schlosspier* ☎ *0385/557–770* ⊕ *www.weisseflotteschwerin.de* ⌦ *€15* ⌫ *Closed Nov.–Mar.*

VISITOR INFORMATION

Contacts Schwerin. ⊠ *Rathaus, Am Markt 14* ☎ *0385/592–5212* ⊕ *www.schwerin.com.*

EXPLORING

Alter Garten (*Old Garden*). The town's showpiece square was the setting for military parades during the years of Communist rule. It's dominated by two buildings: the ornate neo-Renaissance state theater, constructed in 1883–86; and the Kunstsammlungen Schwerin (Schwerin Art Collection). ⊠ *Schwerin.*

Kunstsammlungen Schwerin (*Schwerin Art Collection*). This gallery houses an interesting collection of paintings by Max Liebermann and Lovis Corinth, along with Dutch and Flemish works and sculpture. There are also exhibitions of contemporary art. ⊠ *Alter Garten 3* ☎ *0385/59580* ⊕ *www.museum-schwerin.de* ⌦ *€9* ◔ *Closed Mon.*

Schweriner Dom (*Schwerin Cathedral*). This Gothic cathedral is the oldest building (built 1222–48) in the city. The bronze baptismal font is from the 14th century; the altar was built in 1440. Religious scenes painted on its walls date from the late Middle Ages. Sweeping views of the Old Town and lake await those with the energy to climb the 219 steps to the top of the 320-foot-high cathedral tower. ⊠ *Am Dom 4* ☎ *0385/565–014* ⌦ *Free.*

Schweriner Schloss. On an island near the edge of Lake Schwerin, this meticulously restored palace once housed the Mecklenburg royal family. The original palace dates from 1018 but was enlarged by Henry the Lion when he founded Schwerin in 1160. As it stands now, the palace is surmounted by 15 turrets, large and small, and is reminiscent of a French château. The portions that are neo-Renaissance in style are its many ducal staterooms, which date from between 1845 and 1857. Today, the castle is a seat of parliament. North of the castle's main tower is the **Schlossmuseum.** The Communist government restored and maintained the fantastic opulence of this rambling, 80-room reminder of an absolutist monarchy—and then used it to board kindergarten teachers in training. Antique furniture, objets d'art, silk tapestries, and paintings are sprinkled throughout the salons (the throne room is particularly extravagant), but of special interest are the ornately patterned and highly burnished inlaid wooden floors and wall panels. ⊠ *Lennéstr. 1* ☎ *0385/525–2920 museum* ⊕ *www.schwerin.com* ⌦ *€9* ◔ *Closed Mon.*

If the weather is fine, take a stroll along Wismar's historic harbor.

WHERE TO EAT

$$
GERMAN
✕ **Zum Stadtkrug-Altstadtbrauhaus.** Don't be fooled by the prefab exterior: Schwerin's only brewery is an oasis of great beer and down-to-earth regional and Brauhaus specialties like the *Malzsack* (a pork schnitzel breaded with brewing malt) or Mecklenburger lamb. Wash it down with the house-brewed unfiltered light or dark beer. **Known for:** hearty regional dishes; brewery food; relaxed atmosphere. $ *Average main: €16* ✉ *Wismarsche Str. 126* ☎ *0385/593–6693* ⊕ *www.altstadtbrauhaus.de* ➡ No credit cards.

WHERE TO STAY

$$
HOTEL
⌂ **Hotel Niederländischer Hof.** The city's most elegant hotel has a luxurious interior, decorated in a classic style, along with romantic, airy rooms and the impeccable service. **Pros:** interesting packages include tours, dinner, and more; great location right off a pond and within walking distance to main sights; excellent service. **Cons:** formal atmosphere; English, not German, ambience; small number of rooms. $ *Rooms from: €149* ✉ *Alexandrinnenstr. 12–13* ☎ *0385/591–100* ⊕ *www.niederlaendischer-hof.de* ➡ *23 rooms* ⦿ *Free Breakfast.*

$$
HOTEL
⌂ **Speicher am Ziegelsee.** Only 20 minutes walk from the Old Town and towering seven stories above the old harbor, the Speicher am Ziegelsee was once a grain warehouse. **Pros:** unbeatable location on a lovely lake; very friendly and professional service; lakeside dining. **Cons:** old-style warehouse building; rooms may seem cramped for some travelers; a bit far

from the action. $ *Rooms from: €109* ✉ *Speicherstr. 11* ☎ *0385/50030* 🌐 *www.speicher-hotel.com* 🛏 *79 rooms* 🍴 *Free Breakfast.*

SHOPPING

Antiques and bric-a-brac that have languished in cellars and attics since World War II are still surfacing throughout eastern Germany, and the occasional bargain can be found. The best places to look in Schwerin are on and around Schmiedestrasse, Schlossstrasse, and Mecklenburgstrasse.

BAD DOBERAN

60 km (37 miles) east of Wismar on Rte. 105, 90 km (56 miles) northeast of Schwerin.

Mostly famous for its cathedral, Bad Doberan is a quaint town that also has Germany's oldest sea resort, Heiligendamm. The city is a popular weekend and summer getaway for people from Rostock and Berlin, but it's managed to maintain its laid-back charm.

VISITOR INFORMATION

Contacts Bad Doberan Tourist Office. ✉ *Severinstr. 6* ☎ *038203/62154* 🌐 *www.bad-doberan-heiligendamm.de.*

EXPLORING

Doberaner Münster (*Monastery Church*). Bad Doberan is home to this meticulously restored redbrick church, one of the finest of its kind in Germany. It was built by Cistercian monks between 1294 and 1368 in the northern German brick Gothic style, with a central nave and transept. The main altar dates from the early 14th century. ✉ *Klosterstr. 2* ☎ *038203/62716* 🌐 *www.muenster-doberan.de* 🎟 *Free; guided walks €4.*

FAMILY **Molli.** No visit to this part of the country would be complete without a ride on this narrow-gauge steam train that has been chugging its 16-km (10-mile) route through the streets of Bad Doberan to the nearby beach resorts of **Heiligendamm** and **Kühlungsborn** since 1886. The train was nicknamed after a little local dog that barked its approval every time the smoking iron horse passed by. In summer *Molli* runs 14 times daily between Bad Doberan and Kühlungsborn. ✉ *Am Bahnhof* ☎ *038293/431–331* 🌐 *www.molli-bahn.de* 🎟 *From €10 round-trip.*

WHERE TO STAY

$$$$ HOTEL FAMILY Fodor's Choice ★ 🏨 **Grand Hotel Heiligendamm.** Nestled in five meticulously restored, gleaming white structures on a secluded beach, the hotel displays an almost Californian Bel Air charm and offers timelessly furnished rooms decorated in soft colors. **Pros:** the only real first-class hotel on the Baltic Coast; wide range of sports and activities; wonderful amenities for children up to age 11. **Cons:** very large hotel spread out over somewhat

long distances; service is formal and stiff at times; books up quickly in high season. [$] *Rooms from: €275* ✉ *Prof.-Dr.-Vogel-Str. 16–18, Heiligendamm* ☎ *038203/7400* 🌐 *www.grandhotel-heiligendamm.de* 🛏 *225 rooms* 🍴 *Free Breakfast.*

ROSTOCK

14 km (9 miles) east of Bad Doberan on Rte. 105.

The biggest port and shipbuilding center of the former East Germany, Rostock was founded around 1200. Of all the Hanseatic cities, this once-thriving city suffered the most from the dissolution of the league in 1669. The GDR reestablished Rostock as a major port, but after reunification, shipbuilding all but disappeared. Nevertheless, the city set its sights to the future, retooled its factories and is now a major producer of wind turbines. Ferries from Gedser (Denmark) and Trelleborg (Sweden) come here. The population doubles in the summer due to Baltic cruise ships that dock in Warnemünde. **TIP→ The biggest local annual attraction is Hanse Sail, a week of tallship racing held in August.**

VISITOR INFORMATION

Contacts Rostock Tourist Office. ✉ *Universitätspl. 6* ☎ *0381/381–2222* 🌐 *www.rostock.de.*

EXPLORING

Kröpelinerstrasse. This pedestrian-only shopping street stretches from the Kröpeliner Tor (the old western gate) to the Neuer Markt. Here you'll find the finest examples of late-Gothic and Renaissance houses of rich Hanse merchants. ✉ *Kröpelinerstr.*

Kunsthalle (*Art Gallery*). The Kunsthalle Rostock, once regarded as a prestigious object of GDR cultural policy, features a large collection of modern East German artworks and changing exhibitions of international artists. ✉ *Hamburger Str. 40* ☎ *0381/381–7000* 🌐 *www.kunsthallerostock.de* 🎟 *Free; special exhibitions have fees.*

Neuer Markt (*Town Square*). Here, you'll immediately notice the architectural potpourri of the **Rathaus.** The pink baroque facade from the 18th century hides a wonderful 13th-century Gothic building underneath. The Town Hall spouts seven slender, decorative towers that look like candles on a peculiar birthday cake. Walk around the back to see more of the Gothic elements. Historic gabled houses surround the rest of the square. ✉ *Rostock.*

St. Marienkirche (*St. Mary's Church*). This eight-centuries-old church—Rostock's greatest example of Gothic architecture—contains a bronze baptismal font from 1290 and some interesting baroque features, notably the oak altar (1720) and organ (1770). The huge astronomical clock, dating from 1472, has a calendar extending to 2150. ✉ *Am Ziegenmarkt 4* ☎ *0381/492–3396* 🌐 *www.marienkirche-rostock.de* 🎟 *Free; recommended donation €2.*

Universitätsplatz (*University Square*). The triangular University Square, commemorating the founding of one of northern Europe's oldest universities here in 1419, is home to Rostock University's Italian Renaissance–style main building, finished in 1867. ✉ *Rostock.*

FAMILY **Zoologischer Garten** (*Zoological Garden*). Here you'll find one of the largest collections of exotic animals and birds in northern Germany. This zoo is particularly noted for its polar bears, some of which were bred in Rostock. If you're traveling with children, a visit is a must. A new Polarium opened in fall 2018. ✉ *Barnstorfer Ring 1* ☎ *0381/20820* 🌐 *www.zoo-rostock.de* 🎫 *€16.*

WHERE TO EAT

$$ EUROPEAN 🍴 **Otto's Restaurant und Hafenbar.** Merging an à la carte restaurant with an elegant cocktail bar, Otto's has been shaking up Rostock's dining scene since 2017. Located right on the waterfront inside a pontoon boat, this restaurant also vows with scenic views that stretch from the city harbor to the Old Town. **Known for:** Sunday brunch with buffet; regional and maritime cuisine; romantic dinners for two. [$] *Average main: €18* ✉ *Am Stadthafen 70* ☎ *0160/376–8356* 🌐 *www.ottos-restaurantschiff.de.*

$$ GERMAN 🍴 **Petrikeller.** Once you've crossed the threshold of the Petrikeller, you'll find yourself in the medieval world of Hanseatic merchants, seamen, and wild pirates such as Klaus Störtebecker. The largely meat-centric menu reflects the cuisine of the Middle Ages, when meat and roots were the common daily ration. **Known for:** knights' banquet every Friday and Saturday; rustic atmosphere; relaxed dining (with fingers if you wish like in medieval times). [$] *Average main: €20* ✉ *Harte Str. 27* ☎ *0381/455–855* 🌐 *www.petrikeller.de* 💳 *No credit cards* 🕒 *Closed Mon. No lunch.*

$ SEAFOOD 🍴 **Zur Kogge.** Looking like the cabin of a *Kogge* (a Hanseatic sailing vessel), the oldest sailors' beer tavern in town serves mostly fish. Order the *Fischteller "Schifferhaus,"* consisting of three kinds of fish—depending on the day's catch—served with vegetables, shrimp, and potatoes. **Known for:** local maritime cuisine; seafaring memorabilia; ice cream for dessert. [$] *Average main: €13* ✉ *Wokrenterstr. 27* ☎ *0381/493–4493* 🌐 *www.zur-kogge.de* 🕒 *Closed Sun. No lunch Mon.–Thurs.*

WHERE TO STAY

$$ HOTEL 🏨 **pentahotel Rostock.** A 19th-century mansion, this hotel is a genuine part of Rostock's historic Old Town. **Pros:** good location; very quiet rooms since it's on a back street; excellent gym. **Cons:** restaurant isn't very good; uninspired room design; standard rooms are small. [$] *Rooms from: €104* ✉ *Schwaansche Str. 6* ☎ *0381/49700* 🌐 *www.pentahotels.com* 🛏 *153 rooms* 🍽 *Free Breakfast.*

$ HOTEL 🏨 **Steigenberger Hotel Sonne.** With more than 200 years of history behind it, the "Sun," within the Old Town, is one of the nicest hotels in Rostock. **Pros:** nice view and near many sights; good restaurants, cafés, and bars nearby; sumptuous breakfast. **Cons:** rooms get direct sunlight in summer, and therefore are very warm; traffic over cobblestone road outside can be noisy; no air-conditioning. [$] *Rooms from:*

€97 ⊠ Neuer Markt 2 ☎ 0381/49730 ⊕ www.rostock.steigenberger. de ↷ 111 rooms ⦿ Free Breakfast.

SHOPPING

Echter Rostocker Doppel-Kümmel und -Korn, a kind of schnapps made from various grains and flavored with cumin, is a traditional liquor of the area around Rostock. Fishermen have numbed themselves to the cold for centuries with this 80-proof beverage. A bottle costs €8–€11; Lehment is the best brand of this local moonshine.

WARNEMÜNDE

14

14 km (9 miles) north of Rostock on Rte. 103.

Warnemünde, officially a suburb of Rostock, is a quaint seaside resort town with the best hotels and restaurants in the area, as well as 17 km (11 miles) of beautiful white-sand beach. It's been a popular summer getaway for families in eastern Germany for years.

There are plenty of water sports to do in Warnemünde, but the town also invites pure relaxation. However, Warnemünde is a major cruise-ship terminal. Whenever there is more than one ship at the dock, the town explodes with a county fair–like atmosphere, and shops and restaurants stay open until the ships leave at midnight. The city celebrates its maritime heritage with four port parties annually, which include shantys and fireworks.

GETTING HERE AND AROUND

Thanks to its proximity to Rostock and the A-20, Warnemünde is easily accessible from any major city in the region. Traffic between the seaside district of Rostock and the downtown area can be heavy on summer weekends. The best way to explore the city is by riding a bike or walking.

VISITOR INFORMATION

Contacts Warnemünde Tourist Office. ⊠ *Am Strom 59, at Kirchenstr., Rostock* ☎ *0381/381-2222* ⊕ *www.rostock.de.*

EXPLORING

Alter Strom (*Old Stream*). Inland from the lighthouse is this yacht marina. Once the entry into the port of Warnemünde, it now has bars, plenty of good restaurants, and touristy shops. The fishing boats lining the Strom sell the day's catch, smoked fish, and bags of fried mussels. ⊠ *Rostock.*

Deutsches Bernsteinmuseumm (*German Amber Museum*). In the Deutsches Bernsteinmuseum, which adjoins the main factory, you can see a fascinating exhibit of how this precious "Baltic gold" is collected from the sea and refined to make jewelry. The museum has pieces of amber that are between 35 and 50 million years old. ⊠ *Im Kloster 1–2, Ribnitz-Damgarten ✢ Ribnitz-Damgarten is 30 km (19 miles) northeast of Rostock* ☎ *03821/4622* ⊕ *www.deutsches-bernsteinmuseum.de* 🎫 *€9* ☾ *Closed Mon. Nov.–Mar.*

FAMILY **Leuchtturm.** Children enjoy climbing to the top of the town landmark, a 115-foot-high lighthouse, dating from 1898; on clear days it offers views of the coast and Rostock Harbor. In summer, adults can enjoy a cold beer from the Marlower Brauhaus trailer at the base of the lighthouse. ✉ *Am Leuchtturm, Rostock* 🎟 *Free.*

BEACHES

FAMILY **Warnemünde Beach.** The beach fronting the resort town of Warnemünde is one of Germany's most popular and it can get fairly crowded in summer. The expansive beach, with its soft, clean sand, is fabulous for sunbathing, relaxing, or walking. The pleasant sea breeze invites kite flyers and you can purchase different kinds of kites from the open-air market along the promenade. Food and drinks are available from many vendors and at several supermarkets in the town itself. **Amenities:** food and drink; parking; showers; toilets; water sports. **Best for:** sunrise; sunset; swimming; walking. ✉ *Seepromende 1, Rostock.*

WHERE TO EAT

$ SEAFOOD 🍴 **Fischerklause.** Sailors have stopped in at this restaurant's bar for more than a century. The smoked fish sampler, served on a lazy Susan, is delicious, and the house specialty of fish soup is best washed down with some Rostocker Doppel-Kümmel schnapps. **Known for:** live shantys on the piano Friday and Saturday evenings; locally popular; pierside location. [$] *Average main: €13* ✉ *Am Strom 123, Rostock* ☎ *0381/52516.*

WHERE TO STAY

$ RESORT 🏨 **Landhotel Ostseetraum.** This family-owned hotel, in a thatch-roof farmhouse outside Warnemünde, blends contemporary style with rural architecture. **Pros:** green setting not far away from the sea; friendly and personalized service; very private apartments. **Cons:** old-fashioned interior design in need of updating in some rooms and public areas; outside Warnemünde proper; only small supermarket in vicinity. [$] *Rooms from: €95* ✉ *Stolteraerweg 34b, Rostock* ☎ *0381/519–1848* 🌐 *www.ostseetraum.de* 🛏 *21 rooms* 🍽 *Free Breakfast.*

$$$$ RESORT 🏨 **Yachthafenresidenz Hohe Düne.** The star on the Baltic Coast is this huge, modern resort, comfortably residing on a peninsula between the yacht harbor, a sandy beach, and the port entrance. **Pros:** very well run; stylish hotel with a great ambience and amenities; impressive wellness and spa area. **Cons:** outside Warnemünde; accessible only by 2-minute ferry from the town center; few attractions and restaurants in walking distance. [$] *Rooms from: €227* ✉ *Am Yachthafen 1, Rostock* ☎ *0381/50400* 🌐 *www.hohe-duene.de* 🛏 *368 rooms* 🍽 *Free Breakfast.*

NIGHTLIFE

The pubs in the marina **Alter Strom** are fun gathering places.

Skybar. This bar is open from 8:30 pm until 3 am Friday and Saturday. Roof access gives you the chance to sit under the stars in the highest bar of the region and watch ship lights twinkle on the sea. ⊠ *Neptun Hotel, Seestr. 19, 19th fl., Rostock* ☎ *0381/777–773* ⊕ *www.hotel-neptun.de/sky-bar.html.*

STRALSUND

68 km (42 miles) east of Rostock on Rte. 105.

This jewel of the Baltic has retained its historic city center and parts of its 13th-century defensive wall. The wall was built following an attack by the Lübeck fleet in 1249. In 1815 the Congress of Vienna awarded the city, which had been under Swedish control, to the Prussians.

GETTING HERE AND AROUND

Stralsund is well linked to both Rostock and Berlin by A-20 and A-19. The city is an ideal base for exploring the coast via the well-developed network of Bundesstrassen around it. Inside the city, walking or biking are better options, though, as the dense, historic downtown area makes it difficult to drive.

VISITOR INFORMATION

Contacts Stralsund Tourist Office. ⊠ *Alter Markt 9* ☎ *03831/252–340* ⊕ *www.stralsundtourismus.de.*

EXPLORING

Alter Markt (*Old Market Square*). The Alter Markt has the best local architecture, ranging from Gothic to Renaissance to Baroque. Most homes belonged to rich merchants, notably the late-Gothic **Wulflamhaus,** with 17 ornate, steeply stepped gables. Stralsund's architectural masterpiece, however, is the 14th-century **Rathaus,** considered by many to be the finest secular example of redbrick Gothic. The Rathaus is a mirror image of its counterpart in Lübeck, Stralsund's main rival in the Hanseatic League ⊠ *Stralsund.*

FAMILY **Deutsches Meeresmuseum** (*German Oceanography Museum*). The Stralsund aquarium of Baltic Sea life is part of this three-floor museum, which also displays the skeletons of a giant whale and a hammerhead shark, and a 25-foot-high chunk of coral. ⊠ *Katharinenberg 14–20, entrance on Mönchstr.* ☎ *03831/265–0610* ⊕ *www.meeresmuseum.de* ☞ *€10* ⊗ *Closed Mon. Nov.–Mar.*

FAMILY **Ozeaneum.** The Ozeaneum features 50 aquaria, some of them huge, with 7,000 animals from the Baltic Sea, North Sea, and Atlantic Ocean, as well as the world's largest exhibition of whales. There is also a small Humboldt Penguin colony, a children's favorite. ⊠ *Hafenstr. 11* ☎ *03831/265–0610* ⊕ *www.ozeaneum.de* ☞ *€17* ⊗ *Closed Mon. Nov.–Mar.*

14

Stralsund Museum. This museum, which is located inside the former Dominican Abbey of St Catherine, exhibits diverse artifacts from more than 10,000 years of this coastal region's history. Highlights include a toy collection and 10th-century Viking gold jewelry found on Hiddensee. ⊠ *Mönchstr. 25–28* ☎ *03831/253–617* ⊕ *www.stralsund-museum.de* ⌑ *€6* ⊘ *Closed Mon.*

St. Marienkirche (*St. Mary's Church*). This enormous church is the largest of Stralsund's three redbrick Gothic churches. With 4,000 pipes and intricate decorative figures, the magnificent 17th-century Stellwagen organ (played only during Sunday services) is a delight to see and hear. The view from the church tower of Stralsund's old city center is well worth climbing the 349 steps. ⊠ *Marienstr. 16* ☎ *03831/298–966* ⊕ *www.st-mariengemeinde-stralsund.de* ⌑ *Tour of church tower €4.*

St. Nikolaikirche (*St. Nicholas's Church*). The treasures of the 13th-century Gothic church include a 15-foot-high crucifix from the 14th century, an astronomical clock from 1394, and a famous baroque altar. ⊠ *Auf dem St. Nikolaikirchhof 2* ☎ *03831/297–199* ⊕ *www.hst-nikolai.de* ⌑ *€3 (free Sun.).*

WHERE TO EAT

$$
SEAFOOD
✕ **Wulflamstuben.** This restaurant is on the ground floor of the Wulflamhaus, a 14th-century gabled house on the old market square. In late spring or early summer, get the light and tasty *Ostseescholle* (grilled plaice), fresh from the Baltic Sea, while in winter the hearty *Stralsunder Aalsuppe* (Stralsund eel soup) is a must. **Known for:** historical setting; seafood and meat specialties; small selection of vegan dishes. Ⓢ *Average main: €18* ⊠ *Alter Markt 5* ☎ *03831/291–533* ⊕ *www.wulflamstuben.de.*

$$
GERMAN
✕ **Zum Alten Fritz.** It's worth the trip here just to see the rustic interior and copper brewing equipment. Since the restaurant is owned by the Stralsunder Brewery, all Stralsunder and several Störtebecker beers are on tap, including the rare Störtebecker Roggen-Weizen, a wheat beer made with rye, and Germany's first India Pale Ale. **Known for:** beer garden in summer; redbrick walls and wooden furniture; special beer-based dishes. Ⓢ *Average main: €15* ⊠ *Greifswalder Chaussee 84–85, at B–96a* ☎ *03831/255–500* ⊕ *www.alter-fritz.de.*

WHERE TO STAY

$$
HOTEL
⌂ **Romantik Hotel Scheelehof.** Encompassing five historical buildings built in different centuries, this hotel combines historic architecture with luxurious decor and modern comfort. **Pros:** walking distance to main sights and train station; family rooms with sleeping lofts; dogs welcome. **Cons:** hotel spread across several buildings; rooms all different, so a bit of a lottery; small spa and wellness area. Ⓢ *Rooms from: €140* ⊠ *Fährstr. 23–25* ☎ *03831/283–300* ⊕ *www.scheelehof.com* ⌑ *92 rooms* ⭓◎⭓ *Free Breakfast.*

$
HOTEL
🖵 **Wyndham Stralsund HanseDom Hotel.** This hotel is a modern property with winning amenities and great hospitality at an unbeatable price. **Pros:** top spa; solid and reliable services and amenities; great discounts for early bookings. **Cons:** for Stralsund, this is a large, busy hotel; far away from city center (15 minutes); parking fees. $ *Rooms from: €94* ⊠ *Grünhofer Bogen 18–20* ☎ *030/9780–8888* ⊕ *www.wyndhamstralsund.com* ⤳ *114 rooms* ⟲ *Free Breakfast.*

NIGHTLIFE

Black Pearls. Located in a medieval cellar basement, this bar attracts with creative cocktail creations and soul, funk, and dance music of the last 30 years. Open from 8 pm to 3 am. ⊠ *Ossenreyerstr. 6* ☎ *03831/282–233* ⊕ *www.blackpearls-lounge.de.*

14

SHOPPING

Buddelschiffe (ships in a bottle) are a symbol of the magnificent sailing history of this region. They look easy to build, but they aren't, and they're quite delicate. Expect to pay more than €85 for a 1-liter bottle. Also look for *Fischerteppiche* (fishermen's carpets). Eleven square feet of these traditional carpets take 160 hours to create, which explains why they're meant only to be hung on the wall—and why they cost from €260 to €1,200. They're decorated with traditional symbols of the region, such as the mythical griffin.

RÜGEN ISLAND

4 km (2½ miles) northeast of Stralsund on B-96.

Fodor'sChoice
★
Rügen's diverse and breathtaking landscapes have inspired poets and painters for more than a century. Railways in the mid-19th century brought the first vacationers from Berlin and many of the grand mansions and villas on the island date from this period. The island's main route runs between the **Grosser Jasmunder Bodden** (Big Jasmund Inlet), a giant sea inlet, and a smaller expanse of water, the **Kleiner Jasmunder Bodden** (Little Jasmund Inlet Lake), to the port of Sassnitz. You're best off staying at any of the island's four main vacation centers—Sassnitz, Binz, Sellin, and Göhren.

GETTING HERE AND AROUND
Rügen is an easy two-hour drive from Rostock and a 15-minute drive from Stralsund via the B-96. As there is only one bridge connecting the island to the mainland, the road can get clogged occasionally in summer. On the island, a car is highly recommended to reach the more remote beaches, but watch out for island teenagers and their infatuation with muscle cars; give them a wide berth.

VISITOR INFORMATION
Contacts Sassnitz Tourist Office. ⊠ *Bahnhofstr. 19a, Sassnitz* ☎ *038392/6490* ⊕ *www.insassnitz.de.* **Tourismuszentrale Rügen.** ⊠ *Circus 16, Putbus* ☎ *03838/807–780* ⊕ *www.ruegen.de.*

EXPLORING

Bergen. This small town is the island's administrative capital, founded as a Slavic settlement some 900 years ago. The **Marienkirche** (St. Mary's Church) has geometric murals dating back to the late 1100s and painted brick octagonal pillars. The pulpit and altar are baroque. Outside the front door and built into the church facade is a gravestone from the 1200s. ⊠ *Bergen.*

Binz. The largest resort town on Rügen's east coast, it has white villas and a beach promenade. Four kilometers (2½ miles) north of Binz lies the fascist resort of **Prora**, where the Nazis once planned to provide vacation quarters for up to 20,000 German workers. The complex was never used, except by the East German army. Redevelopment of the site began in 2003 and by 2016 refurbished apartments were available for purchase; there's also a youth hostel. Museums and galleries here today do their best to document the history of the site. ⊠ *Strandpromenade 1, Binz.*

Hiddensee. Just 5 km (3 miles) off the northwest corner of Rügen is a smaller, sticklike island called Hiddensee whose undisturbed solitude has attracted such visitors as Albert Einstein, Thomas Mann, Rainer Maria Rilke, and Sigmund Freud. As Hiddensee is an auto-free zone, leave your car in Schaprode, 21 km (13 miles) west of Bergen, and take a ferry. Reederei Hiddensee (☎ *038300/210* ⊕ *www.reederei-hiddensee. de*) makes the 45-minute trip from Schaprode on Rügen to Vitte on Hiddensee eight times a day, with other departures from Stralsund. They also serve the towns of Kloster and Neuendorf on Hiddensee. Fares start at €15.50. Vacation cottages and restaurants are on the island. ⊕ *www.seebad-hiddensee.de.*

Jagdschloss Granitz. Standing on the highest point of East Rügen, 2 km (1 mile) south of Binz, is the Jagdschloss Granitz, a hunting lodge built in 1836. It offers a splendid view in all directions from its lookout tower and has an excellent hunting exhibit. ⊠ *Binz* ☎ *038393/663–814* ⊕ *www.granitz-jagdschloss.de* ☜ *€6* 🕑 *Closed Mon. Nov.–Mar.*

Jasmund Nationalpark. From Sassnitz, it is an easy walk to the Jasmund Nationalpark, where you can explore the marshes, lush pine forests, and towering chalk cliffs. ⊠ *Stubbenkammer 2 a, Sassnitz* ☎ *038392/35011* ⊕ *www.nationalpark-jasmund.de.*

Kap Arkona. Marking the northernmost point in eastern Germany is the lighthouse at Kap Arkona, a nature lover's paradise filled with blustery sand dunes. The redbrick lighthouse was designed by Karl Friedrich Schinkel, the Prussian court-architect responsible for so many of today's landmarks in Berlin. ⊠ *Putgarten.*

Rasender Roland (*Racing Roland*). This 90-year-old narrow-gauge steam train runs 24 km (16 miles) in the southeast corner of Rügen. Trains leave every two hours from Göhren to Putbus and Binz to Putbus; every hour from Binz to Putbus from May to Oct. The ride takes 70 minutes each way. ⊠ *Binzer Str. 12, Putbus* ☎ *038301/8010* ⊕ *www.ruegensche-baederbahn.de* ☜ *From €23.*

Vacationers sunbathe in Strandkörbe, or on a towel on Ahlbeck's beach.

Sassnitz. This small fishing town is the island's harbor for ferries to Sweden. Sassnitz is surrounded by some of the most pristine nature to be found along the Baltic Coast. Ten kilometers (6 miles) north of Sassnitz are the twin chalk cliffs of Rügen's main attraction, the **Stubbenkammer** headland. From here you can best see the much-photographed white-chalk cliffs called the **Königstuhl,** rising 350 feet from the sea. A steep trail leads down to a beach. ⊠ *Sassnitz.*

BEACHES

FAMILY **Binz Beach.** The rule of the Baltics' most exclusive beach is "see and be seen." The 5-km-long (3-mile-long) and 54-yard-wide beach is the perfect place to sunbathe and swim, as well as stroll—there's a 150-year-old beach path promenade. The somewhat rocky beach is punctuated by the *Seebrücke,* a boardwalk that extends into the sea. **Amenities:** food and drink; lifeguards; parking; showers; toilets; water sports. **Best for:** partiers; surfing; swimming; walking. ⊠ *Strandpromenade, Binz.*

Prora. This is one of the finest beaches on Rügen, and there's probably not another place like it in the world—think fine white beach bordered by a dense pine forest sitting in the shadow of the ruins of a monstrous Nazi beach resort. Prora actually sits in the Prorer Wiek, a pleasant cove with shallow water and plentiful sandbanks. **Amenities:** food and drink; lifeguards; parking; showers; toilets; water sports. **Best for:** nudists; sunset; swimming; walking. ⊠ *Binz.*

Vitte Beach. Tucked away on the west coast of Hiddensee, is a 5-km-long (3-mile-long) beach with shimmering turquoise waters and sand so fine that you might mistake it for the Caribbean. The 50-yard-wide beach is ideal for families with children, but is only accessible by bicycle. The water is quite shallow and it's easy to walk out to the sandbanks. Vitte is divided between a nudist section to the south and a "textile" section to the north. Locals decorate the beach with baskets of flowers in summer. **Amenities:** showers; toilets; water sports. **Best for:** partiers; nudists; swimming; walking. ✉ *Süderende, Vitte.*

WHERE TO EAT

$$ GERMAN 🍴 **Panoramahotel Lohme.** While enjoying fresh fish from local waters, prepared with a light Italian touch, you can watch the sunset over the cliffs of Kap Arkona at this restaurant dubbed "Rügen's balcony." Make a reservation, and insist on a table in the *Fontane-Veranda* (in winter) or the *Arkonablick-Terrasse* (in summer). **Known for:** unbeatable sea views; special year-round herring menu, duck menu in winter; dishes with sea buckthorn. [$] *Average main: €20* ✉ *An der Steilküste 8, Lohme* ☎ *038302/9110* 🌐 *www.panorama-hotel-lohme.de* ⏲ *No lunch.*

WHERE TO STAY

$$ B&B/INN 🏨 **Hotel Godewind.** This small hotel offers food and lodging at reasonable prices. **Pros:** quiet setting; very cozy rooms with nice furniture; near the beach. **Cons:** almost no amenities or services offered; Hiddensee is car-free, so walking everywhere; restaurant often fully booked. [$] *Rooms from: €105* ✉ *Süderende 53, Vitte* ☎ *038300/6600* 🌐 *www.hotelgodewind.de* 💳 *No credit cards* 🛏 *38 rooms* 🍽 *Free Breakfast.*

$ RENTAL 🏨 **Hotel Villa Granitz.** This mostly wooden mansion is a small and quiet retreat for those who want to avoid the masses. **Pros:** cozy hotel in traditional style of the area; very competitive prices for the size and comfort of rooms; intimate and family-run. **Cons:** in the outskirts of the city; a distance from the beach; busy road in front can cause noise in some rooms. [$] *Rooms from: €94* ✉ *Birkenallee 17, Baabe* ☎ *038303/1410* 🌐 *www.villa-granitz.de* 🛏 *58 rooms* 🍽 *Free Breakfast.*

$$$$ HOTEL 🏨 **Travel Charme Kurhaus Binz.** The grand old lady of the Baltic Sea, the neoclassical 19th-century Kurhaus Binz is reviving the splendor of times past, when Binz was called the Nice of the North. **Pros:** extremely clean; highly trained and friendly personnel; all the amenities. **Cons:** lacks the feel of a typical Rügen hotel; not very personal or intimate; no tea or coffeemaker in rooms. [$] *Rooms from: €261* ✉ *Strandpromenade 27, Binz* ☎ *038393/6650* 🌐 *www.travelcharme.com* 🛏 *137 rooms* 🍽 *Free Breakfast.*

USEDOM ISLAND

72 km (45 miles) to Peenebrücke Wolgastbridge from Stralsund.

Fodor's Choice ★ Usedom Island has almost 32 km (20 miles) of sandy shoreline and a string of resorts. Much of the island's untouched landscape is a nature preserve that provides refuge for a number of rare birds, including the giant sea eagle, which has a wingspan of up to 8 feet. Even in summer this island feels more or less deserted and is easy to explore by bicycle.

Due to a fluke in the postwar division of Germany, about one-fifth of the island is actually in Poland.

GETTING HERE AND AROUND

From the west, Usedom is accessed via the causeway at **Wolgast**. The Peenebrücke bridge closes to traffic at times to allow boats to pass through. From the south, the B-110 leads from Anklam to Usedom. In summer, particularly before and after weekends, traffic can be very heavy on both roads. Trains of the Usedomer Bäderbahn traverse the island every 30 minutes; the company also runs an extensive bus network.

Contacts Usedomer Bäderbahn. ⌂ *Am Bahnhof 1, Heringsdorf* ☎ *38378/2710* ⊕ *www.ubb-online.com.*

14

VISITOR INFORMATION

Contacts Usedom Island Tourismus. ⌂ *Hauptstr. 42, Seebad Bansin* ☎ *038375/244–144* ⊕ *www.usedom.de.*

EXPLORING

Ahlbeck. The island's main town is also one of its best resorts. The tidy and elegant resort is one of the three *Kaiserbäder* (imperial baths)—the two others are Heringsdorf and Bansin—where the Emperor Wilhelm II liked to spend his summers in the early 20th century. Noble families and rich citizens followed the emperor, turning Ahlbeck into one of the prettiest summer retreats on the Baltic Coast. Ahlbeck's landmark is the 19th-century wooden pier with four towers. Stroll the beach to the right of the pier and you'll arrive at the Polish border. ⌂ *Kurstr.1, Ahlbeck.*

Historisch-Technisches Museum Peenemünde (*Historical-Technical Museum Peenemünde*). Peenemünde, at the northwest tip of Usedom, is the launch site of the world's first ballistic missiles, the V-1 and V-2, developed by Germany during World War II. At the Historisch-Technisches Museum you can view these rockets as well as models of early airplanes and ships. One exhibit in particular covers the moral responsibility of scientists who develop new technology by focusing on the secret plants where most of the rocket parts were assembled, and where thousands of slave laborers died. ⌂ *Im Kraftwerk, Peenemünde* ☎ *038371/5050* ⊕ *museum-peenemuende.de* ☷ *€8* ◷ *Closed Mon. Nov.–Mar.*

BEACHES

FAMILY **Kaiserbäder.** The Kaiserbäder Strand stretches for more than 12 km (7½ miles) along Usedom Island's northeast coast from Bansin to Heringsdorf to Ahlbeck. A promenade connects the three towns which charm with a mix of 19th-century beach architecture on one side and beach-chair relaxation on the other. A stroll through the windy sea air is said to have magical recuperative powers and locals claim that when the conditions are right, the sand actually sings when the grains rub together. The wide beach bustles with weekend Berliners and long-term visitors in summer. **Amenities:** food and drink; lifeguards; parking;

showers; toilets; water sports. **Best for:** partiers; sunrise; swimming; walking. ✉ *Strandpromenade, Heringsdorf.*

Ückeritz. One of the best-kept secrets on Usedom, this 12-km-long (7½-mile-long) beach is quite busy in the north but almost deserted farther south. The area is quite rustic and the perfect place to feel like you have the beach to yourself. **Amenities:** food and drink; parking. **Best for:** nudists; solitude; sunrise; sunset. ✉ *Uferpromenade, Ückeritz.*

WHERE TO EAT

$$ GERMAN

🍴 **Kaisers Eck.** This friendly restaurant offers a mix of regional and international dishes, all fresh and full of flavor. The small but excellent menu, which has received plaudits from multiple sources, includes crème brûlée with goat cheese, forest honey and tonka beans. **Known for:** top quality at affordable prices; seasonally changing menu; unassuming interior and exterior. [$] *Average main: €20* ✉ *Kaiserstr. 1, Heringsdorf* ☎ *038378/30058* 🌐 *www.kaiserseck.de* 🕓 *Closed Sun.–Tues. in Mar.*

WHERE TO STAY

$$$ HOTEL

🏨 **SEETELHOTEL Ahlbecker Hof.** The grande dame of Ahlbeck, this five-star hotel calls to mind the island's past as a getaway for Prussian nobility in the 19th century. **Pros:** has one of the area's best spas; two gourmet restaurants; near beach. **Cons:** no elevator; some rooms in different building and small; starting to look tired. [$] *Rooms from: €188* ✉ *Dünenstr. 47, Ahlbeck* ☎ *038378/620* 🌐 *www.seetel.de* 🛏 *91 rooms* 🍽 *Free Breakfast.*

BERLIN

WELCOME TO BERLIN

TOP REASONS TO GO

★ **Affordability:** Despite rising costs, Berlin is still one of the better bargains among European capitals. Tickets for the opera, the theater, and museums tend to hover around €12 (though they do go up from there).

★ **Long, creative nights:** The only European city without official closing hours, Berlin's young artists will keep you up all night.

★ **Museum Island (Museuminsel):** The architectural monuments and art treasures here hail from ancient Greece to Egypt to Rome to 18th-century Berlin.

★ **The Reichstag's cupola:** Reserve a coveted spot at the top of Berlin's Parliament to enjoy great city views.

★ **Trace history's path:** The division of Berlin was a major historical event and an anomaly in urban history.

In eastern Germany, almost halfway between Paris and Moscow, Berlin is Germany's largest city. When the city-state of Berlin was incorporated in 1920, it swallowed towns and villages far beyond what had been the downtown area around the two main rivers, the Spree and the Havel. After World War II, Berlin was divided among the conquering powers, and in 1961 the East German government built a wall through the middle of the city, more or less overnight. For the next decades, the city was divided. In November 1989, the wall fell, and a peaceful revolution put an end to the Communist East German regime. In 1999, Berlin became the capital of a reunified Germany, once again.

1 Mitte. Once home to the city's Jewish quarters, after the war Mitte was part of East Berlin. Today, it's the center of the city once again, packed with monuments, museums, and shops.

2 Tiergarten. The neighborhood extends around the Tiergarten (animal garden), Berlin's version of New York's Central Park.

3 Potsdamer Platz. One of the busiest squares in prewar Europe is still the center of commercial action.

4 Friedrichshain. The area's offbeat bars, restaurants, and clubs attract creative types.

5 Kreuzberg. When Berlin was divided, West Berlin's Kreuzberg was right

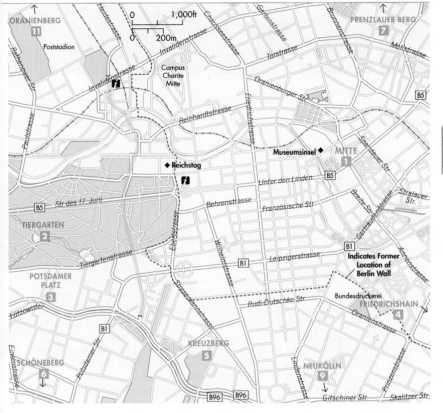

15

alongside the wall. It's still edgy and artsy.

6 Schöneberg. Historically Berlin's gay neighborhood, Schöneberg mixes the alternative vibe of Kreuzberg with the residential feel of West Berlin.

7 Prenzlauer Berg. Once a working-class neighborhood, it's now one of the city's most gentrified areas.

8 Wedding. Berlin's artists are heading to this working-class neighborhood.

9 Neukölln. This area has gone from bleak to chic, and galleries, boutiques, and wine bars have replaced abandoned storefronts.

10 Charlottenburg. This is as elegant as Berlin gets. This beautifully sedate area hasn't changed as much as much of the rest of the city.

11 Wannsee and Oranienburg. The concentration camp in Oranienburg is a somber excursion; Wannsee also has a dark past but offers parks and lakes to explore.

Updated by
Liz Humphreys

Since the fall of the Iron Curtain, no other city in Europe has seen more change than Berlin, the German capital. The two Berlins that had been physically separated for almost 30 years have become one, and the reunited city has become a cutting-edge destination for architecture, culture, entertainment, nightlife, and shopping.

After successfully uniting its own East and West, Berlin now plays a pivotal role in the European Union. But even as the capital thinks and moves forward, history is always tugging at its sleeve. Between the wealth of neoclassical and 21st-century buildings there are constant reminders, both subtle and stark, of the events of the 20th century.

Berlin is quite young by European standards, beginning as two separate entities in 1237 on two islands in the Spree River: Cölln and Berlin. By the 1300s, Berlin was prospering, thanks to its location at the intersection of important trade routes, and rose to power as the seat of the Hohenzollern dynasty. The Great Elector Friedrich Wilhelm, in the nearly 50 years of his reign (1640–88), touched off a cultural renaissance. Later, Frederick the Great (1712–86) made Berlin and Potsdam glorious centers of his enlightened yet autocratic Prussian monarchy.

In 1871, Prussia, ruled by the "Iron Chancellor" Count Otto von Bismarck, unified the many independent German states into the German Empire. Berlin maintained its status as capital for the duration of that Second Reich (1871–1918), through the post–World War I Weimar Republic (1919–33), and also through Hitler's so-called Third Reich (1933–45). The city's golden years were the Roaring Twenties, when Berlin evolved as the energetic center for the era's cultural avant-garde. World-famous writers, painters, and artists met here while the impoverished bulk of its 4 million inhabitants lived in heavily overpopulated quarters. This "dance on the volcano," as those years of political and economic upheaval have been called, came to a grisly and bloody end after January 1933, when Adolf Hitler became chancellor. The Nazis made Berlin their capital but ultimately failed to remake the city into a monument to their power, as they had planned. By World War II's end, 70% of the city lay in ruins, with more rubble than in all other German cities combined.

Along with the division of Germany after World War II, Berlin was partitioned into American, British, and French zones in the West and a Soviet zone in the East. The three western-occupied zones became West Berlin, while the Soviets, who controlled not only Berlin's eastern zone but also all of the east German land surrounding it, tried to blockade West Berlin out of existence. (They failed thanks to the year-long Berlin Airlift [1948–49], during which American airplanes known in German as "raisin bombers," dropped supplies until the blockade lifted.) In 1949 the Soviet Union established East Berlin as the capital of its new satellite state, the German Democratic Republic (GDR). The division of the city was cruelly finalized in concrete in August 1961, when the GDR erected the Berlin Wall, the only border fortification in history built to keep people from leaving rather than to protect them.

For nearly 30 years, the two Berlins served as competing visions of the new world order: Capitalist on one side, Communist on the other. West Berlin, an island of democracy in the Eastern bloc, was surrounded by guards and checkpoints. Nonetheless, thanks in part to being heavily subsidized by Western powers, the city became a haven for artists and freethinkers. Today, with the Wall long relegated to history (most of it was recycled as street gravel), visitors can appreciate the whole city and the anything-goes atmosphere that still pervades.

15

PLANNING

WHEN TO GO

Berlin tends to be gray and cold; it can be warm and beautiful in summer but there's no guarantee, so it's best to always pack a jacket. The best time to visit is from May to early September, though late July and early August can get hot—in which case, everyone heads to one of the city's many lakes. Many open-air events are staged in summer, when the exceedingly green city is at its most beautiful. October and November can be overcast and rainy, though the city occasionally sees crisp blue autumn skies. If you want to get a real feel for Berlin, come during the long winter months, when a host of indoor cultural events combat perpetually gray skies, but bring a heavy winter coat to combat the sleet, icy rain, strong winds, and freezing temperatures.

DISCOUNTS AND DEALS

The **Berlin WelcomeCard** (⊕ *www.visitberlin.de*) entitles one adult and three children up to age six to unlimited travel in Berlin and includes discounted admission at museums and theaters (it does not include state museums unless you pay extra); if you're using public transportation to get to or from the airport and also plan to go to Potsdam, get the card for Zones A, B, and C (€22.90, €30.90, or €35.90 for two, three, or four days, with five- and six-day passes also available; less for just Zones A and B). The Berlin WelcomeCard All-Inclusive costs more but includes admission to 30 Berlin attractions as well as a hop-on, hop-off bus tour. Similarly, the **CityTourCard** (⊕ *www.citytourcard.com*), good for two, three, four, or five days of unlimited travel in the A and B zones, costs €16.90, €23.90, €29.90, and €33.90, respectively, and includes many entertainment discounts; up to three children under age six can accompany an adult. The cost is slightly higher to include Zone C. The difference between the two types of cards are the attractions that are discounted so it's worth doing some research.

Many of the 17 Staatliche Museen zu Berlin (state museums of Berlin) offer several ticket options (children up to 18 are welcomed free of charge). A single ticket ranges €8–€12. A three-day pass (*Tageskarte* or *SchauLust Museen Ticket*) that includes all state museums, plus many others, costs €29.

GETTING HERE AND AROUND

AIRPORT TRANSFERS

Tegel Airport is 6 km (4 miles) from the downtown area. The express X9 airport bus runs at 10-minute intervals between Tegel and Bahnhof Zoologischer Garten (Zoo Station), the center of west Berlin. From here you can connect to bus, train, or subway. The trip takes about 20 minutes; the fare is €2.80. The express bus TXL runs at six-minute intervals between Tegel and Alexanderplatz via Hauptbahnhof and takes about 37 minutes. Alternatively, you can take Bus No. 128 to Kurt Schumacher Platz or Bus No. 109 to Jakob-Kaiser-Platz and change to the U-bahn, where your bus ticket is also valid. Expect to pay around €30 for a taxi from the airport to most destinations in central Berlin. If you rent a car at the airport, follow the signs for the Stadtautobahn into Berlin. The exit to Kurfürstendamm is clearly marked.

At Schönefeld, which is quite a bit farther out, buy an Einzelfahrschein or single ride ticket (€3.40) for the ABC zone from the DB (Deutsche Bahn) office or from an S-bahn platform vending machine (no credit cards) to get you into town. This ticket is good for both the S-bahn and the Airport Express train, which runs about every half-hour from a track that has no vending machine. To take the Airport Express, look for a small dark-blue sign at the foot of the stairs leading to its platform. Bus No. 171 also leaves Schönefeld every 20 minutes for the Rudow U-bahn station. A taxi ride from Schönefeld Airport takes about 40–60 minutes, depending on traffic, and will cost around €50–€60. By car, follow the signs for Stadtzentrum Berlin.

AIR TRAVEL

Major and low-budget airlines serve both Berlin Tegel Airport (TXL) and Berlin Schönefeld Airport, about 24 km (15 miles) outside the center, until Schönefeld is expanded into BBI (Berlin-Brandenburg International, otherwise known as "Willy Brandt"). Long-delayed, the new international airport is now tentatively projected to open in fall 2020—though whether this date is met remains to be seen.

BICYCLE TRAVEL

Berlin is a great city for biking. Particularly in summer, you can get just about anywhere you want by bike. An extensive network of bike paths are generally marked by red pavement or white markings on the sidewalks (when you're walking, try to avoid walking on bike paths if you don't want to have cyclists ring their bells at you). Many stores that rent or sell bikes carry the Berlin biker's atlas, and several places offer terrific bike tours of the city.

Contacts Fahrradstation. ✉ *Dorotheenstr. 30, Mitte* ☎ *0180/510–8000* ⊕ *www.fahrradstation.de.*

CAR TRAVEL

Rush hour is relatively mild in Berlin, but the public transit system is so efficient here that it's best to leave your car at the hotel altogether (or refrain from renting one in the first place). All cars entering downtown Berlin inside the S-bahn ring need to have an environmental certificate. All major rental cars will have these—if in doubt, ask the rental-car agent, as without one you can be fined €40. Daily parking fees at hotels can run up to €18 per day. Vending machines in the city center dispense timed tickets to display on your dashboard; one hour costs €1.

PUBLIC TRANSIT

The city has an efficient public-transportation system, a smoothly integrated network of subway (U-bahn) and suburban (S-bahn) train lines, buses, and trams (almost exclusively in eastern Berlin). Get a map from any information booth. ■ TIP→ **Don't be afraid to try buses and trams— in addition to being well marked, they often cut the most direct path to your destination.**

From Sunday through Thursday, most U-bahn trains stop around 1 am, and S-bahn trains stop by 1:30 am. All-night bus and tram service operates seven nights a week (indicated by the letter *N* next to bus route numbers). On Friday and Saturday night all S-bahn and all U-bahn lines (except U4 and U55) run all night. Buses and trams marked with an *M* for Metro mostly serve destinations without an S-bahn or U-bahn link.

Most visitor destinations are in the broad reach of the fare zones A and B. The €2.80 ticket (fare Zones A and B) and the €3.40 ticket (fare Zones A, B, and C) allow you to make a one-way trip with an unlimited number of changes between trains, buses, and trams. Buy a *Kurzstreckentarif* ticket (€1.70) for short rides of up to six bus or tram stops or three U-bahn or S-bahn stops. The best deal if you plan to travel around the city extensively is the *Tageskarte* (day card for Zones A and B), for €7, good on all transportation until 3 am (added cost for Zones A, B, and C). A *7-Tage-Karte* (seven-day ticket) costs €30, and allows unlimited travel for fare zones A and B (added cost for Zone C).

Tickets are available from vending machines at U-bahn and S-bahn stations. After you purchase a ticket, you are responsible for validating it when you board the train or bus. Both Einzelfahrt and Kurzstreckentarif tickets are good for 120 minutes after validation. If you're caught without a ticket or with an unvalidated one, the fine is €60.

■ TIP→ **The BVG website (www.bvg.de) makes planning any trip on public transportation easier. Enter your origin and destination point into their "Journey Planner" to see a list of your best routes, and a schedule of the next three departure times. If you're not sure which station is your closest, simply type in your current address and the system will tell you (along with the time it takes to walk there).**

15

Most major S-bahn and U-bahn stations have elevators, and most buses have hydraulic lifts. Check the public transportation maps or call the Berliner Verkehrsbetriebe.

Contacts Berliner Verkehrsbetriebe *(BVG)*. ☎ *030/19449* ⊕ *www.bvg.de.* **S-Bahn Berlin GmbH.** ☎ *030/2974–3333* ⊕ *www.s-bahn-berlin.de.*

TAXI TRAVEL

The base rate is €3.90, after which prices vary according to a complex tariff system. Figure on paying around €8–€10 for a ride the length of the Ku'damm. ■TIP➔ If you've hailed a cab on the street and are taking a short ride of up to 2 km (1 mile), ask the driver as soon as you start off for a special fare (€5) called "Kurzstreckentarif." You can also get cabs at taxi stands or order one by calling; there's no additional fee if you call a cab by phone.

BikeTaxi, rickshawlike bicycle taxis, pedal along Kurfürstendamm, Friedrichstrasse, Unter den Linden, and in Tiergarten. Just hail a cab on the street along the boulevards mentioned. The fare is €5 for up to 1 km (½ mile) and €3 for each additional kilometer, and €22.50–€30 for longer tours. Velotaxis operate April through October, daily 10–8. ■TIP➔ Despite these fixed prices, make sure to negotiate the fare before starting the tour.

Contacts Taxis. ☎ *030/210–101, 030/443–322, 030/261–026.*

TRAIN TRAVEL

All long-distance trains stop at the huge and modern central station, Hauptbahnhof, which lies at the northern edge of the government district in central Berlin. Regional trains also stop at the two former "main" stations of the past years: Bahnhof Zoo (in the West) and Ost-bahnhof (in the East), as well as Friedrichstrasse and Alexanderplatz.

VISITOR INFORMATION

There are information center branches in the south wing of the Brandenburg Gate; at Hauptbahnhof (Level 0); at the Central Bus Station in Charlottenburg; in the Europa-Center in West Berlin; at the Hotel Park Inn in Alexanderplatz; and at Tegel Airport (between Terminal A and B). The tourist offices and Berlin's larger transportation offices (BVG) sell the **Berlin WelcomeCard.** Some *Staatliche* (state) museums are closed Monday. A free audio guide is included at all state museums.

Contacts Staatliche Museen zu Berlin *(State Museums of Berlin).* ✉ *Charlottenburg* ☎ *030/2664–24242* ⊕ *www.smb.museum.* **Tourist-Information Center in Prenzlauer Berg.** ✉ *Kulturbrauerei, Schönhauser Allee 36, Prenzlauer Berg* ✛ *Other entrances on Knaackstr. or Sredzkistr.* ☎ *030/4435–2170* ⊕ *www. tic-berlin.de.* **Visit Berlin** *(Berlin Tourist Info).* ☎ *030/2500–2333* ⊕ *www.visitberlin.de.*

TOURS

BOAT TOURS

Tours of central Berlin's Spree and the canals give you up-close views of sights such as Museum Island, Charlottenburg Palace, the Reichstag, and the Berliner Dom. Tours usually depart twice-daily from several bridges and piers in Berlin, such as Schlossbrücke in Charlottenburg;

A boat tour along the Spree River is a lovely way to take in the sights.

Hansabrücke and Haus der Kulturen der Welt in Tiergarten; Friedrich-strasse, Museum Island, and Nikolaiviertel in Mitte; and near the Jannowitzbrücke S-bahn and U-bahn station. Drinks, snacks, and *Wurst* are available during the narrated trips.

BWSG. General city tours and specialized options, like architectural tours, are offered from April to November by this company. ⊠ *Berlin* ⊕ *www.bwsg-berlin.de* ⊠ *From €15.*

Reederei Riedel. One-hour to 90-minute city tours along the Spree take visitors past key city sights, including Museuminsel. ⊠ *Berlin* ☎ *030/6796–1470* ⊕ *www.reederei-riedel.de* ⊠ *From €14.*

BUS TOURS

Several companies, including Berliner Bären Stadtrundfahrten and BEX, offer city tours that run about every 10 minutes. The full circuit takes around two hours, as does the recorded narration listened to through headphones. You can jump on and off at about 18 stops, depending on the company. The bus driver sells tickets. Most companies have tours to Potsdam.

BBS Berliner Bären Stadtrundfahrt (*BBS*). These bright yellow hop-on, hop-off buses tour the city, past the major sights; the purple tour navigates trendy East Berlin, including a stop at the East Side Gallery. It's a great way to get an overview if you have limited time. ⊠ *Berlin* ☎ *030/3519–5255* ⊕ *www.bbsberlin.de* ⊠ *From €14.*

BEX Sightseeing. Hop-on, hop-off tours, as well as themed excursions, are offered by this company. ⊠ *Kurfürstendamm 216, Wilmersdorf* ☎ *030/880–4190* ⊕ *www.bex.de* ⊠ *From €14.*

WALKING AND BIKE TOURS

Getting oriented through a walking tour is a great way to start a Berlin visit. In addition to daily city highlight tours, companies have themed tours such as Third Reich Berlin, Potsdam, and pub crawls. Some companies grant discounts to WelcomeCard and CityCard holders.

Berliner Unterwelten. For a truly memorable experience, check out Berliner Unterwelten, which translates as "Berlin Underworlds." The company offers access to several of Berlin's best-preserved WWII bunkers that are normally closed to the public on intriguing yet eerie tours that take you literally underground. Note that tickets are only available on the day of the tour from the ticket office. ⊠ *Brunnenstr. 105, Wedding* ☎ *030/4991–0527* ⊕ *www.berliner-unterwelten.de* ✉ *From €12.*

Brewer's Berlin Tours. Specialized tours include street art, craft beer and breweries, a food crawl, and queer Berlin, along with a six-hour Best of Berlin tour. ⊠ *Berlin* ☎ *0177/388–1537* ⊕ *www.brewersberlintours. com* ✉ *From €12.*

Fat Tire Bike Tours. Fat Tire Bike Tours rides through Berlin daily March–November (and on Monday, Wednesday, and Saturday, as well as when the weather's nice, December–February), and has a Berlin Wall tour; the 4½-hour city tour includes the bike rental. ⊠ *Panoramastr. 1a, base of TV tower, Mitte* ☎ *030/2404–7991* ⊕ *www.fattiretours. com/berlin* ✉ *From €18.*

Insider Tour. Insider Tours has a "Cold War Berlin" tour about the Soviet era, a Third Reich tour, and a Jewish Berlin tour, among others, plus tours to Potsdam, Dresden, and Sachsenhausen. ⊠ *Bahnhof Zoologischer Garten, outside McDonald's, Charlottenburg* ☎ *030/692–3149* ⊕ *www.insidertour.com* ✉ *From €14.*

Original Berlin Walks. Themed walks include Hitler's Germany; East Berlin; Queer Berlin; Berlin Food Crawl; Craft Beer and Breweries; and visits to Potsdam and the Sachsenhausen concentration camp. ⊠ *Neue Promenade 5, Mitte* ☎ *030/301–9194* ⊕ *www.berlinwalks. de* ✉ *From €14.*

EXPLORING

MITTE

After the fall of the wall, Mitte, which had been in East Germany, once again became the geographic center of Berlin. The area comprises several minidistricts, each with its own distinctive history and flair. Alexanderplatz, home of the iconic TV Tower, was the center of East Berlin. With its Communist architecture, you can still get a feel for the GDR aesthetic here. The nearby Nikolaiviertel is part of the medieval heart of Berlin. The Scheunenviertel, part of the Spandauer Vorstadt, was home to many of the city's Jewish citizens. Today, the narrow streets that saw so much tragedy house art galleries, increasingly excellent restaurants, and upscale shops popular with tourists. Treasures once split between East and West Berlin museums are reunited on Museuminsel, the stunning Museum Island, a UNESCO World Heritage Site.

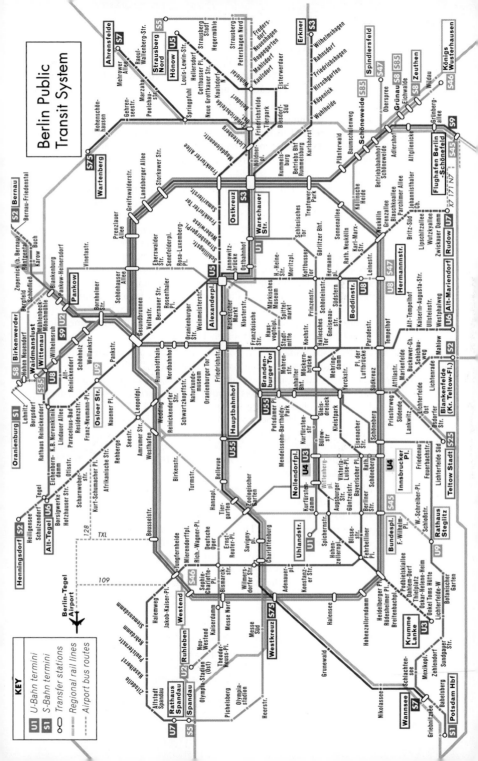

Berlin Public Transit System

KEY
- **U1** U-Bahn termini
- **S1** S-Bahn termini
- ○ Transfer stations
- Regional rail lines
- Airport bus routes

Bordering Tiergarten and the government district are the meticulously restored Brandenburger Tor (Brandenburg Gate), the unofficial symbol of the city, and the Memorial to the Murdered Jews of Europe, whose design and scope engendered many debates.

The historic boulevard Unter den Linden proudly rolls out Prussian architecture and world-class museums—now the site of increased construction related to the extension of U-bahn U5 line, slated to open in 2020. Its major cross street is Friedrichstrasse, revitalized in the mid-1990s with car showrooms (including Bentley and Volkswagen) and upscale malls.

Alexanderplatz. This bleak square, bordered by the train station, the Galeria Kaufhof department store, and the 37-story Park Inn Berlin-Alexanderplatz hotel, once formed the hub of East Berlin and was originally named in 1805 for Czar Alexander I. German writer Alfred Döblin dubbed it the "heart of a world metropolis" (a quote from his 1929 novel *Berlin Alexanderplatz* is written on a building at the northeastern end of the square). Today it's a basic center of commerce and the occasional festival. The unattractive modern buildings are a reminder not just of the results of Allied bombing but also of the ruthlessness practiced by East Germans when they demolished what remained. A famous meeting point in the south corner is the World Time Clock (1969), which even keeps tabs on Tijuana. ⊠ *Mitte.*

Fodor's Choice ★ **Alte Nationalgalerie** (*Old National Gallery*). The permanent exhibit here is home to an outstanding collection of 18th-, 19th-, and early-20th-century paintings and sculpture, by the likes of Cézanne, Rodin, Degas, and one of Germany's most famous portrait artists, Max Liebermann. Its collection has masterpieces from such 19th-century German painters as Karl Friedrich Schinkel and Caspar David Friedrich, the leading members of the German Romantic school. ⊠ *Museumsinsel, Bodestr. 1–3, Mitte* ☎ *30/2664–24242* ⊕ *www.smb.museum* ☒ *€8 (combined ticket for all Museum Island museums €18)* ☉ *Closed Mon.* Ⓜ *Hackescher Markt (S-bahn).*

Altes Museum (*Old Museum*). This red-marble neoclassical building abutting the green Lustgarten was Prussia's first structure purpose-built to serve as a museum. Designed by Karl Friedrich Schinkel, it was completed in 1830. The permanent collection consists of everyday utensils from ancient Greece as well as vases and sculptures from the 6th to 4th century BC. Etruscan art is the highlight here, and there are also a few examples of Roman art. Antique sculptures, clay figurines, and bronze art of the Antikensammlung (Antiquities Collection) are also here (the other part of the collection is in the **Pergamonmuseum**). ⊠ *Museuminsel, Am Lustgarten, Mitte* ☎ *30/2664–24242* ⊕ *www.smb. museum* ☒ *From €10* ☉ *Closed Mon.* Ⓜ *Hackescher Markt (S-bahn).*

Bebelplatz. After he became ruler in 1740, Frederick the Great personally planned the buildings surrounding this square (which has a huge parking garage cleverly hidden beneath the pavement). The area received the nickname "Forum Fridericianum," or Frederick's Forum. On May 10, 1933, Joseph Goebbels, the Nazi minister for propaganda and "public enlightenment," organized one of the nationwide book burnings here.

Berliner Dom (Berlin's Cathedral) is one of the city's landmark buildings, and the vast lawn across from it is a popular gathering spot in nice weather.

The books, thrown on a pyre by Nazi officials and students, included works by Jews, pacifists, and Communists. In the center of Bebelplatz, a modern and subtle memorial (built underground but viewable through a window in the cobblestone pavement) marks where 20,000 books went up in flames. The **Staatsoper Unter den Linden** (State Opera) is on the east side of the square. **St. Hedwigskathedrale** is on the south side of the square. The **Humboldt-Universität** is to the west. ✉ *Mitte* Ⓜ *Französische Strasse (U-bahn), Bhf Hausvogteiplatz (U-bahn).*

Berliner Dom (*Berlin Cathedral*). A church has stood here since 1536, but this enormous version dates from 1905, making it the largest 20th-century Protestant church in Germany. The royal Hohenzollerns worshipped here until 1918, when Kaiser Wilhelm II abdicated and left Berlin for Holland. The massive dome wasn't restored from World War II damage until 1982; the interior was completed in 1993. The climb to the dome's outer balcony is made easier by a wide stairwell, plenty of landings with historic photos and models, and even a couple of chairs. The 94 sarcophagi of Prussian royals in the crypt are significant, but to less-trained eyes can seem uniformly dull. Sunday services include communion. ✉ *Am Lustgarten 1, Mitte* ☎ *030/2026–9136* ⊕ *www. berlinerdom.de* 🎫 *€7; audio guide €4* Ⓜ *Hackescher Markt (S-bahn).*

FAMILY **Berliner Fernsehturm** (*TV Tower*). Finding Alexanderplatz is no problem: just head toward the 1,207-foot-high tower piercing the sky. Built in 1969 as a signal to the West (clearly visible over the Wall, no less) that the East German economy was thriving, it is deliberately higher than both western Berlin's broadcasting tower and the Eiffel Tower in Paris. You can get the best view of Berlin from within the tower's disco

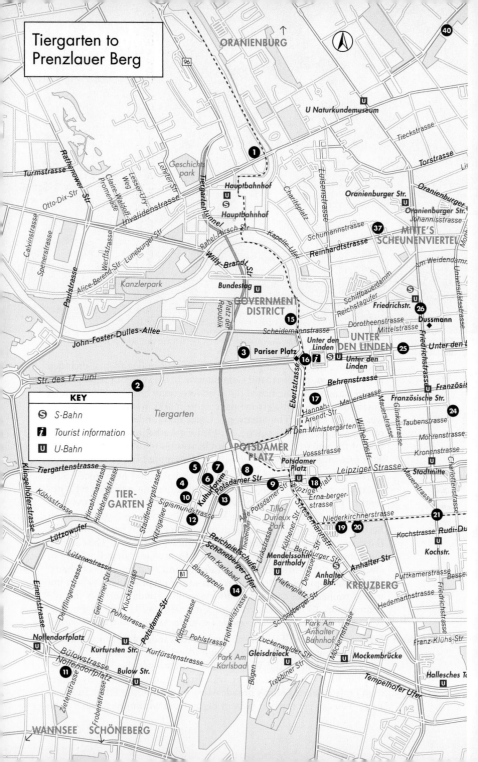

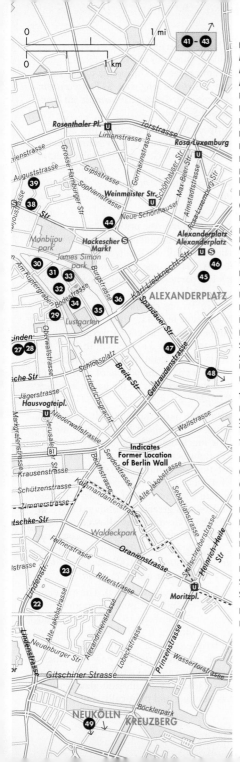

0 ___ 1 mi
0 ___ 1 km

41 – 43

ROSENTHALER PL.
Torstrasse
Rosa-Luxemburg
Weinmeister Str.
Neue Schönhauser
Hackescher Markt
Monbijou park
James Simon park
Alexanderplatz
ALEXANDERPLATZ
MITTE
Lustgarten
Schlossplatz
Hausvogteipl.
Indicates Former Location of Berlin Wall
Waldeckpark
Oranienstrasse
Moritzpl.
NEUKÖLLN
KREUZBERG
Gitschiner Strasse
Böcklerpark

39 **38** **44** **30** **31** **33** **32** **34** **35** **36** **29** **45** **46** **47** **48** **27** **28** **23** **22** **49** B1

ball–like observation level (also home to Berlin's highest bar); on a clear day you can see for 40 km (25 miles). One floor above, the city's highest restaurant rotates for your panoramic pleasure. During the summer season, order fast track tickets online to avoid a long wait. ⊠ *Panoramastr. 1a, Mitte* ☎ *030/247–5750 for restaurant* ⊕ *www.tv-turm.de* ⊠ *From €16* Ⓜ *Alexanderplatz (U-bahn and S-bahn).*

Bode-Museum. At the northern tip of Museum Island is this somber-looking gray edifice graced with elegant columns. The museum is home to the state museum's stunning collection of German and Italian sculptures since the Middle Ages, as well as the Museum of Byzantine Art, and a huge coin collection. ⊠ *Museuminsel, Am Kupfergraben, Mitte* ☎ *030/2664–24242* ⊕ *www.smb.museum* ⊠ *From €12* ⊙ *Closed Mon.* Ⓜ *Hackescher Markt (S-bahn).*

Fodor'sChoice
★

Brandenburger Tor (*Brandenburg Gate*). Once the pride of Prussian Berlin and the city's premier landmark, the Brandenburger Tor was left in a desolate no-man's-land when the Wall was built. Since the Wall's dismantling, the sandstone gateway has become the scene of the city's Unification Day and New Year's Eve parties. This is the sole remaining gate of 14 built by Carl Langhans in 1788–91, designed as a triumphal arch for King Frederick Wilhelm II. Troops paraded through the gate after successful campaigns—the last time in 1945, when victorious Red Army troops took Berlin. The upper part of the gate, together with its chariot and Goddess of Victory, was destroyed in the war. In 1957 the original molds were discovered in West Berlin, and a new quadriga was cast in copper and presented as a gift to the people of East Berlin. A tourist information center is in the south part of the gate. ⊠ *Pariser Pl., Mitte* ⊠ *Free* Ⓜ *Unter den Linden (S-bahn).*

Fodor'sChoice
★

DDR Museum. Half museum, half theme park, the DDR Museum is an interactive and highly entertaining exhibit about life during communism. It's difficult to say just how much the museum benefits from its prime location beside the Spree, right across from the Berliner Dom, but it's always packed, filled with tourists, families, and student groups trying to get a hands-on feel for what the East German experience was really like. Exhibitions include a re-creation of an East German kitchen, all mustard yellows and bilious greens; a simulated drive in a Trabi, the only car the average East German was allowed to own; and a walk inside a very narrow, very claustrophobic interrogation cell. ⊠ *Karl-Liebknecht-Str. 1, at Spree opposite Berliner Dom, Mitte* ☎ *030/8471–23731* ⊕ *www.ddr-museum.de* ⊠ *€10 (€9 online)* Ⓜ *Alexanderplatz (U-bahn and S-bahn), Hackescher Markt (S-bahn).*

Deutsches Historisches Museum (*German History Museum*). The museum is composed of two buildings. The magnificent pink, baroque Prussian arsenal (Zeughaus) was constructed between 1695 and 1730, and is the oldest building on Unter den Linden. It also houses a theater, the Zeughaus Kino, which regularly presents a variety of films, both German and international, historic and modern. The new permanent exhibits offer a modern and fascinating view of German history since the early Middle Ages. Behind the arsenal, the granite-and-glass Pei-Bau building by I. M. Pei holds often stunning and politically controversial

The Brandenburg Gate is one of the most famous landmarks in Germany.

changing exhibits. The museum's café is a great place to stop and restore your energy. ⊠ *Unter den Linden 2, Mitte* ☎ *030/203–040* ⊕ *www.dhm. de* 🖾 *€8* Ⓜ *Französische Strasse (U-bahn), Friedrichstrasse (S-bahn and U-bahn), Hackesher Markt (S-bahn).*

Friedrichstrasse. The once-bustling street of cafés and theaters of prewar Berlin has risen from the rubble of war and Communist neglect to reclaim the crowds with shopping emporiums. North of the train station you will see the rejuvenated heart of the entertainment center of Berlin's Roaring Twenties, including the **Admiralspalast** and the somewhat kitschy **Friedrichstadt Palast.** ⊠ *Mitte* Ⓜ *Französische Strasse (U-bahn), Friedrichstrasse (S-bahn and U-bahn).*

Gendarmenmarkt. This is without a doubt the most elegant square in former East Berlin. Anchored by the beautifully reconstructed 1818 **Konzerthaus** and the **Deutscher Dom** and **Französischer Dom** (German and French cathedrals), it also hosts one of Berlin's classiest annual Christmas markets. ⊠ *Mitte* Ⓜ *Stadtmitte (U-bahn), Hausvogteiplatz (U-bahn).*

Hackesche Höfe (*Hacke Courtyards*). Built in 1905–07, this series of eight connected courtyards is the finest example of art nouveau industrial architecture in Berlin. Most buildings are covered with glazed white tiles, and additional Moorish mosaic designs decorate the main courtyard off Rosenthaler Strasse. Shops, restaurants, the variety theater Chamäleon Varieté, and a movie theater populate the spaces once occupied by ballrooms, a poets' society, and a Jewish girls' club. ⊠ *Rosenthaler Str. 40–41, and Sophienstr. 6, Mitte* ⊕ *www.hackesche-hoefe.com* Ⓜ *Hackescher Markt (S-bahn).*

Fodor's Choice
★ **Hamburger Bahnhof - Museum für Gegenwart** (*Museum of Contemporary Art*). This light-filled, remodeled train station is home to a rich survey of post-1960 Western art. The permanent collection includes installations by German artists Joseph Beuys and Anselm Kiefer, as well as paintings by Andy Warhol, Cy Twombly, Robert Rauschenberg, and Robert Morris. An annex presents the Friedrich Christian Flick Collection, a collection of the latest in the world's contemporary art. The more than 1,500 works rotate, but you're bound to see some by Bruce Naumann, Rodney Graham, and Pipilotti Rist. ✉ *Invalidenstr. 50–51, Mitte* ☎ *030/2664–24242* ⊕ *www.smb.museum* 🖾 *€14 (free 1st Thurs. of month 4–8 pm)* Ⓜ *Naturkundemuseum (U-bahn), Hauptbahnhof (S-bahn).*

The Kennedys. In West Berlin in 1963, John F. Kennedy surveyed the recently erected Berlin Wall and said, "Ich bin ein Berliner" (I am one with the people of Berlin). And with that, he secured his fame throughout Germany. He's honored in this small but intriguing museum, which used to reside opposite the American embassy on Pariser Platz, but has since found a new home in the Ehemalige Jüdische Mädchenschule. With photographs, personal memorabilia, documents, and films, the collection traces the fascination JFK and the Kennedy clan evoked in Berlin and elsewhere. ✉ *Auguststr. 11–13, in Ehemalige Jüdische Mädchenschule, Mitte* ☎ *030/2065–3570* ⊕ *www.thekennedys.de* 🖾 *€5* ☉ *Closed Mon.* Ⓜ *Oranienburger Strasse (S-bahn).*

Fodor's Choice
★ **Memorial to the Murdered Jews of Europe** (*Denkmal für die Ermordeten Juden Europas*). An expansive and unusual memorial dedicated to the 6 million Jews who were killed in the Holocaust, the Memorial to the Murdered Jews of Europe was designed by American architect Peter Eisenman. The stunning place of remembrance consists of a grid of more than 2,700 concrete stelae, planted into undulating ground. The abstract memorial can be entered from all sides and offers no prescribed path. An information center that goes into specifics about the Holocaust lies underground at the southeast corner. Just across Eberstrasse, inside the Tiergarten, is the **Memorial to the Homosexuals Persecuted under the National Socialist Regime**: a large concrete block with a window through which visitors can see a short film depicting a kiss. ✉ *Cora-Berliner-Str. 1, Mitte* ☎ *030/2639–430* ⊕ *www.stiftung-denkmal.de* 🖾 *Free* Ⓜ *Unter den Linden (S-bahn).*

Neue Synagoge (*New Synagogue*). This meticulously restored landmark, built between 1859 and 1866, is an exotic amalgam of styles, the whole faintly Middle Eastern. Its bulbous, gilded cupola stands out in the skyline. When its doors opened, it was the largest synagogue in Europe, with 3,200 seats. The synagogue was damaged on November 9, 1938 (*Kristallnacht*—Night of the Broken Glass), when Nazi looters rampaged across Germany, burning synagogues and smashing the few Jewish shops and homes left in the country. It was destroyed by Allied bombing in 1943, and it wasn't until the mid-1980s that the East German government restored it. The effective exhibit on the history of the building and its congregants includes fragments of the original architecture and furnishings. Sabbath services are held in a modern addition. ✉ *Oranienburger Str. 28–30, Mitte* ☎ *030/8802–8300*

The Pergamonmuseum, on Museumsinsel (Museum Island), is where you'll find a wealth of artifacts from the ancient world, including the Ishtar Gate.

⊕ *www.centrumjudaicum.de* ✉ *€5; English/Hebrew audio guides €3* Ⓜ *Oranienburger Tor (U-bahn), Oranienburger Strasse (S-bahn).*

Neues Museum (*New Museum*). Originally designed by Friedrich August Stüler in 1843–55, the building housing the Neues Museum was badly damaged in World War II and has only in the 21st century been elaborately redeveloped by British star architect David Chipperfield. Instead of completely restoring the Neues Museum, the architect decided to integrate modern elements into the historic landmark, while leaving many of its heavily bombed and dilapidated areas untouched. The result is a stunning experience, considered by many to be one of the world's greatest museums. Home to the Egyptian Museum, including the famous bust of Nefertiti (who, after some 70 years, has returned to her first museum location in Berlin), it also features the Papyrus Collection and the Museum of Prehistory and Early History. ✉ *Museumsinsel, Bodestrasse 1–3, Mitte* ☎ *030/2664–24242* ⊕ *www.smb. museum* ✉ *From €12* Ⓜ *Hackescher Markt (S-bahn).*

Nikolaiviertel (*Nicholas Quarter*). Renovated in the 1980s and a tad concrete-heavy as a result, this tiny quarter grew up around Berlin's oldest parish church, the medieval, twin-spire **St. Nikolaikirche** (St. Nicholas's Church), dating from 1230 and now a museum. The adjacent Fischerinsel (Fisherman's Island) area was the heart of Berlin almost 800 years ago, and retains a bit of its medieval character. At Breite Strasse you'll find two of Berlin's oldest buildings: No. 35 is the **Ribbeckhaus**, the city's only surviving Renaissance structure, dating from 1624, and No. 36 is the early-baroque **Marstall**, built by Michael Matthais between 1666 and 1669. The area feels rather artificial, but draws tourists to

Berlin's Museum Island

Museumsinsel (*Museum Island*). On the site of one of Berlin's two original settlements, this unique complex of five state museums is a UNESCO World Heritage Site and a must-visit in Berlin. The museums are the **Alte Nationalgalerie**, the **Altes Museum** (Old Museum), the **Bode-Museum**, the **Pergamonmuseum**, and the **Neues Museum** (New Museum). If you get tired of antiques and paintings, drop by any of the museums' cafés. A state-of-the-art visitor center is expected to open here in 2019. To avoid standing in long lines (especially during the summer), buy a combined day ticket that covers all Museum Island museums in advance online at ⊕ *www.smb.museum/en* or ⊕ *www.visitberlin.de/en*, or at any of the individual museum ticket offices (the Altes Museum tends to be less busy). ✉ *Museumsinsel, Mitte* ☎ *030/2664–24242* ⊕ *www.visitberlin. de/en/museum-island-in-berlin* 🎟 *€18 combined ticket to all Museum Island museums* Ⓜ *Hackescher Markt (S-bahn).*

its gift stores, cafés, and restaurants. ✉ *Church: Nikolaikirchpl., Mitte* ☎ *030/2400–2162* ⊕ *www.stadtmuseum.de* 🎟 *Nikolaikirche museum €5* Ⓜ *Alexanderplatz (U-bahn and S-bahn).*

Fodor's Choice ★ **Pergamonmuseum.** The Pergamonmuseum is one of the world's greatest museums and its name is derived from its principal display, the Pergamon Altar, a monumental Greek temple discovered in what is now Turkey and dating from 180 BC. The altar was shipped to Berlin in the late 19th century. Equally impressive are the gateway to the Roman town of Miletus, the Ishtar Gate, and the Babylonian processional way. At the end of 2014, the hall with the Pergamon Altar closed for refurbishment and is expected to reopen in 2019; other construction works will be ongoing until at least 2025. That said, the majority of the Pergamonmuseum will continue to be open to the public, and it is still very much worth a visit. ✉ *Museumsinsel, Bodestrasse 1–3, Mitte* ☎ *030/2664–24242* ⊕ *www.smb.museum* 🎟 *From €12* Ⓜ *Hackescher Markt (S-bahn).*

Fodor's Choice ★ **Sammlung Boros.** Both an historic and a modern Berlin attraction all at once, the unique Sammlung Boros houses a private contemporary art collection inside a renovated World War II bunker. Weekend-only visits are only possible by 90-minute guided tour, which are extremely popular and must be booked online months in advance. Tours include both detailed descriptions of the artists and artwork on display, and also the fascinating history and architecture of the bunker itself, which at varying times was used as a war prison, fruit storage facility, and notorious nightclub. ✉ *Reinhardtstr. 20, Mitte* ☎ *030/2759–4065* ⊕ *www. sammlung-boros.de* 🎟 *€15* 𝇈 *Closed Mon.–Thurs.* Ⓜ *Berlin Friedrichstrasse (S-bahn), Oranienburger Tor (U-bahn).*

Staatsoper Unter den Linden (*State Opera*). Frederick the Great was a music lover and he made the Staatsoper Unter den Linden, on the east side of Bebelplatz, his first priority. The lavish opera house was completed in 1743 by the same architect who built Sanssouci in

The dome atop Reichstag is one of the city's top attractions, and a walk inside it offers superb views.

Potsdam, Georg Wenzeslaus von Knobelsdorff. The house reopened in late 2017 after a major seven-year renovation. There are guided tours of the opera house's interior on weekends at 2 and 4 pm (book online), but they are offered in German only. ⊠ *Unter den Linden 7, Mitte* ☎ *030/2035–4555* ⊕ *www.staatsoper-berlin.de* ✉ *Tours €15* Ⓜ *Französische Strasse (U-bahn).*

Unter den Linden. The name of this historic Berlin thoroughfare, between the Brandenburg Gate and Schlossplatz, means "under the linden trees," and it was indeed lined with fragrant and beloved lindens until the 1930s. Imagine Berliners' shock when Hitler decided to fell the trees in order to make the street more parade-friendly. The grand boulevard began as a riding path that the royals used to get from their palace to their hunting grounds (now the central Berlin park called Tiergarten). It is once again lined with linden trees planted after World War II. ⊠ *Mitte.*

TIERGARTEN

The Tiergarten, a bucolic 630-acre park with lakes, meadows, and wide paths, is the "green heart" of Berlin. In the 17th century it served as the hunting grounds of the Great Elector (its name translates as "animal garden"). Now it's the Berliners' backyard for sunbathing and summer strolls.

The government district, Potsdamer Platz, and the embassy district ring the park from its eastern to southern edges. A leisurely walk from Zoo Station through the Tiergarten to the Brandenburger Tor and the Reichstag takes about 90 minutes.

Fodor's Choice **Reichstag** (*Parliament Building*). The Bundestag, Germany's federal
★ parliament, returned to its traditional seat in the spring of 1999 for
the first time since 1933. British architect Sir Norman Foster lightened
up the gray monolith with a glass dome: you can circle up a gently rising ramp while taking in the rooftops of Berlin and the parliamentary
chamber below. At the base of the dome is an exhibit on the Reichstag's history. Completed in 1894, the Reichstag housed the imperial
German parliament and later served a similar function during the
ill-fated Weimar Republic. On the night of February 27, 1933, the
Reichstag burned down in an act of arson, a pivotal event in Third
Reich history. The Reichstag was rebuilt but again badly damaged in
1945. All visitors must register their names and birth dates in advance
and reserve a place on a guided tour, which you can do online. A riv-
erwalk with great views of the government buildings begins behind
the Reichstag. ⊠ *Pl. der Republik 1, Tiergarten* ☏ *030/2273–2152*
⊕ *www.bundestag.de* ⊠ *Free with prior registration online* Ⓜ *Unter
den Linden (S-bahn), Bundestag (U-bahn).*

Sowjetisches Ehrenmal Tiergarten (*Soviet Memorial*). Built immediately
after World War II, this monument stands as a reminder of the Soviet
victory over the shattered German army in Berlin in May 1945. The
Battle of Berlin was one of the deadliest on the European front. A hulking bronze statue of a soldier stands atop a marble plinth taken from
Hitler's former *Reichskanzlei* (headquarters). The memorial is flanked by
what are said to be the first two T-34 tanks to have fought their way into
the city. ⊠ *Str. des 17. Juni, Tiergarten* Ⓜ *Unter den Linden (S-bahn).*

Tiergarten (*Animal Garden*). The quiet greenery of the 210-hectare (520-
acre) Tiergarten is a beloved oasis, with some 23 km (14 miles) of footpaths, meadows, and two beer gardens, making it the third-largest green
space in Germany. The inner park's 6½ acres of lakes and ponds were
landscaped by garden architect Peter Joseph Lenné in the mid-1800s.
⊠ *Tiergarten* Ⓜ *Zoologischer Garten (S-bahn and U-bhan), Bellevue
(S-bahn), Hansaplatz (U-bahn), Potsdamer Platz (U-bahn).*

POTSDAMER PLATZ

The once-divided Berlin is rejoined at Potsdamer Platz, which now
links Kreuzberg with the former East once again. Potsdamer Platz was
Berlin's inner-city center and Europe's busiest plaza before World War
II. Bombings and the Wall left this area a sprawling, desolate lot, where
tourists in West Berlin could climb a wooden platform to peek into East
Berlin's death strip. After the Wall fell, various international companies
made a rush to build their German headquarters on this prime real
estate. In the mid-1990s, Potsdamer Platz became Europe's largest construction site. Today's modern complexes of red sandstone, terra-cotta
tiles, steel, and glass have made it a city within a city.

A few narrow streets cut between the hulking modern architecture,
which includes two high-rise office towers owned by Daimler, one of
which was designed by star architect Renzo Piano. The round atrium of
the Sony Center comes closest to a traditional square used as a public

meeting point. Farther down Potsdamer Strasse are the state museums and cultural institutes of the Kulturforum.

Gemäldegalerie (*Picture Gallery*). The Kulturforum's Gemäldegalerie reunites formerly separated collections from East and West Berlin. It's one of Germany's finest art galleries, and has an extensive selection of European paintings from the 13th to 18th centuries. Seven rooms are reserved for paintings by German masters, among them Dürer, Cranach the Elder, and Holbein. A special collection has works of the Italian masters—Botticelli, Titian, Giotto, Lippi, and Raphael—as well as paintings by Dutch and Flemish masters of the 15th and 16th centuries: Van Eyck, Bosch, Bruegel the Elder, and Van der Weyden. The museum also holds the world's second-largest Rembrandt collection. ⊠ *Kulturforum, Matthäikirchpl., Potsdamer Platz* ☎ *030/2664–24242* ⊕ *www.smb.museum* 🎫 *€10* ⊗ *Closed Mon.* Ⓜ *Potsdamer Platz (U-bahn and S-bahn).*

FAMILY **German Spy Museum** (*Deutsches Spionage Museum*). This museum dedicated to the world of espionage features interactive exhibits from the time of the Bible to the present day, covering topics that include military interrogation techniques and the world of secret services. The museum even touches on celebrated fictional spies, James Bond among them. An exhibit on the Enigma machine and the history of code breaking, as well as a laser maze that visitors can navigate, are two of the museum's biggest draws. ⊠ *Leipziger Pl. 9, Potsdamer Platz* ☎ *030/3982–00451* ⊕ *www.deutsches-spionagemuseum.de* 🎫 *€12* Ⓜ *Potsdamer Platz (U-bahn and S-bahn).*

Fodor'sChoice **Kulturforum** (*Cultural Forum*). This unique ensemble of museums, galleries, and the Philharmonic Hall was long in the making. The first designs were submitted in the 1960s and the last building completed in 1998. Now it forms a welcome modern counterpoint to the thoroughly restored Prussian splendor of Museum Island, although Berliners and tourists alike hold drastically differing opinions on the area's architectural aesthetics. Whatever your opinion, Kulturforum's artistic holdings are unparalleled and worth at least a day of your time, if not more. The Kulturforum includes the **Gemäldegalerie** (Picture Gallery), the **Kunstbibliothek** (Art Library), the **Kupferstichkabinett** (Print Cabinet), the **Kunstgewerbemuseum** (Museum of Decorative Arts), the **Philharmonie**, the **Musikinstrumenten-Museum** (Musical Instruments Museum), the **Staatsbibliothek** (National Library), and the **Neue Nationalgalerie** (New National Gallery), which is closed for renovations until sometime in 2019. ⊠ *Potsdamer Platz* Ⓜ *Potsdamer Platz (U-bahn and S-bahn).*

Kunstbibliothek (*Art Library*). With more than 400,000 volumes on the history of European art, the Kunstbibliothek in the Kulturforum is one of Germany's most important institutions on the subject. It contains art posters and advertisements, examples of graphic design and book design, ornamental engravings, prints and drawings, and a costume library. Visitors can view items in the reading rooms, but many samples from the collections are also shown in rotating special exhibitions. ⊠ *Kulturforum, Matthäikirchpl., Potsdamer Platz* ☎ *030/2664–24242*

⊕ *www.smb.museum* ▣ *Varies according to exhibition* ⊙ *Closed Mon.* Ⓜ *Potsdamer Platz (U-bahn and S-bahn).*

Kunstgewerbemuseum (*Museum of Decorative Arts*). Inside the Kulturforum's Kunstgewerbemuseum are European arts and crafts from the Middle Ages to the present. Among the notable exhibits are the Welfenschatz (Welfen Treasure), a collection of 16th-century gold and silver plates from Nuremberg; a floor dedicated to design and furniture; and extensive holdings of ceramics and porcelain. Though there is a free English-language audio guide, the mazelike museum is difficult to navigate and most signposting is in German. ⊠ *Kulturforum, Herbert-von-Karajan-Str. 10, Potsdamer Platz* ☎ *030/266–2902* ⊕ *www.smb. museum* ▣ *€8* ⊙ *Closed Mon.* Ⓜ *Potsdamer Platz (U-bahn and S-bahn).*

Musikinstrumenten-Museum (*Musical Instruments Museum*). Across the parking lot from the Philharmonie, the Kulturforum's Musikinstrumenten-Museum has a fascinating collection of keyboard, string, wind, and percussion instruments. These are demonstrated during an 11 am tour on Saturday, which closes with a 35-minute Wurlitzer organ concert for an extra fee. ⊠ *Kulturforum, Ben-Gurion-Str. 1, Potsdamer Platz* ☎ *030/254–810* ⊕ *www.sim.spk-berlin.de* ▣ *€6; organ concert €3* ⊙ *Closed Mon.* Ⓜ *Potsdamer Platz (U-bahn and S-bahn).*

Neue Nationalgalerie (*New National Gallery*). Bauhaus member Ludwig Mies van der Rohe originally designed this glass-box structure for Bacardi Rum in Cuba, but Berlin became the site of its realization in 1968. Highlights of the collection of 20th-century paintings, sculptures, and drawings include works by expressionists Otto Dix, Ernst Ludwig Kirchner, and Georg Grosz; special exhibits often take precedence over the permanent collection. The museum is scheduled to reopen in 2019 after four years of renovations. ⊠ *Potsdamer Str. 50, Potsdamer Platz* ☎ *030/2664–24242* ⊕ *www.smb.museum* ▣ *Varies according to exhibition* Ⓜ *Potsdamer Platz (U-bahn and S-bahn).*

Panoramapunkt. Located 300 feet above Potsdamer Platz at the top of one of its tallest towers, the Panoramapunkt (Panoramic Viewing Point) not only features the world's highest-standing original piece of the Berlin wall, but also a fascinating, multimedia exhibit about the dramatic history of Berlin's former urban center. A café and a sun terrace facing west make this open-air viewing platform one of the city's most romantic. Purchase a VIP ticket to bypass the elevator queues. ⊠ *Potsdamer Pl. 1, Potsdamer Platz* ☎ *030/2593–7080* ⊕ *www.panoramapunkt.de* ▣ *From €7.50* Ⓜ *Potsdamer Platz (U-bahn and S-bahn).*

Sony Center. This glass-and-steel construction wraps around a spectacular circular forum. Topping it off is a tentlike structure meant to emulate Mt. Fuji. The architectural jewel, designed by German-American architect Helmut Jahn, is one of the most stunning public spaces of Berlin's new center, filled with restaurants, cafés, movie theaters, and apartments. ⊠ *Potsdamer Platz* ⊕ *www.sonycenter.de* Ⓜ *Potsdamer Platz (U-bahn and S-bahn).*

Staatsbibliothek (*National Library*). The Kulturforum's Staatsbibliothek is one of the largest libraries in Europe, and was one of the Berlin settings in Wim Wenders's 1987 film *Wings of Desire*. ⊠ *Kulturforum,*

Potsdamer Str. 33, Potsdamer Platz ☎ *030/2664–33888* ⊕ *staatsbib-
liothek-berlin.de* Ⓜ *Potsdamer Platz (U-bahn and S-bahn).*

FRIEDRICHSHAIN

The cobblestone streets of Friedrichshain, bustling with bars, cafés,
and shops, have an alternative feel. There's plenty to see here, including Karl-Marx-Allee, a long, monumental boulevard lined by grand
Stalinist apartment buildings (conceived of as "palaces for the people"
that would show the superiority of the Communist system over the
capitalist one); the area's funky parks; the East Side Gallery; and lively
Simon-Dach-Strasse. It's cool, it's hip, it's historical. If you're into street
art, this is a good place to wander.

Fodor'sChoice
★
East Side Gallery. This 1-km (½-mile) stretch of concrete went from
guarded border to open-air gallery within three months. East Berliners
breached the Wall on November 9, 1989, and between February and
June of 1990, 118 artists from around the globe created unique works
of art on its longest remaining section. One of the best-known works,
by Russian artist Dmitri Vrubel, depicts Brezhnev and Honecker (the
former East German leader) kissing, with the caption "My God. Help
me survive this deadly love." The stretch along the Spree Canal runs
between the Warschauer Strasse S- and U-bahn station and Ostbahnhof. The redbrick Oberbaumbrücke (an 1896 bridge) at Warschauer
Strasse makes that end more scenic. ⊠ *Mühlenstr., Friedrichshain*
Ⓜ *Warschauer Strasse (U-bahn and S-bahn), Ostbahnhof (S-bahn).*

KREUZBERG

Hip Kreuzberg, stretching from the West Berlin side of the border crossing at Checkpoint Charlie all the way to the banks of the Spree next
to Friedrichshain, is home base for much of Berlin's famed nightclub
scene and a great place to get a feel for young Berlin. A large Turkish
population shares the residential streets with a variegated assortment
of political radicals and bohemians of all nationalities. In the minds of
most Berliners, it is split into two even smaller sections: Kreuzberg 61 is
a little more upscale, and contains a variety of small and elegant shops
and restaurants, while Kreuzberg 36 has stayed grittier, as exemplified
by the garbage-strewn, drug-infested, but much-beloved Görlitzer Park.
Oranienstrasse, the spine of life in the Kreuzberg 36 district, has mel-
lowed from hard core to funky since reunification. When Kreuzberg
literally had its back against the Wall, West German social outcasts,
punks, and the radical left made this old working-class street their territory. Since the 1970s the population has also been largely Turkish,
and many of yesterday's outsiders have turned into successful owners
of shops and cafés. The most vibrant stretch is between Skalitzer Strasse
and Oranienplatz.

Fodor'sChoice
★
Berlinische Galerie. Talk about site-specific art: all the modern art, photography, and architecture models and plans here, created between
1870 and the present, were made in Berlin (or in the case of architecture competition models, intended for the city). Russians, secessionists,

Berlin Wall Walk

The East German government, in an attempt to keep its beleaguered citizens from fleeing, built the Berlin Wall practically overnight in August 1961. On November 9, 1989, it was torn down, signaling the dawning of a new era. Most of the Wall has been demolished but you can still walk the trail where it used to stand and visualize the 12-foot-tall border that once divided the city.

FOLLOW THE COBBLESTONES

These days, it's hard to believe that Potsdamer Platz used to be a no-man's-land. But in front of the gleaming skyscrapers, next to the S-bahn station, a tiny stretch of the Berlin Wall stands as a reminder of the place's history. Just over on Erna-Berger-Strasse is the last of the hundreds of watchtowers that stood along the Wall.

Today, you can follow the rows of cobblestones on the ground that mark where the Wall used to stand. The path illuminates the effects the Wall had on the city, cutting through streets, neighborhoods, and even through buildings, which were then abandoned.

GO EAST

Walk south along Stresemanstrasse from Potsdamer Platz, then head east along Niederkirchnerstrasse two blocks to Checkpoint Charlie, a border crossing that foreign nationals used to cross between the American and Soviet zones. Niederkirchnerstrasse turns into Zimmerstrasse. Continue east along that to the modest column engraved "He only wanted freedom," in German, at Zimmerstrasse 15, commemorating Peter Fechter, an 18-year-old who was shot and killed while trying to escape to the West.

Follow Zimmerstrasse and turn left on Axel-Springer-Strasse, then right, onto Kommandantenstrasse. Keep walking past Sebastian and Waldemar streets and you'll reach Engelbecken Pond. This is a good place to rest or have lunch at one of the cafés in Kreuzberg.

A DIFFERENT WALL WALK

Potsdamer Platz, Checkpoint Charlie, and the surrounding areas are not the only places to see remnants of the Wall. For another glimpse into the past, head to the border between Mitte and Wedding, just north of Nordbahnhof train station. Starting there, you can follow Bernauer Strasse to the Berlin Wall Memorial (Gedenkstätte Berliner Mauer), in the former "death strip," where a church was once blown up by the East because it was a possible hiding place for those trying to flee.

Follow Bernauer Strasse until you reach the corner of Schwedter Strasse, then take the path that cuts through Mauer Park. The park is now home to one of the city's hippest flea markets, but it used to be the dangerous no-man's land between East and West Berlin. At its northern end, Schwedter Strasse turns into the Schwedter Steg, a footbridge over an impressive chasm of connecting train tracks and S-bahn lines. Turn around for a spectacular view of the TV tower, then descend the steps on your left and continue along Norwegerstrasse. When the path goes under an imposing brick bridge, take the steps that lead up the bridge instead. This is the famous Bornholmer Brücke, where East Berliners overwhelmed the Wall checkpoint and became the first to push through to West Berlin.

The East Side Gallery, the largest surviving section of the Berlin Wall, displays graffiti from artists around the world.

Dadaists, and expressionists all had their day in Berlin, and individual works by Otto Dix, George Grosz, and Georg Baselitz, as well as artists' archives such as the Dadaist Hannah Höch's, are highlights. There's a set price for the permanent collection, but rates vary for special exhibitions, which are usually well attended and quite worthwhile. ⊠ *Alte Jakobstr. 124–128, Kreuzberg* ☎ *030/7890–2600* ⊕ *www.berlinisch-egalerie.de* 🖼 *€8* ⊙ *Closed Tues.* Ⓜ *Kochstrasse (U-bahn).*

FAMILY **Deutsches Technikmuseum** (*German Museum of Technology*). A must if you're traveling with children, this museum will enchant anyone who's interested in technology or fascinated with trains, planes, and automobiles. Set in the remains of Anhalter Bahnhof's industrial yard and enhanced with a glass-enclosed wing, the museum has several floors of machinery, including two airplane rooms on the upper floors crowned with a "Rosinenbomber," one of the beloved airplanes that delivered supplies to Tempelhof Airport during the Berlin Airlift of 1948. Don't miss the train sheds, which are like three-dimensional, walkable timelines of trains throughout history, and the historical brewery, which has a great rooftop view of today's trains, U-bahn lines U1 and U2, converging at the neighboring Gleisdreieck station. ⊠ *Trebbiner Str. 9, Kreuzberg* ☎ *030/902–540* ⊕ *www.sdtb.de* 🖼 *€8* ⊙ *Closed Mon.* Ⓜ *Gleisdreieck (U-bahn), Anhalter Bahnhof (S-bahn).*

Jüdisches Museum Berlin (*Jewish Museum*). The history of Germany's Jews from the Middle Ages through today is chronicled here, from prominent historical figures to the evolution of laws regarding Jews' participation in civil society. A few of the exhibits document the Holocaust itself, but this museum celebrates Jewish life and history far more than it focuses

DID YOU KNOW?

The Sony Center, with its colorful atrium, is Berlin's best example of how traditional squares were used—as a central meeting spot for locals.

on the atrocities committed during WWII. An attraction in itself is the highly conceptual building, designed by Daniel Libeskind, where various physical "voids" in the oddly constructed and intensely personal modern wing of the building represent the idea that some things can and should never be exhibited when it comes to the Holocaust. The museum's permanent collection is closed until 2019, though a variety of temporary exhibitions can still be viewed. ✉ *Lindenstr. 9–14, Kreuzberg* ☎ *030/2599–3300* ⊕ *www.jmberlin.de* 🎫 *€8* Ⓜ *Hallesches Tor (U-bahn).*

Martin-Gropius-Bau. This magnificent palazzo-like exhibition hall first opened in 1881, and once housed Berlin's Arts and Crafts Museum. Its architect, Martin Gropius, was the great-uncle of Walter Gropius, the Bauhaus architect who also worked in Berlin. The international, changing exhibits on art and culture have included archaeology in Germany, Lucien Freud etchings, an expansive Piet Mondrian exhibit, and works from Anish Kapoor and Meret Oppenheim. ✉ *Niederkirchnerstr. 7, Kreuzberg* ☎ *030/254–860* ⊕ *www.gropiusbau.de* 🎫 *Varies with exhibit* ☉ *Closed Tues.* Ⓜ *Kochstrasse (U-bahn), Potsdamer Platz (U-bahn and S-bahn).*

Mauermuseum-Museum Haus am Checkpoint Charlie. Just steps from the famous crossing point between the two Berlins, the somewhat homespun Wall Museum–House at Checkpoint Charlie presents visitors with the story of the Wall and, even more riveting, the stories of those who escaped through, under, and over it. This border crossing for non-Germans was manned by the Soviet military in East Berlin's Mitte district and, several yards south, by the U.S. military in West Berlin's Kreuzberg district. Today the touristy intersection consists of a replica of an American guardhouse and signposting, plus cobblestones that mark the old border. The museum reviews the events leading up to the Wall's construction and, with original tools and devices, plus recordings and photographs, shows how East Germans escaped to the West (one of the most ingenious contraptions was a miniature submarine). Exhibits about human rights and paintings interpreting the Wall round out the experience. Monday, when the state museums are closed, can be particularly crowded. ✉ *Friedrichstr. 43–45, Kreuzberg* ☎ *030/253–7250* ⊕ *www.mauermuseum.com* 🎫 *€15* Ⓜ *Kochstrasse (U-bahn).*

Fodor's Choice **Topographie des Terrors** (*Topography of Terror*). Topographie des Terrors
★ is partially an open-air exhibit, fully exposed to the elements, and partially a stunning indoor exhibition center, where you can view photos and documents explaining the secret state police and intelligence organizations that planned and executed Nazi crimes against humanity. The fates of both victims and perpetrators are given equal attention here. The cellar remains of the Nazis' Reich Security Main Office (composed of the SS, SD, and Gestapo) contains other exhibitions, which typically run from April to October as this section is outdoors. ✉ *Niederkirchnerstr. 8, Kreuzberg* ☎ *030/2545–0950* ⊕ *www.topographie.de* 🎫 *Free* Ⓜ *Kochstrasse (U-bahn), Potsdamer Platz (U-bahn and S-bahn).*

15

SCHÖNEBERG

Long known as Berlin's gay neighborhood, these days Schöneberg also attracts young families. You'll find many stylish shops and cafés in and around Nollendorfplatz, steps away from Winterfeldtplatz, where a weekly food and flea market takes place Wednesday and Saturday.

Urban Nation Museum for Urban Contemporary Art. The largest organized display of street art in the world, this museum features original creations from more than 100 street artists, including well-known names like Shepard Fairey. Outdoors you'll find transportable panels displaying 8,000-square-foot murals that can be rotated regularly. ⊠ *Bülowstr. 7, Schöneberg* ⊕ *urban-nation.com* ☜ *Free* ☉ *Closed Mon.* Ⓜ *Nollendorfplatz (U-bahn).*

PRENZLAUER BERG

Once a spot for edgy art spaces, squats, and all manner of alternative lifestyles, Prenzlauer Berg has morphed into a lively neighborhood filled with jam-packed restaurants and bars, charming clothing stores, and young German and expat couples with baby strollers. That said, it's a lovely place to stroll, with gorgeous prewar buildings shaded by giant chestnut trees. The famous Mauerpark flea market and open-air karaoke attracts throngs of hipsters and tourists every Sunday.

Jüdischer Friedhof Weissensee (*Jewish Cemetery*). More than 150,000 graves make up Europe's largest Jewish cemetery, in Berlin's Weissensee district, near Prenzlauer Berg. The grounds and tombstones are in excellent condition—a seeming impossibility, given its location in the heart of the Third Reich—and wandering through them is like taking an extremely moving trip back in time through the history of Jewish Berlin. Men are required to cover their heads with a kippah, available at the entrance. ⊠ *Herbert-Baum-Str. 45* ☎ *030/925–3330* ⊕ *jewish-cemetery-weissensee.org* ☜ *Free* ☉ *Closed Sat.* Ⓜ *Albertinenstrasse (M4 or M13 tram).*

Kulturbrauerei (*Culture Brewery*). The redbrick buildings of the old Schultheiss brewery are typical of late-19th-century industrial architecture. Parts of the brewery were built in 1842, and at the turn of the 20th century the complex expanded to include the main brewery of Berlin's famous Schultheiss beer, then the world's largest brewery. Today, the multiplex cinema, pubs, clubs, and a concert venue that occupy it make up an arts and entertainment nexus (sadly, without a brewery). Pick up information at the Prenzlauer Berg tourist office here, and come Christmastime, visit the Scandinavian-themed market, which includes children's rides. ⊠ *Schönhauser Allee 36, entry at Sredzkistr. 1 and Knaackstr. 97, Prenzlauer Berg* ☎ *030/4435–2170* ⊕ *www.kulturbrauerei.de* Ⓜ *Eberswalder Strasse (U-bahn).*

FAMILY **Mauerpark.** This former no-man's-land between East and West Berlin (the name translates to "Wall Park") was off-limits to the public from 1961 to 1989, when the Berlin Wall fell. After reconstruction, the area reopened as a park in 1994, and though it's still a bit rough around the edges, it's filled with hipsters, musicians, and tourists on sunny days and for the weekly Sunday flea market. It's also home to the hugely popular open-air Bear Pit Karaoke Show, which runs Sunday afternoon from spring through late fall and attracts a boisterous mix of people of all ages. ⊠ *Prenzlauer Berg* ✚ *Between Gleimstr. to north, Bernauer Str. and Topsstr. to south, Cantianstr. to east, and Graunstr. and Wolliner Str. to west* ⧉ *Free* Ⓜ *Eberswalder Strasse (U-bahn).*

WEDDING

While much of Berlin has gentrified rapidly in recent years, Wedding, north of Mitte, is still an old-fashioned, working-class district. Because rents are still relatively low, it will probably be the next hot spot for artists and other creative types looking for cheap studios and work places. If you want to be on the cutting edge, ferret out an underground show or two in this ethnically diverse neighborhood.

Fodor's Choice
★
Gedenkstätte Berliner Mauer (*Berlin Wall Memorial Site*). This open-air site, located on the former border strip between east and west Berlin, includes a portion of the Berlin Wall and a thorough exhibition on the city's division, which can be viewed 24/7. The creation of the wall was particularly heart-wrenching on Bernauer Strasse, where neighbors and families on opposite sides of the street were separated overnight. The site includes the Reconciliation Chapel, completed in 2000, which replaced the community church dynamited by the Communists in 1985; the church had been walled into the "death strip" and was seen as a hindrance to security patrols. Head into the visitor center for a wealth of images and information, including a film on the history of the wall and a specialized bookstore. ⊠ *Bernauer Str. 111, Wedding* ☎ *030/4679–86666* ⊕ *www.berliner-mauer-gedenkstaette.de* ⧉ *Free, tours €4* ⊗ *Visitor center closed Mon.* Ⓜ *Bernauer Strasse (U-bahn), Nordbahnhof (S-bahn).*

NEUKÖLLN

If you missed Prenzlauer Berg's heyday, you can still get a good feel for its raw charm and creative flair if you head to ultrahip Neukölln. Just southeast of Kreuzberg below the Landwehrkanal, Neukölln was an impoverished, gritty West Berlin neighborhood until the hip crowd discovered it. It's since been almost completely transformed. Makeshift bar-galleries brighten up semi-abandoned storefronts, and vintage café or breakfast spots put a new twist on old concepts. Everything has a salvaged feel, and the crowds are young and savvy. If you're looking for nightlife, there are bars galore.

Fodor's Choice
★
Tempelhofer Feld (*Tempelhofer Park*). Of all Berlin's many transformations, this one—from airport to park—might be the quickest. The iconic airport (it was the site of the 1948–49 Berlin airlift) had its last flight in 2008. Only two years later, it opened as a park, complete with untouched runways. It's now one of the city's most beloved and impressive outdoor spots, where bikers, skaters, kite flyers, urban gardeners, picnickers, and grillers all gather. Although the Nazi-era airport buildings are not open for wandering, you can explore them

15

CLOSE UP

Jewish Berlin Today

As Berlin continues to grapple with the past, important steps toward celebrating Jewish history and welcoming a new generation of Jews to Berlin are in the making.

Somber monuments have been built in memory of victims of the Holocaust and National Socialism. An especially poignant but soft-spoken tribute is the collection of **Stolpersteine** (stumbling blocks) found all over Berlin, embedded in sidewalks in front of the pre-Holocaust homes of Berlin Jews, commemorating former residents simply with names and dates. German artist Gunter Demnig has personally installed these tiny memorials in big cities and small towns across Germany and Austria, and continues to do so as requests come in from communities across Europe.

The **Ronald S. Lauder Foundation** has gone a step further. Along with **Lauder Yeshurun,** Berlin's Jewish communities have been further strengthened by building housing for Jews in the city center, founding a Yeshiva, a rabbinical school, and offering special services for returning Jews.

It's difficult to say how many Jews live in Berlin today, but an official estimate puts the number at 22,000–27,000. About 12,000 members of the Jewish community are practicing Jews, mostly from the former Soviet Union, who belong to one of several synagogues. Berlin is also gaining in popularity among young Israelis, and today, some estimates say there may be as many as 20,000 Israelis who call Berlin home. These numbers don't include the secular and religious Jews who wish to remain anonymous in the German capital.

The government supports Jewish businesses and organizations with funding, keeps close ties with important members of the community, and, perhaps most visibly, provides 24-hour police protection in front of any Jewish establishment that requests it.

on a two-hour tour (book online). ⊠ *Bordered by Columbiadamm and Tempelhoferdamm, Neukölln* ☎ *030/2000–37441* ⊕ *www.thf-berlin.de* ☚ *Park free; airport building guided tour €15* ☉ *No tours Mon. and Tues.* Ⓜ *Tempelhof (S-bahn and U-bahn).*

CHARLOTTENBURG

An important part of former West Berlin but now a western district of the united city, Charlottenburg has retained its old-world charm. Elegance is the keyword here. Whether you're strolling and shopping around Savignyplatz or pausing for a refreshment at the LiteraturHaus, you'll be impressed with the dignity of both the neighborhood's architecture and its inhabitants. Kurfürstendamm (or Ku'damm, as the locals call it) is the central shopping mile, where you'll find an international clientele browsing brand-name designers, or drinking coffee at sidewalk cafés.

FAMILY **Berlin Zoological Garden and Aquarium Berlin.** There are more than 19,000 animals to see here, and more varied species than any other zoo in Europe, including many that are rare and endangered, which the zoo has been successful at breeding. The animals' enclosures are designed to resemble natural habitats, though some structures are ornate, such as the 1910 Arabian-style Zebra House. Pythons, frogs, turtles, invertebrates, Komodo dragons, and an amazing array of strange and colorful fish are part of the three-floor aquarium. Check the feeding times posted to watch creatures such as seals, apes, hippos, penguins, and pelicans during their favorite time of day. ⊠ *Hardenbergpl. 8 and Budapester Str. 32, Tiergarten* ☎ *030/254–010* ⊕ *www.zoo-berlin.de* ☎ *Zoo or aquarium from €16* Ⓜ *Zoologischer Garten (U-bahn and S-bahn).*

Kaiser-Wilhelm-Gedächtnis-Kirche (*Kaiser Wilhelm Memorial Church*). A dramatic reminder of World War II's destruction, the ruined bell tower is all that remains of this once massive church, which was completed in 1895 and dedicated to the emperor, Kaiser Wilhem I. The Hohenzollern dynasty is depicted inside a gilded mosaic whose damage, like that of the building, will not be repaired. The exhibition revisits World War II's devastation throughout Europe. On the hour, the tower chimes out a melody composed by the last emperor's great-grandson, the late Prince Louis Ferdinand von Hohenzollern. In stark contrast to the old bell tower, dubbed the "Hollow Tooth" (under restoration), are the adjoining Memorial Church and Tower, designed by the noted German architect Egon Eiermann and finished in 1961. Church music and organ concerts are presented in the church regularly. ⊠ *Breitscheidpl., Charlottenburg* ⊕ *www.gedaechtniskirche-berlin.de* ☎ *Free* Ⓜ *Zoologischer Garten (U-bahn and S-bahn).*

Käthe-Kollwitz-Museum. Right next door to the Literaturhaus, this small but lovingly curated museum in a formerly private home pays homage to one of Berlin's favorite artists, the female sculptor, printmaker, and painter Käthe Kollwitz. Perhaps best known for her harrowing sculpture of a mother mourning a dead child inside the Neue Wache on Unter den Linden, she also lent her name to one of the city's most beautiful squares, the posh, leafy Kollwitzplatz, which contains a sculpture of her. ⊠ *Fasanenstr. 24, Charlottenburg* ☎ *030/882–5210* ⊕ *www.kaethe-kollwitz.de* ☎ *€7* Ⓜ *Uhlandstrasse (U-bahn).*

Kurfürstendamm. This busy thoroughfare began as a riding path in the 16th century. The elector Joachim II of Brandenburg used it to travel between his palace on the Spree River and his hunting lodge in the Grunewald. The Kurfürstendamm (Elector's Causeway) was transformed into a major route in the late 19th century, thanks to the initiative of Bismarck, Prussia's Iron Chancellor. Even in the 1920s, the Ku'damm was still relatively new and by no means elegant; the Ku'damm's prewar fame was due mainly to its rowdy bars and dance halls, as well as to the cafés where the cultural avant-garde of Europe gathered. Almost half of its 245 late-19th-century buildings were completely destroyed in the 1940s, and the remaining buildings were damaged to varying degrees; what you see today is either restored or newly constructed. Although Ku'damm is still known as the best shopping street in Berlin, many of its establishments have declined in elegance and prestige over the years. Nowadays you'll want to visit just to check it off your list. ⊠ *Charlottenburg* Ⓜ *Kurfürstendamm (U-bahn).*

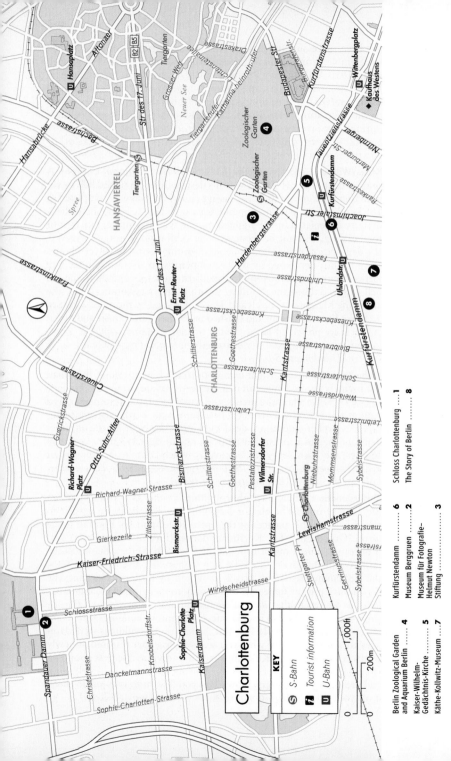

Charlottenburg

KEY

- ⑤ S-Bahn
- ℹ Tourist information
- ⓤ U-Bahn

0	200m
0	1,000ft

Berlin Zoological Garden
and Aquarium Berlin **4**

Kaiser-Wilhelm-
Gedächtnis-Kirche **5**

Käthe-Kollwitz-Museum **7**

Kurfürstendamm **6**

Museum Berggruen **2**

Museum für Fotografie–
Helmut Newton
Stiftung **3**

Schloss Charlottenburg **1**

The Story of Berlin **8**

Museum Berggruen. This small modern-art museum holds works by Matisse, Klee, Giacometti, and Picasso, who is particularly well represented with more than 100 works. Heinz Berggruen (1914–2007), a businessman who left Berlin in the 1930s, collected the excellent paintings. ⊠ *Schlossstr. 1, Charlottenburg* ☎ *030/2664–24242* ⊕ *www.smb. museum* ☜ *€10* ⊙ *Closed Mon.* Ⓜ *Sophie-Charlotte-Platz (U-bahn), Richard-Wagner-Platz (U-bahn).*

Museum für Fotografie–Helmut Newton Stiftung (*Museum of Photography–Helmut Newton Foundation*). Native son Helmut Newton (1920–2004) pledged this collection of 1,000 photographs to Berlin months before his unexpected death. The man who defined fashion photography in the 1960s through the 1980s was an apprentice to Yva, a Jewish fashion photographer in Berlin in the 1930s. Newton fled Berlin with his family in 1938, and his mentor was killed in a concentration camp. The photographs, now part of the state museum collection, are shown on a rotating basis in the huge Wilhelmine building behind the train station Zoologischer Garten. You'll see anything from racy portraits of models to serene landscapes. There are also rotating exhibitions from other photographers, such as Mario Testino and Jean Pigozzi. ⊠ *Jebensstr. 2, Charlottenburg* ☎ *030/6642–4242* ⊕ *www.smb.museum* ☜ *€10* ⊙ *Closed Mon.* Ⓜ *Zoologischer Garten (U-bahn and S-bahn).*

FAMILY **Schloss Charlottenburg** (*Charlottenburg Palace*). A grand reminder of imperial days, this showplace served as a city residence for the Prussian rulers. In the 18th century Frederick the Great made a number of additions, such as the dome and several wings designed in the rococo style. By 1790 the complex had evolved into a massive royal domain that could take a whole day to explore. The **Altes Schloss** is the main building of the Schloss Charlottenburg complex, with the ground-floor suites of Friedrich I and Sophie-Charlotte. Paintings include royal portraits by Antoine Pesne, a noted court painter of the 18th century. The upper floor has the apartments of Friedrich Wilhelm IV, a silver treasury, and Berlin and Meissen porcelain and can be seen on its own. The **Neuer Flügel** (New Building), where Frederick the Great once lived, was designed by Knobbelsdorff, who also built Sanssouci, and houses a ballroom called the Golden Gallery and the Silver Vault with beautiful tableware. The lovely gardens include a mausoleum and the Belvedere tea house, which holds a porcelain collection. ⊠ *Spandauer Damm 20–24, Charlottenburg* ☎ *030/3319–694200* ⊕ *www.spsg.de* ☜ *€17 Tageskarte (day card) for all buildings; gardens free* Ⓜ *Richard-Wagner-Platz (U-bahn).*

FAMILY **The Story of Berlin.** You can't miss this multimedia museum—just look for the airplane wing exhibited in front. It was once part of a "Raisin bomber," a U.S. Air Force DC-3 that supplied Berlin during the Berlin Airlift in 1948 and 1949. Eight hundred years of the city's history, from the first settlers casting their fishing lines to Berliners heaving sledgehammers at the Wall, are conveyed through hands-on exhibits, film footage, and multimedia devices in this unusual venue. The sound of footsteps over broken glass follows your path through the exhibit on the *Kristallnacht* pogrom, and to pass through the section on the Nazis' book-burning on Bebelplatz, you must walk over book bindings.

The modern sculpture on Breitscheidplatz frames the Kaiser-Wilhelm-Gedächtnis-Kirche in the background.

Many original artifacts are on display, such as the stretch Volvo that served as Erich Honecker's state carriage in East Germany. The eeriest relic is the 1974 nuclear shelter, which you can visit by guided tour on the hour. Museum placards are also in English. ⊠ *Ku'damm Karree, Kurfürstendamm 207–208, Charlottenburg* ☎ *030/8872–0100* ⊕ *www. story-of-berlin.de* ⌫ *€12* Ⓜ *Uhlandstrasse (U-bahn).*

WANNSEE

Most tourists come to leafy, upscale Wannsee to see the House of the Wannsee Conference, where the Third Reich's top officials met to plan the "final solution." Beyond this dark historical site, however, there are parks, lakes, and islands to explore. Leave a day for a trip here, especially in warm weather: the Wannsee lake is a favorite spot for a summer dip.

Haus der Wannsee-Konferenz (*House of the Wannsee Conference*). The lovely lakeside setting of this Berlin villa belies the unimaginable Holocaust atrocities planned here. This elegant edifice hosted the fateful conference held on January 20, 1942, at which Nazi leaders and German bureaucrats, under SS leader Reinhard Heydrich, planned the systematic deportation and mass extinction of Europe's Jewish population. Today this so-called "Endlösung der Judenfrage" (final solution of the Jewish question) is illustrated with a chilling exhibit that documents the conference and, more extensively, the escalation of persecution against Jews and the Holocaust itself. A reference library offers source materials in English. ⊠ *Am Grossen Wannsee 56–58, Wannsee* ⊹ *From Wannsee S-bahn station, take Bus 114* ☎ *030/805–0010* ⊕ *www.ghwk.de* ⌫ *Free; tour €3* Ⓜ *Wannsee (S-bahn).*

ORANIENBURG

In this little village a short drive north of Berlin, the Nazis built one of the first concentration camps (neighbors claimed not to notice what was happening there). After the war, the Soviets continued to use it. Only later did the GDR regime turn it into a memorial site. If you feel like you've covered all the main sites in Berlin, this is worth a day trip.

Gedenkstätte und Museum Sachsenhausen (*Sachsenhausen Memorial and Museum*). This concentration camp was established in 1936 and held 200,000 prisoners from every nation in Europe, including British officers and Joseph Stalin's son. It is estimated that tens of thousands died here, among them more than 12,000 Soviet prisoners of war. Between 1945 and 1950 the Soviets used the site as a prison, and malnutrition and disease claimed the lives of 20% of the inmates. The East German government made the site a concentration-camp memorial in April 1961. Many original facilities remain; the barracks and other buildings now hold exhibits. Allow three hours at the memorial, whose exhibits and sites are spread apart. Oranienburg is 35 km (22 miles) north of Berlin's center. ⊠ *Str. der Nationen 22, Oranienburg* ☎ *03301/200–200* ⊕ *www.stiftung-bg.de* ⚑ *Free; audio guide €3* ⊙ *Museum closed Mon. mid-Oct.–mid-Mar.* Ⓜ *Oranienburg (S-bahn).*

15

WHERE TO EAT

Berlin has plenty of unassuming neighborhood restaurants serving old-fashioned German food; but happily, the dining scene in this thriving city has expanded to incorporate all sorts of international cuisine, at all sorts of price points. Italian food is abundant, from relatively mundane "red sauce" pizza and pasta establishments to restaurants offering specific regional Italian delicacies. Asian food, in particular, has made a big entrance, with Charlottenburg's Kantstrasse leading the way as Berlin's unofficial "Asiatown." Turkish food continues to be popular, too, especially *döner kebab* shops that sell pressed lamb or chicken in flatbread pockets with a variety of sauces and salads, which are great for a quick meal. Wurst—especially *Currywurst* (pork sausage served with a mildly curried ketchup)—is also popular if you're looking for a quick meal on the go. At the other end of the spectrum, Berlin now has a good number of sophisticated high-end restaurants serving extensive tasting menus, often accompanied by wine pairings from Germany and elsewhere in Europe.

And as in other big cities around the world, eating local is more and more the rage in Berlin. Restaurants are beginning to understand that although they could import ingredients from other European countries, fresh farm resources are closer to home. Surrounding the city is the rural state of Brandenburg, whose name often comes before *Ente* (duck) on a menu. In spring, *Spargel*, white asparagus from Beelitz, is all the rage, showing up in soups and side dishes.

If you want to experience that old-fashioned German cuisine, Berlin's most traditional four-part meal is *Eisbein* (pork knuckle), always served with sauerkraut, pureed peas, and boiled potatoes. Other old-fashioned

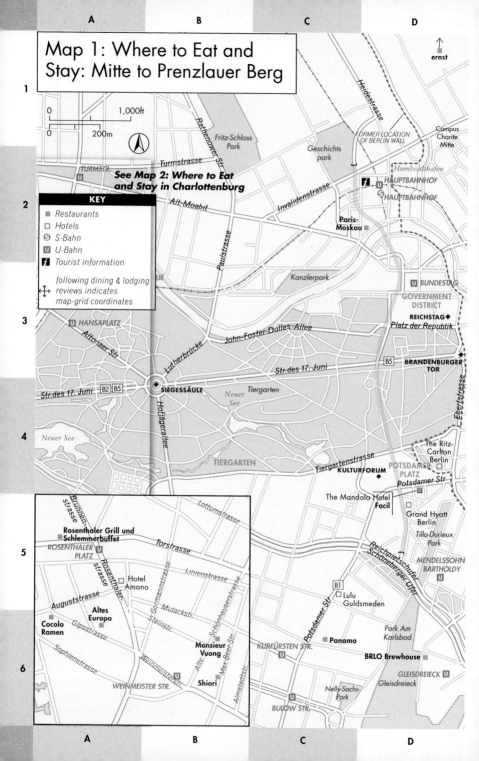

Map 1: Where to Eat and Stay: Mitte to Prenzlauer Berg

ernst

See Map 2: Where to Eat and Stay in Charlottenburg

KEY

- ■ Restaurants
- □ Hotels
- Ⓢ S-Bahn
- Ⓤ U-Bahn
- 🛈 Tourist information

↔ following dining & lodging reviews indicates map-grid coordinates

Fritz-Schloss Park

Geschichts park

FORMER LOCATION OF BERLIN WALL

Campus Charite Mitte

Humboldthafen

HAUPTBAHNHOF

HAUPTBAHNHOF

Turmstrasse

TURMSTR. Ⓤ

Rathenower Str.

Alt-Moabit

Invalidenstrasse

Paulstrasse

Paris-Moskau

Kanzlerpark

Ⓤ BUNDESTAG

GOVERNMENT DISTRICT

REICHSTAG ◆

Platz der Republik

Ⓤ HANSAPLATZ

Altonaer Str.

John-Foster-Dulles-Allee

Lutherbrücke

Str.des 17. Juni

B5 BRANDENBURGER TOR

Str.des 17. Juni B2 B5

SIEGESSÄULE ◆

Neuer See

Tiergarten

Ebertstrasse

Hofjägeralle

Neuer See

TIERGARTEN

Tiergartenstrasse

KULTURFORUM ◆

POTSDAMER PLATZ

The Ritz-Carlton Berlin

Potsdamer Str.

The Mandala Hotel Facil

Grand Hyatt Berlin

Tilla-Durieux Park

Reichpietschufer

Schöneberger Ufer

MENDELSSOHN BARTHOLDY Ⓤ

Lottumstrasse

Brunnen-strasse

Rosenthaler Grill und Schlemmerbüffet ■

ROSENTHALER PLATZ

Torstrasse

Rosenthaler strasse

Linienstrasse

Hotel Amano □

B1 □ Lulu Guldsmeden

Potsdamer Str.

Auguststrasse

Gormannstrasse

Mulackstr.

Steinstr.

Schönhauser strasse

Altes Europa ■

Gipsstrasse

Park Am Karlsbad

Cocolo Ramen ■

Sophienstrasse

Alte Schönhauser Str.

Max-Beer-Str.

Monsieur Vuong ■

KURFÜRSTEN STR. Ⓤ

■ Panama

BRLO Brewhouse ■

GLEISDREIECK Ⓤ

Gleisdreieck

WEINMEISTER STR.

Weinmeisterstr. Ⓤ

Shiori ■

Almstadtstr.

Nelly-Sachs-Park

BÜLOW STR. Ⓤ

0 — 1,000ft
0 — 200m

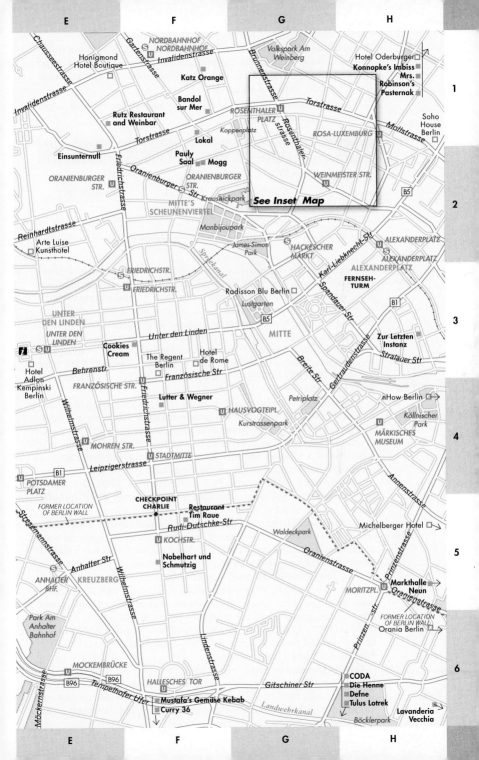

Berlin dishes include *Rouladen* (rolled stuffed beef), *Spanferkel* (suckling pig), *Berliner Schüsselsülze* (potted meat in aspic), and *Hackepeter* (ground beef)—though these are all becoming more difficult to find as the city modernizes and globalizes.

Use the coordinates (✥ 1:B3) at the end of each listing to locate a site on the corresponding map.

WHAT IT COSTS IN EUROS				
	$	$$	$$$	$$$$
AT DINNER	under €15	€15–€20	€21–€25	over €25

Restaurant prices are per person for a main course at dinner.

MITTE

$ GERMAN

🍴 **Altes Europa.** By day, this is a quiet café reminiscent of a classic Viennese coffeehouse (the name means "Old Europe"), with shabby but trendy decor, and fashionable Mitte-ites chatting and paging through newspapers and magazines. At night, it turns into a comfortable but bustling neighborhood pub serving classic Berlin dishes, just crowded enough to look like a scene but never too packed. **Known for:** traditional Berlin dishes like meatballs, schnitzel, and spätzle; daily changing seasonal dishes; being a locals' hangout. [$] *Average main: €12* ✉ *Gipsstr. 11, Mitte* ☎ *030/2809–3840* 🌐 *www.alteseuropa.com* [M] *Hackescher Markt (S-bahn)* ✥ *1:A6.*

$$$$ FRENCH

🍴 **Bandol sur Mer.** This tiny and hip 20-seat eatery serves inspired French cuisine in rotating six- or seven-course menus celebrating a mix of seasonal regional and international ingredients. If you can't get a reservation here, try the sister restaurant next door: the larger and slightly more casual 3 Minutes Sur Mer. **Known for:** casual, industrial setting; creative interpretations of French cooking; well-selected wine pairings. [$] *Average main: €95* ✉ *Torstr. 167, Mitte* ☎ *030/6730–2051* 🌐 *www.bandolsurmer.de* 🕒 *Closed Tues. and Wed. No lunch* [M] *Rosenthaler Platz (U-bahn)* ✥ *1:F1.*

$ JAPANESE

🍴 **Cocolo Ramen.** The narrow, blink-and-you-miss-it ramen joint Cocolo, run by German chef Oliver Prestele, has obviously got it right; the noodle kitchen is packed almost every night of the week and has gained a devoted following—and it doesn't take reservations, so prepare to wait in line. Tasty pork-based broths come in flavors like creamy *tonkotsu* with pork belly, salty *shio* with smoked chicken, or rich *shoyu* with wakame and scallion. **Known for:** authentic-seeming ramen; busy, lively atmosphere; gentle prices. [$] *Average main: €10* ✉ *Gipsstr. 3, Mitte* ☎ *0172/304–7584* 🌐 *kuchi.de/restaurant/cocolo-ramen* 💳 *No credit cards* 🕒 *Closed Sun.* [M] *Rosenthaler Platz, Weinmeisterstrasse (U-bahn), Hackescher Markt (S-bahn)* ✥ *1:A6.*

$$$ VEGETARIAN Fodor's Choice ★

🍴 **Cookies Cream.** The name might have you thinking something different, but this is actually a vegetarian fine-dining restaurant that serves fantastic food (it's above what used to be a club called Cookies, owned by a nightlife mogul by the same moniker); the chef steers away

Locals line up for currywurst at Curry 36.

from "easy" vegetarian dishes like pasta and stir-fries and instead focuses on innovative preparations. The entrance, too, is misleading: the only access is via a dingy alley between the Westin Grand Hotel and the Komische Oper next door, but once you're inside the vibe is industrial-chic, and the service is friendly, casual, and fun. **Known for:** Michelin-starred creative vegetarian cuisine; three- and four-course tasting menus, plus à la carte dishes; interesting organic wine pairings. Ⓢ *Average main: €25* ✉ *Behrenstr. 55, Mitte* ☎ *030/2749–2940* ⊕ *cookiescream.com* ☯ *Closed Sun. and Mon. No lunch* Ⓜ *Friedrichstrasse (S-bahn and U-bahn), Französische Strasse (U-bahn), Brandenburger Tor (S-bahn)* ✛ *1:E3.*

$$$$
GERMAN
Fodor's Choice
★

✗ **Einsunternull.** In a clean and modern Scandinavia-like space done up in woods and light colors, chef Andreas Rieger, formerly of two–Michelin star Reinstoff, aims to serve up German culture on a plate, using all regional ingredients in sometimes nostalgic dishes presented in innovative ways (think back bacon served with dried plums and rose petals). The four- to five-course lunch menu is served upstairs with open kitchen views, while the 10-course dinner is eaten downstairs; natural wines, many from Germany, perfectly balance each plate. **Known for:** German terroir–driven plates, with many foraged and preserved ingredients; inspired wine or alcohol-free beverage pairings; "memories of our childhood" dessert with brown bread and honey. Ⓢ *Average main: €109* ✉ *Hannoversche Str. 1, Mitte* ☎ *030/2757–7810* ⊕ *restaurant-einsunternull.de* ☯ *Closed Sun. and Wed. No lunch Mon.* Ⓜ *Oranienburger Tor (U-bahn)* ✛ *1:E2.*

$$ CONTEMPORARY Fodor's Choice ★ 🍴 **Katz Orange.** This lovely restaurant, hidden in a courtyard off a quiet, residential street, is both elegant enough for a special occasion and homey enough to be a favorite local haunt. Local ingredients are used whenever possible on the inventive menu, and the restaurant is best known for its slow-cooked meats for two: choose pork or lamb, along with fresh vegetable-focused side dishes. **Known for:** beautiful setting with courtyard seating; 12-hour slow-roasted Duroc pork; interesting craft cocktails. [$] *Average main: €20* ✉ *Bergstr. 22, Mitte* ☎ *030/9832–08430* 🌐 *www.katzorange.com* 🕓 *No lunch* [M] *Nordbahnhof (S-bahn)* ⊕ *1:F1.*

$$$ GERMAN 🍴 **Lokal.** This popular restaurant, located on the corner of one of Berlin's prettiest streets, serves locally sourced dishes like Brandenburg wild boar, lake trout, or venison on stylish long wooden tables to an equally stylish crowd. The unfussy German standards have become fast favorites with local gallerists and shop owners, and on warm weekend nights the place opens up to the street, beckoning passersby with the cozy sound of clinking glasses and the low hum of conversation. **Known for:** seasonal, local ingredients; daily changing menus; welcoming, casual vibe. [$] *Average main: €23* ✉ *Linienstr. 160, Mitte* ☎ *030/2844–9500* 🌐 *lokal-berlin.blogspot.de* 🕓 *No lunch* [M] *Oranienburger Tor (U-bahn), Oranienburger Strasse (S-bahn)* ⊕ *1:F1.*

$$$ AUSTRIAN 🍴 **Lutter & Wegner.** The dark-wood-paneled walls, parquet floor, and multiple rooms of this bustling restaurant across from Gendarmenmarkt have an air of 19th-century Vienna, and the food, too, is mostly German and Austrian, with game served in winter and classic dishes offered yearround. In the Weinhandlung, a cozy room lined with wine shelves, meat and cheese plates are served until 1 am. **Known for:** Sauerbraten (marinated pot roast) with red cabbage; Weiner schnitzel with potato and cucumber salad; traditional Austrian apple strudel. [$] *Average main: €25* ✉ *Charlottenstr. 56, Mitte* ☎ *030/2029–5415* 🌐 *www.l-w-berlin.de* [M] *Französische Strasse (U-bahn), Stadtmitte (U-bahn)* ⊕ *1:F4.*

$ CAFÉ 🍴 **Mogg.** In the renovated Ehemalige Jüdische Mädchenschule (Old Jewish Girls' School), this deli-style café serves delicious versions of Jewish deli standards along with regularly changing vegetarian-based salads and mains. The space, with wood floors and tables, blue walls, and low, deep purple banquettes is trendier than any traditional deli. **Known for:** New York–style deli sandwiches, like Reubens and pastrami on rye; chicken liver brûlée with grilled challah; New York cheesecake. [$] *Average main: €12* ✉ *Ehemalige Jüdische Mädchenschule, Auguststr. 11–13, Mitte* ☎ *030/3300–60770* 🌐 *www.moggmogg.com* [M] *Tucholskystrasse (S-bahn)* ⊕ *1:F2.*

$ VIETNAMESE 🍴 **Monsieur Vuong.** This hip Vietnamese eatery is a convenient place to meet before hitting Mitte's galleries or bars, or for a light lunch after browsing the area's popular boutiques. There are only a handful of items and daily specials to choose from, but the delicious curries, *pho* (noodle soup), and noodle salads keep the regulars coming back. **Known for:** lively atmosphere with a nice mix of Berlin locals and tourists; well-prepared and gently priced Vietnamese dishes; tasty shakes, with flavors including mango and raspberry. [$] *Average main: €8* ✉ *Alte Schönhauserstr. 46, Mitte* ☎ *030/9929–6924* 🌐 *www.monsieurvuong.de* [M] *Weinmeisterstrasse (U-bahn), Rosa-Luxemburg-Platz (U-bahn)* ⊕ *1:B6.*

$$$$ ✕**Nobelhart und Schmutzig.** The locavore obsession is taken seriously at
GERMAN this trendy spot that uses only the most local ingredients in the simple
Fodor's Choice but sublime preparations that come from the open kitchen and are
★ served at a long, shared counter. One 10-course menu is served each
evening (dietary restrictions can usually be accommodated) and everything—from the bread and butter through several vegetable, meat, and
fish courses—is gorgeously presented and delicious. **Known for:** one
nightly 10-course tasting menu; all natural wines, best experienced
when paired with each dish; friendly servers who share the stories
behind every plate. Ⓢ*Average main: €95* ✉*Friedrichstr. 218, Mitte*
☎*030/2594–0610* ⊕ *www.nobelhartundschmutzig.com* ☾ *Closed Sun.
and Mon.* Ⓜ*Kochstrasse (U-bahn)* ✛ *1:F5.*

$$$$ ✕**Pauly Saal.** With an airy, high-windowed space in what used to be
GERMAN the school gym of the converted Ehemalige Jüdische Mädchenschule
Fodor's Choice (Old Jewish Girls' School), and outdoor tables taking over the build-
★ ing's expansive courtyard, the setting here alone is a draw, but the
food is also some of the most exquisite in this part of Mitte. The
menu focuses on artful presentation and local ingredients, like meat
from Brandenburg, prawns from Pomerania, and cheese from Bad
Tölz; the lunch prix fixe is a great way to sample the restaurant's
best dishes. **Known for:** only serving 3- to 7-course tasting menus;
extensive wine list; quirky artwork and setting. Ⓢ*Average main:
€100*✉*Ehemalige Jüdische Mädchenschule, Auguststr. 11–13, Mitte*
☎*030/3300–6070* ⊕ *www.paulysaal.com* ☾ *Closed Sun. and Mon.*
Ⓜ*Tucholskystrasse (S-bahn)* ✛ *1:F2.*

$ ✕**Rosenthaler Grill und Schlemmerbuffet.** Döner kebab aficionados love
TURKISH this bright, casual spot for the delicious food—the fact that it's in the
FAMILY middle of the city and open 24 hours a day is an added bonus. The
friendly staff expertly carve paper-thin slices of perfectly cooked meat
from the enormous, revolving spit; if you like things spicy, ask for the
red sauce. **Known for:** döner kebab, either as a meal with salad and
fries, or as a sandwich; other food choices including falafel, chicken,
and even pizza; long hours, open around the clock. Ⓢ*Average main: €5*
✉*Torstr. 125, Mitte* ☎*030/283–2153* ▤ *No credit cards* Ⓜ*Rosenthaler
Platz (U-bahn)* ✛ *1:A5.*

$$$$ ✕**Rutz Restaurant and Weinbar.** The narrow, unassuming facade of
GERMAN this Michelin-starred restaurant, tucked away on a sleepy stretch of
Chausseestrasse, belies the elegant interior and stellar food you'll find
inside. "Inspiration" tasting menus of six or nine courses (limited à la
carte choices are also available for parties of four or fewer) make the
most of ingredients like duck and beef and combine unusual items like
black radishes and mushrooms, or asparagus and wild violets; you can
find more casual and heartier fare at the Weinbar downstairs. **Known
for:** one of the most extensive wine lists in Berlin; mostly adventurous tasting menus using mainly local ingredients; prices on the high
side. Ⓢ*Average main: €64* ✉*Chausseestr. 8, Mitte* ☎*030/2462–8760*
⊕ *www.rutz-restaurant.de* ☾ *Closed Sun. and Mon.* Ⓜ*Oranienburger
Tor (S-bahn)* ✛ *1:E1.*

15

$$$$
JAPANESE

✕ **Shiori.** Sparsely decorated, with a collection of handmade bowls behind the counter, the focus at this Japanese izakaya is solely on the food; there are just 10 seats around a small counter where you can watch the chef Shiori Arai at work. The 10 to 12 exquisitely presented seasonal courses fuse local German ingredients with Japanese technique and can be paired with a small but smart selection of sake for some of the most authentic Japanese cuisine in town. **Known for:** wide-ranging selection of Japanese dishes, from soup to sashimi to tofu; surprisingly affordable prix-fixe menu; cozy atmosphere where diners feel like part of the experience. Ⓢ *Average main: €70* ✉ *Max-Beer-Str. 13, Mitte* ☎ *030/2433–7766* ⊕ *www.shioriberlin.com* ☾ *Closed Sun. No lunch* Ⓜ *Weinmeisterstrasse (U-bahn), Rosa-Luxemburg-Platz (U-bahn)* ✛ *1:B6.*

$$
GERMAN

✕ **Zur Letzten Instanz.** Berlin's oldest restaurant (established in 1621) is half hidden in a maze of medieval streets, though it's welcomed some illustrious diners over the centuries: Napoléon is said to have sat by the tile stove, and Mikhail Gorbachev sipped a beer here in 1989. The small, well-priced menu focuses on some of Berlin's most traditional specialties, including *Eisbein* (pork knuckle), and takes its whimsical dish titles from classic legal jargon—the national courthouse is around the corner, and the restaurant's name is a rough equivalent of the term "at the 11th hour." **Known for:** roasted pork knuckle with red cabbage; meatballs with mashed potatoes; historic setting with charming ambience. Ⓢ *Average main: €18* ✉ *Waisenstr. 14–16, Mitte* ☎ *030/242–5528* ⊕ *www. zurletzteninstanz.de* ☾ *Closed Mon.* Ⓜ *Klosterstrasse (U-bahn)* ✛ *1:H3.*

TIERGARTEN

$$$$
ECLECTIC
Fodor'sChoice
★

✕ **Facil.** One of Germany's top restaurants, Facil is also one of the more relaxed of its class: the elegant, minimalist setting—it's in the fifth-floor courtyard of the Mandala Hotel, with exquisite wall panels and a glass roof that opens in summer—and impeccable service make this feel like something of an oasis in the busy city. Diners can count on a careful combination of German classics and inspiration from across the globe; you can choose from the four- to eight-course set meals, or order à la carte. **Known for:** seasonal tasting menus with mainly regional ingredients; beautiful rooftop setting; extensive wine list. Ⓢ *Average main: €66* ✉ *The Mandala Hotel, Potsdamer Str. 3, Tiergarten* ☎ *030/5900–51234* ⊕ *www.facil.de* ☾ *Closed weekends* Ⓜ *Potsdamer Platz (U-bahn and S-bahn)* ✛ *1:D4.*

$
ECLECTIC
Fodor'sChoice
★

✕ **Panama.** Tucked into a courtyard in the emerging Tiergarten district near galleries and cool boutiques, Panama has a contemporary, artsy decor that perfectly matches its eclectic international cuisine—think small, sharable plates of "leaves and flowers," "grains and vegetables," or "meat and fish." Hip Berliners and in-the-know tourists enjoy seasonal cocktails or a glass of wine with their meal, or you can pop into the sister Tiger Bar next door for a postdinner tipple. **Known for:** well-presented, family-style small plates; inventive, unique flavor combinations; fun vibe with charming waitstaff. Ⓢ *Average main: €14* ✉ *Potsdammer Str. 91, Tiergarten* ☎ *030/9832–08435* ⊕ *oh-panama. com* ☾ *Closed Sun. and Mon. No lunch* Ⓜ *Kurfürstenstrasse (U-bahn), Gleisdreieck (U-bahn), Mendelssohn-Bartholdy-Park (U-bahn)* ✛ *1:C6.*

Hackesche Höfe's eight connected courtyards are an always-buzzing, hip place to hang out in the city.

$$$$
ECLECTIC

🍴 **Paris-Moskau.** If you're looking for a one-of-a-kind dining experience, head to this half-timber house—built more than 100 years ago as a pub and guesthouse along the Paris–Moscow railway—that stands dwarfed by a government complex and the hotels and office buildings around Hauptbahnhof. Today, it serves dishes so intricately prepared they look like works of art, with unique flavor combinations; in addition to the à la carte menu, there is a three-course set menu and a four-course set vegetarian menu in the evening. **Known for:** quaint historic setting; artfully presented international dishes; well-chosen wine list. [$] *Average main: €30* ✉ *Alt-Moabit 141, Tiergarten* ☎ *030/394–2081* 🌐 *www.paris-moskau.de* 🕒 *Closed Sun. No lunch Sat.* [M] *Berlin Hauptbahnhof (S-bahn)* ✥ *1:D2.*

KREUZBERG

$$
ECLECTIC
FAMILY
Fodor's Choice ★

🍴 **BRLO Brwhouse.** A cross between a craft brewery, a hip outdoor beer garden (spring through fall only), and a casual indoor restaurant inside reused shipping containers, BRLO is a quintessential Berlin spot to spend an afternoon drinking and eating. If the weather's nice, grab a striped lounge chair outside and choose from a range of modernized beer snacks at the beer garden, open every day except in winter; otherwise, head indoors for a choice of vegetable-focused mains along with meats cooked in their own smoker. **Known for:** cool, fun outdoor and indoor setting; tasty BBQ and vegetables; beers brewed on-site. [$] *Average main: €18* ✉ *Schöneberger Str. 16, Kreuzberg* ☎ *151/7437–4235* 🌐 *www.brlo-brwhouse.de* 🕒 *Closed Mon. No lunch Tues.–Fri.* [M] *Gleisdreieck (U-bahn)* ✥ *1:D6.*

$ FAST FOOD Fodor's Choice ★ 🍴 **Curry 36.** This Currywurst stand in Kreuzberg has a cult following and just about any time of day or night you'll find yourself amid a crowd of cab drivers, students, and lawyers munching on Currywurst *mit Darm* (with skin) or *ohne Darm* (without skin). Go local and order your sausage with a big pile of crispy fries served *rot-weiss* (red and white)—with curry ketchup and mayonnaise. **Known for:** Berlin's most famous Currywurst; vegan Currywurst for nonmeat eaters; late-night eats (open till 5 am). [$] *Average main: €2* ✉ *Mehringdamm 36, Kreuzberg* ☎ *030/251–7368* 🌐 *www.curry36.de* 💳 *No credit cards* [M] *Mehringdamm (U-bahn)* ✥ *1:F6.*

$$ TURKISH 🍴 **Defne.** In a city full of Turkish restaurants, Defne stands out for its exquisitely prepared food, friendly service, and pleasant setting. Beyond simple kebabs, the fresh and healthy menu here includes a selection of hard-to-find fish dishes from the Bosphorus, such as *acili ahtapot* (spicy octopus served with mushrooms and olives in a white-wine-and-tomato sauce), as well as delicious meze and typical Turkish dishes like "the Imam Fainted," one of many eggplant preparations. **Known for:** large selection of traditional Turkish meat and seafood plates; delicious vegetarian dishes; lovely location on the bank of the Landwehrkanal, with outdoor terrace. [$] *Average main: €15* ✉ *Planufer 92c, Kreuzberg* ☎ *030/8179–7111* 🌐 *www.defne-restaurant.de* 🕒 *No lunch* [M] *Kottbusser Tor (U-bahn)* ✥ *1:H6.*

$ GERMAN Fodor's Choice ★ 🍴 **Die Henne.** The 100-plus-year-old Kreuzberg stalwart has managed to stick around thanks in part to its most famous dish, which is still just about all it serves: a crispy, fried half-chicken. The rest of the menu is short: coleslaw, potato salad, a few *boulette* (meat patty) options, and several beers on tap; for "dessert," look to the impressive selection of locally sourced brandies and fruit schnapps. **Known for:** scrumptious fried chicken; front-yard beer garden; charming historic setting. [$] *Average main: €9* ✉ *Leuschnerdamm 25, Kreuzberg* ☎ *030/614–7730* 🌐 *www.henne-berlin.de* 🕒 *Closed Mon.* [M] *Moritzplatz (U-bahn), Kottbusser Tor (U-bahn)* ✥ *1:H6.*

$ INTERNATIONAL FAMILY Fodor's Choice ★ 🍴 **Markthalle Neun.** Thanks to the efforts of local activists, this century-old market hall was saved from becoming a chain supermarket and instead turned into a center for local food vendors, chefs, wine dealers, and brewers. From Tuesday to Saturday, a large and rotating variety of food and drink is on offer for lunch and all afternoon; Thursday evening is the hugely popular Street Food Thursday; Friday and Saturday find the weekly market with tempting food products for sale, from fruits and vegetables to bread and fish; and the space also hosts a dazzling array of rotating events, so it's best to check what's on before heading there. **Known for:** tasty and varied food choices from local entrepreneurs, from BBQ to crepes to tapas; a fun, hipster scene; a good selection of beer, wine, and coffee. [$] *Average main: €8* ✉ *Eisenbahnstr. 42/43, Kreuzberg* ☎ *030/6107–3473* 🌐 *www.markthalleneun.de* 🕒 *Closed Sun.* [M] *Görlitzer Bahnhof (U-bahn)* ✥ *1:H5.*

$ TURKISH 🍴 **Mustafa's Gemüse Kebab.** For a twist on the traditional döner kebab, head to Mustafa's for mouthwateringly delicious vegetable kebabs (also available with chicken for those who can't resist a bit of protein, but the vegetarian is what people rave about). The line can sometimes stretch down the block, but it's well worth the wait, and this is a traditional street stand, so no seating. **Known for:** toasted pita bread stuffed full of roasted veggies with sauce and feta cheese; döner kebab (seasoned meat in a wrap with salad); long lines at all hours. $ *Average main: €3* ✉ *Mehringdamm 32, Kreuzberg* ☎ *283/2153* ⊕ *www.mustafas.de* ⊟ *No credit cards* ⊙ *Closed Sun.* Ⓜ *Mehringdamm (U-bahn)* ✛ *1:F6.*

$$$$
ASIAN FUSION

✕ **Restaurant Tim Raue.** The conservative decor belies the artistry on offer at this Michelin-starred restaurant from Germany's most famous celebrity chef. Asian ingredients such as wasabi, miso, and dashi find their way into traditional German dishes including veal and pork knuckle, as well as more explicitly fusion dishes; four-, six-, or eight-course tasting menus can be paired with splendid wines from one of the most comprehensive lists in Berlin. **Known for:** Peking duck "TR" (duck three ways); langoustine, wasabi Cantonese-style; yuzu cheesecake with caramel beurre salé. $ *Average main: €66* ✉ *Rudi-Dutschke-Str. 26, Kreuzberg* ☎ *030/2593–7930* ⊕ *tim-raue.com* ⊙ *Closed Sun. and Mon. No lunch Tues.* Ⓜ *Kochstrasse (U-bahn)* ✛ *1:F5.*

$$$$
ECLECTIC
Fodor'sChoice
★

✕ **Tulus Lotrek.** Tucked onto a charming, leafy street, this quirky Michelin-starred restaurant decked out in green jungle wallpaper and wood floral details, with a cozy outdoor terrace, focuses on the "experience" of their food, serving up beautiful and interesting dishes using unusual ingredient combinations. Diners can choose from a six- to eight-course tasting menu, and vivacious co-owner Ilona Scholl will happily suggest (and encourage) whimsical international wine pairings to match. **Known for:** relaxed, fun service; only six- or eight-course tasting menus; large selection of nonstandard wines. $ *Average main: €110* ✉ *Fichtestr. 24, Kreuzberg* ☎ *030/4195–6687* ⊕ *tuluslotrek.de* ⊙ *Closed Wed. and Thurs. No lunch* Ⓜ *Südstern (U-bahn), Schönlein-strasse (U-bahn)* ✛ *1:H6.*

SCHÖNEBERG

$$$
AUSTRIAN
Fodor'sChoice
★

✕ **Café Einstein Stammhaus.** In the historic grand villa of silent movie star Henny Porten, the Einstein is one of the leading coffeehouses in town, and it charmingly recalls the elegant days of the Austro-Hungarian Empire, complete with an artsy, high-brow clientele and slightly snobbish waiters gliding across the parquet floors. Order Austrian delicacies such as Tafelspitz or schnitzel (the small order is plenty large), coffee, and, of course, some cake, best enjoyed in summer in the shady garden behind the villa. **Known for:** schnitzel and Tafelspitz (boiled beef); apple strudel with vanilla sauce; outdoor seating in a beautiful courtyard. $ *Average main: €24* ✉ *Kurfürstenstr. 58, Schöneberg* ☎ *030/263–9190* ⊕ *www.cafeeinstein.com* Ⓜ *Kurfürstenstrasse (U-bahn), Nollendorf-platz (U-bahn)* ✛ *2:C6.*

$
TURKISH

✕ **Hisar Fresh Food.** The lines here are often long, but they move fast and the combination of seasoned, salty meat with crunchy salad and warm bread is unbeatable. Most people come here for a quick döner kebab, line up outside on the sidewalk, and order from the window; there's also a good choice of other Turkish specialties. **Known for:** döner kebabs, made with beef, chicken, or vegetables; beef, chicken, or veggie dürüm (wrapped in Turkish flatbread); quick, easy, and cheap meals. $ *Average main: €3*

15

✉ *Yorckstr. 49, Schöneberg* ☎ *030/216–5125* 🌐 *www.hisarfreshfood.de* 💳 *No credit cards* [M] *Yorckstrasse (U-bahn and S-bahn)* ✥ *2:C6.*

$$ GERMAN 🍴 **Renger-Patzsch.** Black-and-white photographs by the German landscape photographer Albert Renger-Patzsch, the restaurant's namesake, decorate the dark-wood-paneled dining room at this beloved local gathering place that focuses on top-notch ingredients, respecting the classics while also reinventing them. The menu changes daily but might feature blood sausage with lentils or perhaps venison with choucroute, along with lighter bites like a selection of *Flammkuchen* (Alsatian flatbread tarts) that are perfect for sharing. **Known for:** daily changing seasonal specials; Alsatian Flammkuchen in savory and sweet options; lovely outdoor terrace seating. [$] *Average main: €20* ✉ *Wartburgstr. 54, Schöneberg* ☎ *030/784–2059* 🌐 *www.renger-patzsch.com* ⏲ *Closed Sun. No lunch* [M] *Eisenacher Strasse (U-bahn)* ✥ *2:D5.*

PRENZLAUER BERG

$ GERMAN Fodor's Choice ★ 🍴 **Konnopke's Imbiss.** Under the tracks of the elevated U2 subway line is Berlin's most beloved sausage stand. Konnopke's is a family business that's been around since 1930 and though there are several options on the menu, this place is famous for its Currywurst, which is served on a paper tray with a plastic prong that can be used to spear the sauce-covered sausage slices; with french fries and a pilsner, this is one of the quintessential Berlin meals. **Known for:** much-loved Currywurst with fries (there's also a vegan option); throngs of people all day long; quick, cheap eats. [$] *Average main: €4* ✉ *Schönhauser Allee 44b, Prenzlauer Berg* ☎ *030/442–7765* 🌐 *www.konnopke-imbiss.de* 💳 *No credit cards* ⏲ *Closed Sun.* [M] *Eberswalderstrasse (U-bahn)* ✥ *1:H1.*

$$ ECLECTIC Fodor's Choice ★ 🍴 **Mrs. Robinson's.** Intimate and effortlessly cool, this pint-size modern restaurant specializes in creative, affordable small plates with an Asian touch, such as their signature *bao* (filled buns) in varying flavors, served alongside expertly mixed cocktails or inspired wine choices. Snag one of the few tables if you've come with a group, but it's most fun to sit on a bar stool near the kitchen where you can chat with the friendly staff and feel like a part of the action. **Known for:** small, Asian-inflected plates; unusual ingredient combinations; relaxed, fun atmosphere. [$] *Average main: €17* ✉ *Pappelallee 29, Prenzlauer Berg* ☎ *030/5462–2839* 🌐 *www.mrsrobinsons.de* ⏲ *Closed Tues. and Wed. No lunch* [M] *Schönhauser Allee (U-bahn, S-bahn), Eberswalderstrasse (U-bahn)* ✥ *1:H1.*

$$$ RUSSIAN 🍴 **Pasternak.** Russian treats such as dumplings, borscht, *blini* (Russian pancakes), and much more are the mainstays at this casually refined restaurant with a lovely outdoor terrace for when the weather is nice. There are several set menus available for lunch and dinner, but if you come for the weekend brunch buffet you can try just about all of the delicious dishes, as well as dessert, in an extensive buffet. **Known for:** gourmet takes on old-fashioned Russian dishes; charming setting inside and out; very popular Sunday brunch buffet. [$] *Average main: €21* ✉ *Knaackstr. 22/24, Prenzlauer Berg* ☎ *030/441–3399* 🌐 *www.restaurant-pasternak.de* [M] *Senefelder Platz (U-bahn)* ✥ *1:H1.*

WEDDING

$$$$ ECLECTIC
🍴 **ernst.** Hidden behind a metal door in a nondescript part of Wedding, the most talked-about restaurant in town from Canadian wunderkind chef Dylan Watson-Brawn presents a series of roughly 30 small plates foraged, gathered, and purchased from producers he has personally met, mainly in Germany but also from farther afield in Europe. Twelve diners watch the chefs at work right in front of them and hear the stories behind each dish, as well as the tales of the carefully selected all-natural wine pairings chosen to accompany them. **Known for:** deceptively simple farm-to-table cuisine; prepaid dining tickets that must be reserved months in advance; friendly staff happy to chat about their creations. [$] *Average main: €165* ✉ *Gerichtstr. 54, Wedding* 🌐 *www.ernstberlin.de* 🕒 *Closed Mon. and Tues. No lunch* [M] *Wedding (U-bahn, S-bahn)* ✥ *1:D1.*

15

NEUKÖLLN

$$$$ ECLECTIC
🍴 **CODA.** Your childhood dream of having dessert for dinner can come true at this intimate "dessert bar" on a pretty street in trendy Neukölln—except at CODA, many of the desserts are more savory than sweet, and all can be paired with alcoholic beverages, from cocktails to beer to wine. Six-course menus use no white flour and very little added sugar or fat in the dishes, but feature plenty of different textures and beautiful presentations to keep things interesting, even for those without a sweet tooth. **Known for:** small-plate "desserts" using natural flavors; intimate, open-kitchen atmosphere; superlative, unusual cocktails. [$] *Average main: €98* ✉ *Friedelstr. 47, Neukölln* ☎ *030/9149–6396* 🌐 *coda-berlin.com* 🕒 *Closed Sun., Mon., and Wed. No lunch* [M] *Schönleinstrasse (U-bahn), Hermannplatz (U-bahn)* ✥ *1:H6.*

$$$$ ITALIAN
🍴 **Lavanderia Vecchia.** Hidden away in a courtyard off a busy Neukölln street, in a space that used to contain an old laundrette (hence the Italian name), Lavanderia Vecchia offers a prix-fixe-only Italian menu that includes four appetizers, three pasta or risotto *primi,* a meat or fish *secondo,* and dessert, followed by coffee and a digestif; à la carte options, as well as three-course menus, are available at lunchtime only. The white-painted industrial space is decorated with vintage kerchiefs strung along old wash lines. **Known for:** nine-course set dinner menus changing bi-weekly; more affordable daily rotating lunch menus; cool setting in former laundromat. [$] *Average main: €65* ✉ *Flughafenstr. 46, Neukölln* ☎ *030/6272–2152* 🌐 *www.lavanderiavecchia.de* 🕒 *Closed Sun.* [M] *Boddinstrasse (U-bahn), Rathaus Neukölln (U-bahn)* ✥ *1:H6.*

CHARLOTTENBURG

$$ JAPANESE
Fodor's Choice ★
🍴 **893 Ryotei.** Chic foodies frequent this sleek Japanese-Peruvian fusion restaurant from renowned Berlin restaurateur Duc Ngo, which sits behind a graffiti-covered door. The cocktails are top-notch, the sushi and sashimi some of the freshest in town, and the food is wonderfully prepared. **Known for:** tiradito and ceviche (Peruvian marinated raw fish); sashimi taquitos (raw fish rolled into tortillas); enticing cocktail,

sake, and wine list. Ⓢ *Average main: €20* ✉ *Kantstr. 135, Charlotten-burg* ☎ *030/9170–3121* ⊕ *893ryotei.de* ◌ *Closed Sun. and Mon. No lunch* Ⓜ *Savignyplatz (S-bahn)* ✛ *2:B3.*

$$
CHINESE

✕ **Hot Spot.** In a city that's unfortunately full of mediocre pseudo-Asian restaurants that serve bland versions of curries, noodles, and rice dishes, Hot Spot stands out for its daring and authenticity. The menu features recipes from the provinces of Sichuan, Jiangsu, and Shanghai, and the freshest ingredients are guaranteed; *mala* dishes (numbing and spicy) are a specialty here, and the excellent selection of German wines—particularly Riesling—goes well with the spicy food. **Known for:** amazing wine list, unusual to find in an Asian restaurant; much spicier food than normal for Berlin; quick, friendly service. Ⓢ *Average main: €16* ✉ *Eisenzahnstr. 66, Charlottenburg* ☎ *030/8900–6878* ⊕ *www.restaurant-hotspot.de* Ⓜ *Adenauerplatz (U-bahn)* ✛ *2:C1.*

$$
GERMAN

✕ **Lubitsch.** Named after the famous Berlin film director Ernst Lubitsch, this sophisticated restaurant attracts an equally refined crowd with its hearty local fare (and lighter international options) that's hard to find these days. Dishes like *Königsberger Klopse* (German meatballs in a creamy caper sauce), fried calf's liver, and Wiener schnitzel are examples of the home-style German cooking, plus there are frequently rotating seasonal specials, and breakfast on weekends. **Known for:** well-prepared classic German dishes; elegant old-fashioned atmosphere; good location off of lively Savignyplatz. Ⓢ *Average main: €20* ✉ *Bleibtreustr. 47, Charlottenburg* ☎ *030/882–3756* ⊕ *www.restaurant-lubitsch.de* Ⓜ *Savignyplatz (S-bahn)* ✛ *2:C3.*

$$$
AUSTRIAN

✕ **Ottenthal.** This intimate restaurant with white tablecloths is owned by Austrians from the small village of Ottenthal and serves as an homage to their country, with interesting and delicious combinations using many organic ingredients. It's a good option for a leisurely meal before catching a show at Theater des Westens around the corner. **Known for:** huge Wiener schnitzel that extends past the plate's rim; homemade pasta and strudel; excellent Austrian wine list. Ⓢ *Average main: €25* ✉ *Kantstr. 153, Charlottenburg* ☎ *030/313–3162* ⊕ *www.ottenthal.com* ◌ *No lunch* Ⓜ *Zoologischer Garten (U-bahn and S-bahn)* ✛ *2:B4.*

WHERE TO STAY

Berlin's tourism scene is hotter than ever. Though prices in midrange to luxury hotels have increased, Berlin's first-class hotels still tend to be cheaper than their counterparts in Paris, London, or Rome. Many are housed in beautiful historic buildings and, compared to other European cities, most hotel rooms in Berlin are on the large side. Plus there's a nice mix of more intimate boutique properties and larger chain hotels, giving overnighters a wide choice of styles. AirBnBs are also plentiful in all areas of town, tend to be more affordable than in other major European cities, and can be a good choice when traveling with family or a group of friends.

Hotels listed here as "$$$$" often come down to a "$$" level on weekdays or when there is low demand. You often have the option to

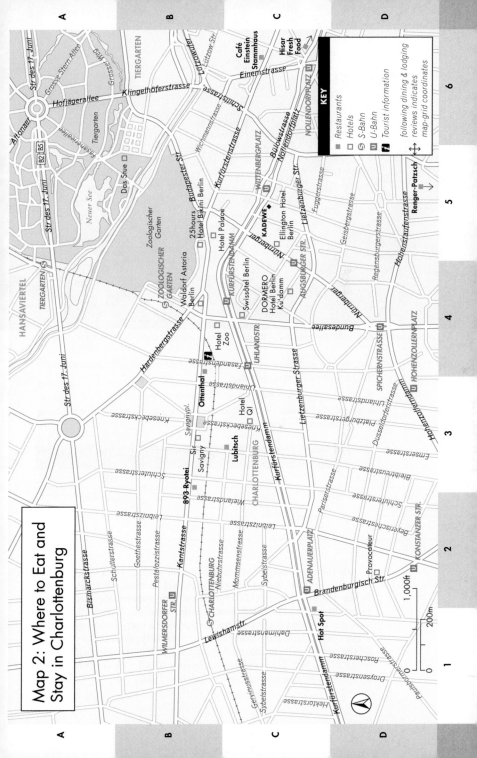

Map 2: Where to Eat and Stay in Charlottenburg

KEY

■ Restaurants
□ Hotels
Ⓢ S-Bahn
Ⓤ U-Bahn
🛈 Tourist information

↔ following dining & lodging reviews indicates map-grid coordinates

Restaurants / Hotels / Landmarks

- Str des 17 Juni
- Grosse Stern Allee
- A Honar
- Hofjägerallee
- TIERGARTEN
- Klingelhöferstrasse
- Lützowufer
- Café Einstein
- Stammhaus
- Hisar Fresh Food
- Einemstrasse
- Schillstrasse
- Wichmannstrasse
- NOLLENDORFPLATZ
- Nollendorfplatz
- Bülowstrasse
- WITTENBERGPLATZ
- Budapester Str.
- 25hours
- Hotel Bikini Berlin
- Hotel Palace
- KADEWE
- Nürnberger Str.
- Nürnbergerplatz
- Ellington Hotel Berlin
- Kleiststrasse
- Tauentzienstr.
- Fuggerstrasse
- Waldorf Astoria Berlin
- KURFÜRSTENDAMM
- Swissôtel Berlin
- DORMERO Hotel Berlin Ku'damm
- AUGSBURGER STR.
- Regensburgerstrasse
- Geisbergstrasse
- Hohenstaufenstrasse
- Renger-Patzsch →
- Hardenbergstrasse
- ZOOLOGISCHER GARTEN
- Zoologischer Garten
- Neuer See
- Dos Stue
- TIERGARTEN
- HANSAVIERTEL
- Str des 17 Juni
- Rastanstrasse
- Kurfürstenstr.
- Nürnberger
- Bundesallee
- HOHENZOLLERNPLATZ
- SPICHERNSTRASSE
- Hotel Zoo
- Fasanenstrasse
- UHLANDSTR.
- Uhlandstrasse
- Lietzenburger Strasse
- Düsseldorferstrasse
- Platzburgerstrasse
- Kantstrasse
- Knesebeckstrasse
- Savigny
- Savignypl.
- Ottenthal
- Hotel Q!
- Knesebeckstrasse
- Sir Savigny
- Lubitsch
- 893 Ryotei
- Wielandstrasse
- CHARLOTTENBURG
- Kurfürstendamm
- Leibnizstrasse
- Pariserstrasse
- Bleibtreustrasse
- Schlüterstrasse
- Bayerischestrasse
- Emserstrasse
- KONSTANZER STR.
- Schlüterstrasse
- Leibnizstrasse
- Bismarckstrasse
- Schillerstrasse
- Goethestrasse
- Pestalozzistrasse
- Mommsenstrasse
- Niebuhrstrasse
- Sybelstrasse
- ADENAUERPLATZ
- Brandenburgisch Str.
- BRANDENBURGISCH STR.
- Provocateur
- WILMERSDORFER STR.
- CHARLOTTENBURG
- Lewishamstr.
- Dahlmannstrasse
- Hol Spot
- Kurfürstendamm
- Gervinusstrasse
- Sybelstrasse
- Hektorstrasse
- Roscherstrasse
- Droysenstrasse
- Paulsbornerstrasse

0   200m
0   1,000ft

A   B   C   D

1   2   3   4   5   6

Berliners look forward to the first warm day of the year to sunbathe in deck chairs on the banks of the Spree River.

decline the inclusion of breakfast, which can save you anywhere from €8 to €30 per person per day.

For expanded hotel reviews, visit Fodors.com.

Use the coordinate (✛ 1:B3) at the end of each listing to locate a site on the corresponding map.

WHAT IT COSTS (IN EUROS)			
$	$$	$$$	$$$$
FOR TWO PEOPLE	Under €100	€100–€175	€176–€225	over €225

MITTE

$ **Arte Luise Kunsthotel.** The Luise is one of Berlin's most original (and
HOTEL most inexpensive) boutique hotels, with each fantastically creative room
in the 1825 building or 2003 built-on wing—facing the Reichstag—
styled by a different artist. **Pros:** central location; historic flair; individually designed rooms. **Cons:** simple rooms with limited amenities;
some rooms share bathrooms down the hallway; can be noisy because
of the nearby rail station. $ *Rooms from: €99* ⊠ *Luisenstr. 19, Mitte*
☎ *030/284–480* ⊕ *www.luise-berlin.com* 🛏 *48 rooms* ⊗ *No meals*
Ⓜ *Friedrichstrasse (U-bahn and S-bahn)* ✛ *1:E2.*

$$$ HOTEL Fodor's Choice ★ 🏨 **Grand Hyatt Berlin.** Stylish guests feel at home at Europe's first Grand Hyatt, which has a feng shui–approved design that combines inspirations from tropical decor, thought-provoking modern art, and the city's history with Bauhaus photographs. **Pros:** large rooms; excellent service; stylish spa and pool area. **Cons:** hotel can be very busy; location is touristy and crowded; pricey breakfast buffet. [$] *Rooms from: €183* ✉ *Marlene-Dietrich-Pl. 2, Mitte* ☎ *030/2553–1234* 🌐 *berlin.grand.hyatt.com* 🛏 *342 rooms* 🍴 *No meals* [M] *Potsdamer Platz (U-bahn and S-bahn)* ⊕ *1:D5.*

$$ HOTEL 🏨 **Honigmond Boutique Hotel.** Inside of a meticulously restored late-19th-century tenement house, this charming, quaint oasis is only a few steps away from the buzzing restaurants and boutiques of Mitte. **Pros:** individually designed rooms; warm, welcoming service; honesty bar for drinks and snacks. **Cons:** some rooms rather small; breakfast buffet is an extra charge; creaky floors, while charming, can be annoying to some. [$] *Rooms from: €106* ✉ *Tieckstr. 12, Mitte* ☎ *030/284–4550* 🌐 *www.honigmond.de* 🛏 *36 rooms* 🍴 *No meals* [M] *Nordbahnhof (S-bahn)* ⊕ *1:E1.*

15

$$$$ HOTEL Fodor's Choice ★ 🏨 **Hotel Adlon Kempinski Berlin.** The Adlon's prime setting adjacent to the Brandenburg Gate, wonderful spa, and highly regarded restaurants (including Michelin-starred Lorenz Adlon) make this one of the top addresses to stay in Berlin. **Pros:** top-notch luxury hotel; surprisingly large rooms; excellent in-house restaurants. **Cons:** sometimes-stiff service with an attitude; rooms off Linden are noisy with the windows open; gym on the small side. [$] *Rooms from: €340* ✉ *Unter den Linden 77, Mitte* ☎ *030/22610* 🌐 *www.kempinski.com/adlon* 🛏 *382 rooms* 🍴 *No meals* [M] *Brandenburger Tor (U-bahn and S-bahn)* ⊕ *1:E3.*

$ HOTEL 🏨 **Hotel Amano.** Built as a "budget design hotel," the basic rooms of the Amano are fairly small, and there is no real restaurant or room service, but stay here and you'll be in the center of the Mitte action. **Pros:** excellent location; happening bar scene; popular, hip roof deck and garden. **Cons:** service can be hit or miss; no restaurant; rooms can feel cramped. [$] *Rooms from: €90* ✉ *Auguststr. 43, Mitte* ☎ *030/809–4150* 🌐 *www.hotel-amano.com* 🛏 *163 rooms* 🍴 *No meals* [M] *Rosenthaler Platz (U-bahn)* ⊕ *1:A5.*

$$$$ HOTEL Fodor's Choice ★ 🏨 **Hotel de Rome.** In a 19th-century former bank, the luxurious Hotel de Rome offers well-designed rooms with fantastic views of Berlin landmarks around Unter den Linden, a unique spa and pool area in the old bank vault, and extremely helpful service. **Pros:** great location near top tourist attractions; large rooms and bathrooms; roof terrace with amazing views. **Cons:** some rooms need minor fixes; expensive compared to other Berlin hotels; service at breakfast can be slow when it's busy. [$] *Rooms from: €310* ✉ *Behrenstr. 37, Mitte* ☎ *030/460–6090* 🌐 *www.roccofortehotels.com/hotels-and-resorts/hotel-de-rome* 🛏 *146 rooms* 🍴 *No meals* [M] *Französische Strasse (U-bahn)* ⊕ *1:F3.*

$$$ HOTEL FAMILY 🏨 **Radisson Blu Berlin.** This full-service business hotel has an ideal location in the heart of Berlin near the Berlin Cathedral, Museum Island, and Unter den Linden boulevard, but the highlight is the view into the courtyard, where the AquaDom—the world's largest cylindrical aquarium—is located. **Pros:** central location; spacious, quiet rooms;

AquaDom is a fun and unique feature. **Cons:** location can be very busy; hotel is fairly big and lacks atmosphere; only Business Class rooms come with Nespresso coffee makers, robes, and slippers. [$] *Rooms from: €177* ✉ *Karl-Liebknecht-Str. 3, Mitte* ☎ *030/238–280* 🌐 *www.radissonblu.com/hotel-berlin* 🛏 *427 rooms* 🍴 *No meals* [M] *Hackescher Markt (S-bahn)* ✣ *1:G3.*

$$$ HOTEL 🏨 **The Regent Berlin.** One of Berlin's most esteemed and exclusive hotels, the Regent pairs the opulence of gilt furniture, thick carpets, marble floors, tasseled settees, and crystal chandeliers with such modern conveniences as flat-screen TVs and Nespresso coffeemakers. **Pros:** old-world elegance and charm; very large rooms; top location off Gendarmenmarkt. **Cons:** some rooms in need of updating; staff not always the friendliest; Internet connection an issue at times. [$] *Rooms from: €196* ✉ *Charlottenstr. 49, Mitte* ☎ *030/20338* 🌐 *www.regenthotels.com/regent-berlin* 🛏 *195 rooms* 🍴 *No meals* [M] *Hausvogteiplatz (U-bahn), Französische Strasse (U-bahn)* ✣ *1:F3.*

$$$ HOTEL 🏨 **The Ritz-Carlton Berlin.** Judging from the outside of this gray, high-rise hotel that soars above Potsdamer Platz, you would never guess that inside it's all luxurious, 19th-century grandeur, with rooms nicely appointed with exquisite furniture, marble bathrooms, and great views of bustling Potsdamer Platz and the Tiergarten. **Pros:** stylish and luxurious interior design; sleek and spacious bathrooms; fabulous cocktails at the Curtain Club and Fragrances bars. **Cons:** rooms surprisingly small for a luxury hotel; not family-friendly (business-oriented atmosphere); basic gym facilities. [$] *Rooms from: €200* ✉ *Potsdamer Pl. 3, Mitte* ☎ *030/337–777* 🌐 *www.ritzcarlton.com* 🛏 *303 rooms* 🍴 *No meals* [M] *Potsdamer Platz (U-bahn and S-bahn)* ✣ *1:D4.*

TIERGARTEN

$$$ HOTEL FAMILY Fodor's Choice ★ 🏨 **Das Stue.** History meets contemporary style on the edge of the leafy Tiergarten, in a building that once housed the Royal Danish Embassy and still retains governmental grandeur—from the classical facade to the dramatic entry staircase—now mixed with warming touches from designer Patricia Uriquola and two restaurants from chef Paco Pérez. **Pros:** quiet location on Tiergarten park and next to the zoo (with direct access); fabulous food at the in-house restaurants; lovely spa, including pool and sauna. **Cons:** can be on the pricey side; a bit far from main Berlin sights and restaurants; touchpad controls in the rooms confusing for some. [$] *Rooms from: €225* ✉ *Drakestr. 1, Tiergarten* ☎ *030/311–7220* 🌐 *www.das-stue.com* 🛏 *80 rooms* 🍴 *No meals* [M] *Tiergarten (S-bahn)* ✣ *2:B5.*

$ HOTEL FAMILY 🏨 **Lulu Guldsmeden.** A dose of hygge in Berlin, this eco-friendly, sustainable outpost of the boho-chic Danish chain effortlessly blends sleek Scandinavian design with exotic Balinese accents, bringing a wholly unique look to the loft-style rooms, and also includes an excellent Nordic restaurant and bar. **Pros:** sustainable philosophy, with bamboo beds and refurbished seating; organic Modern Nordic cuisine in Saeson restaurant; cool location near galleries and restaurants. **Cons:** some rooms feel too small; no air-conditioning; no gym or spa. [$] *Rooms from: €90* ✉ *Potsdamer Str. 67, Tiergarten* ☎ *030/2555–8720* 🌐 *guldsmedenhotels.com/berlin* 🛏 *81 rooms* 🍴 *No meals* [M] *Kurfürstenstrasse (U-bahn)* ✣ *1:C5.*

$$$
HOTEL
Fodor'sChoice
★

⊡ **The Mandala Hotel.** This privately owned luxury hotel exudes a cool, serene, Zen-like ambience, with understated floral arrangements and calming, neutral tones throughout, along with some of the largest rooms in the city, a spa and gym with amazing views, and the elegant Michelin-starred restaurant Facil. **Pros:** free laundry facilities on several floors; relaxing spa area with multiple saunas; fabulous modern restaurant in a stunning setting. **Cons:** in a busy, noisy (though central) Potsdamer Platz location; breakfast on the pricey side; tiny lobby. $ *Rooms from: €198 ⊠ Potsdammer Str. 3, Tiergarten* ☎ *030/5909–50000* ⊕ *www.themandala.de* 🗫 *158 rooms* ⦿| *No meals* Ⓜ *Potsdamer Platz (U-bahn and S-bahn)* ✛ *1:D4.*

FRIEDRICHSHAIN

$
HOTEL

⊡ **Michelberger Hotel.** Started by a group of young Berliners who dreamed of a uniquely designed, artsy space, the Michelberger Hotel, which has an eclectic flea market style, is part budget hotel, part clubhouse, and part bar-restaurant. **Pros:** located at the epicenter of eastern Berlin nightlife; great design and fun atmosphere; affordable prices. **Cons:** on a busy thoroughfare; small rooms; can be noisy at night. $ *Rooms from: €95 ⊠ Warschauer Str. 39–40, Friedrichshain* ☎ *030/2977–8590* ⊕ *michelbergerhotel.com* 🗫 *100 rooms* ⦿| *No meals* Ⓜ *Warschauer Strasse (S-bahn and U-bahn)* ✛ *1:H5.*

$$
HOTEL

⊡ **nHow Berlin.** This ultramodern music-focused hotel, designed by Karim Rashid, is an easy walk to the East Side Gallery and boasts striking rooms, prime Spree river views—especially from the riverside terrace at Fabrics restaurant—and cool features like a small art gallery and the option for guitars or keyboards in your room for your playing pleasure. **Pros:** hip, fun vibe; 24-hour gym and spa; riverfront terrace can't be beat for drinks with a view. **Cons:** pink-and-blue color scheme not to every guest's taste; can be noisy, especially on weekends; a bit far from central Berlin restaurants and attractions. $ *Rooms from: €167 ⊠ Stralauer Allee 3, Friedrichshain* ☎ *030/290–2990* ⊕ *www.nhow-berlin.com* 🗫 *304 rooms* ⦿| *No meals* Ⓜ *Warschauer Strasse (S-bahn and U-bahn)* ✛ *1:H4.*

KREUZBERG

$$
HOTEL

⊡ **Orania.Berlin.** Tucked behind the handsome sandstone facade of a restored 1913 art nouveau building, this upscale boutique property in lively, bar-filled east Kreuzberg offers a warm contemporary design with subtle Asian influences, a sprawling corner restaurant-bar-lounge space, and a top-floor salon and library, featuring live concerts most nights of the week. **Pros:** excellent location in a hip and happening (and hotel poor) area; appealing in-hotel concerts with a variety of music styles; many amenities, including bar, restaurant, and 24-hour gym. **Cons:** restaurant food gets mixed reviews; bathtubs only in suites; hallways quite basic-looking when compared to rooms and other public spaces. $ *Rooms from: €160 ⊠ Oranienstr. 40, Kreuzberg* ☎ *030/6953–9680* ⊕ *orania.berlin* 🗫 *41 rooms* ⦿| *No meals* Ⓜ *Moritzplatz (U-bahn)* ✛ *1:H6.*

15

SCHÖNEBERG

$$ HOTEL 🏨 **Ellington Hotel Berlin.** Tucked away behind the beautiful, historic facade of a grand Bauhaus-style office building—and just around the corner from prime shopping at KaDeWe and Kurfürstendamm—this sleek, modern hotel has small but stylish rooms, accentuated with modern art. **Pros:** stylish interior design with alluring 1920s touches; perfect location for shopping sprees; nice jazz-themed bar. **Cons:** some rooms on the small side; no safe in the rooms; pared-back modern design not to everyone's taste. [$] *Rooms from: €100* ✉ *Nürnbergerstr. 50–55, Schöneberg* ☎ *030/683–150* 🌐 *www.ellington-hotel.com* 🛏 *285 rooms* 🍴 *No meals* [M] *Wittenbergplatz (U-bahn)* ✥ *2:C5.*

PRENZLAUER BERG

$$ HOTEL 🏨 **Hotel Oderberger.** A conversion of a landmarked 19th-century public bathhouse, the palatial stone building in a lovely neighborhood has preserved many of its original details, including the magnificent 65-foot-long indoor pool; former private bathing cabins have been transformed into full-fledged hotel rooms, keeping historic touches like the original numbered wooden doors and subway tiles while adding sleek contemporary artwork. **Pros:** charming location near neighborhood shops and restaurants; gorgeous pool; lovely industrial-chic restaurant. **Cons:** no air-conditioning in the rooms; extra fee to use the pool; some rooms are a hike from the elevator. [$] *Rooms from: €135* ✉ *Oderberger Str. 57, Prenzlauer Berg* ☎ *030/7800–89760* 🌐 *www.hotel-oderberger.berlin* 🛏 *70 rooms* 🍴 *No meals* [M] *Eberswalder Strasse (U-bahn)* ✥ *1:H1.*

$$$ HOTEL Fodor's Choice ★ 🏨 **Soho House Berlin.** The Berlin branch of this luxury hotel–club, inside a grand, restored Bauhaus building, brings the chic atmosphere of London and New York's Soho to the German capital for a moderate price. **Pros:** rooftop pool with skyline views; state-of-the-art gym, plus spa and hammam; buzzy bar and restaurants. **Cons:** food gets mixed reviews; confusing lighting system in rooms; hotel is on a very busy and noisy street corner. [$] *Rooms from: €215* ✉ *Torstr. 1, Prenzlauer Berg* ☎ *030/405–0440* 🌐 *www.sohohouseberlin.com* 🛏 *89 rooms* 🍴 *No meals* [M] *Rosa-Luxemburg-Platz (U-bahn)* ✥ *1:H1.*

CHARLOTTENBURG

$$ HOTEL 🏨 **DORMERO Hotel Berlin Ku'Damm.** On a quiet residential street this turn-of-the-20th-century mansion with lots of modern, Bauhaus-style touches, sleek red-and-black rooms—and elegant in-house restaurant Die Quadriga—that like a hideaway even though Ku'damm is a short walk away. **Pros:** quiet location only steps away from the Ku'damm; large rooms, some with balconies; fitness room with sauna. **Cons:** staff sometimes not helpful; no tea- or coffee-making facilities in the rooms; some showers on the small side. [$] *Rooms from: €120* ✉ *Eislebenerstr. 14, Charlottenburg* ☎ *030/214–050* 🌐 *www.dormero.de/hotel-berlin-kudamm* 🛏 *72 rooms* 🍴 *No meals* [M] *Augsburger Strasse (U-bahn)* ✥ *2:C4.*

$$ HOTEL **Hotel Palace.** This is one of the only nonchain first-class hotels in the heart of the old western downtown, and although it may not look like much from the outside, inside, the friendly staff and spacious rooms make it a popular choice. **Pros:** large rooms; central location close to Kurfürstendamm; impeccable service. **Cons:** interior design outdated in some areas; hotel a bit too business-focused for some; no full-service restaurant. [$] *Rooms from: €149* ✉ *Europa-Center, Budapesterstr. 45, Charlottenburg* ☎ *030/25020* 🌐 *www.palace.de* 🛏 *278 rooms* 🍴 *No meals* [M] *Zoologischer Garten (U-bahn and S-bahn)* ✣ *2:B5.*

$$ HOTEL **Hotel Q!** The Q! has received several international design awards, and the rooms feel like larger-than-life artscapes: they're excruciatingly modern, with clean lines and a modular, innovative use of space (some even have a bathtub right next to the bed). **Pros:** beautiful design; affordable rates; good location for exploring West Berlin. **Cons:** not for families; nightlife makes hotel noisy at times; open-plan bathrooms, some with sinks in the room and visible showers, not appreciated by every guest. [$] *Rooms from: €105* ✉ *Knesebeckstr. 67, Charlottenburg* ☎ *030/810–0660* 🌐 *www.hotel-q.com* 🛏 *77 rooms* 🍴 *No meals* [M] *Uhlandstrasse (U-bahn), Savignyplatz (S-bahn)* ✣ *2:C3.*

15

$$ HOTEL Fodor's Choice ★ **Hotel Zoo.** Tucked inside one of the city's oldest grand hotels, this remodeled property with a 1920s-style elegance is an eclectic clash of New York City design meets Berlin tradition with bare, redbrick walls and a cutting-edge interior design employing objets d'art and oversize mirrors and lamps. **Pros:** multitude of common spaces and even a rooftop terrace; quiet rooms despite central location right on Ku'damm; extremely comfortable beds. **Cons:** dress code to enter the Grace Bar on weekends; edgy photographs in the rooms aren't to everyone's taste; attitude of staff can be an issue at times. [$] *Rooms from: €160* ✉ *Kurfürstendamm 25, Charlottenburg* ☎ *30/884–370* 🌐 *www.hotelzoo.de* 🛏 *144 rooms* 🍴 *No meals* [M] *Kurfürstendamm (U-bahn)* ✣ *2:B4.*

$ HOTEL Fodor's Choice ★ **Provocateur.** This aptly named boutique hotel seduces with its opulent, glamorous, burlesque-style design that pays homage to 1920s Paris, from the common areas to the rooms to the fashionable bar, along with an upscale restaurant, Golden Phoenix, from one of the city's top restauranteurs, Duc Ngo. **Pros:** beautifully designed rooms, with plush velvet furnishings; lively bar with expertly made cocktails; extremely friendly service. **Cons:** edgy style not to everyone's taste; can be noisy in rooms above the bar, especially on weekends; location is a bit far from shopping and other sights. [$] *Rooms from: €98* ✉ *Brandenburgische Str. 21, Charlottenburg* ☎ *030/2205–6060* 🌐 *www.provocateur-hotel.com* 🛏 *58 rooms* 🍴 *No meals* [M] *Konstanzer Strasse (U-bahn)* ✣ *2:D2.*

$$ HOTEL **Sir Savigny.** The first Berlin outpost of the hip European boutique chain appeals to the creative class with its eclectic, arty interiors, urbane vibe, and beautifully designed rooms with plush furnishings. **Pros:** lovely location near shops and restaurants; well-stocked minibars with local specialties; on-site burger restaurant, The Butcher. **Cons:** rooms can be small; light controls in rooms are confusing; no gym or spa. [$] *Rooms from: €153* ✉ *Kantstr. 144, Charlottenburg*

☎ 030/2178–2638 🌐 www.sirhotels.com/savigny 🛏 44 rooms 🍴 No meals [M] Savignyplatz (S-bahn) ✥ 2:B3.

$$ HOTEL 🏨 **Swissôtel Berlin.** At the bustling corner of Ku'damm and Joachimsthaler Strasse, this hotel excels with its reputable Swiss hospitality—from accompanying guests to their floor after check-in to equipping each room with an iron, an umbrella, and a Nespresso coffee machine that preheats the cups—and the unusual, rounded building has a sleek interior with original artwork by Markus Lüpertz. **Pros:** spacious rooms; unobtrusive service; good location for West Berlin shopping and sights. **Cons:** the lobby is on the third floor, with shops on the lower levels; mostly for business travelers; room decor is a bit spare. *[$] Rooms from: €161 ✉ Augsburger Str. 44, Charlottenburg ☎ 030/220–100 🌐 www.swissotel.com/hotels/berlin 🛏 316 rooms 🍴 No meals [M] Kurfürstendamm (U-bahn) ✥ 2:C4.*

$$ HOTEL 🏨 **25hours Hotel Bikini Berlin.** This stylish hotel in a renovated 1950s high-rise next to the Bikini Berlin concept mall features a trendy rooftop bar and restaurant and offers great views of both the zoo and the impressive ruins of the Kaiser Wilhelm Memorial Church. **Pros:** great central location; fun, funky interiors; rooms facing the zoo are very quiet. **Cons:** rooms fairly small by Berlin standards; ambience might be too lively and clubby for some guests; rooms facing city can be noisy if windows are opened. *[$] Rooms from: €150 ✉ Budapester Str. 40, Charlottenburg ☎ 030/1202–21255 🌐 www.25hours-hotels.com 🛏 149 rooms 🍴 No meals [M] Zoologischer Garten (U-bahn and S-bahn) ✥ 2:B5.*

$$$$ HOTEL 🏨 **Waldorf Astoria Berlin.** This impressive skyscraper, a nod to the Waldorf's original New York location, has a chic art deco look, unparalleled service, a suitably glamorous interior, and Germany's first—and only—Guerlain Spa complete with indoor pool. **Pros:** ideal location near posh shopping street Ku'damm; large, luxurious rooms and bathrooms; comprehensive Guerlain spa. **Cons:** service isn't always up to par; extra charge for Wi-Fi; additional fee for spa. *[$] Rooms from: €390 ✉ Hardenbergst. 28, Charlottenburg ☎ 030/814–0000 🌐 www.waldorfastoriaberlin.com 🛏 232 rooms 🍴 No meals [M] Zoologischer Garten (U-bahn and S-bahn) ✥ 2:B4.*

NIGHTLIFE AND PERFORMING ARTS

NIGHTLIFE

Bars in Berlin run the gamut from laid-back to pretentious—those in Charlottenburg and Mitte tend to be more conservative, while the scene in Kreuzberg, Neukölln, Prenzlauer Berg, and Friedrichshain is laid-back and more alternative. Many bars allow smoking inside after 10 pm (some have separate smoking rooms, but many let customers light up in the main area), so if you want to avoid the smoke, consider drinking in the earlier hours. A fun alternative is to hear a jazz concert in one of the many smoke-free jazz clubs throughout town.

Berlin's dance clubs are rightfully famous worldwide. Clubs often switch the music they play from night to night, so crowds and popularity can vary widely. They don't get going until about 12:30 am, but parties labeled "after-work" start as early as 8 pm for professionals looking to socialize during the week.

Berlin's nightspots are open to the wee hours of the morning, but if you stay out after 1 am Sunday through Thursday, you'll have to find a night bus (designated by "N" before the number, which often corresponds to the subway line it is replacing). On Friday and Saturday nights all subway lines (except U-bahn lines 4 and 55) run every 15 minutes and all S-bahn lines run every 30 minutes throughout the night.

MITTE

BARS AND LOUNGES

Newton Bar. This posh bar in Mitte has been around for ages. Helmut Newton's larger-than-life photos of nude women decorate the walls. ⊠ *Charlottenstr. 57, Mitte* ☎ *030/2029–5421* ⊕ *www.newton-bar.de* Ⓜ *Stadtmitte (U-bahn).*

REDWOOD Bar Berlin. Run by a California native, this simple, solid cocktail bar serves near-perfect concoctions that belie the bare wood surroundings. If loud crowds and smoky rooms aren't your thing, this is the place for you—the cocktails are excellent and you'll be able to carry on a conversation in a normal voice. ⊠ *Bergstr. 25, Mitte* ☎ *030/7024–8813* ⊕ *redwoodbar.de* Ⓜ *Nordbahnhof (S-bahn).*

CLUBS

Fodor'sChoice
★
Clärchen's Ballhaus. A night out at Clärchen's Ballhaus (Little Clara's Ballroom) is like a trip back in time; opened in 1913, the club is an impressive sight. On summer nights, lines often stretch out the door, while the front courtyard comes alive with patrons dining alfresco on brick-oven pizzas. The main ballroom features a different style of music every night and there are often dance lessons before the party starts. One of the best things about this place, though, is the variety of people of different ages, nationalities, and social backgrounds. ⊠ *Auguststr. 24, Mitte* ☎ *030/282–9295* ⊕ *www.ballhaus.de* Ⓜ *Oranienburger Strasse (S-bahn).*

Sage Club. Affiliated with nearby Sage Restaurant, this eclectic club is open only on Thursday. Different floors play different music, from rock to electro, so expect to see diverse crowds depending on the vibe (check the program on the website). ⊠ *Köpenicker Str. 76, Mitte* ☎ *030/278–9830* ⊕ *www.sage-club.de* Ⓜ *Heinrich-Heine-Strasse (U-bahn).*

JAZZ CLUBS

Fodor'sChoice
★
b-flat. Young German artists perform most nights at b-flat. The well-known and well-attended Wednesday jam sessions focus on free and experimental jazz, and once a month on Thursday the Berlin Big Band takes over the small stage. ⊠ *Dircksenstr. 40, Mitte* ☎ *030/283–3123* ⊕ *b-flat-berlin.de* Ⓜ *Weinmeisterstrasse (U-bahn), Hackescher Markt (S-bahn).*

Kunstfabrik Schlot. Schlot hosts Berlin jazz scenesters, aspiring musicians playing Monday-night free jazz sessions, and local heavy-hitters. It's a bit hard to find—it's in the cellar of the Edison Höfe—but enter the courtyard via Schlegelstrasse and follow the music. ⊠ *Invalidenstr. 117, entrance at Schlegelstr. 26, Mitte* ☎ *030/448–2160* ⊕ *kunstfabrik-schlot.de* Ⓜ *Nordbahnhof (S-bahn), Naturkundemuseum (U-bahn).*

15

In hip Kreuzberg, you can sip drinks canalside at Freischwimmer.

FRIEDRICHSHAIN

BARS

FAMILY **Holzmarkt Strandbar Pampa.** Constructed of recycled materials on the banks of the Spree, Holzmarkt attracts a range of ages (even families) who come to hang out and chill during Berlin's sunny (and not-so-sunny) afternoons and evenings. ⊠ *Holzmarktstr. 25, Friedrichshain* ☎ *030/4736–1686* ⊕ *www.holzmarkt.com* Ⓜ *Ostbahnhof (S-bahn), Jannowitzbrücke (U-bahn and S-bahn).*

CLUBS

Fodor'sChoice
★ **Berghain.** In an imposing power station in a barren stretch of land between Kreuzberg and Friedrichshain (the name borrows from both neighborhoods), Berghain has achieved international fame as the hedonistic heart of techno music—it was originally a 1990s techno club called Ostgut. It's only open as a club on weekends (for 48-plus hours straight, from midnight on Friday to early Monday), though many international music acts pass through for concert performances during the week. It's become something of a local tradition to arrive on Sunday morning or afternoon and dance until closing. Upstairs, the slightly smaller (but by no means intimate) Panorama Bar opens on Friday at midnight and offers different beats. ⊠ *Am Wriezener Bahnhof, Friedrichshain* ✛ *Exit north from Ostbahnhof and follow Str. der Pariser Kommune, then make right on badly marked Am Wriezener Bahnhof and look for line of clubbers* ☎ *030/2936–0210* ⊕ *www.berghain.de* Ⓜ *Ostbahnhof (S-bahn).*

KREUZBERG

BARS

Bellmann Bar. The candle-lit, rough-wood tables, water-stained walls, and frequent appearances by local musicians just dropping by for a few tunes gives this cozy cocktail bar an artsy old-world feel. Lovingly nicknamed "the Gramophone Bar" for the old gramophone that sits in its window, Bellmann is a place to linger and chat over a glass of wine or a whiskey from the outstanding collection. ⊠ *Reichenbergerstr. 103, Kreuzberg* ☎ *030/6128–0334* Ⓜ *Schlönleinstrasse (U-bahn), Görlitzer Bahnhof (U-bahn).*

Fodor's Choice
★
Wagner Cocktail Bistro. A fine selection of cocktails and natural wines are on offer at this friendly bar, along with seasonal small plates and pleasant outdoor seating. ⊠ *Paul-Lincke-Ufer 22, Kreuzberg* ☎ *030/4996–0932* ⊕ *www.wagnercocktailbistro.com* Ⓜ *Schlönleinstrasse (U-bahn).*

Würgeengel. Named after a 1962 surrealist film by Luis Buñuel (known as *The Exterminating Angel* in English), this classy joint offers an elaborate cocktail menu in a well-designed space off Kottbusser Tor. The bar's loyal fans spill out onto the streets on busy nights, and an evening tapas menu comes from the neighboring restaurant, Gorgonzola Club. ⊠ *Dresdenerstr. 122, Kreuzberg* ☎ *030/615–5560* ⊕ *www.wuergeengel. de* Ⓜ *Kottbusser Tor (U-bahn).*

CLUBS

Watergate. The elegant Watergate is a club for people who usually don't like clubbing. It sits languidly at the base of the Oberbaumbrücke, on the Kreuzberg side, and has two dance floors with bars. The terrace extending over the River Spree is one of the city's best chill-out spaces. In addition to hosting internationally renowned DJs, the club is the beautiful and intimate setting for infrequent but popular classical music nights. ⊠ *Falckensteinstr. 49, Kreuzberg* ☎ *030/6128–0396* ⊕ *water-gate.de* Ⓜ *Schlesisches Tor (U-bahn), Warschauer Strasse (U-bahn and S-bahn).*

GAY AND LESBIAN BARS

Roses. If you don't find any eye candy at tiny Roses there are always the furry red walls and kitschy paraphernalia to admire. It opens at 10 pm and keeps going until very late (and is usually very smoky). ⊠ *Oranienstr. 187, Kreuzberg* ☎ *030/615–6570* Ⓜ *Kottbusser Tor (U-bahn), Görlitzer Bahnhof (U-bahn).*

SCHÖNEBERG

BARS

Green Door. A grown-up crowd focused on conversation and appreciating outstanding cocktails heads to Green Door, a Schöneberg classic (note that smoking is allowed). The decor is retro 1960s style, with gingham walls and stand-alone lamps. ⊠ *Winterfeldstr. 50, Schöneberg* ☎ *030/215–2515* ⊕ *www.greendoor.de* Ⓜ *Nollendorfplatz (U-bahn), Viktoria-Luise-Platz (U-bahn).*

GAY AND LESBIAN BARS

Connection Club. Just south of Wittenbergplatz, the dance club Connection is known for heavy house music and lots of dark corners. ⊠ *Fuggerstr. 33, Schöneberg* ☎ *030/218–1432* ⊕ *www.connectionclub.*

15

de Ⓜ *Bahnhof Wittenbergplatz (U-bahn), Nollendorfplatz (U-bahn), Viktoria-Luise-Platz (U-bahn).*

Hafen. The stylish decor and the energetic crowd at Hafen make it a popular singles hangout. ⊠ *Motzstr. 19, Schöneberg* ☎ *030/211–4118* ⊕ *www.hafen-berlin.de* Ⓜ *Nollendorfplatz (U-bahn), Viktoria-Luise-Platz (U-bahn).*

TREPTOW

CLUBS

Club der Visionaere. It may not be much more than a series of wooden rafts and a few shoddily constructed shacks, but this club is one of the most beloved outdoor venues in town. The place is packed at all hours, either with clubbers on their last stop of the evening, or with locals and tourists soaking up the sunshine on a Sunday morning. ⊠ *Am Flutgraben 1, Treptow* ⊕ *Follow Schlesische Str. east from U-bahn station until you cross two small canals. After second bridge, look left* ☎ *030/6951– 8942* ⊕ *clubdervisionaere.com* Ⓜ *Schlesisches Tor (U-bahn).*

PRENZLAUER BERG

BARS

Fodor's Choice ★ **Prater Biergarten.** Open April to September (though the restaurant's open year-round), this expansive and charming beer garden with 600 seats also serves up Pratwurst, pretzels, and other German snacks (cash only). ⊠ *Kastanienalle 7–9, Prenzlauer Berg* ☎ *030/448–5688* ⊕ *www.praterbiergarten.de* Ⓜ *Eberswalderstrasse (U-bahn).*

CHARLOTTENBURG

BARS

Fodor's Choice ★ **Monkey Bar.** On the rooftop of the 25hours Hotel Bikini Berlin, this often-packed watering hole affords scenic views over Tiergarten Park and an impressive range of well-crafted cocktails. Expect a crowd at the ground-floor entrance (no matter what day of the week)—this place is worth the wait. ⊠ *Budapester Str. 40, Charlottenburg* ☎ *030/1202– 21210* ⊕ *www.25hours-hotels.com* Ⓜ *Zoologischer Garten (U-bahn and S-bahn).*

JAZZ CLUBS

A-Trane. A-Trane in West Berlin has hosted countless greats throughout the years, including Herbie Hancock and Wynton Marsalis. Numerous free events make it a good place to see jazz on a budget. ⊠ *Bleibtreustr. 1, Charlottenburg* ☎ *030/313–2550* ⊕ *www.a-trane.de* Ⓜ *Savignyplatz (S-bahn).*

Quasimodo. To get to Quasimodo, the most established and popular jazz venue in the city, you'll need to descend a small staircase to the basement of the Theater des Westens. Despite its college-town pub feel, the club has hosted many Berlin and international greats. Seats are few, but there's plenty of standing room in the front. ⊠ *Kantstr. 12a, Charlottenburg* ☎ *030/3180–4560* ⊕ *quasimodo.de* Ⓜ *Zoologischer Garten (S-bahn and U-bahn).*

PERFORMING ARTS

For detailed information about events, see *Tip* (⊕ *www.tip-berlin.de*), *Zitty* (⊕ *www.zitty.de*), or *(030)* (⊕ *berlin030.de*). For listings in English, consult the monthly *Ex-Berliner* (⊕ *www.exberliner.com*), which is updated regularly.

Hekticket offices. The Hekticket offices offer discounted and last-minute tickets, including half-price same-day tickets daily at 2 pm. There is a second location in Mitte at Alexanderstrasse 1 open weekdays only. ✉ *Hardenbergpl. 1, off Zoologischer Garten station, Charlottenburg* ☎ *030/230–9930* ⊕ *www.hekticket.de.*

CONCERTS

Fodor'sChoice
★

Berliner Philharmonie. The Berlin Philharmonic Orchestra is one of the world's best and their resident venue is the Philharmonie, comprising the Grosser Saal, or large main hall, and the smaller Kammermusiksaal, dedicated to chamber music. Tickets sell out in advance for the nights when star maestros conduct, but other orchestras and artists appear here as well. Tuesday's free Lunchtime Concerts fill the foyer with eager listeners of all ages at 1 pm. Show up early as these concerts can get very crowded. Daily guided tours (€5) also take place at 1:30 pm. ✉ *Herbert-von-Karajan-Str. 1, Tiergarten* ☎ *030/2548–8999 ticket office* ⊕ *www.berliner-philharmoniker.de.*

Konzerthaus Berlin. The beautifully restored hall at Konzerthaus Berlin is a prime venue for classical music concerts. The box office is open from noon to curtain time. ✉ *Gendarmenmarkt, Mitte* ☎ *030/2030–92101* ⊕ *www.konzerthaus.de.*

DANCE, MUSICALS, AND OPERA

Berlin's three opera houses also host guest productions and companies from around the world, plus the Staatsballett Berlin performs its classic and modern productions at all three venues.

Deutsche Oper Berlin. Of the many composers represented in the repertoire of Deutsche Oper Berlin, Verdi and Wagner are the most frequently presented. ✉ *Bismarckstr. 35, Charlottenburg* ☎ *030/343–8401, 030/343–84343 tickets* ⊕ *www.deutscheoperberlin.de.*

Komische Oper. The operas performed here are sung in their original language (often with English subtitles), but the lavish and at times over-the-top and kitschy staging and costumes make for a fun night even if you don't speak the language. ✉ *Behrenstr. 55–57, Mitte* ☎ *030/4799–7400* ⊕ *www.komische-oper-berlin.de.*

Neuköllner Oper. The small and alternative Neuköllner Oper puts on fun, showy performances of long-forgotten operas as well as humorous musical productions. It also is more likely than other Berlin opera houses to stage productions offering modern social commentary and individual takes on the immigrant experience—which is fitting for this international neighborhood. ✉ *Karl-Marx-Str. 131–133, Neukölln* ☎ *030/6889–0777* ⊕ *www.neukoellneroper.de.*

15

Fodor's Choice **Staatsoper** (*Berlin State Opera*). The premier opera company in Berlin
★ presents both traditional and contemporary productions, often with
international opera stars, in their beautiful concert house on Unter den
Linden, which reopened in 2017 after extensive renovations. ✉ *Staatsoper Unter den Linden, Unter den Linden 7, Mitte* ☎ *030/2035–4555
tickets* ⊕ *www.staatsoper-berlin.de.*

Tanzfabrik. The Tanzfabrik is Berlin's best venue to see young dance
talent and the latest from Europe's avant-garde. Additionally, contemporary artists come to learn and practice here in dance classes
and workshops. The company holds dance festivals at Uferstrasse
8/23 in Wedding on occasion. ✉ *Studio, Möckernstr. 68, Kreuzberg*
☎ *030/786–5861* ⊕ *www.tanzfabrik-berlin.de.*

SHOPPING

What's fashionable in Berlin is creative—either bohemian style or street
style—so designer labels have less appeal here than in Hamburg, Düsseldorf, or Munich. Most young and trendy Berliners step out in vintage and secondhand threads, or some variation on a thrown-together
jeans-and-sneakers look.

MITTE

The finest shops in historic Berlin are along Friedrichstrasse, including
the French department store Galeries Lafayette and the international
luxury department store Departmentstore Quartier 206. Nearby, Unter
den Linden offers a few souvenir shops and a Meissen ceramic showroom, while the area surrounding the picturesque Gendarmenmarkt is
home to top fashion designers and many international brands.

The charming side streets of Mitte's Scheunenviertel area have turned
into a true destination for serious fashion aficionados. The area between
Hackescher Markt, Weinmeister Strasse, and Rosa-Luxemburg-Platz
alternate pricey independent designers with groovy secondhand shops,
and a string of ultrahip flagship stores by the big sports and fashion
designer brands. Neue Schönhauser Strasse meets up with Rosenthaler
Strasse on one end and curves into Alte Schönhauser Strasse on the
other. All three streets are full of stylish and original casual wear. Galleries along Gipsstrasse and Sophienstrasse round out the mix. Most
stores are closed on Sunday.

BOOK STORES

Fodor's Choice **Do You Read Me?** Whether you're looking for something to read on the
★ plane or a special present, this charming bookstore is guaranteed to
have something to pique your literary interests. The wide selection of
magazines and literature—many of the titles are in English—comes
from around the world and spans fashion, photography, architecture,
interior design, and cultural topics. ✉ *Auguststr. 28, Mitte* ☎ *030/6954–
9695* ⊕ *www.doyoureadme.de* Ⓜ *Weinmeisterstrasse (U-bahn), Rosa-Luxemburg-Platz (U-bahn).*

soda. BERLIN. Opened in early 2015, this branch of the Munich bookstore started by Isabell Hummel and Sebastian Steinacker gives the many mainstream and DIY magazines and books carried here plenty of room to breathe. Hummel and Steinacker's goal for their spaces is to offer "curious publications for curious people." Here you'll find plenty of both. ⊠ *Weinbergsweg 1, Mitte* ☏ *030/4373–3700* ⊕ *www.sodabooks.com* Ⓜ *Rosenthaler Platz (U-bahn).*

CLOTHING

A.D. Deertz. This tiny shop on Torstrasse is the flagship menswear outlet for designer Wibke Deertz, who uses fabrics and inspirations from her travels around the world to create a collection of handmade, limited-edition pieces, including pants, shirts, jackets, and accessories. ⊠ *Torstr. 106, Mitte* ☏ *030/9120–6630* ⊕ *www.addeertz.com* Ⓜ *Rosenthaler Platz (U-bahn).*

Apartment. Don't be deterred when you arrive at this seemingly empty storefront: the real treasure lies at the bottom of the black spiral staircase. On the basement level you'll find one of Berlin's favorite shops for local designs and wardrobe staples for both men and women. Think distressed tops, shoes, leather jackets, and skinny jeans. ⊠ *Memhardstr. 8, Mitte* ☏ *030/2804–2251* ⊕ *www.apartmentberlin.de* Ⓜ *Weinmeisterstrasse (U-bahn), Alexanderplatz (U-bahn and S-bahn).*

15

Fodor'sChoice ★ **Baerck.** Baerck artfully displays its mix of European and Berlin men's and women's wear on wheeled structures, allowing them to be rearranged in the store whenever necessary. Along with designers like Henrik Vibskov and Hope, you'll find the store's eponymous accessories line of handbags and scarves, as well as their clothing label NIA for blouses and trousers, and their product line llot llov—a play on the German word *toll* meaning great or cool. ⊠ *Mulackstr. 12, Mitte* ☏ *030/2404–8994* ⊕ *baerck.net* Ⓜ *Weinmeisterstrasse (U-bahn).*

Claudia Skoda. One of Berlin's top avant-garde designers, Claudia Skoda's creations are mostly for women, but there's also a selection of men's knitwear. ⊠ *Mulackstr. 8, Mitte* ☏ *030/4004–1884* ⊕ *www.claudiaskoda.com* Ⓜ *Weinmeisterstrasse (U-bahn), Rosa-Luxemburg-Platz (U-bahn).*

Fodor'sChoice ★ **The Corner Berlin.** In the heart of the stunning Gendarmenmarkt, this luxury concept store sells a contemporary collection of new and vintage clothing from high-end designers like Yves Saint Laurent and Chloé, as well as cosmetics, home furnishings, and art books. There's also a men's shop next door and a second store near Kurfürstendamm. ⊠ *Französischestr. 40, Mitte* ☏ *030/2067–0940* ⊕ *www.thecornerberlin.de* Ⓜ *Französische Strasse (U-bahn).*

Fodor'sChoice ★ **Das Neue Schwarz.** Whether you want a new little black dress or a cool vintage bag to carry around this season, a peek into Das Neue Schwarz (The New Black) is guaranteed to result in some special finds. In the midst of Mitte's fashionista neighborhood of avant-garde designers and exclusive boutiques, this shop holds its own with a collection of secondhand items—many never worn—from big name designers including Vivienne Westwood, Helmut Lang, and Yves Saint Laurent.

✉ *Mulackstr. 38, Mitte* ☎ *030/2787–4467* ⊕ *www.dasneueschwarz.de* Ⓜ *Weinmeisterstrasse (U-bahn), Rosa-Luxemburg-Platz (U-bahn).*

Esther Perbant. An avant-garde pioneer with a penchant for black, Esther Perbant's buzzed-about runway shows during Berlin Fashion Week are as adventurous as the designs sold in her shop. Expect androgynous silhouettes for men and women including tailored trousers, blazers, wrap dresses with generous, draping fabric, and her signature, military-inspired hats. ✉ *Almstadtstr. 3, Mitte* ☎ *030/8853–6791* ⊕ *estherperbandt.com* Ⓜ *Weinmeisterstrasse (U-bahn), Alexanderplatz (U-bahn and S-bahn).*

14 oz. Inside a beautiful old building in the heart of Mitte's Hackescher Markt shopping district, 14 oz. sells high-end denim (Denham the Jeanmaker, Momotaro Jeans, Edwin), along with sneakers, accessories, knitwear, and outerwear. For true VIP treatment, a private shopping area is available on the second floor. ✉ *Neue Schönhauserstr. 13, Mitte* ☎ *030/2804–0514* ⊕ *14oz.com* Ⓜ *Weinmeisterstrasse (U-bahn), Hackescher Markt (S-bahn).*

Fodor'sChoice ★ **Konk.** Since 2003, this Mitte hot spot has nurtured Berlin independent designers who are as visionary in their aesthetics as they are in their production mode: most items are handmade and sustainably sourced. Look for local favorite NCA for hats, and elegant gold earrings and rings by Savoir Joaillerie. ✉ *Kleine Hamburger Str. 15, Mitte* ☎ *030/2809–7839* ⊕ *www.konk-berlin.de* Ⓜ *Oranienburger Strasse (S-bahn), Rosenthaler Platz (U-bahn).*

Lala Berlin. Originally from Tehran, former MTV editor Lelya Piedayesh is one of Berlin's top design talents. Her popular boutique showcases her high-quality fabric scarves, sweaters, and accessories that use the reinterpreted Palestinian keffiyeh pattern she's become known for. ✉ *Alte Schonhauser Str. 3, Mitte* ☎ *030/2576–2924* ⊕ *www.lalaberlin.com* Ⓜ *Weinmeisterstrasse (U-bahn), Rosa-Luxemburg-Platz (U-bahn).*

SOTO. SOTO is the name of the hip, fashion-forward area of Mitte, south of Torstrasse, filled with charming side streets and numerous fashion boutiques. So, it's appropriate that it's also the name of this boutique where you'll find a mix of timeless and trendsetting menswear including brands like Norse Projects and Our Legacy, grooming products, and accessories ranging from cameras to lanyards. ✉ *Torstr. 72, Mitte* ☎ *030/2576–2070* ⊕ *www.sotostore.com* Ⓜ *Rosa-Luxemburg-Platz (U-bahn).*

Thone Negron. From the back of her Linienstrasse atelier, Ettina Berrios-Negron creates some of the most elegant dresses and silk blouses seen in the city. ✉ *Linienstr. 71, Mitte* ☎ *030/5316–1116* ⊕ *www.thonenegron.com* Ⓜ *Rosenthaler Platz (U-bahn).*

DEPARTMENT STORES

Galeries Lafayette. At the corner of Französische Strasse (it means "French Street" and is named for the nearby French Huguenot cathedral) is the French department store Galeries Lafayette. French architect Jean Nouvel included an impressive steel-and-glass funnel at the center of the building, and it's surrounded by four floors of expensive clothing and luxuries as well as an excellent food department with counters offering French cuisine, and a market with some of the best produce in the area. ⊠ *Friedrichstr. 76–78, Mitte* ☎ *030/209–480* ⊕ *www.galerieslafayette.de* Ⓜ *Französische Strasse (U-bahn).*

GIFTS

Ampelmann. This gallery shop opened in the mall-like Hackesche Höfe shopping area in 2001, promoting the red and green Ampelmännchen, the charming symbol used on the former East traffic lights. The brand now operates eight shops in Berlin, and you can find the logo on everything from T-shirts and umbrellas to ice cube trays and candy. ■ TIP→ **It's a perfect stop for souvenirs.** ⊠ *Hackesche Höfe, Hof 5, Rosenthalerstr. 40–41, Mitte* ☎ *030/4472–6438* ⊕ *www.ampelmann.de* Ⓜ *Weinmeisterstrasse (U-bahn), Hackescher Markt (S-bahn).*

ausberlin. This shop near Alexanderplatz provides a wide range of Berlin memories, all designed and manufactured in the city. There is everything from Berlin-themed emergency candy bars and tote bags with city landmark designs to Berlin-produced liquors. ⊠ *Karl-Liebknechtstr. 9, Mitte* ☎ *030/9700–5640* ⊕ *www.ausberlin.de* Ⓜ *Alexanderplatz (U-bahn and S-bahn).*

Bonbonmacherei. Tucked into a small courtyard near the New Synagogue, this charming candy store has been making and selling handmade sweets for more than 100 years. The brightly colored sugar bonbons are pressed on vintage molds into leaf, raspberry, and diamond shapes, and more than 30 different varieties are available. ⊠ *Oranienburgerstr. 32, Mitte* ☎ *030/4405–5243* ⊕ *www.bonbonmacherei.de* Ⓜ *Oranienburger Strasse (U-bahn and S-bahn).*

JEWELRY

Sabrina Dehoff. The flagship store of German jewelry designer Sabrina Dehoff balances bling and minimalism—bright crystals are paired with chunky metals. ⊠ *Auguststr. 26A, Mitte* ☎ *030/9700–4160* ⊕ *www.sabrinadehoff.com* Ⓜ *Rosenthaler Strasse (U-bahn).*

POTSDAMER PLATZ/TIERGARTEN

On the border between the city's former east and west regions, this touristy area is popular thanks to the towering Sony Center, which offers an English-language movie theater as well as restaurants and bars. The main shopping arcade here (also named Potsdamer Platz) offers a wide selection of chain shops, but you'll find a few original shops tucked on the side streets in the trendy Tiergarten neighborhood.

CLOTHING

Fodor'sChoice **Andreas Murkudis.** Inside the former Taggespiegel newspaper office
★ space, you'll find this cool concept store featuring hand-picked men's, women's, and children's clothing, including designs by brother Kostas Murkudis, Dries van Noten, and Christian Haas, as well as accessories, and contemporary homeware. ⊠ *Potsdamer Str. 81e, Potsdamer Platz* ☎ *030/6807–98306* ⊕ *andreasmurkudis.com* Ⓜ *Kurfürstenstrasse (U-bahn).*

15

GIFTS

Fodor'sChoice ★ **Frau Tonis Parfum.** This elegant perfumery will help you create a completely personal scent; choose from vials filled with perfumes like acacia, linden tree blossoms, cedarwood, or pink peppercorns. All the perfumes are produced locally in Berlin, creating a really one-of-a kind gift. ⊠ *Zimmerstr. 13, Potsdamer Platz* ☎ *030/2021–5310* ⊕ *www.frautonis-parfum.com* Ⓜ *Kochstrasse, Checkpoint Charlie (U-bahn).*

PORCELAIN

Königliche Porzellan Manufaktur. Fine porcelain is still produced by Königliche Porzellan Manufaktur, the former Royal Porcelain Manufactory for the Prussians, also called KPM. You can buy this delicate handmade, hand-painted china at KPM's manufactory, where you can learn about the brand's rich history, as well as purchase products directly, with the option to find seconds at reduced prices. ⊠ *Wegelystr. 1, Tiergarten* ☎ *030/3900–9472* ⊕ *www.kpm-berlin.com* Ⓜ *Tiergarten (S-bahn).*

KREUZBERG

Locals love Kreuzberg for its grittier landscape, and the fashion style here is more urban as well. The lively Bergmannstrasse is home to several worthy destinations, as is Mehringdamm. This, along with neighboring Neukölln, is the place to score a unique Berlin find.

CLOTHING

Michael Sontag. You'll see a lot of versatile silk shirts and draping dresses to be worn year-round in Berlin-based Michael Sontag's architecturally striking boutique. Often celebrated by the German fashion press, Sontag thinks in terms of timelessness over seasonality. ⊠ *Muskauerstr. 41, Kreuzberg* ☎ *0179/971–5932* ⊕ *www.michaelsontag.com* Ⓜ *Görlitzer Bahnhof (U-bahn).*

Fodor'sChoice ★ **Voo.** This "super boutique" in a former locksmith's workshop is a Berlin favorite for women's and men's separates, shoes, accessories, and outerwear, often from rare collections around the world. It's also home to Companion Coffee, for when you need a shopping pick-me-up. ⊠ *Oranienstr. 24, Kreuzberg* ☎ *030/6110–1750* ⊕ *www.vooberlin.com* Ⓜ *Kottbusser Tor (U-bahn).*

GIFTS

Hardwax. This iconic record store is run by music veteran Mark Ernestus, who hand-picks all the vinyl and CDs with a heavy focus on techno, electronic, and dubstep. On the third floor of a heavily graffitied building, it's the true essence of Berlin grunge and totally worth a visit for music lovers. ⊠ *Paul-Lincke-Ufer 44a, Kreuzberg* ☎ *030/6113–0111* ⊕ *www.hardwax.com* Ⓜ *Kottbusser Tor (U-bahn).*

Fodor'sChoice ★ **Süper Store.** Located in the charming neighborhood of Kreuzberg known as the Graefekiez, this cute little shop supplies a variety of lovely odds and ends, sourced from all over the world, including Turkey, Italy, and Switzerland, as well as locally produced items. Inside you'll find linens, housewares, pantry items, and jewelry. ⊠ *Dieffenbachstr. 12, Kreuzberg* ☎ *030/9832–7944* ⊕ *www.sueper-store.de* Ⓜ *Schönleinstrasse (U-bahn).*

HOME DECOR

FodorsChoice **Hallesches Haus.** Part playfully curated general store and part café,
★ Hallesches Haus is the brainchild of three ex-Fab and Monoqi staffers. Expect to find terrariums, artfully designed gardening tools, Pendelton blankets, housewares, and gifts with a sense of humor. ⊠ *Tempelhofer Ufer 1, Kreuzberg* ⊕ *www.hallescheshaus.com* Ⓜ *Hallesches Tor (U-bahn).*

PRENZLAUER BERG

Stretching east of Mitte's Rosenthaler Platz, the fashionable boutiques continue into Prenzlauer Berg. This area is well known for its own collection of designer boutiques, secondhand shops, and original designs. The busy Kastanienallee is packed with shops and boutiques, as is the more quiet area around Hemholzpatz.

CLOTHING

15

Dear. A secondhand shop for men is an anomaly in Berlin. Yet this laid-back storefront, on one of Prenzlauer Berg's most charming streets, more than makes up for that fact. You'll find stylish labels like Acne and Nike for him, and there's also a small women's selection of shoes and wardrobe staples. ⊠ *Stargarder Str. 9, Prenzlauer Berg* ☎ *030/4908–1169* Ⓜ *Schönhauser Allee (U-bahn and S-bahn).*

Garments. This chic store offers Prenzlauer Berg's fashion lovers an excellent selection of vintage and secondhand clothing, costume jewelry, and accessories. There is also a branch in Mitte, at Linienstrasse 204–205. ⊠ *Stargarderstr. 12 A, Prenzlauer Berg* ☎ *030/7477–9919* ⊕ *www.garments-vintage.de* Ⓜ *Schönhauser Allee (U-bahn and S-bahn).*

Kauf Dich Glücklich. With an odd assortment of retro furnishings, this ice-cream café and waffle shop takes over the entire corner of a Prenzlauer Berg sidewalk, especially on sunny days. Head to the second story and you'll find a shop that captures young Berliner style, with vintage pieces, bold prints, and skinny fits, as well as shoes and jewelry. There's a second outpost on Odenberger Strasse as well as one in Mitte, plus an outlet shop in Wedding. ⊠ *Kastanienallee 54, Prenzlauer Berg* ☎ *030/4862–3348* ⊕ *www.kaufdichglueclich-shop.de* Ⓜ *Rosenthaler Platz (U-bahn).*

NO WÓDKA. This minimal showroom is offset by a playfully curated selection of Polish art, fashion, and design items. The store's name hints at irony, and indeed no vodka can be found here—just rather covetable contemporary products that reinterpret the meaning of "made in Poland." ⊠ *Pappelallee 10, Prenzlauer Berg* ☎ *030/4862-3086* ⊕ *nowodka.com* Ⓜ *Eberswalder Strasse (U-bahn).*

GIFTS

FodorsChoice **Dr. Kochan Schapskultur.** This small shop embodies traditional German
★ liquor culture; there are schnapps and fruit brandies from family farms and independent distilleries for sale, among other items to pique a tippler's interest. ⊠ *Immanuelkirchstr. 4, Prenzlauer Berg* ☎ *030/3462–4076* ⊕ *www.schnapskultur.de* Ⓜ *Senefelderplatz (U-bahn).*

MARKETS

Markt am Kollwitzplatz. One of the city's best farmers' markets sits on the pretty Kollwitzplatz square in Prenzlauer Berg. During its smaller Thursday and bustling Saturday markets, you'll not only find a superb selection of organic produce, meats, cheeses, and pantry items, but also an array of prepared foods and sellers offering handmade home goods and gifts. ⊠ *Kollwitzpl., Prenzlauer Berg* Ⓜ *Senefelderplatz (U-bahn).*

NEUKÖLLN

Just over the canal from Kreuzberg, the neighborhood of Neukölln is home to a large Turkish population, and brims with Turkish shops, cafés, and restaurants, as well as a lovely weekly market. More and more of the city's young creatives are moving into this area, and it caters to their bohemian lifestyle with a number of secondhand and vintage shops.

CLOTHING

Let Them Eat Cake. A favorite of the vintage shoppers in Neukölln, this delightful shop offers a mixture of handmade pieces and high-quality secondhand clothing for him and her. ⊠ *Weserstr. 164, Neukölln* ☎ *030/6096–5095* Ⓜ *Rathaus Neukölln (U-bahn).*

Shio. This design studio–shop includes items from four designers: the namesake Shio, which stocks new-label sustainable lines, as well as a variety of redesigned secondhand and vintage wear; Treches, which features fun, sustainable clothing in bold colors; Pastperfekt, which refashions recycled materials into jewelry, lamps, furniture, and more; and Pulp Papier, which sells pretty Japanese decorative papers. ⊠ *Weichselstr. 59, Neukölln* ⊕ *www.shiostore.com* Ⓜ *Rathaus Neukölln (U-bahn).*

Sing Blackbird. This Kreuzkölln shop, located on the border between Kreuzberg and Neukölln, has become popular for its carefully edited collection of vintage finds, dating back to the 1960s and '70s. The shop also holds a monthly flea market, as well as occasional movie nights, and is home to a popular café, where a menu of homemade cakes and weekend vegan brunch is served on mismatched vintage china. ⊠ *Sanderstr. 11, Neukölln* ☎ *030/5484–5051* Ⓜ *Schönleinstrasse (U-bahn).*

Vintage Galore. Imagine bringing the midcentury European look home with a walk through this shop, which features a collection of Scandinavian furniture and lamps. The shop also has a limited selection of clothing, bags, and accessories, as well as small housewares like teapots and ceramics, which should all fit more comfortably inside a suitcase. ⊠ *Sanderstr. 12, Neukölln* ☎ *030/6396–3338* ⊕ *www.vintagegalore.de* Ⓜ *Schönleinstrasse (U-bahn).*

CHARLOTTENBURG

Although Ku'damm is still touted as the shopping mile of Berlin, many shops are ho-hum retailers. The best stretch for exclusive fashions, such as Louis Vuitton, Hermès, and Jil Sander, are the three blocks between Leibnizstrasse and Bleibtreustrasse. For home furnishings, gift items, and unusual clothing boutiques, follow this route off Ku'damm: Leibnizstrasse to Mommsenstrasse to Bleibtreustrasse, then on to the ring around Savignyplatz. Fasanenstrasse, Knesebeckstrasse, Schlüterstrasse, and Uhlandstrasse are also fun places to browse.

Ku'damm ends at Breitscheidplatz, but the door-to-door shopping continues along Tauentzienstrasse, which, in addition to international retail stores, offers continental Europe's largest department store, the upscale Kaufhaus des Westens, or KaDeWe.

BOOKSTORES

FodorsChoice ★ **Bucherbogen.** Peek under the rails of Charlottenburg's Savignyplatz and you'll find this much-loved bookstore. The large selection of books, many of them special editions or out of print, include numerous titles on art, design, and architecture, and the international offerings are extensive. ✉ *Stadtbahnbogen 593, Charlottenburg* ☎ *303/3186–9511* ⊕ *www.buecherbogen.com* Ⓜ *Savignyplatz (S-bahn).*

CLOTHING

Jil Sander. The flagship store of German designer Jil Sander carries the newest collections from this iconic, understated brand, including fashions for men. ✉ *Kurfürstendamm 185, Charlottenburg* ☎ *030/886–7020* ⊕ *www.jilsander.com* Ⓜ *Adenauerplatz (U-bahn), Savignyplatz (S-bahn).*

DEPARTMENT STORES

FodorsChoice ★ **Kaufhaus des Westens** (*KaDeWe*). The largest department store in continental Europe, classy Kaufhaus des Westens (KaDeWe) has a grand selection of goods, spread over seven floors, as well as food and deli counters, champagne bars, beer bars, and a beautiful art deco–style atrium café. ✉ *Tauentzienstr. 21–24, Charlottenburg* ☎ *030/21210* ⊕ *www.kadewe.de* Ⓜ *Wittenbergplatz (U-bahn).*

FOOD

FodorsChoice ★ **Paper & Tea.** Enter this serene shop just off Kantstrasse and you'll be stepping into a world of high-quality loose-leaf teas. The stylish store displays its teas in museumlike cases, where you can smell the wares, and there are tasting areas where expert attendants brew and explain the teas. There is also a Mitte shop on Alte Schönhauser Strasse. ✉ *Bleibtreust. 4, Charlottenburg* ☎ *030/5557–98071* ⊕ *www.paperandtea. com* Ⓜ *Savignyplatz (S-bahn).*

FodorsChoice ★ **Wald Königsberger Marzipan.** This third-generation artisan shop offers a taste of the old-world treat marzipan, using a family recipe that dates back to the turn of the 20th century. The vintage-style shop features candy-striped wall paper, vintage tools, and rows of handmade marzipan, all wrapped in delicate packaging. ✉ *Pestalozzistr. 54a, Charlottenburg* ☎ *030/323–8254* ⊕ *www.wald-koenigsberger-marzipan.de* Ⓜ *Sophie-Charlotte-Platz (U-bahn).*

GIFTS

Harry Lehmann. If you want a taste—or rather, a smell—of old Berlin, head to Harry Lehmann. The shopkeeper will greet you in a white lab coat, helpfully explaining the origin and inspiration of the expertly mixed perfumes, which fill large apothecary jars along a mirrored wall.

15

This is definitely old-school—the shop was opened in 1926. ✉ *Kantstr. 106, Charlottenburg* ☎ *030/324–3582* ⊕ *www.parfum-individual.de* Ⓜ *Wilmersdorfer Strasse (U-bahn), Berlin-Charlottenburg (S-bahn).*

MALLS

Fodor's Choice **Bikini Berlin.** At this experimental "concept mall," you can shop local
★ and international design-focused brands or browse through the rotating roster of young labels in the center's pop-up "boxes," plus grab a bite at one of the trendy street-food inspired stalls in the food market. The building used to have an open-air middle floor separating the top and ground levels, giving the appearance of a bikini, hence the name. ✉ *Budapester Str. 38–50, Charlottenburg* ☎ *030/5549–6455* ⊕ *www. bikiniberlin.de* Ⓜ *Zoologischer Garten (S-bahn and U-bahn).*

SIDE TRIP TO POTSDAM

A trip to Berlin wouldn't be complete without paying a visit to Potsdam and its park, which surrounds the important Prussian palaces Neues Palais and Sanssouci. This separate city, the state capital of Brandenburg (the state surrounding Berlin), can be reached within a half hour from Berlin's Zoo Station and most major Berlin S-bahn stations.

Potsdam still retains the imperial character it earned during the many years it served as a royal residence and garrison quarters. The Alter Markt and Neuer Markt show off stately Prussian architecture, and both are easily reached from the main train station by any tram heading into the town center.

GETTING HERE AND AROUND

Potsdam is 20 km (12 miles) southwest of Berlin's center and a half-hour journey by car or bus. From Zoo Station to Potsdam's main train station, the regional train RE-1 takes 17 minutes, and the S-bahn Line No. 7 takes about 30 minutes; use an ABC zone ticket for either service. City traffic is heavy, so a train journey is recommended. Several Berlin tour operators have Potsdam trips.

There are several tours that include Potsdam (most are two or six hours). They leave from the landing across from Berlin's Wannsee S-bahn station between late March and early October. Depending on the various tours on offer, a round-trip ticket costs €7.50–€23.

VISITOR INFORMATION

Contacts Potsdam Tourist Office. ✉ *Babelsberger Str. 16, at Potsdam Haupt-bahnhof, next to platform 6* ☎ *0331/2755–8899* ⊕ *www.potsdam-tourism.com.*

EXPLORING

CITY CENTER

Most visitors to Potsdam come for the castles, but the town itself is picturesque, elegant, and compact enough to be explored in an hour or two. It contains both Alter Markt (Old Market) and Neuer Markt (New Market) squares, which show off stately Prussian architecture, while the Holländisches Viertel (Dutch Quarter) is home to a collection

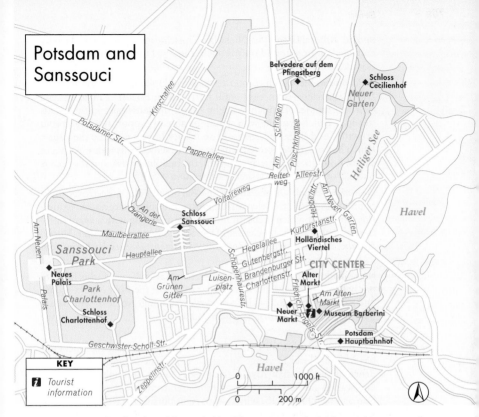

Potsdam and Sanssouci

Belvedere auf dem Pfingstberg

Schloss Cecilienhof

Neuer Garten

Kirschallee

Potsdamer Str.

Pappelallee

Schragen

Am Puschkinallee

Reiter weg

Alleestr

Voltaireweg

An der Orangerie

Schloss Sanssouci

Am Neuen Garten

Heiliger See

Havel

Maulbeerallee

Hebbelstr.

Am Neuen

Hauptallee

Hegelallee

Kurfürstanstr.

Holländisches Viertel

Sanssouci Park

Schopenhauestr.

Gutenbergstr.

Brandenburger Str.

Charlottenstr.

CITY CENTER

Neues Palais

Park Charlottenhof

Am Grünen Gitter

Luisenplatz

Alter Markt

Am Alten Markt

Palais

Schloss Charlottenhof

Neuer Markt

Friedrich-Engels-Str.

Museum Barberini

Potsdam Hauptbahnhof

Geschwister-Scholl-Str.

Havel

Zeppelinstr.

0   1000 ft

0   200 m

KEY

i Tourist information

of redbrick, gable-roofed buildings, many of which now house popular restaurants, boutiques, and cafés. Friedrich-Ebert-Strasse, the town's main thoroughfare, is full of coffee shops and restaurants, and Brandenburger Strasse, the pedestrian walking street, often has outdoor café seating and street musicians. Leafy Hegelallee, to the north, with its tree-lined central pedestrian strip, is where you will find Potsdam's historic gates. Potsdam's city center is easily reached by foot or tram from the main train station.

Alter Markt (*Old Market Square*). The hub of Potsdam's historical center was home to the city's baroque palace for three centuries. The area was heavily damaged by Allied bombing in World War II and then further destroyed by the East German regime in 1960. After reunification, Potsdam decided to rebuild its palace, and the re-created structure, with a combination of modern and historic elements, has housed the state parliament since 2013. Thanks to private donors, a magnificent replica of the Fortunaportal, or Fortune's Gate, now stands proudly at the center of the square. A gilded figure of Atlas tops the tower of the **Altes Rathaus** (Old City Hall), built in 1755 in the model of an Italian palazzo, its dome meant to mimic the Pantheon's in Rome. The **Potsdam Museum** contains a large collection of paintings, photographs, and historical objects. Karl Friedrich Schinkel designed the Alter Markt's domed **Nikolaikirche** (St. Nicholas Church), which was also heavily damaged in the war and only reopened in 1981 after extensive renovations. ⊠ *Alter Markt.*

Holländisches Viertel. The center of the small Holländisches Viertel—the Dutch Quarter—is an easy walk north along Friedrich-Ebert-Strasse to Mittelstrasse. Friedrich Wilhelm I built the settlement in the 1730s to entice Dutch artisans who would be able to support the city's rapid growth. The 134 gabled, mansard-roof brick houses make up the largest Dutch housing development outside of the Netherlands today. Antiques shops, boutiques, and restaurants fill the buildings now, and the area is one of Potsdam's most visited. ⊠ *Potsdam.*

Museum Barberini. On the site of the Barberini Palace, destroyed by a bombing in 1945, this elegant art museum displays large-scale exhibitions, many of which focus on Impressionism, along with a small selection of works from the German Democratic Republic. ⊠ *Alter Markt, Humboldtstr. 5–6* ☎ *0331/2360–14499* ⊕ *www.museum-barberini.com* ⏎ *€14* ⊙ *Closed Tues.*

Neuer Markt (*New Market Square*). Neuer Markt (New Market) square has baroque-style architecture similar to that of the Alter Markt square and a handful of the city's best-preserved buildings, some of which date back to the 18th century. ⊠ *Neuer Markt.*

SANSSOUCI PARK

Fodor's Choice
★

The main attraction for Potsdam visitors, the sprawling Sanssouci Park has been a World Heritage Site since 1990. The former summer residence of the Prussian royals, the park is home to numerous palaces, landscaped gardens, and eye-catching architecture. Your best bet is to hop on Bus 695 or X15, which stops right outside the train station and will get you to the park in 10 minutes. Otherwise it's about a half-hour walk. Note that if you want to see many of the palaces inside the park, your best bet is to buy a sanssouci+ ticket, which includes timed entry to Sanssouci Palace and anytime-entry to the others; buy it in advance online or at any of the palaces or visitor centers on-site.

FAMILY
Fodor's Choice
★

Neues Palais (*New Palace*). A larger and grander palace than Sanssouci, the Neues Palais stands at the end of the long avenue that runs through Sanssouci Park. It was built after the Seven Years' War (1756–63). Impressive interiors include the Grotto Hall with walls and columns set with shells, coral, and other aquatic decorations. The royals' upper apartments have paintings by 17th-century Italian masters. You can tour the palace yourself, with an audio guide, from April through October; the rest of the year you must be accompanied by a tour guide. All visits are at scheduled times when you buy a ticket. ⊠ *Sanssouci Park* ☎ *0331/969–4200* ⊕ *www.spsg.de* ⏎ *€8* ⊙ *Closed Tues.*

FAMILY

Schloss Charlottenhof. After Frederick the Great died in 1786, the ambitious Sanssouci building program ground to a halt, and the park fell into neglect. It was 50 years before another Prussian king, Friedrich Wilhelm IV, restored Sanssouci's earlier glory, engaging the great Berlin architect Karl Friedrich Schinkel to build the small **Schloss Charlottenhof** for the crown prince. Schinkel's demure interiors are preserved, and the most fanciful room is the bedroom, decorated like a Roman tent, with walls and ceiling draped in striped canvas. Friedrich Wilhelm IV also commissioned the **Römische Bäder** (Roman Baths), about a five-minute walk north of Schloss Charlottenhof. It was also designed by Schinkel, and built between 1829 and 1840. Like many other structures in Potsdam, this one is more romantic than authentic. Half Italian villa, half Greek temple, it is nevertheless a charming addition to the park. ⊠ *Geschwister-Scholl-Str. 34a* ☏ *0331/969–4200* ⊕ *www.spsg. de* ✉ *Schloss Charlottenhof €6 with guided tour; Roman Baths €5; combination ticket €8* ☉ *Closed Nov.–Apr., and Mon. May–Oct.*

FAMILY **Schloss Sanssouci.** Prussia's most famous king, Friedrich II—Frederick
Fodor's Choice the Great—spent more time at his summer residence, **Schloss Sans-**
★ **souci,** than in the capital of Berlin. Executed according to Frederick's impeccable French-influenced taste, the palace, which lies on the northeastern edge of Sanssouci Park, was built between 1745 and 1747. It is extravagantly rococo, with scarcely a patch of wall left unadorned. Visits to the palace are only allowed at fixed times scheduled when tickets are purchased. During peak tourist months, timed tickets can sell out before noon, so book online in advance. From Schloss Sanssouci, you can wander down the extravagant terraced gardens, filled with climbing grapevines, trellises, and fountains to reach the Italianate **Friedenskirche**, or "Peace Church," which was completed in 1854, and houses a 13th-century Byzantine mosaic taken from an island near Venice. ⊠ *Park Sanssouci* ☏ *0331/969–4200* ⊕ *www.spsg.de* ✉ *Schloss Sanssouci €12; Friedenskirche free* ☉ *Schloss Sanssouci closed Mon. Friedenskirche closed weekdays Nov.–mid-Mar.*

NEUER GARTEN

Just north of the city center, the Neuer Garten (New Garden) is along the west shore of the Heiliger See (Holy Lake), with beautiful views. The park is home to the Marmorpalais (Marble Palace) and Schloss Cecilienhof, the last palace built by the Prussian Hohenzollern family. To get here from the Potsdam train station, take Tram 92 and then walk 10–15 minutes; another option is to take a taxi.

Belvedere auf dem Pfingstberg. Commissioned by King Friedrich Wilhelm IV, the Belvedere on Pfingstberg was built in the Italian Renaissance style with grand staircases, colonnades, and perfect symmetry. It served as a pleasure palace and lofty observation platform for the royals, and the towers still offer one of the best views of Potsdam. ⊠ *Am Pfingstberg* ☏ *0331/2005–7930* ⊕ *www.pfingstberg.de* ✉ *€5* ☉ *Closed weekdays Nov.–Mar.*

Schloss Cecilienhof (*Cecilienhof Palace*). Resembling a rambling Tudor manor house, Schloss Cecilienhof was built for Crown Prince Wilhelm in 1913, on what was then the newly laid-out stretch of park called the Neuer Garten. It was here, in the last palace built by the Hohenzollerns, that the leaders of the allied forces—Stalin, Truman, and Churchill (later Attlee)—hammered out the fate of postwar Germany at the 1945 Potsdam Conference. ⊠ *Im Neuen Garten 11* ☏ *0331/969–4200* ⊕ *www.spsg.de* ✉ *From €8.*

15

WHERE TO EAT

$$$ ✕ **Der Butt.** Potsdam is surrounded by lakes and rivers so the fish served
SEAFOOD here is almost always local—try the rainbow trout or the eel, fresh
from the Havel River; the house beer is brewed in Potsdam. It's just
a block from the busy pedestrian shopping area, and has a casual,
friendly atmosphere that makes this an excellent spot for a light meal.
Known for: fresh fish from the Havel; sustainable seafood; local wines
and beers. $ *Average main: €21* ✉ *Gutenbergstr. 25* ☎ *0331/200–6066*
⊕ *www.der-butt.de.*

$$$$ ✕ **Restaurant Juliette.** Potsdam is proud of its past French influences, and
FRENCH the highly praised French food at this intimate restaurant on the edge
of the Dutch Quarter is served in a lovely space, with brick walls and
a fireplace. Restaurant Juliette is affiliated with four other more casual
French restaurants in Potsdam, including a creperie and a café. **Known
for:** three- to six-course tasting menus, plus à la carte choices; starter
plate of seasonal foie-gras preparations; more than 120 wines from
Germany and France. $ *Average main: €26* ✉ *Jägerstr. 39* ☎ *0331/270–
1791* ⊕ *www.restaurant-juliette.de* ☾ *Closed Mon. and Tues.*

$$$ ✕ **Speckers Landhaus.** This restored Tudor-style cottage is a 10-minute
GERMAN walk from the town center, and well worth a visit for its charming
historic architecture and relaxing, farmhouse-style dining room. The
menu is unfailingly local, emphasizing produce like white asparagus
in spring and pumpkin in fall. **Known for:** monthly changing dishes
with regional ingredients; homemade pastas, local game, and German
specialties; three spacious guest rooms decorated in a simple, country-
home style. $ *Average main: €25* ✉ *Jägerallee 13* ☎ *0331/280–4311*
⊕ *www.speckers.de* ☾ *Closed Sun. and Mon. No lunch.*

SAXONY, SAXONY-ANHALT, AND THURINGIA

WELCOME TO SAXONY, SAXONY-ANHALT, AND THURINGIA

TOP REASONS TO GO

★ **Following the path of Martin Luther:** Trace the path of the ultimate medieval rebel in Wittenberg, Erfurt, Eisenach, and the Wartburg, and gain valuable insight into the mind and culture of a person whose ideas helped change the world.

★ **Frauenkirche in Dresden:** Rising like a majestic baroque phoenix, the church is a worthy symbol of a city destroyed and rebuilt from its ashes.

★ **Görlitz:** This architectural gem is relatively undiscovered; you'll feel as if you have the whole town to yourself.

★ **Weimar:** The history of Germany seems to revolve around this small town, whose past residents include Goethe, Schiller, Bach, Liszt, and Gropius.

★ **Wine tasting in the Salle-Unstrut:** The castle-topped, rolling hills covered in terraced vineyards are perfect for biking, hiking, and horseback riding.

These three states hold several of Germany's most historical and beautiful cities: Dresden, Leipzig, and Weimar.

1 Leipzig. A major cultural center with a long history of print and book-making. Johann Sebastian Bach was a choirmaster here, Martin Luther preached here, and Richard Wagner was born here. It's also a center of art nouveau architecture.

2 Dresden. The capital of Saxony since the 15th century was mostly destroyed during World War II, but most of the city's Altstadt has been restored, and the Frauenkirche remains a baroque masterpiece, along with the famous Zwinger museums.

3 Meissen. Best known as a center for porcelain-making, the city is overlooked by a looming castle, the Albrechtsburg.

4 Görlitz. Having survived with little damage from World War II, this historic city on the Polish border is rich in examples of multiple styles of architecture.

5 Lutherstadt-Wittenberg. This is the city where Martin Luther nailed his 95 These to the door of the Schlosskirche; it remains a

protestant stronghold and celebrates its favorite son.

6 Dessau. This city is most famous for over 300 buildings designed by Walter Gropius in the Bauhaus style.

7 Naumberg. With a famous Romanesque/Gothic cathedral, this city has a history going back some 1000 years.

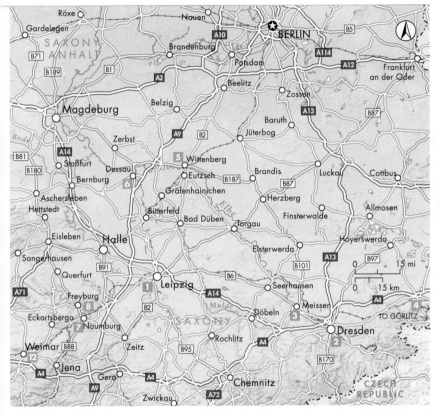

16

16

8 Freyburg. The sleepy town is best known for its wine.

9 Quedlinburg. With more half-timber houses than any other German city, Quedlinburg's Altstadt is a UNESCO World Heritage Site.

10 Eisenach. A center for car-making, Eisenbach was also the birthplace of Johann Sebastian Bach, but it's most notable for the towering Wartburg Castle, built by Hermann I, the count of Thuringia.

11 Erfurt. This beautiful town escaped destruction during World War II; it has the longest surviving Renaissance-era bridge in Europe.

12 Weimar. Not particularly large, Weimar nevertheless has had outsized importance in German cultural and political history, with its connections to Goethe, Schiller, Bach, and (in modern times) Walter Gropius and the Bauhaus movement.

FOLLOWING MARTIN LUTHER

Saxony-Anhalt and Thuringia are currently celebrating the "Luther decade," center on the Protestant Reformation's 500th anniversary. A drive between the "Lutherstädte" (Luther Cities) allows for a deeper understanding of Martin Luther and the Reformation.

(above) Lutherhaus in Eisenach, where he lived as a student (upper right) Martin Luther (lower right) Memorial for Martin Luther in Eisleben

Dissatisfaction with the Catholic Church was already brewing when Martin Luther (1483–1546) spoke out in Germany. His 95 Theses, which he brashly nailed to a church door, called for a return to faith in the Bible's teachings over papal decrees, and an end to the sale of indulgences (letters from the pope purchased by wealthy Christians to absolve them of sins). But Luther's greatest feat was translating the Bible into German, making it accessible to everyone who could read, a process that codified the High German that almost everyone speaks today. Despite his so-called heretical beginnings and excommunication, Luther continued to preach, building a family with Katharina von Bora, a former nun he married after "rescuing" her from a convent. After his death, Lutheranism spread across Europe as an accepted branch of Christianity.

LUTHER QUOTES

"I am more afraid of my own heart than of the pope and all his cardinals. I have within me the great pope, Self."

"When the Devil ... sees men use violence to propagate the gospel, he ... says with malignant looks and frightful grin: 'Ah, how wise these madmen are to play my game! Let them go on; I shall reap the benefit ... '"

ON THE TRAIL OF MARTIN LUTHER

Start in the town of Wittenberg, the unofficial capital of the Reformation. The comprehensive **Lutherhaus** museum is in the Augustinian monastery where Luther lived twice, first as a monk and later with his family. This multilevel, bilingual museum will convince the skeptics that Luther is worth remembering. From the museum, it's a short walk down the main thoroughfare Collegienstrasse to two churches that felt the influence of his teachings. The first is **Stadtkirche St. Marien** (Parish Church of St. Mary), where Luther often preached. The second, **Schlosskirche** (Castle Church), is where Luther changed history by posting his 95 Theses. The original wooden doors were destroyed in a 1760 fire, now replaced by bronze doors with the Latin text of the 95 Theses. On the way from one church to the other, stop to admire the statues of Luther and his friend and collaborator Philipp Melanchthon—they are buried next to each other in Schlosskirche.

In the nearby town of Eisleben, the houses where Luther was born, the **Luthers Geburtshaus,** and died, **Luthers Sterbehaus,** lie 10 minutes from each other. From there, it's easy to spot the steeples of two churches: **St. Petri-Pauli-Kirche** (*Church of Sts. Peter and Paul*) and **St. Andreaskirche** (*St. Andrew's Church*). The first was Luther's place of baptism, while the second houses the pulpit where Luther gave his last four sermons. His funeral was also held here before his body was taken back to Wittenberg.

Continuing southwest the stunning medieval castle **Wartburg** is in the hills high above the town of Eisenach. Luther took refuge here after he was excommunicated by the pope and outlawed by a general assembly called the Diet of Worms, famously translating the New Testament from the original Greek into German.

REFORMATION TIMELINE

1517: Luther nails his 95 Theses to Wittenberg's Schlosskirche.

1521: Luther is excommunicated.

1537: Denmark's Christian III declares Lutheranism the state religion.

1555: Charles V signs Peace of Augsburg, ending open hostilities between Catholicism and Lutheranism. Due to the rise of Calvinism, conflict again bubbles under the surface.

1558: Queen Elizabeth I of England supports the establishment of the English Protestant Church.

1577: The Formula of Concord ends disputes between sects, strengthening and preserving Lutheranism.

1618: Religious tensions explode in Bohemia, thrusting Europe into the Thirty Years' War. At war's end, much of Central Europe is in ruins.

1650s and beyond: Lutheran explorers and settlers bring their beliefs to the New World.

16

Updated by
Lee A. Evans

Germany's traditional charm is most evident in the former East German states of Saxony, Saxony-Anhalt, and Thuringia. The region's rolling hills, terraced vineyards, and wonderfully restored cities speak to an area reborn and reestablished as the German heartland. The region can be a little gritty at times, but a uniquely unspoiled German state of mind predominates.

Eastern Germans resolutely cling to their German heritage. They proudly preserve their connections with such national heroes as Luther, Goethe, Schiller, Bach, Handel, Wagner, and the Hungarian-born Liszt. Towns in the regions of the Thüringer Wald (Thuringian Forest) or the Harz Mountains—long considered the haunt of witches—are drenched in history and medieval legend. The area hides a fantastic collection of rural villages and castles unparalleled in other parts of the country.

Many cities, such as Erfurt, escaped World War II relatively unscathed, and the East Germans extensively rebuilt towns damaged by bombing. Although historical city centers were faithfully restored to their past glory, there are also plenty of eyesores of industrialization and stupendously bland housing projects, which the Germans refer to as *Bausünden* (architectural sins). Famous palaces and cultural wonders—the rebuilt historical center of Dresden, the Wartburg at Eisenach, the Schiller and Goethe houses in Weimar, Luther's Wittenberg, as well as the wonderfully preserved city of Görlitz—are waiting to have their subtle and extravagant charms discovered.

MAJOR REGIONS

The people of **Saxony** identify themselves more as Saxon than German. Their hardworking and rustic attitudes, their somewhat peripheral location on the border with the Czech Republic and Poland, and their almost incomprehensible dialect are the targets of endless jokes and puns. However, Saxon pride rebuilt **Dresden** and **Leipzig** magnificently as the showcase cities of eastern Germany after World War II.

The region also contains romantic Meissen, well-preserved Bautzen, and Görlitz, on the Neisse River, which was also rebuilt after the war. The central state of **Saxony-Anhalt** is a region rich in history and natural beauty, almost completely undiscovered by modern visitors. In the Altmark, on the edge of the Harz Mountains, fields of grain and sugar beets stretch to the horizon. In the mountains themselves are the deep gorge of the Bode River and the stalactite-filled caves of Rubeland. The songbirds of the Harz are renowned, and though pollution has taken its toll, both the flora and the fauna of the Harz National Park (which encompasses much of the region) are coming back. Atop the Brocken, the Harz's highest point, legend has it that witches convene on Walpurgis Night (the night between April 30 and May 1). It's also a place of historical importance. Protestantism was born in the town of **Lutherstadt-Wittenberg**; Dessau was the 1920s home of architect Walter Gropius; **Halle** is a surprisingly pretty city that was once the center of the salt trade; **Naumberg** is famous for its Romanesque-Gothic cathedral; **Freyburg** is famous for its vineyards; **Quedlinburg** is a medieval town that largely escaped damage during World War II.

Unlike other eastern states, unassuming **Thuringia** was not taken from the Slavs by wandering Germanic tribes but has been German since before the Middle Ages. It's the land of Goethe and Schiller. The hilly countryside is mostly rural and forested, and it preserves a rich cultural past in countless small villages, medieval cities, and country palaces. In the 14th century traders used the 168-km (104-mile) Rennsteig ("fast trail") through the dark depths of the Thuringian Forest, and cities such as Erfurt and Eisenach evolved as major commercial hubs. Today the forests and the Erzgebirge Mountains are a remote paradise for hiking and fishing. **Eisenach** is a car-making center and has a mighty medieval castle; **Erfurt** is an attractive city that avoided destruction during World War II; **Weimar** is one of Europe's old cultural centers, where Germany attempted its first go at a true democracy in 1918. Nearby is one of the Third Reich's most notorious concentration camps: Buchenwald.

16

PLANNING

WHEN TO GO
Winters in this part of Germany can be cold, wet, and dismal, so unless you plan to ski in the Harz Mountains or the Thüringer Wald, visit in late spring, summer, or early autumn. Avoid Leipzig at trade-fair times, particularly in March and April. In summer every city, town, and village has a festival, with streets blocked and local culture spilling out into every open space. In the run-up to Christmas the region slows down to enjoy wine and food at some of Germany's most traditional markets.

GETTING HERE AND AROUND
AIR TRAVEL
It's easiest, and usually cheapest, to fly into Berlin or Frankfurt and rent a car from there. Dresden and Leipzig both have international airports that are primarily operated by budget carriers serving European destinations. Dresden Flughafen is about 10 km (6 miles) north

of Dresden, and Leipzig's Flughafen Leipzig-Halle is 12 km (8 miles) northwest of the city.

Contacts Dresden Flughafen. ✉ *Flughafenstr., Dresden* ☎ *0351/881–3360* ⊕ *www.dresden-airport.de.* **Flughafen Leipzig-Halle.** ✉ *Termanalring 11, Schkeuditz* ☎ *0341/224–1155* ⊕ *www.leipzig-halle-airport.de.*

BUS TRAVEL

Long-distance buses travel to Dresden and Leipzig. Bus service within the area is frequent and connects most major cities. Check schedules carefully at central bus stations.

CAR TRAVEL

Expressways connect Berlin with Dresden (A-13) and Leipzig (A-9). Both journeys take about two hours. The A-4 stretches east–west across the southern portion of Thuringia and Saxony.

A road-construction program in eastern Germany is ongoing, and you should expect traffic delays on any journey of more than 300 km (186 miles). The Bundesstrassen throughout eastern Germany are narrow, tree-lined country roads, often jammed with traffic. Roads in the western part of the Harz Mountains are better and wider.

Cars can be rented at the Dresden and Leipzig airports, at train stations, and through all major hotels. Be aware that you are not allowed to take rentals into Poland or the Czech Republic.

TRAIN TRAVEL

The fastest and least expensive way to explore the region is by train. East Germany's rail infrastructure is exceptional; trains serve even the most remote destinations with astonishing frequency. Slower S, RB, and RE trains link smaller towns, while Leipzig, Dresden, Weimar, Erfurt, Naumburg, and Wittenberg are all on major InterCity Express (ICE) lines. Some cities—Dresden and Meissen, for example—are linked by commuter trains.

From Dresden a round-trip ticket to Leipzig costs about €43 (a 1½-hour journey one-way); to Görlitz it's about €38 (a 1½-hour ride). Trains connect Leipzig with Halle (a 30-minute ride, €10), Erfurt (a 1-hour ride, €28), and Eisenach (a 1½-hour journey, €28). The train ride between Dresden and Eisenach (2½ hours) costs €56 one-way.

■ TIP→ Consider using a Länder-Ticket: a €24 (plus €7 per person up to five people) regional day ticket from the German Railroad that covers local train travel in the respective state (for example, within Saxony, Saxony-Anhalt, or Thuringia).

Contacts German Railroad (Deutsche Bahn). ☎ *0180/599–6633* ⊕ *www.bahn.de.*

HOTELS

Hotels in eastern Germany are up to international standards and, due to economic subsidies in the 1990s, often far outshine their West German counterparts. In the East it's quite normal to have a major international hotel in a 1,000-year-old house or restored mansion. Smaller, family-run hotels are more charming local options, and often include a good restaurant. Most big hotels offer special weekend or activity-oriented packages that aren't found in the western part of the country. All hotels include breakfast, unless indicated otherwise.

During the trade fairs and shows of the **Leipziger Messe,** particularly in March and April, most Leipzig hotels increase their prices.

RESTAURANTS

Enterprising young managers and chefs are well established in the East, so look for new, usually small, trendy restaurants. People in the region are extremely particular about their traditional food (rumor has it that one can be deported for roasting Mützbraten over anything other than birch). Some new creative chefs successfully blend contemporary regional German with international influences. Medieval-themed restaurants and "experience dining," complete with entertainment, are all the rage in the East, and, despite being often quite kitschy, warrant at least one try. As the region slowly rediscovers its tremendous beer heritage, microbreweries and brewpubs have sprouted up in almost every city. Pubs are a good bet for meeting locals.

Prices in restaurant reviews are the average cost of a main course at dinner, or if dinner is not served, at lunch. Prices in hotel reviews are the lowest cost of a standard double room in high season.

16

WHAT IT COSTS IN EUROS			
$	$$	$$$	$$$$
Restaurants	under €15	€15–€20	€21–€25	over €25
Hotels	under €100	€100–€175	€176–€225	over €225

TOURS

With two luxury ships, Viking K–D operates a full program of cruises on the Elbe River, from Hamburg as far as Prague. They run up to eight days from mid-April until late October. All the historic cities of Saxony and Thuringia are ports of call—including Dresden, Meissen, Wittenberg, and Dessau. There are also popular narrow-gauge train tours.

Harzer Schmalspurbahnen GmbH. The famous steam locomotive *Harzquerbahn* connects Nordhausen-Nord with Wernigerode and Gernerode in the Harz Mountains. The most popular track of this line is the *Brockenbahn,* a special narrow-gauge train transporting tourists to the top of northern Germany's highest mountain. See website for schedule and further information. ⊠ *Friedrichstr. 151, Wernigerode* ☎ *03943/5580* ⊕ *www.hsb-wr.de.*

Lössnitzgrundbahn. In Saxony, historic narrow-gauge steam trains still operate on a regular schedule. The *Lössnitzgrundbahn,* which connects Ost-Radebeul-Ost and Radeburg is perfect for taking in some of Saxony's romantic countryside. A round-trip ticket is between about €7 and €11, depending on the length of the ride. For schedule and information, contact Deutsche Bahn's regional Dresden office. ⊠ *Geyersdorfer Str. 32, Annaberg-Buchholz* ☎ *0351/46165–63684* ⊕ *www. loessnitzgrundbahn.de* ⛟ *From €7.*

Sächsische Dampfschiffahrt. Weisse Flotte's historic paddle-steam tours depart from and stop in Dresden, Meissen, Pirna, Pillnitz, Königstein, and Bad Schandau. Besides tours in the Dresden area, boats also go into the Czech Republic. ✉ *Hertha-Lindner-Str. 10, Dresden* ☎ *0351/866–090* ⊕ *www.saechsische-dampfschiffahrt.de* 💶 *From €16.*

LEIPZIG

184 km (114 miles) southwest of Berlin.

Leipzig is one of the coolest cities in Europe—but not so cool as to be pretentious. With its world-renowned links to Bach, Schubert, Mendelssohn, Martin Luther, Goethe, Schiller, and the fantastic Neue-Leipziger-Schule art movement, Leipzig is one of the great German cultural centers. It has impressive art nouveau architecture, an incredibly clean city center, meandering narrow streets, and the temptations of coffee and cake on every corner. In *Faust*, Goethe describes Leipzig as "a little Paris"; in reality it's more reminiscent of Vienna, while remaining a distinctly energetic Saxon town.

Leipzig's musical past includes Johann Sebastian Bach (1685–1750), who was organist and choir director at Leipzig's Thomaskirche, and the 19th-century composer Richard Wagner, who was born in the city in 1813. Today's Leipzig continues the cultural focus with extraordinary offerings of music, theater, and opera, not to mention fantastic nightlife.

Wartime bombs destroyed much of Leipzig's city center, but reconstruction efforts have uncovered one of Europe's most vibrant cities. Leipzig's art nouveau flair is best discovered by exploring the countless alleys, covered courtyards, and passageways. Some unattractive buildings from the postwar period remain, but only reinforce Leipzig's position on the line between modernity and antiquity.

With a population of about 535,000, Leipzig is the third-largest city in eastern Germany (after Berlin and Dresden) and has long been a center of printing and bookselling. Astride major trade routes, it was an important market town in the Middle Ages, and it continues to be a trading center, thanks to the Leipziger *Messe* (trade and fair shows) throughout the year that bring together buyers from East and West.

Unfortunately, Leipzig has a tendency to underwhelm first-time visitors. If you take Leipzig slow and have some cake, its subtle, hidden charms may surprise you.

GETTING HERE AND AROUND

Leipzig is an hour from Berlin by train. Leipzig-Halle airport serves many European destinations, but no North American ones.

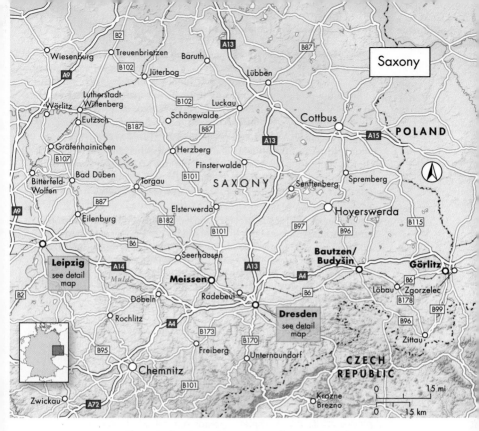

Contacts **Leipzig Tourismus und Marketing.** ✉ *Augustuspl. 9* ☎ *0341/710–4260, 0341/710–4301* ⊕ *www.leipzig.travel.*

EXPLORING

Bach-Museum im Bach-Archiv Leipzig (*Bach Museum at the Bach Archives Leipzig*). The Bach family home, the old Bosehaus, stands opposite the Thomaskirche, and is now a museum devoted to the composer's life and work. The exhibition offers several interactive displays; arranging the instrumental parts of Bach's hymns is by far the most entertaining. ✉ *Thomaskirchhof 16* ☎ *0341/913–7200* ⊕ *www.bach-leipzig.de* 🎫 *€8; free 1st Thurs. of month* ⊘ *Closed Mon.*

Grassi Museum für Angewandte Kunst (*Museum of Applied Art*). This museum showcases 2,000 years of works from Leipzig's and eastern Germany's proud tradition of handicrafts, such as exquisite porcelain, fine tapestry art, and modern Bauhaus design. ✉ *Johannispl. 5–11* ☎ *0341/222–9100* ⊕ *www.grassimuseum.de* 🎫 *From €8* ⊘ *Closed Mon.*

Grassi Museum für Musikinstrumente (*Musical Instruments Museum*). Historical musical instruments, mostly from the Renaissance, include the world's oldest clavichord, constructed in 1543 in Italy. There are also spinets, flutes, and lutes. Recordings of the instruments can be heard at the exhibits. ⊠ *Johannispl. 5–11* ☎ *0341/973–0750* ⊕ *www.grassimuseum.de* 💳 *From €6* ⊙ *Closed Mon.*

Grassi Museum für Völkerkunde (*Ethnological Museum*). Presenting arts and crafts from all continents and various eras, this museum includes a thrilling collection of Southeast Asian antique art and the world's only Kurile Ainu feather costume, in the Northeast Asia collection. ⊠ *Johannispl. 5–11* ☎ *0341/973–1300* ⊕ *www.grassimuseum.de* 💳 *From €8* ⊙ *Closed Mon.*

Hauptbahnhof. With 26 platforms, Leipzig's main train station is Europe's largest railhead. It was built in 1915 and is now a protected monument, but modern commerce rules in its bi-level shopping mall, the Promenaden. The only thing the complex is missing is a pub. Many of the shops and restaurants stay open until 10 pm and are open on Sunday. Thanks to the historic backdrop, this is one of the most beautiful shopping experiences in Saxony. ⊠ *Willy-Brandt-Pl.* ☎ *0341/141–270 for mall, 0341/9968–3275 for train station.*

Leipziger Universitätsturm (*Leipzig University Tower*). Towering over Leipzig's city center is this 470-foot-high structure, which houses administrative offices and lecture rooms. Dubbed the "jagged tooth" or "wisdom tooth" by some University of Leipzig students, it supposedly represents an open book. Students were also largely responsible for changing the university's name, replacing its postwar title, Karl Marx University, with the original one. Best viewed from the viewing platform, the **Augustusplatz** spreads out below the university tower like a space-age campus. ⊠ *Augustuspl. 9* ⊕ *www.panorama-leipzig.de.*

Mädlerpassage (*Mädler Mall*). The ghost of Goethe's Faust lurks in every marble corner of Leipzig's finest shopping arcade. One of the scenes in *Faust* is set in the famous Auerbachs Keller restaurant, at No. 2. A bronze group of characters from the play, sculpted in 1913, beckons you down the stone staircase to the restaurant. Touching the statues' feet is said to bring good luck. A few yards away is a delightful art nouveau bar called *Mephisto.* ⊠ *Grimmaische Str.*

Markt. Leipzig's showpiece is its huge, old market square. One side is completely occupied by the Renaissance town hall, the **Altes Rathaus.** ⊠ *Marktpl., Böttchergässchen 3.*

Mendelssohn Haus (*Mendelssohn House*). The only surviving residence of the composer Felix Mendelssohn-Bartholdy is now Germany's only museum dedicated to him. Mendelssohn's last residence and the place of his death has been preserved in its original 19th-century state. Concerts are held every Sunday at 11. ⊠ *Goldschmidtstr. 12* ☎ *0341/127–0294* ⊕ *www.mendelssohn-stiftung.de* 💳 *€8.*

Fodor'sChoice
★

Museum der Bildenden Künste (*Museum of Fine Arts*). The city's leading art gallery is modernist minimalism incarnate, set in a huge concrete cube encased in green glass in the middle of Sachsenplatz Square. The museum's collection of more than 2,700 paintings and sculptures

represents everything from the German Middle Ages to the modern Neue Leipziger Schule. Especially notable are the collections focusing on Lucas Cranach the Elder and Caspar David Friedrich. Be sure to start at the top and work your way down. Don't miss Max Klinger's Beethoven as Zeus statue. ⊠ *Katharinenstr. 10* ☏ *0341/216–990* ⊕ *www.mdbk.de* ⛁ *€10* ☉ *Closed Mon.*

Museum in der Runden Eck (*Museum in the Round Corner*). This building once served as the headquarters of the city's detachment of the communist secret police, the dreaded *Staatssicherheitsdienst*. The exhibition *Stasi—Macht und Banalität* (Stasi—Power and Banality) presents not only the Stasi's offices and surveillance work, but also hundreds of documents revealing the magnitude of its interests in citizens' private lives. Though the material is in German, the items and atmosphere convey an impression of what life under the regime might have been like. The exhibit about the death penalty in the GDR is particularly chilling. For a detailed tour of the Revolutions of 1989, be sure to download the museum's app. ⊠ *Dittrichring 24* ☏ *0341/961–2443* ⊕ *www.runde-ecke-leipzig.de* ⛁ *Free; English-language tour €5 (by appointment only).*

Museum zum Arabischen Kaffeebaum (*Arabic Coffee Tree Museum*). This museum and café-restaurant tells the fascinating history of coffee culture in Europe, particularly in Saxony. The café is one of the oldest on the continent, and once proudly served coffee to such luminaries as Gotthold Lessing, Schumann, Goethe, and Liszt. The museum features many paintings, Arabian coffee vessels, and coffeehouse games. It also explains the basic principles of roasting coffee. The café is divided into traditional Viennese, French, and Arabian coffeehouses, but no coffee is served in the Arabian section, which is only a display. The cake is better and the seating more comfortable in the Viennese part. ⊠ *Kleine Fleischerg. 4* 🕾 *0341/960–2632* ⊕ *www.coffe-baum.de* 🖃 *Free* ☉ *Closed Mon.*

Nikolaikirche (*St. Nicholas Church*). This church with its rough undistinguished facade was center stage during the demonstrations that helped bring down the communist regime. Every Monday for months before the government collapsed, thousands of citizens gathered in front of the church chanting "Wir sind das Volk" (We are the people). Inside are a soaring Gothic choir and nave. Note the unusual patterned ceiling supported by classical pillars that end in palm-tree-like flourishes. Martin Luther is said to have preached from the ornate 16th-century pulpit. The prayers for peace that began the revolution in 1989 are still held on Monday at 5 pm. ⊠ *Nikolaikirchhof* 🕾 *0341/960–5270* 🖃 *Free.*

Stadtgeschichtliches Museum. Inside the Altes Rathaus, this museum documents Leipzig's past. The entrance is behind the Rathaus. The museum's extended collection continues behind the Museum for Applied Arts. ⊠ *Böttchergässchen 3* 🕾 *0341/965–130* ⊕ *www.stadtgeschichtliches-museum-leipzig.de* 🖃 *€6* ☉ *Closed Mon.*

Thomaskirche (*St. Thomas's Church*). Bach served as choirmaster at this Gothic church for 27 years, and Martin Luther preached here on Whitsunday 1539, signaling the arrival of Protestantism in Leipzig. Originally the center of a 13th-century monastery, the tall church (rebuilt in the 15th century) now stands by itself. Bach wrote most of his cantatas for the church's famous boys' choir, the Thomanerchor, which was founded in the 13th century. Today, the church continues to serve as the choir's home as well as a center of Bach tradition; the composer is buried here. You can listen to the famous boys' choir during the *Motette,* a service with a special emphasis on choral music. Bach's 12 children and Richard Wagner were baptized here; Karl Marx and Friedrich Engels also stood before this same font. In front of the church is a memorial to Felix Mendelssohn, rebuilt with funds collected by the Leipzig Citizens Initiative. The Nazis destroyed the original in front of the Gewandhaus. ⊠ *Thomaskirchhof* 🕾 *0341/222–240* ⊕ *www.thomaskirche.org* 🖃 *Free; Motette €2.*

Völkerschlachtdenkmal (*Memorial to the Battle of the Nations*). In the fall of 1813, Prussian, Austrian, Russian, and Swedish forces defeated Napoléon in the Battle of the Nations. This was the first in a series of losses that served as a prelude to the French general's defeat two years later at Waterloo. An enormous, 300-foot-high monument erected on the site in 1913 commemorates the battle. Despite its massiveness, the site is well worth a visit, if only to wonder at the lengths—and

Bach was choirmaster at the Thomaskirche and is buried here. Bach wrote cantatas for the boys' choir, which you can still hear performed.

heights—to which a newfound sense of German nationalism went to celebrate their military victories, and to take in the view from a windy platform (provided you can climb the 500 steps to get there). The Prussians did make one concession to Napoléon in designing the monument: a stone marks the spot where he stood during the three-day battle. An exhibition hall explains the history of the memorial, which can be reached via Streetcar 15 or 2 or by the S1 or S3 commuter train (leave the tram or the train at the Völkerschlachtdenkmal station). ✉ *Str. des 18 Oktober 100* ☎ *0341/878–0471* 🌐 *www.stadtgeschichtliches-museum-leipzig.de* 🎟 *€8.*

Zeitgeschichtliches Forum Leipzig (*Museum of Contemporary History Leipzig*). This excellent history museum focuses on issues surrounding the division and reunification of Germany after World War II. ✉ *Grimmaische Str. 6* ☎ *0341/225–0500* 🌐 *www.hdg.de* 🎟 *Free* 🕒 *Closed Mon.*

WHERE TO EAT

$$ GERMAN Fodor's Choice ★

🍴 **Auerbachs Keller.** The most famous of Leipzig's restaurants is actually two restaurants: one that's upscale, international, and gourmet (down the stairs to the right) and a rowdy beer cellar (to the left) specializing in hearty Saxon fare, mostly roasted meat dishes. Goethe immortalized one of the vaulted historic rooms in his *Faust,* and Bach was a regular here because of the location halfway between the Thomaskirche and the Nikolaikirche. **Known for:** one of the oldest restaurants on the continent; tasting menu worth the splurge; extensive wine list. [$] *Average main: €20* ✉ *Mädlerpassage, Grimmaische Str. 2–4* ☎ *0341/216–100* 🌐 *www.auerbachs-keller-leipzig.de* 🕒 *Closed Mon.*

$$ GERMAN 🍴 **Barthels Hof.** The English-language menu at this restaurant explains not only the cuisine but the history of Leipzig. Waitresses wear traditional *Trachten* dresses may serve some of the finest Leipzig regional cuisine, but the restaurant itself is quite modern. **Known for:** massive breakfast buffet; Leipziger Allerlei (vegetables and crayfish in beef bouillon); serves Bauer Gose. [$] *Average main: €15* ✉ *Hainstr. 1* ☎ *0341/141–310.*

$$ GERMAN 🍴 **Gasthaus & Gosebrauerei Bayrischer Bahnhof.** Hidden on the far southeast edge of the city center, the Bayrischer Bahnhof was the terminus of the first rail link between Saxony and Bavaria. The brewery here is at the heart of a cultural renaissance and is the only place currently brewing Gose in Leipzig. **Known for:** Leipzig's best Gose beer; beer-inspired dishes; dinner in the Römertopf (a terra-cotta baking dish that originated with the ancient Romans). [$] *Average main: €15* ✉ *Bayrischer Pl. 1* ☎ *0341/124–5760* 🌐 *www.bayerischer-bahnhof.de* 💳 *No credit cards.*

$ CAFÉ 🍴 **Kaffeehaus Riquet.** The restored art nouveau house dates from 1908 and houses a pleasant Viennese-style coffeehouse upstairs—the best views are had from up here—and a noisier and more active café downstairs. Riquet is a company that has had dealings in the coffee trade in Africa and East Asia since 1745, as indicated by the large elephant heads adorning the facade of the building. **Known for:** the best place for coffee and cake in Leipzig; Leipzig Medowlark pastry; people-watching from the second floor. [$] *Average main: €5* ✉ *Schulmachergässchen 1* ☎ *0341/961–0000* 💳 *No credit cards* 🕒 *No dinner.*

$$ GERMAN 🍴 **Thüringer Hof.** One of Germany's oldest restaurants and pubs (dating back to 1454) served its hearty Thuringian and Saxon fare to Martin Luther and the like—who certainly had more than a mere pint of the beers on tap. The menu in the reconstructed, cavernous, and always buzzing dining hall doesn't exactly offer gourmet cuisine, but rather an impressively enormous variety of game, fish, and Bratwurst dishes. **Known for:** traditional Thuringian cuisine; Thuringian sausages served with either sauerkraut and boiled potatoes or onions and mashed potatoes; Sauerbraten (sour roast beef). [$] *Average main: €16* ✉ *Burgstr. 19* ☎ *0341/994–4999* 🌐 *www.thueringer-hof.de.*

$$ GERMAN 🍴 **Zill's Tunnel.** The "tunnel" refers to the barrel-ceiling ground-floor restaurant, where foaming glasses of excellent Gose beer are served with a smile. The friendly staff will also help you decipher the Old Saxon descriptions of the menu's traditional dishes. **Known for:** the best pan-seared Rinderrouladen (a filled beef roll) in the city; cozy upper-level wine restaurant; traditional Saxon cuisine. [$] *Average main: €17* ✉ *Barfussgässchen 9* ☎ *0341/960–2078* 🌐 *www.zillstunnel.de.*

WHERE TO STAY

$$ HOTEL Fodor's Choice ★ 🏨 **Hotel Fürstenhof Leipzig.** The city's grandest hotel is inside the renowned Löhr-Haus, a revered old mansion 500 yards from the main train station on the ring road surrounding the city center. **Pros:** an elegant full-service hotel with stunning rooms; safes big enough for a laptop; pleasant wine bar in the lobby. **Cons:** the ring road can be noisy at night, especially on Friday and Saturday; not inside the city center; expensive Wi-Fi. [$] *Rooms from: €140* ✉ *Tröndlinring 8* ☎ *0341/140–370* 🌐 *www.*

hotelfuerstenhofleipzig.com ⤴ *80 rooms, 12 suites* ⦿*No meals.*

$ **Park Hotel-Seaside Hotel Leipzig.** A
HOTEL few steps from the central train station, this hotel is primarily geared to the business traveler. **Pros:** pleasant swimming-pool area; Orient Express–themed restaurant; centrally located. **Cons:** not the place for romantic weekends; impersonal business hotel; uninspired rooms. $*Rooms from: €95* ✉ *Richard-Wagner-Str. 7* ☎*0341/98520* ⊕ *www.parkhotelleipzig.de* ⤴*290 rooms* ⦿*Free Breakfast.*

$ **Ringhotel Adagio Leipzig.** The
HOTEL quiet Adagio, tucked away behind the facade of a 19th-century city mansion, is centrally located between the Grassi Museum and the Neues Gewandhaus. **Pros:** large rooms with luxurious bathrooms; breakfast available all day; small, personal hotel. **Cons:** room decor is slightly bland; hotel not built to accommodate guests with disabilities; lacks the amenities of a larger property. $*Rooms from: €80* ✉*Seeburgstr. 96* ☎*0341/216–690* ⊕ *www.hotel-adagio.de* ⤴*33 rooms* ⦿*Free Breakfast.*

> **GOSE**
>
> Bismark once remarked that "Gose isn't a beer, it is a way of viewing the world." The top-fermented sour wheat beer, which originated in Goslar, is flavored with coriander and salt and then inoculated with lactobacillus bacteria after the boil. Gose came to Leipzig in 1738, and was so popular that by the end of the 1800s it was considered the local brewing style. It's extremely difficult to make, and after beer production stopped during the war (due to grain shortages), the tradition seemed lost. Today, Lothar Goldhahn is producing Gose again at the Bayrischer Bahnhof and the Bauer Brewery in Leipzig.

16

NIGHTLIFE AND PERFORMING ARTS

NIGHTLIFE

With a vast assortment of restaurants, cafés, and clubs to match the city's exceptional musical and literary offerings, Leipzig is a fun city at night. The *Kneipenszene* (pub scene) is centered on the **Drallewatsch** (a Saxon slang word for "going out"), the small streets and alleys around Grosse and Kleine Fleischergasse and the Barfussgässchen.

Schauhaus. A favorite hangout among the city's business elite, this stylish bar serves great cocktails. ✉ *Bosestr. 1* ☎*0341/960–0596.*

Spizz Keller. This hip place is one of the city's top dance clubs. ✉ *Markt 9* ☎*0341/960–8043.*

Tanzpalast. In the august setting of the *Schauspielhaus* (city theater), the Tanzpalast attracts a thirtysomething crowd. This was *the* place to be seen in GDR Leipzig. ✉ *Bosestr. 1* ☎*0341/960–0596.*

Weinstock. This upscale bar, pub, and restaurant in a Renaissance building offers a huge selection of good wines. ✉ *Markt 7* ☎*0341/1406–0606.*

PERFORMING ARTS

Krystallpalast. This variety theater features a blend of circus, vaudeville, and comedy that is fairly accessible for non-German speakers. ✉ *Magazing. 4* ☎*0341/140–660* ⊕ *www.krystallpalast.de.*

EATING WELL IN SAXONY

The cuisine of the region is hearty and seasonal, and almost every town has a unique specialty unavailable outside the immediate area. Look for *Sächsische Sauerbraten* (marinated sour beef roast), spicy *Thüringer Bratwurst* (sausage), *Schlesische Himmelreich* (ham and pork roast smothered in baked fruit and white sauce, served with dumplings), *Teichlmauke* (mashed potato in broth), *Blauer Karpfe* (blue carp, marinated in vinegar), and *Raacher Maad* (grated and boiled potatoes fried in butter and served with blueberries). Venison and wild boar are standards in forest and mountainous areas, and lamb from Saxony-Anhalt is particularly good. In Thuringia, *Klösse* (potato dumplings) are virtually a religion.

Eastern Germany is experiencing a renaissance in the art of northern German brewing. The first stop for any beer lover should be the Bayrische Bahnhof in Leipzig, to give Gose a try. Dresden's Brauhaus Watzke, Quedlinburg's Lüddebräu, and even the Landskron Brauerei in Görlitz are bringing craft brewing back to a region inundated with mass-produced brew.

Saxony has cultivated vineyards for more than 800 years, and is known for its dry red and white wines, among them Müller-Thurgau, Weissburgunder, Ruländer, and the spicy Traminer. The Sächsische Weinstrasse (Saxon Wine Route) follows the course of the Elbe River from Diesbar-Seusslitz (north of Meissen) to Pirna (southeast of Dresden). Meissen, Radebeul, and Dresden have upscale wine restaurants, and wherever you see a green seal with the letter S and grapes depicted, good local wine is being served. One of the best-kept secrets in German wine making is the Salle-Unstrut region, which produces spicy Silvaner and Rieslings.

Neues Gewandhaus. This uninspired touch of socialist architecture is home to an undeniably splendid orchestra. Tickets to concerts are difficult to obtain unless you reserve well in advance. Sometimes spare tickets are available at the box office a half hour before the evening performance. ✉ *Augustuspl. 8* ☎ *0341/127–0280* ⊕ *www.gewandhaus.de.*

SHOPPING

Small streets leading off the Markt attest to Leipzig's rich trading past. Tucked in among them are glass-roof arcades of surprising beauty and elegance, including the wonderfully restored **Specks Hof, Barthels Hof, Jägerhof,** and the **Passage zum Sachsenplatz.** Invent a headache and step into the *Apotheke* (pharmacy) at Hainstrasse 9—it is spectacularly art nouveau, with finely etched and stained glass and rich mahogany. For more glimpses into the past, check out the antiquarian bookstores of the nearby **Neumarkt Passage.** Leipzig's **Hauptbahnhof** has more than 150 shops, restaurants, and cafés, all open Monday through Saturday 9:30 am–10 pm; many are also open on Sunday, with the same hours.

DRESDEN

25 km (16 miles) southeast of Meissen, 140 km (87 miles) southeast of Leipzig, 193 km (120 miles) south of Berlin.

Sitting in baroque splendor on a wide sweep of the Elbe River, Dresden has been the capital of Saxony since the 15th century, although most of its architectural masterpieces date from the enlightenment of the 18th century and the reigns of Augustus the Strong and his son, Frederick Augustus II. Today the city's yellow and pale-green facades are enormously appealing, and their mere presence is even more overwhelming when you compare what you see with photographs of Dresden from February 1945. That's when Allied bombing destroyed almost all of the Altstadt (Old City). Today, Dresden has risen from these ashes; a tribute to its reputation as "the Florence on the Elbe."

Although parts of the old city center still look stuck between demolition and construction, the city's rebuilding is an enormous tribute to Dresdeners' skill, dedication, and thoroughness. The resemblance of today's riverside to Dresden cityscapes painted by Canaletto in the mid-1700s is remarkable. Unfortunately, war-inflicted gaps in other parts of the city were so massive that reconstruction will progress into the foreseeable future. The Main sights are all contained within the Altstadt. On the other side of the river, the Neustadt (New City), which escaped wartime destruction, is the place to go out at night.

GETTING HERE AND AROUND

Dresden is two hours from Berlin on the Hamburg-Berlin-Prague-Vienna train line. The city's international airport serves mostly European destinations with budget airlines. The newly completed Norman Foster train station is a short walk along the Prager Strasse from the city center. Streetcars are cheap and efficient.

Dresden bus tours (in German and English, run by the Dresdner Verkehrsbetriebe) leave from Postplatz daily at 10, 11:30, and 3; the Stadtrundfahrt Dresden bus tours (also in German and English) leave from Theaterplatz/Augustusbrücke (April–October, daily 9:30–5, every 30 minutes; November–March, daily 10–3, every hour) and stop at most sights.

LEIPZIGER LERCHE

As far back as the 18th century, Leipzig was known for a bizarre culinary specialty: roast meadowlark in crust. The dish was so popular that Leipzig consumed more than 400,000 meadowlarks every month. When the king of Saxony banned lark hunting in 1876, Leipzig's industrious bakers came up with a substitute: a baked short-crust pastry filled with almonds, nuts, and strawberries. Today, the substitute Meadowlark, when prepared correctly, is a delicious treat—found only in Leipzig.

16

VISITOR INFORMATION

Contacts **Dresdner Verkehrsbetriebe AG.** ⊠ *Service Center, Postpl. 1* ☎ *0351/857–2201.* **Stadtrundfahrt Dresden.** ⊠ *Theaterpl.* ☎ *0351/899–5650.*

Visitor Information Dresden Tourist. ⊠ *Schlossstr. 1, inside the Kulturpalast* ☎ *0351/491–920* ⊕ *www.dresden.de.*

EXPLORING

Albertinum. Named after Saxony's King Albert, who between 1884 and 1887 converted a royal arsenal into a suitable setting for the treasures he and his forebears had collected, this massive, imperial-style building houses one of the world's great galleries featuring works from the romantic period to the modern. The Galerie Neue Meister (New Masters Gallery) has an extensive collection ranging from Caspar David Friedrich and Gauguin to Ernst Kirchner and Georg Baselitz. ⊠ *Am Neumarkt, Brühlsche Terrasse* ☎ *0351/49849–14973* ⊕ *www.skd. museum* ☒ *€12* ⊙ *Closed Tues.*

Altmarkt (*Old Market Square*). Although dominated by the nearby unappealing Kulturpalast (Palace of Culture), the Altmarkt is a fascinating concrete leftover from the 1970s (check out the "workers and peasants" GDR mosaic), and the broad square and its surrounding streets are the true center of Dresden. The colonnaded beauty (from the Stalinist-era architecture of the early 1950s) survived the efforts of city planners to turn it into a huge outdoor parking lot. The rebuilt **Rathaus** (Town Hall) is here (go around the front to see bullet holes in the statuary), as is the yellow-stucco, 18th-century Landhaus, which contains the Stadtmuseum Dresden im Landhaus. Dresdeners joke that you should never park your car here because the square is under almost constant construction and you might never find it again. ⊠ *Dresden.*

Deutsches Hygiene-Museum Dresden. This unique (even in a country with a national tendency for excessive cleanliness) and unfortunately named museum relates the history of public health and science. The permanent exhibit offers lots of hands-on activities. The building itself once housed the Nazi eugenics program, and the special exhibit on this period is not recommended for children under 12. ⊠ *Lingnerpl. 1* ☎ *0351/48460* ⊕ *www.dhmd.de* ☒ *€9* ⊙ *Closed Mon.*

Fodor'sChoice **Frauenkirche** (*Church of Our Lady*). This masterpiece of baroque
★ church architecture was completed in 1743 but was almost completely destroyed during the bombing of Dresden in 1945. For the following five decades the remains of the church, a pile of rubble, remained a gripping memorial to the horrors of war. In a move shocking to the East German authorities, who organized all public demonstrations, a group of young people spontaneously met here on February 13, 1982, for a candlelight vigil for peace. It wasn't until the reunification of Germany that Dresden began to seriously consider reconstruction. In the early 1990s a citizens' initiative, joined by the Lutheran Church of Saxony and the city of Dresden, decided to rebuild the church using the original stones. The goal of completing the church by 2006, Dresden's 800th anniversary, seemed insurmountable but was completed on Sunday,

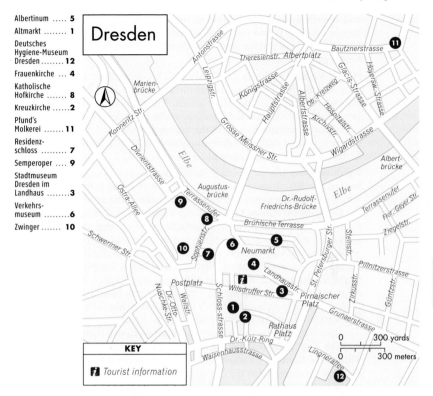

October 30, 2005 (almost a year ahead of schedule). Dresden's skyline became a little more complete with the consecration of the Frauenkirche. ⊠ *An der Frauenkirche* ☎ *0351/498–1131* ⊕ *www.frauenkirche-dresden.org* ⊠ *Free; cupola and tower €8; audio guides in English €3.*

Katholische Hofkirche (*Catholic Court Church*). The largest Catholic church in Saxony is also known as the Cathedral of St. Trinitatis. Frederick Augustus II (who reigned 1733–63) brought architects and builders from Italy to construct a Catholic church in a city that had been the first large center of Lutheran Protestantism (like his father, Frederick Augustus II had to convert to Catholicism to be eligible to wear the Polish crown). Inside, the treasures include a beautiful stone pulpit by the royal sculptor Balthasar Permoser and a painstakingly restored 250-year-old organ, said to be one of the finest ever to come from the mountain workshops of the famous Silbermann family. In the cathedral's crypt are the tombs of 49 Saxon rulers and a reliquary containing the heart of Augustus the Strong, which is rumored to start beating if a beautiful woman comes near. ⊠ *Schlosspl.* ☎ *0351/484–4712* ⊠ *Free.*

Kreuzkirche (*Cross Church*). Soaring high above the Altmarkt, the richly decorated tower of the baroque Kreuzkirche dates back to 1792, but Dresden's main Protestant church has graced this spot for more than 800 years. The church's massive exterior is punctuated by a very simple and dignified nave. Lutherans celebrated their first mass in Saxony here in 1539. A famous boys' choir, the Kreuzchor, performs regularly (check website or call for times). ⊠ *Altmarkt* ☎ *0351/439–390* ⊕ *www. kreuzkirche-dresden.de* ☜ *Tower €2.*

Pfund's Molkerei (*Pfund's Dairy Shop*). This decorative 19th-century shop has been a Dresden institution since 1880, and offers a wide assortment of cheese and other goods. The shop is renowned for its intricate tile mosaics on the floor and walls. Pfund's is also famous for introducing pasteurized milk to the industry; it invented milk soap and specially treated milk for infants as early as 1900. ⊠ *Bautzener Str. 79* ☎ *0351/808–080* ⊕ *www.pfunds.de.*

Residenzschloss (*Royal Palace*). Restoration work is still under way behind the Renaissance facade of this former royal palace, much of which was built between 1709 and 1722. Some of the finished rooms in the **Georgenbau** (Count George Wing) hold historical exhibits, among them an excellent one on the reconstruction of the palace itself. The palace's main gateway, the Georgentor, has an enormous statue of the fully armed Saxon count George. The main attraction in the Royal Palace, though, is the world-famous **Historisches Grünes Gewölbe** (Historic Green Vault), named after a green room in the palace of Augustus the Strong and visited by appointment only (reserve in person, online, or by phone), which contains the crown jewels. The **Neues Grünes Gewölbe** has a wide variety of exhibits including the drinking cup of Ivan the Terrible. The palace also houses the **Münzkabinett** (Coin Museum) and the **Kupferstichkabinett** (Museum of Prints and Drawings). The **Türckische Cammer** (Turkish Chamber) comprises a huge number of Ottoman artifacts collected by Saxon dukes over centuries. It's worth going just to see the six carved Arabian horses, bedecked with jeweled armor. ⊠ *Schlosspl.* ☎ *0351/491–4619, 0351/4919–2285 Historic Green Vault tours* ⊕ *www.skd.museum* ☜ *All museums and collections except Historic Green Vault €12; Historic Green Vault €12; combination ticket €21* ☉ *Closed Tues.*

Semperoper (*Semper Opera House*). One of Germany's best-known and most popular theaters, this magnificent opera house saw the premieres of Richard Wagner's *Rienzi, Der Fliegende Holländer,* and *Tannhäuser* and Richard Strauss's *Salome, Elektra,* and *Der Rosenkavalier.* The Dresden architect Gottfried Semper built the house in 1838–41 in Italian Renaissance style, then saw his work destroyed in a fire caused by a careless lamplighter. Semper had to flee Dresden after participating in a democratic uprising, but his son Manfred rebuilt the theater in the neo-Renaissance style you see today, though even Manfred Semper's version had to be rebuilt after the devastating bombing raid of February 1945. On the 40th anniversary of that raid—February 13, 1985— the Semperoper reopened with a performance of *Der Freischütz,* by Carl Maria von Weber, the last opera performed in the building before its destruction. Guided tours must be reserved in advance, and are offered daily depending on the opera's rehearsal schedule. ⊠ *Theaterpl. 2* ☎ *0351/491–1496* ⊕ *www.semperoper-erleben.de* ☜ *Tour €18.*

The Frauenkirche was painstakingly rebuilt after it was reduced to rubble in the bombing of Dresden.

Stadtmuseum Dresden im Landhaus (*Dresden City Museum at the Landhaus*). The city's small but fascinating municipal museum tells the ups and downs of Dresden's turbulent past—from the dark Middle Ages to the bombing of Dresden in February 1945. There are many peculiar exhibits on display, such as an American 250-kilogram bomb and a stove made from an Allied bomb casing. The building has the most interesting fire escape in the city. ⊠ *Wilsdruffer Str. 2* ☎ *0351/656–480* ⊕ *www.stmd.de* 🖃 *€5* ⊙ *Closed Mon.*

Verkehrsmuseum (*Transportation Museum*). At one time the royal stables, the 16th-century **Johanneum** now displays a collection of historic conveyances, including vintage automobiles and engines. The former stable exercise yard, behind the Johanneum and enclosed by elegant Renaissance arcades, was used during the 16th century as an open-air festival ground. A ramp leading up from the courtyard made it possible for royalty to reach the upper story to view the jousting below without having to dismount. On the outside wall of the Johanneum (behind the building on the Auguststrasse) is a remarkable example of porcelain art: a 336-foot-long Meissen tile mural of a royal procession. More than 100 members of the royal Saxon house of Wettin, half of them on horseback, are represented on the giant mosaic, known as the **Procession of Princes,** which is made of 25,000 porcelain tiles, painted in 1904–07 after a design by Wilhelm Walther. The representations are in chronological order: at 1694, Augustus the Strong's horse is trampling a rose, the symbol of Martin Luther and the Protestant Reformation. The Johanneum is reached by steps leading down from the Brühlsche Terrasse. ⊠ *Am Neumarkt at Augustusstr. 1* ☎ *0351/86440* ⊕ *www.verkehrsmuseum-dresden.de* 🖃 *€9* ⊙ *Closed Mon.*

Fodor's Choice ★ **Zwinger** (*Bailey*). Dresden's magnificent baroque showpiece is entered by way of the mighty **Kronentor** (Crown Gate), off Ostra-Allee. Augustus the Strong hired a small army of artists and artisans to create a "pleasure ground" worthy of the Saxon court on the site of the former bailey, part of the city fortifications. The Zwinger is quite a scene—a riot of garlands, nymphs, and other baroque ornamentation and sculpture. Wide staircases beckon to galleried walks and to the romantic Nymphenbad, a coyly hidden courtyard where statues of nude women perch in alcoves to protect themselves from a fountain that spits unexpectedly. It once had an open view of the riverbank, but the Semper Opera House now occupies that side. The museum holds three collections, the **Gemäldegalerie Alte Meister** (with works by Dürer, Van Eyck, Vermeer, Titian, Canaletto, and Watteau), the **Porzellansammlung** (with a focus on Dresden and Meissen china), and the **Rüstkammer** armor collection. ✉ *Ostra-Allee* 🌐 *www.skd.museum* 🎫 *€12* ⏲ *Closed Mon.*

DRESDEN'S STRIEZELMARKT

Northern Germany's most famous Christmas market dates back to 1434, and is named after the city's famous *Stollen*, a buttery Christmas fruitcake often made with marzipan and sprinkled with powdered sugar. The market hosts a festival in its honor, complete with a 9,000-pound Stollen, on the Saturday of the second weekend of Advent. Traditional wooden toys produced in the nearby Erzgebirge mountains are the other major draw.

WHERE TO EAT

$$$ GERMAN 🍴 **Alte Meister.** In the historic mansion of the architect who rebuilt the Zwinger—and named after the school of medieval painters that includes Dürer, Holbein, and Rembrandt—the Alte Meister has a sophisticated old-world flair that charms locals and tourists alike. **Known for:** light German nouvelle cuisine with careful touches of Asian spices; grand view of the Opera; relaxing before or after the opera. [$] *Average main: €22* ✉ *Theaterpl. 1a* ☎ *0351/481–0426.*

$$ GERMAN 🍴 **Sophienkeller.** One of the liveliest restaurants in town re-creates an 18th-century beer cellar in the basement of the Taschenberg Palace. The furniture and porcelain are as rustic as the food is traditional. **Known for:** Saxon Gesindeessen (panfried rye bread with mustard, slices of pork, and mushrooms, baked with cheese); traditional old-Saxony fare; bread bakery at the entrance. [$] *Average main: €15* ✉ *Taschenbergpalais, Taschenberg 3* ☎ *0351/497–260.*

$ GERMAN 🍴 **Watzke Brauereiausschank am Goldenen Reiter.** The Watzke microbrewery operates this brewhouse with the same beer and hearty menu, directly across from the Goldene Reiter statue of Augustus the Strong. **Known for:** Watzke beer; daily specials, like pork knuckle; popular with locals and beer enthusiasts. [$] *Average main: €14* ✉ *Hauptstr. 11* ☎ *0351/810–6820* 🌐 *www.watzke.de.*

WHERE TO STAY

$ HOTEL **art'otel Dresden.** This hotel is all modern, designed by Italian interior architect Denis Santachiara, and is decorated with more than 600 works of art by Dresden-born painter and sculptor A. R. **Pros:** art elements make the hotel fun; genuine first-class appeal at reasonable prices; trendy cocktail lounge and restaurant. **Cons:** bathrooms have an opaque window into the room; some find the heavily styled rooms a bit much; streetside rooms can be noisy. [$] *Rooms from: €75* ✉ *Ostra-Allee 33* ☎ *0351/49220* 🌐 *www.artotels.com* 🛏 *174 rooms* 🍴 *Free Breakfast.*

$ HOTEL **Hotel Bülow-Residenz.** One of the most intimate first-class hotels in eastern Germany, the Bülow-Residenz is in a baroque palace built in 1730 by a wealthy Dresden city official. **Pros:** extremely helpful staff; verdant courtyard for romantic summer dining; Caroussel restaurant, serving a variety of sophisticated fish and game dishes. **Cons:** air-conditioning can be noisy; hotel is located in Neustadt, a 10-minute walk across the river to the city center; expensive parking. [$] *Rooms from: €75* ✉ *Rähnitzg. 19* ☎ *0351/80030* 🌐 *www.buelow-residenz.de* 🛏 *30 rooms* 🍴 *No meals.*

$ HOTEL **Hotel Elbflorenz.** This centrally located hotel contains Italian-designed rooms bathed in red and yellow and arranged alongside a garden courtyard. **Pros:** extraordinary breakfast buffet; great restaurant, Quattro Cani della Citta, serves delicious Italian seafood and other specialties; fine sauna and relaxation area. **Cons:** in need of renovation; located at edge of city center; spotty Wi-Fi. [$] *Rooms from: €77* ✉ *Rosenstr. 36* ☎ *0351/86400* 🌐 *www.hotel-elbflorenz.de* 🛏 *227 rooms* 🍴 *Free Breakfast.*

$$$ HOTEL **Kempinski Hotel Taschenbergpalais Dresden.** Rebuilt after wartime bombing, the historic Taschenberg Palace—the work of Zwinger architect Matthäus Daniel Pöppelmann—is Dresden's premier address and the last word in luxury, as befits the former residence of the Saxon crown princes. **Pros:** central location in the Altstadt; concierge knows absolutely everything about Dresden; palatial rooms. **Cons:** breakfast costs extra; expensive Internet access; somewhat oblivious service. [$] *Rooms from: €185* ✉ *Taschenberg 3* ☎ *0351/49120* 🌐 *www.kempinski-dresden.de* 🛏 *213 rooms* 🍴 *No meals.*

NIGHTLIFE AND PERFORMING ARTS

NIGHTLIFE

Dresdeners are known for their industriousness and efficient way of doing business, but they also know how to spend a night out. Most of Dresden's pubs and *Kneipen* (bars) are in the **Neustadt** district, across the river from most sights, and along the buzzing **Münzgasse** (between the Frauenkirche and the Brühlsche Terrasse).

Aqualounge. This groovy and hip place is one of the best bars in town. ✉ *Louisenstr. 56* ☎ *0351/810–6116* 🌐 *www.aqualounge.de.*

Bärenzwinger. Folk and rock music are regularly featured here. ✉ *Brühlscher Garten* ☎ *0351/495–1409* 🌐 *www.baerenzwinger.de.*

The Semperoper Dresden (Semper Opera House) saw the openings of several of Richard Wagner's and Richard Strauss's best-loved operas. Its plush interiors are rich with velvet and brocade.

Planwirtschaft. The name ironically refers to the planned socialist economic system; it attracts an alternative crowd. ✉ *Louisenstr. 20* ☎ *0351/801–3187.*

Tonne Jazz Club. Jazz musicians perform most nights of the week at this friendly, laid-back club. ✉ *Waldschlösschen, Am Brauhaus 3* ☎ *0351/802–6017.*

PERFORMING ARTS

Philharmonie Dresden (*Philharmonic Orchestra Dresden*). Dresden's fine orchestra takes center stage in the city's annual music festival, from mid-May to early June. ✉ *Kulturpalast am Altmarkt* ☎ *0351/486–6286* ⊕ *en.dresdnerphilharmonie.de.*

Semperoper Dresden (*Semper Opera House*). The opera in Dresden holds an international reputation largely due to its opera house. Destroyed during the war, the building has been meticulously rebuilt and renovated. Tickets are reasonably priced but also hard to come by; they're often included in package tours. Try reserving tickets on the website, or stop by the box office (just left of the main entrance) about a half hour before the performance. If that doesn't work, take one of the opera-house tours, a nice consolation that gets you into the building. ✉ *Theaterpl.* ☎ *0351/491–1705 evening box office* ⊕ *www.semperoper.de.*

MEISSEN

25 km (15 miles) northwest of Dresden.

This romantic city with its imposing castle looming over the Elbe River is known the world over for Europe's finest porcelain, emblazoned with its trademarked crossed blue swords. The first European porcelain was made in this area in 1708, and in 1710 the Royal Porcelain Workshop was established in Meissen, close to the local raw materials.

The story of how porcelain came to be produced here reads like a German fairy tale: the Saxon elector Augustus the Strong, who ruled from 1694 to 1733, urged his court alchemists to find the secret of making gold, something he badly needed to refill a state treasury depleted by his extravagant lifestyle. The alchemists failed to produce gold, but one of them, Johann Friedrich Böttger, discovered a method for making something almost as precious: fine hard-paste porcelain. Already a rapacious collector of Oriental porcelains, the prince put Böttger and a team of craftsmen up in a hilltop castle, Albrechtsburg, and set them to work.

THE ORIGINS OF THE MEISSEN FUMMEL

At the beginning of the 18th century, the Great Elector of Saxony routinely sent proclamations by messenger to his subjects in Meissen. The messengers were known to chase women and behave poorly, often drinking so much of the famous Meissen wine that their horses were the only ones who remembered the way back to Dresden. To curb this behavior, the elector charged the bakers of Meissen with creating an extremely fragile cake, which the messengers would have to remain sober enough to deliver to the elector intact. Today, the Meissner Fummel remains a local specialty.

GETTING HERE AND AROUND

Meissen is an easy 45-minute train ride, an ideal day-trip, from Dresden. On arrival, exit the station and walk to the left; as you turn the corner there is a beautiful view of Meissen across the river. Trains run about every 30 minutes.

VISITOR INFORMATION

Contacts **Tourist-Information Meissen.** ⊠ *Markt 3* ☎ *03521/4670* ⊕ *www. touristinfo-meissen.de.*

EXPLORING

Albrechtsburg. The story of Meissen porcelain actually began high above Old Meissen. Towering over the Elbe River, this 15th-century castle is Germany's first truly residential one, a complete break with the earlier style of fortified bastions. In the central *Schutzhof*, a typical Gothic courtyard protected on three sides by high rough-stone walls, is an exterior spiral staircase, the **Wendelstein,** a masterpiece of early masonry hewn in 1525 from a single massive stone block. The ceilings of the castle halls are richly decorated, although many date only from a restoration in 1870. Adjacent to the castle is an early Gothic cathedral. It's a bit of a climb up Burgstrasse and Amtsstrasse to the castle, but a bus runs regularly up the hill from the Marktplatz. ⊠ *Meissen* ☎ *03521/47070* ⊕ *www.albrechtsburg-meissen.de* ⌛ *€8.*

Altes Brauhaus (*Old Brewery*). Near the Frauenkirche, the Altes Brauhaus dates to 1460 and is graced by a Renaissance gable. It now houses city offices. ⊠ *An der Frauenkirche 3.*

Franziskanerkirche (*St. Francis Church*). The city's medieval past is recounted in the museum of this former monastery. ⊠ *Heinrichspl. 3* ☎ *03521/458–857* ⌛ *€3.*

Frauenkirche (*Church of Our Lady*). A set of porcelain bells at the late-Gothic Frauenkirche, on the central Marktplatz, was the first of its kind anywhere when installed in 1929. ⊠ *An der Frauenkirche.*

Nikolaikirche (*St. Nicholas Church*). Near the porcelain works, this church holds the largest set of porcelain figures ever crafted (8¼ feet tall) as well as the remains of early Gothic frescoes. ⊠ *Neumarkt 29.*

Staatliche Porzellan–Manufaktur Meissen (*Meissen Porcelain Works*). Outgrowing its castle workshop in the mid-19th century, today's porcelain factory is on the southern outskirts of town. One of its buildings has a demonstration workshop and a museum whose Meissen collection rivals that of Dresden's Porzellansammlung. ⊠ *Talstr. 9* ☎ *03521/468–208* ⊕ *www.meissen.de* ⌛ *€10, including workshop and museum.*

WHERE TO EAT

$$
GERMAN
✕ **Domkeller.** Part of the centuries-old complex of buildings ringing the town castle, this ancient and popular hostelry is a great place to enjoy the view from the large dining room and tree-shaded terrace. **Known for:** hearty German cuisine; fine wines; sensational view of the Elbe Valley. Ⓢ *Average main: €15* ⊠ *Dompl. 9* ☎ *03521/457–676.*

$$
GERMAN
✕ **Restaurant Vincenz Richter.** Tucked away in a yellow wooden-beam house, this historic restaurant has been painstakingly maintained by the Richter family since 1873. The dining room is adorned with rare antiques, documents, and medieval weapons, as well as copper and tin tableware. **Known for:** exquisite Saxon-German menu; personally produced white wines; wild game. Ⓢ *Average main: €17* ⊠ *An der Frauenkirche 12* ☎ *03521/453–285* ☉ *Closed Mon. No dinner Sun.*

PERFORMING ARTS

Concerts. Regular concerts are held at the Albrechtsburg castle, and in early September the *Burgfestspiele*—open-air evening performances—are staged in the castle's romantic courtyard. ⊠ *Meissen* ☎ *03521/47070.*

Dom. Meissen's cathedral, the Dom, has a yearlong music program, with organ and choral concerts every Saturday in summer. ⊠ *Dompl. 7* ☎ *03521/452–490.*

SHOPPING

Sächsische Winzergenossenschaft Meissen. To wine connoisseurs, the name "Meissen" is associated with vineyards producing top-quality white wines much in demand throughout Germany. Müller-Thurgau, Kerner, and Goldriesling are worthy choices and can be bought directly from the producer, Sächsische Winzergenossenschaft Meissen. ⊠ *Bennoweg 9* ☏ *03521/780–970* ⊕ *www.winzer-meissen.de.*

Staatliche Porzellan–Manufaktur Meissen. Meissen porcelain is available directly from the porcelain works as well as in every china and gift shop in town. ⊠ *Talstr. 9* ☏ *03521/468–700.*

BAUTZEN/BUDYŠIN

53 km (33 miles) east of Dresden.

Bautzen has perched high above a deep granite valley formed by the River Spree for more than 1,000 years. Its almost-intact city walls hide a remarkably well-preserved city with wandering back alleyways and fountain-graced squares. Bautzen is definitely a German city, but it is also the administrative center of Germany's only indigenous ethnic minority, the Sorbs.

In the area, the Sorb language enjoys equal standing with German in government and education, and Sorbs are known for their colorful folk traditions. As in all Slavic cultures, Easter Sunday is the highlight of the calendar, when ornately decorated eggs are hung from trees and when the traditional *Osterreiten,* a procession of Catholic men on horseback who carry religious symbols and sing Sorbian hymns, takes place.

GETTING HERE AND AROUND

Bautzen is halfway between Dresden and Görlitz. Trains leave both cities once every hour; travel time is about an hour.

VISITOR INFORMATION

Contacts Tourist-Information Bautzen-Budyšin. ⊠ *Hauptmarkt 1, Bautzen* ☏ *03591/42016, 03591/327–629* ⊕ *www.tourismus-bautzen.de.*

EXPLORING

Alte Wasserkunst (*Old Waterworks*). Erected in 1558, the Alte Wasserkunst served as part of the town's defensive fortifications, but its true purpose was to pump water from the Spree into 86 cisterns spread throughout the city. It proved so efficient that it provided the city's water supply until 1965. It is now a technical museum. ⊠ *Wendischer Kirchhof 7, Bautzen* ☏ *03591/41588* ⊕ *www.altewasserkunstbautzen. de* ⌨ *€3.*

Dom St. Petri (*St. Peter's Cathedral*). Behind the Rathaus is one of Bautzen's most interesting sights: Dom St. Petri is Eastern Germany's only *Simultankirche,* or "simultaneous church." An early effort to avoid the violence that often occurred during the Reformation, St. Peter's has a Protestant side and a Roman Catholic side in the same church. A short fence, which once reached a height of 13 feet, separates the two congregations. The church was built in 1213 on the sight of a Milzener (the forerunners of the Sorbs) parish church. ✉ *An der Petrikirche 6, Bautzen* ☎ *03591/31180* 🌐 *www.dompfarrei-bautzen.de* 🎟 *Free.*

Hexenhäuser (*Witches' Houses*). Below the waterworks and outside the walls, these three reddish houses were the only structures to survive all the city's fires—leading Bautzeners to conclude that they could only be occupied by witches. ✉ *Fischergasse, Bautzen.*

Rathaus. Bautzen's main market square is actually two squares, the **Hauptmarkt** (Main Market) and the **Fleischmarkt** (Meat Market), separated by the yellow, baroque Rathaus. The current town hall dates from 1705, but there has been a town hall in this location since 1213. Bautzen's friendly tourist-information center, next door, has a great Bautzen-in-two-hours walking-tour map and an MP3 guide to the city. ✉ *Fleischmarkt 1, Bautzen.*

Reichenturm (*Rich Tower*). Bautzen's city walls have a number of gates and towers. This one, at the end of Reichenstrasse, is the most impressive. Although the tower base dates from 1490, it was damaged in four city fires (in 1620, 1639, 1686, and 1747) and rebuilt, hence its baroque cupola. The reconstruction caused the tower to lean, however, and its foundation was further damaged in 1837. The "Leaning Tower of Bautzen" currently sits about 5 feet off center. The view from the top is a spectacular vista of Bautzen and the surrounding countryside. ✉ *Reichenstr. 1, Bautzen* ☎ *03591/460–431* 🎟 *€2.*

16

WHERE TO EAT

$ EASTERN EUROPEAN

🍴 **Wjelbik.** The name of Bautzen's best Sorbian restaurant means "pantry." Very popular on Sorb holidays, Wjelbik uses exclusively regional produce. The restaurant is in a 600-year-old building near the cathedral. **Known for:** historic setting; Sorbisches Hochzeitsmenu (traditional Sorb wedding meal of roast beef with horseradish sauce); seasonal specialties such as lamb and white asparagus. [$] *Average main: €14* ✉ *Kornstr. 7, Bautzen* ☎ *03591/42060* 🌐 *www.wjelbik.de.*

GÖRLITZ

48 km (30 miles) east of Bautzen, 60 km (38 miles) northeast of Dresden.

Tucked away in the country's easternmost corner (bordering Poland), Görlitz's quiet, narrow cobblestone alleys and exquisite architecture make it one of Germany's most beautiful cities. It emerged from the destruction of World War II relatively unscathed. As a result it has more than 4,000 historic houses in styles including Gothic, Renaissance, baroque, rococo, Wilhelminian, and art nouveau. Although the city has impressive museums, theater, and music, it's the ambience created by the casual dignity of these buildings, in their jumble of styles, that makes Görlitz so attractive. Notably absent are the typical socialist eyesores and the glass-and-steel modernism found in many eastern German towns.

The Gothic Dicker Turm (Fat Tower) guards the entrance to the city; it's the oldest tower in Görlitz, and its walls are 5 meters (6½ feet) thick.

GETTING HERE AND AROUND
Görlitz can be reached by hourly trains from Dresden (1½ hours) and from Berlin (3 hours, with a change in Cottbus). Görlitz's train station (a wonderful neoclassical building with an art nouveau interior) is a short tram ride outside town.

VISITOR INFORMATION
Contacts Görlitz-Information und Tourist-Service. ⊠ *Obermarkt 32* ☎ *03581/47570, 03581/475–747* ⊕ *www.goerlitz.de.*

EXPLORING

Biblical House. This house is interesting for its Renaissance facade decorated with sandstone reliefs depicting biblical stories. The Catholic Church banned religious depictions on secular buildings, but by the time the house was rebuilt after a fire in 1526, the Reformation had Görlitz firmly in its grip. ⊠ *Neissestr. 29.*

Dreifaltigkeitskirche (*Church of the Holy Trinity*). On the southeast side of the market lies this pleasant Romanesque church with a Gothic interior, built in 1245. The interior houses an impressive Gothic triptych altarpiece. The clock on the thin tower is set seven minutes fast in remembrance of a trick played by the city guards on the leaders of a rebellion. In 1527 the city's disenfranchised cloth makers secretly met to plan a rebellion against the city council and the powerful guilds. Their plans were uncovered, and by setting the clock ahead the guards fooled the rebels into thinking it was safe to sneak into the city. As a result they were caught and hanged. ⊠ *Obermarkt* ☎ *€4.*

Karstadt. Dating 1912–13, Germany's only original art nouveau department store has a main hall with a colorful glass cupola and several stunning freestanding staircases. The store dominates the Marienplatz, a small square outside the city center that serves as Görlitz's transportation hub. It's next to the 15th-century Frauenkirche, the parish church for the nearby hospital and the poor condemned to live outside the city walls. Though the department store is closed, you can peek inside through the perfume shop. ⊠ *An der Frauenkirche 5–7.*

Kirche St. Peter und Paul (*St. Peter and Paul Church*). Perched high above the river is one of Saxony's largest late-Gothic churches, dating to 1423. The real draw is the church's famous one-of-a-kind organ, built in 1703 by Eugenio Casparini. The Sun Organ gets its name from the circularly arranged pipes and not from the golden sun at the center. Its full and deep sound, as well as its birdcalls, can be heard on Sunday and Wednesday afternoons. ⊠ *Bei der Peterkirche 5* ☎ *03581/409–590* ☎ *Free.*

Landskron Braumanufaktur (*Landskron Brewery*). Germany's easternmost Brauhaus is one of the few breweries left that uses open fermentation and gives tours. Founded in 1869, Landskron isn't very old by German standards, but it's unique in that it hasn't been gobbled up by a huge brewing conglomerate. *Görlitzer* are understandably proud of their own

Görlitz's Untermarkt contains the Rathaus and also building No. 14, where all goods coming into the city were weighed and taxed.

Premium Pilsner, but the brewery also produces good dark, Silesian, and winter beers. Landskron Hefeweizen is one of the best in the country. ⊠ *An der Landskronbrauerei* ☎ *03581/465–121* ⊕ *www.landskron.de* ⊠ *Tours €8–€25.*

Obermarkt (*Upper Market*). The richly decorated Renaissance homes and warehouses on the Obermarkt are a vivid legacy of the city's wealthy past. During the late Middle Ages the most common merchandise here was cloth, which was bought and sold from covered wagons and on the ground floors of many buildings. Napoléon addressed his troops from the balcony of the house at No. 29. ⊠ *Görlitz.*

Untermarkt (*Lower Market*). One of Europe's most impressive squares, this market is a testament to the prosperity brought by the cloth trade. It's built up in the middle, and the most important building is No. 14, which formerly housed the city scales. The duty of the city scale masters, whose busts adorn the Renaissance facade of the Gothic building, was to weigh every ounce of merchandise entering the city and to determine the taxes due. The square's most prominent building is the Rathaus. Its winding staircase is as peculiar as its statue of the goddess of justice, whose eyes—contrary to European tradition—are not covered. The corner house on the square, the Alte Ratsapotheke (Old Council Pharmacy), has two intricate sundials on the facade, painted in 1550. ⊠ *Görlitz.*

Verrätergasse (*Traitors' Alley*). On Verrätergasse, across the Obermarkt square from the church, is the **Peter-Liebig-Haus,** where the initials of the first four words of the rebels' meeting place, *Der verräterischen Rotte Tor* (the treacherous gang's gate), are inscribed above the door.

The Obermarkt is dominated by the **Reichenbach Turm,** a tower built in the 13th century, with additions in 1485 and 1782. Until 1904 the tower housed the city watchmen and their families. The apartments and armory are now a museum. There are great views of the city from the tiny windows at the top. The massive **Kaisertrutz** (Emperor's Fortress) once protected the western city gates, and now houses late-Gothic and Renaissance art from the area around Görlitz, as well as some impressive historical models of the city. Both buildings are part of the Kulturhistorisches Museum. ✉ *Görlitz* ☎ *03581/671–355* 🌐 *www.museum-goerlitz.de* 🎫 *€5* 🕒 *Closed Mon.*

GÖRLITZ'S SECRET ADMIRER

After German unification, Görlitz was a run-down border town, but renovations costing upward of €400 million returned the city to much of its former splendor. In 1995 it got an additional boost when an anonymous philanthropist pledged to the city a yearly sum of 1 million marks. Every March, Görlitz celebrates the arrival in its coffers of the mysterious Altstadt-Million (albeit, with the change in currency, now €511,000).

Zgorzelec. In 1946 everything on the eastern side on the Neisse River was ceded to Poland and Görlitz lost its eastern suburb. A walk across the river is like a trip back in time. Zgorzelec certainly isn't as well off as Görlitz, but there are some nice patrician houses and wide parks whose decay resembles the state of Görlitz in the 1980s. For a stroll through, cross the Altstadtbrücke (Old Town Bridge) behind the Peterskirche, turn right, and walk approximately a kilometer (half mile), then cross back into Germany at the former official border crossing. Great Polish food is in plentiful supply at the **Piwnica Staromiejska** at Wrocławska 1, just across the bridge. ✉ *Zgorzelec.*

WHERE TO EAT

$ GERMAN 🍴 **Die Destille.** This small family-run establishment overlooks the Nikolaiturm, one of the towers of the city's wall. The restaurant offers good solid Silesian fare. **Known for:** regional Silesian cuisine; the best Schlesische Himmelreich (ham and pork roast smothered in baked fruit and white sauce, served with dumplings); pleasant location. [$] *Average main: €12* ✉ *Nikolaistr. 6* ☎ *03581/405–302* 💳 *No credit cards* 🕒 *Closed some days in Sept.*

WHERE TO STAY

$ HOTEL 🏨 **Hotel Bon-Apart.** The name says it all: this hotel is an homage to Napoléon, whose troops occupied Görlitz, and it's a splendid departure from a typical hotel, which offers large rooms, some with kitchenettes. **Pros:** large rooms, most with kitchens; artistically decorated bathrooms; huge breakfast buffet. **Cons:** eclectic design may not appeal to everyone; neighboring market can be noisy in the morning; no elevator. [$] *Rooms from: €95* ✉ *Elisabethstr. 41* ☎ *03581/48080* 🌐 *www.bon-apart.de* 🛏 *20 rooms* 🍽 *Free Breakfast.*

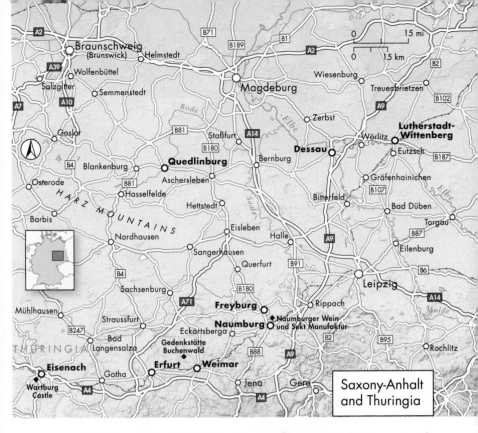

$ **Romantik-Hotel Tuchmacher.** The city's best hotel is also its most mod-
HOTEL ern accommodation in antique disguise, a mansion dating to 1528,
offering guest rooms with wooden floors and thick ceiling beams that
are sparsely furnished with modern, dark cherrywood furniture. **Pros:**
luxury hotel in the heart of the pedestrian zone; historical rooms and
building; good restaurant with Saxon specialties. **Cons:** limited parking
near the hotel; lots of church bells; sometimes too colorful. $ *Rooms*
from: €94 ⊠ *Peterstr. 8* ☎ *03581/47310* ⊕ *www.tuchmacher.de* ⪢ *43*
rooms ⦿ *Free Breakfast.*

LUTHERSTADT-WITTENBERG

107 km (62 miles) southwest of Berlin, 67 km (40 miles) north of
Leipzig.

Protestantism was born in the little town of Wittenberg (officially called
Lutherstadt-Wittenberg). In 1508 the fervently idealistic young Martin
Luther, who had become a priest only a year earlier, arrived to study and
teach at the new university founded by Elector Frederick the Wise. Nine
years later, enraged that the Roman Catholic Church was pardoning sins
through the sale of indulgences, Luther attacked the policy by posting
his *Ninety-Five Theses* on the door of the Schlosskirche (Castle Church).

Martin Luther is still the center of attention in Wittenberg, and sites associated with him are marked with plaques and signs. You can see virtually all of historic Wittenberg on a 2-km (1-mile) stretch of Collegienstrasse and Schlossstrasse that begins at the railroad tracks and ends at the Schlosskirche.

GETTING HERE AND AROUND

Lutherstadt-Wittenberg is approximately halfway between Berlin and Leipzig, and is served by regional and ICE trains. The station is slightly outside the city center, a pleasant walking distance away.

FESTIVALS

Luthers Hochzeit (*Luther's Wedding*). The best time to visit Wittenberg is during this citywide festival that commemorates (and reenacts) Martin Luther's marriage to Katharina von Bora. On the second weekend in June the city center goes back in time to 1525, with period costumes and entertainment. ⊕ *www.lutherhochzeit.de.*

VISITOR INFORMATION

Contacts **Tourist-Information Lutherstadt Wittenberg.** ✉ *Schlosspl. 2, Wittenberg* ☎ *03491/498–610, 03491/498–611* ⊕ *www.wittenberg.de.*

EXPLORING

Ersten Cranachhaus (*First Cranach House*). Lucas Cranach the Elder—court painter, printer, mayor, pharmacist, friend of Luther's, and probably the wealthiest man in Wittenberg—lived in two houses during his years in town. This Cranachhaus is believed to have been the first one. His son, the painter Lucas Cranach the Younger, was born here. Some of the interior has been restored to its 17th-century condition. It's now a gallery with exhibits about Cranach's life and work. Check out the goldsmith and potter that are occasionally on hand demonstrating their crafts in the courtyard. ✉ *Markt 4, Wittenberg* ☎ *03491/420–190* ▢ €6 ☉ *Closed Mon. Dec.–Mar.*

Haus der Geschichte (*House of History*). This museum makes a valiant attempt to evaluate the history of the GDR. It provides fascinating insight into the day-to-day culture of East Germans through the re-creation of a typical East German apartment, and a display of more than 20,000 objects, including detergent packaging and kitchen appliances. A special section deals with Germans and Russians in the Wittenberg region. ✉ *Schlossstr. 6, Wittenberg* ☎ *03491/409–004* ⊕ *www.pflug-ev. de* ▢ €6 ☉ *Closed Mon. in Jan. and Feb.*

Luthereiche (*Luther Oak*). In a small park, the Luthereiche marks the spot where, in 1520, Luther burned the papal bull excommunicating him for his criticism of the Church. The present oak was planted in the 19th century. ✉ *Weserstr. and Collegienstr., Wittenberg.*

Fodor'sChoice **Lutherhaus** (*Luther's House*). Within Lutherhhaus is the Augustinian
★   monastery where Martin Luther lived both as a teacher-monk and later, after the monastery was dissolved, as a married man. Today it's a museum dedicated to Luther and the Reformation. Visitors enter through a garden and an elegant door with a carved stone frame; it was a gift to Luther from his wife, Katharina von Bora. Be sure to visit the

Martin Luther taught in the Lecture Hall within Lutherhaus, which is now a museum dedicated to Martin Luther and the Reformation.

monks' refectory, where works by the painter Lucas Cranach the Elder, Luther's contemporary, are displayed. The room that remains closest to the original is the dark, wood-paneled Lutherstube. The Luthers and their six children used it as a living room, study, and meeting place for friends and students. Prints, engravings, paintings, manuscripts, coins, and medals relating to the Reformation and Luther's translation of the Bible into the German vernacular are displayed throughout the house. ⊠ *Collegienstr. 54, Wittenberg* ☎ *03491/42030* ⊕ *www.martinluther. de* 🎫 *€8* ⊘ *Closed Mon. Dec.–Mar.*

Marktplatz (*Market Square*). Two statues are the centerpiece here: an 1821 statue of Luther by Johann Gottfried Schadow, designer of the quadriga and Victory atop Berlin's Brandenburg Gate, and an 1866 statue of Melanchthon by Frederick Drake. Gabled Renaissance houses containing shops line part of the square. ⊠ *Wittenberg.*

Melanchthonhaus (*Melanchthon House*). In this elegantly gabled Renaissance home, the humanist teacher and scholar Philipp Melanchthon corrected Luther's translation of the New Testament from Greek into German. Luther was hiding in the Wartburg in Eisenach at the time, and as each section of his manuscript was completed it was sent to Melanchthon for approval. (*Melanchthon* is a Greek translation of the man's real name, Schwarzerdt, which means "black earth"; humanists routinely adopted such classical pseudonyms.) The second-floor furnishings have been painstakingly re-created after period etchings. ⊠ *Collegienstr. 60, Wittenberg* ☎ *03491/420–3171* ⊕ *www.martinluther.de* 🎫 *€5* ⊘ *Closed Mon. Nov.–Mar.*

Rathaus. The handsome, white High Renaissance town hall forms the backdrop for the Marktplatz's two statues. ⊠ *Markt 26, Wittenberg* ☎ *03491/421–720.*

Fodor's Choice **Schlosskirche** (*Castle Church*). In 1517 an indignant Martin Luther
★ nailed his *Ninety-Five Theses*, which attacked the Roman Catholic Church's policy of selling indulgences, to this church's doors. Written in Latin, the theses might have gone unnoticed had not someone—without Luther's knowledge—translated them into German and distributed them. In 1521 the Holy Roman Emperor Charles V summoned Luther to Worms when Luther refused to retract his position. On the way home from his confrontation with the emperor, Luther was "captured" by his protector, Elector Frederick the Wise, and hidden from papal authorities in Eisenach for the better part of a year. Today the theses hang in bronze on the door, while inside, simple bronze plaques mark the burial places of Luther and his contemporary, Philipp Melanchthon. ⊠ *Schlosspl. 1, Wittenberg* ☎ *03491/402–585* 🕮 *Free; tower €2.*

Stadtkirche St. Marien (*Parish Church of St. Mary*). From 1514 until his death in 1546, Martin Luther preached two sermons a week in the twin-tower Stadtkirche St. Marien. He and Katharina von Bora were married here (Luther broke with monasticism in 1525 and married the former nun). The altar triptych by Lucas Cranach the Elder includes a self-portrait, as well as portraits of Luther wearing the knight's disguise he adopted when hidden at the Wartburg; Luther preaching; Luther's wife and one of his sons; Melanchthon; and Lucas Cranach the Younger. Also notable is the 1457 bronze baptismal font by Herman Vischer the Elder. On the church's southeast corner is a discomforting juxtaposition of the two **monuments** dedicated to Wittenberg's Jews; a 1304 mocking caricature called the Jewish Pig, erected at the time of the expulsion of the town's Jews, and, on the cobblestone pavement, a contemporary memorial to the the city's Jews murdered by the Nazis. ⊠ *Kirchpl., Wittenberg* ☎ *03491/404–415* 🕮 *€2, including tour.*

Wittenberg English Ministry. English-speaking visitors can worship in the churches where Martin Luther conducted his ministry thanks to *this* ministry. During the summer months it brings English-speaking pastors from the United States to provide Lutheran worship services in the Schlosskirche and Stadtkirche St. Marien. Services follow German Protestant tradition (albeit in English) and conclude with singing Luther's "A Mighty Fortress Is Our God," accompanied on the organ. Tours of Wittenberg and other Luther sites are also offered. ⊠ *Schlosspl. 2, Wittenberg* ☎ *03491/498–610* ⊕ *www.wittenberg-english-ministry.com.*

Zweiten Cranachhaus (*Second Cranach House*). In the second Wittenberg home of Cranach the Elder, the Renaissance man not only lived and painted but also operated a print shop, which has been restored. The courtyard, where it's thought he did much of his painting, remains much as it was in his day. Local children attend the *Malschule* (painting school) next to the apothecary. ⊠ *Schlossstr. 1, Wittenberg* ☎ *03491/410–912* 🕮 *Free* ⊙ *Closed Sun.*

WHERE TO EAT

$ ✕ **Brauhaus Wittenberg.** This historic brewery-cum-restaurant is the per-
GERMAN fect stop for a cold beer after a long day of sightseeing. In the Old
Town's magnificent Beyerhof courtyard, the Brauhaus still produces
local beer such as Wittenberger Kuckucksbier. **Known for:** hand-crafted
beer; southern German brewery cuisine; smoked fish (eel, trout, halibut)
from the Brauhaus smokery. $ *Average main: €13* ✉ *Markt 6, Witten-
berg* ☎ *03491/433–130* ⊕ *www.brauhaus-wittenberg.de.*

$ ✕ **Schlosskeller.** At the back of the Schlosskirche, this restaurant's four
GERMAN dining rooms are tucked away in a basement with 16th-century stone
walls and barrel-vaulted ceilings. The kitchen specializes in German
dishes, such as *Kümmelfleisch mit Senfgurken* (caraway beef with mus-
tard-seed pickles). **Known for:** specialty Luther-beer in massive stone
mugs; regional German cuisine with local ingredients; pleasant location
with vaulted ceilings near the Castle Church. $ *Average main: €12*
✉ *Schlosspl. 1, Wittenberg* ☎ *03491/480–805.*

DESSAU

16

35 km (22 miles) southwest of Wittenberg.

The name "Dessau" is known to students of modern architecture as
the epicenter of architect Walter Gropius's highly influential Bauhaus
school of design. During the 1920s, Gropius hoped to replace the dark
and inhumane tenement architecture of the 1800s with standardized
yet spacious and bright apartments. His ideas and methods were used
in building 316 villas in the city's Törten neighborhood in the 1920s.

GETTING HERE AND AROUND

Dessau makes an excellent day trip from Berlin or Leipzig and the Bauhaus is really the only reason to make the journey. The direct Regional
Express train leaves Berlin every hour, and the trip takes 90 minutes.
Direct trains leave Leipzig every hour; the journey takes less than an
hour.

VISITOR INFORMATION

Contacts Tourist-Information Dessau. ✉ *Zerbster Str. 2c* ☎ *0340/204–1442,
0340/220–3003* ⊕ *www.dessau-rosslau-tourismus.de.*

EXPLORING

Bauhaus Building. The architecture and design school is still operating in
this building, where artists conceived styles that influenced the appearance of such cities as New York, Chicago, and San Francisco. Other
structures designed by Gropius and the Bauhaus architects, among them
the Meisterhäuser, are also open for inspection off Ebertallee and Elbal-
lee. ✉ *Gropiusallee 38* ☎ *0340/650–8251* ⊕ *www.bauhaus-dessau.de*
⛶ *From €9.*

Georgkirche (*St. George's Church*). Like other older buildings in downtown Dessau, this Dutch-baroque church, built in 1712, is quite a contrast to the no-nonsense Bauhaus architecture. ✉ *Georgenstr. 15.*

Technikmuseum Hugo Junkers (*Hugo Junkers Technical Museum*). The Bauhaus isn't the only show in town. Professor Hugo Junkers, one of the most famous engineers-cum-inventors of the 20th century, was at the forefront of innovation in aircraft and industrial design until his inventions were expropriated by the Nazis in 1933. The star of the museum is a completely restored JU-52/3—the ubiquitous German passenger airplane transformed into military transport. The museum also houses a fascinating collection of industrial equipment, machinery, engines, and the original Junkers wind tunnel. ⊠ *Kühnauerstr. 161a* ☎ *0340/661–1982* ⊕ *www.technikmuseum-dessau.de* ⊡ €6.

NAUMBURG

60 km (65 miles) south of Halle.

Once a powerful mercantile and ecclesiastical city, 1,000-year-old Naumburg is the cultural center of the Salle-Unstrut. Although the city is most famous for its Romanesque-Gothic cathedral, it hides a well-preserved collection of patrician houses, winding back alleys, and a marketplace so distinctive that it warrants the appellation "Naumburger Renaissance."

GETTING HERE AND AROUND

From the train station the fun way to get into the city is to take the Naumburger Historical Tram, which runs every 30 minutes. A single ride on Europe's smallest tramway, in antique streetcars, costs €1.50.

VISITOR INFORMATION

Contacts Tourist und Tagungsservice Naumburg. ⊠ *Markt 12* ☎ *03445/273–125, 03445/273–128* ⊕ *www.naumburg-tourismus.de.*

EXPLORING

Dom St. Peter und Paul (*St. Peter and Paul Cathedral*). Perched high above the city and dominating the skyline, this cathedral is the symbol of Naumburg. For the most part constructed during the latter half of the 13th century, it's considered one of the masterpieces of the late Romanesque period. What makes the cathedral unique, however, is the addition of a second choir in the Gothic style less than 100 years later. The Gothic choir is decorated with statues of the cathedral's benefactors from the workshop of the Naumburger Meister. Be sure to find Neo Rauch's red triptych windows in the St. Elisabeth Chapel. The most famous statues are of Uta and Ekkehard, the city's most powerful patrons. Uta's tranquil face is everywhere, from postcards to city maps. ⊠ *Dompl. 16* ☎ *03445/23010* ⊡ €7.

Marientor. Naumburg was once ringed by a defensive city wall with five gates. The only remaining one, the Marientor, is a rare surviving example of a dual-portal gate, called a *barbican*, from the 14th century. The museum inside the gate provides a brief history of the city's defenses. A pleasant walk along the remaining city walls from Marienplatz to the Weingarten is the easiest way to explore the last intact section of

Naumburg's wall, moat, and defensive battlements. ✉ *Marienpl.* 🎫 *€1 turnstile at entrance.*

Marktplatz. Naumburg's historic market square lies strategically at the intersection of two medieval trade routes. Although the market burned in 1517, it was painstakingly rebuilt in Renaissance and baroque styles. ✉ *Naumburg.*

Kaysersches Haus (*Imperial House*). Supported by seven Gothic gables, the Kaysersches Haus has a carved oak doorway from the Renaissance. ✉ *Markt 10.*

Rathaus. Naumburg's town hall, rebuilt in 1523, incorporates the remnants of the original building destroyed by fire. ✉ *Markt 1.*

Schlösschen (*Little Castle*). The Schlösschen houses the offices of Naumburg's first and only Protestant bishop, Nikolaus von Amsdorf, who was consecrated by Martin Luther in 1542. ✉ *Markt 2.*

Naumburger Wein und Sekt Manufaktur (*Naumburg Wine and Sparkling Wine*). Producing fine still and sparkling wines on the bank of the Salle River, this winery in a 200-year-old monastery is a pleasant 2-km (1-mile) walk or bike ride from Naumburg's city center. Tours of the production rooms and the vaulted cellar, with wine tastings, take place whenever a group forms and last about an hour. The wine garden is a pleasant place to relax on the bank of the river and the restaurant serves small snacks. Larger appetites find relief across the street at the Gasthaus Henne. ✉ *Blütengrund 35* 📞 *03445/202–042* ⊕ *www.naumburger.com* 🍷 *Tours with tasting €6* 🕐 *Closed Sun. in Jan. and Feb.*

16

Nietzsche Haus Museum. The philosopher Friedrich Nietzsche's family lived in Naumburg from 1858 to 1897, in a small classical house in the Weingarten. The Nietzsche Haus Museum documents the life and times of one of Naumburg's most controversial residents. The exhibition does not delve too deeply into Nietzsche's philosophy, but focuses a great deal on his bizarre relationship with his sister and her manipulation of his manuscripts. ✉ *Weingarten 18* 📞 *03445/703–503* ⊕ *www.mv-naumburg.de* 🎫 *€4* 🕐 *Closed Mon.*

St. Wenceslas. The parish church of St. Wenceslas dominates the southern end of the Markt. A church has stood on this spot since 1218, but the current incarnation dates from 1426, with interior renovations in 1726. The church is most famous for its huge Hildebrandt Organ, which was tested and tuned by J. S. Bach in 1746. Fans of Lucas Cranach the Elder get their due with two of his paintings, *Suffer the*

> **SALLE-UNSTRUT: WINE COUNTRY**
>
> The Salle-Unstrut is Europe's northernmost wine-producing region, and with more than 30 different grape varieties one of the most diverse. The region stretches from Halle to Eisleben, and has more than 700 vintners operating on a mere 1,600 acres. Grapes are grown on the terraced slopes of rolling hills, guarded by numerous castles and fortresses. The area is easy to explore by the regional train that meanders through the Unstrut Valley once every hour or the bicycle path that stretches along the banks of both rivers.

Little Children Come Unto Me and the *Adoration of the Three Magi*. The 240-foot-tall tower belongs to the city, *not* the church, and was used as a watchtower for the city guards, who lived there until 1994. ✉ *Topfmarkt* ☎ *03445/208–401* 🎫 *Free; tower €2.*

WHERE TO EAT

$ GERMAN 🍴 **Alt-Naumburg.** Enjoy simple but tasty regional specialties directly in front of the Marientor. The beer garden is a good place to relax away from the action of the city center. **Known for:** local specialties; pleasant beer garden; exclusively local wines. [$] *Average main: €12* ✉ *Marienpl. 13* ☎ *03445/234–425* 💳 *No credit cards.*

WHERE TO STAY

$ HOTEL 🏨 **Hotel Stadt Aachen.** Many of the simply decorated rooms overlook the central market at this pleasant hotel in a medieval house. **Pros:** central location on the market square; excellent restaurant, Carolinus Magnus; locked bicycle room, useful if cycling in the area. **Cons:** market is sometimes noisy; somewhat inattentive staff; simple decor. [$] *Rooms from: €85* ✉ *Markt 11* ☎ *03445/2470* 🌐 *www.hotel-stadt-aachen.de* 🛏 *38 rooms* 🍽 *No meals.*

FREYBURG

10 km (6 miles) north of Naumburg.

Stepping off the train in the sleepy town of Freyburg, it is not difficult to see why locals call the area "the Tuscany of the North." With clean, wandering streets, whitewashed buildings, and a huge castle perched on a vine-terraced hill, Freyburg is a little out of place. The town owes its existence to Schloss Neuenburg, which was built by the same Thuringian count who built the Wartburg. Although most visitors head straight for the wine, the historic Old Town and castle certainly warrant a visit.

Freyburg is surrounded by a ¾-mile-long, almost completely intact city wall. The **Ekstädter Tor** was the most important gate into the city and dates from the 14th century. The gate is dominated by one of the few remaining barbicans in central Germany.

GETTING HERE AND AROUND

Hourly trains connect Naumburg and Freyburg in nine minutes. Bike paths along the Unstrut River are a pleasure to cycle. The most serene way to reach Freyburg is to take a small steamboat.

VISITOR INFORMATION

Contacts Freyburger Fremdenverkehrsverein. ✉ *Markt 2* ☎ *034464/27260, 034464/273–760* 🌐 *www.freyburg-info.de.*

EXPLORING

Rotkäppchen Sektkellerei (*Little Red Riding Hood Sparkling Wine*). Freyburg is the home of one of Europe's largest producers of sparkling wine, a rare eastern German product with a significant market share in the West. Hour-long tours of the production facility include the world's largest wooden wine barrel. ✉ *Sektkellereistr. 5* ☎ *034464/340* 🌐 *www.rotkaeppchen.de* 🎫 *€5.*

St. Marien Kirche (*St. Mary's Church*). In 1225 the Thuringian count Ludwig IV erected the St. Marien Kirche as a triple-naved basilica and the only church within the city walls. The coquina limestone building, which resembles the cathedral in Naumburg, was renovated in the 15th century into its current form as a single-hall structure. The great carved altarpiece also dates from the 15th century and the baptistery from 1592. ✉ *Markt 2.*

Schloss Neuenburg (*Neuenburg Castle*). Since its foundation was laid in 1090 by the Thuringian Ludwig I, this castle has loomed protectively over Freyburg. The spacious residential area and huge towers date from the 13th century, when Neuenburg was a part of Thuringia's eastern defenses. The spartan Gothic double-vaulted chapel from 1190 is one of the few rooms that evoke an early medieval past, since most of the castle was renovated in the 15th century. ✉ *Schloss 1* ☎ *34464/35530* 🌐 *www.schloss-neuenburg.de* 🎫 *€7* 🕒 *Closed Mon. Nov.–Mar.*

Winzervereinigung-Freyburg (*Freyburg Vintner's Association*). The best way to try Salle-Unstrut wine is with this trade group. Its 500 members produce some of Germany's finest wines, both white and red, mostly pure varietals, with some limited blends. (A wonderful light red from a hybrid of the Blauer Zweigelt and St. James grapes, called Andre, may change how you think about German red wine.) Tastings and tours must be arranged in advance—with options ranging from a simple tour of one of Germany's largest barrel cellars to the grand tasting (€16)—or you can simply show up on Friday at 1 (€12). The association goes out of its way to cater to the tastes of its guests, and bread, cheese, and water are always in plentiful supply. ✉ *Querfurter Str. 10* ☎ *034464/30623* 🌐 *www.winzervereinigung-freyburg.de.*

WHERE TO EAT

$ GERMAN 🍴 **Burgwirtschaft.** Where better than a castle serenely overlooking the village of Freyburg for a medieval restaurant? Everything is prepared according to historical recipes with ingredients from the region. **Known for:** medieval-style roast meats, like chicken with honey; views of the Unstrut Valley; spacious beer garden. [$] *Average main: €10* ✉ *Schloss 1* ☎ *034464/66200* 🌐 *www.burgwirtschaft.de.*

QUEDLINBURG

95 km (59 miles) northwest of Leipzig.

This medieval Harz town has more half-timber houses than any other town in Germany: more than 1,600 of them line the narrow cobblestone streets and squares. The town escaped destruction during World War II and was treasured in GDR days, though not very well preserved. Today the nicely restored town is a UNESCO World Heritage Site.

For nearly 200 years Quedlinburg was a favorite imperial residence and site of imperial diets, beginning with the election in 919 of Henry the Fowler (Henry I) as the first Saxon king of Germany. It became a major trading city and a member of the Hanseatic League, equal in stature to Cologne (Köln).

GETTING HERE AND AROUND

Quedlinburg lies on a spur rail line between Magdeburg and Thale. Despite being difficult to reach by train, it is still well worth the trouble. The train station is 1 km (½ mile) from the city center. Quedlinburg is an easy drive, 80 km (50 miles), from both Dessau (along the B-71) or from Halle (following the B-80).

VISITOR INFORMATION

Contacts Quedlinburg Tourismus-Marketing GmbH. ⊠ *Markt 2* ☎ *03946/905–624, 03946/905–629* ⊕ *www.quedlinburg.de.*

EXPLORING

Lyonel Feininger Gallery. This sophisticated, modern gallery is placed behind half-timber houses so as not to affect the town's medieval feel. When the art of American-born painter Lyonel Feininger, a Bauhaus teacher in both Weimar and Dessau, was declared "decadent" by the Hitler regime in 1938, the artist returned to America. Left behind with a friend were engravings, lithographs, etchings, and paintings. The most comprehensive Feininger print collection in the world is displayed here. ⊠ *Finkenherd 5a* ☎ *03946/2238* ⊕ *www.feininger-galerie.de* 🖾 *€6* ⊗ *Closed Tues.*

Marktplatz. The Altstadt (Old Town) is full of richly decorated half-timber houses, particularly along Mühlgraben, Schuhof, the Hölle, Breitestrasse, and Schmalstrasse. Notable on the Marktplatz are the Renaissance **Rathaus,** with a 14th-century statue of Roland signifying the town's independence, and the baroque 1701 **Haus Grünhagen.** Street and hiking maps and guidebooks (almost all in German) are available in the information office at the Rathaus. ⊠ *Markt 2* ☎ *03946/90550* 🖾 *Free.*

Schlossmuseum (*Castle Museum*). Quedlinburg's largely Renaissance castle buildings perch on top of the Schlossberg (Castle Hill), with a terrace overlooking woods and valley. The grounds include the Schlossmuseum, which has exhibits on the history of the town and castle, artifacts of the Bronze Age, and the wooden cage in which a captured 14th-century robber baron was put on public view. Restored 17th- and 18th-century rooms give an impression of castle life at that time. ⊠ *Schlossberg 1* ☎ *03946/2730* 🖾 *€5.*

Adorable Quedlinburg has 1,600 half-timber houses: that's more than any other town in Germany.

Ständerbau Fachwerkmuseum (*Half-Timber House*). The oldest half-timber house in Quedlinburg, built about 1310, is now a museum. ⊠ *Wordg. 3* ☎ *03946/3828* ⌨ *€3* ☉ *Closed Mon. and Tues.*

Stiftskirche St. Servatius (*Collegiate Church of St. Servatius*). This simple, graceful church is one of the most important and best-preserved 12th-century Romanesque structures in Germany. Henry I and his wife Mathilde are buried in its crypt. The renowned Quedlinburg Treasure of 10th-, 11th-, and 12th-century gold and silver and bejeweled manuscripts is also kept here (what's left of it). Nazi SS leader Heinrich Himmler made the church into a shrine dedicated to the SS, insisting that it was only appropriate, since Henry I was the founder of the first German Reich. ⊠ *Schlossberg 1* ☎ *03946/709–900* ⌨ *€5* ☉ *Closed Mon.*

WHERE TO EAT

$ ✕ **Lüdde Bräu.** Brewing *Braunbier* (a hoppy, top-fermented beer) has been
GERMAN a Quedlinburg tradition for several centuries, and this brewpub offers both locally made beer and food to go with it. The Lüdde brewery traces its history to 1807, when Braunbier breweries dotted the Harz Mountains, and it was the last surviving brewery when it closed its doors in 1966, reopening after German reunification. **Known for:** Braunbier called Pubarschknall; incredible beer-based game dishes; pleasant beer garden. $ *Average main: €12* ⊠ *Carl-Ritter-Str. 1* ☎ *03946/901–481* ⊕ *www.hotel-brauhaus-luedde.de.*

WHERE TO STAY

$ HOTEL **Hotel Zum Brauhaus.** In a beautifully restored half-timber house, many of the rooms feature bare load-bearing timbers and have pleasant views of the castle. **Pros:** friendly staff; location next to Lüdde brewery; traditional Quedlinburg half-timber house. **Cons:** a little rough around the edges; upper rooms get hot in summer; noise from restaurant and beer garden. [$] *Rooms from: €89* ✉ *Carl-Ritter-Str. 1* ☎ *03946/901–481* 🌐 *www.hotel-brauhaus-luedde.de* *51 rooms* 🍴 *Free Breakfast.*

$ HOTEL **Hotel Zur Goldenen Sonne.** Rooms in this baroque half-timber inn have modern amenities but are furnished in a pleasing, rustic fashion. **Pros:** beautiful half-timber house with modern conveniences; reasonable rates; cozy restaurant. **Cons:** the clock on the square strikes every 15 minutes; rooms in the modern section not quite as nice as the ones in the half-timber house; weekday breakfast not as plentiful as on the weekends. [$] *Rooms from: €79* ✉ *Steinweg 11* ☎ *03946/96250* 🌐 *www.hotelzurgoldenensonne.de* *27 rooms* 🍴 *Free Breakfast.*

EISENACH

140 km (90 miles) southwest of Quedlinburg, 95 km (59 miles) northeast of Fulda.

Standing in Eisenach's ancient market square it's difficult to imagine this half-timber town as a refuge during the Reformation and an important center of the East German automobile industry. Yet this is where Wartburgs (very tiny, noisy, and cheaply produced cars, which are now collector's items) were made. The cars were named after the Wartburg, the famous castle that broods over Eisenach from atop one of the foothills of the Thuringian Forest. Today West German automaker Opel continues the tradition by building one of Europe's most modern car-assembly lines on the outskirts of town.

GETTING HERE AND AROUND

Hourly trains connect Eisenach with Leipzig (two hours) and Dresden (three hours). There are frequent connections to Weimar and Erfurt. Eisenach is about 160 km (100 miles) south of Goslar.

VISITOR INFORMATION

Contacts Eisenach-Information. ✉ *Markt 24* ☎ *03691/79230, 03691/792–320* 🌐 *www.eisenach.de.*

EXPLORING

Bachhaus. Johann Sebastian Bach was born in Eisenach in 1685. The Bachhaus has exhibits devoted to the entire lineage of the musical Bach family and includes a collection of historical musical instruments. It is the largest collection of Bach memorabilia in the world, and displays a bust of the composer built using forensic science from a cast of his skull. The price of admission includes a 20-minute recital using historical instruments, held once per hour. ✉ *Frauenplan 21* ☎ *03691/79340* 🌐 *www.bachhaus.de* 🎫 *€10.*

Lutherhaus. This downtown house has many fascinating exhibits illustrating the life of Martin Luther, who lived here as a student. ✉ *Lutherpl. 8* ☎ *03691/29830* 🌐 *www.lutherhaus-eisenach.de* 🎫 *From €6* ⏲ *Closed Mon. Nov.–Mar.*

Narrowest house. Built in 1890, this is said to be the narrowest house in eastern Germany. Its width is just over 6 feet, 8 inches; its height, 24½ feet; and its depth, 34 feet. ✉ *Johannespl. 9.*

Reuter-Wagner-Museum. Composer Richard Wagner gets his due at this museum, which has the most comprehensive exhibition on Wagner's life and work outside Bayreuth. Monthly concerts take place in the old **Teezimmer** (tearoom), a hall with wonderfully restored French wallpaper. The Erard piano, dating from the late 19th century, is occasionally rolled out. ✉ *Reuterweg 2* ☎ *03691/743–293* 🎫 *€4* ⏲ *Closed Mon.*

Fodor's Choice ★ **Wartburg Castle.** Begun in 1067, this mighty castle has hosted a parade of German celebrities. Legend has it that this is where Walther von der Vogelweide, the greatest lyric poet of medieval Germany, prevailed in the celebrated *Minnesängerstreit* (minnesinger contest), which is featured in Richard Wagner's *Tannhäuser.* Frederick the Wise (1463–1525) shielded Martin Luther here from papal proscription, giving Luther time to finish the first translation of the New Testament from Greek into German. You can peek into the simple study in which Luther worked and see the place where he supposedly saw the devil and threw an inkwell at him. Lucas Cranach the Elder's portraits of Luther and his wife are on view. The 13th-century great hall is breathtaking; it's here that the minstrels sang for courtly favors. Don't leave without climbing the belvedere for a panoramic view of the Harz Mountains and the Thuringian Forest. The only way into the interior of the castle is to take a guided tour (in English daily at 1:30). ✉ *Auf der Wartburg 1* ☎ *03691/2500* 🌐 *www.wartburg-eisenach.de* 🎫 *€10, including guided tour.*

16

WHERE TO EAT

$ GERMAN 🍴 **Brunnenkeller.** This comfortable restaurant serves hearty Thuringian specialties made from local ingredients under medieval vaulted ceilings; the outdoor tables are the perfect place to recharge after exploring the castle. **Known for:** hearty Thuringian cuisine; comfortable vaulted halls; large portions. [$] *Average main: €13* ✉ *Am Markt 10* ☎ *3691/212358* 🌐 *www.brunnenkeller-eisenach.de.*

WHERE TO STAY

$$$$ HOTEL 🏨 **Hotel auf der Wartburg.** In this castle hotel, where Martin Luther, Johann Sebastian Bach, and Richard Wagner were guests, you'll get a splendid view over the town and the countryside. **Pros:** medieval music and fireplaces in the lobby; shuttle bus to the train station; stunning views of the Wartburg. **Cons:** it's a hike to and from the city center; isolated from Eisenach; visitor traffic during the day. [$] *Rooms from: €300* ✉ *Wartburg* ☎ *03691/7970* 🌐 *www.wartburghotel.de* 🛏 *35 rooms* 🍽 *Free Breakfast.*

$ [icon] **Hotel Glockenhof.** At the base of Wartburg Castle, this former church-
HOTEL run hostel has blossomed into a handsome hotel, cleverly incorporating
the original half-timber city mansion into a modern extension. **Pros:**
out of the hustle and bustle of the downtown; plenty of parking; an
incredible breakfast buffet. **Cons:** uphill walk from the station is strenuous; location is a bit far from the city center; some rooms are plain and
somewhat spartan. [$] *Rooms from: €99 ⊠ Grimmelg. 4 ☎ 03691/2340
⊕ www.glockenhof.de ↩ 40 rooms ⵔⵔ Free Breakfast.*

ERFURT

55 km (34 miles) east of Eisenach.

The city of Erfurt emerged from World War II relatively unscathed, with
most of its innumerable towers intact. Of all the cities in the region,
Erfurt is the most evocative of its prewar self, and it's easy to imagine
that many of the towns in northern Germany would look like this
had they not been destroyed. The city's highly decorative and colorful
facades are easy to admire on a walking tour. ■TIP→ Downtown Erfurt
is a photographer's delight, with narrow, busy, ancient streets dominated by a magnificent 14th-century Gothic cathedral, the Mariendom.

GETTING HERE AND AROUND

Hourly trains connect Erfurt with Leipzig (two hours) and Dresden
(three hours). There are frequent connections to Weimar (twice per
hour, 15 minutes) and Eisenach (hourly, 50 minutes). Erfurt is easily
walkable from the train station and the streetcar is easy to use.

VISITOR INFORMATION

Contacts Erfurt Tourist-Information. ⊠ *Benediktspl. 1 ☎ 0361/66400,
0361/664–0290 ⊕ www.erfurt-tourist-info.de.*

EXPLORING

The Anger. Erfurt's main transportation hub and pedestrian zone, the
Anger developed as a result of urban expansion due to the growth of the
railroad in Thuringia in the early 19th century. With some exceptions,
the houses are all architecturally historicized, making them look much
older than they really are. The **Hauptpostgebäude** was erected in 1892
in a mock Gothic style. ⊠ *Erfurt.*

Domplatz (*Cathedral Square*). Erfurt's most picturesque square is bordered by houses dating from the 16th century and dominated by twin
churches. ⊠ *Erfurt.*

Klein Venedig (*Little Venice*). The area around the Krämerbrücke, criss-
crossed with old streets lined with picturesque, often crumbling, homes
and shops, is known as Little Venice because of the recurrent flooding
it endures. ⊠ *Erfurt.*

FodorśChoice **Krämerbrücke** (*Merchant's Bridge*). Behind the predominantly neo-
★ Gothic Rathaus, Erfurt's most outstanding attraction spans the Gera
River. This Renaissance bridge, similar to the Ponte Vecchio in Florence,
is the longest of its kind in Europe and the only one north of the Alps.
Built in 1325 and restored in 1967–73, the bridge served for centuries

as an important trading center. Today antiques shops fill the majority of the timber-frame houses built into the bridge, some dating from the 16th century. The bridge comes alive on the third weekend of June for the Krämerbrückenfest. ✉ *Erfurt.*

Mariendom (*St. Mary's Cathedral*). This cathedral's Romanesque origins (foundations can be seen in the crypt) are best preserved in the choir's glorious stained-glass windows and beautifully carved stalls, and its biggest bell, the Gloriosa, is the largest free-swinging bell in the world. Cast in 1497, it took three years to install in the tallest of the three sharply pointed towers, painstakingly lifted inch by inch with wooden wedges. No chances are taken with this 2-ton treasure; its deep boom resonates only on special occasions, such as Christmas and New Year's. The Mariendom is reached by way of a broad staircase from the expansive Cathedral Square. ✉ *Dompl.* ☎ *0361/646–1265* 🎫 *Free; tour €6.*

St. Augustin Kloster (*St. Augustine Monastery*). The young Martin Luther studied the liberal arts as well as law and theology at Erfurt University from 1501 to 1505. After a personal revelation, Luther asked to become a monk in the St. Augustin Kloster on July 17, 1505. He became an ordained priest here in 1507, and remained at the Kloster until 1511. Today the Kloster is a seminary and retreat hotel. ✉ *Augustinerstr. 10* ☎ *0361/576–600* 🌐 *www.augustinerkloster.de.*

St. Severus. This Gothic church has an extraordinary font, a masterpiece of intricately carved sandstone that reaches practically to the ceiling. It's linked to the cathedral by a 70-step open staircase. ✉ *Dompl.*

16

WHERE TO EAT

$$$$ GERMAN

🍴 **Clara.** This restaurant in the historic, elegant Kaisersaal edifice is the jewel in Erfurt's small gourmet crown. Thuringia native chef Maria Gross has worked in top restaurants around Germany and developed her own minimalist style. **Known for:** traditional Thuringian cuisine with modern interpretations; massive wine list; locally sourced ingredients. [$] *Average main: €107* ✉ *Futterstr. 1, 15–16* ☎ *0361/568–8207* 🌐 *www.restaurant-clara.de* 🕒 *Closed Sun. and Mon. No lunch.*

$ GERMAN FAMILY

🍴 **Luther Keller.** Head down the straw-covered stairs in front of Clara restaurant, and you'll find yourself transported to the Middle Ages. The Luther Keller offers simple but tasty medieval cuisine in a candlelit vaulted cellar. **Known for:** pure kitsch, but completely worthwhile medieval experience; magicians, minnesingers, jugglers, and other players; roast wild boar. [$] *Average main: €14* ✉ *Futterstr. 15* ☎ *0361/568–8205* 🌐 *www.lutherkeller.de* 🕒 *Closed Sun. and Mon. No lunch.*

$ GERMAN

🍴 **Zum Goldenen Schwan.** Beer lovers rejoice: in addition to the Braugold brewery, Erfurt has six brewpubs, among which the Golden Swan is by far the best. The house beer is a pleasant unfiltered *Kellerbier,* and the constantly changing seasonal menu is a step above normal brewpub fare. **Known for:** constantly changing seasonal brews; Thuringian regional cuisine; Germany's best Sauerbraten. [$] *Average main: €12* ✉ *Michaelisstr. 9* ☎ *0361/262–3742* 🌐 *www.zum-goldenen-schwan.de.*

WHERE TO STAY

$$ HOTEL **Radisson Blu Hotel Erfurt.** Since the SAS group gave the ugly high-rise Kosmos a face-lift, the socialist-realist look of the GDR years no longer intrudes on Hotel Erfurt. **Pros:** clean and safe; the hotel has one of Erfurt's best restaurants; centrally located. **Cons:** rather characterless business hotel; sporadic Wi-Fi; small rooms. [$] *Rooms from: €105* ✉ *Juri-Gagarin-Ring 127* ☎ *0361/55100* 🌐 *www.radissonblu.com* *285 rooms* 🍴 *Free Breakfast.*

WEIMAR

21 km (13 miles) east of Erfurt.

Sitting prettily in the geographical center of Thuringia, Weimar occupies a place in German political and cultural history completely disproportionate to its size (population 63,000). It's not even particularly old by German standards, with a civic history that started as late as 1410. Yet by the early 19th century the city had become one of Europe's most important cultural centers, where poets Goethe and Schiller wrote, Johann Sebastian Bach played the organ for his Saxon patrons, Carl Maria von Weber composed some of his best music, and Franz Liszt was director of music, presenting the first performance of *Lohengrin* here. In 1919 Walter Gropius founded his Staatliches Bauhaus here, and behind the classical pillars of the National Theater the German National Assembly drew up the constitution of the Weimar Republic, the first German democracy. As the Weimar Republic began to collapse in 1926, Hitler chose the little city as the site for the second national congress of his Nazi party, where he founded the Hitler Youth. On the outskirts of Weimar the Nazis built—or forced prisoners to build for them—the infamous Buchenwald concentration camp. In 2019, the Bauhaus celebrates its 100th anniversary. Be sure to look for the many events in Weimar, Dessau, and Berlin.

GETTING HERE AND AROUND

Weimar is on the InterCity Express (ICE) line between Dresden/Leipzig and Frankfurt. InterCity (IC) trains link the city with Berlin. Weimar has an efficient bus system, but most sights are within walking distance in the compact city center. If you plan on visiting four or more of Weimar's fine collection of museums and cultural sites, consider using the 48-hour WeimarCard (€29.90), which is valid for the city buses as well.

VISITOR INFORMATION

Contacts Tourist-Information Weimar. ✉ *Markt 10* ☎ *03643/7450, 03643/745–420* 🌐 *www.weimar.de.*

EXPLORING

Bauhaus Museum. Walter Gropius founded the Staatliches Bauhaus (Bauhaus design school) in Weimar in 1919, which has relocated and will open in a new location in April 2019. It was Germany's most influential and avant-garde design school, and it ushered in the era of modern architecture and design just before the start of World War II. Although the school moved to Dessau in 1925, Weimar's Bauhaus Museum is a modest, yet superb collection of the works of Gropius, Johannes Itten, and Henry van de Velde. ✉ *Stéphane-Hessel-Pl. 1* ☎ *03643/545–400* ⊕ *www.bauhausmuseumweimar.de* ⌑ *€10* ⊙ *Closed Mon.*

Bauhaus University. Although the current name, Bauhaus University, only dates from 1996, Walter Gropius renamed the former Great Ducal Saxon Art School as the Bauhaus in 1919. His goal was to challenge the status quo and create a more humanized modernity that fused art and design into architecture and city planning. Henry van de Velde, who suggested Gropius for his position in Weimar, completed what is now the main administrative building of the university in 1911. Although it was conceived as an art nouveau structure, Van de Velde's studio is one of the best-preserved Bauhaus buildings in Germany—be sure to look for the free-standing staircase in the foyer of the building. Van de Velde also designed the horseshoe-shape gable of the Art Faculty in 1906. ✉ *Geschwister-Scholl-Str. 8* ⊕ *www.uni-weimar.de.*

Gedenkstätte Buchenwald (*Buchenwald Memorial*). Just north of Weimar, amid the natural beauty of the Ettersberg hills that once served as Goethe's inspiration, sits the blight of Buchenwald, one of the most infamous Nazi concentration camps. Fifty-six thousand men, women, and children from 35 countries met their deaths here through forced labor, starvation, disease, and gruesome medical experiments. Each is commemorated by a small stone placed on the outlines of the barracks, which have long since disappeared from the site, and by a massive memorial tower. In an especially cruel twist of fate, many liberated inmates returned to the camp as political prisoners of the Soviet occupation; they are remembered in the exhibit *Soviet Special Camp #2.* Besides exhibits, tours are available. To reach Buchenwald by public transportation, take Bus 6 (in the direction of Buchenwald, not Ettersburg), which leaves every 10 minutes from Goetheplatz in downtown Weimar. The one-way fare is €1.90. ✉ *Gedenkstätte Buchenwald ⊹ 10 km (6.2 miles) northwest of Weimar* ☎ *03643/430–200* ⊕ *www.buchenwald.de* ⌑ *Free* ⊙ *Closed Mon.*

Fodor's Choice ★ **Goethe Nationalmuseum** (*Goethe National Museum*). Goethe spent 57 years in Weimar, 47 of them in a house two blocks south of Theaterplatz that has since become a shrine attracting millions of visitors. The Goethe Nationalmuseum consists of several houses, including the **Goethehaus,** where Goethe lived. It shows an exhibit about life in Weimar around 1750 and contains writings that illustrate not only the great man's literary might but also his interest in the sciences, particularly medicine, and his administrative skills (and frustrations) as minister of state and Weimar's exchequer. You'll see the desk at which Goethe stood to write (he liked to work standing up) and the modest bed in which he died. The rooms are dark and often cramped, but an almost palpable intellectual intensity seems to illuminate them. ✉ *Frauenplan 1* ☎ *03643/545–320* ⊕ *www.klassik-stiftung.de* ⌑ *€13* ⊙ *Closed Mon.*

Goethes Gartenhaus (*Garden House*). Goethe's beloved Gartenhaus is a modest country cottage where he spent many happy hours, wrote much poetry, and began his masterly classical drama *Iphigenie.* The house is

16

Take a carriage ride through Weimar to absorb the city's impressive history.

set amid meadowlike parkland on the bank of the River Ilm. Goethe is said to have felt very close to nature here, and you can soak up the same rural atmosphere on footpaths along the peaceful little river. ⊠ *Im Park an der Ilm, Hans-Wahl-Str. 4* ☎ *03643/545–400* ⊕ *www.klassik-stiftung.de* ⤳ *€7* ⊘ *Closed Mon.*

Haus am Horn. This modest, cubical structure designed by Georg Muche for the 1923 Bauhaus exhibition is the first structure constructed using the Bauhaus's new philosophy of functional modernity. The house is a small cubist structure comprised of concrete and stone walls with a flat roof. All of the furniture was created specifically for the house by students of the Bauhaus design school. ⊠ *Am Horn 61* ☎ *03643/904–056.*

Herderkirche (*Herder Church*). The Marktplatz's late-Gothic church has a large winged altar started by Lucas Cranach the Elder and finished by his son in 1555. The elder Cranach lived in a nearby house (two blocks east of Theaterplatz) during his last years, 1552–53. Its wide, imposing facade is richly decorated and bears the coat of arms of the Cranach family. It now houses a modern art gallery. ⊠ *Herderpl. 8* ⊕ *www.ek-weimar.de.*

Historischer Friedhof (*Historic Cemetery*). Goethe and Schiller are buried in this leafy cemetery, where virtually every gravestone commemorates a famous citizen of Weimar. Their tombs are in the vault of the classical-style chapel. The cemetery is a short walk past Goethehaus and Wieland Platz. ⊠ *Am Poseckschen Garten* ☎ *03643/545–400* ⤳ *Goethe-Schiller vault €4.*

Neues Museum Weimar (*New Museum Weimar*). The city is proud of eastern Germany's first museum exclusively devoted to contemporary art, which is under renovation and expected to reopen in April 2019, in time for the 100th anniversary of Bauhaus. The building, dating from 1869, was carefully restored and converted to hold collections of American minimalist and conceptual art and works by German installation-artist Anselm Kiefer and American painter Keith Haring. In addition, it regularly presents international modern-art exhibitions. ✉ *Jorge-Semprún-Pl. 5* ☎ *03643/545–400* 🌐 *www.klassik-stiftung.de* 🎫 *€8* 🕒 *Closed Mon.*

Schillerhaus. This green-shuttered residence, part of the Goethe Nationalmuseum, is on a tree-shaded square not far from Goethe's house. Schiller and his family spent a happy, all-too-brief three years here (he died here in 1805). Schiller's study is tucked underneath the mansard roof, a cozy room dominated by his desk, where he probably completed *Wilhelm Tell*. Much of the remaining furniture and the collection of books were added later, although they all date from around Schiller's time. ✉ *Schillerstr. 17* ☎ *03643/545–400* 🌐 *www.klassik-stiftung.de* 🎫 *€8* 🕒 *Closed Mon.*

Theaterplatz. A statue on this square, in front of the National Theater, shows Goethe placing a paternal hand on the shoulder of the younger Schiller. ✉ *Weimar.*

16

Wittumspalais (*Wittum Mansion*). Much of Weimar's greatness is owed to its patron, the widowed countess Anna Amalia, whose home, the Wittumspalais, is surprisingly modest. In the late 18th century the countess went talent hunting for cultural figures to decorate the glittering court her Saxon forebears had established. She discovered Goethe, and he served the countess as a counselor, advising her on financial matters and town design. Schiller followed, and he and Goethe became valued visitors to the countess's home. Within this exquisite baroque house you can see the drawing room in which she held soirées, complete with the original cherrywood table at which the company sat. The east wing of the house contains a small museum that's a fascinating memorial to those cultural gatherings. ✉ *Am Theaterpl.* ☎ *03643/545–377* 🎫 *€6* 🕒 *Closed Mon.*

WHERE TO EAT

$ GERMAN 🍴 **Felsenkeller.** When Ludwig Deinhard purchased the Weimar Stadtbrauerei in 1875, Felsenkeller was already 100 years old. Beer has been brewed here in small batches ever since. **Known for:** changing seasonal local beers; hearty Thuringian brewery cuisine; good value. [$] *Average main: €11* ✉ *Humboldtstr. 37* ☎ *03643/414–741* 💳 *No credit cards* 🕒 *Closed Mon.*

$ GERMAN 🍴 **Ratskeller.** This is one of the region's most authentic town hall–cellar restaurants. Its whitewashed, barrel-vaulted ceiling and spectacular art nouveau skylight have witnessed centuries of tradition. **Known for:** Weimar's best Sauerbraten; roast venison, when in season; wild game. [$] *Average main: €12* ✉ *Am Markt 10* ☎ *03643/850–573.*

$ GERMAN FAMILY 🍴 **Scharfe Ecke.** If *Klösse* (dumplings) are a Thuringia religion, this restaurant is their cathedral. Thuringia's traditional Klösse are at their best here, but be patient—they're made to order and can take up to 20 minutes. **Known for:** Thuringian dumplings; Roast game; local beer and wine. [$] *Average main: €12* ✉ *Eisfeld 2* ☎ *03643/202–430* 💳 *No credit cards* 🕒 *Closed Mon.*

WHERE TO STAY

$ HOTEL **Amalienhof VCH Hotel.** Book far ahead to secure a room at this friendly little hotel central to Weimar's attractions. **Pros:** surprisingly good value; rooms are often upgraded to the highest available category at check-in; massive Breakfast buffet. **Cons:** street noise can be bothersome; some rooms can be somewhat spartan; rooms need more electrical outlets. [$] *Rooms from: €95* ✉ *Amalienstr. 2* ☎ *03643/5490* 🌐 *www.amalienhof-weimar.de* 🛏 *32 rooms* 🍴 *Free Breakfast.*

$$ HOTEL Fodor's Choice ★ **Grand Hotel Russischer Hof.** This historic, classical hotel, once the haunt of European nobility and intellectual society, continues to be a luxurious gem in the heart of Weimar—it's one of Germany's finest hotels. **Pros:** quiet location in the city center; service is impeccable; good restaurant Anastasia ($$) serves fine Austrian-Thuringian fusion cuisine. **Cons:** rooms are on the small side; rooms have thin walls; some rooms overlook an unsightly back courtyard. [$] *Rooms from: €135* ✉ *Goethepl. 2* ☎ *03643/7740* 🌐 *www.russischerhof.com* 🛏 *125 rooms* 🍴 *No meals.*

$$ HOTEL Fodor's Choice ★ **Hotel Elephant.** The historic Elephant, dating from 1696, has long been famous for its charm—even through the Communist years. **Pros:** beautiful art deco–bauhaus hotel; directly in the city center; attentive staff. **Cons:** no air-conditioning; rooms in the front are sometimes bothered by the town clock if windows are open; often completely booked. [$] *Rooms from: €150* ✉ *Markt 19* ☎ *03643/8020* 🌐 *www.hotelelephantweimar.com* 🛏 *99 rooms* 🍴 *Free Breakfast.*

TRAVEL SMART GERMANY

GETTING HERE AND AROUND

Germany's transportation infrastructure is extremely well developed, so all areas of the country are well connected to each other by road, rail, and air. The autobahns are an efficient system of highways, although they can get crowded during holidays. In winter you may have to contend with closed passes in the Alps or difficult driving on smaller roads in the Black Forest and the Saarland region. High-speed trains are perhaps the most comfortable way of traveling. Munich to Hamburg, for example, a trip of around 966 km (600 miles), takes 5½ hours. Many airlines offer extremely cheap last-minute flights, but you have to be fairly flexible.

∎ AIR TRAVEL

Flying time to Frankfurt, one of Europe's biggest and busiest airports, is 1½ hours from London, 7½ hours from New York, 10 hours from Chicago, and 12 hours from Los Angeles.

AIRLINES

Lufthansa is Germany's leading carrier and has shared mileage plans and flights with Air Canada and United, as well as all members of the Star Alliance.

Germany's internal air network is excellent, with flights linking all major cities in, at most, little more than an hour. A handful of smaller airlines (Germanwings, EasyJet, and TUIfly) compete with low-fare flights within Germany and to other European cities. These companies are reliable, do business almost exclusively over the Internet (since talking to an actual person drives the price of the ticket up astronomically), and often beat the German rail fares. The earlier you book, the cheaper the fare.

∎TIP➔ **Although a budget airfare may not be refundable, new EU regulations require that all other supplemental fees and taxes are. That means that when the**

€1 fare from Berlin to Munich turns out to cost €70 with fuel surcharges and the like, you only lose €1. Refund procedures vary between airlines.

Major Airlines Air Canada. ☎ 888/247–2262 in Canada and U.S. ⊕ www.aircanada.com. **American Airlines.** ☎ 800/433–7300 ⊕ www. aa.com. **British Airways.** ☎ 800/247–9297 ⊕ www.ba.com. **Delta Air Lines.** ☎ 800/241– 4141 ⊕ www.delta.com. **Lufthansa.** ☎ 800/645–3880 in U.S. ⊕ www.lufthansa.com. **United Airlines.** ☎ 800/864–8331 for U.S. reservations, 800/538–2929 for international reservations ⊕ www.united.com.

Airlines Within Germany EasyJet. ⊕ www. easyjet.com. **Germanwings.** ⊕ www.german-wings.com. **TUIfly.** ⊕ www.tuifly.com.

AIRPORTS

Frankfurt is Germany's primary air hub. The large airport has the convenience of its own long-distance train station, but if you're transferring between flights, don't dawdle or you could miss your connection.

Munich is Germany's second air hub, with many services to North America and Asia. The airport is like a minicity, with plenty of activities to keep you entertained during a long layover. Experience a true German tradition and have a beer from the world's first airport brewery at the Hofbräuhaus here. For a more active layover, play miniature golf, beach volleyball, or soccer, or ice-skate in winter. There's also a playground. Live concerts and 150 shops with downtown prices draw locals to the airport as well. If you're an airplane aficionado (and German speaker), you can take advantage of a small cinema showing movies on aviation themes or take a bus tour of the airport's facilities, including maintenance hangars and engine-testing facilities. Looking for some R&R? The airport offers massages at the gate, relaxation zones, and "napcabs" (soundproof minirooms to nap in). Munich's S-bahn railway connects the airport with the city center; trips take about 40 minutes, and trains leave every 10 minutes.

United has nonstop service between New York and Berlin-Tegel. Major airlines, like Lufthansa, fly in and out of Berlin-Tegel, while most budget airlines use Berlin-Schönefeld. Once the Berlin Brandenburg airport finally opens—it was originally slated to open in 2011, but it likely won't open until late 2020—both Tegel and Schönefeld will close.

United also has nonstop service between New York and Hamburg. There are a few nonstop services from North America to Düsseldorf. Stuttgart is convenient to the Black Forest. Also convenient to the Black Forest is the EuroAirport Freiburg-Basel-Mulhouse, which is used by many airlines for European destinations and as a stopover.

CONTACTS
Berlin Berlin Schönefeld (*SXF*). ⊕ *www. berlin-airport.de.* Berlin Tegel (*TXL*). ⊕ *www. berlin-airport.de.* EuroAirport Freiburg-Basel-Mulhouse (*MLH*). ⊕ *www.euroairport. com.* Flughafen Düsseldorf (*DUS*). ⊕ *www. dus.com.* Flughafen Frankfurt Main (*FRA*). ☎ ⊕ *www.frankfurt-airport.de.* Hamburg International Airport (*HAM*). ⊕ *www.hamburg. airport.de.* Flughafen Köln/Bonn (*CGN*). ⊕ *www.koeln-bonn-airport.de.* Flughafen München (*MUC*). ⊕ *www.munich-airport.de.* Flughafen Stuttgart (*STR*). ⊕ *www.flughafen-stuttgart.de.*

▌ BOAT TRAVEL

Eurailpasses and German Rail Passes are honored by KD Rhine Line on the Rhine River and on the Mosel River between Trier and Koblenz. (If you use the fast hydrofoil, a supplementary fee is required.) The rail lines follow the Rhine and Mosel rivers most of their length, meaning you can go one way by ship and return by train. Cruises generally operate between April and October. If you are planning to visit Denmark or Sweden

after Germany, note that Scandlines ferries offer discounts for Eurailpass owners.
Information KD Rhine Line. ☎ *0221/208-8318* ⊕ *www.k-d.com.* Scandlines. ☎ *0381/7788-7766 in Germany* ⊕ *www. scandlines.de.*

▌ BUS TRAVEL

Germany has good local and long-distance bus service. Many cities are served by BerlinLinien Bus or MeinFernBus. Deutsche Touring, a subsidiary of the Deutsche Bahn, has offices and agents countrywide, and travels from Germany to cities elsewhere in Europe. It offers one-day tours along the Castle Road and the Romantic Road. The Romantic Road route is between Würzburg (with connections to and from Frankfurt) and Füssen (with connections to and from Munich, Augsburg, and Garmisch-Partenkirchen). With a Eurailpass or German Rail Pass you get a 20% discount on this route. Buses, with an attendant on board, travel in each direction between April and October.

All towns of any size have local buses, which often link up with trams (streetcars) and electric railway (S-bahn) and subway (U-bahn) services. Fares sometimes vary according to distance, but a ticket usually allows you to transfer freely between the various forms of transportation.

Bus Information Deutsche Touring. ☎ *069/719126-100* ⊕ *www.touring-travel.eu.* Flixbus/MeinFernBus. ☎ *030/3001-37300* ⊕ *www.flixbus.de.* IC Bus (Deutsche Bahn's long-distance bus). ☎ *01806/996-633 in Germany* ⊕ *www.bahn.com.*

▌ CAR TRAVEL

Entry formalities for motorists are few: all you need is proof of insurance; an international car-registration document; and a U.S., Canadian, Australian, or New Zealand driver's license. If you are or your car is from an EU country, Norway, or Switzerland, all you need is your domestic license and proof of insurance. *All* foreign cars must have a country sticker. There are no toll roads in Germany, except for a few Alpine mountain passes, although the autobahn may change to a toll system in 2017. Many large German cities require an environmental sticker on the front windshield. If your rental car doesn't have one, it's likely you'll be required to pay the fine.

CAR RENTAL

It is easy to rent a car in Germany, but not always cheap. You will need an International Driving Permit (IDP); it's available from the American Automobile Association (AAA) and the National Automobile Club. These international permits are universally recognized, and having one in your wallet may save you problems with the local authorities. In Germany you usually must be 21 to rent a car. Nearly all agencies allow you to drive into Germany's neighboring countries. It's frequently possible to return the car in another West European country, but not in Poland or the Czech Republic, for example.

Rates with the major car-rental companies begin at about €55 per day and €300 per week for an economy car with a manual transmission and unlimited mileage. It is invariably cheaper to rent a car in advance from home than to do it on the fly in Germany. Most rentals are manual, so if you want an automatic, be sure to request one in advance. If you're traveling with children, don't forget to ask for a car seat when you reserve. Note that in some major cities, even automobile-producing Stuttgart, rental firms are prohibited from placing signs at major pickup and drop-off locations, such as the main train station. If dropping a car off in an unfamiliar city, you might have to guess your way to the station's underground parking garage; once there, look for a generic sign such as *Mietwagen* (rental cars). The German railway system, Deutsche Bahn, offers discounts on rental cars.

Depending on what you would like to see, you may or may not need a car for all or part of your stay. Most parts of Germany are connected by reliable rail service, so it might be a better plan to take a train to the region you plan to visit and rent a car only for side trips to out-of-the-way destinations.

Major Rental Agencies Avis. ☎ 800/633–3469 *in U.S.* ⊕ *www.avis.com.* **Budget.** ☎ 800/472–3325 *international reservations* ⊕ *www.budget.com.* **Europcar.** ⊕ *www.europcar.com.* **Hertz.** ☎ 800/654–3001 *in U.S.* ⊕ *www.hertz.com.*

Car Rental Comparison Sites Auto Europe. ☎ 888/223–5555 ⊕ *www.autoeurope.com.* **Avanti Destinations.** ☎ 800/422–5053 ⊕ *www.avantidestinations.com.* **Kemwel.** ☎ 877/820–0668 ⊕ *www.kemwel.com.*

GASOLINE

Gasoline costs are around €1.30 per liter—which is higher than in the United States. Some cars use diesel fuel, which is about €0.20 cheaper. If you're renting a car, find out which fuel the car takes. German filling stations are highly competitive, and bargains are often available if you shop around, but *not* at autobahn filling stations. Self-service, or *SB-Tanken,* stations are cheapest. Pumps marked *Bleifrei* contain unleaded gas.

PARKING

Daytime parking in cities and small, historic towns is difficult to find. Restrictions are not always clearly marked and can be hard to understand even when they are. Rental cars come with a "time wheel," which you can leave on your dashboard when parking signs indicate free, limited-time allowances. Larger parking lots have parking meters (*Parkautomaten*). After depositing enough change in a meter, you will be issued a timed ticket to display on your dashboard. Parking-meter spaces are free at night. In German garages you must pay immediately on returning to retrieve your car, not when driving out. Put the ticket you got on arrival into the machine and pay the amount displayed. Retrieve the ticket, and upon exiting the garage, insert the ticket in a slot to raise the barrier. ■TIP→ **You must lock your car when it is parked. Failure to do so risks a €25 fine and liability for anything that happens if the car is stolen.**

ROAD CONDITIONS

Roads are generally excellent. *Bundesstrassen* are two-lane state highways, abbreviated "B," as in B-38. Autobahns are high-speed thruways abbreviated with "A," as in A-7. If the autobahn should be blocked for any reason, you can take an exit and follow little signs bearing a "U" followed by a number. These are official detours.

ROADSIDE EMERGENCIES

The German automobile clubs ADAC and AvD operate tow trucks on all autobahns. "Notruf" signs every 2 km (1 mile) on autobahns (and country roads) indicate emergency telephones. Help is free (with the exception of materials).

Emergency Services Roadside assistance. ☎ *01802/222-222.*

RULES OF THE ROAD

There *are* posted speed limits on most of the autobahns, and they advise drivers to keep below 130 kph (80 mph) or 110 kph (65 mph). A sign saying "Richtgeschwindigkeit and the speed indicates this. Slower traffic should stay in the right lane of the autobahn, but speeds under 80 kph (50 mph) are not permitted. Speed limits on country roads vary from 70 kph to 100 kph (43 mph to 62 mph) and are usually 50 kph (30 mph) through small towns.

Don't enter a street with a signpost bearing a red circle with a white horizontal stripe—it's a one-way street. Blue "Einbahnstrasse" signs indicate you're headed the correct way down a one-way street. The blood-alcohol limit for driving in Germany is very low (0.05%), and passengers, but not the driver, are allowed to consume alcoholic beverages in the car. Note that seatbelts must be worn at all times by front- *and* back-seat passengers.

German drivers tend to drive fast and aggressively. There is no right turn at a red light in Germany. Though prohibited, tailgating is the national pastime on German roads.

You may not use a handheld mobile phone while driving.

■ CRUISE SHIP TRAVEL

River cruises are popular in Germany. You can go on a multiday voyage with a company like Viking River Cruises tours; the Rhine, Mosel, Elbe, and Danube are all popular rivers. Day cruises on the Köln–Düsseldorfer Deutsche Rheinschiffahrt (KD Rhine Line) are offered between Easter and October on the Rhine between Cologne and Mainz, and between May and October on the Mosel between Koblenz and Cochem.

Cruise Lines KD Rhine Line. ☎ *0221/208–8318* ⊕ *www.k-d.com.* **Viking River Cruises.** ☎ *800/706–1483 in U.S.* ⊕ *www.vikingrivercruises.com.*

■ TRAIN TRAVEL

Deutsche Bahn (DB—German Rail) is a very efficient, semi-privatized railway. Its high-speed InterCity Express (ICE), InterCity (IC), and EuroCity (EC) trains make journeys between the centers of many cities (Munich–Frankfurt, for example) faster by rail than by air. All InterCity and InterCity Express trains have restaurant cars and trolley service. RE, RB, and IRE trains are regional trains. It's also possible to sleep on the train and save a day of your trip: a decreasing number of CityNightLine (CNL) trains serving domestic destinations and neighboring countries have sleepers, couches, and recliners.

Once on your platform or *Bahnsteig*—the area between two tracks—you can check the notice boards that give details of the layout of trains (*Wagenstandanzeiger*) arriving on that track (*Gleis*). They show the locations of first- and second-class cars and the restaurant car, as well as where they will stop, relative to the lettered sectors, along the platform. Large railroad stations have English-speaking staff handling information inquiries.

For fare and schedule information, the Deutsche Bahn information line connects you to a live operator; you may have to wait a few moments before someone can help you in English. The automated number is toll-free and gives schedule information. Deutsche Bahn has an excellent website (⊕ *www.bahn.de*), available in English. To calculate the fare, enter your departure and arrival points, any town you wish to pass through, and whether you have a bike. The fare finder will tell you which type of train you'll be riding on—which could be important if you suffer from motion sickness. The ICE, the French TGV, the Swiss ICN, and the Italian Cisalpino all use "tilt technology" for a less jerky ride. One side effect, however, is that some passengers might feel queasy, especially if the track is curvy. An over-the-counter drug for motion sickness should help.

BAGGAGE

Most major train stations have luggage lockers (in four sizes) that cost between €2 and €5 (exact change required).

Throughout Germany, Deutsche Bahn can deliver your baggage from a private residence or hotel to another or even to one of six airports: Berlin, Frankfurt, Leipzig-Halle, Munich, Hamburg, or Hannover. You must have a valid rail ticket. Buy a *Kuriergepäck* ticket at any DB ticket counter, at which time you must schedule a pickup three workdays before your flight. The service costs €38 for a medium suitcase up to 31 kg (68 pounds).

DISCOUNTS

Deutsche Bahn offers many discount options with specific conditions, so do your homework on its website or ask about options at the counter before paying for a full-price ticket. For round-trip travel you can save 25% if you book at least three days in advance, 50% if you stay over a Saturday night and book at least three to seven days in advance.

However, there's a limited number of seats sold at any of these discount prices, so book as early as possible, at least a week in advance, to get the savings. A discounted rate is called a *Sparpreis*. If you change your travel plans after booking, you will have to pay a fee. The surcharge for tickets bought on board is 10% of the ticket cost, or a minimum of €5. Most local, RE, and RB services do not allow purchasing tickets on board. Not having a ticket is considered *Schwarzfahren* (riding black) and is usually subject to a €60 fine. Tickets booked at a counter always cost more than over the Internet or from an automated ticket machine.

Children under 15 travel free when accompanied by a parent or relative on normal, discounted, and some, but not all, special-fare tickets. However, you must indicate the number of children traveling with you when you purchase the ticket; to ride free, the child (or children) must be listed on the ticket. If you have a ticket with 25% or 50% off, a *Mitfahrer-Rabatt* allows a second person to travel with you for a 50% discount (minimum of €15 for a second-class ticket). The *Schönes Wochenend Ticket* (Happy Weekend Ticket) provides unlimited travel on regional trains on weekends for up to five persons for €42 (€40 if purchased online or at a vending machine). Groups of six or more should inquire about *Gruppen & Spar* (group) savings. Each German state, or *Land*, has its own *Länder-Ticket*, which lets up to five people travel from 9 am to 3 am for around €25.

If you plan to travel by train within a day after your flight arrives, purchase a heavily discounted "Rail and Fly" ticket for DB trains at the same time you book your flight. Trains connect with 14 German airports and two airports outside Germany, Basel and Amsterdam.

FARES

A first-class seat is approximately 55% more than a second-class seat. For this premium you get a bit more legroom and the convenience of having meals (not included) delivered directly to your seat. Many regional trains offer an upgrade to first class for as little as €4. This is especially helpful on weekends when local trains are stuffed with cyclists and day-tripping locals. ICs and the later-generation ICE trains are equipped with electrical outlets for laptops and other gadgets.

Tickets purchased through Deutsche Bahn's website can be retrieved from station vending machines. Always check that your ticket is valid for the type of train you are planning to take, not just for the destination served. If you have the wrong type of ticket, you will have to pay the difference on the train, in cash or by credit card. If you book an online ticket and print it yourself, you must present the credit card used to pay for the ticket to the conductor for the ticket to be valid.

The ReisePacket service is for travelers who are inexperienced, elderly, disabled, or just appreciative of extra help. It costs €11 and provides, among other things, help boarding, disembarking, and transferring on certain trains that serve major cities and vacation areas. It also includes a seat reservation and a voucher for an onboard snack. Purchase the service at least one day before travel.

PASSES

A German Rail Pass allows 3 to 10 days of unlimited first- or second-class travel within a one-month period on any DB train, up to and including the ICE. A Twin Pass saves two people traveling together 50% off one person's fare. A Youth Pass (ages 12–25) is for second-class travel only. Passes can be used on some KD Rhine Line (see Cruise Ship Travel) routes. Prices begin at $304 per person in second class. Twin Passes begin at $338 for two people in second class, and Youth Passes begin at $180. Additional days may be added to either pass, but only at the time of purchase and not once the pass has been issued.

Germany is one of 21 countries in which you can use a Eurailpass, which provides unlimited first-class rail travel in all participating countries for the duration of the pass. Two adults traveling together can pay either €580 each for 15 consecutive days of travel or €746 each for 21 consecutive days of travel. The youth fare is €379 for 15 consecutive days and €446 for 10 days within two months. Eurailpasses are available from most travel agents and directly from ⊕ www.eurail.com.

Eurailpasses and some of the German Rail Passes should be purchased before you leave for Europe. You can purchase a Eurailpass and 5- or 10-day German Rail Passes at the Frankfurt airport and at some major German train stations, but the cost will be higher (a youth ticket for five days of travel is just under €149). When you buy your pass, consider purchasing rail-pass insurance in case you lose it during your travels.

In order to comply with the strict rules about validating tickets before you begin travel, read the instructions carefully. Some tickets require that a train official validate your pass, while others require you to write in the first date of travel.

Rail passes do not guarantee you a seat. You may also need to book a seat reservation, which is required on some European trains, particularly high-speed trains; they're a good idea in summer, on national holidays, and on popular routes. If you board the train without a reserved seat, you risk having to stand. You'll also need a reservation if you purchase sleeping accommodations. Seat reservations on InterCity trains cost €6, and a reservation is absolutely necessary for the ICE-Sprinter trains (€12 for second class). There are no reservations on regional trains.

Contacts Deutsche Bahn (German Rail). ☎ 01806/996–633 in Germany ⊕ www.bahn. de. **Eurail.** ⊕ www.eurail.com.

ESSENTIALS

■ ACCOMMODATIONS

The standards of German hotels, down to the humblest inn, are very high. You can nearly always expect courteous and polite service and clean and comfortable rooms. In addition to hotels proper, the country has numerous *Gasthöfe* or *Gasthäuser* (country inns that serve food and also have rooms). At the lowest end of the scale are *Fremdenzimmer*, meaning simply "rooms," normally in private houses. Look for the sign reading "Zimmer frei" (room available) or "zu vermieten" (to rent) on a green background; a red sign reading "besetzt" means there are no vacancies.

If you are looking for a very down-to-earth experience, try an *Urlaub auf dem Bauernhof*, a farm that has rooms for travelers. This can be especially exciting for children. You can also opt to stay at a winery's *Winzerhof*.

Room rates are by no means inflexible and depend very much on supply and demand. You can save money by inquiring about deals: many resort hotels offer substantial discounts in winter, for example. Likewise, many $$$$ and $$$ hotels in cities cut their prices dramatically on weekends and when business is quiet. Major events like Munich's Oktoberfest and the Frankfurt Book Fair will drive prices through the roof.

Tourist offices will make bookings for a nominal fee, but they may have difficulty doing so after 4 pm in high season and on weekends, so don't wait until too late in the day to begin looking for your accommodations. If you do get stuck, ask someone—like a mail carrier, police officer, or waiter, for example—for directions to a house renting a Fremdenzimmer or to a Gasthof.

APARTMENT AND HOUSE RENTALS

If you are staying in one region, renting an apartment is an affordable alternative to a hotel or B&B. *Ferienwohnungen*, or vacation apartments, are especially popular in more rural areas. They range from simple rooms with just the basics to luxury apartments with all the trimmings. Some even include breakfast. It may seem low tech, but the best way to find an apartment is through the local tourist office or the website of the town or village where you would like to stay. Be aware, though, that in some cities like Berlin there are draconian rules limiting vacation apartments (which are seen as accelerating gentrification).

International Agencies AirBnB. ⊕ *www. airbnb.com.* **Forgetaway.** ⊕ *www.forgetaway.com.* **Home Away.** ⊕ *www.homeaway. com.* **Interhome.** ☎ *800/882–6864* ⊕ *www. interhomeusa.com.* **Suzanne B. Cohen & Associates.** ☎ *207/200–2255* ⊕ *www. villaeurope.com.* **Vacation Home Rentals Worldwide.** ☎ *201/767–9393, 800/633–3284* ⊕ *www.vhrww.com.* **Villas & Apartments Abroad.** ☎ *212/213–6435* ⊕ *www.vaanyc. com.* **Villas International.** ☎ *415/499–9490, 800/221–2260* ⊕ *www.villasintl.com.* **Villas of Distinction.** ☎ *800/289–0900* ⊕ *www. villasofdistinction.com.* **Wimco.** ☎ *888/997–4326 in U. S.* ⊕ *www.wimco.com.*

CASTLE-HOTELS

Staying in a historic castle, or *Schloss*, is a great experience. The simpler ones may lack character, but most combine four-star luxury with antique furnishings, four-poster beds, and a baronial atmosphere. Some offer all the facilities of a resort. Euro-Connection can advise you on castle-hotel packages, including four-to six-night tours.

Contacts Euro-Connection. ☎ *800/645–3876* ⊕ *www.euro-connection.com.*

FARM VACATIONS

Almost every regional tourist office has a brochure listing farms that offer bed-and-breakfasts, apartments, and entire farmhouses to rent (*Ferienhöfe*). The German Agricultural Association provides an illustrated brochure, *Urlaub auf dem Bauernhof* (*Vacation Down on the Farm*), that covers more than 2,000 inspected and graded farms, from the Alps to the North Sea. It costs €9.90 and is also sold in bookstores.

Contacts DLG Reisedienst, Agratour
(*German Agricultural Association*). ☎ 069/2478–8450 ⊕ www.dlg-landtourismus.de.

HOTELS

Most hotels in Germany do not have air-conditioning, nor do they need it, given the climate and the German style of building construction that uses thick walls and recessed windows to help keep the heat out. Smaller hotels do not provide much in terms of bathroom amenities. Except in four- and five-star hotels, you won't find a washcloth. Hotels often have no-smoking rooms or even nonsmoking floors, so it's always worth asking for one when you reserve. Beds in double rooms often consist of two twin mattresses placed side by side within a frame. When you arrive, if you don't like the room you're offered, ask to see another.

Among the most delightful places to stay—and eat—in Germany are the aptly named Romantik Hotels and Restaurants. The Romantik group has more than 100 members in Germany. All are in atmospheric and historic buildings—a condition for membership—and are run by the owners with the emphasis on excellent amenities and service. Prices vary considerably, but in general they are a good value.

Contacts Romantik Hotels and Restaurants. ☎ 0800/6612–3400 in Germany ⊕ www.romantikhotels.com.

SPAS

Taking the waters in Germany, whether for curing the body or merely pampering, has been popular since Roman times. More than 300 health resorts, mostly equipped for thermal or mineral-water, mud, or brine treatments, are set within pleasant country areas or historic communities. The word *Bad* before or within the name of a town means it's a spa destination, where many patients reside in health clinics for two to three weeks of doctor-prescribed treatments.

Saunas, steam baths, and other hot-room facilities are often used "without textiles" in Germany—in other words, nude. Wearing a bathing suit is sometimes even prohibited in saunas, but sitting on a towel is always required. (You may need to bring your own towels.) The Deutsche Heilbäderverband has information, but it is in German only.

Contacts Deutsche Heilbäderverband (*German Health Resort and Spa Association*). ☎ 030/2463–6920 ⊕ www.deutscher-heilbaederverband.de.

▌ COMMUNICATIONS

INTERNET

Wireless Internet (Wi-Fi, sometimes called WLAN in Germany) is more and more common in even the most average hotel. The service is not always free, however. Sometimes you must purchase blocks of time from the front desk or online using a credit card. The cost is fairly high, usually around €4 for 30 minutes.

There are alternatives. Some hotels have an Internet room for guests needing to check their email. Otherwise, Internet cafés can still be found, and many bars and restaurants let you surf the Web for free.

PHONES

The country code for Germany is 49. When dialing a German number from abroad, drop the initial "0" from the local area code.

Many companies have service lines beginning with 0180. The cost of these calls averages €0.28 per call. Numbers that begin with 0190 can cost €1.85 per minute and more.

CALLING WITHIN GERMANY

The German telephone system is very efficient, so it's unlikely you'll have to use an operator unless you're seeking information. For information in English, dial ☏ *11837* for numbers within Germany and ☏ *11834* for numbers elsewhere. But first look for the number in the phone book or online (⊕ *www. teleauskunft.de*), because directory assistance is costly. Calls to 11837 and 11834 cost at least €0.50, more if the call lasts more than 30 seconds.

CALLING OUTSIDE GERMANY

The country code for the United States is 1.

Access Codes AT&T Direct. ☏ *0800/225–5288.* **MCI WorldPhone.** ☏ *0800/888–8000.* **Sprint International Access.** ☏ *0800/888–0013.*

MOBILE PHONES

You can buy an inexpensive unlocked mobile phone and a SIM card at almost every corner shop and even at the supermarket. Most shops require identification to purchase a SIM card, but you can avoid this by purchasing a card at any number of phone centers or call shops, usually located near train stations. This is the best option if you just want to make local calls. If you bring a phone from abroad, your provider may have to unlock it for you to use a different SIM card and a prepaid service plan in the destination. You'll then have a local number and can make local calls at local rates. If your trip is extensive, you could also simply buy a new cell phone in your destination, as the initial cost will be offset over time.

Many prepaid plans, like Blau World, offer calling plans to the United States and other countries, starting at €0.03 per minute. Many Germans use these SIM cards to call abroad, as the rates are much cheaper than from landlines.

If you have a multiband phone (some countries use different frequencies from what's used in the United States) and your service provider uses the world-standard GSM network (as do T-Mobile, AT&T, and Verizon), you can probably use your phone abroad. Roaming fees can be steep, however: 99¢ a minute is considered reasonable. And overseas you normally pay the toll charges for incoming calls. It's almost always cheaper to send a text message than to make a call, because text messages have a very low set fee (often less than 5¢).

Cellular Abroad rents and sells GMS phones and sells SIM cards that work in many countries. Mobal rents mobiles and sells GSM phones (starting at $49) that will operate in 140 countries. Planet Fone rents cell phones, but the per-minute rates are expensive.

■TIP→ If you travel internationally frequently, save one of your old mobile phones or buy a cheap one on the Internet; ask your cell phone company to unlock it for you, and take it with you as a travel phone, buying a new SIM card with pay-as-you-go service in each destination.

Contacts Cellular Abroad. ☏ *800/287-5072 in U.S., 00800/3623-3333 in Germany* ⊕ *www. cellularabroad.com.* **Mobal.** ☏ *888/888-9162* ⊕ *www.mobalrental.com.* **Planet Fone.** ☏ *888/988-4777* ⊕ *www.planetfone.com.*

▌CUSTOMS AND DUTIES

German Customs and Border Control is fairly simple and straightforward. The system works efficiently and professionally, and 99% of all travelers will have no real cause to interact with them.

You're always allowed to bring goods of a certain value back home without having to pay any duty or import tax, but there's a limit on the amount of tobacco and liquor you can bring back duty-free, and some countries have separate limits for perfumes. For exact figures, check with your customs department. The values of so-called duty-free goods are included in these amounts. When you shop abroad, save all your receipts, as customs inspectors may ask to see them as well as the items you purchased. If the total value of your goods is more than the duty-free limit, you'll have to pay a tax (most often a flat percentage) on the value of everything beyond that limit.

For anyone entering Germany from outside the EU, the following limitations apply: (1) 200 cigarettes or 100 cigarillos or 50 cigars or 250 grams of tobacco; (2) 2 liters of still table wine; (3) 1 liter of spirits over 22% alcohol by volume (ABV) or 2 liters of spirits under 22% ABV (fortified and sparkling wines) or 2 more liters of table wine; (4) 50 grams of perfume and 250 milliliters of eau de toilette; (5) 500 grams of roasted coffee or 200 grams of instant coffee; (6) other goods to the value of €175.

If you have questions regarding customs or bringing a pet into the country, contact the Zoll-Infocenter.

Contacts Zoll-Infocenter. ☎ *0800/8007–5452 toll-free, 0351/44834–555* ⊕ *www.zoll.de.*

U.S. Information U.S. Customs and Border Protection. ☎ *202/325–8000 outside U.S., 877/227–5511 in U.S.* ⊕ *www.cbp.gov.*

∎ EATING OUT

Almost every street in Germany has its *Gaststätte,* a sort of combination restaurant and pub, and every village its *Gasthof,* or inn. The emphasis in either is on simple food at reasonable prices. A *Bierstube* (pub) or *Weinstube* (wine cellar) may also serve light snacks or meals.

Service can be slow, but you'll never be rushed out of your seat. Something else that may seem jarring at first: people can, and do, join other parties at a table in a casual restaurant if seating is tight. It's common courtesy to ask first, though.

Since Germans don't generally drink from the tap, water always costs extra and comes as still or sparkling mineral water.

BUDGET EATING TIPS

Imbiss (snack) stands can be found in almost every busy shopping street, in parking lots, train stations, and near markets. They serve *Würste* (sausages), grilled, roasted, or boiled, and rolls filled with cheese, cold meat, or fish. Many stands sell Turkish-style wraps called *döner kebab.* Prices range from €1.50 to €2.50 per portion. It's acceptable to bring sandwich fixings to a beer garden so long as you order a beer there; just be sure not to sit at a table with a tablecloth.

Butcher shops, known as *Metzgereien,* often serve warm snacks or very good sandwiches. Try *warmer Leberkäs mit Kartoffelsalat,* a typical Bavarian specialty, which is a sort of baked meat loaf with mustard and potato salad. In northern Germany try *Bouletten,* small meatballs, or *Currywurst,* sausages in a piquant curry sauce. Thuringia has a reputation for its *Bratwurst,* which is usually broken in two and packed into a roll with mustard. Up north, the specialty snack is a herring sandwich with onions.

Restaurants in department stores are especially recommended for appetizing and inexpensive lunches. Kaufhof, Karstadt, Wertheim, and Horton are names to note. Germany's vast numbers of Turkish, Italian, Greek, Chinese, and Balkan restaurants are often inexpensive.

MEALS AND MEALTIMES

Most hotels serve a buffet-style breakfast (*Frühstück*) of rolls, cheese, cold cuts, eggs, cereals, yogurt, and spreads, which is often included in the price of a room. Cafés, especially the more trendy ones, offer breakfast menus sometimes including pancakes, omelets, muesli, or even Thai rice soup. By American standards, a cup (*Tasse*) of coffee in Germany is very petite, and you don't get free refills. Order a *Pot* or *Kännchen* if you want a larger portion.

For lunch (*Mittagessen*), you can get sandwiches from most cafés and bakeries, and many fine restaurants have special lunch menus that make the gourmet experience much more affordable. Dinner (*Abendessen*) is usually accompanied by a potato or *Spätzle* side dish. A salad sometimes comes with the main dish.

Gaststätten normally serve hot meals from 11:30 am to 9 pm; many places stop serving hot meals between 2 pm and 6 pm, although you can still order cold dishes. If you feel like a hot meal, look for a restaurant advertising *durchgehend geöffnet,* or look for a pizza parlor.

Once most restaurants have closed, your options are limited. Take-out pizza parlors and Turkish eateries often stay open later. Failing that, your best option is a train station or a gas station with a convenience store. Many bars serve snacks.

Unless otherwise noted, the restaurants listed are open daily for lunch and dinner.

PAYING

Credit cards are generally accepted only in moderate to expensive restaurants, so check before sitting down. You will need to ask for the bill (say "Die Rechnung, bitte.") in order to get it from the waiter, the idea being that the table is yours for the evening. Round up the bill 5% to 10% and pay the waiter directly rather than leaving any money or tip on the table. The waiter will likely wait at the table for you to pay after he has brought the check. He will also wear a money pouch and make change out of it at the table. If you don't need change, say "Stimmt so" (Keep the change); otherwise tell the waiter how much change you want back, adding in the tip. Meals are subject to 19% tax (abbreviated as "MwSt" on your bill).

RESERVATIONS AND DRESS

Regardless of where you are, it's a good idea to make a reservation if you can. In most fine-dining establishments it's expected. We only mention them specifically when reservations are essential (there's no other way you'll ever get a table) or when they are not accepted. For popular restaurants, book as far ahead as you can (often 30 days), and reconfirm as soon as you arrive. (Parties of more than four should always call ahead to check the reservations policy.) We mention dress only when men are required to wear a jacket or a jacket and tie.

Note that even when Germans dress casually, their look is generally crisp and neat. Jeans are acceptable for most social occasions, unless you're meeting the president.

SMOKING

For such an otherwise health-conscious nation, Germans do smoke. A lot. New antismoking laws came into effect in 2008, effectively banning smoking in all restaurants and many pubs, but many Germans, particularly in Berlin and Hamburg, tend to ignore them. Many hotels have nonsmoking rooms and even nonsmoking floors. However, a smoker will find it intrusive if you ask him or her to refrain.

WINES, BEER, AND SPIRITS

Wines of Germany promotes the wines of all thirteen German wine regions and can supply you with information on wine festivals and visitor-friendly wineries. It also arranges six-day guided winery tours in spring and fall in conjunction with the German Wine Academy.

It's legal to drink beer from open containers in public (even in the passenger seat of a car), and having a beer at one's midday break is nothing to raise an eyebrow at. Bavaria is not the only place to try beer. While Munich's beers have achieved world fame (Löwenbräu and Paulaner, for example), beer connoisseurs will really want to travel to places farther north like Alpirsbach, Bamberg, Erfurt, Cologne, or Görlitz, where smaller breweries produce top-notch brews. Berlin is at the center of a beer revolution that makes it one of the most interesting beer cities in Germany.

ELECTRICITY

The electrical current in Germany is 220 volts, 50 cycles alternating current (AC); wall outlets take Continental-type plugs, with two round prongs.

EMERGENCIES

Throughout Germany call ☎ *110* for police, ☎ *112* for an ambulance or the fire department.

Foreign Embassies U.S. Embassy. ✉ *Pariser Pl. 2, Berlin* ☎ *030/83050 in case of emergency, 030/8305–1200 for U.S. citizens (2–4 pm only)* ⊕ *www.usembassy.de.*

ETIQUETTE

CUSTOMS OF THE COUNTRY
Being on time for appointments, even casual social ones, is very important. There is no "fashionably late" in Germany. Germans are more formal in addressing each other than Americans. Always address acquaintances as Herr (Mr.) or Frau (Mrs.) plus their last name; do not call them by their first name unless invited to do so. The German language has informal and formal pronouns for "you": formal is *Sie,* and informal is *du.* Even if adults are on a first-name basis with one another, they may still keep to the *Sie* form.

Germans are less formal when it comes to nudity: a sign that reads "freikörper" or "fkk" indicates a park or beach that allows nude sunbathing. At a sauna or steam bath, you will often be asked to remove all clothing.

GREETINGS
The standard "Guten Tag" is the way to greet people throughout the country. When you depart, say "Auf Wiedersehen." "Hallo" is also used frequently, as is "Hi" among the younger crowd. A less formal leave-taking is "Tschüss" or "ciao." You will also hear regional differences in greetings.

LANGUAGE
English is spoken in most hotels, restaurants, airports, museums, and other places of interest. However, English is not widely spoken in rural areas or by people over 40; this is especially true of the eastern part of Germany. Learning the basics before going is always a good idea, especially *bitte* (please) and *danke* (thank you). Apologizing for your poor German before asking a question in English will make locals feel respected and begins all communication on the right foot.

A phrase book and language-tape set can help get you started.

■ TIP → Under no circumstances use profanity or pejoratives. Germans take these very seriously, and a slip of the tongue can result in expensive criminal and civil penalties. Calling a police officer a "Nazi" or using vulgar finger gestures can cost you up to €10,000 and two years in jail.

HEALTH

Warm winters have recently caused an explosion in the summertime tick population, which often causes outbreaks of Lyme disease. If you intend to do a lot of hiking, especially in the southern half of the country, be aware of the danger of ticks spreading Lyme disease. There is no vaccination against them, so prevention is important. Wear high shoes or boots, long pants, and light-color clothing. Use a good insect repellent, and check yourself for ticks after outdoor activities, especially if you've walked through high grass.

OVER-THE-COUNTER REMEDIES
All over-the-counter medicines, even aspirin, are only available at an *Apotheke* (pharmacy): the German term *Drogerie,* or drugstore, refers to a shop for sundry items.

Apotheken are open during normal business hours, with those in train stations or airports open later and on weekends. Apotheken are plentiful, and there is invariably one within a few blocks. Every district has an emergency pharmacy that is open after hours. These are listed as

Apotheken Notdienst or *Apotheken-Bere-itschaftsdienst* on the window of every other pharmacy in town, often with directions for how to get there. Pharmacies will have a bell you must ring to enter. Most pharmacists in larger cities speak enough English to help. Some drugs have different names: acetaminophen—or Tylenol—is called *Paracetomol.*

HOURS OF OPERATION

Business hours are inconsistent throughout the country and vary from state to state and even from city to city. Banks are generally open weekdays from 8:30 or 9 am to 3 or 4 pm (5 or 6 pm on Thursday), sometimes with a lunch break of about an hour at smaller branches. Some banks close by 2:30 on Friday afternoon. Banks at airports and main train stations open as early as 6:30 am and close as late as 10:30 pm.

Most museums are open from Tuesday to Sunday 10–6. Some close for an hour or more at lunch. Many stay open until 8 pm or later one day a week, usually Thursday. In smaller towns or in rural areas, museums may be open only on weekends or just a few hours a day.

All stores are closed Sunday, with the exception of those in or near train stations. Larger stores are generally open from 9:30 or 10 am to 8 or 9 pm on weekdays and close between 6 and 8 pm on Saturday. Smaller shops and some department stores in smaller towns close at 6 or 6:30 on weekdays and as early as 4 on Saturday. German shop owners take their closing times seriously. If you come in five minutes before closing, you may not be treated like royalty. Apologizing profusely and making a speedy purchase will help.

Along the autobahn and major highways, as well as in larger cities, gas stations and their small convenience shops are often open late, if not around the clock.

HOLIDAYS

The following national holidays are observed in Germany: January 1; January 6 (Epiphany—Bavaria, Saxony-Anhalt, and Baden-Württemberg only); Good Friday; Easter Monday; May 1 (Workers' Day); Ascension; Pentecost Monday; Corpus Christi (southern Germany only); Assumption Day (Bavaria and Saarland only); October 3 (German Unity Day); November 1 (All Saints' Day—Baden-Württemberg, Bavaria, North Rhine-Westphalia, Rhineland-Pfalz, and Saarland); December 24–26 (Christmas).

Pre-Lenten celebrations in Cologne and the Rhineland are known as Karneval, and for several days before Ash Wednesday work grinds to a halt as people celebrate with parades, banquets, and general debauchery. Farther south, in the state of Baden-Württenburg, the festivities are called Fasching, and tend to be more traditional. In either area, expect businesses to be closed both before and after "Fat Tuesday."

MAIL

A post office in Germany (*Postamt*) is recognizable by the postal symbol, a black bugle on a yellow background. In some villages you will find one in the local supermarket. Stamps (*Briefmarken*) can also be bought at some news agencies and souvenir shops. Post offices are generally open weekdays 8–6, Saturday 8–noon.

Airmail letters and postcards to anywhere outside Germany, even to the United Kingdom and within Europe cost €0.80. These rates apply to standard-size envelopes and postcards. Letters take approximately 3–4 days to reach the United Kingdom, 5–7 days to the United States, and 7–10 days to Australia and New Zealand.

You can arrange to have mail (letters only) sent to you in care of any German post office; have the envelope marked "Postlagernd." This service is free, and the mail will be held for seven days. Or you can have mail sent to any American Express office in Germany. There's no charge to cardholders, holders of American Express traveler's checks, or anyone who has booked a vacation with American Express.

SHIPPING PACKAGES

Most major stores that cater to tourists will also ship your purchases home. You should check your insurance for coverage of possible damage.

The Deutsche Post has an express international service that will deliver your letter or package the next day to countries within the EU, within one to two days to the United States, and slightly longer to Australia. A letter or package to the United States weighing less than 5 kg costs €99. You can drop off your mail at any post office, or it can be picked up for an extra fee. Deutsche Post works in cooperation with DHL. International carriers tend to be slightly cheaper (€35–€45 for the same letter) and provide more services.

Express Services Deutsche Post.
☎ *0028/433–3112* ⊕ *www.deutschepost.de.*
DHL. ⊕ *www.dhl.de.*

▌ MONEY

Credit cards are not usually accepted by most businesses, but you probably won't have to use cash for payment in high-end hotels and restaurants. Many businesses on the other end of the spectrum don't accept them, however. It's a good idea to check in advance if you're staying in a budget lodging or eating in a simple country inn.

Prices throughout *this guide* are given for adults. Substantially reduced fees are almost always available for children, students, and senior citizens.

▌TIP→ **Banks almost never have every foreign currency on hand, and it may take as long as a week to order. If you're planning to exchange funds before leaving home, don't wait until the last minute.**

ATMS AND BANKS

Twenty-four-hour ATMs (*Geldautomaten*) can be accessed with Plus or Cirrus credit and banking cards. Your own bank will probably charge a fee for using ATMs abroad, and some German banks exact €3–€5 fees for use of their ATMs. Nevertheless, you'll usually get a better rate of exchange via an ATM than you will at a currency-exchange office or even when changing money in a bank. And extracting funds as you need them is a safer option than carrying around a large amount of cash. Since some ATM keypads show no letters, know the numeric equivalent of your password. Always use ATMs inside the bank.

▌TIP→ **PINs with more than four digits are not recognized at ATMs in many countries. If yours has five or more, remember to change it before you leave.**

CREDIT CARDS

Most credit cards issued in Europe are now "chip-and-PIN" credit cards that store user information on a computer chip embedded in the card. In the United States, all credit cards switched to "chip-and-signature" cards in fall 2015. While European cardholders are expected to know and use their PIN number for all transactions rather than signing a charge slip, U.S. chip-and-signature cards usually still require users to sign the charge slip. (Very few U.S. issuers offer a PIN along with their cards, except for cash withdrawals at an ATM, though this is expected to change in the future.) The good news: unlike the old magnetic-strip cards that gave American travelers in Europe so much trouble, the new chip-and-signature cards are accepted at many more locations, including in many cases at machines that sell train tickets, machines that process automated motorway tolls at unmanned booths, and automated gas stations—even without a signature or PIN. The bad news: not all European locations will accept the chip-and-signature cards, and you won't know until you try, so it's a good idea to carry enough cash to cover small purchases.

All major U.S. credit cards are accepted in Germany. The most frequently used are MasterCard and Visa. American Express is used less frequently, and Diners Club even less. Since the credit-card companies demand fairly substantial fees, some businesses will not accept credit cards for small purchases. Cheaper restaurants and lodgings often do not accept credit cards. Many credit-card companies charge substantial foreign transaction fees—typically about 3% on every transaction. You can save money by applying for a no-fee credit card well ahead of your departure.

It's a good idea to inform your credit-card company before you travel, especially if you're going abroad and don't travel internationally very often. Otherwise, the credit-card company might put a hold on your card owing to unusual activity—not a good thing halfway through your trip. Record all your credit-card numbers—as well as the phone numbers to call if your cards are lost or stolen—in a safe place, via email, or in the Cloud, so you're prepared should something go wrong.

If you plan to use your credit card for cash advances, you'll need to apply for a PIN at least two weeks before your trip. Although it's usually cheaper (and safer) to use a credit card abroad for large purchases (so you can cancel payments or be reimbursed if there's a problem), note that some credit-card companies *and* the banks that issue them add substantial percentages to all foreign transactions, whether they're in a foreign currency or not. Check on these fees before leaving home, so there won't be any surprises when you get the bill.

■ TIP→ **Before you charge something, ask the merchant whether he or she plans to do a dynamic currency conversion (DCC). In such a transaction the credit-card processor (shop, restaurant, or hotel, not Visa or MasterCard) converts the currency and charges you in dollars. In most cases you'll pay the merchant a 3% fee for this service in addition to any credit-card company and issuing-bank foreign-transaction surcharges.**

Dynamic currency conversion programs are becoming increasingly widespread. Merchants who participate in them are supposed to ask whether you want to be charged in dollars or the local currency, but they don't always do so. And even if they do offer you a choice, they may well avoid mentioning the additional surcharges. The good news is that you *do* have a choice. And if this practice really gets your goat, you can avoid it entirely thanks to American Express; with its cards, DCC simply isn't an option.

Reporting Lost Cards American Express.
☎ *800/528–4800 in U.S., 069/9797–1000 in Germany* ⊕ *www.americanexpress.com.* **Diners Club.** ☎ *800/234–6377 in U.S., 514/877–1577 collect from abroad, 069/900–15014 in Germany* ⊕ *www.dinersclub.com.* **Master-Card.** ☎ *800/627–8372 in U.S., 636/722–7111 collect from abroad, 0800/819–1040 in Germany* ⊕ *www.mastercard.com.* **Visa.** ☎ *800/847–2911 in U.S., 303/967–1096 collect from abroad, 0800/811–8440 in Germany* ⊕ *www.visa.com.*

CURRENCY AND EXCHANGE

Germany uses the euro (€), shared with 18 other countries: Austria, Belgium, Cyprus, Estonia, Finland, France, Greece, Ireland, Italy, Latvia, Lithuania, Luxembourg, Malta, the Netherlands, Portugal, Slovakia, Slovenia, and Spain. The euro is divided into 100 cents. There are bills of 5, 10, 20, 50, 100, and 500 euros and coins of €1 and €2, and 1, 2, 5, 10, 20, and 50 cents. Many businesses and restaurants do not accept €200 and €500 notes. It is virtually impossible to pay for anything in U.S. dollars, but you should have no problem exchanging currency. The large number of banks and exchange services means that you can shop around for the best rate, if you're so inclined. But the cheapest and easiest way to go is using your ATM card.

■ TIP→ Even if a currency-exchange booth has a sign promising no commission, rest assured that there's some kind of huge, hidden fee. (Oh ... that's right. The sign didn't say no fee.) And as for rates, you're almost always better off getting foreign currency at an ATM or exchanging money at a bank.

■ PACKING

For visits to German cities, pack as you would for an American city: dressy outfits for formal restaurants and nightclubs, casual clothes elsewhere. Jeans are as popular in Germany as anywhere else, and are perfectly acceptable for sightseeing and informal dining. In the evening, men will probably feel more comfortable wearing a jacket in more expensive restaurants, although it's almost never required. Many German women wear stylish outfits to restaurants and the theater, especially in the larger cities.

Winters can be bitterly cold; summers are warm but with days that suddenly turn cool and rainy. In summer, take a warm jacket or heavy sweater if you are visiting the Bavarian Alps or the Black Forest, where the nights can be chilly even after hot days. In Berlin and on the Baltic, it is windy, which can be quite pleasant in summer but a complete bear in winter. To discourage purse snatchers and pickpockets, carry a handbag with long straps that you can sling across your body bandolier style and with a zippered compartment for money and other valuables.

For stays in budget hotels, pack your own soap. Many provide no soap at all or only a small bar.

■ PASSPORTS AND VISAS

Visitors from the United States and Canada, including children, are required to have a passport to enter the EU for a period of up to 90 days. There are no official passport controls at any of Germany's land borders, although random spot checks and customs checks are becoming more frequent. Most travelers will only show their documents on entering and leaving the EU. Your passport should be valid for up to six months after your trip ends or this will raise questions at the border. EU citizens can enter Germany with a national identity card or passport. Traveling with children can be problematic. Single parents traveling with their own children rarely face any hassle, but overzealous border guards have been known to ask children about their relationship with the other parent. If you are a parent or grandparent traveling with a child, it helps to have a signed and notarized power of attorney in order to dispel any questions.

■ RESTROOMS

Public restrooms in Germany typically require you to pay a small fee of €0.20–€0.70 to the bathroom attendant. Train stations are increasingly turning to McClean, a privately run enterprise that demands €0.60 to €1.10. These facilities, staffed by attendants who clean almost constantly, sparkle. You won't find them in smaller stations, however. Most gas stations on highb

■ SAFETY

Germany has one of the lowest crime rates in Europe. There are some areas, such as the neighborhoods around train stations and the streets surrounding red-light districts, where you should keep an eye out for potential dangers. The best advice is to take the usual precautions. Secure your valuables in the hotel safe. Don't wear flashy jewelry, and keep expensive electronics out of sight when you are not using them. Carry shoulder bags or purses so that they can't be easily snatched, and never leave them hanging on the back of a chair at a café or restaurant. Avoid walking alone at night, even in relatively safe neighborhoods. Due to increasing incidents of violence in Berlin, Hamburg, and Munich, use caution late at night in the subway.

When withdrawing cash, don't use an ATM in a deserted area or one that is outside. It is best to avoid freestanding ATMs in subway stations and other locations away from a bank. Make sure that no one is looking over your shoulder when you enter your PIN. And never use a machine that appears to have been tampered with.

■TIP→ **Distribute your cash, credit cards, IDs, and other valuables between a deep front pocket, an inside jacket or vest pocket, and a hidden money pouch. Don't reach for the money pouch once you're in public.**

▌TAXES

Most prices you see on items already include Germany's 19% value-added tax (V.A.T.). Some goods, such as food, books, and antiquities, carry a 7% V.A.T. as a percentage of the purchase price. A physical item must cost at least €25 to qualify for a V.A.T. refund.

When making a purchase, ask for a V.A.T. refund form and find out whether the merchant gives refunds—not all stores do, nor are they required to. Have the form stamped like any customs form by customs officials when you leave the country or, if you're visiting several European Union countries, when you leave the EU. After you're through passport control, take the form to a refund-service counter for an on-the-spot refund (which is usually the quickest and easiest option), or mail it to the address on the form (or the envelope with it) after you arrive home. You receive the total refund stated on the form, but the processing time can be long, especially if you request a credit-card adjustment.

Global Refund is a Europe-wide service with 225,000 affiliated stores and more than 700 refund counters at major airports and border crossings. Its refund form, called a Tax Free Check, is the most common across the European continent.

The service issues refunds in the form of cash, check, or credit-card adjustment.

V.A.T. REFUNDS AT THE AIRPORT

If you're departing from Terminal 1 at Frankfurt Airport, where you bring your purchases to claim your tax back depends on how you've packed the goods. If the items are in your checked luggage, check in as normal, but let the ticket counter know you have yet to claim your tax refund. They will give you your luggage back to bring to the customs office in Departure Hall B, Level 2. For goods you are carrying on the plane with you, go to the customs office on the way to your gate. After you pass through passport control, there is a Global Refund office.

If you're departing from Terminal 2, bring goods in luggage to be checked to the customs office in Hall D, Level 2 (opposite the Delta Airlines check-in counters). For goods you are carrying on the plane with you, see the customs office in Hall E, Level 3 (near security control).

At Munich's airport, the Terminal 2 customs area is on the same level as check-in. If your V.A.T. refund items are in your luggage, check in first, and then bring your bags to the customs office on Level 04. From here your bags will be sent to your flight, and you can go to the Global Refund counter around the corner. If your refund items are in your carry-on, go to the Global Refund office in the customs area on Level 05 south. Terminal 1 has customs areas in modules C and D, Level 04.

V.A.T. Refunds Global Refund. ☏ *800/566-9828* ⊕ *www.globalblue.com.*

▌ TIME

All of Germany is on Central European Time, which is six hours ahead of Eastern Standard Time and nine hours ahead of Pacific Standard Time. Daylight Saving Time begins on the last Sunday in March and ends on the last Sunday in October. Timeanddate.com can help you figure out the correct time anywhere.

Germans use the 24-hour clock, or "military time" (1 pm is indicated as 13:00), and write the date before the month, so October 3 will appear as 03.10.

Time Zones Timeanddate.com. ⊕ *www. timeanddate.com/worldclock.*

▌ TIPPING

Tipping is done at your own discretion. All restaurants include a service charge, but you tip the waiter a bit more on top of that. Give the tip to the waiter in cash as you pay the bill (even if you use a credit card); don't leave it on the table, as that's considered rude. Tour guides, bartenders, and taxi drivers are also usually tipped. Rounding off bills to the next highest sum is customary for bills under €10. Above that sum you should add a little more, but rarely more than 5%–10% because Germans are not big tippers. Do give bellhops, hotel doormen, room-service waiters, maids €1.

▌ VISITOR INFORMATION

Staff at the smaller visitor information offices might not speak English. Many offices keep shorter hours than normal businesses, and you can expect some to close during weekday lunch hours and as early as noon on Friday. Almost all German cities and towns have an Internet presence under ⊕ *www.cityname.de,* for example ⊕ *www.berlin.de.* The Internet portal Deutschland.de has lots of information about the country's best-known sights, as well as those that are often overlooked.

Contacts Deutschland.de. ⊕ *www.deutsch- land.de.* **German National Tourist Board.** ⊕ *www.germany.travel.*

INDEX

A

Aachen, 498–501
Accommodations, 772–773
Adolf Wagner ✕, 371
Affenberg, 264
Ahlbeck, 633
Air travel, 28, 766–767
Bavarian Alps, 127
Berlin, 640
Black Forest, 283–284
Bodensee, 249
Fairy-Tale Road, 511
Franconia and the German
 Danube, 209
Frankfurt, 351
Hamburg, 554
Heidelberg and the Neckar
 Valley, 315
Munich, 49
Pfalz and Rhine Terrace, 392
Rhineland, 432
Romantic Road, 163
Saxony, Saxony-Anhalt, and
 Thuringia, 717–718
Schleswig-Holstein and the
 Baltic Coast, 603
Albertinum, 730
Albrecht-Dürer-Haus, 226
Albrechtsburg, 738–739
Alemannenmuseum, 269
Alexanderplatz (Berlin), 646
Alken, 462
Alpirsbach, 298
Alps. ⇨ See Bavarian Alps
Alster Lakes, 558–559
Alte Brücke, 318
Alte Kanzlei ✕, 336
Alte Kapelle, 233
Alte Mainbrücke, 198
Alte Nationalgalerie, 646
Alte Oper, 354
Alte Pinakothek, 70
Alte Universität, 318
Alte Wasserkunst, 740
Alter Garten, 620
Alter Friedhof, 480
Alter Jüdisher Friedhof, 359
Alter Markt (Köln), 488
Alter Markt (Potsdam), 707
Alter Markt (Stralsund), 627
Alter Strom, 625
Altes Brauhaus, 739
Altes Museum, 646
Altes Rathaus (Bamberg), 219
Altes Rathaus (Bonn), 481
Altes Rathaus (Göttingen), 530
Altes Rathaus (Hannover), 536

Altes Rathaus (Köln), 488–489
Altes Rathaus (Konstanz), 272
Altes Rathaus (Lindau), 253
Altes Rathaus (Munich), 57
Altes Rathaus (Nürnberg), 226
Altes Rathaus (Potsdam),
 707–708
Altes Rathaus (Regensburg),
 233–234
Altes Rathaus (Überlingen), 264
Altes Schloss (Meersburg), 261
Altes Schloss (Stuttgart), 334
Altmarkt (Dresden), 730
Altona, 571, 595
Altpörtel, 405
Altstadt (Düsseldorf), 502
Altstadt (Frankfurt), 354–355,
 358–359
Altstadt (Hamburg), 558–563,
 593–594
Altstadt (Lübeck), 614
Altstadt (Munich), 56–64,
 85–87, 90–91, 95–97,
 103–104
Altstadt (Wiesbaden), 434
Ammersee, 117–119
Amphitheater, 475
Andechs Monastery, 118
Andreas Murkudis (shop), 701
Anger, The (Erfurt), 758
Apartment and house rentals,
 772
Apfelwein, 367
Archaologisches Museum
 (Frankfurt), 354
Asamkirche, 57
ATMs, 779
Au, 73, 94, 106–107
Auerbachs Keller ✕, 725
Augsburg, 181–183
Augsburg Puppenkiste, 180
Augustiner Keller Biergarten,
 106
Augustinermuseum, 305

B

Bacharach, 448–449
Bachhaus, 756
Bachmair Weissach ☲, 149
Bach-Museum im Bach-Archiv
 Leipzig, 721
Bad Bergzabern, 394
Bad Doberan, 622–623
Bad Dürkheim, 410–412
Bad Homburg, 382–384
Bad Karlshafen, 527–528
Bad Mergentheim, 195–196
Bad Staffelstein, 223–224
Bad Tölz, 146–147

Bad Wimpfen, 330–331
Badisches Landesmuseum, 287
Baiersbronn, 294–296
Ballet
 Berlin, 698
 Frankfurt, 378–379
 Hamburg, 591–592
 Munich, 109
BallinStadt, 572
Baltic Coast. ⇨ See
 Schleswig-Holstein and the
 Baltic Coast
Bamberg, 219–223
Banks, 779
Baerck (shop), 699
Barockgalerie, 332
Basilika St. Martin, 446
Bauhaus Building (Dessau), 749
Bauhaus Museum, 760–761
Bauhaus University, 761
Bautzen/Budyšin, 740–741
Bavaria Statue, 68
Bavaria Filmstadt, 73, 82
Bavarian Alps, 122–158
 dining, 128, 133, 137, 140–141,
  143–144, 146, 148–149, 151
 discounts and deals, 129–130
 festivals and seasonal events,
  140, 141–142, 149
 lodging, 128, 133–134, 137,
  141, 144, 147, 149, 151–152,
  156
 nightlife and the arts, 134,
  141–142, 147, 149
 prices, 129
 shopping, 145
 sports and the outdoors,
  124–125, 134–135, 142,
  144–145, 147, 150, 152–153,
  156–157
 timing the visit, 127
 tours, 131, 136, 140, 154
 transportation, 127–128, 136,
  143, 146, 147–148, 150,
  153, 158
 visitor information, 131, 143,
  146, 148, 150, 154
Bayerischer Hof ☲, 95
Bayerisches Kunstgewer-
 be-Verein, 111
Bayerisches Nationalmuseum,
 64–65
Bayreuth, 215–218
Beaches, 600–601, 608, 626,
 631–632, 633–634
Bebelplatz (Berlin), 646–647
Bebenhausen, 339–340

PHOTO CREDITS

Cover: Stefano Politi Markovina / AWL Images Ltd [Spitalgasse street, Rothenburg ob der Tauber, Bavaria, Germany]. Back cover, from left to right: Rudi1976 | Dreamstime.com, gary718/Shutterstock, mkrberlin/Shutterstock. Spine: Tiberiu Stan/Shutterstock. Massimiliano Pieraccini/Shutterstock (1). Wolfgang Kaehler / age fotostock (2,3). Minnystock | Dreamstime.com (4,5). Bildgigant/Shutterstock (5). Foottoo/Shutterstock (5). Mariia Golovianko/Shutterstock (6). Werner Dieterich / Alamy Stock Photo (6). Pecold/Shutterstock (7). S-F/Shutterstock (8). linerpics/Shutterstock (8). Anna Pustynnikova/Shutterstock (8). sma1050/Shutterstock (8). Janniswerner | Dreamstime.com (9). Sahachatz/Shutterstock (9). Traveller Martin/Shutterstock (9). Yuri Turkov/Shutterstock (9). Pecold/Shutterstock (10). canadastock/Shutterstock (10). NaughtyNut/Shutterstock (10). hlphoto/Shutterstock (10). Yury Dmitrienko/Shutterstock (11). Sean Pavone/Shutterstock (12). stockcreations/Shutterstock (12). Val Thoermer/Shutterstock (12). Prasit Rodphan/Shutterstock (12). Minnystock | Dreamstime.com (13). ilolab/Shutterstock (13). McPhoto PWI / age fotostock (15). **Chapter 1: Experience Germany:** BerlinPictures/Shutterstock (20,21). **Chapter 2: Munich:** Scanrail | Dreamstime.com (43). B. Roemmelt/ Munich Tourist Office (46). Jay Tong/Flickr, [CC BY-ND 2.0] (47). Jay Tong/Flickr, [CC BY-ND 2.0] (47). Public Domain (48). Noppasinw | Dreamstime.com (50,51). Manfred Bail / age fotostock (63). Deutsches Museum (69). Borgese Maurizio/age fotostock (73). McPhoto PWI / age fotostock (74,75). Pierre Adenis/GNTB (75). Mirenska Olga/Shutterstock (76). Fabian von Poser / age fotostock (77). sebastian-julian/iStockphoto (77). chirapbogdan/Shutterstock (77). Pierre Adenis/GNTB (78). Marco Maccarini/iStockphoto (79). Abhijeet Rane/Flickr, [CC BY-ND 2.0](80). Karussell by digital cat/ Flickr, [CC BY-ND 2.0] (81). gary718/Shutterstock (84). Tory Marie / 500px (112). **Chapter 3: The Bavarian Alps:** Charles Bowman/age fotostock (121). Andreas Strauss/age fotostock (124). Kaster, Andreas/GNTB (125). Andreas Strauss / age fotostock (125). Alexander Mertz/iStockphoto (126). St. Nick/Shutterstock (129). Andreas Strauss / age fotostock (137). St. Nick/Shutterstock (139). juergen2008/iStockphoto (152). Priyendu Subashchandran/iStockphoto (157). **Chapter 4: The Romantic Road:** Cowin, Andrew/GNTB (159). Adrian Zenz/Shutterstock (162). Thonig / age fotostock (170). bilwissedition com / age fotostock (171). yannick luthy / Alamy (171). jean-pierre lescourre / age fotostock (172). McPhoto PWI / age fotostock(173). digital cat/Flickr, [CC BY-ND 2.0](173). Ashutosh Garg/Flickr, [CC BY-ND 2.0] (174). Public domain (175). Werner Otto / age fotostock (175, 176). Dainis Derics/Shutterstock (177). AYArktos/Wikimedia Commons (177). Hubertus Blume / age fotostock (185). Stella / age fotostock (186). Martin Siepmann / age fotostock (195). Martin Moxter / age fotostock (200). **Chapter 5: Franconia and the German Danube:** Walter Bibikow / age fotostock (203). Cowin, Andrew/GNTB (206). Congress & Tourismus Zentrale Nürnberg/GNTB (207). hsvrs/ iStockphoto (207). Cowin, Andrew/Deutsche Zentrale für Tourismus e.V./GNTB (208). Martin Siepmann / age fotostock (217). Sunny Celeste / age fotostock (222). Germanisches Nationalmuseum, Nuremberg (229). Cowin, Andrew/GNTB (230). Spectral-Design/Shutterstock (235). Rudi1976 | Dreamstime.com (237). Walter Bibikow / age fotostock (242). **Chapter 6: The Bodensee:** Dr. Heinz Linke/iStockphoto (245). Mainau GmbH/GNTB (248). xyno/iStockphoto (260). Bildagentur RM / age fotostock (265). Clemens v. Vogelsang/Wikimedia Commons (268). Ralf Brunner/GNTB (273). parasola / age fotostock (276). **Chapter 7: The Black Forest:** Juergen Stumpe / age fotostock (279). Elke Wetzig (Elya)/Wikimedia Commons (282). Cowin, Andrew/GNTB (295). Blaine Harrington / age fotostock (305). Europa-Park Rust/GNTB (307). **Chapter 8: Heidelberg and The Neckar Valley:** Esbin-Anderson / age fotostock (311). Cowin, Andrew/GNTB (314). Kai Koehler/iStockphoto (329). Michael Weber / age fotostock (334). Sabine Lubenow / age fotostock (337). Matthias Hauser / age fotostock (342,343). **Chapter 9: Frankfurt:** F WagnerF1online / age fotostock (345). Shawn Hempel / age fotostock. (348). esemelwe/iStockphoto (349). Dontworry/Wikimedia Commons (349). Jochen Keute/Frankfurt am Main/GNTB (350). Carlo Morucchio / age fotostock (358). Raimund Kutter / age fotostock (361). Ingolf Pompe / age fotostock (363). H Leue / age fotostock (366). Martin Moxter / age fotostock (373). Michael Zegers / age fotostock (379). McPhoto / age fotostock (380). **Chapter 10: The Pfalz and Rhine Terrace:** Neustadt a.d. Weinstraße, Tourist, Kongress- und Saalbau GmbH/ GNTB (385). ultimathule/Shutterstock (388). Wolfgang Eichentopf/Shutterstock (389). Neustadt a.d. Weinstraße, Tourist, Kongress- und Saalbau GmbH/GNTB (390). Sabine Lubenow / age fotostock (398). Public Domain (401). Werner Dieterich / age fotostock (403). Martin Moxter / age fotostock (419). Sascha Kopp/Landeshauptstadt Mainz (424). **Chapter 11: The Rhineland:** Hubertus Blume / age fotostock (427). interlight/Shutterstock (430). Martin Moxter / age fotostock (442). Rainer Martini / age fotostock (445). Superstock (452). Werner Otto / age fotostock (461). Norman Steinmetz/Weingut Dr. Pauly Bergweiler (466). Galli Max / age fotostock (466,467). Jeff Kavanagh (468). Rob & Lisa Meehan/Flickr, [CC BY-ND 2.0] (468). Kerpen (469). Weingut Karp-Schreiber (469). Weingut Karp-Schreiber (469). Heinz-Dieter Falkenst / age fotostock (470). Jeff Kavanagh (470).

Public Domain (478). Heinz-Dieter Falkenst / age fotostock (482). Sabine Lubenow / age fotostock (492, 502). **Chapter 12: The Fairy-Tale Road:** HA Hessen Agentur GmbH/GNTB (507). Saladauskas/ Foto Graf/iStockphoto (510). One and Only/Shutterstock (516). Santi Roman / age fotostock (522). Arco/b Bönsch / age fotostock (526). Marcus Siebert / age fotostock (532). Charles Mahaux / age fotostock (537). Siegfried Kuttig / age fotostock (542). **Chapter 13: Hamburg:** Justus de Cuveland / age fotostock (547). Ivan Zupic / Alamy (550). Elzbieta Sekowska/iStockphoto (551). Igor Stevanovic/ iStockphoto (551). temporalata/Flickr, [CC BY-ND 2.0] (552). Anandoart (557). Stuart Forster / age fotostock (563). Yadid Levy / age fotostock (567). Industryandtravel I Dreamstime.com (570). Mauritus / age fotostock (576). **Chapter 14: Schleswig-Holstein and The Baltic Coast:** Siegfried Kuttig / age fotostock (597). Hans Peter Merten /GNTB (600). Lars Goldenbogen/Flickr, [CC BY-ND 2.0] (601). LianeM/Shutterstock (601). Andreas Bauer/iStockphoto (602). Sabine Lubenow / age fotostock (609). Ivan Vdovin / age fotostock (616). Wismar, Tourismus Zentrale/GNTB (621). Kuttig - Travel / Alamy (631). **Chapter 15: Berlin:** Nikada/iStockphoto (635). anweber/Shutterstock (638). Ontour / age fotostock (643). F Herrmann / age fotostock (647). kapitaen/iStockphoto (651). Hans Peter Merten / GNTB (653). Lucas Vallecillos / age fotostock (655). Tupungato I Dreamstime.com (661). Ingenui/ iStockphoto (662). Günter Flegar/imageBroker / age fotostock (670). ilovebutter/Flickr, [CC BY-ND 2.0] (675). Atlantide SNC / age fotostock (679). Iain Masterton / age fotostock (686). Held Jargen / age fotostock (694). **Chapter 16: Saxony, Saxony-Anhalt, and Thuringia:** Nico Stengert / age fotostock (711). Robert Scarth//Flickr, [CC BY-ND 2.0] (714). Public domain (715). fotosol / age fotostock (715). ilovebutter/Flickr, [CC BY-ND 2.0] (716). Wojtek Buss / age fotostock (725). Scirocco340/ Shutterstock (733). Wojtek Buss / age fotostock (735). Ernst Wrba / age fotostock (737). Bildarchiv Monheim GmbH / Alamy (743). fotosol / age fotostock (747). T W P / age fotostock (755). F1online digitale Bildagentur GmbH / Alamy (762). About Our Writers: All photos are courtesy of the writers.

NOTES

ABOUT OUR WRITERS

Joe Baur is a travel author (*Talking Tico*) and the editor of *trivago Magazine*. He's constantly looking to go off the beaten path in search of new stories and enjoys few things more than a hoppy beer and chorizo in good company. You can follow him at joebaur.com and at Without A Path. He updated the Rhineland for this edition.

Born and raised in Communist East Germany, Wibke Carter grew up in a world filled with pioneer uniforms, Trabants, and Vita Cola. After reunification, she caught the travel bug early on, living for some years in New Zealand, New York, and, currently, London. Writing for international newspapers and magazines, she visits her old Heimat several times a year in search of hidden corners and untold stories. She updated Hamburg and Schleswig-Holstein & the Baltic Coast.

Jennifer Ceaser has been a freelance writer and editor for 20 years. A former New Yorker and editor at the *New York Post*, Jennifer now splits her time between Germany and Spain. She regularly contributes to *Condé Nast Traveler, AFAR, New York* magazine, *Evening Standard UK, Time Out,* and a number of other U.S. and UK publications. She updated Munich.

Christie Dietz moved from London to Wiesbaden in 2010 to join her German husband. A food and travel writer, she has since busied herself exploring Riesling country and learned to cook all manner of traditional German dishes. She has written for various online publications and documents her culinary adventures at ⊕ *www.asausagehastwo.com.* For this edition, Christie updated the chapter on her favorite region for food and drink, the Pfalz and Rhine Terrace.

Lee A. Evans witnessed firsthand the revolutions that swept the Eastern bloc in 1989. Since then, he's had a front-row seat as his favorite city, Berlin, has transformed into one of the cultural epicenters of Europe. He has worked extensively as a travel writer and tour manager. He lives happily with his wife and daughter in quiet, bucolic Charlottenburg and maintains the web site ⊕ *www.berlinandbeyond.de.* He updated the Franconia & the German Danube and Saxony, Saxony-Anhalt, and Thuringia.

Liz Humphreys made the move to the creative hub of Berlin in 2017 after spending several years in Amsterdam and London. Before that, she lived in New York City, where she worked in editorial for Condé Nast, Time Inc., and other media companies. She currently writes and edits for publications including *Condé Nast Traveler, Time Out International,* and Forbes. Liz updated the Berlin chapter for this edition.

Evelyn Kanter is a NYC-based travel and automotive journalist who visits Germany often, where she eats sausages, prowls car museums, and visits relatives Munich and Frankfurt. A former on-air consumer reporter for ABC News and CBS News in New York, Sshe writes for airline in-flights and AAA magazines, and for Fodors.com. Evelyn also writes two websites—NYC on the Cheap and ecoXplorer. She updated the Frankfurt and Heidelberg & the Neckar Valley.

Chantal Panozzo moved to Switzerland in 2006, pleased to discover a country where people can actually pronounce her name. She is the author of *Swiss Life: 30 Things I Wish I'd Known,* and has also written for CNN Travel, *Brain, Child* magazine, and *The Christian Science Monitor,* among others. For this edition, she updated the Bodensee.

Courtney Tenz came to Germany in 2005 as a Fulbright recipient and has lived in Cologne, Germany, ever since. She is a culture editor at *Deutsche Welle* and writes frequently about German culture and the arts. For this edition, she toured Bavaria to update the Bavarian Alps and Romantic Road chapters, as well as those on the Black Forest and Fairy-Tale Road.